Date Due

FEB 1			
MAR 15			
MAR 30			
MAY 9			
MAY 29			
FEB 28			
FEB 25			
MAR 19			
APR 3			
APR 30			
May 14			
OCT 30			
FEB 27			
AUG 6 '70			

No. 293   DEMCO-MADISON-WIS

CASES

ON

INTERNATIONAL LAW

BY

CHARLES G. FENWICK

PROFESSOR OF POLITICAL SCIENCE, BRYN MAWR COLLEGE
AUTHOR OF ''THE NEUTRALITY LAWS OF THE UNITED STATES,''
''INTERNATIONAL LAW,'' ETC.

NATIONAL CASE BOOK SERIES

CHICAGO
CALLAGHAN AND COMPANY
1935

PREFACE

The purpose which a collection of cases on international law may serve in the curriculum of law schools or universities is much more limited than that served by collections of cases on the various branches of national law. Even in the field of national law, whether constitutional law or the customary divisions of private law, it is generally recognized that a collection of cases can only hope to present outstanding examples of the application of principle to concrete issues. No collection of a few hundred cases can state the whole law upon a broad subject. The citation of other cases in point may help to prevent the impression that the instant case has a wider application than it really has; but only an encyclopedic digest of reported cases can assure the student that he has the materials for making an adequate statement of the law. In the field of international law it has been the custom to include in a compilation of cases not only the awards of international tribunals and mixed claims commissions but the decisions of national courts applying the rules of international law as incidental to the interpretation of national law. No collection, however complete, of cases confined strictly to the relatively small number of judicial controversies between states could give any but the narrowest indication of the scope of international law. It would still be necessary, in order to present an adequate picture of the subject, to supplement these strictly international cases by a formidable array of treaties and multipartite conventions and of diplomatic correspondence between the foreign offices of the different nations. The result would be not a "case book" but a treatise in many volumes, suited rather to the uses of the Department of State than to those of the ordinary practicing attorney.

In consequence, collections of cases on international law have generally sought a narrower object, namely, to introduce the law student to those aspects of international law which are met with in controversial cases before domestic courts. Strictly speaking, such cases are not international cases, but are national cases involving international law—they are the municipal court's interpretation of international law as applied to conflicts of private rights and to the enforcement of the statutes of national law. It is, however, with just such cases that the practicing attorney is apt to be concerned. Arguments before international tribunals are rare; arguments before national courts on points of international law indirectly raised are quite common.

iii

But while cases of this latter type are prominent in this as in other collections, strictly international cases must also be given their due place as examples of the final appeals to which the decisions of national courts or the acts of national officers may lead when they are not regarded by another government as expressing the correct principles of international law. The present collection includes, therefore, decisions and advisory opinions of the Permanent Court of International Justice, awards of the Hague Permanent Court of Arbitration and of special arbitration tribunals, and the decisions of mixed claims commissions, in sufficient number to illustrate both the law and the procedure of international adjudication. Cases involving suits between states of the United States are also included as illustrating the application of principles of international law to the relations of members of a federal union and suggesting a like application to current international controversies. While it has been found desirable to reduce greatly the number of cases on War and Neutrality appearing in earlier collections of cases, enough space has been assigned to those topics to give the student an idea of their importance in the development of international law and of the difficulties attending the attempt, recently being renewed, to define in terms of law relationships as abnormal and paradoxical as those created by war.

A somewhat novel feature of the collection is the series of introductory notes which precede each chapter subdivision. In these notes the general principle of the law is first stated and then queries are raised indicating the issue presented by the particular case. By this means the student is made aware of his problem and is saved the loss of time due to the obscurity of so many international cases. While the introductory notes are not intended to dispense with reference to one or other of the standard treatises on international law where time permits, they should nevertheless serve to give definiteness to class discussions and to permit a wider range of topics to be covered.

As a practical matter it has been found necessary to confine the decisions of national courts almost entirely to American and British cases. In like manner limitations of space have necessitated the abridgment of cases by the omission of points not closely related to the main issue and of footnotes accompanying the case. As far as possible the facts of the individual case have been left as stated in the opinion of the court, in spite of the space that might have been saved by condensation. The object here has been to accustom the student to read the case in the light of the particular facts before the court, much harm being done, it is believed, by quotations out of their context. Additional cases have been summarized in footnotes at the close of chapter subdivisions. It must always be remembered by the student that a case book is not meant to be a substitute for the original texts of the decisions—it is only a convenient manual of class-room discussion, not a source book of final authority.

For the same reason no effort has been made to reprint the bibliographies that may be found in the leading treatises on international law or the extended lists of citations to be found in the various digests available in a law library. As for the captions under which the cases are listed, the editor is aware that they may in many instances give rise to the criticism that the same case is equally illustrative of other points of law. Nevertheless it is hoped that they may prove helpful to the student in locating himself in a field which has thus far not been laid out in accordance with any agreed system of classification. The texts of the decisions have been checked against the original sources and are printed literatim, except that the unusual typographical form of early cases has been brought more into accord with modern usage. In view of the lack of standards of typography in the printing of court cases at the present day, the student must be warned not to expect consistency in the use of capitals or italics or in the citation of authorities.

The thanks of the editor are due to his many colleagues who at Conferences of Teachers of International Law and on other occasions have discussed with him the proper content of a collection of cases on international law; and in particular to Professor Reeves of the University of Michigan and to Professor Garner of the University of Illinois who have made helpful suggestions for the improvement of this collection, as well as to Ruth C. Lawson, Fellow at Bryn Mawr College, who assisted in the task of gathering the material. While the determination of what constitutes a "leading" case has been made chiefly on the basis of the citation of such cases by the courts themselves, the editor has been to some extent guided by earlier collections of cases by Scott, Bentwich, Cobbett, Dickinson and Hudson, and recognition of their help is gratefully made.

C. G. FENWICK

Bryn Mawr College
April 10, 1935

TABLE OF CONTENTS

CHAPTER VII

JURISDICTION OVER PERSONS: ALIENS

CHAPTER VIII

SPECIAL JURISDICTIONAL OBLIGATIONS TOWARDS FOREIGN STATES

CHAPTER IX

JURISDICTION OVER PRIVATE AND PUBLIC VESSELS

CHAPTER X

SPECIAL PROTECTIVE JURISDICTION ON THE HIGH SEAS

CHAPTER XV

INTERNATIONAL TREATIES

CHAPTER XVI

AGENTS OF INTERNATIONAL INTERCOURSE

CHAPTER XVII

ARBITRAL AND JUDICIAL PROCEDURE FOR THE SETTLEMENT OF INTERNATIONAL DISPUTES

TABLE OF CASES

[REFERENCES ARE TO PAGES]

CASES

ON

INTERNATIONAL LAW

CHAPTER I

THE NATURE OF INTERNATIONAL LAW [1]

A. Precedence of established law over new rules.

International law may be defined as the body of rules regarded by nations as binding upon them in their relations with one another. It is a law deriving its authority from certain generally recognized principles of justice and from other concrete rules expressed in customs and treaties. Query, at what point does a new principle or a growing custom come to constitute a rule of law for all nations? Has one state the right to enforce against the vessels of another state on the high seas new rules of conduct believed by it to be more in accord with the general principles of moral obligation as they develop from generation to generation? Would it make any difference in such case whether the action of the vessel was contrary to the law of the state whose flag it was flying? Is the consent of the individual state required in order that a new rule contrary to established custom should become binding upon it? [United States v. La Jeune Eugenie; The Antelope.]

UNITED STATES v. THE SCHOONER LA JEUNE EUGENIE, RAIBAUD AND LABATUT, CLAIMANTS.

United States, Circuit Court, First Circuit, 1822.

2 Mason, 409.

STORY J. This is a libel brought against the schooner La Jeune Eugenie, which was seized by Lieut. Stockton, on the coast of Africa,

---

[1] For a more detailed study of this subject, see Fenwick, International Law, 2nd ed., Chap. II; Oppenheim, International Law, 4th ed., Vol. I, §§ 1–19; Brierly, The Law of Nations, I; Lauterpacht, Private Law Sources and Analogies of International Law; Reeves, J. S., "International Society and International Law," Am. Journal Int. Law, XV (1921), 361.

1

for being employed in the slave trade. The allegation asserts the offence in two forms; first, as against the slave trade acts of the United States; and secondly, as against the general law of nations. A claim has been given in by the French consul, in behalf of the claimants, who are subjects of France, resident in Basseterre, in the island of Guadaloupe, as owners of the schooner; and there is also a Protest filed by the French consul against the jurisdiction of the court, upon the ground, that this is a French vessel, owned by French subjects, and, as such, exclusively liable to the jurisdiction of the French tribunals, if she shall turn out, upon the evidence, to have been engaged in this dishonorable traffic. . . .

Standing, then, as this cause does, I am not satisfied, that the property is owned as claimed; and before it would be restored, even if all other difficulties were overcome, I should feel myself bound to require further proof of proprietary interest. If there were nothing more in the cause, I should pass such an order without hesitation.

But supposing the vessel to be established to be French, sailing under French papers, and employed in the African slave trade, the more important question is, whether this court is at liberty to entertain jurisdiction of the cause, or is bound to restore the property without any farther inquiry, remitting the party to the domestic forum. It is contended on behalf of the plaintiffs, that this court has a right to entertain jurisdiction, and is bound to reject the claim of the defendants; First, because the African Slave Trade is repugnant to the law of nations; Secondly, because it is prohibited by the municipal laws of France. On the other side it is contended, that the trade is not repugnant to the law of nations; and if prohibited by the laws of France, it is a municipal regulation, which the tribunals of France are alone competent to inquire into and punish. . . .

Having adverted to these preliminary considerations, I may now be permitted to proceed to the great points in controversy.

And the first question naturally arising out of the asserted facts is, whether the African slave trade be prohibited by the law of nations; for, if it be so, it will not, I presume, be denied, that confiscation of the property ought to follow; for that is the proper penalty denounced by that law for any violation of its precepts; and the same reasons, which enforce that penalty ordinarily, apply with equal force to employment in this trade.

I shall take up no time in the examination of the history of slavery, or of the question, how far it is consistent with the natural rights of mankind. That it may have a lawful existence, at least by way of punishment for crimes, will not be doubted by any persons, who admit the general right of society to enforce the observance of its laws by adequate penalties. That it has existed in all ages of the world, and has been tolerated by some, encouraged by others, and sanctioned by most, of the enlightened and civilized nations of the earth in former ages, admits of no reasonable question. That it has interwoven itself into the municipal institutions of some countries, and forms the foundation of large masses of property in a portion of our own country, is known to all of us. Sitting, therefore, in an American court of judicature, I am not permitted to deny, that under some circumstances it may have a lawful existence; and that the practice may be justified by the condition, or wants, of society; or may form a part of the domestic policy of a nation. It would be unbecoming in me here to assert, that the state of slavery cannot have a legitimate existence, or that it stands condemned by the unequivocal testimony of the law of nations.

But this concession carries us but a very short distance towards the decision of this cause. It is not, as the learned counsel for the government have justly stated, on account of the simple fact, that the traffic necessarily involves the enslavement of human beings, that it stands reprehended by the present sense of nations; but that it necessarily carries with it a breach of all the moral duties, of all the maxims of justice, mercy and humanity, and of the admitted rights, which independent christian nations now hold sacred in their intercourse with each other. What is the fact as to the ordinary, nay, necessary course, of this trade? It begins in corruption, and plunder, and kidnapping. It creates and stimulates unholy wars for the purpose of making captives. It desolates whole villages and provinces for the purpose of seizing the young, the feeble, the defenceless, and the innocent. It breaks down all the ties of parent, and children, and family, and country. It shuts up all sympathy for human suffering and sorrows. It manacles the inoffensive females and the starving infants. It forces the brave to untimely death in defence of their humble homes and firesides, or drives them to despair and self-immolation. It stirs up the worst passions of the human soul, darkening the spirit of revenge, sharpening the greediness of avarice, brutalizing the selfish, envenoming the cruel, famishing the weak, and crushing to death the broken hearted. This is but the beginning of the evils. Before the unhappy captives arrive at the destined market, where the traffic ends, one quarter part at least in the ordinary course of events perish in cold blood under the inhuman, or thoughtless treatment of their oppressors. . . .

It is of this traffic, thus carried on, and necessarily carried on, beginning in lawless wars, and rapine, and kidnapping, and ending in disease, and death, and slavery,—it is of this traffic in the aggregate of its accumulated wrongs, that I would ask, if it be consistent with the law of nations? It is not by breaking up the elements of the case into fragments, and detaching them one from another, that we are to be asked of each separately, if the law of nations prohibits it. We are not to be told, that war is lawful, and slavery lawful, and plunder lawful, and the taking away of life is lawful, and the selling of human beings is lawful. Assuming that they are so under circumstances, it establishes nothing. It does not advance one jot to the support of the proposition, that a traffic, that involves them all, that is unnecessary, unjust, and inhuman, is countenanced by the eternal law of nature, on which rests the law of nations.

Now the law of nations may be deduced, first, from the general principles of right and justice, applied to the concerns of individuals, and thence to the relations and duties of nations; or, secondly, in things indifferent or questionable, from the customary observances and recognitions of civilized nations; or, lastly, from the conventional or positive law, that regulates the intercourse between states. What, therefore, the law of nations is, does not rest upon mere theory, but may be considered as modified by practice, or ascertained by the treaties of nations at different periods. It does not follow, therefore, that because a principle cannot be found settled by the consent or practice of nations at one time, it is to be concluded, that at no subsequent period the principle can be considered as incorporated into the public code of nations. Nor is it to be admitted, that no principle belongs to the law of nations, which is not universally recognized, as such, by all civilized communities, or even by those constituting, what may be called, the christian states of Europe. Some doctrines, which we, as well as Great Britain, admit to belong to the law of nations, are of but recent origin and application, and have not, as yet, received any public or general sanction in other nations; and yet they are founded in such a just view of the duties and rights of nations, belligerent and neutral, that we have not hesitated to enforce them by the penalty of confiscation. There are other doctrines, again, which have met the decided hostility of some of the European states, enlightened as well as powerful, such as the right of search, and the rule, that free ships do not make free goods, which, nevertheless, both Great Britain and the United States maintain, and in my judgment with unanswerable arguments, as settled rules in the Law of Prize, and scruple not to apply them to the ships of all other nations. And yet, if the general custom of nations in modern times, or even in the present age, recognized an opposite doctrine, it could not, perhaps, be affirmed, that that practice did not constitute a part, or, at least, a modification, of the law of nations.

But I think it may be unequivocally affirmed, that every doctrine, that may be fairly deduced by correct reasoning from the rights and duties of nations, and the nature of moral obligation, may theoretically be said to exist in the law of nations; and unless it be relaxed or waived by the consent of nations, which may be evidenced by their general practice and customs, it may be enforced by a court of justice, whenever it arises in judgment. And I may go farther and say, that no practice whatsoever can obliterate the fundamental distinction between right and wrong, and that every nation is at liberty to apply to another the correct principle, whenever both nations by their public acts recede from such practice, and admit the injustice or cruelty of it.

Now in respect to the African slave trade, such as it has been described to be, and in fact is, in its origin, progress, and consummation, it cannot admit of serious question, that it is founded in a violation of some of the first principles, which ought to govern nations. It is repugnant to the great principles of christian duty, the dictates of natural religion, the obligations of good faith and morality, and the eternal maxims of social justice. When any trade can be truly said to have these ingredients, it is impossible, that it can be consistent with any system of law, that purports to rest on the authority of reason or revelation. And it is sufficient to stamp any trade as interdicted by public law, when it can be justly affirmed, that it is repugnant to the general principles of justice and humanity.

Now there is scarcely a single maritime nation of Europe, that has not in the most significant terms, in the most deliberate and solemn conferences, acts, or treaties, acknowledged the injustice and inhumanity of this trade; and pledged itself to promote its abolition. I need scarcely advert to the conferences at Vienna, at Aix-la-Chapelle, and at London, on this interesting subject, as they have been cited at the argument of this cause, and authenticated by our own government, to shew what may be emphatically called the sense of Europe upon this point. . . . Our own country, too, has firmly and earnestly pressed forward in the same career. The trade has been reprobated and punished, as far as our authority extended, from a very early period of the government; and by a very recent statute, to mark at once its infamy and repugnance to the law of nations, it has been raised in the catalogue of public crimes to the bad eminence of piracy. I think, therefore, that I am justified in saying, that at the present moment the traffic is vindicated by no nation, and is admitted by almost all commercial nations as incurably unjust and inhuman. It appears to me, therefore, that in an American court of judicature, I am bound to consider the trade an offence against the universal law of society and in all cases, where it is not protected by a foreign government, to deal with it as an offence carrying with it the penalty of confiscation.

And I cannot but think, notwithstanding the assertion at the bar to the contrary, that this doctrine is neither novel nor alarming. That it stands on principles of sound sense and general policy, and, above all, of moral justice. And I confess, that I should be somewhat startled, if any nation, sincerely anxious for the abolition, and earnest in its duty, should interpose its influence to arrest its universal adoption.

There is an objection urged against the doctrine, which is here asserted, that ought not to be passed over in silence; and that is, if the

African slave trade is repugnant to the law of nations, no nation can rightfully permit its subjects to carry it on, or exempt them from obedience to that law; for it is said, that no nation can privilege itself to commit a crime against the law of nations by a mere municipal regulation of its own. In a sense the proposition is true, but not universally so. No nation has a right to infringe the law of nations, so as thereby to produce an injury to any other nation. But if it does, this is understood to be an injury, not against all nations, which all are bound or permitted to redress; but which concerns alone the nation injured. The independence of nations guarantees to each the right of guarding its own honor, and the morals and interests of its own subjects. No one has a right to sit in judgment generally upon the actions of another; at least to the extent of compelling its adherence to all the principles of justice and humanity in its domestic concerns. If a nation were to violate as to its own subjects in its domestic regulation the clearest principles of public law, I do not know, that that law has ever held them amenable to the tribunals of other nations for such conduct. It would be inconsistent with the equality and sovereignty of nations, which admit no common superior. No nation has ever yet pretended to be the *custos morum* of the whole world; and though abstractedly a particular regulation may violate the law of nations, it may sometimes, in the case of nations, be a wrong without a remedy. . . .

After listening to the very able, eloquent, and learned arguments delivered at the bar on this occasion—after weighing the authorities, which bear on the case, with mature deliberation,—after reflecting anxiously and carefully upon the general principles, which may be drawn from the law of nations to illustrate or confirm them, I have come to the conclusion, that the slave trade is a trade prohibited by universal law, and by the law of France, and that, therefore, the claim of the asserted French owners must be rejected. That claim being rejected, I feel myself at perfect liberty, with the express consent of our own government, to decree, that the property be delivered over to the consular agent of the King of France, to be dealt with according to his own sense of duty and right. . . . [1]

---

[1] The attempt of the court in this and other cases to enforce new principles of law against the vessels of other states led to a disclaimer from Secretary Adams, on February 22, 1822, of any right to search French vessels in the future and to the subsequent payment of an indemnity for the seizures. See Moore, Digest of Int. Law, II, p. 920.

THE ANTELOPE, THE VICE-CONSULS OF SPAIN AND PORTUGAL, LIBELLANTS.

United States, Supreme Court, 1825.

10 Wheaton, 66. [6 L. ed. 268.]

Appeal from the Circuit Court of Georgia.

These cases were allegations filed by the Vice-Consuls of Spain and Portugal, claiming certain Africans as the property of subjects of their nation. The material facts were as follows: A privateer, called the Colombia, sailing under a Venezuelan commission, entered the port of Baltimore in the year 1819; clandestinely shipped a crew of thirty or forty men; proceeded to sea, and hoisted the Artegan flag, assuming the name of the Arraganta, and prosecuted a voyage along the coast of Africa; her officers and the greater part of her crew being citizens of the United States. Off the coast of Africa she captured an American vessel, from Bristol, in Rhode Island, from which she took twenty-five Africans; she captured several Portuguese vessels, from which she also took Africans; and she captured a Spanish vessel, called the Antelope, in which she also took a considerable number of Africans. The two vessels then sailed in company to the coast of Brazil, where the Arraganta was wrecked, and her master, Metcalf, and a great part of his crew, made prisoners; the rest of the crew, with the armament of the Arraganta, were transferred to the Antelope, which, thus armed, assumed the name of the General Ramirez, under the command of John Smith, a citizen of the United States; and on board this vessel were all the Africans, which had been captured by the privateer in the course of her voyage. This vessel, thus freighted, was found hovering near the coast of the United States, by the revenue cutter, Dallas, under the command of Captain Jackson, and finally brought into the port of Savannah for adjudication. The Africans, at the time of her capture, amounted to upwards of two hundred and eighty. On their arrival, the vessel, and the Africans, were libelled, and claimed by the Portuguese and Spanish Vice-Consuls reciprocally. They were also claimed by John Smith, as captured *jure belli*. They were claimed by the United States, as having been transported from foreign parts by American citizens, in contravention to the laws of the United States, and as entitled to their freedom by those laws, and by the law of nations. Captain Jackson, the master of the revenue cutter, filed an alternative claim for the bounty given by law, if the Africans should be adjudged to the United States; or to salvage, if the whole subject should be adjudged to the Portuguese and Spanish Consuls.

The Court dismissed the libel and claim of John Smith. They dismissed the claim of the United States, except as to that portion of the Africans which had been taken from the American vessel. The residue was divided between the Spanish and Portuguese claimants. . . .

MR. CHIEF JUSTICE MARSHALL delivered the opinion of the Court, and, after stating the case, proceeded as follows:

In prosecuting this appeal, the United States assert no property in themselves. They appear in the character of guardians, or next friends, of these Africans, who are brought, without any act of their own, into the bosom of our country, insist on their right to freedom, and submit their claim to the laws of the land, and to the tribunals of the nation.

The Consuls of Spain and Portugal, respectively, demand these Africans as slaves, who have, in the regular course of legitimate commerce, been acquired as property by the subjects of their respective sovereigns, and claim their restitution under the laws of the United States.

In examining claims of this momentous importance; claims in which the sacred rights of liberty and of property come in conflict with each other; which have drawn from the bar a degree of talent and of eloquence, worthy of the questions that have been discussed; this Court must not yield to feelings which might seduce it from the path of duty, and must obey the mandate of the law.

That the course of opinion on the slave trade should be unsettled, ought to excite no surprise. The Christian and civilized nations of the world, with whom we have most intercourse, have all been engaged in it. However abhorrent this traffic may be to a mind whose original feelings are not blunted by familiarity with the practice, it has been sanctioned in modern times by the laws of all nations who possess distant colonies, each of whom has engaged in it as a common commercial business which no other could rightfully interrupt. It has claimed all the sanction which could be derived from long usage, and general acquiescence. That trade could not be considered as contrary to the law of nations which was authorized and protected by the laws of all commercial nations; the right to carry on which was claimed by each, and allowed by each.

The course of unexamined opinion, which was founded on this inveterate usage, received its first check in America; and, as soon as these States acquired the right of self-government, the traffic was forbidden by most of them. In the beginning of this century, several humane and enlightened individuals of Great Britain devoted themselves to the cause of the Africans; and, by frequent appeals to the nation, in which the enormity of this commerce was unveiled, and exposed to the public eye, the general sentiment was at length roused against it, and the feelings of justice and humanity, regaining their long lost ascendency, prevailed so far in the British parliament as to obtain an act for its abolition. The utmost efforts of the British government, as well as of that of the United States, have since been assiduously employed in its suppression. It has been denounced by both in terms of great severity, and those concerned in it are sub-

jected to the heaviest penalties which law can inflict. In addition
to these measures operating on their own people, they have used all
their influence to bring other nations into the same system, and to
interdict this trade by the consent of all.

Public sentiment has, in both countries, kept pace with the measures
of government; and the opinion is extensively, if not universally
entertained, that this unnatural traffic ought to be suppressed. While
its illegality is asserted by some governments, but not admitted by all;
while the detestation in which it is held is growing daily, and even
those nations who tolerate it in fact, almost disavow their own conduct, and rather connive at, than legalize, the acts of their subjects;
it is not wonderful that public feeling should march somewhat in
advance of strict law, and that opposite opinions should be entertained on the precise cases in which our own laws may control and
limit the practice of others. Indeed, we ought not to be surprised, if,
on this novel series of cases, even Courts of justice should, in some
instances, have carried the principle of suppression farther than a
more deliberate consideration of the subject would justify. . . . [1]

In the United States, different opinions have been entertained in the
different Circuits and Districts; and the subject is now, for the first
time, before this Court.

The question, whether the slave trade is prohibited by the law of
nations has been seriously propounded, and both the affirmative and
negative of the proposition have been maintained with equal earnest-
ness.

That it is contrary to the law of nature will scarcely be denied. That
every man has a natural right to the fruits of his own labour, is generally admitted; and that no other person can rightfully deprive him of
those fruits, and appropriate them against his will, seems to be the
necessary result of this admission. But from the earliest times war has
existed, and war confers rights in which all have acquiesced. Among
the most enlightened nations of antiquity, one of these was, that the

---

[1] The court here cites, among other cases, Le Louis [Great Britain, High Court
of Admiralty, 2 Dodson 210 (1817)], in which a French vessel engaged in the
slave trade was captured by a British cruiser off the coast of Africa. The court
held the only ground upon which a right of search of foreign vessels might be
exercised in time of peace was that of suspicion of piracy or "some new ground"
forming an exception to the general rule. Piracy being excluded, the court
further found that the slave trade was not a crime at international law. The
court, said the opinion, "must look to the legal standard of morality; and upon a
question of this nature, that standard must be found in the law of nations as
fixed and evidenced by general and ancient and admitted practice, by treaties
and by the general tenor of the laws and ordinances, and the formal transactions
of civilized states; and looking to those authorities, I find a difficulty in maintaining that the traffic is legally criminal." For other aspects of this case, see
below, pp. 67, 369.

victor might enslave the vanquished. This, which was the usage of all, could not be pronounced repugnant to the law of nations, which is certainly to be tried by the test of general usage. That which has received the assent of all, must be the law of all.

Slavery, then, has its origin in force; but as the world has agreed that it is a legitimate result of force, the state of things which is thus produced by general consent, cannot be pronounced unlawful.

Throughout Christendom, this harsh rule has been exploded, and war is no longer considered as giving a right to enslave captives. But this triumph of humanity has not been universal. The parties to the modern law of nations do not propagate their principles by force; and Africa has not yet adopted them. Throughout the whole extent of that immense continent, so far as we know its history, it is still the law of nations that prisoners are slaves. Can those who have themselves renounced this law, be permitted to participate in its effects by purchasing the beings who are its victims?

Whatever might be the answer of a moralist to this question, a jurist must search for its legal solution, in those principles of action which are sanctioned by the usages, the national acts, and the general assent, of that portion of the world of which he considers himself as a part, and to whose law the appeal is made. If we resort to this standard as the test of international law, the question, as has already been observed, is decided in favour of the legality of the trade. Both Europe and America embarked in it; and for nearly two centuries, it was carried on without opposition, and without censure. A jurist could not say, that a practice thus supported was illegal, and that those engaged in it might be punished, either personally, or by deprivation of property.

In this commerce, thus sanctioned by universal assent, every nation had an equal right to engage. How is this right to be lost? Each may renounce it for its own people; but can this renunciation affect others?

No principle of general law is more universally acknowledged, than the perfect equality of nations. Russia and Geneva have equal rights. It results from this equality, that no one can rightfully impose a rule on another. Each legislates for itself, but its legislation can operate on itself alone. A right, then, which is vested in all by the consent of all, can be devested only by consent; and this trade, in which all have participated, must remain lawful to those who cannot be induced to relinquish it. As no nation can prescribe a rule for others, none can make a law of nations; and this traffic remains lawful to those whose governments have not forbidden it.

If it is consistent with the law of nations, it cannot in itself be piracy. It can be made so only by statute; and the obligation of the statute cannot transcend the legislative power of the state which may enact it.

If it be neither repugnant to the law of nations, nor piracy, it is almost superfluous to say in this Court, that the right of bringing in for adjudication in time of peace, even where the vessel belongs to a nation which has prohibited the trade, cannot exist. The Courts of no country execute the penal laws of another; and the course of the American government on the subject of visitation and search, would decide any case in which that right had been exercised by an American cruiser, on the vessel of a foreign nation, not violating our municipal laws, against the captors.

It follows, that a foreign vessel engaged in the African slave trade, captured on the high seas in time of peace, by an American cruiser, and brought in for adjudication, would be restored.

The general question being disposed of, it remains to examine the circumstances of the particular case. . . .

Had the Arraganta been a regularly commissioned cruiser, which had committed no infraction of the neutrality of the United States, her capture of the Antelope must have been considered as lawful, and no question could have arisen respecting the rights of the original claimants. The question of prize or no prize belongs solely to the Courts of the captor. But, having violated the neutrality of the United States, and having entered our ports, not voluntarily, but under coercion, some difficulty exists respecting the extent of the obligation to restore, on the mere proof of former possession, which is imposed on this government.

If, as is charged in the libels of both the Consuls, as well as of the United States, she was a pirate, hovering on the coast with intent to introduce slaves in violation of the laws of the United States, our treaty requires that property rescued from pirates shall be restored to the Spanish owner on his making proof of his property.

Whether the General Ramirez, originally the Antelope, is to be considered as the prize of a commissioned belligerent ship of war unlawfully equipped in the United States, or as a pirate, it seems proper to make some inquiry into the title of the claimants.

In support of the Spanish claim, testimony is produced, showing the documents under which the Antelope sailed from the Havana on the voyage on which she was captured; that she was owned by a Spanish house of trade in that place; that she was employed in the business of purchasing slaves, and had purchased and taken on board a considerable number, when she was seized as prize by the Arraganta.

Whether, on this proof, Africans brought into the United States, under the various circumstances belonging to this case, ought to be restored or not, is a question on which much difficulty has been felt. It is unnecessary to state the reasons in support of the affirmative or negative answer to it, because the Court is divided on it, and, consequently, no principle is settled. So much of the decree of the Circuit Court as directs restitution to the Spanish claimant of the Africans found on board the Antelope when she was captured by the Arraganta, is affirmed. . . .

[The claim of the Portuguese Vice-Consul being found invalid, the Court ordered the rest of the slaves to be delivered up to the United States to be disposed of according to law.]

B. Sources of international law.

The great body of international law was until recent years embodied in usages and customs which gave expression to a recognition that a particular practice was so well established that it was no longer optional but had become a rule of obligation. Query, how is the existence of such a usage or custom to be determined? What are the primary evidences of customary law? How far are the works of publicists of value in determining the existence of a binding custom? [The Paquete Habana.]

Established custom may be set aside by formal consent of the nations, and this may occasionally happen, as in the case of maritime law, by the individual adoption of uniform national codes. Query, would such individual national action be sufficient of itself to change the customary law so as to affect adversely a vessel operating under the regulations of the older law? [The Scotia.]

The more common method of setting aside established custom or of creating new obligations where none were recognized previously is by the formal procedure of entering into treaties or conventions. Where treaties are merely bilateral in character they do no more than set up a new rule of conduct for the two parties and can not strictly be said to be sources of international law. On the other hand the numerous multilateral conventions of recent years constitute what may fairly be called "international legislation," since they create obligations for all the signatories of the convention.[1]

THE PAQUETE HABANA.

THE LOLA.

United States, Supreme Court, 1900.

175 U. S. 677. [44 L. ed. 320; 20 S. Ct. 290.]

MR. JUSTICE GRAY delivered the opinion of the court.

These are two appeals from decrees of the District Court of the United States for the Southern District of Florida condemning two fishing vessels and their cargoes as prize of war.

---

[1] Compare the collection of multipartite conventions in Hudson, International Legislation, Vols. I–IV (1919–1929).

Each vessel was a fishing smack, running in and out of Havana, and regularly engaged in fishing on the coast of Cuba; sailed under the Spanish flag; was owned by a Spanish subject of Cuban birth, living in the city of Havana; . . . . Her cargo consisted of fresh fish, . . . Until stopped by the blockading squadron she had no knowledge of the existence of the war or of any blockade. . . .

Both fishing vessels were brought by their captors into Key West. . . . On May 30, 1898, a final decree of condemnation and sale was entered, "the court not being satisfied, that, as a matter of law, without any ordinance, treaty, or proclamation, fishing vessels of this class are exempt from seizure." . . .

We are then brought to the consideration of the question whether, upon the facts appearing in these records, the fishing smacks were subject to capture by the armed vessels of the United States during the recent war with Spain.

By an ancient usage among civilized nations, beginning centuries ago, and gradually ripening into a rule of international law, coast fishing vessels, pursuing their vocation of catching and bringing in fresh fish, have been recognized as exempt, with their cargoes and crews, from capture as prize of war.

This doctrine, however, has been earnestly contested at the bar; and no complete collection of the instances illustrating it is to be found, so far as we are aware, in a single published work, although many are referred to and discussed by the writers on international law, notably in 2 Ortolan, Reglès Internationales et Diplomatie de la Mer, (4th ed.) lib. 3, c. 2, pp. 51–56; in 4 Calvo, Droit International (5th ed.) sections 2367–2373; in De Boeck, Propriété Privée Ennemie sous Pavillon Ennemi, §§ 191–196; and in Hall, International Law, (4th ed.) § 148. It is therefore worth the while to trace the history of the rule, from the earliest accessible sources, through the increasing recognition of it, with occasional setbacks, to what we may now justly consider as its final establishment in our own country and generally throughout the civilized world.

The earliest acts of any government on the subject, mentioned in the books, either emanated from, or were approved by, a King of England.

In 1403 and 1406 Henry IV. issued orders to his admirals and other officers, entitled "Concerning Safety for Fishermen—*De Securitate pro Piscatoribus*." By an order of October 26, 1403, reciting that it was made pursuant to a treaty between himself and the King of France; and for the greater safety of the fishermen of either country, and so that they could be, and carry on their industry, the more safely on the sea, and deal with each other in peace; and that the French King had consented that English fishermen should be treated likewise; it was ordained that French fishermen might, during the then pending season for the herring fishery, safely fish for herrings and all other fish, from the harbor of Gravelines and the island of Thanet to the mouth of the Seine and the harbor of Hautoune. . . .

The treaty made October 2, 1521, between the Emperor Charles V. and Francis I. of France, through their ambassadors, recited that a great and fierce war had arisen between them, because of which there had been, both by land and sea, frequent depredations and incursions on either side, to the grave detriment and intolerable injury of the innocent subjects of each; and that a suitable time for the herring fishery was at hand, and, by reason of the sea being beset by the enemy, the fishermen did not dare to go out, whereby the subject of their industry, bestowed by heaven to allay the hunger of the poor, would wholly fail for the year, unless it were otherwise provided,—*quo fit, ut piscaturae commoditas, ad pauperum levandam famem a coelesti numine concessa, cessare hoc anno omnino debeat, nisi aliter provideatur.* . . .

France, from remote times, set the example of alleviating the evils of war in favor of all coast fishermen. In the compilation entitled "Us et Coutumes de la Mer," published by Cleirac in 1661, and in the third part thereof, containing "Maritime or Admiralty Jurisdiction,—*la Jurisdiction de la Marine ou d'Admirauté*—as well in time of peace, as in time of war," article 80 is as follows: "The admiral may in time of war accord fishing truces—*tresves pescheresses*—to the enemy and to his subjects; provided that the enemy will likewise accord them to Frenchmen." Cleirac, 544. . . . And Cleirac adds, in a note, this quotation from Froissart's Chronicles: "Fishermen on the sea, whatever war there were in France and England, never did harm to one another; so they are friends, and help one another at need. . . ."

The same custom would seem to have prevailed in France until towards the end of the seventeenth century. . . . But by the ordinances of 1681 and 1692 the practice was discontinued, because, Valin says, of the faithless conduct of the enemies of France, who, abusing the good faith with which she had always observed the treaties, habitually carried off her fishermen, while their own fished in safety. . . .

The doctrine which exempts coast fishermen, with their vessels and cargoes, from capture as prize of war, has been familiar to the United States from the time of the War of Independence.

On June 5, 1779, Louis XVI., our ally in that war, addressed a letter to his admiral, informing him that the wish he had always had of alleviating, as far as he could, the hardships of war, had directed his attention to that class of his subjects which devoted itself to the trade of fishing, and had no other means of livelihood; . . . and that he had therefore given orders to the commanders of all his ships not to disturb English fishermen. . . .

In the treaty of 1785 between the United States and Prussia, article 23 (which was proposed by the American Commissioners, John Adams, Benjamin Franklin, and Thomas Jefferson, and is said to have been drawn up by Franklin), provided that, if war should arise between the contracting parties, "all women and children, scholars of every faculty, cultivators of the earth, artisans, manufacturers, and fishermen, unarmed and inhabiting unfortified towns, villages, or places, and in general all others whose occupations are for the common subsistence and benefit of mankind, shall be allowed to continue their respective employments. . . ."

Since the United States became a nation, the only serious interruptions, so far as we are informed, of the general recognition of the exemption of coast fishing vessels from hostile capture, arose out of the mutual suspicions and recriminations of England and France during the wars of the French Revolution. . . .

Lord Stowell's judgment in The Young Jacob and Johanna, 1 C. Rob. 20, above cited, was much relied on by the counsel for the United States, and deserves careful consideration.

The vessel there condemned is described in the report as "a small Dutch fishing vessel taken April, 1798, on her return from the Dogger bank to Holland"; and Lord Stowell, in delivering judgment, said: "In former wars it has not been usual to make captures of these small fishing vessels; but this rule was a rule of comity only, and not of legal decision; it has prevailed from views of mutual accommodation between neighboring countries, and from tenderness to a poor and industrious order of people. In the present war there has, I presume, been sufficient reason for changing this mode of treatment." . . .

Both the capture and the condemnation were within a year after the order of the English government of January 24, 1798, instructing the commanders of its ships to seize French and Dutch fishing vessels, and before any revocation of that order. Lord Stowell's judgment shows that his decision was based upon the order of 1798, as well as upon strong evidence of fraud. . . . Nothing more was adjudged in the case.

. . . The opinion begins by admitting the known custom in former wars not to capture such vessels; adding, however, "but this was a rule of comity only, and not of legal decision." . . . The word "comity" was apparently used by Lord Stowell as synonymous with courtesy or goodwill. But the period of a hundred years which has since elapsed is amply sufficient to have enabled what originally may have rested in custom or comity, courtesy or concession, to grow, by the general assent of civilized nations, into a settled rule of international law. . . .

The French prize tribunals, both before and after Lord Stowell's decision, took a wholly different view of the general question. . . .

The English government, soon afterwards, more than once unqualifiedly prohibited the molestation of fishing vessels employed in catching and bringing to market fresh fish. . . .

Wheaton, in his Digest of the Law of Maritime Captures and Prizes, published in 1815, wrote: "It has been usual in maritime wars to exempt from capture fishing boats and their cargoes, both from views of mutual accommodation between neighboring countries, and from tenderness to a poor and industrious order of people. This custom, so honorable to the humanity of civilized nations, has fallen into disuse; and it is remarkable that both France and England mutually reproach each other with that breach of good faith which has finally abolished it." Wheaton on Captures, c. 2, § 18.

This statement clearly exhibits Wheaton's opinion that the custom had been a general one, as well as that it ought to remain so. His assumption that it had been abolished by the differences between France and England at the close of the last century was hardly justified by the state of things when he wrote, and has not since been borne out.

During the wars of the French Empire, as both French and English writers agree, the coast fisheries were left in peace. 2 Ortolan, 54; De Boeck, § 193; Hall, § 148. De Boeck quaintly and truly adds, "and the incidents of 1800 and of 1801 had no morrow,—*n'eurent pas de lendemain.*"

In the war with Mexico in 1846, the United States recognized the exemption of coast fishing boats from capture. . . .

France in the Crimean war in 1854, and in her wars with Austria in 1859 and with Germany in 1870, by general orders, forbade her cruisers to trouble the coast fisheries, or to seize any vessel or boat engaged therein, unless naval or military operations should make it necessary. Calvo, § 2372; Hall, § 148; 2 Ortolan, (4th ed.) 449; 10 Revue de Droit International, (1878) 399. . . .

International law is part of our law, and must be ascertained and administered by the courts of justice of appropriate jurisdiction, as often as questions of right depending upon it are duly presented for their determination. For this purpose, where there is no treaty, and no controlling executive or legislative act or judicial decision, resort must be had to the customs and usages of civilized nations; and, as evidence of these, to the works of jurists and commentators, who by years of labor, research, and experience, have made themselves peculiarly well acquainted with the subjects of which they treat. Such works are resorted to by judicial tribunals, not for the speculations of their authors concerning what the law ought to be, but for trustworthy evidence of what the law really is. Hilton v. Guyot, 159 U. S. 113, 163, 164, 214, 215.

Wheaton places among the principal sources of international law, "Text-writers of authority, showing what is the approved usage of nations, or the general opinion respecting their mutual conduct, with the definitions and modifications introduced by general consent." As to these he forcibly observes: "Without wishing to exaggerate the importance of these writers, or to substitute, in any case, their authority for the principles of reason, it may be affirmed that they are generally impartial in their judgment. They are witnesses of the sentiments and usages of civilized nations, and the weight of their testimony increases every time that their authority is invoked by statesmen, and every year that passes without the rules laid down in their works being impugned by the avowal of contrary principles." Wheaton's International Law, (8th ed.), § 15.

Chancellor Kent says: "In the absence of higher and more authoritative sanctions, the ordinances of foreign states, the opinions of eminent statesmen, and the writings of distinguished jurists, are regarded as of great consideration on questions not settled by conventional law. In cases where the principal jurists agree, the presumption will be very great in favor of the solidity of their maxims; and no civilized nation that does not arrogantly set all ordinary law and justice at defiance will venture to disregard the uniform sense of the established writers on international law." 1 Kent, Com. 18. . . .

This review of the precedents and authorities on the subject appears to us abundantly to demonstrate that at the present day, by the general consent of the civilized nations of the world, and independently of any express treaty or other public act, it is an established rule of international law, founded on considerations of humanity to a poor and industrious order of men, and of the mutual convenience of belligerent states, that coast fishing vessels, with their implements and supplies, cargoes and crews, unarmed and honestly pursuing their peaceful calling of catching and bringing in fresh fish, are exempt from capture as prize of war. . . .

This rule of international law is one which prize courts administering the law of nations are bound to take judicial notice of, and to give effect to, in the absence of any treaty or other public act of their own government in relation to the matter. . . .

By the practice of all civilized nations, vessels employed only for the purposes of discovery or science are considered as exempt from the contingencies of war, and therefore not subject to capture. It has been usual for the government sending out such an expedition to give notice to other powers; but it is not essential. 1 Kent, Com. 91, note; Halleck, c. 20, § 22; Calvo, § 2376; Hall, § 138. . . .

The position taken by the United States during the recent war with Spain was quite in accord with the rule of international law, now generally recognized by civilized nations, in regard to coast fishing vessels.

Upon the facts proved in either case, it is the duty of this court, sitting as the highest prize court of the United States, and administering the law of nations, to declare and adjudge that the capture was unlawful and without probable cause; and it is therefore, in each case,

Ordered, that the decree of the District Court be reversed, and the proceeds of the sale of the vessel, together with the proceeds of any sale of her cargo, be restored to the claimant, with damages and costs.

[In a dissenting opinion Chief Justice Fuller and two other justices held that the alleged custom was not so well established as to exempt the vessels "as matter of law" and that the exemption, to be valid, should be specifically designated by the Executive Department of the government.]

THE SCOTIA.

United States, Supreme Court, 1872.

14 Wallace, 170. [20 L. ed. 822.]

[In 1863 the British Government adopted a series of regulations for preventing collisions at sea. In 1864 the American Congress adopted practically the same regulations, as did, within a short time after, the governments of almost all maritime countries. Under these conditions the Scotia, a British steamer, collided in mid-ocean with the Berkshire, an American sailing ship, which was not carrying the lights required by the new regulations. As a result of the collision the Berkshire was sunk. The owners of the Berkshire filed their libel in the United States District Court in New York, alleging that the collision occurred through the fault of the Scotia, and arguing that the respective rights and duties of the two vessels were determined by the general maritime law as it existed before the British legislation of 1863. The District Court dismissed the libel, and the Circuit Court having affirmed that decree an appeal was taken to the Supreme Court. It was argued by counsel for the Berkshire that the questions in controversy were to be determined without reference to the municipal laws of either nation and solely according to the general maritime law which could not be changed by the isolated action of individual states].

Mr. Justice Strong delivered the opinion of the court. . . .

It must be conceded, however, that the rights and merits of a case may be governed by a different law from that which controls a court in which a remedy may be sought. The question still remains, what was the law of the place where the collision occurred, and at the time when it occurred. Conceding that it was not the law of the United States, nor that of Great Britain, nor the concurrent regulations of the two governments, but that it was the law of the sea, was it the ancient maritime law, that which existed before the commercial nations of the world adopted the regulations of 1863 and 1864, or the law changed after those regulations were adopted? Undoubtedly, no single nation can change the law of the sea. That law is of universal obligation, and no statute of one or two nations can create obligations for the world. Like all the laws of nations, it rests upon the common consent of civilized communities. It is of force, not because it was prescribed by any superior power, but because it has been generally accepted as a rule of conduct. Whatever may have been its origin, whether in the usages of navigation or in the ordinances of maritime states, or in both, it has become the law of the sea only by the concurrent sanction of those nations who may be said to constitute the commercial world. Many of the usages which prevail, and which have the force of law, doubtless originated in the positive prescriptions of some single state, which were at first of limited effect, but which when generally accepted became of universal obligation. The Rhodian law is supposed to have been the earliest system of marine rules. It was a code for Rhodians only, but it soon became of general authority because accepted and assented to as a wise and desirable system by other maritime nations. The same may be said of the Amalphitan table, of the ordinances of the Hanseatic League, and of parts of the marine ordinances of Louis XIV. They all became the law of the sea, not on account of their origin, but by reason of their acceptance as such. And it is evident that unless general assent is efficacious to give sanction to international law, there never can be that growth and development of maritime rules which the constant changes in the instruments and necessities of navigation require. Changes in nautical rules have taken place. How have they been accomplished, if not by the concurrent assent, express or understood, of maritime nations? When, therefore, we find such rules of navigation as are mentioned in the British orders in council of January 9th, 1863, and in our act of Congress of 1864, accepted as obligatory rules by more than thirty of the principal commercial states of the world, including almost all which have any shipping on the Atlantic Ocean, we are constrained to regard them as in part at least, and so far as relates to these vessels, the laws of the sea, and as having been the law at the time when the collision of which the libellants complain took place.

This is not giving to the statutes of any nation extraterritorial effect. It is not treating them as general maritime laws, but it is recognition of the historical fact that, by common consent of mankind, these rules have been acquiesced in as of general obligation. Of that fact we think we may take judicial notice. Foreign municipal laws must indeed be proved as facts, but it is not so with the law of nations.

The consequences of this ruling are decisive of the case before us. The violation of maritime law by the Berkshire in carrying a white light (to say nothing of her neglect to carry colored lights), and her carrying it on deck instead of at her masthead, were false representations to the Scotia. They proclaimed that the Berkshire was a steamer, and such she was manifestly taken to be. The movements of the Scotia were therefore entirely proper, and she was without fault.

Decree affirmed, with costs.[1]

_____

C. Sanctions of international law.

Unlike municipal law, international law rests not upon the command of a political superior, but upon the mutual recognition by nations of the binding force of certain rules of conduct. Down to the year 1920 the only international sanction of the law, apart from the right of the individual state to go to war in defense of its claims, was the force of public opinion among the nations, which exercised a very uncertain restraint upon individual states in times of crisis. While, however, it was not always possible for members of the international community to enforce the observance of the law by direct means, it was at least in their power to refuse to enforce unlawful decrees of another state when such decrees were presented to them indirectly in the course of judicial proceedings arising in consequence of them. Query, if in time of war a belligerent were to issue a declaration in violation of established customary law, would the declaration be recognized as valid by the courts of a neutral country in passing upon the contract rights of private parties entered into in contemplation of the law set aside by the declaration? [The Prometheus.]

_____

[1] In numerous cases national and international courts have commented obiter upon the nature and sources of international law when presented with concrete issues calling for the application of general principles. A century ago when there were fewer international conventions the courts naturally fell back upon "reason" as a source of international law to supplement and develop those principles of natural justice believed to be applicable to nations equally as to individual men. A statement by Chief Justice Marshall in the case of Thirty Hogsheads of Sugar (Bentzon, Claimant) v. Boyle, 9 Cranch, 191 (1815), showing the transition from abstract to applied reason has become almost classic. The question before the court was whether a rule laid down by the British courts which identified the national character of the owner of produce with that of the soil which produced it (Bentzon, a Danish subject, had shipped the produce of his plantation in Santa Cruz then under occupation by the British) would be followed by the courts of the United States. "The law of nations," said the court, "is the great source from which we derive those rules, respecting belligerent and neutral rights, which are recognized by all civilized and commercial states throughout Europe and America. This law is in part unwritten, and in part conventional. To ascertain that which is unwritten, we resort to the great principles of reason and justice: but, as these principles will be differently understood by different nations under different circumstances, we consider them as being, in some degree, fixed and rendered stable by a series of judicial decisions. The decisions of the Courts of every country, so far as they are founded upon a law common to every country, will be received, not as authority, but with respect. The decisions of the Courts of every country show how the law of nations, in the given case, is understood in that country, and will be considered in adopting the rule which is to prevail in this."

IN THE MATTER OF AN ARBITRATION BETWEEN THE OSAKA SHOSEN KAISHA AND THE OWNERS OF THE STEAMSHIP PROMETHEUS.

Hong Kong, Supreme Court, 1906.

2 Hong Kong L. R. 207.

[The Osaka Shosen Kaisha, a Japanese steamship company, and the agents of the owners of the Norwegian steamship Prometheus signed on Feb. 10, 1904, a charter-party at Hong Kong by which the steamship Prometheus was chartered to the Japanese company for six months. By clause 37 of the contract it was expressly agreed that "in case of war steamer not to be directed to any blockaded port nor to carry any contraband of war." When the charter-party was signed, hostilities had already broken out between Russia and Japan, but this was not known to the signers of the contract, although the contract was made in anticipation of war. On February 14, the government of Russia published the list of articles which it declared to be contraband, which list concluded with the words, "In general, all articles intended for war, on sea or land, such as rice, provisions, horses, beasts of burden and others which can be of use in war, if they are carried for an enemy or to an enemy destination." While the Prometheus was at Kobe loading with a cargo for Formosa, the owners telegraphed the master of the vessel to "decline rice and provisions between Japanese ports." In consequence of the refusal of the master to accept the cargo of rice, sugar and provisions, on the ground that they were contraband within the meaning of clause 37 of the charter-party, the steamship could not be used in the trade for which it was hired, and the Osaka Shosen Kaisha brought an action for breach of contract. The arbitrator who found the facts submitted to the court several questions, the first of which was, whether the cargo offered for shipment at Kobe was contraband under the terms of Russia's declaration, and if so, whether that declaration was binding upon neutrals.]

THE CHIEF JUSTICE [SIR HENRY BERKELEY] : . . .

What then is the meaning of the expression "contraband of war" in its primary sense? Mr. Wharton, in his "Law Lexicon," defines contraband of war as meaning in its primary sense that which according to international law cannot be supplied to a hostile belligerent except at the risk of seizure and condemnation by the aggrieved belligerent. That seems to me a sound definition if you understand the word "risk" to mean that risk which is contemplated and recognized by the law of nations. Broadly stated then "contraband of war" is that which is so considered by the law of nations. The question which naturally follows is "What do you mean by the law of nations?" I answer that the law of nations is that system of rules respecting belligerent and neutral rights established by consent among the civilized and commercial nations of the world, partly written and partly arising out of custom and rendered stable by judicial decisions from time to time.

In my opinion, the expression contraband of war has a well-known and accepted meaning among the civilized commercial powers of the world. If that were not so we should not, as we do, find the expression used without definition in solemn treaties between the powers. The expression "contraband of war" is used without any definition of its meaning in the Treaty of Paris of the 16th April, 1856. The inference from that fact is, to my mind, irresistible that there was no definition needed, because the expression had the same definite meaning in the minds of all the plenipotentiaries of the Powers parties to that treaty.

. . . . What then was the meaning which it must fairly be assumed the Plenipotentiaries attached to the expression "contraband of war" as used by them in the Treaty of Paris? It seems to me that the Plenipotentiaries had in their minds the meaning which at the time attached to the expression "contraband of war" resulting from the decisions of the courts of law of the nations of Europe and America; principally indeed the decisions in the English Courts on cases arising during the Napoleonic War. What then is the result of those decisions? What meaning has been thereby attached to the expression "contraband of war"? The result has been to attach to that expression the following twofold meaning:—(1) Absolute contraband of war—which includes everything useful for war only; (2) That which is conditional contraband of war—which includes all things which though useful for both peace and war become contraband if destined for the purposes of war: excluding from the meaning of contraband of war such things as are useful for the purposes of peace only. "Provisions," consequently, come within the definition of conditional contraband only, if and when destined for the enemy's forces; otherwise they are excluded from the definition. That is, in my opinion, the true meaning to be attached to the expression "contraband of war," and that is the sense which, in my opinion, that expression bears on a true construction of the Declaration of the Plenipotentiaries who signed the Treaty of Paris of 1856.

That is, in my opinion, the sense in which the parties to the charter of the ship Prometheus must be taken to have understood the expression "contraband of war" when they agreed by clause 37, that the ship Prometheus was not to "carry any contraband of war." To construe that expression as meaning whatever might at any time, that is to say from time to time, be declared by Russia to be contraband, as the learned counsel for the owner contended I should, would be to import into the contract between the parties an element of uncertainty where none need exist. The contract was made in Hongkong, and therefore in the absence of evidence to the contrary which I could act upon the parties must be taken to have used the expression "contraband of war" in the sense in which it is understood in British courts of law, which is its sense in international law. It cannot be successfully contended that provisions would be regarded by British courts of law as unconditional contraband of war, or that there is any likelihood that they will ever take that view. Had this court been asked at any time between the signing of the charter party on the 10th February, 1904, and the issuing of the Russian declaration to construe the meaning of the words contraband of war it cannot be doubted that it would have excluded provisions from the category of unconditional contraband.

It is contended, however, that the court ought to place a different meaning on that expression, after, and in view of, the terms of the Russian declaration, inasmuch as Russia being a sovereign independent power has a prerogative right to declare whatever she pleases to be contraband of war in any war in which she may be engaged, and that the effect of the Russian declaration having been to make provisions unconditionally contraband the master of the ship Prometheus was excused from loading them on his ship. In this contention I am unable to concur. In the view which I take of the effect of the Declaration under the Treaty of Paris of 1856, and of the undertaking by the several powers signatory thereto, given in the Protocol No. 24, not to depart from the principles enunciated in the Declaration, I think that Russia was not at liberty to declare provisions unconditional contraband of war; and that her declaration in that respect could not affect the contract between the parties to this charter party, even supposing it could be held that contraband of war means, as used in the charter party, whatever Russia may consider as such: for Russia having been a party to the solemn declaration of "fixed principles" under the Treaty of Paris was not at liberty to disregard those principles and was therefore bound to recognize, and act upon, the generally accepted rule of international law that provisions are not unconditional contraband. In this view I am supported by the decision in the case of Pollard v. Bell, 8 T. R. 434, where it was laid down that it is not competent to one nation to add to the law of nations by its own arbitrary ordinances without the concurrence of other nations! . . .

Applying the principle of that case to the present case, I say that the Russian declaration including provisions among the list of articles absolutely contraband and as departing from the recognized custom of nations had no binding effect upon other nations, and consequently could not excuse the non-performance of the contract under the charter party between the Osaka Shosen Kaisha and the owners of the s. s. Prometheus. It was contended on behalf of the owners of the Prometheus that the term "law" as applied to this recognized system of principles and rules known as international law is an inexact expression, that there is, in other words, no such thing as international law; that there can be no such law binding upon all nations inasmuch as there is no sanction for such law, that is to say that there is no means by which obedience to such law can be imposed upon any given nation refusing obedience thereto. I do not concur in that contention. In my opinion a law may be established and become international, that is to say binding upon all nations, by the agreement of such nations to be bound thereby, although it may be impossible to enforce obedience thereto by any given nation party to the agreement. The resistance of a nation to a law to which it has agreed does not derogate from the authority of the law because that resistance cannot, perhaps, be overcome. Such resistance merely makes the resisting nation a breaker of the law to which it has given its adherence, but it leaves the law, to the establishment of which the resisting nation was a party, still subsisting. Could it be successfully contended that because any given person or body of persons possessed for the time being power to resist an established municipal law such law had no existence? The answer to such a contention would be that the law still existed, though it might not for the time being be possible to enforce obedience to it. My answer to the first question put to me by the arbitrator must therefore, for the reasons I have given, be (1) that the cargo intended to be loaded by the charterers on the steamship Prometheus was not contraband of war within the meaning of the charter party; (2) that the Russian declaration constituting provisions unconditional contraband was not binding upon neutrals who were no party thereto, and consequently has no bearing upon the construction of the charter party between the Osaka Shosen Kaisha and the owners of the ship Prometheus. . . . [1]

---

[1] Whether the court interpreted the charter-party correctly in this case is of course open to question. It would appear that it was the intention of the owners of the vessel that it should not be used for a purpose that would make it liable to capture, and this would suggest that the term "contraband" should have been liberally interpreted. This issue, however, has no bearing upon the principle of international law upon which the case was decided.

For the more recent development of "sanctions" in international law, see Fenwick, *op. cit.*, 40, 428.

CHAPTER II

THE RELATION OF INTERNATIONAL LAW TO NATIONAL LAW [1]

A. Precedence given to statute law by national courts.

International law is a law between states. As such it is binding upon each particular state and therefore upon all official departments of its government. At the same time, however, the government of the particular state is responsible to its own constitution and laws. In a conflict between the obligations of national constitutional law and those of international law the latter must, of practical necessity, give way to the former in so far as the domestic administration of the state is concerned. Query, what if in the application of statute law by national courts a rule of customary international law should be violated incidentally? [Mortensen v. Peters.] What if statute law were to conflict with the specific provisions of a treaty, would the national courts enforce the statute without regard to the international obligations created by the treaty? [Head Money Cases.] In either case the adverse decision of the national court would obviously not close the question; and the foreign state whose rights were affected, either directly or indirectly through the losses sustained by one of its nationals, might then bring its claims before the foreign office of the other state where the question of international law would be settled by diplomatic negotiation.

MORTENSEN v. PETERS.

Scotland, High Court of Justiciary, 1906.

14 Scots L. T. R. 227.

Lord Justice-General.—The facts of this case are that the appellant being a foreign subject, and master of a vessel registered in a foreign

---

[1] For a more detailed study of this subject, see Fenwick, *op. cit.*, Chap. IV; Oppenheim, *op. cit.*, Vol. I, §§ 20–25; Masters, International Law in National Courts; Wright, The Enforcement of International Law through Municipal Law in the United States; Picciotto, The Relation of International Law to the Law of England; Q. Wright, "International Law in Its Relation to Constitutional Law," Am. Journal, XVII (1923), 234; P. B. Potter, "Relative Authority of International and National Law," ibid., XIX (1925), 315; E. D. Dickinson, "Changing Concepts and the Doctrine of Incorporation," ibid., XXVI (1932), 239.

country, exercised the method of fishing known as otter-trawling at a point within the Moray Firth, more than three miles from the shore, but to the west of a line drawn from Duncansby Head, in Caithness, to Rattray Point in Aberdeenshire; that being thereafter found within British territory, to wit, at Grimsby, he was summoned to the Sheriff Court at Dornoch to answer to a complaint against him for having contravened the 7th section of the Herring Fishery Act, 1889, and the byelaw of the Fishery Board, thereunder made, and was convicted. . . .

I apprehend that the question is one of construction, and of construction only. In this Court we have nothing to do with the question of whether the Legislature has or has not done what foreign powers may consider a usurpation in a question with them. Neither are we a tribunal sitting to decide whether an act of the legislature is *ultra vires* as in contravention of generally acknowledged principles of international law. For us an Act of Parliament duly passed by Lords and Commons and assented to by the King, is supreme, and we are bound to give effect to its terms. The counsel for the appellant advanced the proposition that statutes creating offences must be presumed to apply (1) to British subjects; and (2) to foreign subjects in British territory; but that short of express enactment their application should not be further extended. The appellant is admittedly not a British subject, which excludes (1); and he further argued that the *locus delicti*, being in the sea beyond the three-mile limit, was not within British territory; and that consequently the appellant was not included in the prohibition of the statute. Viewed as general propositions the two presumptions put forward by the appellant may be taken as correct. This, however, advances the matter but little, for like all presumptions they may be redargued, and the question remains whether they have been redargued on this occasion.

The first thing to be noted is that the prohibition here, a breach of which constitutes the offence, is not an absolute prohibition against doing a certain thing, but a prohibition against doing it in a certain place. Now, when a Legislature, using words of admitted generality—"It shall not be lawful," &c., "Every person who," &c.—conditions an offence by territorial limits, it creates, I think, a very strong inference that it is, for the purpose specified, assuming a right to legislate for that territory against all persons whomsoever. . . .

It is said by the appellant that all this must give way to the consideration that International Law has firmly fixed that a *locus* such as this is beyond the limits of territorial sovereignty; and that consequently it is not to be thought that in such a place the Legislature could seek to affect any but the King's subjects.

It is a trite observation that there is no such thing as a standard of International Law, extraneous to the domestic law of a kingdom, to which appeal may be made. International Law, so far as this Court is concerned, is the body of doctrine regarding the international rights and duties of States which has been adopted and made part of the Law of Scotland. Now can it be said to be clear by the law of Scotland that the *locus* here is beyond what the Legislature may assert right to affect by legislation against all whomsoever for the purpose of regulating methods of fishing?

I do not think I need say anything about what is known as the three-mile limit. It may be assumed that within the three miles the territorial sovereignty would be sufficient to cover any such legislation as the present. It is enough to say that that is not a proof of the counter proposition that outside the three miles no such result could be looked for. The locus, although outside the three-mile limit, is within the bay known as the Moray Firth, and the Moray Firth, says the respondent, is *intra fauces terrae*. Now, I cannot say that there is any definition of what *fauces terrae* exactly are. But there are at least three points which go far to shew that this spot might be considered as lying therein.

1st. The *dicta* of the Scottish institutional writers seem to show that it would be no usurpation, according to the law of Scotland, so to consider it.

Thus, Stair, II, i. 5: "The vast ocean is common to all mankind as to navigation and fishing, which are the only uses thereof, because it is not capable of bounds; but when the sea is inclosed in bays, creeks, *or otherwise is capable of any bounds or meiths as within the points of such lands,* or within the view of such shores, then it may become proper, but with the reservation of passages for commerce as in the land." And Bell, Pr. Sec. 639: "The Sovereign . . . is proprietor of the narrow seas within cannon shot of the land, and the *firths*, gulfs, and bays around the Kingdom."

2nd. The same statute puts forward claims to what are at least analogous places. If attention is paid to the Schedule appended to section 6, many places will be found far beyond the three-mile limit— e. g., the Firth of Clyde near its mouth. I am not ignoring that it may be said that this in one sense is proving *idem per idem,* but none the less, I do not think the fact can be ignored.

3rd. There are many instances to be found in decided cases where the right of a nation to legislate for waters more or less landlocked or landembraced, although beyond the three-mile limit, has been admitted.

. . .

It seems to me therefore, without laying down the proposition that the Moray Firth is for every purpose within the territorial sovereignty, it can at least be clearly said that the appellant cannot make out his proposition that it is inconceivable that the British legislature should attempt for fishery regulation to legislate against all and sundry in such a place. And if that is so, then I revert to the considerations already stated which as a matter of construction make me think that it did so legislate. . . . [1]

HEAD MONEY CASES. EDYE AND ANOTHER v. ROBERTSON, COLLECTOR; CUNARD STEAMSHIP CO. v. SAME.

United States, Supreme Court, 1884.

112 U. S. 580. [28 L. ed. 798; 5 S. Ct. 247.]

These suits were brought to recover back sums collected at various times as duties on immigrants arriving in the United States, under the provision of the act of August 3, 1882, 23 Stat. 214, "that there shall be levied, collected, and paid a duty of fifty cents for each and every passenger not a citizen of the United States, who shall come by steam or sail vessel from a foreign port to any 'port within the United States." Protests were filed against each payment, and all other steps required as foundations for the actions were taken. In the Edye Case there was a trial, jury being waived, a finding of facts, a judgment, and exceptions. 18 Fed. Rep. 135. In the Cunard Cases judgment was entered in favor of the collector on demurrer to the complaints. The causes were brought here on writs of error. . . .

Mr. Justice Miller delivered the opinion of the court. . . .

Another objection to the validity of this act of Congress, is that it violates provisions contained in numerous treaties of our government with friendly nations. And several of the articles of these treaties are annexed to the careful brief of counsel. We are not satisfied that this act of Congress violates any of these treaties, on any just construction of them. Though laws similar to this have long been enforced by the State of New York in the great metropolis of foreign trade, where four-fifths of these passengers have been landed, no complaint has been made by any foreign nation to ours, of the violation of treaty obligations by the enforcement of those laws.

But we do not place the defence of the act of Congress against this objection upon that suggestion.

We are of opinion that, so far as the provisions in that act may be found to be in conflict with any treaty with a foreign nation, they must prevail in all the judicial courts of this country. We had supposed that the question here raised was set at rest in this court by the deci-

---

[1] While the court in this case had no alternative but to apply the act of Parliament, the British Government acknowledged the undue extension of authority beyond the three-mile limit and remitted the fine imposed upon Mortensen.

sion in the case of The Cherokee Tobacco, 11 Wall. 616. It is true, as suggested by counsel, that three judges of the court did not sit in the case, and two others dissented. But six judges took part in the decision, and the two who dissented placed that dissent upon the ground that Congress did not *intend* that the tax on tobacco should extend to the Cherokee tribe. They referred to the existence of the treaty which would be violated if the statute was so construed as persuasive against such a construction, but they nowhere intimated that, if the statute was correctly construed by the court, it was void because it conflicted with the treaty, which they would have done if they had held that view. On the point now in controversy it was therefore the opinion of all the judges who heard the case. See United States v. McBratney, 104 U. S. 621–3.

The precise question involved here, namely, a supposed conflict between an act of Congress imposing a customs duty, and a treaty with Russia on that subject, in force when the act was passed, came before the Circuit Court for the District of Massachusetts in 1855. It received the consideration of that eminent jurist, Mr. Justice Curtis of this court, who in a very learned opinion exhausted the sources of argument on the subject, holding that if there were such conflict the act of Congress must prevail in a judicial forum. Taylor v. Morton, 2 Curtis, 454. And Mr. Justice Field, in a very recent case in the Ninth Circuit, that of Ah Lung, 18 Fed. Rep. 28, on a writ of habeas corpus, has delivered an opinion sustaining the same doctrine in reference to a statute regulating the immigration of Chinamen into this country. In the Clinton Bridge Case, Woolworth, 150, 156, the writer of this opinion expressed the same views as did Judge Woodruff, on full consideration, in Ropes v. Clinch, 8 Blatchford, 304, and Judge Wallace, in the same circuit, in Bartram v. Robertson, 15 Fed. Rep. 212.

It is very difficult to understand how any different doctrine can be sustained.

A treaty is primarily a compact between independent nations. It depends for the enforcement of its provisions on the interest and the honor of the governments which are parties to it. If these fail, its infraction becomes the subject of international negotiations and reclamations, so far as the injured party chooses to seek redress, which may in the end be enforced by actual war. It is obvious that with all this the judicial courts have nothing to do and can give no redress. But a treaty may also contain provisions which confer certain rights upon the citizens or subjects of one of the nations residing in the territorial limits of the other, which partake of the nature of municipal law, and which are capable of enforcement as between private parties in the courts of the country. An illustration of this character is found in treaties, which regulate the mutual rights of citizens and subjects of the contracting nations in regard to rights of property by descent or inheritance, when the individuals concerned are aliens. The Constitution of the United States places such provisions as these in the same category as other laws of Congress by its declaration that "this Constitution and the laws made in pursuance thereof, and all treaties made or which shall be made under authority of the United States, shall be the supreme law of the land." A treaty, then, is a law of the land as an act of Congress is, whenever its provisions prescribe a rule by which the rights of the private citizen or subject may be determined. And when such rights are of a nature to be enforced in a court of justice, that court resorts to the treaty for a rule of decision for the case before it as it would to a statute.

But even in this aspect of the case there is nothing in this law which makes it irrepealable or unchangeable. The Constitution gives it no superiority over an act of Congress in this respect, which may be repealed or modified by an act of a later date. Nor is there anything in its essential character, or in the branches of the government by which the treaty is made, which gives it this superior sanctity.

A treaty is made by the President and the Senate. Statutes are made by the President, the Senate and the House of Representatives. The addition of the latter body to the other two in making a law certainly does not render it less entitled to respect in the matter of its repeal or modification than a treaty made by the other two. If there be any difference in this regard, it would seem to be in favor of an act in which all three of the bodies participate. And such is, in fact, the case in a declaration of war, which must be made by Congress, and which, when made, usually suspends or destroys existing treaties between the nations thus at war.

In short, we are of opinion that, so far as a treaty made by the United States with any foreign nation can become the subject of judicial cognizance in the courts of this country, it is subject to such acts as Congress may pass for its enforcement, modification, or repeal. . . .

The judgment of the Circuit Court in all the cases is

Affirmed.[1]

---

[1] SUPPLEMENTARY CASES. In the case of Murray v. The Charming Betsy, 2 Cranch 64 (1804), involving the application of the Non-Intercourse Act of 1800 in respect to the property of a native American citizen which, by reason of his long residence abroad had lost the national character belonging to its owner by birth, Chief Justice Marshall stated that "an act of Congress ought never to be construed to violate the law of nations if any other possible construction remains." (See below, p. 737, n. 1.) The condition attached to the statement clearly indicates the supremacy of national law before the national courts.

In the case of Cunard Steamship Co. v. Mellon, 262 U. S. 100 (1923) involving the application of the Eighteenth Amendment and the National Prohibition Act of 1919 to foreign vessels in port (see below, p. 316), the court was unwilling to read into the law an exception in favor of such vessels in spite of the established custom, recognized in a dissenting opinion, against interference by the local government with the internal affairs of the vessel.

B. Recognition by national courts of customary international law.

In cases where there is no constitutional provision or statute or special treaty conflicting with the general principles or established customs of international law, the courts of Great Britain and the United States have in general practice enforced the rule of international law as they interpreted it, and this policy has led them to announce broadly that international law was "part of the law of the land." The statement can be taken only in a restricted sense. It originated at a time when international law was far narrower in its scope than at the present day, consisting then of such broad general principles, based in part upon established customs and in part upon deductions from the "law of nature," that the occasion for a conflict with national law was not likely to arise. Hence a British court on one occasion went so far as to say that a particular statute was merely "declaratory" of what was already the law of the land. [Triquet v. Bath.] Within more recent years the relation of customary international law to national statute law has been more clearly defined; and while customary law is still applied in cases where there is no treaty or statute controlling the case the field of its application has grown steadily narrower in the presence of the increasing body of international conventions.

TRIQUET AND OTHERS v. BATH.

Great Britain, Court of King's Bench, 1764.

3 Burrow, 1478.

Mr. Blackstone, Mr. Thurlow, and Mr. Dunning, on behalf of the plaintiffs, shewed cause why the bill of Middlesex in each of these causes should not be set aside, and the bail-bond be cancelled.

The rule was made upon affidavits "Of the defendant's being a domestic servant of a foreign minister; and having taken all the proper steps to intitle him to the privilege of such domestics."

The only question was, "Whether the defendant (Chrispher Bath) was really and truly and *bona fide* a domestic servant of Count Haslang, the Bavarian minister"; or, "Whether his service was only colourable, and a mere sham and pretence calculated to protect him from the just demands of his creditors." . . .

Lord Mansfield.—This privilege of foreign ministers and their domestic servants depends upon the law of nations. The act of parliament of 7 Ann c. 12. is declaratory of it. All that is new in this act, is the clause which gives a summary jurisdiction for the punishment of the infractors of this law.

The act of parliament was made upon occasion of the Czar's ambassador being arrested. If proper application had been immediately made for his discharge from the arrest, the matter might and doubtless would have been set right. Instead of that, bail was put in, before any complaint was made. An information was filed by the then attorney general against the persons who were thus concerned, as infractors of the law of nations: and they were found guilty; but never brought up to judgment.

The Czar took the matter up, highly. No punishment would have been thought, by him an adequate reparation. Such a sentence as the Court could have given, he might have thought a fresh insult.

Another expedient was fallen upon and agreed to: this act of parliament passed, as an apology and humiliation from the whole nation. It was sent to the Czar, finely illuminated by an ambassador extraordinary, who made excuses in a solemn oration.

A great deal relative to this transaction and negotiation, appears in the annals of that time; and from a correspondence of the secretary of state there printed.

But the act was not occasioned by any doubt "Whether the law of nations, particularly the part relative to public ministers, was not part of the law of England; and the infraction, criminal; nor intended to vary, an iota from it."

I remember in a case before Lord Talbot, of Buvot v. Barbut [Cas. t. Talb. 281 (1737)], upon a motion to discharge the defendant, (who was in execution for not performing a decree,) "Because he was agent of commerce, commissioned by the king of Prussia, and received here as such;" the matter was very elaborately argued at the bar; and a solemn deliberate opinion given by the court. These questions arose and were discussed.—"Whether a minister could, by any act or acts, wave his privilege."—"Whether being a trader was any objection against allowing privilege to a minister, personally."—"Whether an agent of commerce, or even a consul, was intitled to the privileges of a public minister."—"What was the rule of decision: the act of parliament; or, the law of nations." Lord Talbot declared a clear opinion—"That the law of nations, in its full, extent, was part of the law of England."— "That the act of parliament was declaratory; and occasioned by a particular incident."—"That the law of nations was to be collected from the practice of different nations, and the authority of writers." Accordingly, he argued and determined from such instances, and the authority of Grotius, Barbeyrac, Binkershoek, Wiquefort, &c; there being no English writer of eminence, upon the subject.

I was counsel in this case; and have a full note of it.

I remember, too, Lord Hardwicke's declaring his opinion to the same effect; and denying, that Lord Chief Justice Holt ever had any doubt as to the law of nations being part of the law of England, upon the occasion of the arrest of the Russian ambassador.

Mr. Blackstone's principles are right: but as to the facts in the present case, the affidavits on the part of the defendant have out-sworn those on the part of the plaintiffs. . . . Lord Mansfield observed also, that the defendant was employed in the service of Monsieur Haslang, before the plaintiff took out his writ.

It was not to be expected, he said, that every particular act of the service should be particularly specified: it is enough, if an actual *bona fide* service be proved. And if such a service be sufficiently proved by affidavit, we must not, upon bare suspicion only, suppose it to have been merely colourable and collusive. . . .

Per Cur'.—Both Rules were made absolute; but without costs, by reason of the suspicious circumstances of this case.[1]

C. Judicial attitude towards alleged rules of customary law.

In the latter part of the nineteenth century, when the questions of international law presented to national courts came to deal with more specific issues, it was but natural that courts should inquire more carefully into the existence of an alleged rule of law upon which the determination of the case depended. Query, would mere citations from jurists and text-books be sufficient to indicate that the alleged rule of customary international law had been accepted as a binding rule by Great Britain in the absence of some more definite expression of the recognition of the rule by the government? Suppose that it could be shown that the alleged rule had been generally adopted by other nations, would that raise the presumption that it was binding upon a country which had not expressly adopted it? [West Rand Central Gold Mining Co. v. The King.]

WEST RAND CENTRAL GOLD MINING CO., LTD., v. THE KING.

Great Britain, King's Bench Division, 1905.

L. R. [1905] 2 K. B. 391.

Petition of right by the West Rand Central Gold Mining Company, Limited. . . .

LORD ALVERSTONE, C. J. In this case the Attorney-General, on behalf of the Crown, demurred to a petition of right presented in the month of June, 1904, by the West Rand Central Gold Mining Company, Limited. The petition of right alleged that two parcels of gold, amounting in all to the value of 3804 l., had been seized by officials of

---

[1] In the case of the Paquete Habana (above, p. 12) the court recognized the force of international custom (in respect to the exemption of fishing vessels from capture) even where there was no act of Congress prescribing a special exception of the kind. The statement made in that case of the relations between national and international law has since become almost classic.

the South African Republic—1104 l. on October 2 in course of transit from Johannesburg to Cape Town, and 2700 l. on October 9, taken from the bank premises of the petitioners. No further statement was made in the petition of the circumstances under which, or the right by which, the government of the Transvaal Republic claimed to seize the gold; but it was stated in paragraph 6: "That the gold was in each case taken possession of by, and on behalf of, and for the purposes of, the then existing government of the said Republic, and that the said government, by the laws of the said Republic, was under a liability to return the said gold, or its value, to your suppliants. None of the said gold has been returned to your suppliants, nor did the said government make any payment in respect thereof." The petition then alleged that a state of war commenced at 5 p. m. on October 11, 1899, that the forces of the late Queen conquered the Republic, and that by a proclamation of September 1, 1900, the whole of the territories of the Republic were annexed to, and became part of, Her Majesty's dominions, and that the government of the Republic ceased to exist. The petition then averred that by reason of the conquest and annexation Her Majesty succeeded to the sovereignty of the Transvaal Republic, and became entitled to its property; and that the obligation which vested in the government was binding upon his present Majesty the King.

Before dealing with the questions of law which were argued before us, we think it right to say that we must not be taken as acceding to the view that the allegations in the petition disclosed a sufficient ground for relief. The petition appears to us demurrable for the reason that it shews no obligation of a contractual nature on the part of the Transvaal government. For all that appears in the petition the seizure might have been an act of lawless violence. . . .

Lord Robert Cecil argued that all contractual obligations incurred by a conquered state, before war actually breaks out, pass upon annexation to the conqueror, no matter what was their nature, character, origin, or history. . . . His main proposition was divided into three heads: First, that, by international law, the sovereign of a conquering state is liable for the obligations of the conquered; secondly, that international law forms part of the law of England; and, thirdly, that rights and obligations, which were binding upon the conquered state, must be protected and can be enforced by the municipal courts of the conquering state.

In support of his first proposition Lord Robert Cecil cited passages from various writers on international law. In regard to this class of authority it is important to remember certain necessary limitations to its value. There is an essential difference, as to certainty and definiteness, between municipal law and a system or body of rules in regard to international conduct, which, so far as it exist at all (and its existence is assumed by the phrase "international law"), rests upon a concensus of civilized States, not expressed in any code or pact, nor possessing, in case of dispute, any authorized or authoritative interpreter; and capable, indeed, of proof, in the absence of some express international agreement, only by evidence of usage to be obtained from the action of nations in similar cases in the course of their history. It is obvious that, in respect of many questions that may arise, there will be room for difference of opinion as to whether such a consensus could be shown to exist. Perhaps it is in regard to the extraterritorial privileges of ambassadors, and in regard to the system of limits as to territorial waters, that it is least open to doubt or question. The views expressed by learned writers on international law have done in the past, and will do in the future, valuable service in helping to create the opinion by which the range of the consensus of civilized nations is enlarged. But in many instances their pronouncements must be regarded rather as the embodiments of their views as to what ought to be, from an ethical standpoint, the conduct of nations *inter se,* than the enunciation of a rule or practice so universally approved or assented to as to be fairly termed, even in the qualified sense in which that word can be understood in reference to the relations between independent political communities, ''law.'' The reference which these writers not infrequently make to stipulations in particular treaties as acceptable evidence of international law is as little convincing as the attempt, not unknown to our Courts, to establish a trade custom which is binding without being stated, by adducing evidence of express stipulations to be found in a number of particular contracts. . . .[1]

The second proposition urged by Lord Robert Cecil, that international law forms part of the law of England, requires a word of explanation and comment. It is quite true that whatever has received the common consent of civilized nations must have received the assent of our country, and that to which we have assented along with other nations in general may properly be called international law, and as such will be acknowledged and applied by our municipal tribunals when legitimate occasion arises for those tribunals to decide questions to which doctrines of international law may be relevant. But any doctrine so invoked must be one really accepted as binding between nations, and the international law sought to be applied must, like anything else, be proved by satisfactory evidence, which must shew either that the particular proposition put forward has been recognised and acted upon by our own country, or that it is of such a nature, and has been so widely and generally accepted, that it can hardly be supposed that any civilized State would repudiate it. The mere opinions of jurists, however eminent or learned, that it ought to be so recognised, are not in them-

---

[1] An omitted part of the opinion, dealing with the general principle of the alleged succession of a conquering state to the obligations of the conquered, is reproduced below, p. 105.

selves sufficient. They must have received the express sanction of international agreement, or gradually have grown to be part of international law by their frequent practical recognition in dealings between
various nations. We adopt the language used by Lord Russell of Kil-
lowen in his address at Saratoga in 1896 on the subject of international
law and arbitration: "What, then, is international law? I know no
better definition of it than that it is the sum of the rules or usages which
civilized States have agreed shall be binding upon them in their dealings with one another." In our judgment, the second proposition for
which Lord Robert Cecil contended in his argument before us ought to
be treated as correct only if the term "international law" is understood in the sense, and subject to the limitations of application, which
we have explained. The authorities which he cited in support of the
proposition are entirely in accord with and, indeed, well illustrate our
judgment upon this branch of the arguments advanced on behalf of the
suppliants; for instance, Barbuit's Case [Cas. t. Talb. 281], Triquet v.
Bath [3 Burr. 1478], and Heathfield v. Chilton [4 Burr. 2016] are cases
in which the Courts of law have recognised and have given effect to the
privilege of ambassadors as established by international law. But the
expressions used by Lord Mansfield when dealing with the particular
and recognised rule of international law on this subject, that the law
of nations forms part of the law of England, ought not to be construed
so as to include as part of the law of England opinions of text-writers
upon a question as to which there is no evidence that Great Britain has
ever assented, and *a fortiori* if they are contrary to the principles of her
laws as declared by her Courts. The cases of Wolff v. Oxholm [6 M. & S.
92] and Rex v. Keyn [2 Ex. D. 63] are only illustrations of the same
rule—namely, that questions of international law may arise, and may
have to be considered in connection with the administration of municipal law. . . .

We are of opinion, for the reasons given, that no right on the part
of the suppliants is disclosed by the petition which can be enforced as
against His Majesty in this or in any municipal Court; and we therefore allow the demurrer, with costs.[1]

---

[1] In the case of Queen v. Keyn (below, p. 485), involving the jurisdiction of
the local criminal court to try an alien for alleged manslaughter committed
within the three-mile limit, the higher court, on appeal, held by a majority that
the court had no jurisdiction in the absence of an act of Parliament. The case
has been frequently cited as indicating that the court did not regard the established custom with respect to the territorial character of the marginal sea as
forming "part of the law of the land"; but in fact the majority of the court
reached its conclusion upon points of constitutional rather than international
law. The existence of the alleged custom was even questioned by several of the
majority.

CHAPTER III

STATES AS SUBJECTS OF INTERNATIONAL LAW [1]

A. Kinds of states.

International law recognizes a distinction between states on the one hand, and semi-sovereign states, protectorates and dependencies on the other. The terms "sovereign" and "semi-sovereign" are a relic of traditional political thought and have little theoretical justification to-day. They were, however, in common use during the nineteenth century and they are still on occasion referred to as a basis of classification. A sovereign state holds full membership in the community of nations and possesses all the rights and duties of a state without any substantial qualification or limitation. If there be question of the exemption of its property from the jurisdiction of a foreign state, or a question of the privileges to be accorded to its diplomatic representatives, the sovereign state may claim the full benefit of the established rules of international law. On the other hand semi-sovereign states, protectorates, dependencies may claim only in a limited degree, if at all, the rights of such membership. Query, is the head of a semi-sovereign state entitled to personal exemption from the jurisdiction of the courts of a foreign state and is his property likewise immune from suit? The decision would depend in part upon the relationship existing between the two states and would be determined upon political rather than legal grounds. [The Charkieh.]

International law recognizes that *de facto* communities in revolt against the state of which they were formerly a part, whether as colonial dependencies or as members of a federal state, may, under certain circumstances, be accorded a temporary legal status pending the final determination of their *de jure* status. It is, moreover, left to each existing state to determine for itself its policy with respect to such inchoative states, subject to the general rule that the recognition of their *de facto* status shall not prejudice the rights of the state against which they are in rebellion. Query, may the rights of belligerents be accorded to *de facto* states during the period of their transitional status? To what extent would the domestic governmental functions of such "states," such

---

[1] For a more detailed study of this subject, see Fenwick, *op. cit.,* Chap. VI, pp. 86–106; Chap. VII, pp. 107–114; Oppenheim, *op. cit.,* Vol. I, §§ 85–101; Moore, Digest of International Law, Vol. I, Chap. III, §§ 27–42; Hyde, International Law, Vol. I, §§ 12–29; 36–42.

as the laws governing the validity of contracts, be given recognition by third states, notably the state of which they were formerly a part, in the event that their *de facto* status should fail to become *de jure*? [Thorington v. Smith.]

THE CHARKIEH.

Great Britain, High Court of Admiralty, 1873.

L. R. 4 Adm. and Eccl. 59.

SIR ROBERT PHILLIMORE. This is a cause instituted on behalf of the Netherlands Steamship Company, the owners of the steamship Batavier, and on behalf of the master, crew, and passengers thereof, against the screw steamship Charkieh and her freight, for damages arising out of a collision between the Batavier and the Charkieh in the river Thames, on the 19th of October, 1872.

The cause was instituted and the Charkieh was arrested by a warrant from this Court on the 21st of October.

No appearance was at that time entered on behalf of the owners of the Charkieh, but in the month of November an application was made on behalf of his Highness Ismail Pacha, Khedive of Egypt, to the Court of Queen's Bench for a prohibition to restrain this Court from proceeding further in the suit, and a rule nisi was granted, which rule was, after argument, on the 23rd of January, 1873, discharged. [Law Rep. 8 Q. B. 197.]

It appears from the report that the Court of Queen's Bench expressed no opinion upon the question which it was sought to raise on the application for a prohibition, deciding only that the question was one upon which this Court was specially qualified to adjudicate. Since this decision an appearance has been entered under protest for his Highness Ismail Pacha, the Khedive of Egypt, the owner of the Charkieh, and Admiral Latif Pacha, Minister of Marine of the government of Egypt. The pleadings on protest have been filed; they consist of a petition on behalf of his Highness the Khedive, an answer on behalf of the owners of the Batavier, a reply, and a conclusion. The petition concludes with a prayer to this Court—[His lordship here read the prayer of the petition].

The principal averments of fact and law in the petition are the following: That the Charkieh is the property of his Highness Ismail Pacha, the Khedive of Egypt, as reigning sovereign of the state of Egypt, and is a public vessel of the government and semi-sovereign state of Egypt. . . .

The answer, in substance, sets up that the Charkieh came to England on the footing of an ordinary merchant vessel, and was so treated without objection in all respects by the proper public authorities of England. That she was regularly advertised as a merchant vessel when about to leave Alexandria for England, and when again about to return, on the former occasion carrying cargo on the terms of ordinary bills of lading. It appears from the evidence that she was chartered to an English subject for the voyage to Alexandria.

The answer further submits that the Khedive "is not such a reigning sovereign as to entitle him or the government of Egypt to have accorded to the Charkieh by the comity of nations or otherwise the privileges or immunities of a public vessel of war of an independent sovereign or state, or the privilege of freedom from arrest and process in this suit." . . .

From these averments in the pleadings, and these facts in the evidence, the following questions arise:

1. Is the international status of the Khedive that of sovereign prince of Egypt?

2. Is he entitled by virtue of that status to claim the exemption of this ship from the jurisdiction of this Court?

3. If he be entitled to this privilege, has he waived or forfeited it?

I proceed to consider these questions in their order, and first, as to the international status of His Highness the Khedive. Very scanty evidence as to this status of the Khedive was produced before me at the hearing of the case. I was told by the counsel for his Highness that it was considered improper to offer evidence upon this subject, that it was my duty to take official cognisance of that status, and to obtain, by reference to the Foreign Office, any information which I might think necessary. Whether this was, or was not, the right course on the part of counsel to adopt, I do not now stop to inquire. I have endeavoured to inform myself, and have had recourse to the following sources of knowledge:

1. The general history of the government of Egypt.

2. The firmans which contain the public law of the Ottoman Empire on this subject.

3. The European treaties, which concern the relations between Egypt and the Porte.

4. The answer which the Foreign Office has furnished to an inquiry which I thought it my duty to make. . . .

What were the relations at this epoch [1806–1832] existing between the Khedive and the Porte, and what was the nature and character of the authority of the former, so far as foreign states are connected with these considerations? Did they entitle the Khedive to the privilege of the sovereign of an independent state? These are questions which must be answered, like all others appertaining to international jurisprudence, by a reference to usage, authority, and the reason of the thing.

Many accredited writers and jurists have drawn a distinction, which seems not to have escaped the framer of the Khedive's petition on protest now before me—between a sovereignty absolute and pure, and that less complete and perfect dominion to which the name of half-sovereignty (demi-souverain) has been given. I am inclined to think that the sovereign of a state in the latter category may be entitled to require from foreign states the consideration and privileges which are unquestionably incident to the sovereign of a state who is in the former category. There are also certain acts of feudal homage, or, as jurists say, *servitutes juris gentium,* which do not disentitle the state obliged to them to an international existence as a separate state.

Some examples of half sovereignties are to be found in history. Some of the smaller states (halb souverain) of the German confederation, before it was virtually destroyed by Napoleon's confederation of the Rhine, and formally extinguished by the abdication of the Emperor Francis in 1806, also furnished examples of states cum imminutione imperii—to borrow the expression of Grotius . . . —but entitled to be treated as states by foreign powers. The old feudal relations of the Dukes of Burgundy, Normandy, and Brittany to France did not, I believe, prevent these princes from being considered as sovereigns at home and abroad, and from being entitled to be represented by ambassadors at foreign courts. . . .

It may, moreover, be that, if such a status existed *de facto,* it would not be the province of the tribunals of a foreign state to look beyond the fact, or to inquire minutely or at all into the history of its establishment. International law has no concern with the form, character, or power of a state, if, through the medium of a government, it has such an independent existence as to render it capable of entertaining international relations with other states. An apt illustration of this position is furnished by the status accorded by European Powers in more modern times to what were once commonly called the Barbary States. . . .

If, at this period, I had been obliged to decide whether the Pacha of Egypt was entitled to the privilege of a sovereign in this country, my decision would have been influenced by a regard to the *de facto* sovereign rights apparently exercised at this period by his Highness; and perhaps the analogy of an European state having absolute dominion over its own subjects with feudal subordination to another state might have been cited with effect.

Though, even in this crisis of the history of Egypt, when the independence of that country was so nearly established, it must be observed that no attempt appears to have been made on behalf of the Pacha to exercise the principal international attribute of sovereignty, namely, the jus legationis, to be represented by an ambassador or diplomatic agent at the court of foreign sovereigns; nor is there any reason to believe that such an attempt, if made, would have been successful.

But in the interval between 1833 A. D. and 1841 A. D. the scene is greatly changed. The actors remain, but play very different parts.

Nor is it unimportant to observe, with reference to the question immediately before me, that the stream of Egyptian political history, . . . has ever since this epoch been greatly affected by the currents of European diplomacy. . . . Mohammed Ali and Ibrahim, in 1834 A. D., pursued the scheme of uniting all the provinces belonging to the caliphate under their Government; . . . But in 1840 A. D., Mohammed Ali was made aware that the European powers would not allow an Arab empire to be established on the ruins of the Ottoman state.

England sent an agent to warn the Pacha of his danger, and, in answer to a statement of his rights, the following language was used: "I have to instruct you," said Lord Palmerston to Colonel Hodges, the agent employed, "on the next occasion on which Mohammed Ali shall speak to you of his rights, to say to his highness, that you are instructed by your Government to remind him that he has no rights except such as the Sultan has conferred upon him; that the only legitimate authority which he possesses is the authority which has been delegated to him by the Sultan over a portion of the Sultan's dominions, and which has been entrusted to him for the sole purpose of being used in the interest and in obedience to the orders of the Sultan; . . . " (Correspondence relating to the affairs of the Levant presented to Parliament in 1841. pt. 1. p. 592).

And on the 18th of July, 1840, Lord Palmerston wrote to Colonel Hodges as follows: "You will see that orders have been given to the British fleet to act at once, by cutting off the communication between Syria and Egypt, and by helping the Syrians. If Mehemet Ali should complain of this, and of its being done without notice, you will remind him civilly that we are the allies of the Sultan, and have a right to help the faithful subjects of the Sultan in maintaining their allegiance, and to assist the Sultan against those of his subjects who are in revolt against him, as Mehemet Ali is; and that Mehemet Ali, not being an independent sovereign with whom the Four Powers have any political relations, those Powers are not bound to give him any notice of their intended proceedings" (*Ibid.*, pt. 2, p. 5). . . .

Have events subsequent to this epoch made this claim, then untenable, capable of being sustained? Surely not; for the principles of international policy enunciated in these despatches were fully carried into execution by the convention of the 15th of July, 1840, . . . by which Austria, England, Prussia, and Russia concurred in the determination to protect the Porte by coercive measures, if necessary, against the Pacha. Whether the Pacha should be a sovereign prince or a subject, however powerful, of the Porte, seems to have depended on the result of this war. But the consequence of this European intervention was the rapid overthrow of the Pacha's power in Syria; after which the Sultan issued to the Pacha the firman of the 13th of February, 1841, . . .

The first firman of the 13th of February, 1841 (of which I have only the French translation) begins by reciting the act of submission (l'acte de soumission) by the Pacha, and the experience which he has acquired during the time he has occupied the position of "Gouverneur de L' Égypte," and proceeds:—"Je t'accorde le gouvernement de l' Égypte dans ses anciennes limites, avec le privilége additionnel de l'hérédité." Certain conditions are added as to the succession of his heir in the direct male line, on the failure of which the Porte is to confer the government on some other person (Correspondence relating to the affairs of the Levant, pt. 3, p. 436). And then follows this important qualification (at p. 437): "Bien que les Pachas d'Égypte ayent obtenu le privilége de l' hérédité, ils doivent cependant être considérés quant à la préséance comme étant sur un pied d' égalité avec les autres Vizirs, ils seront traités comme les autres Vizirs de ma Sublime Porte, et recevront les mêmes titres que l' on donne aux autres Vizirs quand on leur écrit."

All the treaties concluded, or to be concluded, between the Porte and friendly powers "seront complétement mis à l' exécution dans la province de l' Égypte aussi;" so also the fundamental laws contained in the Hatti-Sheriff of Gulhané (3rd of November, 1839, State Papers, vol. 31, p. 1239). All taxes are to be imposed and received in the name of the Sultan, and "attendu que les Égyptiens aussi sont les sujets de ma Sublime Porte," certain regulations are to be made to prevent their being harassed by the manner of their imposition. The amount of annual tribute is to be fixed. The army is not to exceed 18,000 men, "Mais vu que les troupes de terre et de mer de l'Égypte sont instituées pour le service de ma Sublime Porte, il sera permis, en temps de guerre, de les porter au nombre qui aura été jugé convenable par ma Sublime Porte."

The troops are to carry the same colours as those of the Porte. . . .

The Court of Chancery, when a plaintiff averred in his bill that a certain republic in Central America had been recognised as an independent government, put itself in communication with the Foreign Office, and after such communication, declared itself authorized to state that the republic in question had never been recognized by the government of this country, and on the ground that what was pleaded was "historically false," allowed a demurrer to the bill: Taylor v. Barclay. [2 Sim. 213.] I have communicated with the Foreign Office, and have received the following answer to my questions, viz.: "that the Khedive has not been and is not now recognised by Her Majesty as reigning sovereign of the state of Egypt." "He is recognised by Her Majesty's government as the hereditary ruler of the province of Egypt under the supremacy of the Sultan of Turkey."

Upon all these facts I have arrived at the conclusion that, independently of any other consideration, his Highness the Khedive has failed

to establish his claim to exempt his vessel from the process of this
Court. . . .

Upon all grounds therefore, namely,

First, that his highness the Khedive, however exalted his position and
distinguished his rank, has failed to establish that he is entitled to the
privileges of a sovereign prince, according to the criteria of sovereignty
required by the reason of the thing, and by the usage and practice of
nations as expounded by accredited writers upon international jurisprudence;

Secondly, that, on the assumption he is entitled to such privilege, it
would not oust the jurisdiction of this Court in the particular proceeding which has been instituted against this ship; [1]

And, thirdly, that, assuming the privilege to exist, it has been waived
with reference to this ship by the conduct of the person who claims it;

I pronounce against the protest, and I think I must in justice to the
suitor give him the costs of these proceedings.

Having regard to the importance of the case, if any leave of the Court
be required in order to appeal from this decision, I will readily give
the requisite permission.

THORINGTON v. SMITH.

United States, Supreme Court, 1868.

8 Wallace, 1. [19 L. ed. 361.]

Appeal from the District Court for the Middle District of Alabama,
the case being this:

In November, 1864, Thorington being the owner of a piece of land
adjoining the city of Montgomery, Alabama, sold it to Smith and
Hartley, all parties being then resident of Montgomery. At the time
of this sale the late rebellion was still in active operation and had been
so for more than three years. Alabama, or this part of it, was at the
time in the occupation of the military and civil authorities of the rebel
States, and the Federal government exercised no authority there. There
was no gold or silver coin in use, nor any notes of the United States, such
as made the circulation of the loyal portion of the country. The only
currency in any ordinary use, or in which current daily business could
be at all carried on, were treasury notes of the Confederate States, notes
in form and general aspect like bank bills, and by which the Confederate States of America promised to pay the bearer the sum named

---

[1] The dictum of the court on this point, that a proceeding *in rem* against a
public owned vessel engaged in trade would not violate any established immunity is not in accord with subsequent decisions. See below, p. 326.

in them, "two years after the ratification of a treaty of peace between the Confederate States and the United States of America." . . .

The price agreed to be paid by Smith and Hartley, for the land which they purchased was $45,000. Of this sum $35,000 were paid at the execution of the deed in Confederate States treasury notes; and for the residue a note was executed thus:

Montgomery, November 28th, 1864.

$10,000.

One day after date, we, or either of us, promise to pay Jack Thorington, or bearer, ten thousand dollars, for value received in real estate, sold and delivered by said Thorington to us this day, as per his deed to us of this date: this note, part of the same transaction, is hereby declared as a lien or mortgage on said real estate situate and adjoining the city of Montgomery.

W. D. SMITH.
J. H. HARTLEY.

The rebellion being suppressed in 1865, the Confederate States treasury notes became, of course, worthless, and Thorington, in 1867, filed a bill in the court below against his purchasers, who were still in possession, for the enforcement of the vendor's lien, claiming the $10,000 in the only money now current, to wit, lawful money of the United States. . . .

The court below, admitting the evidence to prove that the note was in fact made for payment in Confederate States treasury notes, and sustaining, apparently, the view of the purchasers that the contract was illegal because to be paid in such notes, dismissed the bill.

The questions before this court upon the appeal, were these:

1. Can a contract for the payment of Confederate notes, made during the late rebellion, between parties residing within the so-called Confederate States, be enforced at all in the courts of the United States?

2. Can evidence be received to prove that a promise expressed to be for the payment of dollars was, in fact, made for the payment of any other than lawful dollars of the United States? . . . .

THE CHIEF JUSTICE [CHASE] delivered the opinion of the court. . . .

The first question is by no means free from difficulty. It cannot be questioned that the Confederate notes were issued in furtherance of an unlawful attempt to overthrow the government of the United States, by insurrectionary force. Nor is it a doubtful principle of law that no contracts made in aid of such an attempt can be enforced through the courts of the country whose government is thus assailed. But, was the contract of the parties to this suit a contract of that character? Can it be fairly described as a contract in aid of the rebellion?

In examining this question the state of that part of the country in which it was made must be considered. It is familiar history, that early in 1861 the authorities of seven States, supported, as was alleged, by popular majorities, combined for the overthrow of the National Union, and for the establishment, within its boundaries, of a separate and independent confederation. A governmental organization, representing these States, was established at Montgomery in Alabama, first under a provisional constitution, and afterwards under a constitution intended to be permanent. In the course of a few months, four other States acceded to this confederation, and the seat of the central authority was transferred to Richmond, in Virginia. It was, by the central authority thus organized, and under its direction, that civil war was carried on upon a vast scale against the government of the United States for more than four years. Its power was recognized as supreme in nearly the whole of the territory of the States confederated in insurrection. It was the actual government of all the insurgent States, except those portions of them protected from its control by the presence of the armed forces of the National government.

What was the precise character of this government in contemplation of law?

It is difficult to define it with exactness. Any definition that may be given may not improbably be found to require limitation and qualification. But the general principles of law relating to *de facto* government will, we think, conduct us to a conclusion sufficiently accurate.

There are several degrees of what is called *de facto* government.[1]

Such a government, in its highest degree, assumes a character very closely resembling that of a lawful government. This is when the usurping government expels the regular authorities from their customary seats and functions, and establishes itself in their place, and so becomes the actual government of a country. The distinguishing characteristic of such a government is, that adherents to it in war against the government *de jure* do not incur the penalties of treason; and under certain limitations, obligations assumed by it in behalf of the country, or otherwise, will, in general, be respected by the government *de jure* when restored. . . .

It is very certain that the Confederate government was never acknowledged by the United States as a *de facto* government in this sense [referring to instances cited by the court from English history]. Nor was it acknowledged as such by other powers. No treaty was made by it with any civilized state. No obligations of a National character were created by it, binding after its dissolution, on the States which it represented, or on the National government. From a very early period of

---

[1] The student should note that throughout this opinion the word "government" is used when in point of international law the word "state" should have been used. There was no revolt on the part of the separate Confederate states against the individual state governments under whose authority contracts such as the one in question were entered into. The revolt was against the larger Federal union from which the smaller group was seeking to detach itself.

the civil war to its close, it was regarded as simply the military representative of the insurrection against the authority of the United States.

But there is another description of government, called also by publicists a government *de facto,* but which might, perhaps, be more aptly denominated a government of paramount force. Its distinguishing characteristics are (1), that its existence is maintained by active military power, within the territories, and against the rightful authority of an established and lawful government; and (2), that while it exists, it must necessarily be obeyed in civil matters by private citizens who, by acts of obedience, rendered in submission to such force, do not become responsible, as wrong-doers, for those acts, though not warranted by the laws of the rightful government. Actual governments of this sort are established over districts differing greatly in extent and conditions. They are usually administered directly by military authority, but they may be administered, also, by civil authority, supported more or less directly by military force.

One example of this sort of government is found in the case of Castine, in Maine, reduced to British possession during the war of 1812. From the 1st of September, 1814, to the ratification of the treaty of peace in 1815, according to the judgment of this court in United States v. Rice, [4 Wheaton, 253] "the British government exercised all civil and military authority over the place." "The authority of the United States over the territory was suspended, and the laws of the United States could no longer be rightfully enforced there, or be obligatory upon the inhabitants who remained and submitted to the conqueror. By the surrender, the inhabitants passed under a temporary allegiance to the British government, and were bound by such laws, and such only, as it chose to recognize and impose." It is not to be inferred from this that the obligations of the people of Castine as citizens of the United States were abrogated. They were suspended merely by the presence, and only during the presence, of the paramount force. A like example is found in the case of Tampico, occupied during the war with Mexico by the troops of the United States. It was determined by this court, in Fleming v. Page, [9 Howard, 614] that, although Tampico did not become a port of the United States in consequence of that occupation, still, having come, together with the whole State of Tamaulipas, of which it was part, into the exclusive possession of the National forces, it must be regarded and respected by other nations as the territory of the United States. These were cases of temporary possession of territory by lawful and regular governments at war with the country of which the territory so possessed was part.

The central government established for the insurgent States differed from the temporary governments at Castine and Tampico in the circumstance, that its authority did not originate in lawful acts of regular war, but it was not, on that account, less actual or less supreme. And we think that it must be classed among the governments of which these are examples. It is to be observed that the rights and obligations of a belligerent were conceded to it, in its military character, very soon after the war began, from motives of humanity and expediency by the United States. The whole territory controlled by it was thereafter held to be enemies' territory, and the inhabitants of that territory were held, in most respects, for enemies. To the extent, then, of actual supremacy, however unlawfully gained, in all matters of government within its military lines, the power of the insurgent government cannot be questioned. That supremacy did not justify acts of hostility to the United States. How far it should excuse them must be left to the lawful government upon the re-establishment of its authority. But it made obedience to its authority, in civil and local matters, not only a necessity but a duty. Without such obedience, civil order was impossible.

It was by this government exercising its power throughout an immense territory, that the Confederate notes were issued early in the war, and these notes in a short time became almost exclusively the currency of the insurgent States. As contracts in themselves, except in the contingency of successful revolution, these notes were nullities; for, except in that event, there could be no payer. They bore, indeed, this character upon their face, for they were made payable only "after the ratification of a treaty of peace between the Confederate States and the United States of America." While the war lasted, however, they had a certain contingent value, and were used as money in nearly all the business transactions of many millions of people. They must be regarded, therefore, as a currency, imposed on the community by irresistible force.

It seems to follow as a necessary consequence from this actual supremacy of the insurgent government, as a belligerent, within the territory where it circulated, and from the necessity of civil obedience on the part of all who remained in it, that this currency must be considered in courts of law in the same light as if it had been issued by a foreign government, temporarily occupying a part of the territory of the United States. Contracts stipulating for payments in this currency, cannot be regarded for that reason only, as made in aid of the foreign invasion in the one case, or of the domestic insurrection in the other. They have no necessary relations to the hostile government, whether invading or insurgent. They are transactions in the ordinary course of civil society, and, though they may indirectly and remotely promote the ends of the unlawful government, are without blame, except when proved to have been entered into with actual intent to further invasion or insurrection. We cannot doubt that such contracts should be enforced in the courts of the United States, after the restoration of peace, to the extent of their just obligation. The first question, therefore, must receive an affirmative answer.

The second question, Whether evidence can be received to prove that a promise, made in one of the insurgent States, and expressed to be for the payment of dollars, without qualifying words, was in fact made for the payment of any other than lawful dollars of the United States? is next to be considered.

It is quite clear that a contract to pay dollars, made between citizens of any State of the Union, while maintaining its constitutional relations with the National government, is a contract to pay lawful money of the United States, and cannot be modified or explained by parol evidence. But it is equally clear, if in any other country, coins or notes denominated dollars should be authorized of different value from the coins or notes which are current here under that name, that, in a suit upon a contract to pay dollars, made in that country, evidence would be admitted to prove what kind of dollars were intended, and, if it should turn out that foreign dollars were meant, to prove their equivalent value in lawful money of the United States. Such evidence does not modify or alter the contract. It simply explains an ambiguity, which, under the general rules of evidence, may be removed by parol evidence.

We have already seen that the people of the insurgent States, under the Confederate government were, in legal contemplation, substantially in the same condition as inhabitants of districts of a country occupied and controlled by an invading belligerent. The rules which would apply in the former case would apply in the latter; and, as in the former case, the people must be regarded as subjects of a foreign power, and contracts among them be interpreted and enforced with reference to the conditions imposed by the conqueror, so in the latter case, the inhabitants must be regarded as under the authority of the insurgent belligerent power actually established as the government of the country, and contracts made with them must be interpreted and enforced with reference to the condition of things created by the acts of the governing power.

. . . Our answer to the second question is, therefore, also in the affirmative. We are clearly of opinion that such evidence must be received in respect to such contracts, in order that justice may be done between the parties, and that the party entitled to be paid in these Confederate dollars can recover their actual value at the time and place of the contract, in lawful money of the United States. . . .

It follows that the decree of the Circuit Court must be *reversed*, and the cause remanded, for further hearing and decree, in conformity with this opinion.[1]

---

[1] SUPPLEMENTARY CASES. During the eighteenth and the early part of the nineteenth century the status of the Barbary Pirates, as they were called, Morocco, Algiers, Tunis and Tripoli, presented problems for judicial determination. In the case of the Helena, 4 C. Rob. 3 (1801), the court had to determine the validity of a title to the vessel obtained by purchase from the Dey of Algiers who had captured the vessel from the original British owner. The original owner claimed that the Algerines were no more than pirates and that no legal conversion of property could be "derived from their piratical seizure." The court held that "although their [the Algerines'] notions of justice, to be

observed between nations, differ from those which we entertain, we do not, on
that account, venture to call in question their public acts"; and finding that "the
act of capture and condemnation was not a mere private act of depredation"
the court refused under the circumstances to annul the several acts of transfer.

Query, would the limited recognition frequently given to *de facto* states extend
so far as to accept as valid a law confiscating the property of enemy aliens?
In Williams v. Bruffy, 96 U. S. 176 (1878), involving an action of assumpsit
brought by Williams, a resident of Pennsylvania, against the administrator of
Bruffy's estate for goods sold to Bruffy, a resident of Virginia, in March 1861,
the Supreme Court overruled the plea of the administrator that, in consequence
of a law of the Confederate States of August 30, 1861, Bruffy had been forced
to pay into the Confederate treasury the debt owing to Williams. But while
the court was unwilling to recognize any validity in the legislation of the Confederate States, explaining away Thorington v. Smith in that respect, it observed
that the legislation of the individual states of the Confederacy stood "on very
different grounds." "As far," said the court, "as the acts of the States did not
impair, or tend to impair the supremacy of the national authority, or the just
rights of citizens under the Constitution, they are, in general, to be treated as
valid and binding." In Keith v. Clark, 97 U. S. 454 (1878), involving a suit by
Keith to recover from the collector of taxes a sum of lawful money paid under
protest when the collector refused to receive in payment notes of the Bank of
Tennessee issued during the period of insurrection, the Supreme Court held that
the constitutional amendment, adopted by Tennessee in 1865, declaring the issues
in question void and forbidding their receipt in payment of taxes, was in violation of the obligation of the charter of the bank granted in 1838 in which it
was agreed that the state should receive all of the issues of circulating notes in
payment of taxes. "The political society," said the court, "which in 1796 became
a State of the Union by the name of the State of Tennessee, is the same which is
now represented as one of those States in the Congress of the United States.
Not only is it the same body politic now, but it has always been the same. There
has been perpetual succession and perpetual identity." Hence the court held
that as the bank was not shown to have been engaged during the insurrection in
other than a legitimate banking business it was entitled to the protection of the
Constitution.

In the earlier case of Texas v. White, 7 Wall. 700 (1869) the court, in maintaining that Texas was still a State of the Union in spite of the part it took in
the war of the rebellion, held that while her "acts of ordinary legislation were
valid" it was otherwise in regard to the delivery of the bonds to White in payment for military supplies. A distinction was drawn between "acts necessary
to peace and good order among citizens" and "acts in furtherance or support of
rebellion."

In addition to the recognition of the *de facto* status of belligerent communities
the United States has on occasion recognized a "status of insurgency" the effect
of which has been to bring into operation the neutrality laws of the United
States without, however, conceding to the insurgents the right of visit and search
at sea. In the case of the Three Friends, 166 U. S. 1 (1897), forfeiture proceedings were instituted against a vessel which had been fitted out with supplies
for the Cuban insurgents then in rebellion against Spain. The libel alleged a
violation of Rev. Stat. 5283 in that the vessel had been fitted out with intent
that she should be employed "in the service of any foreign prince or state, or of
any colony, district or people" to commit hostilities against a foreign prince or
state with which the United States was at peace. The Supreme Court, reversing
the decision of the lower court, held that the word "people," taken in connection
with the words "colony" and "district" covered in their judgment "any insurgent

or insurrectionary 'body of people acting together, undertaking and conducting hostilities,' although its belligerency has not been recognized." The neutrality laws were therefore held applicable and the vessel was condemned.

Query, what was the international status of Cuba during the period of American occupation of the island following the treaty of peace with Spain? In Neely v. Henkel, 180 U. S. 109 (1901), involving the extradition of a fugitive criminal from the United States to Cuba during the period of military occupation by the United States, the Supreme Court held that in spite of the relinquishment by Spain of sovereignty over the island and its occupation by the United States it was not "in any constitutional, legal or international sense, a part of the territory of the United States." "It is true," said the court, "that as between Spain and the United States—indeed, as between the United States and all foreign nations—Cuba, upon the cessation of hostilities with Spain and after the Treaty of Paris was to be treated as if it were conquered territory. But as between the United States and Cuba that Island is territory held in trust for the inhabitants of Cuba to whom it rightfully belongs and to whose exclusive control it will be surrendered when a stable government shall have been established by their voluntary action." Neely was therefore extradited to Cuba as being a "foreign country" under the statute.

The status of the "native states" of India has presented a number of problems to the British courts. While these "states" are definitely not states at international law, they have been as a general rule accorded that status under British law. In the case of Mighell v. Sultan of Johore, [1894] 1 Q. B. 149, decided in 1893, involving an action against the Sultan, under the name of Albert Baker, for breach of promise of marriage the court held that the defendant was "an independent sovereign" and that such a sovereign was entitled to immunity from the jurisdiction of British courts beyond all question. In the case of Duff Development Co. v. Government of Kelantan, [1924] A. C. 797, involving the question whether execution of an arbitral award could be issued against the defendant state in the British courts, the House of Lords stated the case as follows:

"The question put was as to the status of the ruler of Kelantan. It is obvious that for sovereignty there must be a certain amount of independence, but it is not in the least necessary that for sovereignty there should be complete independence. It is quite consistent with sovereignty that the sovereign may in certain respects be dependent upon another Power; the control, for instance, of foreign affairs may be completely in the hands of a protecting Power, and there may be agreements or treaties which limit the powers of the sovereign even in internal affairs without entailing a loss of the position of a sovereign Power. In the present case it is obvious that the Sultan of Kelantan is to a great extent in the hands of His Majesty's Government. We were asked to say that it is for the Court and for this House in its judicial capacity to decide whether these restrictions were such that the Sultan had ceased to be a sovereign. We have no power to enter into any such inquiry. The reply of the Colonial Office to Master Jelf on October 9, 1922, states that Kelantan is an independent State in the Malay Peninsula and that the Sultan is the sovereign ruler, that His Majesty's Government does not exercise or claim any rights of sovereignty or jurisdiction over Kelantan, and that the Sultan makes laws, dispenses justice through Courts, and generally speaking, exercises without question the usual attributes of sovereignty."

Query, what is the international status of a territory placed under a mandate in accordance with Article 22 of the Covenant of the League of Nations and with the terms of the treaty creating the mandate? See, in illustration, the Mavrommatis Concessions Case, below, p. 643.

B.   Recognition of new states.

States acquire international personality upon their formal admission into the community of nations.   Prior to their admission they may possess the legal personality of states, but they are not subjects of international rights and duties in the strict sense.   The older states which were in existence at the time international law began to take definite shape in the 17th century might be called the "charter members" of the international community.   Then, beginning with the United States in 1783, a number of new states came to be formed by breaking off from the mother country and successfully asserting their independence.   In such cases it becomes a question whether the older states should accord to the revolting community the recognition of its separate statehood. The decision has generally been made on the basis of the demonstrated ability of the revolting community to maintain its *de facto* existence. Query, whether pending such recognition the government in control of the revolting territory has any legal status in relation to third states, so that a contract between a neutral citizen and an officer of the revolutionary government would be recognized as having legal validity? [Kennett v. Chambers.]   It is a point of constitutional, as distinct from international law, what evidence the courts of a particular state shall accept as indicating that the executive department has recognized the new state.   [The Gagara.]

KENNETT ET AL. v. CHAMBERS.

United States, Supreme Court, 1852.

14 Howard, 38.   [14 L. ed. 316.]

Mr. Chief Justice Taney delivered the opinion of the court.

This is an appeal from the decree of the District Court of the United States for the District of Texas.

The appellants filed a bill in that court against the appellee, to obtain the specific execution of an agreement which is set out in full in the bill; and which they allege was executed at the city of Cincinnati, in the State of Ohio, on or about the 16th of September, 1836.   Some of the complainants claim as original parties to the contract, and the others as assignees of original parties, who have sold and assigned to them their interest.

The contract, after stating that it was entered into on the day and year above mentioned, between General T. Jefferson Chambers, of the Texan army, of the first part, and Morgan Neville and six others, who are named in the agreement, of the city of Cincinnati, of the second part, proceeds to recite the motives and inducements of the parties in the following words:—

"That the said party of the second part, being desirous of assisting the said General T. Jefferson Chambers, who is now engaged in raising, arming, and equipping volunteers for Texas, and who is in want of means therefor; and, being extremely desirous to advance the cause of freedom and the independence of Texas, have agreed to purchase of the said T. Jefferson Chambers, of his private estate, the lands hereinafter described."

And after this recital follows the agreement of Chambers, to sell and convey to them the land described in the agreement, situated in Texas, for the sum of twelve thousand five hundred dollars, which he acknowledged that he had received in their notes, payable in equal instalments of four, six, and twelve months, and he covenanted that he had a good title to this land, and would convey it with general warranty. . . .

After setting out the contract at large, the bill avers, that the notes given, as aforesaid, were all paid; and sets forth the manner in which the complainants, who were not parties to the original contract, had acquired their interest as assignees; and charges that, notwithstanding the full payment of the money, Chambers, under different pretexts, refuses to convey the land, according to the terms of his agreement. . . .

To this bill the respondent (Chambers) demurred, and the principal question which arises on the demurrer is, whether the contract was a legal and valid one, and such as can be enforced by either party in a court of the United States. It appears on the face of it, and by the averments of the appellants in their bill, that it was made in Cincinnati, with a general in the Texan army who was then engaged in raising, arming, and equipping volunteers for Texas, to carry on hostilities with Mexico; and that one of the inducements of the appellants, in entering into this contract and advancing the money, was to assist him in accomplishing these objects.

The District Court decided that the contract was illegal and void, and sustained the demurrer and dismissed the bill; and we think that the decision was right.

The validity of this contract depends upon the relation in which this country then stood to Mexico and Texas; and the duties which these relations imposed upon the government and citizens of the United States.

Texas had declared itself independent a few months previous to this agreement. But it had not been acknowledged by the United States; and the constituted authorities charged with our foreign relations, regarded the treaties we had made with Mexico as still in full force, and obligatory upon both nations. By the treaty of limits, Texas had been admitted by our government to be a part of the Mexican territory; and by the first article of the treaty of amity, commerce, and navigation, it was declared, "that there should be a firm, inviolable, and universal peace, and a true and sincere friendship between the United States of America and the United Mexican States, in all the extent of their possessions and territories, and between their people and citizens respectively, without distinction of persons or place." These treaties, while they remained in force, were, by the Constitution of the United States, the supreme law, and binding not only upon the government, but upon every citizen. No contract could lawfully be made in violation of their provisions.

Undoubtedly, when Texas had achieved her independence, no previous treaty could bind this country to regard it as a part of the Mexican territory. But it belonged to the government, and not to individual citizens, to decide when that event had taken place. And that decision, according to the laws of nations, depended upon the question whether she had or had not a civil government in successful operation, capable of performing the duties and fulfilling the obligations of an independent power. It depended upon the state of the fact, and not upon the right which was in contest between the parties. And the President, in his message to the Senate, of December 22, 1836, in relation to the conflict between Mexico and Texas, which was still pending, says: "All questions relative to the government of foreign nations, whether of the old or the new world, have been treated by the United States as questions of fact only, and our predecessors have cautiously abstained from deciding upon them until the clearest evidence was in their possession, to enable them not only to decide correctly, but to shield their decision from every unworthy imputation." Senate Journal of 1836, 37, p. 54.

Acting upon these principles, the independence of Texas was not acknowledged by the Government of the United States until the beginning of March, 1837. Up to that time, it was regarded as a part of the territory of Mexico. The treaty which admitted it to be so, was held to be still in force and binding on both parties, and every effort made by the government to fulfill its neutral obligations, and prevent our citizens from taking part in the conflict. This is evident from an official communication from the President to the Governor of Tennessee, in reply to an inquiry in relation to a requisition for militia, made by General Gaines. The despatch is dated in August, 1836; and the President uses the following language: "The obligations of our treaty with Mexico, as well as the general principles which govern our intercourse with foreign powers, require us to maintain a strict neutrality in the contest which now agitates a part of that republic. So long as Mexico, fulfils her duties to us, as they are defined by the treaty, and violates none of the rights which are secured by it to our citizens, any act on the part of the Government of the United States, which would tend to foster a spirit of resistance to her government and laws, whatever may be their character or form, when administered within her own limits and jurisdiction, would be unauthorized and highly improper." Ex. Doc. 1836, 1837, Vol. 1, Doc. 2, p. 58.

And on the very day on which the agreement of which we are speaking was made, (September 16, 1836,) Mr. Forsyth, the Secretary of State, in a note to the Mexican Minister, assured him that the government had taken measures to secure the execution of the laws for preserving the neutrality of the United States, and that the public officers were vigilant in the discharge of that duty. Ex. Doc. Vol. 1, Doc. 2, pages 63–64.

And still later, the President, in his message to the Senate of Dec. 22, 1836, before referred to, says: "The acknowledgment of a new State as independent, and entitled to a place in the family of nations, is at all times an act of great delicacy and responsibility; but more especially so when such a State has forcibly separated itself from another, of which it formed an integral part, and which still claims dominion over it." And, after speaking of the policy which our government had always adopted on such occasions, and the duty of maintaining the established character of the United States for fair and impartial dealing, he proceeds to express his opinion against the acknowledgment of the independence of Texas, at that time, in the following words:—

"It is true, with regard to Texas, the civil authority of Mexico has been expelled, its invading army defeated, the chief of the republic himself captured, and all present power to control the newly organized Government of Texas annihilated within its confines. But, on the other hand, there is, in appearance at least, an immense disparity of physical force on the side of Mexico. The Mexican republic, under another executive, is rallying its forces under a new leader, and menacing a fresh invasion to recover its lost dominion. Upon the issue of this threatened invasion, the independence of Texas may be considered as suspended; and, were there nothing peculiar in the relative situation of the United States and Texas, our acknowledgment of its independence at such a crisis would scarcely be regarded as consistent with that prudent reserve with which we have heretofore held ourselves bound to treat all similar questions." . . .

This being the attitude in which the government stood, and this its open and avowed policy, upon what grounds can the parties to such a contract as this, come into a court of justice of the United States and ask for its specific execution? It was made in direct opposition to the policy of the government, to which it was the duty of every citizen to conform. And, while they saw it exerting all its power to fulfil in good faith its neutral obligations, they made themselves parties to the war, by furnishing means to a general of the Texan army, for the avowed purpose of aiding and assisting him in his military operations.

It might indeed fairly be inferred, from the language of the contract and the statements in the appellants' bill, that the volunteers were to be raised, armed, and equipped within the limits of the United States.

The language of the contract is: "That the said party of the second part, (that is the complainants,) being desirous of assisting the said General T. Jefferson Chambers, who is now engaged in raising, arming, and equipping volunteers for Texas, and is in want of means therefor." And as General Chambers was then in the United States, and was, as the contract states, actually engaged at that time in raising, arming, and equipping volunteers, and was in want of means to accomplish his object, the inference would seem to be almost irresistible that these preparations were making at or near the place where the agreement was made, and that the money was advanced to enable him to raise and equip a military force in the United States. . . .

If this be the correct interpretation of the agreement, the contract is not only void, but the parties who advanced the money were liable to be punished in a criminal prosecution, for a violation of the neutrality laws of the United States. And certainly, with such strong indications of a criminal intent, and without any averment in the bill from which their innocence can be inferred, a court of chancery would never lend its aid to carry the agreement into specific execution, but would leave the parties to seek their remedy at law. And this ground would of itself be sufficient to justify the decree of the District Court dismissing the bill.

But the decision stands on broader and firmer ground, and this agreement cannot be sustained either at law or in equity. The question is not whether the parties to this contract violated the neutrality laws of the United States or subjected themselves to a criminal prosecution; but whether such a contract, made at that time, within the United States, for the purposes stated in the contract and the bill of complaint, was a legal and valid contract, and such as to entitle either party to the aid of the courts of justice of the United States to enforce its execution.

The intercourse of this country with foreign nations, and its policy in regard to them, are placed by the Constitution of the United States in the hands of the government, and its decisions upon these subjects are obligatory upon every citizen of the Union. He is bound to be at war with the nation against which the war-making power has declared war, and equally bound to commit no act of hostility against a nation with which the government is in amity and friendship. This principle is universally acknowledged by the laws of nations. It lies at the foundation of all government, as there could be no social order or peaceful relations between the citizens of different countries without it. It is, however, more emphatically true in relation to citizens of the United States. For as the sovereignty resides in the people, every citizen is a portion of it, and is himself personally bound by the laws which the representatives of the sovereignty may pass, or the treaties into which they may enter, within the scope of their delegated authority. And when that authority has plighted its faith to another nation that there shall be peace and friendship between the citizens of the two countries, every citizen of the United States is equally and personally pledged. The compact is made by the department of the government upon which he himself has agreed to confer the power. It is his own personal compact as a portion of the sovereignty in whose behalf it is made. And he can do no act, nor enter into any agreement to promote or encourage revolt or hostilities against the territories of a country with which our government is pledged by treaty to be at peace, without a breach of his duty as a citizen, and the breach of the faith pledged to the foreign nation. And if he does so he cannot claim the aid of a court of justice to enforce it. The appellants say, in their contract, that they were induced to advance the money by the desire to promote the cause of freedom. But our own freedom cannot be preserved without obedience to our own laws, nor social order preserved if the judicial branch of the government countenanced and sustained contracts made in violation of the duties which the law imposes, or in contravention of the known and established policy of the political department, acting within the limits of its constitutional power. . . .

This is not a new question. It came before the court in the case of Rose v. Himely, 4 Cr., 272, and again in Gelston v. Hoyt, 3 Wheat. 324. And in both of these cases the court said, that it belongs exclusively to governments to recognize new states in the revolutions which may occur in the world; and until such recognition, either by our own government or the government to which the new state belonged, courts of justice are bound to consider the ancient state of things as remaining unaltered. . . .

Nor can the subsequent acknowledgment of the independence of Texas, and her admission into the Union as a sovereign State, affect the question. The agreement being illegal and absolutely void at the time it was made, it can derive no force or validity from events which afterwards happened. . . .

We therefore hold this contract to be illegal and void, and affirm the decree of the District Court.

MR. JUSTICE DANIEL and MR. JUSTICE GRIER dissented.

THE GAGARA.

Great Britain, Court of Appeal, 1919.

L. R. [1919] Probate, 95.

Appeal from a decision of Hill, J., sitting in Admiralty, setting aside a writ in rem and all subsequent proceedings against the steamship Gagara.

The facts, as found by the learned judge, were as follows: The plaintiffs, described in the writ as the West Russian Steamship Company, Limited, on January 1, 1919, procured to be issued out of the Admiralty Court a writ in rem against "the steamship Gagara, now sailing under the name of the Kajak, and the parties interested in the said steamship." . . . On January 9 appearance under protest was entered and a summons was taken out asking that the writ, service, and all subsequent proceedings be set aside on the ground that the owners of the Gagara were the Esthonian Government. . . .

It appeared from the affidavits filed on behalf of the plaintiffs that the plaintiff company purchased the Gagara in 1914, and she was registered in the name of the company as owners at Petrograd under the Russian merchant flag. During the earlier part of the war the vessel was under some form of requisition in the service of the Imperial Government, and afterwards, by arrangement with the company, in the service of the succeeding Government. The Bolshevik Government having come into power, on June 21, 1918, declared the whole of the Russian mercantile fleet to be national property and ordered the Gagara, then lying at Petrograd, to be repaired. In the autumn of 1918 the Bolshevik Government loaded a cargo of wood on the vessel, and sent her on a voyage to Copenhagen under the captain who had originally been appointed by the company together with some of the old crew and others put on board by the Bolshevik Government. In the course of this voyage it appeared that the Gagara put into Reval, where she was captured by the Esthonians.

From the affidavits filed on behalf of the Esthonian Government it appeared that the Gagara was flying the red flag of the Bolshevik Government and she was accordingly condemned as prize of war, not by bringing her before a Prize Court, but by a decree of the Government. She was then, under the name of the Kajak, registered at Reval as of Esthonian nationality and subject to the ownership of the Esthonian Republic. A new master was appointed by the Esthonian Provisional Government, and by their instructions a bill of lading, dated December 13, 1918, was signed by him for the cargo shipped by that Government to be delivered in London to their representative. The vessel, manned by a crew appointed by the Esthonian Government, then left under the Esthonian flag for London, where she arrived late in December. . . .

When the motion to set aside the writ came before the Court on January 20 the learned judge invited the assistance of the Foreign Office for information as to the status of the Esthonian Government. The law officers attended on January 27, and informed his lordship that His Majesty's Government had (as indeed appeared from the correspondence between the Foreign Office and the Esthonian representatives, exhibited to the defendants' affidavits) for the time being, provisionally and with all necessary reservations as to the future, recognized the Esthonian National Council as a de facto independent body; and His Majesty's Government had accordingly received certain gentlemen as the informal diplomatic representatives of the Esthonian Provisional Government. Further, it was the view of His Majesty's Government, without in any way binding itself as to the future, that the Esthonian Government was such a Government as could, if it thought fit, set up a Prize Court. . . .

BANKES, L. J. This is an appeal from a decision of Hill, J., which was given in the following circumstances: An action was brought *in rem* by the West Russian Steamship Co., Ld., against the steamship Gagara, now sailing under the name of the Kajak, and the parties interested in the steamship. There was a second action, also brought by the same plaintiffs, against the freight. The plaintiffs alleged that they were the owners of the steamship. They claimed a declaration to that effect, and an injunction against persons removing the ship or her cargo, or permitting the same to be removed, and a decree condemning the defendants in costs and damages.

An appearance was entered under protest. A motion was then made in the Admiralty Court to set aside the writ and all subsequent proceedings, on the ground that the Court had no jurisdiction to entertain the action. (His Lordship stated the grounds set out in the notice of motion, and continued:) Hill J. dealt with the case in reference to the claim that the vessel was the property of the Esthonian Government, and had been lawfully condemned as prize by a decree of that Government, and he gave no decision in reference to the point that the dispute was between two foreigners as to a foreign ship. From that decision this appeal is made.

The question which Hill J. decided, and which we have to decide, is whether the Esthonian National Council has been recognized by the Government of this country as having the status of a foreign Sovereign. If it has been so recognized it is not disputed that the Courts of this country would not allow that Council to be impleaded in any of these courts. The principle upon which that practice proceeds was laid down in the case of The Parlement Belge [(1880) 5 P. D. 197, 214], and the passage I am going to read is quoted by Lord Esher in the case of Mighell v. Sultan of Johore [[1894] 1 Q. B. 149, 159]: "The principle to be deduced from all these cases is that, as a consequence of the absolute independence of every sovereign authority, and of the international comity which induces every sovereign State to respect the independence and dignity of every other sovereign State, each and every one declines to exercise by means of its Courts any of its territorial jurisdiction over the person of any sovereign or ambassador of any other State, or over the public property of any State which is destined to public use, or over the property of any ambassador, though such sovereign, ambassador, or property be within its territory, and therefore, but for the common agreement, subject to its jurisdiction."

It appears from that passage that the principle arises from international comity, and the rule is there laid down with reference to matters in respect of which the Court will not exercise its territorial jurisdiction. In giving judgment, Hill J. indicated the reasons why he thought this particular case came within the rule so laid down. In a passage in his judgment which I will read, he says: "In the first place the Esthonian Government is in actual possession of the ship, and that Government states that the ship is being used by it for public purposes. The plaintiffs invite the Court to take that possession away by arrest of the ship and ultimately by decree to transfer it to the plaintiffs. But to permit the arrest is to compel the Esthonian Government either to submit to the jurisdiction of the Court or to lose their *de facto* possession, and to compel the Esthonian Government to submit to this Court the question of the ownership of the Gagara. In accordance with the principles laid down in The Parlement Belge and The Broadmayne [[1916] P. 64], I conceive I cannot compel the Esthonian Government to submit to the jurisdiction. But if that difficulty could be got over, there remains this further difficulty. The Esthonian Government seized the ship *jure belli,* and condemned her as the property of their enemy, the Bolshevist Government."

On these grounds Hill J. came to the conclusion that the case was one with reference to which the Court would not exercise jurisdiction, provided the Court was satisfied that the foreign Government were recognized by our Government as a foreign sovereign. With that part of his judgment I entirely agree.

The question therefore which remains is whether the learned judge was right in coming to the conclusion that the evidence before him was such that he ought to come to the conclusion that the Esthonian National Council had been recognized as having the status of a foreign sovereign. Upon that point I desire to refer to a passage in Lord Esher's judgment in Mighell v. Sultan of Johore [[1894] 1 Q. B. 149, 158, 161], and to a passage in the judgment of Kay L. J., as to the materials upon which the Court is justified in acting and the materials on which the Court is constrained to act in such a matter. Lord Esher says: "I am of opinion that . . . when once there is the authoritative certificate of the Queen through her minister of state as to the status of another sovereign, that in the Courts of this country is decisive. Therefore this letter is conclusive that the defendant is an independent sovereign."
. . .

In the present case the statement is in the fullest sense authoritative. It emanates from the Foreign Office, and it was presented to Hill J. by His Majesty's Attorney-General. The only question is whether it amounts to a statement that the Esthonian National Council has the status of a foreign independent sovereign. Upon that the materials before the Court consist partly of certain letters which passed between the Foreign Office and some gentlemen who addressed the Foreign

Office as being the authorized representatives of Esthonia, and partly of a statement by the Attorney-General and by junior counsel for the Treasury at the Bar before·Hill J.

The submission of counsel for the appellants, as I understand it, is that, so far as the statements in the letters of the Foreign Office are concerned, they are deliberately ambiguous statements of a benevolent character, and not such an emphatic and deliberate statement of fact as the Court should require. Further, he says that no statement as to the recognition of a sovereign state can be sufficient unless it appears that the recognition is irrevocable; and on that last point he cited two passages from Westlake's International Law and Oppenheim's International Law. He has also cited passages from Hall, Halleck, and Wheaton. It does not appear, however, that these writers are entirely agreed on that particular point. At any rate, the statements of these writers have reference to conditions very different from the exceptional conditions existing as regards the status of States in Europe at the time this dispute arose.

I read the letters of the Foreign Office as being statements which do recognize, and recognize to the full, the sovereignty of Esthonia, but with the limitation that in the exceptional conditions due to the setting up of the Peace Conference no undertaking could be given to continue the recognition if conditions altered; and, speaking for myself, I think that that would be a sufficient statement to require and compel the Court to decline jurisdiction in reference to any matter which comes within the principles laid down in the passage which I have read from the judgment in The Parlement Belge. But, however that may be, I am of opinion that the statements which were made by the law officers of the Crown are free from the objections that counsel suggested were to be found in the letters of the Foreign Office. The Attorney-General says that: "Our own Government—and looking at the affidavits in this case I see the statement is no less true whether of the Government of France or the Government of Italy—has for the time being provisionally, and with all necessary reservations as to the future, recognized the Esthonian National Council as a *de facto* independent body, and accordingly has received a certain gentleman as the informal diplomatic representative of that Provisional Government. The state of affairs is of necessity provisional and transitory. The matter remains to be determined in the way that has been described." Junior counsel for the Treasury, at a later stage, said: "If it will assist the Court—I am sorry the Attorney-General is not here now—but I have had the opportunity of putting to him the point which has arisen, and I have his authority for stating to the Court that, in the present view of His Majesty's Government, and without in any way binding itself as to the future, the Esthonian Government is such a Government as could, if it thought fit, set up a Prize Court."

Reading these deliberate statements of the Law Officers of the Crown, as expressing the attitude of the Government towards this Esthonian National Council, I cannot but feel that if the Court claimed to exercise, and did exercise, jurisdiction in respect of such a dispute as arises in this action, they would not be acting in accordance with what was pointed out in the Parlement Belge as being the principle of international comity, and that there would be a divergence of action as between the Courts of this country and the statements that have been made by the Government of the country as to the attitude which this country was prepared to take.

On these grounds, in my opinion, the view taken by Hill J. was right.

WARRINGTON, L. J. I am of the same opinion, for the same reasons, and have nothing to add.

DUKE, L. J. I entirely agree.

Appeal dismissed.[1]

C. Loss of international personality.

The international personality of a state may be lost by the voluntary incorporation of the state into a federal union, as in the case of the admission of Texas to the United States in 1845, or by the voluntary dissolution of a union of states, such as that of Norway and Sweden in 1905. Again, international personality may be lost by the enforced annexation of a state, as in the case of Korea to Japan in 1910; or by the enforced dissolution of a union of states, such as that of Austria and Hungary in 1919. Extinction brings to an end all treaties concluded by the state with other states, although the substance of the rights and obligations provided for by such treaties may, under certain circumstances, pass to the state or states which succeeded to the extinct state. Query, would the relationship, such as that between Austria and Hungary before 1919, technically known as a "real union," argue in favor of a distributive or a joint liability, following their separation, for wrongs committed during their union? [United States, Austria and Hungary: Tripartite Claims Commission.]

---

[1] SUPPLEMENTARY CASES. In the cases of the Annette and the Dora, L. R. [1919] Probate 105, involving warrants of arrests against two Russian vessels, brought by two Esthonian subjects claiming to be the owners, and motions on the part of those operating the vessels to set aside the warrants on the ground that the vessels had been requisitioned by the Provisional Government of Northern Russia and were its property, the Admiralty court observed that the statement from the Foreign Office read into the record indicated that, while Great Britain was at the time "cooperating with the Provisional Government in the opposition which that Government is making to the forces of the Russian Soviet Government," formal recognition had not been given to the Provisional Government as a sovereign power. The motions to set aside the warrants were therefore dismissed.

UNITED STATES, AUSTRIA, AND HUNGARY: TRIPARTITE CLAIMS COMMISSION

Administrative Decision No. 1.

Announcing definitions and general governing principles and dealing with the functions and jurisdiction of the commission. 1927.

Am. Journal of International Law, XXI (1927), 599.

. . . FUNCTIONS OF COMMISSION

[EDWIN B. PARKER, Commissioner.] This Commission was constituted and exists in pursuance of the terms of the Tripartite Agreement between the United States and Austria and Hungary which became effective on December 12, 1925. Therein are found the source of, and the limitations upon, the Commission's powers and jurisdiction in the discharge of its task of determining the amount to be paid by Austria and/or Hungary in satisfaction of their financial obligations to the United States and to American nationals falling within the terms of the Treaties of Vienna and/or Budapest respectively. Article I of the Tripartite Agreement provides that the Commissioner shall determine the amounts to be paid to the United States by Austria and by Hungary in satisfaction of claims embraced within the terms of the said treaties "including the following categories":

(1) Claims of American citizens arising since July 31, 1914, in respect of damage to or seizure of their property, rights and interests, including any company or association in which they are interested, within the territories of either the former Austrian Empire or the former Kingdom of Hungary as they respectively existed on August 1, 1914;

(2) Other claims for loss or damage to which the United States or its nationals have been subjected with respect to injuries to or death of persons, or with respect to property, rights and interests, including any company or association in which American nationals are interested, since July 31, 1914, as a consequence of the war;

(3) Debts owing to American citizens by the Austrian and/or the Hungarian Governments or by their nationals.

The financial obligations of Austria and/or Hungary which this Commission is empowered to determine arise out of claims presented by the United States falling within the several categories specified in the Tripartite Agreement and more particularly defined or described in the Treaties of Vienna and of Budapest. American nationals who acquired rights under these treaties are without a remedy to enforce them save through the United States. As a part of the means of supplying that remedy this Commission was, by the Tripartite Agreement, created as the forum for determining the amount of the obligations of Austria and of Hungary. These treaties fix those obligations and prescribe what Austria and/or Hungary shall pay for. The Tripartite Agreement neither adds to nor subtracts from the rights or the obligations thus fixed but clothes this Commission with jurisdiction over all claims of the United States and its nationals based on the terms of the treaties and lays on the Commissioner the duty of applying those terms to the claims presented and of determining the amount, if any, due to the several claimants thereunder. . . .

Apportionment of Compensation in Reparation Claims and in Claims for Damages Resulting from Acts of Austro-Hungary

The Commissioner decides that the compensation for damages suffered by American nationals (1) falling within the reparation provisions of the treaties, or (2) resulting from acts of Austro-Hungary or its agents during the period of American neutrality, will be borne 63.6 per cent by Austria and 36.4 per cent by Hungary and awards made accordingly. The reasons for this decision follow.

Prior to the war the former Austrian Empire and the former Kingdom of Hungary were separate and distinct states. Each had its own governmental machinery, including a parliament. The citizenship of each was distinct from the other. Austro-Hungarian citizenship did not exist. An Austrian citizen could abandon his Austrian citizenship and acquire Hungarian citizenship and *vice versa*.

In 1867 a *de facto* and constitutional union with limited powers was formed whereby each of these states delegated to the Austro-Hungarian Dual Monarchy the power to act for them in common administration of (1) foreign affairs, (2) the common army and navy (excluding the special army of each state), and (3) matters of finance in so far as concerned joint expenditures for state purposes. This union was expressed in the common head who bore the title "Emperor of Austria and Apostolic King of Hungary." These joint expenditures were apportioned between the former Austrian Empire and the former Kingdom of Hungary by the Austro-Hungarian law of December 30, 1907 (B. L. I., No. 278), on the basis of 63.6 per cent to be borne by Austria and 36.4 per cent to be borne by Hungary. This was the basis upon which contributions were made by the former Austrian Empire and the former Kingdom of Hungary to the Imperial and Royal Austro-Hungarian Government enabling it to wage war against the United States.

The former Austrian Empire and the former Kingdom of Hungary while existing as independent states had no international status. It was against the Imperial and Royal Austro-Hungarian Government that the United States waged war (see resolutions of Congress effective

December 7, 1917, and July 2, 1921). Following the armistice that government ceased to exist (see recitations in preambles to the Treaties of Vienna and of Budapest). In pursuance of the terms of the several treaties entered into between the opposing Powers after the armistice, not only was the Austro-Hungarian Dual Monarchy dismembered but substantial parts of the territories of the former Austrian Empire and of the former Kingdom of Hungary were ceded some to new and some to existing states. The Austria and the Hungary dealt with by the United States in entering into the Treaties of Vienna and of Budapest respectively not only bore little resemblance either to the government or the territory of the Dual Monarchy with which the United States had been at war but differed essentially from the former Austrian Empire and the former Kingdom of Hungary. Unlike the Treaty of Berlin *"restoring* friendly relations" between the United States and Germany, these treaties in terms *"establish"* for the first time such relations between Austria and the United States and between Hungary and the United States.

The questions here presented are, What existing government or governments are liable for the acts of the Austro-Hungarian Government or its agents resulting in damage to American nationals, is that liability joint or several, and what is its extent?

The answer must be found in the provisions of the Treaties of Vienna and of Budapest. It will not be profitable to examine the divergent views maintained by European continental writers on international law as compared with those of Great Britain and the United States with respect to the liability of a successor state for the obligations either *ex contractu* or *ex delicto* of a dismembered state. It is, however, interesting to note in passing that while one group maintains that such obligations pass with succession and are apportioned between the successor states, and while the other group maintains that the obligations do not pass with succession, neither group maintains that a joint liability rests upon two or more successor states where the territory of a dismembered state has been divided between them.

Under the financial clauses (Part IX of the treaties) elaborate provision is made for the apportionment between the successor states, including Austria and Hungary as they now exist, of the pre-war indebtedness, secured and unsecured, of the former Austro-Hungarian Monarchy, the former Austrian Empire, and the former Kingdom of Hungary, fixing sole responsibility on each successor state for the proportion of such indebtedness allocated to it.

All of the successor states other than Austria and Hungary are classed as "Allied or Associated Powers" and under the treaties it is entirely clear that none of them is held liable for any damages suffered by American nationals resulting from acts of the Austro-Hungarian Government or its agents during either the period of American neutrality or American belligerency.

By Article 178 (162) of the treaty Austria (Hungary) undertakes that she will make compensation for damage done, as defined in the annex thereto, to the civilian population of the United States and to their property by the aggression of Austro-Hungary and her allies. The language is the same in both treaties. There is an undertaking by Austria to make compensation for specified damage and a separate undertaking by Hungary to make compensation for the same damage. Obviously it was not intended that double compensation should be made. Neither is there a joint undertaking. . . .

Having in mind the pre-war and war relationship between the former Austrian Empire and the former Kingdom of Hungary and their respective responsibilities for the acts of the Austro-Hungarian Monarchy, the Tripartite Agreement under which this Commission is constituted was executed. It recites that all three of the parties are "desirous of determining the amounts to be paid by Austria and by Hungary" under the Treaties of Vienna and of Budapest respectively and provides that the Commissioner "shall determine the amounts to be paid to the United States by Austria and by Hungary." This language imports a distributive and not a joint liability and a purpose to apportion damages for which both may be liable, allocating to each a definite amount. The notes exchanged between the United States and Austria during the negotiation of this agreement clearly reflect this purpose. This is in harmony with the spirit of the treaties considered as a whole which indicates a purpose not to create joint obligations as between Austria and Hungary as they now exist but to divide and to allocate to each its separate liabilities.

The Reparation Commission, which under the Treaties of St. Germain and Trianon is clothed with the power to fix the amount of compensation to be paid by Austria and Hungary respectively under the reparation provisions of the treaties, has not as yet directly dealt with this question of apportionment as between them. That commission, however, acting within its jurisdiction has in a number of instances considered questions of credits on their reparation accounts to Austria and to Hungary respectively for warships, mine layers, abandoned war material, and other property formerly belonging to the Austro-Hungarian Government and passing under the treaties through the Reparation Commission or otherwise to the Allied and Associated Powers. The Reparation Commission in apportioning these credits as between Austria and Hungary accorded to Austria 63.6 per cent and to Hungary 36.4 per cent of the aggregate amount thereof, this being the basis on which the former Austrian Empire and the former Kingdom of Hungary respectively contributed to the acquisition of the ceded property by the Austro-Hungarian Government. It is believed that the rule applicable to the apportionment of credits to which Austria and Hungary are respectively entitled under the reparation provisions of the treaties is equally applicable to the apportionment of their liabilities thereunder. The Governments of Austria and of Hungary in the agreement of June 1, 1926, adopted as between themselves a division of liabilities in harmony with the rule here announced.

While this decision, in so far as applicable, will control the preparation, presentation, and ·decision of all claims submitted to the Commission falling within its scope, nevertheless should the American Agent, the Austrian Agent, and/or the Hungarian Agent be of the opinion that the peculiar facts of any case take it out of the rules here announced such facts with the differentiation believed to exist will be called to the attention of the Commissioner in the presentation of that case.[1]

D. Equality of states.

It has long been affirmed by jurists that all states, large and small, are legally equal, but there is considerable difference of opinion as to the precise application of the principle of legal equality so asserted. It would seem, however, to be accepted that the same principles of conduct are binding upon all states; the same general rights may be asserted by them and the same general obligations must be recognized. Query, what of the adoption of new rules of law? Is each state, irrespective of its size, on a par with others in accepting new obligations? Is the acceptance of the new rule by each particular state a condition of its binding force in respect to that state? [Le Louis.]

---

[1] SUPPLEMENTARY CASES. In the case of Terlinden v. Ames, 184 U. S. 270 (1902), involving the question whether a treaty of extradition entered into by the United States with Prussia in 1852 necessarily terminated by reason of the formation of the German Empire so as to preclude the extradition of Terlinden to Prussia as a member of the Empire, the court held that it did not necessarily follow from the fact of the formation of the German Empire "that the Kingdom of Prussia lost its identity as such, or that treaties theretofore entered into by it could not be performed either in the name of its king or that of the Emperor." As a matter of international law Prussia became extinct, and the emphasis should have been put upon the succession of the German Empire to the position of Prussia as a party to the treaty. In this instance it should be noted that the United States was ready to accept the obligations of the treaty on its side, not seeking to press them against an unwilling other party to the treaty.

LE LOUIS, FOREST [MASTER].

Great Britain, High Court of Admiralty, 1817.

2 Dodson, 210.

[A French vessel, Le Louis, was captured off the coast of Africa in 1816 and carried to Sierra Leone where she was proceeded against in the vice admiralty court of that colony and condemned for being engaged in the slave trade. From the decision of the lower court condemning the vessel, an appeal was taken to the High Court of Admiralty. In addition to a variety of disputed acts the court had to determine whether the act of engaging in the slave trade was of itself a violation of international law apart from a possible violation of the internal law of France and of a treaty between Great Britain and France. The resistance to search offered by the vessel raised the preliminary question of a "right of search" in time of peace.]

SIR WILLIAM SCOTT. . . .

Assuming the fact, which is indistinctly proved, that there was a demand, and a resistance producing the deplorable results here described, I think that the natural order of things compels me to inquire first, whether the party who demanded had a right to search; for if not, then not only was the resistance to it lawful, but likewise the very fact on which the other ground of condemnation rests is totally removed. . . . Supposing, however, that it should appear that he had a right to visit and search, and therefore to avail himself of all the information he so acquired, the question would then be, whether that information has established all the necessary facts? The first is, that this was a French ship intentionally employed in the slave trade, which, I have already intimated, appears to be sufficiently shown. The second is, that such a trading is a contravention of the French law; for it has been repeatedly admitted that the court, in order to support this sentence of condemnation, must have the foundation of the trade being prohibited by the law of the country to which the party belongs.

Upon the first question, whether the right of search exists in time of peace, I have to observe, that two principles of public law are generally recognized as fundamental. One is the perfect equality and entire independence of all distinct states. Relative magnitude creates no distinction of right; relative imbecility, whether permanent or casual, gives no additional right to the more powerful neighbor; and any advantage seized upon that ground is mere usurpation. This is the great foundation of public law, which it mainly concerns the peace of mankind, both in their politic and private capacities, to preserve inviolate. The second is, that all nations being equal, all have an equal right to the uninterrupted use of the unappropriated parts of the ocean for their navigation. In places where no local authority exists, where the subjects of all states meet upon a footing of entire equality and independence, no one state, or any one of its subjects, has a right to assume or exercise authority over the subjects of another. I can find no authority that gives the right of interruption to the navigation of states in amity upon the high seas, excepting that which the rights of war give to both belligerents against neutrals.[1, 2]

---

[1] For other parts of the opinion dealing with the suppression of the slave trade, see below, p. 369.

[2] Supplementary Cases. In the case of the Antelope, 10 Wheaton 66 (1825), involving a substantially similar issue (see above, p. 7) the court used the following language: "No principle of general law is more universally acknowledged, than the perfect equality of nations. Russia and Geneva have equal rights. It results from this equality that no one can rightfully impose a rule on another."

In the Sambiaggio Arbitration between Italy and Venezuela (Ralston, Venezuelan Arbitrations of 1903, p. 679), involving the responsibility of Venezuela for losses incurred by an Italian national from revolutionary forces, the arbitrator refused to depart from the general rules of liability applicable to other nations, asserting that "it is his deliberate opinion that as between two nations through whose joint action he exercises his functions he can indulge in no presumption which could be regarded as lowering to either. He is bound to assume equality of position and equality of right."

In The Schooner Exchange v. M'Faddon, below, p. 326, involving the immunity from suit of a foreign public vessel in the territorial waters of the United States, the Supreme Court, in recognizing the immunity referred to it as originating in the "perfect equality and absolute independence of sovereigns."

CHAPTER IV

THE CONTINUITY OF STATE PERSONALITY [1]

A. Effect of changes in the government of a state.

It is a well-established rule of international law that once a state becomes a member of the international community it retains the same international personality, the same corporate legal character, notwithstanding any changes that may take place in its internal organization and government. [The Sapphire.]

When, however, changes in the form of a government are sudden and abrupt, such as the transition from a monarchy to a republic, or when, without change of constitutional form, a change in the personnel of the government takes place by revolution or by violence, it is the right and practice of other states to refuse or to delay recognition of the new government until such time as it appears to be sufficiently well established to be able to speak with authority in the name of the state and to be answerable for its obligations. Once, however, a *de facto* government has been duly recognized by other states as *de jure*, it acquires by such recognition the right to maintain claims due to the state and the state, in turn, becomes responsible for the acts of its new agent. Query, if the new *de jure* government were to be overthrown in turn by a succeeding revolution, would the obligations incurred by it remain binding upon the state in the same way as would the obligations of a government whose *de jure* character had never been questioned? [Republic of Peru v. Dreyfus Brothers.]

Query, would the fact that a state is represented by a *de facto* government, which for various reasons has not been given formal recognition by a particular state, deprive the former of its exemption from suit in the courts of the latter, or does the exemption belong to the state as such, irrespective of its existing government? [Wulfsohn v. R. S. F. S. R.] Would the *de facto* but unrecognized government be precluded on its part from suing before the courts of the state denying it recognition if a question should arise involving the property of the state it represents? [R. S. F. S. R. v. Cibrario.]

---

[1] For a more detailed study of this subject, see Fenwick, *op. cit.*, Chap. VII, pp. 114–120; Hyde, *op. cit.*, Vol. I, §§ 43–50; Oppenheim, *op. cit.*, Vol. I, §§ 75–77; Hervey, Legal Effects of Recognition in International Law; E. D. Dickinson, "Recent Recognition Cases," Am. Journal of Int. Law, XIX (1925), 263; "Recognition Cases, 1925–1930," *ibid.*, XXV (1931) 214; E. M. Borchard, "The Unrecognized Government in American Courts," *ibid.*, XXVI (1932), 261.

THE SAPPHIRE.

United States, Supreme Court, 1871.

11 Wallace, 164.   [20 L. ed. 127.]

This was an appeal from the Circuit Court of the United States for the District of California.

[Following a collision between the American ship Sapphire and the French transport Euryale, in the harbor of San Francisco, a libel was filed against the Sapphire in the name of the Emperor Napoleon III, then Emperor of the French, as owner of the Euryale which had been damaged in the collision. The decree of the District Court in favor of the libellant, awarding him $15,000, the total amount claimed, was affirmed by the Circuit Court, from which an appeal was taken in July, 1869. In September, 1870, the Emperor Napoleon was deposed. The case was argued before the Supreme Court in February, 1871.]

MR. JUSTICE BRADLEY delivered the opinion of the court.

The first question raised is as to the right of the French Emperor to sue in our courts. On this point not the slightest difficulty exists. A foreign sovereign, as well as any other foreign person, who has a demand of a civil nature against any person here, may prosecute it in our courts. To deny him this privilege would manifest a want of comity and friendly feeling. Such a suit was sustained in behalf of the King of Spain in the third circuit by Justice Washington and Judge Peters in 1810. The Constitution expressly extends the judicial power to controversies between a State, or citizens thereof, and *foreign States,* citizens, or subjects, without reference to the subject-matter of the controversy. Our own government has largely availed itself of the like privilege to bring suits in the English courts in cases growing out of our late civil war. Twelve or more of such suits are enumerated in the brief of the appellees, brought within the last five years in the English law, chancery, and admiralty courts. There are numerous cases in the English reports in which suits of foreign sovereigns have been sustained, though it is held that a sovereign cannot be forced into court by suit.

The next question is, whether the suit has become abated by the recent deposition of the Emperor Napoleon. We think it has not. The reigning sovereign represents the national sovereignty, and that sovereignty is continuous and perpetual, residing in the proper successors of the sovereign for the time being. Napoleon was the owner of the Euryale, not as an individual, but as sovereign of France. This is substantially averred in the libel. On his deposition the sovereignty does not change, but merely the person or persons in whom it resides. The foreign state is the true and real owner of its public vessels of war. The reigning Emperor, or National Assembly, or other actual person or party in power, is but the agent and representative of the national sovereignty. A change in such representative works no change in the national sovereignty or its rights. The next successor recognized by our government is competent to carry on a suit already commenced and receive the fruits of it. A deed to or treaty with a sovereign as such inures to his successor in the government of the country. If a substitution of names is necessary or proper it is a formal matter, and can be made by the court under its general power to preserve due symmetry in its forms of proceeding. No allegation has been made that any change in the real and substantial ownership of the Euryale has occurred by the recent devolution of the sovereign power. The vessel has always belonged and still belongs to the French nation.[1]

If a special case should arise in which it could be shown that injustice to the other party would ensue from a continuance of the proceedings after the death or deposition of a sovereign, the court, in the exercise of its discretionary power, would take such order as the exigency might require to prevent such a result. . . .

Decree of the Circuit Court reversed. . . .

REPUBLIC OF PERU v. DREYFUS BROTHERS.

Supreme Court of Judicature, Chancery Division, 1888.

L. R. 38 C. D. 348.

[In the year 1869 Messrs. Dreyfus and Co., who were French subjects carrying on business in Paris, entered into a contract with the Government of Peru. In 1879, while disputes arising under the contract were still unsettled, Señor Nicolas di Pierola made himself Dictator of Peru, overthrowing the existing government. In 1880 after he had been recognized by England and France and other European states as supreme ruler of Peru, he entered into negotiations with Messrs. Dreyfus for the purpose of raising more money for the Government of Peru, then at war with Chile. A clause in the original contract calling for the submission to the courts of Peru of disputes arising under the contract was waived by the government and an amount was then agreed upon in settlement of the claims. In November, 1881, Señor Pierola resigned, and in June, 1886, the Government of Peru was reconstituted in the form in which it had existed previously to the dictatorship, whereupon

---

[1] The student should note carefully the distinction between the recognition of new *governments* and the recognition of new states discussed in the preceding chapter. While the test of *de facto* control is more or less the same in the two cases, in the recognition of a new government there is no issue of the legal position or rights of the state itself, but merely the issue as to who is competent to speak in the name of the state.

the Congress of the Republic passed an act declaring void all the internal acts of the Government done by Señor Pierola. In the meantime Dreyfus Brothers had brought an action against the Peruvian Guano Company for cargoes of guano assigned to them by the Pierola Government and had obtained judgment. The new Government of Peru, in pursuance of the act of Congress, brought an action claiming an injunction to restrain Dreyfus Brothers from taking out of court the funds standing to the credit of their action against the Peruvian Guano Company.]

KAY, J.:—. . . It is difficult to see how this [the legality of the arrangement with Pierola's Government] can be determined by the law of Peru. It is a question of international law of the highest importance whether or not the citizens of a foreign State may safely have such dealings as existed in this case with a Government which such State has recognized. If they may not, of what value to the citizens of a foreign State is such recognition by its Government? There have been successive Governments in European countries—usurpations of the power of previous Governments overthrown—altering the Constitution essentially. These have in turn been recognised by this and other nations. When the Government of this country recognised the third Emperor of the French, if any Englishman entered into contracts with his Government, could it be maintained that the validity of such contracts must depend upon the law of France as settled by decree of the Republic which was established on his deposition? Obviously it would follow that no Englishman could safely contract with the present Government of France, or, indeed, with any existing Government, lest it in turn should be displaced by another Government which might treat its acts as void.

There is no authority for any such proposition. I must take the law to be that an Englishman or Frenchman might safely contract with Señor Pierola's Government, if not before, at any rate after, it was recognised by the Governments of England and France respectively. . . .

The decisions on the subject are completely in accordance with the law as I have stated it. I prefer to look somewhat further than the few cases cited at the bar; but all the authorities to which I shall refer are within the last 100 years. There have been in the history of the world during that period many revolutions and usurpations of supreme power among civilised nations who recognise international law. The Plaintiffs' counsel have been unable to cite, nor can I find, any authority whatever in favour of their contention. . . .

In Gelston v. Hoyt [3 Wheat. 246, 324], in the Supreme Court of the United States, the law is stated thus: "No doctrine is better established, than that it belongs exclusively to Governments to recognise new States in the revolutions which may occur in the world; and until such recognition, either by our own Government or the Government to which the new State belonged, Courts of Justice are bound to consider the ancient state of things as remaining unaltered. This was expressly held by this Court in the case of Rose v. Himely [4 Cranch, 241], and to that decision on this point we adhere. . . ."

[Finally, the Court held that the existing Peruvian Government could not recover the proceeds of the cargoes in question unless the Government of Pierola could have done so, and that Pierola's Government could not have recovered them in violation of its own contract.]

MAX WULFSOHN ET AL., RESPONDENTS, v. RUSSIAN SOCIALIST FEDERATED SOVIET REPUBLIC, APPELLANT.

United States, Court of Appeals of New York, 1923.

234 N. Y. 372.

Appeal, by permission, from an order of the Appellate Division of the Supreme Court in the second judicial department, entered July 21, 1922, which affirmed an order of Special Term denying a motion to vacate a warrant of attachment.

The following question was certified: "Can the defendant, which has not been recognized as a sovereign state by the United States government, be sued in the courts of this state as a foreign corporation?" . . .

ANDREWS, J. The Russian Federated Soviet Republic is the existing *de facto* government of Russia. This is admitted by the plaintiff. Otherwise there is no proper party defendant before the court. It is claimed by the defendant. The Appellate Division states that it is a matter of common knowledge. It has not been recognized by the government of the United States. The plaintiffs owned a quantity of furs. They were stored in Russia and they were confiscated by the Russian government. Treating this act as a conversion the present action is brought. The litigation is not, therefore, with regard to title to property situated within the jurisdiction of our courts where the result depends upon the effect to be given to the action of some foreign government. Under such circumstances it might be that the theory of the comity of nations would have a place. (The Annette, L. R. Pro. Div. [1919] 105; The Nueva Anna, 6 Wheat. 193; Oetjen v. Central Leather Co., 246 U. S. 297; Luther v. Sagor & Co., 1 K. B. 1921, 456; S. C., 3 K. B. 1921, 532.) A different case is presented to us. The government itself is sued for an exercise of sovereignty within its own territories on the theory that such an act if committed by an individual here would be a tort under our system of municipal law.

It is said that because of non-recognition by the United States such an action may be maintained. There is no relation between the premise and the conclusion.

The result we reach depends upon more basic considerations than recognition or non-recognition by the United States. Whether or not a government exists clothed with the power to enforce its authority within its own territory, obeyed by the people over whom it rules, capable of performing the duties and fulfilling the obligations of an independent power, able to enforce its claims by military force, is a fact not a theory. For it recognition does not create the state although it may be desirable. So only are diplomatic relations permitted. Treaties made with the government which it succeeds may again come into effect. It is a testimony of friendly intentions. Also in the country granting the recognition that act is conclusive as to the existence of the government recognized. (Taylor v. Barclay, 2 Sim. 213; Republic of Peru v. Dreyfus Bros. & Co., L. R. 38 Ch. Div. 348; Republic of Peru v. Peruvian Guano Co., L. R. 36 Ch. Div. 489.) Again recognition may become important where the actual existence of a government created by rebellion or otherwise becomes a political question affecting our neutrality laws, the recognition of the decrees of prize courts and similar questions. But except in such instances the fact of the existence of such a government whenever it becomes material may probably be proved in other ways. (Yrisarri v. Clement, 3 Bing. 432; The Charkieh, L. R. 4 A. & E. 59, but see Mighell v. Sultan of Johore, [1894] 1 Q. B. 158; Luther v. Sagor, 1 K. B. 1921, 456, 474.) Here, however, we need no proof. The fact is conceded. We have an existing government sovereign within its own territories. There necessarily its jurisdiction is exclusive and absolute. It is susceptible of no limitation not imposed by itself. This is the result of its independence. It may be conceded that its actions should accord with natural justice and equity. If they do not, however, our courts are not competent to review them. They may not bring a foreign sovereign before our bar, not because of comity, but because he has not submitted himself to our laws. Without his consent he is not subject to them. Concededly that is so as to a foreign government that has received recognition. (The Schooner Exchange v. McFaddon, 7 Cranch, 116; Porto Rico v. Rosaly, 227 U. S. 270; Oetjen v. Central Leather Co., 246 U. S. 297; Underhill v. Hernandez, 168 U. S. 250; American Banana Co. v. United Fruit Co., 213 U. S. 347; Ricaud v. American Metal Co., 246 U. S. 304; Hassard v. United States of Mexico, 29 Misc. Rep. 511; affd., 173 N. Y. 645; Mason v. Intercolonial Railway, 197 Mass. 349; Wadsworth v. Queen of Spain, 17 Q. B. 171; Vavasseur v. Krupp, L. R. 9 Ch. Div. 351; Strousborg v. Costa Rica, 44 L. T. 199.) But whether recognized or not the evil of such an attempt would be the same. "To cite a foreign potentate into a municipal court for any complaint against him in his public capacity is contrary to the law of nations and an insult which he is entitled to resent.'' (De Haber v. Queen of Portugal, 17 Q. B. 171.) In either case to do so would ''vex the peace of nations.'' In either case the hands of the state department would be tied. Unwillingly it would find itself involved in disputes it might think unwise. Such is not the proper method of redress if a citizen of the United States is wronged. The question is a political one, not confided to the courts but to another department of government. Whenever an act done by a sovereign in his sovereign character is questioned it becomes a matter of negotiation, or of reprisals or of war.

If the complaint and the affidavits upon which the warrant of attachment was based in the case before us clearly indicate that the plaintiffs must ultimately fail the warrant should be vacated. It does so appear in this case.

The orders, therefore, appealed from should be reversed, with costs in all courts, and motions to vacate attachment granted, with costs, and the question certified to us should be answered in the negative.

HISCOCK, CH. J., HOGAN, CARDOZO, POUND and MCLAUGHLIN, JJ., concur; CRANE, J., dissents.

Ordered accordingly.

RUSSIAN SOCIALIST FEDERATED SOVIET REPUBLIC, APPELLANT, v. JACQUES R. CIBRARIO ET AL., RESPONDENTS.

United States, Court of Appeals of New York, 1923.

235 N. Y. 255.

Appeal from a judgment of the Appellate Division of the Supreme Court in the first judicial department, entered May 16, 1922, affirming a judgment in favor of the defendants, entered upon an order of Special Term sustaining a demurrer to and directing a dismissal of the complaint.

ANDREWS, J. In Wulfsohn v. Russian Federated Soviet Republic, (234 N. Y. 372) we held that our courts would not entertain jurisdiction of an action brought without its consent against an existing foreign government, in control of the political and military power within its own territory, whether or not such government had been recognized by the United States. We have now to determine whether such a government may itself become a plaintiff here.

If recognized, undoubtedly it may. (Republic of Honduras v. Soto, 112 N. Y. 310; United States of America v. Wagner, L. R. 2 Ch. App. 582; King of Spain v. Machado, 4 Russ. 560; King of Prussia v. Kuepper,

22 Mo. 550.) Conceivably this right may depend on treaty. But if no treaty to that effect exists the privilege rests upon the theory of international comity. This is so with regard to all foreign corporations. (Hollis v. Drew Theological Seminary, 95 N. Y. 166; Bank of Augusta v. Earle, 13 Pet. 519; National Telephone Mfg. Co. v. Du Bois, 165 Mass. 117.) Their power to sue may be regulated as is done by section 15 of our General Corporation Law (Consol. Laws, c. 23). (Paul v. Virginia, 75 U. S. [8 Wall.] 168.) And except as limited by constitutional provisions the same thing is true of those not citizens of our state. Much more true is it that the right of a foreign government to sue is likewise based upon the same consideration. Neither a natural person nor a corporation, ordinarily we would not recognize it as a proper party plaintiff. (W. & A. R. R. Co. v. Dalton Marble Works, 122 Ga. 774.) It represents, however, the general interests of the nation over which it has authority. We permit it to appear and protect those interests as a body analogous to one possessing corporate rights, but solely because of comity. (Republic of Honduras v. Soto, 112 N. Y. 310, 19 N. E. 845; Hullet & Co. v. King of Spain, 1 Dow & Clark, 169, 175; Duke of Brunswick v. King of Hanover, 6 Beav. 1, 37; The Sapphire, 78 U. S. [11 Wall.] 164.)

Comity may be defined as that reciprocal courtesy which one member of the family of nations owes to the others. It presupposes friendship. It assumes the prevalence of equity and justice. Experience points to the expediency of recognizing the legislative, executive, and judicial acts of other powers. We do justice that justice may be done in return. "What is termed the comity of nations is the formal expression and ultimate result of that mutual respect accorded throughout the civilized world by the representatives of each sovereign power to those of every other, in considering the effects of their official acts. Its source is a sentiment of reciprocal regard, founded on identity of position and similarity of institutions." (Fisher, Brown & Co. v. Fielding, 67 Conn. 91, 108.) As defined by Webster, comity "is in general terms that there are between nations at peace with one another rights both national and individual resulting from the comity or courtesy due from one friendly nation to another. Among these is the right to sue in their courts respectively." (6 Webster Works, 117.) It may, however, not be demanded as a right. It is yielded as a favor. Not an arbitrary favor; nor is it the favor of the courts. "It is not the comity of the courts, but the comity of the nation which is administered." (Bank of Augusta v. Earle, 13 Pet. 519.) Rules of comity are a portion of the law that they enforce. Precedents mark the line that they should follow. Both in England and in the United States so universally and for such a length of time have actions by alien corporations and individuals been allowed that the right to bring them in a proper case has become fixed. Unless restrained by legislative fiat no court may

now deny it.   (Hollis v. Drew Theological Seminary, 95 N. Y. 166, 175;
Stone v. Penn Yan, K. P. & B. Ry. Co., 197 N. Y. 279, 90 N. E. 843;
Christian Union v. Yount, 101 U. S. 352.)   So long as the plaintiff does
not reside in a country at war with the United States we inquire no
further. The original basis of the right has fallen into the background.
If trade is permitted between him and ourselves we do not ask whether
he comes from Mexico or from France. But no like current of authority
controls us in the case before us. Undisturbed the rule of comity is
our only guide. This rule is always subject, however, to one consideration. There may be no yielding, if to yield is inconsistent with our
public policy. We might give effect to the French decree in Gould v.
Gould (235 N. Y. 14) only because it was consonant with our theories
of marriage and divorce. Such public policy may be interpreted by
the courts. It is fixed by general usage and morality or by executive
or legislative declaration. Especially is the definition of our relations
to foreign nations confided not to the courts, but to another branch of
the government. That branch determines our policy toward them. It
only remains for the courts to enforce it.

The use of the word "comity" as expressing the basis of jurisdiction
has been criticized. It is, however, a mere question of definition. The
principles lying behind the word are recognized. Whether or not we
sum them up by one expression or another, the truth remains that jurisdiction depends upon the law of the forum, and this law in turn depends
upon the public policy disclosed by the acts and declarations of the
political departments of the government.

Does any rule of comity, then, require us to permit a suit by an unrecognized power? In view of the attitude of our government, should we
permit an action to be brought by the Soviet government? To both
queries we must give a negative answer.

We may state at the outset that we find no precedent that a power
not recognized by the United States may seek relief in our courts. Such
intimations as exist are to the contrary. Statements are that "a recognized government may be a plaintiff."   (Republic of Honduras v.
Soto, ·112 N. Y. 310; United States v. Wagner, L. R. 2 Ch. App. 582,
589.)   In King of Spain v. Oliver (14 Fed. Cas. 577) the Circuit Court
noted the question, but refused to decide it. In City of Berne v. Bank
of England (9 Ves. Jr. 347) Lord Eldon expressed great doubt. So in
Dolder v. Lord Huntingfield (11 Ves. Jr. 283). In The Penza (D. C.)
(277 Fed. Rep. 91) the present plaintiff was refused relief.

What, then, is the meaning and effect of recognition in its relation to
comity? It is difficult to find a clear discussion of this question, either
in reports or in text-books. Where a new government has seized power,
"no official intercourse is possible between the powers refusing recognition and the state concerned." "Through recognition the other states
declare that they are ready to negotiate with such individual (a new

ruler) as the highest organ of his state." (Oppenheim, International
Law [3d Ed.] vol. 1, sections 77, 342.) Speaking of the recognition of
a new state, Wheaton (International Law [2d Ed.] p. 39) says: "So
long, indeed, as the new state confines its action to its own citizens and
to the limits of its own territory, it may well dispense with such recognition. But if it desires to enter into the great society of nations, all
the members of which recognize rights to which they are mutually entitled, and duties which they may be called upon reciprocally to fulfil,
such recognition becomes essentially necessary to the complete participation of the new state in all the advantages of this society. . . .
The new state becomes entitled to the exercise of its external sovereignty
as to those states only by whom that sovereignty has been recognized."
In Hyde's International Law (Vol. 1, § 37) is the statement that "the
mode of recognition is not material, provided there be an unequivocal
act indicating clearly that the new state is dealt with as such and is
deemed to be entitled to exercise the privileges of statehood in the
society of nations."

More assistance may be found in the reasons underlying various decisions of the courts as to the effect to be given to the acts of foreign governments. This effect depends upon our acknowledgment of the comity
of nations. "The principle that the conduct of one independent government cannot be successfully questioned in the courts of another is as applicable to a case involving the title to property brought within the
custody of a court, such as we have here, as it was held to be to the cases
cited, in which claims for damages were based upon acts done in a foreign country, for it rests at last upon the highest considerations of international comity and expediency." (Oetjen v. Central Leather Co.,
246 U. S. 297, 303; Mighell v. Sultan of Johore, 1 Q. B. 1894, p. 149;
The Parlement Belge, 5 Pro. Div. 1880, p. 197.) Therefore where comity
exists between two nations, and no question of public policy arises, this
rule is invariable. Yet in specific cases the question of recognition is
thought controlling—recognition existing at the time the alleged wrongful act was done, or recognition later, which relates back to that time.
(Oetjen v. Central Leather Co., supra; Underhill v. Hernandez, 168 U. S.
250; Ricaud v. American Metal Co., 246 U. S. 304; The Gagara, [1919]
Pro. Div. 95; The Annette, [1919] Pro. Div. 105.) A most interesting
case is Luther v. Sagor, [1921] 3 K. B. 532. The Soviet Republic seized
personal property belonging to the plaintiff. Then sold to the defendant,
it was imported into England. There the plaintiff brought an action to
recover it. The plaintiff succeeded in the lower court, there being no
proof of the recognition of the Russian government. Later such recognition occurred, and the judgment because of that fact was reversed on
appeal. In the course of his opinion Scrutton, L. J., says the title to
the goods coming into the hands of a purchaser from the Russian gov-.
ernment cannot be questioned. "This immunity follows from recogni-

tion as a sovereign state. Should there be any government which appropriates other people's property without compensation, the remedy appears to be to refuse to recognize it as a sovereign state. Then the courts could investigate the title without infringing the comity of nations.'' Why? Obviously because in the absence of recognition no comity exists.

We reach the conclusion, therefore, that a foreign power brings an action in our courts not as a matter of right. Its power to do so is the creature of comity. Until such government is recognized by the United States no such comity exists. The plaintiff concededly has not been so recognized. There is, therefore, no proper party before us. We may add that recognition, and, consequently, the existence of comity, is purely a matter for the determination of the legislative or executive departments of the government. Who is the sovereign of a territory is a political question. In any case where that question is in dispute the courts are bound by the decision reached by those departments. (Jones v. U. S., 137 U. S. 202; Luther v. Sagor, *supra*, 556.) It is not for the courts to say whether the present governments of Russia or Mexico or Great Britain should or should not be recognized. They are or they are not. That is as far as we may inquire. Nor is anything here decided inconsistent with Wulfsohn v. Soviet Republic *(supra)*. Upon the facts in that case, if the defendant was not an existing government it might not be sued. There was no party before the court. If it were, as was alleged and admitted, the same result followed, not because of comity, but because an independent government is not answerable for its acts to our courts.

We are the more ready to reach this conclusion because to hold otherwise might tend to nullify the rule that public policy must always prevail over comity. More than once during the last seventy years our relations with one or another existing but unrecognized government have been of so critical a character that to permit it to recover in our courts funds which might strengthen it or which might even be used against our interests would be unwise. We should do nothing to thwart the policy which the United States has adopted. Yet, unless recognition is the test of the right to sue, we do not see why Maximilian, as emperor of Mexico, might not have maintained an action here.

With regard to the present Russian government the case is still stronger, even did comity not depend on recognition. We not only refuse to recognize it. Our State Department gives the reasons. Secretary Colby has stated them in an official note, dated August 10, 1920. He begins by saying that our government will not participate in any plan for the expansion of the armistice negotiations between Russia and Poland into a general European conference, ''which would in all probability involve two results, from both of which this country strongly recoils, viz.: The recognition of the Bolshevist régime, and a settlement of the Russian problem almost inevitably upon the basis of a dismemberment of Russia.'' . . .

Our government has not receded from this position. Secretary Hughes, in rejecting trade proposals of the Soviet, said on March 25, 1921, ''It is only in the productivity of Russia that there is any hope for the Russian people, and it is idle to expect resumption of trade until the economic bases of production are securely established. Production is conditioned upon the safety of life, the recognition by firm guaranties of private property, the sanctity of contract and the rights of free labor,'' and he postpones any consideration of trade relations until such time as our government has convincing evidence of fundamental changes that will fulfill these conditions.

In the face of these declarations it is impossible to hold that to-day any such relations exist between the United States and Russia as call upon our courts to enforce rules in favor of the latter depending on the comity of nations.

The judgment appealed from should be affirmed, with costs.[1]

B. Status of de facto governments.

The question as to the extent to which the acts of a *de facto* government may be given legal validity by reason of the fact that, although the government is not recognized, it is actually in control of the territory and exercising the functions of government, is one to be decided by the circumstances. As a rule, the normal business relations of private citizens living under the *de facto* government are legal transactions and enforceable as such, whether or not the *de facto* government succeeds in surviving. [United States (re Hopkins) v. Mexico.] Query, does the fact that a particular state has failed to recognize the new *de facto* government preclude it from pressing the claims of its nationals arising out of governmental acts of the *de facto* government? [Great Britain and Costa Rica: Tinoco Arbitration.]

---

[1] SUPPLEMENTARY CASES. Query, what effect upon a pending suit by a *de jure* government in the courts of a foreign state would result from the displacement of the *de jure* government by a new *de facto* but unrecognized government? In the case of Lehigh Valley Railroad Co. v. State of Russia, 21 F. (2d) 396 (1927), involving the question whether an action begun by the Russian Imperial Government in 1916 might be continued in 1927 by a representative of the old government recognized by the United States in spite of the fact that a different government was in *de facto* control in Russia, the Circuit Court of Appeals held that the old recognized government might carry on the suit, at least until the new government became accredited by recognition by the political departments of the United States. See below, p. 601.

UNITED STATES ON BEHALF OF GEORGE .W. HOPKINS, CLAIMANT v. UNITED MEXICAN STATES.

General Claims Commission, 1926.

Opinions of Commissioners under the Convention Concluded September 8, 1923, between the United States and Mexico, p. 42.

[By the Commission, VAN VOLLENHOVEN, PARKER, MACGREGOR.] This case is before this Commission on the Mexican Agent's motion to dismiss.

1. It is put forward by the United States of America on behalf of George W. Hopkins, who was born and has ever remained an American national. The claim is based on six postal money orders aggregating 1,013.40 pesos alleged to have been purchased by the claimant from the Mexican Government at its postoffices of Mazatlan, Sinaloa, and Guaymas, Sonora, between April 27, 1914, and June 8, 1914, inclusive. It is alleged that all of these money orders were in due time presented to the Mexican authorities and payment was refused by them. The ground of the motion to dismiss is that these money orders were issued by the Huerta administration, which was illegal, that the acts of such administration did not bind Mexico, and that therefore these orders can not be made the basis of a claim before this Commission against the United Mexican States.

Status of Huerta administration

2. In considering the character and the status of the Huerta régime this international tribunal will look to the substance rather than its form, a substance which is not difficult to discover notwithstanding the flimsy garb of constitutional power under which it undertook to masquerade. There is no room to doubt but that the assumption of power by Huerta was pure usurpation. From being the military commander of the capital, charged with the protection of the administration of President Madero against the revolutionary activities of Generals Reyes and Díaz to overthrow it, Huerta went over to Madero's enemies (February 18, 1913); he declared himself provisional president while Madero lawfully was in power (February 18, 1913, at 2 p. m. and 9 p. m.); he imprisoned both President Madero and Vice-President Bino Suárez and compelled them to tender their resignations (February 19, 1913, about 8 a. m.); he forced the provisional acting president, Lascurain, to appoint him, Huerta, the ranking minister in office (February 19, 1913, at 10 a. m.), and immediately thereafter forced him to resign (February 19, 1913, at 11 a. m.); he had his arbitrary acts confirmed by a congress from which his antagonists had fled and which could not muster a quorum (February 19, 1913, at 11:20 a. m.); and he contrived to procure recognition in some quarters as the constitutional provisional president through the suppression of press news so that the manner of

his forcibly seizing the reins of government should not be known. The supreme court felicitated Huerta on his assuming office prior to the assassination of Madero and his associates and before the court could have known of the methods used to seize the office. The governors of the States which recognized Huerta were, most of them, either the partisans of Reyes and Díaz with whom Huerta conspired or had been placed in power by Huerta directly after the state stroke. It is not for an international tribunal to assume that events so abhorrent as these are only to be viewed from their "legal" aspect and that uncovering the real facts means an intrusion of "moral" or "sentimental" considerations on the sacred ground of law. Nor is there reason for alleging that in so judging the Commission infringes upon Mexico's sovereignty over its domestic affairs, for the Mexican Government itself, through its Agency, invites the Commission to do so.

3. Before considering the question of the validity or nullity of acts done by or contracts entered into with a government administration of this character it is necessary to state at once the impossibility of treating alike all acts done by such an administration or all transactions entered into by an individual with it. There seems to be a tendency both in jurisprudence and in literature to do so, to declare that all acts of a given administration, the legality of which is doubtful, must have been either valid or void. Facts and practice, however, point in a different direction.

4. The greater part of governmental machinery in every modern country is not affected by changes in the higher administrative officers. The sale of postage stamps, the registration of letters, the acceptance of money orders and telegrams (where post and telegraph are government services), the sale of railroad tickets (where railroads are operated by the government), the registration of births, deaths, and marriages, even many rulings by the police and the collection of several types of taxes, go on, and must go on, without being affected by new elections, government crises, dissolutions of parliament, and even state strokes.
. . .

5. The difficulty of distinguishing between the government itself and the administration of that government arises at the point where the voluntary dealings and relations between the individual and the government agencies assume a personal character in support of the particular agencies administering the government for the time being. To this class belong voluntary undertakings to provide a revolutionary administration with money or arms or munitions and the like. But the ordinary agencies, departments, and bureaus of the government must continue to function notwithstanding its principal administrative offices may be in the hands of usurpers, and in such a case the sale and delivery to these necessary and legitimate agencies of supplies, merchandise, and the like, to enable the government itself in its unperson-

al aspect to function is a very different transaction from one having for its object the support of an individual or group of individuals seeking to maintain themselves in office. The character of each transaction must be judged and determined by the facts of the particular case. . . .

7. Facts and practice, as related to the Huerta administration in Mexico, illustrate the necessity of a cleavage in determining the validity or nullity of its acts.

8. In the field of international relations the distinction is apparent. Where preexisting relations with government agencies continued under such circumstances as not to imply either approval or disapproval of the new administration or recognition of its authority, these transactions must be treated as government transactions and binding on it as such rather than transactions had with a particular administration. The routine diplomatic and consular business of the nation continued to be transacted with the agencies assuming to act for the government and which were in control of the foreign office, the treasury, and the embassies, legations, and consulates abroad. Even the United States, though placing its stamp of disapproval in the most unmistakable manner on the act of Huerta in usurping authority, kept its embassy in Mexico City open for the transaction of routine business, entrusting it to a chargé of d'affaires, and maintained its consulates throughout Mexico. Such relations, so maintained were entirely unpersonal; they constituted relations with the United Mexican States, with its Government as such, without respect to the status of the individual assuming to act for the Government.

9. This distinction was recognized in the decisions made by the Carranza administration as to the legality of the acts of the Huerta administration. Such acts as the registration of births, deaths, and marriages were practically undisturbed, because they were performed in the orderly functioning of the government quite independent of the recognition or non-recognition of the individuals exercising authority. These were unpersonal acts of the Government itself as an abstract entity. It does not matter for the present argument, and it is not for the Commission to decide, whether the terms of the Carranza decree of July 11, 1916, are or not in all things to be commended; it is noticed here only to point out that it recognized the distinction between transactions with and by the Government itself and transactions with and by the Huerta administration. . . .

11. It is clear that the sale by the Mexican Government to and the purchase by the claimant Hopkins of postal money orders falls within the category of purely government routine having no connection with or relation to the individuals administering the Government for the time being. The facts as developed in the memorial and the briefs, which are not contested by the Mexican Agent, aptly illustrate the necessity of the distinction here made between acts of the Huerta admin-

istration in its personal character and acts of the Government itself in its unpersonal character. . . . At no time [during the Huerta administration] did the Government machinery cease to function, notwithstanding the change in the personnel of some members of its executive branch. To the extent that this machinery acted in the discharge of its usual and ordinary functions or to the extent that it received benefits from transactions of an unusual nature, Mexico is bound. . . .

14. From the foregoing the Commission concludes that Hopkins' contracts are unaffected by the legality or illegality of the Huerta administration as such, that they bind the Government of Mexico, that they have not been nullified by any decree issued by Carranza, and that they have not been and can not be nullified by any unilateral act of the Government of Mexico.

Nonrecognition as an estoppel

15. Has the American Government forfeited its right to espouse Hopkins' claim because in 1913 it warned its citizens against the "usurper" Huerta and never recognized his administration? The Commission holds that such warnings and such failure to recognize the Huerta administration can not affect the vested rights of an American citizen or act as an estoppel of the right of the American Government to espouse the claim of such citizen before this Commission. (See the award of Honorable William H. Taft, Sole Arbitrator between Great Britain and Costa Rica, October 18, 1923, reported in 18 American Journal of International Law, at pages 155–157.) The position assumed by the American Government under the administration of President Wilson was purely political and was binding, even on that administration, only so long as it was not modified. It was an executive policy, which, so long as it remained unmodified and unrevoked, would close to the American Government the avenue of diplomatic interposition and intervention with the Huerta administration. It temporarily, therefore, rendered this remedy—diplomatic interposition or intervention—unavailable to an American citizen but it did not affect a vested *right* of such citizen. But non-recognition of the Huerta administration by the American Government under the Wilson administration was not dependent upon Huerta's paramountcy in Mexico. It meant that, even if it were paramount, it came into power through force by methods abhorrent to the standards of modern civilization, that it was not "elected by legal and constitutional means," and hence, while the *Government* of Mexico continued to exist and to function, its *administration* was not entitled to recognition. . . .

Decision

17. From the foregoing opinion it follows, and the Commission decides, that the allegations contained in the memorial filed herein bring

this claim within the jurisdiction of this Commission. Assuming that such allegations are true, the Government of Mexico is bound to pay the claimant the postal money orders declared upon. The motion of the Mexican Agent to dismiss is therefore overruled.

GREAT BRITAIN AND COSTA RICA: THE TINOCO ARBITRATION.

Arbitration under the Agreement of January 12, 1922. 1923.

American Journal of International Law, XVIII (1924), 147.

TAFT, Arbitrator. This is a proceeding under a treaty of arbitration between Great Britain and Costa Rica. . . .

In January, 1917, the Government of Costa Rica, under President Alfredo Gonzalez, was overthrown by Frederico Tinoco, the Secretary of War. Gonzalez fled. Tinoco assumed power, called an election, and established a new constitution in June, 1917. His government continued until August, 1919, when Tinoco retired, and left the country. His government fell in September following. After a provisional government under one Barquero, the old constitution was restored and elections held under it. The restored government is a signatory to this treaty of arbitration.

On the 22d of August, 1922, the Constitutional Congress of the restored Costa Rican Government passed a law known as Law of Nullities No. 41. It invalidated all contracts between the executive power and private persons, made with or without approval of the legislative power between January 27, 1917 and September 2, 1919, covering the period of the Tinoco government. It also nullified the legislative decree No. 12 of the Tinoco government, dated June 28, 1919, authorizing the issue of the fifteen million colones currency notes. The colon is a Costa Rican gold coin or standard nominally equal to forty-six and one-half cents of an American dollar, but it is uncoined and the exchange value of the paper colon actually in circulation is much less. The Nullities Law also invalidated the legislative decree of the Tinoco government of July 8, 1919, authorizing the circulation of notes of the nomination of 1,000 colones, and annulled all transactions with such colones bills between holders and the state, directly or indirectly, by means of negotiation or contract, if thereby the holders received value as if they were ordinary bills of current issue.

The claim of Great Britain is that the Royal Bank of Canada and the Central Costa Rica Petroleum Company are Britain corporations whose shares are owned by British subjects; that the Banco Internacional of Costa Rica and the Government of Costa Rica are both indebted to the Royal Bank in the sum of 998,000 colones, evidenced by 998,000 colones bills held by the Bank; that the Central Costa Rica Petroleum Company owns, by due assignment, a grant by the Tinoco government in 1918 of the right to explore for and exploit oil deposits in Costa Rica, and that both the indebtedness and the concession have been annulled without right by the Law of Nullities and should be excepted from its operation. She asks an award that she is entitled on behalf of her subjects to have the claim of the bank paid, and the concession recognized and given effect by the Costa Rican Government.

The Government of Costa Rica denies its liability for the acts or obligations of the Tinoco government and maintains that the Law of Nullities was a legitimate exercise of its legislative governing power. It further denies the validity of such claims on the merits, unaffected by the Law of Nullities.

It is convenient to consider first the general objections to both claims of Great Britain, urged by Costa Rica, and then if such general objections cannot prevail, to consider the merits of each claim and Costa Rica's special defenses to it.

Coming now to the general issues applicable to both claims, Great Britain contends, first, that the Tinoco government was the only government of Costa Rica *de facto* and *de jure* for two years and nine months; that during that time there is no other government disputing its sovereignty, that it was in peaceful administration of the whole country, with the acquiescence of its people.

Second, that the succeeding government could not by legislative decree avoid responsibility for acts of that government affecting British subjects, or appropriate or confiscate rights and property by that government except in violation of international law; that the Act of Nullities is as to British interests, therefore itself a nullity, and is to be disregarded, with the consequence that the contracts validly made with the Tinoco government must be performed by the present Costa Rican Government, and that the property which has been invaded or the rights nullified must be restored.

To these contentions the Costa Rican Government answers: First, that the Tinoco government was not a *de facto* or *de jure* government according to the rules of international law. This raises an issue of fact.

Second, that the contracts and obligations of the Tinoco government, set up by Great Britain on behalf of its subjects, are void, and do not create a legal obligation, because the government of Tinoco and its acts were in violation of the constitution of Costa Rica of 1871.

Third, that Great Britain is estopped by the fact that it did not recognize the Tinoco government during its incumbency, to claim on behalf of its subjects that Tinoco's was a government which could confer rights binding on its successor. . . .

Dr. John Bassett Moore, now a member of the Permanent Court of International Justice, in his Digest of International Law, Volume I, p. 249, announces the general principle which has had such universal acquiescence as to become well settled international law:

"Changes in the government or the internal policy of a state do not as a rule affect its position in international law. A monarchy may be transformed into a republic or a republic into a monarchy; absolute principles may be substituted for constitutional, or the reverse; but, though the government changes, the nation remains, with rights and obligations unimpaired. . . .

"The principle of the continuity of states has important results. The state is bound by engagements entered into by governments that have ceased to exist; the restored government is generally liable for the acts of the usurper. The governments of Louis XVIII and Louis Philippe so far as practicable indemnified the citizens of foreign states for losses caused by the government of Napoleon; and the King of the Two Sicilies made compensation to citizens of the United States for the wrongful acts of Murat."

Again Dr. Moore says:

"The origin and organization of government are questions generally of internal discussion and decision. Foreign powers deal with the existing *de facto* government, when sufficiently established to give reasonable assurance of its permanence, and of the acquiescence of those who constitute the state in its ability to maintain itself, and discharge its internal duties and its external obligations."

The same principle is announced in Professor Borchard's new work on The Diplomatic Protection of Citizens Abroad. . . .

First, what are the facts to be gathered from the documents and evidence submitted by the two parties as to the *de facto* character of the Tinoco government?

In January, 1917, Frederico A. Tinoco was Secretary of War under Alfredo Gonzalez, the then President of Costa Rica. On the ground that Gonzalez was seeking re-election as President in violation of a constitutional limitation, Tinoco used the army and navy to seize the government, assume the provisional headship of the Republic and become Commander-in-Chief of the army. Gonzalez took refuge in the American Legation, thence escaping to the United States. Tinoco constituted a provisional government at once and summoned the people to an election for deputies to a constituent assembly on the first of May, 1917. At the same time he directed an election to take place for the Presidency and himself became a candidate. An election was held. Some 61,000 votes were cast for Tinoco and 259 for another candidate. Tinoco then was inaugurated as the President to administer his powers under the former constitution until the creation of a new one. A new constitution was adopted June 8, 1917, supplanting the constitution of 1871. For a full two years Tinoco and the legislative assembly under him peaceably administered the affairs of the Government of Costa Rica, and there was no disorder of a revolutionary character during that interval. No other government of any kind asserted power in the country. The courts sat, Congress legislated, and the government was duly administered. Its power was fully established and peaceably exercised. The people seemed to have accepted Tinoco's government with great good will when it came in, and to have welcomed the change. . . .

Though Tinoco came in with popular approval, the result of his two years administration of the law was to rouse opposition to him. Conspiracies outside of the country were projected to organize a force to attack him. But this did not result in any substantial conflict or even a nominal provisional government on the soil until considerably more than two years after the inauguration of his government, and did not result in the establishment of any other real government until September of that year, he having renounced his Presidency in August preceding, on the score of his ill health, and withdrawn to Europe. The truth is that throughout the record as made by the case and counter case, there is no substantial evidence that Tinoco was not in actual and peaceable administration without resistance or conflict or contest by anyone until a few months before the time when he retired and resigned. . . .

It is true that action of the supporters of those seeking to restore the former government was somewhat delayed by the influence of the United States with Gonzalez and his friends against armed action, on the ground that military disturbances in Central America during the World War would be prejudicial to the interests of the Allied Powers. It is not important, however, what were the causes that enabled Tinoco to carry on his government effectively and peaceably. The question is, must his government be considered a link in the continuity of the Government of Costa Rica? I must hold that from the evidence that the Tinoco government was an actual sovereign government.

But it is urged that many leading Powers refused to recognize the Tinoco government, and that recognition by other nations is the chief and best evidence of the birth, existence and continuity of succession of a government. Undoubtedly recognition by other Powers is an important evidential factor in establishing proof of the existence of a government in the society of nations. What are the facts as to this? The Tinoco government was recognized by Bolivia on May 17, 1917; by Argentina on May 22, 1917; by Chile on May 22, 1917; by Haiti on May 22, 1917; by Guatemala on May 28, 1917; by Switzerland on June 1, 1917; by Germany on June 10, 1917; by Denmark on June 18, 1917; by Spain on June 18, 1917; by Mexico on July 1, 1917; by Holland on July 11, 1917; by the Vatican on June 9, 1917; by Columbia on August 9, 1917; by Austria on August 10, 1917; by Portugal on August 14, 1917; by El Salvador on September 12, 1917; by Roumania on November 15, 1917; by Brazil on November 28, 1917; by Peru on December 15, 1917; and by Ecuador on April 23, 1917.

What were the circumstances as to the other nations? . . .

The United States, on February 9, 1917, two weeks after Tinoco had assumed power, took this action:

"The Government of the United States has viewed the recent overthrow of the established government in Costa Rica with the gravest concern and considers that illegal acts of this character tend to disturb the peace of Central America and to disrupt the unity of the American continent. In view of its policy in regard to the assumption of power through illegal methods, clearly enunciated by it on several occasions during the past four years, the Government of the United States desires to set forth in an emphatic and distinct manner its present position in regard to the actual situation in Costa Rica which is that it will not give recognition or support to any government which may be established unless it is clearly proven that it is elected by legal and constitutional means."

And again on February 24, 1917:

"In order that citizens of the United States may have definite information as to the position of this Government in regard to any financial aid which they may give to, or any business transaction which they may have with those persons who overthrew the constitutional Government of Costa Rica by an act of armed rebellion, the Government of the United States desires to advise them that it will not consider any claims which may in the future arise from such dealings, worthy of its diplomatic support." . . .

Probably because of the leadership of the United States in respect to a matter of this kind, her then Allies in the war, Great Britain, France and Italy, declined to recognize the Tinoco government. Costa Rica was, therefore, not permitted to sign the Treaty of Peace at Versailles, although the Tinoco government had declared war against Germany.

The merits of the policy of the United States in this non-recognition it is not for the arbitrator to discuss, for the reason that in his consideration of this case, he is necessarily controlled by principles of international law, and however justified as a national policy non-recognition on such a ground may be, it certainly has not been acquiesced in by all the nations of the world, which is a condition precedent to considering it as a postulate of international law.

The non-recognition by other nations of a government claiming to be a national personality, is usually appropriate evidence that it has not attained the independence and control entitling it by international law to be classed as such. But when recognition *vel non* of a government is by such nations determined by inquiry, not into its *de facto* sovereignty and complete governmental control, but into its illegitimacy or irregularity of origin, their non-recognition loses something of evidential weight on the issue with which those applying the rules of international law are alone concerned. What is true of the non-recognition of the United States in its bearing upon the existence of a *de facto* government under Tinoco for thirty months is probably in a measure true of the non-recognition by her Allies in the European War. Such non-recognition for any reason, however, cannot outweigh the evidence disclosed by this record before me as to the *de facto* character of Tinoco's government, according to the standard set by international law.

Second. It is ably and earnestly argued on behalf of Costa Rica that the Tinoco government cannot be considered a *de facto* government, because it was not established and maintained in accord with the constitution of Costa Rica of 1871. To hold that a government which establishes itself and maintains a peaceful administration, with the acquiescence of the people for a substantial period of time, does not become a *de facto* government unless it conforms to a previous constitution would be to hold that within the rules of international law a revolution contrary to the fundamental law of the existing government cannot establish a new government. This cannot be, and is not, true. The change by revolution upsets the rule of the authorities in power under the then existing fundamental law, and sets aside the fundamental law in so far as the change of rule makes it necessary. To speak of a revolution creating a *de facto* government, which conforms to the limitations of the old constitution is to use a contradiction in terms. The same government continues internationally, but not the internal law of its being. The issue is not whether the new government assumes power or conducts its administration under constitutional limitations established by the people during the incumbency of the government it has overthrown. The question is, has it really established itself in such a way that all within its influence recognize its control, and that there is no opposing force assuming to be a government in its place? Is it discharging its functions as a government usually does, respected within its own jurisdiction? . . .

Third. It is further objected by Costa Rica that Great Britain by her failure to recognize the Tinoco government is estopped now to urge claims of her subjects dependent upon the acts and contracts of the Tinoco government. The evidential weight of such non-recognition against the claim of its *de facto* character I have already considered and admitted. The contention here goes further and precludes a government which did not recognize a *de facto* government from appearing in an international tribunal in behalf of its nationals to claim any rights based on the acts of such government.

To sustain this view a great number of decisions in English and American courts are cited to the point that a municipal court cannot, in litigation before it, recognize or assume the *de facto* character of a foreign government which the executive department of foreign affairs of the government of which the court is a branch has not recognized. This is clearly true. It is for the executive to decide questions of foreign policy and not courts. It would be most unseemly to have a conflict of opinion in respect to foreign relations of a nation between its department charged with the conduct of its foreign affairs and its judicial branch. But such cases have no bearing on the point before us. Here the executive of Great Britain takes the position that the Tinoco government which it did not recognize, was nevertheless a *de facto* government that could create rights in British subjects which it now seeks to protect. Of course, as already emphasized, its failure to recognize the *de facto* government can be used against it as evidence to disprove the character it now attributes to that government, but this does not bar it from changing its position. Should a case arise in one of its own courts after it has changed its position, doubtless that court would feel it incumbent upon it to note the change in its further rulings. . . .

There are other estoppels recognized in municipal law than those which rest on equitable considerations. They are based on public policy. It may be urged that it would be in the interest of the stability of governments and the orderly adjustment of international relations, and so a proper rule of international law, that a government in recognizing or refusing to recognize a government claiming admission to the society of nations should thereafter be held to an attitude consistent with its deliberate conclusion on this issue. Arguments for and against such a rule occur to me; but it suffices to say that I have not been cited to text writers of authority or to decisions of significance indicating a general acquiescence of nations in such a rule. Without this, it cannot be applied here as a principle of international law. . . .

A consideration of the issues before us, therefore, recurs to the merits of the two claims. The decision of them must be governed by the answer to the question whether the claims would have been good against the Tinoco government as a government, unaffected by the Law of Nullities, and unaffected by the Costa Rican Constitution of 1871. . . . [1]

My award, therefore, is that the Law of Nullities in its operation upon the validity of the 998 one thousand colones bills and the claim in behalf of the Royal Bank, will work no injury of which Great Britain can complain, if Costa Rica assigns all her interest in the mortgage for $100,000 upon Jose Joaquin Tinoco's estate executed by his widow, together with all interest paid thereon to the Royal Bank, and that, upon Costa Rica's executing this assignment and delivering the mortgage, the Royal Bank should deliver to the Government of Costa Rica the 998 one thousand colones bills held by it.

---

[1] The arbitrator found that there were irregularities in the acceptance by the Royal Bank of the deposits to the credit of the Tinoco government and in the payments made against them. He also found that the Costa Rican government had, after the fall of the Tinoco government, prosecuted a suit against the widow of Tinoco's brother based on the payment to him by the Royal Bank of the sum of $100,000, and that the suit had been compromised by a mortgage given by the widow against her husband's estates.

My award further is that the Law of Nullities in decreeing the invalidity of the Amory concession worked no injury to the Central Costa Rica Petroleum Company, Ltd., the assignee of the concession, and the British Controlled Oil Fields, Ltd., its sole stockholder, of which Great Britain can complain, because the concession was in fact invalid under the Constitution of 1917. . . . [1]

---

[1] SUPPLEMENTARY CASES. In the case of Sokoloff v. National City Bank, 239 N. Y. 158 (1924), the plaintiff had in June, 1917, deposited funds in the bank against which the bank was to open an account in its Petrograd branch. Upon the subsequent confiscation of the bank's Russian assets by decree of the Soviet government the bank sought to plead the acts of the Soviet government in discharge of its obligation to the plaintiff. The Court of Appeals held that, while under certain circumstances effect might be given to the ordinances of an unrecognized but notoriously *de facto* government, in the instant case there was no injustice in holding the bank liable to make payment since the bank was not acting as bailee for the plaintiff nor were any of its confiscated assets earmarked to the plaintiff's use.

In the case of Russian Reinsurance Co. v. Stoddard, 240 N. Y. 149 (1925) a Russian company, incorporated under the government of the Czar, had deposited funds with a New York trust company as a condition of doing business in the state. Having been put out of business by the Soviet government and its property confiscated, the company, then domiciled in Paris, sued to recover the funds on deposit in New York. The court denied the suit, holding that while the failure of the United States to recognize the Soviet government resulted in depriving its decrees of confiscation of the force which those of a recognized sovereign government would have, yet it was necessary for the court to take into account the changed situation in Russia and the fact that other nations recognized the validity of the Russian decrees even if the United States did not. The court therefore refused to recognize the plaintiff as the party entitled to bring suit.

In the case of Russian Volunteer Fleet v. United States, 282 U. S. 481 (1931) the Supreme Court, in construing federal legislation dealing with claims against the United States for compensation for the requisitioning by United States Shipping Board Emergency Fleet Corporation of contracts for the construction of vessels, held that an alien friend might bring suit in spite of the fact that citizens of the United States were not entitled to prosecute claims against the government of the alien's country in its courts or that the United States had not recognized the régime (in this case the Soviet government) which was functioning in that country. "The provision that private property shall not be taken for public use without just compensation," said the court, "establishes a standard for our government which the Constitution does not make dependent upon the standards of other governments."

In the case of Salimoff & Co. v. Standard Oil Co., 262 N. Y. 220 (1933) the Court of Appeals of New York followed the principle laid down in the Sokoloff case (that cognizance might be taken of the acts and decrees of an unrecognized foreign government "if violence to fundamental principles of justice or to our own policy might otherwise be done") and held that the defendants, in purchasing oil from the Soviet government after it had confiscated the oil lands formerly owned by the plaintiffs, could not be held for an accounting in New York, the Soviet confiscation decrees having completely divested the interest asserted by the former owners.

C. Collateral effects of the recognition of new governments.

When an insurgent group, having overthrown an established government and set up a *de facto* government, comes to be formally recognized
as the *de jure* government of the state, the validity of acts performed by
it during the period of the revolution dates back to the commencement
of its *de facto* existence. Query, would the creation of this retroactive
responsibility go so far as to give personal immunity to an officer of
the insurgent government for official acts performed by him during
the revolution? [Underhill v. Hernandez.] Would it validate contracts entered into by such an officer or other governmental representative during the revolution? [Oetjen v. Central Leather Co.]
Would the recognition of a *de facto* government by a foreign state give
to the new *de jure* government the right to continue a suit in the courts
of a foreign state to which a plea in abatement had been previously sustained on ground of non-recognition? [Republic of China v. Merchants'
Fire Assurance Corporation.]

UNDERHILL v. HERNANDEZ.

United States, Supreme Court, 1897.

168 U. S. 250. [42 L. ed. 456; 18 S. Ct. 83.]

In the early part of 1892 a revolution was initiated in Venezuela,
against the administration thereof, which the revolutionists claimed had
ceased to be the legitimate government. The principal parties to this conflict were those who recognized Palacio as their head, and those who followed the leadership of Crespo. General Hernandez belonged to the anti-
administration party, and commanded its forces in the vicinity of Ciudad
Bolivar. On the 8th of August, 1892, an engagement took place between the armies of the two parties at Buena Vista, some seven miles
from Bolivar, in which the troops under Hernandez prevailed; and, on
the 13th of August, Hernandez entered Bolivar, and assumed command
of the city. All of the local officials had in the meantime left, and the vacant positions were filled by General Hernandez, who from that date, and
during the period of the transactions complained of was the civil and
military chief of the city and district. In October the party in revolt had
achieved success generally, taking possession of the capital of Venezuela,
October 6th; and on October 23, 1892, the Crespo government, so called,
was formally recognized as the legitimate government of Venezuela by
the United States.

George F. Underhill was a citizen of the United States, who had constructed a waterworks system for the city of Bolivar, under a contract
with the government, and was engaged in supplying the place with water; and he also carried on a machinery repair business. Some time after

the entry of General Hernandez, Underhill applied to him, as the officer in command, for a passport to leave the city. Hernandez refused this request, and requests made by others in Underhill's behalf, until October 18th, when a passport was given, and Underhill left the country.

This action was brought to recover damages for the detention caused by reason of the refusal to grant the passport, for the alleged confinement of Underhill to his own house, and for certain alleged assaults and affronts by the soldiers of Hernandez's army.

The cause was tried in the Circuit Court of the United States for the Eastern District of New York, and on the conclusion of plaintiff's case the Circuit Court ruled that upon the facts plaintiff was not entitled to recover, and directed a verdict for defendant, on the ground that "because the acts of defendant were those of a military commander, representing a *de facto* government in the prosecution of a war, he was not civilly responsible therefor." Judgment having been rendered for defendant, the case was taken to the Circuit Court of Appeals, and by that court affirmed, upon the ground "that the acts of the defendant were the acts of the government of Venezuela, and as such are not properly the subject of adjudication in the courts of another government." 26 U. S. App. 573. Thereupon the cause was brought to this court on certiorari.

MR. CHIEF JUSTICE FULLER, after stating the case, delivered the opinion of the court.

Every sovereign state is bound to respect the independence of every other sovereign state, and the courts of one country will not sit in judgment on the acts of the government of another, done within its own territory. Redress of grievances by reason of such acts must be obtained through the means open to be availed of by sovereign powers as between themselves.

Nor can the principle be confined to lawful or recognized governments, or to cases where redress can manifestly be had through public channels. The immunity of individuals from suits brought in foreign tribunals for acts done within their own states, in the exercise of governmental authority, whether as civil officers or as military commanders, must necessarily extend to the agents of governments ruling by paramount force as matter of fact. Where a civil war prevails (that is, where the people of a country are divided into two hostile parties, who take up arms and oppose one another by military force), generally speaking, foreign nations do not assume to judge of the merits of the quarrel. If the party seeking to dislodge the existing government succeeds, and the independence of the government it has set up is recognized, then the acts of such government, from the commencement of its existence, are regarded as those of an independent nation. If the political revolt fails of success, still, if actual war has been waged, acts of legitimate warfare cannot be made the basis of individual liability. United States v. Rice, 4 Wheat. 246; Fleming v. Page, 9 How. 603; Thorington v. Smith, 8 Wall. 1; Williams v. Bruffy, 96 U. S. 176; Ford v. Surget, 97 U. S. 594; Dow v. Johnson, 100 U. S. 158; and other cases.

Revolutions or insurrections may inconvenience other nations, but by accommodation to the facts the application of settled rules is readily reached. And, where the fact of the existence of war is in issue in the instance of complaint of acts committed within foreign territory, it is not an absolute prerequisite that that fact should be made out by an acknowledgment of belligerency, as other official recognition of its existence may be sufficient proof thereof. The Three Friends, 166 U. S. 1.

In this case the archives of the State Department show that civil war was flagrant in Venezuela from the spring of 1892, that the revolution was successful, and that the revolutionary government was recognized by the United States as the government of the country; it being, to use the language of the Secretary of State in a communication to our minister to Venezuela, "accepted by the people, in the possession of the power of the nation, and fully established."

That these were facts of which the court is bound to take judicial notice, and for information as to which it may consult the Department of State, there can be no doubt. Jones v. United States, 137 U. S. 202; Mighell v. Sultan of Johore [1894] 1 Q. B. 149.

It is idle to argue that the proceedings of those who thus triumphed should be treated as the acts of banditti or mere mobs.

We entertain no doubt, upon the evidence that Hernandez was carrying on military operations in support of the revolutionary party. It may be that adherents of that side of the controversy in the particular locality where Hernandez was the leader of the movement entertained a preference for him as the future executive head of the nation, but that is beside the question. The acts complained of were the acts of a military commander representing the authority of the revolutionary party as a government, which afterwards succeeded, and was recognized by the United States. We think the Circuit Court of Appeals was justified in concluding "that the acts of the defendant were the acts of the government of Venezuela, and as such are not properly the subject of adjudication in the courts of another government."

The decisions cited on plaintiff's behalf are not in point. Cases respecting arrests by military authority in the absence of the prevalence of war, or the validity of contracts between individuals entered into in aid of insurrection, or the right of revolutionary bodies to vex the commerce of the world on its common highway without incurring the penalties denounced on piracy, and the like, do not involve the questions presented here.

We agree with the Circuit Court of Appeals that "the evidence upon the trial indicated that the purpose of the defendant in his treatment of the plaintiff was to coerce the plaintiff to operate his waterworks and his repair works for the benefit of the community and the revolutionary forces,'' and that ''it was not sufficient to have warranted a finding by the jury that the defendant was actuated by malice or any personal or private motive,'' and we concur in its disposition of the rulings below. The decree of the circuit court is affirmed.

OETJEN v. CENTRAL LEATHER COMPANY.

United States, Supreme Court, 1918.

246 U. S. 297. [62 L. ed. 726; 38 S. Ct. 309.]

Mr. Justice Clarke delivered the opinion of the court.

These two cases involving the same question, were argued and will be decided together. They are suits in replevin and involve the title to two large consignments of hides, which the plaintiff in error claims to own as assignee of Martinez & Company, a partnership engaged in business in the City of Torreon, Mexico, but which the defendant in error claims to own by purchase from the Finnegan-Brown Company, a Texas corporation, which it is alleged purchased the hides in Mexico from General Francisco Villa, on January 3, 1914.

The cases were commenced in a Circuit Court of New Jersey, in which judgments were rendered for the defendants, which were affirmed by the Court of Errors and Appeals, and they are brought to this court on the theory, that the claim of title to the hides by the defendant in error is invalid because based upon a purchase from General Villa, who, it is urged, confiscated them contrary to the provisions of the Hague Convention of 1907 respecting the laws and customs of war on land; that the judgment of the state court denied to the plaintiff in error this right which he ''set up and claimed'' under the Hague Convention or treaty; and that this denial gives him the right of review in this court.

A somewhat detailed description will be necessary of the political conditions in Mexico prior to and at the time of the seizure of the property in controversy by the military authorities. It appears in the record, and is a matter of general history, that on February 23, 1913, Madero, President of the Republic of Mexico, was assassinated; that immediately thereafter General Huerto declared himself Provisional President of the Republic and took the oath of office as such; that on the twenty-sixth day of March following General Carranza, who was then Governor of the State of Coahuila, inaugurated a revolution against the claimed authority of Huerta and in a ''Manifesto addressed to the Mexican Nation'' proclaimed the organization of a constitutional government under ''The Plan of Guadalupe,'' and that civil war was at once entered upon between the followers and forces of the two leaders. When General Carranza assumed the leadership of what were called the Constitutionalist forces he commissioned General Villa his representative, as "Commander of the North," and assigned him to an independent command in that part of the country. Such progress was made by the Carranza forces that in the autumn of 1913 they were in military possession, as the record shows, of approximately two-thirds of the area of the entire country, with the exception of a few scattered towns and cities, and after a battle lasting several days the City of Torreon in the State of Coahuila was captured by General Villa on October 1 of that year. Immediately after the capture of Torreon, Villa proposed levying a military contribution on the inhabitants, for the support of his army, and thereupon influential citizens, preferring to provide the required money by an assessment upon the community to having their property forcibly seized, called together a largely attended meeting and, after negotiations with General Villa as to the amount to be paid, an assessment was made on the men of property of the city, which was in large part promptly paid. Martinez, the owner from whom the plaintiff in error claims title to the property involved in this case, was a wealthy resident of Torreon and was a dealer in hides in a large way. Being an adherent to Huerta, when Torreon was captured Martinez fled the city and failed to pay the assessment imposed upon him, and it was to satisfy this assessment that, by order of General Villa, the hides in controversy were seized and on January 3, 1914, were sold in Mexico to the Finnegan-Brown Company. They were paid for in Mexico, and were thereafter shipped into the United States and were replevied, as stated.

This court will take judicial notice of the fact that, since the transactions thus detailed and since the trial of this case in the lower courts, the Government of the United States recognized the Government of Carranza as the *de facto* government of the Republic of Mexico, on October 19, 1915, and as the *de jure* government on August 31, 1917. Jones v. United States, 137 U. S. 202; Underhill v. Hernandez, 168 U. S. 250.

On this state of fact the plaintiff in error argues that the "Regulations" annexed to the Hague Convention of 1907 "Respecting Laws and Customs of War on Land" constitute a treaty between the United States and Mexico; that these "Regulations" forbid such seizure and sale of property as we are considering in this case; and that, therefore, somewhat vaguely, no title passed by the sale made by General Villa and the property may be recovered by the Mexican owner or his assignees when found in this country.

It would, perhaps, be sufficient answer to this contention to say that the Hague Conventions are international in character, designed and adapted to regulate international warfare, and that they do not, in terms or in purpose, apply to a civil war. Were it otherwise, however, it might be effectively argued that the declaration relied upon that "private property cannot be confiscated" contained in Article 46 of the Regulations does not have the scope claimed for it, since Article 49 provides that "money contributions" . . . "for the needs of the army" may be levied upon occupied territory, and Article 52 provides that "Requisitions in kind and services shall not be demanded . . . except for the needs of the army of occupation," and that contributions in kind shall, as far as possible, be paid for in cash, and when not so paid for a receipt shall be given and payment of the amount due shall be made as soon as possible. And also for the reason that the "Convention" to which the "Regulations" are annexed, recognizing the incomplete character of the results arrived at, expressly provides that until a more complete code is agreed upon, cases not provided for in the "Regulations" shall be governed by the principles of the law of nations.

But, since claims similar to the one before us are being made in many cases in this and in other courts, we prefer to place our decision upon the application of three clearly settled principles of law to the facts of this case as we have stated them.

The conduct of the foreign relations of our Government is committed by the Constitution to the Executive and Legislative—"the political"— Departments of the Government, and the propriety of what may be done in the exercise of this political power is not subject to judicial inquiry or decision. United States v. Palmer, 3 Wheat. 610; Foster v. Neilson, 2 Pet. 253, 307, 309; Garcia v. Lee, 12 Pet. 511, 517, 520; Williams v. Suffolk Ins. Co., 13 Pet. 415, 420; In re Cooper, 143 U. S. 472, 499. It has been specifically decided that "Who is the sovereign, *de jure* or *de facto,* of a territory is not a judicial, but is a political question, the determination of which by the legislative and executive departments of any government conclusively binds the judges, as well as all other officers, citizens and subjects of that government. This principle has always been upheld by this court, and has been affirmed under a great variety of circumstances." Jones v. United States, 137 U. S. 202, 212.

It is also the result of the interpretation by this court of the principles of international law that when a government which originates in revolution or revolt is recognized by the political department of our government as the *de jure* government of the country in which it is established, such recognition is retroactive in effect and validates all the actions and conduct of the government so recognized from the commencement of its existence. Williams v. Bruffy, 96 U. S. 176, 186; Underhill v. Hernandez, 168 U. S. 250, 253. See s. c. 65 Fed. Rep. 577.

To these principles we must add that: "Every sovereign State is bound to respect the independence of every other sovereign State, and the courts of one country will not sit in judgment on the acts of the government of another done within its own territory. Redress of grievances by reason of such acts must be obtained through the means open to be availed of by sovereign powers as between themselves." Underhill v. Hernandez, 168 U. S. 250, 253; American Banana Co. v. United Fruit Co., 213 U. S. 347.

Applying these principles of law to the case at bar, we have a duly commissioned military commander of what must be accepted as the legitimate government of Mexico, in the progress of a revolution, and when conducting active independent operations, seizing and selling in Mexico, as a military contribution, the property in controversy, at the time owned and in the possession of a citizen of Mexico, the assignor of the plaintiff in error. Plainly this was the action, in Mexico, of the legitimate Mexican government when dealing with a Mexican citizen, and, as we have seen, for the soundest reasons, and upon repeated decisions of this court such action is not subject to reëxamination and modification by the courts of this country.

The principle that the conduct of one independent government cannot be successfully questioned in the courts of another is as applicable to a case involving the title to property brought within the custody of a court, such as we have here, as it was held to be to the cases cited, in which claims for damages were based upon acts done in a foreign country, for it rests at last upon the highest considerations of international comity and expediency. To permit the validity of the acts of one sovereign State to be reëxamined and perhaps condemned by the courts of another would very certainly "imperil the amicable relations between governments and vex the peace of nations."

It is not necessary to consider, as the New Jersey court did, the validity of the levy of the contribution made by the Mexican commanding general, under rules of international law applicable to the situation, since the subject is not open to reëxamination by this or any other American court.

The remedy of the former owner, or of the purchaser from him, of the property in controversy, if either has any remedy, must be found in the courts of Mexico or through the diplomatic agencies of the political department of our Government. The judgments of the Court of Errors and Appeals of New Jersey must be affirmed.

REPUBLIC OF CHINA v. MERCHANTS' FIRE ASSURANCE CORPORATION OF NEW YORK.

SAME v. GREAT AMERICAN INSURANCE COMPANY.

United States, Circuit Court of Appeals, Ninth Circuit, 1929.

30 F. (2d) 278.

Appeals from the United States Court for China. . . .

Actions by the Republic of China against the Merchants' Fire Assurance Corporation of New York and against the Great American Insurance Company. From judgments of dismissal, plaintiff appeals. . . .

RUDKIN, Circuit Judge.   The Republic of China commenced an action in the United States Court for China to recover a fire loss under a policy issued by the Merchants' Fire Assurance Corporation of New York to the Chinese Government Telephone Administration at Wuchang, a department of the Republic of China, covering a building occupied by the Telephone Administration.   After the policy issued and after the fire loss occurred, the military forces of the national government captured the city of Wuchang and became the custodian of the policy and the property covered thereby.   At the time of the commencement of this action, the National Government was in control in 15 of the 18 provinces of China, comprising about three-fourths of its total area, but had not as yet been recognized by the United States.   The insurance company appeared specially in the court below, and filed a plea in abatement on the ground that the plaintiff was not the Republic of China, but was a revolutionary organization known as the National Government of China, unrecognized by the government of the United States of America and was without legal capacity to sue. The plea in abatement was sustained, and from the judgment of dismissal this appeal is prosecuted.

The courts of this country cannot recognize the existence of a government which originates in revolution or revolt, until it has first been recognized by the political department of the government, and inasmuch as there had been no such recognition of the National Government of China at the time of the trial in the court below, it would seem to follow that that government had no existence in contemplation of law and no legal capacity to sue in the courts of this country.   But since the trial below, there has been a material change in the situation, and of this change we must take judicial notice.   Jones v. United States, 137 U. S. 202, 11 S. Ct. 80, 34 L. Ed. 691.

On July 25, 1928, the Envoy Extraordinary and Minister Plenipotentiary to China, appointed by the President of the United States, and the Minister of Finance, appointed by the National Government of the Republic of China, entered into a treaty of commerce; and while this treaty has not as yet been ratified by the Senate, it contains a clear recognition by the Executive Department of this government of both the National Government of the Republic of China and of its accredited representative.   This recognition by the Executive Department would seem to satisfy the requirements of the law; but, if this is not enough, we have been advised by a telegram from the Secretary of State that the Minister Plenipotentiary and Envoy Extraordinary of the National Government of China has been officially received by this government, so that the recognition of the former is now settled beyond question.   "Recognition is not necessarily express; it may be implied, as when a state enters into negotiations with the new state, sends its diplomatic agents, receives such agents officially, gives ex-

equaturs to its consuls, forms with it conventional relations.'' Moore's
Digest of International Law, p. 73.

The judgment of the court below must therefore be reversed. The
appellant contends that it is entitled to a reversal and to a judgment in
its favor; but with this latter contention we are unable to agree. The
plea in abatement was sustained at the threshold, and the defendant was
never called upon to answer to the merits.

The judgment will therefore be reversed, and the cause remanded
for further proceedings. Inasmuch as the cause of reversal arose since
the trial in the court below, the reversal will be without costs to either
party. . . . [1]

---

[1] SUPPLEMENTARY CASES. In the case of State of Yucatan v. Argumedo, 92
Misc. Rep. 547 (1915), the governor of Yucatan sued for an accounting from
the defendant Argumedo who as insurgent governor of Yucatan during a brief
period had levied a forced loan and had subsequently fled from the country
taking with him a large part of the money and depositing it to his own account
in Havana and in New York City. The Supreme Court of New York held that
the recognition accorded by the United States to General Carranza in 1915 involved the recognition that his government was in "effective control" of the
State of Yucatan, so that the governor who held under his authority in Yucatan
might sue in the name of that state. The fact that the suit was begun before
the recognition was immaterial, "for the recognition of the Carranza government relates back to its inception, and all acts of the plaintiff government of
Yucatan, such as the bringing of this action, are ratified."

In the case of Luther v. Sagor, [1921] 3 K. B. 532, the plaintiffs, a Russian
company incorporated in 1898, whose lumber had been confiscated by the Soviet
decrees of 1918, brought suit to obtain title to a part of the lumber that had been
sold by the Soviet government to the defendants. The lower court, finding upon
the evidence submitted that Great Britain had not recognized the Soviet government, gave judgment for the plaintiffs. The Court of Appeal, presented with
evidence that in the meantime recognition had been given to the Soviet government as the *de facto* government of Russia, reversed the judgment and found the
title of the purchasers of the lumber valid. No weight was given to the point
that the recognition had been given to the Soviet government as merely *de facto*.
"The government of this country," said the court, "having, to use the language
just quoted, recognized the Soviet Government as the government really in
possession of the powers of sovereignty in Russia, the acts of that government
must be treated by the Courts of this country with all the respect due to the
acts of a duly recognized foreign sovereign State."

CHAPTER V

STATE SUCCESSION [1]

A. Universal succession following annexation of one state by another.

It is a general rule of international law that when one state annexes another state and thereby destroys its international personality entirely it succeeds to certain of the rights and obligations of the annexed state towards third states. The personal obligations of the extinct state which are executory in character, such as treaties of extradition and of amity and commerce, are in general wiped out and third states lose whatever benefits they may have enjoyed under such treaties. On the other hand the obligations of the extinct state, which during its lifetime had the effect of creating vested interests on the part of third states, such as contractual liabilities, concessions and debts, must be assumed by the annexing state, while at the same time the annexing state acquires the right to assert any claims of the extinct state of a similar character. Both obligations and claims are naturally assumed under the conditions under which they existed at the time the extinct state lost its legal personality. [United States v. Prioleau.] The rule of succession, however, is not so absolute as to have prevented a British court on one occasion from refusing to apply it in a case involving the claims of a former corporation of an extinct state which had acquired British nationality by reason of annexation of the territory. [West Rand Central Gold Mining Co. v. The King.] Query, is the state which succeeds to the extinct state under an international duty to assume obligations in tort incurred by the extinct state? [United States and Great Britain: Robert E. Brown Claim.] Query, should a new state be allowed to succeed to the property of an alleged *de facto* state subsequently become extinct, when there is no legal continuity between the two, although the territory of the former coincides approximately with the territory of the latter? [Irish Free State v. Guaranty Trust Co.]

---

[1] For a more detailed study of this subject, see Fenwick, Chap. VII, pp. 122–127; Oppenheim, Vol. I, §§ 80–84; Hyde, *op. cit.*, Vol. I, §§ 120–133; Feilchenfeld, Public Debts and State Succession.

UNITED STATES OF AMERICA v. PRIOLEAU.

Great Britain, High Court of Chancery, 1865.

2 Hemming & Miller, 559.[1]

Certain of the component States of the United States of America having seceded, and established a *de facto* Government under the style of the Confederate States of America, the Confederate Government raised funds by voluntary contributions and taxes, and thereby became possessed, as public property of their Government, of certain cotton.

By an agreement dated the 7th of July, 1864, between the defendant, Prioleau, one of the members of a firm of Fraser, Trenholm & Co., carrying on business in Liverpool, of the one part, and McCrae, who was an agent of the Confederate Government, of the other part, it was agreed as follows. Prioleau was to build eight steam-vessels, to be let out to hire to McCrae, and to be employed in the transport of cotton from the Confederate States. The cargoes were to be consigned to Prioleau, to be sold by him according to instructions. Out of the proceeds all expenses of sailing the ships and otherwise in respect thereof were to be recouped and commission paid, and of the balance one-half was to be applied as McCrae should direct, and the other half to be retained by Prioleau until the gross purchase-money of the vessels should be made up, and the vessels were then to be transferred to McCrae as purchaser. The purchase-money was to be 20 per cent. in addition to the cost of building. McCrae was to guarantee the safety of the ships, and pay damages for any that might be lost. The members of Fraser, Trenholm & Co., were Americans, but Prioleau was naturalized as a British subject.

Certain of the cotton before mentioned was shipped at Galveston in Texas, one of the Confederate States, by the agent of the Confederate Government, and taken to Havana, where the cotton was delivered to an agent of Prioleau's firm. He caused it to be reshipped in the Aline, one of the eight ships the subject of the agreement, and consigned to Fraser & Co. in Liverpool, where the ship had recently arrived, and was lying in the Mersey Docks. The ship Aline was consigned to the Defendants, Malcolmson and others. The Aline had left Havana before the submission of the Confederate armies in Texas, but after the conquest of other portions of the Confederate States.

The Plaintiffs by their bill claimed to have the cotton delivered up to them, and prayed an injunction to restrain the Defendants from dealing with it, and a receiver.

The case now came on upon motion for a receiver and injunction. It appeared in the evidence that the cotton was worth about £40,000, and that Fraser & Co. had incurred expenses in sailing the ships of

---

[1] Also reported, with slight variations, in 35 L. J. Ch. (N. S.) 7.

about £20,000, which remained unsatisfied, independently of the cost of building. Some of the ships had not gone to sea, and had not been taken from the builders' yard at the time of the subjection of the Confederate Government. . . .

VICE CHANCELLOR SIR W. PAGE WOOD:—The first point raised as to the rights of the United States Government, was whether they could take the cotton, except subject to the agreement between the Defendants and the Confederate Government. The title of the United States to what was once the property of the *de facto* Government of the so-called Confederate States is scarcely disputed. That Government raised funds (it scarcely matters whether by voluntary contribution or by taxation, though it is not denied that compulsory means were used), and this cotton is the produce of the funds so raised.

The *de facto* Government has been displaced, and the authority of the Government of the United States has been restored. This cotton was clearly acquired by the *de facto* Government, including several States, and not by the State of Texas alone. It is therefore public property of the people of the United States, and belongs as such to the Plaintiffs. The case of the King of the Two Sicilies and other authorities establish the principle that where a *de facto* Government has, as such, obtained possession of property, the Government which displaces it succeeds to all its rights.

Then upon the second point, as to the claim of the Defendants under the agreement: I confess I do not see much room to doubt that the United States must take subject to the agreement. That was the result of a negotiation between the *de facto* Government and certain persons in England (one of them, as it appears, being naturalized), who had a perfect right to deal with the *de facto* Government. It is not, as was said, a taking of the Plaintiffs' property with notice of their rights. If the transactions were regarded in that light, the result would be that no dealing with a *de facto* Government would ever be possible. That Government exercised the power of levying taxes, and enjoyed belligerent rights against what, the Plaintiffs say, was the only lawful Government. Other nations cannot enter into that question, but must protect their subjects, and cannot allow a Government which succeeds to the property of a *de facto* Government to displace rights acquired by their people. If this were otherwise, the Plaintiffs might equally have insisted that Confederate vessels lying in our ports during the war, should have been handed over by the authority of English tribunals to the Government of the United States, as being their property.

If the case had been that of a body of mere robbers devastating and plundering the territories of the United States, our Courts might have interfered to restore property so acquired; but then the rightful claimants would have been not the United States Government, but the persons who had been robbed. It is only because the money was raised by a *de facto* Government that the United States can come here to claim at all. Had the money been obtained by mere robbery it would never have become public property. It only acquired that character because it was levied by an authority exercising rights of Government.

I have so little doubt upon this point that I cannot put the Defendants upon any terms which would abridge their rights under the contract. It may be contended that the measure of damages should be ascertained on this principle. The Defendants to take out of the gross proceeds the expenses of sailing the ships, and then to divide the balance and carry one-half to the account of the purchase-money of the eight ships, and upon that the Plaintiffs to be entitled to the eight ships (other than those lost within the meaning of the last clause of the agreement). The only liability sworn to by the Defendants is a sum of £20,000 for expenses, and subject to the results of an account. I must treat them at this stage of the cause as entitled to that. Of the remaining £20,000, the Plaintiffs seem to be entitled to one-half and the Defendants to retain the other half, but only on the terms of giving up the ships. I do not now decide any of these questions; but, under the circumstances, the proper course will be to appoint the Defendant, Prioleau, receiver, he either giving security for £20,000, or else paying that amount into Court on or before the 1st of November.

WEST RAND CENTRAL GOLD MINING COMPANY, LIMITED, v. THE KING.

Great Britain, King's Bench Division, 1905.

L. R. [1905] 2 K. B. 391.

[Petition of right which alleged that before the outbreak of the South African War, gold, the produce of a mine in the South African Republic owned by the suppliants, had been seized by officials of that Republic, which gold or its value, under the laws of the Republic, the government thereof was bound to return. The suppliants contended that by reason of the conquest and annexation of the territories of the Republic by Her late Majesty, Queen Victoria, the obligation of the government thereof towards the suppliant was now binding upon His Majesty the King.] [1]

LORD ALVERSTONE, C. J. In this case the Attorney-General, on behalf of the Crown, demurred to a petition of right presented in the month of June, 1904, by the West Rand Central Gold Mining Company, Limited.

. . .

The Attorney-General for the Crown, as well as Lord Robert Cecil for the suppliants, desired that we should deal with the case as if any neces-

---

[1] For further details, see above, p. 33, where other parts of the case, bearing on the judicial attitude towards alleged rules of customary law, are reproduced.

sary amendment had been made, and decide the question whether all the contractual obligations of a State annexed by Great Britain upon conquest are imposed as a matter of course, and in default of express reservations, upon Great Britain, and can be enforced by British municipal law against the Crown in the only way known to British municipal law, that is by a petition of right. We have no hesitation in answering this question in the negative, but, inasmuch as it is one of great importance, and we have had the advantage of hearing very able argument upon both sides, we think it right to give our reasons in some detail.

Lord Robert Cecil argued that all contractual obligations incurred by a conquered State, before war actually breaks out, pass upon annexation to the conqueror, no matter what was their nature, character, origin, or history. . . . His main proposition was divided into three heads. First, that, by international law, the Sovereign of a conquering State is liable for the obligations of the conquered; secondly, that international law forms part of the law of England; and, thirdly, that rights and obligations, which were binding upon the conquered State, must be protected and can be enforced by the municipal Courts of the conquering State.

In support of his first proposition, Lord Robert Cecil cited passages from various writers on international law. . . . Before, however, dealing with the specific passages in the writings of jurists upon which the suppliants rely, we desire to consider the proposition, that by international law the conquering country is bound to fulfil the obligations of the conquered, upon principle; and upon principle we think it cannot be sustained. When making peace the conquering Sovereign can make any conditions he thinks fit respecting the financial obligations of the conquered country, and it is entirely at his option to what extent he will adopt them. It is a case in which the only law is that of military force. This, indeed, was not disputed by counsel for the suppliants; but it was suggested that although the Sovereign when making peace may limit the obligations to be taken over, if he does not do so they are all taken over, and no subsequent limitation can be put upon them. What possible reason can be assigned for such a distinction? Much inquiry may be necessary before it can be ascertained under what circumstances the liabilities were incurred, and what debts should *in foro conscientiae* be assumed. There must also be many contractual liabilities of the conquered State of the very existence of which the superior Power can know nothing, and as to which persons having claims upon the nation about to be vanquished would, if the doctrine contended for were correct, have every temptation to concealment—others, again, which no man in his senses would think of taking over. A case was put in argument which very well might occur. A country has issued obligations to such an amount as wholly to destroy the national credit, and the war, which ends in annexation of the country by another Power, may have been brought about by the very state of insolvency to which the conquered country has been reduced by its own misconduct. Can any valid reason be suggested why the country which has made war and succeeded should take upon itself the liability to pay out of its own resources the debts of the insolvent State, and what difference can it make that in the instrument of annexation or cessation of hostilities matters of this kind are not provided for? We can well understand that, if by public proclamation or by convention the conquering country has promised something that is inconsistent with the repudiation of particular liabilities, good faith should prevent such repudiation. We can see no reason at all why silence should be supposed to be equivalent to a promise of universal novation of existing contracts with the Government of the conquered State. It was suggested that a distinction might be drawn between obligations incurred for the purpose of waging war with the conquering country and those incurred for general State expenditure. What municipal tribunal could determine, according to the laws of evidence to be observed by that tribunal, how particular sums had been expended, whether borrowed before or during the war? It was this and cognate difficulties which compelled Lord Robert Cecil ultimately to concede that he must contend that the obligation was absolute to take over all debts and contractual obligations incurred before war had been actually declared.

Turning now to the text-writers, we may observe that the proposition we have put forward that the conqueror may impose what terms he thinks fit in respect of the obligations of the territory, and that he alone must be the judge in such a matter, is clearly recognized by Grotius: see "War and Peace," book iii. chap. 8, s. 4, and the Notes to Barbeyrac's edition of 1724, vol. ii. p. 632. For the assertion that a line is to be drawn at the moment of annexation, and that the conquering Sovereign has no right at any later stage to say what obligations he will or will not assume, we venture to think that there is no authority whatever. A doctrine was at one time urged by some of the older writers that to the extent of the assets taken over by the conqueror he ought to satisfy the debts of the conquered State. It is, in our opinion, a mere expression of the ethical views of the writers; but the proposition now contended for is a vast extension even of that doctrine. It has been urged that in numerous cases, both of peace and of cession of territories, special provision has been made for the discharge of obligations by the country accepting the cession or getting the upper hand in war; but, as we have already pointed out, conditions the result of express mutual consent between two nations afford no support to the argument that obligations not expressly provided for are to follow the course, by

no means uniform, taken by such treaties. See as to this, s. 27 of the
4th edition of Hall's International Law, and the opinion of Lord Clarendon there cited. Lord Robert Cecil cited a passage from Mr. Hall's book,
4th ed. p. 105, in which he states that the annexing Power is liable for
the whole of the debts of the State annexed. It cannot, however, be
intended as an exhaustive or unqualified statement of the practice of
nations, whatever may have been the opinion of the writer as to what
should be done in such cases. It is not, in our opinion, directed to the
particular subject now under discussion. The earlier parts of the
same chapter contain passages inconsistent with any such view. We
would call attention particularly to s. 27 on pp. 98 and 99 of the 4th
edition, where the question as to the extent to which obligations do not
pass is discussed, and the passages on pp. 101 and 102, referring to the
discussion between England and the United States in 1854, in which
Lord Clarendon's contention that Mexico did not inherit the obligations or rights of Spain is approved of by Mr. Hall. In the same way
the passage from Halleck, s. 25 of chap. 34 (Sir Sherston Baker's edition
of 1878), cited by Lord Robert Cecil, cannot be construed as meaning to
lay down any such general proposition. It is cited from a chapter in
which other sections contain passages inconsistent with the view that
the legal obligation to fulfil all contracts passed to the conquering
State. The particular section is in fact directed to the obligations of
the conquering or annexing State upon the rights of private property
of the individual—the point which formed the subject of discussion in
the American cases upon which the suppliants relied and with which we
shall deal later on. The passage from Wheaton (Atlay's ed. p. 46, s. 30)
shews that the writer was only expressing an opinion respecting the duty
of a succeeding State with regard to public debts, and, as the note to
the passage shows, it is really based upon the fact that many treaties
have dealt with such obligations in different ways. We have already
pointed out how little value particular stipulations in treaties possess
as evidence of that which may be called international common law.
We have not had the opportunity of referring to the edition of Calvo,
cited by Lord Robert Cecil, but the sections of the 8th book of the edition published in 1872 contain a discussion as to the circumstances under
which certain obligations should be undertaken by the conquering State.
The distinction between the obligations of the successor with regard to
the private property of individuals on the one hand, and the debts of
the conquered State on the other, is clearly pointed out, and paragraphs 1005 and 1010 are quite inconsistent with any recognition by
the author of the proposition contended for by the suppliants. The
same observations apply to Heffter, another work upon which reliance
was placed. As regards Max Huber's work on State Succession, published in 1898, there is no doubt, as appears from Mr. Westlake's recent

book on international law, published last year, and from other criticisms, that Huber does attempt to press the duty of a succeeding or conquering State to recognize the obligations of its predecessor to a greater extent than previous writers on international law, but the extracts cited by the Attorney-General in his reply and other passages in Huber's book show that even his opinion falls far short of the proposition for which the suppliants contend. But whatever may be the view taken of the opinions of these writers, they are, in our judgment, inconsistent with the law as recognised for many years in the English Courts; and it is sufficient for us to cite the language of Lord Mansfield in Campbell v. Hall [1 Cowp. 204, 209] in a passage the authority of which has, so far as we know, never been called in question: "It is left by the Constitution to the King's authority to grant or refuse a capitulation. . . . If he receives the inhabitants under his protection and grants them their property he has a power to fix such terms and conditions as he thinks proper. He is entrusted with making the treaty of peace; he may yield up the conquest or retain it upon what terms he pleases. These powers no man ever disputed, neither has it hitherto been controverted that the King might change part or the whole of the law or political form of government of a conquered dominion." And so, much earlier, in the year 1722 (2nd Peere Williams, p. 75), it is said by the Master of the Rolls to have been determined by the Lords of the Privy Council that "where the King of England conquers a country it is a different consideration, for there the conqueror by saving the lives of the people conquered gains a right and property in such people, in consequence of which he may impose upon them what laws he pleases." References were made to many cases of cession of territory not produced by conquest, and the frequent assumption in such cases of the liabilities of the territory ceded by the State accepting the cession was referred to. They may be dismissed in a sentence. The considerations which applied to peaceable cession raise such different questions from those which apply to conquest that it would answer no useful purpose to discuss them in detail. . . .

We pass now to consider the third proposition upon which the success of the suppliants in this case must depend—namely, that the claims of the suppliants based upon the alleged principle that the conquering State is bound by the obligations of the conquered can be enforced by petition of right. It is the consideration of this part of the case which brings out in the strongest relief the difficulties which exist in the way of the suppliants. It is not denied on the suppliants' behalf that the conquering State can make whatever bargain it pleases with the vanquished; and a further concession was made that there may be classes of obligations that it could not be reasonably contended that the conquering State would by annexation take upon itself, as, for instance, obligations to repay money used for the purposes of the war. We asked more than once during the course of the argument by what rule, either of law or equity, which could be applied in municipal Courts could those Courts decide as to the obligations which ought or ought not to be discharged by the conquering State. To refer again to the instance given in the commencement of this judgment—the obligation incurred by the conquered State by which their credit has been ruined may have been contracted for insufficient consideration or under circumstances which would make it perfectly right from every point of view for the conquering State to repudiate it in whole or in part. No answer was, or could be, given. Upon this part of the case there is a series of authorities from the year 1793 down to the present time holding that matters which fall properly to be determined by the Crown by treaty or as an act of State are not subject to the jurisdiction of the municipal Courts, and that rights supposed to be acquired thereunder cannot be enforced by such Courts. It is quite unnecessary to refer in detail to them all. . . .

It must not be forgotten that the obligations of conquering states with regard to private property of private individuals, particularly land as to which the title had already been perfected before the conquest or annexation, are altogether different from the obligations which arise in respect of personal rights by contract. As is said in more cases than one, cession of territory does not mean the confiscation of the property of individuals in that territory. If a particular piece of property has been conveyed to a private owner or has been pledged, or a lien has been created upon it, considerations arise which are different from those which have to be considered when the question is whether the contractual obligation of the conquered state towards individuals is to be undertaken by the conquering state. The English cases on which reliance was placed were United States v. Prioleau [2 H. & M. 559], in which a claim was made by the United States government to cotton which had been the property of the Confederate States; United States v. Macrae [L. R. 8 Eq. 69], which recognised the right of the government suppressing rebellion to all moneys, goods, and treasures which were public property at the time of the outbreak; Republic of Peru v. Peruvian Guano Co. [36 Ch. D. 489] and Republic of Peru v. Dreyfus [38 Ch. D. 348]. The only principle, however, which can be deduced from these cases is that a government claiming rights of property and rights under a contract cannot enforce those rights in our courts without fulfilling the terms of the contract as a whole. They have, in our judgment, no bearing upon the propositions which we have been discussing. We are aware that we have not commented upon all the cases which were cited before us—we have not failed to consider them; and any arguments which could be founded upon them seem to us to be covered by the observations already made. We are of opinion, for the reasons given, that no right on the part of the suppliants is disclosed by the petition which can be enforced as against His Majesty in this or in any municipal court; and we therefore allow the demurrer, with costs.

Judgment for the Crown.[1]

UNITED STATES AND GREAT BRITAIN: ROBERT E. BROWN CLAIM.

Claims Arbitration under the Special Agreement of August 18, 1910. 1923.

Nielsen's Report, pp. 162, 187.

Arbitrators: HENRI FROMAGEOT, EDWARD A. MITCHELL INNES, ROBERT E. OLDS.

The United States claims £330,000, with interest, from Great Britain on account of the alleged denial of certain real property rights [mining claims] contended to have been acquired in 1895, by one Robert E. Brown [an American citizen] in the territory of the South African Republic which was conquered and annexed by Great Britain on September 1, 1900. . . .

Two main questions arise on these facts:

First, whether there was a denial of justice in any event; and

Second, whether in case a denial of justice is found, any claim for damages based upon it can be made to lie against the British Government.

On the first point we are of opinion that Brown had substantial rights of a character entitling him to an interest in real property or to damages for the deprivation thereof, and that he was deprived of these rights by the Government of the South African Republic in such manner and under such circumstances as to amount to a denial of justice within the settled principles of international law. . . .

On this branch of the case we are satisfied, therefore, that there was a real denial of justice, and that if there had never been any war, or annexation by Great Britain, and if this proceeding were directed against the South African Republic, we should have no difficulty in awarding damages on behalf of the claimant.

Passing to the second main question involved, we are equally clear that this liability never passed to or was assumed by the British Government. Neither in the terms of peace granted at the time of the surrender of the Boer forces (Answer, p. 192), nor in the Proclamation

---

[1] The decision of the court in this case has been criticized by a number of jurists. Had the plaintiff been a citizen of another state there is little doubt but that the latter might have taken up its claim and pressed it through diplomatic channels, although the arbitral decision in the case next following does not suggest that the outcome would have been successful.

of Annexation (Answer, p. 191), can there be found any provision referring to the assumption of liabilities of this nature. It should be borne in mind that this was simply a pending claim for damages against certain officials and had never become a liquidated debt of the former State. Nor is there, properly speaking, any question of state succession here involved. The United States plants itself squarely on two propositions: first, that the British Government, by the acts of its own officials with respect to Brown's Case, has become liable to him; and, second, that in some way a liability was imposed upon the British Government by reason of the peculiar relation of suzerainty which is maintained with respect to the South African Republic.

The first of these contentions is set forth in the Reply as follows:

"The United States reaffirms that Brown suffered a denial of justice at the hands of authorities of the South African Republic. Had it not been for this denial of justice, it may be assumed that a diplomatic claim would not have arisen. But it does not follow that, as is contended in His Majesty's Government's Answer, it is incumbent on the United States to show that there is a rule of international law imposing liability on His Majesty's Government for the tortious acts of the South African Republic. Occurrences which took place during the existence of the South African Republic are obviously relevant and important in connection with the case before the Tribunal, but the United States contends that acts of the British Government and of British officials and the general position taken by them with respect to Brown's case have fixed liability on His Majesty's Government." (Reply, p. 2.)

Again on page 8 of the Reply it is said:

"The succeeding British authorities to whom Brown applied for the licenses to which he had been declared entitled by the Court also refused to grant the licenses, and therefore refused to carry out the decree of the Court which the United States contends was binding on them. And they have steadfastly refused to make compensation to Brown in lieu of the licenses to which the Court declared Brown to be entitled, failing the granting of the licenses."

The American Agent quoted these passages in his oral argument (transcript of 17th sitting, November 9, 1923, pp. 337, 338), and disclaimed any intention of maintaining "that there is any general liability for torts of a defunct State" (Id. p. 339). We have searched the record for any indication that the British authorities did more than leave this matter exactly where it stood when annexation took place. They did not redress the wrong which had been committed, nor did they place any obstacles in Brown's path; they took no action one way or the other. No British official nor any British court undertook to deny Brown justice or to perpetuate the wrong. The Attorney General of the Colony, in his opinion, declared that the courts were still open to the claimant. The contention of the American Agent amounts to an assertion that a succeeding State acquiring a territory by conquest without any undertaking to assume such liabilities is bound to take affirmative steps to right the wrongs done by the former state. We cannot indorse this doctrine.

The point as to suzerainty is likewise not well taken. It is not necessary to trace the vicissitudes of the South African State in its relation to the British Crown, from the Sand River Convention of 1852, through the annexation of 1877, the Pretoria Convention of 1881, and the London Convention of 1884, to the definitive annexation in 1900. We may grant that a special relation between Great Britain and the South African State, varying considerably in its scope and significance from time to time, existed from the beginning. No doubt Great Britain's position in South Africa imposed upon her a peculiar status and responsibility. She repeatedly declared and asserted her authority as the so-called paramount power in the region; but the authority which she exerted over the South African Republic certainly at the time of the occurrences here under consideration, in our judgment fell far short of what would be required to make her responsible for the wrong inflicted upon Brown. Concededly, the general relation of suzerainty created by the Pretoria Convention of 1881 (Reply, p. 26), survived after the concluding of the London Convention of 1884 (Reply, p. 37). Nevertheless the specific authority of the suzerain power was materially changed, and under the 1884 Convention it is plain that Great Britain as suzerain, reserved only a qualified control over the relations of the South African Republic with foreign powers. The Republic agreed to conclude no "treaty or engagement" with any State or nation other than the Orange Free State, without the approval of Great Britain, but such approval was to be taken for granted if the latter did not give notice that the treaty was in conflict with British interests within six months after it was brought to the attention of Her Majesty's Government. Nowhere is there any clause indicating that Great Britain had any right to interest herself in the internal administration of the country, legislative, executive or judicial; nor is there any evidence that Great Britain ever did undertake to interfere in this way. Indeed the only remedy which Great Britain ever had for mal-administration affecting British subjects and those of other Powers residing in the South African Republic was, as the event proved, the resort to war. If there had been no South African war, we hold that the United States Government would have been obliged to take up Brown's claim with the Government of the Republic and that there would have been no ground for bringing it to the attention of Great Britain. The relation of suzerain did not operate to render Great Britain liable for the acts complained of.

Now therefore:

The decision of the Tribunal is that the claim of the United States Government be disallowed.

IRISH FREE STATE AND OTHERS, PLAINTIFFS, v. GUARANTY
SAFE DEPOSIT COMPANY AND OTHERS, DEFENDANTS.

United States, New York Supreme Court, New York County, 1927.

129 Misc. Rep. 551.

PETERS, J. This is an action in equity wherein the plaintiff Irish
Free State seeks a judgment adjudging that it is the owner of and entitled to the possession of funds and property hereinafter described, and
that the defendants Stephen M. O'Mara and Eamonn De Valera render
an account of said funds and property, together with an account of all
other funds and property received by them under a certain trust agreement. The funds and property in question consist of moneys on deposit with the defendant Harriman National Bank and certain securities
contained in safe deposit boxes, all within the jurisdiction of this court.
Said funds and property represent the proceeds of the balance of subscriptions to two certain loans of an organization which was seeking to
set up by force in Ireland a Republic of Ireland which would be free
and independent of any allegiance whatsoever to the government of
Great Britain and Ireland. Sums aggregating something over $6,000,-
000 were subscribed by citizens or inhabitants of this country. The
greater portion of the amounts subscribed was transferred to Ireland and
used for the purposes for which they were subscribed. The balance not
so transferred amounts in the aggregate to approximately $2,500,000,
and it is this balance which is the subject of this action. Each sub-
scriber to the loans subsequently received a printed form of bond certificate in the amount subscribed, which read as follows:

"Republic of Ireland. Bond Certificate & —— To ——: I, Eamonn
De Valera, President of the Elected Government of the Republic of Ireland, acting in the name of and by the authority of the elected representatives of the Irish Nation, issue this certificate in acknowledgment
of your subscription of $—— to the first national loan of the Republic
of Ireland. This certificate is not negotiable but is exchangeable if
presented at the Treasury of the Republic of Ireland one month after
the international recognition of the said Republic for one $—— Gold
Bond of the Republic of Ireland. Said Bond to bear interest at five
per cent per annum from the first day of the seventh month after the
freeing of the territory of the Republic of Ireland from Britain's military control, and said Bond to be redeemable at par within one year
thereafter.

"EAMONN DE VALERA,
"President."

The uncontradicted purport of the testimony is to the effect that these
moneys were loaned for the purpose of establishing a free and independent Republic of Ireland. It is admitted, of course, that no such republic

was established and the court must now determine in this action the title to these unexpended moneys.

The plaintiff Irish Free State claims possession of the funds by title paramount, contending that it succeeded the organization called the "Irish Republic," whether this court decides that such organization constituted a *de facto* government or whether it was merely an organized rebellion against the authority of the duly constituted government of Great Britain and Ireland. The defendant trustees deny that title and claim that they have a right to continue in possession of the funds. . . .

By the Act of Union of 1800, enacted by the King and Parliaments of Great Britain and of Ireland, Ireland formed a part of the United Kingdom of Great Britain and Ireland with one parliament called the Parliament of the United Kingdom of Great Britain and Ireland, consisting of a House of Lords and a House of Commons, and sitting at Westminster, Eng. From time to time efforts were made by some of the people of Ireland to establish a free nation, at times by parliamentary means and at other times through armed resistance to the government. The events upon which the decision of this case must be founded began on April 24, 1916, when there occurred in Dublin what is known in Irish history as the "Easter Uprising," by an armed force known as the "Irish Volunteers." Independence was declared and the Republic of Ireland proclaimed. This uprising was short-lived, being sternly suppressed by the military forces of the British government. The Irish Volunteers continued in existence, reorganized their forces and engaged in Irish political activities. In or about 1918 an Irish political party known as the "Sinn Fein Party," adopted the policy of sending forward candidates for parliamentary elections in Ireland on a pledge that if elected they would not attend the Parliament at Westminster, but would assemble in Ireland and constitute themselves a parliament for Ireland, and as such would take over the government of the country. In December, 1918, the British Parliament was duly dissolved and new elections were ordered for members in the House of Commons. At this election the constituencies in Ireland were entitled to elect 105 members to the House of Commons to sit in the British Parliament. The Sinn Fein party took advantage of the election machinery to elect candidates who had pledged themselves as aforesaid. All members elected at said election in Ireland were summoned to a meeting to be held at the official residence of the Lord Mayor, known as the "Mansion House," in Dublin on the 21st of January, 1919, . . . and all, . . . except those who were in the custody of the British military forces or abroad on political missions, assembled at the appointed place . . . and constituted themselves a parliament for Ireland, to which they gave the name of "Dail Eireann," . . . hereinafter called the "First Dail." . . . This First Dail issued a proclamation of independence, adopted a provisional constitution and standing rules and orders and set up a ministry, and attempted to perform varied governmental functions in Ireland. This Dail on April 1, 1919, elected the defendant De Valera Prime Minister, and on April 10, 1919, authorized a loan of £1,000,000, £500,000 to be offered for immediate subscription, £250,000 for subscription at home and £250,000 for subscription abroad. The plaintiff, Rev. Michael Fogarty, the defendant De Valera and one James O'Mara were appointed trustees for one year for the funds to be raised and subsequently executed a trust agreement in respect of such funds. A further loan of $23,750,000 was authorized by the Dail in August, 1919. The trustees were reappointed for the succeeding year. After the formation of the Dail Eireann organization the military forces of the British government became active in the work of suppressing the revolt. The activities of the First Dail will now be noted. This Dail set up ministries and a civil service for offices.

A force of unpaid volunteers was maintained, any members of which captured by the British in action or with arms even if not in action, were almost invariably executed after summary military trial. The force was small and active and because it was small it had to strike frequently at different points. Its real nature, however, is shown by the testimony that it was housed, fed and *concealed* by the population generally. Courts were set up which in fact first became effective after the treaty hereinafter mentioned. The British local boards were largely ousted. The Dail organization maintained no post offices, printed no stamps, exercised no supervision over railroads which were maintained by the British government, issued no money or currency, had no school system and raised no taxes. It maintained a secret police force, appointed consular agents who had no official status in the countries to which they were sent. It set up a land commission and passed decrees. The uncontradicted testimony is that throughout the period of the First Dail and the hereinafter described Second Dail and until the treaty hereinafter mentioned, though persons were appointed to ministerial positions and staffs were appointed to help them, it was impossible for them to have any permanent location for the reason that during the entire period everyone connected with the Dail was hunted down by the British and all office equipment was of a portable character capable of instantaneous removal at the approach of the British military forces. An entire department might find it necessary to make a hurried removal through a skylight or down a drainpipe at a moment's notice.

The courts tentatively set up were, like the ministry, continuously "on the run." They sat in private houses; sometimes in fields, cellars and wherever it was possible to congregate for a sufficient length of time. The Dail did not maintain jails. Occasionally persons were held by the Dail authorities, but only for short periods, and they generally had to be "on the run" with their captors. Records were always in danger of seizure. This Dail organization was never recognized by any foreign country. Another indication of the nature of the Dail organization, upon the question whether it was a *de facto* government, is apparent from a provision in the trust deed, before mentioned, which devolved the duty of disbursing the Dail funds upon the trustees or "such of them as may be *free* to act" in the event that neither a quorum of the Dail or the ministry were available or able to meet. From all the foregoing it is apparent that the Dail organization was never a *de facto* government but simply an organization fostering a rebellion or revolt against the British government in Ireland.

In an attempt to bring peace and quiet to the Irish people a statute called the "Government of Ireland Act" was enacted by the King and Parliament of Great Britain and Ireland in the year 1920, which was designed to confer upon Ireland a measure of home rule. This act provided for a separate government for six counties and two boroughs in the northeast of Ireland, defined in the act as Northern Ireland, and a separate government for the rest of Ireland, defined in the act as Southern Ireland. To make this act effective, elections were ordered for the election of members of the Parliaments of Northern and Southern Ireland, respectively, by a proclamation of the King of England, to take place in May and June, 1921. The first Dail adopted a resolution to the effect that said election should be regarded as an election of members to the Dail, and that that body would automatically dissolve on the meeting of the new body. In other words, the De Valera organization again took advantage of the British election machinery in Ireland for the election of members to a new assembly which is hereinafter called the Second Dail. Candidates of the Sinn Fein party made the same pledges as in the election of 1918. Candidates elected were summoned to meet at the Mansion House, Dublin, and on August 16, 1921, 120 members elected on a Sinn Fein program assembled at the appointed place and constituted themselves the Second Dail Eireann under the constitution adopted by the First Dail. Candidates elected to the House of Commons and to the Senate for Northern Ireland made and constituted a government under the aforesaid Government of Ireland Act. The Parliament of Southern Ireland, which was provided for by said act, was summoned to meet on June 28, 1921. The House of Commons met on that day. The First Dail ignored the two Parliaments provided for by the Government of Ireland Act.

On July 11, 1921, a truce was declared between the forces of the British government and the volunteer forces of Dail Eireann. On August 26, 1921, a new ministry was elected by the Second Dail, with the defendant De Valera as president; a further loan of $20,000,000 in the United States was authorized, and the three trustees of the loan funds were elected for the years 1921–1922. On September 14, 1921, the Second Dail appointed plenipotentiaries to treat with the British government in an effort to secure permanent peace for Ireland. These plenipotentiaries entered into negotiations at London with the British delegates headed by D. Lloyd-George, Prime Minister of England. The great obstacle to peace throughout these negotiations was the insistence by the Irish delegates on independence for Ireland and the insistence on the other hand on the part of Lloyd-George that independence would never be granted Ireland. . . .

It is apparent that the British government never recognized the De Valera organization, and never receded from the position that it was the only duly constituted government within the territory comprising Ireland.

In this last letter Lloyd-George invited a meeting of the delegates with a view to ascertaining how an association of Ireland with the community of nations known as the British Empire might best be reconciled with Irish national aspirations, which invitation was accepted. . . .

On December 6, 1921, articles of agreement were signed at London by the British and Irish delegations, which provided that Ireland should have the same constitutional status in the community of nations known as the British Empire as the Dominion of Canada, the Commonwealth of Australia and the Dominion of New Zealand, with a Parliament having power to make laws for the order and good government of Ireland, and an executive responsible to that Parliament, and should be styled and known as the Irish Free State. The position of the Irish Free State with relation to the British Parliament and government was to be similar to that of the Dominion of Canada. . . .

It was further provided that the treaty should be submitted by the British government for the *approval* of the British Parliament and by the Irish signatories *to a meeting summoned for the purpose of the members elected to sit in the House of Commons of Southern Ireland.* If approved, the treaty was to be ratified by the necessary legislation. . . .

Pursuant to the provisions of the treaty a meeting of the members elected to sit in the *Parliament of Southern Ireland* was held on January 14, 1922, the treaty was approved and a provisional government set up. The Second Dail met for the last time on June 8, 1922. . . .

The British Parliament on March 31, 1922, passed the Irish Free State Agreement Act, thus ratifying and enacting into law said agreement. The act provided that the articles of agreement should have the force of law as from the date of the passing of the act. The act further provided that within four months the Parliament of Southern Ireland should be dissolved and that steps should be taken for the holding of an election to the provisional Parliament from the constituencies which would have been entitled to elect members to the Parliament of Southern Ireland, and the members so elected were to constitute the House of Parliament to which the provisional government should be responsible. The British government, on April 1, 1922, pursuant to the treaty agreement, by an order in council, provided for the transfer of functions in connection with the administration of public services in Southern Ireland theretofore performed by the existing *British* government departments and offices to the provisional government constituted under the treaty. The Constitution of the Irish Free State was adopted by that government on October 25, 1922, and on December fifth of the same year the British Parliament enacted the Irish Free State Constitution Act, thus creating plaintiff, the Irish Free State, which is now a government consisting of the King, an Irish Parliament called the "Oireachtas," consisting of an upper house, the Seanad Eireann, and a lower house, the Dail Eireann, and a ministry called the executive council. On December 6, 1922, the Constitution of the Irish Free State was declared to be in operation by a proclamation by the King made pursuant to the Irish Free State Constitution Act.

It is manifest from the foregoing that the object or the purpose for which the moneys were subscribed by the so-called bondholders, that is, the establishment of a Republic of Ireland free and independent of any allegiance to Great Britain, was never accomplished, and it follows, therefore, that if it were not for the claim of the plaintiffs the said subscribers would be entitled to a return in proportion to the amounts of their subscriptions of the funds and property within the jurisdiction of this court. Manifestly, the trustees would not have any legal title to the funds, holding such funds merely as such.

It is, therefore, necessary to consider the propositions advanced by the plaintiffs' counsel to support their claim of title.

Plaintiffs' first contention is that the Irish Free State is the successor of the original *de facto* government which raised the money. As hereinbefore shown, and held in this opinion, the so-called Irish Republic never existed as a *de facto* government.

Plaintiffs next contend that (a) if the *de facto* status has not been established then the Irish Free State is the successor of the revolutionary group which raised the money; (b) the Irish Free State is also in fact the continuation of the very Dail Eireann which raised the money and to which the trustees admitted they were responsible.

With these contentions this court cannot agree. The De Valera group, organized as the Dail Eireann, were engaged in a revolt against the only lawful government existing in Ireland, which was the government of Great Britain and Ireland formed under the act of 1800, as modified by the Government of Ireland Act of 1920. This was the *de jure* government existing in the territory of Ireland up to the time of the formation of the Irish Free State.

England did not crush this rebellion or revolution with military force, but set up, with the consent of the governed, a *new* government to take the place of the *existing* government in Ireland. This consent, so far as Southern Ireland was concerned, consisted of the approval of the treaty *by the duly constituted Parliament for Southern Ireland* as provided for by that instrument. The treaty absolutely ignored the Second Dail and, as before stated, the approval by that body was wholly voluntary and without any legal effect. This government of the Irish Free State was, therefore, set up by the English government with the consent of the people of Southern Ireland.

As the government of Great Britain and Ireland was the only existing government in Ireland, with a revolt on its hands in the form of the Dail Eireann organization, how can it be said that the new government set up by England succeeded the revolt and not the legal existing government? Such a conclusion would be an assertion that the new government succeeded an unsuccessful rebellious organization and not the existing government of Ireland.

In the case of The King of the Two Sicilies v. Willcox (1 Sim. [N. S.] 301) the court said: "Every government, in its dealings with others, necessarily partakes, in many respects, of the character of a corporation. It must, of necessity, be treated as a body having perpetual succession." In short, when a revolt succeeds so far as to become a *de facto* government which displaces a *de jure* government, this change merely affects the character of the government, but does not interrupt its perpetual succession. If, therefore, the Dail Eireann had succeeded in displacing the *de jure* government of Great Britain and Ireland and had become a *de facto* government, while the nature of the government of Ireland would have changed, such change would not have interrupted the perpetual succession of the government. The *de facto* government would merely have succeeded the *de jure* government previously existing, and the Irish Free State would have succeeded the *de facto* government, thus preserving the continuity of the government of Ireland. As the Dail Eireann did not succeed in establishing a *de facto* government, it, therefore, did not displace the existing *de jure* government. It follows, therefore, that the Irish Free State succeeded the only government in existence in Ireland at the time it came into being, to wit, the *de jure* government of Great Britain and Ireland. . . .

As the plaintiff Irish Free State succeeded the *de jure* government of Great Britain and Ireland, and not the revolutionary organization known as Dail Eireann, said plaintiff has no title either paramount or derivative to the funds in question, and the complaint must, therefore, be dismissed. Even if this conclusion be incorrect the complaint must be dismissed upon the authority of the McRae case, for said plaintiff claims by paramount title and not by derivative title offering to adopt the contracts.

The defendant trustees have no title as owners of the funds in question, and their demand that they be left in possession of the same must, therefore, be denied. No good purpose could result from leaving them in possession of the trustees, for the reason that the Irish Republic was never formed and the terms of the subscription, *i. e.,* the issuance of bonds of the Irish Republic, cannot be complied with.

With the complaint dismissed on the ground that the plaintiff Irish Free State has not title to the funds in question, and as the government of Great Britain and Ireland has made no claim to the funds, the only parties entitled to the possession of the money are the original subscribers, and the two bondholder committees in their answers have set up counterclaims demanding judgment for the funds. The demand of the Noonan Committee that the funds be awarded to the Irish Free State upon condition that that government issue bonds to the full extent of the original subscriptions cannot, in view of the foregoing opinion, be granted.

As the purpose or object for which the funds in question were advanced has become impossible of fulfillment (Thomas v. Hartshorne, 45 N. J. Eq. 215), the relief demanded by the Hearn Committee should be granted to the extent that a judgment be entered decreeing that these defendants and all other subscribers to the two loans in the United States are entitled to receive, in proportion to their subscriptions, the proceeds of the money and securities in question, together with accumulated interest, after payment of all proper charges and disbursements taxed or allowed by the court.[1]

B. Partial succession following upon transfer of territory.

Principles similar to those governing universal succession are applied in the case of a state which takes over a part of the territory of another state without destroying the international personality of the latter. Query, does such *partial* succession go so far as to include a duty to assume the contractual obligations existing between the government of

---

[1] SUPPLEMENTARY CASES. In United States v. McRae, L. R. 8 Eq. 69 (1869), involving a suit brought by the United States in Great Britain against McRae for an accounting of money received by him from the sale of goods consigned to him by the Confederate Government during the American Civil War, the court held that while upon the suppression of a rebellion the legitimate government was entitled as of right to what had been public property of the suppressed government at the time of the outbreak, in respect to property or rights subsequently acquired by the insurrectionary government the legitimate government was entitled to it not by title paramount but as successory only and must therefore take it subject to the same rights and obligations "as if that [insurrectionary] government had not been displaced and was itself proceeding against the agent." Since the United States was unwilling to recognize the authority of the Confederate States to that extent, the suit was dismissed with costs.

In Terlinden v. Ames (above, p. 66, n. 1) the court made the mistake of considering that Prussia, after its incorporation in the German Empire in 1871, might continue to be a party to a treaty entered into in 1852, instead of looking upon the German Empire as the legal successor to Prussia's obligations.

the annexed territory and a public utility corporation chartered in a third state? [Eastern Extension, Australasia and China Telegraph Co. v. United States.] Must the obligations of a municipal corporation operating under the former government of the transferred territory be assumed by a municipal corporation embracing the same inhabitants but chartered under the new laws of the annexing state? [Vilas v. City of Manila.]

THE EASTERN EXTENSION, AUSTRALASIA AND CHINA TELE-GRAPH COMPANY v. THE UNITED STATES.

United States, Court of Claims, 1912.

48 Ct. of Claims, 33.

PEELE, Ch. J. delivered the opinion of the court: . . .

The petition avers substantially that prior to the War with Spain the claimant herein, a British corporation, had by separate grants and concessions entered into contracts with the Spanish Government for the construction and operation at its own expense of certain submarine cables and telegraph land lines communicating between the Island of Luzon and certain other islands in the Philippine Archipelago and Hongkong, China, for which the Spanish Government agreed to pay the claimant an annual subsidy of £4,500, payable monthly at Manila by the chief treasury office of those islands.

That prior to December, 1898, the Philippine Archipelago, including the islands referred to, was under the control and sovereignty of the Government of Spain, but by Article III of the treaty of Paris of that date (30 Stat. L., 1754), ceding the Philippine Archipelago to the United States, the control and sovereignty of Spain passed to the control and sovereignty of the United States, who thereupon took possession of said islands and, as averred, assumed "jurisdiction and control over all property and property rights in and upon said Philippine Islands, including the several lines of submarine cable and telegraph land lines established, constructed, and operated by the claimant, and availed itself of all the benefits and advantages thereof, using said lines of cable and telegraph for its governmental and other purposes, which it has continued to do ever since and still continues to do" without the payment of said annual subsidy of £4,500 so theretofore agreed to be paid by the Spanish Government.

By Article VIII of the treaty all buildings, wharves, public highways, forts, and all public property which by law belong to the public domain, and as such to the Crown of Spain, were ceded or relinquished to the United States, for which it is understood $20,000,000 were paid; and it was therein provided that the relinquishment or cession "can not in any respect impair the property or rights which by law belong to the peaceful possession of property of all kinds, of Provinces, municipalities, public or private establishments, ecclesiastical or civic bodies, or any other associations having legal capacity to acquire and possess property in the aforesaid territories renounced or ceded, or of private individuals, of whatsoever nationality such individuals may be.''

Upon investigation it will be found that the foregoing is the usual stipulation in treaties and is in effect a declaration of the rights of the inhabitants under international law. (United States v. de la Arredondo, 6 Pet., 691, 712.) . . .

In the case of Cessna v. United States (169 U. S., 165, 186) the court observed: ''It is the duty of a nation receiving a cession of territory to respect all rights of property as those rights were recognized by the nation making the cession, but it is no part of its duty to right the wrongs which the grantor may have theretofore committed.''

This, however, in the absence of a stipulation in the treaty therefor, does not mean that the United States assumed the personal obligations or debts of the Spanish Government to individuals or corporations unless under the rules of international law they thereby became liable. When the United States succeeded to the sovereignty of Spain over the islands they were under no more obligation to continue the contracts for public or private service of individuals or corporations than they were to continue in office officials appointed by the Spanish Government. (Sanchez v. United States, 42 C. Cls. 458; affirmed 216 U. S., 167.)

The cables so constructed under the grants or contracts aforesaid were not public property belonging to the Crown of Spain, and therefore did not pass to the United States by the treaty, but were the private property of the claimant, and, so far as the averments of the petition show, were so recognized by the United States. . . .

It is not averred that the Government seized or took physical possession of the cables or that, as sovereign over the islands, it did other than assume jurisdiction and control over all property and property rights therein, including the submarine cable and telegraph lines of the claimant, using the latter for its governmental and other purposes, for which it made compensation.

There is no averment that the rights of the claimant in and to the ownership and control of its cable and telegraph lines were in any way interrupted or interfered with by the officers of the Government other than for the transmission of messages, for which compensation was made; and if they were, such acts would constitute a tort, over which this court would have no jurisdiction. . . .

The obligation of Spain to the claimant was not the obligation of the Philippine Archipelago, though the Spanish Government saw fit to pay the subsidy out of the revenues of the islands; but if we were to assume that it was, the United States, in the absence of treaty stipulation, such as is referred to in Hall's International Law, sec. 28, p. 104, would not be liable therefor. If we were to assume that the obligations of Spain to the claimant was a general debt of the Spanish Government, it would be a personal one, as laid down in Hall's International Law, p. 99, note; and being a personal obligation would not in the absence of a treaty stipulation therefor, attach to the United States. . . .

The court is without jurisdiction . . . and therefore the demurrer must be sustained, . . . and the petition dismissed.[1]

VILAS v. CITY OF MANILA.

United States, Supreme Court, 1911.

220 U. S. 345.   [55 L. ed. 491; 31 S. Ct. 416.]

Error to and appeals from the Supreme Court of the Philippine Islands.

MR. JUSTICE LURTON delivered the opinion of the court.

The plaintiffs in error,[2] who were plaintiffs below, are creditors of the city of Manila as it existed before the cession of the Philippine Islands to the United States by the treaty of Paris, December 10, 1898. Upon the theory that the city under its present charter from the government of the Philippine Islands is the same juristic person and liable upon the obligations of the old city, these actions were brought against it. The Supreme Court of the Philippine Islands denied relief, holding that the present municipality is a totally different corporate entity, and in no way liable for the debts of the Spanish municipality.

The fundamental question is whether, notwithstanding the cession of the Philippine Islands to the United States, followed by a reincorporation of the city, the present municipality is liable for the obligations of the city incurred prior to the cession to the United States. . . .

The city as now incorporated has succeeded to all of the property rights of the old city and to the right to enforce all of its causes of action. There is identity of purpose between the Spanish and American charters and substantial identity of municipal powers. The area and the inhabitants incorporated are substantially the same. But for the change of sovereignty which has occurred under the treaty of Paris, the

---

[1] The decision of the Court of Claims as to jurisdiction was reversed by the Supreme Court, 231 U. S. 326 (1913), and the case remanded for further proceedings on the merits, subject to certain limitations. In 251 U. S. 355 (1920), the Supreme Court affirmed a judgment of the Court of Claims dismissing the claim. A different claim on behalf of the same company was at issue in an arbitration between the United States and Great Britain, below, p. 231.

[2] Including Trigas and Aguado whose cases were decided at the same time.

question of the liability of the city under its new charter for the debts
of the old city would seem to be of easy solution. The principal question
would therefore seem to be the legal consequence of the cession referred
to upon the property rights and civil obligations of the city incurred
before the cession. And so the question was made to turn in the court
below upon the consequence of a change in sovereignty and a reincorporation of the city by the substituted sovereignty. . . .

The historical continuity of a municipality embracing the inhabitants
of the territory now occupied by the city of Manila is impressive. Before the conquest of the Philippine Islands by Spain, Manila existed.
The Spaniards found on the spot now occupied a populous and fortified
community of Moros. In 1571 they occupied what was then and is now
known as Manila, and established it as a municipal corporation. In 1574
there was conferred upon it the title of "Illustrious and ever loyal city
of Manila." From time to time there occurred amendments, and, on
January 19, 1894, there was reorganization of the city government under a royal decree of that date. Under the charter there was power to
incur debts for municipal purposes and power to sue and be sued. The
obligations here in suit were incurred under the charter referred to, and
are obviously obligations strictly within the provision of the municipal
power. To pay judgments upon such debt it was the duty of the
Ayuntamiento of Manila, which was the corporate name of the old city,
to make provision in its budget.

The contention that the liability of the city upon such obligations was
destroyed by a mere change of sovereignty is obviously one which is
without a shadow of moral force, and, if true, must result from settled
principles of rigid law. While the contracts from which the claims in
suit resulted were in progress, war between the United States and Spain
ensued. On August 13, 1898, the city was occupied by the forces of this
Government and its affairs conducted by military authority. On July 31,
1901, the present incorporating act was passed, and the city since that
time has been an autonomous municipality. The charter in force is act
183 of the Philippine Commission and now may be found as chapters 68
to 75 of the Compiled Acts of the Philippine Commission. . . .

The charter contains no reference to the obligations or contracts of the
old city.

If we understand the argument against the liability here asserted, it
proceeds mainly upon the theory that inasmuch as the predecessor of
the present city, the Ayuntamiento of Manila, was a corporate entity
created by the Spanish government, when the sovereignty of Spain in
the islands was terminated by the treaty of cession, if not by the capitulation of August 13, 1908, the municipality *ipso facto* disappeared for
all purposes. This conclusion is reached upon the supposed analogy to
the doctrine of principal and agent, the death of the principal ending
the agency. So complete is the supposed death and annihilation of a

municipal entity by extinction of sovereignty of the creating State that it was said in one of the opinions below that all of the public property of Manila passed to the United States, "for a consideration, which was paid," and that the United States was therefore justified in creating an absolutely new municipality and endowing it with all of the assets of the defunct city, free from any obligation to the creditors of that city. And so the matter was dismissed in the Trigas Case by the Court of First Instance, by the suggestion that "the plaintiff may have a claim against the crown of Spain, which has received from the United States payment for that done by the plaintiff."

We are unable to agree with the argument. It loses sight of the dual character of municipal corporations. They exercise powers which are governmental and powers which are of a private or business character. In one character a municipal corporation is a governmental sub-division, and for that purpose exercises by delegation a part of the sovereignty of the State. In the other character it is a mere legal entity or juristic person. In the latter character it stands for the community in the administration of local affairs wholly beyond the sphere of the public purposes for which its governmental powers are conferred. . . .

In view of the dual character of municipal corporations there is no public reason for presuming their total dissolution as a mere consequence of military occupation or territorial cession. The suspension of such governmental functions as are obviously incompatible with the new political relations thus brought about may be presumed. But no such implication may be reasonably indulged beyond that result.

Such a conclusion is in harmony with the settled principles of public law as declared by this and other courts and expounded by the text books upon the laws of war and international law. Taylor, International Public Law, § 578.

That there is a total abrogation of the former political relations of the inhabitants of the ceded region is obvious. That all laws theretofore in force which are in conflict with the political character, constitution or institutions of the substituted sovereign lose their force, is also plain. Alvarez v. United States, 216 U. S. 167. But it is equally settled in the same public law that that great body of municipal law which regulates private and domestic rights continues in force until abrogated or changed by the new ruler. In Chicago, Rock Island & Pacific Railway Co. v. McGlinn, 114 U. S. 524, 546, it was said:

"It is a general rule of public law, recognized and acted upon by the United States, that whenever political jurisdiction and legislative power over any territory are transferred from one nation or sovereign to another, the municipal laws of the country, that is, laws which are intended for the protection of private rights, continue in force until abrogated or changed by the new government or sovereign. By the cession public property passes from one government to the other, but private property remains as before, and with it those municipal laws which are designed to secure its peaceful use and enjoyment. As a matter of course, all laws, ordinances, and regulations in conflict with the political character, institutions and constitution of the new government are at once displaced. Thus, upon a cession of political jurisdiction and legislative power—and the latter is involved in the former—to the United States, the laws of the country in support of an established religion, or abridging the freedom of the press, or authorizing cruel and unusual punishments, and the like, would at once cease to be of obligatory force without any declaration to that effect; and the laws of the country on other subjects would necessarily be superseded by existing laws of the new government upon the same matters. But with respect to other laws affecting the possession, use and transfer of property, and designed to secure good order and peace in the community, and promote its health and prosperity, which are strictly of a municipal character, the rule is general, that a change of government leaves them in force until, by direct action of the new government, they are altered or repealed. . . ."

That the United States might, by virtue of its situation under a treaty ceding full title, have utterly extinguished every municipality which it found in existence in the Philippine Islands may be conceded. That it did so in view of the practice of nations to the contrary is not to be presumed and can only be established by cogent evidence. . . .[1]

C. Effect of succession upon private rights.

Transfers of territory from one state to another frequently raise questions as to the private rights and obligations of residents of the transferred territory. On occasion it is stipulated in the treaty effecting the

---

[1] SUPPLEMENTARY CASES. In Virginia v. West Virginia, 220 U. S. 1 (1911), the Supreme Court held that West Virginia was liable to pay an equitable portion of the public debt of Virginia as it stood January 1, 1861, some months before the formation of the new State of West Virginia. But in this case the decision was based upon a compact between the existing state (or rather a rump convention recognized by the Government of the United States as the State of Virginia) and a constituent convention of persons favoring the new state. The law of state succession did not, strictly speaking, enter into the decision.

The problem of the partial succession of a newly-formed state to the public obligations of the parent state presents many difficulties. In the suit between Greece and Great Britain in the matter of the Mavrommatis Concessions, Publications of the Court, Series A, No. 2 (1924), the Permanent Court of International Justice held that the granting by Great Britain, after obtaining the mandate over Palestine, of concessions overlapping those granted by the Ottoman Empire before the war to Mavrommatis, a Greek subject, constituted a breach of the mandate. The decision, however, was reached by application of the provisions of the mandate rather than by those of the law of succession. See below, p. 643.

transfer that certain specific protection shall be given to them. Query, do property rights of individual inhabitants of transferred territory remain unaffected by the transfer? [United States v. Percheman.] Is continued residence in the territory a necessary condition of the enjoyment of property rights within it? [United States v. Repentigny.]

THE UNITED STATES, APPELLANTS, v. JUAN PERCHEMAN, APPELLEE.

United States, Supreme Court, 1833.

7 Peters, 51. [8 L. ed. 604.]

Appeal from the superior court for the eastern district of Florida. On the 17th of September, 1830, Juan Percheman filed in the clerk's office of the superior court for the eastern district of Florida, a petition, setting forth his claim to a tract of land containing two thousand acres, within the district of East Florida. . . . The petitioner stated that he derived his title to the said tract of land under a grant made to him on the 12th day of December, 1815, by governor Estrada, then Spanish governor of East Florida, and whilst East Florida belonged to Spain. . . . The court . . . adjudged . . . "that the grant is valid, . . . and . . . it is confirmed." The United States appealed to this court.

MR. CHIEF JUSTICE MARSHALL delivered the opinion of the court. . . .

Florida was a colony of Spain, the acquisition of which by the United States was extremely desirable. It was ceded by a treaty concluded between the two powers at Washington, on the 22d day of February, 1819.

The second article contains the cession, and enumerates its objects. The eighth contains stipulations respecting the titles to lands in the ceded territory.

It may not be unworthy of remark, that it is very unusual, even in cases of conquest, for the conqueror to do more than to displace the sovereign and assume dominion over the country. The modern usage of nations, which has become law, would be violated; that sense of justice and of right which is acknowledged and felt by the whole civilized world would be outraged, if private property should be generally confiscated, and private rights annulled. The people change their allegiance; their relation to their ancient sovereign is dissolved; but their relations to each other, and their rights of property, remain undisturbed. If this be the modern rule even in cases of conquest, who can doubt its application to the case of an amicable cession of territory? Had Florida changed its sovereign by an act containing no stipulation respecting the property of individuals, the right of property in all those who became subjects or citizens of the new government would have been unaffected by the change. It would have remained the same as under the ancient sovereign. The language of the second article conforms to this general principle. "His catholic majesty cedes to the United States in full property and sovereignty, all the territories which belong to him situated to the eastward of the Mississippi, by the name of East and West Florida." A cession of territory is never understood to be a cession of the property belonging to its inhabitants. The king cedes that only which belonged to him. Lands he had previously granted were not his to cede. Neither party could so understand the cession. Neither party could consider itself as attempting a wrong to individuals, condemned by the practice of the whole civilized world. The cession of a territory by its name from one sovereign to another, conveying the compound idea of surrendering at the same time the lands and the people who inhabit them, would be necessarily understood to pass the sovereignty only, and not to interfere with private property. If this could be doubted, the doubt would be removed by the particular enumeration which follows. "The adjacent islands dependent on said provinces, all public lots and squares, vacant land, public edifices, fortifications, barracks and other buildings which are not private property, archives and documents which relate directly to the property and sovereignty of the said provinces, are included in this article." . . .

This state of things ought to be kept in view when we construe the eighth article of the treaty, and the acts which have been passed by congress for the ascertainment and adjustment of titles acquired under the Spanish government. That article in the English part of it is in these words: "All the grants of land made before the 24th of January, 1818, by his catholic majesty, or by his lawful authorities, in the said territories ceded by his majesty to the United States, shall be ratified and confirmed to the persons in possession of the lands, to the same extent that the said grants would be valid if the territories had remained under the dominion of his catholic majesty."

This article is apparently introduced on the part of Spain, and must be intended to stipulate expressly for that security to private property which the laws and usages of nations would, without express stipulation, have conferred. . . . Without it, the titles of individuals would remain as valid under the new government as they were under the old; and those titles, so far at least as they were consummate, might be asserted in the courts of the United States, independently of this article. . . .

The decree is affirmed.

UNITED STATES v. REPENTIGNY.

United States, Supreme Court, 1866.

5 Wallace, 211. [18 L. ed. 627.]

Appeal by the United States from a decree of the District Court of the United States decreeing to the representatives of the Chevalier de Repentigny and of Captain Louis De Bonne, a large tract of land at the Saut de St. Marie, under a grant from the French government, in the year 1751. . . . .

MR. JUSTICE NELSON delivered the opinion of the court.

The bill in this case was filed in the court below to recover possession of a large tract of land of six leagues square, fronting on the River St. Marie, at the Saut, which connects the waters of Lake Superior with those of Lake Huron, in the State of Michigan. The grant of the land was made on the 18th October, 1750, by the governor and intendant-general of Canada (then called New France), to Louis De Bonne, a captain of infantry, and Count Repentigny, an ensign, in the French army. The complainants derive title under them. It was confirmed by the King of France the next year, on the 24th June, 1751.

The grant was to De Bonne and Repentigny, their heirs and assigns, "in perpetuity by title of feof and seigniory," with all the customary rights belonging to that species of estate. Repentigny went into possession about the date of the grant, at the Saut, having about the same time received an appointment to command the military post established there. He constructed a small stockade fort, and made some improvements in connection with it, such as the clearing of a few acres of land and the erection of huts for the people with him, and continued thus engaged till 1754. When war broke out between France and England he was called away into active military service of the government, and never afterwards returned. De Bonne never took personal possession, or possession of any other character, except that derived from the transient occupation of his co-tenant.

The bill was filed on the 9th January, 1861, one hundred and ten years since the date of the grant.

We will now refer to the act of Congress, passed April 19th, 1860, under which the bill was filed. . . . .

This act of 1860, which authorizes the institution of these proceedings, was passed in pursuance of petitions to Congress by the representatives of the original grantees. The first notice to this government of any claim to the lands on their behalf was in the year 1825 or 1826, some seventy-five years after the date of the grant. Since then the subject has, from time to time, been brought to the attention of Congress, and finally disposed of by the passage of the act in question. The act, as we have seen, refers the claimants to the judiciary for relief, and prescribes the principles which shall govern it in hearing and adjudicating upon the case. They are—

1. The law of nations.
2. The laws of the country from which the title was derived.
3. The principles of justice.
4. The stipulations of treaties.

In the light of these principles, we shall proceed to an examination of the claim; and, first, as to the claim of the representatives of Repentigny. He was a native of Canada, and a captain in the French army at the close of the war, which terminated in the surrender of that province to the British forces, in 1760. His family was among the earliest emigrants to the country after possession had been taken by the King of France, and held high and influential positions in the government. Soon after the execution of the definitive treaty of peace of 1763, the Governor of Canada opened a correspondence with Repentigny to induce him to remain in the province, and become a subject of Great Britain, promising him protection and advancement in his profession. . . . But he declined all the advances made to him, and soon after left the country, by order of his superior officer, to take a command on the Island of Newfoundland, where the Indians were disturbing the settlers, and spent the rest of his life in the military service of France, . . . He died in 1786, leaving a son, Gaspard, an officer in the French naval service, from whom the present claimants descended, and who reside in the Island of Guadaloupe. The preliminary treaty of the 3d November, 1762, at the surrender of Canada, provided in the second article, in behalf of his Britannic majesty, that the French inhabitants, or others who would have been subjects of the Most Christian King, in Canada, may retire in all safety and freedom, wherever they please, and may sell their estates, provided it be to his Britannic majesty's subjects, and transport their effects, as well as their persons, without being restrained in their emigration, under any pretence whatsoever, except debts or criminal prosecutions,—the term limited for this emigration being the space of eighteen months, to be computed from the day of the ratification of the definitive treaty. The definitive treaty of the 10th February of 1763 contained a similar article.

The articles of capitulation at Montreal, dated 8th September, 1760, when the Canadas were given up to the British forces, secured to the inhabitants their property movable and immovable; and the proclamation of the king, under date of 7th October, 1763, pledged to his loving subjects of Canada his paternal care for the security of the liberty and property of those who are, or should become, inhabitants thereof. These pledges, both before and after the treaty, were but the recognition of the modern usages of civilized nations which have acquired the force of law, even in the case of an absolute and unqualified conquest of the enemy's country. But the rule is limited, as in the pledge of the king, in his proclamation to the inhabitants of the conquered territory, to those who remain and become the subjects or citizens of the victorious sovereign,—those who, in the language of Chief Justice Marshall, change their allegiance, and where the relations to their ancient sovereign are dissolved. Speaking of the cession of Florida, he observed: "Had Florida changed its sovereign by an act containing no stipulation respecting the property of individuals, the right of property in all those who became subjects or citizens of the new government would have been unaffected by the change." [United States v. Percheman, 7 Pet. 51, 87.] . . .

Now, in view of these principles, it is apparent that Repentigny, having refused to continue an inhabitant of Canada, and to become a subject of Great Britain, but, on the contrary, elected to adhere in his allegiance to his native sovereign, and to continue in his service, deprived himself of any protection or security of his property, except so far as it was secured by the treaty. That protection, as we have seen, was limited to the privilege of sale or sales to British subjects, and to carry with him his effects, at any time within eighteen months from its ratification. Whatever property was left unsold was abandoned to the conqueror. Repentigny acted upon this view of his rights. . . .

Repentigny was a gentleman of education and high intelligence. He rose to the rank of general in the army, and aspired to that of Marshall of France; was Governor of Senegal and its dependencies, and, as is obvious from his correspondence with his government, comprehended fully the principles of public law which forfeited all his property left unsold at the time he retired from Canada, under the provisions of the treaty.

He died in 1786, twenty-three years after the date of the treaty; and, during all this time, not only set up no claim to this seigniory, but, on the contrary, repeatedly, as we have seen, urged the patriotic sacrifice of it to his government, as a merit for her favorable consideration of himself and family. And we may add that his only son, an officer in the French navy, and who died in 1808, at the age of fifty-five, also never set up any claim or right to it to this government, and the first notice she had of it, so far as the record discloses, was in 1824 or 1825, from the descendants of this son residing in the Island Guadaloupe, and who are the complainants in the suit. . . .

Upon the whole we are quite satisfied that, consistent with the principles, in the light of which we are directed by the act of Congress to examine into the validity of this title, the complainants have failed to establish it. We have felt justified in applying to the case these principles with reasonable strictness and particularity, as it is nearly, if not wholly, destitute of merit.

Decree of the court below reversed, and case remanded with directions to dismiss the bill.[1]

---

[1] SUPPLEMENTARY CASES. In American Insurance Co. v. Canter, 1 Peters 511 (1828), involving the validity of a sale of cotton ordered by a local court constituted in 1823 by the territorial legislature of Florida, the Supreme Court, in upholding the competence of the territorial legislature to enact the law, rejected the suggestion that the provisions of the Constitution applied automatically to the new territory. "The usage of the world," said the court, "is, if a nation be not entirely subdued, to consider the holding of conquered territory as a mere military occupation, until its fate shall be determined at the treaty of peace. If it be ceded by the treaty, the acquisition is confirmed, and the ceded territory becomes a part of the nation to which it is annexed, either on the terms stipulated in the treaty of cession, or on such as its new master shall impose. On such transfer of territory, it has never been held that the relations of the inhabitants with each other undergo any change. Their relations with their former sovereign are dissolved, and new relations are created between them and the government which has acquired their territory. The same act which transfers their country, transfers the allegiance of those who remain in it; and the law, which may be denominated political, is necessarily changed, although that which regulates the intercourse and general conduct of individuals, remains in force until altered by the newly created power of the state."

Query, would a contract right to a public office be regarded as a property right which a state obtaining territory by transfer from another would be obligated to respect? In O'Reilly de Camara v. Brooke, 209 U. S. 45 (1908), the Supreme Court held that the plaintiff had no property right to the perpetual and hereditary office of high sheriff of Havana which he had purchased from the government of Spain at public auction. The same conclusion was reached in Alvarez v. United States, 216 U. S. 167 (1910) in respect to a claim to a public office in Porto Rico that had been purchased for a valuable consideration.

In the dispute between Germany and Poland, submitted by the Council of the League of Nations to the Permanent Court of International Justice in 1923 for an advisory opinion (Publications of the Court, Series B, No. 6), involving the obligations of Poland under the treaty of June 28, 1919, in respect to the recognition of contracts known as Rentengutsverträge (holdings in perpetuity upon payment of a fixed rental) and Pachtverträge (leases for a term of years) made by the German government with individuals before the transfer of German territory to Poland by the treaty of Versailles, the court held that the attempt of Poland to cancel certain of the contracts was not in conformity with its international obligations. The basis of the decision was, however, primarily the specific provisions of the treaty and only incidentally "the principle that, in the case of a change of sovereignty, private rights are to be respected."

CHAPTER VI

JURISDICTION OVER PERSONS: NATIONALS [1]

A. Nationality by birth.

International law recognizes that states have special claims over the persons who form their citizen body and are attached to them by the bond of allegiance. Query, is the individual state free under all conditions to determine whether a particular person or class of persons shall be admitted to its citizen body? [United States v. Wong Kim Ark.] To what extent may a state, having accepted a particular person as its national, undertake to protect him within the jurisdiction of a foreign state as against the claim of the foreign state that he is also one of its nationals? [Italy and Peru: Canevaro Case.] It is a well-established rule that a state may claim exclusively as its nationals persons born upon its soil (*jus soli*) of parents who are themselves nationals of the state (*jus sanguinis*). Conflicts of claims may arise when one state makes a claim *jure soli* and another *jure sanguinis*, and again when one state makes a claim based upon birth and another a claim based upon naturalization. Occasionally the operation of the ordinary rules is set aside in favor of special treaty provisions. [Great Britain and France: Nationality Decrees in Tunis and Morocco.]

UNITED STATES v. WONG KIM ARK.

United States, Supreme Court, 1898.

169 U. S. 649. [42 L. ed. 890; 18 S. Ct. 456.]

MR. JUSTICE GRAY, after stating the case, delivered the opinion of the court.

The facts of this case, as agreed by the parties, are as follows: Wong Kim Ark was born in 1873 in the city of San Francisco, in the State of California and United States of America, and was and is a laborer. His father and mother were persons of Chinese descent, and subjects of the Emperor of China; they were at the time of his birth domiciled residents

---

[1] For a more detailed study of this subject, see Fenwick, *op. cit.*, pp. 176–189; Hyde, *op. cit.*, Vol. I, §§ 342–393; Oppenheim, Vol. I, §§ 288–313; Research in International Law: Draft Conventions on Nationality, Responsibility of States, Territorial Waters; Flournoy and Hudson, Nationality Laws; J. B. Scott, "Nationality," Am. Journal of Int. Law, XXIV (1930), 556.

of the United States, having previously established and still enjoying a permanent domicil and residence therein at San Francisco; they continued to reside and remain in the United States until 1890, when they departed for China; and during all the time of their residence in the United States they were engaged in business, and were never employed in any diplomatic or official capacity under the Emperor of China. Wong Kim Ark, ever since his birth, has had but one residence, to wit, in California, within the United States, and has there resided, claiming to be a citizen of the United States, and has never lost or changed that residence, or gained or acquired another residence; and neither he, nor his parents acting for him, ever renounced his allegiance to the United States, or did or committed any act or thing to exclude him therefrom. In 1890 (when he must have been about seventeen years of age) he departed for China on a temporary visit and with the intention of returning to the United States, and did return thereto by sea in the same year, and was permitted by the collector of customs to enter the United States, upon the sole ground that he was a native-born citizen of the United States. After such return, he remained in the United States, claiming to be a citizen thereof, until 1894, when he (being about twenty-one years of age, but whether a little above or a little under that age does not appear) again departed for China on a temporary visit and with the intention of returning to the United States; and he did return thereto by sea in August, 1895, and applied to the collector of customs for permission to land; and was denied such permission, upon the sole ground that he was not a citizen of the United States.

It is conceded that, if he is a citizen of the United States, the acts of Congress, known as the Chinese Exclusion Acts, prohibiting persons of the Chinese race, and especially Chinese laborers, from coming into the United States, do not and cannot apply to him.

The question presented by the record is whether a child born in the United States, of parents of Chinese descent, who, at the time of his birth, are subjects of the Emperor of China, but have a permanent domicil and residence in the United States, and are there carrying on business, and are not employed in any diplomatic or official capacity under the Emperor of China, becomes at the time of his birth a citizen of the United States, by virtue of the first clause of the Fourteenth Amendment of the Constitution, "All persons born or naturalized in the United States, and subject to the jurisdiction thereof, are citizens of the United States and of the State wherein they reside."

I. In construing any act of legislation, whether a statute enacted by the legislature, or a constitution established by the people as the supreme law of the land, regard is to be had, not only to all parts of the act itself, and of any former act of the same law-making power, of which the act in question is an amendment; but also to the condition, and to the history, of the law as previously existing, and in the light of which the new act must be read and interpreted.

The Constitution of the United States, as originally adopted, uses the words "citizen of the United States," and "natural-born citizen of the United States." By the original Constitution, every representative in Congress is required to have been "seven years a citizen of the United States," and every Senator to have been "nine years a citizen of the United States;" and "no person except a natural-born citizen, or a citizen of the United States at the time of the adoption of this Constitution, shall be eligible to the office of President." The Fourteenth Article of Amendment, besides declaring that "all persons born or naturalized in the United States, and subject to the jurisdiction thereof, are citizens of the United States and of the State wherein they reside," also declares that "no State shall make or enforce any law which shall abridge the privileges or immunities of citizens of the United States; nor shall any State deprive any person of life, liberty or property, without due process of law; nor deny to any person within its jurisdiction the equal protection of the laws." And the Fifteenth Article of Amendment declares that "the right of citizens of the United States to vote shall not be denied or abridged by the United States, or by any State, on account of race, color or previous condition of servitude."

The Constitution nowhere defines the meaning of these words, either by way of inclusion or of exclusion, except in so far as this is done by the affirmative declaration that "all persons born or naturalized in the United States, and subject to the jurisdiction thereof, are citizens of the United States." In this, as in other respects, it must be interpreted in the light of the common law, the principles and history of which were familiarly known to the framers of the Constitution. Minor v. Happersett, 21 Wall. 162; Ex parte Wilson, 114 U. S. 417, 422; Boyd v. United States, 116 U. S. 616, 624, 625; Smith v. Alabama, 124 U. S. 465. The language of the Constitution, as has been well said, could not be understood without reference to the common law. 1 Kent Com. 336; Bradley, J., in Moore v. United States, 91 U. S. 270, 274. . . .

II. The fundamental principle of the common law with regard to English nationality was birth within the allegiance, also called "ligealty," "obedience," "faith" or "power," of the King. The principle embraced all persons born within the King's allegiance and subject to his protection. Such allegiance and protection were mutual—as expressed in the maxim, *protectio trahit subjectionem, et subjectio protectionem*—and were not restricted to natural-born subjects and naturalized subjects, or to those who had taken an oath of allegiance; but were predicable of aliens in amity, so long as they were within the kingdom. Children, born in England, of such aliens, were therefore natural-born subjects. But the children, born within the realm, of foreign ambassadors, or the children of alien enemies, born during and within their hostile occupation of part of the King's dominions, were not natural-born subjects, because not born within the allegiance, the obedience, or the power, or, as would be said at this day, within the jurisdiction of the King. . . .

It thus clearly appears that by the law of England for the last three centuries, beginning before the settlement of this country, and continuing to the present day, aliens, while residing in the dominions possessed by the Crown of England, were within the allegiance, the obedience, the faith or loyalty, the protection, the power, the jurisdiction, of the English Sovereign; and therefore every child born in England of alien parents was a natural-born subject, unless the child of an ambassador or other diplomatic agent of a foreign State, or of an alien enemy in hostile occupation of the place where the child was born.

III. The same rule was in force in all the English Colonies upon this continent down to the time of the Declaration of Independence, and in the United States afterwards, and continued to prevail under the Constitution as originally established. . . .

That all children, born within the dominion of the United States, of foreign parents holding no diplomatic office, became citizens at the time of their birth, does not appear to have been contested or doubted until more than fifty years after the adoption of the Constitution, when the matter was elaborately argued in the Court of Chancery of New York, and decided upon full consideration by Vice Chancellor Sandford in favor of their citizenship. Lynch v. Clarke, (1844) 1 Sandf. Ch. 583.

The same doctrine was repeatedly affirmed in the executive departments, as, for instance, by Mr. Marcy, Secretary of State, in 1854, 2 Whart. Int. Dig. (2d ed.) p. 394; by Attorney General Black in 1859, 9 Opinions, 373; and by Attorney General Bates in 1862, 10 Opinions, 328, 382, 394, 396.

Chancellor Kent, in his Commentaries, speaking of the "general division of the inhabitants of every country, under the comprehensive title of aliens and natives," says: "Natives are all persons born within the jurisdiction and allegiance of the United States. This is the rule of the common law, without any regard or reference to the political condition or allegiance of their parents, with the exception of the children of ambassadors, who are in theory born within the allegiance of the foreign power they represent." . . . 2 Kent Com. (6th ed.) 39. And he elsewhere says: "And if, at common law, all human beings born within the ligeance of the King, and under the King's obedience, were natural-born subjects, and not aliens, I do not perceive why this doctrine does not apply to these United States, in all cases in which there is no express constitutional or statute declaration to the contrary." "Subject and citizen are, in a degree, convertible terms as applied to natives; and though the term citizen seems to be appropriate to republican freemen, yet we are, equally with the inhabitants of all other countries, *subjects*, for we are equally bound by allegiance and subjection to the government and law of the land." 2 Kent Com. 258, note. . . .

IV. It was contended by one of the learned counsel for the United States that the rule of the Roman law, by which the citizenship of the child followed that of the parent, was the true rule of international law, as now recognized in most civilized countries, and had superseded the rule of the common law, depending on birth within the realm, originally founded on feudal considerations.

But at the time of the adoption of the Constitution of the United States in 1789, and long before, it would seem to have been the rule in Europe generally, as it certainly was in France, that, as said by Pothier, "citizens, true and native-born citizens, are those who are born within the extent of the dominion of France," and "mere birth within the realm gives the rights of a native-born citizen, independently of the origin of the father or mother, and of their domicil;" and children born in a foreign country, of a French father who had not established his domicil there nor given up the intention of returning, were also deemed Frenchmen, as Laurent says, by "a favor, a sort of fiction," and Calvo, "by a sort of fiction of exterritoriality, considered as born in France, and therefore invested with French nationality." . . . The Code Napoleon of 1807 [1803] changed the law of France, and adopted, instead of the rule of country of birth, *jus soli*, the rule of descent or blood, *jus sanguinis,* as the leading principle; but an eminent commentator has observed that the framers of that code "appear not to have wholly freed themselves from the ancient rule of France, or rather, indeed, ancient rule of Europe—*de la vieille règle française, ou plutôt même de la vieille règle européenne*—according to which nationality had always been, in former times, determined by the place of birth." 1 Demolombe *Cours de Code Napoleon*, (4th ed.) no. 146.

The later modifications of the rule in Europe rest upon the constitutions, laws or ordinances of the various countries, and have no important bearing upon the interpretation and effect of the Constitution of the United States. . . .

There is, therefore, little ground for the theory that, at the time of the adoption of the Fourteenth Amendment of the Constitution of the United States, there was any settled and definite rule of international law, generally recognized by civilized nations, inconsistent with the ancient rule of citizenship by birth within the dominion.

Nor can it be doubted that it is the inherent right of every independent nation to determine for itself, and according to its own constitution and laws, what classes of persons shall be entitled to its citizenship.

Both in England and in the United States, indeed, statutes have been passed, at various times, enacting that certain issue born abroad of English subjects, or of American citizens, respectively, should inherit, to some extent at least, the rights of their parents. But those statutes applied only to cases coming within their purport; and they have never been considered, in either country, as affecting the citizenship of persons born within its dominion. . . .

V. In the fore front, both of the Fourteenth Amendment of the Constitution, and of the Civil Rights Act of 1866, the fundamental principle of citizenship by birth within the dominion was reaffirmed in the most explicit and comprehensive terms. . . .

The first section of the Fourteenth Amendment of the Constitution begins with the words, "All persons born or naturalized in the United States, and subject to the jurisdiction thereof, are citizens of the United States and of the State wherein they reside." As appears upon the face of the amendment, as well as from the history of the times, this was not intended to impose any new restrictions upon citizenship, or to prevent any persons from becoming citizens by the fact of birth within the United States, who would thereby have become citizens according to the law existing before its adoption. It is declaratory in form, and enabling and extending in effect. Its main purpose doubtless was, as has been often recognized by this court, to establish the citizenship of free negroes, which had been denied in the opinion delivered by Chief Justice Taney in Dred Scott v. Sandford, (1857) 19 How. 393; and to put it beyond doubt that all blacks, as well as whites, born or naturalized within the jurisdiction of the United States, are citizens of the United States. The Slaughterhouse Cases, (1873) 16 Wall. 36, 73; Strauder v. West Virginia, (1879) 100 U. S. 303, 306; Ex parte Virginia, (1879) 100 U. S. 339, 345; Neal v. Delaware, (1880) 103 U. S. 370, 386; Elk v. Wilkins, (1884) 112 U. S. 94, 101. But the opening words, "All persons born," are general, not to say universal, restricted only by place and jurisdiction, and not by color or race—as was clearly recognized in all the opinions delivered in The Slaughterhouse Cases, above cited. . . .

This sentence of the Fourteenth Amendment is declaratory of existing rights, and affirmative of existing law, as to each of the qualifications therein expressed—"born in the United States," "naturalized in the United States," and "subject to the jurisdiction thereof"—in short, as to everything relating to the acquisition of citizenship by facts occurring within the limits of the United States. But it has not touched the acquisition of citizenship by being born abroad of American parents; and has left that subject to be regulated, as it had always been, by Congress, in the exercise of the power conferred by the Constitution to establish an uniform rule of naturalization. . . .

The foregoing considerations and authorities irresistibly lead us to these conclusions: The Fourteenth Amendment affirms the ancient and fundamental rule of citizenship by birth within the territory, in the allegiance and under the protection of the country, including all children here born of resident aliens, with the exceptions or qualifications (as old as the rule itself) of children of foreign sovereigns or their ministers, or born on foreign public ships, or of enemies within and during a hostile occupation of part of our territory, and with the single additional exception of children of members of the Indian tribes owing direct allegiance to their several tribes. The Amendment, in clear words and in manifest intent, includes the children born, within the territory of the United States, of all other persons, of whatever race or color, domiciled within the United States. Every citizen or subject of another country, while domiciled here, is within the allegiance and the protection, and consequently subject to the jurisdiction, of the United States. His allegiance to the United States is direct and immediate, and, although but local and temporary, continuing only so long as he remains within our territory, is yet, in the words of Lord Coke, in Calvin's Case, 7 Rep. 6a, "strong enough to make a natural subject, for if he hath issue here, that issue is a natural-born subject:" and his child, as said by Mr. Binney in his essay before quoted, "if born in the country, is as much a citizen as the natural-born child of a citizen, and by operation of the same principle." . . .

To hold that the Fourteenth Amendment of the Constitution excludes from citizenship the children, born in the United States, of citizens or subjects of other countries, would be to deny citizenship to thousands of persons of English, Scotch, Irish, German or other European parentage, who have always been considered and treated as citizens of the United States.

VI. Whatever considerations, in the absence of a controlling provision of the Constitution, might influence the legislative or the executive branch of the Government to decline to admit persons of the Chinese race to the status of citizens of the United States, there are none that can constrain or permit the judiciary to refuse to give full effect to the peremptory and explicit language of the Fourteenth Amendment, which declares and ordains that "All persons born or naturalized in the United States, and subject to the jurisdiction thereof, are citizens of the United States." . . .

The Fourteenth Amendment of the Constitution, in the declaration that "all persons born or naturalized in the United States, and subject to the jurisdiction thereof, are citizens of the United States and of the State wherein they reside," contemplates two sources of citizenship, and two only: birth and naturalization. Citizenship by naturalization can only be acquired by naturalization under the authority and in the forms of law. But citizenship by birth is established by the mere fact of birth under the circumstances defined in the Constitution. Every person born in the United States, and subject to the jurisdiction thereof, becomes at once a citizen of the United States, and needs no naturalization. A person born out of the jurisdiction of the United States can only become a citizen by being naturalized, either by treaty, as in the case of the annexation of foreign territory; or by authority of Congress, exercised either by declaring certain classes of persons to be citizens, as in the enactments conferring citizenship upon foreign-born children of citizens, or by enabling foreigners individually to become citizens by proceedings in the judicial tribunals, as in the ordinary provisions of the naturalization acts. . . .

The fact, therefore, that acts of Congress or treaties have not permitted Chinese persons born out of this country to become citizens by naturalization, cannot exclude Chinese persons born in this country from the operation of the broad and clear words of the Constitution, "All persons born in the United States, and subject to the jurisdiction thereof, are citizens of the United States."

VII. Upon the facts agreed in this case, the American citizenship which Wong Kim Ark acquired by birth within the United States has not been lost or taken away by anything happening since his birth. No doubt he might himself, after coming of age, renounce this citizenship, and become a citizen of the country of his parents, or of any other country; for by our law, as solemnly declared by Congress, "the right of expatriation is a natural and inherent right of all people," and "any declaration, instruction, opinion, order or direction of any officer of the United States, which denies, restricts, impairs or questions the right of expatriation, is declared inconsistent with the fundamental principles of the Republic." Rev. Stat. § 1999, reënacting act of July 27, 1868, c. 249, § 1; 15 Stat. 223, 224. Whether any act of himself, or of his parents, during his minority, could have the same effect, is at least doubtful. But it would be out of place to pursue that inquiry; inasmuch as it is expressly agreed that his residence has always been in the United States, and not elsewhere; that each of his temporary visits to China, the one for some months when he was about seventeen years old, and the other for something like a year about the time of his coming of age, was made with the intention of returning, and was followed by his actual return, to the United States; and "that said Wong Kim Ark has not, either by himself or his parents acting for him, ever renounced his allegiance to the United States, and that he has never done or committed any act or thing to exclude him therefrom."

The evident intention, and the necessary effect, of the submission of this case to the decision of the court upon the facts agreed by the parties, were to present for determination the single question, stated at the beginning of this opinion, namely, whether a child born in the United States, of parents of Chinese descent, who, at the time of his birth, are subjects of the Emperor of China, but have a permanent domicil and residence in the United States, and are there carrying on business, and are not employed in any diplomatic or official capacity under the Emperor of China, becomes at the time of his birth a citizen of the United States. For the reasons above stated, this court is of opinion that the question must be answered in the affirmative.

Order affirmed.

MR. CHIEF JUSTICE FULLER, with whom concurred MR. JUSTICE HARLAN, dissenting. . . .

ITALY AND PERU: CANEVARO CASE.

Tribunal of the Permanent Court of Arbitration, 1912.

Scott, Hague Court Reports (1916), p. 284.

The claim of the Italian Government against Peru on behalf of Napoléon, Carlos and Rafael Canevaro originated as follows: It appears that on December 12, 1880, N. de Pierola, at the time dictator of Peru, issued a decree by virtue of which there were created, under date of December 23, 1880, pay checks (*bons de paiement, libramientos*) to the order of the firm of José Canevaro & Sons for the sum of 77,000 pounds sterling, payable at different periods; that these pay checks were not paid as they fell due; that in 1885, the father having died in 1883, the firm was reorganized with José Francisco, César and Rafael Canevaro, Peruvian citizens, as copartners, forming a Peruvian corporation; that in 1885 the Peruvian Government paid 35,000 pounds sterling on account, leaving due and oustanding to the firm the sum of 43,140 pounds sterling; that the firm remained in existence until it was dissolved in 1900 by the death of José Francisco Canevaro; and that the pay checks (*bons de paiement*) finally passed into possession of Napoléon and Carlos Canevaro, Italian subjects, and Rafael Canevaro, whose claim to Italian nationality was contested by Peru.

Differences arose between the claimants and Peru as to whether the pay checks should be paid in coin, or in one per cent bonds in accordance with the provisions of the Peruvian domestic debt law of June 12, 1889, as to the amount which the claimants had a right to demand, and as to the nationality of Rafael Canevaro. Peru contended that the debt was contracted by Peru with a Peruvian corporation and that therefore its settlement was entirely a domestic matter, but, finally, on April 25, 1910, as the result of diplomatic negotiations with Italy, a compromis was signed, submitting the questions in dispute to a tribunal of the Permanent Court of Arbitration at The Hague. . . .

[THE TRIBUNAL—RENAULT, FUSINATO, CALDERON.] Whereas, by a compromis dated April 25, 1910, the Italian and Peruvian Governments agreed to submit the following questions to arbitration:

Should the Peruvian Government pay in cash, or in accordance with the provisions of the Peruvian law of June 12, 1889, on the domestic debt, the bills of exchange (*cambiali, libramientos*) now in the possession of the brothers Napoléon, Carlos, and Rafael Canevaro, which were drawn by the Peruvian Government to the order of the firm of José Canevaro & Sons for the sum of 43,140 pounds sterling, plus the legal interest on the said amount?

Have the Canevaro brothers a right to demand the total amount claimed?

Has Count Rafael Canevaro a right to be considered as an Italian claimant? . . .

Whereas, in order to simplify the following statement it is deemed best to pass first upon the third question contained in the compromis, that is, the question of the status of Rafael Canevaro;

Whereas, according to Peruvian legislation (Article 34 of the Constitution), Rafael Canevaro is a Peruvian by birth because born on Peruvian territory,

And, whereas, on the other hand, according to Italian legislation (Article 4 of the Civil Code) he is of Italian nationality because born of an Italian father;

Whereas, as a matter of fact, Rafael Canevaro has on several occasions acted as a Peruvian citizen, both by running as a candidate for the Senate, where none are admitted except Peruvian citizens and where he succeeded in defending his election, and, particularly, by accepting the office of Consul General for the Netherlands, after having secured the authorization of both the Peruvian Government and the Peruvian Congress;

Whereas, under these circumstances, whatever Rafael Canevaro's status as a national may be in Italy, the Government of Peru has a right to consider him a Peruvian citizen and to deny his status as an Italian claimant. . . .

And whereas, according to the above decision in regard to the status of Rafael Canevaro, the tribunal is to pass judgment only in regard to his two brothers; . . .

Therefore, the arbitral tribunal decides that the Peruvian Government shall, on July 31, 1912, deliver to the Italian Legation at Lima, on account of the brothers Napoléon and Carlos Canevaro [specified bonds and a sum of gold] . . .

FRANCE AND GREAT BRITAIN: NATIONALITY DECREES IN TUNIS AND MOROCCO.

Permanent Court of International Justice, 1923.

Publications of the Court, Series B, No. 4.

[This dispute had its origin [1] in a decree promulgated on November 8, 1921 by the Bey of Tunis, the first article of which was as follows:

"With the exception of citizens, subjects or nationals of the Protecting Power (other than our own subjects), every person born in the territory of our Kingdom of parents one of whom was also born there, is a Tunisian, subject to the provisions of conventions or treaties binding the Tunisian Government."

---

[1] See Publications of the Court, Series E, No. 1, p. 195.

On the same date, the President of the French Republic issued a Decree of which the first article was as follows:

"Every person born in the Regency of Tunis of parents of whom one, justiciable as a foreigner in the French Courts of the Protectorate, was also born there, is French."

Similar legislation was introduced at the same time in Morocco (French Zone).

The British Ambassador in Paris protested to the French Government against the application to British subjects of the decrees promulgated in Tunis, and also stated that his Government was unable to recognize that the decrees put into force in the French Zone of Morocco were applicable to persons entitled to British nationality. As it was not found possible to adjust the divergence of views, the British Government proposed to the French that the matter should be referred to the Court, invoking amongst other things, the Franco-British Arbitration Convention of October 14th, 1903. The French Government refused to submit the matter to arbitral or judicial settlement, whereupon the British Government stated, on July 14th, 1922, that it had no alternative but to submit the dispute to the Council of the League of Nations, relying on Articles 13 and 15 of the Covenant. The Quai d'Orsay replied that the question was not one for consideration by the Council of the League of Nations, having regard to the reservation made in paragraph 8 of Article 15 of the Covenant concerning questions which by international law are solely within the domestic jurisdiction of one Party.

The Governments concerned then came to an agreement, under the auspices of the Council, to the effect that the latter should request the Court to give an advisory opinion on this question of jurisdiction, *viz.* whether the dispute is or is not, by international law, solely a matter of domestic jurisdiction.]

[By the Court] . . . III. The question before the Court for advisory opinion is as follows:

"*Whether the dispute between France and Great Britain as to the Nationality Decrees issued in Tunis and Morocco (French zone) on November 8th, 1921, and their application to British subjects, is or is not, by international law, solely a matter of domestic jurisdiction (Article 15, paragraph 8, of the Covenant).*" . . .

IV. Under the terms of sub-section (a) of the Council's resolution, the Court, in replying to the question stated above, has to give an opinion upon the nature and not upon the merits of the dispute, which, under the terms of sub-section (c) may, in certain circumstances, form the subject of a subsequent decision. . . .

The paragraph to which sub-section (a) of the Council's resolution expressly refers is as follows:

(*English text*).

"If the dispute between the parties is claimed by one of them, and is found by the Council, to arise out of a matter which by international law is solely within the domestic jurisdiction of that party, the Council shall so report, and shall make no recommendation as to its settlement." . . .

Special attention must be called to the word "*exclusive*" in the French text, to which the word "solely" (within the domestic jurisdiction) corresponds in the English text. The question to be considered is not whether one of the parties to the dispute is or is not competent in law to take or to refrain from taking a particular action, but whether the jurisdiction claimed belongs *solely* to that party.

From one point of view, it might well be said that the jurisdiction of a State is *exclusive* within the limits fixed by international law—using this expression in its wider sense, that is to say, embracing both customary law and general as well as particular treaty law. But a careful scrutiny of paragraph 8 of Article 15 shows that it is not in this sense that exclusive jurisdiction is referred to in that paragraph.

The words "solely within the domestic jurisdiction" seem rather to contemplate certain matters which, though they may very closely concern the interests of more than one State, are not, in principle, regulated by international law.[1] As regards such matters, each State is sole judge.

The question whether a certain matter is or is not solely within the jurisdiction of a State is an essentially relative question; it depends upon the development of international relations. Thus, in the present state of international law, questions of nationality are, in the opinion of the Court, in principle within this reserved domain.

For the purpose of the present opinion, it is enough to observe that it may well happen that, in a matter which, like that of nationality, is not, in principle, regulated by international law, the right of a State to use its discretion is nevertheless restricted by obligations which it may have undertaken towards other States. In such a case, jurisdiction which, in principle, belongs solely to the State, is limited by rules of international law. Article 15, paragraph 8, then ceases to apply as regards those States which are entitled to invoke such rules, and the dispute as to the question whether a State has or has not the right to take certain measures becomes in these circumstances a dispute of an international character and falls outside the scope of the exception contained in this paragraph. To hold that a State has not exclusive jurisdiction does not in any way prejudice the final decision as to whether that State has a right to adopt such measures.

This interpretation follows from the actual terms of paragraph 8 of Article 15 of the Covenant, and, in the opinion of the Court, it is also in harmony with that Article taken as a whole.

Article 15, in effect, establishes the fundamental principle that any dispute likely to lead to a rupture which is not submitted to arbitration

---

[1] This statement is somewhat misleading. What is really meant is that there *is* a rule of international law on the subject and that rule is that each state has complete liberty of action in respect to that subject. See below, p. 149, n. 1.

in accordance with Article 13 shall be laid before the Council. The reservations generally made in arbitration treaties are not to be found in this Article.

Having regard to this very wide competence possessed by the League of Nations, the Covenant contains an express reservation protecting the independence of States; this reservation is to be found in paragraph 8 of Article 15. Without this reservation, the internal affairs of a country might, directly they appeared to affect the interests of another country, be brought before the Council and form the subject of recommendations by the League of Nations. Under the terms of paragraph 8, the League's interest in being able to make such recommendations as are deemed just and proper in the circumstances with a view to the maintenance of peace must, at a given point, give way to the equally essential interest of the individual State to maintain intact its independence in matters which international law recognises to be solely within its jurisdiction.

It must not, however, be forgotten that the provision contained in paragraph 8, in accordance with which the Council, in certain circumstances, is to confine itself to reporting that a question is, by international law, solely within the domestic jurisdiction of one Party, is an exception to the principles affirmed in the preceding paragraphs and does not therefore lend itself to an extensive interpretation.

This consideration assumes especial importance in the case of a matter which, by international law, is, in principle, solely within the domestic jurisdiction of one Party, but in regard to which the other Party invokes international engagements which, in the opinion of that Party, are of a nature to preclude in the particular case such exclusive jurisdiction. . . .

V. The main arguments developed by the Parties in support of their respective contentions are as follows:

1. A. The French Decrees relate to persons born, not upon the territory of France itself, but upon the territory of the French Protectorates of Tunis and of the French zone of Morocco. Granted that it is competent for a State to enact such legislation within its national territory, the question remains to be considered whether the same competence exists as regards protected territory.

The extent of the powers of a protecting State in the territory of a protected State depends, first, upon the Treaties between the protecting State and the protected State establishing the Protectorate, and, secondly, upon the conditions under which the Protectorate has been recognised by third Powers as against whom there is an intention to rely on the provisions of these Treaties. In spite of common features possessed by Protectorates under international law, they have individual legal characteristics resulting from the special conditions under which they were created, and the stage of their development. . . .

The question whether the exclusive jurisdiction possessed by a protecting State in regard to nationality questions in its own territory extends to the territory of the protected State depends upon an examination of the whole situation as it appears from the standpoint of international law. The question therefore is no longer solely one of domestic jurisdiction as defined above. (See Part IV.)

B. The French Government contends that the public powers (*puissance publique*) exercised by the protecting State, taken in conjunction with the local sovereignty of the protected State, constitute full sovereignty equivalent to that upon which international relations are based, and that therefore the protecting State and the protected State may, by virtue of an agreement between them, exercise and divide between them within the protected territory the whole extent of the powers which international law recognises as enjoyed by sovereign States within the limits of their national territory. This contention is disputed by the British Government.

The Court observes that, in any event, it will be necessary to have recourse to international law in order to decide what the value of an agreement of this kind may be as regards third States, and that the question consequently ceases to be one which, by international law, is solely within the domestic jurisdiction of a State, as that jurisdiction is defined above.

2. A. Great Britain denies that the Decrees of November 8th, 1921, are applicable to British subjects, and relies in support of her contention upon the Treaties concluded by her with the two States which were subsequently placed under protectorate (Treaty between Great Britain and Morocco dated December 9th, 1856, and Treaty between Great Britain and Tunis dated July 19th, 1875). By virtue of these Treaties, persons claimed as British subjects would enjoy a measure of extra-territoriality incompatible with the imposition of another nationality.

According to the French contention, as developed in the course of the oral statements, these Treaties, which were concluded for an indefinite period, that is to say, in perpetuity, have lapsed by virtue of the principle known as the *clausula rebus sic stantibus* because the establishment of a legal and judicial regime in conformity with French legislation has created a new situation which deprives the capitulatory regime of its *raison d'être*.

It is clearly not possible to make any pronouncement upon this point without recourse to the principles of international law concerning the duration of the validity of treaties. It follows, therefore, that in this respect also the question does not, by international law, fall solely within the domestic jurisdiction of a State, as that jurisdiction is defined above.

B. As regard Tunis more especially, France contends that, following upon negotiations between the French and British Governments, Great Britain formally renounced her rights of jurisdiction in the Regency

(Note from Lord Granville to M. Tissot dated June 20th, 1883, British Case, Appendix No. 6; French Counter-case page 82; Order in Council of December 31st, 1883), and that by the Franco-British Arrangement of September 18th, 1897, she accepted a new basis for the relations between France and herself in Tunis. It appears from the Cases and Counter-Cases that the two Governments take different views with regard to the scope of the declarations made by Great Britain in this respect and also with regard to the construction to be placed upon the Arrangement of 1897.

The appreciation of these divergent points of view involves, owing to the very nature of the divergence, the interpretation of international engagements. The question therefore does not, according to international law, fall solely within the domestic jurisdiction of a single State, as that jurisdiction is defined above.

C. As far as Morocco is concerned, it is certain that Great Britain still exercises there her consular jurisdiction. France argues that Great Britain, by consenting to the Franco-German Convention of November 4th, 1911, with regard to Morocco, agreed to renounce her capitulatory rights as soon as the new judicial system contemplated by the Convention had been introduced.

The British Government, on the contrary, contends that the Franco-German Convention of 1911—its adhesion to which was conditional upon the internationalisation of the town and district of Tangiers, a condition which has not yet been fulfilled—was not an agreement for the suppression of the capitulatory regime: in this respect, the relations between France and Great Britain are, it is said, still governed by the second of the Secret Articles of the Anglo-French Declaration of April 8th, 1904 (British Counter-Case, Appendix No. 7).

In the case of Morocco also, therefore, as in the case of Tunis, there is a difference with regard to the interpretation of international engagements. The international character of the legal situation follows not only from the fact that the two governments concerned place a different construction upon the obligations undertaken, but also from the fact that Great Britain exercises capitulatory rights in the territory of the French Protectorate in Morocco. Again, from this standpoint, the question does not, according to international law, fall solely within the domestic jurisdiction of a State, as that jurisdiction is defined above

. . .

4. According to the French Government, paragraph 2 of Article 1 of the Arrangement of September 18th, 1897, should be interpreted as a formal recognition by Great Britain of the competence of France to legislate with regard to the situation of persons in Tunis, and more particularly with regard to their nationality, under the same conditions as in France. This construction is disputed by the British Government. . . .

In the opinion of the Court, these facts suffice, even when considered separately, to prove that the dispute arises out of a matter which, by international law, is not solely within the domestic jurisdiction of France as such jurisdiction is defined in this opinion.

For these reasons:

The court is of opinion that the dispute referred to in the Resolution of the Council of the League of Nations of October 4th, 1922, is not, by international law, solely a matter of domestic jurisdiction (Article 15, paragraph 8, of the Covenant), and therefore replies to the question submitted to it in the negative. . . . [1,2]

---

[1] While the chief issue in this case was the interpretation of a treaty, it is valuable to the student for its incidental discussion of the exclusive control by a state, under normal conditions, of the nationality of persons born within its territories. The issue with respect to "domestic jurisdiction" under Article 15 is somewhat confused by the phrasing of the article. In the numerous jurisdictional disputes that have arisen between nations "domestic questions" might be described as questions which are definitely subject to the decision of the state within whose territory they arise. This does not mean, strictly speaking, that there is no rule of international law upon the subject, but rather that international law on that point recognizes the right of the individual state to be free in determining its own policy. See Fenwick, *op. cit.* 176, 177, n. 2.

[2] SUPPLEMENTARY CASES. In Lynch v. Clarke, 1 Sandford 583 (1844), involving the right of Julia Lynch, born in the State of New York during the temporary sojourn of her parents in the United States, to inherit the property of her uncle, the Court of Chancery of New York held that the rule of the common law of England, that "persons born within the ligeance of the crown of England, were natural born subjects, without reference to the status or condition of their parents" was also, since the adoption of the Constitution, the common law of the United States and therefore the law of the State of New York. Hence the New York law that aliens could not inherit had no application in her case.

In the case of In re Lam Mow, 19 F. (2d) 951 (1927), involving the citizenship by birth of a child born to Chinese parents on an American ship in which they were returning to the United States from China, the District Court held that a merchant ship was not part of the territory of the country whose flag it flies in any such physical sense as to make birth on board the vessel constitute birth "in the United States" in the sense of the Fourteenth Amendment. Affirmed in Lam Mow v. Nagle, 24 F. (2d) 316 (1928).

Query, in the case of a person born outside the territory of the United States of parents who are citizens of the United States what acts would be necessary to divest him of the citizenship belonging to him *jure sanguinis?* In State of Vermont v. Jackson, 79 Vermont 504 (1907) involving the citizenship of Jackson as a necessary condition of his holding the office of state's attorney, the Supreme Court of Vermont held that the great-grandfather of the respondent was a citizen of the United States by reason of continued residence in the country after the Declaration of Independence, the grandfather was a citizen by birth and had not lost it by residence in Canada, the father, although born in Canada, was a citizen by reason of parentage and subsequent residence in the United States, and the son, whose citizenship was at issue, was, although born in Canada, a citizen by reason of parentage and subsequent residence in the United States.

In the dispute between Germany and Poland, referred by the Council of the League of Nations to the Permanent Court of International Justice in 1923 for

B. Nationality by naturalization.

International law recognizes that a state may acquire the right to protect certain persons as its nationals when they have been admitted to its citizenship by the procedure of naturalization.[1] It is not settled, however, to what extent naturalization in one country dissolves or modifies the nationality attaching to a person by birth, and conflicts may arise between a state making claims based upon birth and another making claims based upon naturalization. The older rule of indelible allegiance [MacDonald's Case; Williams' Case] has given way to a more liberal policy in accordance with which many states accept the fact of the naturalization of one of their citizens in another state as an automatic release of the citizen from his former allegiance. The procedure of naturalization may, however, be more strictly construed when one state is pressing the claims of its alleged nationals against another state. [United States (re Hilson) v. Germany.]

PROCEEDINGS AGAINST ÆNEAS MACDONALD, ALIAS ANGUS MACDONALD, FOR HIGH TREASON.

Great Britain, Court of Kings Bench, 1747.

18 Howell's State Trials, 857.

In the year 1747, a bill of indictment was found against him under the special commission in Surrey for the share he had in the late rebellion. . . .

The overt acts charged in the indictment were sufficiently proved. And also that the prisoner was apprehended and in custody before the 1st of January 1746–7.

The counsel for the prisoner insisted that he was born in the dominions of the French king, and on this point they put his defence.

But apprehending that the weight of the evidence might be against them, as indeed it was, with regard to the place of the prisoner's birth,

---

an advisory opinion (Publications of the Court, Series B, No. 7, 1923), involving the nationality of persons born in the territory transferred by Germany to Poland, the court held that the terms of the treaty of June 28, 1919, interpreted in the light of the precedents supplied by international practice, indicated an intention to combine "both the principle of habitual residence and the principle of origin"; so that while it was necessary that the persons in question, to become automatically Polish citizens, should have been born in the territory of parents habitually resident there at the time of the birth of the individual, it was not necessary that the parents should also have been habitually resident there on the day of the coming into force of the treaty.

[1] In the United States naturalization is limited by law to "white persons" and to "persons of African descent," and the statutes have been interpreted as excluding Chinese, Japanese and other persons of the brown and yellow races. In respect to the Japanese, see Ozawa v. United States, 260 U. S. 178 (1922).

they endeavoured to captivate the jury and bystanders, by representing the great hardship of a prosecution of this kind against a person, who, admitting him to be a native of Great Britain, had received his education from his early infancy in France; and had spent his riper years in a profitable employment in that kingdom, where all his hopes centered. And speaking of the doctrine of natural allegiance, they represented it as a slavish principle, not likely to prevail in these times; especially as it seemed to derogate from the principles of the Revolution.

Here the Court interposed, and declared, that the mentioning the case of the Revolution as a case any way similar to that of the prisoner, supposing him to have been born in Great Britain, can serve no purpose but to bring an odium on that great and glorious transaction. It never was doubted that a subject born, taking a commission from a foreign prince, and committing high treason, may be punished as a subject for that treason, notwithstanding his foreign commission. (Dyer, 298. 300. 1 Hale, 68. 96.) It was so ruled in doctor Storey's case. [1 How. St. Tr. 1087.] And that case was never yet denied to be law. It is not in the power of any private subject to shake off his allegiance, and to transfer it to a foreign prince. Nor is it in the power of any foreign prince by naturalizing or employing a subject of Great Britain to dissolve the bond of allegiance between that subject and the crown.

However, as the prisoner's counsel had mentioned his French commission as a circumstance tending in their opinion to prove his birth in France, the Court permitted it to be read, the attorney general consenting. It was dated the 1st of June 1745, and appointed the prisoner commissary of the troops of France, which were then intended to embark for Scotland.

The Court, with the consent of the counsel for the crown, permitted the cartel between France and Great Britain for the exchange or ransom of prisoners likewise to be read. And observed, that as it relateth barely to the exchange or ransom of prisoners of war, it can never extend to the case of the prisoner at the bar, supposing him to be a subject born. Because by the laws of all nations, subjects taken in arms against their lawful prince, are not considered as prisoners of war, but as rebels; and are liable to the punishments ordinarily inflicted on rebels.

Lord Chief Justice Lee in his direction to the jury, told them that the overt acts laid in the indictment being fully proved, and not denied by the prisoner, or rather admitted by his defence, the only fact they had to try was, whether he was a native of Great Britain? If so, he must be found guilty. And as to that point, he said the presumption in all cases of this kind is against the prisoner, and the proof of his birth out of the king's dominions, where the prisoner putteth his defence on that issue, lieth upon him. But whether the evidence that had been given in the present case (which he summed up very minutely) did or did not amount to such proof he left to their consideration.

The jury found him Guilty, but recommended him to mercy. He received sentence of death as in cases of high treason; but was afterwards pardoned upon the conditions mentioned afterwards [banishment].

WILLIAMS' CASE.

United States, Circuit Court for the District of Connecticut, 1799.

Wharton's State Trials, 652. [Fed. Cas. No. 17,708.] [1]

. . . On the trial, it was admitted on the part of Williams, that he had committed the facts alleged against him in the indictment, but, in his defence, he offered to prove that, in the year 1792, he received from the Consul-General of the French Republic, a warrant, appointing him third-lieutenant on board the Jupiter, a French seventy-four gun ship; that, pursuant to this appointment, he went on board the Jupiter, and took the command to which he was appointed; that the Jupiter soon after sailed for France, and arrived at Rochefort, in France, in the autumn of the same year; that at Rochefort he was duly naturalized in the various Bureaux in that place, the same autumn, renouncing his allegiance to all other countries, particularly to America, and taking an oath of allegiance to the Republic of France, all according to the laws of said republic; that immediately after said naturalization he was duly commissioned by the Republic of France appointing him a second-lieutenant on board a French frigate called the Charont; and that before the ratification of the treaty of amity and commerce between the United States and Great Britain, he was duly commissioned by the French Republic a second-lieutenant on board a seventy-four gun ship, in the service of said republic; and that he has ever continued under the government of the French Republic down to the present time, and the most of said time actually resident in the dominions of the French Republic; that during said period he was not resident in the United States more than six months, which was in the year 1796, when he came to this country for the purpose merely of visiting his relations and friends; that, for about three years past, he has been domiciliated in the island of Guadaloupe, within the dominions of the French Republic, and has made that place his fixed habitation, without any design of again returning to the United States for permanent residence. The Attorney for the District conceded the above mentioned statement to be true; but objected that it ought not to be admitted as evidence to the jury, because it could have no operation in law to justify the prisoner in committing the facts alleged against him in the indictment. This question was

---

[1] Also reported, in less detail, in 2 Cranch 88, note a.

argued on both sides by Mr. Pierpont Edwards for the United States, and Mr. David Daggett for the prisoner.

Judge LAW (district judge) expressed doubts as to the legal operation of the evidence; and gave it as his opinion, that the evidence, and the operation of law thereon, be left to the consideration of the jury.

Judge ELLSWORTH, the Chief Justice of the United States, stated his views nearly in the following language:

The common law of this country remains the same as it was before the Revolution. The present question is to be decided by two great principles; one is, that all the members of civil community are bound to each other by compact. The other is, that one of the parties to this compact cannot dissolve it by his own act. The compact between our community and its members is, that the community will protect its members; and on the part of the members, that they will at all times be obedient to the laws of the community, and faithful in its defence. This compact distinguishes our government from those which are founded in violence or fraud. It necessarily results, that the members cannot dissolve this compact, without the consent or default of the community. There has been here no consent—no default. Default is not pretended. Express consent is not claimed; but it has been argued, that the consent of the community is implied by its policy—its conditions, and its acts.

In countries so crowded with inhabitants that the means of subsistence are difficult to be obtained, it is reason and policy to permit emigration. But our policy is different; for our country is but sparsely settled, and we have no inhabitants to spare.

Consent has been argued from the condition of the country; because we were in a state of peace. But though we were in peace the war had commenced in Europe. We wished to have nothing to do with the war; but the war would have something to do with us. It has been extremely difficult for us to keep out of this war; the progress of it has threatened to involve us. It has been necessary for our government to be vigilant in restraining our own citizens from those acts which would involve us in hostilities. The most visionary writers on this subject do not contend for the principle in the unlimited extent, that a citizen may at any and at all times renounce his own and join himself to a foreign country. Consent has been argued from the acts of our own government, permitting the naturalization of foreigners. When a foreigner presents himself here, and proves himself to be of a good moral character, well affected to the Constitution and Government of the United States, and a friend to the good order and happiness of civil society, if he has resided here the time prescribed by law, we grant him the privilege of a citizen. We do not inquire what his relation is to his own country; we have not the means of knowing, and the inquiry would be indelicate; we leave him to judge of that. If he embarrasses himself by contracting contradictory obligations, the fault and the folly are his own. But this implies no consent of the government, that our own citizens should expatriate themselves. Therefore, it is my opinion that these facts which the prisoner offers to prove in his defence, are totally irrelevant; they can have no operation in law; and the jury ought not to be embarrassed or troubled with them; but by the constitution of the court the evidence must go to the jury. . . .

[The prisoner was found guilty, fined and imprisoned.][1]

UNITED STATES OF AMERICA ON BEHALF OF EDWARD A. HILSON v. GERMANY.

United States—Germany, Mixed Claims Commission, 1925.

Decisions and Opinions, 1925, p. 231.

Parker, Umpire, rendered the decision of the Commission.

This case is before the Umpire for decision on a certificate of the National Commissioners certifying their disagreement.

The record discloses that Edward A. Hilson, a British national, was employed as a radio operator on the American Steamship Columbian when she was captured by a German submarine on November 7, 1916, and on the following day torpedoed and sunk. He with other members of the ship's crew eventually reached the coast of Spain after rowing in an open boat some twenty or twenty-five miles through a rough sea. A claim is put forward by the United States on claimant's behalf for personal injuries alleged to have been suffered by him through exposure to the elements and also for the value of his personal effects lost when the Columbian was sunk.

Prior thereto the claimant had, in pursuance of the naturalization statutes of the United States, made formal declaration of his intention to become an American citizen, but this intention had not matured into citizenship and he remained a citizen and subject of Great Britain. Section 2174 of the Revised Statutes of the United States, in effect at that time and the substance of which is in effect now, provides that "Every seaman, *being a foreigner,* who declares his intention of becoming a citizen of the United States" shall be admitted to citizenship after three years' service on board a merchant vessel of the United States subsequent to such declaration "but such seaman shall, *for all purposes of protection* as an American citizen, be deemed such, after the filing of his declaration of intention to become such citizen."

The claimant on July 5, 1918, became through naturalization and has since remained an American citizen. The question presented is the narrow one, Is Germany under the terms of the Treaty of Berlin obligated

---

[1] Compare the act of July 27, 1868, and subsequent legislation.

to pay such damages as may have been suffered by claimant during November, 1916?

It will be constantly borne in mind that the Treaty of Berlin constitutes a contract by which Germany accorded to the United States, as one of the conditions of peace, rights on behalf of *American nationals*. Many of the claims against Germany arising under the reparation provisions of the Treaty of Versailles and presented to this Commission by the United States on behalf of its nationals could not have been maintained under the rules of international law but were created by and are based exclusively on the contract terms of the Treaty of Berlin. The obligations thus assumed by Germany, and the reparation claims with which this Commission is empowered to deal, are manifestly limited to such as are embraced within the Treaty terms, which are enumerated in this Commission's Administrative Decision No. I. As heretofore pointed out it results from that decision that no claim "falls within the Treaty unless it is based on a loss, damage, or injury *suffered by* an American national—that is, it must be American in its origin."

The term American national as used in the Treaty and the decisions of this Commission has been defined by this Commission in its Administrative Decision No. I as "a person wheresoever domiciled owing permanent allegiance to the United States of America." The decision was concurred in by the American Commissioner, and while the German Commissioner did not concur in the decision as a whole he and the Government of Germany did concur in this definition and he and the Government of Germany have accepted the decision as a whole as binding on both Governments.

This definition of an American national is taken from that part of the Joint Resolution of the Congress of the United States approved July 2, 1921, which is carried into and forms the basis of the Treaty of Berlin. There the claims, for the satisfaction of which it is stipulated that Germany shall make suitable provision, are limited to those "of all persons, wheresoever domiciled, who owe permanent allegiance to the United States of America and who have suffered . . . loss, damage, or injury to their persons or property," etc. The phrase "who owe permanent allegiance to the United States of America" was manifestly used advisedly. It has a well defined meaning in American jurisprudence. It broadens the term "American citizens" to embrace, not only citizens of the United States, but Indians and members of other aboriginal tribes or native peoples of the United States and of its territories and possessions. But on the other hand it *expressly limits* American citizenship for all purposes of the Treaty to those who owed *permanent allegiance* to the United States.

It is not contended that Hilson owed permanent allegiance to the United States at the time he suffered the damages complained of. On the contrary the very statute above quoted invoked to afford to him the protection of an American citizen describes the class to which he belonged as "every seaman, being a foreigner." He was at the time of the sinking of the Columbian a citizen and subject of Great Britain. He owed allegiance to the United States while serving on an American ship. But such allegiance was limited to the duration of his service and was of a temporary nature. At the time of suffering the damages complained of the claimant was a British subject. The personal injuries of which he complains were injuries suffered by a British subject. The personal effects which he lost were impressed with his British nationality. The fact that the United States had through its statutes extended to claimant, an alien seaman, the same measure of protection for the duration of his service on an American ship as that extended to an American citizen does not change the nationality status of claimant, and Germany's obligations arising under the Treaty of Berlin are limited, so far as non-government-owned claims are concerned, to claims which were in point of origin suffered by American nationals.

An expression of an intention to become a citizen does not make such declarant a citizen. The status of a declarant has sometimes been described as "inchoate citizenship." The term between the filing of the declaration and the admission to citizenship has sometimes been referred to as "a probationary period." But it has never been held that the mere declaration of an *intention* to become an American citizen constituted a tie *permanently* binding the declarant to the United States, to which he should thenceforth owe permanent allegiance. The allegiance which a declarant owes to the United States is at most of a temporary nature. His declaration is a step toward the transfer of his allegiance, which is completed only when he has matured his "intention" to become a citizen by complying with all the requirements of the statutes of the United States. Then, but not until then, does his allegiance become permanent. . . .

But whatever may have been the reason of the rule adopted by the Congress of the United States and carried into the Treaty of Berlin, restricting Germany's obligations to pay damages to such as were suffered by persons owing permanent allegiance to the United States, the rule itself is clearly expressed and has been definitely followed by this Commission in its Administrative Decision No. I, which, as before pointed out, is the law of this case. The limitation is written into the Treaty, and must be so applied as to give its ordinary and obvious meaning full force and effect.

The American Commissioner expresses the opinion that claims of the character here dealt with "are recognized under international law as properly presentable internationally." This may be conceded. He expresses the further opinion that "under the laws of the United States this claim, on the facts stated, must be treated as a claim of American nationality at the time of its origin." This Commission is concerned only with claims falling within the terms of the Treaty of Berlin, and that Treaty does not deal with claims of *alien seamen* on American vessels which the United States had undertaken to protect, but only with claims of *American nationals* who were such when they suffered the loss, damage, or injury complained of. The sole question is what rights the United States may assert on behalf of its nationals under the Treaty, not what claims it might have presented internationally under the rules of international law.

This Commission can not in construing the Treaty give weight to any considerations of national policy or to the duty of protection owing by the United States to the claimant and others similarly situated as expressed by the acts of the Congress or otherwise. This Commission can consider not what the Congress and the parties to the Treaty might or could have said or done but only what they did say and do. Germany's obligations are fixed by contract as expressed in the Treaty of Berlin. Her obligations to make compensation are by that contract limited to such damages as were suffered by those owing permanent allegiance to the United States. The sole question presented, therefore, is the narrow one, Did claimant owe permanent allegiance to the United States within the meaning of the Treaty of Berlin both at the time he suffered the damages complained of and at the time the Treaty became effective? Manifestly he did not. Therefore Germany is not obligated to compensate for the damages suffered by him.

Applying the rules in Administrative Decision No. V and in the other decisions of this Commission to the facts as disclosed by the record herein, the Commission decrees that under the Treaty of Berlin of August 25, 1921, and in accordance with its terms the Government of Germany is not obligated to pay to the Government of the United States any amount on behalf of the claimant herein.

C. Nationality of married women and of children.

International law is in a state of transition with respect to the nationality of married women. In the case of the United States the earlier judicial recognition of the independent status of a married woman gave way to legislation making the nationality of the married woman follow that of her husband [Mackenzie v. Hare] ; while recent legislation, the Cable Act of 1922, has put the married woman in a position independent of her husband. In the United States the acquisition of citizenship by minor children in consequence of the naturalization of their parents commences when such children begin to reside permanently in the country; whereas the acquisition of citizenship *jure sanguinis* is dependent upon the residence of the parents in the country at some time before the birth of the child. [Weedin v. Chin Bow.]

MACKENZIE v. HARE ET AL., BOARD OF ELECTION OF SAN FRANCISCO.

United States, Supreme Court, 1915.

239 U. S. 299.   [60 L. ed. 297; 36 S. Ct. 106.]

Mr. Justice McKenna delivered the opinion of the court.

Mandamus prosecuted by plaintiff in error as petitioner against defendants in error, respondents, as and composing the board of election commissioners of the city and county of San Francisco, to compel her registration as a qualified voter of the city and county, in the appropriate precinct therein.

An alternative writ was issued, but a permanent writ was denied upon demurrer to the petition.

The facts are not in dispute and are stated by Mr. Justice Shaw, who delivered the opinion of the court, as follows:

"The plaintiff was born and ever since has resided in the state of California. On August 14, 1909, being then a resident and citizen of this state and of the United States, she was lawfully married to Gordon Mackenzie, a native and subject of the kingdom of Great Britain. He had resided in California prior to that time, still resides here, and it is his intention to make this state his permanent residence. He has not become naturalized as a citizen of the United States and it does not appear that he intends to do so. Ever since their marriage the plaintiff and her husband have lived together as husband and wife. On January 22, 1913, she applied to the defendants to be registered as a voter. She was then over the age of twenty-one years and had resided in San Francisco for more than ninety days. Registration was refused to her on the ground that, by reason of her marriage to Gordon Mackenzie, a subject of Great Britain, she thereupon took the nationality of her husband and ceased to be a citizen of the United States."

Plaintiff in error claims a right as a voter of the state under its Constitution and the Constitution of the United States.

The Constitution of the state gives the privilege of suffrage to "every native citizen of the United States," and it is contended that under the Constitution of the United States every person born in the United States is a citizen thereof. The latter must be conceded, and if plaintiff has not lost her citizenship by her marriage, she has the qualification of a voter prescribed by the Constitution of the state of California. The question then is, Did she cease to be a citizen by her marriage?

On March 2, 1907, that is, prior to the marriage of plaintiff in error, Congress enacted a statute the third section of which provides: "That any American woman who marries a foreigner shall take the nationality of her husband. At the termination of the marital relation she may resume her American citizenship, if abroad, by registering as an

American citizen within one year with a consul of the United States, or by returning to reside in the United States, or, if residing in the United States at the termination of the marital relation, by continuing to reside therein.''

Plaintiff contends that ''such legislation, if intended to apply to her, is beyond the authority of Congress.'' . . .

An earnest argument is presented to demonstrate its invalidity. Its basis is that the citizenship of plaintiff was an incident to her birth in the United States, and, under the Constitution and laws of the United States, it became a right, privilege, and immunity which could not be taken away from her except as a punishment for crime or by her voluntary expatriation.

The argument to support the contention and the argument to oppose it take a wide range through the principles of the common law and international law and their development and change. Both plaintiff and defendants agree that under the common law originally allegiance was immutable. They do not agree as to when the rigidity of the principle was relaxed. Plaintiff in error contests the proposition which she attributes to defendants in error, ''that the doctrine of perpetual allegiance maintained by England was accepted by the United States,'' but contends ''that the prevalent doctrine of this country always has been that a citizen had a right to expatriate himself,'' and cites cases to show that expatriation is a natural and inherent right.

Whether this was originally the law of this country or became such by inevitable evolution it is not important to inquire. The first view has certainly high authority for its support. In Shanks v. Dupont, 3 Pet. 242, 246, Mr. Justice Story, delivering the judgment of the court, said: ''The general doctrine is, that no persons can by any act of their own, without the consent of the government, put off their allegiance, and become aliens.'' And Kent, in his Commentaries, after a historical review of the principle and discussion in the Federal courts, declares that ''the better opinion would seem to be, that a citizen cannot renounce his allegiance to the United States without the permission of government to be declared by law; and that, as there is no existing legislative regulation on the case, the rule of the English common law remains unaltered.'' 2 Kent, 14th Ed. 49. The deduction would seem to have been repelled by the naturalization laws, and it was certainly opposed to executive opinion; and, we may say, popular sentiment, so determined that it sought its vindication by war. Further discussion would lead us far afield, and, besides, would only have historical interest. The condition which Kent suggested has occurred; there is a legislative declaration. In 1868 Congress explicitly declared the right of expatriation to have been and to be the law. And the declaration was in effect said to be the dictate of necessity. The act recites that emigrants have been received and invested with citizenship in recognition of the principle of the right of expatriation and that there should be a prompt and final disavowal of the claim "that such American citizens, with their descendants, are subjects of foreign states." Rev. Stat. § 1999.

But plaintiff says, "Expatriation is evidenced only by emigration, coupled with other acts indicating an intention to transfer one's allegiance." And all the acts must be voluntary, "the result of a fixed determination to change the domicil and permanently reside elsewhere, as well as to throw off the former allegiance, and become a citizen or subject of a foreign power."

The right and the condition of its exercise being thus defined, it is said that the authority of Congress is limited to giving its consent. . . . It will thus be seen that plaintiff's contention is in exact antagonism to the statute. Only voluntary expatriation, as she defines it, can devest a woman of her citizenship, she declares; the statute provides that, by marriage with a foreigner, she takes his nationality.

It would make this opinion very voluminous to consider in detail the argument and the cases urged in support of or in attack upon the opposing conditions. Their foundation principles, we may assume, are known. The identity of husband and wife is an ancient principle of our jurisprudence. It was neither accidental nor arbitrary, and worked in many instances for her protection. There has been, it is true, much relaxation of it, but in its retention as in its origin it is determined by their intimate relation and unity of interests, and this relation and unity may make it of public concern in many instances to merge their identity, and give dominance to the husband. It has purpose, if not necessity, in purely domestic policy; it has greater purpose, and, it may be, necessity, in international policy. And this was the dictate of the act in controversy. Having this purpose, has it not the sanction of power?

Plaintiff contends, as we have seen, that it has not, and bases her contention upon the absence of an express gift of power. But there may be powers implied, necessary or incidental to the expressed powers. As a government, the United States is invested with all the attributes of sovereignty. As it has the character of nationality it has the powers of nationality, especially those which concern its relations and intercourse with other countries. We should hesitate long before limiting or embarrassing such powers. But monition is not necessary in the present case. There need be no dissent from the cases cited by plaintiff; there need be no assertion of very extensive power over the right of citizenship or of the imperative imposition of conditions upon it. It may be conceded that a change of citizenship cannot be arbitrarily imposed, that is, imposed without the concurrence of the citizen. The law in controversy does not have that feature. It deals with a condition voluntarily entered into, with notice of the consequences. We concur with counsel that citizenship is of tangible worth, and we sympathize with plaintiff in her desire to retain it and in her earnest assertion of it. But there is involved more than personal considerations. As we have seen, the legislation was urged by conditions of national moment. And this is an answer to the apprehension of counsel that our construction of the legislation will make every act, though lawful, as marriage, of course, is, a renunciation of citizenship. The marriage of an American woman with a foreigner has consequences of like kind, may involve national complications of like kind, as her physical expatriation may involve. Therefore, as long as the relation lasts, it is made tantamount to expatriation. This is no arbitrary exercise of government. It is one which, regarding the international aspects, judicial opinion has taken for granted would not only be valid, but demanded. It is the conception of the legislation under review that such an act may bring the government into embarrassments, and, it may be, into controversies. It is as voluntary and distinctive as expatriation and its consequence must be considered as elected.

Judgment affirmed.[1]

WEEDIN, COMMISSIONER OF IMMIGRATION, v. CHIN BOW.

United States, Supreme Court, 1927.

274 U. S. 657. [71 L. ed. 1284; 47 S. Ct. 772.]

MR. CHIEF JUSTICE TAFT delivered the opinion of the Court.

This is a writ of certiorari to review a judgment of the United States Circuit Court of Appeals for the Ninth Circuit, affirming an order of the District Court for the Western District of Washington allowing a writ of habeas corpus for Chin Bow, a Chinese boy ten years of age, and granting him a discharge. . . .

Chin Bow applied for admission to the United States at Seattle. The board of special inquiry of the Immigration Bureau at that place denied him admission on the ground that, though his father is a citizen, he is not a citizen, because at the time of his birth in China his father had never resided in the United States. Chin Bow was born March 29, 1914, in China. His father, Chin Dun was also born in China on March 8, 1894, and had never been in this country until July 18, 1922. Chin Dun was the son of Chin Tong, the respondent's grandfather. Chin Tong is forty-nine years old and was born in the United States.

The Secretary of Labor affirmed the decision of the board of inquiry, and the deportation of the respondent was ordered. He secured a writ of *habeas corpus* from the District Court. Upon a hearing, an order discharging him was entered without an opinion. On appeal by the United States, the Circuit Court of Appeals affirmed the judgment of

---

[1] Compare the provisions of the Cable Act of 1922. Fenwick, *op. cit.,* p. 185.

the District Court, 7 F. (2d) 369, holding him to be a citizen under the provisions of § 1993 of the Revised Statutes, which is as follows:

"All children heretofore born or hereafter born out of the limits and jurisdiction of the United States, whose fathers were or may be at the time of their birth citizens thereof, are declared to be citizens of the United States; but the rights of citizenship shall not descend to children whose fathers never resided in the United States."

The rights of Chin Bow are determined by the construction of this section. The Secretary of Labor, April 27, 1916, asked the opinion of Attorney General Gregory whether a rule of the Chinese regulations of his Department, which denied citizenship to foreign-born children of American Chinese, was a valid one. He advised that it was not, because § 1993 applied to all children and therefore included Chinese children as well. The second question was whether foreign-born children of American-born Chinese fathers were entitled to enter the United States as citizens thereof, when they had continued to reside for some time in China after reaching their majorities, without any affirmative action on their part indicating an intention to remain citizens of the United States, and the Attorney General advised that they were, in spite of these circumstances, entitled to enter the United States as citizens thereof. 30 Op. A. G. 529.

The United States contends that the proviso of section 1993, "but the rights of citizenship shall not descend to children whose fathers never resided in the United States," must be construed to mean that only the children whose fathers have resided in the United States before their birth become citizens under the section. It is claimed for the respondent that the residence of the father at any time in the United States before his death entitles his son whenever born to citizenship. These conflicting claims make the issue to be decided. . . .

It is very clear that the proviso in § 1993 has the same meaning as that which Congress intended to give it in the Act of 1790, except that it was then retrospective as it was in the Act of 1802, while in the Act of 1855 it was intended to be made prospective as well as retrospective. What was the source of the peculiar words of the proviso there seems to be no way of finding out, as the report of the discussion of the subject is not contained in any publication brought to our attention. It is evident, however, from the discussion in the First Congress, already referred to, that there was a strong feeling in favor of the encouragement of naturalization. There were some congressmen, although they did not prevail, who were in favor of naturalization by the mere application and taking of the oath. The time required for residence to obtain naturalization was finally limited to two years. In the Act of 1795 this was increased to five years, with three years for declaration of intention. Congress must have thought that the questions of naturalization and of the conferring of citizenship on sons of American citizens born abroad were related. . . .

Only two constructions seem to us possible, and we must adopt one or the other. The one is that the descent of citizenship shall be regarded as taking place at the birth of the person to whom it is to be transmitted, and that the words, "have never been resident in the United States," refer in point of time to the birth of the person to whom the citizenship is to descend. This is the adoption of the rule of *jus sanguinis* in respect to citizenship, and that emphasizes the fact and time of birth as the basis of it. We think the words, "the right of citizenship shall not descend to persons whose fathers have never been resident in the United States," are equivalent to saying that fathers may not have the power of transmitting by descent the right of citizenship until they shall become residents in the United States. The other view is that the words, "have never been resident in the United States," have reference to the whole life of the father until his death, and therefore that grandchildren of native-born citizens, even after they, having been born abroad, have lived abroad to middle age and without residing at all in the United States, will become citizens, if their fathers born abroad and living until old age abroad shall adopt a residence in the United States just before death. We are thus to have two generations of citizens who have been born abroad, lived abroad, the first coming to old age, and the second to maturity, and bringing up of a family without any relation to the United States at all until the father shall in his last days adopt a new residence. We do not think that such a construction accords with the probable attitude of Congress at the time of the adoption of this proviso into the statute. Its construction extends citizenship to a generation whose birth, minority, and majority, whose education, and whose family life have all been out of the United States and naturally within the civilization and environment of an alien country. The beneficiaries would have evaded the duties and responsibilities of American citizenship. They might be persons likely to become public charges or afflicted with disease; yet they would be entitled to enter as citizens of the United States. Van Dyne, Citizenship of the United States, p. 34.

As between the two interpretations, we feel confident that the first one was more in accord with the views of the First Congress. . . .

In answer to the reasons which influence us to the conclusion already indicated, counsel for the respondent say, first, that the hypothesis that the foreign-born fathers and sons may all live abroad from birth to middle age and bring up families without any association with the United States, and that the sons may then become citizens by the ultimate residence of their fathers in the United States, is not a possible one, because such children must have signified their intention to become citizens when they reached eighteen years of age or at majority at any rate. But these provisions with respect to election of citizenship by those coming to majority were not in the statute when the proviso was enacted, and we must construe it as of 1790 with reference to the views that Congress may be thought to have had at that time.

Then it is urged that the State Department has held that section 1993 refers only to children and not to adults. This would be a narrow construction of the proviso as it was intended to operate in 1790 when the act was passed, and, although this was suggested as a possible view by Secretary of State Bayard, it would limit too much the meaning of the word "children" at a time when no provision had been made by law for election of citizenship by those coming of age. Nor does it seem to be in accord with Attorney General Gregory's opinion already referred to. 30 Op. A. G. 529.

It is said that it would be illogical and unnatural to provide that the father, having begotten children abroad before he lived in the United States at all, and then having gone to the United States and resided there and returned and had more children abroad, should have a family part aliens and part citizens. As this is entirely within the choice of the father, there would seem to be no reason why such a situation should be anomalous. As the father may exercise his option in accordance with the law, so citizenship will follow that option. . . .

It would seem then that the question before us is one that has really not been authoritatively decided except by two Circuit Courts of Appeals—that of the Ninth Circuit, which is here under review, and that of the Circuit Court of Appeals for the First Circuit (Johnson v. Sullivan, 8 F. (2d) 988), which adopted the view of the Ninth Circuit Court and followed it.

The opinion in the Ninth Circuit says (page 369):

"The statute refers to the descent of the rights of citizenship. The term 'descend' has a well-defined meaning in law. As defined by Webster, it means: 'To pass down, as from generation to generation, or from ancestor to heir.' If the term 'descend' is given that meaning in this connection, the status of the appellee would not become definitely fixed until his father became a resident of the United States or died without becoming such. In the former event he would become vested with all the rights of citizenship as soon as his father became a resident, while in the latter event his claim to citizenship would be forever lost."

The expression, "the rights of citizenship shall descend," cannot refer to the time of the death of the father, because that is hardly the time when they do descend. The phrase is borrowed from the law of property. The descent of property comes only after the death of the ancestor. The transmission of right of citizenship is not at the death of the ancestor but at the birth of the child, and it seems to us more natural to infer that the conditions of the descent contained in the limiting proviso, so far as the father is concerned, must be perfected and have been performed at that time.

This leads to a reversal of the judgment of the Circuit Court of Appeals and a remanding of the respondent.

Reversed.[1]

D. Nationality of business associations.

As a general rule incorporated companies are recognized as having the nationality of the state in which they have received their charter of incorporation, while unincorporated companies have the nationality of the state in which they are constituted or in which their directors are normally resident. Query, would the fact that the alien directors of an incorporated company have, by the outbreak of war, become enemy aliens prevent the company from bringing suit in the state in which it is incorporated on the ground that the payment of a debt to the company would constitute trading with the enemy, forbidden by law? [Daimler Co. v. Continental Tyre and Rubber Co.]

---

[1] SUPPLEMENTARY CASES. In Shanks v. Dupont, 3 Peters 242 (1830), involving the citizenship of an American woman who had married a British officer in 1781 and had moved to England in 1782, the Supreme Court held that she had not lost her citizenship by the fact of her marriage but that she had lost it by removal to Great Britain under the terms of the treaty of 1783. "Neither did the marriage with Shanks," said the court, "produce that effect [change of allegiance]; because marriage with an alien, whether a friend or an enemy, produces no dissolution of the native allegiance of the wife. It may change her civil rights, but it does not affect her political rights or privileges. The general doctrine is, that no persons can, by any act of their own, without the consent of the government, put off their allegiance and become aliens. If it were otherwise, then a *feme* alien would by her marriage become, *ipso facto,* a citizen, and would be dowable of the estate of her husband; which are clearly contrary to law."

Query, would a child born in the United States lose its citizenship by reason of acquiring Canadian citizenship in virtue of a Canadian statute naturalizing the child of a father who had removed with her to Canada and acquired Canadian citizenship during her minority? In the case of In re Reid, 6 F. Supp. 800 (1934), involving the petition of a native-born American woman, who had married a Canadian citizen in 1919, to be repatriated under the Cable Act of 1922 facilitating the naturalization of "a woman who has lost her United States citizenship by reason of her marriage to an alien," the court held that the terms of the treaty with Great Britain of 1870 by which the United States agreed to recognize the British citizenship of citizens of the United States who became naturalized within the British dominions could not deprive the petitioner of her Amercan citizenship of birth which could not be lost by involuntary expatriation. The petitioner was held, therefore, to have been an American citizen at the time of her marriage and entitled to the benefits of the Cable Act.

DAIMLER CO., LTD., APPELLANTS, v. CONTINENTAL TYRE &
RUBBER CO., LTD., RESPONDENTS.

Great Britain, House of Lords, 1916.

L. R. [1916] 2 A. C. 307.

Appeal from a decision of the Court of Appeal [[1915] 1 K. B. 893]
affirming an order of Scrutton, J., in chambers. . . .

On October 23, 1914, an action was commenced in the name of the
respondent company by specially indorsed writ for 5605 l. 16s. alleged
to be due from the appellants for principal, interest, and notarial
charges on three bills of exchange drawn by the respondents and accepted by the appellants in payment for goods supplied to them by the
respondents prior to the outbreak of the war with Germany. The writ
was issued by the solicitors of the respondent company upon the instructions of the secretary. On October 30, 1914, a summons was taken
out on behalf of the respondent company under Order XIV for leave
to sign judgment for the amount of the claim with interest and costs.
This summons was opposed by the appellants on the grounds that the
company and its officers were alien enemies and that consequently the
company was incapable of instituting these proceedings or of giving a
good and valid discharge for the amount claimed; and, further, that
the appellants, in paying that amount, would be acting in contravention of the Trading with the Enemy Act, 1914. The appellants therefore contended that the proceedings were wrongly instituted and that
unconditional leave to defend should be given to them.

The respondent company was incorporated under the Companies Acts
on March 29, 1905, with a capital of 10,000 l. subsequently increased
to 25,000 l., in fully paid £1 shares, and had its registered office in
London. It was formed for the purpose of selling in the United Kingdom motor car tyres made in Germany by a company incorporated in
that country under German law. At the date of the writ the German
company held 23,398 shares in the respondent company, and the remaining shares, except one, were held by subjects of the German Empire. The one share was registered in the name of Mr. Wolter, the
secretary of the company, who was born in Germany, but resided in
this country and in 1910 became a naturalized subject of the Crown.
All the directors were subjects of the German Empire, and three of
the four directors were resident in Germany when war was declared;
the fourth, who had previously resided in England, left this country
for Germany on the outbreak of the war.

The master made an order that the respondent company be at liberty
to sign final judgment in the action. This order was affirmed by Scrutton, J., in chambers, and the order of the learned judge was affirmed
by the Court of Appeal. . . .

LORD PARKER OF WADDINGTON. .· . . My Lords, in my opinion this appeal ought to be allowed.

When the action was instituted all the directors of the plaintiff company were Germans resident in Germany. In other words, they were the King's enemies, and as such incapable of exercising any of the powers vested in them as directors of a company incorporated in the United Kingdom. They were incapable, therefore, of authorizing the institution of this action. The contention that the secretary of the company could authorize such institution is untenable. The resolution by which he was appointed secretary would confer on him such powers only as were incident to the performance of his secretarial duties. It is true that the directors of the company might by a proper resolution in that behalf have conferred on him a power to authorize the institution of proceedings in the company's name, but they did not do so. Their conduct in holding him out as a person having this power, if they in fact so hold him out, may in particular cases have operated to estop the company from denying the authority of a solicitor whom he retained, but it could not confer the power in question.

It follows that this action was instituted without authority from the company, and in my opinion the Court having notice of the fact should have refused relief. . . .

My Lords, under these circumstances, it is, strictly speaking, unnecessary to consider whether a company incorporated in the United Kingdom can under any and what circumstances be an enemy or assume an enemy character. The question has, however, been so elaborately argued both here and in the Court of Appeal, and is of such general importance, that it would not be right to ignore it.

The principle upon which the judgment under appeal proceeds is that trading with an incorporated company cannot be trading with an enemy where the company is registered in England under the Companies Acts and carries on its business here. Such a company it calls an "English company," and obviously likens to a natural-born Englishman, and accordingly holds that payment to it of a debt which is due to it, and of money which is its own, cannot be trading with the enemy, be its corporators who they may. The view is that an English company's enemy officers vacate their office on becoming enemies and so affect it no longer, and that its enemy shareholders, being neither its agents nor its principals, never in law affect it at all.

My Lords, much of the reasoning by which this principle is supported is quite indisputable. No one can question that a corporation is a legal person distinct from its corporators; that the relation of a shareholder to a company, which is limited by shares, is not in itself the relation of principal and agent or the reverse; that the assets of the company belong to it and the acts of its servants and agents are its acts, while its shareholders, as such, have no property in the assets and no personal responsibility for those acts. The law on the subject is clearly laid down in a passage in Lord Halsbury's judgment in Salomon v. Salomon & Co. [[1897] A. C. 22, 30]: "I am simply here," he says, "dealing with the provisions of the statute, and it seems to me to be essential to the artificial creation that the law should recognise only that artificial existence—quite apart from the motives or conduct of individual corporators. . . . Short of such proof"—i. e., proof in appropriate proceedings that the company had no real legal existence—"it seems to me impossible to dispute that once the company is legally incorporated it must be treated like any other independent person with its rights and liabilities appropriate to itself, and that the motives of those who took part in the formation of the company are absolutely irrelevant in discussing what those rights and liabilities are." I do not think, however, that it is a necessary corollary of this reasoning to say that the character of its corporators must be irrelevant to the character of the company; and this is crucial, for the rule against trading with the enemy depends upon enemy character.

A natural person, though an English-born subject of His Majesty, may bear an enemy character and be under liability and disability as such by adhering to His Majesty's enemies. If he gives them active aid, he is a traitor; but he may fall far short of that and still be invested with enemy character. If he has what is known in prize law as a commercial domicil among the King's enemies, his merchandise is good prize at sea, just as if it belonged to a subject of the enemy Power. Not only actively, but passively, he may bring himself under the same disability. Voluntary residence among the enemy, however passive or pacific he may be, identifies an English subject with His Majesty's foes. I do not think it necessary to cite authority for these well-known propositions, nor do I doubt that, if they had seemed material to the Court of Appeal, they would have been accepted.

How are such rules to be applied to an artificial person, incorporated by forms of law? As far as active adherence to the enemy goes, there can be no difference, except such as arises from the fact that a company's acts are those of its servants and agents acting within the scope of their authority. An illustration of the application of such rules to a company (as it happens a company of neutral incorporation, which is an *a fortiori* case) is to be found in Netherlands South African Ry. Co. v. Fisher [18 Times L. R. 116].

In the case of an artificial person what is the analogue to voluntary residence among the King's enemies? Its impersonality can hardly put it in a better position than a natural person and lead to its being unaffected by anything equivalent to residence. It is only by a figure of speech that a company can be said to have a nationality or residence at all. If the place of its incorporation under municipal law fixes its residence, then its residence cannot be changed, which is almost a contradiction in terms, and in the case of a company residence must correspond to the birthplace and country of natural allegiance in the case of a living person, and not to residence or commercial domicil. Nevertheless, enemy character depends on these last. It would seem, therefore, logically to follow that, in transferring the application of the rule against trading with the enemy from natural to artificial persons, something more than the mere place or country of registration or incorporation must be looked at. . . .

My Lords, having regard to the foregoing considerations, I think the law on the subject may be summarized in the following propositions:—

(1) A company incorporated in the United Kingdom is a legal entity, a creation of law with the status and capacity which the law confers. It is not a natural person with mind or conscience. To use the language of Buckley, L. J., "it can be neither loyal nor disloyal. It can be neither friend nor enemy."

(2) Such a company can only act through agents properly authorized, and so long as it is carrying on business in this country through agents so authorized and residing in this or a friendly country it is *prima facie* to be regarded as a friend, and all His Majesty's lieges may deal with it as such.

(3) Such a company may, however, assume an enemy character. This will be the case if its agents or the persons in *de facto* control of its affairs, whether authorized or not, are resident in an enemy country, or, wherever resident, are adhering to the enemy or taking instructions from or acting under the control of enemies. A person knowingly dealing with the company in such a case is trading with the enemy.

(4) The character of individual shareholders cannot of itself affect the character of the company. This is admittedly so in times of peace, during which every shareholder is at liberty to exercise and enjoy such rights as are by law incident to his status as shareholder. It would be anomalous if it were not so also in a time of war, during which all such rights and privileges are in abeyance. The enemy character of individual shareholders and their conduct may, however, be very material on the question whether the company's agents, or the persons in *de facto* control of its affairs, are in fact adhering to, taking instructions from, or acting under the control of enemies. This materiality will vary with the number of shareholders who are enemies and the value of their holdings. The fact, if it be the fact, that after eliminating the enemy shareholders the number of shareholders remaining is insufficient for the purpose of holding meetings of the company or appointing directors or other officers may well raise a presumption in this respect. For example, in the present case, even if the secretary had been fully authorized to manage the affairs of the company and to institute legal proceedings on its behalf, the fact that he held one share only out of 25,000 shares, and was the only shareholder who was not an enemy, might well throw on the company the onus of proving that he

was not acting under the control of, taking his instructions from, or adhering to the King's enemies in such manner as to impose an enemy character on the company itself. It is an *a fortiori* case when the secretary is without authority and necessarily depends for the validity of all he does on the subsequent ratification of enemy shareholders. The circumstances of the present case were, therefore, such as to require close investigation and preclude the propriety of giving leave to sign judgment under Order XIV, r. 1.

(5) In a similar way a company registered in the United Kingdom, but carrying on business in a neutral country through agents properly authorized and resident here or in the neutral country, is *prima facie* to be regarded as a friend, but may, through its agents or persons in *de facto* control of its affairs, assume an enemy character.

(6) A company registered in the United Kingdom but carrying on business in an enemy country is to be regarded as an enemy.

My Lords, the foregoing propositions are not only consistent with the authorities cited in argument, and in particular with what was said in this House in Janson v. Driefontein Consolidated Mines [[1902] A. C. 484], but they have, I think, the advantage of affording convenient and intelligible guidance to the public on questions of trading with the enemy. It would be a misfortune if the law were such that during war every one proposing to deal with a British company had to examine the character of its shareholders and decide whether the number of the enemy shareholders coupled with the value of their holdings were such as to impose an enemy character on the company itself. It would be still more unfortunate if this question were a question for the jury in each particular case. No one could maintain that a company had assumed an enemy character merely because it had a few enemy shareholders. It might possibly be contended that it assumed an enemy character when its enemy shareholders amounted to (say) one-half, three-fifths, or five-eighths of the whole, but how if the one-half, three-fifths, or five-eighths held only one-sixth, one-fifth, or one-fourth of the shares? The Legislature might, but no Court could possibly, lay down a hard and fast rule, and, if no such rule were laid down, how could any one proposing to deal with the company ascertain whether he was or was not proposing to deal with the enemy? . . .

[Opinions of other justices omitted.]

Order of the Court of Appeal reversed and action dismissed, and all orders made therein discharged.

E. Jurisdiction over nationals in respect to acts outside national territory.

While the exercise by a state of effective jurisdiction over its citizens is contingent upon the presence of the citizen within territorial boundaries, international law recognizes that a state may assert legal claims over the citizen in respect to acts committed abroad and in respect to duties owing to the state irrespective of the residence of the citizen abroad. Query, may such claims be enforced against any property owned by the absentee citizen within the national domain? [Blackmer v. United States.]

HARRY M. BLACKMER v. UNITED STATES OF AMERICA.

United States, Supreme Court, 1932.

284 U. S. 421.   [76 L. ed. 375; 52 S. Ct. 252.]

MR. CHIEF JUSTICE HUGHES delivered the opinion of the Court.

The petitioner, Harry M. Blackmer, a citizen of the United States resident in Paris, France, was adjudged guilty of contempt of the Supreme Court of the District of Columbia for failure to respond to subpoenas served upon him in France and requiring him to appear as a witness on behalf of the United States at a criminal trial in that court. Two subpoenas were issued, for appearances at different times, and there was a separate proceeding with respect to each. The two cases were heard together, and a fine of $30,000 with costs was imposed in each case, to be satisfied out of the property of the petitioner which had been seized by order of the court. The decrees were affirmed by the Court of Appeals of the District, 49 F. (2d) 523, and this Court granted writs of certiorari.

The subpoenas were issued and served, and the proceedings to punish for contempt were taken, under the provisions of the Act of July 3, 1926, C. 762, 44 Stat. 835, U. S. C., Tit. 28, §§ 711–718. The statute provides that whenever the attendance at the trial of a criminal action of a witness abroad, who is "a citizen of the United States or domiciled therein," is desired by the Attorney General, or any assistant or district attorney acting under him, the judge of the court in which the action is pending may order a subpoena to issue, to be addressed to a consul of the United States and to be served by him personally upon the witness with a tender of traveling expenses. §§ 2, 3. Upon proof of such service and of the failure of the witness to appear, the court may make an order requiring the witness to show cause why he should not be punished for contempt, and upon the issue of such an order the court may direct that property belonging to the witness and within the United States may be seized and held to satisfy any judgment which may be rendered against him in the proceeding. §§ 4, 5. Provision is made for personal service of the order upon the witness and also for its publication in a newspaper of general circulation in the district where the court is sitting. § 6. If, upon the hearing, the charge is sustained, the court may adjudge the witness guilty of contempt and impose upon him a fine not exceeding $100,000, to be satisfied by a sale of the property seized. § 7. This statute and the proceedings against the petitioner are assailed as being repugnant to the Constitution of the United States.

First. The principal objections to the statute are that it violates the due process clause of the Fifth Amendment. These contentions are (1) that the "Congress has no power to authorize United States consuls to serve process except as permitted by treaty;" (2) that the Act does not provide "a valid method of acquiring judicial jurisdiction to render personal judgment against defendant and judgment against his property;" (3) that the Act "does not require actual or any other notice to defendant of the offense or of the Government's claim against his property;" (4) that the provisions "for hearing and judgment in the entire absence of the accused and without his consent" are invalid; and (5) that the Act is "arbitrary, capricious and unreasonable."

While it appears that the petitioner removed his residence to France in the year 1924, it is undisputed that he was, and continued to be, a citizen of the United States. He continued to owe allegiance to the United States. By virtue of the obligations of citizenship, the United States retained its authority over him, and he was bound by its laws made applicable to him in a foreign country. Thus, although resident abroad, the petitioner remained subject to the taxing power of the United States. Cook v. Tait, 265 U. S. 47, 54, 56. For disobedience to its laws through conduct abroad he was subject to punishment in the courts of the United States. United States v. Bowman, 260 U. S. 94, 102. With respect to such an exercise of authority, there is no question of international law, but solely of the purport of the municipal law which establishes the duties of the citizen in relation to his own government. While the legislation of the Congress, unless the contrary intent appears, is construed to apply only within the territorial jurisdiction of the United States, the question of its application, so far as citizens of the United States in foreign countries are concerned, is one of construction, not of legislative power. American Banana Co. v. United Fruit Co., 213 U. S. 347, 357; United States v. Bowman, 260 U. S. 94, *supra;* Robertson v. Railroad Labor Board, 268 U. S. 619, 622. Nor can it be doubted that the United States possesses the power inherent in sovereignty to require the return to this country of a citizen, resident elsewhere, whenever the public interest requires it, and to penalize him in case of refusal. Compare Bartue & Duchess of Suffolk's Case, 2 Dyer, 176b, 73 Eng. Rep. 388; Knowles v. Luce, Moore, 109, 72 Eng. Rep. 473. What in England was the prerogative of the sovereign in this respect pertains under our constitutional system to the national authority which may be exercised by the Congress by virtue of the legislative power to prescribe the duties of the citizens of the United States. It is also beyond controversy that one of the duties which the citizen owes to his government is to support the administration of justice by attending its courts and giving his testimony whenever he is properly summoned. Blair v. United States, 250 U. S. 273, 281. And the Congress may provide for the performance of this duty and prescribe penalties for disobedience.

In this present instance, the question concerns only the method of enforcing the obligation. The jurisdiction of the United States over its absent citizen, so far as the binding effect of its legislation is concerned, is a jurisdiction *in personam*, as he is personally bound to take notice of the laws that are applicable to him and to obey them. United States v. Bowman, 260 U. S. 94, *supra*. But for the exercise of judicial jurisdiction *in personam*, there must be due process, which requires appropriate notice of the judicial action and an opportunity to be heard. For this notice and opportunity the statute provides. The authority to require the absent citizen to return and testify necessarily implies the authority to give him notice of the requirement. As his attendance is needed in court, it is appropriate that the Congress should authorize the court to direct the notice to be given and that it should be in the customary form of a subpoena. Obviously, the requirement would be nugatory, if provision could not be made for its communication to the witness in the foreign country. The efficacy of an attempt to provide constructive service in this country would rest upon the presumption that the notice would be given in a manner calculated to reach the witness abroad. McDonald v. Mabee, 243 U. S. 90, 92. The question of the validity of the provision for actual service of the subpoena in a foreign country is one that arises solely between the Government of the United States and the citizen. The mere giving of such a notice to the citizen in the foreign country of the requirement of his government that he shall return is in no sense an invasion of any right of the foreign government and the citizen has no standing to invoke any such supposed right. While consular privileges in foreign countries are the appropriate subjects of treaties, it does not follow that every act of a consul, as, *e. g.*, in communicating with citizens of his own country, must be predicated upon a specific provision of a treaty. The intercourse of friendly nations, permitting travel and residence of the citizens of each in the territory of the other, presupposes and facilitates such communications. In selecting the consul for the service of the subpoena, the Congress merely prescribed a method deemed to assure the desired result but in no sense essential. The consul was not directed to perform any function involving consular privileges or depending upon any treaty relating to them, but simply to act as any designated person might act for the Government in conveying to the citizen the actual notice of the requirement of his attendance. The point raised by the petitioner with respect to the provision for the service of the subpoena abroad is without merit.

As the Congress could define the obligation, it could prescribe a penalty to enforce it. And as the default lay in disobedience to an authorized direction of the court, it constituted a contempt of court and the Congress could provide for procedure appropriate in contempt cases. The provision of the statute for punishment for contempt is applicable only "upon proof being made of the service and default." § 4. That proof affords a proper basis for the proceeding, and provision is made for personal service upon the witness of the order to show cause why he should not be adjudged guilty. For the same reasons as those which sustain the service of the subpoena abroad, it was competent to provide for the service of the order in like manner. It is only after a hearing pursuant to the order to show cause, and upon proof sustaining the charge, that the court can impose the penalty. The petitioner urges that the statute does not require notice of the offense, but the order to show cause is to be issued after the witness has failed to obey the subpoena demanding his attendance and the order is to be made by the court before which he was required to appear. This is sufficient to apprise the witness of the nature of the proceeding and he has full opportunity to be heard. The further contention is made that, as the offense is a criminal one, it is a violation of due process to hold the hearing, and to proceed to judgment, in the absence of the defendant. The argument misconstrues the nature of the proceeding. "While contempt may be an offense against the law and subject to appropriate punishment, certain it is that since the foundation of our government proceedings to punish such offenses have been regarded as *sui generis* and not 'criminal prosecutions' within the Sixth Amendment or common understanding." Myers v. United States, 264 U. S. 95, 104, 105. See also Bessette v. W. B. Conkey Co., 194 U. S. 324, 336, 337; Michaelson v. United States, 266 U. S. 42, 65, 66; *Ex parte* Grossman, 267 U. S. 87, 117, 118. The requirement of due process in such a case is satisfied by suitable notice and adequate opportunity to appear and to be heard. Cf. Cooke v. United States, 267 U. S. 517, 537.

The authorization of the seizure of the property belonging to the defaulting witness and within the United States, upon the issue of the order to show cause why he should not be punished for contempt (§ 5), affords a provisional remedy, the propriety of which rests upon the validity of the contempt proceeding. As the witness is liable to punishment by fine if, upon the hearing, he is found guilty of contempt, no reason appears why his property may not be seized to provide security for the payment of the penalty. The proceeding conforms to familiar practice where absence or other circumstance makes a provisional remedy appropriate. See Cooper v. Reynolds, 10 Wall. 308, 318. The order that is to be served upon the witness contains the direction for the seizure. The property is to be held pending the hearing and is to be applied to the satisfaction of the fine if imposed and unless it is paid. Given the obligation of the witness to respond to the subpoena, the showing of his default after service, and the validity of the provision for a fine in case default is not excused, there is no basis for objection to the seizure upon constitutional grounds. The argument that the statute creates an unreasonable classification is untenable. The disobedience of the defaulting witness to a lawful requirement of the court, and not the fact that he owns property, is the ground of his liability. He is not the subject of unconstitutional discrimination simply because he has property which may be appropriated to the satisfaction of a lawful claim. . . .

Decrees affirmed.[1]

---

[1] Supplementary Cases. Query, does the absence of a national from his country preclude a suit from being brought against him in personam? In Douglas v. Forrest, 4 Bingham, 686 (1828), involving an action against the executor of the deceased who after contracting a debt in Scotland left the country and never returned, the plaintiffs resting their claim upon decrees of a Scottish court rendered in the absence of the defendant and without his having notice of the proceedings, the Court of Common Pleas of Great Britain held that the action could be maintained on the Scottish judgments when they were "perfectly consistent with the principles of justice." "A natural-born subject of any country," said the court, "quitting that country, but leaving property under the protection of its law, even during his absence, owes obedience to those laws, particularly when those laws enforce a moral obligation." Compare Schibsby v. Westenholz, L. R. 6 Q. B. 155 (1870), and Grubel v. Nassauer, below, p. 429, n. 1.

In American Banana Co. v. United Fruit Co., 213 U. S. 347 (1909), involving a suit on the part of the plaintiff to obtain damages under the Sherman Anti-Trust Act by reason of acts of the defendant committed in Costa Rica and in part with the coöperation of the Costa Rican government, the Supreme Court held that acts committed outside the jurisdiction of the United States were not within the scope of the statute. While there were exceptions, said the court, "the general and almost universal rule is that the character of an act as lawful or unlawful must be determined wholly by the law of the country where the act is done. . . . A conspiracy in this country to do acts in another jurisdiction does not draw to itself those acts and make them unlawful, if they are permitted by the local law." Compare United States v. Sisal Sales Corporation, 274 U. S. 268 (1927) where the conspiracy, although relating to a monopoly over a product produced in a foreign country, was made effective by acts done within the United States and was therefore within the jurisdiction of the court.

In Cook v. Tait, 265 U. S. 47 (1924), involving an income tax levied by the United States upon the property of Cook, a native citizen of the United States, who at the time the income was received was permanently resident and domiciled in the city of Mexico, the income being from real and personal property located in Mexico, the Supreme Court held that the basis of the power to tax was not dependent upon the situs of the property in all cases nor upon the domicil of the citizen, but upon the relation of the person as citizen to the United States. The tax was therefore held to be legal.

CHAPTER VII

JURISDICTIÓN OVER PERSONS: ALIENS [1]

A. The admission and expulsion of aliens.

International law recognizes the general principle that a state may forbid the entrance of aliens into its territory or admit them subject to such restrictions as, in its sole judgment, the circumstances may call for. No serious difficulties have arisen where the restrictions on the immigration of aliens have been applied to all nations equally. Discrimination against the nationals of particular countries has, however, presented controversial issues, notably in regard to the exclusion of Chinese and Japanese from the United States. [Chae Chan Ping v. United States.] The right of expelling undesirable aliens who have already been admitted is as well established as the right of exclusion. Query, may the state of which the expelled person is a national inquire into the grounds for his expulsion and enter protest in case these grounds do not appear to it to be reasonable? [Great Britain and Belgium: Tillett's Case.]

THE CHINESE EXCLUSION CASE:
CHAE CHAN PING v. UNITED STATES.

United States, Supreme Court, 1889.

130 U. S. 581. [32 L. ed. 1068; 9 S. Ct. 623.]

[The appellant, a subject of the Emperor of China, had resided in the United States from 1875 to 1887, when he went to China, having in his possession a certificate which under the treaties and statutes then in force entitled him to return to the United States. Upon his arrival in San Francisco in 1888 the Collector of the Port refused to allow him to land on the ground that his certificate had been annulled by the act of Congress of October 1, 1888. The lower court had issued an order refusing to release the appellant, on a writ of habeas corpus, from his

---

[1] For a more detailed study of this subject, see Fenwick, *op. cit.*, pp. 189–210; Hyde, *op. cit.*, Vol. I, §§ 270–309; Borchard, The Diplomatic Protection of Citizens Abroad; Eagleton, The Responsibility of States in International Law; Research in International Law: Draft Conventions on Nationality, Responsibility of States, Territorial Waters; Dunn, The Protection of Nationals.

alleged unlawful detention by the master of the ship. The appellant argued that the act was invalid (1) because it contravened the provisions of the treaty between the United States and China and (2) because it violated rights vested in citizens of China by earlier statutes.]

MR. JUSTICE FIELD delivered the opinion of the court. . . .

There being nothing in the treaties between China and the United States to impair the validity of the act of Congress of October 1, 1888, was it on any other ground beyond the competency of Congress to pass it? If so, it must be because it was not within the power of Congress to prohibit Chinese laborers who had at the time departed from the United States, or should subsequently depart, from returning to the United States. Those laborers are not citizens of the United States; they are aliens. That the government of the United States through the action of the legislative department, can exclude aliens from its territory is a proposition which we do not think open to controversy. Jurisdiction over its own territory to that extent is an incident of every independent nation. It is a part of its independence. If it could not exclude aliens it would be to that extent subject to the control of another power. As said by this court in the case of The Exchange, 7 Cranch, 116, 136, speaking by Chief Justice Marshall: "The jurisdiction of the nation within its own territory is necessarily exclusive and absolute. It is susceptible of no limitation not imposed by itself. Any restriction upon it, deriving validity from an external source, would imply a diminution of its sovereignty to the extent of the restriction, and an investment of that sovereignty to the same extent in that power which could impose such restriction. All exceptions, therefore, to the full and complete power of a nation within its own territories, must be traced up to the consent of the nation itself. They can flow from no other legitimate source."

While under our Constitution and form of government the great mass of local matters is controlled by local authorities, the United States, in their relation to foreign countries and their subjects or citizens are one nation, invested with powers which belong to independent nations, the exercise of which can be invoked for the maintenance of its absolute independence and security throughout its entire territory. The powers to declare war, make treaties, suppress insurrection, repel invasion, regulate foreign commerce, secure republican governments to the States, and admit subjects of other nations to citizenship, are all sovereign powers, restricted in their exercise only by the Constitution itself and considerations of public policy and justice which control, more or less, the conduct of all civilized nations. As said by this court in the case of Cohens v. Virginia, 6 Wheat. 264, 413, speaking by the same great Chief Justice: "That the United States form, for many, and for most important purposes, a single nation, has not yet been denied. In war, we are one people. In making peace we are one people. In all commercial regulations, we are one and the same people. In many other respects, the American people are one; and the government which is alone capable of controlling and managing their interests in all these respects, is the government of the Union. It is their government, and in that character they have no other. America has chosen to be in many respects, and to many purposes, a nation; and for all these purposes her government is complete; to all these objects, it is competent. The people have declared, that in the exercise of all powers given for these objects, it is supreme. It can then in effecting these objects legitimately control all individuals or governments within the American territory. The constitution and laws of a State, so far as they are repugnant to the Constitution and laws of the United States, are absolutely void. These States are constituent parts of the United States. They are members of one great empire—for some purposes sovereign, for some purposes subordinate.'' The same view is expressed in a different form by Mr. Justice Bradley, in Knox v. Lee, 12 Wall. 457, 555, where he observes that ''the United States is not only a government, but it is a national government, and the only government in this country that has the character of nationality. It is invested with power over all the foreign relations of the country, war, peace and negotiations and intercourse with other nations; all of which are forbidden to the state governments.'' . . .

The control of local matters being left to local authorities, and national matters being entrusted to the government of the Union, the problem of free institutions existing over a widely extended country, having different climates and varied interests, has been happily solved. For local interests the several States of the Union exist, but for national purposes, embracing our relations with foreign nations, we are but one people, one nation, one power.

To preserve its independence, and give security against foreign aggression and encroachment, is the highest duty of every nation, and to attain these ends nearly all other considerations are to be subordinated. It matters not in what form such aggression and encroachment come, whether from the foreign nation acting in its national character or from vast hordes of its people crowding in upon us. The government possessing the powers which are to be exercised for protection and security, is clothed with authority to determine the occasion on which the powers shall be called forth; and its determination, so far as the subjects affected are concerned, are necessarily conclusive upon all its departments and officers. If, therefore, the government of the United States, through its legislative department, considers the presence of foreigners of a different race in this country, who will not assimilate with us, to be dangerous to its peace and security, their exclusion is not to be stayed because at the time there are no actual hostilities with the nation of which the foreigners are subjects. The existence of war would render the necessity of the proceeding only more obvious and pressing. The same necessity, in a less pressing degree, may arise when war does not exist, and the same authority which adjudges the necessity in one case must also determine it in the other. In both cases its determination is conclusive upon the judiciary. If the government of the country of which the foreigners excluded are subjects is dissatisfied with this action it can make complaint to the executive head of our government, or resort to any other measure which, in its judgment, its interests or dignity may demand; and there lies its only remedy.

The power of the government to exclude foreigners from the country whenever, in its judgment, the public interests require such exclusion, has been asserted in repeated instances, and never denied by the executive or legislative departments. . . . In a dispatch to Mr. Fay, our minister to Switzerland, in March, 1856, Mr. Marcy, Secretary of State under President Pierce, writes: "Every society possesses the undoubted right to determine who shall compose its members, and it is exercised by all nations, both in peace and war." "It may always be questionable whether a resort to this power is warranted by the circumstances, or what department of the government is empowered to exert it; but there can be no doubt that it is possessed by all nations, and that each may decide for itself when the occasion arises demanding its exercise." In a communication in September, 1869, to Mr. Washburne, our minister to France, Mr. Fish, Secretary of State under President Grant, uses this language: "The control of the people within its limits, and the right to expel from its territory persons who are dangerous to the peace of the State, are too clearly within the essential attributes of sovereignty to be seriously contested. Strangers visiting or sojourning in a foreign country voluntarily submit themselves to its laws and customs, and the municipal laws of France, authorizing the expulsion of strangers, are not of such recent date, nor has the exercise of the power by the government of France been so infrequent, that sojourners within her territory can claim surprise when the power is put in force." In a communication to Mr. Foster, our minister to Mexico, in July, 1879, Mr. Evarts, Secretary of State under President Hayes, referring to the power vested in the constitution of Mexico to expel objectionable foreigners, says: "The admission that, as that constitution now stands and is interpreted, foreigners who render themselves harmful or objectionable to the general government must expect to be liable to the exercise of the power adverted to, even in time of peace, remains, and no good reason is seen for departing from that conclusion now. But, while there may be no expedient basis on which to found objection, on principle and in advance of a special case thereunder, to the constitutional right thus asserted by Mexico, yet the manner of carrying out such asserted right may be highly objectionable. You would be fully justified in making earnest remonstrances should a citizen of the United States be expelled from Mexican territory without just steps to assure the grounds of such expulsion, and in bringing the fact to the immediate knowledge of the Department." In a communication to Mr. W. J. Stillman, under date of August 3, 1882, Mr. Frelinghuysen, Secretary of State under President Arthur, writes: "This government cannot contest the right of foreign governments to exclude, on police or other grounds, American citizens from their shores." Wharton's International Law Digest, § 206.

The exclusion of paupers, criminals and persons afflicted with incurable diseases, for which statutes have been passed, is only an application of the same power to particular classes of persons, whose presence. is deemed injurious or a source of danger to the country. As applied to them, there has never been any question as to the power to exclude them. The power is constantly exercised; its existence is involved in the right of self-preservation. . . .

The power of exclusion of foreigners being an incident of sovereignty belonging to the government of the United States, as a part of those sovereign powers delegated by the Constitution, the right to its exercise at any time when, in the judgment of the government, the interests of the country require it, cannot be granted away or restrained on behalf of any one. The powers of government are delegated in trust to the United States, and are incapable of transfer to any other parties. They cannot be abandoned or surrendered. Nor can their exercise be hampered, when needed for the public good, by any considerations of private interest. The exercise of these public trusts is not the subject of barter or contract. Whatever license, therefore, Chinese laborers may have obtained, previous to the act of October 1, 1888, to return to the United States after their departure, is held at the will of the government, revocable at any time, at its pleasure. Whether a proper consideration by our government of its previous laws, or a proper respect for the nation whose subjects are affected by its action, ought to have qualified its inhibition and made it applicable only to persons departing from the country after the passage of the act, are not questions for judicial determination. If there be any just ground of complaint on the part of China, it must be made to the political department of our government, which is alone competent to act upon the subject. . . .

Order affirmed.

GREAT BRITAIN AND BELGIUM:
CASE OF ALDERMAN BEN TILLETT.

Arbitration under the Convention of March 19, 1898.

British Parliamentary Papers [C. 9235], Commercial No. 2 (1899), p. 33.

ARTHUR DESJARDINS, Arbitrator. In discharge of the functions of Arbitrator conferred on me, with the authority of the French Government, by virtue of the Convention of the 19th March, 1898, concluded between the Government of His Majesty the King of the Belgians and the Government of Her Brittanic Majesty, on the subject of the international dispute occasioned by the expulsion of Mr. Ben Tillett, a British subject, from Belgian territory.

Having carefully examined and maturely weighed the documents that have been produced on either side concerning the indemnity claimed by the Government of Her Brittanic Majesty from the Government of His Majesty the King of the Belgians on behalf of Mr. Ben Tillett.

Having, moreover, proceeded to Antwerp on the 15th August, 1898, in order, by means of a full knowledge of the case, to solve certain questions which seemed doubtful to me, and having held an inquiry in the Antwerp prison itself,

I pronounce the following award of arbitration:

(A) On the right of expulsion from the point of view of principle.

Whereas, the right of a State to exclude from its territory foreigners when their dealings or presence appears to compromise its security cannot be contested;

Whereas, moreover, the State in the plenitude of its sovereignty judges the scope of the acts which lead to this prohibition;

(B) As to the watch kept on the person of Ben Tillett in consequence of the meeting of the 21st August, 1896, and up to the confinement of this British subject in the lock-up at Antwerp;

Whereas, if the right of the State to expel be recognized, the means of insuring the execution of its injunctions in that regard cannot be denied to it;

Whereas, the State should have the power to keep a watch on foreigners whose presence seems dangerous to public order, and, if it fears lest those to whom it forbids its territory should escape this vigilance, it may keep them in view;

Whereas, in fact, Ben Tillett repaired to Belgium to organize the international federation of dockers there, and to foment a strike which was considered by the Royal Government to be at once prejudicial to the interests of the port of Antwerp and dangerous to the public tranquility;

Whereas, the Belgian Government had plausible reasons for thinking that Ben Tillett had already harangued the dock labourers at the

"Werker" Club on the evening of the 22d July, 1896, and after this speech, had cleverly eluded the search of the police;

Whereas, that Government did not overstep its functions or exceed its right in endeavouring not to lose sight of Ben Tillett on the afternoon of the 21st August, and in subsequently securing his person after the meeting held in the courtyard of Schram's inn;

Whereas, no measure of expulsion had, it is true, yet been taken against Ben Tillett at the time of his being conducted to the police station about 4 o'clock in the afternoon of the 21st August, 1896; but whereas, the Ministerial despatch of the 9th July, 1896 (referred to in the requisition of the Commissary of Police of Antwerp, Fifth Southern Section, dated the 21st August), relative to foreigners arriving at Antwerp for the purpose of holding meetings there on behalf of a universal union of sailors and dock labourers, left no doubt as to the wishes of the central power; and whereas, the Antwerp police could not, without disobeying these instructions, fail to detain, on behalf of the Government, foreigners who came to take an active part in the agitation set on foot since June 1896, for the organization of the international federation;

Whereas, moreover, according to the papers produced in the case, and, in particular, a report of the Assistant Commissary Bucan, dated the 31st August, 1896, Ben Tillett had been formally advised of the instructions given by the Minister; whereas, according to the deposition of the aforesaid Bucan, taken by me on oath on the 15th August, 1898, Ben Tillett knew perfectly well what he had to expect; he had been officially informed, directly he had landed, that if he meant to hold the public meeting loudly announced in the "Seaman's Chronicle" of the 8th August, 1896, "he must quit Belgian territory; otherwise he would render himself liable to be arrested and conducted under escort to the frontier;"

Whereas, in this condition of things, the agents of the Executive were entitled to detain Ben Tillett at the police station rather more than three hours with a view to insuring the execution of a measure of expulsion which had been decreed in principle by the Government in Council, and which was shortly to become an accomplished fact;

Whereas, decrees of expulsion do not generally precede the events which call for them; and, whereas, if forcible means may not be employed to hold in safe-keeping for a few hours a foreigner whose conduct has become a cause of trouble, until this measure is officially taken, this person will have time to evade the police, and the Government will find itself powerless;

(C) On the imprisonment in a lock-up;

Whereas, the British Government reproach the Belgian authorities with having taken Ben Tillett from the police station to conduct him to a prison, where he found himself mixed up with men under sentence for, or accused of, common law offences;

Whereas, as a matter of fact, Ben Tillett was entered in the books at the Antwerp lock-up at 8 o'clock in the evening of the 21st August, 1896, in order, according to the requisition of the 21st August, 1896, to be "kept at the disposal of the gendarmerie," and thence "conducted out of the kingdom";

Whereas, the Belgian authorities undoubtedly conformed to the rule of this penitentiary establishment, according to which the lock-up is intended not only for accused persons, but also for "foreigners detained on behalf of the Administrator of Public Safety, and for those whose extradition is demanded by foreign Governments;" and whereas, the sole question at issue is whether the Royal Government has not infringed an obligation of international propriety in imprisoning Ben Tillett in quarters simultaneously devoted to these different classes of prisoners.

But whereas, in fact, on the one hand, Ben Tillett was confined in two cells of this building successively;

And whereas, in law, on the other hand, it is impossible to compel a Sovereign State either to construct special establishments exclusively designed for the provisional detention of foreigners between the time of their arrest and the moment when the measure of expulsion can be carried out, or even to reserve them special quarters in houses already constructed; whereas, the Belgian Government satisfied the exigencies of international courtesy by isolating Ben Tillett, and thereby preventing him from coming into contact with persons awaiting their trial;

(D) On the duration of the whole detention;

Whereas, in fact, Ben Tillett, having been entered in the books of the Antwerp prison at 8 o'clock in the evening of the 21st August, was not taken out till 6 o'clock in the evening of the next day, the 22d August, in order to be taken on board the Harwich boat which left for England at 7 o'clock; and whereas, twenty-six [twenty-two?] hours thus elapsed from the moment when this English subject was consigned to the police station until the time when he was put in a position to go back to his country;

But whereas, the Belgian Government could not be compelled to send Ben Tillett away by the Harwich boat at 7 P. M. on the 21st August; whereas, the Antwerp police had to concert with the Government, and consequently communicate with Brussels; and whereas, the instructions awaited by the witness Winne, assistant to the Police Commissary at Antwerp, heard by us on oath, had not reached him at 7 o'clock;

Whereas, it is impossible to maintain that these instructions ought necessarily to have reached the Antwerp police agents by 7 o'clock, without considering with excessive strictness the manner in which the representatives of the Belgian Government use their time;

Whereas, other boats, it is true, left for England both on the night of the 21st-22d August and in the morning of the 22d August; and whereas, the British Government asks us in its second Memorandum why one of these various means of transport was not made use of;

But whereas, it appears from the documents produced and from the depositions taken by us in the prison at Antwerp on the 15th August, 1898:

1. That Ben Tillett, when he embarked for Antwerp on the Harwich boat, had taken a return ticket which was available for thirty days.

2. That, in order to utilize the ticket in question, he intended to make use of the same line of steamers on his return voyage;

3. That he had expressly informed the witness Winne of his intention of returning by the Harwich boat;

That under these circumstances the Belgian Government were guilty of no error in sending Ben Tillett on board the Harwich boat at 7 o'clock on the 22nd August, this being the earliest time of sailing of that vessel; . . .

For these reasons:

I decide that the demand for compensation put forward by Her Majesty's Government has no basis, and I declare them non-suited;

I condemn them in costs, in virtue of article 5 of the Convention of the 19th March, 1898, assuming that there are costs to be paid; but at the same time I declare that, as far as I myself am concerned, I make no claim to fees or reimbursement of expenses.[1]

B. Privileges conceded to resident aliens.

International law records the gradual widening of the privileges conceded by states to resident, or domiciled, aliens. The earlier right to engage in business has been extended in most states to the practice of the professions and to the ownership of real property, but each state is free to determine the restrictions on these privileges which it may believe to be necessary in the general interest. Query, taking the due process of law clause of the Fourteenth Amendment of the United States Constitution as representing the American standard of the minimum due to the resident alien, would it be consistent with that standard for a state of the Union to limit the right of employers to engage aliens to work in private establishments? [Truax v. Raich.] Would it be consistent with that standard for a state of the Union to deny to aliens

---

[1] Supplementary Cases. In the case of Nishimura Ekiu v. United States, 142 U. S. 651 (1892), involving a writ of habeas corpus issued on behalf of a Japanese woman who had been denied entry into the country by the immigration authorities, the Supreme Court laid down the rule of exclusion as follows: "It is an accepted rule of international law, that every sovereign nation has the power, as inherent in sovereignty, and essential to self-preservation, to forbid the entrance of foreigners within its dominions, or to admit them only in such cases and upon such conditions as it may see fit to prescribe."

the right to own or lease land unless such alien should have declared his intention to become a citizen? [Terrace v. Thompson.] Whatever the restrictions, the unequal or discriminatory application of them would, of course, give rise to complaint by the foreign state on behalf of its nationals. Many of the privileges normally granted to aliens are specifically provided for in treaties. In the United States it has been held that treaties stipulating that certain privileges be accorded to aliens should be liberally interpreted. [Jordan v. Tashiro.]

TRUAX AND THE ATTORNEY GENERAL OF THE STATE OF ARIZONA v. RAICH.

United States, Supreme Court, 1915.

239 U. S. 33. [60 L. ed. 131; 36 S. Ct. 7.]

Mr. Justice Hughes delivered the opinion of the court.

Under the initiative provision of the constitution of Arizona (Art. IV, § 1), there was adopted the following measure which was proclaimed by the Governor as a law of the State on December 14, 1914:

"An act to protect the citizens of the United States in their employment against non-citizens of the United States, in Arizona, and to provide penalties and punishment for the violation thereof,

"Be it enacted by the People of the State of Arizona:

"Section 1. Any company, corporation, partnership, association or individual who is, or may hereafter become an employer of more than five (5) workers at any one time, in the State of Arizona, regardless of kind or class of work, or sex of workers, shall employ not less than eighty (80) per cent qualified electors or native born citizens of the United States or some sub-division thereof.

"Sec. 2. Any company, corporation, partnership, association or individual, their agent or agents, found guilty of violating any of the provisions of this Act shall be guilty of a misdemeanor, and, upon conviction thereof, shall be subject to a fine of not less than one hundred ($100.00) dollars, and imprisoned for not less than thirty (30) days.

"Sec. 3. Any employé who shall misrepresent, or make false statement, as to his or her nativity or citizenship, shall, upon conviction thereof, be subject to a fine of not less than one hundred ($100.00) dollars, and imprisoned for not less than thirty (30) days." Laws of Arizona, 1915. Initiative Measure, p. 12.

Mike Raich (the appellee), a native of Austria, and an inhabitant of the State of Arizona but not a qualified elector, was employed as a cook by the appellant William Truax, Sr., in his restaurant in the City of Bisbee, Cochise County. Truax had nine employés, of whom seven were neither "native-born citizens" of the United States nor qualified electors. After the election at which the act was passed Raich was informed by his employer that when the law was proclaimed, and solely by reason of its requirements and because of the fear of the penalties that would be incurred in case of its violation, he would be discharged. Thereupon, on December 15, 1914, Raich filed this bill in the District Court of the United States for the District of Arizona, asserting among other things that the act denied to him the equal protection of the laws and hence was contrary to the Fourteenth Amendment of the Constitution of the United States. Wiley E. Jones, the attorney general of the State, and W. G. Gilmore, the county attorney of Cochise County, were made defendants in addition to the employer Truax, upon the allegation that these officers would prosecute the employer unless he complied with its terms and that in order to avoid such a prosecution the employer was about to discharge the complainant. Averring that there was no adequate remedy at law, the bill sought a decree declaring the act to be unconstitutional and restraining action thereunder.

Soon after the bill was filed, an application was made for an injunction *pendente lite*. After notice of this application, Truax was arrested for a violation of the act, upon a complaint prepared by one of the assistants in the office of the County Attorney of Cochise County, and as it appeared that by reason of the determination of the officers to enforce the act there was danger of the complainant's immediate discharge from employment, the district judge granted a temporary restraining order.

The allegations of the bill were not controverted. The defendants joined in a motion to dismiss upon the grounds (1) that the suit was against the State of Arizona without its consent; (2) that it was sought to enjoin the enforcement of a criminal statute; (3) that the bill did not state facts sufficient to constitute a cause of action in equity; and (4) that there was an improper joinder of parties and the plaintiff was not entitled to sue for the relief asked. The application for an interlocutory injunction and the motion to dismiss were then heard before three judges, as required by § 266 of the Judicial Code. The motion to dismiss was denied and an interlocutory injunction restraining the defendants, the attorney general and the county attorney, and their successors and assistants, from enforcing the act against the defendant Truax, was granted. 219 Fed. Rep. 273. This direct appeal has been taken.

As the bill is framed upon the theory that the act is unconstitutional, and that the defendants who are public officers concerned with the enforcement of the laws of the State are about to proceed wrongfully to the complainant's injury through interference with his employment, it is established that the suit cannot be regarded as one against the State. Whatever doubt existed in this class of cases was removed by the decision in Ex parte Young, 209 U. S. 123, 155, 161, which has repeatedly been followed. . . .

It is also settled that while a court of equity, generally speaking, has "no jurisdiction over the prosecution, the punishment or the pardon of crimes or misdemeanors" (In re Sawyer, 124 U. S. 200, 210) a distinction obtains, and equitable jurisdiction exists to restrain criminal prosecutions under unconstitutional enactments, when the prevention of such prosecutions is essential to the safeguarding of rights of property. . . . The right to earn a livelihood and to continue in employment unmolested by efforts to enforce void enactments should similarly be entitled to protection in the absence of adequate remedy at law. It is said that the bill does not show an employment for a term, and that under an employment at will the complainant could be discharged at any time for any reason or for no reason, the motive of the employer being immaterial. The conclusion, however, that is sought to be drawn is too broad. The fact that the employment is at the will of the parties, respectively, does not make it one at the will of others. The employé has manifest interest in the freedom of the employer to exercise his judgment without illegal interference or compulsion and, by the weight of authority, the unjustified interference of third persons is actionable although the employment is at will. . . . It is further urged that the complainant cannot sue save to redress his own grievance (McCabe v. Atchison, Topeka & Santa Fe Ry., 235 U. S. 151, 162); that is, that the servant cannot complain for the master, and that it is the master who is subject to prosecution, and not the complainant. But the act undertakes to operate directly upon the employment of aliens and if enforced would compel the employer to discharge a sufficient number of his employés to bring the alien quota within the prescribed limit. It sufficiently appears that the discharge of the complainant will be solely for the purpose of meeting of the requirements of the act and avoiding threatened prosecution under its provisions. It is, therefore, idle to call the injury indirect or remote. It is also entirely clear that unless the enforcement of the act is restrained the complainant will have no adequate remedy, and hence we think that the case falls within the class in which, if the unconstitutionality of the act is shown, equitable relief may be had.

The question then is whether the act assailed is repugnant to the Fourteenth Amendment. Upon the allegations of the bill, it must be assumed that the complainant, a native of Austria, has been admitted to the United States under the Federal law. He was thus admitted with the privilege of entering and abiding in the United States, and hence of entering and abiding in any State in the Union. (See Gegiow v. Uhl, Commissioner, decided October 25, 1915, ante, p. 3.) Being lawfully an inhabitant of Arizona, the complainant is entitled under the Fourteenth Amendment to the equal protection of its laws. The description—"any person within its jurisdiction"—as it has frequently been held, includes aliens. "These provisions," said the court in Yick Wo v.

Hopkins, 118 U. S. 356, 369 (referring to the due process and equal protection clauses of the Amendment), "are universal in their application, to all persons within the territorial jurisdiction, without regard to any differences of race, of color, or of nationality; and the equal protection of the laws is a pledge of the protection of equal laws." See also Wong Wing v. United States, 163 U. S. 228, 242; United States v. Wong Kim Ark, 169 U. S. 649, 695. The discrimination defined by the act does not pertain to the regulation or distribution of the public domain, or of the common property or resources of the people of the State, the enjoyment of which may be limited to its citizens as against both aliens and the citizens of other States. Thus in McCready v. Virginia, 94 U. S. 391, 396, the restriction to the citizens of Virginia of the right to plant oysters in one of its rivers was sustained upon the ground that the regulation related to the common property of the citizens of the State, and an analogous principle was involved in Patsone v. Pennsylvania, 232 U. S. 138, 145, 146, where the discrimination against aliens upheld by the court had for its object the protection of wild game within the States with respect to which it was said that the State could exercise its preserving power for the benefit of its own citizens if it pleased. The case now presented is not within these decisions, or within those relating to the devolution of real property (Hauenstein v. Lynham, 100 U. S. 483; Blythe v. Hinckley, 180 U. S. 333, 341, 342); and it should be added that the act is not limited to persons who are engaged on public work or receive the benefit of public moneys. The discrimination here involved is imposed upon the conduct of ordinary private enterprise.

The act, it will be observed, provides that every employer (whether corporation, partnership, or individual) who employs more than five workers at any one time "regardless of kind or class of work, or sex of workers" shall employ "not less than eighty per cent. qualified electors or native born citizens of the United States or some subdivision thereof." It thus covers the entire field of industry with the exception of enterprises that are relatively very small. Its application in the present case is to employment in a restaurant the business of which requires nine employés. The purpose of an act must be found in its natural operation and effect (Henderson v. Mayor, 92 U. S. 259, 268; Bailey v. Alabama, 219 U. S. 219, 244), and the purpose of this act is not only plainly shown by its provisions, but it is frankly revealed in its title. It is there described as "An act to protect the citizens of the United States in their employment against non-citizens of the United States, in Arizona." As the appellants rightly say, there has been no subterfuge. It is an act aimed at the employment of aliens, as such, in the businesses described. Liberally, its terms might be taken to include with aliens those naturalized citizens who by reason of change of residence might not be at the time qualified electors in any subdivision of the United States, but we are dealing with the main purpose of the statute, definitely stated, in the execution of which the complainant is to be forced out of his employment as a cook in a restaurant, simply because he is an alien.

It is sought to justify this act as an exercise of the power of the State to make reasonable classifications in legislating to promote the health, safety, morals and welfare of those within its jurisdiction. But this admitted authority, with the broad range of legislative discretion that it implies, does not go so far as to make it possible for the State to deny to lawful inhabitants, because of their race or nationality, the ordinary means of earning a livelihood. It requires no argument to show that the right to work for a living in the common occupations of the community is of the very essence of the personal freedom and opportunity that it was the purpose of the Amendment to secure. Butchers' Union Co. v. Crescent City Co., 111 U. S. 746, 762; Barbier v. Connolly, 113 U. S. 27, 31; Yick Wo v. Hopkins, *supra*; Allgeyer v. Louisiana, 165 U. S. 578, 589, 590; Coppage v. Kansas, 236 U. S. 1, 14. If this could be refused solely upon the ground of race or nationality, the prohibition of the denial to any person of the equal protection of the laws would be a barren form of words. It is no answer to say, as it is argued, that the act proceeds upon the assumption that "the employment of aliens unless restrained was a peril to the public welfare." The discrimination against aliens in the wide range of employments to which the act relates is made an end in itself and thus the authority to deny to aliens, upon the mere fact of their alienage, the right to obtain support in the ordinary fields of labor is necessarily involved. It must also be said that reasonable classification implies action consistent with the legitimate interests of the State, and it will not be disputed that these cannot be so broadly conceived as to bring them into hostility to exclusive Federal power. The authority to control immigration—to admit or exclude aliens—is vested solely in the Federal Government. Fong Yue Ting v. United States, 149 U. S. 698, 713. The assertion of an authority to deny to aliens the opportunity of earning a livelihood when lawfully admitted to the State would be tantamount to the assertion of the right to deny them entrance and abode, for in ordinary cases they cannot live where they cannot work. And, if such a policy were permissible, the practical result would be that those lawfully admitted to the country under the authority of the acts of Congress, instead of enjoying in a substantial sense and in their full scope the privileges conferred by the admission, would be segregated in such of the States as chose to offer hospitality.

It is insisted that the act should be supported because it is not "a total deprivation of the right of the alien to labor"; that is, the restriction is limited to those businesses in which more than five workers are employed, and to the ratio fixed. It is emphasized that the employer in any line of business who employs more than five workers may employ aliens to the extent of twenty per cent. of his employés. But the fallacy of this argument at once appears. If the State is at liberty to treat the employment of aliens as in itself a peril requiring restraint regardless of kind or class of work, it cannot be denied that the authority exists to make its measures to that end effective. Otis v. Parker, 187 U. S. 606; Silz v. Hesterburg, 211 U. S. 31; Purity Co. v. Lynch, 226 U. S. 192. If the restriction to twenty per cent. now imposed is maintainable the State undoubtedly has the power if it sees fit to make the percentage less. We have nothing before us to justify the limitation to twenty per cent. save the judgment expressed in the enactment, and if that is sufficient, it is difficult to see why the apprehension and conviction thus evidenced would not be sufficient were the restriction extended so as to permit only ten per cent. of the employés to be aliens or even a less percentage, or were it made applicable to all businesses in which more than three workers were employed instead of applying to those employing more than five. We have frequently said that the legislature may recognize degrees of evil and adapt its legislation accordingly (St. Louis Consol. Coal Co. v. Illinois, 185 U. S. 203, 207; McLean v. Arkansas, 211 U. S. 539, 551; Miller v. Wilson, 236 U. S. 373, 384); but underlying the classification is the authority to deal with that at which the legislation is aimed. The restriction now sought to be sustained is such as to suggest no limit to the State's power of excluding aliens from employment if the principle underlying the prohibition of the act is conceded. No special public interest with respect to any particular business is shown that could possibly be deemed to support the enactment, for as we have said it relates to every sort. 'The discrimination is against aliens as such in competition with citizens in the described range of enterprises and in our opinion it clearly falls under the condemnation of the fundamental law.

The question of rights under treaties was not expressly presented by the bill, and, although mentioned in the argument, does not require attention in view of the invalidity of the act under the Fourteenth Amendment.

Order affirmed.

MR. JUSTICE McREYNOLDS dissenting. . . .

TERRACE ET AL. v. THOMPSON, ATTORNEY GENERAL OF THE STATE OF WASHINGTON.

United States, Supreme Court, 1923.

263 U. S. 197. [68 L. ed. 255; 44 S. Ct. 15.]

MR. JUSTICE BUTLER delivered the opinion of the Court.

Appellants brought this suit to enjoin the Attorney General of Washington from enforcing the Anti-Alien Land Law of that State, c. 50,

Laws, 1921, on the grounds that it is in conflict with the due process and equal protection clauses of the Fourteenth Amendment; with the treaty between the United States and Japan, and with certain provisions of the constitution of the State.

The appellants are residents of Washington. The Terraces are citizens of the United States and of Washington. Nakatsuka was born in Japan of Japanese parents and is a subject of the Emperor of Japan. The Terraces are the owners of a tract of land in King County which is particularly adapted to raising vegetables, and which for a number of years had been devoted to that and other agricultural purposes. The complaint alleges that Nakatsuka is a capable farmer and will be a desirable tenant of the land; that the Terraces desire to lease their land to him for the period of five years; that he desires to accept such lease, and that the lease would be made but for the act complained of. And it is alleged that the defendant, as Attorney General, has threatened to and will take steps to enforce the act against the appellants if they enter into such lease, and will treat the leasehold interest as forfeited to the State, and will prosecute the appellants criminally for violation of the act; that the act is so drastic and the penalties attached to its violation are so great that neither of the appellants may make the lease even to test the constitutionality of the act, and that, unless the court shall determine its validity in this suit, the appellants will be compelled to submit to it, whether valid or invalid, and thereby will be deprived of their property without due process of law and denied the equal protection of the laws.

The Attorney General made a motion to dismiss the amended complaint upon the ground that it did not state any matters of equity or facts sufficient to entitle the appellants to relief. The District Court granted the motion and entered a decree of dismissal on the merits. The case is here on appeal from that decree.

Section 33 of Article II of the Constitution of Washington prohibits the ownership of land by aliens other than those who in good faith have declared intention to become citizens of the United States, except in certain instances not here involved. The act provides in substance that any such alien shall not own, take, have or hold the legal or equitable title, or right to any benefit of any land as defined in the act, and that land conveyed to or for the use of aliens in violation of the state constitution or of the act shall thereby be forfeited to the State. And it is made a gross misdemeanor, punishable by fine or imprisonment or both, knowingly to transfer land or the right to the control, possession or use of land to such an alien. It is also made a gross misdemeanor for any such alien having title to such land or the control, possession or use thereof, to refuse to disclose to the Attorney General or the prosecuting attorney the nature and extent of his interest in the land. The Attorney General and the prosecuting attorneys of the several counties are charged with the enforcement of the act. . . .

2. Is the act repugnant to the due process clause or the equal protection clause of the Fourteenth Amendment?

Appellants contend that the act contravenes the due process clause in that it prohibits the owners from making lawful disposition or use of their land, and makes it a criminal offense for them to lease it to the alien, and prohibits him from following the occupation of farmer; and they contend that it is repugnant to the equal protection clause in that aliens are divided into two classes,—those who may and those who may not become citizens, one class being permitted, while the other is forbidden, to own land as defined.

Alien inhabitants of a State, as well as all other persons within its jurisdiction, may invoke the protection of these clauses. Yick Wo v. Hopkins, 118 U. S. 356, 369; Truax v. Raich, *supra,* 39. The Fourteenth Amendment, as against the arbitrary and capricious or unjustly discriminatory action of the State, protects the owners in their right to lease and dispose of their land for lawful purposes and the alien resident in his right to earn a living by following ordinary occupations of the community, but it does not take away from the State those powers of police that were reserved at the time of the adoption of the Constitution. Barbier v. Connolly, 113 U. S. 27, 31; Mugler v. Kansas, 123 U. S. 623, 663; Powell v. Pennsylvania, 127 U. S. 678, 683; In re Kemmler, 136 U. S. 436, 449; Lawton v. Steel, 152 U. S. 133, 136; Phillips v. Mobile, 208 U. S. 472, 479; Hendrick v. Maryland, 235 U. S. 610, 622, 623. And in the exercise of such powers the State has wide discretion in determining its own public policy and what measures are necessary for its own protection and properly to promote the safety, peace and good order of its people.

And, while Congress has exclusive jurisdiction over immigration, naturalization and the disposal of the public domain, each State, in the absence of any treaty provision to the contrary, has power to deny to aliens the right to own land within its borders. Hauenstein v. Lynham, 100 U. S. 483, 484, 488; Blythe v. Hinckley, 180 U. S. 333, 340. . . .

State legislation applying alike and equally to all aliens, withholding from them the right to own land, cannot be said to be capricious or to amount to an arbitrary deprivation of liberty or property, or to transgress the due process clause.

This brings us to a consideration of appellants' contention that the act contravenes the equal protection clause. That clause secures equal protection to all in the enjoyment of their rights under like circumstances. In re Kemmler, *supra;* Giozza v. Tiernan, 148 U. S. 657, 662. But this does not forbid every distinction in the law of a State between citizens and aliens resident therein. In Truax v. Corrigan, 257 U. S. 312, this Court said (p. 337):

"In adjusting legislation to the need of the people of a State, the legislature has a wide discretion and it may be fully conceded that perfect uniformity of treatment of all persons is neither practical nor desirable, that classification of persons is constantly necessary. . . . Classification is the most inveterate of our reasoning processes. We can scarcely think or speak without consciously or unconsciously exercising it. It must therefore obtain in and determine legislation; but it must regard real resemblances and real differences between things, and persons, and class them in accordance with their pertinence to the purpose in hand.''

The rights, privileges and duties of aliens differ widely from those of citizens; and those of alien declarants differ substantially from those of nondeclarants. Formerly in many of the States the right to vote and hold office was extended to declarants, and many important offices have been held by them. But these rights have not been granted to nondeclarants. By various acts of Congress, declarants have been made liable to military duty, but no act has imposed that duty on nondeclarants. The fourth paragraph of Article I of the treaty invoked by the appellants, provides that the citizens or subjects of each shall be exempt in the territories of the other from compulsory military service either on land or sea, in the regular forces, or in the national guard, or in the militia; also from all contributions imposed in lieu of personal service, and from all forced loans or military exactions or contributions. The alien's formally declared bona fide intention to renounce forever all allegiance and fidelity to the sovereignty to which he lately has been a subject, and to become a citizen of the United States and permanently to reside therein markedly distinguishes him from an ineligible alien or an eligible alien who has not so declared.

By the statute in question all aliens who have not in good faith declared intention to become citizens of the United States, as specified in § 1 (a), are called ''aliens,'' and it is provided that they shall not ''own'' ''land,'' as defined in clauses (d) and (b) of § 1 respectively. The class so created includes all, but is not limited to, aliens not eligible to become citizens. Eligible aliens who have not declared their intention to become citizens are included, and the act provides that unless declarants be admitted to citizenship within seven years after the declaration is made, bad faith will be presumed. This leaves the class permitted so to own land made up of citizens and aliens who may, and who intend to, become citizens, and who in good faith have made the declaration required by the naturalization laws. The inclusion of good faith declarants in the same class with citizens does not unjustly discriminate against aliens who are ineligible or against eligible aliens who have failed to declare their intention. The classification is based on eligibility and purpose to naturalize. Eligible aliens are free white persons and persons of African nativity or descent. Congress is not trammeled, and it may grant or withhold the privilege of naturalization upon any ground or without any reason, as it sees fit. But it is not to be supposed that its acts defining eligibility are arbitrary or unsupported by reasonable considerations of public policy. The State properly may assume that the considerations upon which Congress made such classification are substantial and reasonable. Generally speaking, the natives of European countries are eligible. Japanese, Chinese and Malays are not. Appellants' contention that the state act discriminates arbitrarily against Nakatsuka and other ineligible aliens because of their race and color is without foundation. All persons of whatever color or race who have not declared their intention in good faith to become citizens are prohibited from so owning agricultural lands. Two classes of aliens inevitably result from the naturalization laws,—those who may and those who may not become citizens. The rule established by Congress on this subject, in and of itself, furnishes a reasonable basis for classification in a state law withholding from aliens the privilege of land ownership as defined in the act. We agree with the court below (274 Fed. 841, 849) that:

"It is obvious that one who is not a citizen and cannot become one lacks an interest in, and the power to effectually work for the welfare of, the state, and, so lacking, the state may rightfully deny him the right to own and lease real estate within its boundaries. If one incapable of citizenship may lease or own real estate, it is within the realm of possibility that every foot of land within the state might pass to the ownership or possession of noncitizens."

And we think it is clearly within the power of the State to include nondeclarant eligible aliens and ineligible aliens in the same prohibited class. Reasons supporting discrimination against aliens who may but who will not naturalize are obvious.

Truax v. Raich, *supra,* does not support the appellants' contention. In that case, the Court held to be repugnant to the Fourteenth Amendment an act of the legislature of Arizona making it a criminal offense for an employer of more than five workers at any one time, regardless of kind or class of work, or sex of workers, to employ less than eighty per cent. qualified electors or native born citizens of the United States. In the opinion it was pointed out that the legislation there in question did not relate to the devolution of real property, but that the discrimination was imposed upon the conduct of ordinary private enterprise covering the entire field of industry with the exception of enterprises that were relatively very small. It was said that the right to work for a living in the common occupations of the community is a part of the freedom which it was the purpose of the Fourteenth Amendment to secure.

In the case before us, the thing forbidden is very different. It is not an opportunity to earn a living in common occupations of the community, but it is the privilege of owning or controlling agricultural land within the State. The quality and allegiance of those who own, occupy and use the farm lands within its borders are matters of highest importance and affect the safety and power of the State itself.

The Terraces, who are citizens, have no right safeguarded by the Fourteenth Amendment to lease their land to aliens lawfully forbidden to take or have such lease. The state act is not repugnant to the equal protection clause and does not contravene the Fourteenth Amendment. . . .

The decree of the District Court is affirmed.

MR. JUSTICE MCREYNOLDS and MR. JUSTICE BRANDEIS think there is no justiciable question involved and that the case should have been dismissed on that ground.

MR. JUSTICE SUTHERLAND took no part in the consideration or decision of this case.

JORDAN, SECRETARY OF STATE OF CALIFORNIA, ET AL. v. TASHIRO ET AL.

United States, Supreme Court, 1928.

278 U. S. 123. [73 L. ed. 214; 49 S. Ct. 47.]

MR. JUSTICE STONE delivered the opinion of the Court.

The respondents, subjects of Japan residing in California, presented for filing in the office of the secretary of state of California, one of the petitioners, proposed articles of incorporation of the "Japanese Hospital of Los Angeles." The articles provided for the creation of a business corporation with a share capital of $100,000. They purported to authorize the corporation to construct and operate in Los Angeles a general hospital with a home for nurses and resident physicians, and to lease land for that purpose.

Although the articles complied with all provisions of the California statutes governing the organization of a corporation for such purposes, the petitioners refused to file them on the ground that, as the respondents were citizens of Japan, the Alien Land Law of the state (Statutes of 1921, p. lxxxiii) did not permit an incorporation by them for the purposes named. The respondents then brought, in the Supreme Court of California, a proceeding in mandamus to compel the petitioners to file the proposed articles and to issue a certificate of incorporation to the hospital. The mandamus petition set up that the treaty of commerce and navigation between the government of the United States and the empire of Japan, proclaimed April 5, 1911, 37 Stat. 1504, and now in force, conferred on citizens and subjects of the empire of Japan the right to incorporate in the United States for the purposes named in the proposed articles.

The state court granted the writ as prayed basing its determination on the construction of the treaty. Tashiro v. Jordan, 201 Cal. 236. This

court granted the petition of the secretary of state of California for certiorari, 277 U. S. 580.

Section 2 of the Alien Land Law of California, as amended by the
Act of the Legislature approved June 20, 1923, Stats. 1923, p. 1020,
provides that aliens of a class in which respondents are included may
acquire, possess and enjoy real estate within the state "in the manner
and to the extent, and for the purposes prescribed by any treaty now
existing between the government of the United States and the nation or
country of which such alien is a citizen or subject, and not otherwise."
Section 3, in like terms, permits (a) acquisition of land by a corporation,
the majority of whose stockholders are aliens; and (b) the purchase by
aliens of stock in corporations owning or leasing land, only for purposes prescribed by such a treaty.

The statutes of California do not otherwise forbid the organizing of
a corporation by citizens of Japan residing in the state, and by these
enactments there was effected perfect harmony in the operation of the
statute and of the treaty. What the treaty prescribes the statute authorizes. There is thus no possibility of conflict between the exercise of the
treaty-making power of the federal government and the reserved powers
of the state such as that suggested in Geofroy v. Riggs, 133 U. S. 258,
267, on which petitioners placed reliance on the argument.

The Supreme Court of California, in passing upon the application for
mandamus, granted the relief prayed, not as a matter of statutory construction, but because it thought the conduct of a hospital by Japanese
citizens through the instrumentality of a corporation, organized under
the laws of the state, was a privilege secured to the respondents by the
treaty which the state statute did not purport to withhold. The privilege challenged by petitioners is one specially set up or claimed under a
treaty of the United States and sustained by the state court and the case
is thus one within the jurisdiction of this court conferred by § 237 (b) of
the Judicial Code. Compare Red Cross Line v. Atlantic Fruit Co., 264
U. S. 109, 120.

The question presented is one of the construction of the treaty, the
relevant portions of which are printed in the margin. It in terms authorizes the citizens of Japan to carry on trade within the United States and
"to lease land for residential and commercial purposes, and generally
to do anything incident to or necessary for trade upon the same terms
as native citizens or subjects, submitting themselves to the laws and
regulations there established."

The petitioners insist that the construction and operation of a hospital
is not one of the purposes prescribed by the treaty, which, it is argued,
are limited so far as "trade" and "commerce" are concerned to the purchase and sale or exchange of goods and commodities, and that, in any
case, the treaty does not confer upon Japanese subjects, resident in California, the privilege of forming a corporation under the laws of Cali-

fornia or of leasing lands through a corporate agency for such a purpose.

The principles which should control the diplomatic relations of nations, and the good faith of treaties as well, require that their obligations should be liberally construed so as to effect the apparent intention of the parties to secure equality and reciprocity between them. See Geofroy v. Riggs, *supra;* Tucker v. Alexandroff, 183 U. S. 424, 437; Wright v. Henkel, 190 U. S. 40, 57; In re Ross, 140 U. S. 453, 475. Upon like ground, where a treaty fairly admits of two constructions, one restricting the rights that may be claimed under it and the other enlarging them, the more liberal construction is to be preferred. Asakura v. Seattle, 265 U. S. 332; Tucker v. Alexandroff, *supra;* Geofroy v. Riggs, *supra*.

While in a narrow and restricted sense the terms "commerce," or "commercial," and "trade" may be limited to the purchase and sale or exchange of goods and commodities, they may connote, as well, other occupations and other recognized forms of business enterprise which do not necessarily involve trading in merchandise. Asakura v. Seattle, *supra*. And although commerce includes traffic in this narrower sense, for more than a century it has been judicially recognized that in a broad sense it embraces every phase of commercial and business activity and intercourse. See Gibbons v. Ogden, 9 Wheat. 1, 189.

Considerations which led this court to conclude that the terms "trade" and "commerce" as used in this treaty do not include agriculture, and the circumstances attending the making of the treaty which were deemed to exclude from the operation of its broad language any grant of the privilege of acquiring and using lands within the United States for agricultural purposes, were discussed in the opinions in Terrace v. Thompson, 263 U. S. 197, 223; Webb v. O'Brien, 263 U. S. 313, 323; Frick v. Webb, 263 U. S. 326, 333, and need not now be detailed. But in Asakura v. Seattle, *supra,* it was held that the language of this treaty securing to Japanese citizens the privilege of carrying on trade within the United States was broad enough to comprehend all classes of business which might reasonably be embraced in the word "trade," and included the privilege of carrying on the business of a pawnbroker. In Clarke v. Deckebach, 274 U. S. 392, 396, in considering the treaty with Great Britain of July 3, 1815, 8 Stat. 228, and August 6, 1827, 8 Stat. 361, granting reciprocal liberty of commerce between the United States and Great Britain, and in holding that the guarantee that ". . . the merchants and traders of each nation, respectively, shall enjoy the most complete protection and security for their commerce," did not extend to a British subject engaged in keeping a poolroom within the United States, we took occasion to point out that the language of the present treaty with Japan was of broader scope than that then before the court.

Giving to the terms of the treaty, as we are required by accepted principles, a liberal rather than a narrow interpretation, we think, as the state court held, that the terms "trade" and "commerce," when used in conjunction with each other and with the grant of authority to lease land for "commercial purposes" are to be given a broader significance than that pressed upon us, and are sufficient to include the operation of a hospital as a business undertaking; that this is a commercial purpose for which the treaty authorizes Japanese subjects to lease lands.

It is said that the elimination from the original draft of this clause of the treaty of words authorizing the leasing of land for "industrial, manufacturing and other lawful" purposes (see Terrace v. Thompson, *supra*, p. 223) leads to the conclusion that land might not be leased for hospital purposes by Japanese subjects, even though under the other provisions of the treaty they might be permitted to operate such an institution. But as the leasing of land for a hospital is obviously not for an industrial or manufacturing purpose, this argument presupposes that the phrase "commercial purposes" is limited to merchandising businesses, which for reasons already stated we deem inadmissible. Moreover, a construction which concedes the authority of Japanese subjects to operate a hospital but would deny to them an appropriate means of controlling so much of the earth's surface as is indispensable to its operation, does not comport with a reasonable, to say nothing of a liberal, construction. The Supreme Court of California has reached a like conclusion in State of California v. Tagami, 195 Cal. 522, holding that this treaty secured to a Japanese subject the privilege of leasing land within the state for the purpose of using and occupying it for the maintenance of a health resort and sanitarium.

The contention that the treaty does not permit the exercise of the privileges secured by it through a corporate agency requires no extended consideration. The employment of such an agency is incidental to the exercise of the granted privilege. But it is not an incident which enlarges the privilege by annexing to the permitted business another class of business otherwise excluded from the grant, as would have been the case in Terrace v. Thompson, *supra*, had the business of farming been deemed an incident to the business of trading in farm products.

The principle of liberal construction of treaties would be nullified if a grant of enumerated privileges were held not to include the use of the usual methods and instrumentalities of their exercise. Especially would this be the case where the granted privileges relate to trade and commerce and the use of land for commercial purposes. It would be difficult to select any single agency of more universal use or more generally recognized as a usual and appropriate means of carrying on commerce and trade than the business corporation. And it would, we think, be a narrow interpretation indeed, which, in the absence of restrictive language, would lead to the conclusion that the treaty had secured to citizens of

Japan the privilege of engaging in a particular business, but had denied to them the privilege of conducting that business in corporate form. But here any possibility of doubt would seem to be removed by the clause which confers on citizens and subjects of the high contracting parties the right " . . . to do anything generally incident to or necessary for trade upon the same terms as native citizens or subjects, submitting themselves to the laws and regulations there established."

Affirmed.[1]

C. **Jurisdiction over aliens in respect to acts taking effect in national territory.**[2]

Controversial issues have arisen in cases where states have sought to exercise over aliens entering their territory a jurisdiction based upon acts committed outside the territory of the state but taking effect within it. Query, would such jurisdiction properly extend to a libel published outside the state and taking only moral effect within the territory? [The Cutting Case.] Would it properly extend to an act taking effect on a national vessel on the high seas when committed by a person on board a foreign vessel? [France and Turkey: Case of the "Lotus."] Would it extend to a conspiracy entered into outside the national territory to commit illegal acts within the national territory? [Ford v. United States.]

----

[1] SUPPLEMENTARY CASES. Compare Asakura v. Seattle, 265 U. S. 332 (1924), below p. 576, holding an ordinance of the city of Seattle, which provided that no license to engage in the business of pawnbroker should be issued unless the applicant was a citizen of the United States, to be in violation of the treaty between the United States and Japan.

Query, does a resident alien owe allegiance to the government of the state of which he is a resident as against the claims of his national state? In De Jager v. Attorney-General of Natal, L. R. [1907] A. C. 326, involving an appeal from a conviction of high treason by a British court of a burgher of the South African Republic resident in the British colony of Natal, who when the town in which he resided was temporarily occupied by the Boer forces in 1899 was compelled to join the Boer forces and assisted them in various ways, the Judicial Committee of the Privy Council, on appeal, sustained the conviction. "It is an old law," said the court, "that an alien resident within British territory owes allegiance to the Crown, and may be indicted for high treason, though not a subject. . . . Their Lordships consider that the duty of a resident alien is so to act that the Crown shall not be harmed by reason of its having admitted him as a resident."

[2] See Research in International Law: Draft Convention on Jurisdiction with Respect to Crime.

THE CUTTING CASE.

Mexico, Bravos District Court, Chihuahua, 1886.

Report on Extraterritorial Crime and The Cutting Case [J. B. Moore], p. 9.

Zubia, J.　In view of the present suit instituted against A. K. Cutting, who declares himself to be unmarried, 40 years of age, a native of the state of New York, a resident of this town, and editor of the Newspaper El Centinela, for the offense of defamation:

In view of the preliminary statement of the accused, the petition of the district attorney, the statement made by the complainant, Emigdio Medina (the civil party to the suit), the defense of the prisoner's attorney, Jesus E. Islas, and all else which appears from the proceedings and was proper to be seen:

It appears, 1. That in No. 14 of the newspaper called El Centinela, published in this place, under date of the 6th of June last, there appeared a local item in English, in which there was criticised as fraudulent a prospectus published in El Paso, Texas, announcing the appearance of a newspaper called Revista Internacional.

It appears, 2. That Emigdio Medina, considering himself alluded to and aggrieved by that paragraph, appeared before the second alcalde, acting in turn as criminal judge in this town, and asked for a judgment of conciliation against A. K. Cutting, as responsible editor of El Centinela.

It appears, 3. That the parties being present before the mediating judge, agreed on the publication in the same newspaper, El Centinela, of a retraction which was written by Medina and corrected by Cutting, the publication to be made four times in English, and, if Mr. A. N. Daguerre, an associate editor of the paper, would allow it, also in Spanish.

It appears, 4. That Cutting, instead of complying with the agreement as stipulated in the conciliation, published on the 20th of the same month of June a retraction only in English in El Centinela, in small type and with material errors that rendered it almost unintelligible, and published on the same day a notice or communication in the El Paso Sunday Herald, in which he ratified and enlarged the defamatory statements which were published against Medina, and denounced as contemptible the agreement of conciliation which had taken place before the second alcalde of this town.

It appears, 5. That the plaintiff then appeared and in due form accused Cutting of the penal offense of defamation, in conformity with articles 643 and 646, section 2 of the Penal Code, for which cause the corresponding order of arrest was issued.

It appears, 6. That on the 22d of the same month the plaintiff enlarged the accusation, stating that although the newspaper, the El Paso

Sunday Herald, is published in Texas, Cutting had had circulated a great number in this town and in the interior of the Republic, it having been read by more than three persons, for which reason an order had been issued to seize the copies that were still in the office of the said Cutting.

' It appears, 7. That according to law the preliminary statement of the accused was taken, in which he denied the jurisdiction of the court, on the ground that the act had been committed in Texas, placing himself under the protection of the consul of the United States, and the warrant for his arrest in due form was ordered to be issued and communicated to the proper parties. . . .

Considering, therefore, 1. That, in conformity with article 121 of the Code of Criminal Procedure, the foundation of the criminal proceeding is the proof of the act which the law accounts a penal offense, and that in the present case the existence of this fact is fully proved, as it consists of the publication appearing in El Centinela on the 6th of June last, characterizing as fraudulent the prospectus which was issued to announce the publication of the Revista Internacional.

Considering, 2. That although it is true that there was in regard to this matter an act of conciliation, which would have satisfied the plaintiff if it had been carried out, it is also true that the terms of this act were not complied with, and that, for this reason, the responsibility of the penal offense remains the same.

Considering, 3. That the proof of the lack of fulfillment of the compromise entered into in the judgment of conciliation is actually in the communication published by Cutting in the El Paso Sunday Herald, in which he ratified the original assertion that Emigdio Medina was a fraud and a swindler, and at the same time in the article published in El Centinela of the same date, leaving out all the capital letters and putting the name of Medina in microscopic type in order to make the reading of it difficult.

Considering, 4. That ratification, according to the dictionary of Escriche, is the confirmation and sanction of what has been said or done, it is retroactive and by consequence does not constitute an act different from that to which it refers: "Ratihabitio retrotrahitur ad initium," nor does new responsibility, distinct from that which originally existed, arise therefrom.

Considering, 5. That this being so, the criminal responsibility of Cutting arose from the article published in El Centinela, issued in this town, which article was ratified in the Texas newspaper, which ratification, however, did not constitute a new penal offense to be punished with a different penalty from that which was applicable to the first publication.

Considering, 6. That even on the supposition, not admitted, that the defamation arose from the communication published on the 20th of June in the El Paso Sunday Herald, article 186 of the Mexican Penal Code provides that—

"Penal offenses committed in a foreign country by a Mexican against Mexicans or foreigners, or by a foreigner against Mexicans," may be punished in the Republic and according to its laws, subject to the following conditions: 1. That the accused be in the Republic, whether he came voluntarily or has been brought by extradition proceedings; 2. that if the offended party be a foreigner, he shall have made proper legal complaint; 3. that the accused shall not have been definitely tried in the country where the offense was committed, or, if tried, that he shall not have been acquitted, included in an amnesty, or pardoned; 4. that the breach of law of which he is accused shall have the character of a penal offense both in the country in which it was committed and in the Republic; 5. that by the laws of the Republic the offense shall be subject to a severer penalty than that of "arresto mayor"—requisites which have been fully met in the present case: for Cutting was arrested in the territory of the Republic; there is complaint from a proper legal source—that of Medina, who presented his complaint in the form prescribed by law; the accused has not been definitely tried, nor acquitted, nor included in an amnesty, nor pardoned in the country in which he committed the offense; the penal offense of which Cutting is accused has that character in the country in which it was committed and in the Republic, as can be seen in the penal code in force in the State of Texas, articles 616, 617, 618, and 619, and in the Penal Code of the State of Chihuahua, articles 642 and 646; and according to this latter article, section 2, the breach of law in question is subject to a heavier penalty than that of "arresto mayor."

Considering, 7. That according to the rule of law, *"Judex non de legibus, sed secundum leges debet judicare,"* it does not belong to the judge who decides to examine the principle laid down in said article 186, but to apply it fully, it being the law in force in the State. . . .

Considering, 9. That the said article 186 of the Penal Code, far from being contrary to the supreme law or to the treaties made by the President of the Republic, has for its object, as is seen in the expository part of the same code, page 38, "the free operation of the principle on which the right to punish is founded, to wit, justice united to utility."

Considering, 10. That even supposing, without conceding it, that the penal offense of defamation was committed in the territory of Texas, the circumstance that the newspaper, El Paso Sunday Herald, was circulated in this town, of which circumstance Medina complained, and which was the ground of ordering the seizure of the copies which might be found in the office of Cutting, in this same town, properly constituted the consummation of the crime, conformably to article 644 of the Penal Code. . . .

Considering, 12. That the publication by Cutting in El Centinela, ratified subsequently in the El Paso Sunday Herald and in the Evening Tribune, on file in the case attacks the private life of Emigdio Medina by attributing to him the penal offense of fraud and of swindling, and is therefore comprised in the restriction placed on the liberty of the press by the said article of the constitution.

Considering, 13. That as acts consummated in the territory of the Canton of Bravos, State of Chihuahua, are in question, it is incumbent on the judge, whose name is hereto subscribed, to pass upon them conformably to the laws in force in the said State, especially in view of the fact that the accused resides in this town, where he has had his domicil for more than two years, as appears from the declarations made on folios 20, 21, and 22 of this case, a statement not contradicted by Cutting, who on folio 19 declares that he resides on both sides, that is, in Paso del Norte, Mexico, and in El Paso, Texas, without a fixed residence on either of the two sides.

Considering, 14. That to show this more fully, Cutting expressly recognized the jurisdiction of the authorities of this town by appearing before the second alcalde, acting in turn as criminal judge, and answering the demand for conciliation, which was made against him by Medina for defamation.

Considering, 15. That the responsibility of Cutting is fully proved, since it appears in credible documents which have in no wise been contradicted by their author; and, if any doubt should exist respecting the malicious intent with which the first publication was made, it would disappear in view of the subsequent ratifications made in the El Paso Sunday Herald and in the Evening Tribune, in which Cutting expressly says that Emigdio Medina is a fraud, swindler, coward and thief; the requisites specified in article 391 of the Code of Criminal Proceedings being thus fully met.

Considering, 16. That in order to fix the penalty which ought to be enforced, it must be borne in mind that, although the charge imputed to the offended party causes him dishonor and serious prejudice, and there are no extenuating circumstances, the crime under consideration is of a private character between two editors, in which the only aggravating circumstances that exist are those referred to in the seventh and eleventh sections of article 44 and articles 656 and 657 section 4 of the Penal Code, it does not appear that the other aggravating circumstances mentioned by the district attorney are fully proved; for, although it is true that the present case has caused great alarm in the community, this is not attributable to the penal offense imputed to Cutting, but to the inadequate means which have been taken for his defense; this being exactly the case provided for in the final part of article 66 of the said code; . . .

In view of the foregoing article 646, section 2, and articles 661, 119 and 218, of the said code, it is ordered and adjudged as follows:

First. For the penal offense of defamation committed against the person of Emigdio Medina, A. K. Cutting is sentenced to serve a year at hard labor and pay a fine of $600, or, in default thereof, endure additional imprisonment of a hundred days.

Second. He is also sentenced to pay the civil indemnity, to be fixed according to the provisions of article 313 of the Penal Code.

Third. Let the defendant be admonished not to repeat the offense for which he is sentenced, and advised of the penalties to be incurred in that event. . . .

Fifth. The case shall be sent to the supreme court of justice, for the purposes to which the final part of the petition of the district attorney refers, relative to the intervention of the American consul in this suit.

Sixth. Let the interested parties be notified, and the prisoner be advised of the length of time he has to appeal from this sentence.

FRANCE AND TURKEY:
THE CASE OF THE S. S. "LOTUS."

Permanent Court of International Justice, 1927.

Publications of the Court, Series A, No. 10.

[BY THE COURT.] By a special agreement signed at Geneva on October 12th, 1926, between the Governments of the French and Turkish Republics and filed with the Registry of the Court, in accordance with Article 40 of the Statute and Article 35 of the Rules of Court, on January 4th, 1927, by the diplomatic representatives at The Hague of the aforesaid Governments, the latter have submitted to the Permanent Court of International Justice the question of jurisdiction which has arisen between them following upon the collision which occurred on August 2nd, 1926, between the steamships Boz-Kourt and Lotus.

According to the special agreement, the Court has to decide the following questions:

"(1) Has Turkey, contrary to Article 15 of the Convention of Lausanne of July 24th, 1923, respecting conditions of residence and business and jurisdiction, acted in conflict with the principles of international law—and if so, what principles—by instituting, following the collision which occurred on August 2nd, 1926, on the high seas between the French steamer Lotus and the Turkish steamer Boz-Kourt and upon the arrival of the French steamer at Constantinople—as well as against the captain of the Turkish steamship—joint criminal proceedings in pursuance of Turkish law against M. Demons, officer of the watch on board the Lotus at the time of the collision, in consequence of the loss of the Boz-Kourt having involved the death of eight Turkish sailors and passengers?

"(2) Should the reply be in the affirmative, what pecuniary reparation is due to M. Demons, provided, according to the principles of international law, reparation should be made in similar cases?" . . .

On August 2nd, 1926, just before midnight, a collision occurred between the French mail steamer Lotus, proceeding to Constantinople, and the Turkish collier Boz-Kourt, between five and six nautical miles to the north of Cape Sigri (Mitylene). The Boz-Kourt, which was cut in two, sank, and eight Turkish nationals who were on board perished. After having done everything possible to succour the shipwrecked persons, of whom ten were able to be saved, the Lotus continued on its course to Constantinople, where it arrived on August 3rd.

At the time of the collision, the officer of the watch on board the Lotus was Monsieur Demons, a French citizen, lieutenant in the merchant service and first officer of the ship, whilst the movements of the Boz-Kourt were directed by its captain, Hassan Bey, who was one of those saved from the wreck.

As early as August 3rd the Turkish police proceeded to hold an enquiry into the collision on board the Lotus; and on the following day, August 4th, the captain of the Lotus handed in his master's report at the French Consulate-General, transmitting a copy to the harbour master.

On August 5th, Lieutenant Demons was requested by the Turkish authorities to go ashore to give evidence. The examination, the length of which incidentally resulted in delaying the departure of the Lotus, led to the placing under arrest of Lieutenant Demons—without previous notice being given to the French Consul-General—and Hassan Bey, amongst others. This arrest, which has been characterized by the Turkish Agent as arrest pending trial (*arrestation préventive*), was effected in order to ensure that the criminal prosecution instituted against the two officers, on a charge of manslaughter, by the Public Prosecutor of Stamboul, on the complaint of the families of the victims of the collision, should follow its normal course.

The case was first heard by the Criminal Court of Stamboul on August 28th. On that occasion, Lieutenant Demons submitted that the Turkish Courts had no jurisdiction; the Court, however, overruled his objection. When the proceedings were resumed on September 11th, Lieutenant Demons demanded his release on bail: this request was complied with on September 13th, the bail being fixed at 6,000 Turkish pounds.

On September 15th, the Criminal Court delivered its judgment, the terms of which have not been communicated to the Court by the Parties. It is, however, common ground, that it sentenced Lieutenant Demons to eighty days' imprisonment and a fine of twenty-two pounds, Hassan Bey being sentenced to a slightly more severe penalty.

It is also common ground between the Parties that the Public Prosecutor of the Turkish Republic entered an appeal against this decision, which had the effect of suspending its execution until a decision upon the appeal had been given; that such decision has not yet been given; but that the special agreement of October 12th, 1926, did not have the effect of suspending "the criminal proceedings . . . now in progress in Turkey."

The action of the Turkish judicial authorities with regard to Lieutenant Demons at once gave rise to many diplomatic representations and other steps on the part of the French Government or its representatives in Turkey, either protesting against the arrest of Lieutenant Demons or demanding his release, or with a view to obtaining the transfer of the case from the Turkish Courts to the French Courts.

As a result of these representations, the Government of the Turkish Republic declared on September 2nd, 1926, that "it would have no objection to the reference of the conflict of jurisdiction to the Court at The Hague."

The French Government having, on the 6th of the same month, given "its full consent to the proposed solution," the two Governments appointed their plenipotentiaries with a view to the drawing up of the special agreement to be submitted to the Court; this special agreement was signed at Geneva on October 12th, 1926, as stated above, and the ratifications were deposited on December 27th, 1926. . . .

5.—The prosecution was instituted in pursuance of Turkish legislation. The special agreement does not indicate what clause or clauses of that legislation apply. No document has been submitted to the Court indicating on what article of the Turkish Penal Code the prosecution was based; the French Government however declares that the Criminal Court claimed jurisdiction under Article 6 of the Turkish Penal Code, and far from denying this statement, Turkey, in the submissions of her Counter-Case, contends that that article is in conformity with the principles of international law. It does not appear from the proceedings whether the prosecution was instituted solely on the basis of that article.

Article 6 of the Turkish Penal Code, Law No. 765 of March 1st, 1926 (Official Gazette No. 320 of March 13th, 1926), runs as follows:

[Translation] "Any foreigner who, apart from the cases contemplated by Article 4, commits an offence abroad to the prejudice of Turkey or of a Turkish subject, for which offence Turkish law prescribes a penalty involving loss of freedom for a minimum period of not less than one year, shall be punished in accordance with the Turkish Penal Code provided that he is arrested in Turkey. The penalty shall however be reduced by one third and instead of the death penalty, twenty years of penal servitude shall be awarded. . . ."

Even if the Court must hold that the Turkish authorities had seen fit to base the prosecution of Lieutenant Demons upon the above-mentioned

Article 6, the question submitted to the Court is not whether that article is compatible with the principles of international law; it is more general. The Court is asked to state whether or not the principles of international law prevent Turkey from instituting criminal proceedings against Lieutenant Demons under Turkish law. Neither the conformity of Article 6 in itself with the principles of international law nor the application of that article by the Turkish authorities constitutes the point at issue; it is the very fact of the institution of proceedings which is held by France to be contrary to those principles. . . .

II. Having determined the position resulting from the terms of the special agreement, the Court must now ascertain which were the principles of international law that the prosecution of Lieutenant Demons could conceivably be said to contravene.

It is Article 15 of the Convention of Lausanne of July 24th, 1923, respecting conditions of residence and business and jurisdiction, which refers the contracting Parties to the principles of international law as regards the delimitation of their respective jurisdiction.

This clause is as follows:

"Subject to the provisions of Article 16, all questions of jurisdiction shall, as between Turkey and the other contracting Powers, be decided in accordance with the principles of international law."

The French Government maintains that the meaning of the expression "principles of international law" in this article should be sought in the light of the evolution of the Convention. . . . The French Government deduces from these facts that the prosecution of Demons is contrary to the intention which guided the preparation of the Convention of Lausanne.

. . . Now the Court considers that the words "principles of international law," as ordinarily used, can only mean international law as it is applied between all nations belonging to the community of States. . . . the principles which are in force between all independent nations and which therefore apply equally to all the contracting Parties. . . .

III. The Court, having to consider whether there are any rules of international law which may have been violated by the prosecution in pursuance of Turkish law of Lieutenant Demons, is confronted in the first place by a question of principle which, in the written and oral arguments of the two Parties, has proved to be a fundamental one. The French Government contends that the Turkish Courts, in order to have jurisdiction, should be able to point to some title to jurisdiction recognized by international law in favour of Turkey. On the other hand, the Turkish Government takes the view that Article 15 allows Turkey jurisdiction whenever such jurisdiction does not come into conflict with a principle of international law.

The latter view seems to be in conformity with the special agreement itself, No. 1 of which asks the Court to say whether Turkey has acted contrary to the principles of international law and, if so, what principles. According to the special agreement, therefore, it is not a question of stating principles which would permit Turkey to take criminal proceedings, but of formulating the principles, if any, which might have been violated by such proceedings.

This way of stating the question is also dictated by the very nature and existing conditions of international law.

International law governs relations between independent States. The rules of law binding upon States therefore emanate from their own free will as expressed in conventions or by usages generally accepted as expressing principles of law and established in order to regulate the relations between these co-existing independent communities or with a view to the achievement of common aims. Restrictions upon the independence of States cannot therefore be presumed. . . .

IV. The Court will now proceed to ascertain whether general international law, to which Article 15 of the Convention of Lausanne refers, contains a rule prohibiting Turkey from prosecuting Lieutenant Demons.

. . .

The arguments advanced by the French Government, other than those considered above, are, in substance, the three following:

(1) International law does not allow a State to take proceedings with regard to offences committed by foreigners abroad, simply by reason of the nationality of the victim; and such is the situation in the present case because the offence must be regarded as having been committed on board the French vessel.

(2) International law recognizes the exclusive jurisdiction of the State whose flag is flown as regards everything which occurs on board a ship on the high seas.

(3) Lastly, this principle is especially applicable in a collision case.

. . .

. . . the Court does not think it necessary to consider the contention that a State cannot punish offences committed abroad by a foreigner simply by reason of the nationality of the victim. For this contention only relates to the case where the nationality of the victim is the only criterion on which the criminal jurisdiction of the State is based. Even if that argument were correct generally speaking—and in regard to this the Court reserves its opinion—it could only be used in the present case if international law forbade Turkey to take into consideration the fact that the offence produced its effects on the Turkish vessel and consequently in a place assimilated to Turkish territory in which the application of Turkish criminal law cannot be challenged, even in regard to offences committed there by foreigners. But no such rule of international law exists. No argument has come to the knowledge of the Court from which it could be deduced that States recognize themselves to be under an obligation towards each other only to have regard to the place where the author of the offence happens to be at the time of the offence. On the contrary, it is certain that the courts of many countries, even of countries which have given their criminal legislation a strictly territorial character, interpret criminal law in the sense that offences, the authors of which at the moment of commission are in the territory of another State, are nevertheless to be regarded as having been committed in the national territory, if one of the constituent elements of the offence, and more especially its effects, have taken place there. French courts have, in regard to a variety of situations, given decisions sanctioning this way of interpreting the territorial principle. Again, the Court does not know of any cases in which governments have protested against the fact that the criminal law of some country contained a rule to this effect or that the courts of a country construed their criminal law in this sense: Consequently, once it is admitted that the effects of the offence were produced on the Turkish vessel, it becomes impossible to hold that there is a rule of international law which prohibits Turkey from prosecuting Lieutenant Demons because of the fact that the author of the offence was on board the French ship. Since, as has already been observed, the special agreement does not deal with the provision of Turkish law under which the prosecution was instituted, but only with the question whether the prosecution should be regarded as contrary to the principles of international law, there is no reason preventing the Court from confining itself to observing that, in this case, a prosecution may also be justified from the point of view of the so-called territorial principle. . . .

The second argument put forward by the French Government is the principle that the State whose flag is flown has exclusive jurisdiction over everything which occurs on board a merchant ship on the high seas.

It is certainly true that—apart from certain special cases which are defined by international law—vessels on the high seas are subject to no authority except that of the State whose flag they fly. In virtue of the principle of the freedom of the seas, that is to say, the absence of any territorial sovereignty upon the high seas, no State may exercise any kind of jurisdiction over foreign vessels upon them. Thus, if a war vessel, happening to be at the spot where a collision occurs between a vessel flying its flag and a foreign vessel, were to send on board the latter an officer to make investigations or to take evidence, such an act would undoubtedly be contrary to international law.

But it by no means follows that a State can never in its own territory exercise jurisdiction over acts which have occurred on board a foreign ship on the high seas. A corollary of the principle of the freedom of the seas is that a ship on the high seas is assimilated to the territory of the State the flag of which it flies, for, just as in its own territory, that

State exercises its authority upon it, and no other State may do so. All that can be said is that by virtue of the principle of the freedom of the seas, a ship is placed in the same position as national territory; but there is nothing to support the claim according to which the rights of the State under whose flag the vessel sails may go farther than the rights which it exercises within its territory properly so called. It follows that what occurs on board a vessel on the high seas must be regarded as if it occurred on the territory of the State whose flag the ship flies. If, therefore, a guilty act committed on the high seas produces its effects on a vessel flying another flag or in foreign territory, the same principles must be applied as if the territories of two different States were concerned, and the conclusion must therefore be drawn that there is no rule of international law prohibiting the State to which the ship on which the effects of the offence have taken place belongs, from regarding the offence as having been committed in its territory and prosecuting, accordingly, the delinquent.

This conclusion could only be overcome if it were shown that there was a rule of customary international law which, going further than the principle stated above, established the exclusive jurisdiction of the State whose flag was flown. The French Government has endeavoured to prove the existence of such a rule, having recourse for this purpose to the teachings of publicists, to decisions of municipal and international tribunals, and especially to conventions which, whilst creating exceptions to the principle of the freedom of the seas by permitting the war and police vessels of a State to exercise a more or less extensive control over the merchant vessels of another State, reserve jurisdiction to the courts of the country whose flag is flown by the vessel proceeded against.

In the Court's opinion, the existence of such a rule has not been conclusively proved. . . .

On the other hand, there is no lack of cases in which a State has claimed a right to prosecute for an offence, committed on board a foreign ship, which it regarded as punishable under its legislation. Thus Great Britain refused the request of the United States for the extradition of John Anderson, a British seaman who had committed homicide on board an American vessel, stating that she did not dispute the jurisdiction of the United States but that she was entitled to exercise hers concurrently. This case, to which others might be added, is relevant in spite of Anderson's British nationality, in order to show that the principle of the exclusive jurisdiction of the country whose flag the vessel flies is not universally accepted.

The cases in which the exclusive jurisdiction of the State whose flag was flown has been recognized would seem rather to have been cases in which the foreign State was interested only by reason of the nationality of the victim, and in which, according to the legislation of that State itself or the practice of its courts, that ground was not regarded as sufficient to authorize prosecution for an offence committed abroad by a foreigner.

Finally, as regards conventions expressly reserving jurisdiction exclusively to the State whose flag is flown, it is not absolutely certain that this stipulation is to be regarded as expressing a general principle of law rather than as corresponding to the extraordinary jurisdiction which these conventions confer on the state-owned ships of a particular country in respect of ships of another country on the high seas. Apart from that, it should be observed that these conventions relate to matters of a particular kind, closely connected with the policing of the seas, such as the slave trade, damage to submarine cables, fisheries, etc., and not to common-law offences. Above all it should be pointed out that the offences contemplated by the conventions in question only concern a single ship; it is impossible therefore to make any deduction from them in regard to matters which concern two ships and consequently the jurisdiction of two different States.

The Court therefore has arrived at the conclusion that the second argument put forward by the French Government does not, any more than the first, establish the existence of a rule of international law prohibiting Turkey from prosecuting Lieutenant Demons.

It only remains to examine the third argument advanced by the French Government and to ascertain whether a rule specially applying to collision cases has grown up, according to which criminal proceedings regarding such cases come exclusively within the jurisdiction of the State whose flag is flown. . . .

As regards the Franconia case (R. v. Keyn 1877, L. R. 2 Ex. Div. 63) upon which the Agent for the French Government has particularly relied, it should be observed that the part of the decision which bears the closest relation to the present case is the part relating to the localization of the offence on the vessel responsible for the collision.

But, whatever the value of the opinion expressed by the majority of the judges on this particular point may be in other respects, there would seem to be no doubt that if, in the minds of these judges, it was based on a rule of international law, their conception of that law, peculiar to English jurisprudence, is far from being generally accepted even in common-law countries. This view seems moreover to be borne out by the fact that the standpoint taken by the majority of the judges in regard to the localization of an offence, the author of which is situated in the territory of one State whilst its effects are produced in another State, has been abandoned in more recent English decisions (R. v. Nillins, 1884, 53 L. J. 157; R. v. Godfrey, L. R. 1923, 1 K. B. 24). This development of English case-law tends to support the view that international law leaves States a free hand in this respect. . . .

The conclusion at which the Court has therefore arrived is that there is no rule of international law in regard to collision cases to the effect that criminal proceedings are exclusively within the jurisdiction of the State whose flag is flown. . . .

V.—Having thus answered the first question submitted by the special agreement in the negative, the Court need not consider the second question, regarding the pecuniary reparation which might have been due to Lieutenant Demons.

For these reasons, the Court, having heard both Parties, gives, by the President's casting vote—the votes being equally divided—, judgment to the effect

(1) that, following the collision which occurred on August 2nd, 1926, on the high seas between the French steamship Lotus and the Turkish steamship Boz-Kourt, and upon the arrival of the French ship at Stamboul, and in consequence of the loss of the Boz-Kourt having involved the death of eight Turkish nationals, Turkey, by instituting criminal proceedings in pursuance of Turkish law against Lieutenant Demons, officer of the watch on board the Lotus at the time of the collision, has not acted in conflict with the principles of international law, contrary to Article 15 of the Convention of Lausanne of July 24th, 1923, respecting conditions of residence and business and jurisdiction;

(2) that, consequently, there is no occasion to give judgment on the question of the pecuniary reparation which might have been due to Lieutenant Demons if Turkey, by prosecuting him as above stated, had acted in a manner contrary to the principles of international law. . . .

Done at the Peace Palace, The Hague, this seventh day of September, nineteen hundred and twenty-seven, in three copies, one of which is to be placed in the archives of the Court, and the others to be transmitted to the Agents of the respective Parties. . . .

MM. Loder, former President, Weiss, Vice-President, and Lord Finlay, MM. Nyholm and Altamira, Judges, declaring that they are unable to concur in the judgment delivered by the Court and availing themselves of the right conferred on them by Article 57 of the Statute, have delivered the separate opinions which follow hereafter.

Mr. Moore, dissenting from the judgment of the Court only on the ground of the connection of the criminal proceedings in the case with Article 6 of the Turkish Penal Code, also delivered a separate opinion.[1]

---

[1] Judge Loder's dissenting opinion argued that "the place where an offense has been committed is necessarily that where the guilty person is when he commits the act." It may be justifiable to assume that an act and its effect are indistinguishable "when there is a direct relation between them; for instance, a shot fired at a person on the other side of a frontier"; but this "legal fiction" does not hold in the case of unintentional acts, such as the collision in question.

In general, on this important case, see J. L. Brierly, "The Lotus Case," 44 Law Quart. Rev. (1928), 154; W. E. Beckett, "Criminal Jurisdiction over Foreigners," British Year Book, VIII (1927), 108; Sir J. F. Williams, "L'Affaire du 'Lotus,'" Rev. Gen. de Droit Int. Public, XXXV (1928), 361; J. W. H. Verzijl, "L'Affaire du 'Lotus,'" Rev. de Droit Int. et de Leg. Comp., IX (1928), 1.

FORD ET AL. v. UNITED STATES.

United States, Supreme Court, 1927.

273 U. S. 593. [71 L. ed. 793; 47 S. Ct. 531.]

MR. CHIEF JUSTICE TAFT delivered the opinion of the Court.

This is a review by certiorari of the conviction of George Ford, George Harris, J. Evelyn, Charles H. Bellanger and Vincent Quartararo, of a conspiracy, contrary to § 37 of the Criminal Code, to violate the National Prohibition Act, Title II, §§ 3 and 29, c. 85, 41 Stat. 305, 308, 316, and the Tariff Act of 1922, § 593 (b), c. 356, 42 Stat. 858, 982. The trial and conviction resulted largely from the seizure of the British vessel Quadra, hovering in the high seas off the Farallon Islands, territory of the United States, twenty-five miles west from San Francisco. The ship, her officers, her crew and cargo of liquor were towed into the port of San Francisco. The seizure was made under the authority of the treaty between Great Britain and the United States, proclaimed by the President May 22, 1924, 43 Stat. 1761, as a convention to aid in the prevention of the smuggling of intoxicating liquors into the United States.

The main questions presented are, first, whether the seizure of the vessel was in accordance with the treaty; second, whether the treaty prohibits prosecution of the persons, subjects of Great Britain, on board the seized vessel brought within the jurisdiction of the United States upon the landing of such vessel, for illegal importation of liquor; third, whether the treaty authorizes prosecution of such persons, not only for the substantive offense of illegal importation or attempt to import, but also for conspiracy to effect it; and, fourth, whether such persons, without the United States, conspiring and coöperating to violate its laws with other persons who are within the United States and to commit overt acts therein, can be prosecuted therefor when thereafter found in the United States.

The petitioners and fifty-five others were indicted in November, 1924, for carrying on a continuous conspiracy at the Bay of San Francisco, in the jurisdiction of the United States, from January 1, 1924 to November of that year, the date of the indictment, to commit offenses against the laws of the United States, first, by introducing into and transporting in the United States intoxicating liquor, in violation of the National Prohibition Act; second, by importing liquor into the United States, in violation of § 593, sub-division (b), of the Tariff Act of 1922, making it a penal offense to introduce merchandise into the United States in violation of law; and, third, by violation of the terms of the treaty. It charged as overt acts: the loading of 12,000 cases of liquor on the Quadra at Vancouver, British Columbia, her proceeding on September 10, 1924, to a point less than twelve miles from the Farallon Islands,—a distance which could be traversed in less than an hour by the Quadra and by the motor boats, 903 B, C-55, Marconi, California, Ocean Queen and divers others, by which the liquor was then delivered from her and imported into the United States; that on the 29th of September, 1924, the defendants landed from the steamer Quadra a barrel containing 100 gallons of whiskey, and, at another time, on October 11, 1924, a large variety of alcohol, gin, brandy, whiskey, and vermouth; and that, at another time, on October 12th, the day of the seizure, they attempted to land 89 sacks of whiskey, but that two of the defendants, who were on the small craft C-55, were arrested and were prevented from carrying out their purpose. Two defendants pleaded guilty. Of twenty-nine defendants tried, nineteen, including all the crew of the Quadra were acquitted, and ten, including the captain and the first and second officers of the Quadra, were convicted. Of these ten, five, including the three officers, are now before the Court as petitioners. The convictions were affirmed by the Circuit Court of Appeals of the Ninth Circuit. 10 Fed. (2d) 339. . . .

[In a part of the opinion reproduced below, p. 504, the court considered objections to the validity of the indictment based chiefly upon the location of the vessel at the time of seizure, discussed the meaning of the treaty of 1924, and held that the treaty permitted seizure for the offense of conspiring to import liquor illegally as well as for the substantive offense of importing or attempting to import.]

The next objection of the defendants taken from the Quadra is that on all the evidence they were entitled to a directed verdict of not guilty. They argue that they are charged with a conspiracy illegally to import or to attempt to import liquor into the United States, when they were corporeally at all times during the alleged conspiracy out of the jurisdiction of the United States, and so could commit no offense against it. What they are charged with is conspiring "at the Bay of San Francisco" with the defendants Quartararo and Belanger illegally to import liquor, and the overt acts of thus smuggling and attempting to smuggle it. The conspiracy was continuously in operation between the defendants in the United States and those on the high seas adjacent thereto, and of the four overt acts committed in pursuance thereof, three were completed and took effect within the United States, and the fourth failed of its effect only by reason of the intervention of the federal officers. In other words, the conspiring was directed to violation of the United States law within the United States, by men within and without it, and everything done was at the procuration and by the agency of each for the other in pursuance of the conspiracy and the intended illegal importation. In such a case all are guilty of the offense of conspiring to violate the United States law whether they are in or out of the country.

In Strassheim v. Daily, 221 U. S. 280, Daily had been convicted of procuring Armstrong, a public official of Michigan, to pay bills presented to the State which Armstrong knew to be fraudulent. It was objected that, during the whole period of the crime, Daily was in Chicago, Illinois, and could not be punished under an indictment found in Michigan for such an offense. This Court denied the claim, saying (pp. 284, 285):

"If a jury should believe the evidence and find that Daily did the acts that led Armstrong to betray his trust, deceived the Board of Control, and induced by fraud the payment by the State, the usage of the civilized world would warrant Michigan in punishing him, although he never had set foot in the State until after the fraud was complete. Acts done outside a jurisdiction, but intended to produce and producing detrimental effects within it, justify a State in punishing the cause of the harm as if he had been present at the effect, if the State should succeed in getting him within its power. Commonwealth v. Smith, 11 Allen 243, 256, 259; Simpson v. State, 92 Georgia 41; American Banana Co. v. United Fruit Co., 213 U. S. 347, 356; Commonwealth v. Macloon, 101 Mass. 1, 6, 18. We may assume therefore that Daily is a criminal under the laws of Michigan."

Other cases in this Court which sustain the same view are Benson v. Henkel, 198 U. S. 1; Re Palliser, 136 U. S. 257; Horner v. United States, 143 U. S. 207; Burton v. United States, 202 U. S. 344, 387; and Lamar v. United States, 240 U. S. 60, 65, 66.

There has been much discussion of this general principle, and its application has been varied in some courts because of certain rules of the common law with respect to principals and accessories; but in the consideration of such a case as this, we are not controlled by such considerations and regard the principle as settled, as in the passage quoted. It is supported by other authorities: Commonwealth v. Gillespie, 7 Sargent & Rawle 469, 478; Rex v. Brisac and Scott, 4 East, 164; State v. Piver, 74 Wash. 96; Weil v. Black, 76 W. Va. 685, 694.

In Regina v. Garrett, Dearsly's Crown Cases Reserved, 232, 241, Lord Campbell said:

"I do not proceed upon the ground that the offense was committed beyond the jurisdiction of the Court"—which was the fact there—"for if a man employ a conscious or unconscious agent in this country, he may be amenable to the laws of England, although at the time he was living beyond the jurisdiction."

It will be found among the earlier cases that the principle is sometimes qualified by saying that the person out of the State can not be held for a crime committed within the State by his procuration unless it is done by an innocent agent or a mechanical one; but the weight of authority is now against such limitation. Generally the cases show that jurisdiction exists to try one who is a conspirator whenever the conspiracy is in whole or in part carried on in the country whose laws are conspired against. In Hyde v. United States, 225 U. S. 347; Brown v. Elliott, 225 U. S. 392, the question was whether a conspiracy could be tried, not where it was carried on, but in a place where only an overt act under it was performed by one conspirator. There was strong diversity of opinion among the Justices, though a majority sustained the venue following the Court of King's Bench in Rex v. Brisac and Scott, 4 East, 164. But we have no such ground for difference here, for the conspiracy was being carried on all the time by communications exchanged between the conspirators in San Francisco and on the high seas just beyond the three-mile limit near San Francisco Bay, and the overt acts were in both places.

The whole question was fully considered from the international standpoint in a learned opinion by John Bassett Moore, now Judge of the Permanent Court of International Justice, while he was Assistant Secretary in the State Department, to be found in Moore's International Law Digest, vol. 2, p. 244. The report was made in view of controversy between this Government and the Government of Mexico in reference to the arrest and imprisonment of one Cutting for a libel charged to have been committed by Cutting in the publication of an article in a newspaper in the State of Texas.[1] The prosecution was under Article 186 of the Mexican Penal Code. That code provided that penal offences committed in a foreign country against a Mexican might be punished in Mexico. Our government maintained that it could not recognize the validity of a prosecution in Mexico of an American citizen who happened thereafter to be there, for an offense committed in the United States, merely because it was committed against a Mexican. In the course of the examination of this question, Mr. Moore, recognizing the principle already stated, said:

"The principle that a man who outside of a country wilfully puts in motion a force to take effect in it is answerable at the place where the evil is done, is recognized in the criminal jurisprudence of all countries. And the methods which modern invention has furnished for the performance of criminal acts in that manner has made this principle one of constantly growing importance and of increasing frequency of application.

"Its logical soundness and necessity received early recognition in the common law. Thus it was held that a man who erected a nuisance in one county which took effect in another was criminally liable in the county in which the injury was done. (Bulwer's case, 7 Co. 2 b. 3 b.; Com. Dig. Action, N. 3, 11.) So, if a man, being in one place, circulates a libel in another, he is answerable at the latter place. (Seven Bishops' Case, 12 State Trials, p. 331; Rex v. Johnson, 7 East. 65.)"

After referring to the doctrine of innocent agent and its dependence on the distinctions between accessories and principal in crime, Judge Moore says (p. 249):

"But, as has been shown, the doctrine of accessoryship has been abolished by statute in many jurisdictions in which it formerly prevailed,

---

[1] See above, p. 200.

and is condemned by many writers as unnecessary and unsound. Referring to accessories before the fact, Mr. Bishop says:

" 'The distinction between such accessory and a principal rests solely in authority, being without foundation either in natural reason or in the ordinary doctrines of the law. The general rule of the law is, that what one does through another's agency is to be regarded as done by himself.'

"And on this point he cites Broom's Legal Maxims, 2d ed., p. 643; Co. Lit. 258a; and the opinion of Hosmer, C. J., in Barkhamsted v. Parsons, 3 Conn. 1, that 'the principle of common law, *Qui facit per alium, facit per se,* is of universal application, both in criminal and civil cases.' "

The overt acts charged in the conspiracy to justify indictment under § 37 of the Criminal Code were acts within the jurisdiction of the United States, and the conspiracy charged, although some of the conspirators were corporeally on the high seas, had for its object crime in the United States and was carried on partly in and partly out of this country, and so was within its jurisdiction under the principles above settled. . . .

The judgment of conviction of the Court of Appeals is affirmed.

D. Special exemption of aliens from jurisdiction in non-Christian countries.

During the nineteenth century a system of "extraterritorial jurisdiction," which had earlier been established in Turkey and other Mohammedan countries, came to be extended to the non-Christian states of the Far East, in accordance with which the consuls of the "treaty powers" exercised both civil and criminal jurisdiction over the citizens of their respective countries. [In re Ross.]

IN RE ROSS, PETITIONER.

United States, Supreme Court, 1891.

140 U. S. 453. [35 L. ed. 581; 11 S. Ct. 897.]

Appeal from the Circuit Court of the United States for the Northern District of New York.

The petitioner below, the appellant here, is imprisoned in the penitentiary at Albany, in the state of New York. He was convicted on the 20th of May, 1880, in the American consular tribunal in Japan, of the crime of murder committed on board of an American ship in the harbor of Yokohama in that empire, and sentenced to death.

On the 6th of August following, his sentence was commuted by the President to imprisonment for life in the penitentiary at Albany, and to that place he was taken, and there he has ever since been confined. . . .

On the 9th of May, 1880, the appellant, John M. Ross, was one of the crew of the American ship Bullion, then in the waters of Japan, and lying at anchor in the harbor of Yokohama. On that day, on board of the ship, he assaulted Robert Kelly, its second mate, with a knife, inflicting in his neck a mortal wound, of which in a few minutes afterwards he died on the deck of the ship. Ross was at once arrested by direction of the master of the vessel and placed in irons, and on the same day he was taken ashore and confined in jail at Yokohama. On the following day, May 10th, the master filed with the American consul general at that place, Thomas B. Van Buren, a complaint against Ross, charging him with the murder of the mate. . . .

Previously to its being filed, the accused appeared with counsel before the consul general, and, the complaint being read to him, he presented an affidavit stating that he was a subject of Great Britain, a native of Prince Edward's Island, a dependency of the British empire. . . . Upon this affidavit he contended that the court was without jurisdiction over him, by reason of his being a subject of Great Britain, and he prayed that he be discharged. . . .

The court held that, as the accused was a seaman on an American vessel, he was subject to its jurisdiction, and overruled the objection. The counsel of the accused then moved that the charge against him be dismissed, on the ground that he could not be held for the offense except upon the presentment or indictment of a grand jury; but this motion was also overruled.

Four associates were drawn, as required by statute and the consular regulations, to sit with the consul general on the trial of the accused, and, being sworn to answer questions as to their eligibility, the accused stated that he had no questions to ask them on that subject. They were then sworn in to try the cause "in accordance with court regulations." A motion for a jury on the trial was also made, and denied. . . . The court found him guilty of murder, and he was sentenced to suffer death in such manner and at such time and place as the United States minister should direct. . . . The President subsequently directed the issue to the prisoner of a pardon on condition that he be imprisoned at hard labor for the term of his natural life in the penitentiary at Albany, and it was accepted by him on that condition. His sentence was accordingly commuted, and he was removed to the Albany penitentiary.

The Circuit Court, after hearing argument of counsel and full consideration of the subject, made an order on January 21, 1891, denying the motion of the prisoner for his discharge, and remanding him to the penitentiary, and the custody of its superintendent. 44 Fed. Rep. 185. From that order the case is brought here on appeal.

MR. JUSTICE FIELD . . . delivered the opinion of the court.

The Circuit Court did not refuse to discharge the petitioner upon any independent conclusion as to the validity of the legislation of Congress establishing the consular tribunal in Japan, and the trial of Americans for offenses committed within the territory of that country, without the indictment of a grand jury, and without a trial by a petit jury, but placed its decision upon the long and uniform acquiescence by the executive, administrative, and legislative departments of the government in the validity of the legislation. Nor did the Circuit Court consider whether the status of the petitioner as a citizen of the United States, or as an American within the meaning of the treaty with Japan, could be questioned, while he was a seaman of an American ship, under the protection of the American flag, but simply stated the view taken on that subject by the minister to Japan, the State Department, and the President. . . .

The practice of European governments to send officers to reside in foreign countries, authorized to exercise a limited jurisdiction over vessels and seamen of their country, to watch the interests of their countrymen, and to assist in adjusting their disputes and protecting their commerce, goes back to a very early period, even preceding what are termed the Middle Ages. During those ages these commercial magistrates, generally designated as consuls, possessed to some extent a representative character, sometimes discharging judicial and diplomatic functions. In other than Christian countries they were, by treaty stipulations, usually clothed with authority to hear complaints against their countrymen, and to sit in judgment upon them when charged with public offenses. After the rise of Islamism, and the spread of its followers over western Asia and other countries bordering on the Mediterranean, the exercise of this judicial authority became a matter of great concern. The intense hostility of the people of Moslem faith to all other sects, and particularly to Christians, affected all their intercourse, and all proceedings had in their tribunals. Even the rules of evidence adopted by them placed those of different faith on unequal grounds in any controversy with them. For this cause, and by reason of the barbarous and cruel punishments inflicted in those countries, and the frequent use of torture to enforce confession from parties accused, it was a matter of deep interest to Christian governments to withdraw the trial of their subjects, when charged with the commission of a public offense, from the arbitrary and despotic action of the local officials. Treaties conferring such jurisdiction upon these consuls were essential to the peaceful residence of Christians within those countries, and the successful prosecution of commerce with their people.

The treaty-making power vested in our government extends to all proper subjects of negotiation with foreign governments. It can, equally with any of the former or present governments of Europe, make treaties providing for the exercise of judicial authority in other countries by its officers appointed to reside therein.

We do not understand that any question is made by counsel as to its power in this respect. His objection is to the legislation by which such treaties are carried out, contending that, so far as crimes of a felonious character are concerned, the same protection and guaranty against an undue accusation or an unfair trial secured by the constitution to citizens of the United States at home should be enjoyed by them abroad. In none of the laws which have been passed by Congress to give effect to treaties of the kind has there been any attempt to require indictment by a grand jury before one can be called upon to answer for a public offense of that grade committed in those countries, or to secure a jury on the trial of the offense. Yet the laws on that subject have been passed without objection to their constitutionality. Indeed, objection on that ground was never raised in any quarter, so far as we are informed, until a recent period.

It is now, however, earnestly pressed, by counsel for the petitioner, but we do not think it tenable. By the Constitution a government is ordained and established "for the United States of America," and not for countries outside of their limits. The guaranties it affords against accusation of capital or infamous crimes, except by indictment or presentment by a grand jury, and for an impartial trial by a jury when thus accused, apply only to citizens and others within the United States, or who are brought there for trial for alleged offenses committed elsewhere, and not to residents or temporary sojourners abroad. Cook v. United States, 138 U. S. 157, 181. The Constitution can have no operation in another country. When, therefore, the representatives or officers of our government are permitted to exercise authority of any kind in another country, it must be on such conditions as the two countries may agree; the laws of neither one being obligatory upon the other. The deck of a private American vessel, it is true, is considered, for many purposes, constructively as territory of the United States; yet persons on board of such vessels, whether officers, sailors, or passengers, cannot invoke the protection of the provisions referred to until brought within the actual territorial boundaries of the United States. And, besides, their enforcement abroad in numerous places, where it would be highly important to have consuls invested with judicial authority, would be impracticable from the impossibility of obtaining a competent grand or petit jury. The requirement of such a body to accuse and to try an offender would, in a majority of cases, cause an abandonment of all prosecution. The framers of the Constitution, who were fully aware of the necessity of having judicial authority exercised by our consuls in non-Christian countries, if commercial intercourse was to be had with their people, never could have supposed that all the guaranties in the administration of the law upon criminals at home were to be transferred to such consular establishments, and applied before an American who had committed a felony there could be accused and tried. They must have known that such a requirement would defeat the main purpose of investing the consul with judicial authority. While, therefore, in one aspect the American accused of crime committed in those countries is deprived of the guaranties of the Constitution against unjust accusation and a partial trial, yet in another aspect he is the gainer, in being withdrawn from the procedure of their tribunals, often arbitrary and oppressive, and some times accompanied with extreme cruelty and torture. Letter of Mr. Cushing to Mr. Calhoun of September 29, 1844, accompanying President's message communicating abstract of treaty with China, Senate Doc. 58, 28th Cong. 2d Sess.; Letter on Judicial Extraterritorial Rights by Secretary Frelinghuysen to Chairman of Senate Committee on Foreign Relations of April 29, 1882, Senate Doc. 89, 47th Cong. 1st Sess.; Phillimore on Int. Law, vol. 2, part 7; Halleck on Int. Law, c. 41. . . .

The position that the petitioner, being a subject of Great Britain, was not within the jurisdiction of the consular court, is more plausible, but admits, we think, of a sufficient answer. The national character of the petitioner, for all the purposes of the consular jurisdiction, was determinable by his enlistment as one of the crew of the American ship Bullion. By such enlistment he became an American seaman,—one of an American crew on board of an American vessel,—and as such entitled to the protection and benefits of all the laws passed by Congress on behalf of American seamen, and subject to all their obligations and liabilities. Although his relations to the British government are not so changed that, after the expiration of his enlistment on board of the American ship, that government may not enforce his obligation of allegiance, and he, on the other hand, may not be entitled to invoke its protection as a British subject, that relation was changed during his service of seaman on board of the American ship under his enlistment. He could then insist upon treatment as an American seaman, and invoke for his protection all the power of the United States which could be called into exercise for the protection of seamen who were native born. He owes for that time to the country to which the ship on which he is serving belongs a temporary allegiance, and must be held to all its responsibilities. The question has been treated more as a political one for diplomatic adjustment than as a legal one to be determined by the judicial tribunals, and has been the subject of correspondence between our government and that of Great Britain. . . .

We are satisfied that the true rule of construction in the present case was adopted by the Department of State in the correspondence with the English government, and that the action of the consular tribunal in taking jurisdiction of the prisoner Ross, though an English subject, for the offense committed, was authorized. While he was an enlisted seaman on the American vessel, which floated the American flag, he was, within the meaning of the statute and the treaty, an American, under the protection and subject to the laws of the United States equally with the seaman who was native born. As an American seaman, he could have demanded a trial before the consular court as a matter of right, and must therefore be held subject to it as a matter of obligation.

We have not overlooked the objection repeatedly made and earnestly pressed by counsel, that the consular tribunal is a court of limited jurisdiction. It is undoubtedly a court of that character, limited by the treaty and the statutes passed to carry it into effect, and its jurisdiction cannot be extended beyond their legitimate meaning; but their construction is not, therefore, to be so restricted as to practically defeat the purposes to be accomplished by the treaty, but rather so as to give it full operation, in order that it may not be a vain and nugatory act.

It is true that the occasion for consular tribunals in Japan may hereafter be less than at present, as every year that country progresses in civilization, and in the assimilation of its system of judicial procedure to that of Christian countries, as well as in the improvement of its penal statutes; but the system of consular tribunals which have a general similarity in their main provisions is of the highest importance; and their establishment in other than Christian countries, where our people may desire to go in pursuit of commerce, will often be essential for the protection of their persons and property.

We have not considered the objection to the discharge of the prisoner on the ground that he accepted the conditional pardon of the President. If his conviction and sentence were void for want of jurisdiction in the consular tribunal, it may be doubtful whether he was estopped, by his acceptance of the pardon, from assailing their validity; but into that inquiry we need not go, for, the consular court having had jurisdiction to try and sentence him, there can be no question as to the binding force of the acceptance.

Order affirmed.[1]

---

[1] SUPPLEMENTARY CASES. In Dainese v. Hale, 91 U. S. 13 (1875), involving an action by Dainese to recover goods attached by order of Hale when the latter was acting as consul-general of the United States in Egypt, the Supreme Court held that while "the general fact that public ministers and consuls of Christian States in Turkey exercise jurisdiction in civil matters between their fellow-citizens or subjects might be assumed as sufficiently attested by the works on international law and the acts and instructions of our own government," yet the precise extent of that jurisdiction was unknown to the court, so that the defendant was called upon to amend his plea (that he was invested with judicial functions) and show the laws and usages of Turkey which permitted the jurisdiction at issue.

In Dainese v. United States, 15 Court of Claims 64 (1880), involving a claim by the plaintiff for extra pay in consequence of the performance, as vice-consul at Constantinople, of "judicial duties," the court held that the exercise of such duties by foreign consuls within the jurisdiction of the Ottoman Porte was so far a part of the customary law of nations as to imply their possible exercise by the plaintiff from the fact of appointment to the office. In this case, however, it was found that the plaintiff had not been duly invested with the office.

E.   Protection due to resident aliens.

In admitting aliens within its territory a state impliedly recognizes its obligation to give to them a degree of protection, in respect to their persons and their property, which is in general represented by the protection given by the state to its own citizens. [Mexico (re Galván) v. United States.]   When, however, the local standard of justice has been below that of the more advanced countries, claims have frequently been made on the basis of the higher standard which has been asserted to be the "international standard."   Query, what if a revolt should occur or revolution break out and the property of aliens, along with that of citizens, should be destroyed by the insurgents or revolutionists? [United States and Salvador: Claim of Rosa Gelbtrunk.] Would negligence on the part of the state in suppressing the revolt constitute ground for a claim on the part of a foreign state on behalf of its nationals? [United States and Great Britain: Home Missionary Society Case.] What if the property of the alien were injured as the result of military operations in time of war? [Great Britain and United States: Eastern Extension, Australasia and China Telegraph Company Case.]   In cases where contracts have been entered into between the state and aliens, would the fact that the alien had signed a clause, known in Latin America as the Calvo Clause, expressly waiving the right to appeal to his home government, operate to prevent his home government from taking up his case if it believed that justice had been denied him? [United States (Re North American Dredging Co.) v. Mexico.]

THE UNITED MEXICAN STATES ON BEHALF OF SALOMÉ LERMA VDA. DE GALVÁN, CLAIMANT, v. THE UNITED STATES OF AMERICA.

General Claims Commission, 1926.

Opinions of Commissioners under the Convention Concluded September 8, 1923, between the United States and Mexico, p. 408.

Nielsen, Commissioner:

1. Claim is made in this case in the amount of 50,000 pesos, by the United Mexican States, in behalf of Salomé Lerma de Galván, mother of Adolfo Pedro Galván, a Mexican citizen, who was killed in August, 1921, at Driscoll, Texas, by an American citizen named Hugh K. Kondall. The facts in the case as disclosed by the record may be briefly summarized.

2. Kondall and Galván were employed as foreman and laborer, respectively, in the construction of a bridge at a point about a half mile north of the depot at Driscoll. On the morning of August 25, 1921, Galván had a slight altercation with the son of Kondall who supplied

drinking water to the workmen. It appears that Kondall was angered when he learned of the episode and proceeded to his house where he probably procured a pistol. He thereupon returned to the place where Galván was working. There is evidence that the latter, when he knew that Kondall was armed with a pistol, proceeded with a raised hammer in his hand toward the spot where Kondall and another man were standing, and that Kondall thereupon twice shot Galván who died shortly thereafter.

3. Kondall was immediately taken into custody by the local authorities and charged with murder. On August 29, 1921, he was given a preliminary hearing before a justice of the peace at which several eye witnesses of the shooting were examined. The accused was required to give a bond in the amount of $25,000 for his appearance before the Criminal District Court of Nueces County, at its October, 1921, term. No indictment was returned against Kondall at that term of the court, but in the following March an indictment was found against him, charging him with the murder of Galván, and trial was set for April 20, 1922. Subsequently the accused was admitted to bail in the sum of $5,000.

4. Accompanying the American Answer is a copy of the criminal court docket in this case from which the following is an extract:

"April 7, 1922. Case set for Thursday April 13, 1922, 10 A. M. Venire of fifty ordered for that date and hour. Writ returnable Tuesday.

"April 17, 1922. Case continued by agreement.

"December 14, 1922. Continued by operation of law.

"4/30/23. Set for May 14. Special venire of 60 ordered.

"5/14/23. Set for May 21.

"5/22/23. Continued by agreement.

"11/12/23. Set for 11/21.

"6/5/24. Continued by operation of law.

"5/8/25. Set for May 20. Venire of 50 men.

"5/20/25. Continued illness of parties."

5. From additional evidence filed by the United States it is shown that the trial of Kondall was further continued at the instance of the State "because of a defaulting witness" and set for hearing at the term of court beginning on October 25, 1926, and still further continued at that term of court until April, 1927, on account of absence of material witnesses for the State.

6. The record contains an affidavit executed on November 24, 1925, by George C. Westervelt, District Attorney for the Counties of Nueces, Kleberg, Kenedy, Willacy and Cameron, Texas. It is stated in this affidavit that several subpoenas were issued for the appearance at the several terms of court of Louis F. Johnston, an eye witness to the shooting of Galván, and that the State could not safely and successfully go to trial without the production of this witness.

7. It is alleged in behalf of Mexico that there was an unnecessary delay in the prosecution of a person charged with a capital crime, and that under international law the United States should make compensation in satisfaction of a denial of justice. This case presents no difficulties. The question at issue is whether it reveals a failure of compliance with the general principle of international law requiring authorities to take proper measures to apprehend and punish a person who appears to be guilty of a crime against an alien. The Commission is bound to conclude that there was a clear failure on the part of the authorities of the state of Texas to act in conformity with this principle. There was no difficulty in the apprehension of Kondall, and a preliminary trial was promptly held. At this trial testimony was given from which it seems to be obvious that a grand jury could not properly fail to return an indictment for murder against Kondall. An indictment was found by a grand jury in March, 1922. After that it is plain that the authorities failed to take the proper steps to try the accused. There is no satisfactory explanation of continuances of the proceedings from time to time. Justification for the failure to bring the accused to justice cannot be found on the ground stated in the affidavit made by the District Attorney as late as November 24, 1925, that a certain eye witness had not been located. There is no reason to suppose that the legal machinery of the state of Texas is so defective that in a case in which a preliminary trial reveals that there were at least five eye witnesses to the shooting of Galván the authorities during a period of six years after the shooting found themselves unable to conduct a proper prosecution. If any such defect had existed it would not be an adequate defence to the claim presented by Mexico. If witnesses actually disappeared during the course of the long delay in the trial, then as argued by counsel for Mexico, that would be evidence of the evils incident to such delay. It may be observed that the argument in behalf of the United States appeared to be directed more to the question of the measure of damages than to a justification of the delay in the proceedings against the accused.

8. I am of the opinion that in the light of the principles underlying decisions rendered by the Commission in the past an award may properly be made in this case in the sum of $10,000.

VAN VOLLENHOVEN, Presiding Commissioner: I concur in Commissioner Nielsen's opinion.

FERNÁNDEZ MACGREGOR, Commissioner: I concur in Commissioner Nielsen's opinion.

Decision. The Commission decides that the Government of the United States of America shall pay to the Government of the United Mexican States in behalf of Salomé Lerma de Galván the sum of $10,000 (ten thousand dollars) without interest.

UNITED STATES AND SALVADOR:
CLAIM OF ROSA GELBTRUNK.

Arbitration under Special Agreement of March 1, 1902, submitting claim to Arbitration Tribunal constituted under Agreement of December 19, 1901.

U. S. Foreign Relations, 1902, pp. 874, 877.

Opinion of Sir HENRY STRONG:

In 1898 Maurice Gelbtrunk & Co., a partnership firm composed of Maurice Gelbtrunk and Isidore Gelbtrunk, both of whom were American citizens, were engaged in carrying on a mercantile business in the Central American Republic of Salvador.

In November, 1898, there was a revolution in Salvador and a revolutionary force occupied the city of Sensuntepeque, where a quantity of merchandise of the value (in silver) of $22,000 and upward, belonging to the firm of Gelbtrunk & Co., was stored. There is no dispute as to the value of these goods or as to the fact of their being the property of Gelbtrunk & Co. The soldiers of the revolutionary army possessed themselves of the goods—"looted" them, in short—and sold, appropriated, or destroyed them. It does not appear that this was done in carrying out the orders of any officer in authority or as an act of military necessity, but, so far as it appears, it was an act of lawless violence on the part of the soldiery. The firm of Maurice Gelbtrunk & Co. having assigned their claim against the Republic of Salvador to the present claimant, Rosa Gelbtrunk, the wife of Isidore Gelbtrunk, Mrs. Gelbtrunk (who, following the status as regards nationality of her husband, was also an American citizen) appealed to the Government of the United States to intervene on her behalf in claiming indemnity for the property lost. The Government did so intervene, and having failed to bring about a satisfactory settlement by diplomatic negotiation, it was agreed by the United States and Salvador to refer this claim to the arbitrators to whom another claim by the United States against Salvador had already been referred. The arbitrators in question were Hon. Don M. Dickinson, Don José Rosa Pacas, a citizen of Salvador, and myself. After having read the evidence and documents produced by the parties and heard the learned and able arguments of counsel, we came unanimously to the conclusion that the United States had failed to establish a right to indemnity on behalf of the claimant.

I now write this opinion, not on behalf of my brother arbitrators, but as stating exclusively my own personal reasons for the conclusion arrived at.

There is no dispute as to facts. It is admitted, or can not be denied, that the members of the firm of Gelbtrunk & Co. were American citizens; that the merchandise looted or destroyed in respect of which the claim is made was of the actual value stated; and, further, that it was stolen or destroyed by the soldiers as alleged. The only point for decision is that principally argued, namely, the right, upon established principles of international law, of the United States to reclaim indemnity for a loss accruing to its citizens upon the facts stated.

The principle which I hold to be applicable to the present case may be thus stated: A citizen or subject of one nation who, in the pursuit of commercial enterprise, carries on trade within the territory and under the protection of the sovereignty of a nation other than his own is to be considered as having cast in his lot with the subjects or citizens of the State in which he resides and carries on business. Whilst on the one hand he enjoys the protection of that State, so far as the police regulations and other advantages are concerned, on the other hand, he becomes liable to the political vicissitudes of the country in which he thus has a commercial domicile in the same manner as the subjects or citizens of that State are liable to the same. The State to which he owes national allegiance has no right to claim for him as against the nation in which he is resident any other or different treatment in case of loss by war—either foreign or civil—revolution, insurrection, or other internal disturbance caused by organized military force or by soldiers, than that which the latter country metes out to its own subjects or citizens.

This I conceive to be now the well-established doctrine of international law. The authorities on which it has been so established consist of the writings of publicists and diplomats, the decisions of arbitrators —especially those of mixed commissions—and the text of writers on international law. Without proposing to present an exhaustive array of authorities, I may refer to some of these. . . .

These citations might be largely added to, but those already made are sufficient to show that the rule that aliens share the fortunes of citizens in case of loss by military force or by the irregular acts of soldiers in a civil war is firmly established.

It is, however, not to be assumed that this rule would apply in a case of mob violence which might, if due diligence had been used, have been prevented by civil authorities alone or by such authorities aided by an available military force. In such case of spoliation by a mob, especially where the disorder has arisen in hostility to foreigners, a different rule may prevail. It would, however, be irrelevant to the present case now to discuss such a question. It therefore appears that all we have to do now is to inquire whether citizens of the United States, in the matter of losses incurred by military force or by the irregular acts of the soldiery in the revolution of November, 1898, in Salvador, were treated less favorably or otherwise than the citizens of Salvador.

To this inquiry there can be but one answer: They were not in any way discriminated against, for the legislature of the Republic in providing indemnity for such losses applied the same as well to foreigners as to the citizens of Salvador.

For these reasons I am of opinion that we have no alternative but to reject this claim.

[The other arbitrators concurred.]

UNITED STATES AND GREAT BRITAIN: HOME MISSIONARY SOCIETY CASE.

Claims Arbitration under the Special Agreement of August 18, 1910. 1920.

Nielsen's Report, pp. 421, 423.

Arbitrators: HENRI FROMAGEOT, SIR CHARLES FITZPATRICK, CHANDLER P. ANDERSON.

This is a claim for $78,068.15, together with interest thereon from May 30, 1898, presented by the United States Government on behalf of an American religious body known as the "Home Frontier and Foreign Missionary Society of the United Brethren in Christ." The claim is in respect of losses and damages sustained by that body and some of its members during a native rebellion in 1898 in the British Protectorate of Sierra Leone.

The facts are few and simple.

In 1898 the collection of a tax newly imposed on the natives of the Protectorate and known as the "hut tax" was the signal for a serious and widespread revolt in the Ronietta District. The revolt broke out on April 27, and lasted for several days. As is common in the more uncivilized parts of Africa it was marked by every circumstance of cruelty and by undiscriminating attacks on the persons and properties of all Europeans.

In the Ronietta District, which was the centre of the rebellion, the Home Missionary Society had several establishments—the Bompeh Mission at Rotofunk and Tiama, Sherbro-Mendi Mission at Shengeh, Avery Mission at Avery, and Imperreh Mission at Danville and Momaligli.

In the course of the rebellion all these missions were attacked, and either destroyed or damaged, and some of the missionaries were murdered.

The rising was quickly suppressed, and law and order enforced with firmness and promptitude. In September, October, and November such of the guilty natives as could be caught were prosecuted and punished. (British Answer, Annexes 15, 16 and 17.)

A Royal Commissioner was appointed by the British Government to inquire into the circumstances of the insurrection and into the general position of affairs in the Colony and Protectorate.

On the receipt of his report, as well as of one from the Colonial Governor, the Secretary of State for the Colonies came to the conclusion that though some mistakes might have been made in its execution, the line of policy pursued was right in its main outlines and that the scheme of administration, as revised in the light of experience, would prove a valuable instrument for the peaceful development of the Protectorate and the civilization and well being of its inhabitants. (British Blue Book, Sierra Leone, C. 9388 and 1899, part 1, p. 175.)

On February 21, 1899, the United States Government (British Answer, Annex 39), through its Embassy in London, brought the fact of the losses sustained by the Home Missionary Society to the attention of the British Government. In his reply on October 14, 1899, Lord Salisbury repudiated liability on behalf of the British Government with an expression of regret that sensible as it was of the worth of the services of the American missionaries, there was no fund from which, as an act of grace, compensation could be awarded.

The contention of the United States Government before this Tribunal is that the revolt was the result of the imposition and attempted collection of the "hut tax"; that it was within the knowledge of the British Government that this tax was the object of deep native resentment; that in the face of the native danger the British Government wholly failed to take proper steps for the maintenance of order and the protection of life and property; that the loss of life and damage to property was the result of this neglect and failure of duty, and therefore that it is liable to pay compensation.

Now, even assuming that the "hut tax" was the effective cause of the native rebellion, it was in itself a fiscal measure in accordance not only with general usage in colonial administration, but also with the usual practice in African countries. (Wallis, "Advance of Our West African Empire," p. 40.)

It was a measure to which the British Government was perfectly entitled to resort in the legitimate exercise of its sovereignty, if it was required. Its adoption was determined by the course of its policy and system of administration. Of these requirements it alone could judge.

Further, though it may be true that some difficulty might have been foreseen, there was nothing to suggest that it would be more serious than is usual and inevitable in a semi-barbarous and only partially colonized protectorate, and certainly nothing to lead to any apprehension of widespread revolt.

It is a well-established principle of international law that no government can be held responsible for the act of rebellious bodies of men committed in violation of its authority, where it is itself guilty of no breach of good faith, or of no negligence in suppressing insurrection. (Moore's International Law Digest, Vol. VI, p. 956; VII, p. 957; Moore's Arbitrations, pp. 2991–92; British Answer, p. 1.)

The good faith of the British Government can not be questioned, and as to the conditions prevailing in the Protectorate there is no evidence to support the contention that it failed in its duty to afford adequate protection for life and property. As has been said with reference to circumstances very similar, "It would be almost impossible for any government to prevent such acts of omnipresence by its forces." (Sir Edward Thornton, Moore's Arbitrations, pp. 3–38.)

It is true that the Royal Commissioner criticized in his report the mode of application of certain measures. But there is no evidence of any criticisms directed at the police organization, or the measures taken for the protection of Europeans. On the contrary, it is clear that from the outbreak of the insurrection the British Authorities took every measure available for its repression. Despite heavy losses, the troops in the area of revolt were continually increased. But communication was difficult; the risings occurred simultaneously in many districts remote from one another and from any common centre; and it was impossible at a few days' or a few hours' notice to afford full protection to the building and properties in every isolated and distant village. It is impossible to judge the system of police and protection of life and property in force in the savage regions of Africa by the standard of countries or cities which enjoy the social order, the respect for authority, and the settled administration of a high civilization. A government can not be held liable as the insurer of lives and property under the circumstances presented in this case. (See Wipperman Case, Ralston's International Law and Procedure, No. 491, p. 231.)

No lack of promptitude or courage is alleged against the British troops. On the contrary the evidence of eye-witnesses proves that under peculiarly difficult and trying conditions they did their duty with loyalty and daring, and upheld the highest traditions of the British army.

Finally it is obvious that the Missionary Society must have been aware of the difficulties and perils to which it exposes itself in its task of carrying Christianity to so remote and barbarous a people. The contempt for difficulty and peril is one of the noblest sides of their missionary zeal. Indeed, it explains why they are able to succeed in fields which mere commercial enterprise cannot be expected to enter.

For these reasons, the Tribunal is of opinion that the claim presented by the United States Government on behalf of the Home Missionary Society has no foundation in law and must be dismissed.

But if His Brittanic Majesty's Government in consideration of the service which the Home Missionary Society has rendered and is still rendering in the peaceful development of the Protectorate and the civilization of its inhabitants, and of the support its activities deserve, can avail itself of any fund from which to repair as far as possible

the losses sustained in the native revolt, it would be an act of grace
which this Tribunal cannot refrain from recommending warmly to the
generosity of that Government.

For these reasons and subject to this recommendation,

The Tribunal decides that this claim must be dismissed.

GREAT BRITAIN AND UNITED STATES: EASTERN EXTENSION, AUSTRALASIA & CHINA TELEGRAPH COMPANY CASE.

Claims Arbitration under the Agreement of August 18, 1910. 1923.

Nielsen's Report, pp. 40, 73.

Arbitrators: HENRI FROMAGEOT, EDWARD A. MITCHELL INNES, ROBERT
E. OLDS.

This is a claim presented by His Britannic Majesty's Government on
behalf of the Eastern Extension, Australasia and China Telegraph Company, Limited, a British corporation, for a sum of £912 5s. 6d., being
the amount which this company had to expend upon the repair of the
Manila-Hong Kong and the Manila-Capiz submarine telegraph cables
which had been cut by the United States naval authorities during the
Spanish-American war in 1898.

The facts are as follows:

Under concessions granted by the Spanish Government and dated,
respectively, December 14, 1878, and April 14, 1897, the Eastern Extension Company had laid down certain submarine telegraph cables connecting Manila and Hong Kong and Manila and Capiz, which the Company was operating in 1898.

In April, 1898, war broke out between the United States and Spain,
and on May 1, 1898, the United States naval forces, under the command of Commodore, afterwards Admiral, Dewey, entered Manila Bay
and destroyed or captured the Spanish warships lying in that harbour.
On the same day (United States Answer, p. 14, Exhibit 5) Commodore
Dewey, through the British consul at Manila, proposed to the Spanish
Captain General that both the United States and the Spanish authorities should be allowed to transmit messages by cable to Hong Kong.
That proposition having been refused, on the morning of the following
day, viz., on May 2, 1898, the Manila-Hong Kong cable was cut by
order of the American Commodore, this cutting being effected within
Manila Bay and consequently within the territorial waters of the
enemy.

On May 10 the Company, acting on a formal order of the Spanish
Government under the provisions of the concession above referred to,
sealed the end of the cable at Hong Kong, thereby preventing any use

of the cable by the United States forces. Subsequently, the United States Navy Department proposed to the Company to re-establish cable communication between Manila and Hong Kong, and the Company refused, informing the American Navy Department that the Company was under the orders of the Spanish Government and that the transmission of messages from the Philippine Islands to Hong Kong had been prohibited by that Government (United States Answer, p. 12, Exhibit 2). Furthermore, as appears from the oral argument on behalf of His Brittanic Majesty's Government (Notes of the 11th Sitting, p. 251), the British Government themselves, acting in the interest of shipping, subsequently asked the Madrid Government if they would consent to the reopening of the cables; but the Spanish Government refused to accede to this request, except on terms which the United States could not accept.

On May 23 the Manila-Capiz cable was cut, also inside Manila Bay.

These facts are not contested; and further it is admitted on behalf of Great Britain that the severance of the cable between Manila and Hong Kong, as well as between Manila and Capiz, was a proper military measure on the part of the United States, taken with the important object of interrupting communication whether with other parts of the Spanish possessions in the Philippine Islands or with the Spanish Government and the outside world.

The question is whether or not the United States Government is bound to pay to the Company, as damages, the cost incurred by the Company in repairing the cables.

The British Government admits that there was not in existence in 1898 any treaty or any rule of international law imposing on the United States the legal obligation to pay compensation for the cutting of these cables; but they contend that, under article 7 of the Special Agreement establishing this Tribunal, such compensation may be awarded on the ground of equity, and that the United States Government, having paid compensation to some other foreign cable company for similar cuttings during the same war, is, therefore, legally bound to compensate the British company, and, finally, that in the absence of any rule of international law on the point, it is within the powers, if it be not the duty, of this Tribunal to lay down such a rule.

The United States Government contends that the cutting of the cables by its naval authorities was a necessity of war giving rise to no obligation to make compensation therefor; that the United States were entitled to treat the said cables as having the character of enemy property, on the ground that their terminals were within enemy territory and under the control of the enemy's military authorities, and that the sealing of the terminal at Hong Kong, on neutral territory, was a hostile act of itself impressing this cable with enemy character. Further, the United States Government contends that there is no rule of international law imposing any legal liability on the United States, but that, on the contrary, the action of the United States naval authorities and the refusal to pay compensation are justified by international law and that the United States Government is not bound to pay compensation to the British Company merely because more favourable treatment was meted out to another foreign company, the facts underlying whose claim were, in any case, different. Further, the United States Government say that it is not the duty, nor within the power, of this Tribunal to lay down any new rule of international law, but only to construe and apply such rules or principles as existed at the time of the cutting of these cables.

It may be said that article 15 of the International Convention for the Protection of Submarine Cables of 1884, enunciating the principle of the freedom of Governments in time of war, had thereby recognised that there was no special limitation, by way of obligatory compensation or otherwise, to their right of dealing with submarine cables in time of war. In our opinion, however, even assuming that there was in 1898 no treaty and no specific rule of international law formulated as the expression of a universally recognised rule governing the case of the cutting of cables by belligerents, it can not be said that there is no principle of international law applicable. International law, as well as domestic law, may not contain, and generally does not contain, express rules decisive of particular cases; but the function of jurisprudence is to resolve the conflict of opposing rights and interests by applying, in default of any specific provision of law, the corollaries of general principles, and so to find—exactly as in the mathematical sciences—the solution of the problem. This is the method of jurisprudence; it is the method by which the law has been gradually evolved in every country resulting in the definition and settlement of legal relations as well between States as between private individuals.

Now, it is almost unnecessary to recall that principle of international law which recognises that the legitimate object of sea warfare is to deprive the enemy of those means of communication, which the high seas, in their character as "res nullius" or "res communis" afford to every nation. The user by the enemy of that communication by sea, every belligerent, if he can, is entitled to prevent, subject to a due respect for innocent neutral trade; he is even entitled to prevent its user by neutrals, who use it to afford assistance to the enemy either by carrying contraband, by communicating with blockaded coasts, or by transporting hostile despatches, troops, enemy agents, and so on. In such cases the neutrals do not, properly speaking, lose their neutral character; but their action itself loses that character, such action being, as it is said, impressed with a hostile character. Thus it may be said that a belligerent's principal object in maritime warfare is to deprive the enemy of communication over the high seas while preserving it unimpeded for himself.

It is difficult to contend in the same breath that a belligerent is justified by international law in depriving the enemy of the benefit of the freedom of the high seas, but is not justified in depriving him of the use of the seas by means of telegraphic cables.

Not only does the cutting of cables appear not to be prohibited by the rules of international law applicable to sea warfare, but such action may be said to be implicitly justified by that right of legitimate defense which forms the basis of the rights of any belligerent nation.

It is contended, however, that the cutting, however legitimate, may create an obligation to compensate the neutral owner of the cable; and various instances are, or may be, given of legitimate acts which, it is said, do create such an obligation. We do not think that the instances given furnish a just analogy. In those instances, the right is not absolute but limited, and is in reality only itself acquired in consideration of the payment of compensation, and has no existence as a right apart from the obligation to make compensation. Such is the case in respect of requisition, either for the purpose of ownership or user, of expropriations, or, to take a case from maritime law, of the exercise of the right of angary.

As to the contention that, having regard to the terms of article 7 of the Special Agreement providing for the settlement of these claims, this Tribunal is to decide "in accordance with treaty rights and with the principles of international law and of equity," compensation in this case should be paid on the ground of equity, the following observations may be made:

If the strict application of a treaty or of a specific rule of international law conduct to a decision which, however, justified from a strictly legal point of view, will result in hardship, unjustified having regard to the special circumstances of the case, then it is the duty of this Tribunal to do their best to avoid such a result, so far as it may be possible, by recommending for instance some course of action by way of grace on the part of the respondent Government.

In this case it is to be observed that the Eastern Extension Company was well aware of its own risk in Spanish territory. As has been shown, their concessions expressly provided for it. The various advantages, privileges, exemptions, and subsidies accorded them by the Spanish Government, form the consideration in exchange for which the Company assumed the risk of being treated in time of war as a Spanish public service with all the consequences which that position implied.

In the opinion of this Tribunal, there is no ground of equity, upon which the United States should be adjudged to pay compensation for the materialization of this risk in the form of an act of war the legitimacy of which is admitted.

The British Government contend that, as a matter of right, the Eastern Extension Company is entitled to receive compensation because some other foreign cable company, viz., La Compagnie française des Câbles télégraphiques, working cables between the United States of America, Haiti, and Cuba, received from the United States Government compensation for the cutting of its cables. It is urged that, when acts of war by a belligerent have resulted in personal injury to individuals in certain territory or in damage to their property in that territory, if the Government of that territory pays the claims of the nationals of one country, it must also pay the claims of the nationals of other countries without discrimination (Oral Argument, pp. 261 and 262); and further, as the argument would seem to imply (Oral Argument, p. 264), that, if it be established that a Government has paid compensation to its own citizens, then it is bound to pay compensation to foreigners whose person or property was damaged; and authority is said to be found for the last proposition in cases arising out of the Mexican insurrection.

Whether viewed as a general principle, or in its particular application to the facts of this claim, such a proposition appears to us to be impossible of acceptance. It is perfectly legitimate for a Government, in the absence of any special agreement to the contrary, to afford to subjects of any particular Government treatment which is refused to the subjects of other Governments, or to reserve to its own subjects treatment which is not afforded to foreigners. Some political motive, some service rendered, some traditional bond of friendship, some reciprocal treatment in the past or in the present, may furnish the ground for discrimination. . . .

As to the contention of the British Government that, in the absence of any rule governing the matter of cable cutting, it is the duty of this Tribunal to frame a new rule, we desire to say:

First, the duty of this Tribunal, in our opinion, under article 7 of the Special Agreement, is not to lay down new rules. Such rules could not have retroactive effect, nor could they be considered as being anything more than a personal expression of opinion by members of a particular tribunal, deriving its authority from only two Governments;

Secondly, in any case this Tribunal, as has been already stated, is of opinion that the principles of international law, applicable to maritime warfare, existing in 1898, are sufficient to enable us to decide this case.

Now therefore:

The Tribunal decides that the claim of His Britannic Majesty's Government be disallowed. . . .

THE UNITED STATES OF AMERICA ON BEHALF OF NORTH AMERICAN DREDGING COMPANY OF TEXAS, CLAIMANT, v. THE UNITED MEXICAN STATES.

General Claims Commission, 1926.

Opinions of Commissioners under the Convention Concluded September 8, 1923, between the United States and Mexico, p. 21.

[By the Commission: C. VAN VOLLENHOVEN, Presiding Commissioner, and G. FERNANDEZ MACGREGOR, Commissioner.]

This case is before this Commission on a motion of the Mexican Agent to dismiss. It is put forward by the United States of America on behalf of North American Dredging Company of Texas, an American corporation, for the recovery of the sum of $233,523.30 with interest thereon, the amount of losses and damages alleged to have been suffered by claimant for breaches of a contract for dredging at the port of Salina Cruz, which contract was entered into between the claimant and the Government of Mexico November 23, 1912. The contract was signed at Mexico City. The Government of Mexico was a party to it. It had for its subject matter services to be rendered by the claimant in Mexico. Payment therefor was to be made in Mexico. Article 18, incorporated by Mexico as an indispensable provision, not separable from the other provisions of the contract, was subscribed to by the claimant for the purpose of securing the award of the contract. Its translation by the Mexican Agent reads as follows:

"The contractor and all persons who, as employees or in any other capacity, may be engaged in the execution of the work under this contract either directly or indirectly, shall be considered as Mexicans in all matters, within the Republic of Mexico, concerning the execution of such work and the fulfillment of this contract. They shall not claim, nor shall they have, with regard to the interests and the business connected with this contract, any other rights or means to enforce the same than those granted by the laws of the Republic to Mexicans, nor shall they enjoy any other rights than those established in favor of Mexicans. They are consequently deprived of any rights as aliens, and under no conditions shall the intervention of foreign diplomatic agents be permitted, in any matter related to this contract."

1. The jurisdiction of the Commission is challenged in this case on the grounds (first) that claims based on an alleged nonperformance of contract obligations are outside the jurisdiction of this Commission and (second) that a contract containing the so-called Calvo clause deprives the party subscribing said clause of the right to submit any claims connected with his contract to an international commission.

2. The Commission, in its decision this day rendered on the Mexican motion to dismiss the Illinois Central Railroad Company case, Docket No. 432 [See page 15], has stated the reasons why it deems contractual

claims to fall within its jurisdiction. It is superfluous to repeat them. The first ground of the motion is therefore rejected.

The Calvo clause.

3. The Commission is fully sensible of the importance of any judicial decision either sustaining in whole or in part, or rejecting in whole or in part, or construing the so-called "Calvo clause" in contracts between nations and aliens. It appreciates the legitimate desire on the part of nations to deal with persons and property within their respective jurisdictions according to their own laws and to apply remedies provided by their own authorities and tribunals, which laws and remedies in no wise restrict or limit their international obligations, or restrict or limit or in any wise impinge upon the correlative rights of other nations protected under rules of international law. The problem presented in this case is whether such legitimate desire may be accomplished through appropriate and carefully phrased contracts; what form such a contract may take; what is its scope and its limitations; and does clause 18 of the contract involved in this case fall within the field where the parties are free to contract without violating any rule of international law?

4. The Commission does not feel impressed by arguments either in favor of or in opposition to the Calvo clause, in so far as these arguments go to extremes. The Calvo clause is neither upheld by all outstanding international authorities and by the soundest among international awards nor is it universally rejected. The Calvo clause in a specific contract is neither a clause which must be sustained to its full length because of its contractual nature nor can it be discretionarily separated from the rest of the contract as if it were just an accidental postscript. The problem is not solved by saying yes or no; the affirmative answer exposing the rights of foreigners to undeniable dangers, the negative answer leaving to the nations involved no alternative except that of exclusion of foreigners from business. The present stage of international law imposes upon every international tribunal the solemn duty of seeking for a proper and adequate balance between the sovereign right of national jurisdiction, on the one hand, and the sovereign right of national protection of citizens on the other. No international tribunal should or may evade the task of finding such limitations of both rights as will render them compatible within the general rules and principles of international law. By merely ignoring world-wide abuses either of the right of national protection or of the right of national jurisdiction no solution compatible with the requirements of modern international law can be reached.

5. At the very outset the Commission rejects as unsound a presentation of the problem according to which if article 18 of the present contract were upheld Mexico or any other nation might lawfully bind all

foreigners by contract to relinquish all rights of protection by their
governments.   It is quite possible to recognize as valid some forms of
waiving the right of foreign protection without thereby recognizing as
valid and lawful every form of doing so.

6. The Commission also denies that the rules of international public
law apply only to nations and that individuals can not under any
circumstances have a personal standing under it.   . . .

7. It is well known how largely the increase of civilization, intercourse, and interdependence as between nations has influenced and mod-
erated the exaggerated conception of national sovereignty.   As civilization has progressed individualism has increased; and so has the right
of the individual citizen to decide upon the ties between himself and
his native country.   There was a time when governments and not individuals decided if a man was allowed to change his nationality or
his residence, and when even if he had changed either of them his
government sought to lay burdens on him for having done so.   To
acknowledge that under the existing laws of progressive, enlightened
civilization a person may voluntarily expatriate himself but that short
of expatriation he may not by contract, in what he conceives to be his
own interest, to any extent loosen the ties which bind him to his country
is neither consistent with the facts of modern international intercourse
nor with corresponding developments in the field of international law
and does not tend to promote good will among nations.

Lawfulness of the Calvo clause.

8.   The contested provision, in this case, is part of a contract and
must be upheld unless it be repugnant to a recognized rule of international law.   What must be established is not that the Calvo clause
is universally accepted or universally recognized, but that there exists
a generally accepted rule of international law condemning the Calvo
clause and denying to an individual the right to relinquish to any
extent, large or small, and under any circumstances or conditions, the
protection of the government to which he owes allegiance.[1] . . .   It is as
little doubtful nowadays as it was in the day of the Geneva Arbitration that international law is paramount to decrees of nations and to
municipal law; but the task before this Commission precisely is to

---

[1] The commission here refers to an alleged parallel between the Calvo clause
and a statute of the State of Arkansas providing for the revocation of a license
to do business within the state in case a foreign corporation, so licensed, should
resort to the Federal courts in the event of a suit brought against it or by it.
In Terral v. Burke Construction Co., 257 U. S. 529 (1922) the Supreme Court
held the statute to be in violation of the constitutional right of the citizens of
one state to resort to Federal courts in another state.   The commission here
sees no parallel between the two cases unless there can be established a generally
accepted rule of international law condemning the Calvo clause.

ascertain whether international law really contains a rule prohibiting contract provisions attempting to accomplish the purpose of the Calvo clause.

9. The commission does not hesitate to declare that there exists no international rule prohibiting the sovereign right of a nation to protect its citizens abroad from being subject to any limitation whatsoever under any circumstances. The right of protection has been limited by treaties between nations in provisions related to the Calvo clause. While it is true that Latin-American countries—which are important members of the family of nations and which have played for many years an important and honorable part in the development of international law— are parties to most of these treaties, still such countries as France, Germany, Great Britain, Sweden, Norway, and Belgium, and in one case at least even the United States of America (Treaty between the United States and Peru dated September 6, 1870, Volume 2, Malloy's United States Treaties, at page 1426; article 37) have been parties to treaties containing such provisions.

10. What Mexico has asked of the North American Dredging Company of Texas as a condition for awarding it the contract which it sought is, "If all of the means of enforcing your rights under this contract afforded by Mexican law, even against the Mexican Government itself, are wide open to you, as they are wide open to our own citizens, will you promise not to ignore them and not to call directly upon your own Government to intervene in your behalf in connection with any controversy, small or large, but seek redress under the laws of Mexico through the authorities and tribunals furnished by Mexico for your protection?" and the claimant, by subscribing to this contract and seeking the benefits which were to accrue to him thereunder, has answered, "I promise."

11. Under the rules of international law may an alien lawfully make such a promise? The Commission holds that he may, but at the same time holds that he can not deprive the government of his nation of its undoubted right of applying international remedies to violations of international law committed to his damage. Such government frequently has a larger interest in maintaining the principles of international law than in recovering damage for one of its citizens in a particular case, and manifestly such citizen can not by contract tie in this respect the hands of his government. But while any attempt to so bind his government is void, the Commission has not found any generally recognized rule of positive international law which would give to his government the right to intervene to strike down a lawful contract, in the terms set forth in the preceding paragraph 10, entered into by its citizen. The obvious purpose of such a contract is to prevent abuses of the right to protection, not to destroy the right itself— abuses which are intolerable to any self-respecting nation and are pro-

lific breeders of international friction. The purpose of such a contract is to draw a reasonable and practical line between Mexico's sovereign right of jurisdiction within its own territory, on the one hand, and the sovereign right of protection of the government of an alien whose person or property is within such territory, on the other hand. Unless such line is drawn and if these two coexisting rights are permitted constantly to overlap, continual friction is inevitable.

12. It being impossible to prove the illegality of the said provision, under the limitations indicated, by adducing generally recognized rules of positive international law, it apparently can only be contested by invoking its incongruity to the law of nature (natural rights) and its inconsistency with inalienable, indestructible, unprescriptible, uncurtailable rights of nations. The law of nature may have been helpful, some three centuries ago, to build up a new law of nations, and the conception of inalienable rights of men and nations may have exercised a salutary influence, some one hundred and fifty years ago, on the development of modern democracy on both sides of the ocean; but they have failed as a durable foundation of either municipal or international law and can not be used in the present day as substitutes for positive municipal law, on the one hand, and for positive international law, as recognized by nations and governments through their acts and statements, on the other hand. Inalienable rights have been the cornerstones of policies like those of the Holy Alliance and of Lord Palmerston; instead of bringing to the world the benefit of mutual understanding, they are to weak or less fortunate nations an unrestrained menace.

Interpretation of the Calvo clause in the present contract.

13. What is the true meaning of article 18 of the present contract? It is essential to state that the closing words of the article should be combined so as to read: "being deprived, in consequence, of any rights as aliens in any matter connected with this contract, and without the intervention of foreign diplomatic agents being in any case permissible in any matter connected with this contract." Both the commas and the phrasing show that the words "in any matter connected with this contract" are a limitation on either of the two statements contained in the closing words of the article.

14. Reading this article as a whole, it is evident that its purpose was to bind the claimant to be governed by the laws of Mexico and to use the remedies existing under such laws. The closing words "in any matter connected with this contract" must be read in connection with the preceding phrase "in everything connected with the execution of such work and the fulfillment of this contract" and also in connection with the phrase "regarding the interests or business connected with this contract." In other words, in executing the contract, in fulfilling the contract, or in putting forth any claim "regarding the interests or

business connected with this contract,'' the claimant should be governed by those laws and remedies which Mexico had provided for the protection of its own citizens. But this provision did not, and could not, deprive the claimant of his American citizenship and all that that implies. It did not take from him his undoubted right to apply to his own Government for protection if his resort to the Mexican tribunals or other authorities available to him resulted in a denial or delay of justice as that term is used in international law. In such a case the claimant's complaint would be not that his contract was violated but that he had been denied justice. The basis of his appeal would be not a construction of his contract, save perchance in an incidental way, but rather an internationally illegal act.

15. What, therefore, are the rights which claimant waived and those which he did not waive in subscribing to article 18 of the contract? (a) He waived his right to conduct himself as if no competent authorities existed in Mexico; as if he were engaged in fulfilling a contract in an inferior country subject to a system of capitulations; and as if the only real remedies available to him in the fulfillment, construction, and enforcement of this contract were international remedies. All these he waived and had a right to waive. (b) He did not waive any right which he possessed as an American citizen as to any matter not connected with the fulfillment, execution, or enforcement of this contract as such. (c) He did not waive his undoubted right as an American citizen to apply to his Government for protection against the violation of international law (internationally illegal acts) whether growing out of this contract or out of other situations. (d) He did not and could not affect the right of his Government to extend to him its protection in general or to extend to him its protection against breaches of international law. But he did frankly and unreservedly agree that in consideration of the Government of Mexico awarding him this contract, he did not need and would not invoke or accept the assistance of his Government with respect to the fulfillment and interpretation of his contract and the execution of his work thereunder. The conception that a citizen in doing so impinges upon a sovereign, inalienable, unlimited right of his government belongs to those ages and countries which prohibited the giving up of his citizenship by a citizen or allowed him to relinquish it only with the special permission of his government. . . .

The Calvo clause and the claimant.

18. If it were necessary to demonstrate how legitimate are the fears of certain nations with respect to abuses of the right of protection and how seriously the sovereignty of those nations within their own boundaries would be impaired if some extreme conceptions of this right were recognized and enforced, the present case would furnish an illuminating example. The claimant, after having solemnly promised in writing that

it would not ignore the local laws, remedies, and authorities, behaved from the very beginning as if article 18 of its contract had no existence in fact. It used the article to procure the contract, but this was the extent of its use. It has never sought any redress by application to the local authorities and remedies which article 18 liberally granted it and which, according to Mexican law, are available to it, even against the Government, without restrictions, both in matter of civil and of public law. It has gone so far as to declare itself freed from its contract obligations by its *ipse dixit* instead of having resort to the local tribunals to construe its contract and its rights thereunder. And it has gone so far as to declare that it was not bound by article 7 of the contract and to forcibly remove a dredge to which, under that article, the Government of Mexico considered itself entitled as security for the proper fulfillment of its contract with claimant. While its behavior during the spring and summer of 1914, the latter part of the Huerta administration, may be in part explained by the unhappy conditions of friction then existing between the two countries in connection with the military occupation of Veracruz by the United States, this explanation can not be extended from the year 1917 to the date of the filing of its claim before this Commission, during all of which time it has ignored the open doors of Mexican tribunals. The record before this Commission strongly suggests that the claimant used article 18 to procure the contract with no intention of ever observing its provisions. . . .

Extent of the present interpretation of the Calvo clause.

22. Manifestly it is impossible for this Commission to announce an all-embracing formula to determine the validity or invalidity of all clauses partaking of the nature of the Calvo clause, which may be found in contracts, decrees, statutes, or constitutions, and under widely varying conditions. Whenever such a provision is so phrased as to seek to preclude a Government from intervening, diplomatically or otherwise, to protect its citizen whose rights of any nature have been invaded by another Government in violation of the rules and principles of international law, the Commission will have no hesitation in pronouncing the provision void. . . .

23. Even so, each case involving application of a valid clause partaking of the nature of the Calvo clause will be considered and decided on its merits. Where a claim is based on an alleged violation of any rule or principle of international law, the Commission will take jurisdiction notwithstanding the existence of such a clause in a contract subscribed by such claimant. But where a claimant has expressly agreed in writing, attested by his signature, that in all matters pertaining to the execution, fulfillment, and interpretation of the contract he will have resort to local tribunals, remedies, and authorities, and then wil-

fully ignores them by applying in such matters to his Government, he will be held bound by his contract and the Commission will not take jurisdiction of such claim. . . .

Decision.

25. The Commission decides that the case as presented is not within its jurisdiction and the motion of the Mexican Agent to dismiss it is sustained and the case is hereby dismissed without prejudice to the claimant to pursue his remedies elsewhere or to seek remedies before this Commission for claims arising after the signing of the Treaty of September 8, 1923.[1]

---

[1] Supplementary Cases. Compare the "El Triunfo Company" case [Salvador Commercial Co. v. Salvador], U. S. Foreign Relations, 1902, pp. 838 ff., in which the United States obtained damages from Salvador for the cancellation of a franchise and the resulting destruction of a concession given to a Salvador corporation whose stockholders were American citizens. Compare also the Delagoa Bay Railway case, Moore, Int. Arbitrations, II, 1865 ff., in which the United States obtained damages on behalf of one of its citizens for the seizure by the Portuguese government of a railway built under a concession.

In the Sambiaggio case between Italy and Venezuela, arbitrated under the Protocol of 1903 (Ralston, Venezuelan Arbitrations of 1903, p. 679), involving a claim by Sambiaggio, an Italian citizen resident in Venezuela, for losses sustained at the hands of Venezuelan revolutionists who failed of success, the arbitrator laid it down as a general rule that "the very existence of a flagrant revolution presupposes that a certain set of men have gone temporarily or permanently beyond the power of the authorities; and unless it clearly appear that the government has failed to use promptly and with appropriate force its constituted authority, it can not reasonably be said that it should be responsible for a condition of affairs created without its volition"; and he refused to discriminate against Venezuela on the ground that it was on a lower plane of civilization and as such responsible "in derogation of the general principles of international law."

The dispute between France and Jugoslavia over the Serbian loans, Publications of the Permanent Court of International Justice, Series A, No. 20, involved action by France on behalf of French holders of Serbian bonds issued at different dates between 1895 and 1913, the loan in each case being designated as a "gold loan" or as being for a sum of "gold francs," Serbia claiming that in view of the depreciation of the French gold franc the standard of payment had changed, and payment should be made in current French francs. The court held that the bonds must be paid in gold francs as contemplated by the contract.

Compare Feist v. Société Intercommunale Belge d'Électricité, [1934] A. C. 161, involving the obligation of a Belgian corporation on bonds payable as to principal and interest in London in sterling "in gold coin of the United Kingdom of or equal to the standard of weight and fineness existing on September 1, 1928." The House of Lords, reversing the decision of both of the lower courts, construed the gold clause not as constituting the mode of payment, which was now forbidden by law, but as describing and measuring the company's obligation which must be met; and held that the bondholder was entitled to receive

F.   Taxation of property of non-resident aliens.

It frequently happens that the securities of public and private corporations are owned by non-resident aliens. Query, may a state tax such securities when they are physically within its jurisdiction? [Burnet v. Brooks.]

BURNET, COMMISSIONER OF INTERNAL REVENUE, v. BROOKS, ET AL., EXECUTORS.

United States, Supreme Court, 1933.

288 U. S. 378.   [77 L. ed. 844; 53 S. Ct. 457.]

MR. CHIEF JUSTICE HUGHES delivered the opinion of the Court.

Respondents contested the determination of the Commissioner of Internal Revenue in including in the gross estate of decedent certain intangible property. Decedent, who died in October, 1924, was a subject of Great Britain and a resident of Cuba. He was not engaged in business in the United States. The property in question consisted of securities, viz., bonds of foreign corporations, bonds of foreign governments, bonds of domestic corporations and of a domestic municipality, and stock in a foreign corporation, and also of a balance of a cash deposit. Some of the securities, consisting of a stock certificate and bonds, were in the possession of decedent's son in New York City, who collected the income and placed it to the credit of decedent in a New York bank. Other securities were in the possession of Lawrence Turnure & Company in New York City who collected the income and credited it to decedent's checking account, which showed the above mentioned balance in his favor. None of the securities was pledged or held for any indebtedness. Finding these facts, the Board of Tax Appeals decided that the property should not be included in the decedent's gross estate for the purpose of the Federal Estate Tax (22 B. T.

"such a sum in sterling as represents the gold value of the nominal amount" due on the bonds.

Compare, further, Perry v. United States, decided February 18, 1935, in which the Supreme Court of the United States held that the Resolution of Congress of June 5, 1933, declaring the gold clause contrary to public policy and providing that payment might be made in any currency that was legal tender, was unconstitutional so far as it applied to obligations of the United States and that in consequence damages were due to Perry for breach of contract. The further statement made by the Court that Perry had failed to show cause of action for actual damages, taking into consideration the purchasing power of the dollars that he had received on his bond, left open the inference that the foreign bondholder, whose dollars had suffered in foreign exchange by reason of the change in the gold content of the dollar, might sue successfully or might seek the intermediation of his government if the Court of Claims denied him relief.

A. 71), and the decision was affirmed by the Circuit Court of Appeals. 60 F. (2d) 890. This Court granted certiorari in 287 U. S. 594.

The provisions governing the imposition of the tax are found in the Revenue Act of 1924, c. 234, 43 Stat. 253, 303–307, and are set forth in the margin. Two questions are presented,—(1) whether the property in question is covered by these provisions, and (2) whether, if construed to be applicable, they are valid under the Fifth Amendment of the Federal Constitution. The decisions below answered the first question in the negative.

First. The first question is one of legislative intention. In the case of a nonresident of the United States, that part of the gross estate was to be returned and valued "which at the time of his death is situated in the United States." In interpreting this clause, regard must be had to the purpose in view. . . .

Second. The question of power to lay the tax. As a nation with all the attributes of sovereignty, the United States is vested with all the powers of government necessary to maintain an effective control of international relations. Fong Yue Ting v. United States, 149 U. S. 698, 711; Knox v. Lee, 12 Wall. 457, 555, 556. "We should hesitate long," we said in Mackenzie v. Hare, 239 U. S. 299, 311, "before limiting or embarrassing such powers." So far as our relation to other nations is concerned, and apart from any self-imposed constitutional restriction, we cannot fail to regard the property in question as being within the jurisdiction of the United States,—that is, it was property within the reach of the power which the United States by virtue of its sovereignty could exercise as against other nations and their subjects without violating any established principle of international law. This view of the scope of the sovereign power in the matter of the taxation of securities physically within the territorial limits of the sovereign is sustained by high authority and is a postulate of legislative action in other countries. The subject was considered by the House of Lords in Winans v. Attorney-General, [1910] A. C. 27. The question was as to the liability to estate duty, under the British Finance Act, 1894, of bonds and certificates when these were physically situated in the United Kingdom at the death of the owner, who was a citizen of the United States and domiciled here. The securities were payable to bearer, marketable on the London Stock Exchange, and passed by delivery. The executors insisted that "the property did not pass by the law of the United Kingdom but by the law of the deceased's domicile;" that "the presence in the United Kingdom of the documents of title to the property did not create a liability to estate duty;" that "all the debtors on the bonds and certificates were at the time of the death and all material times outside the United Kingdom and beyond its jurisdiction;" that "the marketability of a piece of paper in the United Kingdom was not sufficient to make the debt of which it was evidence liable to estate duty;'' and that ''the property was not situate in the United Kingdom.'' The House of Lords was not convinced by these contentions. The Lord Chancellor observed that ''the property received the full protection of British laws—which is a constant basis of taxation—and can only be transferred from the deceased to other persons by the authority of a British Court.'' Id. p. 30. Lord Atkinson referred to the status of the securities under international law. ''Being physically situated in England at the time of their owner's death,'' said his Lordship, ''they were subject to English law and the jurisdiction of English Courts, and taxes might therefore *prima facie* be leviable upon them. . . . There does not appear, *a priori*, to be anything contrary to the principles of international law, or hurtful to the policy of nations, in a State's taxing property physically situated within its borders, wherever its owner may have been domiciled at the time of his death.'' Id. p. 31. And Lord Shaw of Dunfermline summed up the application of the British acts as follows: ''In the case of an English citizen all his property 'wheresoever situate,' subject to the exception in the Act, is aggregated, and into that aggregation—to confine oneself to the matter in hand—all personal property situate out of the United Kingdom must come, unless legacy or succession duty would not have been payable in respect thereof. In the case of the foreign citizen no taxation, of course, falls, except upon property situate within the United Kingdom, and I know no reason either under the law of nations, by the custom of nations, or in the nature of things why property within the jurisdiction of this country, possessed and held under the protection of its laws, should not, upon transfer from the dead to the living, pay the same toll which would have been paid by property enjoying the same protection but owned by a deceased British subject.'' Id. pp. 47, 48. In this view, the securities were held to be subject to the estate duty. . . .

As jurisdiction may exist in more than one government, that is, jurisdiction based on distinct grounds—the citizenship of the owner, his domicile, the source of income, the situs of the property—efforts have been made to preclude multiple taxation through the negotiation of appropriate international conventions. These endeavors, however, have proceeded upon express or implied recognition, and not in denial, of the sovereign taxing power as exerted by governments in the exercise of jurisdiction upon any one of these grounds. For many years this subject has been under consideration by international committees of experts and drafts of conventions have been proposed, the advantages of which lie in the mutual concessions or reciprocal restrictions to be voluntarily made or accepted by Powers freely negotiating on the basis of recognized principles of jurisdiction. In its international relations, the United States is as competent as other nations to enter into such negotiations, and to become a party to such conventions, without any disadvantage due to limitation of its sovereign power, unless that limitation is necessarily found to be imposed by its own Constitution.

Respondents urge that constitutional restriction precluding the Federal estate tax in question is found in the due process clause of the Fifth Amendment. . . . Respondents' reliance is upon the decisions of this Court with respect to the limitation of the taxing power of the States under the due process clause of the Fourteenth Amendment. . . . They insist that the like clause of the Fifth Amendment imposes a corresponding restriction upon the taxing power of the Federal Government.

The argument is specious, but it ignores an established distinction. Due process requires that the limits of jurisdiction shall not be transgressed. That requirement leaves the limits of jurisdiction to be ascertained in each case with appropriate regard to the distinct spheres of activity of State and Nation. The limits of State power are defined in view of the relation of the States to each other in the Federal Union. The bond of the Constitution qualifies their jurisdiction. This is the principle which underlies the decisions cited by respondents. These decisions established that proper regard for the relation of the States in our system required that the property under consideration should be taxed in only one State and that jurisdiction to tax was restricted accordingly. . . .

. . . The decisive point is that the criterion of state taxing power by virtue of the relation of the States to each other under the Constitution is not the criterion of the taxing power of the United States by virtue of its sovereignty in relation to the property of non-residents. The Constitution creates no such relation between the United States and foreign countries as it creates between the States themselves.

Accordingly, in what has been said, we in no way limit the authority of our decisions as to state power. We determine national power in relation to other countries and their subjects by applying the principles of jurisdiction recognized in international relations. Applying those principles we cannot doubt that the Congress had the power to enact the statute, as we have construed and applied it to the property in question. The securities should be included in the gross estate of the decedent; the inclusion of the balance of the cash deposit will depend, under the statute, upon the finding to be made with respect to the nature of the business of the concern with which the deposit was made.

The judgment is reversed and the cause is remanded for further proceedings in conformity with this opinion.

Reversed.

Mr. Justice Butler is of opinion that the statute does not extend to the transfer of the foreign or other securities effected by the death of decedent, Ernest Augustus Brooks, a British subject resident of and dying in Cuba, and that the conclusions of the Board of Tax Appeals and Circuit Court of Appeals are right and should be affirmed.

CHAPTER VIII [1]

SPECIAL JURISDICTIONAL OBLIGATIONS TOWARDS FOREIGN STATES

A. Prevention of acts injurious to foreign states.

The jurisdiction of a state over all persons and property within its territory gives rise to the duty of preventing certain uses of its territory by individuals which might be directly injurious to the governmental interests of foreign states. The specific obligations which this general duty entails are reflected in the judicial and legislative action of national governments. Query, is a state under an obligation to afford the protection of its municipal law to a foreign state seeking an injunction to prevent the printing of notes intended to be circulated subsequently as public paper money in pursuance of a movement involving the overthrow of the existing government? [Emperor of Austria v. Day and Kossuth.] Does the power to "define and punish . . . offenses against the law of Nations" given to Congress by the Constitution of the United States extend to the punishing of the act of counterfeiting the securities of a foreign state? [United States v. Arjona.] In the decision of a case arising between two states of the United States involving an alleged public nuisance committed by one against the other, would the Supreme Court of the United States take into account the principles of international law applicable between independent sovereignties? [Missouri v. Illinois.]

THE EMPEROR OF AUSTRIA v. DAY AND KOSSUTH.

Great Britain, High Court of Chancery, 1861.

2 Giffard, 628.

[On February 28, 1861, counsel on behalf of the Emperor moved for an injunction that Messers. Day and Sons might be restrained from printing or delivering to Louis Kossuth documents purporting to be notes of the Hungarian state or notes with the royal arms of Hungary printed thereon. The bill, which was supported by an affidavit of

---

[1] For a more detailed study of this subject, see Fenwick, *op. cit.*, pp. 210–216; Hyde, *op. cit.*, §§ 244–249; Harvard Draft, Competence of Courts in Regard to Foreign States; Allen, The Position of Foreign States before National Courts.

248

Count Apponyi, alleged that the plaintiff was King of Hungary, and as such had the exclusive right of authorizing the issue in Hungary of notes to be circulated in Hungary as money, and also the exclusive right of authorizing the royal arms of Hungary to be affixed to any document intended to be circulated in that country. That nearly the whole of the circulation of Hungary consisted of notes of the National Bank of Austria, issued under the authority of the Plaintiff as Emperor of Austria and King of Hungary, which circulated in Hungary as money, and were for various sums from one florin upwards. That the defendants Day & Sons (the well-known lithographers) had by the direction of the defendant Kossuth prepared plates for printing notes purporting to be notes of the Hungarian nation or state, for various sums of money, and which were intended to be circulated as money in Hungary, and that they were engaged by the direction of Kossuth in printing such notes from the plates.

That the body of each note was in the Hungarian language, and had on the border, in the German and Sclavonian and other languages, the amount for which it purported to be a note, and at the bottom a print of the royal arms of Hungary. The body of a one florin note, when translated, was as follows:

"One florin. This monetary note will be received in every Hungarian state and public pay office as one florin in silver. Three zwanzigers being one florin, and its whole nominal value is guaranteed by the state.

"In the name of the nation, Kossuth, Louis."

That the total amount of these notes which was being prepared was upwards of 100,000,000 florins. That Day & Sons had in their possession a large quantity of them entirely or nearly completed, and, unless restrained by the Court, would deliver them to Kossuth. That Kossuth intended, as soon as he received them, to send them to Hungary and endeavour to introduce some of them into circulation there, and use the remainder for other purposes in Hungary, in violation of the rights and prerogative of the Plaintiff as king of that country, and, amongst other purposes, for the promotion of revolution and disorder there. That the Plaintiff had never authorized the manufacture of the notes or the use of the royal arms of Hungary thereon; and that the introduction of the notes into Hungary would create a spurious circulation there, and by that and other means cause great detriment to the state and the subjects of the Plaintiff. That Day & Sons had notice of the purpose for which the notes were intended, and of Kossuth's want of authority to prepare or issue them.

The bill prayed (besides the injunction) that Messers. Day might be decreed to deliver up to the plaintiff, to be destroyed, the plates and any documents printed or lithographed therefrom, and any other documents purporting to be notes of the Hungarian state or nation, or notes with the royal arms of Hungary printed thereon.]

THE VICE-CHANCELLOR [SIR JOHN STUART] :—

The plaintiff sues in his sovereign character, as King of Hungary. He asks the assistance of the Court to prevent an injury, of a public kind, to what he asserts to be his legal rights. These rights he claims as the acknowledged possessor of the sovereign power in a foreign state at peace with this kingdom.

It appears that the defendants have manufactured and prepared in this country a vast quantity of printed paper, purporting to represent public paper money of Hungary, such as could be lawfully issued by the sovereign power. What they have thus prepared is intended to be circulated at some future time as the public paper money of Hungary. This paper has been thus made and prepared, not only without the license of the plaintiff, but as in exercise of some contemplated power hostile to that of the plaintiff, and intended to supersede it.

What the Court has now to decide is the question, whether the defendants can, by the law of England, be allowed to continue in possession, or to be protected in the possession, of this large quantity of printed paper, manufactured and held by them for such a purpose; or whether, on the other hand, the plaintiff is entitled to have the right of which he claims to be in possession, protected against the invasion of the defendants, and to have delivered up to him what has been thus prepared, and made ready to be used, for a purpose hostile to his existing right.

For the defendants, it has been argued, that this Court has no jurisdiction in such a case; that what is complained of is a public wrong, not cognizable by the law of England, because it relates merely to the public and political affairs of a foreign nation. The defendant's counsel have admitted that a foreign sovereign may have relief in this court, when he sues in his public character to recover public property within the jurisdiction of this Court. But they insist that, what is in question in this cause is not any right of property, but a mere public and political right, which, by the constitution of Hungary, is not absolute in the Sovereign, but subject to the control and direction of the Diet of that kingdom. Such a right, they say, is beyond the jurisdiction of this Court.

If the question related merely to an affair of state, it would be a question, not of law, but for mere political discussion. But the regulation of the coin and currency of every State is a great prerogative right of the sovereign power. It is not a mere municipal right, or a mere question of municipal law. Money is the medium of commerce between all civilized nations; therefore, the prerogative of each sovereign state as to money is but a great public right recognised and protected by the law of nations. A public right, recognised by the law of nations, is a legal right; because the law of nations is part of the common law of England.

These propositions are supported by unquestionable authority. In the modern version of Blackstone's Commentaries (4 Steph. Com. 282), it is laid down (and it has so always been held in our courts) that the law of nations, wherever any question arises, which is properly the object of its jurisdiction, is adopted in its full extent by the common law of England, and held to be part of the law of the land. Acts of Parliament, which have been from time to time made to enforce this universal law, or to facilitate the execution of its decisions, are not considered as introductive of any new rule, but merely declaratory of the old fundamental constitution of the kingdom, without which it must cease to be part of the civilized world.

To apply these acknowledged principles of the law of nations and law of England to the present case, it appears that the British Parliament, by the Act 11 Geo. 4 & 1 Wm. 4, c. 66, has enacted, that the forgery or counterfeiting the paper money of any foreign sovereign or state is a felony punishable by the law of England. This statute is a legislative recognition of the general right of the sovereign authority in foreign states to the assistance of the laws of this country, to protect their rights as to the regulation of their paper money as well as their coin, and to punish, by the law of England, offences against that power.

The friendly relations between civilized countries require, for their safety, the protection by municipal law of an existing sovereign right of this kind recognised by the law of nations. It appears from the evidence of the defendant Kossuth himself, that the present plaintiff is in possession of the supreme power in Hungary, and that the property now in question, which this defendant has caused to be manufactured in order, at some future time, to issue it as the public paper money of the State of Hungary, is not intended to be immediately used for that purpose, because of the existing power of the plaintiff. But it also appears, that the paper so manufactured is now in the possession and power of both the defendants, ready to be used, when the defendant Kossuth shall think fit, for a purpose adverse to the existing right of the plaintiff.

The manufactured paper in question, therefore, is property which has been made for no other purpose, and can be used for no other purpose, except one hostile to the sovereign rights of the plaintiff. It is not property of a kind which, like warlike weapons or other property, may be lawfully used for other purposes. And if the avowed and single purpose, for which this property is now in the hands of the defendants, be a purpose hostile to the plaintiff's rights, if this Court were to refuse its interference, the refusal would amount to a decision that it has no jurisdiction to protect the legal right of the plaintiff—a legal right recognised by the law of nations, and, therefore, by the law of England.

But it has been said, that the right of the plaintiff is not an absolute right, but is subject to the control of the Diet of Hungary. The prerogative rights of the Crown of England are all directly or indirectly subject to control of Parliament, and the sovereign rights in most other nations are subject to some control or limitation, yet they are not therefore the less actual rights; and it is at the suit of the sovereign that they are to be protected by the law.

Then, it is said, that the defendant Kossuth contemplates the overthrow of the existing right of the plaintiff, and that when it is overthrown, and the power transferred to himself or to some other body, which shall sanction the use of this paper as the current money of the kingdom of Hungary, he will then be entitled to use it; and therefore, that this Court ought not now to interfere.

To this argument the answer is, that this Court, like other public tribunals, can deal only with existing laws and existing governments. Obedience to existing laws and to existing governments, by which alone the laws can be enforced, are purposes essential to the distribution of justice, and to the maintenance of civil society. Therefore, if by the existing laws the plaintiff has the right which he asserts, and if the defendants have made and have now in their possession the property in question, which has been made and now is in their hands for no other purpose than one hostile to the legal rights of the plaintiff, the legal right of the plaintiff ought to be protected by the interference of this Court. This right of the plaintiff is clear on principle, unless the Court is to abandon its protective jurisdiction. It is clear, also, upon authority. In the case of Farina v. Silverlock [1 K. & J. 509], an injunction was granted against a printer, who had made and printed papers which he had in his possession, merely because they might be used, and were ready to be used, in such a manner as to violate the legal right of the plaintiff, although they were not in fact actually used for that purpose.

Foreign States at peace with this country have always been held entitled to the assistance of the law of England to vindicate and protect their rights, and to punish offenders against those acknowledged public privileges recognised by the law of nations. Even the sovereign power, under a revolutionary government recognized for the time by the Crown of England as an existing government, has had its rights protected, and offenders against those rights punished by prosecution in the courts of England. The prosecution and conviction of M. Peltier, for a libel on the First Consul of France, proceeded on this principle. In earlier times, Lord George Gordon was tried and convicted for a libel on the Queen of France.

These rights of foreign powers may be for a time suppressed, and the law may be silent during the flagrance of rebellion and revolution, when rights, both public and private, are overturned and destroyed during the crimes and calamities of civil war.

But where, as in the present case, the existing rights of the plaintiff, as Sovereign of Hungary, are recognised by the Crown of England, the relief which he seeks in this cause, is for the protection of a legal right of universal public importance against the acts of the defendants.

That protection can only be effectually afforded by the relief prayed for in this suit; and there must be a decree against the defendants, according to the prayer of the bill.

EMPEROR OF AUSTRIA v. DAY AND KOSSUTH.

Great Britain, Court of Appeal in Chancery, 1861.

3 De Gex, Fisher & Jones, 217.

[For the facts of the case, see the same case in the High Court of Chancery. Both decisions are given because they reached the same conclusion by different reasoning.]

This was an appeal from the whole of a decree of Vice-Chancellor Stuart, restraining the Defendants from making notes purporting to be notes of the Hungarian State, and ordering them to deliver up to the Plaintiff the notes already made and the plates used for printing them.

The case made by the bill was in substance as follows: . . .

Vice-Chancellor Stuart having made a decree according the prayer of the bill, the defendants Kossuth and Day & Sons severally appealed.

THE LORD CHANCELLOR [LORD CAMPBELL.] . . . I will now consider the objections to the decree appealed against, which appear to me to be chiefly relied upon by the Appellant's counsel in the very learned and very able arguments which we have had the advantage of hearing from them.

In the first place, they deny the right of the Plaintiff as a sovereign prince to maintain this suit, and if the suit were instituted merely to support his political power and prerogatives, or for any alleged wrong sanctioned by the government of England, I should acquiesce in that position. But the King of Spain v. Hullett [(1833) 7 Bligh, N. S. 359], The King of the Two Sicilies v. Willcox [(1851) 1 Simons N. S. 301], and various other authorities show that by the law of England a foreign sovereign may sue in our Courts for a wrong done to him by an English subject unauthorized by the English government, in respect of property belonging to the foreign sovereign, either in his individual or in his corporate capacity.

Then comes the great question, whether this is a subject over which the Court of Chancery has jurisdiction by injunction? . . . I consider that this Court has jurisdiction by injunction to protect property from an act threatened, which if completed would give a right of action. I by no means say that in every such case an injunction may be demanded as of right, but if the party applying is free from blame and promptly applies for relief, and shows that by the threatened wrong his property would be so injured that an action for damages would be no adequate redress, the injunction will be granted.

Although an action arising purely ex delicto for an injury to property may not have been brought by a foreign sovereign against an English subject in an English Court, on principle I cannot doubt that such action would be maintainable. . . .

I rather think that the decree ought to be varied with respect to prohibiting M. Kossuth from the use of the royal arms of Hungary; for it would appear that they may be innocently used by all Hungarians, and, I presume, by all mankind.

With this variation, I am of opinion that the decree appealed against ought to be affirmed, and that the appeal must be dismissed.

[Concurring opinion of Knight Bruce, L. J., omitted.]

TURNER, L. J. . . . This brings us to the question, whether the infringement of the prerogative rights of a foreign sovereign constitutes a ground of suit in this Court. The case was very much argued upon this point. It was urged for the plaintiff that the right of coining money, the jus cudendæ monetæ, was universally acknowledged to be a prerogative of sovereigns vested in them for the benefit of their subjects,—that this prerogative right extended no less to the creation of paper money than to the stamping of coin,—that it was acknowledged by all nations and recognized by international law, and that, international law being part of the law of England, this Court would interfere in favor of the rights recognized by and founded upon it. That the right of coining money is the prerogative of a sovereign is laid down by all the writers on international law, and I see no reason to doubt that the prerogative right reaches to the issue of paper money. Burlamaqui [Vol. 3, p. 241] indeed, mentions and treats of it as so extending. To this extent, therefore, I agree with the argument on the part of the plaintiff, but the argument failed to satisfy my mind that this Court can or ought to interfere in aid of the prerogatives of a foreign sovereign. The prerogative rights of sovereigns seem to me, as at present advised, to stand very much upon the same footing as acts of state and matters of that description, with which the municipal Courts of this country do not and cannot interfere. Such acts and matters are recognized by international law no less than the prerogative rights of sovereigns; but the municipal Courts of this country have disclaimed all right to interfere with respect to them. If the subject of one state infringes the prerogative of the sovereign of another state, the remedy, as I apprehend, lies in an appeal by the offended sovereign to the sovereign of the state to which the offender belongs, and if redress be unjustly refused, the refusal may, as I apprehend, even be made the ground of war. This, I think, may be gathered from Vattel, and it seems to me important to be adhered to; for the prerogative of peace and war belongs to the sovereign of every state, and it can hardly be denied that the interference of the municipal Courts in such matters may tend very much to embarrass if not to fetter the free exercise of these latter prerogatives. The same reasoning which applies to the prerogative rights of sovereigns seems to me to apply also to the political rights of nations; and so far, therefore, as this bill is founded upon the prerogative rights of the plaintiff, or upon the political rights of his subjects, my present opinion, speaking with all respect of what fell from the Vice-Chancellor in the course of his judgment, is against the decree which he has made.

The conclusion to which I have come in this case does not, however, depend upon these points; and I do not think it necessary, therefore, to enter more fully into them, or into the arguments bearing upon them; nor do I wish to be understood as giving any final opinion upon them. This case, as it seems to me, may and ought to be decided upon the third ground on which the case is rested by the bill—the injury to the subjects of the Plaintiff by the introduction of a spurious circulation. I take it to be now well settled, although upon looking into the authorities I have been surprised to find that the point was doubted even in the time of Lord Loughborough, that a foreign sovereign may sue in the Courts of this country, and that he may sue in this Court on the behalf of his subjects; and this bill, if it does not require, certainly admits the construction, that it is filed by the Plaintiff in his representative character on behalf of the subjects of his kingdom, for it distinctly alleges a case of injury to them. We must consider, then, what is the nature of this injury. I think it is an injury not to the political but to the private rights of the Plaintiff's subjects. What is proposed to be done is to introduce into the kingdom of Hungary an enormous number of notes which, on the face of them, purport that they will be received in the public offices of the state and that they are guaranteed by the state, and which purport also to be signed in the name of the nation by the defendant Louis Kossuth. That the effect of this introduction will be to disturb the circulation of the kingdom cannot, in my opinion, be doubted; and what will be the effect of that disturbance? Surely to endanger, to prejudice and to deteriorate the value of the existing circulating medium, and thus to affect directly all the holders of Austrian bank notes, and indirectly, if not directly, all the holders of property in the state. The same great authority to which I have referred has very clearly pointed out these consequences. [Vattel, book 1, chap. 10.] But it is said that the acts proposed to be done are not the subject of equitable jurisdiction, or that if they are, the jurisdiction ought not to be exercised until a trial at law shall have been had. To neither of these propositions can I give my assent. I agree that the jurisdiction of this Court in a case of this nature rests upon injury to property actual or prospective, and that this Court has no jurisdiction to prevent the commission of acts which are merely criminal or merely illegal, and do not affect any rights of property, but I think there are here rights of property quite sufficient to found jurisdiction in this Court. I do not agree to the proposition, that there is no remedy in this Court if there be no remedy at law, and still less do I agree to the proposition that this Court is bound to send a matter of this description to be tried at law. . . . If the property of an individual is affected by an undue and unauthorized use of his name, the law would no doubt give a remedy. I am not satisfied that the law would not give the same remedy in the case of the undue and unauthorized use of the name of a nation or state; but whether it would do so or not, and if not, whether it would be prevented from doing so by the absence of positive law or by mere formal impediments as to the right to sue, I think the authority to which I have referred, and the instance which I have mentioned of the application of it, warrant me in saying that the case falls within the jurisdiction of this Court. It was said, on the part of the Defendants, that the Court has only interfered in cases of this nature where there was a right at law, or where there was trust or confidence; but if the jurisdiction exists, the extent of it cannot be limited by the instances in which it has been applied. It was also attempted to be argued on the part of the Defendants, that, assuming the existence of the jurisdiction, there was no sufficient case for the exercise of it. But upon this point I have felt no doubt. The jurisdiction of this Court is preventive as well as remedial, and the affidavit of the Defendant Kossuth himself quite satisfies my mind that there is a proper case for the exercise of it. Subject, therefore, to the qualification to which the Lord Chancellor has adverted, I think that this decree must stand.

UNITED STATES v. ARJONA.

United States, Supreme Court, 1887.

120 U. S. 479. [30 L. ed. 728; 7 S. Ct. 628.]

[On a certificate of division of opinion between the Judges of the Circuit Court of the United States for the Southern District of New York.]

MR. CHIEF JUSTICE WAITE delivered the opinion of the court:

This is an indictment containing three counts against Ramon Arjona, for violations of §§ 3 and 6, of the Act of May 16, 1884, c. 52, 23 Stat. 22, "to prevent and punish the counterfeiting within the United States of notes, bonds and other securities of foreign governments." The first and second counts were found under § 6 of the statute, and the third under § 3. . . .

The first count of the indictment charges Arjona with having "in his control and custody a certain metallic plate from which there might then and there be printed in part a counterfeit note in the likeness and similitude in part of the notes theretofore issued by a foreign bank, to wit, the bank known as El Banco del Estado de Bolivar, which said bank was then and there a bank authorized by the laws of a foreign state, to wit, the state of Bolivar; said state being then and there one of the states of the United States of Colombia." . . .

In the third count, the charge is that he, "unlawfully and with intent to defraud, did cause and procure to be falsely made a certain note in the similitude and resemblance of the notes theretofore issued by a bank of a foreign country; to wit, the bank known as El Banco del Estado de Bolivar, . . . and the notes issued by the said bank being then and by the usage of the said state of Bolivar intended to circulate as money." . . .

Congress has power to make all laws which shall be necessary and proper to carry into execution the powers vested by the Constitution in the Government of the United States, Art. I, sec. 8, clause 18; and the Government of the United States has been vested exclusively with the power of representing the nation in all its intercourse with foreign countries. It alone can "regulate commerce with foreign Nations," Art. I, sec. 8, clause 3; make treaties, and appoint ambassadors and other public ministers and consuls. Art. II, sec. 2, clause 2. A state is expressly prohibited from entering into any "treaty, alliance, or confederation." Art. I, sec. 10, clause 1. Thus all official intercourse between a state and foreign nations is prevented, and exclusive authority for that purpose given to the United States. The national government is in this way made responsible to foreign nations for all violations by the United States of their international obligations, and because of this Congress is expressly authorized "to define and punish . . . offenses against the law of nations." Art. I, sec. 8, clause 10.

The law of nations requires every national government to use "due diligence" to prevent a wrong being done within its own dominion to another nation with which it is at peace, or to the people thereof; and because of this the obligation of one nation to punish those who, within its own jurisdiction, counterfeit the money of another nation has long been recognized. Vattel, in his Law of Nations, which was first printed at Neuchâtel in 1758, and was translated into English and published in England in 1760, uses this language: "From the principles thus laid down, it is easy to conclude that if one Nation counterfeits the money of another, or if she allows and protects false coiners who presume to do it, she does that Nation an injury." When this was written money was the chief thing of this kind that needed protection, but still it was added: "There is another custom more modern, and of no less use to commerce than the establishment of coin; namely, *exchange*, or the traffic of bankers, by means of which a merchant remits immense sums from one end of the world to the other, at very trifling expense, and, if he pleases, without risk. For the same reason that Sovereigns are obliged to protect commerce, they are obliged to support this custom, by good laws, in which every merchant, whether citizen or foreigner, may find security. In general, it is equally the interest and duty of every nation to have wise and equitable commercial laws established in the country." Vattel, Law of Nations, Phil. ed., 1876, Book I, chap. 10, pages 46, 47. In a note by Mr. Chitty in his London edition of 1834 it is said: "This is a sound principle, which ought to be extended so as to deny effect to any fraud upon a foreign nation or its subjects." Id. 47, note 50.

This rule was established for the protection of nations in their intercourse with each other. If there were no such intercourse, it would be a matter of no special moment to one nation that its money was counterfeited in another. Its own people could not be defrauded if the false coin did not come among them; and its own sovereignty would not be violated if the counterfeit could not under any circumstances be made to take the place of the true money. But national intercourse includes commercial intercourse between the people of different nations. It is as much the duty of a nation to protect such an intercourse as it is any other, and that is what Vattel meant when he said: "For the same reason that sovereigns are obliged to protect commerce, they are obliged to support this custom"; "namely, *exchange,* or the traffic of bankers, by means of which a merchant remits immense sums from one end of the world to the other," "by good laws, in which every merchant, whether citizen or foreigner, may find security."

In the time of Vattel certificates of the public debt of a nation, government bonds, and other government securities, were rarely seen in any other country than that in which they were put out. Banks of issue were not so common as to need special protection for themselves or the public against forgers and counterfeiters elsewhere than at home; and the great corporations, now so numerous and so important, established by public authority for the promotion of public enterprises, were almost unknown, and certainly they had not got to be extensive borrowers of money wherever it could be had, at home or abroad, on the faith of their *quasi* public securities. Now, however, the amount of national and corporate debt and of corporate property represented by bonds, certificates, notes, bills and other forms of commercial securities, which are bought and sold in all the money markets of the world, both in and out of the country under whose authority they were created, is something enormous.

Such being the case, it is easy to see that the same principles that developed, when it became necessary, the rule of national conduct which was intended to prevent, as far as might be, the counterfeiting of the money of one nation within the dominion of another, and which, in the opinion of so eminent a publicist as Vattel, could be applied to the foreign exchange of bankers, may with just propriety be extended to the protection of this more recent custom among bankers of dealing in foreign securities, whether national or corporate, which have been put out under the sanction of public authority at home, and sent abroad as the subjects of trade and commerce. And especially is this so of bank notes and bank bills issued under the authority of law, which, from their very nature, enter into and form part of the circulating medium of exchange—the money—of a country. Under such circumstances, every nation has not only the right to require the protection, as far as possible, of its own credit abroad against fraud, but the banks and other great commercial corporations which have been created within its own jurisdiction for the advancement of the public good may call on it to see that their interests are not neglected by a foreign government to whose dominion they have, in the lawful prosecution of their business, become to some extent subjected.

No nation can be more interested in this question than the United States. Their money is practically composed of treasury notes or certificates issued by themselves, or of bank bills issued by banks created under their authority and subject to their control. Their own securities, and those of the States, the cities, and the public corporations, whose interests abroad they alone have the power to guard against foreign national neglect, are found on sale in the principal money markets of Europe. If these securities, whether national, municipal, or corporate, are forged and counterfeited with impunity at the places where they are sold, it is easy to see that a great wrong will be done to the United States and their people. Any uncertainty about the genuineness of the security necessarily depreciates its value as a merchantable commodity; and against this, international comity requires that national protection shall, as far as possible, be afforded. If there is neglect in that, the United States may, with propriety, call on the proper government to provide for the punishment of such an offense, and thus secure the restraining influences of a fear of the consequences of wrongdoing. A refusal may not, perhaps, furnish sufficient cause for war, but it would certainly give just ground of complaint, and thus disturb that harmony between the governments which each is bound to cultivate and promote.

But if the United States can require this of another, that other may require it of them, because international obligations are of necessity reciprocal in their nature. The right, if it exists at all, is given by the law of nations; and what is law for one is, under the same circumstances, law for the other. A right secured by the law of nations to a nation or its people, is one the United States as the representatives of this nation are bound to protect. Consequently, a law which is necessary and proper to afford this protection is one that is needed to carry into execution a power conferred by the Constitution on the Government of the United States exclusively. There is no authority in the United States to require the passage and enforcement of such a law by the States. Therefore, the United States must have the power to pass it and enforce it themselves, or be unable to perform a duty which they may owe to another nation, and which the law of nations has imposed on them as part of their international obligations. This, however, does not prevent a State from providing for the punishment of the same thing, for here, as in the case of counterfeiting the coin of the United States, the act may be an offense against the authority of a State as well as that of the United States. . . .

It remains only to consider those questions which present the point whether, in enacting a statute to define and punish an offense against the law of nations, it is necessary, in order "to define" the offense, that it be declared in the statute itself to be "an offense against the law of nations." This statute defines the offense, and if the thing made punishable is one which the United States are required by their international obligations to use due diligence to prevent, it is an offense against the law of nations. . . . Whether the offense as defined is an offense against the law of nations depends on the thing done, not on any declaration to that effect by Congress. . . .

MISSOURI v. ILLINOIS AND THE SANITARY DISTRICT OF CHICAGO.

United States, Supreme Court, 1906.

200 U. S. 496. [50 L. ed. 572; 26 S. Ct. 268.]

Mr. Justice Holmes delivered the opinion of the court.

This is a suit brought by the state of Missouri to restrain the discharge of the sewage of Chicago through an artificial channel into the Desplaines River, in the State of Illinois. That river empties into the Illinois river, and the latter empties into the Mississippi at a point about forty-three miles above the city of St. Louis. It was alleged in the bill that the result of the threatened discharge would be to send 1,500 tons of poisonous filth daily into the Mississippi, to deposit great quantities of the same upon the part of the bed of the last-named river belonging to the plaintiff, and so to poison the water of that river, upon which various of the plaintiff's cities, towns, and inhabitants depended, as to make it unfit for drinking, agricultural, or manufacturing purposes. It was alleged that the defendant Sanitary District was acting in pursuance of a statute of the State of Illinois, and as an agency of that state. The case is stated at length in 180 U. S. 208, where a demurrer to the bill was overruled. A supplemental bill alleges that since the filing of the original bill the drainage canal has been opened and put into operation, and has produced and is producing all the evils which were apprehended when the injunction first was asked. The answers deny the plaintiff's case, allege that the new plan sends the water of the Illinois River into the Mississippi much purer than it was before, that many towns and cities of the plaintiff along the Missouri and Mississippi discharge their sewage into those rivers, and that if there is any trouble the plaintiff must look nearer home for the cause. . . .

. . . The nuisance set forth in the bill was one which would be of international importance—a visible change of a great river from a pure stream into a polluted and poisoned ditch. The only question presented was whether, as between the States of the Union, this court was competent to deal with a situation which, if it arose between independent sovereignties, might lead to war. Whatever differences of opinion there might be upon matters of detail, the jurisdiction and authority of this court to deal with such a case as that is not open to doubt. But the evidence now is in, the actual facts have required for their establishment the most ingenious experiments, and for their interpretation the most subtle speculations, of modern science, and therefore it becomes necessary at the present stage to consider somewhat more nicely than heretofore how the evidence in it is to be approached.

The first question to be answered was put in the well known case of the Wheeling bridge. Pennsylvania v. Wheeling & Belmont Bridge Co., 13 How. 518. In that case, also, there was a bill brought by a State to restrain a public nuisance, the erection of a bridge alleged to obstruct navigation, and a supplemental bill to abate it after it was erected. The question was put most explicitly by the dissenting judges, but it was accepted by all as fundamental. The Chief Justice observed that if the bridge was a nuisance, it was an offense against the sovereignty whose laws had been violated, and he asked what sovereignty that was. 13 How. 561; Daniel, J., 13 How. 599. See also Kansas v. Colorado, 185 U. S. 125. It could not be Virginia, because that state had purported to authorize it by statute. The Chief Justice found no prohibition by the United States. 13 How. 580. No third source of law was suggested by anyone. The majority accepted the Chief Justice's postulate, and found an answer in what Congress had done.

It hardly was disputed that Congress could deal with the matter under its power to regulate commerce. The majority observed that although Congress had not declared in terms that a state should not obstruct the navigation of the Ohio by bridges, yet it had regulated navigation upon that river in various ways, and had sanctioned the compact between Virginia and Kentucky when Kentucky was let into the Union. By that compact the use and navigation of the Ohio, so far as the territory of either state lay thereon, was to be free and common to the citizens of the

United States. The compact, by the sanction of Congress, had become a law of the Union. A state law which violated it was unconstitutional. Obstructing the navigation of the river was said to violate it, and it was added that more was not necessary to give a civil remedy for an injury done by the obstruction. 13 How. 565, 566. At a later stage of the case, after Congress had authorized the bridge, it was stated again in so many words that the ground of the former decision was that "the act of the legislature of Virginia afforded no authority or justification. It was in conflict with the acts of Congress, which were the paramount law." 18 How. 421, 429.

In the case at bar, whether Congress could act or not, there is no suggestion that it has forbidden the action of Illinois. The only ground on which that state's conduct can be called in question is one which must be implied from the words of the Constitution. The Constitution extends the judicial power of the United States to controversies between two or more states, and between a state and citizens of another state, and gives this court original jurisdiction in cases in which a state shall be a party. Therefore, if one state raises a controversy with another, this court must determine whether there is any principle of law, and, if any, what, on which the plaintiff can recover. But the fact that this court must decide does not mean, of course, that it takes the place of a legislature. Some principles it must have power to declare. For instance, when a dispute arises about boundaries, this court must determine the line; and, in doing so, must be governed by rules explicitly or implicitly recognized. Rhode Island v. Massachusetts, 12 Pet. 657, 737. It must follow and apply those rules, even if legislation of one or both of the states seems to stand in the way. But the words of the Constitution would be a narrow ground upon which to construct and apply to the relations between states the same system of municipal law in all its details which would be applied between individuals. If we suppose a case which did not fall within the power of Congress to regulate, the result of a declaration of rights by this court would be the establishment of a rule which would be irrevocable by any power except that of this court to reverse its own decision, an amendment of the Constitution, or possibly an agreement between the States, sanctioned by the legislature of the United States.

The difficulties in the way of establishing such a system of law might not be insuperable, but they would be great and new. Take the question of prescription in a case like the present. The reasons on which prescription for a public nuisance is denied or may be granted to an individual as against the sovereign power to which he is subject have no application to an independent state. See 1 Oppenheim, International Law, 293, §§ 242, 243. It would be contradicting a fundamental principle of human nature to allow no effect to the lapse of time, however long, Davis v. Mills, 194 U. S. 451, 457, yet the fixing of a definite time usually belongs to the legislature rather than the courts. The courts did fix a time in the rule against perpetuities, but the usual course, as in the instances of statutes of limitation, the duration of patents, the age of majority, etc., is to depend upon the lawmaking power.

It is decided that a case such as is made by the bill may be a ground for relief. The purpose of the foregoing observations is not to lay a foundation for departing from that decision, but simply to illustrate the great and serious caution with which it is necessary to approach the question whether a case is proved. It may be imagined that a nuisance might be created by a State upon a navigable river like the Danube, which would amount to a *casus belli* for a State lower down, unless removed. If such a nuisance were created by a State upon the Mississippi, the controversy would be resolved by the more peaceful means of a suit in this court. But it does not follow that every matter which would warrant a resort to equity by one citizen against another in the same jurisdiction equally would warrant an interference by this court with the action of a State. It hardly can be that we should be justified in declaring statutes ordaining such action void in every instance where the circuit court might intervene in a private suit, upon no other ground than analogy to some selected system of municipal law, and the fact that we have jurisdiction over controversies between States.

The nearest analogy would be found in those cases in which an easement has been declared in favor of land in one state over land in another. But there the right is recognized on the assumption of a concurrence between the two states, the one, so to speak, offering the right, the other permitting it to be accepted. Mannville Co. v. Worcester, 138 Massachusetts, 89. But when the State itself is concerned, and by its legislation expressly repudiates the right set up, an entirely different question is presented.

Before this court ought to intervene, the case should be of serious magnitude, clearly and fully proved, and the principle to be applied should be one which the court is prepared deliberately to maintain against all considerations on the other side. See Kansas v. Colorado, 185 U. S. 125.

As to the principle to be laid down, the caution necessary is manifest. It is a question of the first magnitude whether the destiny of the great rivers is to be the sewers of the cities along their banks or to be protected against everything which threatens their purity. To decide the whole matter at one blow by an irrevocable fiat would be at least premature. If we are to judge by what the plaintiff itself permits, the discharge of sewage into the Mississippi by cities and towns is to be expected. We believe that the practice of discharging into the river is general along its banks, except where the levees of Louisiana have led to a different course. The argument for the plaintiff asserts it to be proper within certain limits. These are facts to be considered. Even in cases between individuals, some consideration is given to the practical course of events. In the black country of England parties would not be expected to stand upon extreme rights. St. Helen's Smelting Co. v. Tipping, 11 H. L. C. 642. See Boston Ferrule Co. v. Hills, 159 Massachusetts, 147, 150. Where, as here, the plaintiff has sovereign powers, and deliberately permits discharges similar to those of which it complains, it not only offers a standard to which the defendant has the right to appeal, but, as some of those discharges are above the intake of St. Louis, it warrants the defendant in demanding the strictest proof that the plaintiff's own conduct does not produce the result, or at least so conduce to it, that courts should not be curious to apportion the blame.

We have studied the plaintiff's statement of the facts in detail, and have perused the evidence, but it is unnecessary for the purposes of decision to do more than give the general result in a very simple way. . . .

We might go more into detail, but we believe that we have said enough to explain our point of view and our opinion of the evidence as it stands. What the future may develop, of course we cannot tell. But our conclusion upon the present evidence is that the case proved falls so far below the allegations of the bill that it is not brought within the principles heretofore established in the cause.

Bill dismissed without prejudice.[1]

B.   Jurisdictional immunities of foreign states.

It is a long standing rule of customary international law that a foreign state may not be sued in the courts of another state. The rule orig-

---

[1] Supplementary Cases. Query, is a government under the obligation to deny the use of its courts to enforce contracts by which private individuals may seek to raise loans on behalf of unrecognized insurgents at war with the *de jure* government? In De Wutz v. Hendricks, 2 Bing. 314 (1824), involving a suit by De Wutz for the return of papers deposited with the defendant in connection with a proposed loan for the Greeks in arms against the government of the Ottoman Porte, the Court of Common Pleas of Great Britain held that it was "contrary to the law of nations . . . for persons in England to enter into engagements to raise money to support the subjects of a government in amity with our own, in hostilities against their government, and that no right of action could arise out of such a transaction." A similar conclusion was reached by the Supreme Court of the United States in 1852 in Kennett v. Chambers, above, p. 51.

States are obviously under the same obligation to refrain in their corporate capacity from committing acts injurious to a neighboring state as they are under to prevent the acts of unauthorized individuals. In New Jersey v. City of New York, 283 U. S. 473 (1931) involving a prayer by New Jersey for an injunction restraining the city of New York from dumping garbage into the ocean off the coast of New Jersey, the Supreme Court held that the fact that the dumping took place at points from 10 to 22 miles from shore and therefore outside the jurisdiction of the court did not preclude the granting of the injunction when the property alleged to have been injured by the dumping was within the jurisdiction of the court.

inated in the personal exemption of a foreign sovereign from suit, but it was later extended to the sovereign as representative of the interests and property of his state. In modern times numerous complications have arisen in consequence of the extent to which one state may happen to own property which is temporarily or permanently within the territory of another state. Can the property of a foreign sovereign, in the form of moneys and other effects, be attached in the hands of a garnishee at the suit of a creditor of the foreign state? [De Haber v. Queen of Portugal.] Could property in the form of goods purchased by the foreign sovereign be attached by a citizen on the ground that the goods were manufactured in violation of patent rights? [Vavasseur v. Krupp.] Could the personal property of a foreign government be attached by a citizen as a means of satisfying claims against the foreign government having no connection with the title of the foreign government to the property? [Hassard v. United States of Mexico.] If a foreign government appears in court as a plaintiff, may the defendant file a counterclaim or set-off? [Kingdom of Norway v. Federal Sugar Refining Co.] Must such counterclaim arise out of the same action or may it relate to another and distinct matter? [South African Republic v. Compagnie Franco-Belge.]

DE HABER v. THE QUEEN OF PORTUGAL.

Court of Queen's Bench, 1851.

17 Q. B. 196.

LORD CAMPBELL, C. J. . . .

We are of opinion that the rule for a prohibition in this case ought to be made absolute.

The plaintiff has commenced an action of debt in the Court of the Lord Mayor of London against "Her most faithful Majesty Doña Maria da Gloria, Queen of Portugal, as reigning Sovereign and supreme head of the nation of Portugal": and, by an affidavit laid before us, it appears that the plaintiff's alleged cause of action is in respect of a sum of Portuguese money equivalent to 12,136 l. sterling, which he had in the hands of one Francisco Ferreiri of Lisbon, banker, at the period when Don Miguel, pretending to the Crown of Portugal, was driven out of that country, and which was by the said Francisco Ferreiri paid over to the Portuguese Government now represented by the royal defendant. The plaintiff, having entered his plaint, proceeded according to the custom of foreign attachment in the city of London, as if the defendant were subject to the jurisdiction of the Lord Mayor's Court and the cause of action had arisen within that jurisdiction; and he sued out a summons for the defendant to appear and answer the plaintiff in the plea aforesaid. . . . The defendant being solemnly called, and not appearing before the Lord Mayor, the plaintiff alleged, by his attorney, that Senhor Guilherne Candida Xavier de Brito, of the city of London, the garnishee, had money, goods and effects of the defendant in his hands, and prayed process . . . to attach the said defendant by the said money. . . . Thereupon the Judge presiding in the Court awarded an attachment against the defendant as prayed, leaving with the garnishee a notice in the terms following. . . . "Take notice that, by virtue of an action . . . against her most faithful Majesty . . . Queen of Portugal, . . . I do attach all such moneys, goods and effects as you now have . . . of the said defendant, to answer the plaintiff in the plea aforesaid." . . .

Let us see what has been done by the Lord Mayor of London. On a plaint being entered in his Court against "Doña Maria da Gloria, as reigning Sovereign and supreme head of the nation of Portugal," for what she had done "for and on behalf of the said nation," he summons her to appear before him; and, she being solemnly called and making default, he, with full knowledge that she was so sued, issues an attachment against her for this default, to compel her to appear. Under this attachment, all her money, goods and effects within the City and liberties of London are ordered to be seized; if she does not obey the mandate within a year and a day, these funds are to be confiscated or applied to the satisfaction of the plaintiff's demand, without any proof of its being justly due; and she can only get rid of the attachment by giving bail, to pay the sum which the plaintiff may recover, or to render herself to prison that she may be committed to the Poultry or Giltspur Street Compter. . . .

In the first place, it is quite certain, upon general principles, and upon the authority of the case of The Duke of Brunswick v. The King of Hanover, 2 H. L. Cas. 1 [affirming the decree of the Master of the Rolls in s. c., 6 Beav. 1], recently decided in the House of Lords, that an action cannot be maintained in any English Court against a foreign potentate, for anything done or omitted to be done by him in his public capacity as representative of the nation of which he is the head; and that no English court has jurisdiction to entertain any complaints against him in that capacity. Redress for such complaints affecting a British subject is only to be obtained by the laws and tribunals of the country which the foreign potentate rules, or by the representations, remonstrances or acts of the British Government. To cite a foreign potentate in a municipal court, for any complaint against him in his public capacity, is contrary to the law of nations, and an insult which he is entitled to resent.

The statute 7 Anne, c. 12, passed on the arrest of the Russian Ambassador, to appease the Czar, has always been said to be merely declaratory of the law of nations, recognized and enforced by our municipal law; and it provides (section 3) that all process, whereby the person of any ambassador, or of his domestic servant, may be arrested, or his goods distrained or seized, shall be utterly null and void. On the occasion of the outrage which gave rise to the statute, Lord Holt was present as a Privy Councillor to advise the Government as to the fit steps to be taken; and, with his sanction, seventeen persons, who had been concerned in arresting the ambassador, were committed to prison that they might be prosecuted by information at the suit of the Attorney General. Can we doubt that, in the opinion of that great Judge, the Sovereign himself would have been considered entitled to the same protection, immunity and privilege as the minister who represents him? . . .

We have now to consider whether we can grant the prohibition on the application of the Queen of Portugal before she appears in the Lord Mayor's Court. The plaintiff's counsel argue that, before she can be heard, she must appear and be put in bail, in the alternative, to pay or to render. It would be very much to be lamented if, before doing justice to her, we were obliged to impose a condition upon her which would be a further indignity, and a further violation of the law of nations. If the rule were that the application for a prohibition can only be by the defendant after appearance, we should have had little scruple in making this an exception to the rule. But we find it laid down in books of the highest authority that, where the court to which the prohibition is to go has no jurisdiction, a prohibition may be granted upon the request of a stranger, as well as of the defendant himself; . . . Therefore this court, vested with the power of preventing all inferior courts from exceeding their jurisdiction to the prejudice of the Queen or her subjects, is bound to interfere when duly informed of such an excess of jurisdiction. What has been done in this case by the Lord Mayor's Court must be considered as peculiarly in contempt of the Crown, it being an insult to an independent sovereign, giving that sovereign just cause of complaint to the British Government, and having a tendency to bring about a misunderstanding between our own gracious Sovereign and her ally the Queen of Portugal.

Therefore, upon the information and complaint of the Queen of Portugal, either as the party grieved, or as a stranger, we think we are bound to correct the excess of jurisdiction brought to our notice, and to prohibit the Lord Mayor's Court from proceeding further in this suit.

Rule absolute.

VAVASSEUR v. KRUPP.

Great Britain, Court of Appeal, 1878.

L. R. [1878] 9 Ch. D. 351.

Josiah Vavasseur, the plaintiff in this case, had brought an action against F. Krupp, of Essen, in Germany, Alfred Longsden, his agent in England, and Ahrens & Co., described as agents for the Government of

Japan, claiming an injunction and damages for the infringement of the plaintiff's patent for making shells and other projectiles. The shells in question had been made at Essen, in Germany, had been there bought for the Government of Japan, had been brought to this country and landed here in order to be put on board three ships of war which were being built here for the Government of Japan, and to be used as ammunition for the guns of those ships.

On the 18th of January, 1878, an injunction was, without prejudice to any question, granted, restraining the defendants and the owners of the wharf where the shells lay from selling or delivering the shells to the Government of Japan, or to any person on their behalf, or otherwise from parting with, selling, or disposing of the shells and projectiles.

On the 11th of May an application to the Court was made on behalf of the Mikado of Japan and his Envoy Extraordinary in this country, that, notwithstanding the injunction, the Mikado and his agents might be at liberty to remove the shells, and that if and so far as might be necessary the Mikado and his Envoy should for the purposes of making and being heard upon such application be added as Defendants in the suit. Upon this application an order was made by the Master of the Rolls that on the Mikado by his counsel submitting to the jurisdiction of this Court and desiring to be made a defendant, and on payment into Court by the Mikado of £100 as security for costs, the name of the Mikado be added as a party Defendant in the action.

Notice of motion was then given on the part of the Mikado that the injunction might be dissolved, and that the Mikado might be at liberty to take possession, and remove out of the jurisdiction of the Court the shells in question the property of his Imperial Majesty.

The motion was heard before the Master of the Rolls on the 29th of June.

Jessel, M. R. . . . I propose to make an order that, without prejudice to any question, notwithstanding the injunction, the Mikado shall be at liberty to take out of the jurisdiction the shells which belong to him.

The Plaintiff expressed his intention at once to appeal, and the appeal came on at once for hearing, on the 3rd of July, without any order having been drawn up or any formal notice of appeal having been given. . . .

James, L. J. I am of opinion that this attempt on the part of the Plaintiff to interfere with the right of a foreign sovereign to deal with his public property is one of the boldest I have ever heard of as made in any Court in this country.

It is an undoubted and admitted fact that the Mikado of Japan, who is a sovereign prince, bought in Germany a certain quantity of shells, which shells were lawfully made in Germany, although they were, as alleged, made upon the same principle as something which is the subject of a patent in this country. Those shells were bought by the Mikado for the purpose of his government. He brought them into this country on the way to Japan, and he asks to be allowed to remove them from this country, that is to say, he asks that he shall not, by reason of something which was done between the Plaintiff and some other persons, be interfered with in his removal of them to his own country. It seems to me that to refuse him that leave would be a very dangerous proceeding. If a tribunal of any foreign country were to deal with the ammunition of a British man of war under those circumstances, or refuse to permit the captain of a British man of war to remove his ammunition and shells, or anything else, I think that our country would consider it a very serious matter, and possibly demand reparation.

The objection made is this. The Plaintiff says, "True it is that these shells were your property; you had brought them to this country *in transitu* to Japan, and you had no doubt a right so to bring them. But some persons in this country, either with or without your authority— with your authority it may be, but at all events having possession of these things as your agents—were minded to make, and did make, a use of these shells which was inconsistent with our patent, that is to say, they were making a profitable use of them." If they were doing so, then they are liable in an action for damages, and the plaintiff may recover any damages that he may be entitled to. But that does not interfere with the rights of the sovereign of Japan, who now asks to be allowed to take his property. It was his property. It is now in the shape in which it was when he lawfully bought it in Germany, where it was lawfully made, and he asks to be allowed to take it out of this country in that shape.

I cannot conceive it possible how any doubt could arise or could be suggested as to the right of the Mikado to do this. I suppose that there is a notion that in some way these shells became tainted or affected through the breach or attempted breach of the patent; but even then a foreign sovereign cannot be deprived of his property because it has become tainted by the infringement of somebody's patent. He says, "It is my public property, and I ask you for it." That seems to me to be the whole of the case.

It is, however, said that the Mikado has submitted to the jurisdiction. No doubt he submitted to the jurisdiction, but in this way only, and for this purpose only. In certain circumstances (which it is not necessary for us now to inquire into) Mr. Ahrens and others were ordered by a Court of municipal jurisdiction not to deliver certain shells and other things to the Mikado, that is to say, treating them as property, these persons were ordered not to deliver them to the Mikado, but entirely without prejudice. It could never be supposed that that order was to deprive him of any right or property which he had in them. Then when he himself applied to these persons and said, "Give me my property, let me take my property out of this country to my own country," they said, "We do not claim the property, we know it is yours, but there is an injunction of this Court, and we may be liable to punishment by this Court if we give you up your property." Upon which the Mikado, for the purpose of making an application to relieve his own property from a fetter which had been put upon it (I think inadvertently, if I may venture to say so), by the injunction of the Court, does come and say, "I will submit to the jurisdiction of the Court," which means "I will submit to the jurisdiction of the Court as to discovery, as to process, and as to costs." He never meant, "I shall submit my public property to be dealt with by a Court of municipal jurisdiction in another country, and in violation of my rights." The whole effect of that proceeding was that he made himself a suitor liable to the ordinary consequences, so far as they can be enforced against a sovereign as to costs and otherwise, and in that character he made a deposit of £100 to provide for the costs of the proceedings. The order he obtained does not prevent his saying, as is the truth, "This is my property, it was lawfully bought by me and paid for by me, and it is public property. Whether anybody else has done anything right or wrong with it, is a question with which I have nothing to do. No Court of municipal jurisdiction has any right to interfere with my property, and be good enough to remove your hands from it." The Master of the Rolls, who granted the injunction and heard the whole matter, as soon as he learnt what was the state of things, said of course that he could not keep hands on a property which he had no right to interfere with; and he made the order which is complained of.

[Opinions of Brett and Cotton, L. JJ., omitted.]

This appeal is dismissed with costs.

HAHN H. HASSARD, PLAINTIFF, v. THE UNITED STATES OF MEXICO, ET AL., DEFENDANTS.

United States, Supreme Court of New York, New York Special Term, 1899.

29 Misc. Rep. 511.

Motion to vacate attachment.

BOOKSTAVER, J. This motion is made by the United States Attorney for the Southern District of New York, under instructions from the Attorney-General of the United States, to vacate an attachment obtained by the plaintiff against the defendants and to dismiss the complaint upon the ground that this court has no jurisdiction of the subject-matter. The action is against the Republic of Mexico and States of Tamaulipas and San Luis Potosi, the latter two being subordinate divisions of the former. The amount claimed is $3,075,000, with interest at seven per cent from September 1, 1865, which is alleged to be the sum due upon 3,075 bonds of the amount of $1,000 each, issued by the defendants on or about July 4, 1865. The United States District Attorney disclaims appearing by any authority from the defendants, but only on instructions from the Attorney-General, and as *amicus curiae*, to call the attention of the court to its want of jurisdiction in the premises.

That the court is without jurisdiction seems to be a proposition beyond serious dispute. The principal defendant is an independent sovereign nation, having treaty relations with this country, and the other defendants are subordinate divisions thereof. It is an axiom of international law, of long-established and general recognition, that a sovereign State cannot be sued in its own courts, or in any other, without its consent and permission. For applications of this doctrine see Schooner Exchange v. McFaddon, 7 Cranch, 116; Manning v. State of Nicaragua, 14 How. Pr. 517; Beers v. State of Arkansas, 20 How. (U. S.) 527.

This principle extends so far that a sovereign State, by coming into court as a suitor, does not thereby abandon its sovereignty and subject itself to an affirmative judgment upon a counterclaim. People v. Dennison, 84 N. Y. 272; United States v. Eckford, 6 Wall. 490.

So far as this doctrine is applied to foreign powers, it is obviously based upon sound considerations of international comity and peace, and it is significant that this country is so solicitous on this point that it has, by its Constitution, article 3, section 2, subdivision 2, conferred upon its highest judicial tribunal original jurisdiction in all cases affecting ambassadors or other public ministers and consuls, and by section 687 of the United States Revised Statutes, that jurisdiction is made exclusive and is extended even to domestics or domestic servants of such foreign representatives.

That State courts scrupulously recognize their own lack of jurisdiction is illustrated in Valarino v. Thompson, 7 N. Y. 576, where it was held that the exemption was a privilege, not of the representative, but of his sovereign, and that he could not waive it. It was also there stated that the court will put a stop to the proceedings at any stage on its being shown that they have no jurisdiction. So far as jurisdiction is concerned, there is no difference between suits against a sovereign directly and suits against its property. Stanley v. Schwalby, 147 U. S. 508; United States v. Lee, 106 *id.* 196.

The plaintiff's attorney strenuously combats the right of the district attorney to intervene, and points out that section 682 of the Code provides expressly the only methods by which a motion to vacate an attachment can be made, and that the district attorney has no standing under these provisions. The fault of this argument lies in the fact that section 682 makes no provision for vacating an attachment of this kind, because the legislators never contemplated the issuance of such an attachment. Properly speaking, this is not a proceeding to vacate a thing that ever had validity, but rather to revoke what was the result of an inadvertence in an *ex parte* proceeding and a nullity *ab initio* and to set the court right on its own records and in the eyes of the world. The motion should be granted.

Motion granted.[1]

KINGDOM OF NORWAY v. FEDERAL SUGAR REFINING CO.

United States, District Court, Southern District of New York, 1923.

286 Fed. 188.

At Law. Action by the Kingdom of Norway against the Federal Sugar Refining Company. On motion by plaintiff to restrict answer and counterclaim. Denied.

MACK, Circuit Judge. These three cases[2] involve the question of the existence and extent of the right of cross-libel and counterclaim in legal proceedings instituted by or on behalf of a sovereign state. . . .

Case III is a suit at law by the plaintiff, the kingdom of Norway, a sovereign state, for money had and received in the alleged sum of $165,000, on the ground that the defendant has been unjustly enriched by the receipt of money which equitably is alleged to belong to the plaintiff. The complaint may be briefly summarized: The kingdom of Norway had, through its Food Commission, contracted with the defendant, the Federal Sugar Refining Company, to purchase 4,500 tons of refined sugar at $6.60 per hundredweight. Although the plaintiff was in great need of sugar to feed its people, it was prevented from receiving sugar under its contract, by reason of the embargo placed on the export of sugar by the United States government. On account of this embargo it was agreed between the plaintiff and the defendant that the time for the performance of their contract should be extended, and that the price should equal that fixed by the government for the market at the time delivery was actually made. It is alleged that the United States Sugar Equalization Board, Inc., a corporation organized and controlled by the Food Administration of the United States, which owned and held all the capital stock thereof, procured the government of the United States to refuse to license the export of sugar under the plaintiff's contract with

---

[1] Affirmed by the Appellate Division of the Supreme Court of New York, 61 N. Y. S. 939.

[2] The other two suits against The Gloria and The Thekla, for collision, were in admiralty.

the defendant, and that in the meantime the market price as fixed by the government rose to $8.12 per hundredweight. The United States Sugar Equalization Board is alleged to have taken advantage of the necessities of the plaintiff, and to have sold the plaintiff 4,500 tons of refined sugar at $11 per hundredweight, an extortionate price, $2.88 per hundredweight above the price fixed by the government. It is stated that the defendant herein, the Federal Sugar Refining Company, brought suit against the United States Sugar Equalization Board for tortious interference with its contract with the kingdom of Norway, and that on demurrer it was held by this court (Federal Sugar Refining Co. v. U. S. Sugar Equalization Board, 268 Fed. 575) that the complaint stated a good cause of action. Before trial a settlement was effected, and the kingdom of Norway contends that $165,000 collected by the defendant from the Equalization Board represented the money unjustly exacted from the plaintiff by the Equalization Board when it took advantage of the plaintiff's necessities to extort an unfair and improper price for its sugar. It is maintained that the defendant in fact did not suffer the loss or damage for which the compensation was paid, and that the sum of $165,000 collected from the Equalization Board is money had and received to the use of the plaintiff, to which money the plaintiff is equitably entitled.

The defendant has filed a counterclaim, setting up that the plaintiff, the kingdom of Norway, has, without legal excuse, failed to perform its contract for the purchase of 4,500 tons of sugar, whereby the defendant sustained damage in the sum of $219,000, for which judgment is asked. The case is now before the court on the motion of the plaintiff, the kingdom of Norway, to restrict the answer and counterclaim to such matters and to such amount as may properly be pleaded as a set-off to the plaintiff's cause of action. Although counsel for the defendant has contended that under section 266 of the New York Civil Practice Act, printed in the footnote, . . . he is not limited, even in filing a counterclaim against a friendly sovereign state, to a cause of action arising out of the contract or transaction as set forth in the complaint as the foundation of the plaintiff's claim or connected with the subject of the action, still it would seem clear that, if it were necessary that the counterclaim arise out of the same transaction as the original complaint, under a fair and liberal construction of the act, this counterclaim could be regarded as so arising.

The principle of immunity of a sovereign state from suit without its consent has a long history in our law, yet there are many new and unsettled problems in regard to its application in modern law to-day. Precedent and logic, while important, afford no infallible guide to the correct solution of these. All the important interests involved must be carefully weighed and balanced. The Pesaro (D. C.) 277 Fed. 473.

With respect to the specific questions here to be decided, it must be remembered that the law of set-off and counterclaim is of relatively recent development. Recoupment only was known to the common law, and a restricted right of set-off first developed in equity. Even the limited right of set-off, properly so called, was never recognized at common law, but was introduced by the statute of 2 Geo. II, c. 22, § 13, made permanent by the statute of 8 Geo. II, c. 24, §§ 4 and 5. Cf. also earlier St. 4 and 5 Anne, c. 17, authorizing set-off in bankruptcy. The broader right of counterclaim and affirmative relief was an even more modern innovation. The right of counterclaim and set-off having been first introduced as a part of our procedural law, halting recognition is just beginning to be given to the fact that the right as between litigants is something more than a procedural convenience and is really a requirement of substantive justice. That the right of set-off and counterclaim is regarded in our law to-day as affecting, in important aspects, the substantive relations between the parties, is clearly seen in the rules as to the assignment of choses in action being subject to existing set-offs or counterclaims. It is interesting to note that in Roman law, too, the right of set-off was at first grudgingly recognized as part of the adjective law and only gradually accepted as a part of the substantive law. Girard, Manuel Elementaire de Droit Romain (4th Ed.) pp. 701–708; Buckland, A Text-Book of Roman Law, pp. 696–700.

If the right of set-off and counterclaim be regarded as a mere matter of procedure, there would seem to be no reason why a right against a sovereign state should be recognized by set-off or counterclaim, which could not be set up in an independent suit. On the other hand, if the right of set-off or counterclaim is to be regarded as affecting the substantive relations between the litigants, the question presented assumes an entirely different aspect. It would be only natural for one to expect, in the development of the law of set-off and counterclaim, to find decisions refusing to recognize anything but a right of recoupment in respect of the transaction in suit in a proceeding begun by a sovereign state. Cf. People v. Dennison, 84 N. Y. 272.

On the other hand, as the right of set-off and counterclaim gradually comes to be regarded as affecting the substantive rights of the litigants, one would expect to find courts reluctant to give judgment in favor of a sovereign state, where judgment would, in the circumstances, be denied a private litigant because of the right of set-off or .counterclaim. Once the first hurdle is past, and it is recognized that the defendant in suit brought by a sovereign state is not limited in his defense to strict common-law recoupment, but may assert the broader right of set-off, it may be expected that a modern court of equity, of admiralty, or even of law will be impatient of any restrictions on its jurisdiction to determine judicially all questions involved in the controversy or controversies submitted. While a court may have no power to enforce an affirmative judgment against a sovereign state, still if, as a defense to a suit instituted by a sovereign state, a counterclaim or set-off is asserted, it would seem only proper that the court determine all issues fairly before it, even though it involve a finding that the plaintiff state was indebted to the defendant. A modern court should strive to do complete justice; a partial and incomplete adjudication tends only to protract and complicate litigation to the detriment of all concerned. A partial and incomplete adjudication leaves all parties in grave doubt as to their status and rights, and leads to a multiplicity of suits.

A sovereign state, generally speaking, is not obliged to go into court; but, if it seeks the assistance of the court, it would seem to be in accord with the best principles of modern law that it should be obliged to submit to the jurisdiction of the court in respect of **any set**-off or counterclaim properly assertable as a defense in a similar suit between private litigants. Although, perhaps, the defendant should not be permitted to assert any counterclaim which would not be, in whole or part, a defense to the action brought by the state, yet, if it is necessary to examine a counterclaim for the purpose of determining whether there is a defense to the original action, it would seem inconsistent with the duty of a court of general jurisdiction to do complete justice for the court not to determine the whole nature and extent of the counterclaim, even though it involved incidentally a determination that a sovereign state was indebted or obligated to the defendant.

There is no principle of public law exempting a sovereign state from its obligations under the law. It should not be assumed that a state desires to deny or evade its obligations. There may be sound reasons of public policy why a state should be immune from the harrassment of litigation in forums and under conditions not agreeable to the state. But, once the state has chosen its forum, there seems little reason in law or policy why it should not be subject to the substantive requirements of law and justice.

It is believed that a careful analysis of the English decisions and the decisions of our Supreme Court justify the views herein expressed.

. . .

It is true that there have been some federal decisions, which follow the earlier decisions of the Supreme Court, the later decisions apparently having been overlooked by counsel, and in others there are dicta to the same effect. See U. S. v. Nipissing Mines Co., 206 F. 431, 124 C. C. A. 313 (C. C. A. 2); Kingdom of Roumania v. Guaranty Trust Co., 250 F. 341, 162 C. C. A. 411, Ann. Cas. 1918 E, 524 (C. C. A. 2, semble); French Republic v. Inland Navigation Co. (D. C.) 263 F. 410; Barendrecht Steamship Co., Ltd., v. U. S. (U. S. Dist. Ct. for S. D. N. Y.) 286 F. 386, decided by Judge Ward on January 27, 1922. While there are intimations and dicta in some of the opinions hereinabove cited contrary to the views herein expressed, the actual decisions in those cases which are binding upon this court are, I believe, distinguishable. In the Kingdom of Roumania Case, it was a third party, not the defendant, who asserted the counterclaim; in the Nipissing Case, the construction of the statute in reference to set-offs allowed by accounting officers was involved. It is also true that the decisions in the state courts, taken at large, do not seem as yet to have reached the same stage of development as has been reached in the federal Supreme Court. See cases collected in 33 L. R. A. (N. S.) 376, and in French Republic v. Inland Navigation Co., *supra.* It is interesting to note, however, the recent tendency away from limiting the set-off or counterclaim to the same transactions. French Republic v. Inland Navigation Co., *supra.* In New York, however, People v. Dennison, 84 N. Y. 272, so limiting the right of set-off or counterclaim, apparently has not been overruled. See Republic of France v. Pittsburgh Steel Export Co., Inc., 112 Misc. Rep. 688, 184 N. Y. S. 280. . . .

This field of law, it may be noted, seems also to be in a stage of flux and development in continental Europe. There appears to be considerable conflict among the doctrinal writers, and the course of decisions does not seem firmly settled. The German jurisprudence seems to favor the broad right of counterclaim, while the French possibly tends to the more restricted view. See Van Praag, Jurisdiction et Droit International Public, § 105. . . .

Case III is complicated by the fact that, the proceedings being at law, the procedure should conform with the state practice. The counterclaim filed, however, appears to arise out of the same transaction as the original suit, and would seem, therefore, to be properly entertainable under the state practice. It may be that, under the law of the state of New York an affirmative judgment should not be rendered against the kingdom of Norway, even though the final determination of the controverted issues would justify the same, if the suit were between private litigants. The New York precedents may preclude the rendering of an affirmative judgment, but they do not clearly necessarily preclude a complete determination of the issues raised, short of a judgment. There is, therefore, no necessity at this stage to grant the motion of the kingdom of Norway to restrict the answer and counterclaim to such matters and to such amount as may properly be pleaded as a set-off to the plaintiff's causes of action.

Plaintiff's motion is denied.

SOUTH AFRICAN REPUBLIC v. LA COMPAGNIE FRANCO-BELGE DU CHEMIN DE FER DU NORD.

Great Britain, Supreme Court of Judicature, Chancery Division, 1897.

L. R. [1898] 1 Ch. 190.

The defendant company were a Belgian corporation constituted in 1882 for the purpose of acquiring and working a concession from the plaintiffs, the South African Republic, to make a railway in the territory of the plaintiffs. The concession was granted to the defendants, and under its terms they had power, with the sanction of the plaintiff Government, to issue bonds to the amount of 1,500,000l., the payment of interest on which was guaranteed by the plaintiff Government. In June, 1894, such bonds to the amount of 500,000l. having been already issued, the defendant company negotiated with the plaintiff Republic for sanction to issue the rest of the bonds, and obtained such sanction on the basis of the following term contained in a letter written on their behalf: "That the proceeds of the issue shall be placed on deposit in the joint names of Mr. Baelaerts van Blokland and a trustee named by the company, so that all moneys required for the construction, etc., can only be drawn on the joint signatures of the two trustees." Under this arrangement large sums arising from the issue of such debentures were deposited with two London banks in the names of Baelaerts van Blokland, the commissioner in Europe of the plaintiff Republic, and Baron Robert Oppenheim as trustee for the defendant company.

Baelaerts van Blokland died on March 14, 1896. The defendants thereupon claimed a right to deal as they pleased with the funds then standing in the sole name of their nominee: and in March, 1897, the plaintiffs commenced this action against the defendant company, the two banks, and Baron Oppenheim. By their writ they claimed (*inter alia*) an injunction to restrain the defendants dealing with the funds till trial of the action.

The action was brought on on motion for an injunction, the money on deposit was paid into court, and the defendant bankers were dismissed. The plaintiffs put in a statement of claim by which they claimed a declaration that they were entitled to nominate a trustee in the place of Blokland; the appointment of such a trustee on their nomination; and the transfer of the funds in court to the trustees when the new trustee had been appointed.

The defendant company put in a statement of defence and counterclaim by which they alleged various breaches by the plaintiff Government of the terms of the concession; the writing of a letter by an agent of the plaintiffs asserted to be libellous: and that the plaintiffs were unjustly and in bad faith taking proceedings in the Transvaal courts to avoid the concession.

By the counter-claim the company claimed (1.) payment of three several sums of 60,000*l.*, 1800*l.*, and 147,000*l.* as damages for alleged breaches of the terms of the concession; (2.) 100,000*l.* damages for libel; and (3.) that the plaintiff Republic might be restrained from taking or continuing proceedings in the courts of the South African Republic for the purpose of having the said concession declared void and its property expropriated, or, in the alternative, 500,000*l.* damages.

On July 26, 1897, North J., on summons by the plaintiffs, made an order in chambers to strike out the allegations in the counter-claim as to libel and the second head of the defendant company's claim. The defendants appealed, and the Court of Appeals affirmed the order of North J.: see South African Republic v. La Compagnie Franco-Belge, etc. [[1897] 2 Ch. 487].

This was a summons, brought on as a motion, on the part of the plaintiff Republic to strike out the rest of the counter-claim.

NORTH J. . . . I think that the application to strike out the whole counter-claim is well founded. The second paragraph in the prayer of that counter-claim has been already dealt with by me in chambers and in the Court of Appeal. . . .

They have applied now that the other portion of the counter-claim may be struck out too. They say that a foreign Government coming here to sue can be met by defence or counter-claim with respect to the matters incident to the subject-matter of the action brought by the foreign Government; but the plaintiffs deny, and the defendants allege that, by the foreign Government coming here as plaintiffs, they have submitted to the general jurisdiction of the Court, so as to be capable of being caught and sued here in respect of any matter which would be a proper subject of litigation between them if the two parties were private individuals, both resident in this country, and subject to the jurisdiction of its Courts.

Now, on that, several cases were cited as to the position of a foreign Government coming here to sue. There are only two or three that I need refer to very shortly. The first is Duke of Brunswick v. King of Hanover [6 Beav. 38], where Lord Langdale says—I need only read a few lines of a very long judgment—"The cases which we have upon this point go no further than this; that where a foreign Sovereign files a bill, or prosecutes an action in this country, he may be made a defendant to a cross-bill or bill of discovery in the nature of a defence to the proceeding, which the foreign Sovereign has himself adopted. There is no case to shew that, because he may be plaintiff in the courts of this country for one matter, he may therefore be made a defendant in the courts of this country for another and quite a distinct matter; and the question to be now determined is independent of the fact stated at the bar, that the King of Hanover is or was himself plaintiff in a suit for an entirely distinct matter in this court." It is clear that Lord Langdale considered the law settled. There may be a proceeding against a foreign government plaintiff by way of counter-proceeding, by cross-bill, or, what I take to be not the same as a cross-bill, a bill of discovery—it might be either a bill of discovery, if necessary, or a cross-bill—in the nature of a defence to the proceedings set up by the plaintiff; but not a proceeding setting up against the Sovereign another claim in respect of another and entirely distinct matter.

Then there was a case—Strousberg v. Republic of Costa Rica, [29 W. R. 125]—where the Republic of Costa Rica had sued Strousberg in this country, and judgment had been recovered in that action for them. There had been a final judgment for the payment of large sums of money; there had been no cross-bill apparently, or cross-action, pending that action; but, after it was disposed of, and final judgment had been recovered, Strousberg sought to sue the Government of Costa Rica in this country for the purpose of setting up a claim to meet the claim of the Government under the judgment. That proceeding was clearly wrong. If he could have taken any step, it ought to have been to stay proceedings in the action under which the judgment had been recovered; but in the course of the judgment both the Master of the Rolls and James L. J. made certain observations, not essential for the judgment, but arising out of the matter before the Court, that are useful to be considered. Pollock B. had made an order in chambers allowing service of the writ in this new action upon the ground that it was in the nature of a cross-action. Thereupon the Government entered a conditional appearance and moved to discharge the order. The Court of Appeal decided that the order ought not to have been made, and ought to be discharged. The Master of the Rolls pointed out it was made under a misunderstanding. He said, the learned judge "was told, and he seems to have adopted the statement without sufficient knowledge of the prior proceedings, that it was in the nature of a counter-claim or cross-action, and in that case, no doubt,"—that is to say, if it was a counter-claim or cross-action— "you can make a Sovereign State a defendant, with a view of doing justice in the original action brought by the Sovereign State"—not settling every possible matter in dispute between the parties, but doing justice in the original action. Then James L. J. says: "It appears to me that it is due from one nation to another, that one Sovereign should not assume or usurp jurisdiction over another Sovereign. It is a violation of the respect due to a foreign Sovereign or State to issue the process of our Courts against such Sovereign or State. There is but one exception, if it can be called an exception, to the rule, and that is where a foreign Sovereign or State comes into the Courts of this country for the purpose of obtaining some remedy; then by way of defence to that proceeding, the person sued here may file a cross-claim against that Sovereign or State for enabling complete justice to be done between

them. The defendant in that case is, in fact, only giving to the foreign
Sovereign's attorney or solicitor notice of the proceedings—for that is,
in substance, what it comes to—so as to bring in whatever defence or
counter-claim there might be as a set-off. We went recently very fully,
in the case of The Parlement Belge [5 P. D. 197], into the question of
the extent to which the Courts of this country ought to go, even as to
property of a foreign Sovereign found here, and I have no hesitation,
having fully considered the matter, in arriving at the conclusion I have
now stated." Then he said there was one other case in which a foreign
Sovereign might be joined as defendant to an action, and that was where
he was, or was alleged to be, one of several claimants upon a fund over
which the Court had jurisdiction. I do not read the part of the judgment relating to that, because it is not material to the case here.

Now, I believe the law is still exactly as it was stated to be at the
time Lord Langdale laid it down in the way in which he did. Here the
defendant has brought in a counter-claim, and there seem to me to be two
questions on it, first of all, whether it is a case in which, having regard
to the action in which the foreign Government has submitted to the
jurisdiction, this is a case in which a counter-claim such as this can
properly be put in; and, secondly, if it is, whether as a matter of convenience, assuming the Court could allow it, it is more convenient that the
subject-matter should be dealt with in a separate action, or in this
action.

The great object of the defendants in getting it joined in this action is
this. In ordinary cases it probably would not matter very much whether
they proceeded by counter-claim or cross-action; but if there has to be a
cross-action, it cannot be served upon a foreign Government in this
country. They want to get a counter-claim to enable them to serve it
upon the plaintiffs in the action, and so get jurisdiction against them
in respect of these matters. Now, it is a remarkable thing that neither
in the statement of claim nor in the defence, so far as my attention
has been called to it, and certainly not in the counter-claim, is there any
suggestion that the Court has to deal with this fund by executing the
trusts of it, or that it is for the Court to try the question whether the
fund has or has not properly been applied. Proceedings of that sort
have been commenced in the country where the property is situated,
which is, prima facie, certainly the proper tribunal before which these
matters must come, and it is conceded that that part of the counter-claim
which asks me to restrain the plaintiff Government from taking proceedings in the Courts of their own country cannot be supported. There is
also a claim either for such an injunction or 500,000l. damages; but,
in my opinion, that fails absolutely and entirely, and I do not think that
claim to the alternative damages has really been seriously pressed. The
more important matter is as to the three sums of money which are the
subject of the first head of the counter-claim. There are three sums in

respect of which it has been pointed out in various paragraphs of the counter-claim that the Government are alleged to be indebted to the defendants; but they are not sums with respect to which the defendants have any claim whatever upon the fund in question itself. The claim, if any, is against the Government for particular sums, which would have to be paid by the Government 'out of its general revenues, and for which there is no claim on the fund in question in any way. That being so, I do not see how the claim to recover those sums against the Government can be right, having regard to the passages which I have read from those two cases, and passages similar to which may be found in many other cases. It is a pure pecuniary claim against the Government, entirely outside of and independent of the subject-matter of the present action. It is not in reality a defence at all to the case set up by the Government in that action.

Under these circumstances, it seems to me that these sums are not sums which can be made the subject of counter-claim against the Government; in other words, I do not think the Government can be sued in respect of these matters by way of counter-claim; but even if they could, I certainly think they are so foreign to the subject-matter of the present action that it would not by any means be convenient to unite these matters with the subject-matters of the action at all. Under these circumstances, the counter-claim must be struck out; but without costs, because I see no reason why the two applications to strike out parts of the counter-claim should not have been combined in one.[1]

---

[1] SUPPLEMENTARY CASES. Query, as to personal immunities of sovereigns of protected states. In Statham v. Statham and the Gaekwar of Baroda, [1912] Probate 92, involving a suit against the Gaekwar as corespondent in proceedings for divorce, the British examined the status of the Gaekwar and found that his position as reigning sovereign entitled him to immunity from suit. While the court stated that its decision was based upon "international law" and quoted from Grotius and Vattel, its conclusions would not have been supported had the suit been brought outside of the British Empire. Compare Mighell v. Sultan of Johore, above, p. 50. In the case of Duff Development Co. v. Kelantan, above, p. 50, the British House of Lords was unwilling to read into the terms of a contract between a foreign state and a British corporation, in accordance with which immunity from suit was waived by the foreign state in respect to the execution of the contract, such "consent" between the foreign state and the court as would warrant assumption of jurisdiction.

Query, as to limitations upon counterclaims in answer to the suit of a foreign sovereign? In French Republic v. Inland Navigation Co., 263 F. 410 (1920), involving a suit by the plaintiff to recover $330,000 paid as part payment upon a contract to which the defendant entered a counterclaim for $600,000 for breach of the same contract, the court held that, while the defendant might set off the plaintiff's demand by pleading "so much of a demand as may serve as a defense, . . . yet no affirmative judgment can be sustained as upon a counterclaim against the sovereign, whereby the sovereign shall be compelled or adjudged to pay money or any other thing of value." Kingdom of Roumania v. Guaranty Trust Co., 250 F. 341 (1918), involved a suit by the Kingdom of

Roumania to recover money deposited with the defendant and an attempt on the part of the defendant, who was at the same time being sued by a third party, Arditti, claiming the same money, to have Arditti substituted as defendant and itself discharged on payment into court of the funds in question. The Court of Appeals, reversing the ruling of the District Court which sustained the motion of the Trust Co. held that the defendant could not "avail himself of any counter-claim or set-off, except perhaps a set-off arising out of the same transaction. Under no circumstances can he obtain an affirmative judgment. . . . We are clear that the action by the Kingdom of Roumania to recover a debt owed it by the Guaranty Trust Company was not a waiver of its immunity as a sovereign to be sued by other parties. If this be not so, the immunity can be frittered away either by interpleader or attachment in any case when a foreign sovereign undertakes to collect a debt owed it."

Query as to suits by foreign sovereigns to recover unpaid taxes? In Queen of Holland v. Drukker, L. R. [1928] 1 Ch. Div. 877, involving a suit by the Queen against the executor of the estate of a Dutch subject to enforce payment of a succession tax on personal property left in England by the deceased, the Court of Chancery held that "there is a well recognized rule, which has been enforced for at least 200 years or thereabouts, under which these Courts will not collect the taxes of foreign States for the benefit of the sovereigns of those foreign States; and this is one of those actions which these Courts will not entertain. . . . The statement of claim must therefore be struck out and the action dismissed; and, as the sovereign State has submitted to jurisdiction by coming here, I am in a position to order the sovereign State to pay the costs of the action."

Query, as to the effect of possession of property in suits involving the property of sovereigns? In The Johnson Lighterage Co. No. 24, 231 F. 365 (1916), in-volving a suit for salvage against the Lighterage Co. and consequent seizure of the vessel and its cargo of munitions, the latter being the property of the Russian government, the court held that while an action could not be entertained against the property of a friendly foreign nation if the property was "in its possession and devoted or destined to be devoted to the public use," where such property was not in the actual possession of the Russian government but in the possession of the charterer of the vessel a proceeding in rem might be brought to enforce a lien for salvage services.

Query, as to the status of governmental agents acting in excess of their authority? In Pilger v. United States Steel Corporation and Public Trustee, 98 N. J. Eq. 665 (1925), involving a suit by Pilger, a German subject, for the transfer of shares of stock upon the books of the Steel Corporation and the surrender of certificates seized in Great Britain by the Public Trustee as Cus-todian of Enemy Property during the war, the court held that the Public Trustee could not, as representative of the British government, claim immunity from suit when acting outside the scope of his authority and might therefore be joined with the Steel Corporation as party defendant in a suit to determine the ownership of shares of stock. "An instrumentality of government," said the court, "whether corporate or not, although created for purposes of the very greatest importance, does not cease to be personally answerable for acts done under color of the authority conferred upon it, but, in fact, in excess of that authority and without legal justification. The immunity of a sovereign against suits arising out of the unlawful acts of its representatives does not extend to those who acted in its name, and cannot be set up by them as a bar to suits brought against them for the doing of such unlawful acts."

Query, may a state by adopting and approving an act of one of its citizens as an "act of state" require the dismissal of a criminal prosecution brought

C. Suits against individual states of the United States: necessity of consent.

The question whether the political subdivisions of a nation, whatever be their designation—"states," provinces, colonies, counties or municipalities, are entitled to the immunity from suit which belongs to the nation of which they are a part, is one to which no definite answer can be given, the precedents being too few and the attitudes of national governments too varying. While there would seem to be logical ground for distinguishing such subdivisions from the nation itself, practical constitutional difficulties would in many cases stand in the way. [Monaco v. Mississippi.]

---

against such citizen in a foreign jurisdiction? In People v. McLeod, 25 Wendell 483 (1841), involving the indictment of McLeod for a murder committed in connection with the destruction of the Caroline in the Niagara River in 1837, the Supreme Court of New York held that the approval of the act by a foreign sovereign could "take nothing from the criminality of the principal offender," so that the prisoner was remanded to take his trial in the ordinary forms of law. McLeod was, however, acquitted when put on trial and the affair led to the passage of an act of Congress providing for the issuance by the federal courts of writs of habeas corpus where a prisoner, "being a subject or citizen of a foreign state, and domiciled therein, is in custody for an act done or omitted under any alleged right, title, authority, privilege, protection, or exemption claimed under the commission, or order, or sanction of any foreign state, or under color thereof, the validity and effect whereof depend upon the law of nations." Rev. Stat., § 753 (28 USCA § 453).

In Arce v. State, 83 Tex. Cr. 292 (1918), involving a conviction for the murder of an American soldier committed by soldiers belonging to the army of General Carranza when the army crossed the border into Texas in 1916, the court reversed the judgment of the lower court on the ground that a "state of warfare" existed.

See, on the question of state responsibility for acts of its officers, the references given under Chapter VII. Also E. C. S. Wade, "Act of State in English Law," British Year Book, XV (1934), 98.

Query, would the defense by a public officer that his act was an "act of state" be valid before the national courts on the ground that the injured party was a resident alien? In Johnstone v. Pedlar, L. R. [1921] 2 A. C. 262 involving a suit brought by Pedlar, a naturalized American citizen of Irish birth, against Johnstone, Chief Commissioner of the Dublin Metropolitan Police, for the return of funds taken from his person when arrested for illegal drilling, the British House of Lords held that the defense of an "act of state" could not prevail. Lord Phillimore quoted Walker v. Baird, [1892] A. C. 491, to the effect that "between Her Majesty and one of her subjects there can be no such thing as an act of State," and argued that the individual hostility of an alien friend did not entitle him to the character of an alien enemy and that his residence gave him "the same rights for the protection of his person and property as a natural born or naturalized subject."

PRINCIPALITY OF MONACO v. MISSISSIPPI.

United States, Supreme Court, 1934.

292 U. S. 313. [78 L. ed. 1282; 54 S. Ct. 745.]

Mr. Chief Justice Hughes delivered the opinion of the Court.

The Principality of Monaco asks leave to bring suit in this Court against the State of Mississippi upon bonds issued by the State and alleged to be the absolute property of the Principality.

The proposed declaration sets forth four causes of action. Two counts are upon bonds known as Mississippi Planters' Bank Bonds, dated March 1, 1833, the first count being upon eight bonds of $1000 each, due March 1, 1861, and the second count upon two bonds of $1000 each, due March 1, 1866, all with interest at six per cent. per annum. The remaining two counts are upon bonds known as Mississippi Union Bank Bonds, the third count being on twenty bonds of $2000 each, dated June 7, 1838, due February 5, 1850, and the fourth count upon twenty-five bonds of $2000 each, dated June 6, 1838, due February 5, 1858, all with interest at five per cent. per annum. In each count it was alleged that the bonds were transferred and delivered to the Principality at its legation in Paris, France, on or about September 27, 1933, as an absolute gift. Accompanying the declaration and made a part of it is a letter of the donors, dated September 26, 1933, stating that the bonds had "been handed down from their respective families who purchased them at the time of their issue by the State of Mississippi;" that the State had "long since defaulted on the principal and interest of these bonds, the holders of which have waited for some 90 years in the hope that the State would meet its obligations and make payment;" that the donors had been advised that there was no basis upon which they could maintain a suit against Mississippi on the bonds, but that "such a suit could only be maintained by a foreign government or one of the United States;" and that in these circumstances the donors were making an unconditional gift of the bonds to the Principality to be applied "to the causes of any of its charities, to the furtherance of its internal development or to the benefit of its citizens in such manner as it may select."

The State of Mississippi, in its return to the rule to show cause why leave should not be granted, raises the following objections: (1) that the Principality of Monaco is not a "foreign State" within the meaning of § 2, Article III, of the Constitution of the United States, and is therefore not authorized to bring a suit against a State; (2) that the State of Mississippi has not consented and does not consent that she be sued by the Principality of Monaco and that without such consent the State cannot be sued; (3) that the Constitution by § 10, clause 3, Article I, "forbids the State of Mississippi without the consent of Congress to enter into any compact or agreement with the Principality of Monaco, and no compact, agreement or contract has been entered into by the

State with the Principality;" (4) that the proposed litigation is an attempt by the Principality "to evade the prohibitions of the Eleventh Amendment of the Constitution of the United States;" (5) that the proposed declaration does not state a controversy which is "justiciable under the Constitution of the United States and cognizable under the jurisdiction of this Court;" (6) that the alleged right of action "'has long since been defeated and extinguished" by reason of the completion of the period of limitation of action prescribed by the statutes of Mississippi; that the plaintiff and its predecessors in title have been guilty of laches, and that the right of action, if any, is now and for a long time has been stale. . . .

[The court here recites the several statutes of 1833, 1871 and 1873 conferring and restricting the right to sue upon the bonds, and the constitutional provisions of 1876 and 1890 specifically prohibiting the State from making payment upon them.]

In reply to these objections, the Principality asserts that she is a foreign State recognized as such by the Government of the United States; that the consent of the State of Mississippi is not necessary to give the Court jurisdiction; that the obligation of the State of Mississippi to pay her bonds is not an agreement or a compact with a foreign power within § 10, Clause 3, Article I, of the Constitution; that the action is not a subterfuge to evade the Eleventh Amendment; that the cause of action is justiciable; that no statute of limitations has run against the plaintiff or its predecessors and that neither has been guilty of laches. Upon the last-mentioned points the Principality urges that under the provisions of the statutes of Mississippi, holders of her bonds never had an enforceable remedy which could be said to be barred by the running of any state statute of limitations, and that the Principality will be prepared in the course of the suit to meet the defense of laches by showing the history of the efforts of the holders of the bonds to procure payment.

These contentions have been presented in oral argument as well as upon briefs. We find it necessary to deal with but one, that is, the question whether this Court has jurisdiction to entertain a suit brought by a foreign State against a State without her consent. That question, not hitherto determined, is now definitely presented.

The Principality relies upon the provisions of § 2 of Article III of the Constitution of the United States that the judicial power shall extend to controversies "between a State, or the Citizens thereof, and foreign States, Citizens or Subjects" (Clause one), and that in cases "in which a State shall be Party" this Court shall have original jurisdiction (Clause two). The absence of qualification requiring the consent of the State in the case of a suit by a foreign State is asserted to be controlling. And the point is stressed that the Eleventh Amendment of the Constitution, providing that the judicial power shall not be construed to extend to any suit against one of the United States "by Citizens of another State, or by Citizens or Subjects of any Foreign State," contains no reference to a suit brought by a foreign State.

The argument drawn from the lack of an express requirement of consent to be sued is inconclusive. Thus there is no express provision that the United States may not be sued in the absence of consent. Clause one of § 2 of Article III extends the judicial power "to Controversies to which the United States shall be a Party." Literally, this includes such controversies, whether the United States be party plaintiff or defendant. Williams v. United States, 289 U. S. 553, 573. But by reason of the established doctrine of the immunity of the sovereign from suit except upon consent, the provision of Clause one of § 2 of Article III does not authorize the maintenance of suits against the United States. Williams v. United States, *supra*; compare Cohens v. Virginia, 6 Wheat. 264, 411, 412; Minnesota v. Hitchcock, 185 U. S. 373, 384, 386; Kansas v. United States, 204 U. S. 331, 341, 342. And while Clause two of § 2 of Article III gives this Court original jurisdiction in those cases in which "a State shall be Party," this Court has no jurisdiction of a suit by a State against the United States in the absence of consent, Kansas v. United States, *supra*. Clause two merely distributes the jurisdiction conferred by Clause one, and deals with cases in which resort may be had to the original jurisdiction of this Court in the exercise of the judicial power as previously given. Duhne v. New Jersey, 251 U. S. 311, 314.

Similarly, neither the literal sweep of the words of Clause one of § 2 of Article III nor the absence of restriction in the letter of the Eleventh Amendment, permits the conclusion that in all controversies of the sort described in Clause one, and omitted from the words of the Eleventh Amendment, a State may be sued without her consent. Thus Clause one specifically provides that the judicial Power shall extend "to *all* Cases, in Law and Equity, arising under this Constitution, the Laws of the United States, and Treaties made, or which shall be made, under their Authority." But, although a case may arise under the Constitution and laws of the United States, the judicial power does not extend to it if the suit is sought to be prosecuted against a State, without her consent, by one of her own citizens. Hans v. Louisiana, 134 U. S. 1; Duhne v. New Jersey, *supra*, p. 311. The requirement of consent is necessarily implied. . . .

Manifestly, we cannot rest with a mere literal application of the words of § 2 of Article III, or assume that the letter of the Eleventh Amendment exhausts the restrictions upon suits against non-consenting States. Behind the words of the constitutional provisions are postulates which limit and control. There is the essential postulate that the controversies, as contemplated, shall be found to be of a justiciable character. There is also the postulate that States of the Union, still possessing attributes of sovereignty, shall be immune from suits, without their consent, save where there has been "a surrender of this immunity in the plan of the convention." The Federalist, No. 81. The question is whether the plan of the Constitution involves the surrender of immunity when the suit is brought against a State, without her consent, by a foreign State.

The debates in the Constitutional Convention do not disclose a discussion of this question. But Madison, in the Virginia Convention, answering objections to the ratification of the Constitution, clearly stated his view as to the purpose and effect of the provision conferring jurisdiction over controversies between States of the Union and foreign States. That purpose was suitably to provide for adjudication in such cases if consent should be given but not otherwise. Madison said: "The next case provides for disputes between a foreign state and one of our states, should such a case ever arise; and between a citizen and a foreign citizen or subject. I do not conceive that any controversy can ever be decided, in these courts, between an American state and a foreign state, without the consent of the parties. If they consent, provision is here made." 3 Elliot's Debates, 533.

Marshall, in the same Convention, expressed a similar view. Replying to an objection as to the admissibility of a suit by a foreign state, Marshall said: "He objects, in the next place, to its jurisdiction in controversies between a state and a foreign state. Suppose, says he, in such a suit, a foreign state is cast; will she be bound by the decision? If a foreign state brought a suit against the commonwealth of Virginia, would she not be barred from the claim if the federal judiciary thought it unjust? The previous consent of the parties is necessary; and, as the federal judiciary will decide, each party will acquiesce." 3 Elliot's Debates, 557.

Hamilton, in The Federalist, No. 81, made the following emphatic statement of the general principle of immunity: "It is inherent in the nature of sovereignty not to be amenable to the suit of an individual *without its consent*. This is the general sense and the general practice of mankind; and the exemption, as one of the attributes of sovereignty, is now enjoyed by the government of every State in the Union. Unless, therefore, there is a surrender of this immunity in the plan of the convention, it will remain with the States, and the danger intimated must be merely ideal. . . . "

It is true that, despite these cogent statements of the views which prevailed when the Constitution was ratified, the Court held, in Chisholm v. Georgia, 2 Dall. 419, over the vigorous dissent of Mr. Justice Iredell, that a State was liable to suit by a citizen of another State or of a foreign country. But this decision created such a shock of surprise that the Eleventh Amendment was at once proposed and adopted. As the Amendment did not in terms apply to a suit against a State by its own citizens, the Court had occasion, when that question was presented in Hans v. Louisiana, *supra* (a case alleged to arise under the Constitution of the United States), to give elaborate consideration to the application of the general principle of the immunity of States from suits brought against them without their consent. . . . The Court said (134 U. S. pp. 12 *et seq.*): "Looking back from our present standpoint at the decision in Chisholm v. Georgia, we do not greatly wonder at the effect which it had upon the country. Any such power as that of authorizing the federal judiciary to entertain suits by individuals against the States, had been expressly disclaimed, and even resented, by the great defenders of the Constitution, whilst it was on its trial before the American people." . . .

"The truth is, that the cognizance of suits and actions unknown to the law, and forbidden by the law, was not contemplated by the Constitution when establishing the judicial power of the United States. . . .

"The suability of a State without its consent was a thing unknown to the law. This has been so often laid down and acknowledged by courts and jurists that it is hardly necessary to be formally asserted. . . . "

The question of that immunity, in the light of the provisions of Clause one of § 2 of Article III of the Constitution, is thus presented in several distinct classes of cases, that is, in those brought against a State (a) by another State of the Union; (b) by the United States; (c) by the citizens of another State or by the citizens or subjects of a foreign State; (d) by citizens of the same State or by federal corporations; and (e) by foreign States. Each of these classes has its characteristic aspect, from the standpoint of the effect, upon sovereign immunity from suits, which has been produced by the constitutional scheme.

1. The establishment of a permanent tribunal with adequate authority to determine controversies between the States, in place of an inadequate scheme of arbitration, was essential to the peace of the Union. The Federalist, No. 80; Story on the Constitution, § 1679. With respect to such controversies, the States by the adoption of the Constitution, acting "in their highest sovereign capacity, in the convention of the people," waived their exemption from judicial power. The jurisdiction of this Court over the parties in such cases was thus established "by their own consent and delegated authority" as a necessary feature of the formation of a more perfect Union. . . .

2. Upon a similar basis rests the jurisdiction of this Court of a suit by the United States against a State, albeit without the consent of the latter. While that jurisdiction is not conferred by the Constitution in express words, it is inherent in the constitutional plan. . . .

3. To suits against a State, without her consent, brought by citizens of another State or by citizens or subjects of a foreign State, the Eleventh Amendment erected an absolute bar. . . .

4. Protected by the same fundamental principle, the States, in the absence of consent, are immune from suits brought against them by their own citizens or by federal corporations, although such suits are not within the explicit prohibitions of the Eleventh Amendment. . . .

5. We are of the opinion that the same principle applies to suits against a State by a foreign State. The decision in Cherokee Nation v. Georgia, 5 Pet. 1, is not opposed, as it rested upon the determination that the Cherokee nation was not a "foreign State" in the sense in which the term is used in the Constitution. The question now before us necessarily remained an open one. We think that Madison correctly interpreted Clause one of § 2 of Article III of the Constitution as making provision for jurisdiction of a suit against a State by a foreign State in the event of the State's consent but not otherwise. In such a case, the grounds of coercive jurisdiction which are present in suits to determine controversies between States of the Union, or in suits brought by the United States against a State, are not present. The foreign State lies outside the structure of the Union. The waiver or consent, on the part of a State, which inheres in the acceptance of the constitutional plan, runs to the other States who have likewise accepted that plan, and to the United States as the sovereign which the Constitution creates. We perceive no ground upon which it can be said that any waiver or consent by a State of the Union has run in favor of a foreign State. As to suits brought by a foreign State, we think that the States of the Union retain the same immunity that they enjoy with respect to suits by individuals whether citizens of the United States or citizens or subjects of a foreign State. The foreign State enjoys a similar sovereign immunity and without her consent may not be sued by a State of the Union.

The question of the right of suit by a foreign State against a State of the Union is not limited to cases of alleged debts or of obligations issued by a State and claimed to have been acquired by transfer. Controversies between a State and a foreign State may involve international questions in relation to which the United States has a sovereign prerogative. One of the most frequent occasions for the exercise of the jurisdiction granted by the Constitution over controversies between States of the Union has been found in disputes over territorial boundaries. See Rhode Island v. Massachusetts, *supra*, p. 737. Questions have also arisen with respect to the obstruction of navigation, South Carolina v. Georgia, 93 U. S. 4; the pollution of streams, Missouri v. Illinois, 180 U. S. 208; 200 U. S. 496; and the diversion of navigable waters, Wisconsin v. Illinois, 278 U. S. 367; 289 U. S. 395, 400. But in the case of such a controversy with a foreign power, a State has no prerogative of adjustment. No State can enter "into any Treaty, Alliance, or Confederation" or, without the consent of Congress, "into any Agreement or Compact with a foreign Power." Const. Art. 1, § 10. The National Government, by virtue of its control of our foreign relations is entitled to employ the resources of diplomatic negotiations and to effect such an international settlement as may be found to be appropriate, through treaty, agreement of arbitration, or otherwise. It cannot be supposed that it was the intention that a controversy growing out of the action of a State, which involves a matter of national concern and which is said to affect injuriously the interests of a foreign State, or a dispute arising from conflicting claims of a State of the Union and a foreign State as to territorial boundaries, should be taken out of the sphere of international negotiations and adjustment through a resort by the foreign State to a suit under the provisions of § 2 of Article III.   In such a case, the State has immunity from suit without her consent and the National Government is protected by the provision prohibiting agreements between States and foreign powers in the absence of the consent of the Congress.   While, in this instance, the proposed suit does not raise a question of national concern, the constitutional provision which is said to confer jurisdiction should be construed in the light of all its applications.

We conclude that the Principality of Monaco, with respect to the right to maintain the proposed suit, is in no better case than the donors of the bonds, and that the application for leave to sue must be denied.

Rule discharged and leave denied.[1]

---

[1] For comments upon the case, see J. S. Reeves, "The Principality of Monaco v. The State of Mississippi," Am. Journal Int. Law, XXVIII (1934), 739.

CHAPTER IX

JURISDICTION OVER PRIVATE AND PUBLIC VESSELS [1]

A. Territorial character of national vessels.

The earlier theory offered in explanation of the jurisdiction exercised by a state over merchant vessels flying its national flag was that they were "floating portions" of its territory. This fiction of the "exterritoriality" of vessels has now largely given way to a more practical position which sees in the rules governing the status of merchant vessels on the high seas and in foreign ports nothing more than rules of convenience mutually accepted by nations. Jurisdiction over acts performed or committed on board a merchant vessel may be based upon the national character of the vessel, upon the nationality of the person committing the act, and again it may be based upon the presence of the vessel in territorial waters. Query, what if a crime be committed by a citizen of one state on board a national vessel of a second state within the territorial waters of a third state? [Regina v. Anderson.] Would an act committed on a national vessel within the territorial waters of a foreign state with the express sanction of the local authorities be punishable under the laws of the home state when the vessel returns again within its jurisdiction? [Regina v. Leslie.] In countries following the territorial principle of criminal jurisdiction would an exception be made in respect to acts committed on board national vessels in foreign ports? [United States v. Flores.]

REGINA v. JAMES ANDERSON.

Great Britain, Court of Criminal Appeal, 1868.

11 Cox's Criminal Cases, 198.

Case reserved by Byles, J., at the October Sessions of the Central Criminal Court, 1868, for the opinion of this court.

James Anderson, an American citizen, was indicted for murder on board a vessel, belonging to the port of Yarmouth in Nova Scotia. She was registered in London, and was sailing under the British flag.

---

[1] For a more detailed study of this subject, see Fenwick, *op. cit.*, 217–230; Hyde, *op. cit.*, §§ 250–257; Oppenheim, I, §§ 447–451a; Jessup, Law of Territorial Waters and Maritime Jurisdiction, Chap. III; Harvard Draft: Territorial Waters; J. W. Garner, "Immunities of State-owned Ships Employed in Commerce," British Year Book, VI (1925), 128.

At the time of the offence committed the vessel was in the river Garonne, within the boundaries of the French empire, on her way up to Bordeaux, which city is by the course of the river about ninety miles from the open sea. The vessel had proceeded about half-way up the river, and was at the time of the offence about three hundred yards from the nearest shore, the river at that place being about half a mile wide.

The tide flows up to the place and beyond it.

No evidence was given whether the place was or was not within the limits of the port of Bordeaux.

It was objected for the prisoner that the offence having been committed within the empire of France, the vessel being a colonial vessel, and the prisoner an American citizen, the Court had no jurisdiction to try him.

I expressed an opinion unfavorable to the objection, but agreed to grant a case for the opinion of this Court.

The prisoner was convicted of manslaughter.

J. BARNARD BYLES.

BOVILL, C. J.   There is no doubt that the place where the offence was committed was within the territory of France, and that the prisoner was therefore subject to the laws of France, which the local authorities of that realm might have enforced if so minded; but at the same time, in point of law, the offence was also committed within British territory, for the prisoner was a seaman on board a merchant vessel, which, as to her crew and master, must be taken to have been at the time under the protection of the British flag, and, therefore, also amenable to the provisions of the British law.   It is true that the prisoner was an American citizen, but he had with his own consent embarked on board a British vessel as one of the crew.   Although the prisoner was subject to the American jurisprudence as an American citizen, and to the law of France as having committed an offence within the territory of France, yet he must also be considered as subject to the jurisdiction of British law, which extends to the protection of British vessels, though in ports belonging to another country.   From the passage in the treatise of Ortolan, already quoted, it appears that, with regard to offences committed on board of foreign vessels within the French territory, the French nation will not assert their police law unless invoked by the master of the vessel, or unless the offence leads to a disturbance of the peace of the port; and several instances where that course was adopted are mentioned.   Among these are two cases where offences were committed on board American vessels—one at the port of Antwerp, and the other at Marseilles—and where, on the local authorities interfering, the American Court claimed exclusive jurisdiction.   As far as America herself is concerned, it is clear that she, by the statutes of the 23d of March, 1825, has made regulations for persons on board her vessels in foreign parts, and we have adopted the same course of legislation. Our vessels must be subject to the laws of the nation at any of whose ports they may be, and also to the laws of our country, to which they belong. As to our vessels when going to foreign parts we have the right, if we are not bound, to make regulations. America has set us a strong example that we have the right to do so. In the present case, if it were necessary to decide the question on the 17 & 18 Vict. c. 104, I should have no hesitation in saying that we now not only legislate for British subjects on board of British vessels, but also for all those who form the crews thereof, and that there is no difficulty in so construing the statute; but it is not necessary to decide that point now. Independently of that statute, the general law is sufficient to determine this case. Here the offence was committed on board a British vessel by one of the crew, and it makes no difference whether the vessel was within a foreign port or not. If the offence had been committed on the high seas it is clear that it would have been within the jurisdiction of the Admiralty, and the Central Criminal Court has now the same extent of jurisdiction. Does it make any difference because the vessel was in the river Garonne halfway between the sea and the head of the river? The place where the offence was committed was in a navigable part of the river below bridge, and where the tide ebbs and flows, and great ships do lie and hover. An offence committed at such a place, according to the authorities, is within the Admiralty jurisdiction, and it is the same as if the offence had been committed on the high seas. On the whole I come to the conclusion that the prisoner was amenable to the British law, and that the conviction was right.

Byles, J. I am of the same opinion. I adhere to the opinion that I expressed at the trial. A British ship is, for the purposes of this question, like a floating island; and, when a crime is committed on board a British ship, it is within the jurisdiction of the Admiralty Court, and therefore of the Central Criminal Court, and the offender is as amenable to British law as if he had stood on the Isle of Wight and committed the crime. Two English and two American cases decide that a crime committed on board a British vessel in a river like the one in question, where there is the flux and reflux of the tide, and wherein great ships do hover, is within the jurisdiction of the Admiralty Court; and that is also the opinion expressed in Kent's Commentaries. The only effect of the ship being within the ambit of French territory is that there might have been concurrent jurisdiction had the French claimed it. I give no opinion on the question whether the case comes within the enactment of the Merchant Shipping Act.

BLACKBURN, J. I am of the same opinion. It is not necessary to decide whether the case comes within the Merchant Shipping Act. If the offence could have been properly tried in any English court, then the Central Criminal Court had jurisdiction to try it. It has been decided by a number of cases that a ship on the high seas, carrying a national flag, is part of the territory of that nation whose flag she carries; and all persons on board her are to be considered as subject to the jurisdiction of the laws of that nation, as much so as if they had been on land within that territory. From the earliest times it has been held that the maritime courts have jurisdiction over offences committed on the high seas where great ships go, which are, as it were, common ground to all nations, and that the jurisdiction extends over ships in rivers or places where great ships go as far as the tide extends. In this case the vessel was within French territory, and subject to the local jurisdiction, if the French authorities had chosen to exercise it. Our decisions establish that the Admiralty jurisdiction extends at common law over British ships on the high seas, or in waters where great ships go as far as the tide ebbs and flows. The cases Rex v. Allen, [1 Moo. C. C. 494] and Rex v. Jemot [Old Baily, 1812, MS.] are most closely in point, and establish that offences committed on board British ships in places where great ships go are within the jurisdiction of the Court of Admiralty, and consequently of the Central Criminal Court. In America it appears, from the case of The United States v. Wiltberger, [5 Wheaton, 76] that it was held that the United States had no jurisdiction in the case of the crime of manslaughter committed on board a United States vessel in the river Tigris in China; but, as I understand the American cases of Thomas v. Lane [2 Sumner, 1] and The United States v. Coombes [12 Peters, 71], a rule more in conformity with the English decisions was laid down; and upon those authorities I take it that the American courts would agree with us. It is clear, therefore, that a person on board a British ship is amenable to the British law just as much as a British person on board an American ship is subject to the American law. My view is, that when a person is on board a vessel sailing under the British flag, and commits a crime, that nation has a right to punish him for the crime committed by him; and clearly the same doctrine extends to those who are members of the crew of the vessel.

Conviction affirmed.

[BARON CHANNEL and JUSTICE LUSH delivered concurring opinions.]

REGINA v. WILLIAM LESLIE.

Great Britain, Court of Criminal Appeal, Crown Cases Reserved, 1860.

8 Cox's Criminal Cases, 269.[1]

Case reserved by Watson, B., at the Christmas Assizes at Liverpool.

The prisoner was the master of the British ship Louisa Braginton, and the charge against him was for the false imprisonment of several Chilian subjects during a voyage from Valparaiso to Liverpool.

These persons having been ordered to be banished from Chili by the Government of that country, were brought by force, guarded by soldiers of that state, on board the ship, whence the prisoner, under a contract (a copy accompanies this case) with the Chilian Government, carried and conveyed these Chilian subjects to Liverpool.

On this evidence I [Watson, B.] directed a verdict of guilty, reserving the question of law, whether or not the defendant was liable to an indictment in this country, under the circumstances, for the opinion of this court. . . .

ERLE, C. J. In this case the question is, whether a conviction for false imprisonment can be sustained upon the following facts: The prosecutor and others being in Chili, and subjects of that state, were banished by the Government from Chili to England. The defendant, being master of an English merchant vessel lying in the territorial waters of Chili, near Valparaiso, contracted with that Government to take the prosecutor and his companions from Valparaiso to Liverpool, and they were accordingly brought on board the defendant's vessel by the officers of the Government, and carried to Liverpool by the defendant under his contract. Then can the conviction be sustained for that which was done in Chilian waters? We answer, no. We assume that in Chili the act of Government towards its subjects was lawful; and although an English ship in some respects carries with it the laws of her country in the territorial waters of a foreign state, yet in other respects it is subject to the laws of that state as to acts done to the subjects thereof. We assume that the Government could justify all that it did within its own territory, and we think it follows that the defendant can justify all that he did there as agent for the Government, and under its authority. In Dobree v. Napier (2 Bing. N. C. 781) the defendant, on behalf of the Queen of Portugal, seized the plaintiff's vessel for violating a blockade of a Portuguese port in the time of war. The plaintiff brought trespass, and judgment was for the defendant, because the Queen of Portugal in her own territory had a right to seize the vessel and to employ whom she would to make the seizure, and therefore the defendant,

---

[1] The case is also reported in Bell's Crown Cases, p. 220, where the name is spelled Lesley.

although an Englishman, seizing an English vessel, could justify the act under the employment of the Queen. We think that the acts of the defendant in Chili become lawful on the same principle, and are therefore no ground for the conviction.

The further question remains, can the conviction be sustained for that which was done out of the Chilian territory? and we think that it can. It is clear that an English ship on the high seas, out of any foreign territory, is subject to the laws of England, and persons, whether foreign or English, on board such ship are as much amenable to English law as they would be on English soil. In Reg. v. Sattler (7 Cox Crim. Cas. 431), this principle was acted on so as to make the prisoner, a foreigner, responsible for murder on board an English ship at sea. The same principle has been laid down by foreign writers on international law, among which it is enough to cite Ortolan sur la Diplomatie de la Mer, liv. 2, cap. 13. The Merchant Shipping Act (17 & 18 Vict. c. 104, s. 267), makes the master and seamen of a British ship responsible for all offences against property or person, committed on the seas out of Her Majesty's dominions, as if they had been committed within the jurisdiction of the Admiralty of England. Such being the law, if the act of the defendant amounted to a false imprisonment, he was liable to be convicted. Now, as the contract of the defendant was to receive the prosecutor and the others as prisoners on board his ship, and to take them without their consent over the sea to England, although he was justified in first receiving them in Chili, yet that justification ceased when he passed the line of Chilian jurisdiction, and after that it was a wrong which was intentionally planned and executed in pursuance of the contract, amounting in law to a false imprisonment. It may be that transportation to England is lawful by the law of Chili, and that a Chilian ship might so lawfully transport Chilian subjects, but for an English ship the laws of Chili out of the state are powerless, and the lawfulness of the acts must be tried by English law. For these reasons, to the extent above mentioned, the conviction is affirmed.

Conviction affirmed.

UNITED STATES OF AMERICA v. FLORES.

United States, Supreme Court, 1933.

289 U. S. 137. [77 L. ed. 1086; 53 S. Ct. 580.]

MR. JUSTICE STONE delivered the opinion of the Court.

By indictment found in the District Court for Eastern Pennsylvania, it was charged that appellee, a citizen of the United States, murdered another citizen of the United States upon the S. S. "Padnsay," an American vessel, while at anchor in the Port of Matadi, in the Belgian

Congo, a place subject to the sovereignty of the Kingdom of Belgium, and that appellee, after the commission of the crime, was first brought into the Port of Philadelphia, a place within the territorial jurisdiction of the District Court. By stipulation it was conceded, as though stated in a bill of particulars, that the "Padnsay," at the time of the offense charged, was unloading, being attached to the shore by cables, at a point two hundred and fifty miles inland from the mouth of the river.

The District Court, following its earlier decision in United States ex rel. Maro v. Mathues, 21 F. (2d) 533, affirmed, 27 F. (2d) 518, sustained a demurrer to the indictment and discharged the prisoner on the ground that the court was without jurisdiction to try the offense charged. The case comes here by direct appeal under the Act of March 2, 1907, c. 2564, 34 Stat. 1246, 18 U. S. C. § 682 and § 238 of the Judicial Code, as amended by Act of February 13, 1925, 28 U. S. C. § 345, the court below certifying that its decision was founded upon its construction of § 272 of the Criminal Code, 18 U. S. C. § 451.

Sections 273 and 275 of the Criminal Code, 18 U. S. C. §§ 452, 454, define murder and fix its punishment. Section 272, upon the construction of which the court below rested its decision, makes punishable offenses defined by other sections of the Criminal Code, among other cases, "when committed within the admiralty and maritime jurisdiction of the United States and out of the jurisdiction of any particular state, on board any vessel belonging in whole or in part to the United States" or any of its nationals. And by § 41 of the Judicial Code, 28 U. S. C. § 102, venue to try offenses "committed upon the high seas or elsewhere out of the jurisdiction of any particular State or district," is "in the district where the offender is found or into which he is first brought." As the offense charged here was committed on board a vessel lying outside the territorial jurisdiction of a state, see Wynne v. United States, 217 U. S. 234; United States v. Rodgers, 150 U. S. 249, 265, and within that of a foreign sovereignty, the court below was without jurisdiction to try and punish the offense unless it was within the admiralty and maritime jurisdiction of the United States.

Two questions are presented on this appeal, first, whether the extension of the judicial power of the Federal government "to all cases of admiralty and maritime jurisdiction," by Art. III, § 2 of the Constitution confers on Congress power to define and punish offenses perpetrated by a citizen of the United States on board one of its merchant vessels lying in navigable waters within the territorial limits of another sovereignty; and second, whether Congress has exercised that power by the enactment of § 272 of the Criminal Code under which the indictment was found.

The court below thought, as appellee argues, that as § 8 of Art. I of the Constitution specifically granted to Congress the power "to define and punish piracies and felonies committed on the high seas, and offenses against the law of nations," and "to make rules concerning captures on land and water," that provision must be regarded as a limitation on the general provision of § 2 of Art. III, that the judicial power shall extend "to all cases of admiralty and maritime jurisdiction;" that as the specific grant of power to punish offenses outside the territorial limits of the United States was thus restricted to offenses occurring on the high seas, the more general grant could not be resorted to as extending either the legislative or judicial power over offenses committed on vessels outside the territorial limits of the United States and not on the high seas. . . .

This section has been consistently interpreted as adopting for the United States the system of admiralty and maritime law, as it had been developed in the admiralty courts of England and the Colonies, and, by implication, conferring on Congress the power, subject to well recognized limitations not here material, to alter, qualify, or supplement it as experience or changing conditions may require. . . .

In view of the history of the two clauses and the manner of their adoption, the grant of power to define and punish piracies and felonies on the high seas cannot be deemed to be a limitation on the powers, either legislative or judicial, conferred on the national government by Article III, § 2. . . .

As we cannot say that the specific grant of power to define and punish felonies on the high seas operated to curtail the legislative or judicial power conferred by Art. III, § 2, we come to the question principally argued, whether the jurisdiction over admiralty and maritime cases, which it gave, extends to the punishment of crimes committed on vessels of the United States while in foreign waters. As was pointed out by Mr. Justice Story, in the course of an elaborate review of the history of admiralty jurisdiction, in DeLovio v. Boit, 7 Fed. Cas. 418, 438, admiralty "from the highest antiquity has exercised a very extensive criminal jurisdiction and punished offenses by fine and imprisonment." The English courts have consistently held that jurisdiction is not restricted to vessels within the navigable waters of the realm, but follows its ships upon the high seas and into ports and rivers within the territorial jurisdiction of foreign sovereigns. Queen v. Carr & Wilson, 10 Q. B. Div. 76; Queen v. Anderson, L. R. 1 Crown Cases Reserved 161; Rex v. Allen, 1 Moody, C. C. 494; see Rex v. Jemot, 1 Russell on Crimes, 4th ed. 153.

The criminal jurisdiction of the United States is wholly statutory, see United States v. Hudson, 7 Cranch, 32, but it has never been doubted that the grant of admiralty and maritime jurisdiction to the federal government includes the legislative power to define and punish crimes committed upon vessels lying in navigable waters of the United States. From the very organization of the government, and without intermission, Congress has also asserted the power, analogous to that exercised by English courts of admiralty, to punish crimes committed on vessels of the United States while on the high seas or on navigable waters not within the territorial jurisdiction of a state. The Act of April 30, 1790, c. 9, § 8, 1 Stat. 112, 113, provided for the punishment of murder committed "upon the high seas or in any river, haven, basin or bay out of the jurisdiction of any particular state," and provided for the trial of the offender in the district where he might be apprehended or "into which he may first be brought." Section 12 of this Act dealt with manslaughter, but only when committed upon the high seas. It is true that in United States v. Bevans, 3 Wheat. 336, the prisoner, charged with murder on a warship in Boston Harbor, was discharged, as was one charged with manslaughter committed on a vessel on a Chinese river in United States v. Wiltberger, 5 Wheat. 76. But the judgments were based not upon a want of power in Congress to define and punish the crimes charged, but upon the ground that the statute did not apply, in the one case, for the reason that the place of the offense was not out of the jurisdiction of a state, and in the other, because the offense, manslaughter, was not committed on the high seas.

The Act of March 3, 1825, c. 65, § 4, 4 Stat. 115, provided for the punishment of any person committing murder "upon the high seas or in any arm of the sea or in any river, haven, creek, basin or bay, within the admiralty and maritime jurisdiction of the United States and out of the jurisdiction of any particular state," and § 22 provided for the punishment of assault with a dangerous weapon, committed under similar circumstances. The provisions of the latter section, carried into § 5346 of the Revised Statutes, U. S. C. title 18, § 455, were upheld in United States v. Rodgers, *supra,* as a constitutional exercise of the power of Congress to define and punish offenses occurring in American vessels while within territorial waters of another sovereignty. Rodgers had been convicted of assault with a dangerous weapon, committed on a vessel of the United States lying in the Detroit River within the territorial jurisdiction of Canada, and his conviction was sustained by this Court. It was assumed that the statute was applicable only with respect to offenses committed on the high seas and waters tributary to them, and the decision turned on whether the Great Lakes were to be deemed "high seas" within the meaning of the statute. It was held that they were, and the power of Congress to punish offenses committed on an American vessel within the territorial waters of Canada, tributary to the Lakes, was expressly affirmed.

As the offense charged here appears to have been committed on an American vessel while discharging cargo in port, the jurisdiction is not affected by the fact that she was then at a point on the Congo remote from the sea, where it does not affirmatively appear that the water is salt or tidal. On this point also United States v. Rodgers, *supra,* is controlling, for there the offense committed within a foreign territorial jurisdiction was upon non-tidal fresh water.

The appellee insists that even though Congress has power to define and punish crimes on American vessels in foreign waters, it has not done so by the present statute, since the criminal jurisdiction of the United States is based upon the territorial principle and the statute cannot rightly be interpreted to be a departure from that principle. But the language of the statute making it applicable to offenses committed on an American vessel outside the jurisdiction of a state "within the admiralty and maritime jurisdiction of the United States" is broad enough to include crimes in the territorial waters of a foreign sovereignty. For Congress, by incorporating in the statute the very language of the constitutional grant of power, has made its exercise of the power co-extensive with the grant. Compare The Hine v. Trevor, 4 Wall. 555.

It is true that the criminal jurisdiction of the United States is in general based on the territorial principle, and criminal statutes of the United States are not by implication given an extra-territorial effect. United States v. Bowman, 260 U. S. 94, 98; compare Blackmer v. United States, 284 U. S. 421. But that principle has never been thought to be applicable to a merchant vessel which, for purposes of the jurisdiction of the courts of the sovereignty whose flag it flies to punish crimes committed upon it, is deemed to be a part of the territory of that sovereignty, and not to lose that character when in navigable waters within the territorial limits of another sovereignty. . . . This qualification of the territorial principle in the case of vessels of the flag was urged by Mr. Webster while Secretary of State, in his letter to Lord Ashburton of August 1, 1842, quoted with approval in United States v. Rodgers, *supra*, 264, 265. Subject to the right of the territorial sovereignty to assert jurisdiction over offenses disturbing the peace of the port, it has been supported by writers on international law, and has been recognized by France, Belgium, and other continental countries, as well as by England and the United States. See 2 Moore, International Law Digest, Vol. 2, 287, 297; Fiore, International Law Codified, translated by E. M. Borchard, 192, 193; Wheaton, International Law, Vol. I, 245; Hall, International Law, 8th ed. 253–258; Jessup, The Law of Territorial Waters, 144–193.

In view of the wide recognition of this principle of extra-territorial jurisdiction over crimes committed on merchant vessels and its explicit adoption in United States v. Rodgers, *supra,* we cannot say that the language of the present statute punishing offenses on United States vessels out of the jurisdiction of a state, "when committed within the admiralty and maritime jurisdiction of the United States," was not intended to give effect to it. If the meaning of the statute were doubtful, the doubt would be resolved by the report on these sections by the Special Joint Committee on the Revision of the Laws, 60th Congress,

1st Sess., Rep. 10, part 1, p. 10, in which it was pointed out that the jurisdiction extends to vessels of the United States when on navigable waters within the limits of a foreign state, and ''all cases arising on board such vessels while on any such waters, are clearly cases within the admiralty and maritime jurisdiction of the United States.''

A related but different question, not presented here, may arise when jurisdiction over an offense committed on a foreign vessel is asserted by the sovereignty in whose waters it was lying at the time of its commission, since for some purposes, the jurisdiction may be regarded as concurrent, in that the courts of either sovereignty may try the offense.

There is not entire agreement among nations or the writers on international law as to which sovereignty should yield to the other when the jurisdiction is asserted by both. See Jessup, the Law of Territorial Waters, 144–193. The position of the United States, exemplified in Wildenhus's Case (Mali v. Keeper of Common Jail) 120 U. S. 1, has been that at least in the case of major crimes, affecting the peace and tranquillity of the port, the jurisdiction asserted by the sovereignty of the port must prevail over that of the vessel. . . .

. . . In the absence of any controlling treaty provision, and any assertion of jurisdiction by the territorial sovereign, it is the duty of the courts of the United States to apply to offenses committed by its citizens on vessels flying its flag, its own statutes, interpreted in the light of recognized principles of international law. So applied the indictment here sufficiently charges an offense within the admiralty and maritime jurisdiction of the United States and the judgment below must be reversed.[1]

---

[1] Supplementary Cases. In Crapo v. Kelly, 16 Wallace 610 (1873), involving a conflict between an assignment executed in favor of Crapo by the insolvent court of Massachusetts, covering a vessel registered at a port of Massachusetts but on the high seas at the time of the execution of the assignment, and an attachment issued in New York upon the arrival of the vessel in that port, the Supreme Court held that while the vessel was upon the high seas she was in law within the territory of Massachusetts. "We are of the opinion," said the court, "for the purpose we are considering, that the ship Arctic was a portion of the territory of Massachusetts, and the assignment by the insolvent court of that State passed the title to her, in the same manner and with the like effect as if she had been physically within the bounds of that State when the assignment was executed."

In Queen v. Carr, L. R. 10 Q. B. Div. (1882), involving the conviction in Great Britain of persons who had received stolen property on board a British vessel which at the time lay in the Maas moored to a quay, the court held, citing Regina v. Anderson, that since the place was within the old description of a place within the ebb and flow of the tide "where great ships do go" it was within the jurisdiction of the court, and that it was of no consequence that the offender was not a member of the crew. "The true principle," said the court, "is, that a person who comes on board a British ship, where English law is reigning, places himself under the protection of the British flag, and as a

B.   Jurisdiction over foreign privately-owned vessels in national ports.

Both by custom and by treaty the extent to which a state may exercise jurisdiction over foreign vessels within its territorial waters has been fairly clearly determined. Query, would the local authorities be justified in going on board a foreign ship and interfering with the personal relations and property rights of the officers and passengers of the ship? [United States and Great Britain: The Creole.] Would the commission of a crime on board the vessel be justification for the intervention of the local authorities? [Wildenhus' Case.] Would the local authorities be justified in enforcing, in favor of seamen on board a foreign ship, local laws which are in conflict with the laws of the flag state? [Strathearn Steamship Co. v. Dillon.] What if a state should attempt to apply its sumptuary laws so as to interfere with the internal discipline of the foreign ship in matters having no relation to the peace of the port? [Cunard Steamship Company v. Mellon.]

UNITED STATES AND GREAT BRITAIN: THE CREOLE.

Claims Arbitration under the Agreement of February 8, 1853. 1855.

Report of Decisions, p. 241.

BATES, Umpire: . . .

The American brig Creole, Captain Ensor, sailed from Hampton Roads, in the State of Virginia, on the 27th October, 1841, having on board one hundred and thirty-five slaves bound for New Orleans. On the 7th of November, at nine o'clock in the evening, a portion of the slaves rose against the officers, crew, and passengers, wounding severely the captain, the chief mate and two of the crew, and murdering one of the passengers; the mutineers, having got complete possession of the vessel, ordered the mate, under threat of instant death should he disobey or deceive them, to steer for Nassau, in the island of New Providence, where the brig arrived on the 9th November, 1841.

The American consul was apprised of the situation of the vessel, and requested the governor to take measures to prevent the escape of the slaves, and to have the murderers secured. The consul received reply from the governor, stating that under the circumstances he would comply with the request.

The consul went on board the brig, placed the mate in command in place of the disabled master, and found the slaves all quiet.

About noon twenty African soldiers, with an African sergeant and corporal, commanded by a white officer, came on board. The officer

---

correlative, if he thus becomes entitled to our law's protection, he becomes amenable to its jurisdiction, and liable to the punishments it inflicts upon those who there infringe its requirements."

was introduced by the consul to the mate as commanding officer of the vessel.

The consul, on returning to the shore, was summoned to attend the governor and council, who were in session, who informed the consul that they had come to the following decision:

"1st. That the courts of law have no jurisdiction over the alleged offences.

"2d. That, as an information had been lodged before the governor, charging that the crime of murder had been committed on board said vessel while on the high seas, it was expedient that the parties, implicated in so grave a charge, should not be allowed to go at large, and that an investigation ought therefore to be made into the charges, and examinations taken on oath; when, if it should appear that the original information was correct, and that a murder had actually been committed, that all the parties implicated in such crime, or other acts of violence, should be detained here until reference could be made to the Secretary of State to ascertain whether the parties should be delivered over to the United States government; if not, how otherwise to dispose of them.

"3d. That as soon as such examinations should be taken, all persons on board the Creole, not implicated in any of the offences alleged to have been committed on board that vessel, must be released from further restraint."

Then two magistrates were sent on board. The American consul went also. The examination was commenced on Tuesday, the 9th, and was continued on Wednesday, the 10th, and then postponed until Friday, on account of the illness of Captain Ensor. On Friday morning it was abruptly, and without any explanation, terminated.

On the same day, a large number of boats assembled near the Creole, filled with colored persons armed with bludgeons. They were under the immediate command of the pilot who took the vessel into the port, who was an officer of the government, and a colored man. A sloop or larger launch was also towed from the shore and anchored near the brig. The sloop was filled with men armed with clubs, and clubs were passed from her to the persons in the boats. A vast concourse of people were collected on shore opposite the brig.

During the whole time the officers of the government were on board they encouraged the insubordination of the slaves.

The Americans in port determined to unite and furnish the necessary aid to forward the vessel and negroes to New Orleans. The consul and the officers and crews of two other American vessels had, in fact, united with the officers, men, and passengers of the Creole to effect this. They were to conduct her first to Indian quay, Florida, where there was a vessel of war of the United States.

On Friday morning, the consul was informed that attempts would be made to liberate the slaves by force, and from the mate he received information of the threatening state of things. The result was, the attorney general and other officers went on board the Creole. The slaves, identified as on board the vessel concerned in the mutiny, were sent on shore, and the residue of the slaves were called on deck by direction of the attorney general, who addressed them in the following terms: "My friends," or "my men, you have been detained a short time on board the Creole for the purpose of ascertaining what individuals were concerned in the murder. They have been identified, and will be detained. The rest of you are free, and at liberty to go on shore, and wherever you please."

The liberated slaves, assisted by the magistrates, were then taken on board the boats, and when landed were conducted by a vast assemblage to the superintendent of police, by whom their names were registered. They were thus forcibly taken from the custody of the master of the Creole, and lost to the claimants.

I need not refer to authorities to show that slavery, however odious and contrary to the principles of justice and humanity, may be established by law in any country; and, having been so established in many countries, it cannot be contrary to the law of nations.

The Creole was on a voyage, sanctioned and protected by the laws of the United States, and by the law of nations. Her right to navigate the ocean could not be questioned, and as growing out of that right, the right to seek shelter or enter the ports of a friendly power in case of distress or any unavoidable necessity.

A vessel navigating the ocean carries with her the laws of her own country, so far as relates to the persons and property on board, and to a certain extent, retains those rights even in the ports of the foreign nations she may visit. Now, this being the state of the law of nations, what were the duties of the authorities at Nassau in regard to the Creole? It is submitted that mutineers could not be tried by the courts of that island, the crime having been committed on the high seas. All that the authorities could lawfully do, was to comply with the request of the American consul, and keep the mutineers in custody until a conveyance could be found for sending them to the United States.

The other slaves, being perfectly quiet, and under the command of the captain and owners, and on board an American ship, the authorities should have seen that they were protected by the law of nations; their rights under which cannot be abrogated or varied, either by the emancipation act or any other act of the British Parliament.

Blackstone, 4th volume, speaking of the law of nations, states: "Whenever any question arises, which is properly the object of its jurisdiction, such law is here adopted in its full extent by the common law."

The municipal law of England cannot authorize a magistrate to violate the law of nations by invading with an armed force the vessel of a friendly nation that has committed no offence, and forcibly dissolving the relations which by the laws of his country the captain is bound to preserve and enforce on board.

These rights, sanctioned by the law of nations—viz: the right to navigate the ocean, and to seek shelter in case of distress or other unavoidable circumstances, and to retain over the ship, her cargo, and passengers, the laws of her own country—must be respected by all nations; for no independent nation would submit to their violation.

Having read all the authorities referred to in the arguments on both sides, I have come to the conclusion that the conduct of the authorities at Nassau was in violation of the established law of nations, and that the claimants are justly entitled to compensation for their losses. I therefore award to the undermentioned parties, their assigns, or legal representatives, the sums set opposite their names, due on the 15th of January, 1855.

WILDENHUS' CASE.[1]

United States, Supreme Court, 1887.

120 U. S. 1. [30 L. ed. 565; 7 S. Ct. 383.]

Appeal from the Circuit Court of the United States for the District of New Jersey.

This appeal brought up an application made to the circuit court of the United States for the District of New Jersey, by Charles Mali, the "consul of his majesty the king of the Belgians, for the States of New York and New Jersey, in the United States," for himself, as such consul, "and in behalf of one Joseph Wildenhus, one Gionviennie Gobnbosich, and John J. Ostenmeyer," for the release, upon a writ of *habeas corpus*, of Wildenhus, Gobnbosich, and Ostenmeyer from the custody of the keeper of the common jail of Hudson county, New Jersey, and their delivery to the consul, "to be dealt with according to the law of Belgium." The facts on which the application rests are thus stated in the petition for the writ:

"*Second.* That on or about the sixth day of October, 1886, on board the Belgian steamship Noordland, there occurred an affray between the said Joseph Wildenhus and one Fijens, wherein and whereby it is charged that the said Wildenhus stabbed with a knife and inflicted upon the said Fijens a mortal wound, of which he afterwards died.

---

[1] Also reported as Charles Mali, Consul of His Majesty the King of the Belgians, and Joseph Wildenhus, et al., Appellants v. The Keeper of the Common Jail of Hudson County, New Jersey.

"*Third.* That the said Wildenhus is a subject of the kingdom of Belgium, and has his domicile therein, and is one of the crew of the said steamship Noordland, and was such when the said affray occurred.

"*Fourth.* That the said Fijens was also a subject of Belgium, and had his domicile and residence therein, and at the time of the said affray, as well as at the time of his subsequent death, was one of the crew of the said steamship.

"*Fifth.* That, at the time said affray occurred, the said steamship Noordland was lying moored at the dock of the port of Jersey City, in said state of New Jersey.

"*Sixth.* That the said affray occurred and ended wholly below the deck of the said steamship, and that the tranquillity of the said port of Jersey City was in nowise disturbed or endangered thereby.

"*Seventh.* That said affray occurred in the presence of several witnesses, all of whom were and still are of the crew of the said vessel, and that no other person or persons except those of the crew of said vessel were present or near by.

"*Eighth.* Your petitioner therefore respectfully shows unto this honorable court that the said affray occurred outside of the jurisdiction of the said state of New Jersey.

"*Ninth.* But, notwithstanding the foregoing facts, your petitioner respectfully further shows that the police authorities of Jersey City, in said state of New Jersey, have arrested the said Joseph Wildenhus, and also the said Gionviennie Gobnbosich and John J. Ostenmeyer, of the crew of the said vessel (one of whom is a quartermaster thereof), and that said Joseph Wildenhus has been committed by a police magistrate, acting under the authority of the said state, to the common jail of the county of Hudson, on a charge of an indictable offense under the laws of the said state of New Jersey, and is now held in confinement by the keeper of the said jail, and that the others of the said crew, arrested as aforesaid, are also detained in custody and confinement as witnesses to testify in such proceedings as may hereafter be had against the said Wildenhus." . . .

Article XI of a Convention between the United States and Belgium "concerning the rights, privileges, and immunities of consular officers," concluded March 9, 1880, and proclaimed by the President of the United States, March 1, 1881, 21 Stat. 776, 781, is as follows:

"The respective consuls general, consuls, vice-consuls, and consular agents shall have exclusive charge of the internal order of the merchant vessels of their nation, and shall alone take cognizance of all differences which may arise, either at sea or in port, between the captains, officers, and crews, without exception, particularly with reference to the adjustment of wages and the execution of contracts. The local authorities shall not interfere, except when the disorder that has arisen is of such a nature as to disturb tranquillity and public order on shore or in the port, or when a person of the country, or not belonging to the crew, shall be concerned therein.

"In all other cases, the aforesaid authorities shall confine themselves to lending aid to the consuls and vice-consuls or consular agents, if they are requested by them to do so, in causing the arrest and imprisonment of any person whose name is inscribed on the crew list, whenever, for any cause, the said officers shall think proper."

The claim of the consul is that, by the law of nations and the provisions of this treaty, the offense with which Wildenhus has been charged is "solely cognizable by the authority of the laws of the kingdom of Belgium," and that the state of New Jersey is without jurisdiction in the premises. The circuit court refused to deliver the prisoners to the consul, and remanded them to the custody of the jailer. 28 Fed. Rep. 924. To reverse that decision this appeal was taken.

Mr. Chief Justice Waite, after stating the case as above reported, delivered the opinion of the court.

By §§ 751 and 753 of the Revised Statutes the courts of the United States have power to issue writs of *habeas corpus* which shall extend to prisoners in jail when they are in "custody in violation of the Constitution or a law or treaty of the United States," and the question we have to consider is, whether these prisoners are held in violation of the provisions of the existing treaty between the United States and Belgium.

It is part of the law of civilized nations that when a merchant vessel of one country enters the ports of another for the purposes of trade, it subjects itself to the law of the place to which it goes, unless by treaty or otherwise the two countries have come to some different understanding or agreement; for, as was said by Chief Justice Marshall in The Exchange, 7 Cranch, 116, 144, "it would be obviously inconvenient and dangerous to society, and would subject the laws to continual infraction, and the government to degradation, if such . . . merchants did not owe temporary and local allegiance, and were not amenable to the jurisdiction of the country." United States v. Diekelman, 92 U. S. 520; 1 Phillimore's Int. Law, 3d ed. 483, § 351; Twiss' Law of Nations in Time of Peace, 229, § 159; Creasy's Int. Law, 167, § 176; Halleck's Int. Law, 1st ed. 171. And the English judges have uniformly recognized the rights of the courts of the country of which the port is part to punish crimes committed by one foreigner on another in a foreign merchant ship. Regina v. Cunningham, Bell C. C. 72; S. C. 8 Cox C. C. 104; Regina v. Anderson, 11 Cox C. C. 198, 204; S. C. L. R. 1 C. C. 161, 165; Regina v. Keyn, 13 Cox C. C. 403, 486, 525; S. C. 2 Ex. Div. 63, 161, 213. As the owner has voluntarily taken his vessel for his own private purposes to a place within the dominion of a government other than his own, and from which he seeks protection during his stay, he owes that government such allegiance for the time being as is due for the protection to which he becomes entitled.

From experience, however, it was found long ago that it would be beneficial to commerce if the local government would abstain from interfering with the internal discipline of the ship, and the general regulation of the rights and duties of the officers and crew towards the vessel or among themselves. And so by comity it came to be generally understood among civilized nations that all matters of discipline and all things done on board which affected only the vessel or those belonging to her, and did not involve the peace or dignity of the country, or the tranquillity of the port, should be left by the local government to be dealt with by the authorities of the nation to which the vessel belonged as the laws of that nation or the interests of its commerce should require. But if crimes are committed on board of a character to disturb the peace and tranquillity of the country to which the vessel has been brought, the offenders have never by comity or usage been entitled to any exemption from the operation of the local laws for their punishment, if the local tribunals see fit to assert their authority. Such being the general public law on this subject, treaties and conventions have been entered into by nations having commercial intercourse, the purpose of which was to settle and define the rights and duties of the contracting parties with respect to each other in these particulars, and thus prevent the inconvenience that might arise from attempts to exercise conflicting jurisdictions.

The first of these conventions entered into by the United States after the adoption of the Constitution was with France, on the 14th of November, 1788, 8 Stat. 106, "for the purpose of defining and establishing the functions and privileges of their respective consuls and vice-consuls," Art. VIII of which is as follows:

"The consuls or vice-consuls shall exercise police over all the vessels of their respective nations, and shall have on board the said vessels all power and jurisdiction in civil matters, in all the disputes which may there arise; they shall have an entire inspection over the said vessels, their crew, and the changes and substitutions there to be made; for which purpose they may go on board the said vessels whenever they may judge it necessary. Well understood that the functions hereby allowed shall be confined to the interior of the vessels, and that they shall not take place in any case which shall have any interference with the police of the ports where the said vessels shall be."

It was when this convention was in force that the cases of The Sally and The Newton arose, an account of which is given in Wheaton's Elements of International Law (3d ed.) 153, and in 1 Phillimore's International Law (3d ed.) 484 and (2d ed.) 407. The Sally was an American merchant vessel in the port of Marseilles, and The Newton a vessel of a similar character in the port of Antwerp, then under the dominion

.of France. In the case of The Sally, the mate, in the alleged exercise of discipline over the crew, had inflicted a severe wound on one of the seamen, and in that of The Newton one seaman had made an assault on another seaman in the vessel's boat. In each case the proper consul of the United States claimed exclusive jurisdiction of the offence, and so did the local authorities of the port; but the Council of State, a branch of the political department of the government of France to which the matter was referred, pronounced against the local tribunals, "considering that one of these cases was that of an assault committed in the boat of the American ship Newton, by one of the crew upon another, and the other was that of a severe wound inflicted by the mate of the American ship Sally upon one of the seamen for having made use of the boat without leave." This was clearly because the things done were not such as to disturb "the peace or tranquillity of the port." Wheaton's Elements Int. Law, 3d ed. 154. The case of The Sally was simply a quarrel between certain of the crew while constructively on board the vessel, and that of The Newton grew out of a punishment inflicted by an officer on one of the crew for disobedience of orders. Both were evidently of a character to affect only the police of the vessel, and thus within the authority expressly granted to the consul by the treaty. . . .

The form of the provision found in the present convention with Belgium first appeared in a convention with Austria concluded in 1870, Art. XI, 17 Stat. 827, and it is found now in substantially the same language in all the treaties and conventions which have since been entered into by the United States on the same subject. See the conventions with the German Empire in 1871, Art. XIII, 17 Stat. 927; with the Netherlands in 1878, Art. XI, 21 Stat. 668; with Italy in 1881, Art. I, 22 Stat. 832; with Belgium in 1881, as stated above; and with Roumania the same year, Art. XI, 23 Stat. 714.

It thus appears that at first provision was made only for giving consuls police authority over the interior of the ship and jurisdiction in civil matters arising out of disputes or differences on board, that is to say, between those belonging to the vessel. Under this police authority the duties of the consuls were evidently confined to the maintenance of order and discipline on board. This gave them no power to punish for crimes against the peace of the country. In fact, they were expressly prohibited from interfering with the local police in matters of that kind. The cases of The Sally and The Newton are illustrative of this position. That of The Sally related to the discipline of the ship, and that of The Newton to the maintenance of order on board. In neither case was the disturbance of a character to affect the peace or the dignity of the country.

In the next conventions consuls were simply made judges and arbitrators to settle and adjust differences between those on board. This clearly related to such differences between those belonging to the vessel as are capable of adjustment and settlement by judicial decision or by arbitration, for it simply made the consuls judges or arbitrators in such matters. That would of itself exclude all idea of punishment for crimes against the State which affected the peace and tranquillity of the port; but, to prevent all doubt on this subject, it was expressly provided that it should not apply to differences of that character.

Next came a form of convention which in terms gave the consuls authority to cause proper order to be maintained on board and to decide disputes between the officers and crew, but allowed the local authorities to interfere if the disorders taking place on board were of such a nature as to disturb the public tranquillity, and that is substantially all there is in the convention with Belgium which we have now to consider. This treaty is the law which now governs the conduct of the United States and Belgium towards each other in this particular. Each nation has granted to the other such local jurisdiction within its own dominion as may be necessary to maintain order on board a merchant vessel, but has reserved to itself the right to interfere if the disorder on board is of a nature to disturb the public tranquillity.

The treaty is part of the supreme law of the United States, and has the same force and effect in New Jersey that it is entitled to elsewhere. If it gives the consul of Belgium exclusive jurisdiction over the offence which it is alleged has been committed within the territory of New Jersey, we see no reason why he may not enforce his rights under the treaty by writ of *habeas corpus* in any proper court of the United States. This being the case, the only important question left for our determination is whether the thing which has been done—the disorder that has arisen—on board this vessel is of a nature to disturb the public peace, or, as some writers term it, the "public repose" of the people who look to the state of New Jersey for their protection. If the thing done—"the disorder," as it is called in the treaty—is of a character to affect those on shore or in the port when it becomes known, the fact that only those on the ship saw it when it was done is a matter of no moment. Those who are not on the vessel pay no special attention to the mere disputes or quarrels of the seamen while on board, whether they occur under deck or above. Neither do they as a rule care for anything done on board which relates only to the discipline of the ship, or to the preservation of order and authority. Not so, however, with crimes which from their gravity awaken a public interest as soon as they become known, and especially those of a character which every civilized nation considers itself bound to provide a severe punishment for when committed within its own jurisdiction. In such cases inquiry is certain to be instituted at once to ascertain how or why the thing was done, and the popular excitement rises or falls as the news spreads and the facts become known. It is not alone the publicity of the act, or the noise and clamor which attends it, that fixes the nature of the crime, but the act itself. If that is of a character to awaken public interest when it becomes known, it is a "disorder" the nature of which is to affect the community at large, and consequently to invoke the power of the local government whose people have been disturbed by what was done. The very nature of such an act is to disturb the quiet of a peaceful community, and to create, in the language of the treaty, a "disorder" which will "disturb tranquillity and public order on shore or in the port." The principle which governs the whole matter is this: Disorders which disturb only the peace of the ship or those on board are to be dealt with exclusively by the sovereignty of the home of the ship, but those which disturb the public peace may be suppressed, and, if need be, the offenders punished by the proper authorities of the local jurisdiction. It may not be easy at all times to determine to which of the two jurisdictions a particular act of disorder belongs. Much will undoubtedly depend on the attending circumstances of the particular case, but all must concede that felonious homicide is a subject for the local jurisdiction, and that if the proper authorities are proceeding with the case in a regular way, the consul has no right to interfere to prevent it. That, according to the petition for the *habeas corpus,* is this case.

This is fully in accord with the practice in France, where the government has been quite as liberal towards foreign nations in this particular as any other, and where, as we have seen in the cases of The Sally and The Newton, by a decree of the Council of State, representing the political department of the government, the French courts were prevented from exercising jurisdiction. But afterwards, in 1859, in the case of Jally, the mate of an American merchantman, who had killed one of the crew and severely wounded another on board the ship in the port of Havre, the Court of Cassation, the highest judicial tribunal of France, upon full consideration held, while the Convention of 1853 was in force, that the French courts had rightful jurisdiction, for reasons which sufficiently appear in the following extract from its judgment:

"Considering that it is a principle of the law of nations that every state has sovereign jurisdiction throughout its territory;

"Considering that by the terms of Article 3 of the Code Napoleon the laws of police and safety bind all those who inhabit French territory, and that consequently foreigners, even *transeuntes,* find themselves subject to those laws;

"Considering that merchant vessels entering the port of a nation other than that to which they belong cannot be withdrawn from the territorial jurisdiction, in any case in which the interest of the state of which that port forms part finds itself concerned, without danger to good order and to the dignity of the government;

"Considering that every state is interested in the repression of crimes and offences that may be committed in the ports of its territory, not only by the men of the ship's company of a foreign merchant vessel towards men not forming part of that company, but even by men of the ship's company among themselves, whenever the act is of a nature to compromise the tranquillity of the port, or the intervention of the local authority is invoked, or the act constitutes a crime by common law,'' (*droit commun,* the law common to all civilized nations,) ''the gravity of which does not permit any nation to leave it unpunished, without impugning its rights of jurisdictional and territorial sovereignty, because that crime is in itself the most manifest as well as the most flagrant violation of the laws which it is the duty of every nation to cause to be respected in all parts of its territory.'' 1 Ortolan Diplomatie de la Mer (4th ed.), pp. 455, 456; Sirey (N. S.), 1859, p. 189.

The judgment of the Circuit Court is affirmed.

STRATHEARN STEAMSHIP COMPANY, LIMITED, v. DILLON.

United States, Supreme Court, 1920.

252 U. S. 348.   [64 L. ed. 607; 40 S. Ct. 350.]

MR. JUSTICE DAY delivered the opinion of the court.

This case presents questions arising under the Seamen's Act of March 4, 1915, c. 153, 38 Stat. 1164. It appears that Dillon, the respondent, was a British subject, and shipped at Liverpool on the eighth of May, 1916, on a British vessel. The shipping articles provided for a voyage of not exceeding three years, commencing at Liverpool and ending at such port in the United Kingdom as might be required by the master, the voyage including ports of the United States. The wages which were fixed by the articles were made payable at the end of the voyage. At the time of the demand for one-half wages, and at the time of the beginning of the action, the period of the voyage had not been reached. The articles provided that no cash should be advanced abroad or liberty granted other than at the pleasure of the master. This, it is admitted, was a valid contract for the payment of wages under the laws of Great Britain. The ship arrived at the Port of Pensacola, Florida, on July 31, 1916, and while she was in that port, Dillon, still in the employ of the ship, demanded from her master one-half part of the wages theretofore earned, and payment was refused. Dillon had received nothing for about two months, and after the refusal of the master to comply with his demand for one-half wages, he filed in the District Court of the United States a libel against the ship, claiming $125.00, the amount of wages earned at the time of demand and refusal.

The District Court found against Dillon upon the ground that his demand was premature. The Circuit Court of Appeals reversed this decision, and held that Dillon was entitled to recover. 256 Fed. Rep.

631. A writ of certiorari brings before us for review the decree of the Circuit Court of Appeals.

In Sandberg v. McDonald, 248 U. S. 185, and Neilson v. Rhine Shipping Co., 248 U. S. 205, we had occasion to deal with § 11 of the Seamen's Act, and held that it did not invalidate advancement of seamen's wages in foreign countries when legal where made. The instant case requires us to consider now § 4 of the same act. That section amends § 4530, Rev. Stats., and so far as pertinent provides: "Sec. 4530. Every seaman on a vessel of the United States shall be entitled to receive on demand from the master of the vessel to which he belongs one-half part of the wages which he shall have then earned at every port where such vessel, after the voyage has been commenced, shall load or deliver cargo before the voyage is ended and all stipulations in the contract to the contrary shall be void: *Provided,* such a demand shall not be made before the expiration of, nor oftener than once in five days. Any failure on the part of the master to comply with this demand shall release the seaman from his contract, and he shall be entitled to full payment of wages earned. . . . *And provided further,* that this section shall apply to seamen on foreign vessels while in harbors of the United States, and the courts of the United States shall be open to such seamen for its enforcement."

This section has to do with the recovery of wages by seamen, and by its terms gives to every seaman on a vessel of the United States the right to demand one-half the wages which he shall have then earned at every port where such vessel, after the voyage has been commenced, shall load or deliver cargo before the end of the voyage, and stipulations in the contract to the contrary are declared to be void. A failure of the master to comply with the demand releases the seaman from his contract and entitles him to recover full payment of the wages, and the section is made applicable to seamen on foreign vessels while in harbors of the United States, and the courts of the United States are open to such seamen for enforcement of the act.

This section is an amendment of § 4530 of the Revised Statutes, it was intended to supplant that section, as amended by the Act of December 21, 1898, c. 28, 30 Stat. 756, which provided: "Every seaman on a vessel of the United States shall be entitled to receive from the master of the vessel to which he belongs one-half part of the wages which shall be due him at every port where such vessel, after the voyage has been commenced, shall load or deliver cargo before the voyage is ended unless the contrary be expressly stipulated in the contract," etc.

The section, of which the statute now under consideration is an amendment, expressly excepted from the right to recover one-half of the wages those cases in which the contract otherwise provided. In the amended section all such contract provisions are expressly rendered void, and the right to recover is given the seamen notwithstanding contractual obligations to the contrary. The language applies to all seamen on vessels of the United States, and the second proviso of the section as it now reads makes it applicable to seamen on foreign vessels while in harbors of the United States. The proviso does not stop there, for it contains the express provision that the courts of the United States shall be open to seamen on foreign vessels for its enforcement. The latter provision is of the utmost importance in determining the proper construction of this section of the act. It manifests the purpose of Congress to give the benefit of the act to seamen on foreign vessels, and to open the doors of the federal courts to foreign seamen. No such provision was necessary as to American seamen for they had the right independently of this statute to seek redress in the courts of the United States, and, if it were the intention of Congress to limit the provision of the act to American seamen, this feature would have been wholly superfluous.

It is said that it is the purpose to limit the benefit of the act to American seamen, notwithstanding this provision giving access to seamen on foreign vessels to the courts of the United States, because of the title of the act in which its purpose is expressed "to promote the welfare of American seamen in the merchant marine of the United States." But the title is more than this, and not only declares the purposes to promote the welfare of American seamen but further to abolish arrest and imprisonment as a penalty for desertion and to secure the abrogation of treaty provisions in relation thereto; and to promote safety at sea. But the title of an act cannot limit the plain meaning of its text, although it may be looked to to aid in construction in cases of doubt. Cornell v. Coyne, 192 U. S. 418, 530, and cases cited. Apart from the text, which we think plain, it is by no means clear that if the act were given a construction to limit its application to American seamen only, the purposes of Congress would be subserved, for such limited construction would have a tendency to prevent the employment of American seamen, and to promote the engagement of those who were not entitled to sue for one-half wages under the provisions of the law. But, taking the provisions of the act as the same are written, we think it plain that it manifests the purpose of Congress to place American and foreign seamen on an equality of right in so far as the privileges of this section are concerned, with equal opportunity to resort to the courts of the United States for the enforcement of the act. Before the amendment, as we have already pointed out, the right to recover one-half the wages could not be enforced in face of a contractual obligation to the contrary. Congress, for reasons which it deemed sufficient, amended the act so as to permit the recovery upon the conditions named in the statute. In the case of Sandberg v. McDonald, 248 U. S. 185, *supra*, we found no purpose manifested by Congress in section 11 to interfere with wages advanced in foreign ports under contracts legal where made. That section dealt with advancements, and contained no provision such as we find in § 4. Under § 4 all contracts are avoided which run counter to the purposes of the statute. Whether consideration for contractual rights under engagements legally made in foreign countries would suggest a different course is not our province to inquire. It is sufficient to say that Congress has otherwise declared by the positive terms of this enactment, and if it had authority to do so, the law is enforceable in the courts.

We come then to consider the contention that this construction renders the statute unconstitutional as being destructive of contract rights. But we think this contention must be decided adversely to the petitioner upon the authority of previous cases in this court. The matter was fully considered in Patterson v. Bark Eudora, 190 U. S. 169, in which the previous decisions of this court were reviewed, and the conclusion reached that the jurisdiction of this Government over foreign merchant vessels in our ports was such as to give authority to Congress to make provisions of the character now under consideration; that it was for this Government to determine upon what terms and conditions vessels of other countries might be permitted to enter our harbors, and to impose conditions upon the shipment of sailors in our own ports, and make them applicable to foreign as well as domestic vessels. Upon the authority of that case, and others cited in the opinion therein, we have no doubt as to the authority of Congress to pass a statute of this sort, applicable to foreign vessels in our ports and controlling the employment and payment of seamen as a condition of the right of such foreign vessels to enter and use the ports of the United States.

But, it is insisted, that Dillon's action was premature as he made a demand upon the master within less than five days after the vessel arrived in an American port. This contention was sustained in the District Court, but it was ruled otherwise in the Court of Appeals. . . .

We agree with the Circuit Court of Appeals of the Fifth Circuit, whose judgment we are now reviewing, that the demand was not premature. It is true that the Circuit Court of Appeals for the Second Circuit held in the case of The Italier, 257 Fed. Rep. 712, that demand, made before the vessel had been in port for five days, was premature; this was upon the theory that the law was not in force until the vessel had arrived in a port of the United States. But, the limitation upon demand has no reference to the length of stay in the domestic port. The right to recover wages is controlled by the provisions of the statute and includes wages earned from the beginning of the voyage. It is the right to demand and recover such wages with the limitation of the intervals of demand as laid down in the statute, which is given to the seaman while the ship is in a harbor of the United States.

We find no error in the decree of the Circuit Court of Appeals and the same is affirmed.

CUNARD STEAMSHIP COMPANY, LTD., ET AL. v. MELLON, SECRETARY OF THE TREASURY, ET AL.

United States, Supreme Court, 1923.

262 U. S. 100. [67 L. ed. 894; 43 S. Ct. 504.]

Appeals from decrees of the District Court dismissing, on the merits, as many suits brought by the appellant steamship companies for the purpose of enjoining officials of the United States from seizing liquors carried by the appellants' passenger ships as sea stores and from taking other proceedings against the companies and their vessels, under the National Prohibition Act. . . .

MR. JUSTICE VAN DEVANTER delivered the opinion of the Court.

These are suits by steamship companies operating passenger ships between United States ports and foreign ports to enjoin threatened application to them and their ships of certain provisions of the National Prohibition Act. The defendants are officers of the United States charged with the act's enforcement. In the first ten cases the plaintiffs are foreign corporations and their ships are of foreign registry, while in the remaining two the plaintiffs are domestic corporations and their ships are of United States registry. All the ships have long carried and now carry, as part of their sea stores, intoxicating liquors intended to be sold or dispensed to their passengers and crews at meals and otherwise for beverage purposes. Many of the passengers and crews are accustomed to using such beverages and insist that the ships carry and supply liquors for such purposes. By the laws of all the foreign ports at which the ships touch this is permitted and by the laws of some it is required. The liquors are purchased for the ships and taken on board in the foreign ports and are sold or dispensed in the course of all voyages, whether from or to those ports. . . .

October 6, 1922, the Attorney General, in answer to an inquiry by the Secretary of the Treasury, gave an opinion to the effect that the National Prohibition Act, construed in connection with the Eighteenth Amendment to the Constitution, makes it unlawful (a) for any ship, whether domestic or foreign, to bring into territorial waters of the United States, or to carry while within such waters, intoxicating liquors intended for beverage purposes, whether as sea stores or cargo, and (b) for any domestic ship even when without those waters to carry such liquors for such purposes either as cargo or sea stores. The President thereupon directed the preparation, promulgation and application of new instructions conforming to that construction of the act. Being advised of this and that under the new instructions the defendants would seize all liquors carried in contravention of the act as so construed and would proceed to subject the plaintiffs and their ships to penalties provided in the act, the plaintiffs brought these suits.

The hearings in the District Court were on the bills or amended bills, motions to dismiss and answers, and there was a decree of dismissal on the merits in each suit. 284 Fed. 890; 285 Fed. 79. Direct appeals under Judicial Code, § 238, bring the cases here.

While the construction and application of the National Prohibition Act is the ultimate matter in controversy, the act is so closely related to the Eighteenth Amendment, to enforce which it was enacted, that a right understanding of it involves an examination and interpretation of the Amendment. The first section of the latter declares, 40 Stat. 1050, 1941:

"Section 1. After one year from the ratification of this article the manufacture, sale, or transportation of intoxicating liquors within, the importation thereof into, or the exportation thereof from the United States and all territory subject to the jurisdiction thereof for beverage purposes is hereby prohibited."

These words, if taken in their ordinary sense, are very plain. The articles proscribed are intoxicating liquors for beverage purposes. The acts prohibited in respect of them are manufacture, sale and transportation within a designated field, importation into the same, and exportation therefrom. And the designated field is the United States and all territory subject to its jurisdiction. There is no controversy here as to what constitutes intoxicating liquors for beverage purposes; but opposing contentions are made respecting what is comprehended in the terms "transportation," "importation" and "territory."

Some of the contentions ascribe a technical meaning to the words "transportation" and "importation." We think they are to be taken in their ordinary sense, for it better comports with the object to be attained. In that sense transportation comprehends any real carrying about or from one place to another. It is not essential that the carrying be for hire, or by one for another; nor that it be incidental to a transfer of the possession or title. If one carries in his own conveyance for his own purposes it is transportation no less than when a public carrier at the instance of a consignor carries and delivers to a consignee for a stipulated charge. See United States v. Simpson, 252 U. S. 465. Importation, in a like sense, consists in bringing an article into a country from the outside. If there be an actual bringing in it is importation regardless of the mode in which it is effected. Entry through a custom house is not of the essence of the act.

Various meanings are sought to be attributed to the term "territory" in the phrase "the United States and all territory subject to the jurisdiction thereof." We are of opinion that it means the regional areas—of land and adjacent waters—over which the United States claims and exercises dominion and control as a sovereign power. The immediate context and the purport of the entire section show that the term is used in a physical and not a metaphorical sense,—that it refers to areas or districts having fixity of location and recognized boundaries. See United States v. Bevans, 3 Wheat. 336, 390.

It now is settled in the United States and recognized elsewhere that the territory subject to its jurisdiction includes the land areas under its dominion and control, the ports, harbors, bays and other enclosed arms of the sea along its coast and a marginal belt of the sea extending from the coast line outward a marine league, or three geographic miles. Church v. Hubbart, 2 Cranch, 187, 234; The Ann, 1 Fed. Cas., p. 926; United States v. Smiley, 27 Fed. Cas., p. 1132; Manchester v. Massachusetts, 139 U. S. 240, 257–258; Louisiana v. Mississippi, 202 U. S. 1, 52. . . . This, we hold, is the territory which the Amendment designates as its field of operation; and the designation is not of a part of this territory but of "all" of it.

The defendants contend that the Amendment also covers domestic merchant ships outside the waters of the United States, whether on the high seas or in foreign waters. But it does not say so, and what it does say shows, as we have indicated, that it is confined to the physical territory of the United States. In support of their contention the defendants refer to the statement sometimes made that a merchant ship is a part of the territory of the country whose flag she flies. But this, as has been aptly observed, is a figure of speech, a metaphor. Scharrenberg v. Dollar S. S. Co., 245 U. S. 122, 127; In re Ross, 140 U. S. 453, 464; . . .[1] The jurisdiction which it is intended to describe arises out of the nationality of the ship, as established by her domicile, registry and use of the flag, and partakes more of the characteristics of personal than of territorial sovereignty. See The Hamilton, 207 U. S. 398, 403; American Banana Co. v. United Fruit Co., 213 U. S. 347, 355; 1 Oppenheim International Law, 3d ed., §§ 123–125, 128. It is chiefly applicable to ships on the high seas, where there is no territorial sovereign; and as respects ships in foreign territorial waters it has little application beyond what is affirmatively or tacitly permitted by the local sovereign. . . .

The defendants further contend that the Amendment covers foreign merchant ships when within the territorial waters of the United States. Of course, if it were true that a ship is a part of the territory of the country whose flag she carries, the contention would fail. But, as that is a fiction, we think the contention is right.

A merchant ship of one country voluntarily entering the territorial limits of another subjects herself to the jurisdiction of the latter. The jurisdiction attaches in virtue of her presence, just as with other objects within those limits. During her stay she is entitled to the protection of the laws of that place and correlatively is bound to yield obedience to

---

[1] Compare In re Lam Mow, above, p. 149, where the court quoted these words in holding that birth on a merchant vessel flying the American flag was not equivalent to birth "in the United States" in the sense of the Fourteenth Amendment.

them. Of course, the local sovereign may out of considerations of public policy choose to forego the exertion of its jurisdiction or to exert the same in only a limited way, but this is a matter resting solely in its discretion.[1]

In principle, therefore, it is settled that the Amendment could be made to cover both domestic and foreign merchant ships when within the territorial waters of the United States. And we think it has been made to cover both when within those limits. It contains no exception of ships of either class and the terms in which it is couched indicate that none is intended. Such an exception would tend to embarrass its enforcement and to defeat the attainment of its obvious purpose, and therefore cannot reasonably be regarded as implied. . . .

With this understanding of the Amendment, we turn to the National Prohibition Act, c. 85, 41 Stat. 305, which was enacted to enforce it. . . .

As originally enacted the act did not in terms define its territorial field, but a supplemental provision afterwards enacted declares that it "shall apply not only to the United States but to all territory subject to its jurisdiction," which means that its field coincides with that of the Eighteenth Amendment. There is in the act no provision making it applicable to domestic merchant ships when outside the waters of the United States, nor any provision making it inapplicable to merchant ships, either domestic or foreign, when within those waters, save in the Panama Canal. There is a special provision dealing with the Canal Zone which excepts "liquor in transit through the Panama Canal or on the Panama Railroad." The exception does not discriminate between domestic and foreign ships, but applies to all liquor in transit through the canal, whether on domestic or foreign ships. Apart from this exception, the provision relating to the Canal Zone is broad and drastic like the others. . . .

Examining the act as a whole, we think it shows very plainly, first, that it is intended to be operative throughout the territorial limits of the United States, with the single exception stated in the Canal Zone provision; secondly, that it is not intended to apply to domestic vessels when outside the territorial waters of the United States; and, thirdly, that it is intended to apply to all merchant vessels, whether foreign or domestic, when within those waters, save as the Panama Canal Zone exception provides otherwise. . . .

The plaintiffs invite attention to data showing the antiquity of the practice of carrying intoxicating liquors for beverage purposes as part of a ship's sea stores, the wide extent of the practice and its recognition in a congressional enactment, and argue therefrom that neither the amendment nor the act can have been intended to disturb that practice. But in

---

[1] The court here quotes at length from The Schooner Exchange v. M'Faddon, below, p. 326.

this they fail to recognize that the avowed and obvious purpose of both the amendment and the act was to put an end to prior practices respecting such liquors, even though the practices had the sanction of antiquity, generality and statutory recognition. Like data could be produced and like arguments advanced by many whose business, recognized as lawful theretofore, was shut down or curtailed by the change in national policy. In principle the plaintiffs' situation is not different from that of the innkeeper whose accustomed privilege of selling liquor to his guests is taken away, or that of the dining-car proprietor who is prevented from serving liquor to those who use the cars which he operates to and fro across our northern and southern boundaries. . . .

It therefore is of no importance that the liquors in the plaintiffs' ships are carried only as sea stores. Being sea stores does not make them liquors any the less; nor does it change the incidents of their use as beverages. But it is of importance that they are carried through the territorial waters of the United States and brought into its ports and harbors. This is prohibited transportation and importation in the sense of the Amendment and the act.[1]

Our conclusion is that in the first ten cases—those involving foreign ships—the decrees of dismissal were right and should be affirmed, and in the remaining two—those involving domestic ships—the decrees of dismissal were erroneous and should be reversed with directions to enter

---

[1] The court here refers to the cases of Grogan v. Walker & Sons and Anchor Line v. Aldridge, 259 U. S. 80, involving respectively the question whether carrying liquor in bond by rail from Canada to Mexico through the United States was prohibited "transportation" and the question whether the transshipment of liquor from one British vessel to another in the harbor of New York was similarly prohibited. In both cases the answer was in the affirmative. "The Eighteenth Amendment," said the court, "meant a great revolution in the policy of this country, and presumably and obviously meant to upset a good many things on as well as off the statute book. It did not confine itself in any meticulous way to the use of intoxicants in this country. It forbade export for beverage purposes elsewhere. True this discouraged production here, but that was forbidden already, and the provision applied to liquors already lawfully made. See Hamilton v. Kentucky Distilleries & Warehouse Co., 251 U. S. 146, 151, n. 1. It is obvious that those whose wishes and opinions were embodied in the Amendment meant to stop the whole business. They did not want intoxicating liquor in the United States and reasonably may have thought that if they let it in some of it was likely to stay. When, therefore, the Amendment forbids not only importation into and exportation from the United States but transportation within it, the natural meaning of the words expresses an altogether probable intent. The Prohibition Act only fortifies in this respect the interpretation of the Amendment itself. The manufacture, possession, sale and transportation of spirits and wine for other than beverage purposes are provided for in the act, but there is no provision for transshipment or carriage across the country from without. When Congress was ready to permit such a transit for special reasons, in the Canal Zone, it permitted it in express words."

decrees refusing any relief as respects the operations of the ships within the territorial waters of the United States and awarding the relief sought as respects operations outside those waters. . . .

Mr. Justice McReynolds dissents.

Mr. Justice Sutherland, dissenting.

I agree with the judgment of the Court in so far as it affects domestic ships, but I am unable to accept the view that the Eighteenth Amendment applies to foreign ships coming into our ports under the circumstances here disclosed.

It would serve no useful purpose to give my reasons at any length for this conclusion. I therefore state them very generally and briefly.

The general rule of international law is that a foreign ship is so far identified with the country to which it belongs that its internal affairs, whose effect is confined to the ship, ordinarily are not subjected to interference at the hands of another State in whose ports it is temporarily present, 2 Moore, Int. Law Dig., p. 292; United States v. Rodgers, 150 U. S. 249, 260; Wildenhus's Case, 120 U. S. 1, 12; and, as said by Chief Justice Marshall, in Murray v. Schooner Charming Betsy, 2 Cranch, 64, 118: ". . . an act of Congress ought never to be construed to violate the law of nations, if any other possible construction remains. . . ."

That the Government has full power under the Volstead Act to prevent the landing or transshipment from foreign vessels of intoxicating liquors or their use in our ports is not doubted, and, therefore, it may provide for such assurances and safeguards as it may deem necessary to those ends. Nor do I doubt the power of Congress to do all that the Court now holds has been done by that act, but such power exists not under the Eighteenth Amendment, to whose provisions the act is confined, but by virtue of other provisions of the Constitution, which Congress here has not attempted to exercise. With great deference to the contrary conclusion of the Court, due regard for the principles of international comity, which exist between friendly nations, in my opinion, forbids the construction of the Eighteenth Amendment and of the act which the present decision advances. Moreover, the Eighteenth Amendment, it must not be forgotten, confers concurrent power of enforcement upon the several States, and it follows that if the General Government possesses the power here claimed for it under that Amendment, the several States within their respective boundaries, possess the same power. It does not seem possible to me that Congress, in submitting the Amendment or the several States in adopting it, could have intended to vest in the various seaboard States a power so intimately connected with our foreign relations and whose exercise might result in international confusion and embarrassment.

In adopting the Eighteenth Amendment and in enacting the Volstead Act the question of their application to foreign vessels in the circumstances now presented does not appear to have been in mind. If, upon consideration, Congress shall conclude that when such vessels, in good faith carrying liquor among their sea stores, come temporarily into our ports their officers should, *ipso facto*, become liable to drastic punishment and the ships themselves subject to forfeiture, it will be a simple matter for that body to say so in plain terms. But interference with the purely internal affairs of a foreign ship is of so delicate a nature, so full of possibilities of international misunderstandings and so likely to invite retaliation that an affirmative conclusion in respect thereof should rest upon nothing less than the clearly expressed intention of Congress to that effect, and this I am unable to find in the legislation here under review.[1]

C. Jurisdiction in salvage and collision cases.

In suits arising out of collisions between vessels of different states, no question of jurisdiction is raised when the defendant vessel is sued in the courts of the state whose flag it flies. Query, what if a suit were brought by a vessel of one state against a vessel of a second state in the courts of a third state within whose territorial waters both vessels happen to be? [The Belgenland.]

THE BELGENLAND.

United States, Supreme Court, 1885.

114 U. S. 355. [29 L. ed. 152; 5 S. Ct. 860.]

Appeal from the Circuit Court of the United States for the Eastern District of Pennsylvania.

This case grew out of a collision which took place on the high seas between the Norwegian barque Luna and the Belgian steamship Belgen-

---

[1] Supplementary Cases. In the case of Brown v. Duchesne, 19 Howard 183 (1856), involving an action for infringement of a patent brought by the plaintiff against the French master of a French vessel which happened to be temporarily in port and whose gaffs were the occasion of the alleged infringement, the Supreme Court held that the proper construction of the patent laws was that they did not extend the rights of the patentee to a foreign vessel in port when the equipment in question was placed upon her in a foreign port in accordance with the laws of the foreign country.

In Patterson v. Bark Eudora, 190 U. S. 169 (1903), involving the question whether the provisions of the act of 1898 prohibiting advance payment of wages to seamen were applicable to seamen shipping in a port of the United States on a foreign vessel, the Supreme Court in holding that they were applicable argued that, since the implied consent of the government to leave jurisdiction over the internal affairs of foreign merchant vessels in our harbors to the nations to which those vessels belonged might be wholly withdrawn, it might be extended upon such terms and conditions as the government saw fit to impose.

land by which the former was run down and sunk. Part of the crew of the Luna, including the master, were rescued by the Belgenland and brought to Philadelphia. The master immediately libelled the steamship on behalf of the owners of the Luna and her cargo, and her surviving crew, in a cause civil and maritime. . . . The District Court decided in favor of the libellant, . . . An appeal was taken to the Circuit Court, . . . A decree was thereupon entered, affirming the decree of the District Court. . . . A reargument was then had on the question of jurisdiction, and the court held and decided that the Admiralty Courts of the United States have jurisdiction of collisions occurring on the high seas between vessels owned by foreigners of different nationalities; and overruled the plea to the jurisdiction.

MR. JUSTICE BRADLEY delivered the opinion of the court. . . .

The first question to be considered is that of the jurisdiction of the District Court to hear and determine the cause.

It is unnecessary here, and would be out of place, to examine the question which has so often engaged the attention of the common law courts, whether, and in what cases, the courts of one country should take cognizance of controversies arising in a foreign country, or in places outside of the jurisdiction of any country. . . . We shall content ourselves with inquiring what rule is followed by Courts of Admiralty in dealing with maritime causes arising between foreigners and others on the high seas.

This question is not a new one in these courts. Sir William Scott had occasion to pass upon it in 1799. An American ship was taken by the French on a voyage from Philadelphia to London, and afterwards rescued by her crew, carried to England, and libelled for salvage; and the court entertained jurisdiction. The crew, however, though engaged in the American ship, were British born subjects, and weight was given to this circumstance in the disposition of the case. The judge, however, made the following remarks: "But it is asked, if they were American seamen, would this court hold plea of their demands? It may be time enough to answer this question whenever the fact occurs. In the meantime, I will say without scruple that I can see no inconvenience that would arise if a British court of justice was to hold plea in such a case; or conversely, if American courts were to hold pleas of this nature respecting the merits of British seamen on such occasions. For salvage is a question of *jus gentium,* and materially different from the question of a mariner's contract, which is a creature of the particular institutions of the country, to be applied and construed and explained by its own particular rules. There might be good reason, therefore, for this court to decline to interfere in such cases and to remit them to their own domestic forum; but this is a general claim, upon the general ground of *quantum meruit,* to be governed by a sound discretion, acting on general principles; and I can see no reason why one country should be afraid to trust to the equity of the courts of another on such a question, of such a nature, so to be determined." The Two Friends, 1 Ch. Rob., 271, 278.

The law has become settled very much in accord with these views. That was a case of salvage; but the same principles would seem to apply to the case of destroying or injuring a ship, as to that of saving it. Both, when acted on the high seas, between persons of different nationalities, come within the domain of the general law of nations, or *communis juris*, and are *prima facie* proper subjects of inquiry in any Court of Admiralty which first obtains jurisdiction of the rescued or offending ship at the solicitation in justice of the meritorious, or injured, parties.

The same question of jurisdiction arose in another salvage case which came before this court in 1804, Mason v. The Blaireau, 2 Cranch, 240. There a French ship was saved by a British ship, and brought into a port of the United States; and the question of jurisdiction was raised by Mr. Martin, of Maryland, who, however, did not press the point, and referred to the observations of Sir William Scott in The Two Friends. Chief Justice Marshall, speaking for the court, disposed of the question as follows:—"A doubt has been suggested," said he, "respecting the jurisdiction of the court, and upon reference to the authorities, the point does not appear to have been ever settled. These doubts seem rather founded on the idea that upon principles of general policy, this court ought not to take cognizance of a case entirely between foreigners, than from any positive incapacity to do so. On weighing the considerations drawn from public convenience, those in favor of the jurisdiction appear much to overbalance those against it, and it is the opinion of this court, that, whatever doubts may exist in a case where the jurisdiction may be objected to, there ought to be none where the parties assent to it." . . .

But, although the courts will use a discretion about assuming jurisdiction of controversies between foreigners in cases arising beyond the territorial jurisdiction of the country to which the courts belong, yet where such controversies are *communis juris*, that is, where they arise under the common law of nations, special grounds should appear to induce the court to deny its aid to a foreign suitor when it has jurisdiction of the ship or party charged. The existence of jurisdiction in all such cases is beyond dispute; the only question will be, whether it is expedient to exercise it. See 2 Parsons Ship. and Adm., 226, and cases cited in the notes. In the case of The Jerusalem, 2 Gall. 191, . . . Justice Story examined the subject very fully, and came to the conclusion that, wherever there is a maritime lien on the ship, an Admiralty Court can take jurisdiction on the principle of the civil law, that in proceedings *in rem* the proper forum is the *locus rei sitæ*. He added: "With reference, therefore, to what may be deemed the public law of Europe, a proceeding *in rem* may well be maintained in our courts where the property of a foreigner is within our jurisdiction. Nor am I able to perceive how the exercise of such judicial authority clashes with any principles of public policy." . . .

Justice Story's decision in this case was referred to by Dr. Lushington with strong approbation in the case of The Golubchick, 1 W. Rob., 143, decided in 1840, and was adopted as authority for his taking jurisdiction in that case.

In 1839, a case of collision on the high seas between two foreign ships of different countries (the very case now under consideration) came before the English Admiralty. The Johann Friederich, 1 W. Rob. 35. A Danish ship was sunk by a Bremen ship, and on the latter being libelled, the respondents entered a protest against the jurisdiction of the court. But jurisdiction was retained by Dr. Lushington who, amongst other things, remarked: "An alien friend is entitled to sue [in our courts] on the same footing as a British-born subject, and if the foreigner in this case had been resident here, and the cause of action had originated *infra corpus comitatus,* no objection could have been taken." Reference being made to the observations of Lord Stowell in cases of seamen's wages, the judge said: "All questions of collision are questions *communis juris;* but in case of mariners' wages, whoever engages voluntarily to serve on board a foreign ship, necessarily undertakes to be bound by the law of the country to which such ship belongs, and the legality of his claim must be tried by such law. One of the most important distinctions, therefore, respecting cases where both parties are foreigners is, whether the case be *communis juris* or not. . . . If these parties must wait until the vessel that has done the injury returned to its own country, their remedy might be altogether lost, for she might never return, and, if she did, there is no part of the world to which they might not be sent for their redress."

In the subsequent case of The Griefswald, 1 Swabey, 430, decided by the same judge in 1859, which arose out of a collision between a British barque and a Persian ship in the Dardanelles, Dr. Lushington said: "In cases of collision, it has been the practice of this country, and, so far as I know, of the European States and of the United States of America, to allow a party alleging grievance by a collision to proceed *in rem* against the ship wherever found, and this practice, it is manifest, is most conducive to justice, because in very many cases a remedy *in personam* would be impracticable."

The subject has frequently been before our own Admiralty Courts of original jurisdiction, and there has been but one opinion expressed, namely, that they have jurisdiction in such cases, and that they will exercise it unless special circumstances exist to show that justice would be better subserved by declining it.

. . . Indeed, where the parties are not only foreigners, but belong to different nations, and the injury or salvage service takes place on the high seas, there seems to be no good reason why the party injured, or doing the service, should ever be denied justice in our courts. Neither party has any peculiar claim to be judged by the municipal law of his own country, since the case is pre-eminently one *communis juris,* and can generally be more impartially and satisfactorily adjudicated by the court of a third nation having jurisdiction of the *res* or parties, than it could be by the courts of either of the nations to which the litigants belong. As Judge Deady very justly said, in a case before him in the district of Oregon: "The parties cannot be remitted to a home forum, for, being subjects of different governments, there is no such tribunal. The forum which is common to them both by the *jus gentium* is any court of admiralty within the reach of whose process they may both be found." Bernhard v. Greene, 3 Sawyer, 230, 235.

As to the law which should be applied in cases between parties, or ships, of different nationalities, arising on the high seas, not within the jurisdiction of any nation, there can be no doubt that it must be the general maritime law, as understood and administered in the courts of the country in which the litigation is prosecuted. . . .

The decree of the Circuit Court is affirmed. . . .

D. Immunity of foreign government-owned vessels in national ports.

Public and publicly-owned vessels enjoy a specially privileged position when in the ports of a foreign state. Certain of them, such as war-ships or naval auxiliaries, are completely exempt from the local jurisdiction not only with respect to the internal discipline of the vessel but also in respect to acts which may disturb "the peace of the port." Query, may a foreign war-ship be sued before the local courts by persons claiming title to the ship itself? [The Schooner Exchange v. M'Faddon.] May it be sued for salvage? [The Constitution.] What if the government-owned vessel is used for public but non-military functions, such as carrying the mails? [The Parlement Belge.] Could a suit for salvage be brought in the local courts against a government-owned foreign vessel which was engaged in ordinary trade? [The Porto Alexandre; Berizzi Brothers v. The Pesaro.] Would the fact that the vessel, although privately-owned, was engaged in public business be sufficient to obtain for it the exemption accorded to public ships? [The Roseric.]

THE SCHOONER EXCHANGE v. M'FADDON AND OTHERS.

United States, Supreme Court, 1812.

7 Cranch, 116. [3 L. ed. 287.]

[The schooner Exchange, belonging to John M'Faddon and William Greetham, citizens of Maryland, while on a voyage from Baltimore to

Spain in December, 1810, was seized by officers of Napoleon, taken to France, converted into a public vessel, and given the name Balaou. When the vessel put into Philadelphia in July, 1811, her original owners filed a libel praying that she be attached and returned to them. Thereupon the United States District Attorney suggested to the court that the vessel was a public vessel, the property of a power with which the United States was at peace, and consequently it was not within the jurisdiction of the court. The decision of the District Court dismissing the libel having been reversed by the Circuit Court, an appeal was taken to this court.]

Marshall, Ch. J., delivered the opinion of the Court as follows:

This case involves the very delicate and important inquiry, whether an American citizen can assert, in an American court, a title to an armed national vessel, found within the waters of the United States.

The question has been considered with an earnest solicitude, that the decision may conform to those principles of national and municipal law by which it ought to be regulated.

In exploring an unbeaten path, with few, if any aids, from precedents or written law, the court has found it necessary to rely much on general principles, and on a train of reasoning, founded on cases in some degree analogous to this.

The jurisdiction of courts is a branch of that which is possessed by the nation as an independent sovereign power.

The jurisdiction of the nation within its own territory is necessarily exclusive and absolute. It is susceptible of no limitation not imposed by itself. Any restriction upon it, deriving validity from an external source, would imply a diminution of its own sovereignty to the extent of the restriction, and an investment of that sovereignty to the same extent in that power which could impose such restrictions.

All exceptions, therefore, to the full and complete power of a nation within its own territories, must be traced up to the consent of the nation itself. They can flow from no other legitimate source.

This consent may be either expressed or implied. In the latter case, it is less determinate, exposed more to the uncertainties of construction; but, if understood, not less obligatory.

The world being composed of distinct sovereignties, possessing equal rights and equal independence, whose mutual benefit is promoted by intercourse with each other, and by an interchange of those good offices which humanity dictates and its wants require, all sovereigns have consented to a relaxation in practice, in cases under certain peculiar circumstances, of that absolute and complete jurisdiction within their respective territories which sovereignty confers.

This consent may, in some instances, be tested by common usage, and by common opinion, growing out of that usage.

A nation would justly be considered as violating its faith, although that faith might not be expressly plighted, which should suddenly and without previous notice, exercise its territorial powers in a manner not consonant to the usages and received obligations of the civilized world.

This full and absolute territorial jurisdiction being alike the attribute of every sovereign, and being incapable of conferring extra-territorial power, would not seem to contemplate foreign sovereigns nor their sovereign rights as its objects. One sovereign being in no respect amenable to another; and being bound by obligations of the highest character not to degrade the dignity of his nation, by placing himself or its sovereign rights within the jurisdiction of another, can be supposed to enter a foreign territory only under an express license, or in the confidence that the immunities belonging to his independent sovereign station, will be extended to him.

This perfect equality and absolute independence of sovereigns, and this common interest impelling them to mutual intercourse, and an interchange of good offices with each other, have given rise to a class of cases in which every sovereign is understood to waive the exercise of a part of that complete exclusive territorial jurisdiction, which has been stated to be the attribute of every nation.

1st. One of these is admitted to be the exemption of the person of the sovereign from arrest or detention within a foreign territory. . . .

2d. A second case, standing on the same principles with the first, is the immunity which all civilized nations allow to foreign ministers. . . .

3d. A third case in which a sovereign is understood to cede a portion of his territorial jurisdiction is, where he allows the troops of a foreign prince to pass through his dominions.

In such case, without any express declaration waiving jurisdiction over the army to which this right of passage has been granted, the sovereign who should attempt to exercise it would certainly be considered as violating his faith. By exercising it, the purpose for which the free passage was granted would be defeated, and a portion of the military force of a foreign independent nation would be diverted from those national objects and duties to which it was applicable, and would be withdrawn from the control of the sovereign whose power and whose safety might greatly depend on retaining the exclusive command and disposition of this force. The grant of a free passage, therefore, implies a waiver of all jurisdiction over the troops during their passage, and permits the foreign general to use that discipline, and to inflict those punishments which the government of his army may require. . . .

It is obvious that the passage of an army through a foreign territory will probably be at all times inconvenient and injurious, and would often be imminently dangerous to the sovereign through whose dominion it passed. Such a practice would break down some of the most decisive distinctions between peace and war, and would reduce a nation to the necessity of resisting by war an act not absolutely hostile in its character, or of exposing itself to the stratagems and frauds of a power whose integrity might be doubted, and who might enter the country under deceitful pretexts. It is for reasons like these that the general license to foreigners to enter the dominions of a friendly power, is never understood to extend to a military force; and an army marching into the dominions of another sovereign, may justly be considered as committing an act of hostility; and, if not opposed by force, acquires no privileges by its irregular conduct. It may however well be questioned whether any other than the sovereign power of the state be capable of deciding that such military commander is without a license.

But the rule which is applicable to armies, does not appear to be equally applicable to ships of war entering the ports of a friendly power. The injury inseparable from the march of an army through an inhabited country, and the dangers often, indeed generally, attending it, do not ensue from admitting a ship of war, without a special license, into a friendly port. A different rule therefore with respect to this species of military force has been generally adopted. If, for reasons of state, the ports of a nation generally, or any particular ports be closed against vessels of war generally, or the vessels of any particular nation, notice is usually given of such determination. If there be no prohibition, the ports of a friendly nation are considered as open to the public ships of all powers with whom it is at peace, and they are supposed to enter such ports and to remain in them while allowed to remain, under the protection of the government of the place. . . .

If there be no treaty applicable to the case, and the sovereign, from motives deemed adequate by himself, permits his ports to remain open to the public ships of foreign friendly powers, the conclusion seems irresistible, that they enter by his assent. And if they enter by his assent necessarily implied, no just reason is perceived by the Court for distinguishing their case from that of vessels which enter by express assent. . . .

To the Court, it appears, that where, without treaty, the ports of a nation are open to the private and public ships of a friendly power, whose subjects have also liberty without special license, to enter the country for business or amusement, a clear distinction is to be drawn between the rights accorded to private individuals or private trading vessels, and those accorded to public armed ships which constitute a part of the military force of the nation.

The preceding reasoning, has maintained the propositions that all exemptions from territorial jurisdiction, must be derived from the consent of the sovereign of the territory; that this consent may be implied or expressed; and that when implied, its extent must be regulated by the nature of the case, and the views under which the parties requiring and conceding it must be supposed to act.

When private individuals of one nation spread themselves through another as business or caprice may direct, mingling indiscriminately with the inhabitants of that other, or when merchant vessels enter for the purposes of trade, it would be obviously inconvenient and dangerous to society, and would subject the laws to continual infraction, and the government to degradation, if such individuals or merchants did not owe temporary and local allegiance, and were not amenable to the jurisdiction of the country. Nor can the foreign sovereign have any motive for wishing such exemption. His subjects thus passing into foreign countries, are not employed by him, nor are they engaged in national pursuits. Consequently there are powerful motives for not exempting persons of this description from the jurisdiction of the country in which they are found, and no one motive for requiring it. The implied license, therefore, under which they enter can never be construed to grant such exemption.

But in all respects different is the situation of a public armed ship. She constitutes a part of the military force of her nation; acts under the immediate and direct command of the sovereign; is employed by him in national objects. He has many and powerful motives for preventing those objects from being defeated by the interference of a foreign state. Such interference cannot take place without affecting his power and his dignity. The implied license therefore under which such vessel enters a friendly port, may reasonably be construed, and it seems to the Court, ought to be construed, as containing an exemption from the jurisdiction of the sovereign, within whose territory she claims the rites of hospitality.

Upon these principles, by the unanimous consent of nations, a foreigner is amenable to the laws of the place; but certainly in practice, nations have not yet asserted their jurisdiction over the public armed ships of a foreign sovereign entering a port open for their reception.
. . .

It seems then to the Court, to be a principle of public law, that national ships of war, entering the port of a friendly power open for their reception, are to be considered as exempted by the consent of that power from its jurisdiction.

Without doubt, the sovereign of the place is capable of destroying this implication. He may claim and exercise jurisdiction either by employing force, or by subjecting such vessels to the ordinary tribunals. But until such power be exerted in a manner not to be misunderstood, the sovereign cannot be considered as having imparted to the ordinary tribunals a jurisdiction, which it would be a breach of faith to exercise. Those general statutory provisions therefore which are descriptive of the ordinary jurisdiction of the judicial tribunals, which give an individual whose property has been wrested from him, a right to claim that property in the courts of the country, in which it is found, ought not, in the opinion of this Court, to be so construed as to give them jurisdiction in a case, in which the sovereign power has impliedly consented to waive its jurisdiction.

The arguments in favor of this opinion which have been drawn from the general inability of the judicial power to enforce its decisions in cases of this description, from the consideration, that the sovereign power of the nation is alone competent to avenge wrongs committed by a sovereign, that the questions to which such wrongs give birth are rather questions of policy than of law, that they are for diplomatic, rather than legal discussion, are of great weight, and merit serious attention. But the argument has already been drawn to a length, which forbids a particular examination of these points.

The principles which have been stated, will now be applied to the case at bar.

In the present state of the evidence and proceedings, the Exchange must be considered as a vessel which was the property of the Libellants, whose claim is repelled by the fact, that she is now a national armed vessel, commissioned by, and in the service of the emperor of France. The evidence of this fact is not controverted. But it is contended, that it constitutes no bar to an enquiry into the validity of the title, by which the emperor holds this vessel. Every person, it is alleged, who is entitled to property brought within the jurisdiction of our Courts, has a right to assert his title in those Courts, unless there be some law taking his case out of the general rule. It is therefore said to be the right, and if it be the right, it is the duty of the Court, to enquire whether this title has been extinguished by an act, the validity of which is recognized by national or municipal law.

If the preceding reasoning be correct, the Exchange, being a public armed ship, in the service of a foreign sovereign, with whom the government of the United States is at peace, and having entered an American port open for her reception, on the terms on which ships of war are generally permitted to enter the ports of a friendly power, must be considered as having come into the American territory, under an implied promise, that while necessarily within it, and demeaning herself in a friendly manner, she should be exempt from the jurisdiction of the country.

If this opinion be correct, there seems to be a necessity for admitting that the fact might be disclosed to the Court by the suggestion of the Attorney for the United States.

I am directed to deliver it, as the opinion of the Court, that the sentence of the Circuit Court, reversing the sentence of the District Court, in the case of the Exchange be reversed, and that of the District Court, dismissing the libel, be affirmed.

THE CONSTITUTION.

Great Britain, High Court of Justice, Admiralty, 1879.

48 L. J., P. D. and A. 13.

This was a motion for leave to issue warrants of arrest against the United States frigate Constitution grounded near Swanage, and among other vessels which rendered assistance in getting her afloat was the steam-tug Admiral. A sum of 200*l*. was offered to the owner of the Admiral as a reward for such services as his tug had performed, but he declined this offer and claimed 1,500*l*., which the captain of the Constitution refused to give him. The owner of the Admiral gave notice that he would move the Court for leave to issue warrants of arrest in an action of salvage against the Constitution and her cargo respectively. . . .

Sir Robert Phillimore: In this case an application was made to the court to allow a warrant to issue of a peculiar character—a warrant which was to be served upon a ship of war belonging to an independent state at amity with Her Majesty. The court directed the case to stand over, and suggested that it would be proper that notice should be given to his Excellency, the American Minister in London, and to Lord Salisbury, as Secretary for Foreign Affairs. The court has reason to congratulate itself that it took that step, for the result has been that it has had the advantage of hearing the opinion of counsel on behalf of the United States and of the learned gentleman representing the Crown. It appears from telegrams which have passed in the case that a claim has been made by the owner of the tug for 1,500*l*., but that the American Consul at Portsmouth has forwarded simply a cheque for 200*l*., in recognition of the services which the tug has rendered. The owner of the tug was dissatisfied with that amount; and consequently made an application to this court for an order to issue a warrant to arrest the Constitution and her cargo. The question, therefore, which is raised under these proceedings is whether I have any jurisdiction to permit the arrest of a foreign ship of war belonging to an independent state in amity with our sovereign, and I hardly think that it can be denied that if I were to exercise the jurisdiction which is craved in the present case, I should be doing that for which there exists no direct precedent. On the contrary, I have no doubt as to this general proposition—that ships of war belonging to another nation with whom we are at peace are exempt from the civil jurisdiction of the courts of this country; and I have listened in vain for any peculiar circumstances which would take this case out of that general proposition. It has happened to me more than once to have been requested by foreign states to sit as arbitrator, and to make awards in differences which had arisen between them and British subjects. Had such an application been made in the present instance I would have gladly undertaken the duty sought to be imposed upon me; but that is not the state of matters I have now to consider. All that I have now to determine is the simple question of jurisdiction. Various cases have been cited before me in argument, all of which, with one exception, were discussed in the case of the Charkieh, but that was a wholly different case because the Khedive of Egypt was not an independent sovereign, and the Charkieh herself formed one of a fleet of merchantmen. I may in the lengthy judgment which I delivered in that cause, have let drop some expression which may have given rise to an impression that a foreign ship of war is liable to arrest, but, in that case this question, as it is here raised, had not to be decided. Now that it comes before me in this plain and simple form, I feel no doubt that it would be improper for me to accede to the request of the owner of the steam-tug, nor do I think, as I have said above, that the Constitution is liable to the process of this court. In regard to the question of the liability of the cargo, I must say I see no distinction between the issue of a warrant in the case of the ship and in the case of this cargo; it is on board a foreign vessel of war, and is under the charge of a foreign government for public purposes. So that, having no authority to issue either of the warrants prayed for, and as no precedent exists for such a course, I must dismiss this motion with costs.[1]

THE PARLEMENT BELGE.

Great Britain, Court of Appeal, 1880.

L. R. [1880]. 5 P. D. 197.

Brett, L. J. In this case proceedings in rem on behalf of the owners of the Daring were instituted in the Admiralty Division, in accordance with the forms prescribed by the Judicature Act, against the Parlement Belge, to recover redress in respect of a collision. A writ was served in the usual and prescribed manner on board the Parlement Belge. No appearance was entered, but the Attorney-General, in answer to a motion to direct that judgment with costs should be entered for the plaintiffs, and that a warrant should be issued for the arrest of the Parlement Belge, filed an information and protest, asserting that the Court had no jurisdiction to entertain the suit. Upon the hearing of the motion and protest the learned judge of the Admiralty Division overruled the protest and allowed the warrant of arrest to issue. The Attorney-General appealed. The protest alleged that the Parlement Belge was a mail packet running between Ostend and Dover, and one of the packets

---

[1] Compare the case of the Johnson Lighterage Co. No. 24, above, p. 282, n. 1, where the libel to recover for salvage services was brought against an American scow and its cargo of munitions of war belonging to the Russian government.

mentioned in Article 6 of the Convention of the 17th of February, 1876, made between the sovereigns of Great Britain and Belgium; that she was and is the property of his Majesty the King of the Belgians, and in his possession, control, and employ as reigning sovereign of the state, and was and is a public vessel of the sovereign and state, carrying his Majesty's royal pennon, and was navigated and employed by and in the possession of such government, and was officered by officers of the Royal Belgian navy, holding commissions, &c. In answer it was averred on affidavits, which were not contradicted, that the packet boat, besides carrying letters, carried merchandise and passengers and their luggage for hire.

Three main questions were argued before us: (1) Whether, irrespective of the express exemption contained in Article 6 of the Convention, the Court had jurisdiction to seize the Belgian vessel in a suit in rem; (2) whether, if the Court would otherwise have such jurisdiction, it was ousted by Article 6 of the Convention; (3) whether any exemption from the jurisdiction of the Court, which the vessel might otherwise have had, was lost by reason of her trading in the carriage of goods and persons. . . .

The proposition raised by the first question seems to be as follows: Has the Admiralty Division jurisdiction in respect of a collision to proceed in rem against, and, in case of non-appearance or omission to find bail, to seize and sell, a ship present in this country, which ship is at the time of the proceedings the property of a foreign sovereign, is in his possession, control, and employ as sovereign by means of his commissioned officers, and is a public vessel of his state, in the sense of its being used for purposes treated by such sovereign and his advisers as public national services, it being admitted that such ship, though commissioned, is not an armed ship of war or employed as a part of the military force of his country? On the one side it is urged that the only ships exempted from the jurisdiction are armed ships of war, or ships which, though not armed, are in the employ of the government as part of the military force of the state. On the other side it is contended that all moveable property, which is the public property of a sovereign and nation used for public purposes, is exempt from adverse interference by any court of judicature. It is admitted that neither the sovereign of Great Britain nor any friendly sovereign can be adversely personally impleaded in any court of this country. It is admitted that no armed ship of war of the sovereign of Great Britain or of a foreign sovereign can be seized by any process whatever, exercised for any purpose, of any court of this country. But it is said that this vessel, though it is the property of a friendly sovereign in his public capacity and is used for purposes treated by him as public national services, can be seized and sold under the process of the Admiralty Court of this country, because it will, if so seized and sold, be so treated, not in a suit brought against the sovereign personally, but in a suit in rem against the vessel itself. This contention raises two questions: first, supposing that an action in rem is an action against the property only, meaning thereby that it is not a legal proceeding at all against the owner of the property, yet can the property in question be subject to the jurisdiction of the Court? Secondly, is it true to say that an action in rem is only and solely a legal procedure against the property, or is it not rather a procedure indirectly, if not directly, impleading the owner of the property to answer to the judgment of the Court to the extent of his interest in the property?

The first question really raises this, whether every part of the public property of every sovereign authority in use for national purposes is not as much exempt from the jurisdiction of every Court as is the person of every sovereign. Whether it is so or not depends upon whether all nations have agreed that it shall be, or in other words, whether it is so by the law of nations. The exemption of the person of every sovereign from adverse suit is admitted to be a part of the law of nations. An equal exemption from interference by any process of any Court of some property of every sovereign is admitted to be a part of the law of nations. The universal agreement which has made these propositions part of the law of nations has been an implied agreement. Whether the law of nations exempts all the public property of a state which is destined to the use of the state, depends on whether the principle, on which the agreement has been implied, is as applicable to all that other public property of a sovereign or state as to the public property which is admitted to be exempt. If the principle be equally applicable to all public property used as such, then the agreement to exempt ought to be implied with regard to all such public property. If the principle only applies to the property which is admitted to be exempt, then we have no right to extend the exemption.

The first question, therefore, is—What is the principle on which the exemption of the person of sovereigns and of certain public properties has been recognized? "Our king," says Blackstone (B. 1, c. 7), "owes no kind of subjection to any other potentate on earth. Hence it is that no suit or action can be brought against the king, even in civil matters, because no Court can have jurisdiction over him. For all jurisdiction implies superiority of power; authority to try would be vain and idle without an authority to redress, and the sentence of a Court would be contemptible unless the Court had power to command the execution of it, but who shall command the king?" In this passage, which has been often cited and relied on, the reason of the exemption is the character of the sovereign authority, its high dignity, whereby it is not subject to any superior authority of any kind. "The world," says Wheaton, adopting the words of the judgment in the case of The Exchange (7 Cranch, 116), "being composed of distinct sovereignties, possessing equal rights and equal independence, all sovereigns have consented to a relaxation in practice, under certain peculiar circumstances, of that absolute and complete jurisdiction within their respective territories which sovereignty confers." "This perfect equality and absolute independence of sovereigns has given rise to a class of cases in which every sovereign is understood to waive the exercise of a part of that complete exclusive territorial jurisdiction which has been stated to be the attribute of every nation." "One of these is the exemption of the person of the sovereign from arrest or detention within a foreign territory. Why have the whole world concurred in this? The answer cannot be mistaken. A foreign sovereign is not understood as intending to subject himself to a jurisdiction incompatible with his dignity and the dignity of his nation." By dignity is obviously here meant his independence of any superior authority. So Vattel, Lib. 4, c. 7, s. 108, speaking of sovereigns, says:—"*S'il est venu en voyageur, sa dignité seule, et ce qui est dû à la nation qu'il représente et qu'il gouverne, le met à couvert de toute insulte, lui assure des respects et toute sorte d'égards, et l'exempte de toute juridiction.*"

In the case of The Duke of Brunswick v. The King of Hanover [6 Beav. 1], the suit was against the king. There was a demurrer to the jurisdiction. Lord Langdale in an elaborate judgment allowed the demurrer. He rejected the alleged doctrine of a fictitious extraterritoriality; he admitted that there are some reasons which might justify the exemption of ambassadors which do not necessarily apply to a sovereign, but he nevertheless adopted an analogy between the cases of the ambassadors and the sovereign, and allowed the demurrer on the ground that the sovereign character is superior to all jurisdiction. . . .

From all these authorities it seems to us, although other reasons have sometimes been suggested, that the real principle on which the exemption of every sovereign from the jurisdiction of every Court has been deduced is that the exercise of such jurisdiction would be incompatible with his regal dignity,—that is to say, with his absolute independence of every superior authority. By a similar examination of authorities we come to the conclusion, although other grounds have sometimes been suggested, that the immunity of an ambassador from the jurisdiction of the Courts of the country to which he is accredited is based upon his being the representative of the independent sovereign or state which sends him, and which sends him upon the faith of his being admitted to be clothed with the same independence of and superiority to all adverse jurisdiction as the sovereign authority whom he represents would be. . . .

The judgment of Lord Campbell in De Haber v. The Queen of Portugal, 17 Q. B. 171, seems to the same effect, though the decision may fairly be said to apply only to a suit directly brought against the sovereign. . . . The decision therefore is that the immunity of the sovereign is at least as great as the immunity of an ambassador, but as the statute declares that the law is, and always has been, not only that an ambassador is free from personal suit or process, but that his goods are free from such process as distress or seizure, the latter meaning seizure by process of law, it follows that the goods of every sovereign are free from any seizure by process of law.

The latest case on the point seems to be the case of Vavasseur v. Krupp, 9 Ch. D. 351, before this Court. . . .

The principle to be deduced from all these cases is that, as a consequence of the absolute independence of every sovereign authority, and of the international comity which induces every sovereign state to respect the independence and dignity of every other sovereign state, each and every one declines to exercise by means of its Courts any of its territorial jurisdiction over the person of any sovereign or ambassador of any other state, or over the public property of any state which is destined to public use, or over the property of any ambassador, though such sovereign, ambassador or property be within its territory, and, therefore, but for the common agreement, subject to its jurisdiction. . . .

This proposition would determine the first question in the present case in favour of the protest, even if an action in rem were held to be a proceeding solely against property and not a procedure directly or indirectly impleading the owner of the property to answer to the judgment of the Court. But we cannot allow it to be supposed that in our opinion the owner of the property is not indirectly impleaded. . . .
To implead an independent sovereign in such a way is to call upon him to sacrifice either his property or his independence. To place him in that position is a breach of the principle upon which his immunity from jurisdiction rests. We think that he cannot be so indirectly impleaded, any more than he could be directly impleaded. The case is, upon this consideration of it, brought within the general rule that a sovereign authority cannot be personally impleaded in any court.

But it is said that the immunity is lost by reason of the ship having been used for trading purposes. As to this, it must be maintained either that the ship has been so used as to have been employed substantially as a mere trading ship and not substantially for national purposes, or that a use of her in part for trading purposes takes away the immunity, although she is in possession of the sovereign authority by the hands of commissioned officers, and is substantially in use for national purposes. Both these propositions raise the question of how the ship must be considered to have been employed.

As to the first, the ship has been by the sovereign of Belgium, by the usual means, declared to be in his possession as sovereign, and to be a public vessel of the state. It seems very difficult to say that any Court can inquire by contentious testimony whether that declaration is or is not correct. To submit to such an inquiry before the Court is to submit to its jurisdiction. It has been held that if the ship be declared by the sovereign authority by the usual means to be a ship of war that declaration cannot be inquired into. That was expressly decided under very trying circumstances in the case of The Exchange [7 Cranch, 116]. Whether the ship is a public ship used for national purposes seems to come within the same rule. But if such an inquiry could properly be instituted it seems clear that in the present case the ship has been mainly used for the purpose of carrying the mails, and only subserviently to that main object for the purposes of trade. The carrying of passengers and merchandise has been subordinated to the duty of carrying the mails. The ship is not in fact brought within the first proposition. As to the second, it has been frequently stated that an independent sovereign cannot be personally sued, although he has carried on a private trading adventure. It has been held that an ambassador cannot be personally sued, although he has traded; and in both cases because such a suit would be inconsistent with the independence and equality of the state which he represents. If the remedy sought by an action in rem against public property is, as we think it is, an indirect mode of exercising the authority of the Court against the owner of the property, then the attempt to exercise such an authority is an attempt inconsistent with the independence and equality of the state which is represented by such owner. The property cannot upon the hypothesis be denied to be public property; the case is within the terms of the rule; it is within the spirit of the rule; therefore, we are of opinion that the mere fact of the ship being used subordinately and partially for trading purposes does not take away the general immunity. For all these reasons we are unable to agree with the learned judge, and have come to the conclusion that the judgment must be reversed.

Appeal allowed.

THE PORTO ALEXANDRE.

Great Britain, Court of Appeal, 1919.

Law Reports [1920] P. 30.

Appeal from a decision of Hill J. setting aside the writ *in rem* and all subsequent proceedings against the steamship Porto Alexandre. . . .

[The Porto Alexandre, formerly a German-owned steamship, was condemned as prize of war by the Portuguese Government and subsequently employed in ordinary trading earning freight for the government commission which operated it. A writ *in rem* was issued on behalf of the owners of the tugs in respect of the services rendered. Service of the writ was accepted by solicitors for the steamship and appearance was entered "under protest."]

SCRUTTON L. J. In this case the Porto Alexandre came into the Mersey, got on to the mud, and was salved by three Liverpool tugs. On [the owners of the tugs] arresting her to obtain security for the payment of their salvage, the Portuguese Republic, through the Portuguese Chargé d'Affaires, put forward a statement that she was a public vessel of the Portuguese Republic, and was therefore exempt from any process in England. Accordingly the defendants moved to set aside the writ and arrest. Hill J. in the Admiralty Court granted the application and the plaintiffs' appeal to this Court.

Now this state and other states proceed in their jurisprudence on the assumption that sovereign states are equal and independent, and that as a matter of international courtesy no one sovereign independent state will exercise any jurisdiction over the person of the sovereign or the property of any other sovereign state; and now that sovereigns move about more freely than they used to, and do things which they used not to do, and now that states do things which they used not to do, the question arises whether there are any limits to the immunity which international courtesy gives as between sovereign independent states and their sovereigns. I think it has been well settled first of all as to the sovereign that there are no limits to the immunity which he enjoys. His private character is equally free as his public character. If he chooses to come into this country under an assumed name and indulge in privileges not peculiar to sovereigns, of making promises of marriage and breaking them, the English Courts still say on his appearing in his true character of sovereign and claiming his immunity, that he is absolutely free from the jurisdiction of this Court. That is the well-known case of Mighell v. Sultan of Johore [[1894] 1 Q. B. 149]. It has been held, as Mr. Dunlop admits, in The Parlement Belge [5 P. D. 197] that trading on the part of a sovereign does not subject him to any liability to the jurisdiction. His ambassador is in the same position; an ambassador coming here as an ambassador of the sovereign may engage in private trading, but it has been held that his immunity still protects him even from proceedings in respect of his private trading. Jervis C. J. in Taylor v. Best [(1854) 14 C. B. 487, 519], said: ". . . if the privilege does attach, it is not, in the case of an ambassador or public minister, forfeited by the party's engaging in trade, as it would, by virtue of the proviso in the 7 Anne, c. 12, s. 5, in the case of an ambassador's servant. If an ambassador or public minister, during his residence in this country, violates the character in which he is accredited to our Court, by engaging in commercial transactions, that may raise a question between the Government of this country and that of the country by which he is sent; but he does not thereby lose the general privilege which the law of nations has conferred upon persons filling that high character,—the proviso in the statute of Anne limiting the privilege in cases of trading applying only to the servants of the embassy." There being no limitation in the case of the sovereign, and no limitation in the case of the ambassador, is there any limitation in the case of the property? Mr. Dunlop has argued before us that in the case of property of the state there is a limitation, and that—as I understand him—if the property is used in trading that cannot be for the public service of the state. That is not the way in which he expressed it, but it appears to me to be the proposition which emerges from his argument.

We are concluded in this Court by the decision in The Parlement Belge [5 P. D. 197, 217]. Sir Robert Phillimore took the view that trading with the property of a state might render that property liable to seizure; but the Court of Appeal in The Parlement Belge overruled the views of Sir Robert Phillimore, as I understand them. The principle then laid down has been recited by the other members of the Court. Brett L. J. said: "As a consequence of the absolute independence of every sovereign authority and of the international comity which induces every sovereign state to respect the independence of every other sovereign state, each and every one declines to exercise by means of any of its Courts, any of its territorial jurisdiction over the person of any sovereign or ambassador of any other state, or over the public property of any state which is destined to its public use." One of the reasons given seems to me conclusive: the moment property is arrested in the Admiralty Court a proceeding is instituted against the person, and the person is compelled to appear if he wants to protect his property, and by seizing his property the personal rights of the sovereign or the personal rights of the state are interfered with. The position seems to me to be very accurately stated in the 7th edition of Hall's International Law at p. 211, where, after dealing with warships and public vessels so called, Mr. Hall goes on to deal with other vessels employed in the public service and property possessed by the state within foreign jurisdiction, and says: "If in a question with respect to property coming before the Courts a foreign state shows the property to be its own, and claims delivery, jurisdiction at once fails, except in so far as it may be needed for the protection of the foreign state."

I quite appreciate the difficulty and doubt which Hill J. felt in this case, because no one can shut his eyes, now that the fashion of nationalisation is in the air, to the fact that many states are trading, or are about to trade, with ships belonging to themselves; and if these national ships wander about without liabilities, many trading affairs will become difficult; but it seems to me the remedy is not in these Courts. The Parlement Belge [5 P. D. 197, 217] excludes remedies in these Courts. But there are practical commercial remedies. If ships of the state find themselves left on the mud because no one will salve them when the State refuses any legal remedy for salvage, their owners will be apt to change their views. If the owners of cargoes on national ships find that the ship runs away and leaves them to bear all the expenses of salvage, as has been done in this case, there may be found a difficulty in getting cargoes for national ships. These are matters to be dealt with by negotiations between Governments, and not by Governments exercising their power to interfere with the property of other states contrary to the principles of international courtesy which govern the relations between independent and sovereign states. While appreciating the difficulties which Hill J. has felt, I think it is clear that we must, in this Court, stand by the decision already given, and the appeal must be dismissed.

[BANKES L. J. and WARRINGTON L. J. delivered concurring opinions.]

BERIZZI BROTHERS COMPANY v. STEAMSHIP PESARO.

United States, Supreme Court, 1926.

271 U. S. 562. [70 L. ed. 1088; 46 S. Ct. 611.]

Appeal from a decree of the District Court in admiralty dismissing a libel *in rem* against a ship owned, possessed, and operated for trade purposes by the Italian Government, for want of jurisdiction. See 277 Fed. 473. . . .

MR. JUSTICE VAN DEVANTER delivered the opinion of the Court.

This was a libel *in rem* against the steamship ''Pesaro'' on a claim for damages arising out of a failure to deliver certain artificial silk accepted by her at a port in Italy for carriage to the port of New York. The usual process issued, on which the vessel was arrested; and subsequently she was released, a bond being given for her return, or the payment of the libellant's claim, if the court had jurisdiction and the claim was established. In the libel the vessel was described as a general ship engaged in the common carriage of merchandise for hire. The Italian Ambassador to the United States appeared and on behalf of the Italian Government specially set forth that the vessel at the time of her arrest was owned and possessed by that government, was operated by it in its service and interest; and therefore was immune from process of the courts of the United States. At the hearing it was stipulated that the vessel when arrested was owned, possessed and controlled by the Italian Government, was not connected with its naval or military forces, was employed in the carriage of merchandise for hire between Italian ports and ports in other countries, including the port of New York, and was so employed in the service and interest of the whole Italian nation as distinguished from any individual member thereof, private or official; and that the Italian Government never had consented that the vessel be seized or proceeded against by judicial process. On the facts so appearing the court sustained the plea of immunity and on that ground entered a decree dismissing the libel for want of jurisdiction. This direct appeal is from that decree and was taken before the Act of February 13, 1925, became effective.

The single question presented for decision by us is whether a ship owned and possessed by a foreign government, and operated by it in the carriage of merchandise for hire, is immune from arrest under process based on a libel in rem by a private suitor in a federal district court exercising admiralty jurisdiction.

This precise question never has been considered by this Court before. Several efforts to present it have been made in recent years, but always in circumstances which did not require its consideration. The nearest approach to it in this Court's decisions is found in The Exchange, 7 Cranch 116. . . .

It will be perceived that the opinion, although dealing comprehensively with the general subject, contains no reference to merchant ships owned and operated by a government. But the omission is not of special significance, for in 1812, when the decision was given, merchant ships were operated only by private owners and there was little thought of governments engaging in such operations. That came much later.

The decision in The Exchange therefore cannot be taken as excluding merchant ships held and used by a government from the principles there announced. On the contrary, if such ships come within those principles, they must be held to have the same immunity as war ships, in the absence of a treaty or statute of the United States evincing a different purpose. No such treaty or statute has been brought to our attention.

We think the principles are applicable alike to all ships held and used by a government for a public purpose, and that when, for the purpose of advancing the trade of its people or providing revenue for its treasury, a government acquires, mans and operates ships in the carrying trade, they are public ships in the same sense that war ships are. We know of no international usage which regards the maintenance and advancement of the economic welfare of a people in time of peace as any less a public purpose than the maintenance and training of a naval force.

The subsequent course of decision in other courts gives strong support to our conclusion.

In Briggs v. Light Boats, 11 Allen 157, there was involved a proceeding against three vessels to subject them to a lien and to satisfy it through their seizure and sale. The boats had been recently acquired by the United States and were destined for use as floating lights to aid navigation. Whether their ownership and intended use rendered them immune from such a proceeding and seizure was the principal question. In answering it in the affirmative the state court, speaking through

Mr. Justice Gray, afterwards a member of this Court, said (p. 163): "These vessels were not held by the United States, as property might perhaps be held by a monarch, in a private or personal, rather than in a public or political character. . . . They were, in the precise and emphatic language of the plea to the jurisdiction, held and owned by the United States for public uses." And again (p. 165): "The immunity from such interference arises, not because they are instruments of war, but because they are instruments of sovereignty; and does not depend on the extent or manner of their actual use at any particular moment, but on the purpose to which they are devoted."

In The Parlement Belge, L. R. 5 P. D. 197, the question was whether a vessel belonging to Belgium and used by that government in carrying the mail and in transporting passengers and freight for hire could be subjected to a libel *in rem* in the admiralty court of Great Britain. The Court of Appeal gave a negative answer and put its ruling on two grounds, one being that the vessel was public property of a foreign government in use for national purposes. After reviewing many cases bearing on the question, including The Exchange, the court said:

"The principle to be deduced from all these cases is that, as a consequence of the absolute independence of every sovereign authority, and of the international comity which induces every sovereign state to respect the independence and dignity of every other sovereign state, each and every one declines to exercise by means of its Courts any of its territorial jurisdiction over the person of any sovereign or ambassador of any other state, or over the public property of any state which is destined to public use, or over the property of any ambassador, though such sovereign, ambassador, or property be within its territory, and, therefore, but for the common agreement, subject to its jurisdiction."

Sometimes it is said of that decision that it was put on the ground that a libel *in rem* under the British admiralty practice is not a proceeding solely against property, but one directly or indirectly impleading the owner—in that instance the Belgian Government. But this latter was given as an additional and independent ground, as is expressly stated in the opinion at page 217.

The ruling in that case has been consistently followed and applied in England from 1880, when it was made, to the present day. Young v. The Scotia, 1903 A. C. 501; The Jassy, L. R. 1906 P. D. 270; The Gagara, L. R. 1919, P. D. 95; The Porto Alexandre, L. R. 1920, P. D. 30; The Jupiter, L. R. 1924, P. D. 236.

In the lower federal courts there has been some diversity of opinion on the question, but the prevailing view has been that merchant ships owned and operated by a foreign government have the same immunity that warships have. Among the cases so holding is The Maipo, 252 Fed. 627, and 259 Fed. 367. The principal case announcing the other view is The Pesaro, 277 Fed. 473. That was a preliminary decision in the present case, but it is not the one now under review, which came later and was the other way.

We conclude that the general words of section 24, clause 3, of the Judicial Code investing the district courts with jurisdiction of "all civil causes of admiralty and maritime jurisdiction" must be construed, in keeping with the last paragraph before quoted from The Exchange, as not intended to include a libel *in rem* against a public ship, such as the "Pesaro," of a friendly foreign government. It results from this that the court below rightly dismissed the libel for want of jurisdiction.

Decree affirmed.

THE ROSERIC.

United States, District Court, District of New Jersey, 1918.

254 Fed. 154.

In Admiralty. Suit by the McAllister Lighterage Line, Incorporated, against the British steamship Roseric. On suggestion that writ of arrest be quashed, or suit stayed. . . .

Rellstab, District Judge. The libel alleges that on April 16, 1918, the steamship Roseric negligently collided with libelant's barge Mc-Allister Bros. No. 63, in New York Harbor, to its damage. After seizure by the marshal, within the territorial jurisdiction of this court, the steamship was released by the order of libelant upon an undertaking by the owners to bond her, in case the court should hold that she was not immune from process, on grounds to be urged on behalf of the British Ambassador. Thereupon counsel for the British Embassy, appearing by leave of court as amici curiæ, filed a suggestion. . . .

From this suggestion and the deposition of the ship's master, which was not offered in evidence, but produced for the information of the court, it appears that, while the steamship is owned by a British subject and its navigation in charge of the owner's officers and crew, who receive their compensation from such owner, it, as well as the officers and crew, is under the complete control of the British government, and is engaged in its business as an admiralty transport, carrying such cargo, and going to and from such ports, as that government directs. For the time being it is appropriated by the British government for its public use, and was when the collision occurred and the arrest was made.

On the face of the libel, the libelant, an American citizen, has an inchoate lien on the ship, and this court prima facie jurisdiction to perfect it. If the arrest is set aside and the writ quashed, the libelant has no present remedy but in the British courts. If the proceedings to arrest the ship are stayed for as long as it remains in the service of the British government, the libelant's rights will be seriously prejudiced, and in the end it may find itself remediless.

On the other hand, if the right to arrest this ship, so requisitioned, is sustained, the sovereign rights of the British government, at a time when it is engaged in a war, will be subordinated to those of a private claimant. Furthermore, the right to seize one ship so requisitioned means the right to seize any number of ships similarly conditioned, with the result that during the continuance of the war, not only that government, but the United States and other sovereignties, cobelligerents in prosecuting such war against the common enemy, will be seriously hampered in their joint struggle to maintain their sovereign rights. It is of no moment that in this case, by arrangement between the proctors of the libelant and the ship's owner, no prejudicial detention of the ship resulted. The right to arrest involves the right to detain; detention includes the probability of loss to the users of the vessel; and exemption from delay of a vessel engaged exclusively in the public service of a nation is as much the privilege of sovereignty as the vessel's exemption from final condemnation. For present purposes the steamship must be regarded as still subject to or threatened with process of arrest. The Florence H. (D. C.) 248 Fed. 1012.

Libelant asserts that, "if this court drops or stays its jurisdiction, that must be done for reasons which our courts have declared to be not well founded," and that to grant such immunity would go "far beyond the principles which have been laid down by our courts as determining whether a ship shall be immune from process."

In The Exchange, 11 U. S. (7 Cranch) 116, 3 L. Ed. 287, a pioneer in this field of judicial inquiry, it was held that—

"A public vessel of war of a foreign sovereign at peace with the United States, coming into our ports, and demeaning herself in a friendly manner, is exempt from the jurisdiction of the country." . . .

The Exchange is a strong case, but it has always been accepted as law both here and abroad. There the allegation was that libelants had been wrongfully dispossessed of their vessel by the representatives of a foreign sovereign. The inconvenience or possible injustice that may happen to the libelant in the instant case, if the Roseric is held immune from arrest, is incomparable with that apparently sustained by the libelant in the cited case.

The immunity there accorded was not due to a lack of judicial power. The power was assumed, but its exercise was waived out of a due regard for the dignity and independence of a sister sovereignty, with whom this nation was at peace. . . .

. . . The privilege was based on the idea that the sovereign's property devoted to state purposes is free and exempt from all judicial process to enforce private claims. Such idea is as cogently applicable to an unarmed vessel employed by the sovereign in the public service as it is to one of his battleships. The exemption declared in that case was considered in The Santissima Trinidad, 20 U. S. (7 Wheat.) 283, 353, 5 L. Ed. 454, and Mr. Justice Story, who sat in The Exchange, in stating the grounds thereof, referred to them as applicable to foreign public ships.

In Briggs et al. v. Lightboats, 93 Mass. (11 Allen) 157, Justice Gray, in answering the contention that these lightboats, though owned by the United States, were not intended for military service, and therefore were subject to judicial process, stated the ground of exemption as follows:

"The immunity from such interference arises, not because they are instruments of war, but because they are instruments of sovereignty, and does not depend on the extent or manner of their actual use at any particular moment, but on the purpose to which they are devoted." Page 165.

In granting immunity to property devoted by a sovereign to public use, neither its ownership nor the particular public use made of it is treated as important in the British courts.[1]

These cases, in my judgment, must be accepted as declaring the judicial policy to exercise no jurisdiction over a sovereign, whether local or foreign, or over instrumentalities employed by it in the public service, by any proceedings in invitum, regardless of the form or character of the process. The libelant, however, insists that The Johnson Lighterage Co. No. 24 (D. C.) 231 Fed. 365, and The Attualita (C. C. A. 4) 238 Fed. 909, 152 C. C. A. 43, announce a different rule and control the instant case. The Johnson Lighterage Co. Case (decided by this court) was a proceeding to recover for salvage services. Both cargo and vessel were seized. On an order to show cause why such cargo (munitions of war) should not be released from seizure and turned over to the Russian government, who was the owner thereof, it was held that, as the possession of the cargo at the time of its seizure was not in that government, but in the charterer of the vessel, under a contract for transportation, it was within the exception declared in The Davis, 77 U. S. (10 Wall.) 15, 19 L. Ed. 875, and subject to arrest. The lack of actual possession of the property by the government at the time of seizure is the basis of the exception established by the Davis Case, and distinguishes both it and the Lighterage Case from the case at bar.

The contention of libelant that, as the ship's officers and crew operated the Roseric, she was within the exception established by these cases, is not tenable. The British government, in the exercise of its sovereign powers, took the Roseric and devoted it to its own purposes. That no change in the officers and crew took place, and that they continued in the employment of the ship's owner, is unimportant. The ship, its owner, officers, and crew, were under the compulsion of sovereignty.

---

[1] The court here quotes from The Parlement Belge, above, p. 333.

While the fact that the operation of the ship was by the owner's officers and crew may be important on the question of the owner's present, and the ship's ultimate, liability for the negligence charged in the libel, it is immaterial upon the question of the right of a private individual to enforce such liability by seizing the ship while it remains appropriated to the sovereign's public use. Whether the government should operate the ship by the owner's officers and crew or others was for the sovereign's exclusive determination.

The effect of its requisition was to put the ship and its equipment into the public service. The officers and crew, as well as the ship, for the time being became the sovereign's instrumentalities, and whatever possession of the ship they obtained by reason of this employment was the sovereign's possession while the requisition was in force.

In legal effect a ship so subjected to *vis major* is no less in the possession of the sovereign than if he had taken it over by a regular charter or had manned it by his navy. . . .

The Attualita (C. C. A. 4) 238 Fed. 909, 152 C. C. A. 43, is more in point. In that case, notwithstanding the ship had been requisitioned by the Italian government and was engaged in its public service, it was held subject to arrest in a proceeding *in rem* to recover damages for an alleged tort. That case was decided before this country became a co-belligerent with the Italian government in the war against Germany. In all other respects the facts of that case are seemingly identical with those of the case at bar. The District Court had held that the ship was immune from arrest, basing its decision on the ground of international comity. The Circuit Court of Appeals, observing that to allow the immunity would require it to go beyond any of the decided cases, said:

"There are many reasons which suggest the inexpediency and the impolicy of creating a class of vessels for which no one is in any way responsible." 238 Fed. 911, 152 C. C. A. 45. . . .

It seems to me, and I state my judgment with deference, that the decision in that case unduly subordinates the rights of sovereignty to those of the individual. The immunity of the sovereign's instrumentalities devoted to public service from the process of its own courts, as I understand the previous cases, is not based upon the idea that it may be "safely accorded," but on account of its dignity and independence, and because it is necessary, for the well-being of the nation that it serves, that it shall not be hampered or interfered with in the use of such instrumentalities.

In the case of the courts of one sovereignty waiving jurisdiction over another sovereignty's instrumentalities, the thought of safety to private litigants, to my mind, is at least equally irrelevant. The immunity in such cases, as already noted, is based upon the idea that sovereigns are of equal dignity and independence, and that out of regard for such rights, and to maintain and further amicable relations among them, it is, by tacit agreement, recognized as needful, in certain particulars, that one sovereign should decline to exercise some of its prerogatives when to exercise them would necessarily place another sovereign in a subordinate position.

In line with this thought, the following language of Judge Thompson in The Luigi (D. C.) 230 Fed. 495, is pertinent:

"It is far more important for the courts of the United States to recognize the international rule of comity that an independent sovereign cannot be personally sued, because such a suit would be inconsistent with the independence and equality among the nations of the state which he represents, than it is to take cognizance of private rights, if by so doing that rule is violated." Page 496.

If these ideas dominate the question whether immunity should be granted to a foreign sovereign's property devoted to the public service, it logically follows that it is not the ownership or exclusive possession of the instrumentality by the sovereign, but its appropriation and devotion to such service, that exempts it from judicial process. That in such use the owner of the instrumentality, through its servants, is permitted to remain in physical possession thereof, and, in consequence, may become personally liable for its agents' torts, is of no moment, where, as in this case, the ship and its entire equipment is under the absolute dominion of the sovereign. . . .

The only remaining question is whether, in following the British Embassy's suggestion, the writ of arrest should be quashed, or merely that the suit be stayed. While full immunity is to be accorded the British government in the use of the Roseric while she is under its requisition, no good reason calls for the dismissal of the suit, a result which would follow the quashing of the writ.

A decree may be entered, staying all proceedings to arrest or detain the Roseric so long as she continues in the service of the British government.[1]

---

[1] Supplementary Cases. In the case of the Attualita, 238 F. 909 (1916), involving a libel *in rem* filed in the port of Norfolk against an Italian steamship for damages occasioned by the alleged negligent sinking of a Greek vessel in the Mediterranean Sea, the attention of the court was called to a statement of the Italian ambassador that the vessel had been requisitioned by and was in the service of the Italian government. The immunity asked for was refused, the court observing that "there are many reasons which suggest the inexpediency and the impolicy of creating a class of vessels for which no one is in any way responsible. For actions of the public armed ships of a sovereign, and of those, whether armed or not, which are in the actual possession, custody, and control of the nation itself, and are operated by it, the nation would be morally responsible, although without her consent not answerable legally in her own or other courts. For the torts and contracts of an ordinary vessel, it and its owners are liable. But the ship in this case, and there are now

apparently thousands like it, is operated by its owners, and for its actions no government is responsible, at law or in morals.

"The persons in charge of the navigation of the ship remain the servants of the owners and are paid by them. The immunity granted to diplomatic representatives of a sovereignty, to its vessels of war, and under some circumstances to other property in its possession and control, can be safely accorded, because the limited numbers and the ordinarily responsible character of the diplomats or agents in charge of the property in question and the dignity and honor of the sovereignty in whose services they are, make abuse of such immunity rare. There will be no such guaranty for the conduct of the thousands of persons privately employed upon ships which at the time happen by contract or requisition to be under charter to sovereign governments."

In the case of the Tervaete, L. R. [1922] Probate 259, involving a suit *in rem* against the Tervaete for damages sustained in a collision which took place while the vessel was the property of the Belgian government and before it was sold to its private owners at the time of the suit, the Court of Appeal held that since at the time of the collision no proceedings could have been taken against the Belgian government *in personam* or against its ship *in rem* they could not now be taken against the private owners. "To hold that a lien would come into existence," said the court, "if the Government sold the ship to a private purchaser, would be to deprive the Belgian government of part of their property, for such a lien about to arise must reduce the price paid to the Government and so affect the property of the Government."

CHAPTER X

SPECIAL PROTECTIVE JURISDICTION ON THE HIGH SEAS [1]

A. The suppression of piracy.

By custom of immemorial origin pirates have been regarded as *hostes humani generis* and all nations have undertaken to exercise summary jurisdiction over persons taking part in acts of piracy. This jurisdiction has necessitated the visit and search on the high seas of vessels suspected of being guilty of actual or intended piracy. Query, what if a vessel were to resist visit and search and were in consequence to be fired upon by a public ship of another state? Would damages be due if the suspicion of piracy proved to be unfounded? [The Marianna Flora.] Would a person who, with others, had seized a vessel belonging to an insurgent government and had thereupon without commission of any kind proceeded to capture a vessel flying the flag of the country against which the insurgents were at war be guilty of piracy under the terms of a law of the United States? [United States v. Smith.] What if the insurgents were to commit acts of depredation outside the scope of normal warfare? [The Magellan Pirates.] Suppose the insurgents were seeking not to form an independent state by secession from the mother country, but merely to substitute their new government in place of the established government, would the absence of recognition of their belligerent rights make their acts piratical? [The Ambrose Light.]

THE MARIANNA FLORA. THE VICE CONSUL OF PORTUGAL, CLAIMANT.

United States, Supreme Court, 1826.

11 Wheaton, 1. [6 L. ed. 405.]

[In 1821 the American armed schooner Alligator, Lieutenant Stockton commanding, while on a cruise in the Atlantic against pirates and slave-traders, met the Portuguese ship Marianna Flora. When within long shot, the latter opened fire upon the Alligator, and continued firing until

---

[1] For a more detailed study of this subject, see Fenwick, *op. cit.*, pp. 230–236; 320–322; Hyde, *op. cit.*, §§ 230–234; Oppenheim, *op. cit.*, I, §§ 272–285; Harvard Draft: Piracy; E. D. Dickinson, "Is the Crime of Piracy Obsolete?", Harvard Law Review, XXXVIII (1925), 334.

within musket range, when a broadside from the Alligator silenced her. Not until that time did the Marianna Flora hoist her national flag, although the Alligator had hoisted her flag immediately upon the firing of the first shot. The Portuguese master explained his conduct by saying that he thought the Alligator was a piratical cruiser. Lieutenant Stockton took possession of the vessel and sent it to Boston where it was libelled for an alleged piratical aggression attempted or committed against the Alligator. The District Court decreed restitution of the vessel and damages for detention. An appeal was taken to the Circuit Court, pending which the ship was voluntarily restored. The Circuit Court reversed the decree as to damages, and from this an appeal was taken to the Supreme Court.]

MR. JUSTICE STORY delivered the opinion of the Court. . . .

But in the present posture of this cause, the libellants are no longer plaintiffs. The claimants interpose for damages in their turn, and have assumed the character of actors. They contend that they are entitled to damages, first, because the conduct of Lieutenant Stockton, in the approach and seizure of the Marianna Flora, was unjustifiable; and, secondly, because, at all events, the subsequent sending her in for adjudication was without any reasonable cause.

In considering these points, it is necessary to ascertain what are the rights and duties of armed, and other ships, navigating the ocean in time of peace. It is admitted, that the right of visitation and search does not, under such circumstances, belong to the public ships of any nation. This right is strictly a belligerent right, allowed by the general consent of nations in time of war, and limited to those occasions. It is true, that it has been held in the Courts of this country, that American ships, offending against our laws, and foreign ships, in like manner, offending within our jurisdiction, may, afterwards, be pursued and seized upon the ocean, and rightfully brought into our ports for adjudication. This, however, has never been supposed to draw after it any right of visitation or search. The party, in such case, seizes at his peril. If he establishes the forfeiture, he is justified. If he fails, he must make full compensation in damages.

Upon the ocean, then, in time of peace, all possess an entire equality. It is the common highway of all, appropriated to the use of all; and no one can vindicate to himself a superior or exclusive prerogative there. Every ship sails there with the unquestionable right of pursuing her own lawful business without interruption; but, whatever may be that business, she is bound to pursue it in such a manner as not to violate the rights of others. The general maxim in such cases is, *sic utere tuo, ut non alienum laedas.*

It has been argued, that no ship has a right to approach another at sea; and that every ship has a right to draw round her a line of jurisdiction, within which no other is at liberty to intrude. In short, that she may appropriate so much of the ocean as she may deem necessary for her protection, and prevent any nearer approach.

This doctrine appears to us novel, and is not supported by any authority. It goes to establish upon the ocean a territorial jurisdiction, like that which is claimed by all nations within cannon-shot of their shores, in virtue of their general sovereignty. But the latter right is founded upon the principle of sovereign and permanent appropriation, and has never been successfully asserted beyond it. Every vessel undoubtedly has a right to the use of so much of the ocean as she occupies, and as is essential to her own movements. Beyond this, no exclusive right has ever yet been recognized, and we see no reason for admitting its existence. Merchant ships are in the constant habit of approaching each other on the ocean, either to relieve their own distress, to procure information, or to ascertain the character of strangers; and, hitherto, there has never been supposed in such conduct any breach of the customary observances, or of the strictest principles of the law of nations. In respect to ships of war sailing, as in the present case, under the authority of their government, to arrest pirates, and other public offenders, there is no reason why they may not approach any vessels descried at sea, for the purpose of ascertaining their real characters. Such a right seems indispensable for the fair and discreet exercise of their authority; and the use of it cannot be justly deemed indicative of any design to insult or injure those they approach, or to impede them in their lawful commerce. On the other hand, it is clear, that no ship is, under such circumstances, bound to lie, or wait the approach of any other ship. She is at full liberty to pursue her voyage in her own way, and to use all necessary precautions to avoid any suspected sinister enterprise or hostile attack. She has a right to consult her own safety; but, at the same time, she must take care not to violate the rights of others. She may use any precautions dictated by the prudence or fears of her officers; either as to delay, or the progress or course of her voyage; but she is not at liberty to inflict injuries upon other innocent parties, simply because of conjectural dangers. These principles seem to us the natural result of the common duties and rights of nations navigating the ocean in time of peace. Such a state of things carries with it very different obligations and responsibilities from those which belong to public war, and is not to be confounded with it.

The first inquiry, then, is whether the conduct of Lieutenant Stockton was, under all the circumstances preceding and attending the combat, justifiable. There is no pretence to say that he committed the first aggression. That, beyond all question, was on the part of the Marianna Flora; and her firing was persisted in after the Alligator had hoisted her national flag, and, of course, held out a signal of her real pacific character. What, then, is the excuse for this hostile attack?

Was it occasioned by any default or misconduct on the part of the Alligator? It is said, that the Alligator had no right to approach the Marianna Flora, and that the mere fact of approach authorized the attack. This is what the court feels itself bound to deny. Lieutenant Stockton, with a view to the objects of his cruise, had just as unquestionable a right to use the ocean, as the Portuguese ship had; and his right of approach was just as perfect as her right of flight. But, in point of fact, Lieutenant Stockton's approach was not from mere motives of public service, but was occasioned by the acts of the Marianna Flora. He was steering on a course which must, in a short time, have carried him far away from her. She lay to, and showed a signal ordinarily indicative of distress. It was so understood, and, from motives of humanity, the course was changed, in order to afford the necessary relief. There is not a pretence in the whole evidence, that the lying to was not voluntary, and was not an invitation of some sort. The whole reasoning on the part of the claimants is, that it was for the purpose of meeting a supposed enemy by daylight, and, in this way, to avoid the difficulties of an engagement in the night. But how was this to be known on board of the Alligator? How was it to be known that she was a Portuguese ship, or that she took the Alligator for a pirate, or that her object in laying to was a defensive operation? When the vessels were within reach of each other, the first salutation from the ship was a shot fired ahead, and, at the same time, no national flag appeared at the mast-head. The ship was armed, appeared full of men, and, from her manœuvres, almost necessarily led to the supposition, that her previous conduct was a decoy, and that she was either a piratical vessel, or, at least, in possession of pirates. Under such circumstances, with hostilities already proclaimed, Lieutenant Stockton was certainly not bound to retreat; and, upon his advance, other guns, loaded with shot, were fired, for the express purpose of destruction. It was, then, a case of open, meditated hostility, and this, too, without any national flag displayed by the Portuguese ship, which might tend to correct the error, for she never hoisted her flag until the surrender. . . .

But, it is argued, that Lieutenant Stockton was bound to have affirmed his national flag by an appropriate gun; that this is a customary observance at sea, and is universally understood as indispensable to prevent mistakes and misadventures; and that the omission was such a default on his part, as places him *in delicto* as to all the subsequent transactions. This imputation certainly comes with no extraordinary grace from the party by whom it is now asserted. If such an observance be usual and necessary, why was it not complied with on the part of the Marianna Flora? Her commander asserts, that by the laws of his own country, as well as those of France and Spain, this is a known and positive obligation on all armed vessels, which they are not at liberty to disregard. Upon what ground, then, can he claim an exemption from performing it? . . . He left, therefore, according to his own view of the law, his own duty unperformed, and fortified, as against himself the very inference, that his ship might properly be deemed under such circumstances, a piratical cruiser.

But, we are not disposed to admit, that there exists any such universal rule or obligation of an affirming gun, as has been suggested at the bar. It may be the law of the maritime states of the European continent already alluded to, founded in their own usages or positive regulations. But, it does not hence follow, that it is binding upon all other nations. . . . Assuming, . . . that the ceremony might be salutary and proper in periods of war, and suitable to its exigencies, it by no means follows that it is justly to be insisted on at the peril of costs and damages in peace. In any view, therefore, we do not think this omission can avail the claimants.

Again; it is argued, that there is a general obligation upon armed ships, in exercising the right of visitation and search, to keep at a distance, out of cannon shot, and to demean themselves in such a manner as not to endanger neutrals. And this objection, it is added, has been specially provided for, and enforced by the stipulations of many of our own treaties with foreign powers. It might be a decisive answer to this argument, that, here, no right of visitation and search was attempted to be exercised. Lieutenant Stockton did not claim to be a belligerent, entitled to search neutrals on the ocean. His commission was for other objects. He did not approach or subdue the Marianna Flora, in order to compel her to submit to his search, but with other motives. He took possession of her, not because she resisted the right of search, but because she attacked him in a hostile manner, without any reasonable cause or provocation.

Doubtless, the obligation of treaties is to be observed with entire good faith, and scrupulous care. But, stipulations in treaties having sole reference to the exercise of the rights of belligerents in time of war, cannot, upon any reasonable principles of construction, be applied to govern cases exclusively of another nature, and belonging to a state of peace. Another consideration, quite sufficient to establish that such stipulations cannot be applied in aid of the present case, is, that whatever may be our duties to other nations, we have no such treaty subsisting with Portugal. It will scarcely be pretended, that we are bound to Portugal by stipulations to which she is no party, and by which she incurs no correspondent obligation.

Upon the whole, we are of opinion, that the conduct of Lieutenant Stockton, in approaching, and ultimately, in subduing the Marianna Flora, was entirely justifiable. . . .

. . . the decree of the Circuit Court ought to be affirmed. . . .

THE UNITED STATES v. SMITH.

United States, Supreme Court, 1820.

5 Wheaton, 153.   [5 L. ed. 57.]

This was an indictment for piracy against the prisoner Thomas Smith, before the Circuit Court of Virginia, on the act of Congress, of the 3d of March, 1819, c. 76. . . .

The jury found a special verdict as follows: "We of the jury find, that the prisoner, Thomas Smith, in the month of March, 1819, and others, were part of the crew of a private armed vessel, called the Creollo (commissioned by the government of Buenos Ayres, a colony then at war with Spain), and lying in the port of Margaritta; that in the month of March, 1819, the said prisoner and others of the crew mutinied, confined their officers, left the vessel, and in the said port of Margaritta seized by violence a vessel' called the Irresistible, a private armed vessel, lying in that port, commissioned by the government of Artegas, who was also at war with Spain; that the said prisoner and others, having so possessed themselves of the said vessel, the Irresistible, appointed their officers, proceeded to sea on a cruise, without any documents or commission whatever; and while on that cruise, in the month of April, 1819, on the high seas, committed the offence charged in the indictment, by the plunder and robbery of the Spanish vessel therein mentioned. If the plunder and robbery aforesaid be piracy under the act of the Congress of the United States, entitled, 'An act to protect the commerce of the United States, and punish the crime of piracy,' then we find the said prisoner guilty; if the plunder and robbery, above stated, be not piracy under the said act of Congress, then we find him, not guilty."

The Circuit Court divided on the question, whether this be piracy as defined by the law of nations, so as to be punishable under the act of Congress, of the 3d of March, 1819, and thereupon the question was certified to this court for its decision.   . . .

Mr. Justice Story delivered the opinion of the court. The act of Congress upon which this indictment is founded provides, "that if any person or persons whatsoever shall, upon the high seas, commit the crime of piracy, as defined by the law of nations, and such offender or offenders shall be brought into, or found in the United States, every such offender or offenders shall, upon conviction thereof, etc., be punished with death."

The first point made at the bar is, whether this enactment be a constitutional exercise of the authority delegated to Congress upon the subject of piracies. The constitution declares, that Congress shall have power "to define and punish piracies and felonies, committed on the high seas, and offences against the law of nations." The argument which has been urged in behalf of the prisoner is, that Congress is bound to define, in terms, the offence of piracy, and is not at liberty to leave it to be ascertained by judicial interpretation. If the argument be well founded, it seems admitted by the counsel that it equally applies to the 8th section of the act of Congress of 1790, ch. 9, which declares, that robbery and murder committed on the high seas shall be deemed piracy; and yet, notwithstanding a series of contested adjudications on this section, no doubt has hitherto been breathed of its conformity to the constitution. . . . .

It is next to be considered, whether the crime of piracy is defined by the law of nations with reasonable certainty. What the law of nations on this subject is, may be ascertained by consulting the works of jurists, writing professedly on public law; or by the general usage and practice of nations; or by judicial decisions recognizing and enforcing that law. There is scarcely a writer on the law of nations who does not allude to piracy as a crime of a settled and determined nature; and whatever may be the diversity of definitions in other respects, all writers concur in holding that robbery, or forcible depredations upon the sea *animo furandi,* is piracy. The same doctrine is held by all the great writers on maritime law in terms that admit of no reasonable doubt. The common law, too, recognizes and punishes piracy as an offence, not against its own municipal code, but as an offence against the law of nations (which is part of the common law), as an offence against the universal law of society, a pirate being deemed an enemy of the human race. Indeed, until the statute of 28th of Henry VIII., ch. 15, piracy was punishable in England only in the admiralty as a civil law offence; and that statute, in changing the jurisdiction, has been universally admitted not to have changed the nature of the offence. Sir Charles Hedges, in his charge at the admiralty sessions, in the case of Rex v. Dawson, (5 State Trials), declared in emphatic terms that "piracy is only a sea term for robbery, piracy being a robbery committed within the jurisdiction of the admiralty." Sir Leoline Jenkins, too, on a like occasion, declared that "a robbery, when committed upon the sea, is what we call piracy;" and he cited the civil law writers, in proof. And it is manifest from the language of Sir William Blackstone [4 Bl. Comm. 73], in his comments on piracy, that he considered the common-law definition as distinguishable in no essential respect from that of the law of nations. So that, whether we advert to writers on the common law, or the maritime law, or the law of nations, we shall find that they universally treat of piracy as an offence against the law of nations, and that its true definition by that law is robbery upon the sea. And the general practice of all nations in punishing all persons, whether natives or foreigners, who have committed this offence against any persons whatsoever, with whom they are in amity, is a conclusive proof that the offence is supposed to depend, not upon the particular provisions of any municipal code, but upon the law of nations, both for its definition and punishment. We have, therefore, no hesitation in declaring that piracy, by the law of nations, is robbery upon the sea, and that it is sufficiently and constitutionally defined by the fifth section of the act of 1819.

Another point has been made in this case, which is, that the special verdict does not contain sufficient facts upon which the Court can pronounce that the prisoner is guilty of piracy. We are of a different opinion. The special verdict finds that the prisoner is guilty of the plunder and robbery charged in the indictment; and finds certain additional facts from which it is most manifest that he and his associates were, at the time of committing the offence, freebooters upon the sea, not under the acknowledged authority, or deriving protection from the flag or commission of any government. If, under such circumstances, the offence be not piracy, it is difficult to conceive any which would more completely fit the definition.

It is to be certified to the Circuit Court that upon the facts stated the case is piracy, as defined by the law of nations, so as to be punishable under the act of Congress of the 3d of March, 1819.

Mr. Justice Livingstone dissented. . . .

THE MAGELLAN PIRATES.

Great Britain, High Court of Admiralty, 1853.

1 Spink's Eccl. and Adm. Rep. 81.

This was a cause arising under 13 & 14 Vict. c. 26., in pursuance of which the Court was prayed to determine and pronounce that certain persons captured by Her Majesty's sloop "Virago," in the Straits of Magellan, were pirates, and to adjudge the number of them, in order to the usual application being made for the bounty. . . .

These cases have generally been decided in a summary manner on the hearing of the petition; but in the present case the petition was opposed by the Queen's Proctor, the Admiralty Proctor and also a proctor for the owner of the "Eliza Cornish," who asserted an interest, inasmuch as, if the men who seized the "Eliza Cornish" were not pirates, but only revolted subjects of the Chilian Government, his party would then have a claim for damages against that Government; which, if the men were pirates, could not, as he was advised, be supported.

Dr. Lushington. The Court has two questions to determine; first, whether the acts set forth in these proceedings were done by persons falling under the denomination of pirates according to the true construction of the two Acts of Parliament passed upon this subject. I say the two Acts, because, though I am fully aware that the first, viz., 6 Geo. 4. c. 49. is repealed, yet I think that in ascertaining the true meaning of the statute now in existence, viz., 13 & 14 Vict. c. 26., I am bound to look at both Acts.

Should this first question be decided in the affirmative, then it will be necessary to determine as to the number of persons which the Court is to pronounce as having been concerned in this piracy. . . .

Now, the words of the first Act of Parliament are these:—"The actual taking, sinking, or destroying of boats, &c., manned by pirates or persons engaged in acts of piracy;" and the second Act has these words: "After the said 1st day of June, attack or be engaged with any persons alleged to be pirates, afloat or ashore." The words omitted, therefore, in this latter Act, are—"persons engaged in acts of piracy," and the words substituted are, "persons alleged to be pirates." . . .

It may be well, I think, to bear in mind what is the object of both statutes, because, respecting that matter there can be no doubt. The title to the first is, "An Act for the encouraging the Capture or Destruction of Piratical Ships and Vessels," and it must have been the wish and intention of the Legislature to put down piratical acts by whomsoever committed. Now, how am I to determine who are pirates, except by the acts that they have committed? I apprehend that, in the administration of our criminal law, generally speaking, all persons are held to be pirates who are found guilty of piratical acts; and piratical acts are robbery and murder upon the high seas. I do not believe that, even where human life was at stake, our Courts of Common Law ever thought it necessary to extend their inquiries further, if it was clearly proved against the accused that they had committed robbery and murder upon the high seas. In that case they were adjudged to be pirates, and suffered accordingly. Whatever may have been the definition in some of the books, and I have been referred by Her Majesty's advocate to an American Case [United States v. Smith, 5 Wheaton 153], where, I believe, all the authorities bearing on this subject are collected, it was never, so far as I am able to find, deemed necessary to inquire whether parties so convicted of these crimes had intended to rob on the high seas, or to murder on the high seas indiscriminately.

Though the municipal law of different countries may and does differ, in many respects, as to its definition of piracy, yet I apprehend that all nations agree in this: that acts, such as those which I have mentioned, when committed on the high seas, are piratical acts, and contrary to the law of nations.

It is true, that where the subjects of one country may rebel against the ruling power, and commit divers acts of violence with regard to that ruling power, that other nations may not think fit to consider them as acts of piracy. But, however this may be, I do not think it necessary to follow up that disquisition on the present occasion. I think it does not follow that, because persons who are rebels or insurgents may commit against the ruling power of their own country acts of violence, they may not be, as well as insurgents and rebels, pirates also; pirates for other acts committed towards other persons. It does not follow that rebels or insurgents may not commit piratical acts against the subjects of other states, especially if such acts were in no degree connected with the insurrection or rebellion.

Even an independent state may, in my opinion, be guilty of piratical acts. What were the Barbary pirates of olden times? What many of the African tribes at this moment? It is, I believe, notorious, that tribes now inhabiting the African coast of the Mediterranean will send out their boats and capture any ships becalmed upon their coasts. Are they not pirates, because, perhaps, their whole livelihood may not depend on piratical acts? I am well aware that it has been said that a state cannot be piratical; but I am not disposed to assent to such *dictum* as a universal proposition.

It appears to me, therefore, that in affixing a construction to this statute, I am entitled to hold that the intention of the Legislature was, that acts of piracy might constitute men pirates, notwithstanding they were committed by the subjects of a barbarous state, or by insurgents. It appears to me this is true as a general, though, perhaps, not as a universal proposition.

Having thus briefly stated my opinion as to the construction of the statute, I will now advert, with equal brevity, to what appears to have been our own law; and for this purpose: because in considering what is the true meaning of an Act of Parliament where any expression is used, I think the probability is, where nothing appears in the context to the contrary, the term in the Act of Parliament is used in conformity with a similar term known in Common Law, and not in a more general or extensive sense.

Now, I refer to Russell on Crimes, where we find the result of many older authorities. He commences in these words: "The offence of piracy, at Common Law, consists in committing those acts of robbery and depredation upon the high seas, which, if committed upon land, would have amounted to felony there" [Russell on Crimes, book ii. ch. 8. s. 1]: and in a subsequent part I find the following: "If a robbery be committed in creeks, harbours, ports, &c., in foreign countries, the Court of Admiralty indisputably has jurisdiction of it, and such offence is consequently piracy." [*Ibid.* s. 2.] There is a case also stated here which I think applies: "Where a prisoner was indicted for stealing three chests of tea out of the 'Aurora,' of London, on the high seas, and it was proved that the larceny was committed while the vessel lay off Wampa, in the river, twenty or thirty miles from the sea, but there was no evidence as to the tide flowing or otherwise, at the place where the vessel lay; it was held, from the circumstance that the tea was stolen on board the vessel which had crossed the ocean, that there was sufficient evidence that the larceny was committed on the high seas." [*Ibid.*]

Again, it was decided in another case, that where A, standing on the shore of a harbour, fired a loaded musket at a revenue cutter which had struck upon a sand-bank in the sea, about 100 yards from the shore, by which firing a person was maliciously killed on board the vessel, it was piracy. [*Ibid.*]

It appears to me, therefore, that, from the quotations which I have just made, I derive two advantages; one, in being enabled with greater certainty to affix a true meaning to the statute itself; the other, a reference to what I must more particularly consider,—the place where the occurrence happened.

• I will not advert to so much of the facts as will be sufficient to enable me to judge whether the present claim is well-founded.

It appears that, towards the latter end of 1851, there was an insurrection in some of the dominions belonging to the States of Chili. General Cruz was at the head of this insurrection, failed, and retired into the country. There was a Chilian convict settlement at a place called Punta Arenas, the garrison of which consisted of 160 soldiers, and 450 male convicts. An officer in that garrison raised an insurrection against the governor, murdered him, and, in conjunction with those who conspired with him, seized a British vessel, called "The Eliza Cornish," and also an American vessel called the "Florida." They murdered the master of the "Eliza Cornish," and a Mr. Deane, a passenger and part owner, and they also murdered the owner of the "Florida," who was on board. These facts coming to the knowledge of Admiral Thoresby, the commander-in-chief of that station, he despatched the "Virago," a British steamer, under the command of Captain Houston Stewart, to the Straits of Magellan. On the 28th January, 1852, a vessel, which proved to be the "Eliza Cornish," was descried working out of the Straits; chase was made; a shot fired across her bows brought her to; she was boarded and seized by orders of Captain Stewart.

At the time she was so seized she was in possession of a large number of the persons who had raised the insurrection at Punta Arenas. There were found on board her 128 men, 24 women, and 18 children; the guns were loaded and the men were armed. These were under the command of a man named Bruno Brionis, who held a commission from Cambiaso, the leader of the insurrection, and the instigator of the murders and robberies then committed; and these men were afterwards delivered up to the Chilian authorities at Valparaiso. Captain Stewart proceeded in search of Cambiaso and the other insurgents, giving that name to those who had left Punta Arenas. He secured fifty-six at a place called Wood's Bay, and on the 15th February he discovered the "Florida" herself, in the possession of a large number of the same people. It was said that these insurgents had, whilst at sea, risen against Cambiaso and five others, and, with the aid of the American master and crew, brought the vessel to the port where Captain Stewart had found her.

On board the "Florida" was found treasure which had been plundered from the "Eliza Cornish." All the persons on board the "Florida," not American, were delivered up to the Chilian authorities.

As to the general character of these transactions, I really cannot bring myself to entertain a doubt. Even if I could be induced to adopt the distinction, that the acts in question were the acts of insurgents, I should still, even from that, adhere to the opinion that they were piratical acts;—piratical acts, too, in my judgment, in no degree whatsoever connected with the insurrection or rebellion, or with the intention of these parties to go to any other part of the world. They were acts, in one sense, of wanton cruelty, in the murder of foreign subjects, and in the indiscriminate plunder of their property. I am of opinion that the persons who did these acts were guilty of piracy, and were to be deemed pirates, unless some of the other objections which have been urged ought to prevail.

It has been said that these acts were not committed on the high seas, and, therefore, the murder and robbery not properly or legally piratical. This objection well deserves consideration; for it is true that murder and robbery, done upon land, and not by persons notoriously pirates, would not be piracy. Here, as I understand the facts, the "Eliza Cornish" and the "Florida" were seized in port, and the murders committed in port or committed on land, on the persons taken out of the vessels. Had the vessels been recaptured whilst lying in port, there might be raised an argument, though I do not say it would prevail, that these offences, legally speaking, would not be classed as acts of piracy. I say it might be so; though I am not disposed to hold that the doctrine that the port, forming a part of the dominions of the State to which it belongs, ought in all cases to divest robbery and murder done in such port of the character of piracy. I am much more strongly inclined to hold this from the facts quoted from Russell; and I am still more inclined to come to that conclusion for another reason, because the statute expressly contemplates acts done on shore, for these are the words: "Shall, after the said first day of June, attack or be engaged with any persons alleged to be pirates, afloat or ashore," manifestly intending to take cognisance of piratical offences, or offences of that class, when they were committed on shore. It would quite fail if it were not so; because we all know that pirates are not perpetually at sea, but under the necessity of going on shore at various places; and, of course, they must be followed and taken there, or not at all.

In this case, however, the ships were carried away and navigated by the very same persons who originally seized them. Now, I consider the possession at sea to have been a piratical possession; to have been a continuation of the murder and robbery; and the carrying away the ships on the high seas, to have been piratical acts, quite independently of the original seizure. . . .

I cannot conclude my judgment without expressing my opinion that it was for services like these that the Legislature intended to provide a reward; services of great importance to the safe navigation of the seas in that part of the world, and affected by the capture of a band of persons whose acts of murder and plunder, both on land and at sea, rendered their capture and punishment indispensable to the safety of ships of all nations occupied in those waters.

I trust I have not put too latitudinarian a construction on this Act of Parliament, from my high consideration of the services so rendered, and of the decision and promptitude whereby those measures were so successfully taken; and I repeat my opinion, that the persons so taken are justly to be deemed pirates, and were, when captured, within the meaning of the Act. . . .[1]

THE AMBROSE LIGHT.

United States, District Court, Southern District of New York, 1885.

25 Fed. 408.

The libel in this case was filed to procure the condemnation of the brigantine Ambrose Light, which was brought into this port as prize on June 3, 1885, by Lieut. Wright and a prize crew, detached from the United States gunboat Alliance, under Commander Clarke, by whose orders the brigantine had been seized on the twenty-fourth of April. The seizure was made in the Caribbean sea, about 20 miles to the westward of Cartagena. The commander was looking for the insurgent Preston, by whose orders Colon had shortly before been fired, to the great loss and injury of our citizens. Observing the brigantine displaying a strange flag, viz., a red cross on a white ground, he bore down upon her, and brought her to by a couple of shot across her bows. Before coming to she exhibited the Colombian flag. On examination some 60 armed soldiers were found concealed below her decks, and one cannon was aboard, with a considerable quantity of shot, shell, and ammunition. Preston was not found. Her papers purported to commission her as a Colombian man-of-war. . . .

Believing this commission to be irregular, and to show no lawful authority to cruise as a man-of-war on the high seas, Commander Clarke

---

[1] Compare United States v. Cargo of the Brig Malek Adhel, 2 Howard, 210 (1844), involving an interpretation of "piratical" which included not only acts done for purposes of plunder but acts of aggression done "for purposes of hatred, revenge, or wanton abuse of power."

reported her under seizure, in accordance with the naval regulations, to Admiral Jouett, commanding the North Atlantic squadron then cruising in the Central American waters, and the admiral directed the vessel to be taken to New York for adjudication as prize. The vessel was at first supposed to belong to citizens of the United States. The proofs showed that she had been sold to, and legally belonged to, Colente, one of the chief military leaders of the insurgents at Barranquilla. None of her officers or crew were citizens of the United States. She was engaged upon a hostile expedition against Cartagena, and designed to assist in the blockade and siege of that port by the rebels against the established government of the United States of Colombia. She had left Sabanilla on April 20th, bound for Baru, near Cartagena, where she expected the soldiers aboard to disembark. She was under the orders of the colonel of the troops, whose instructions were to shoot the captain if disobedient to his orders. Further instructions were to fight any Colombian vessel not showing the white flag with a red cross. Sabanilla, and a few other adjacent sea-ports, and the province of Barranquilla, including the city of Barranquilla, had been for some months previous, and still were, under the control of the insurgents. The proofs did not show that any other depredations or hostilities were intended by the vessel than such as might be incident to the struggle between the insurgents and the government of Colombia, and to the so-called blockade and siege of Cartagena.

As respects any recognition of the insurgents by foreign powers, it did not appear in evidence that up to the time of the seizure of the vessel on April 24, 1885, a state of war had been recognized as existing, or that the insurgents had ever been recognized as a *de facto* government, or as having belligerent rights, either by the Colombian government, or by our own government, or by any other nation. The claimants introduced in evidence a diplomatic note from our secretary of state to the Colombian minister, dated April 24, 1885, which, it was contended, amounted to a recognition by implication of a state of war. The government claimed the forfeiture of the ship as piratical, under the law of nations, because she was not sailing under the authority of any acknowledged power. The claimants contended that, being actually belligerent, she was in no event piratical by the law of nations; but if so, that the subsequent recognition of belligerency by our government by implication entitles her to a release. . . .

BROWN, J. The legality of the original seizure of the Ambrose Light depends upon the answer to be given to the inquiry whether the cruise of the vessel under the commission of the insurgent leaders, to assist in the so-called blockade of Cartagena, must be regarded, under the circumstances of this case, as lawful warfare or as piratical. She was owned by one of the insurgents that signed her commission. None of her officers or crew were residents of this country. The question must therefore be adjudged according to the law of nations.

Neither the causes, nor the objects, nor the merits of the revolt are understood by the court; nor is its extent or probability of success known. It is said to be, not for independence, nor for any division of the republic, but rather a personal or party struggle for the possession of the reins of government, such as, unhappily, has too often arisen in the southern republics. The few ports and provinces that have passed under the control of the insurgents have been acquired, it is said, partly by force of arms and partly by the former loyal officials recognizing the insurgent leaders as their superior officers. But these circumstances, as well as the general merits or demerits of the struggle, are, in the view of the court, wholly immaterial here; because, as will be seen, it is not within the province of this court to inquire into them, or to take any cognizance of them, except in so far as they have been previously recognized by the political or executive department of the government.

The consideration that I have been able to give to the subject leads me to the conclusion that the liability of the vessel to seizure, as piratical, turns wholly upon the question whether the insurgents had or had not obtained any previous recognition of belligerent rights, either from their own government or from the political or executive department of any other nation; and that, in the absence of recognition by any government whatever, the tribunals of other nations must hold such expeditions as this to be technically piratical. This result follows logically and necessarily, both from the definition of piracy in the view of international law, and from a few well-settled principles. Wheaton defines piracy as "the offense of depredating on the high seas without being authorized by any sovereign state, or with commissions from different sovereigns at war with each other." Dana's Wheat. Int. Law, § 122. Rebels who have never obtained recognition from any other power are clearly not a sovereign state in the eye of international law, and their vessels sent out to commit violence on the high seas are therefore piratical within this definition. The general principles of international right and of self-protection lead to the same conclusion. (1) All nations are entitled to the peaceful pursuit of commerce through the ports of all other civilized nations, unobstructed, save by the incidents of lawful war, or by the just restrictions of the sovereign. (2) Maritime warfare, with its burdens and inconveniences to nations not engaged in it, is the lawful prerogative of sovereigns only. Private warfare is unlawful. International law has no place for rebellion; and insurgents have strictly no legal rights, as against other nations, until recognition of belligerent rights is accorded them. (3) Recognition of belligerency, or the accordance of belligerent rights to communities in revolt, belongs solely to the political and executive departments of each government. (4) Courts cannot inquire into the internal condition of foreign communities in order to determine whether a state of civil war, as distinguished from sedition or armed revolt, exists there or not. They must follow the political and executive departments, and recognize only what those departments recognize; and, in the absence of any recognition by them, must regard the former legal conditions as unchanged.

From these principles it necessarily follows that in the absence of recognition by any government of their belligerent rights, insurgents that send out vessels of war are, in legal contemplation, merely combinations of private persons engaged in unlawful depredations on the high seas; that they are civilly and criminally responsible in the tribunals for all their acts of violence; that in blockading ports which all nations are entitled to enter, they attack the rights of all mankind, and menace with destruction the lives and property of all who resist their unlawful acts; that such acts are therefore piratical, and entitle the ships and tribunals of every nation whose interests are attacked or menaced, to suppress, at their discretion, such unauthorized warfare by the seizure and confiscation of the vessels engaged in it. The right of seizure by other nations arises in such cases, *ex necessitate*, from the very nature of the case. There is no other remedy except open war; and nations are not required to declare *war* against individual rebels whom they are unwilling and are not required to recognize as a belligerent power. Nor are other nations required, for their own security, in such a case, to make any alliance with the parent state. By the right of self-defense, they may simply seize such law-breakers as come in their way and menace them with injury. Without this right, insurgents, though recognition were rightfully refused them, and however insignificant their cause, or unworthy their conduct, might violate the rights of all other nations, harass their commerce, and capture or sink their ships with impunity. The whole significance and importance of the doctrine of recognition of belligerency would be gone, since the absence of recognition could be safely disregarded; the distinction between lawful and unlawful war would be practically abolished; and the most unworthy revolt would have the same immunities for acts of violence on the high seas, without any recognition of belligerent rights, as the most justifiable revolt would have with it. The right to treat unlawful and unauthorized warfare as piratical, seems to me, therefore, clearly imbedded in the very roots of international law.

These considerations seem to me sufficient for the determination of this branch of the case. But as the *right* of the government to treat such acts as piratical is vehemently challenged, and as doubt on this point has been expressed by some recent authors, I proceed to consider the subject more in detail.

It should be first observed that the case is not one where recognition of belligerency has been accorded by the parent government, or by any other nation. . . . The question here arises upon the entire absence of recognition anywhere. In this respect the case is unique in modern times. No rebels, so far as I am aware, have ever attempted to blockade ports, and make an attack on the commerce of other nations, without any previous recognition of their belligerent rights. . . .

Again, this is a suit *in rem* for the condemnation of the vessel only; not a trial upon a criminal indictment of her officers or crew. The two proceedings are wholly independent, and pursued in different courts. Condemnation of the vessel as piratical does not necessarily imply a criminal liability of her officers or crew. The vessel might be condemned for being engaged upon a piratical expedition only, or for attempts at piratical aggression or restraint. In such a case no indictment for piracy would lie, because criminal punishment is inflicted only according to the municipal law of the captors; and our statutes do not make criminally punishable piratical undertakings or aggressions merely. The Marianna Flora, 11 Wheat. 40; The Palmyra, 12 Wheat. 1, 15. Even as regards acts that constitute undoubted piracy, there may be valid personal defenses of the officers and crew, as suggested, though not decided, by Marshall, C. J., in U. S. v. Klintock, 5 Wheat. 144, 149. If an owner should forge a commission from a lawful belligerent, and send his vessel out as a privateer under officers and crew who acted in good faith, supposing her commission to be genuine, the vessel should be condemned, though the officers and crew might be acquitted. So if mere usurpers, knowing that they have no recognized authority, should commission their own ships as vessels of war to blockade loyal ports and to threaten the lawful commerce of all nations, and foreign merchant-men were captured or sunk by them during such a blockade, it is pos-sible that the officers and crew might have accepted the commission upon such a reasonable supposition of its coming from an authorized belliger-ent as to furnish a just defense upon a criminal indictment, though none the less should the vessel and those who commissioned her be held en-gaged in an illegal and piratical expedition. See U. S. v. Gibert, 2 Sum. 19. Here the court has to do only with the character and design of the expedition upon which the Ambrose Light was sent out by the insurgents who owned and commissioned her. And, so far as respects the lawfulness of her seizure, the question is the same as if she had actually captured one of our merchantmen, or sunk her and killed the officers and crew while they were lawfully entering the port at Car-tagena.

1. Piracy has two aspects: (a) As a violation of the common right of nations, punishable under the common law of nations by the seizure and condemnation of the vessel only, in prize courts; (b) its liability to punishment criminally by the municipal law of the place where the of-fenders are tried. Accordingly, the definitions of piracy, aside from "statutory piracy," fall naturally into two classes, according as the

offense is viewed more especially as it affects the rights of nations, or as amenable to criminal punishment under the municipal law. . . .

2. The recognition by foreign states of a state of war in civil strife, or, what is the same thing, a recognition of the belligerent rights of the insurgents, authorizes courts of law to treat the insurgents as lawful combatants. In the language of Burke, "it is an intermediate treaty that puts rebels in possession of the law of nations." It gives them temporarily, and for war purposes, the *status* of an established nation, and all the rights of public war. On the one hand, it is a concession to rebels in the interest of humanity and expediency. On the other hand, since recognition of belligerency is not usually accorded till rebellion rises to the dignity of real war, and in its general aspects is fairly entitled to belligerent rights, notwithstanding the burdens it inflicts on other nations, it may be viewed as an adjustment by foreign nations of their own relations, so as to accord with the just requirements of the actual facts. If recognition be granted, it relieves the parent state from all responsibility for damages for any irregularities or violence committed by the other belligerent. Had the Ambrose Light sunk one of our merchantmen off Cartagena, we should have had claims for damages against Colombia, in the absence of any recognition of the usurpers; but if they had been recognized by us, Colombia would have been released, and the blockade would have been lawful. . . .

It follows that in the absence of any recognition by our government of an existing civil war in Colombia, the commission executed by the insurgents to their own vessel to carry on maritime war, and to blockade Cartagena, has no validity that this court can recognize. Her depredations, or intended depredations, in preventing other nations from pursuing lawful commerce with Cartagena, must be viewed by the court as the acts of mere private, unauthorized persons. The commission is void, and as no commission. The vessel derives no protection from it, and must be held piratical, as she would be held if cruising for similar purposes without any commission at all. In addition to this, there was also the fraudulent exhibition of the Colombian flag when approached by the Alliance; a flag to which the Ambrose Light clearly had no color of right, since the rebels had no color of claim to constitute the established government of the republic of Colombia, but were mere usurpers.

5. But it is urged that her cruise, to be held piratical, must have been such in intent, and that an intent that, like this, is simply belligerent, is not piratical; and that on two grounds: First, because a belligerent vessel is directed against the ships or property of one nation only; and, second, because her acts are not done *animo furandi*, for the sake of plunder, but as acts of war only, *animo belligerandi*. . . .

To constitute a criminal offense, it is only necessary to show, therefore, that the accused committed intentionally, with design to injure another, and without legal excuse, an act which the law makes criminal.

3 Greenl. Ev. §§ 1, 13, 20. The law of nations necessarily makes unlawful the capture or destruction of ships by a vessel sailing without any commission, or without a lawful commission from some recognized power, as well as a capture under a usurped flag. Such captures, considered by themselves, are acts of spoliation and robbery; and when committed knowingly, with intent to injure, and without lawful authority, they are felonious, and therefore piratical, even in its criminal aspect. That such spoliation and capture are done under the name of war, cannot furnish a legal defense, if the court cannot recognize the warfare as *lawful*. . . .

This great weight of authority,[1] drawn from every source that authoritatively makes up the law of nations, seems to me fully to warrant the conclusion that the public vessels of war of all nations, for the preservation of the peace and order of the seas, and the security of their own commerce, have the right to seize as piratical all vessels carrying on, or threatening to carry on, unlawful private warfare to their injury; and that privateers, or vessels of war, sent out to blockade ports, under the commissions of insurgents, unrecognized by the government of any sovereign power, are of that character, and derive no protection from such void commissions. . . .

Whether a foreign nation shall *exercise* its rights only when its own interests are immediately threatened, or under special provocations only, after injuries inflicted by the insurgents, as in this case, at Colon, is a question purely for the executive department. But when a seizure has been made by the navy department, under the regulations, and the case is prosecuted before the court by the government itself, claiming *summum jus*,—its extreme rights,—the court is bound to apply to the case the strict technical rules of international law. The right here asserted may be rarely enforced; the very knowledge that the right exists tends effectually, in most cases, to prevent any violation of it, or at least any actual interference by insurgents with the rights of other nations. But if the right itself were denied, the commerce of all commercial nations would be at the mercy of every petty contest carried on by irresponsible insurgents and marauders under the name of war.

In the absence of any recognition of these insurgents as belligerents, I therefore hold the Ambrose Light to have been lawfully seized, as bound upon an expedition technically piratical.

Second. The additional facts proved show, however, such a subsequent implied recognition by our government of the insurgent forces as a government de facto, in a state of war with Colombia, and entitled to belligerent rights, as should prevent the condemnation of the vessel as prize. . . .

---

[1] The full report contains an exhaustive examination of the authorities and precedents.

Upon these considerations and on these authorities I cannot doubt that in thus notifying the Colombian government, in effect, that the United States would recognize no right in Colombia to close the insurgent ports by virtue of her own sovereignty, but only through the exercise of the belligerent right of blockade, *i. e.*, by war, our government recognized, by necessary implication, the existing insurrection as a state of war, and the insurgent forces as a *de facto* power, having the counter-rights of a belligerent. From this indirect and implied recognition of the belligerency of the insurgents, the conclusion of law follows that their vessels of war cannot be regarded as piratical. . . .

B. The suppression of the slave trade.

Beginning with the opening decades of the nineteenth century a number of states undertook to extend the penalties attached to piracy to vessels engaged in the slave trade. Query, might a public vessel of one state, whose municipal laws prohibited the slave trade, visit and search on the high seas the private vessels of another state on the suspicion of their being engaged in the slave trade and bring them into port for condemnation if the search should show evidence of guilt? [Le Louis.]

LE LOUIS.[1]

Great Britain, High Court of Admiralty, 1817.

2 Dodson, 210.

This was the case of a French vessel which sailed from Martinique on the 30th of January, 1816, destined on a voyage to the coast of Africa and back, and was captured ten or twelve leagues to the southward of Cape Mesurada, by the Queen Charlotte cutter, on the 11th of March in the same year, and carried to Sierra Leone. She was proceeded against in the vice admiralty court of that colony, and the information pleaded,— 1st, that the seizors were duly and legally commissioned to make captures and seizures. 2d, That the seizure was within the jurisdiction of the court. 3d, That the vessel belonged to French subjects or others, and was fitted out, manned and navigated for the purpose of carrying on the African slave-trade, after that trade had been abolished by the internal laws of France, and by the treaty between Great Britain and France. 4th, That the vessel had bargained for twelve slaves at Mesurada, and was prevented by the capture alone from taking them on board.

---

[1] A part of the opinion, dealing with the right of search and laying down the principles of the equality and independence of states and of their equal rights to the use of the high seas, is reproduced above, p. 67.

5th, That the brig being engaged in the slave-trade, contrary to the laws of France, and the law of nations, was liable to condemnation, and could derive no protection from the French or any other flag: 6th, That the crew of the brig resisted the Queen Charlotte, and piratically killed eight of her crew, and wounded twelve others. 7th, That the vessel being engaged in this illegal traffic resisted the king's duly commissioned cruisers, and did not allow of search until overpowered by numbers. And 8t:., That by reason of the circumstances stated, the vessel was out of the protection of any law, and liable to condemnation. The ship was condemned to His Majesty in the Vice-admiralty Court at Sierra Leone, and from this decision an appeal was made to this court. . . .

Sir W. Scott. This ship was taken off Cape Mesurada, on the coast of Africa, on the 11th of March, 1816, by an English colonial armed vessel, after a severe engagement, which followed an attempt to escape. . . .
. . . This right [of search in time of war], incommodious as its exercise may occasionally be to those who are subjected to it, has been fully established in the legal practice of nations, having for its foundation the necessities of self-defense, in preventing the enemy from being supplied with the instruments of war, and from having his means of annoyance augmented by the advantages of maritime commerce. Against the property of his enemy each belligerent has the extreme rights of war. Against that of neutrals, the friends of both, each has the right of visitation and search, and of pursuing an inquiry whether they are employed in the service of his enemy, the right being subject, in almost all cases of an inquiry wrongfully pursued, to a compensation in costs and damages. . . .
. . . If it be asked why the right of search does not exist in time of peace as well as in war, the answer is prompt; that it has not the same foundation on which alone it is tolerated in war,—the necessities of self-defence. They introduced it in war; and practice has established it. No such necessities have introduced it in time of peace, and no such practice has established it. It is true, that wild claims (alluded to in the argument) have been occasionally set up by nations, particularly those of Spain and Portugal, in the East and West Indian seas; but these are claims of a nature quite foreign to the present question, being claims not of a general right of visitation and search upon the high seas unappropriated, but extravagant claims to the appropriation of particular. seas, founded upon some grants of a pretended authority, or upon some ancient exclusive usurpation. Upon a principle much more just in itself and more temperately applied, maritime states have claimed a right of visitation and inquiry within those parts of the ocean adjoining to their shores, which the common courtesy of nations has, for their common convenience, allowed to be considered as parts of their dominions for various domestic purposes, and particularly for fiscal or defensive regu-

lations more immediately affecting their safety and welfare. Such are our hovering laws, which within certain limited distances more or less moderately assigned, subject foreign vessels to such examination. This has nothing in common with a right of visitation and search upon the unappropriated parts of the ocean. A recent Swedish claim of examination on the high seas, though confined to foreign ships bound to Swedish ports, and accompanied in a manner not very consistent or intelligible, with a disclaimer of all right of visitation, was resisted by our government as unlawful, and was finally withdrawn.

The right of visitation being in this present case exercised in time of peace, the question arises, how is it to be legalized? And looking to what I have described as the known existing law of nations evidenced by all authority and all practice, it must be upon the ground that the captured vessel is to be taken *legally* as a pirate, or else some new ground is to be assumed on which this right which has been distinctly admitted not to exist generally in time of peace can be supported. Wherever it has existed, it has existed upon the ground of repelling injury, and as a measure of self-defence. No practice that exists in the world carries it farther.

It is perfectly clear, that this vessel cannot be deemed a pirate from any want of a national character legally obtained. . . . If, therefore, the character of a pirate can be impressed upon her, it must be only on the ground of her occupation as a slave trader; no other act of piracy being imputed. The question then comes to this:—Can the occupation of this French vessel be legally deemed a piracy, inferring, as it must do, if it be so, all the pains and penalties of piracy? . . .

. . . It has not been contended in argument, that the common case of dealing in slaves could be deemed a piracy in law. In all the fervor of opinion which the agitation of all questions relating to this practice has excited in the minds of many intelligent persons in this country, no attempt has ever been thought of, at least with any visible effect, to submit any such question to the judgment of the law by such a prosecution of any form instituted in any Court: and no lawyer, I presume, could be found hardy enough to maintain, that an indictment for piracy could be supported by the mere evidence of a trading in slaves. Be the malignity of the practice what it may, it is not that of *piracy*, in legal consideration.

Piracy being excluded, the court has to look for some new and peculiar ground: but in the first place a new and very extensive ground is offered to it by the suggestion, which has been strongly pressed, that this trade, if not the crime of piracy, is nevertheless *crime*, and that every nation, and indeed every individual has not only a right, but a duty, to prevent in every place the commission of crime. It is a sphere of duty sufficiently large that is thus opened out to communities and to their members. But to establish the consequence required, it is first necessary to establish that the right to interpose by force to prevent the commission of crime, commences not upon the commencement of the overt act, nor upon the evident approach towards it, but on the bare surmise grounded on the mere possibility; for unless it goes that length it will not support the right of forcible inquiry and search. What are the proximate circumstances which confer on you the right of intruding yourself into a foreign ship, over which you have no authority whatever, or of demanding the submission of its crew to your inquiry, whether they mean to deal in the traffic of slaves, not in your country, but in one with which you have no connection? Where is the law that has defined those circumstances and created that right under their existence? Secondly, it must be shown that the act imputed to the parties is unquestionably and legally criminal by the universal law of nations; for the right of search claimed makes no distinctions, and in truth can make none; for till the ship is searched it cannot be known whether she is a slave trader or not, and whether she belongs to a nation which admits the act to be criminal, or to one which maintains it to be simply commercial,—and I say legally criminal, because neither this court nor any other can carry its private apprehensions, independent of law, into its public judgments on the quality of actions. It must conform to the judgment of the law upon that subject; and acting as a court in the administration of law, it cannot attribute criminality to an act where the law imputes none. It must look to the legal standard of morality; and upon a question of this nature, that standard must be found in the law of nations as fixed and evidenced by general and ancient and admitted practice, by treaties and by the general tenor of the laws and ordinances, and the formal transactions of civilized states; and looking to those authorities, I find a difficulty in maintaining that the traffic is legally criminal. . . .

. . . . What is the doctrine of our Courts of the Law of Nations relatively to them? Why, that their practice is to be respected; that their slaves if taken are to be restored to them; and if not taken under innocent mistake, to be restored with costs and damages.—All this surely, upon the ground that such conduct on the part of any state is no departure from the Law of Nations; because, if it were, no such respect could be allowed to it, upon an exemption of its own making; for no nation can privilege itself to commit a crime against the Law of Nations by a mere municipal regulation of its own. And if our understanding and administration of the Law of Nations be, that every nation, independently of treaties, retains a legal right to carry on this traffic, and that the trade carried on under that authority is to be respected by all tribunals, foreign as well as domestic, it is not easy to find any consistent grounds on which to maintain that the traffic, according to our views of that law, is criminal. . . .

It is next said that every country has a right to enforce its own navigation laws; and so it certainly has, so far as it does not interfere with the rights of others. It has a right to see that its own vessels are duly navigated, but it has no right in consequence to visit and search all the apparent vessels of other countries on the high seas, in order to institute an inquiry whether they are not in truth British vessels violating British laws. No such right has ever been claimed, nor can it be exercised without the oppression of interrupting and harassing the real and lawful navigation of other countries; for the right of search when it exists at all, is universal, and will extend to vessels of all countries, whether they tolerate the slave trade or not; and whether the vessels are employed in slave trading or in any other traffic. It is no objection to say that British ships may thus by disguise elude the obligations of British law. The answer of the foreigner is ready, that you have no right to provide against that inconvenience by imposing a burden upon his navigation. If even the question were reduced to this, that either all British ships might fraudulently escape, or all foreign ships be injuriously harassed, Great Britain could not claim the option to embrace the latter branch of the alternative. When you complain that the regulation cannot be enforced without the exercise of such a right, the answer again is, that you ought not to make regulations which you cannot enforce without trespassing on the rights of others. If it were a matter by which your own safety was affected, the necessities of self-defence would fully justify; but in a matter in which your own safety is in no degree concerned, you have no right to prevent a suspected injustice towards another, by committing an actual injustice of your own.

The next argument is, that the legislature must have contemplated the exercise of this right in time of peace; otherwise they have left the remedy incomplete, and peace in Europe will be war in Africa. The legislature must be understood to have contemplated all that was within its power, and no more. It provided for the existing occasion and left to future wisdom to provide for future times. Nothing can be more clear than that it was so understood by the British Government; for the project of the treaty proposed by Great Britain to France, in 1815, is, "that permission should be reciprocally given by each nation to search and bring in the ships of each other;" and when the permission of neutrals to have their ships searched is asked at the commencement of a war, it may then be time enough to admit that the right stands on exactly the same footing in time of war and in time of peace. The fact turned out to be, that such permission was actually refused by France, upon the express ground that she would not tolerate any maritime police to be exercised on her subjects, but by herself. Nor can it be matter of just surprise or resentment, that that people should be willing to retain, what every independent nation must be adverse to part with, the exclusive right of executing their own laws.

It is pressed as a difficulty, what is to be done, if a French ship laden with slaves for a French port is brought in? I answer, without hesitation, restore the possession which has been unlawfully divested:— rescind the illegal act done by your own subject; and leave the foreigner to the justice of his own country. . . .

It is said, and with just concern, that if not permitted in time of peace it will be extremely difficult to suppress the traffic. It will be so, and no man can deny, that the suppression, however desirable, and however sought, is attended with enormous difficulties; difficulties which have baffled the most zealous endeavors of many years. To every man it must have been evident that without a general and sincere concurrence of all maritime states in the principle and in the proper modes of pursuing it, comparatively but little of positive good could be acquired; so far at least, as the interests of the victims of this commerce were concerned in it; and to every man who looks to the rival claims of these states, to their established habit of trades, to their real or pretended wants, to their different modes of thinking, and to their real mode of acting upon this particular subject, it must be equally evident that such a concurrence was matter of very difficult attainment. But the difficulty of the attainment will not legalize measures that are otherwise illegal. To press forward to a great principle by breaking through every other great principle that stands in the way of its establishment; to force the way to the liberation of Africa by trampling on the independence of other states in Europe; in short, to procure an eminent good by means that are unlawful, is as little consonant to private morality as to public justice. Obtain the concurrence of other nations, if you can, by application, by remonstrance, by example, by every peaceable instrument which man can employ to attract the consent of man.

. . . the seizor has entirely failed in the task he has undertaken of proving the existence of a prohibitory law, enacted by the legal government [of France], which can be applied to the present transaction, and therefore upon that ground, as well as upon the other, I think myself called upon to reverse this judgment. . . .[1]

C. Protection of pelagic sealing.

The need of regulating fisheries on the high seas has not been felt except in certain localities and under certain special conditions. Hence there are no customary rules of international law on the subject, but only treaty provisions adopted to meet particular circumstances. Query, in the absence of such treaty provisions could a country, such as the

---

[1] Compare the decision of the Supreme Court of the United States in The Antelope (above, p. 7) and the conflicting decision of the Circuit Court, by Justice Story, in La Jeune Eugenie (above, p. 1).

United States in 1886, undertake to protect from extermination fisheries as valuable as were the seal fisheries of Bering Sea, when to do so necessitated the seizure on the high seas of the vessels of other states? [United States and Great Britain: Seal Fisheries Case; United States and Great Britain: The Wanderer.]

UNITED STATES AND GREAT BRITAIN: SEAL FISHERIES CASE.

Arbitration under the Treaty of February 29, 1892. 1893.

Treaties, Conventions, etc., between the United States and Other Powers, I, 751.

Whereas, by a Treaty between the United States of America and Great Britain, signed at Washington, February 29, 1892, the ratifications of which by the Governments of the two Countries were exchanged at London on May 7, 1892, it was, amongst other things, agreed and concluded that the questions which had arisen between the Government of the United States of America and the Government of Her Britannic Majesty, concerning the jurisdictional rights of the United States in the waters of Behring's [Bering] Sea, and concerning also the preservation of the fur-seal in or habitually resorting to the said sea, and the rights of the citizens and subjects of either country as regards the taking of fur-seals in or habitually resorting to the said waters, should be submitted to a Tribunal of Arbitration to be composed of seven Arbitrators, who should be appointed in the following manner, that is to say: Two should be named by the President of the United States; two should be named by Her Britannic Majesty; His Excellency the President of the French Republic should be jointly requested by the High Contracting Parties to name one; His Majesty the King of Italy should be so requested to name one; His Majesty the King of Sweden and Norway should be so requested to name one; the seven Arbitrators to be so named should be jurists of distinguished reputation in their respective Countries, and the selecting Powers should be requested to choose, if possible, jurists who are acquainted with the English language;

And whereas, it was further agreed by article II of the said Treaty that the Arbitrators should meet at Paris within twenty days after the delivery of the Counter-Cases mentioned in article IV, and should proceed impartially and carefully to examine and decide the questions which had been or should be laid before them as in the said Treaty provided on the part of the Governments of the United States and of Her Britannic Majesty respectively, and that all questions considered by the Tribunal, including the final decision, should be determined by a majority of all the Arbitrators;

And whereas, by article VI of the said Treaty, it was further provided as follows: "In deciding the matters submitted to the said Arbitrators, it is agreed that the following five points shall be submitted to them in order that their award shall embrace a distinct decision upon each of said five points, to wit:

"1. What exclusive jurisdiction in the sea now known as the Behring's Sea, and what exclusive rights in the seal fisheries therein, did Russia assert and exercise prior and up to the time of the cession of Alaska to the United States?

"2. How far were these claims of jurisdiction as to the seal fisheries recognized and conceded by Great Britain?

"3. Was the body of water now known as Behring's Sea included in the phrase *Pacific Ocean,* as used in the Treaty of 1825 between Great Britain and Russia; and what rights, if any in the Behring's Sea were held and exclusively exercised by Russia after said Treaty?

"4. Did not all the rights of Russia as to jurisdiction and as to the seal fisheries in Behring's Sea east of the water boundary, in the Treaty between the United States and Russia of the 30th of March, 1867, pass unimpaired to the United States under that Treaty?

"5. Has the United States any right, and, if so, what right, of protection or property in the fur-seals frequenting the islands of the United States in Behring's Sea when such seals are found outside the ordinary three-mile limit?"

"And whereas, by article VII of the said Treaty, it was further agreed as follows:

"If the determination of the foregoing questions as to the exclusive jurisdiction of the United States shall leave the subject in such position that the concurrence of Great Britain is necessary to the establishment of Regulations for the proper protection and preservation of the fur-seal in, or habitually resorting to the Behring Sea, the Arbitrators shall then determine what concurrent Regulations, outside the jurisdictional limits of the respective Governments, are necessary, and over what waters such Regulations should extend;"

"The High Contracting Parties furthermore agree to co-operate in securing the adhesion of other Powers to such Regulations;" . . .

And whereas, We, the said Arbitrators so named and appointed, having taken upon ourselves the burden of the said Arbitration, and having duly met at Paris, proceeded impartially and carefully to examine and decide all the questions submitted to us the said Arbitrators, under the said Treaty, or laid before us as provided in the said Treaty on the part of the Governments of Her Britannic Majesty and the United States respectively:

Now we, the said Arbitrators, having impartially and carefully examined the said questions, do in like manner by this our Award decide and determine the said questions in the manner following, that is to say: We decide and determine as to the five points mentioned in article VI as to which our Award is to embrace a distinct decision upon each of them:

As to the first of the said five points, we, the said Baron De Courcel, Mr. Justice Harlan, Lord Hannen, Sir John Thompson, Marquis Visconti Venosta, and Mr. Gregers Gram, being a majority of the said Arbitrators, do decide and determine as follows:

By the Ukase of 1821, Russia claimed jurisdiction in the sea now known as the Behring's Sea, to the extent of 100 Italian miles from the coasts and islands belonging to her, but, in the course of the negotiations which led to the conclusion of the Treaties of 1824 with the United States and of 1825 with Great Britain, Russia admitted that her jurisdiction in the said sea should be restricted to the reach of cannon shot from shore, and it appears that, from that time up to the time of the cession of Alaska to the United States, Russia never asserted in fact or exercised any exclusive jurisdiction in Behring's Sea or any exclusive rights in the seal fisheries therein beyond the ordinary limit of territorial waters.

As to the second of the said five points, we, the said Baron De Courcel, Mr. Justice Harlan, Lord Hannen, Sir John Thompson, Marquis Visconti Venosta, and Mr. Gregers Gram, being a majority of the said Arbitrators, do decide and determine that Great Britain did not recognize or concede any claim, upon the part of Russia, to exclusive jurisdiction as to the seal fisheries in Behring Sea, outside of ordinary territorial waters.

As to the third of the said five points, as to so much thereof as required us to decide whether the body of water now known as Behring Sea was included in the phrase "Pacific Ocean" as used in the Treaty of 1825 between Great Britain and Russia, We, the said Arbitrators, do unanimously decide and determine that the body of water now known as the Behring Sea was included in the phrase "Pacific Ocean" as used in the said Treaty.

And as to so much of the said third point as requires us to decide what rights, if any, in the Behring Sea were held and exclusively exercised by Russia after the said Treaty of 1825, We, the said Baron De Courcel, Mr. Justice Harlan, Lord Hannen, Sir John Thompson, Marquis Visconti Venosta, and Mr. Gregers Gram, being a majority of the said arbitrators, do decide and determine that no exclusive rights of jurisdiction in Behring Sea and no exclusive rights as to the seal fisheries therein, were held or exercised by Russia outside of ordinary territorial waters after the Treaty of 1825.

As to the fourth of the said five points, We, the said Arbitrators, do unanimously decide and determine that all the rights of Russia as to jurisdiction and as to the seal fisheries in Behring Sea, east of the water boundary, in the Treaty between the United States and Russia of the 30th of March, 1867, did pass unimpaired to the United States under the said Treaty.

As to the fifth of the said five points, We, the said Baron de Courcel, Lord Hannen, Sir John Thompson, Marquis Visconti Venosta, and Mr. Gregers Gram, being a majority of the said Arbitrators, do decide and determine that the United States has not any right of protection or property in the fur-seals frequenting the islands of the United States in Behring Sea, when such seals are found outside the ordinary three-mile limit. . . .

UNITED STATES AND GREAT BRITAIN: THE WANDERER.

Arbitration under the Agreement of August 18, 1910. 1921.

Nielsen's Report, 459.

Arbitrators: HENRI FROMAGEOT, Sir CHARLES FITZPATRICK, CHANDLER P. ANDERSON.

This is a claim presented by His Britannic Majesty's Government for $17,507.36 and interest from November, 1894, for damages arising out of the seizure and detention of the British sealing schooner Wanderer, and her officers, men, and cargo, by the United States revenue cutter Concord on June 10, 1894.

The Wanderer, a schooner of 25 tons burden, was a British ship registered at the Port of Victoria, B. C.; her owner was Henry Paxton, a British subject and a master mariner. On the 5th of January, 1894, she was chartered for the sealing season of 1894 by the said Paxton to Simon Leiser, a naturalized British subject. . . .

On June 9, 1894, at 8:30 a. m., when the vessel was in latitude 58° north and longitude 150° west, and heading west-southwest, en route for Sand Point, she was hailed by the United States revenue cutter Yorktown, and boarded by an officer who, acting under instructions hereinafter referred to, searched the schooner, placed her sealing implements under seal, and made an entry in the ship's log stating the number of sealskins found on board to be 400.

On the same day, about seven hours later, i. e., at about 4 p. m., the vessel being in latitude 58° 21′ north and longitude 150° 22′ west, heading north, wind astern, she was hailed by another United States revenue cutter, the Concord, and boarded and searched. During his search the officer discovered hidden on board and unsealed one 12-bore shotgun, 39 loaded shells, and 3 boxes primers, one of which was already opened. The United States naval officer took possession of the gun and shells.
. . .

As the sea was rough, the commanding officer of the Concord, at the request of the master of the Wanderer, took her in tow to St. Paul, Kadiak Island. She arrived there towed by the Concord on June 10th. . . . At 4 p. m. the commanding officer of the Concord, Commander

Goodrich, advised the master that his ship and the ship's papers had actually been seized.

The ordinary declaration of seizure was made and notice given that the seizure had been made for the following reasons: "Subsequent to the warning and certificate aforesaid arms and ammunition suitable to the killing of fur seals were discovered concealed on board; . . . and whereas the possession of such unsealed arms and ammunition was in contravention of the Behring Sea Award Act, 1894, clause I, par. 2, and clause III, par. 2, as well as of section 10 in the President's Proclamation. . . ." (United States Answer, Exhibit 5.)

The master of the Wanderer protested against this declaration.

On June 16 Commander Goodrich sent a report to the Commander of the United States Naval Force in the Behring Sea (United States Answer, Exhibit 4) in which he stated:

"My action is based on the last half of Sec. 10 of the Act of Congress April 6; the next to the last sentence in the 'Regulations Governing Vessels, etc.,' the Behring Sea Award Act, and Pars. 1 and 3 of your confidential instructions of May 13th."

To this report were annexed the statements of the officers and men of the Concord, who took part in the search, all of which referred merely to the discovery on board of a gun and ammunition hidden and unsealed. On July 1st, the Wanderer arrived at Dutch Harbor, Unalaska, where she remained under seizure until August 2d, when she was handed over to her Britannic Majesty's ship Pheasant. (United States Answer, Exhibits 12, 13.)

On August 6th the schooner was sent to Victoria, B. C., and after her arrival there, she was released by order of the British Naval Commander in Chief on the Pacific Station. (British Memorial, p. 10.) The evidence does not disclose how long the Wanderer was detained at Victoria by the British authorities before her release was ordered.

The Government of His Britannic Majesty contend that the seizure of the Wanderer was illegal; that the alleged reason for it was wholly insufficient, and that the Government of the United States is responsible for the act of its naval officers.

The United States Government, on the other hand, denies all liability; first, because its officers were acting on behalf of the British Government and not of the United States Government; second, because there was a *bona fide* belief that an infraction of the Behring Sea Award Act, 1894, had been committed; third, because the release of the Wanderer by the British naval authorities without a regular prosecution before a court rendered it impossible to determine in the only competent way whether the seizure was illegal; fourth, because even supposing the seizure was made without probable cause, the liability to pay damages would rest upon His Britannic Majesty's Government; fifth, because the detention of the vessel after July 1, 1894, the date when she arrived at Dutch Harbor, Unalaska, was due to the failure of the British naval authorities to send a vessel there to take charge of the schooner; and, sixth, because there is no basis in law or in fact for the measure of damages.

I. *As to the legality of the seizure and liability of the United States:*

The fundamental principle of the international maritime law is that no nation can exercise a right of visitation and search over foreign vessels pursuing a lawful avocation on the high seas, except in time of war or by special agreement.

The Wanderer was on the high seas. There is no question here of war. It lies therefore on the United States to show that its naval authorities acted under special agreement. Any such agreement being an exception to the general principle, must be construed *stricto jure.*

At the time of the seizure, as the result of the Arbitral Award of Paris, August 15, 1893, and the Regulations annexed thereto, there was in operation between the United States and Great Britain a conventional régime the object of which was the protection of the fur seals in the North Pacific Ocean.

By the Award it was decided, *inter alia:* ''that concurrent regulations outside the jurisdictional limits of the respective governments are necessary and that they should extend over the water hereinafter mentioned.''

By the Regulations above referred to, it was provided that the two Governments should forbid their citizens and subjects, first, to kill, capture, or pursue at any time and in any manner whatever, the fur seals within a zone of sixty miles around the Pribilof Islands; and second, to kill, capture and pursue fur seals in any manner whatever from the first of May to the 31st of July within the zone included between latitude 35° north and the Behring Straits, and eastward of longitude 180°.

Furthermore the same Regulations provide:

''Article 6. The use of nets, firearms and explosives shall be forbidden in the fur-seal fishing. This restriction shall not apply to shot guns when such fishing takes place outside of Behring's Sea during the season when it may be lawfully carried on.''

To comply with the Award and Regulations, an Act of Congress was passed in the United States on April 6, 1894 [28 Stat. 52]. This Act provided:

''Sec. 10. . . . if any licensed vessel shall be found in the waters to which this Act applies, having on board apparatus or implements suitable for taking seals, but forbidden then and there to be used, it shall be presumed that the vessel in the one case and the apparatus or implements in the other was or were used in violation of this Act until it is otherwise sufficiently proved.''

On April 18, 1894, instructions were given to the United States naval authorities, according to which—

"Par. 6. Any vessel or person . . . having on board or in their possession apparatus or implements suitable for taking seal . . . you will order seized." (United States Answer, Exhibit 20.)

On their side the British Government passed an Act dated April 23, 1894, providing:

"Sec. 1. The provisions of the Behring Sea Arbitration Award . . . shall have effect as if those provisions . . . were enacted by this Act." (United States Answer, Exhibit 17.)

The British Act further provides:

"Sec. 3, par. 3. An order in council under this act may provide that such officers of the United States of America as are specified in the order may, in respect of offenses under this act, exercise the like powers under this act as may be exercised by a commissioned officer of Her Majesty in relation to a British ship. . . ." (United States Answer, Exhibit 17.)

As may be observed, the United States Act and the instructions to its naval authorities did not follow the wording of the Award Regulations exactly, and Her Majesty's Government drew attention to the variance, in a letter addressed by their Ambassador in Washington to the Secretary of State on April 30, 1894:

". . . I am directed to draw your attention to paragraph 6 of the draft instructions, so far as it relates to British vessels. The paragraph requires modification in order to bring it, as regards the powers to be exercised by the United States cruisers over British vessels, within the limits prescribed by the British order in Council conferring such powers.

"The Earl of Kimberly desires me to state to you that the order in council which is about to be issued to empower United States cruisers to seize British vessels will only authorize them to make seizures of vessels contravening the provisions of the British act of Parliament, or, in other words, the provisions of the award.

"There is no clause in the British act corresponding with section 10 of the United States act of Congress. United States cruisers can not therefore seize British vessels merely for having on board, while within the area of the award and during the close season, implements suitable for taking seal." (United States Answer, Exhibit 21.)

Meanwhile and on April 30, 1894, a British Order in Council was issued providing:

"Par. 1. The commanding officer of any vessel belonging to the naval or revenue service of the United States of America, and appointed for the time being by the President of the United States for the purpose of carrying into effect the powers conferred by this article, the name of which vessel shall have been communicated by the President of the United States to Her Majesty as being a vessel so appointed as aforesaid, may . . . seize and detain any British vessel which has become liable to be forfeited to Her Majesty under the provisions of the recited act, and may bring her for adjudication before any such British court of admiralty as is referred to in section 103 of 'The Merchant Shipping Act, 1854,' . . . or may deliver her to any such British officer as is mentioned in the said section for the purpose of being dealt with pursuant to the recited act.'' (United States Answer, Exhibit 18.)

It appears from the documents that an exchange of views took place between the two Governments in order to arrive at some agreement as to the regulations. On May 4, 1894, an agreement was reached. The previous United States instructions, dated April 18, 1894, were revoked (53 Cong. 2d Sess. Senate Ex. Doc. No. 67, p. 228) ; a memorandum of the agreement regulations was exchanged (*Ibid.*, p. 120; United States Answer, Exhibit 23), and those regulations were sent by the United States Government to their naval officers (*Ibid.*, pp. 126, 226, 228). From these new regulations of May 4, 1894, the provision concerning the possession of arms was omitted.

In these circumstances, the legal position in the sealing zone at the time of the seizure of the Wanderer may be summarized as follows: The provisions of the Award in their strict meaning, and those provisions only, had been agreed upon as binding upon the vessels, citizens, and subjects of the two countries; and it was only for contravention of those provisions that the United States cruisers were authorized to seize British vessels.

Such being the state of the law, the question to be determined here is whether or not the Wanderer was contravening the aforesaid provisions so as to justify her seizure.

The declaration of seizure does not allege that the Wanderer was killing or pursuing or had killed or pursued fur seals within the prohibited time or zone, but that she was discovered to have certain arms and ammunition unsealed and hidden on board. The offense alleged was the possession of such arms and ammunition (United States Answer, Exhibit 5). The same charge is brought by the notice of the declaration of seizure ''. . . whereas in thus having concealed arms and ammunition on board, you were acting in contravention . . . .'' (United States Answer, Exhibit 6). In the report of the United States authorities, a report of a merely domestic character, the same view is taken. It is explained by the repeated references to the above quoted Section 10 of the United States Act of April 6, 1894.

Inasmuch as it was only *use* and not the mere *possession* of arms and ammunition which was prohibited by the Paris Award and Regulations, it is impossible to say that the Wanderer was acting in contravention of them.

Even if it be admitted that in case of contravention the United States officers were empowered to seize on behalf of Her Majesty's Government under the British Act, it is clear that such a delegation of power only gave them authority to act within the limits of that Act, and as the seizure was made for a reason not provided for by that Act, it is impossible to say that in this case they were exercising that delegated authority.

The *bona fides* of the United States naval officers is not questioned. It is evident that the provisions of section 10 of the Act of Congress constituted a likely cause of error. But the United States Government is responsible for that section, and liable for the errors of judgment committed by its agents. . . .

For these reasons:

The Tribunal decides that the Government of the United States shall pay to the Government of His Britannic Majesty for the claimants the sum of one thousand six hundred and three dollars and five cents ($1,603.05), with interest at four per cent. (4%) on six hundred and three dollars and five cents ($603.05) thereof, from September 6, 1895, to April 26, 1912.[1]

---

[1] Supplementary Cases. In the case of La Ninfa, 75 Fed. 513 (1896), involving a libel brought in 1891 against an American ship for being engaged in the seal fisheries in Bering Sea in violation of statute of 1889, the Circuit Court of Appeals, reversing the decree of the District Court, held that the award of the arbitrators in the Bering Sea Arbitration in 1893 had to be taken into account in the interpretation of the statute. "The duty of courts," said the court, "is to construe and give effect to the latest expression of the sovereign will; hence it follows that, whatever may have been the contention of the government at the time In re Cooper was decided, it has receded therefrom since the award was rendered by an agreement to accept the same 'as a full, complete, and final settlement of all questions referred to by the arbitrators,' and from the further fact that the government since the rendition of the award has passed 'an act to give effect to the award rendered by the tribunal of arbitration.'"

CHAPTER XI

JURISDICTIONAL CO-OPERATION BETWEEN STATES: EXTRADITION OF FUGITIVE CRIMINALS; LETTERS ROGATORY; COMITY [1]

A. Territorial limitations upon criminal jurisdiction.

Since the effective jurisdiction of a state is strictly limited to its territorial boundaries, the punishment of fugitive criminals is dependent in most cases upon the willingness of the state of refuge to apprehend the criminal and return him to the state in which the crime was committed. This willingness is expressed in treaties of extradition stipulating the conditions under which the state is prepared to surrender criminals who take refuge upon its territory. So strictly is the territorial integrity of states construed that under no circumstances whatever may one state exercise the slightest act of jurisdiction within the territory of another without its express permission. Would this rule extend so far as to deny to the officers of one state the right of "hot pursuit" of a criminal across territorial boundaries? Would the escape of a prisoner when in transit through a third state call for the procedure of extradition to effect his return to custody? [France and Great Britain: Savarkar Case.]

FRANCE AND GREAT BRITAIN: THE SAVARKAR CASE.

Tribunal of the Hague Permanent Court of Arbitration, 1911.

Scott, Hague Court Reports, 276.

[BY THE TRIBUNAL.] Whereas, by an agreement dated the 25th October 1910, the Government of the French Republic and the Government of His Britannic Majesty agreed to submit to Arbitration the questions of fact and law raised by the arrest and restoration to the mail-steamer Morea at Marseilles, on the 8th July 1910, of the British Indian Savarkar, who had escaped from that vessel where he was in custody; and the demand made by the Government of the French Republic for the restitution of Savarkar.

---

[1] For a more detailed study of this subject, see Fenwick, *op. cit.*, pp. 237–247; Hyde, *op. cit.*, §§ 310–341; Oppenheim, *op. cit.*, §§ 327–337; Research in International Law: Draft Convention on Extradition.

The arbitral tribunal has been called upon to decide the following question:

Should Vinayak Damodar Savarkar, in conformity with the rules of international law, be restored or not be restored by His Britannic Majesty's Government to the Government of the French Republic?

. . .

Whereas, with regard to the facts which gave rise to the difference of opinion between the two Governments, it is established that, by a letter, dated the 29th June 1910, the Commissioner of the Metropolitan Police in London informed the *Directeur de la Sûreté générale* at Paris, that the British-Indian Vinayak Damodar Savarkar was about to be sent to India, in order to be prosecuted for abetment of murder, etc., and that he would be on board the vessel Morea touching at Marseilles on the 7th or 8th July.

Whereas, in consequence of the receipt of this letter, the Ministry of the Interior informed the Prefect of the *Bouches-du-Rhône,* by a telegram dated the 4th July 1910, that the British Police were sending Savarkar to India on board the steamship Morea. This telegram states that some *"révolutionnaires hindous"* [Hindu revolutionaries] then on the Continent, might take advantage of this to further the escape of this foreigner, and the Prefect was requested to take the measures necessary to guard against any attempt of that kind.

Whereas the *Directeur de la Sûreté générale* replied by a letter dated the 9th July 1910 to the letter of the Commissioner of the Metropolitan Police, stating that he had given the necessary instructions for the purpose of guarding against the occurrence of any incident during the presence at Marseilles of the said Vinayak Damodar Savarkar, on board the steamship Morea.

Whereas, on the 7th July, the Morea arrived at Marseilles. The following morning, between 6 and 7 o'clock, Savarkar, having succeeded in effecting his escape, swam ashore and began to run; he was arrested by a brigadier of the French maritime *gendarmerie* and taken back to the vessel. Three persons who had come ashore from the vessel assisted the brigadier in taking the fugitive back. On the 9th July, the Morea left Marseilles with Savarkar on board.

Whereas, from the statements made by the French brigadier to the police of Marseilles, it appears:

That he saw the fugitive, who was almost naked, get out of a porthole of the steamer, throw himself into the sea and swim to the quay;

That at the same moment some persons from the ship, who were shouting and gesticulating, rushed over the bridge leading to the shore, in order to pursue him;

That a number of people on the quay commenced to shout *"Arrêtez-le;"*

That the brigadier at once went in pursuit of the fugitive and, coming up to him after running above five hundred metres, arrested him.

Whereas the brigadier declares that he was altogether unaware of the identity of the person with whom he was dealing, that he only thought that the man who was escaping was one of the crew, who had possibly committed an offence on board the vessel.

Whereas, with regard to the assistance afforded him by one of the crew and two Indian policemen, it appears from the explanations given on this point, that these men came up after the arrest of Savarkar, and that their intervention was only auxiliary to the action of the brigadier. The brigadier had seized Savarkar by one arm for the purpose of taking him back to the ship, and the prisoner went peaceably with him. The brigadier, assisted by the above mentioned persons, did not relax his hold till he reached the half deck of the vessel.

The brigadier said that he did not know English.

From what has been stated, it would appear that the incident did not occupy more than a few minutes.

Whereas, it is alleged that the brigadier who effected the arrest was not ignorant of the presence of Savarkar on board the vessel, and that his orders, like those of all the French police [agents] and *gendarmes*, were to prevent any Hindoo from coming on board who had not got a ticket.

Whereas, these circumstances show that the persons on board in charge of Savarkar might well have believed that they could count on the assistance of the French police [*agents*].

Whereas, it is established that a *commissaire* of the French police came on board the vessel shortly after her arrival at the port, and in accordance with the orders of the prefect, placed himself at the disposal of the commander in respect of the watch to be kept;

That, in consequence, this *commissaire* was put into communication with the British police officer who, with other police officers, was in charge of the prisoner;

That the prefect of Marseilles, as appears from a telegram dated the 13th July, 1910, addressed to the Minister of the Interior, stated that he had acted in this matter in accordance with instructions given by the *Sûreté générale* to make the necessary arrangements to prevent the escape of Savarkar.

Whereas, having regard to what has been stated, it is manifest that the case is not one of recourse to fraud or force in order to obtain possession of a person who had taken refuge in foreign territory, and that there was not, in the circumstances of the arrest and delivery of Savarkar to the British authorities and of his removal to India, anything in the nature of a violation of the sovereignty of France, and that all those who took part in the matter certainly acted in good faith and had no thought of doing anything unlawful.

Whereas, in the circumstances cited above, the conduct of the brigadier not having been disclaimed by his chiefs before the morning of the 9th July, that is to say before the Morea left Marseilles, the British police might naturally have believed that the brigadier had acted in accordance with his instructions, or that his conduct had been approved.

Whereas, while admitting that an irregularity was committed by the arrest of Savarkar and by his being handed over to the British police, there is no rule of international law imposing, in circumstances such as those which have been set out above, any obligation on the Power which has in its custody a prisoner, to restore him because of a mistake committed by the foreign agent who delivered him up to that Power.

For these reasons: The arbitral tribunal decides that the Government of His Britannic Majesty is not required to restore the said Vinayak Damodar Savarkar to the Government of the French Republic. . . .

B. Treaty stipulations controlling extradition.

While treaties of extradition, upon which the return of fugitive criminals depends, vary widely in respect to the particular offenses for which extradition is granted, there are certain general principles common to most of them. Query, is it obligatory that the fugitive, upon being extradited, be tried for the particular offense stipulated in the request for his extradition? [United States v. Rauscher.] What if the law of the requesting state differs from the law of the requested state (the state of refuge) in respect to the definition of one of the crimes enumerated in the treaty or in respect to the specific offenses that may properly be included under the general definition of a crime? [Factor v. Laubenheimer.] Is the state of refuge privileged to inquire into the evidence submitted in the request for extradition and to refuse to extradite the fugitive if it does not appear that he would have been guilty of the offense under its own law? [Insull Case.] Suppose the fugitive is a national of the state of refuge: may his national state decline on that account to surrender him and proceed to try him according to its own laws? [Charlton v. Kelley.]

UNITED STATES v. RAUSCHER.

United States, Supreme Court, 1886.

119 U. S. 407. [30 L. ed. 425; 7 S. Ct. 234.]

MR. JUSTICE MILLER delivered the opinion of the court. This case comes before us on a certificate of division of opinion between the judges holding the Circuit Court of the United States for the Southern District of New York, arising after verdict of guilty, and before judgment, on a motion in arrest of judgment.

The prisoner, William Rauscher, was indicted by a grand jury for that, on the 9th day of October, 1884, on the high seas, out of the jurisdiction of any particular state of the United States, and within the admiralty and maritime jurisdiction thereof, he, the said William Rauscher, being then and there second mate of the ship J. F. Chapman, unlawfully made an assault upon Janssen, one of the crew of the vessel of which he was an officer, and unlawfully inflicted upon said Janssen cruel and unusual punishment. This indictment was found under § 5347 of the Revised Statutes of the United States.

The statement of the division of opinion between the judges is in the following language: . . .

"First. The prisoner having been extradited upon a charge of murder, on the high seas, of one Janssen, under § 5339, Rev. Stat., had the Circuit Court of the Southern District of New York jurisdiction to put him to trial upon an indictment, under § 5347, Rev. Stat., charging him with cruel and unusual punishment of the same man, he being one of the crew of an American vessel of which the defendant was an officer, and such punishment consisting of the identical acts proved in the extradition proceedings?

"Second. Did or not the prisoner, under the extradition treaty with Great Britain, having been surrendered upon a charge of murder, acquire a right to be exempt from prosecution upon the charge set forth in the indictment, without being first afforded an opportunity to return to Great Britain? . . . ."

The treaty with Great Britain, under which the defendant was surrendered by that government to ours upon a charge of murder, is that of August 9, 1842, styled "A treaty to settle and define the boundaries between the territories of the United States and the possessions of Her Britannic Majesty in North America; for the final suppression of the African slave trade; and for the giving up of criminals, fugitives from justice, in certain cases." 8 Stat. 576.

With the exception of this caption, the tenth article of the treaty contains all that relates to the subject of extradition of criminals. That article is here copied, as follows:

"It is agreed that the United States and Her Britannic Majesty shall, upon mutual requisitions by them, or their ministers, officers, or authorities, respectively made, deliver up to justice all persons who, being charged with the crime of murder, or assault with intent to commit murder, or piracy, or arson, or robbery, or forgery, or the utterance of forged paper, committed within the jurisdiction of either, shall seek an asylum, or shall be found, within the territories of the other: provided that this shall only be done upon such evidence of criminality as, according to the laws of the place where the fugitive or person so charged shall be found, would justify his apprehension and commitment for trial, if the crime or offence had there been committed; and the respective judges and other magistrates of the two Governments shall have power, jurisdiction, and authority, upon complaint made under oath, to issue a warrant for the apprehension of the fugitive or person so charged, that he may be brought before such judges or other magistrates, respectively, to the end that the evidence of criminality may be heard and considered; and if, on such hearing, the evidence be deemed sufficient to sustain the charge, it shall be the duty of the examining judge or magistrate to certify the same to the proper Executive authority, that a warrant may issue for the surrender of such fugitive." . . .

It is only in modern times that the nations of the earth have imposed upon themselves the obligation of delivering up these fugitives from justice to the states where their crimes were committed, for trial and punishment. This has been done generally by treaties made by one independent government with another. Prior to these treaties, and apart from them, it may be stated, as the general result of the writers upon international law, that there was no well-defined obligation on one country to deliver up such fugitives to another; and, though such delivery was often made, it was upon the principle of comity, and within the discretion of the government whose action was invoked; and it has never been recognized as among those obligations of one government towards another which rest upon established principles of international law. . . .

The treaty of 1842 being, therefore, the supreme law of the land, of which the courts are bound to take judicial notice, and to enforce in any appropriate proceeding the rights of persons growing out of that treaty, we proceed to inquire, in the first place, so far as pertinent to the questions certified by the circuit judges, into the true construction of the treaty. We have already seen that, according to the doctrine of publicists and writers on international law, the country receiving the offender against its laws from another country had no right to proceed against him for any other offense than that for which he had been delivered up. This is a principle which commends itself, as an appropriate adjunct, to the discretionary exercise of the power of rendition, because it can hardly be supposed that a government which was under no treaty obligation, nor any absolute obligation of public duty, to seize a person who had found an asylum within its bosom, and turn him over to another country for trial, would be willing to do this, unless a case was made of some specific offense, of a character which justified the government in depriving the party of his asylum. It is unreasonable that the country of the asylum should be expected to deliver up such person to be dealt with by the demanding government without any limitation, implied or otherwise, upon its prosecution of the party. In exercising its discretion, it might be very willing to deliver up offenders against such laws as were essential to the protection of life, liberty, and person, while it would not be willing to do this on account of minor misdemeanors, or of a certain class of political offenses in which it would have no interest or sympathy. Accordingly, it has been the policy of all governments to grant an asylum to persons who have fled from their homes on account of political disturbances, and who might be there amenable to laws framed with regard to such subjects, and to the personal allegiance of the party. In many of the treaties of extradition between the civilized nations of the world there is an express exclusion of the right to demand the extradition of offenders against such laws, and in none of them is this class of offenses mentioned as being the foundation of extradition proceedings. Indeed, the enumeration of offenses in most of these treaties, and especially in the treaty now under consideration, is so specific, and marked by such a clear line in regard to the magnitude and importance of those offenses, that it is impossible to give any other interpretation to it than that of the exclusion of the right of extradition for any others.

It is therefore very clear that this treaty did not intend to depart in this respect from the recognized public law which had prevailed in the absence of treaties, and that it was not intended that this treaty should be used for any other purpose than to secure the trial of the person extradited for one of the offenses enumerated in the treaty. This is not only apparent from the general principle that the specific enumeration of certain matters and things implies the exclusion of all others, but the entire face of the treaty, including the processes by which it is to be carried into effect, confirms this view of the subject. It is unreasonable to suppose that any demand for rendition, framed upon a general representation to the government of the asylum (if we may use such an expression) that the party for whom the demand was made was guilty of some violation of the laws of the country which demanded him, without specifying any particular offense with which he was charged, and even without specifying an offense mentioned in the treaty, would receive any serious attention; and yet such is the effect of the construction that the party is properly liable to trial for any other offense than that for which he was demanded and which is described in the treaty. There would, under that view of the subject, seem to be no need of a description of a specific offense in making the demand. But, so far from this being admissible, the treaty not only provides that the party shall be charged with one of the crimes mentioned, to-wit, murder, assault with intent to commit murder, piracy, arson, robbery, forgery, or the utterance of forged paper, but that evidence shall be produced to the judge or magistrate of the country of which such demand is made of the commission of such an offense, and that this evidence shall be such as, according to the law of that country, would justify the apprehension and commitment for trial of the person so charged. If the proceedings under which the party is arrested in a country where he is peaceably and quietly living, and to the protection of whose laws he is entitled, are to have no influence in limiting the prosecution in the country where the offense is charged to have been committed, there is very little use for this particularity in charging a specific offense, requiring that offense to be one mentioned in the treaty, as well as sufficient evidence of the party's guilt to put him upon trial for it. . . .

If, upon the face of this treaty it could be seen that its sole object was to secure the transfer of an individual from the jurisdiction of one sovereignty to that of another, the argument might be sound; but as this right of transfer, the right to demand it, the obligation to grant it, the proceedings under which it takes place, all show that it is for a limited and defined purpose that the transfer is made, it is impossible to conceive of the exercise of jurisdiction in such a case for any other purpose than that mentioned in the treaty, and ascertained by the proceedings under which the party is extradited, without an implication of fraud upon the rights of the party extradited, and of bad faith to the country which permitted his extradition. No such view of solemn public treaties between the great nations of the earth can be sustained by a tribunal called upon to give judicial construction to them.

The opposite view has been attempted to be maintained in this country upon the ground that there is no express limitation in the treaty of the right of the country in which the offense was committed to try the person for the crime alone for which he was extradited; and that once being within the jurisdiction of that country, no matter by what contrivance or fraud, or by what pretense of establishing a charge provided for by the extradition treaty, he may have been brought within the jurisdiction, he is, when here, liable to be tried for any offense against the laws, as though arrested here originally. This proposition of the absence of express restriction in the treaty of the right to try him for other offenses than that for which he was extradited, is met by the manifest scope and object of the treaty itself. The caption of the treaty, already quoted, declaring that its purpose is to settle the boundary line between the two governments, to provide for the final suppression of the African slave trade, adds, "and for the giving up of criminals, fugitive from justice, *in certain cases*." The treaty, then, requires, as we have already said, that there shall be given up, upon requisitions respectively made by the two governments, all persons charged with any of the seven crimes enumerated; and the provisions giving a party an examination before a proper tribunal, in which, before he shall be delivered up on this demand, it must be shown that the offense for which he is demanded is one of those enumerated, and that the proof is sufficient to satisfy the court or magistrate before whom this examination takes place that he is guilty, and such as the law of the state of the asylum requires to establish such guilt, leave no reason to doubt that the fair purpose of the treaty is that the person shall be delivered up to be tried for that offense, and for no other.　.　.　.

Upon a review of these decisions of the Federal and State courts, to which may be added the opinions of the distinguished writers which we have cited in the earlier part of this opinion, we feel authorized to state that the weight of authority and of sound principle are in favor of the proposition that a person who has been brought within the jurisdiction of the court, by virtue of proceedings under an extradition treaty, can only be tried for one of the offenses described in that treaty, and for the offense with which he is charged in the proceedings for his extradition, until a reasonable time and opportunity have been given him, after his release or trial upon such charge, to return to the country from whose asylum he had been forcibly taken under those proceedings.　.　.　.

The result of these considerations is that the first of the questions certified to us is answered in the negative; the second and third are answered in the affirmative; and it is ordered to be so certified to the judges of the circuit court.

[Opinion of Gray, J., concurring, omitted.]

Mr. Chief Justice Waite dissenting.

I am unable to concur in the decision of this case. A fugitive from justice has no absolute right of asylum in a country to which he flees; and, if he can be got back within the jurisdiction of the country whose laws he has violated, he may be proceeded with precisely the same as if he had not fled, unless there is something in the laws of the country where he is to be tried, or in the way in which he was got back, to prevent. I do not understand this to be denied. All, therefore, depends, in this case on the treaty with Great Britain under which this extradition was effected, and § 5275 of the Revised Statutes. I concede that the treaty is as much a part of the law of the United States as is a statute; and, if there is anything in it which forbids a trial for any other offense than that for which the extradition was made, the accused may use it as a defense to a prosecution on any other charge until a reasonable time has elapsed after his release from custody on account of the crime for which he was sent back. But I have been unable to find any such provision. The treaty requires a delivery up to justice, on demand, of those accused of certain crimes, but says nothing about what shall be done with them after the delivery has been made. It might have provided that they should not be tried for any other offenses than those for which they were surrendered; but it has not. Consequently, as it seems to me, the accused has acquired no new rights under the treaty. He fled from the justice of the country whose laws he violated, and has been got back. The treaty under which he was surrendered has granted him no immunity, and therefore it has not provided him with any new defense.　.　.　.

This is, I think, the true rule; and it is in full accord with the principles applied by this court in The Richmond, 9 Cranch, 102, where it was insisted upon by way of defense that a vessel proceeded against for a violation of the non-intercourse act had been seized within the territorial jurisdiction of Spain. As to this, Chief Justice Marshall said, in delivering the opinion of the court: "The seizure of an American vessel within the territorial jurisdiction of a foreign power is certainly an offense against that power, which must be adjusted between the two governments. This court can take no cognizance of it; and the majority of the court is of opinion that the law does not connect that trespass, if it be one, with the subsequent seizure by the civil authority, under the process of the district court, so as to annul the proceedings of that court against the vessel." If either country should use its privileges under the treaty to obtain a surrender of a fugitive on the pretense of trying him for an offense for which extradition could be claimed, so as to try him for one for which he could not, it might furnish just cause of complaint on the part of the country which had been deceived, but it would be a matter entirely for adjustment between the two countries, and which could in no way inure to the benefit of the accused, except through the instrumentality of the government that had been induced to give him up. . . .

FACTOR v. LAUBENHEIMER, U. S. MARSHALL, ET AL.

United States, Supreme Court, 1933.

290 U. S. 276. [78 L. ed. 315; 54 S. Ct. 191.]

MR. JUSTICE STONE delivered the opinion of the Court.

On complaint of the British Consul, a United States Commissioner for the Northern District of Illinois issued his warrant to hold petitioner in custody for extradition to England, under Article X of the Webster-Ashburton Treaty of 1842 (1 Malloy's Treaties, pp. 650, 655) as supplemented by the Blaine-Pauncefote Convention of 1889 (1 Malloy's Treaties, 740) and certified the evidence in the proceeding before him to the Secretary of State under the provisions of § 651, title 18, U. S. C. A. The application for extradition was based on a charge that petitioner, at London, had "received from Broadstreet Press Limited" certain sums of money, "knowing the same to have been fraudulently obtained." Upon application by the petitioner for writ of *habeas corpus,* and certiorari in its aid, the District Court for Northern Illinois, ordered him released from custody on the ground that the act charged was not embraced within the applicable treaties because not an offense under the laws of Illinois, the state in which he was apprehended and held. On appeal the Court of Appeals for the Seventh Circuit reversed the judgment of the District Court, 61 F. (2d) 626, on the ground that the offense was a crime in Illinois, as had been declared in Kelly v. Griffin, 241 U. S. 6. This Court granted certiorari, 289 U. S. 713, on a petition which presented as ground for the reversal of the judgment below that under the Treaty of 1842 and Convention of 1889, extradition may not be had unless the offense charged is a crime under the law of the state where the fugitive is found, and that "receiving money, knowing the same to have been fraudulently obtained," the crime with which the petitioner was charged, is not an offense under the laws of Illinois.

In support of this contention, petitioner asserts that it is a general principle of international law that an offense for which extradition may be had must be a crime both in the demanding country and in the place where the fugitive is found, and that the applicable treaty provisions, interpreted in the light of that principle, exclude any right of either country to demand the extradition of a fugitive unless the offense with which he is charged is a crime in the particular place of asylum. See Wright v. Henkel, 190 U. S. 40, 61. But the principles of international law recognize no right to extradition apart from treaty. While a government may, if agreeable to its own constitution and laws, voluntarily exercise the power to surrender a fugitive from justice to the country from which he has fled, and it has been said that it is under a moral duty to do so, (see 1 Moore, Extradition, § 14; Clarke, Extradition, 4th ed. p. 14) the legal right to demand his extradition and the correlative duty to surrender him to the demanding country exist only when created by treaty. See United States v. Rauscher, 119 U. S. 407, 411, 412; Holmes v. Jennison, 14 Pet. 540, 569, 582; United States v. Davis, 2 Sumn. 482; Case of Jose Ferreira dos Santos, 2 Brock. 493; Commonwealth ex rel. Short v. Deacon, 10 Serg. & R. 125; 1 Moore, Extradition, §§ 9–13; cf. Matter of Washburn, 4 Johns. Ch. 106, 107; 1 Kent, Com. 37. To determine the nature and extent of the right we must look to the treaty which created it. The question presented here, therefore, is one of the construction of the provisions of the applicable treaties in accordance with the principles governing the interpretation of international agreements.

The extradition provisions of the treaty with Great Britain of 1842 are embodied in Article X which provides that each country "shall . . . deliver up to justice all persons who, being charged with" any of seven named crimes "committed within the jurisdiction of either, shall seek an asylum or shall be found within the territories of the other." The crime charged here is not one of those specified in Article X and is therefore not an offense with respect to which extradition may be demanded, unless made so by the provisions of the supplemental convention of 1889. That convention recites that it is desired by the high contracting parties that the provisions of Article X of the earlier treaty should "embrace certain crimes not therein specified," and agrees by Article I that the provisions of Article X of the earlier treaty shall be made applicable to an added schedule of crimes specified in ten numbered classes of offenses and one unnumbered class. In the case of certain offenses, those enumerated in the classes numbered 4 and 10, and in the unnumbered class, Article X applies only if they are, in the former case, "made criminal" and, in the latter, "punishable," "by the laws of both countries." No such limitation is expressed with respect to the crimes enumerated in the other eight classes, one of which, the third, includes the crime with which petitioner is charged. Thus, like Article X of the earlier treaty, Article I specifies by name those offenses upon accusation of which the fugitive is to be surrendered and it extends to them the obligation of the earlier treaty. But Article I unlike Article X, singles out for exceptional treatment certain of the offenses named, which in terms are brought within the obligation of the treaty only if they are made criminal by the laws of both countries.

Notwithstanding this distinction, appearing on the face of the Convention, petitioner insists that in no case does it require extradition of a fugitive who has sought asylum in the United States unless the criminal act with which he is charged abroad is similarly defined as a crime by the laws of the particular state, district or territory of the United States in which he is found. The only language in the two treaties said to support this contention is the proviso in Article X of the treaty of 1842, following the engagement to surrender fugitives charged with specified offenses, which reads as follows:

"Provided, that this shall only be done upon such evidence of criminality as, according to the laws of the place where the fugitive or person so charged shall be found, would justify his apprehension and commitment for trial if the crime or offence had there been committed; . . ."

It cannot be said that these words give any clear indication that a fugitive charged with acts constituting a crime named in the treaty is not to be subject to extradition unless those acts are also defined as criminal by the laws of the state in which he is apprehended. The proviso would appear more naturally to refer to the procedure to be followed in the country of the asylum in asserting and making effective the obligation of the treaty and particularly to the quantum of proof— the "evidence"—which is to be required at the place of asylum to establish the fact that the fugitive has committed the treaty offense within the jurisdiction of the demanding country. . . .

Were Article X intended to have the added meaning insisted upon by petitioner, that there should be no extradition unless the act charged is one made criminal by the laws of the place of refuge, that meaning would naturally have been expressed in connection with the enumeration of the treaty offenses, rather than in the proviso which, in its whole scope, deals with procedure. That no such meaning can fairly be attributed to the proviso becomes evident when Article X is read, as for present purposes it must be, with the supplementary provisions of the Convention of 1889.

The draftsmen of the latter document obviously treated the proviso as dealing with procedure alone, since they took care to provide in Article I that fugitives should be subject to extradition for certain offenses, only if they were defined as criminal by the laws of both countries, but omitted any such provision with respect to all the others enumerated, including the crime of "receiving," with which petitioner is charged. This was an unnecessary precaution and one not consistently taken if the proviso already precluded extradition when the offense charged is not also criminal in the particular place of asylum. A less strained and entirely consistent construction is that urged by respondent, that the specification of the crime of "receiving," as a treaty offense, without qualification, evidenced an intention to dispense with the restriction applied to other treaty offenses, that they must be crimes "by the laws of both countries."

In choosing between conflicting interpretations of a treaty obligation, a narrow and restricted construction is to be avoided as not consonant with the principles deemed controlling in the interpretation of international agreements. Considerations which should govern the diplomatic relations between nations, and the good faith of treaties, as well, require that their obligations should be liberally construed so as to effect the apparent intention of the parties to secure equality and reciprocity between them. For that reason if a treaty fairly admits of two constructions, one restricting the rights which may be claimed under it, and the other enlarging them, the more liberal construction is to be preferred. Jordan v. Tashiro, 278 U. S. 123, 127; Geofroy v. Riggs, 133 U. S. 258, 271; Re Ross, 140 U. S. 453, 475; Tucker v. Alexandroff, 183 U. S. 424, 437; Asakura v. Seattle, 265 U. S. 332. Unless these principles, consistently recognized and applied by this Court, are now to be discarded, their application here leads inescapably to the conclusion that the treaties, presently involved, on their face require the extradition of the petitioner, even though the act with which he is charged would not be a crime if committed in Illinois. . . .

Other considerations peculiarly applicable to treaties for extradition, and to these treaties in particular, fortify this conclusion. The surrender of a fugitive, duly charged in the country from which he has fled with a non-political offense and one generally recognized as criminal at the place of asylum, involves no impairment of any legitimate public or private interest. The obligation to do what some nations have done voluntarily, in the interest of justice and friendly international relationships, see 1 Moore, Extradition, § 40, should be construed more liberally than a criminal statute or the technical requirements of criminal procedure. Grin v. Shine, 187 U. S. 181, 184; Yordi v. Nolte, 215 U. S. 227, 230. All of the offenses named in the two treaties are not only denominated crimes by the treaties themselves, but they are recognized as such by the jurisprudence of both countries. Even that with which petitioner is charged is a crime under the law of many states, if not in Illinois, punishable either as the crime of receiving money obtained fraudulently or by false pretenses, or as larceny. See United States v. Mulligan, 50 F. (2d) 687. Compare Kelly v. Griffin, *supra*, p. 15. It has been the policy of our own government, as of others, in entering into extradition treaties, to name as treaty offenses only those generally recognized as criminal by the laws in force within its own territory. But that policy, when carried into effect by treaty designation of offenses with respect to which extradition is to be granted, affords no adequate basis for declining to construe the treaty in accordance with its language, or for saying that its obligation, in the absence of some express requirement, is conditioned on the criminality of the offense charged according to the laws of the particular place of asylum. Once the contracting parties are satisfied that an identified offense is generally recognized as criminal in both countries there is no occasion for stipulating that extradition shall fail merely because the fugitive may succeed in finding, in the country of refuge, some state, territory or district in which the offense charged is not punishable. . . .

It is of some significance also that the construction which petitioner urges would restrict the reciprocal operation of the treaty. Under that construction the right to extradition from the United States may vary with the state or territory where the fugitive is found although extradition may be had from Great Britain with respect to all the offenses named in the treaty. While under the laws of Great Britain extradition treaties are not self-executing, and effect must be given to them by an act of Parliament designating the crimes, upon charge of which extradition from Great Britain and its dependencies may be had, all the offenses named in the two treaties have been so designated by Acts of Parliament of 1870, 33 and 34 Victoria, *c.* 52, as amended by Act of 1873, 36 and 37 Victoria, c. 60. . . .

The petitioner also objects that the Dawes-Simon extradition treaty with Great Britain of 1932, 47 Stat. 2122, is now in force; that it does not name as a treaty offense the receiving of money, knowing it to have been fraudulently obtained, the crime with which petitioner is charged, and, that by abrogating the earlier extradition treaties between the two countries it has abated this proceeding and that for the extradition of the petitioner which was brought while the Treaty of 1842 and the Convention of 1889 were in force.

The ratifications of the Dawes-Simon Treaty were announced by presidential proclamation of August 9, 1932, which declared that the treaty was made public to the end that "every article and clause thereof may be observed and fulfilled with good faith" by the United States and its citizens. Article 18 provides that: "The present treaty shall come into force in ten days after its publication in conformity with the forms prescribed by the high contracting parties.'' Under the applicable provisions of the British Extradition Act of 1870, 33 and 34 Victoria, c. 52, as amended by the Act of 1873, 36 and 37 Victoria, c. 60, extradition treaties are carried into effect and given the force of law in Great Britain by publication of an Order-in-Council embodying the terms of the treaty, and directing that the Extradition Act shall apply with respect to the foreign state which has entered into the treaty. As appears from the record, and as is conceded, no Order-in-Council has been promulgated with respect to this treaty, and the State Department appears not to have recognized it as in force in either country. See Doe v. Braden, 16 How. 635, 656.

We find it unnecessary to determine whether or not the treaty, as suggested on the argument, is now in force, and binding on the United States, although not binding on Great Britain until proclaimed by an Order-in-Council. For if we were to arrive at that conclusion, we could not say that its obligation would not extend to the offense with which petitioner is charged, or that its substitution for the earlier treaties would abate the proceeding for the extradition of petitioner or the pending *habeas corpus* proceeding.

Paragraph 18 of Article 3 of the Dawes-Simon Treaty includes among the offenses for which extradition may be demanded ''receiving any money, valuable security or other property, knowing the same to have been stolen or unlawfully obtained.'' It is insisted that ''receiving money,'' knowing the same to have been stolen or unlawfully obtained, is not the equivalent of receiving money, knowing the same to have been fraudulently obtained. . . . This phrase, like all the other words of the treaty, is to be given a meaning, if reasonably possible, and rules of construction may not be resorted to to render it meaningless or inoperative. See Mason v. United States, 260 U. S. 545, 553.

As the crime with which petitioner is charged is an extraditable offense under the Dawes-Simon Treaty, the effective promulgation of that treaty and the consequent abrogation of earlier ones would not abate the pending proceedings. The obligation of the later treaty, by its terms, extends generally to fugitives charged with the several offenses named, without regard to the date of their commission. See In re Giacomo, 12 Blatchf. 391; 1 Moore, Extradition, § 86. It does not purport to exclude from its operation crimes committed before signature or promulgation, as did Article VIII. of the Treaty of 1889. Hence, it did not by mere force of the abrogation of the earlier treaty relinquish the obligation under it to surrender the petitioner, but continued it by making the offense with which he was charged extraditable even though it antedated the treaty.

The extradition proceeding has not come to an end. The petitioner's commitment by order of the commissioner was ''to abide the order of the

Secretary of State," and continues in force so long as the Secretary may lawfully order his extradition. Hence, the new treaty, if in force, is authority for the Secretary to issue his extradition warrant under § 653 of U. S. C. A. Title 18. The detention of the petitioner being lawful under treaty provisions continuously in force since his arrest, the proceeding in *habeas corpus* is not moot and does not abate merely because the obligation to surrender the petitioner for trial upon the offense charged, and for which he is held, originating in one treaty, was continued without change of substance in the other. See Abie State Bank v. Bryan, 282 U. S. 765, 781.

Affirmed.

[MR. JUSTICE BUTLER delivered a dissenting opinion, in which MR. JUSTICE BRANDEIS and MR. JUSTICE ROBERTS joined.][1]

THE INSULL CASE.

Decision of the Greek Court of Appeals on the application of the United States of America for the extradition of Samuel Insull, Sr., 1933.

Am. Journal of Int. Law, XXVIII (1934), 362.

The Council of the Court of Appeals at Athens, . . . upon the report of the Justice Alex. Digenopoulos, rendered the following decision:

I. Whereas, according to the more correct and generally accepted view, extradition does not aim exclusively at rectifying the affront done by the accused to the law of the country demanding his extradition, and can not be granted unless the act for which the accused has been indicted or sentenced is punishable under the law of both countries, *i. e.*, the extraditing country and the country demanding the extradition (see French *Pandects*, s. v., "Extradition," Vol. 31, Nos. 226–231. *Contra*, Bernard, Vol. 2, p. 209). It is, of course, evident that the offense need not bear the same name nor be included in the same category nor be punished by the same penalty in the two sets of laws. It has finally become accepted as a general deduction, that the mere investigation as to whether the offense with which the accused is charged is included in those for which extradition is permitted under the treaty, is not sufficient or in itself satisfies the extraditing country's conception of justice, since that country is under obligation to give the accused person the same lawful protection as to its own citizens, in accordance with the

---

[1] The decision in this case has given rise to controversy. See M. O. Hudson, "The Factor Case and Double Criminality in Extradition" Am. Journal Int. Law, XXVIII (1934), 274; E. M. Borchard, "The Factor Extradition Case," *ibid.*, 742.

unwritten law of protection of the liberty of those who have taken refuge on its soil. And the most modern conceptions on this subject go still further and give the extraditing country the right to examine the substance and basis of the charges against the accused, in order that thereby additional safeguards may be created for personal liberty, without thereby wounding the susceptibilities of the country demanding the extradition, nor creating any doubt of distrust as to the dispensation of justice in the extraditing country, which on general principles is satisfied to have the offender removed out of its territory. It is self-evident that insuperable difficulties would be encountered and often a faulty judgment would be rendered by a judge, if he were forced to judge the facts without investigating them according to the law with which he is familiar and to his conception of the right of personal liberty. These correct principles are embodied in the provisions of Article 3 of Law △∧A' (1912), which, under Article 2 of Law 5554, apply to the Extradition Treaty between Greece and the United States. The latter country has applied for the extradition of the arrested person as having violated within its territory the bankruptcy laws, an offense for which extradition is permitted according to Article 2, Section 25, of the said treaty. And from Article 5 of the treaty, which forbids extradition in case by reason of prescription (under the law of limitations) or for any other lawful reason under the laws of either country, the fugitive from justice escapes the prosecution and the punishment of his offense, the acceptance of the foregoing conclusions is to be deduced.

These conclusions are furthermore clearly recognized by the wording of Article 1 of the treaty, which expressly provides that extradition can not be granted unless and in so far as, according to the laws of the extraditing country, there is sufficient evidence (plainly meaning *indications*) of guilt, justifying the arrest and commitment for trial of the accused if the offense had been committed in the extraditing country itself. Hence, it is clear that, if there has been no offense according to the laws of the extraditing country, extradition is not granted, since in such case the judge hearing the application is usually able to judge correctly of the matter and is called upon without any serious necessity to sacrifice his convictions concerning liberty of the person, derived from the conceptions of law prevailing in his country, without which it becomes impossible to serve the ends of justice, which was the objective of the parties to the treaty. And therefore, to remove any doubts on this point, this principle is expressly stated in connection with Article 2, Sections 22 and 23, of the treaty, treating of special offenses for which extradition is permitted, provided the offense is punishable under the laws of both states. Therefore, this court, being plainly incompetent to examine also the constitutionality of the laws which are quoted in the indictment, as interpreted by the competent authorities of the country demanding the extradition and on which laws the indictment is based, can only examine whether the acts charged in the indictment constitute a violation of the Greek laws on bankruptcy; and the court will then proceed to the estimation of whether the charges are well-founded and whether the evidence furnishes sufficient probabilities to justify the accused's commitment for trial, which is all that Greek law requires for commitment.

II. Whereas, according to the documents produced, the indictment charged the accused with five offenses, all committed by him and others as officers and agents of a corporation that has since gone into bankruptcy, at a time when the said corporation was insolvent, and in contemplation of the possibility of the corporation's bankruptcy, which acts were performed unlawfully, deliberately, and deceitfully, with the intention of frustrating the object of the bankruptcy law of the United States. Of these counts, the second and third, as specified in the indictment, consist in the transfer (delivery) to existing creditors of certain assets (securities) of the bankrupt corporation, for the sole purpose that these assets should serve as additional security for loans already lawfully contracted at a time when there was no doubt (*as to the corporation's solvency*). The fourth count consists in the immediate *partial* payment of $1,000,000 to an existing creditor of the bankrupt corporation, against a debt of $5,000,000 existing at the time of the said payment, although the corporation's total liabilities (according to the indictment) amounted at that time to $59,237,313.80 as against assets amounting to $35,264,445.03. The fifth act, in due consideration of the circumstances set forth in the indictment, also took place at a time when the company's liabilities were in a similar state as described above, and is nothing else than a giving of security in cash, intended as a preferential satisfaction, in the event of bankruptcy, of a real creditor, who had at that time a larger claim, as being a creditor for a sum of $4,000,000, and who received a security of $291,000. Lastly, under the first count, the accused being, together with others, an officer (Chairman of the Board of Directors and member of the Executive Committee) of the bankrupt corporation and well knowing the latter's insolvent condition, etc., handed over out of the corporation's assets and capital a sum of $558,120 to The Northern Trust Company of Chicago, which, acting on the accused's instructions, used this sum for the payment of a dividend to the holders of the company's preferred stock (amongst whom was the accused himself), which dividend was paid, not out of real earnings or surpluses of the company, but really out of its capital, the earnings and surpluses being fictitious and imaginary.

All the foregoing five counts constitute offenses (according to the indictment) against the laws of the United States, and are punishable by imprisonment not exceeding five years, if committed by officers or agents of a person or corporation who, in contemplation of the corporation's bankruptcy or with intent to frustrate the operation of the bankruptcy law, shall conceal or transfer any assets of the corporation or person, whose officers or agents they are, "transfer" being understood, under the official interpretation, to mean any alienation of the property or of its possession, whether absolute or conditional, and if attempted in any manner.

These acts constitute offenses under the Greek bankruptcy laws, as well. Our law specially and restrictively provides for the responsibility of the administrators of a bankrupt company, even to a greater extent than the American law, by Articles 680 (592) and 685 (597) of the Commercial Law. Article 680, Section 2, punishes for simple bankruptcy (in case of the company's bankruptcy) the administrators of the company, if the latter's bankruptcy was brought about through any fault of theirs. . . . It also punishes those who by fraud or through fraudulent acts cause the company's bankruptcy. The danger from the payment to the shareholders of nonexistent dividends by reducing the share of capital is manifest; and such acts are manifestly intended as a snare for the attraction of outside capital to a precarious enterprise, whose only object is the administration of such capital to the profit of the administrators, who thus prolong their benefits (Antonopoulos, Section 52). This payment of dividends manifestly non-existent at the expense of the share capital is in itself fraudulent and it is unnecessary to prove any other more specific definition of fraud. . . .

III. Whereas, after what has been said above on the strength of the evidence produced in the records (*dossier*) and the evidence produced by the defense, all duly considered and developed orally during the hearing, the court now proceeds to the examination of how far the charges against the accused are founded in fact. It has been established that the accused, now of advanced age and suffering from a serious complaint, was primarily an engineer of great enterprise, an assistant of the great inventor Edison; that he contributed in a marked and characteristic manner to the world's industrial progress, by achieving the production of cheaper electricity, whereby electricity was introduced into a variety of domestic and industrial uses. That having built up an electric empire of three billion dollars and created enterprises that were in many ways useful to mankind, he acquired such prestige in America that everybody believed that any enterprise that bore his name must be profitable, and the public hastened to buy his shares for the sole reason that they bore his name. Thus by the year 1929 he controlled a group of 52 companies, most of which are still in existence and in flourishing operation. Under the glamour of this prestige, on October 5, 1929, there was founded under his presidency (for which he received no salary) the "Corporation Securities Company of Chicago," which subsequently went into bankruptcy and out of whose activities the present prosecution has arisen. This company, according to the statutes and to the testimony of Harold Huling (p. 241), was founded to do business in general securities, buying and selling securities or holding such for sale. This object was one fraught with many dangers. A similar company, the "Insull Utilities Investments, Inc.," had already been formed on December 27, 1928, under the presidency of the accused, with exactly the same object. The capital of the Corporation Securities Company of Chicago amounted to about $144,000,000, raised chiefly from the public. According to H. Huling's testimony (p. 238), the accused and his relatives participated in the said Corporation Securities Company to the extent of 7,045,346 common and 45,436 preferred shares. The company's entire capital was invested in shares of the other Insull companies (and especially in Insull Utilities Investments), and finally evaporated, so that on the day of the company's suspension of payments (April 16, 1932), the day before the petition of bankruptcy was filed, the company's position was truly a picture of ruin. On that day the company had no assets or property whatever. According to the testimony (p. 256) of Mr. H. Huling, who carried out a general audit of the books not only of this company but also of the other companies with which it was in close relations, the Corporation Securities Company's assets on that day comprised a small amount in cash and insignificant accounts for collection, and 98 per cent of its assets consisted of company securities, while its liabilities on the same day (see p. 259 of Huling's testimony) exceeded its assets by $45,140,133.31. This was, in truth, one of the biggest failures in history, as the American press described it, and the public's unbounded confidence in the accused created irreparable disasters and many victims. It should not be overlooked that, in justice to the public, the statutes of the Corporation Securities Company of Chicago should have expressly and clearly stated that the funds collected from the sale of its capital shares would be used *exclusively* for the purchase of shares of the companies of the Insull group, as was actually done and seems to have been the real objective of the company. In fact, the object of the company, as stated in the statutes, leaves the suspicion that the company aimed, by the contributions of the public, chiefly at reinforcing the Insull group and especially those of its companies which, by reason of the impending general crisis, could not directly raise fresh capital by loans or new shares. But this in itself does not necessarily imply fraudulent intent on the part of the accused, who was entitled, under the statutes, to invest the company's capital in any securities.

It has been made clear in the present hearing that none of the companies of the Insull group (most of which were operating companies) had as yet suffered any reverses through ill-considered or unsuccessful operations; and the temporary difficulties in which they found themselves gave rise to no reasonable apprehension or even suspicion of impending collapse if affairs had followed their usual and normal course. The accused, in believing in a successful outcome for the companies of

the group and in having participated out of his own property in the
foundation of the Corporation Securities Company of Chicago, was
manifestly not inspired by any malevolent intentions. This is shown by
the early history of the Corporation Securities Company of Chicago,
when the company, under normal conditions, realized a profit of $103,000
through dividends on securities purchased and held by it. But also the
fact that the accused later on borrowed in his personal capacity various
sums for the needs of the company, shows the absence of any underhand
intentions on his part. Moreover, his attitude in the face of a great and
unforeseen general disaster, which swept everything away and spared
nobody, does not appear to have been actuated by any fraudulent intent.
A dispassionate review of the facts leaves the impression that this in-
glorious termination of a great and useful career was as heavy a blow to
him as to any one else.

It is, of course, undeniable that the accused, together with his associates, did not hesitate to commit an act which is forbidden both by the
moral law and the criminal law of all countries. It has been clearly
shown and established by documentary evidence that, for the purpose of
creating a high price for the Corporation Securities Company's shares,
by means of fraudulent and illegal sales and purchases of shares on the
Chicago Stock Exchange, in which there was no change of ownership,
he succeeded in maintaining the Corporation Securities Company's
shares at a high price at a time when these shares had a real value far
below that which, through this Satanic artifice, was registered on the
Stock Exchange bulletins. Huling, the most important of the witnesses,
in his long testimony (especially Vol. I, p. 303) states that from official
documents he was firmly convinced that such fictitious and fraudulent
transactions were performed in the year 1930 to the extent of 19.89 per
cent. and in 1931 of 27.51 per cent. of the whole number of common
shares sold. It is evident that by this artifice the public was deceived
into the belief that the Corporation Securities Company shares had the
value shown in the Stock Exchange bulletins, whereas their liquidating
or real value had declined to zero (Huling, pp. 304, 305). And for
the surer success of the said artifice and the more complete deception of
the public, the Corporation Securities Company used to pay the tax and
broker's commission on every such fictitious transaction. These are
manifestly immoral acts which no self-respecting person can commit;
but unfortunately they are not unusual in the administration of corporations, where the dominant idea is to bolster up the corporation's credit
by any means.

These acts on the part of the accused, constituting, as they do, a violation of written and unwritten law, but bearing no relation to the case
under discussion, and performed at a time when the post-war financial
whirlwind in America was sweeping away everything and overthrowing
in an instant all values, irrespectively of their intrinsic solidity, must

not be judged with the same measure of severity as would apply to normal conditions; and in any case the said acts can not in any way have been the cause of the company's subsequent bankruptcy. There can be no question that the said acts aimed at a contrary result in that they constituted an effort to save the company's credit in an entirely unforeseen emergency, which was bringing everything to the ground, without regard to antecedents. To retain what one has obtained through long years of work and effort is a universal human instinct, wherever man is not a fatalist, prepared to surrender himself without a struggle and to renounce any hope of future recovery. There was no other more legitimate and less drastic means of self-defense open to the accused, who was responsible to those who had shared in his enterprises. Lastly, these acts which tended to avert bankruptcy, aimed at no objective that comes under the bankruptcy laws. . . .

These tactics, which are a very common practice in corporations for maintaining the company's credit at all costs, are not presented in the indictment as a separate offense, and do not seem in any case to have been committed with fraudulent intent on the part of the accused and his associates, who firmly believed in the maintenance of the high prices of the shares against the great and abrupt fluctuations to which they were exposed at that time and which made it impossible to evaluate the assets on the basis of any steady prices. . . .

As regards the transfers on which the remaining four counts are based, which transfers were made in December, 1931, and January, 1932, at a time when the Corporation Securities Company was in a state of insolvency, and which were transfers of securities and cash as additional collateral to existing creditors, and a partial payment to one of these creditors, the following may be said: In the first place, there is not the slightest proof of any private bond by reason of which the accused and his associates gave preferential treatment to these real creditors of the Corporation Securities Company at a time when the company was struggling against insuperable difficulties due entirely to the general financial crisis and when the imminent danger of irreparable disaster to all concerned rendered it necessary to make these preferential transfers in order to avert the immediate collapse of the company, which would have had far-reaching and disastrous consequences.

It is undeniable that the Corporation Securities Company, with a view to a temporary adjustment of things until the storm should have passed away, from which every one was seeking to save himself at any sacrifice, endeavored, by the so-called "Standstill agreement" (see testimony of the witness F. Jackson, p. 83) to obtain the creation of a stationary condition of things. But in this matter the company encountered a categorical refusal on the part of the banks, which unreasonably demanded an immediate settlement, and it was forced to comply with this demand in order to save whatever was possible, in the hope of better days. In so doing the officers of the Corporation Securities Company were actuated by no evil intentions and were not aiming at the frustration of the operation of the Bankruptcy Act, since the latter in any case can annul any such acts without loss to the whole body of creditors, inasmuch as the creditors who were thus given preferential treatment are solvent up to the present day. Any one would have acted thus in order to forestall bankruptcy and would not hesitate to give the additional collateral demanded by the said creditors, whereby, if the situation had developed otherwise, no one would have suffered any loss and a state of things would have been forestalled which no one desired. . . .

Lastly, it must not be overlooked that the petition in bankruptcy (April 16, 1932) was not filed for a long time after the Corporation Securities Company became insolvent, and that it was not until May, 1933, that the prosecution of the accused began, who in the meantime had left the country with the good wishes of a goodly number of his fellow-citizens, after having ceded to his creditors his entire real property in the United States. All these facts show that even in the United States the acts committed by the accused were at first not considered fraudulent or as independent of the general financial crisis.

By all the foregoing considerations, the majority of this court is led to the conclusion that at present there is not sufficient evidence to justify the commitment for trial of the accused.

IV. Whereas, upon the rejection of the application for extradition, the seizure as evidence of things belonging to the accused should be remitted and the said things should be restored to him.

Now therefore, the court refuses the aforesaid application of the United States of America for the extradition of Samuel Insull, Senior, and offers the opinion that there is no lawful ground for his extradition to the United States of America.

It annuls warrant No. 263 issued on August 25, 1933, by the President of this court for the arrest of Samuel Insull, Senior, and provisionally ratified by the Council of this court by its decision No. 118/1933.

It orders the setting at liberty of the said Samuel Insull, Senior, if his detention is not necessary for any other reason. . . .[1]

---

[1] The decision of the Greek court has been the object of much criticism as amounting to a trial of the fugitive rather than an examination of evidence justifying commitment for trial. For comments, see C. C. Hyde, "Extradition Case of Samuel Insull, Sr., in relation to Greece," Am. Journal Int. Law, XXVIII (1934), 307.

Compare the decision of Judge Wilkerson in the United States District Court for the Northern District of Illinois, November 24, 1934, in the proceedings against Samuel Insull for fraudulent use of the mails. — F. (2d) —.

CHARLTON v. KELLY, SHERIFF OF HUDSON COUNTY, NEW JERSEY.

United States, Supreme Court, 1913.

229 U. S. 447. [57 L. ed. 1274; 33 S. Ct. 945.]

Appeal from the Circuit Court of the United States for the District of New Jersey.

This is an appeal from a judgment dismissing a petition for a writ of *habeas corpus* and remanding the petitioner to custody under a warrant for his extradition as a fugitive from the justice of the kingdom of Italy.

The proceedings for the extradition of the appellant were begun upon a complaint duly made by the Italian Vice Consul, charging him with the commission of a murder in Italy. A warrant was duly issued by Hon. John A. Blair, one of the judges of New Jersey, qualified to sit as a committing magistrate in such a proceeding, under § 5270, Rev. Stat. At the hearing, evidence was produced which satisfied Judge Blair that the appellant was a fugitive from justice and that he was the person whose return to Italy was desired, and that there was probable cause for holding him for trial upon the charge of murder, committed there. He thereupon committed the appellant, to be held until surrendered under a warrant to be issued by the Secretary of State. A transcript of the evidence and of the findings was duly certified as required by § 5270, Rev. Stat., and a warrant in due form for his surrender was issued by the Secretary of State. Its execution has, up to this time, been prevented by the *habeas corpus* proceedings in the court below and the pendency of this appeal. . . .

MR. JUSTICE LURTON delivered the opinion of the court. . . . The objections which are relied upon for the purpose of defeating extradition may be conveniently summarized and considered under four heads: . . .[1]

3. That appellant is a citizen of the United States, and that the treaty in providing for the extradition of "persons" accused of crime does not include persons who are citizens or subjects of the nation upon whom the demand is made.

4. That if the word "person" as used in the treaty includes citizens of the asylum country, the treaty, in so far as it covers that subject, has been abrogated by the conduct of Italy in refusing to deliver up its own citizens upon the demand of the United States, and by the enactment of a municipal law, since the treaty, forbidding the extradition of citizens.

We will consider these objections in their order: . . .

3. By Article 1 of the extradition treaty with Italy the two governments mutually agree to deliver up all persons, who, having been con-

---

[1] The first two heads dealt with evidence of the insanity of the accused and the time within which the formal demand for extradition was made after the arrest.

victed of or charged with any of the crimes specified in the following article, committed within the jurisdiction of one of the contracting parties, shall seek an asylum in the other, etc. It is claimed by counsel for the appellant that the word "persons" as used in this article does not include persons who are citizens of the asylum country.

That the word "persons" etymologically includes citizens as well as those who are not, can hardly be debatable. The treaty contains no reservation of citizens of the country of asylum. The contention is that an express exclusion of citizens or subjects is not necessary, as by implication, from accepted principles of public law, persons who are citizens of the asylum country are excluded from extradition conventions unless expressly included. This was the position taken by the Foreign Minister of Italy in a correspondence in 1890 with the Secretary of State of the United States, concerning a demand made by the United States for the extradition of Bevivini and Villella, two subjects of Italy whose extradition was sought, that they might be tried for a crime committed in this country. Their extradition was refused by Italy on account of their Italian nationality. The Foreign Minister of Italy advanced in favor of the Italian position these grounds: (a) That the Italian Penal Code of 1890, in express terms provided that, "the extradition of a citizen is not permitted;" (b) That a crime committed by an Italian subject in a foreign country was punishable in Italy, and, therefore, there was no ground for saying that unless extradited the crime would go unpunished; and (c) That it has become a recognized principle of public international law that one nation will not deliver its own citizens or subjects upon the demand of another, to be tried for a crime committed in the territory of the latter, unless it has entered into a convention expressly so contracting, and that the United States had itself recognized the principle in many treaties by inserting a clause exempting citizens from extradition. (United States Foreign Relations 1890, p. 555.) Mr. Blaine, then Secretary of State of the United States, protested against the position of the Italian government and maintained the view that citizens were included among the persons subject to extradition unless expressly excluded. His defense of the position is full and remarkably able. It is to be found in United States Foreign Relations for 1890, pp. 557, 566.

We shall pass by the effect of the Penal Code in preventing the authorities of Italy from carrying out its international engagements to surrender citizens, for that has no bearing upon the question now under consideration, which is, whether under accepted principles of international law, citizens are to be regarded as not embraced within an extradition treaty unless expressly included. That it has come to be the practice with a preponderant number of nations to refuse to deliver its citizens, is true; but this exception is convincingly shown by Mr. Blaine in his reply to the Foreign Minister of Italy and by the thorough consideration of the whole subject by Mr. John Bassett Moore, in his treatise on extradition, ch. V, pp. 152, 193, to be of modern origin. The beginning of the exemption is traced to the practice between France and the Low Countries in the eighteenth century. Owing to the existence in the municipal law of many nations of provisions prohibiting the extradition of citizens, the United States has in several of its extradition treaties clauses exempting citizens from their obligation. The treaties in force in 1910 may, therefore, be divided into two classes, those which expressly exempt citizens, and those which do not. Those which do contain the limitation are by far the larger number. Among the treaties which provide for the extradition of "persons," without limitation or qualification are the following:

With Great Britain, August 9, 1842, extended July 12, 1889, United States Treaties, 1910, pp. 650 and 740.

With France, November 9, 1843, *supra*, p. 526.

With Italy, February 8, 1868, *supra*, p. 961.

With Venezuela, August 27, 1860, *supra*, p. 1845.

With Ecuador, June 28, 1872, *supra*, p. 436.

With Dominican Republic, February 8, 1867, *supra*, p. 403.

The treaty with Japan of April 29, 1886, *supra*, p. 1025, contains a qualification in these words:

"Art. VII. Neither of the contracting parties shall be bound to deliver up its own citizens or subjects under the stipulations of this convention, but they shall have the power to deliver them up if in their discretion it be deemed proper to do so."

The conclusion we reach is, that there is no principle of international law by which citizens are excepted out of an agreement to surrender "persons," where no such exception is made in the treaty itself. Upon the contrary, the word "persons" includes all persons when not qualified as it is in some of the treaties between this and other nations. That this country has made such an exception in some of its conventions and not in others, demonstrates that the contracting parties were fully aware of the consequences unless there was a clause qualifying the word "persons." This interpretation has been consistently upheld by the United States, and enforced under the several treaties which do not exempt citizens. That Italy has not conformed to this view, and the effect of this attitude will be considered later. But that the United States has always construed its obligation as embracing its citizens is illustrated by the action of the executive branch of the Government in this very instance. A construction of a treaty by the political department of the Government, while not conclusive upon a court called upon to construe such a treaty in a matter involving personal rights, is nevertheless of much weight.

The subject is summed up by Mr. John Bassett Moore in his work on extradition, vol. 1, p. 170, § 138, where he says:

"'Persons' includes citizens. In respect to the persons to be surrendered, the extradition treaties of the United States all employ the general term 'persons,' or 'all persons.' Hence, where no express exception is made, the treaties warrant no distinction as to nationality. Writing on the general subject of the extradition treaties of the United States and the practice thereunder, Mr. Seward said: 'In some of the United States' extradition treaties it is stipulated that the citizens or subjects of the parties shall not be surrendered. Where there is no express reservation of the kind, there would not, it is presumed, be any hesitation in giving up a citizen of the United States to be tried abroad.' Such has been the uniform and unquestioned practice under the treaty with Great Britain of 1842, in which the term 'all persons' is used.''

The effect of yielding to the interpretation urged by Italy would have brought about most serious consequences as to other treaties then in force. One of these was the extradition treaty with Great Britain made as far back as 1843. Inasmuch as under the law of that country, as of this, crimes committed by their citizens within the jurisdiction of another country were punishable only where the crime was committed, it was important that the Italian interpretation should not be accepted. . . .

4. We come now to the contention that by the refusal of Italy to deliver up fugitives of Italian nationality, the treaty has thereby ceased to be of obligation on the United States. The attitude of Italy is indicated by its Penal Code of 1900 which forbids the extradition of citizens, and by the denial in two or more instances to recognize this obligation of the treaty as extending to its citizens. . . .

The attitude of the Italian government indicated by proffering this request for extradition ''in accordance with Article V of the Treaty of 1868,'' is, as shown by the communication of July 1st set out above, substantially this,—

First. That crimes committed by an American in a foreign country were not justiciable in the United States, and must, therefore, go unpunished unless the accused be delivered to the country wherein the crime was committed for trial.

Second: Such was not the case with Italy, since under the laws of Italy, crimes committed by its subjects in foreign lands were justiciable in Italy.

Third: That as a consequence of the difference in the municipal law, ''it was logical that so far as parity in the matter of extraditing their respective citizens or subjects is concerned, each party should, in the absence of specific provisions in the Convention itself, be guided by the spirit of its own legislation.''

This adherence to a view of the obligation of the treaty as not requiring one country to surrender its nationals while it did the other, presented a situation in which the United States might do either of two things, namely: abandon its own interpretation of the word persons as including citizens, or adhere to its own interpretation and surrender the appellant, although the obligation had, as to nationals, ceased to be reciprocal. The United States could not yield its own interpretation of the treaty, since that would have had the most serious consequence on five other treaties in which the word "persons" had been used in its ordinary meaning, as including *all persons,* and, therefore, not exempting citizens. If the attitude of Italy was, as contended, a violation of the obligation of the treaty, which, in international law, would have justified the United States in denouncing the treaty as no longer obligatory, it did not automatically have that effect. If the United States elected not to declare its abrogation, or come to a rupture, the treaty would remain in force. It was only voidable, not void; and if the United States should prefer, it might waive any breach which in its judgment had occurred and conform to its own obligation as if there had been no such breach. 1 Kent's Comm., p. 175. . . . .

In the case of In re Thomas, 12 Blatchf. 370, Mr. Justice Blatchford (then District Judge) said:

"Indeed, it is difficult to see how such a treaty as that between Bavaria and the United States can be abrogated by the action of Bavaria alone, without the consent of the United States. Where a treaty is violated by one of the contracting parties, it rests alone with the injured party to pronounce it broken, the treaty being, in such case, not absolutely void, but voidable, at the election of the injured party, who may waive or remit the infraction committed, or may demand a just satisfaction, the treaty remaining obligatory if he chooses not to come to a rupture." . . .

That the political branch of the Government recognizes the treaty obligation as still existing is evidenced by its action in this case. In the memorandum giving the reasons of the Department of State for determining to surrender the appellant, after stating the difference between the two governments as to the interpretation of this clause of the treaty, Mr. Secretary Knox said:

"The question is now for the first time presented as to whether or not the United States is under obligation under treaty to surrender to Italy for trial and punishment citizens of the United States fugitive from the justice of Italy, notwithstanding the interpretation placed upon the treaty by Italy with reference to Italian subjects. In this connection it should be observed that the United States, although, as stated above, consistently contending that the Italian interpretation was not the proper one, has not treated the Italian practice as a breach of the treaty obligation necessarily requiring abrogation, has not abrogated the treaty or taken any step looking thereto, and has, on the contrary, constantly regarded the treaty as in full force and effect and has answered the obligations imposed thereby and has invoked the rights therein granted. It should, moreover, be observed that even though the action of the Italian Government be regarded as a breach of the treaty, the treaty is binding until abrogated, and therefore the treaty not having been abrogated, its provisions are operative against us.

"The question would, therefore, appear to reduce itself to one of interpretation of the meaning of the treaty, the Government of the United States being now for the first time called upon to declare whether it regards the treaty as obliging it to surrender its citizens to Italy, notwithstanding Italy has not and insists it can not surrender its citizens to us. It should be observed, in the first place, that we have always insisted not only with reference to the Italian extradition treaty, but with reference to the other extradition treaties similarly phrased that the word 'persons' includes citizens. We are, therefore, committed to that interpretation. The fact that we have for reasons already given ceased generally to make requisition upon the Government of Italy for the surrender of Italian subjects under the treaty, would not require of necessity that we should, as a matter of logic or law, regard ourselves as free from the obligation of surrendering our citizens, we laboring under no such legal inhibition regarding surrender as operates against the government of Italy. Therefore, since extradition treaties need not be reciprocal, even in the matter of the surrendering of citizens, it would seem entirely sound to consider ourselves as bound to surrender our citizens to Italy even though Italy should not, by reason of the provisions of her municipal law be able to surrender its citizens to us."

The executive department having thus elected to waive any right to free itself from the obligation to deliver up its own citizens, it is the plain duty of this court to recognize the obligation to surrender the appellant as one imposed by the treaty as the supreme law of the land and as affording authority for the warrant of extradition.

Judgment affirmed.[1]

---

[1] Supplementary Cases. Query, may a fugitive from justice who has been kidnapped in the country of asylum and forcibly brought back to the place where the crime was committed and there convicted enter a plea in abatement on ground of the unlawful character of his arrest? In Ker v. Illinois, 119 U. S. 436 (1886) the court held that the forcible abduction of Ker from Peru without the formality of extradition proceedings was "no sufficient reason why the party should not answer when brought within the jurisdiction of the court which has the right to try him for such an offense." That did not mean, however, that the Government of Peru was without a remedy for the unauthorized seizure or that the prisoner himself could not sue the kidnapper in an action of trespass and false imprisonment. Compare State v. Brewster, 7 Vt. 118 (1835), where the fugitive was forcibly brought back from Canada by citizens of the United States. The court held that it was not for it "to inquire by what means, or in what precise manner, he may have been brought within the reach of justice." The fugitive himself had no claim to protection, and if a wrong was done to the foreign sovereignty that was a matter which concerned "the political relations of the two countries." See also Ex parte Lopez, 6 F. Supp. 342 (1934), where the court denied a writ of habeas corpus on behalf of a person who had been abducted from Mexico to be tried in the United States for violation of the narcotic laws. The intervention of the Mexican Government on behalf of

C. Scope of "political offenses."

Practically all treaties of extradition make exception of offenses of a "political character." This is consistent with the principle that the offense must be one which is regarded as a crime in both countries; but it raises a question as to what are to be considered "political" crimes? Would a murder committed in a riot having as its object the overthrow of the government be a political crime? [In re Castioni.] Would the death of an innocent bystander due to the explosion of a bomb by an anarchist seeking to destroy government property be a "political offense" within the meaning of an extradition treaty? [In re Meunier.]

IN RE CASTIONI.

Great Britain, Queen's Bench Division, 1890.

L. R. [1891] 1 Q. B. 149.

Application for habeas corpus. The motion was made on behalf of Angelo Castioni, for an order nisi calling upon the Solicitor to the Treasury, Franklin Lushington, Esq., a metropolitan police magistrate, and the consul general of Switzerland, as representatives of the Swiss Republic, to show cause why a writ of habeas corpus should not issue to bring up the body of Castioni in order that he might be discharged from custody.

The prisoner Castioni had been arrested in England on the requisition of the Swiss government, and brought before the magistrate at the police court at Bow Street, and by him committed to prison for the purpose of extradition, on a charge of willful murder, alleged to have been committed in Switzerland. . . .

The prisoner was charged with the murder of Luigi Rossi, by shooting him with a revolver on September 11, 1890, in the town of Bellinzona, in the canton of Ticino in Switzerland. The deceased, Rossi, was a member of the State Council of the canton of Ticino, and was about twenty-six years of age. The prisoner, Castioni, was a citizen of the same canton; he had resided for seventeen years in England, and arrived at Bellinzona on September 10, 1890. For some time previous to this date much dissatisfaction had been felt and expressed by a large number of the inhabitants of Ticino at the mode in which the political party then in power were conducting the government of the canton. A request was pre-

---

the prisoner was a matter which might "well be presented to the Executive Department" but of which the court had no jurisdiction.

In the case of Dominguez v. State, 90 Tex. Cr. 92 (1921), the court held that the rule that a person extradited may not be tried for any crime other than that for which the requisition was granted was applicable to a person who had been captured by United States troops on foreign soil when in hot pursuit of bandits.

sented to the Government for a revision of the constitution of the canton, under art. 15 of the constitution, which provides that "The constitution of the canton may be revised wholly or partially . . . (b) at the request of 7000 citizens presented with the legal formalities. In this case the Council shall within one month submit to the people the question whether or not they wish to revise the constitution," and a law of May 9, 1877, prescribes the course to be adopted for the execution of letter (b) of art. 15. The Government having declined to take a popular vote on the question of the revision of the constitution, on September 11, 1890, a number of the citizens of Bellinzona, among whom was Castioni, seized the arsenal of the town, from which they took rifles and ammunition, disarmed the gendarmes, arrested, and bound or handcuffed, several persons connected with the Government, and forced them to march in front of the armed crowd to the municipal palace. Admission to the palace was demanded in the name of the people, and was refused by Rossi and another member of the Government, who were in the palace. The crowd then broke open the outer gate of the palace, and rushed in, pushing before them the Government officials whom they had arrested and bound; Castioni, who was armed with a revolver, was among the first to enter. A second door, which was locked, was broken open, and at this time, or immediately after, Rossi, who was in the passage, was shot through the body with a revolver, and died very soon afterwards. Some other shots were fired, but no one else was injured. Two witnesses, who were present when the shot was fired, and were called before the magistrate at Bow Street, identified Castioni as the person who fired the shot. One of the witnesses called for the prisoner was an advocate named Bruni, who had taken a leading part in the attack on the municipal palace. In cross-examination he said: "The death of Rossi was a misfortune, and not necessary for the rising." There was no evidence that Castioni had any previous knowledge of Rossi. The crowd then occupied the palace, disarmed the gendarmes who were there, and imprisoned several members of the Government. A provisional government was appointed, of which Bruni was a member, and assumed the government of the canton, which it retained until dispossessed by the armed intervention of the Federal Government of the Republic.

The magistrate was of opinion that the identification of Castioni was sufficient, and held upon the evidence that the bar to extradition specified in s. 3 of the Extradition Act, 1870 did not exist, and committed Castioni to prison. . . .

DENMAN, J. . . . I am unable to entertain a doubt that this is a case in which we ought to order that the prisoner be discharged. . . .

There has been no legal decision as yet upon the meaning of the words contained in the Act of 1870, upon the true meaning of which this case mainly depends. . . . I do not think it is necessary or desirable that we should attempt to put into language, in the shape of an exhaustive definition, exactly the whole state of things, or every state of things which might bring a particular case within the description of an offence of a political character. I wish, however, to express an opinion as to one matter upon which I entertain a very strong opinion. That is, that if the description given by Mr. John Stuart Mill, ["Any offence committed in the course of or furthering of civil war, insurrection, or political commotion,"] were to be construed in the sense that it really means any act which takes place in the course of a political rising without reference to the object and intention of it, and other circumstances connected with it, I should say that it was a wrong definition and one which could not be legally applied to the words in the Act of Parliament. Sir Charles Russell suggested that "in the course of" was to be read with the words following, "or in furtherance of," and that "in furtherance of" is equivalent to "in the course of." I cannot quite think that this was the intention of the speaker, or is the natural meaning of the expression; but I entirely concur with the observation of the Solicitor-General that in the other sense of the words, if they are not to be construed as merely equivalent expressions, it would be a wrong definition. I think that in order to bring the case within the words of the Act and to exclude extradition for such an act as murder, which is one of the extradition offences, it must at least be shown that the act is done in furtherance of, done with the intention of assistance, as a sort of overt act in the course of acting in a political matter, a political rising, or a dispute between two parties in the State as to which is to have the government in its hands, before it can be brought within the meaning of the words used in the Act. . . .

It seems to me that it is a question of mixed law and fact—mainly indeed of fact—as to whether the facts are such as to bring the case within the restriction of s. 3, and to show that it was an offence of a political character. I do not think it is disputed, or that now it can be looked upon as in controversy, that there was at this time existing in Ticino a state of things which would certainly show that there was more than a mere small rising of a few people against the law of the State. I think it is clearly made out by the facts of this case, that there was something of a very serious character going on—amounting, I should go so far as to say, in that small community, to a state of war. There was an armed body of men who had seized arms from the arsenal of the State; they were rushing into the municipal council chamber in which the Government of the State used to assemble; they demanded admission; admission was refused; some firing took place; the outer gate was broken down; and I think it also appears perfectly plain from the evidence in the case that Castioni was a person who had been taking part in that movement at a much earlier stage. He was an active party in the movement; he had taken part in the binding of one member of the

Government. Some time before he arrived with his pistol in his hand at the seat of government, he had gone with multitudes of men, armed with arms from the arsenal, in order to attack the seat of government, and I think it must be taken that it is quite clear that from the very first, he was an active party, one of the rebellious party who was acting and in the attack against the Government. . . . At the moment at which Castioni fired the shot, the reasonable presumption is, not that it is a matter of absolute certainty (we cannot be absolutely certain about anything as to men's motives), but the reasonable assumption is that he, at the moment knowing nothing about Rossi, having no spite or ill-will against Rossi, as far as we know, fired that shot—that he fired it thinking it would advance and that it was an act which was in furtherance of, and done intending it to be in furtherance of, the very object which the rising had taken place in order to promote, and to get rid of the Government, who, he might, until he had absolutely got into the place, have supposed were resisting the entrance of the people to that place. . . . There is evidence that there was great confusion; there is evidence of shots fired after the shot which Castioni fired; and all I can say is, that looking at it as a question of fact, I have come to the conclusion that at the time at which that shot was fired he acted in the furtherance of the unlawful rising to which at that time he was a party, and an active party—a person who had been doing active work from a very much earlier period, and in which he was still actively engaged. That being so, I think the writ ought to issue, and that we should be acting contrary to the spirit of this enactment, and to the fair meaning of it, if we were to allow him to be detained in custody longer.

Hawkins, J. I am of the same opinion. . . .

Now, I entirely dissent, and I think all reasonable persons would dissent, from the proposition that any act done in the course of a political rising, or in the course of any insurrection, is necessarily of a political character. Everybody would agree, I think, with this—that it is not everything done during the period during which a political rising exists that could be said to be of a political character. A man might be joining in an insurrection, joining in a rising, joining in that which in itself is a pure political matter, but notwithstanding that he were engaged in a political rising, if he were deliberately, for a matter of private revenge or for the purpose of doing injury to another, to shoot an unoffending man, because he happened himself to be one of an insurgent crowd and had a revolver in his hand, no reasonable man would question that he was guilty of the crime of murder, because that offence so committed by him could not be said to have any relation at all to a political crime, namely, a crime which in law ought to be punished with the punishment awarded for such a crime.

Now, what is the meaning of crime of a political character? I have thought over this matter very much indeed, and I have thought whether any definition can be given of the political character of the crime—I mean to say, in language which is satisfactory. I have found none at all, and I can imagine for myself none so satisfactory, and to my mind so complete, as that which I find in a work which I have now before me, and the language of which for the purpose of my present judgment I entirely adopt, and that is the expression of my brother Stephen in his History of the Criminal Law of England in vol. ii., pp. 70, 71. I will not do more than refer to the interpretations, other than those with which he agrees, which have been given upon this expression, "political character"; but I adopt his definition absolutely. "The third meaning which may be given to the words, and which I take to be the true meaning, is somewhat more complicated than either of those I have described. An act often falls under several different definitions. For instance, if a civil war were to take place, it would be high treason by levying war against the Queen. Every case in which a man was shot in action would be murder. Whenever a house was burnt for military purposes arson would be committed. To take cattle, &c., by requisition would be robbery. According to the common use of language, however, all such acts would be political offences, because they would be incidents in carrying on a civil war. I think, therefore, that the expression in the Extradition Act ought (unless some better interpretation of it can be suggested) to be interpreted to mean that fugitive criminals are not to be surrendered for extradition crimes, if those crimes were incidental to and formed a part of political disturbances. I do not wish to enter into details before hand on a subject which might at any moment come under judicial consideration." The question has come under judicial consideration, and having had the opportunity before this case arose of carefully reading and considering the views of my learned brother, having heard all that can be said upon the subject, I adopt his language as the definition that I think is the most perfect to be found or capable of being given as to what is the meaning of the phrase which is made use of in the Extradition Act.

Now, was this act done by Castioni of a political character? . . . I find no evidence which satisfies me that his object in firing at Rossi was to take that poor man's life, or to pay off any old grudge which he had against him, or to revenge himself for anything in the least degree which Rossi or any one of the community had ever personally done to him. When it is said that he took aim at Rossi, there is not a particle of evidence that Rossi was even known to him by name. I cannot help thinking that everybody knows there are many acts of a political character done without reason, done against all reason; but at the same time, one cannot look too hardly and weigh in golden scales the acts of men hot in their political excitement. We know that in heat and in heated blood men often do things which are against and contrary to reason; but none the less an act of this description may be done for the purpose of furthering and in furtherance of a political rising, even though it is an act which may be deplored and lamented, as even cruel and against all reason, by those who can calmly reflect upon it after the battle is over.

For the reasons I have expressed, I am of opinion that . . . the prisoner ought to be discharged.

[Stephen, J., delivered a concurring opinion.]

IN RE MEUNIER.

Great Britain, High Court of Justice, Queen's Bench Division, 1894.

L. R. [1894] 2 Q. B. 415.

Application for a writ of habeas corpus to bring up and discharge a prisoner named Meunier, who had been committed by Sir John Bridge, the Chief Magistrate at Bow Street, for surrender to the French Government under the Extradition Acts, 1870 and 1873 (33 & 34 Vict. c. 52; 36 & 37 Vict. c. 60).

The prisoner was charged with wilfully causing two explosions in France, one at the Café Véry in Paris, which caused the death of two persons, and the other at certain barracks. It was proved by the witnesses whose depositions were taken in France, as well as by a statement voluntarily made by the prisoner himself to the inspector of police who arrested him in London, that the prisoner was an anarchist.

The application was made in vacation by summons at chambers, which Kennedy, J., referred to the Court.

The grounds of the application were four: (1.) that there was no evidence that the prisoner Meunier, who was brought up and committed at Bow Street, was the same person as Meunier, who was charged with the offences committed in France, and was referred to in the depositions taken in France; (2.) that the evidence relied on to connect the prisoner with the offences charged was the evidence of an accomplice, and was not corroborated; (3.) that two separate and distinct offences were included in one committal; (4.) that the explosion at the barracks was an offense of a political character, within the meaning of the Extradition Act, 1870 (33 & 34 Vict. c. 52) s. 3, sub-s. 1, and therefore the prisoner was not liable to be surrendered in respect of that offence.

Cave, J. I am of opinion that this application for a writ of habeas corpus must be refused. . . .

The last point [1] taken is, that, so far as regards the outrage at the barracks, the offence charged is one of a political character, and therefore the accused is not liable to be surrendered under the Extradition Acts; for it is said that the outrage was an attack on Government property, and was an attempt to destroy the quarters occupied by the troops of the French Government. It appears to me that, in order to constitute an offence of a political character, there must be two or more parties in the State, each seeking to impose the Government of their own choice on the other, and that, if the offence is committed by one side or the other in pursuance of that object, it is a political offence, otherwise not. In the present case there are not two parties in the State, each seeking to impose the Government of their own choice on the other; for the party with whom the accused is identified by the evidence, and by his own voluntary statement, namely, the party of anarchy, is the enemy of all Governments. Their efforts are directed primarily against the general body of citizens. They may, secondarily and incidentally, commit offences against some particular Government; but anarchist offences are mainly directed against private citizens. I agree, as to this question also, with the view taken by Sir John Bridge; and I am of opinion that the crime charged was not a political offence within the meaning of the Extradition Act.

For these reasons I am of opinion that the contention on behalf of the prisoner fails on all grounds, and that the application for a writ of habeas corpus must be refused.

COLLINS, J. I am of the same opinion, and on the same grounds. Application refused.

D. Letters rogatory.

It has become a common practice for the courts of justice of different countries to give mutual aid in the administration of justice by compelling persons within their jurisdiction to appear and give their depositions to be used as testimony in the courts of a foreign country. A request from the foreign court for such a deposition is known as a "letter rogatory," informing the local court of the action that is pending and of the testimony desired. Query, what if the request were to go so far as to ask the local court to serve process upon a person so as to compel him to answer to a suit brought against him in the foreign country? [In re Letters Rogatory out of First Civil Court of City of Mexico.]

---

[1] Other points dealt with the identity of the prisoner, the evidence of guilt, and the form of committal.

IN RE LETTERS ROGATORY OUT OF FIRST CIVIL COURT OF CITY OF MEXICO.

United States, District Court, Southern District of New York, 1919.

261 Fed. 652.

AUGUSTUS N. HAND, District Judge. This is a motion to vacate an order directing the service of a summons within this district upon a resident to answer to a suit brought against him in the republic of Mexico for the payment of rent and redelivery of certain property which is claimed by virtue of a contract of lease made in the city of Mexico for the term of one year, from June, 1914, to June, 1915. The process was accompanied by a request from the judge of the court having jurisdiction in the city of Mexico that process of that court be served upon defendant in New York. This judicial request is said to come within the definition of letters rogatory in the civil law, is addressed to any one who may be a judge having jurisdiction over a civil case in the city of New York, and, as translated, reads as follows:

"In order that such decisions may be accomplished in the name of the national sovereignty existing between the two nations, allow me the honor of sending this requisitorial letter, begging that, when you get it, do me the favor of deciding to accomplish it in its terms, and, when it is made, send it back to this court, assuring you my reciprocity in similar cases at your request."

I am referred to the following articles of the Civil Code of Mexico deemed to be applicable to the situation:

"Art. 25. Both Mexicans and foreigners residing in the federal district or in (Lower) California may be sued in the courts of this country, on obligations contracted with Mexicans or foreigners within or without the republic.

"Art. 26. They may also be sued in said courts, even though they do not reside in said places, if they have property which is affected by any obligations contracted or if the same are to be performed in said places."

By reason of the foregoing provisions, it is apparently possible through the aid of this court to render the person sought to be served subject to a personal judgment in Mexico, because the contract sued upon was to be performed there. Such a result is contrary to our own system of jurisprudence, which treats the legal jurisdiction of a court as limited to persons and property within its territorial jurisdiction. Pennoyer v. Neff, 95 U. S. 714, 24 L. Ed. 565. It is undesirable, in my opinion, to aid a process which may require residents of this district to submit to the burden of defending foreign suits brought in distant countries, where they have no property, or as an alternative to suffer a personal judgment by default, which will be enforceable against them personally whenever they may enter the foreign territory. As a matter of policy, the matter would be quite different, if the effect of the service would only be a judgment enforceable against property of the defendant in Mexico.

While this court has power to execute letters rogatory in the sense in which the term is used in the American and English law, neither it nor, so far as I can discover from the reported decisions, any other American or English court, has by an order directing the service of process aided a foreign tribunal to acquire jurisdiction over a party within the United States. Letters rogatory have been so long familiar to our courts, and so exclusively limited by understanding and in practice to proceedings in the nature of commissions to take depositions of witnesses at the request of a foreign court, that I should hardly feel inclined to assume such a novel jurisdiction as is proposed without statutory authority, even if I regarded the case as one where, as a matter of sound policy, aid should be given to the foreign tribunal.

The New York Supreme Court reached a similar conclusion to the one I have arrived at, for much the same reasons that I have given, in the Matter of Romero, 56 Misc. Rep. 319, 107 N. Y. Supp. 621.

It is unnecessary to discuss whether the general power of this court to execute letters rogatory is inherent in it as a court, or is derived solely from section 875 of the Revised Statutes (Comp. St. § 1486). In re Letters Rogatory (C. C.) 36 Fed. 306; In re Pacific Railway Commission (C. C.) 32 Fed. 256; De Villeneuve v. Morning Journal Ass'n (D. C.) 206 Fed. 70.

The motion to vacate the order is granted, both on the ground that the judicial aid invoked is without precedent, and also because it is contrary to the ideas of American courts as to the limits of judicial jurisdiction.

E. Comity in matters of jurisdiction.

In the administration of justice in cases involving either citizens or resident aliens it frequently happens that national courts are called upon to apply the provisions of foreign laws under which the acts involved in the dispute were performed. The body of rules that has developed from this practice is known as the "conflict of laws," and its content is a matter of national law; while the practice by which nations give such mutual recognition to foreign legislative, executive and judicial acts is known as "comity." Query, is reciprocity an essential condition upon which full faith and credit will be given by one state to the judgments of a foreign court? [Hilton v. Guyot.]

HILTON v. GUYOT.

United States, Supreme Court, 1895.

159 U. S. 113.   [40 L. ed. 95; 16 S. Ct. 139.]

In Error to [and Appeal from] the Circuit Court of the United States for the Southern District of New York.

The first of these two cases was an action at law, brought December 18, 1885, in the Circuit Court of the United States for the Southern District of New York, by Gustave Bertin Guyot, as official liquidator of the firm of Charles Fortin & Co., and by the surviving members of that firm, all aliens and citizens of the republic of France, against Henry Hilton and William Libbey, citizens of the United States and of the state of New York, and trading as copartners, in the cities of New York and Paris, and elsewhere, under the firm name of A. T. Stewart & Co. The action was upon a judgment recovered in a French court at Paris, in the republic of France, by the firm of Charles Fortin & Co., all of whose members were French citizens, against Hilton & Libbey, trading as copartners, as aforesaid, and citizens of the United States and of the state of New York. . . .

The complaint further alleged that between March 1, 1879, and December 1, 1882, five suits were brought by Fortin & Co. against Stewart & Co. for sums alleged to be due, and three suits by Stewart & Co. against Fortin & Co., in the tribunal of commerce of the department of the Seine, a judicial tribunal or court, organized and existing under the laws of France, sitting at Paris, and having jurisdiction of suits and controversies between merchants or traders growing out of commercial dealings between them; that Stewart & Co. appeared by their authorized attorneys in all those suits; and that . . . final judgment was rendered on January 20, 1883, that Fortin & Co. recover of Stewart & Co. various sums, arising out of the dealings between them, amounting to 660,847 francs, with interest, . . .

The complaint further alleged that appeals were taken by both parties from that judgment to the court of appeals of Paris, . . . and that the said court of appeal, by a final judgment, rendered March 19, 1884, . . . confirmed the judgment of the lower court in favor of the plaintiffs, and ordered, upon the plaintiffs' appeal, that they recover the additional sum of 152,528 francs, with 182,849 francs for interest on all the claims allowed, and 12,559 francs for costs and expenses.

The complaint further alleged that Guyot had been duly appointed . . . official liquidator of the firm of Fortin & Co., with full powers, according to law and commercial usage, for the verification and realization of its property, both real and personal, and to collect and cause to be executed the judgments aforesaid. . . .

The defendants, in their answer, set forth in detail the original contracts and transactions in France between the parties, and the subsequent dealings between them, modifying those contracts, and alleged that the plaintiffs had no just claim against the defendants, but that, on the contrary, the defendants, upon a just settlement of the accounts, were entitled to recover large sums from the plaintiffs. . . .

The answer further alleged that the tribunal of commerce of the department of the Seine was a tribunal whose judges were merchants, ship captains, stockbrokers, and persons engaged in commercial pursuits, and of which Charles Fortin had been a member until shortly before the commencement of the litigation. . . .

The answer further alleged that pending that litigation the defendants discovered gross frauds in the accounts of Fortin & Co., that the arbitrator and the tribunal declined to compel Fortin & Co. to produce their books and papers for inspection, and that, if they had been produced, the judgment would not have been obtained against the defendants. . . .

The answer further alleged . . . .

"That the construction given to said statutes [of France] by the judicial tribunals of France is such that no comity is displayed towards the judgments of tribunals of foreign countries against the citizens of France, when sued upon in said courts of France, and the merits of the controversies upon which the said judgments are based are examined anew, unless a treaty to the contrary effect exists between the said Republic of France and the country in which such judgment is obtained. That no treaty exists between the said Republic of France and the United States, by the terms or effect of which the judgments of either country are prevented from being examined anew upon the merits, when sued upon in the courts of the country other than that in which it is obtained. That the tribunals of the Republic of France give no force and effect, within the jurisdiction of the said country, to the duly rendered judgments of courts of competent jurisdiction of the United States against citizens of France, after proper personal service of the process of said courts is made thereon in this country." . . .

The defendants, on June 22, 1888, filed a bill in equity against the plaintiffs, setting forth the same matters as in their answer to the action at law, and praying for a discovery, and for an injunction against the prosecution of the action. To that bill a plea was filed, setting up the French judgments, and upon a hearing the bill was dismissed. 42 Fed. Rep. 249. From the decree dismissing the bill an appeal was taken, which is the second case now before this court.

The action at law afterwards came on for trial by a jury, and the plaintiffs put in the records of the proceedings and judgments in the French courts, . . .

The records of the judgments of the French courts, put in evidence by the plaintiffs, showed that all the matters now relied on to show fraud were contested in and considered by those courts. . . .

The court . . . directed a verdict for the plaintiffs in the sum of $277,775.44, being the amount of the French judgment and interest. The defendants, having duly excepted to the rulings and direction of the court, sued out a writ of error. . . .

Mr. Justice Gray . . . delivered the opinion of the court.

These two cases—the one at law and the other in equity—of Hilton v. Guyot, and the case of Ritchie v. McMullen, which has been under advisement at the same time, present important questions relating to the force and effect of foreign judgments, not hitherto adjudicated by this court, which have been argued with great learning and ability, and which require for their satisfactory determination a full consideration of the authorities. To avoid confusion in indicating the parties, it will be convenient first to take the case at law of Hilton v. Guyot.

International law, in its widest and most comprehensive sense,—including not only questions of right between nations, governed by what has been appropriately called the "law of nations," but also questions arising under what is usually called "private international law," or the "conflict of laws," and concerning the rights of persons within the territory and dominion of one nation, by reason of acts, private or public, done within the dominions of another nation,—is part of our law, and must be ascertained and administered by the courts of justice as often as such questions are presented in litigation between man and man, duly submitted to their determination.

The most certain guide, no doubt, for the decision of such questions is a treaty or a statute of this country. But when, as is the case here, there is no written law upon the subject, the duty still rests upon the judicial tribunals of ascertaining and declaring what the law is, whenever it becomes necessary to do so, in order to determine the rights of parties to suits regularly brought before them. In doing this, the courts must obtain such aid as they can from judicial decisions, from the works of jurists and commentators, and from the acts and usages of civilized nations. Fremont v. United States, 17 How. 542, 557; The Scotia, 14 Wall. 170, 188; Respublica v. De Longchamps, 1 Dall. 111, 116; Moultrie v. Hunt, 23 N. Y. 394, 396.

No law has any effect, of its own force, beyond the limits of the sovereignty from which its authority is derived. The extent to which the law of one nation, as put in force within its territory, whether by executive order, by legislative act, or by judicial decree, shall be allowed to operate within the dominion of another nation, depends upon what our greatest jurists have been content to call "the comity of nations." Although the phrase has been often criticised, no satisfactory substitute has been suggested.

"Comity," in the legal sense, is neither a matter of absolute obligation, on the one hand, nor of mere courtesy and good will, upon the other. But it is the recognition which one nation allows within its territory to the legislative, executive, or judicial acts of another nation, hav g due regard both to international duty and convenience, and to the rights of its own citizens, or of other persons who are under the protection of its laws. . . .

In order to appreciate the weight of the various authorities cited at the bar, it is important to distinguish different kinds of judgments. Every foreign judgment, of whatever nature, in order to be entitled to any effect, must have been rendered by a court having jurisdiction of the cause, and upon regular proceedings, and due notice. In alluding to different kinds of judgments, therefore, such jurisdiction, proceedings, and notice will be assumed. It will also be assumed that they are untainted by fraud, the effect of which will be considered later.

A judgment *in rem,* adjudicating the title to a ship or other movable property within the custody of the court, is treated as valid everywhere. As said by Chief Justice Marshall: ''The sentence of a competent court, proceeding *in rem,* is conclusive with respect to the thing itself, and operates as an absolute change of the property. By such sentence the right of the former owner is lost, and a complete title given to the person who claims under the decree. No court of co-ordinate jurisdiction can examine the sentence. The question, therefore, respecting its conformity to general or municipal law can never arise, for no co-ordinate tribunal is capable of making the inquiry.'' Williams v. Armroyd, 7 Cranch, 423, 432. The most common illustrations of this are decrees of courts of admiralty and prize, which proceed upon principles of international law. Croudson v. Leonard, 4 Cranch, 434; Williams v. Armroyd, above cited; Ludlow v. Dale, 1 Johns. Cas. 16. But the same rule applies to judgments *in rem* under municipal law. Hudson v. Guestier, 4 Cranch, 293; Ennis v. Smith, 14 How. 400, 430; Wisconsin v. Pelican Ins. Co., 127 U. S. 265, 291; Scott v. McNeal, 154 U. S. 34, 46; Castrique v. Imrie, L. R. 4 H. L. 414; Monroe v. Douglas, 4 Sandf. Ch. 126.

A judgment affecting the status of persons, such as a decree confirming or dissolving a marriage, is recognized as valid in every country, unless contrary to the policy of its own law. . . . It was of a foreign sentence of divorce that Lord Chancellor Nottingham, in the House of Lords, in 1688, in Cottington's Case, above cited, said: ''It is against the law of nations not to give credit to the judgments and sentences of foreign countries till they be reversed by the law, and according to the form, of those countries wherein they were given; for what right hath one kingdom to reverse the judgment of another? And how can we refuse to let a sentence take place till it be reversed? And what confusion would follow in Christendom, if they should serve us so abroad, and give no credit to our sentences!'' . . .

The extraterritorial effect of judgments *in personam,* at law, or in equity may differ according to the parties to the cause. A judgment of that kind between two citizens or residents of the country, and thereby subject to the jurisdiction in which it is rendered, may be held conclusive as between them everywhere. So, if a foreigner invokes the jurisdiction by bringing an action against a citizen, both may be held bound by a judgment in favor of either; and if a citizen sues a foreigner, and judgment is rendered in favor of the latter, both may be held equally bound. . . .

The effect to which a judgment, purely executory, rendered in favor of a citizen or resident of the country, in a suit there brought by him against a foreigner, may be entitled in an action thereon against the latter in his own country, as is the case now before us, presents a more difficult question, upon which there has been some diversity of opinion.

Early in the last century it was settled in England that a foreign judgment on a debt was considered, not like a judgment of a domestic court of record, as a record or a specialty, a lawful consideration for which was conclusively presumed, but as a simple contract only. . . .

The law upon this subject as understood in the United States at the time of their separation from the mother country was clearly set forth by Chief Justice Parsons, speaking for the supreme judicial court of Massachusetts, in 1813, and by Mr. Justice Story in his Commentaries on the Constitution of the United States, published in 1833. Both those eminent jurists declared that by the law of England the general rule was that foreign judgments were only *prima facie* evidence of the matter which they purported to decide; and that by the common law, before the American Revolution, all the courts of the several colonies and states were deemed foreign to each other, and consequently judgments rendered by any one of them were considered as foreign judgments, and their merits re-examinable in another colony, not only as to the jurisdiction of the court which pronounced them, but also as to the merits of the controversy, to the extent to which they were understood to be re-examinable in England. And they noted that, in order to remove that inconvenience, statutes had been passed in Massachusetts, and in some of the other colonies, by which judgments rendered by a court of competent jurisdiction in a neighboring colony could not be impeached. Bissell v. Briggs, 9 Mass. 462, 464, 465; Mass. St. 1773–74, c. 16, 5 Prov. Laws, 323, 369; Story on the Constitution, (1st Ed.) §§ 1301, 1302; (4th Ed.) §§ 1306, 1307.

It was because of that condition of the law, as between the American colonies and states, that the United States, at the very beginning of their existence as a nation, ordained that full faith and credit should be given to the judgments of one of the states of the Union in the courts of another of those states. . . .

In view of all the authorities upon the subject, and of the trend of judicial opinion in this country and in England, following the lead of Kent and Story, we are satisfied that where there has been opportunity for a full and fair trial abroad before a court of competent jurisdiction, conducting the trial upon regular proceedings, after due citation or voluntary appearance of the defendant, and under a system of jurisprudence likely to secure an impartial administration of justice between the citizens of its own country and those of other countries, and there is nothing to show either prejudice in the court, or in the system of laws under which it was sitting, or fraud in procuring the judgment, or any other special reason why the comity of this nation should not allow it full effect, the merits of the case should not, in an action brought in this country upon the judgment, be tried afresh, as on a new trial or an appeal, upon the mere assertion of the party that the judgment was erroneous in law or in fact. The defendants, therefore, cannot be permitted, upon that general ground, to contest the validity or the effect of the judgment sued on. . . .

When an action is brought in a court of this country, by a citizen of a foreign country against one of our own citizens, to recover a sum of money adjudged by a court of that country to be due from the defendant to the plaintiff, and the foreign judgment appears to have been rendered by a competent court, . . . it should be held conclusive upon the merits tried in the foreign court, unless some special ground is shown for impeaching the judgment, as by showing that it was affected by fraud or prejudice, or that by the principles of international law, and by the comity of our own country, it should not be given full credit and effect.

There is no doubt that both in this country, as appears by the authorities already cited, and in England, a foreign judgment may be impeached for fraud. . . .

By the law of France, settled by a series of uniform decisions of the Court of Cassation, the highest judicial tribunal, for more than half a century, no foreign judgment can be rendered executory in France without a review of the judgment *au fond*—to the bottom, including the whole merits of the cause of action on which the judgment rests. . . .

The Court of Cassation has ever since constantly affirmed the same view. . . . In Clunet, 1894, p. 913, note, it is said to be "settled by judicial decisions—*il est de jurisprudence*—that the French courts are bound, in the absence of special diplomatic treaties, to proceed to the revision on the whole merits—*au fond*—of foreign judgments, execution of which is demanded of them"; citing, among other cases, a decision of the court of cassation on February 2, 1892, by which it was expressly held to result from the articles of the Codes above cited "that judgments rendered in favor of a foreigner against a Frenchman, by a foreign court, are subject, when execution of them is demanded in France, to the revision of the French tribunals which have the right and the duty to examine them, both as to the form and as to the merits.'' Sirey, 1892, 1, 201. . . .

It appears, therefore, that there is hardly a civilized nation on either continent which, by its general law, allows conclusive effect to an executory foreign judgment for the recovery of money. In France and in a few smaller states—Norway, Portugal, Greece, Monaco, and Hayti— the merits of the controversy are reviewed, as of course, allowing to the foreign judgment, at the most, no more effect than of being *prima facie* evidence of the justice of the claim. In the great majority of the countries on the continent of Europe,—in Belgium, Holland, Denmark, Sweden, Germany, in many cantons of Switzerland, in Russia and Poland, in Roumania, in Austria and Hungary, (perhaps in Italy), and in Spain—as well as in Egypt, in Mexico, and in a great part of South America, the judgment rendered in a foreign country is allowed the same effect only as the courts of that country allow to the judgments of the country in which the judgment in question is sought to be executed.

The prediction of Mr. Justice Story (in § 618 of his Commentaries on the Conflict of Laws, already cited), has thus been fulfilled, and the rule of reciprocity has worked itself firmly into the structure of international jurisprudence.

The reasonable, if not the necessary, conclusion appears to us to be that judgments rendered in France, or in any other foreign country, by the laws of which our own judgments are reviewable upon the merits, are not entitled to full credit and conclusive effect when sued upon in this country, but are *prima facie* evidence only of the justice of the plaintiffs' claim.

In holding such a judgment, for want of reciprocity, not to be conclusive evidence of the merits of the claim, we do not proceed upon any theory of retaliation upon one person by reason of injustice done to another, but upon the broad ground that international law is founded upon mutuality and reciprocity, and that by the principles of international law recognized in most civilized nations, and by the comity of our own country, which it is our judicial duty to know and to declare, the judgment is not entitled to be considered conclusive. . . .

If we should hold this judgment to be conclusive, we should allow it an effect to which, supposing the defendants' offers to be sustained by actual proof, it would, in the absence of a special treaty, be entitled in hardly any other country in Christendom, except the country in which it was rendered. If the judgment had been rendered in this country, or in any other outside of the jurisdiction of France, the French courts would not have executed or enforced it, except after examining into its merits. The very judgment now sued on would be held inconclusive in almost any other country than France. In England, and in the Colonies subject to the law of England, the fraud alleged in its procurement would be a sufficient ground for disregarding it. In the courts of nearly every other nation, it would be subject to reëxamination, either merely because it was a foreign judgment, or because judgments of that nation would be reëxaminable in the courts of France.

For these reasons, in the action at law, the

Judgment is reversed, and the cause remanded to the Circuit Court, with directions to set aside the verdict and to order a new trial.

For the same reasons, in the suit in equity between these parties, the foreign judgment is not a bar, and, therefore, the

Decree dismissing the bill is reversed, the plea adjudged bad, and the cause remanded to the Circuit Court for further proceedings not inconsistent with this opinion.

Mr. Chief Justice Fuller, with whom concurred Mr. Justice Harlan, Mr. Justice Brewer, and Mr. Justice Jackson, dissenting. . . .[1]

---

[1] Supplementary Cases. Query, will comity induce a court to respect a foreign judgment obtained without personal service of process against a citizen of a foreign country who at the time the judgment was rendered had his domicil in the state which is asked to enforce the judgment? In Grubel v. Nassauer, 210 N. Y. 149 (1913), the court refused to enforce against Nassauer a judgment obtained against him by Grubel in the courts of Bavaria on an obligation alleged to have been incurred by Nassauer before his departure from Bavaria.

CHAPTER XII

JURISDICTION OVER TERRITORY: MODES OF ACQUIRING TITLE [1]

A. Discovery and occupation.

States obtain title to territory either through the acquisition of land not hitherto belonging to any other state or through the transfer of land from one state already in possession to another. The former method of acquisition confers an original title, the latter a derivative title. In the sixteenth and seventeenth centuries original titles to territory were frequently asserted on the basis of the mere discovery of the land; but by the eighteenth century discovery alone ceased to be a valid title and occupation came to be regarded as necessary to the assertion of a claim that would hold against other states. But whether title was claimed by discovery or by occupation the natives of the territory were not regarded as having any rights in international law, so that grants of land made by them to individuals need not be recognized as having validity. [Johnson and Graham's Lessee v. M'Intosh.] In cases where a claim based upon discovery came into conflict with a claim based upon occupation, evidence of occupation might be found in treaties made with native chiefs even though these were powerless of themselves to confer title. [United States and The Netherlands: Island of Palmas Case.] Query, would the occupation of arctic regions call for as extensive acts of settlement as the occupation of a more habitable country? [Denmark and Norway: Eastern Greenland Case.]

JOHNSON AND GRAHAM'S LESSEE v. WILLIAM M'INTOSH.

United States, Supreme Court, 1823.

8 Wheaton, 543. [5 L. ed. 681.]

Error to the District Court of Illinois. This was an action of ejectment for lands in the State and District of Illinois, claimed by the plaintiffs under a purchase and conveyance from the Piankeshaw Indians, and by the defendant, under a grant from the United States. It

---

[1] For a more detailed study of this subject, see Fenwick, *op. cit.*, pp. 248–272; Hyde, *op. cit.*, §§ 98–119; Oppenheim, *op. cit.*, I, §§ 209–247; Wambaugh, Plebiscites since the World War.

came up on a case stated, upon which there was a judgment below for the defendant. . . .

Mr. Chief Justice Marshall delivered the opinion of the Court. The plaintiffs in this cause claim the land, in their declaration mentioned, under two grants, purporting to be made, the first in 1773, and the last in 1775, by the chiefs of certain Indian tribes, constituting the Illinois and the Piankeshaw nations; and the question is, whether this title can be recognised in the Courts of the United States?

The facts, as stated in the case agreed, show the authority of the chiefs who executed this conveyance, so far as it could be given by their own people; and likewise show, that the particular tribes for whom these chiefs acted were in rightful possession of the land they sold. The inquiry, therefore, is, in a great measure, confined to the power of Indians to give, and of private individuals to receive, a title which can be sustained in the Courts of this country.

As the right of society, to prescribe those rules by which property may be acquired and preserved is not, and cannot be drawn into question; as the title to lands, especially, is and must be admitted to depend entirely on the law of the nation in which they lie; it will be necessary, in pursuing this inquiry, to examine, not singly those principles of abstract justice, which the Creator of all things has impressed on the mind of his creature man, and which are admitted to regulate, in a great degree, the rights of civilized nations, whose perfect independence is acknowledged; but those principles also which our own government has adopted in the particular case, and given us as the rule for our decision.

On the discovery of this immense continent, the great nations of Europe were eager to appropriate to themselves so much of it as they could respectively acquire. Its vast extent offered an ample field to the ambition and enterprise of all; and the character and religion of its inhabitants afforded an apology for considering them as a people over whom the superior genius of Europe might claim an ascendency. The potentates of the old world found no difficulty in convincing themselves that they made ample compensation to the inhabitants of the new, by bestowing on them civilization and Christianity, in exchange for unlimited independence. But, as they were all in pursuit of nearly the same object, it was necessary, in order to avoid conflicting settlements, and consequent war with each other, to establish a principle, which all should acknowledge as the law by which the right of acquisition, which they all asserted, should be regulated as between themselves. This principle was, that discovery gave title to the government by whose subjects, or by whose authority, it was made, against all other European governments, which title might be consummated by possession.

The exclusion of all other Europeans, necessarily gave to the nation making the discovery the sole right of acquiring the soil from the natives, and establishing settlements upon it. It was a right with which no Europeans could interfere. It was a right which all asserted for themselves, and to the assertion of which, by others, all assented.

Those relations which were to exist between the discoverer and the natives, were to be regulated by themselves. The rights thus acquired being exclusive, no other power could interpose between them.

In the establishment of these relations, the rights of the original inhabitants were, in no instance, entirely disregarded; but were necessarily, to a considerable extent, impaired. They were admitted to be the rightful occupants of the soil, with a legal as well as just claim to retain possession of it, and to use it according to their own discretion; but their rights to complete sovereignty, as independent nations, were necessarily diminished, and their power to dispose of the soil at their own will, to whomsoever they pleased, was denied by the original fundamental principle, that discovery gave exclusive title to those who made it.

While the different nations of Europe respected the right of the natives, as occupants, they asserted the ultimate dominion to be in themselves; and claimed and exercised, as a consequence of this ultimate dominion, a power to grant the soil, while yet in possession of the natives. These grants have been understood by all, to convey a title to the grantees, subject only to the Indian right of occupancy.

The history of America, from its discovery to the present day, proves, we think, the universal recognition of these principles.

Spain did not rest her title solely on the grant of the Pope. Her discussions respecting boundary, with France, with Great Britain, and with the United States, all show that she placed it on the rights given by discovery. Portugal sustained her claim to the Brazils by the same title.

France, also, founded her title to the vast territories she claimed in America on discovery. However conciliatory her conduct to the natives may have been, she still asserted her right of dominion over a great extent of country not actually settled by Frenchmen, and her exclusive right to acquire and dispose of the soil which remained in the occupation of Indians. . . .

The States of Holland also made acquisitions in America, and sustained their right on the common principle adopted by all Europe. . . .

No one of the powers of Europe gave its full assent to this principle, more unequivocally than England. The documents upon this subject are ample and complete. So early as the year 1496, her monarch granted a commission to the Cabots, to discover countries then unknown to Christian people, and to take possession of them in the name of the king of England. Two years afterwards, Cabot proceeded on this voyage, and discovered the continent of North America, along which he sailed as far south as Virginia. To this discovery the English trace their title.

In this first effort made by the English government to acquire territory on this continent, we perceive a complete recognition of the principle which has been mentioned. The right of discovery given by this commission, is confined to countries "then unknown to all Christian people;" and of these countries Cabot was empowered to take possession in the name of the king of England. Thus asserting a right to take possession, notwithstanding the occupancy of the natives, who were heathens, and, at the same time, admitting the prior title of any Christian people who may have made a previous discovery. . . .

Thus, all the nations of Europe, who have acquired territory on this continent, have asserted in themselves, and have recognised in others, the exclusive right of the discoverer to appropriate the lands occupied by the Indians. . . .

The United States, then, have unequivocally acceded to that great and broad rule by which its civilized inhabitants now hold this country. They hold, and assert in themselves, the title by which it was acquired. They maintain, as all others have maintained, that discovery gave an exclusive right to extinguish the Indian title of occupancy, either by purchase or by conquest; and gave also a right to such a degree of sovereignty, as the circumstances of the people would allow them to exercise.

. The power now possessed by the government of the United States to grant lands, resided, while we were colonies, in the crown, or its grantees. The validity of the titles given by either has never been questioned in our Courts. It has been exercised uniformly over territory in possession of the Indians. The existence of this power must negative the existence of any right which may conflict with, and control it. An absolute title to lands cannot exist, at the same time, in different persons, or in different governments. An absolute, must be an exclusive title, or at least a title which excludes all others not compatible with it. All our institutions recognise the absolute title of the crown, subject only to the Indian right of occupancy, and recognise the absolute title of the crown to extinguish that right. This is incompatible with an absolute and complete title in the Indians. . . .

After bestowing on this subject a degree of attention which was more required by the magnitude of the interest in litigation, and the able and elaborate arguments of the bar, than by its intrinsic difficulty, the Court is decidedly of opinion, that the plaintiffs do not exhibit a title which can be sustained in the Courts of the United States; and that there is no error in the judgment which was rendered against them in the District Court of Illinois.

Judgment affirmed, with costs.

UNITED STATES AND THE NETHERLANDS: ISLAND OF PALMAS CASE.

Tribunal of the Permanent Court of Arbitration, 1928.

Publication of the International Bureau of the Permanent Court of Arbitration (1928), as reprinted in Scott, Hague Court Reports, Second Series, 84.

[HUBER, Arbitrator.] . . . II. The *subject of the dispute* is the sovereignty over the Island of Palmas (or Miangas). The Island in question is indicated with precision in the preamble to the Special Agreement, its latitude and longitude being specified. . . .

It results from the evidence produced by either side that Palmas (or Miangas) is a single, isolated island, not one of several islands clustered together. It lies about half way between Cape San Augustin (Mindanao, Philippine Islands) and the most northerly island of the Nanusa (Nanoesa) group (Netherlands East Indies).

The *origin of the dispute* is to be found in the visit paid to the Island of Palmas (or Miangas) on January 21st, 1906, by General Leonard Wood, who was then Governor of the Province of Moro. . . .

This visit led to the statement that the Island of Palmas (or Miangas), undoubtedly included in the "archipelago known as the Philippine Islands," as delimited by Article III of the Treaty of Peace between the United States and Spain, dated December 10th, 1898 (hereinafter also called "Treaty of Paris") and ceded in virtue of the said article to the United States, was considered by the Netherlands as forming part of the territory of their possessions in the East Indies. There followed a diplomatic correspondence, beginning on March 31st, 1906, and leading up to the conclusion of the special agreement of January 23d, 1925.
. . . .

Titles of acquisition of territorial sovereignty in present-day international law are either based on an act of effective apprehension, such as occupation or conquest, or, like cession, presuppose that the ceding and the cessionary Power or at least one of them, have the faculty of effectively disposing of the ceded territory. In the same way natural accretion can only be conceived of as an accretion to a portion of territory where there exists an actual sovereignty capable of extending to a spot which falls within its sphere of activity. It seems therefore natural that an element which is essential for the constitution of sovereignty should not be lacking in its continuation. So true is this, that practice, as well as doctrine, recognizes—though under different legal formulæ and with certain differences as to the conditions required—that the continuous and peaceful display of territorial sovereignty (peaceful in relation to other States) is as good as a title. The growing insistence with which international law, ever since the middle of the 18th century, has demanded that the occupation shall be effective would be inconceivable, if effectiveness were required only for the act of acquisition and not equally for the maintenance of the right. If the effectiveness has above all been insisted on in regard to occupation, this is because the question rarely arises in connection with territories in which there is already an established order of things. Just as before the rise of international law, boundaries of lands were necessarily determined by the fact that the power of a State was exercised within them, so too, under the reign of international law, the fact of peaceful and continuous display is still one of the most important considerations in establishing boundaries between States.

Territorial sovereignty, as has already been said, involves the exclusive right to display the activities of a State. This right has as corollary a duty: the obligation to protect within the territory the rights of other States, in particular their right to integrity and inviolability in peace and in war, together with the rights which each State may claim for its nationals in foreign territory. Without manifesting its territorial sovereignty in a manner corresponding to circumstances, the State cannot fulfil this duty. Territorial sovereignty cannot limit itself to its negative side, i. e. to excluding the activities of other States; for it serves to divide between nations the space upon which human activities are employed, in order to assure them at all points the minimum of protection of which international law is the guardian.

Although municipal law, thanks to its complete judicial system, is able to recognize abstract rights of property as existing apart from any material display of them, it has none the less limited their effect by the principles of prescription and the protection of possession. International law, the structure of which is not based on any super-State organisation, cannot be presumed to reduce a right such as territorial sovereignty, with which almost all international relations are bound up, to the category of an abstract right, without concrete manifestations.

The principle that continuous and peaceful display of the functions of State within a given region is a constituent element of territorial sovereignty is not only based on the conditions of the formation of independent States and their boundaries (as shown by the experience of political history) as well as on an international jurisprudence and doctrine widely accepted; this principle has further been recognized in more than one federal State, where a jurisdiction is established in order to apply, as need arises, rules of international law to the interstate relations of the States members. . . .

It may suffice to quote among several non-dissimilar decisions of the Supreme Court of the United States of America that in the case of the State of Indiana v. State of Kentucky (136 U. S. 479) 1890, where the precedent of the case of Rhode Island v. Massachusetts (4 How. 591, 639) is supported by quotations from Vattel and Wheaton, who both admit prescription founded on length of time as a valid and incontestable title.

Manifestations of territorial sovereignty assume, it is true, different forms, according to conditions of time and place. Although continuous in principle, sovereignty cannot be exercised in fact at every moment on every point of a territory. The intermittence and discontinuity compatible with the maintenance of the right necessarily differ according as inhabited or uninhabited regions are involved, or regions enclosed within territories in which sovereignty is uncontestably displayed or again regions accessible from, for instance, the high seas. It is true that neighbouring States may by convention fix limits to their own sovereignty, even in regions such as the interior of scarcely explored continents where such sovereignty is scarcely manifested, and in this way each may prevent the other from any penetration of its territory. The delimitation of Hinterland may also be mentioned in this connection.

If, however, no conventional line of sufficient topographical precision exists or if there are gaps in the frontiers otherwise established, or if a conventional line leaves room for doubt, or if, as e. g. in the case of an island situated in the high seas, the question arises whether a title is valid *erga omnes,* the actual continuous and peaceful display of state functions is in case of dispute the sound and natural criterium of territorial sovereignty. . . .

III. The *title alleged by the United States of America* as constituting the immediate foundation of its claim is that of cession, brought about by the Treaty of Paris, which cession transferred all rights of sovereignty which Spain may have possessed in the region indicated in Article III of the said Treaty and therefore also those concerning the Island of Palmas (or Miangas).

It is evident that Spain could not transfer more rights than she herself possessed. . . .

Whilst there existed a divergence of views as to the extension of the cession to certain Spanish islands outside the treaty limits, it would seem that the cessionary power never envisaged that the cession, in spite of the sweeping terms of Article III, should comprise territories on which Spain had not a valid title, though falling within the limits traced by the Treaty. It is evident that whatever may be the right construction of a treaty, it cannot be interpreted as disposing of the rights of independent third Powers. . . .

The essential point is therefore whether the island of Palmas (or Miangas) at the moment of the conclusion and coming into force of the treaty of Paris formed a part of the Spanish or Netherlands territory. The United States declares that Palmas (or Miangas) was Spanish territory and denies the existence of Dutch sovereignty; the Netherlands maintain the existence of their sovereignty and deny that of Spain. . . .

It is admitted by both sides that international law underwent profound modifications between the end of the Middle-Ages and the end of the 19th century, as regards the rights of discovery and acquisition of uninhabited regions or regions inhabited by savages or semi-civilised peoples. Both Parties are also agreed that a juridical fact must be appreciated in the light of the law contemporary with it, and not of the law in force at the time when a dispute in regard to it arises or falls to be settled. The effect of discovery by Spain is therefore to be determined by the rules of international law in force in the first half of the 16th century—or (to take the earliest date) in the first quarter of it, i. e. at the time when the Portuguese or Spaniards made their appearance in the Sea of Celebes.

If the view most favourable to the American arguments is adopted—with every reservation as to the soundness of such view—that is to say, if we consider as positive law at the period in question the rule that discovery as such, i. e. the mere fact of seeing land, without any act, even symbolical, of taking possession, involved *ipso jure* territorial sovereignty and not merely an "inchoate title," a *jus ad rem*, to be completed eventually by an actual and durable taking of possession within a reasonable time, the question arises whether sovereignty yet existed at the critical date, i. e. the moment of conclusion and coming into force of the Treaty of Paris.

As regards the question which of different legal systems prevailing at successive periods is to be applied in a particular case (the so-called intertemporal law), a distinction must be made between the creation of rights and the existence of rights. The same principal which subjects the act creative of a right to the law in force at the time the right arises, demands that the existence of the right, in other words its continued manifestation, shall follow the conditions required by the evolution of law. International law in the 19th century, having regard to the fact that most parts of the globe were under the sovereignty of States members of the community of nations, and that territories without a master had become relatively few, took account of a tendency already existing and especially developed since the middle of the 18th century, and laid down the principle that occupation, to constitute a claim to territorial sovereignty, must be effective, that is, offer certain guarantees to other States and their nationals. It seems therefore incompatible with this rule of positive law that there should be regions which are neither under the effective sovereignty of a State, nor without a master, but which are reserved for the exclusive influence of one State, in virtue solely of a title of acquisition which is no longer recognized by existing law, even if such a title ever conferred territorial sovereignty. For these reasons, discovery alone, without any subsequent act, cannot at the present time suffice to prove sovereignty over the Island of Palmas (or Miangas); and in so far as there is no sovereignty, the question of an abandonment properly speaking of sovereignty by one State in order that the sovereignty of another may take its place does not arise.

If on the other hand the view is adopted that discovery does not create a definitive title of sovereignty, but only an "inchoate" title, such a title exists, it is true, without external manifestation. However, according to the view that has prevailed at any rate since the 19th century, an inchoate title of discovery must be completed within a reasonable period by the effective occupation of the region claimed to be discovered. This principle must be applied in the present case, for the reasons given above in regard to the rules determining which of successive legal systems is to be applied (the so-called intertemporal law). Now, no act of occupation nor, except as to a recent period, any exercise of sovereignty at Palmas by Spain has been alleged. But even admitting that the Spanish title still existed as inchoate in 1898 and must be considered as included in the cession under Article III of the Treaty of Paris, an inchoate title could not prevail over the continuous and peaceful display of authority by another State; for such display may prevail even over a prior, definitive title put forward by another State. This point will be considered, when the Netherlands argument has been examined and the allegations of either Party as to the display of their authority can be compared. . . .

. . . IV. The *Netherlands' arguments* contend that the East India Company established Dutch sovereignty over the Island of Palmas (or Miangas) as early as the seventeenth century, by means of conventions with the princes of Tabukan (Taboekan) and Taruna (Taroena), two native chieftains of the Island of Sangi (Groot Sangihe), the principal island of the Talautse Isles (Sangi Islands), and that sovereignty has been displayed during the past two centuries.

In the annexes to the Netherland memorandum the texts of conventions concluded by the Dutch East India Company (and, after 1795, by the Netherlands State), in 1677, 1697, 1720, 1758, 1828, 1885 and 1899 with the Princes, Radjas or Kings, as they are indiscriminately called, of Tabukan, Taruna and Kandahar (Kandhar)-Taruna. . . .

. . . The questions to be solved in the present case are the following:

Was the Island of Palmas (or Miangas) in 1898 a part of territory under Netherlands sovereignty?

Did this sovereignty actually exist in 1898 in regard to Palmas (or Miangas) and are the facts proved which were alleged on this subject? . . .

Before beginning to consider the facts alleged by the Netherlands in support of their arguments, there are two preliminary points, in regard to which the parties also put forward different views, which require elucidation. These relate to questions raised by the United States: firstly the power of the East India Company to act validly under international law, on behalf of the Netherlands, in particular by concluding so-called political contracts with native rulers; secondly the identity or non-identity of the island in dispute with the island to which the allegations of the Netherlands as to display of sovereignty would seem to relate.

The acts of the *East India Company* (General Geoctroyeerde Nederlandsch Oost-Indische Compagnie), in view of occupying or colonizing the regions at issue in the present affair must, in international law, be entirely assimilated to acts of the Netherlands State itself. From the end of the sixteenth till the nineteenth Century, companies formed by individuals and engaged in economic pursuits (Chartered Companies), were invested by the States to whom they were subject with public powers for the acquisition and administration of colonies. The Dutch East India Company is one of the best known. Article V of the Treaty of Münster and consequently also the Treaty of Utrecht clearly show that the East and West India Companies were entitled to create situations recognized by international law; for the peace between Spain and the Netherlands extends to "tous Potentats, nations et peuples" with whom the said companies, in the name of the States of the Netherlands, "entre les limites de leurdits Octroys sont en Amitié et Alliance." The conclusion of conventions, even of a political nature, was, by Article XXXV of the Charter of 1602, within the powers of the Company. It is a question for decision in each individual case whether a contract concluded by the Company falls within the range of simple economic transactions or is of a political and public administrative nature.

As regards *contracts between a State* or a Company such as the Dutch East India Company and *native princes or chiefs of peoples* not recognized as members of the community of nations, they are not, in the international law sense, treaties or conventions capable of creating rights and obligations such as may, in international law, arise out of treaties. But, on the other hand, contracts of this nature are not wholly void of indirect effects on situations governed by international law; if they do not constitute titles in international law, they are none the less facts of which that law must in certain circumstances take account. From the time of the discoveries until recent times, colonial territory has very often been acquired, especially in the East Indies, by means of contracts with the native authorities, which contracts leave the existing organization more or less intact as regards the native population, whilst granting to the colonizing Power, besides economic advantages such as monopolies or navigation and commercial privileges, also the exclusive direction of relations with other Powers, and the right to exercise public authority in regard to their own nationals and to foreigners. The form of the legal relations created by such contracts is most generally that of suzerain and vassal, or of the so-called colonial protectorate.

In substance, it is not an agreement between equals; it is rather a form of internal organization of a colonial territory, on the basis of autonomy for the natives. In order to regularize the situation as regards other states, this organization requires to be completed by the establishment of powers to ensure the fulfillment of the obligations imposed by international law on every state in regard to its own territory. And thus suzerainty over the native state becomes the basis of territorial sovereignty as towards other members of the community of nations. It is the sum-total of functions thus allotted either to the native authorities or to those of the colonial Power which decides the question whether at any certain period the conditions required for the existence of sovereignty are fulfilled. It is a question to be decided in each case whether such a régime is to be considered as effective or whether it is essentially fictitious, either for the whole or a part of the territory. There always remains reserved the question whether the establishment of such a system is not forbidden by the pre-existing rights of other States.

The point of view here adopted by the Arbitrator is—at least in principle—in conformity with the attitude taken up by the United States in the note already quoted above, from the Secretary of State to the Spanish Minister, dated January 7, 1900 and relating to two small islands lying just outside the line drawn by the Treaty of Paris, but claimed by the United States under the said treaty. The note states that the two islands ''have not hitherto been directly administered by Spain, but have been successfully claimed by Spain as a part of the dominions of her subject, the Sultan of Sulu. As such they have been administered by Sulu agencies, under some vague form of resident supervision by Spanish agencies, which latter have been withdrawn as a result of the recent war.''

This system of contracts between colonial Powers and native princes and chiefs is even expressly approved by Article V of the Treaty of Münster quoted above; for, among the ''Potentates, Nations and Peoples,'' with whom the Dutch State or Companies may have concluded treaties of alliance and friendship in the East and West Indies, are necessarily the native princes and chiefs.

The arbitrator can therefore not exclude the contracts invoked by the Netherlands from being taken into consideration in the present case.

. . .

V   The conclusions to be derived from the above examination of the arguments of the Parties are the following:

The claim of the United States to sovereignty over the Island of Palmas (or Miangas) is derived from Spain by way of cession under the Treaty of Paris. The latter Treaty, though it comprises the island in dispute within the limits of cession, and in spite of the absence of any reserves or protest by the Netherlands as to these limits, has not created in favour of the United States any title of sovereignty such as was not already vested in Spain. The essential point is therefore to decide whether Spain had sovereignty over Palmas (or Miangas) at the time of the coming into force of the Treaty of Paris.

The United States base their claim on the titles of discovery, or recognition by treaty and of contiguity, i. e. titles relating to acts or circumstances leading to the acquisition of sovereignty; they have however not established the fact that sovereignty so acquired was effectively displayed at any time.

The Netherlands on the contrary found their claim to sovereignty essentially on the title of peaceful and continuous display of state authority over the island. Since this title would in international law prevail over a title of acquisition of sovereignty not followed by actual display of state authority, it is necessary to ascertain in the first place, whether the contention of the Netherlands is sufficiently established by evidence, and, if so, for what period of time.

In the opinion of the Arbitrator the Netherlands have succeeded in establishing the following facts:

a. The Island of Palmas (or Miangas) is identical with an island designated by this or a similar name, which has formed, at least since 1700, successively a part of two of the native States of the Island of Sangi (Talautse Isles).

b. These native States were from 1677 onwards connected with the East India Company, and thereby with the Netherlands, by contracts of suzerainty, which conferred upon the suzerain such powers as would justify his considering the vassal state as a part of his territory.

c. Acts characteristic of State authority exercised either by the vassal state or by the suzerain Power in regard precisely to the Island of Palmas (or Miangas) have been established as occurring at different epochs between 1700 and 1898, as well as in the period between 1898 and 1906. . . .

It is not necessary that the display of sovereignty should be established as having begun at a precise epoch; it suffices that it had existed at the critical period preceding the year 1898. It is quite natural that the establishment of sovereignty may be the outcome of a slow evolution, of a progressive intensification of state control. This is particularly the case, if sovereignty is acquired by the establishment of the suzerainty of a colonial power over a native State, and in regard to outlying possessions of such a vassal state.

Now the evidence relating to the period after the middle of the 19th century makes it clear that the Netherlands Indian Government considered the island distinctly as a part of its possessions and that, in the years immediately preceding 1898, an intensification of display of sovereignty took place. . . .

There is moreover no evidence which would establish any act of display of sovereignty over the island by Spain or another Power, such as might counter-balance or annihilate the manifestations of Netherlands sovereignty. As to third Powers, the evidence submitted to the Tribunal does not disclose any trace of such action, at least from the middle of the 17th century onwards. These circumstances, together with the absence of any evidence of a conflict between Spanish and Netherlands authorities during more than two centuries as regards Palmas (or Miangas), are an indirect proof of the exclusive display of Netherlands sovereignty. . . .

The display has been open and public, that is to say that it was in conformity with usages as to exercise of sovereignty over colonial states. A clandestine exercise of state authority over an inhabited territory during a considerable length of time would seem to be impossible. An obligation for the Netherlands to notify to other Powers the establishment of suzerainty over the Sangi States or of the display of sovereignty in these territories did not exist. . . .

The conditions of acquisition of sovereignty by the Netherlands are therefore to be considered as fulfilled. It remains now to be seen whether the United States as successors of Spain are in a position to bring forward an equivalent or stronger title. This is to be answered in the negative.

The title of discovery, if it had not been already disposed of by the Treaties of Münster and Utrecht would, under the most favourable and most extensive interpretation, exist only as an inchoate title, as a claim to establish sovereignty by effective occupation. An inchoate title however cannot prevail over a definite title founded on continuous and peaceful display of sovereignty. . . .

The Netherlands title of sovereignty, acquired by continuous and peaceful display of state authority during a long period of time going probably back beyond the year 1700, therefore holds good. . . .

This is the conclusion reached on the ground of the relative strength of the titles invoked by each Party, and founded exclusively on a limited part of the evidence concerning the epoch immediately preceding the rise of the dispute.

This same conclusion must impose itself with still greater force if there be taken into consideration—as the Arbitrator considers should be done—all the evidence which tends to show that there were unchallenged acts of peaceful display of Netherlands sovereignty in the period from 1700 to 1906, and which—as has been stated above—may be regarded as sufficiently proving the existence of Netherlands sovereignty.

For these reasons the Arbitrator, in conformity with Article I of the special agreement of January 23rd, 1925 decides that: The Island of Palmas (or Miangas) forms in its entirety a part of Netherlands territory. . . .

THE ROYAL DANISH GOVERNMENT AND THE ROYAL NORWEGIAN GOVERNMENT: LEGAL STATUS OF EASTERN GREENLAND.

Permanent Court of International Justice, 1933.

Publications of the Court, Series A/B, No. 53.

The Court . . . delivers the following judgment:

By an Application instituting proceedings, filed with the Registry of the Court on July 12th, 1931, in accordance with Article 40 of the Statute and Article 35 of the Rules of Court, the Royal Danish Government, relying on the optional clause of Article 36, paragraph 2, of the Statute, brought before the Permanent Court of International Justice a suit against the Royal Norwegian Government on the ground that the latter Government had, on July 10th, 1931, published a proclamation declaring that it had proceeded to occupy certain territories in Eastern Greenland, which, in the contention of the Danish Government, were subject to the sovereignty of the Crown of Denmark. The Application . . . proceeds . . . to formulate the claim by asking the Court for judgment to the effect that "the promulgation of the above-mentioned declaration of occupation and any steps taken in this respect by the Norwegian Government constitute a violation of the existing legal situation and are accordingly unlawful and invalid." . . .

According to the royal Norwegian proclamation of July 10th, 1931, which gave rise to the present dispute, the "country" the "taking possession" of which "is officially confirmed" and which is "placed under Norwegian sovereignty" is "situated between Carlsberg Fjord on the South and Bessel Fjord on the North, in Eastern Greenland," and extends from latitude 71° 30′ to 75° 40′ N.

By "Eastern Greenland" is meant the eastern coast of Greenland. . . .

The climate and character of Greenland are those of an Arctic country. The "Inland Ice" is difficult to traverse, and parts of the coast—particularly of the East coast—are for months together difficult of access owing to the influence of the Polar current and the stormy winds on the icebergs and the floe ice and owing to the frequent spells of bad weather.

According to the information supplied to the Court by the Parties, it was about the year 900 A. D. that Greenland was discovered. The country was colonized about a century later. The best known of the colonists was Eric the Red, who was an inhabitant of Iceland of Norwegian origin; it was at that time that two settlements called Eystribygd and Vestribygd were founded towards the southern end of the western coast. These settlements appear to have existed as an independent State for some time, but became tributary to the kingdom of Norway in the XIIIth century. These settlements had disappeared before 1500.

. . . .

In 1380, the kingdoms of Norway and Denmark were united under the same Crown; the character of this union, which lasted until 1814, changed to some extent in the course of time, more particularly as a result of the centralization at Copenhagen of the administration of the various countries which were under the sovereignty of the Dano-Norwegian Crown. This evolution seems to have obliterated to some extent the separation which had existed between them from a constitutional standpoint. On the other hand, there is nothing to show that during this period Greenland, in so far as it constituted a dependency of the Crown, should not be regarded as a Norwegian possession. . . .

The Napoleonic era profoundly affected the international status of the Scandinavian countries, and also that of Greenland. After Sweden had ceded Finland to Russia (1809), the policy of the Allies against France made it possible for Sweden to obtain the cession of the kingdom of Norway which until then had been united to Denmark, who had supported France. . . . After the Franco-Danish alliance had been renewed on July 10th, 1813, and war had broken out between Denmark, on the one hand, and Sweden and her allies, on the other, the battle of Leipzig (October 1813) led to the triumph of the Allied cause and the Swedish army compelled Denmark to sign the Peace Treaty of Kiel, dated January 14th, 1814, the fourth Article of which provided for the cession to Sweden of the kingdom of Norway, excluding however Greenland, the Faeroe Isles and Iceland. . . .

In the course of the XIXth century and the early years of the XXth, the coasts of Greenland were entirely explored. For the purposes of the present case, it is only necessary to note two dates: first, in 1822 the Scottish whaler Scoresby made the first landing by a European in the territory covered by the Norwegian declaration of occupation; secondly, about 1900, thanks to the voyages of the American Peary, the insular character of Greenland was established. It is admitted by Norway that from the time of Scoresby's landing the East coast forms part of the known portion of Greenland. . . .

In 1905, a Decree was issued by the Danish Minister of the Interior, fixing the limits of the territorial waters round Greenland. The limits within which the fishing was stated to be reserved for Danish subjects were to be drawn at a distance of three marine miles along the whole coast of Greenland.

In 1908, a law was promulgated by Denmark relating to the administration of Greenland. The colonies on the West coast were divided into two districts, a northern and a southern.

In 1921, a Decree was issued, running as follows:

"In pursuance of His Majesty's authority dated the 6th instant, . . . know all men that Danish Trading, Mission and Hunting Stations have been established on the East and West coasts of Greenland, with the result that the whole of that country is henceforth linked up with Danish colonies and stations under the authority of the Danish Administration of Greenland.'' . . .

This Decree was notified to the Powers during June and July. It was followed on June 16th, 1921, by a Proclamation (Notice to Mariners) concerning navigation in the seas around Greenland, to the effect that the closing of the island to Danish and foreign ships extended to ''the whole of the coasts and islands pertaining to Greenland.'' . . .

Throughout this period and up to the present time, the practice of the Danish Government in concluding bilateral commercial conventions or when participating in multilateral conventions relating to economic questions—such as those concluded since 1921 under the auspices of the League of Nations—has been to secure the insertion of a stipulation excepting Greenland from the operation of the convention. Only in one case—that of the conventions concluded with Japan on February 12th, 1912—is the exception or the reservation otherwise than in favor of ''Greenland'' or the ''territory of Greenland'' without qualification; in the conventions with Japan, the exception is in favour of ''the Danish colonies in Greenland.'' . . .

In 1920, the Danish Government approached the Governments in London, Paris, Rome and Tokyo with a view to obtaining assurances from these Governments on the subject of the recognition of Denmark's sovereignty over the whole of Greenland. Each of those Governments replied in terms which satisfied the Danish Government—which thereupon, in 1921, approached the Swedish and Norwegian Governments as the only other Governments interested. The communication to the Swedish Government was dated January 13th, and that to the Norwegian Government January 18th.

The Swedish Government made no difficulty. The Norwegian Government was not prepared to adopt the same attitude unless it received an undertaking from the Danish Government that the liberty of hunting and fishing on the East coast (outside the limits of the colony of Angmagssalik), which Norwegians had hitherto enjoyed, should not be interfered with. This undertaking the Danish Government was unwilling to give, as it alleges that it would have involved a reversal of the policy which Denmark had hitherto followed of endeavouring to shield the Eskimo people of Greenland on grounds of health from uncontrolled contact with white races; such a policy could not be maintained unless control could be exercised over those having access to the territory. . . .

On July 9th, 1924, the latter signed a Convention applicable to the whole eastern coast of Greenland, excepting the district of Angmagssalik (and, in a certain eventuality, that of Scoresby Sound); the Convention was to come into force as from July 10th, 1924, for a first period of twenty years.

Under Article 2, ships were to have free access to the East coast, and their crews and persons on board were given the right to land, to winter in the territory and to hunt and fish. Under Article 5, the erection of meteorological, telegraphic and telephonic stations was authorized.

Simultaneously with the Convention, notes were signed by each Government to the effect that it signed the Convention in order to avoid disputes and to strengthen friendly relations between the two Powers, and that it reserved its opinion on questions concerning Greenland not dealt with in the Convention, so that by the Convention nothing was prejudged, abandoned or lost. . . .

The chief points that these notes had in view were: the Danish contention that Denmark possessed full and entire sovereignty over the whole of Greenland and that Norway had recognized that sovereignty, and the Norwegian contention that all the parts of Greenland which had not been occupied in such a manner as to bring them effectively under the administration of the Danish Government were in the condition of *terrae nullius,* and that if they ceased to be *terrae nullius* they must pass under Norwegian sovereignty. . . .

On April 1st, 1925, the Danish Government promulgated a law "on fishing and hunting in Greenland waters," etc.; this was followed, on April 18th, by a law "concerning the administration of Greenland." . . .

Subsequently, the question of Danish sovereignty over the eastern coast of Greenland appears not to have been raised for nearly five years. But, in the summer of 1930, the Norwegian Government conferred police powers on certain Norwegian nationals "for the inspection of the Norwegian hunting stations in Eastern Greenland." Denmark became uneasy at this action, and intimated to the Norwegian Government, at first verbally, and afterwards—on December 26th, 1930—in writing, that she could not countenance the granting of regular police powers to Norwegian nationals in territories situated in Greenland, seeing that these territories were, in the Danish view, subject to Danish sovereignty. On January 6th, 1931, the Norwegian Government replied that, in accordance with the standpoint which it had reserved in its note of July 9th, 1924, Eastern Greenland constituted a *terra nullius,* and that, consequently, it was "fully entitled" to invest Norwegian nationals in this territory with police powers in respect of Norwegian nationals and other persons domiciled in Norway. . . .

Finally, on July 10th, 1931, in a *note verbale* addressed by the Norwegian Minister for Foreign Affairs to the Danish Minister at Oslo, the Norwegian Government stated that, "having regard to the legal position of Norway in the proceedings before the Court," it "had felt obliged to proceed, in virtue of a Royal Resolution of the same date, to the occupation of the territories in Eastern Greenland situated between latitude 71° 30′ and 75° 40′ N." . . .

The territory covered by this Resolution was denominated by Norway "Eirik Raudes Land."

The contents of the Resolution were notified to the Powers whom Norway regarded as being interested.

On the following day—July 11th, 1931—the Danish Government informed the Norwegian Government that it had "submitted the question" on the same day "to the Permanent Court of International Justice." The Danish Application instituting proceedings was filed with the Registry, as already stated, on July 12th, 1931.

The Danish submission in the written pleading, that the Norwegian occupation of July 10th, 1931, is invalid, is founded upon the contention that the area occupied was at the time of the occupation subject to Danish sovereignty; that the area is part of Greenland, and at the time of the occupation Danish sovereignty existed over all Greenland; consequently it could not be occupied by another Power.

In support of this contention, the Danish Government advances two propositions. The first is that the sovereignty which Denmark now enjoys over Greenland has existed for a long time, has been continuously and peacefully exercised and, until the present dispute, has not been contested by any Power. This proposition Denmark sets out to establish as a fact. The second proposition is that Norway has by treaty or otherwise herself recognized Danish sovereignty over Greenland as a whole and therefore cannot now dispute it.

The Norwegian submissions are that Denmark possessed no sovereignty over the area which Norway occupied on July 10th, 1931, and that at the time of the occupation the area was *terra nullius*. Her contention is that the area lay outside the limits of the Danish colonies in Greenland and that Danish sovereignty extended no further than the limits of these colonies. . . .

The Danish claim is not founded upon any particular act of occupation but alleges—to use the phrase employed in the Palmas Island decision of the Permanent Court of Arbitration, April 4th, 1928—a title "founded on the peaceful and continuous display of State authority over the island." It is based upon the view that Denmark now enjoys all the rights which the King of Denmark and Norway enjoyed over Greenland up till 1814. Both the existence and the extent of these rights must therefore be considered, as well as the Danish claim to sovereignty since that date. . . .

The conclusion to which the Court is led is that, bearing in mind the absence of any claim to sovereignty by another Power, and the Arctic and inaccessible character of the uncolonized parts of the country, the King of Denmark and Norway displayed during the period from the founding of the colonies by Hans Egede in 1721 up to 1814 his authority to an extent sufficient to give his country a valid claim to sovereignty, and that his rights over Greenland were not limited to the colonized area.

Up to the date of the Treaty of Kiel of 1814, the rights which the King possessed over Greenland were enjoyed by him as King of Norway. It was as a Norwegian possession that Greenland was dealt with in Article 4 of that Treaty, whereby the King ceded to the King of Sweden the Kingdom of Norway, *"la Groënlande . . . non comprise . . . ."* The result of the Treaty was that what had been a Norwegian possession remained with the King of Denmark and became for the future a Danish possession. Except in this respect, the Treaty of Kiel did not affect or extend the King's rights over Greenland. . . .

In view of the above facts, when taken in conjunction with the legislation she had enacted applicable to Greenland generally, the numerous treaties in which Denmark, with the concurrence of the other contracting Party, provided for the non-application of the treaty to Greenland in general, and the absence of all claims to sovereignty over Greenland by any other Power, Denmark must be regarded as having displayed during this period of 1814 to 1915 her authority over the uncolonized part of the country to a degree sufficient to confer a valid title to the sovereignty.

The application which the Danish Government addressed to foreign governments between 1915 and 1921, seeking the recognition of Denmark's position in Greenland, have played so large a part in the arguments addressed to the Court that it is necessary to deal with them in some detail. The point at issue between the Parties is whether Denmark was seeking a recognition of an existing sovereignty extending over all Greenland, as has been urged by her Counsel, or, as maintained by Counsel on behalf of Norway, whether she was trying to persuade the Powers to agree to an extension of her sovereignty to territory which did not as yet belong to her. . . .

The conclusion which the Court has reached is that the view upheld by the Danish Government in the present case is right and that the object which that Government was endeavouring to secure was an assurance from each of the foreign governments concerned that it accepted the Danish point of view that all Greenland was already subject to Danish sovereignty and was therefore content to see an extension of Denmark's activities to the uncolonized parts of Greenland. . . .

The period subsequent to the date when the Danish Government issued the Decree of May 10th, 1921, referred to above, witnessed a considerable increase in the activity of the Danish Government on the eastern coast of Greenland. . . .

Even if the period from 1921 to July 10th, 1931, is taken by itself and without reference to the preceding period, the conclusion reached by the Court is that during this time Denmark regarded herself as possessing sovereignty over all Greenland and displayed and exercised her sovereign rights to an extent sufficient to constitute a valid title to sovereignty. When considered in conjunction with the facts of the preceding periods, the case in favour of Denmark is confirmed and strengthened.

It follows from the above that the Court is satisfied that Denmark has succeeded in establishing her contention that at the critical date, namely, July 10th, 1931, she possessed a valid title to the sovereignty over all Greenland.

This finding constitutes by itself sufficient reason for holding that the occupation of July 10th, 1931, and any steps taken in this connection by the Norwegian Government, were illegal and invalid.

For these reasons, The Court, by twelve votes to two, (1) decides that the declaration of occupation promulgated by the Norwegian Government on July 10th, 1931, and any steps taken in this respect by that Government, constitute a violation of the existing legal situation and are accordingly unlawful and invalid; . . .[1]

B. Accretion.

Accretion is the slow addition made to land by the action of rivers flowing past it or by the action of the ocean on the coast. When a delta

---

[1] SUPPLEMENTARY CASES. In the Clipperton Island Case, submitted by France and Mexico to the arbitration of the King of Italy by a convention of March 2, 1909, involving title to an uninhabitable coral reef situated 670 miles southwest from the coast of Mexico, the arbitrator held, January 28, 1931, Am. Journal Int. Law, XXVI (1932), 390, that, in view of the failure of Mexico to prove any actual exercise of sovereignty over the island on the part of Spain or on its own part, "the legal status of the island [in November, 1858] was that of a *territorium nullius* and was therefore open to occupation;" further, that the document by which the French government on November 17, 1858, proclaimed and declared sovereignty over the island was followed by such "occupation" as the uninhabited character of the island called for which need not be more than the announcement of an intention to take possession and the continuous assertion of title.

The principle that, in point of constitutional law in the United States, the determination of the sovereignty over disputed territory rests with the legislative and the executive departments of the government and not with the judiciary, has been laid down in numerous cases, notably in Williams v. Suffolk Insurance Co., 13 Peters, 415 (1839), involving the sovereignty of the Falkland Islands and the issue whether the violation by an American vessel of regulations respecting seal fisheries issued by the government of Buenos Aires invalidated an insurance policy issued by the defendant; and in Jones v. United States, 137 U. S. 202 (1890), involving the jurisdiction of the Circuit Court of the United States for the District of Maryland to try the plaintiff in error for a murder committed on the Island of Navassa in the Caribbean Sea which the United States claimed as its territory under the Guano Islands Act of 1856.

is formed at the mouth of a river the ownership of the main land carries with it the ownership of the delta. Query, whether the three-mile limit of the maritime belt should be measured from the mainland or from the mud islands forming the delta? [The Anna.]

THE ANNA, LA PORTE [MASTER].

Great Britain, High Court of Admiralty, 1805.

5 C. Rob. 373.

This was the case of a ship under American colours, with a cargo of logwood, and about 13,000 dollars on board, bound from the Spanish main to New Orleans, and captured by the Minerva privateer near the mouth of the River Mississippi. A claim was given under the direction of the American Ambassador for the ship and cargo, "as taken within the territory of the United States, at the distance of a mile and a half from the western shore of the principal entrance of the Mississippi, and within view of a post protected by a gun, and where is stationed an officer of the United States." . . .

SIR WILLIAM SCOTT.— . . .
When the ship was brought into this country, a claim was given of a grave nature, alledging a violation of the territory of the United States of America. This great leading fact has very properly been made a matter of much discussion, and charts have been laid before the Court to shew the place of capture, though with different representations from the adverse parties. The capture was made, it seems, at the mouth of the River Mississippi, and, as it is contended in the claim, within the boundaries of the United States. We all know that the rule of law on this subject is "*terræ dominium finitur, ubi finitur armorum vis,*" and since the introduction of fire arms, that distance has usually been recognized to be about three miles from the shore. But it so happens in this case, that a question arises as to what is to be deemed the shore, since there are a number of little mud islands composed of earth and trees drifted down by the River, which form a kind of portico to the main land. It is contended that these are not to be considered as any part of the territory of America, that they are a sort of "*no mans land,*" not of consistency enough to support the purposes of life, uninhabited, and resorted to, only, for shooting and taking birds nests. It is argued that the line of territory is to be taken only from the Balise, which is a fort raised on made land by the former *Spanish* possessors. I am of a different opinion; I think that the protection of territory is to be reckoned from these islands; and that they are the natural appendages of the coast on which they border, and from which indeed they are formed.

Their elements are derived immediately from the territory, and on the principle of alluvium and increment, on which so much is to be found in the books of law, *Quod vis fluminis de tuo prædio detraxerit, & vicino prædio attulerit, palam tuum remanet,* even if it had been carried over to an adjoining territory. Consider what the consequence would be if lands of this description were not considered as appendant to the main land, and as comprized within the bounds of territory. If they do not belong to the United States of America, any other power might occupy them; they might be embanked and fortified. What a thorn would this be in the side of America! It is physically possible at least that they might be so occupied by European nations, and then the command of the River would be no longer in America, but in such settlements. The possibility of such a consequence is enough to expose the fallacy of any arguments that are addressed to shew, that these islands are not to be considered as part of the territory of America. Whether they are composed of earth or solid rock, will not vary the right of dominion, for the right of dominion does not depend upon the texture of the soil.

I am of opinion that the right of territory is to be reckoned from those islands. That being established, it is not denied that the actual capture took place within the distance of three miles from the islands, and at the very threshold of the river.[1] . . .

. . . The conduct of the captors has on all points been highly reprehensible. Looking to all the circumstances of previous misconduct, I feel myself bound to pronounce, that there has been a violation of territory, and that as to the question of property, there was not sufficient ground of seizure; and that these acts of misconduct have been further aggravated, by bringing the vessel to England, without any necessity that can justify such a measure. In such a case it would be falling short of the justice due to the violated rights of America, and to the individuals who have sustained injury by such misconduct, if I did not follow up the restitution which has passed on the former day, with a decree of costs and damages.

C. Prescription.

Prescription is the acquisition of property by an adverse holding continued through a long term of years. It presumes the abandonment of the territory by the original owner, so that the rules relating to prescription are closely related to those governing *occupation*. Its

----

[1] The court here considered the question whether the doctrine of hot pursuit into territorial waters was applicable and found the authority of Bynkershoek in its favor, but refused to apply it in view of the objectionable conduct of the captors.

legal basis is the recognition of the necessity of not disturbing situations that have been allowed to continue so long as to give rise to vested interests. [Rhode Island v. Massachusetts; Maryland v. West Virginia.]

THE STATE OF RHODE ISLAND, COMPLAINANT, v. THE STATE OF MASSACHUSETTS, DEFENDANT.

United States, Supreme Court, 1846.

4 Howard, 591. [11 L. ed. 1116.]

MR. JUSTICE McLEAN delivered the opinion of the court.

We approach this case under a due sense of the dignity of the parties, and of the importance of the principles which it involves.

The jurisdiction of the court having been settled at a former term,[1] we have now only to ascertain and determine the boundary in dispute. This, disconnected with the consequences which follow, is a simple question, differing little, if any, in principle from a disputed line between individuals. It involves neither a cession of territory, nor the exercise of a political jurisdiction. In settling the rights of the respective parties, we do nothing more than ascertain the true boundary, and the territory up to that line on either side necessarily falls within the proper jurisdiction.

James the First, on the 3d of November, 1620, granted to the Council established at Plymouth the territory on the Atlantic lying between forty and forty-eight degrees of north latitude, extending westward to the sea. And on the 19th of March, 1628, the Council of Plymouth granted to Henry Roswell and others the territory of Massachusetts, which was confirmed by Charles the First, the 4th of March, 1629. This grant was limited to the territory "lying within the space of three English miles on the south part of Charles River, or of any or every part thereof; and also all and singular the lands and hereditaments whatsoever, lying and being within the space of three English miles to the southward of the southernmost part of Massachusetts Bay; and also all those lands and hereditaments whatsoever, which lie and be within the space of three English miles to the northward of the Merrimack River, or to the northward of any and every part thereof," extending westward the same breadth to the sea. . . .

The Council of Plymouth surrendered its charter to the king the 7th of June, 1635. . . .

---

[1] See 12 Peters, 657. The case was also before the Supreme Court on various points in 7 Peters, 651; 11 Peters, 226; 12 Peters, 755; 13 Peters, 23; 14 Peters, 210; 15 Peters, 233.

The charter of Rhode Island was granted the 8th of July, 1663, by Charles the Second, limited on the north by the southerly line of Massachusetts.

It thus appears that the disputed line is the common boundary between Massachusetts and Rhode Island; the latter lying south of the line, and the former north of it. The true location of this line settles this controversy.

More than two hundred years have elapsed since the emanation of the Massachusetts charter, calling for this boundary; and more than one hundred and eighty years, since the date of the Rhode Island charter. In looking at transactions so remote, we must, as far as practicable, view things as they were seen and understood at the time they transpired. There is no other test of truth and justice, which applies to the variable condition of all human concerns.

The words of the Massachusetts charter, "lying within the space of three English miles on the south part of Charles River, or of any or every part thereof," do not convey so clear and definite an idea as to be susceptible of but one construction. Whether the measurement of the three miles shall be from the body of the river, or from the head-waters of the streams which fall into it, are questions which different minds may not answer in the same way. That the tributary streams of a river, in one sense, constitute a part of it, is clear; but whether they come within the meaning of the charter is the matter in controversy. The early exposition of this instrument by those who claimed under it is not to be disregarded, though it may not be conclusive.

This line is said to have been often a matter of controversy between the Plymouth colony and Massachusetts, as early as 1638, and that in that year Nathaniel Woodward took an observation upon part of Charles River, 41° 50' north latitude. In 1642, the southern bounds of Massachusetts were ascertained by the said Woodward and Solomon Saffrey, who fixed a station three miles south of the southernmost part of Charles River. And in 1664, a line was run by commissioners from each colony, and their return was accepted by the General Court of Massachusetts, and ordered to be recorded; and it may fairly be presumed that the return was also accepted by Plymouth. This was a construction of the charter by Massachusetts, and assented to by Plymouth, that the three miles were to be measured not from the main channel of Charles River, but from the head-waters of one of its tributaries. . . .

Serious difficulties occurred between the border inhabitants of Massachusetts and Rhode Island, on account of conflicting grants, and the establishment of towns. And after much correspondence and legislative action on the subject by the respective parties, it was finally agreed to appoint commissioners to settle the line. . . .

The commissioners of both colonies met at Roxbury, January 19th, 1710–11, and after stating the authority under which they acted, and having "examined the several charters and letters patent relating to the line betwixt the said respective governments, and being desirous to remove and take away all occasions of dispute and controversy," &c., "they agree that the stake set up by Nathaniel Woodward and Solomon Saffrey [. . .] be accounted and allowed on both sides the commencement of the line between the Massachusetts and the colony of Rhode Island." . . . In March, 1711, the Rhode Island legislature sanctioned this agreement, by authorizing the line to be run in pursuance thereof, and the agreement was accepted and approved of by Massachusetts. . . .

The complainant's counsel rely mainly upon two grounds:—

1. The misconstruction of the charter.

2. The mistake as to the true location of the Woodward and Saffrey station.

If the first be ruled against the complainant, the second must fall as a consequence. And as regards the first ground, little need be added to what has already been said. The charter is of doubtful construction, and may, without doing violence to its language, be construed in favor of or against the position of the complainant. In this view, the construction of the charter by Massachusetts, assented to by the old colony of Plymouth, many years before Connecticut or Rhode Island had a political organization, is an important fact in the case. . . .

This dispute is between two sovereign and independent states. It originated in the infancy of their history, when the question in contest was of little importance. And fortunately steps were early taken to settle it, in a mode honorable and just, and one most likely to lead to a satisfactory result. There is no objection to the joint commission in this case, as to their authority, capacity, or the fairness of their proceeding. An innocent mistake is all that is alleged against their decision. And as has been shown, this mistake is not clearly established, either in the construction of the charter, or as to the location of the Woodward and Saffrey station. But if the mistake were admitted as broadly and fully as charged in the bill, could the court give the relief asked by the complainant.

In 1754, William Murray, then attorney-general, afterwards Lord Mansfield, was consulted by Connecticut, whether the agreement with Massachusetts respecting their common boundary, in 1713, would be set aside by a commission appointed by the crown. To which Mr. Murray replied,—"I am of opinion, that, in settling the above-mentioned boundary, the crown will not disturb the settlement by the two provinces so long ago as 1713. I apprehend His Majesty will confirm their agreement, which of itself is not binding on the crown, but neither province should be suffered to litigate such an amicable compromise of doubtful boundaries. If the matter was open, the same construction already made in the case of Merrimack River must be put upon the same words in the same charter applied to Charles River. As to Jack's Brook, it is impossible to say whether it is part of Charles River, without a view, at least without an exact plan, and knowing how it has been reputed.''

From the settlement referred to up to the time this opinion was given by Mr. Murray, forty-one years only had elapsed. And if that time was sufficient to protect that agreement, with how much greater force does the principle apply to the agreements under consideration, which are protected by the lapse of more than a century and a quarter. More than two centuries have passed since Massachusetts claimed and took possession of the territory up to the line established by Woodward and Saffrey. This possession has ever since been steadily maintained, under an assertion of right. It would be difficult to disturb a claim thus sanctioned by time, however unfounded it might have been in its origin.

The possession of the respondent was taken not only under a claim of right, but that right in the most solemn form has been admitted by the complainant and by the other colonies interested in opposing it. Forty years elapsed before a mistake was alleged, and since such allegation was made nearly a century has transpired. If in the agreements there was a departure from the strict construction of the charter, the commissioners of Rhode Island acted within their powers, for they were authorized ''to agree and settle the line between the said colonies in the best manner they can, as near agreeable to the royal charter as in honor they can compromise the same.'' Under this authority, can the complainant insist on setting aside the agreements, because the words of the charter were not strictly observed? It is not clear that the calls of the charter were deviated from by establishing the station of Woodward and Saffrey. But if in this respect there was a deviation, Rhode Island was not the less bound, for its commissioners were authorized to compromise the dispute. Surely this, connected with the lapse of time, must remove all doubt as to the right of the respondent under the agreements of 1711 and 1718. No human transactions are unaffected by time. Its influence is seen on all things subject to change. And this is peculiarly the case in regard to matters which rest in memory, and which consequently fade with the lapse of time, and fall with the lives of individuals. For the security of rights, whether of states or individuals, long possession under a claim of title is protected. And there is no controversy in which this great principle may be involved with greater justice and propriety than in a case of disputed boundary. . . . .

STATE OF MARYLAND v. STATE OF WEST VIRGINIA.

Supreme Court of the United States, 1910.

217 U. S. 1.　[54 L. ed. 645; 30 S. Ct. 268.]

Original.　In Equity.

Mr. Justice Day delivered the opinion of the court. . . .

It is true there has been more or less contention as to the true boundary line between these States. Attempts have been made to settle and adjust the same, some of which we have referred to, and the details of which may be found in the very interesting document to which we have already made reference, the report of the committee of the Maryland Historical Society. In the proposed settlements, for many years, Virginia and West Virginia have consistently adhered to the Fairfax Stone as a starting point for the disputed boundary. When West Virginia passed the act of 1887, ratifying the Michler line, it was upon condition that Virginia titles granted between the Michler line and the old Maryland line should be validated. Maryland, in the act of 1852, recognized the same starting point.

And the fact remains that after the Deakins survey in 1788 the people living along the line generally regarded that line as the boundary line between the States at bar. In the acts of the legislatures of the two States, to which we have already referred, resulting in the survey and running of the Michler line, it is evident from the language used that the purpose was not to establish a new line, but to retrace the old one, and we are strongly inclined to believe that had this been done at that time the controversy would have been settled.

A perusal of the record satisfies us that for many years occupation and conveyance of the lands on the Virginia side has been with reference to the Deakins line as the boundary line. The people have generally accepted it and have adopted it, and the facts in this connection cannot be ignored. In the case of Virginia v. Tennessee, 148 U. S. 503, 522, 523, Mr. Justice Field, speaking for the court, had occasion to make certain comments which are pertinent in this connection, wherein he said:

"Independently of any effect due to the compact as such, a boundary line between States or provinces, as between private persons, which has been run out, located and marked upon the earth, and afterwards recognized and acquiesced in by the parties for a long course of years, is conclusive, even if it be ascertained that it varies somewhat from the courses given in the original grant; and the line so established takes effect, not as an alienation of territory, but as a definition of the true and ancient boundary. Lord Hardwicke in Penn v. Lord Baltimore, 1 Vesey Sen. 444, 448; Boyd v. Graves, 4 Wheat. 513; Rhode Island v. Massachusetts, 12 Pet. 657, 734; United States v. Stone, 2 Wall. 525, 537; Kellogg v.

Smith, 7 Cush. 375, 382; Chenery v. Waltham, 8 Cush. 327; Hunt on Boundaries (3d ed.), 396.

"As said by this court in the recent case of the State of Indiana v. Kentucky, 136 U. S. 479, 510, 'it is a principle of public law, universally recognized, that long acquiescence in the possession of territory, and in the exercise of dominion and sovereignty over it, is conclusive of the nation's title and rightful authority.' In the case of Rhode Island v. Massachusetts, 4 How. 591, 639, this court, speaking of the long possession of Massachusetts, and the delays in alleging any mistake in the action of the commissioners of the colonies, said: 'Surely this, connected with the lapse of time, must remove all doubts as to the right of the respondent under the agreements of 1711 and 1718.' . . ."

And quoting from Vattel on the Law of Nations to the same effect (Sec. 149, p. 190):

"The tranquillity of the people, the safety of States, the happiness of the human race do not allow that the possessions, empire, and other rights of nations should remain uncertain, subject to dispute and ever ready to occasion bloody wars. Between nations, therefore, it becomes necessary to admit prescription founded on length of time as a valid and incontestable title."

And adds from Wheaton on International Law (Sec. 164, p. 260):

"The writers on natural law have questioned how far that peculiar species of presumption, arising from the lapse of time, which is called prescription, is justly applicable as between nation and nation; but the constant and approved practice of nations shows that by whatever name it be called, the uninterrupted possession of territory or other property for a certain length of time by one State excludes the claim of every other in the same manner, as, by the law of nature and the municipal code of every civilized nation, a similar possession by an individual excludes the claim of every other person to the articles or property in question."

And it was said:

"There are also moral considerations which should prevent any disturbance of long recognized boundary lines; considerations springing from regard to the natural sentiments and affections which grow up for places on which persons have long resided; the attachments to the country, to home and to family, on which is based all that is dearest and most valuable in life."

In Louisiana v. Mississippi, 202 U. S., 1, 53, this court said:

"The question is one of boundary, and this court has many times held that, as between the States of the Union, long acquiescence in the assertion of a particular boundary and the exercise of dominion and sovereignty over the territory within it, should be accepted as conclusive, whatever the international rule might be in respect of the acquisition by prescription of large tracts of country claimed by both."

An application of these principles cannot permit us to ignore the conduct of the States and the belief of the people concerning the purpose of the boundary line known as the old state, or Deakins, line, and to which their deeds called as the boundary of their farms, in recognition of which they have established their allegiance as citizens of the State of West Virginia, and in accordance to which they have fixed their homes and habitations. . . .

The effect to be given to such facts as long continued possession "gradually ripening into that condition which is in conformity with international order," depends upon the merit of individual cases as they arise. 1 Oppenheim International Law, Sec. 243. In this case we think a right, in its nature prescriptive, has arisen, practically undisturbed for many years, not to be overthrown without doing violence to principles of established right and justice equally binding upon States and individuals. Rhode Island v. Massachusetts, 12 Pet. 657. . . .

D. Cession.

Title by cession in international law corresponds in a general way to title by deed of transfer in private law. It is usually carried out by means of a treaty between the two parties, describing the territory to be transferred and the conditions under which the transfer is to take place. Query, would the mere signature of a treaty, without any formal proclamation or other public act signifying that the transfer of the territory has taken place, be sufficient to change the national status of the inhabitants of the territory in question? [The Fama.]

THE FAMA, BUTLER [MASTER].

Great Britain, High Court of Admiralty, 1804.

5 C. Rob. 106.

This was a question respecting the national character of Louisiana, whether it was, at the time of capture, May 1803, to be considered as a Spanish settlement, or as belonging to France, by reason of the treaty of Idelfonso, 1796, by which it was ceded to that country. The question arose on the claim of Mr. ——, a merchant, resident at New Orleans, for property taken, May 1803, on a voyage from New Orleans to Havre le Grace. . . .

SIR W. SCOTT.—The present question is a general one, respecting the situation, in which the people of a distant settlement are placed, by a Treaty of the State to which they undoubtedly belong, and by which they are stipulated to be transferred to another power. The case proceeded for a considerable time without dispute as to principle, on a mere enquiry into the fact of possession; under an understanding, as I apprehended, that if possession *had not* been taken by France, the French character could not be deemed to have attached. The question has however now been fully argued as to the principle of law, whether the Treaty did not in itself confer full sovereignty and right of dominion, and whether the inhabitants were not so ceded by that Treaty, as to become immediately French subjects. . . .

It is to be observed then, that all corporeal property depends very much upon occupancy. With respect to the origin of property, this is the Sole foundation, *Quod nullius est ratione naturali occupanti conceditur.* So with regard to transfer also, it is universally held in all systems of jurisprudence, that to consummate the right of property, a person must unite the *right of the thing with possession.* A question has been made indeed by some writers, whether this necessity proceeds from what they call the natural law of nations, or from that which is only conventional. Grotius seems to consider it as proceeding only from civil institutions. Puffendorf and Pothier go farther. All concur, however, in holding it to be a necessary principle of jurisprudence, that to complete the right of property, *the right to the thing*, and *the possession of the thing* itself, should be united; or, according to the technical expression, borrowed either from the civil law, or as Barbeyrac explains it, from the commentators on the Canon Law, that there should be both the *jus in rem*, and the *jus in re.*—This is the general law of property, and applies, I conceive, no less to the right of territory than to other rights. Even in newly discovered countries, where a title is meant to be established, *for the first time*, some act of possession is usually done and proclaimed as a notification of the fact. In transfer, surely, where the former rights of others are to be superseded, and extinguished, it cannot be less necessary that such a change should be indicated by some public acts, that all who are deeply interested in the event, as the inhabitants of such settlements, may be informed under whose dominion, and under what laws they are to live. This I conceive to be the general propriety of principle on the subject, and no less applicable to cases of territory, than to property of every other description.

It will be only necessary to enquire then, whether the practice has been conformable to what we might conceive to be the true principle of law. On this point no doubt can be entertained. The *Corps Diplomatique* is full of instances of this kind: Where stipulations of Treaties for ceding particular countries are to be carried into execution, solemn instruments of cession are drawn up, and adequate powers are formally given to the persons, by whom the actual delivery is to be made. In modern times, more especially, such a proceeding is become almost a matter of necessity, with regard to the colonial establishments of the States of Europe in the new world. The Treaties by which they are affected may not be known to them for months after they are made. Many articles must remain *executory* only, and not executed, till carried into effect; and until that is done by some public act, the former sovereignty must remain. Amongst the instances that might be cited to shew what the practice has been on this subject, I will mention only a few. On the cession of Nova Scotia to France by Treaty, 21st *July*, 1667, the act of cession, which purports to be made in consequence of the Treaty, was not drawn up till February 1668, when full powers were sent out to deliver up the *settlement to the person who should be empowered to take possession, under the great* seal of *France.*—Another instance, which comes nearer to the present question, is to be found in the proceedings which took place when this very settlement of Louisiana was ceded by France to Spain in 1762. It passed by act of cession drawn up in solemn form, and dated more than a year after the Treaty itself. Indeed modern history abounds in such instances. If to these it were necessary to add the authority of a judicial recognition of the principle, I think the case of Wroughton against Mann, to which I alluded on the former day, is strongly in point. That was a case before the delegates on appeal in a revenue cause. The Act of Court pleaded, "that East Florida was ceded to Spain by Treaty of 1803, and that eighteen months were allowed for emigration. 2dly. That notwithstanding the Treaty, the English laws continued till the Spanish Government arrived and received delivery from General Tonin; and the formal instruments, under which possession was afterwards taken, were exhibited." The offence charged was an act of importation contrary to the British Revenue Laws, long after the ratification of the Treaty, but before the arrival of the Spanish Governor, and the actual delivery. Objections were taken to the allegation, similar to the arguments which have been urged in the present case, *viz.* "That the country had passed to Spain by virtue of the Treaty; that the continuance of British possession was but an usurpation; and that the offence was no longer amenable to the British laws. If that could have been sustained, the plea must have been bad; but it was not so held. The Court of Delegates were of opinion, that the contract was merely *executory,* and till it was carried into execution, the British possession, and the British laws," continued in full force. On this ground the allegation was admitted. The cause proceeded, and went off afterwards on failure of proof as to the fact; but the opinion of the Court, as to the law, was fully declared by the admission of such a plea. I am of opinion, therefore, that on all the several grounds of reason or practice, and judicial recognition, until possession was actually taken, the inhabitants of New Orleans continued under the former sovereignty of Spain. . . .

. . . In this situation of things, it appears to me, upon the grounds before stated, that the colony must be considered as continuing, at the time of capture, under the dominion of Spain, and consequently that these persons, as Spanish subjects, are entitled to restitution.[1]

E. Conquest.

As a technical form of acquiring title to territory conquest consists in the occupation of the enemy territory in time of war and the retention of the territory at the close of the war without mention of it in the treaty of peace if one be signed. Query, could an enemy vessel, captured by the British in territorial waters held at the time by conquest from the enemy, be said to have been captured within the dominions of the Crown when there had been no formal annexation of the territory? [The Foltina.]

THE FOLTINA, JULINS [MASTER].

Great Britain, High Court of Admiralty, 1814.

1 Dodson, 450.

This was the case of a ship and cargo seized on the 15th of December, 1811, whilst lying at anchor in the roadstead of Heligoland, which island had been surrendered to his Majesty's forces on the 5th of September, 1807. The question was, whether the ship and cargo should be condemned as droits of admiralty or otherwise.[2]

---

[1] SUPPLEMENTARY CASES. In Davis v. The Police Jury of the Parish of Concordia, 9 Howard 280 (1850), involving the validity of a franchise granted by authority of the Spanish government in 1801, four months after the signing of the treaty of St. Ildefonso by which Spain retroceded to France the province of Louisiana, the Supreme Court held that while after the treaty was made possession continued in Spain until Louisiana was delivered to France, yet the sovereignty over the territory ceased with the signature of the treaty. "All of our proceedings respecting Louisiana" said the court, "have been done upon the principle, that the law of nations does not recognize in a nation ceding a territory the continuance of supreme power over it after the treaty has been signed, or any other exercise of sovereignty than that which is necessary for social order and for commercial purposes, and to keep the cession in an unaltered value, until a delivery of it has been made. Such being the extent of sovereignty under such circumstances, is not the grant of a perpetual ferry franchise attached to land as much prohibited as a grant of land?" The case of the Fama was cited as coinciding with the views of the court.

[2] The question at issue, while one of constitutional rather than of international law, gave rise to interesting obiter dicta showing the effects of conquest. According to the location of the ship at the time of the capture the condemnation had

SIR W. SCOTT.—This is the case of a vessel which was taken in the roadstead of Heligoland, not at the time of the surrender of the island, but afterwards, and the seizure is represented to have taken place within the *harbour*. The locality of the transaction is, I think, sufficiently described by the term made use of by the witnesses, who must be understood to mean that portion of the sea to which vessels are carried for the purpose of landing their cargoes at Heligoland; and whether the same portion of the sea is more or less enclosed, whether it is completely land-locked or not, does not appear to be material to the issue in the present case. The Gazette, too, describes the place as a *haven*, a compliment to which it is certainly not, in strictness, entitled; but it is used as a haven, and may, therefore, fairly be considered as such, at least, for the purposes of the present question. There is certainly no reason for saying that the property is not within the grant of the Crown to the Lord High Admiral, so far as the locality of the seizure is concerned; for it is the ordinary rule, that ships, taken in such places during the existence of hostilities, become droits of Admiralty.

But the chief point to be considered is, whether, at the time this seizure was made, Heligoland formed part of the dominions of the crown of Great Britain or not. The island, it appears, had been conquered and taken possession of by British forces, but the conquest had not been confirmed to this country by a treaty of peace. It was a firm capture in war, but was still subject to a kind of latent title in the enemy, by which he might have recovered it at the conclusion of the war, provided this country would have consented to its restitution.

It is somewhat extraordinary that, in the course of the numerous and long wars in which this country has been engaged, no case should have been determined which might serve as a guide to the court in the decision of the present question. It does not appear that any case of the kind has hitherto occurred, with the solitary exception of that which has been mentioned in the argument, (The Esperanza,) and that is admitted to have passed with very little notice, and without opposition. A cause thus passing *sub silentio* cannot be considered of great weight in point of authority. I observe that the grant from the crown to the Lord High Admiral applies to the king's dominions generally, and that there is nothing which points to a distinction between those parts of the king's dominions over which the crown has *plenum dominium* or otherwise. No point is more clearly settled in courts of common law than that a conquered country forms immediately part of the king's dominions. (Campbell v. Hall, Cowper's Rep. 208.) In a late instance, we know

to be in favor of the Admiral or of others. The Order in Council under which the conclusion was reached provided that enemy ships and goods coming into any "port, creek, or road of this his Majesty's Kingdom of England or Ireland" by stress of weather or in ignorance of hostilities were to belong to the Lord High Admiral.

that an island so acquired (Guadaloupe) was transferred to a third power, subject, undoubtedly, to the shadowy right of the former proprietor. It is said, that a conquest of this kind may be re-acquired *flagranti bello* by the state from which it was taken; but so may any other possession, though forming part of the original and established dominions of the crown of this country, if the enemy has it in his power to make the conquest. The same observation is applicable to the Isle of Wight, as well as to Heligoland, for the enemy has the same right to make a conquest of the one as the other. It is said that the enemy may recover back the island of Heligoland when peace takes place; but it is equally true that the conqueror may retain it if he can; and, if nothing is said about it in the treaty, it remains with the possessor, whose title cannot afterwards be called in question. The distinction between the two species of territories is, in fact, rather more formal than real and substantial, at least I must profess my inability to see any distinction between them that can materially affect the present question. The power of the British Government was full and complete; and, though the Lords Commissioners of the Admiralty might not have interposed the particular authority with which they are invested, yet the Crown had exercised its authority, and the Admiralty, as the grantee of the Crown, would succeed to its rights. It might have erected a court there, for the exercise of Admiralty jurisdiction; and, if it did not, I presume that it only refrained from so doing because it was not thought that public convenience required it. The enemy certainly had no right to say that a Court of that kind should not be there erected. Under the circumstances, I think there is no solid ground for the distinction that has been taken; and though I am by no means disposed, at this time of day, to enlarge the bounds of the ancient grant from the Crown to the Lord High Admiral, which is now become of less consequence, yet it is the duty of the Court to maintain ancient landmarks. I shall pronounce for the claim of the Admiralty, and condemn this ship as droits of Admiralty.

CHAPTER XIII

JURISDICTION OVER TERRITORY: NATIONAL BOUNDARIES AND TERRITORIAL WATERS [1]

A. Rivers.

The present boundary lines between nations have for the most part not been determined upon any principle of economic or social utility but have been the result of conflicts of national interest brought to a conclusion by treaties of peace. As a matter of geographical convenience, and in certain cases because of their strategic value, rivers have frequently been incorporated into the boundary-lines of states. Query, would a cession of territory lying on the further side of a river leave the ownership of the entire river in the possession of the state making the cession? [Handly's Lessee v. Anthony.] In the more normal case where the boundary-line follows the middle of the river, does this mean the surveyor's line or the middle of the main channel of navigation? [Iowa v. Illinois.] May the formula of the thalweg be applied to the settlement of a present controversy even though the formula was not a rule of international law at the time of the historical origin of the controversy? [New Jersey v. Delaware.] What are the effects of slow accretion and sudden avulsion upon boundary-lines following the middle of rivers? [Nebraska v. Iowa.]

HANDLY'S LESSEE v. ANTHONY ET AL.

Supreme Court of the United States, 1820.

5 Wheaton, 374. [5 L. ed. 113.]

Mr. Chief Justice Marshall delivered the opinion of the Court. This was an ejectment brought in the Circuit Court of the United States for the District of Kentucky, to recover land which the plaintiff claims under a grant from the State of Kentucky, and which the defend-

---

[1] For a more detailed study of this subject, see Fenwick, *op. cit.*, pp. 273–287; Hyde, *op. cit.*, §§ 134–151; Oppenheim, *op. cit.*, I, §§ 172–202; Jessup, Law of Territorial Waters and Maritime Jurisdiction; Masterson, Jurisdiction in Marginal Seas; Harvard Draft: Territorial Waters; P. M. Brown, "Protective Jurisdiction over Marginal Waters," Proceedings, Am. Society Int. Law, 1923, pp. 15–31.

ants hold under a grant from the United States as being part of Indiana. The title depends upon the question whether the lands lie in the State of Kentucky, or in the State of Indiana.

At this place, as appears from the plat and surveyor's certificate, the Ohio turns its course, and runs southward for a considerable distance, and then takes a northern direction, until it approaches within less than three miles, as appears from the plat, of the place where its southern course commences. A small distance above the narrowest part of the neck of land which is thus formed, a channel, or what is commonly termed in that country a bayou, makes out of the Ohio, and enters the same river a small distance below the place where it resumes its westward course. This channel, or bayou, is about nine miles by its meanders, three miles and a half in a straight line, and from four to five poles wide. The circuit made by the river appears to be from fifteen to twenty miles. About midway of the channel two branches empty into it from the northwest, between six and seven hundred yards from each other; the one of which runs along the channel at low water, eastward, and the other westward, until they both enter the main river. Between them is ground over which the waters of the Ohio do not pass until the river has risen about ten feet above its lowest state. It rises from forty to fifty feet, and all the testimony proves that this channel is made by the waters of the river, not of the creeks which empty into it. The people who inhabit this peninsula, or island, have always paid taxes to Indiana, voted in Indiana, and been considered as within its jurisdiction, both while it was a Territory, and since it has become a State. The jurisdiction of Kentucky has never been extended over them.

The question whether the lands in controversy lie within the State of Kentucky or of Indiana, depends chiefly on the land law of Virginia, and on the cession made by that State to the United States.

Both Kentucky and Indiana were supposed to be comprehended within the charter of Virginia at the commencement of the war of our revolution. At an early period of that war, the question whether the immense tracts of unsettled country which lay within the charters of particular States, ought to be considered as the property of those States, or as an acquisition made by the arms of all, for the benefit of all, convulsed our confederacy, and threatened its existence. It was probably with a view to this question that Virginia, in 1779, when she opened her land office, prohibited the location or entry of any land "on the northwest side of the river Ohio."

In September, 1780, Congress passed a resolution, recommending "to the several States having claims to waste and unappropriated lands in the western country, a liberal cession to the United States, of a portion of their respective claims, for the common benefit of the Union." And in January, 1781, the Commonwealth of Virginia yielded to the United

States "all right, title, and claim, which the said Commonwealth had to the territory northwest of the river Ohio, subject to the conditions annexed to the said act of cession." One of these conditions is, "that the ceded territory shall be laid out and formed into States." Congress accepted this cession, but proposed some small variation in the conditions, which was acceded to; and in 1783 Virginia passed her act of confirmation, giving authority to her members in Congress to execute a deed of conveyance.

It was intended then by Virginia, when she made this cession to the United States, and most probably when she opened her land office, that the great river Ohio should constitute a boundary between the States which might be formed on its opposite banks. This intention ought never to be disregarded in construing this cession. . . .

The two exceptions [taken by the plaintiff] present substantially the same questions to the Court, and may therefore be considered together. They are, whether land is properly denominated an island of the Ohio, unless it be surrounded with the water of the river, when low? and whether Kentucky was bounded on the west and northwest by the low-water mark of the river, or at its middle state? or, in other words, whether the State of Indiana extends to low-water mark, or stops at the line reached by the river when at its medium height?

In pursuing this inquiry, we must recollect that it is not the bank of the river, but the river itself, at which the cession of Virginia commences. She conveys to Congress all her right to the territory "situate, lying, and being to the northwest of the river Ohio." And this territory, according to express stipulation, is to be laid off into independent States. These States, then, are to have the river itself, wherever that may be, for their boundary. This is a natural boundary, and in establishing it, Virginia must have had in view the convenience of the future population of the country.

When a great river is the boundary between two nations or states, if the original property is in neither, and there be no convention respecting it, each holds to the middle of the stream. But when, as in this case, one State is the original proprietor, and grants the territory on one side only, it retains the river within its own domain, and the newly created State extends to the river only. The river, however, is its boundary.

"In case of doubt," says Vattel, "every country lying upon a river, is presumed to have no other limits but the river itself; because nothing is more natural than to take a river for a boundary, when a state is established on its border; and wherever there is a doubt, that is always to be presumed which is most natural and most probable."

"If," says the same author, "the country which borders on a river, has no other limits than the river itself, it is in the number of territories that have natural or indetermined limits, and it enjoys the right of alluvion.'' [L. 1, c. 22, § 268.]

Any gradual accretion of land, then, on the Indiana side of the Ohio, would belong to Indiana, and it is not very easy to distinguish between land thus formed, and land formed by the receding of the water.

If, instead of an annual and somewhat irregular rising and falling of the river, it was a daily and almost regular ebbing and flowing of the tide, it would not be doubted that a country bounded by the river would extend to low-water mark. This rule has been established by the common consent of mankind. It is founded on a common convenience. Even when a State retains its dominion over a river which constitutes the boundary between itself and another State, it would be extremely inconvenient to extend its dominion over the land on the other side, which was left bare by the receding of the water. And this inconvenience is not less where the rising and falling is annual, than where it is diurnal. Wherever the river is a boundary between States, it is the main, the permanent river, which constitutes that boundary; and the mind will find itself embarrassed with insurmountable difficulty in attempting to draw any other line than the low-water mark.

When the State of Virginia made the Ohio the boundary of States, she must have intended the great river Ohio, not a narrow bayou into which its waters occasionally run. All the inconvenience which would result from attaching a narrow strip of country lying on the northwest side of that noble river to the States on its southeastern side, would result from attaching to Kentucky, the State on its southeastern border, a body of land lying northwest of the real river, and divided from the mainland only by a narrow channel, through the whole of which the waters of the river do not pass, until they rise ten feet above the low-water mark.

The opinions given by the Court must be considered in reference to the case in which they were given. The sole question in the cause respected the boundary of Kentucky and Indiana; and the title depended entirely upon that question. The definition of an island which the court was requested to give, was either an abstract proposition, which it was unnecessary to answer, or one which was to be answered according to its bearing on the facts in the cause. The definition of an island was only material so far as that definition might aid in fixing the boundary of Kentucky. In the opinion given by the court on the motion made by the counsel for the defendants, they say that ''no land can be called an island of the Ohio, unless it be surrounded by the waters of that river at low-water mark.'' We are not satisfied that this definition is incorrect, as respected the subject before the court; but it is rendered unimportant, by the subsequent member of the sentence, in which they say, ''that to low-water mark only, on the western and northwestern side of the Ohio, does the State of Kentucky extend.''

So, in the motion made by the counsel for the plaintiff, the court was requested to say, that if the waters of the Ohio flowed in the channel, in its middle and usual state, it was not only an island, but "within the State of Kentucky."

If the land was not within the State of Kentucky, the court could not give the direction which was requested. The court gave an instruction substantially the same with that which had been given on the motion of the defendant's counsel.

If it be true, that the river Ohio, not its ordinary bank, is the boundary of Indiana, the limits of that State can be determined only by the river itself. The same tract of land cannot be sometimes in Kentucky, and sometimes in Indiana, according to the rise and fall of the river. It must be always in the one State, or the other.

There would be little difficulty in deciding, that in any case other than land which was sometimes an island, the State of Indiana would extend to low-water mark. Is there any safe and secure principle, on which we can apply a different rule to land which is sometimes, though not always, surrounded by water?

So far as respects the great purposes for which the river was taken as the boundary, the two cases seem to be within the same reason, and to require the same rule. It would be as inconvenient to the people inhabiting this neck of land, separated from Indiana only by a bayou or ravine, sometimes dry for six or seven hundred yards of its extent, but separated from Kentucky by the great river Ohio, to form a part of the last-mentioned State, as it would for the inhabitants of a strip of land along the whole extent of the Ohio, to form a part of the State on the opposite shore. Neither the one nor the other can be considered as intended by the deed of cession.

If a river, subject to tides, constituted the boundary of a State, and at flood the waters of the river flowed through a narrow channel, round an extensive body of land, but receded from that channel at ebb, so as to leave the land it surrounded at high water, connected with the main body of the country; this portion of territory would scarcely be considered as belonging to the State on the opposite side of the river, although that State should have the property of the river. The principle that a country bounded by a river extends to low-water mark, a principle so natural, and of such obvious convenience as to have been generally adopted, would, we think, apply to that case. We perceive no sufficient reason why it should not apply to this.

The case is certainly not without its difficulties; but in great questions which concern the boundaries of States, where great natural boundaries are established in general terms, with a view to public convenience, and the avoidance of controversy, we think the great object, where it can be distinctly perceived, ought not to be defeated by those technical perplexities which may sometimes influence contracts between individuals. The State of Virginia intended to make the great river Ohio, throughout its extent, the boundary between the territory ceded to the United States and herself. When that part of Virginia, which is now Kentucky, became a separate State, the river was the boundary between the new States erected by Congress in the ceded territory, and Kentucky. Those principles and considerations which produced the boundary, ought to preserve it. They seem to us to require, that Kentucky should not pass the main river, and possess herself of lands lying on the opposite side, although they should, for a considerable portion of the year, be surrounded by the waters of the river flowing into a narrow channel.

It is a fact of no inconsiderable importance in this case, that the inhabitants of this land have uniformly considered themselves, and have been uniformly considered, both by Kentucky and Indiana, as belonging to the last-mentioned State. No diversity of opinion appears to have existed on this point. The water on the northwestern side of the land in controversy, seems not to have been spoken of as a part of the river, but as a bayou. The people of the vicinage, who viewed the river in all its changes, seem not to have considered this land as being an island of the Ohio, and as a part of Kentucky, but as lying on the northwestern side of the Ohio, and being a part of Indiana.

The compact with Virginia, under which Kentucky became a State, stipulates, that the navigation of, and jurisdiction over, the river, shall be concurrent between the new States, and the States which may possess the opposite *shores* of the said river. This term seems to be a repetition of the idea under which the cession was made. The shores of a river border on the water's edge.

Judgment affirmed, with costs.

IOWA v. ILLINOIS.

United States, Supreme Court, 1893.

147 U. S. 1. [37 L. ed. 55; 13 S. Ct. 239.]

MR. JUSTICE FIELD delivered the opinion of the court.

The Mississippi River flows between the States of Iowa and Illinois. It is a navigable stream and constitutes the boundary between the two States; and the controversy between them is as to the position of the line between its banks or shores which separates the jurisdiction of the two States for the purposes of taxation and other purposes of government.

The complainant, the State of Iowa, contends that, for taxation, and for all other purposes, the boundary line is the middle of the main body of the river, taking the middle line between its banks or shores without regard to the "steamboat channel," as it is termed, or deepest part of the stream, and that, to determine the banks or shores, the measurements must be taken when the water is in its natural or ordinary stage, neither swollen by floods nor shrunk by droughts.

On the other hand, the defendant, the State of Illinois, claims that, for taxation and all other purposes, its jurisdiction extends to the middle of "the steamboat channel" of the river, wherever that may be, whether on its east or west bank—the channel upon which commerce on the river by steamboats or other vessels is usually conducted, and which for that reason is sometimes designated as "the channel of commerce."

The State of Iowa in its bill alleges: That prior to and at the time of the treaty between England, France and Spain, in 1763, 3 Jenkinson's Treaties, 177, the territory now comprising the State of Iowa was under the dominion of France, and the territory now comprising the State of Illinois was under the dominion of Great Britain, and that, by the treaty named, the middle of the river Mississippi was made the boundary line between the British and French possessions in North America.

That by the treaty of Paris between Great Britain and the United States, which was concluded September 3, 1783, 3 Jenkinson's Treaties, 410, Art. II, and 8 Stat. 80, the territory comprising the State of Illinois passed to the United States; and that by the purchase of Louisiana from France, under the treaty of April 30, 1803, 8 Stat. 200, the territory comprising the State of Iowa passed to the United States.

That the boundary between the territory comprising the States of Illinois and Iowa remained the middle of the river Mississippi, as fixed by the treaty of 1763.

That by the act of Congress of April 18, 1818, known as the act enabling the people of Illinois to form a State constitution, (3 Stat. 428, c. 67,) the northern and western boundaries of Illinois were defined as follows: Starting in the middle of Lake Michigan, at north latitude forty-two degrees and thirty minutes, "then e west to the middle of the Mississippi River, and thence down along the middle of that river to its confluence with the Ohio River," and that the constitutions of Illinois of 1818, 1848 and 1870 defined the boundaries in the same way.

. . .

When a navigable river constitutes the boundary between two independent States, the line defining the point at which the jurisdiction of the two separates is well established to be the middle of the main channel of the stream. The interest of each State in the navigation of the river admits of no other line. The preservation by each of its equal right in the navigation of the stream is the subject of paramount interest. It is, therefore, laid down in all the recognized treatises on international law of modern times that the middle of the channel of the stream marks the true boundary between the adjoining States up to which each State will on its side exercise jurisdiction. In international law, therefore, and by the usage of European nations, the term "middle of the stream," as applied to a navigable river, is the same as the middle of the channel of such stream, and in that sense the terms are used in the treaty of peace between Great Britain, France and Spain, concluded at Paris in 1763. By the language, "a line drawn along the middle of the river Mississippi from its source to the river Iberville," as there used, is meant along the middle of the channel of the river Mississippi. Thus Wheaton, in his Elements of International Law, (8th ed. § 192,) says:

"Where a navigable river forms the boundary of conterminous States, the middle of the channel, or *Thalweg,* is generally taken as the line of separation between the two States, the presumption of law being that the right of navigation is common to both; but this presumption may be destroyed by actual proof of prior occupancy and long undisturbed possession, giving to one of the riparian proprietors the exclusive title to the entire river."

And in § 202, whilst thus stating the rule as to the boundary line of the Mississippi River being the middle of the channel, he states that the channel is remarkably winding, "crossing and recrossing perpetually from one side to the other of the general bed of the river."

Mr. Creasy, in his First Platform on International Law, § 231, p. 222, expresses the same doctrine. He says:

"It has been stated that, where a navigable river separates neighboring States, the *Thalweg,* or middle of the navigable channel, forms the line of separation. Formerly a line drawn along the middle of the water, the *medium filum aquæ,* was regarded as the boundary line; and still will be regarded *prima facie* as the boundary line, except as to those parts of the river as to which it can be proved that the vessels which navigate those parts keep their course habitually along some channel different from the *medium filum.* When this is the case, the middle of the channel of traffic is now considered to be the line of demarcation."

Mr. Creasy also refers to the language of Dr. Twiss on the same subject, who observes that "Grotius and Vattel speak of *the middle of the river* as the line of demarcation between two jurisdictions, but modern publicists and statesmen prefer the more accurate and more equitable boundary of the navigable Midchannel. If there be more than one channel of a river, the deepest channel is the Midchannel for the purposes of territorial demarcation; and the boundary line will be the line drawn along the surface of the stream corresponding to the line of deepest depression in its bed. . . . The islands on either side of the Midchannel are regarded as appendages to either bank; and if they have once been taken possession of by the nation to whose bank they are appendant, a change in the Midchannel of the river will not operate to

deprive that nation of its possession, although the water-frontier line
will follow the change of the Midchannel.''

Halleck in his Treatise on International Law, c. 6, § 23, is to the
same effect. He says: ''Where the river not only separates the conterminous States, but also their territorial jurisdictions, the *thalweg*, or
middle channel, forms the line of separation through the bays and
estuaries through which the waters of the river flow into the sea. As a
general rule, this line runs through the middle of the deepest channel,.
although it may divide the river and its estuaries into two very unequal
parts. But the deeper channel may be less suited, or totally unfit for
the purposes of navigation, in which case the dividing line would be in
the middle of the one which is best suited and ordinarily used for that
object.''

Woolsey in his International Law, § 58, repeats the same doctrine and
says: ''Where a navigable river forms the boundary between two States,
both are presumed to have free use of it, and the dividing line will
run in the middle of the channel, unless the contrary is shown by long
occupancy or agreement of the parties. If a river changes its bed, the
line through the old channel continues, but the equitable right to the
free use of the stream seems to belong, as before, to the State whose
territory the river has forsaken.''

The middle of the channel of a navigable river between independent
States is taken as the true boundary line from the obvious reason that
the right of navigation is presumed to be common to both in the absence
of a special convention between the neighboring States, or long use of
a different line equivalent to such a convention.

Phillimore, in his Commentaries on International Law, in the chapter
upon acquisitions, (c. xii,) speaks of decisions upon the law of property
as incident to neighborhood proceeding upon the principle that ''midchannel'' is the line of demarcation between the neighbors. (Vol. 1,
239.)

The reason and necessity of the rule of international law as to the
midchannel being the true boundary line of a navigable river separating
independent States may not be as cogent in this country, where neighboring States are under the same general government, as in Europe, yet
the same rule will be held to obtain unless changed by statute or usage
of so great a length of time as to have acquired the force of law.

As we have stated, in international law and by the usage of European
nations, the terms ''middle of the stream'' and ''midchannel'' of a
navigable river are synonymous and interchangeably used. The enabling
act of April 18, 1818, (3 Stat. 428, c. 67,) under which Illinois adopted a
constitution and became a State and was admitted into the Union, made
the middle of the Mississippi River the western boundary of the State.
The enabling act of March 6, 1820, (3 Stat. c. 22, § 2, p. 545,) under
which Missouri became a State and was admitted into the Union, made

the middle of *the main channel of the Mississippi River* the eastern boundary, so far as its boundary was conterminous with the western boundary of Illinois. The enabling act of August 6, 1846, (9 Stat. 56, c. 89,) under which Wisconsin adopted a constitution and became a State and was admitted into the Union, gives the western boundary of that State, after reaching the river St. Croix, as follows: "Thence down the main channel of said river to the Mississippi, thence down the centre of the main channel of that" (Mississippi) "river to the northwest corner of the State of Illinois." The northwest corner of the State of Illinois must therefore be in the middle of the main channel of the river which forms a portion of its western boundary. It is very evident that these terms, "middle of the Mississippi River," and "middle of the main channel of the Mississippi River," and "the centre of the main channel of that river," as thus used, are synonymous. It is not at all likely that the Congress of the United States intended that those terms, as applied to the Mississippi River separating Illinois and Iowa, should have a different meaning when applied to the Mississippi River separating Illinois from Missouri or a different meaning when used as descriptive of a portion of the western boundary of Wisconsin. They were evidently used as signifying the same thing. . . .

The opinions in both of these cases are able and present, in the strongest terms, the different views as to the line of jurisdiction between neighboring States, separated by a navigable stream; but we are of opinion that the controlling consideration in this matter is that which preserves to each State equality in the right of navigation in the river. We therefore hold, in accordance with this view, that the true line in navigable rivers between the States of the Union which separates the jurisdiction of one from the other is the middle of the main channel of the river. Thus the jurisdiction of each State extends to the thread of the stream, that is, to the "midchannel," and, if there be several channels, to the middle of the principal one, or, rather, the one usually followed.

It is therefore ordered, adjudged and declared that the boundary line between the State of Iowa and the State of Illinois is the middle of the main navigable channel of the Mississippi River. And, as the counsel of the two States both desire that this boundary line be established at the places where the several bridges mentioned in the pleadings—nine in number—cross the Mississippi River, it is further ordered that a commission be appointed to ascertain and designate at said places the boundary line between the two States, such commission, consisting of three competent persons, to be named by the court upon suggestion of counsel, and be required to make the proper examination and to delineate on maps prepared for that purpose the true line as determined by this court, and report the same to the court for its further action.

STATE OF NEW JERSEY v. STATE OF DELAWARE.

United States, Supreme Court, 1934.

291 U. S. 361. [78 L. ed. 847; 54 S. Ct. 407.]

Mr. Justice Cardozo delivered the opinion of the Court.

Invoking our original jurisdiction, New Jersey brings Delaware into this court and prays for a determination of the boundary in Delaware Bay and River.

The controversy divides itself into two branches, distinct from each other in respect of facts and law. The first branch has to do with the title to the bed or subaqueous soil of the Delaware River within a circle of twelve miles about the town of New Castle. Delaware claims to be the owner of the entire bed of the river within the limits of this circle up to low water mark on the east or New Jersey side. New Jersey claims to be the owner up to the middle of the channel. The second branch of the controversy has to do with the boundary line between the two states in the river below the circle and in the bay below the river. In that territory as in the river above, New Jersey bounds her title by the *Thalweg*. Delaware makes the division at the geographical centre, an irregular line midway between the banks or shores.

The Special Master appointed by this court in January, 1930 (280 U. S. 529) has now filed his report. As to the boundary within the circle, his report is in favor of Delaware. To that part of the report exceptions have been filed by New Jersey. As to the boundary in the bay and in the river below the circle, his report is in favor of New Jersey. To that part exceptions have been filed by Delaware. The two branches of the controversy will be separately considered here.

First. The boundary within the circle.

Delaware traces her title to the river bed within the circle through deeds going back two and a half centuries and more.

On August 24, 1682, the Duke of York delivered to William Penn a deed of feoffment for the twelve mile circle whereby he conveyed to the feoffee "ALL THAT the Towne of Newcastle otherwise called Delaware and All that Tract of Land lying within the Compass or Circle of Twelve Miles about the same scituate lying and being upon the River Delaware in America And all Islands in the same River Delaware and the said River and Soyle thereof lying North of the Southermost part of the said Circle of Twelve Miles about the said Towne." On October 28, 1682, there was formal livery of seisin of the lands and waters within the twelve mile circle. John Moll and Ephriam Herman, attorneys appointed in the deed of feoffment, gave possession and seisin "by delivery of the fort of the sd Town and leaving the sd William Penn in quiet and peaceable possession thereof and allso by the delivery of turf and twig and water and Soyle of the River of Delaware." "We did deliver allso unto him one turf with a twigg upon it a porringer with River water and Soyle in part of all what was specified in the sd Indentures or deeds.''

By force of these acts there was conveyed to the feoffee any title to the river bed within the circle that then belonged to the feoffor. New Jersey insists, however, that the feoffor, the Duke of York, was not then the owner of any territory west of the easterly side of the Delaware River, and hence at the time of the feoffment had no title to convey. Letters patent from Charles II, dated May 12, 1664, had granted to the Duke full title to and government of a large territory in America, embracing much of New England and in particular ''all the land from the west side of Connecticut River to the east side of Delaware Bay,'' not including, however, lands or waters to the west. True the Duke had gone into possession of lands westward of the grant, including land within the circle, and through his delegates and deputies was exercising powers of government. His acts in that behalf were the outcome of conflicts with the Dutch. What is now the State of Delaware had been subject to the government of the Dutch until 1664, when with the victory of the English arms it became an English colony. From that time until August 24, 1682, the date of the deed of feoffment, Delaware was governed (with the exception of a brief period from July, 1763, to February 9, 1764) as a dependency of the Government and Colony of New York through governors commissioned by the Duke of York and Albany. Upon the delivery of the deed to Penn, the Duke was the *de facto* overlord of the land within the circle, though title at that time was still vested in the Crown. . . .

We uphold the title of Delaware to the land within the circle.

Second. The boundary below the circle in the lower river and the bay.

Below the twelve mile circle there is a stretch of water about five miles long, not different in its physical characteristics from the river above, and below this is another stretch of water forty-five miles long where the river broadens into a bay.

The title to the soil of the lower river and the bay is unaffected by any grant to the Duke of York or others. The letters patent to James do not affect the ownership of the bed below the circle. Up to the time when New Jersey and Delaware became independent states, the title to the soil under the waters below the circle was still in the Crown of England. When independence was achieved, the precepts to be obeyed in the division of the waters were those of international law. Handly's Lessee v. Anthony, 5 Wheat. 374, 379.

International law today divides the river boundaries between states by the middle of the main channel, when there is one, and not by the geographical centre, half way between the banks. Iowa v. Illinois, 147 U. S. 1, 7, 8, 9; Keokuk & H. Bridge Co. v. Illinois, 175 U. S. 626, 631; Louisiana v. Mississippi, 202 U. S. 1, 49; Arkansas v. Tennessee, 246 U. S. 158, 169, 170; Arkansas v. Mississippi, 250 U. S. 39; Minnesota v. Wis-

consin, 252 U. S. 273, 282. It applies the same doctrine, now known as
the doctrine of the *Thalweg*, to estuaries and bays in which the dominant
sailing channel can be followed to the sea. Louisiana v. Mississippi,
supra; and compare 1 Halleck, International Law, 4th ed., p. 182; 1
Moore, Digest International Law, p. 617; Matter of Devoe Mfg. Co., 108
U. S. 401; The Fame, 8 Fed. Cas. 984, Story, J.; The Open Boat, 18
Fed. Cas. 751, Ware, J. The *Thalweg*, or downway, is the track taken
by boats in their course down the stream, which is that of the strongest
current. 1 Westlake, International Law, p. 144; Orban, Etude de Droit
Fluvial International, p. 343; Kaeckenbeck, International Rivers, p. 176;
Hyde, Int. Law, p. 244; Fiore, Int. Law Codified, § 1051; Calvo, Dic-
tionnaire de Droit International. Delaware makes no denial that this
is the decisive test whenever the physical conditions define the track
of navigation. Her position comes to this, that the bay is equally navigable in all directions, or at all events was so navigable in 1783, and
that in the absence of a track of navigation the geographical centre becomes the boundary, not of choice, but of necessity. As to the section of
the river between the bay and the circle, the same boundary is to be
accepted, we are told, as a matter of convenience.

The findings of the Special Master, well supported by the evidence,
overcome the argument thus drawn from physical conditions. He finds
that ''as early as Fisher's Chart of Delaware Bay (1756) there has been
a well-defined channel of navigation up and down the Bay and River,'' in
which the current of water attains its maximum velocity; that ''Delaware River and Bay, on account of shoals, are not equally navigable in
all directions, but the main ship channel must be adhered to for safety
in navigation;'' that the Bay, according to the testimony, ''is only an
expansion of the lower part of the Delaware River,'' and that the fresh
water of the river does not spread out uniformly when it drains into
the bay, but maintains a continuing identity through its course into the
ocean. ''The record shows the existence of a well-defined deep water
sailing channel in Delaware River and Bay constituting a necessary
track of navigation, and the boundary between the States of Delaware
and New Jersey in said bay is the middle of said channel.''

The underlying rationale of the doctrine of the *Thalweg* is one of
equality and justice. ''A river,'' in the words of Holmes, J. (New Jersey
v. New York, 283 U. S. 336, 342), ''is more than an amenity, it is a treasure.'' If the dividing line were to be placed in the centre of the stream
rather than in the centre of the channel, the whole track of navigation
might be thrown within the territory of one state to the exclusion of the
other. Considerations such as these have less importance for common-
wealths or states united under a general government than for states
wholly independent. Per Field, J. in Iowa v. Illinois, *supra,* p. 10.
None the less, the same test will be applied in the absence of usage or
convention pointing to another. Iowa v. Illinois, *supra.* Indeed, in 1783,

the equal opportunity for use that was derived from equal ownership may have had a practical importance for the newly liberated colonies, still loosely knit together, such as it would not have today. They were not taking any chances in affairs of vital moment. Bays and rivers are more than geometrical divisions. They are the arteries of trade and travel.

The commentators tell us of times when the doctrine of the *Thalweg* was still unknown or undeveloped. Anciently, we are informed, there was a principle of co-dominion by which boundary streams to their entire width were held in common ownership by the proprietors on either side. 1 Hyde, International Law, p. 243, § 137. Then, with Grotius and Vattel, came the notion of equality of division (Nys, Droit International, vol. 1, pp. 425, 426; Hyde, *supra*, p. 244, citing Grotius, De Jure Belli ac Pacis, and Vattel, Law of Nations), though how this was to be attained was still indefinite and uncertain, as the citations from Grotius and Vattel show. Finally, about the end of the eighteenth century, the formula acquired precision, the middle of the "stream" becoming the middle of the "channel." There are statements by the commentators that the term *Thalweg* is to be traced to the Congress of Rastadt in 1797 (Englehardt, Du Régime Conventionnel des Fleuves Internationaux, p. 72; Koch, Histoire des Traités de Paix, vol. 5, p. 156), and the Treaty of Lunéville in 1801. Hyde, *supra*, pp. 245, 246; Kaeckenbeck, International Rivers, p. 176; Adami, National Frontiers, translated by Behrens, p. 17. If the term was then new, the notion of equality was not. There are treaties before the Peace of Lunéville in which the boundary is described as the middle of the channel, though, it seems, without thought that in this there was an innovation, or that the meaning would have been different if the boundary had been declared to follow the middle of the stream. Hyde, *supra*, p. 246. Thus, in the Treaty of October 27, 1795, between the United States and Spain (Article IV), it is "agreed that the western boundary of the United States which separates them from the Spanish colony of Louisiana is in the middle of the channel or bed of the River Mississippi." Miller, Treaties and other International Acts of the United States of America, vol. 2, p. 321. There are other treaties of the same period in which the boundary is described as the middle of the river without further definition, yet this court has held that the phrase was intended to be equivalent to the middle of the channel. Iowa v. Illinois; Arkansas v. Tennessee; and Arkansas v. Mississippi, *supra*. See, e. g., the Treaty of 1763 between Great Britain, France and Spain, which calls for "a line drawn along the middle of the River Mississippi." The truth plainly is that a rule was in the making which was to give fixity and precision to what had been indefinite and fluid. There was still a margin of uncertainty within which conflicting methods of division were contending for the mastery. Conceivably that is true today in unusual situations of avulsion or erosion. Hyde, *supra*, pp. 246, 247.

Even so there has emerged out of the flux of an era of transition a working principle of division adapted to the needs of the international community. Through varying modes of speech the law has been groping for a formula that will achieve equality in substance, and not equality in name only. Unless prescription or convention has intrenched another rule (1 Westlake, International Law, p. 146), we are to utilize the formula that will make equality prevail.

In 1783, when the Revolutionary War was over, Delaware and New Jersey began with a clean slate. There was no treaty or convention fixing the boundary between them. There was no possessory act nor other act of dominion to give to the boundary in bay and river below the circle a practical location, or to establish a prescriptive right. In these circumstances, the capacity of the law to develop and apply a formula consonant with justice and with the political and social needs of the international legal system is not lessened by the fact that at the creation of the boundary the formula of the *Thalweg* had only a germinal existence. The gap is not so great that adjudication may not fill it. Lauterpacht, The Function of Law in the International Community, pp. 52, 60, 70, 85, 100, 110, 111, 255, 404, 432. Treaties almost contemporaneous, which were to be followed by a host of others, were declaratory of a principle that was making its way into the legal order. Hall, International Law, 8th ed. p. 7. International law, or the law that governs between states, has at times, like the common law within states, a twilight existence during which it is hardly distinguishable from morality or justice, till at length the *imprimatur* of a court attests its jural quality. Lauterpacht, *supra*, pp. 110, 255; Hall, *supra*, pp. 7, 12, 15, 16; Jenks, The New Jurisprudence, pp. 11, 12. "The gradual consolidation of opinions and habits" (Vinogradoff, Custom and Right, p. 21) has been doing its quiet work.

It is thus with the formula of the *Thalweg* in its application to the division between Delaware and New Jersey. We apply it to that boundary, which goes back to the Peace of Paris, just as we applied it to the boundary between Illinois and Iowa, which derives from a treaty of 1763 (Iowa v. Illinois; Keokuk & H. Bridge Co. v. Illinois; Arkansas v. Tennessee; Arkansas v. Mississippi, 250 U. S. 39, 63 L. ed. 832, 39 S. Ct. 422, *supra*), or to that between Louisiana and Mississippi (202 U. S. 1, 16), which goes back to 1812, or between Minnesota and Wisconsin (252 U. S. 273), going back to 1846. Indeed, counsel for Delaware make no point that the result is to be affected by difference of time. In requests submitted to the Master they have asked for a finding that "there was in 1783 no well defined channel in the Delaware Bay constituting a necessary track of navigation and the boundary line between the States of Delaware and New Jersey in said bay is the geographical center thereof." The second branch of the request is dependent on the first. This is clear enough upon its face, but is made doubly clear by the exceptions to the report and by the written and oral arguments. The line of division is to be the centre of the main channel unless the physical conditions are of such a nature that a channel is unknown.

We have seen that even in the bay the physical conditions are consistent with a track of navigation, which is also the course of safety. Counsel do not argue that such a track is unknown in the five miles of river between the bay and the circle. The argument is, however, that the geographical centre is to be made the boundary in the river as a matter of convenience, since otherwise there will be need for a sharp and sudden turn when the river meets the bay. Inconvenient such a boundary would unquestionably be, but the inconvenience is a reason for following the *Thalweg* consistently through the river and the bay alike instead of abandoning it along a course where it can be followed without trouble. If the boundary be taken to be the geographical centre, the result will be a crooked line, conforming to the indentations and windings of the coast, but without relation to the needs of shipping. Minnesota v. Wisconsin, *supra*. If the boundary be taken to be the *Thalweg*, it will follow the course furrowed by the vessels of the world.

The report will be confirmed, and a decree entered accordingly, which, unless agreed to by the parties, may be settled upon notice.

Within the twelve mile circle, the river and the subaqueous soil thereof up to low water mark on the easterly or New Jersey side will be adjudged to belong to the State of Delaware, subject to the Compact of 1905.

Below the twelve mile circle, the true boundary between the complainant and the defendant will be adjudged to be the middle of the main ship channel in Delaware River and Bay.

The costs of the suit will be equally divided.

It is so ordered.

NEBRASKA v. IOWA.

United States, Supreme Court, 1892.

143 U. S. 359. [36 L. ed. 186; 12 S. Ct. 396.]

This is an original suit, brought in this court by the State of Nebraska against the State of Iowa, the object of which is to have the boundary line between the two States determined. Iowa was admitted into the Union in 1846, and its western boundary, as defined by the act of admission, was the middle of the main channel of the Missouri River. Nebraska was admitted in 1867, and its eastern boundary was likewise the middle of the channel of the Missouri River. Between 1851 and 1877, in the vicinity of Omaha, there were marked changes in the course of this channel, so that in the latter year it occupied a very different bed from that through which it flowed in the former year. Out of these changes has come this litigation, the respective States claiming jurisdiction over the same tract of land. To the bill filed by the State of Nebraska the State of Iowa answered, alleging that this disputed ground was part of its territory; and also filed a cross-bill praying affirmative relief, establishing its jurisdiction thereof, to which cross-bill the State of Nebraska answered. Replications were duly filed and proofs taken.

Mr. Justice Brewer delivered the opinion of the court.

It is settled law that when grants of land border on running water, and the banks are changed by that gradual process known as "accretion," the riparian owner's boundary line still remains the stream, although, during the years, by this accretion, the actual area of his possessions may vary. In New Orleans v. United States, 10 Pet. 662, 717, this court said: "The question is well settled at common law, that the person whose land is bounded by a stream of water which changes its course gradually by alluvial formations shall still hold by the same boundary, including the accumulated soil. No other rule can be applied on just principles. Every proprietor whose land is thus bounded is subject to loss by the same means which may add to his territory; and, as he is without remedy for his loss in this way, he cannot be held accountable for his gain." . . .

It is equally well settled that where a stream, which is a boundary, from any cause suddenly abandons its old and seeks a new bed, such change of channel works no change of boundary; and that the boundary remains as it was, in the center of the old channel, although no water may be flowing therein. This sudden and rapid change of channel is termed, in the law, "avulsion." In Gould on Waters, sec. 159, it is said: "But if the change is violent and visible, and arises from a known cause, such as a freshet, or a cut through which a new channel is formed, the original thread of the stream continues to mark the limits of the two estates." . . .

These propositions, which are universally recognized as correct where the boundaries of private property touch on streams, are in like manner recognized where the boundaries between States or nations are, by prescription or treaty, found in running water. Accretion, no matter to which side it adds ground, leaves the boundary still the center of the channel. Avulsion has no effect on boundary, but leaves it in the center of the old channel. In volume 8, Opinions of Attorneys General, 175, 177, this matter received exhaustive consideration. A dispute arose between our government and Mexico in consequence of changes in the Rio Bravo. The matter having been referred to Attorney General Cushing, he replied at length. We quote largely from that opinion. After stating the case, he proceeds:

"With such conditions, whatever changes happen to either bank of the river by accretion on the one or degradation of the other,—that is by the gradual, and, as it were, insensible, accession or abstraction of mere particles,—the river as it runs continues to be the boundary. One country may, in process of time, lose a little of its territory, and the other gain a little, but the territorial relations cannot be reversed by such imperceptible mutations in the course of the river. The general aspect of things remains unchanged. And the convenience of allowing the river to retain its previous function, notwithstanding such insensible changes in its course, or in either of its banks, outweighs the inconveniences, even to the injured party, involved in a detriment, which, happening gradually, is inappreciable in the successive moments of its progression.

"But, on the other hand, if, deserting its original bed, the river forces for itself a new channel in another direction, then the nation through whose territory the river thus breaks its way suffers injury by the loss of territory greater than the benefit of retaining the natural river boundary, and that boundary remains in the middle of the deserted river-bed. For, in truth, just as a stone pillar constitutes a boundary, not because it is a stone, but because of the place in which it stands, so a river is made the limit of nations, not because it is running water bearing a certain geographical name, but because it is water flowing in a given channel, and within given banks, which are the real international boundary. . . ."

Vattel states the rule thus (Book I, c. 22, secs. 268, 269, 270):

"If a territory which terminates on a river has no other boundary than that river, it is one of those territories that have natural or indeterminate bounds (*territoria arcifinia*), and it enjoys the right of alluvion; that is to say, every gradual increase of soil, every addition which the current of the river may make to its bank on that side, is an addition to that territory, stands in the same predicament with it, and belongs to the same owner. For, if I take possession of a piece of land, declaring that I will have for its boundary the river which washes its side, or if it is given to me upon that footing, I thus acquired beforehand the right of alluvion; and, consequently, I alone may appropriate to myself whatever additions the current of the river may insensibly make to my land. I say 'insensibly,' because, in the very uncommon case called 'avulsion,' when the violence of the stream separates a considerable part from one piece of land and joins it to another, but in such manner that it can still be identified, the property of the soil so removed naturally continues vested in its former owner. The civil laws have thus provided against and decided this case when it happens between individual and individual. They ought to unite equity with the welfare of the state, and the care of preventing litigations.

"In case of doubt, every territory terminating on a river is presumed to have no other boundary than the river itself, because nothing is more natural than to take a river for a boundary, when a settlement is made; and wherever there is a doubt, that is always to be presumed which is most natural and most probable.

"As soon as it is determined that a river constitutes the boundary line between two territories, whether it remains common to the inhabitants on each of its banks, or whether each shares half of it, or, finally, whether it belongs entirely to one of them, their rights, with respect to the river, are in no wise changed by the alluvion. If, therefore, it happens that, by a natural effect of the current, one of the two territories receives an increase, while the river gradually encroaches on the opposite bank, the river still remains the natural boundary of the two territories, and, notwithstanding the progressive changes in its course, each retains over it the same rights which it possessed before; so that, if, for instance, it be divided in the middle between the owners of the opposite banks, that middle, though it changes its place, will continue to be the line of separation between the two neighbors. The one loses, it is true, while the other gains; but nature alone produces this change; she destroys the land of the one, while she forms new land for the other. The case cannot be otherwise determined, since they have taken the river alone for their limits.

"But if, instead of a gradual and progressive change of its bed, the river, by an accident merely natural, turns entirely out of its course, and runs into one of the two neighboring states, the bed which it has abandoned, becomes, thenceforward, their boundary, and remains the property of the former owner of the river, (Sec. 267,) the river itself is, as it were, annihilated in all that part, while it is reproduced in its new bed, and there belongs only to the State in which it flows."

The result of these authorities puts it beyond doubt that accretion on an ordinary river would leave the boundary between two states the varying center of the channel, and that avulsion would establish a fixed boundary, to-wit, the center of the abandoned channel. It is contended, however, that the doctrine of accretion has no application to the Missouri river, on account of the rapid and great changes constantly going on in respect to its banks; but the contrary has already been decided by this court in Jefferis v. Land Company, 134 U. S. 178, 189. . . .

The case before us is presented on testimony, and not on allegation. But what are the facts apparent from that testimony? The Missouri River is a winding stream, coursing through a valley of varying width, the substratum of whose soil, a deposit of distant centuries, is largely of quicksand. In building the bridge of the Union Pacific Railway Company across the Missouri River in the vicinity of the tracts in controversy, the builders went down to the solid rock, 65 feet below the surface, and there found a pine log a foot and a half in diameter,—of course, a deposit made in the long ago. The current is rapid, far above the average of ordinary rivers; and by reason of the snows in the mountains there are two well-known rises in the volume of its waters, known as the April and June rises. The large volume of water pouring down at the time of these rises, with the rapidity of its current, has great and rapid action upon the loose soil of its banks. Whenever it impinges with direct attack upon the bank at a bend of the stream, and that bank is of the loose sand obtaining in the valley of the Missouri, it is not strange that the abrasion and washing away is rapid and great. Frequently, where above the loose substratum of sand there is a deposit of comparatively solid soil, the washing out of the underlying sand causes an instantaneous fall of quite a length and breadth of the superstratum of soil into the river; so that it may, in one sense of the term, be said, that the diminution of the banks is not gradual and imperceptible, but sudden and visible. Notwithstanding this, two things must be borne in mind, familiar to all dwellers on the banks of the Missouri river, and disclosed by the testimony : that, while there may be an instantaneous and obvious dropping into the river of quite a portion of its banks, such portion is not carried down the stream as a solid and compact mass, but disintegrates and separates into particles of earth borne onward by the flowing water, and giving to the stream that color, which, in the history of the country, has made it known as the "muddy" Missouri; and also that, while the disappearance, by reason of this process, of a mass of bank may be sudden and obvious, there is no transfer of such a solid body of earth to the opposite shore, or anything like an instantaneous and visible creation of a bank on that shore. The accretion, whatever may be the fact in respect to the diminution, is always gradual, and by the imperceptible deposit of floating particles of earth. There is, except in such cases of avulsion as may be noticed hereafter, in all matter of increase of bank, always a mere gradual and imperceptible process. There is no heaping up at an instant, and while the eye rests upon the stream, of acres or rods on the forming side of the river. No engineering skill is sufficient to say where the earth in the bank washed away and disintegrating into the river finds its rest and abiding place. The falling bank has passed into the floating mass of earth and water, and the particles of earth may rest one or fifty miles below, and upon either shore. There is, no matter how rapid the process of subtraction or addition, no detachment of earth from the one side and deposit of the same upon the other. The only thing which distinguishes this river from other streams, in the matter of accretion, is in the rapidity of the change, caused by the velocity of the current, and this in itself, in the very nature of things, works no change in the principle underlying the rule of law in respect thereto.

Our conclusions are that, notwithstanding the rapidity of the changes in the course of the channel, and the washing from the one side and onto the other, the law of accretion controls on the Missouri River as elsewhere; and that not only in respect to the rights of individual landowners, but also in respect to the boundary lines between States. The boundary, therefore, between Iowa and Nebraska is a varying line, so far as affected by these changes of diminution and accretion in the mere washing of the waters of the stream.

It appears, however, from the testimony, that in 1877 the river above Omaha, which had pursued a course in the nature of an ox-bow, suddenly cut through the neck of the bow and made for itself a new channel. This does not come within the law of accretion, but of that of avulsion. By this selection of a new channel the boundary was not changed, and it remained, as it was prior to the avulsion, the center line of the old channel; and that, unless the waters of the river returned to their former bed, became a fixed and unvarying boundary, no matter what might be the changes of the river in its new channel.

We think we have, by these observations, indicated as clearly as is possible the boundary between the two states, and upon these principles the parties may agree to a designation of such boundary, and such designation will pass into a final decree. If no agreement is possible, then the court will appoint a commission to survey and report in accordance with the views herein expressed. . . .[1]

---

[1] SUPPLEMENTARY CASES. The rule laid down in Handly's Lessee v. Anthony as to the low-water mark where a boundary follows one or other side of a river is further illustrated in Vermont v. New Hampshire, 289 U. S. 593 (1933), where the Supreme Court, in holding against the claim of New Hampshire that the bound should extend to the top of the west bank of the Connecticut River, argued *inter alia* that the early document upon which the determination of the boundary depended should be interpreted "with a view to public convenience and the avoidance of controversy." If the contention of New Hampshire were to prevail an abutting property owner in Vermont "could not cross the bank to the water without trespass." Compare, also, Indiana v. Kentucky, 136 U. S. 479 (1889), holding that the boundary between the two states ran to low-water mark on the north side of the channel of the Ohio River in the area under dispute.

The meaning of the thalweg as a boundary line is further discussed in Louisiana v. Mississippi, 202 U. S. 1 (1906); and in Minnesota v. Wisconsin, 252 U. S. 273 (1920). Washington v. Oregon, 211 U. S. 127 (1908) dealt with the problem of a river (the Columbia) having two channels, each of which was at different times the main channel.

In Arkansas v. Tennessee, 246 U. S. 158 (1918) involving the determination of the boundary line between the two states along a portion of the bed of the Mississippi River that had been left dry as the result of an avulsion in 1876, the Supreme Court, citing Nebraska v. Iowa, held that the effect of the avulsion was to leave the former boundary unchanged, namely, the middle of the channel of the river as it was prior to the avulsion. The claim of Tennessee that the effect of the avulsion was to press back the boundary to an earlier fixed line of 1823 which had been gradually changed by erosions between 1823 and 1876 was rejected. See also, Missouri v. Nebraska, 196 U. S. 23 (1904).

In the Chamizal Arbitration case between the United States and Mexico, Am. Journal of Int. Law V (1911), 785, involving a dispute as to territory lying between the old bed of the Rio Grande, as it was surveyed in 1852, and the new bed, as it existed in 1910, the commission held that the true construction of the boundary treaties of 1848 and 1853 was that they created an arcifinious, or natural, boundary, as contended by the United States, rather than an artificial and invariable one, as contended by Mexico, and that the subsequent treaty of 1884 as applied to the changes occurring after 1852 warranted the award of a part of the disputed tract, representing the result of slow and gradual erosion and accretion, to the United States, and the remaining part, representing changes caused by the flood of 1864, to Mexico.

B. The marginal sea.

It is a well-established rule of customary international law that the jurisdiction of a state extends to a certain distance from the shore. The precise extent of this maritime belt or marginal sea is not clearly defined, but it is agreed that it extends at least three miles from the shore, that distance representing approximately the range of cannon in the middle of the seventeenth century. Query, may a state exercise criminal jurisdiction over the captain of a foreign vessel passing through territorial waters when in consequence of his negligence a collision takes place in those waters? [Queen v. Keyn.]

THE QUEEN v. KEYN [THE FRANCONIA].

Great Britain, Court for Crown Cases Reserved, 1876.

L. R. 2 Exch. Div. 63.

The following judgments were delivered:—

SIR R. PHILLIMORE. The prisoner was indicted at the Central Criminal Court for the manslaughter of Jessie Dorcas Young on the high seas, and within the jurisdiction of the Admiralty of England.

The deceased was a passenger on board the Strathclyde, a British steam-vessel bound from London to Bombay.

This vessel, when at a distance of one mile and nine-tenths of a mile S.S.E. from Dover pier-head, and within two and a half miles from Dover beach, was run into by the Franconia, a German steamer, in consequence of which she sank, and the deceased woman was drowned.

The Franconia was carrying the German mails from Hamburg to St. Thomas in the West Indies.

The prisoner, being the officer in command of the Franconia, was convicted of manslaughter, but a question of law was reserved for this Court of Criminal Appeal. An objection was taken on the part of the prisoner that, inasmuch as he was a foreigner, in a foreign vessel, on a foreign voyage, sailing upon the high seas, he was not subject to the jurisdiction of any Court in this country. The contrary position maintained on the part of the Crown is that, inasmuch as at the time of the collision both vessels were within the distance of three miles from the English shore, the offence was committed within the realm of England, and is triable by the English Court. The case has been most ably conducted on both sides, and the Court has derived very great assistance from the arguments of counsel.

Before I consider the principal question, whether the offence committed on board the foreign vessel be triable here, it may be well to take notice of a subsidiary contention put forward on behalf of the Crown, namely, that the person injured was on board an English ship at the time when she received the injury which was the immediate and direct result of the collision, and that in fact the offence was committed on board an English ship. It seems expedient to deal with this contention in the first place, because, if it be valid, the inquiry as to the jurisdiction of the English Court over a foreign ship would be unnecessary. I am of opinion that this contention cannot be sustained. Looking at the facts stated by the learned judge who tried the case, as well as the indictment, it appears that the prisoner had no intention to injure the Strathclyde or any person on board of her. He was guilty of negligence, and want of nautical skill, and of presence of mind in the management of his vessel, and thereby caused the collision, but the act by which the woman died was not his act, nor was it a consequence immediate or direct of his act. He never left the deck of his own ship, nor did he send any missile from it to the other ship; neither in will nor in deed can he be considered to have been on board the British vessel. He can no more be considered by intendment of law to have been on board the British vessel than he would have been if his bad navigation had caused the Strathclyde to impale herself upon the Franconia, and so to sink. The jurisdiction of the English Court, therefore, cannot be founded on this contention. . . .[1]

With these preliminary observations, I proceed to inquire what is the nature and extent of the jurisdiction over the high seas, which international law confers upon or concedes to the sovereign of the adjacent territory.

Whatever may have been the claims asserted by nations in times past—and perhaps no nation has been more extravagant than England in this matter—it is at the present time an unquestionable proposition of international jurisprudence, that the high seas are of right navigable by the ships of all states. Whether the reasons upon which this liberty of navigation rests be, as some jurists say, that the open sea is incapable of continuous occupation and insusceptible of permanent appropriation, or, as other jurists say, that the use of it is inexhaustible, and, therefore, common to all mankind; or, whether it rests upon both these, or upon other reasons also, it is unnecessary to inquire. This liberty of navigation is a fact recognised by all civilized states.

An important corollary of this proposition is that the merchant vessel (with ships of war we are not now concerned) on the open sea is subject only to the law of her flag, that is, the law of the state to which she belongs.

The next proposition, though it be of an elementary kind, to which attention should be drawn, is, that every state is entitled to exclusive

---

[1] The student may compare on this point the decision of the Permanent Court of International Justice in the case of the Lotus, above, p. 204. The position taken by Phillimore was rejected by two of the minority justices.

dominion over its own territory, that is, not only over the soil and over all subjects, but over all foreigners commorant therein. . . .[1]

The question as to dominion over portions of the seas inclosed within headlands or contiguous shores, such as the King's Chambers, is not now under consideration. It is enough to say that within this term "territory" are certainly comprised the ports and harbours, and the space between the flux and reflux of tide, or the land up to the furthest point at which the tide recedes. But it is at this point that the difficulty presented by the case before us begins, and here the following questions present themselves for solution:—

1. Is a state entitled to any extension of dominion beyond low-water mark?

2. If so, how far does this territory, or do these territorial waters, as they are usually called, extend?

3. Has a state the same dominion over these territorial waters as over the territory of her soil and in her ports, or is it of a more limited character and confined to certain purposes?

With respect to the first of these questions the answer may be given without doubt or hesitation, namely, that a state is entitled to a certain extension of territory, in a certain sense of that word, beyond low-water mark.

With respect to the second question, the distance to which the territorial waters extend, it appears on an examination of the authorities that the distance has varied (setting aside even more extravagant claims) from 100 to 3 miles, the present limit. . . .[2]

The third question, though touched upon in the preceding citations, remains to be substantively considered; it is one of much importance, viz., whether, admitting that the state has a dominion over three miles of adjacent water, it is the same dominion which the possessor has over her land and her ports, or is it of a more limited character—limited to the purpose of protecting the adjacent shore, for which it was granted, and not extending to a general sovereignty over all passing vessels, and therefore not improbably [? improperly] called ligne de respect? . . .

The sound conclusions which result from the investigation of the authorities which have been referred to appear to me to be these:—

The consensus of civilised independent states has recognised a maritime extension of frontier to the distance of three miles from low-water mark, because such a frontier or belt of water is necessary for the defence and security of the adjacent state.

It is for the attainment of these particular objects that a dominium has been granted over this portion of the high seas.

---

[1] The learned justice here quotes from the opinion of Chief Justice Marshall in Schooner Exchange v. M'Faddon, above, p. 326.

[2] The learned justice here reviews the authorities, citing Grotius, Bynkershoek, Wolff, Vattel, Azuni, Kent, Wheaton, and Massé.

This proposition is materially different from the proposition contended for, namely, that it is competent to a state to exercise within these waters the same rights of jurisdiction and property which appertain to it in respect to its lands and its ports. There is one obvious test by which the two sovereignties may be distinguished.

According to modern international law, it is certainly a right incident to each state to refuse a passage to foreigners over its territory by land, whether in time of peace or war. But it does not appear to have the same right with respect to preventing the passage of foreign ships over this portion of the high seas.

In the former case there is no jus transitus; in the latter case there is.

The reason of the thing, that is, the defence and security of the state, does not require or warrant the exclusion of peaceable foreign vessels from passing over these waters; and the custom and usage of nations has not sanctioned it.

Consequences fraught with mischief and injustice might flow from the opposite doctrine, which would render applicable to a foreign vessel while in itinere from one foreign port to another, passing over these waters, all the criminal law of the adjacent territory. No single instance has been brought to our notice of the practical exercise by any nation of this jurisdiction. . . .

Upon the whole, I am of opinion that the Court had no jurisdiction over this foreigner for an offence committed on board a foreign ship on the high seas, though within three miles of the coast; that he is governed by the law of the state to which his flag belongs; and that the conviction cannot be sustained. . . .

BRETT, J. A. The prisoner was at the Central Criminal Court convicted of manslaughter, that is to say, he was found to have been guilty of acts and their results which amount, according to the law of England, to the crime of manslaughter. The prisoner was a German subject.

The question reserved is, whether the Court which tried him had jurisdiction so to do. All are agreed that it had none, unless by reason of the locality in which the crime was committed. It was committed on the open sea, but within three miles of the coast of England. It is suggested that it was also committed on board an English ship. In either case it is urged it was committed in a locality or place subject to the criminal law of England, and to the jurisdiction of the Central Criminal Court. It was argued on the one side that the open sea within three miles of the coast of England is a part of the territory of England as much and as completely as if it were land a part of England; that the criminal law of England, unless expressly restricted, applies to every crime, by whomsoever committed, within the territory of England; that there is no express restriction as to the crime in question; that the criminal law, therefore, is to be applied to the present case. It was further argued that at all events the crime was committed on board an English ship, and, therefore, although by a foreigner, it is by statute to be tried according to the criminal law of England. It was answered that the open sea within three miles of the coast of England is not in any sense a part of the territory of England or within the jurisdiction of the Crown of England; that if it be within the jurisdiction of the Crown, so that the Sovereign or Parliament of England might, by constituting a Court to do so, have properly taken cognizance of the crime, yet no such Court has been constituted, and, therefore, the Central Criminal Court had no jurisdiction. It was further argued that even though the open sea within three miles be a part of the territory of England, yet the crime was committed on board a foreign ship, and, therefore, could not be tried in England.

The questions raised by these arguments seem to me to be: First, is the open sea within three miles of the coast a part of the territory of England as much and as completely as if it were land a part of England? Secondly, if it is, has the Central Criminal Court any jurisdiction to try alleged crimes there committed, by whomsoever committed? Thirdly, can the crime be properly said to have been committed on board of an English ship so as thereby to give jurisdiction to an English Court, although the sea in question be not a part of England? Fourthly, can it be properly said to have been committed on board of the German ship; and if so, is jurisdiction thereby ousted from an English Court, although the sea in question be a part of English territory? As to the first part, the argument does not deny that it is an axiom of law that the criminal law of England runs everywhere within England, so as to be applicable to every crime by whomsoever therein committed. If the three miles of open sea are a part of the territory of England, it was not denied,—nay it was expressly admitted,—that unless there be an exception in favour of a crime committed on board of a foreign passing ship, and this crime was committed on board of such a ship, the criminal law of England might of right be applied to the crime. What was denied upon this hypothesis, as to the three miles of open sea, was that the Central Criminal Court, or indeed any Court hitherto constituted by the sovereign authority, had had jurisdiction given to it to apply the criminal law to such a case. The great question argued was, whether the three miles of open sea next the coast are or are not a part of the territory of England, meaning thereby a territory in which its law is paramount and exclusive. . . . The only evidence suggested in this case is, that by the law of nations every country bordered by the sea is to be held to have, as part of its territory, meaning thereby a territory in which its law is paramount and exclusive, the three miles of open sea next to its coast; and, therefore, that England among others has such territory. The question on both sides has been made to depend on whether such is or is not proved to be the law of nations. On the one side it is said there is evidence and authority on which the Court ought to hold that such is the law of nations; on the other side it is said there is no such evidence or authority. The evidence relied on for the Crown is an alleged common acquiescence by recognized jurists of so many countries, as to be substantially of all countries, and declarations of statesmen, and similar declarations of English judges in court in the course of administering law. On the other side it is said that the declarations cited of the judges were opinions only, and not decisions; that there is no common acquiescence of jurists to the alleged effect, or declarations of statesmen; and that if there were, such acquiescence or declarations are not sufficient; that there should be acquiescence by governments declared in treaties or evidenced by acts of government. It is admitted that there is no such acquiescence by any general treaty or by unequivocal acts of many, if of any, governments. Main reliance is placed by the one side on the alleged common agreement of jurists. Their acquiescence or agreement in fact is denied by the other side, and, further, their authority is denied, if such acquiescence or agreement is held to exist. . . .

The next questions are whether there is, by reason of such or other evidence, proof of a common consent of nations to any propositions, and if to any, to what proposition, with regard to the three miles of open sea which are adjacent to any country. . . .

After citing this long list of authorities, I make the following observations. I have done so because it seems to me that the whole question depends entirely upon authority. There is no reason, founded on the axiomatic rules of right and wrong, why the three miles should or should not be considered as a part of the territory of the adjacent country. They may have been so treated by general consent; they might equally well have not been so treated. If they have been so treated by such consent, the authority for the alleged ownership is sufficient. The question is, whether such a general consent has in this case been proved by sufficient evidence. I have cited the assertions of a large number of writers, recognised as able writers on international law, of different countries and different periods. I have cited assertions of statesmen, and opinions of great judges, and the decisions of some judges, and the assertion made on behalf of a great government. As there is no common court of nations, and no common legislature, none of these are, in the usual sense, binding on this Court. As the opinions of the judges are manifestly founded on the opinions of the writers, I think the principal evidence is that of the writers. I have already said that, in my opinion, a general consent of recognised writers of different times and different countries to a reasonable proposition is sufficient evidence of a general consent of nations to that proposition. Such a general consent establishes the proposition as one of international law. In this case I think there is a general consent to a proposition with regard to the three miles of open sea adjacent to the shores of sovereign states. I do not think that such general consent, as to a distance of three miles, is impeached by shewing that there has been a difference as to a claim by some with regard to a greater distance than three miles. The question is, what is the proposition to which such general consent as to the three miles is given? The dispute is whether, by the consent of all, certain limited rights are given to the adjacent country, such as a right that the waters should be treated as what is called a neutral zone, or whether the water is, by consent of all, given to the adjacent country as its territory, with all rights of territory, it being agreed by such country with all others, that all shall have a free right of navigation or way over such waters for harmless passage and some other rights. If the first be true, it is impossible, according to the reasoning of Vattel and Marshall, C. J.,—which reasoning, I think, is irresistible—that it can be properly said that the adjacent country has any proprietary right in the three miles, or any dominion, or any sovereignty, or any sovereign jurisdiction. If the latter be correct, the adjacent country has the three miles, as its property, as under its dominion and sovereignty. If so, that three miles are its territorial waters, subject to its rights of property, dominion, and sovereignty. Those are all the rights, and the same rights which a nation has, or can have, over its land territory. If, then, such be its rights over the three miles of sea, that sea is as much a part of its country or territory as its land.

Considering the authorities I have cited, the terms used by them, wholly inconsistent, as it seems to me, with the idea that the adjacent country has no property, no dominion, no sovereignty, no territorial right; and considering the necessary foundation of the admitted rights and duties of the adjacent country as to neutrality, which have always been made to depend on a right and duty as to its territory, I am of opinion that it is proved that, by the law of nations, made by the tacit consent of substantially all nations, the open sea within three miles of the coast is a part of the territory of the adjacent nation, as much and as completely as if it were land a part of the territory of such nation. By the same evidence which proves this proposition, it is equally proved that every nation which possesses this water territory has agreed with all other nations that all shall have the right of free navigation to pass through such water territory, if such navigation be with an innocent or harmless intent or purpose. This right of free navigation cannot, according to ordinary principles, be withdrawn without common consent; but it by no means derogates from the sovereign authority over all its territory of the state which has agreed to grant this liberty, or easement, or right to all the world. . . .

. . . I think it therefore proved that the offence committed, though it was committed by a foreigner, was within the cognizance of the English criminal law, because it was committed within English territory, unless there be an exceptional privilege in favour of crimes committed on board foreign ships by foreigners, as such ships are passing through the water territory of England, and this crime was committed on board the foreign ship. Now if this exception exists, it is alleged to be proved by the same evidence, to the same effect, as the right of territory and the right of free passage or navigation have been proved. They are proved, as I have said, by a common consent, found in the common consent of the great body of recognised writers, and in the opinions or decisions of great judges of different nations. I can only say of this exception that, although there are one or two expressions by some writers which may be alleged in argument as in support of it, it is not expressed in clear terms by any one. I do not think there is really any evidence of a common assent to it. It follows that, even if the offence could properly be said to have been committed on board the foreign passing ship, still it would be an offense committed within British territory, and therefore cognizable by the British criminal law. . . .

It follows, therefore, in my opinion, that the Central Criminal Court has jurisdiction to try all crimes made cognizable in general terms by English law which may be committed . . . by any foreigner or British subject in any ship, British or foreign, on the open sea within three miles of the coast of Great Britain. . . .

COCKBURN, C. J. The defendant has been convicted of the offence of manslaughter on the high seas, on a trial had at the Central Criminal Court, under the statute 4 & 5 Wm. 4, c. 36, s. 22, which empowers the judges sitting there to hear and determine offences "committed on the high seas and other places within the jurisdiction of the Admiralty of England." The facts were admittedly such as to warrant the conviction, if there was jurisdiction to try the defendant as amenable to English law. Being in command of a steamship, the Franconia, and having occasion to pass the Strathclyde, a British ship, the defendant brought his ship unnecessarily close to the latter, and then, by negligence in steering, ran into the Strathclyde and broke a hole in her, in consequence of which she filled with water and sank, when the deceased, whose death the accused is charged with having occasioned, being on board the Strathclyde, was drowned.

That the negligence of which the accused was thus guilty, having resulted in the death of the deceased, amounts according to English law to manslaughter can admit of no doubt. The question is, whether the accused is amenable to our law, and whether there was jurisdiction to try him? . . .

Now, no proposition of law can be more incontestable or more universally admitted than that, according to the general law of nations, a foreigner, though criminally responsible to the law of a nation not his own for acts done by him while within the limits of its territory, cannot be made responsible to its law for acts done beyond such limits:—

"Leges cujusque imperii," says Huber de Conflictu legum citing Dig. de jurisdictione, l. ult., "Vim habent intra terminos ejusdem reipublicae, omnesque ei subjectos obligant, nec ultra." "*Extra territorium jus dicenti impune non paretur*" is an old and well-established maxim. "No sovereignty," says Story (Conflict of Laws, s. 539), "can extend its process beyond its own territorial limits, to subject either persons or property to its judicial decisions. Every exertion of authority of this sort beyond this limit is a mere nullity, and incapable of binding such persons or property in any other tribunals." "The power of this country," says Dr. Lushington in the case of The Zollverein [1 Sw. Adm. 96], "is to legislate for its subjects all the world over, and as to foreigners within its jurisdiction, but no further." . . .

According to the general law, therefore, a foreigner who is not residing permanently or temporarily in British territory, or on board a British ship, cannot be held responsible for an infraction of the law of this country. Unless, therefore, the accused, Keyn, at the time the offence of which he has been convicted was committed, was on British territory or on board a British ship, he could not be properly brought to trial under English law, in the absence of express legislation. . . .

Now, it may be asserted without fear of contradiction that the position that the sea within a belt or zone of three miles from the shore, as distinguished from the rest of the open sea, forms part of the realm or territory of the Crown is a doctrine unknown to the ancient law of England, and which has never yet received the sanction of an English criminal Court of justice. It is true that from an early period the kings of England, possessing more ships than their opposite neighbours, and being thence able to sweep the Channel, asserted the right of sovereignty over the narrow seas, as appears from the commissions issued in the fourteenth century, of which examples are given in the 4th Institute, in the chapter on the Court of Admiralty, and others are to be found in Selden's Mare Clausum, Book 2. At a later period still more extravagant pretensions were advanced. Selden does not scruple to assert the sovereignty of the King of England over the sea as far as the shores of Norway, in which he is upheld by Lord Hale in his treatise *De jure maris:* Hargrave's Law Tracts, p. 10.

In the reign of Charles II. Sir Leoline Jenkins, then the judge of the Court of Admiralty, in a charge to the grand jury at an Admiralty sessions at the Old Bailey, not only asserted the King's sovereignty within the four seas, and that it was his right and province "to keep the public peace on these seas"—that is, as Sir Leoline expounds it, "to preserve his subjects and allies in their possessions and properties upon these seas, and in all freedom and security to pass to and fro on them, upon their lawful occasions," but extended this authority and jurisdiction of the King.

"To preserve the public peace and to maintain the freedom and security of navigation all the world over; so that not the utmost bound of the Atlantic Ocean, nor any corner of the Mediterranean, nor any part of the South or other seas, but that if the peace of God and the King be violated upon any of his subjects, or upon his allies or their subjects, and the offender be afterwards brought up or laid hold of in any of His Majesty's ports, such breach of the peace is to be inquired of and tried in virtue of a commission of oyer and terminer as this is, in such county, liberty, or place as His Majesty shall please to direct—so long an arm hath God by the laws given to his vicegerent, the King.''

To be sure, the learned civilian, as regards these distant seas, admits that other sovereigns have a concurrent jurisdiction, which, however, he by no means concedes to them in these so-called British seas. In these the refusal by a foreign ship to strike the flag and lower the topsail to a King's ship he treats as amounting to piracy.

Venice, in like manner, laid claim to the Adriatic, Genoa to the Ligurian Sea, Denmark to a portion of the North Sea. The Portuguese claimed to bar the ocean route to India and the Indian Seas to the rest of the world, while Spain made the like assertion with reference to the West.

All these vain and extravagant pretensions have long since given way to the influence of reason and common sense. If, indeed, the sovereignty thus asserted had a real existence, and could now be maintained, it would of course, independently of any question as to the three-mile zone, be conclusive of the present case. But the claim to such sovereignty, at all times unfounded, has long since been abandoned. No one would now dream of asserting that the sovereign of these realms has any greater right over the surrounding seas than the sovereigns on the opposite shores; or that it is the especial duty and privilege of the Queen of Great Britain to keep the peace in these seas; or that the Court of Admiralty could try a foreigner for an offence committed in a foreign vessel in all parts of the Channel. . . . That it is out of this extravagant assertion of sovereignty that the doctrine of the three-mile jurisdiction, asserted on the part of the Crown, and which, the older claim being necessarily abandoned, we are now called upon to consider, has sprung up, I readily admit. Let me endeavour to trace its origin and growth. . . .

From the review of these authorities we arrive at the following results. There can be no doubt that the suggestion of Bynkershoek, that the sea surrounding the coast to the extent of cannon-range should be treated as belonging to the state owning the coast, has, with but very few exceptions, been accepted and adopted by the publicists who have followed him during the last two centuries. But it is equally clear that, in the practical application of the rule, in respect of the particular of distance, as also in the still more essential particular of the character and degree of sovereignty and dominion to be exercised, great difference of opinion and uncertainty have prevailed, and still continue to exist. . . .

Some of these authors,—for instance, Professor Bluntschli,—make a most important distinction between a commorant and a passing ship. According to this author, while the commorant ship is subject to the general law of the local state, the passing ship is liable to the local jurisdiction only in matters of ''military and police regulations, made for the safety of the territory and population of the coast.'' None of these writers, it should be noted, discuss the question, or go the length of asserting that a foreigner in a foreign ship, using the waters in question for the purpose of navigation solely, on its way to another country, is liable to the criminal law of the adjoining country for an offence committed on board. . . .

In the result, looking to the fact that all pretension to sovereignty or jurisdiction over foreign ships in the narrow seas has long since been wholly abandoned—to the uncertainty which attaches to the doctrine of the publicists as to the degree of sovereignty and jurisdiction which may be exercised on the so-called territorial sea—to the fact that the right of absolute sovereignty therein, and of penal jurisdiction over the subjects of other states, has never been expressly asserted or conceded among independent nations, or, in practice, exercised and acquiesced in, except for violation of neutrality or breach of revenue or fishery laws, which, as has been pointed out, stand on a different footing—as well as to the fact that, neither in legislating with reference to shipping, nor in respect of the criminal law, has parliament thought proper to assume territorial sovereignty over the three-mile zone, so as to enact that all offences committed upon it, by foreigners in foreign ships, should be within the criminal law of this country, but, on the contrary, wherever it was thought right to make the foreigner amenable to our law, has done so by express and specific legislation—I cannot think that, in the absence of all precedent, and of any judicial decision or authority applicable to the present purpose, we should be justified in holding an offence, committed under such circumstances, to be punishable by the law of England, especially as in so holding we must declare the whole body of our penal law to be applicable to the foreigner passing our shores in a foreign vessel on his way to a foreign port. . . .

Conviction quashed.[1,2]

---

[1] The decision in this case was reached by a majority of seven to six, eleven of the thirteen judges rendering separate opinions. The opinions in all cover some 176 pages of the Reports and contain a wealth of learning upon the general subject. The opinions of Sir R. Phillimore and Chief Justice Cockburn are the two most important majority opinions. In addition to the minority opinion of Justice Brett here printed, five other justices rendered opinions upholding the jurisdiction of the court, Lord Coleridge, C. J., and Justice Denman basing their opinions also on the ground that the offense of Captain Keyn was committed on board the vessel on which the act took effect and therefore on British territory. The opinion of the majority was sharply criticised at the time and was followed shortly after by the Territorial Waters Jurisdiction Act of 1878 in accordance with which "an offense committed by a person, whether he is or is not a subject of Her Majesty, on the open sea within the territorial waters of Her Majesty's dominions, is an offence within the jurisdiction of the Admiral, although it may have been committed on board or by means of a foreign ship, and the person who committed such offence may be arrested, tried, and punished accordingly."

[2] SUPPLEMENTARY CASES. Query, does the doctrine of "hot pursuit" justify the seizure within its own national territorial waters of a foreign vessel which

C. Limited extension of jurisdiction beyond the marginal sea.

The general principle that a state may protect its shores by extending its jurisdiction out into the sea has resulted in the assertion by states of a jurisdiction greater than three miles in the exercise of police measures to prevent smuggling. Query, has this assertion found recognition by states as a rule of customary law? [Church v. Hubbart.] Would a state be justified in seizing a foreign vessel which remained outside the three-mile limit and unloaded its illegal cargo into smaller vessels which were to carry it within the three-mile limit? [The Grace and Ruby.] Would persons conspiring on the high seas to violate the laws of a foreign country lose their immunity from prosecution if the vessel upon which they are engaged in their conspiracy were to lose its immunity from seizure by reason of special treaty provisions? [Ford v. United States.]

CHURCH v. HUBBART.

United States, Supreme Court, 1804.

2 Cranch, 187. [2 L. ed. 249.]

Error from the Circuit Court for the district of Massachusetts, in an action on the case, upon two policies of assurance, whereby John Barker Church, junior caused to be insured twenty thousand dollars upon the cargo of the brigantine Aurora, Nathaniel Shaler, master, at and from New-York to one or two Portuguese ports on the coast of Brazil, and at and from thence back to New-York. At the foot of one of the policies was the following clause: *"The insurers are not liable for seizure by the Portuguese for illicit trade;"* and in the body of the other was inserted the following: *"N. B. The insurers do not take the risk of illicit trade with the Portuguese."*

The vessel was cleared out for the Cape of Good Hope, and Mr. Church went out in her as supercargo. On the 18th of April she arrived at Rio Janeiro, where she obtained a permit to remain fifteen days, and where Mr. Church sold goods to the amount of about 700 dollars, which were delivered in open day, and in the presence of the guard which had been previously put on board, and to all appearance with the approba-

---

has committed an offense within the territorial waters of the pursuing state and has been unsuccessfully pursued upon the high seas? In the case of the Itata [South American Steamship Co. v. United States], Moore, Int. Arbitrations, III, 3067, the United States-Chile Claims Commission established under the Convention of August 7, 1892, held that the pursuit of the vessel by a public armed ship of the United States into Chilean territorial waters and its seizure there was in violation of international law and an act for which the United States was liable in damages. For the issue as to the alleged violation of the neutrality laws of the United States by the Itata, see United States v. Trumbull, 48 Fed. 99 (1891) and The Itata, 56 Fed. 505 (1893).

tion of the officers of the customs. On the 6th of May she sailed from Rio Janeiro bound to the port of Para on the coast of Brazil, and on the 12th, fell in with the Schooner Four Sisters of New-York, Peleg Barker, master, bound to the same port, who agreed to keep company, and on the 12th of June they came to anchor about four or five leagues from the land, off the mouth of the river Para, in the bay of Para, about west and by north from Cape Baxos and about two miles to the northward of the Cape "on a meridian line drawn from east to west."—The land to the westward could not be observed from the deck, but might be seen from the mast-head.

The destination of the vessel after her departure from Rio Janeiro, was by the master kept secret from the crew, at the request of Mr. Church, and the master assigned as a reason why they came to anchor off the river Para, that they were in want of water and wood, which was truly the case, the greater part of the water on board having been caught a night or two before, and the crew had been on an allowance of water for ten days.

After the vessels had come to anchor, Mr. Church with two of the seamen of the brig, and the mate of the schooner with two of her seamen, went off in the schooner's long boat to speak a boat seen in shore, to endeavour to obtain a pilot to carry the vessels up the river that they might procure a supply of wood and water, and, if permitted, sell their cargo. . . .

Mr. Church, and the others who went on shore with him, . . . were seized and imprisoned; and on the 14th of June, both the brig and schooner were taken possession of by a body of armed men, on board of three armed boats, and carried into Para. The masters and crews were imprisoned, and underwent several examinations, the principal object of which seemed to be to ascertain whether they were not employed by some of the belligerent powers to examine the boats, &c. whether they had not come with intention to trade; whether they had not traded at Rio Janeiro, and why they had kept so close along the coast. They denied the intention to trade, but alleged that they were obliged to put in for wood and water, and to refit. . . .

The defendant, to prove that the trade was illicit, offered a copy of a law of Portugal, entitled "A law by which foreign vessels are prohibited from entering the ports of India, Brazil, Guinea, and Islands, and other provinces of Portugal." . . .

To prove that the vessel was *seized for illicit trade*, the defendant produced the following paper, purporting to be a copy of "the sentence of the governor of the capital of Para, on the brig Aurora." . . .

[The circuit court instructed the jury to find for the defendant on the ground that the property had been seized on account, in part at least, of prohibited trade falling within the exceptions of the policies.]

Marshall, C. J. delivered the opinion of the court. . . . If the proof is sufficient to show that the loss of the vessel and cargo was occasioned by attempting an illicit trade with the Portuguese; that an offence was actually committed against the laws of that nation, and that they were condemned by the government on that account, the case comes fairly within the exception of the policies, and the risk was one not intended to be insured against. . . .

For the plaintiff it is contended, that the terms used require an actual traffic between the vessel and inhabitants, and a seizure in consequence of that traffic, or at least that the vessel should have been brought into port, in order to constitute a case which comes within the exception of the policy. But such does not seem to be the necessary import of the words. The more enlarged and liberal construction given to them by the defendants, is certainly warranted by common usage; and wherever words admit of a more extensive or more restricted signification, they must be taken in that sense which is required by the subject matter, and which will best effectuate what it is reasonable to suppose, was the real intention of the parties.

In this case, the unlawfulness of the voyage was perfectly understood by both parties. That the crown of Portugal excluded, with the most jealous watchfulness, the commercial intercourse of foreigners with their colonies, was probably a fact of as much notoriety as that foreigners had devised means to elude this watchfulness, and to carry on a gainful but very hazardous trade with those colonies. If the attempt should succeed it would be very profitable, but the risk attending it was necessarily great. It was this risk which the underwriters, on a fair construction of their words, did not mean to take upon themselves. "They are not liable," they say, "for seizure by the Portuguese for illicit trade." "They do not take the risk of illicit trade with the Portuguese;" now this illicit trade was the sole and avowed object of the voyage, and the vessel was engaged in it from the time of her leaving the port of New-York. The risk of this illicit trade, is separated from the various other perils to which vessels are exposed at sea, and excluded from the policy. Whenever the risk commences the exception commences also, for it is apparent that the underwriters meant to take upon themselves no portion of that hazard which was occasioned by the unlawfulness of the voyage.

If it could have been presumed by the parties to this contract, that the laws of Portugal, prohibiting commercial intercourse between their colonies and foreign merchants, permitted vessels to enter their ports, or to hover off their coasts for the purposes of trade, with impunity, and only subjected them to seizure and condemnation after the very act had been committed, or if such are really their laws, then indeed the exception might reasonably be supposed to have been intended to be as limited in its construction as is contended for by the plaintiff. If the danger did not commence till the vessel was in port, or till the act of bargain and sale, without a permit from the governor, had been committed, then it would be reasonable to consider the exception as only contemplating that event. But this presumption is too extravagant to have been made. If indeed the fact itself should be so, then there is an end of presumption, and the contract will be expounded by the law; but as a general principle, the nation which prohibits commercial intercourse with its colonies, must be supposed to adopt measures to make that prohibition effectual. They must therefore, be supposed to seize vessels coming into their harbours or hovering on their coasts, in a condition to trade, and to be afterwards governed in their proceedings with respect to those vessels by the circumstances which shall appear in evidence. That the officers of that nation are induced occasionally to dispense with their laws, does not alter them, or legalize the trade they prohibit. As they may be executed at the will of the governor, there is always danger that they will be executed, and that danger the insurers have not chosen to take upon themselves.

That the law of nations prohibits the exercise of any act of authority over a vessel in the situation of the Aurora, and that this seizure is, on that account, a mere marine trespass, not within the exception, cannot be admitted. To reason from the extent of protection a nation will afford to foreigners to the extent of the means it may use for its own security does not seem to be perfectly correct. It is opposed by principles which are universally acknowledged. The authority of a nation within its own territory is absolute and exclusive. The seizure of a vessel within the range of its cannon by a foreign force is an invasion of that territory, and is a hostile act which it is its duty to repel. But its power to secure itself from injury, may certainly be exercised beyond the limits of its territory. Upon this principle the right of a belligerent to search a neutral vessel on the high seas for contraband of war, is universally admitted, because the belligerent has a right to prevent the injury done to himself by the assistance intended for his enemy: so too a nation has a right to prohibit any commerce with its colonies. Any attempt to violate the laws made to protect this right, is an injury to itself which it may prevent, and it has a right to use the means necessary for its prevention. These means do not appear to be limited within any certain marked boundaries, which remain the same at all times and in all situations. If they are such as unnecessarily to vex and harass foreign lawful commerce, foreign nations will resist their exercise. If they are such as are reasonable and necessary to secure their laws from violation, they will be submitted to.

In different seas and on different coasts, a wider or more contracted range, in which to exercise the vigilance of the government, will be assented to. Thus in the channel, where a very great part of the commerce to and from all the north of Europe, passes through a very narrow sea, the seizure of vessels on suspicion of attempting an illicit trade, must necessarily be restricted to very narrow limits, but on the coast of South America, seldom frequented by vessels but for the purpose of illicit trade, the vigilance of the government may be extended somewhat further; and foreign nations submit to such regulations as are reasonable in themselves, and are really necessary to secure that monopoly of colonial commerce, which is claimed by all nations holding distant possessions.

If this right be extended too far, the exercise of it will be resisted. It has occasioned long and frequent contests, which have sometimes ended in open war. The English, it will be well recollected, complained of the right claimed by Spain to search their vessels on the high seas, which was carried so far that the *guarda costas* of that nation, seized vessels not in the neighbourhood of their coasts. This practice was the subject of long and fruitless negotiations, and at length of open war. The right of the Spaniards was supposed to be exercised unreasonably and vexatiously, but it never was contended that it could only be exercised within the range of the cannon from their batteries. Indeed the right given to our own revenue cutters, to visit vessels four leagues from our coast, is a declaration that in the opinion of the American government, no such principle as that contended for, has a real existence.

Nothing then is to be drawn from the laws or usages of nations, which gives to this part of the contract before the court the very limited construction which the plaintiff insists on, or which proves that the seizure of the Aurora, by the Portuguese governor, was an act of lawless violence.

The argument that such act would be within the policy, and not within the exception, is admitted to be well founded. That the exclusion from the insurance of "the risk of illicit trade with the Portuguese," is an exclusion only of that risk, to which such trade is by law exposed, will be readily conceded.

It is unquestionably limited and restrained by the terms "illicit trade." No seizure, not justifiable under the laws and regulations established by the crown of Portugal, for the restriction of foreign commerce with its dependencies, can come within this part of the contract, and every seizure which is justifiable by those laws and regulations must be deemed within it. . . .

The edicts of Portugal, then, not having been proved, ought not to have been laid before the jury. . . .

The judgment must be reversed with costs, and the cause remanded to be again tried in the circuit court, with instructions not to permit the copies of the edicts of Portugal and the sentence in the proceedings mentioned to go to the jury, unless they be authenticated according to law.

THE GRACE AND RUBY.

United States, District Court, District of Massachusetts, 1922.

283 Fed. 475.

MORTON, District Judge.   These are libels for the forfeiture of the schooner Grace and Ruby for smuggling liquor in violation of Rev. St. §§ 2872, 2874 (Comp. St. §§ 5563, 5565), and the National Prohibition Act (41 Stat. 305).   They were heard upon exceptions to the libels, raising solely the question of jurisdiction.   The facts are settled by stipulation of the parties.   Those essential to a decision may be briefly stated as follows:

The Grace and Ruby was a British vessel owned and registered in Yarmouth, Nova Scotia, and commanded by one Ross, a British subject. She sailed from the Bahama Islands, British West Indies, with a St. John, N. B., clearance, on February 10, 1922, having a cargo of liquor, part of which was owned by one Sullivan, of Salem, Mass., who was on board.   From the Bahamas she proceeded directly to a point about six miles off Gloucester, Mass., where Sullivan was set on shore and the schooner stood off and on, keeping always more than three miles from land.   Two days later Sullivan came out to her in motorboat Wilkin II, owned in Gloucester and manned by two men, to bring provisions to the schooner and to take on shore part of her cargo.   At that time the schooner was about ten miles from the nearest land.   About 8,000 bottles of whiskey and some other liquors were there transferred from the Grace and Ruby into the motorboat and taken to shore at night.   Three members of the crew of the schooner, as well as Sullivan, went in the Wilkin II, and a dory belonging to the schooner was towed along, presumably for use in landing the liquor, or to enable the men to return to the schooner after the liquor was landed.   The attempt to land the liquor was discovered by revenue officers, and Wilkin II and her cargo were seized.

The next day the revenue cutter Tampa was ordered to find the Grace and Ruby and bring her into port.   Two days later, on February 23d, she discovered the schooner, and after some show of resistance on her part, which was overcome by a display of force by the cutter, the schooner was seized and brought into the port of Boston by the Tampa. At the time of the seizure the Grace and Ruby was about four miles from the nearest land.   She had on board the balance of her cargo of liquor.   Her master in no way assented to the seizure.   After the schooner was brought into Boston the present libels were filed, a warrant for her arrest issued, and she was taken into custody by the United States marshal.

From the agreed facts it is clearly inferable that the master of the Grace and Ruby knew that she was engaged in an enterprise forbidden by the laws of the United States; that he knew her cargo was contraband; that she was lying off the coast beyond the three-mile limit, but within the four-league limit, for the purpose of having her cargo taken ashore in other boats; and that before her seizure part of her cargo had been transferred to Wilkin II for the purpose, as her master knew, of being smuggled into this country, with the assistance of the schooner's crew and boat. There is nothing to suggest any intent on his part, if that be material, that the Grace and Ruby herself should go within the territorial jurisdiction of this country, and so far as appears she never did. She was hovering on the coast for the purpose of landing contraband goods, and had actually sent, at night, a part of her cargo ashore, with her boat and three of her men to assist in landing it.

While the question is not free from doubt, and no decision upon the point has come to my notice, it seems to me that this action on her part constituted an unlawful unlading by the Grace and Ruby at night within the territorial limits of the United States, in violation of Rev. St. §§ 2872, 2874. See 1 Wheaton, Criminal Law (11th Ed.) §§ 324, 330, 341, for a discussion of the principles involved and a collection of cases. The act of unlading, although beginning beyond the three-mile limit, continued until the liquor was landed, and the schooner was actively assisting in it by means of her small boat and three of her crew, who were on the motorboat for that purpose. It was none the less an unlawful unlading, within the section referred to, because by the transfer to the motorboat an offense was committed under section 2867, which rendered the motorboat and liquor liable to seizure and forfeiture, and the persons who aided and assisted liable to a penalty for so doing. The two classes of offenses are substantially different. I am aware that there has been a difference of judicial opinion about the scope of these sections. See U. S. v. The Hunter (1806) Fed. Cas. No. 15428; The Industry (1812) Fed. Cas. No. 7028; The Betsy, Fed. Cas. No. 1365; The Harmony, Fed. Cas. No. 6081; The Active, Fed. Cas. No. 33. I follow the opinion of Mr. Justice Story, both because it is the law of this circuit and because it seems to me to be the sounder view.

The case, then, is that the Grace and Ruby, having violated our law and laid herself liable to forfeiture under it if she could be reached, was forcibly taken four miles off the coast by an executive department of the government and brought within our jurisdiction. The present question is whether on such facts this court has jurisdiction of a libel brought by the government for the forfeiture of the vessel. It is to be noticed that the schooner is held in these proceedings on the arrest made by the marshal under the warrant that was issued on the filing of the libels, and not under the seizure made by the cutter, when the schooner was taken and brought into Boston. Whether she could have been seized beyond the three-mile limit for an offense committed wholly beyond that limit is not the present question.

The high seas are the territory of no nation; no nation can extend its laws over them; they are free to the vessels of all countries. But this has been thought not to mean that a nation is powerless against vessels offending against its laws which remain just outside the three-mile limit. . . .[1]

These expressions have been questioned by writers on international law, and are perhaps not entirely consistent with views which have been expressed by our State Department. . . . But Church v. Hubbart has never been overruled, and I am bound by it until the law is clearly settled otherwise. Moreover, the principle there stated seems to me such a sensible and practical rule for dealing with cases like the present that it ought to be followed until it is authoritatively repudiated. This is not to assert a right generally of search and seizure on the high seas, but only a limited power, exercised in the waters adjacent to our coasts, over vessels which have broken our laws.

The mere fact, therefore, that the Grace and Ruby was beyond the three-mile limit, does not of itself make the seizure unlawful and establish a lack of jurisdiction.

As to the seizure: The line between territorial waters and the high seas is not like the boundary between us and a foreign power. There must be, it seems to me, a certain width of debatable waters adjacent to our coasts. How far our authority shall be extended into them for the seizure of foreign vessels which have broken our laws is a matter for the political departments of the government rather than for the courts to determine.

It is a question between governments; reciprocal rights and other matters may be involved. In re Cooper, 143 U. S. 472, 503, 12 S. Ct. 453; The Kodiak (D. C.) 53 F. 126, 130. In the case of The Cagliari, Dr. Twiss advised the Sardinian government that:

"In ordinary cases, where a merchant ship has been seized on the high seas, the sovereign whose flag has been violated waives his privilege, considering the offending ship to have acted with mala fides towards the other state with which he is in amity, and to have consequently forfeited any just claim to his protection."

He considered the revenue regulations of many states authorizing visit and seizure beyond their waters to be enforceable at the peril of such states, and to rest on the express or tacit permission of the states whose vessels may be seized. 1 Moore's Internat. Law Digest, pp. 729, 730.

It seems to me that this was such a case. The Grace and Ruby had committed an offense against our law, if my view as to the unlading is right, and was lying just outside the three-mile limit for purposes relating to her unlawful act. In directing that she be seized there and

---

[1] The court here quotes from Church v. Hubbart, above, p. 496.

brought into the country to answer for her offense, I am not prepared to say that the Treasury Department exceeded its power.

An order may be entered, overruling the exceptions to each libel alleging lack of jurisdiction.[1]

FORD [ET AL.] v. UNITED STATES.

United States, Supreme Court, 1927.

273 U. S. 593.   [71 L. ed. 793; 47 S. Ct. 531.]

[The latter part of the case, dealing with the question whether persons could commit the offense of conspiracy to violate the prohibition laws when they were at all times corporeally out of the jurisdiction of the United States, is reproduced above, p. 213.]

Mr. Chief Justice Taft delivered the opinion of the Court: . . .

The case on the evidence made by the government was as follows:

On October 12, 1924, the United States Coast Guard cutter Shawnee, on the lookout for vessels engaged in the illicit importation into the United States of intoxicating liquor, saw the Quadra, a British steamer of Canadian register, near the Farallon Islands. As the Shawnee bore down on her to investigate, she turned and began to move off shore. The captain of the Shawnee signaled her to stop, and she complied. As the Shawnee approached her, a motor boat, C–55, was seen just after the boat had left the Quadra. The Shawnee captain signaled the boat to stop, and, because it did not do so, fired a shot across its bow, whereupon it rounded about and came alongside. It had two men and a number of sacks of intoxicating liquor, as well as a partly filled case of beer bottles. It was made fast to the Shawnee, and the two men were placed under arrest. The Shawnee captain then sent two officers aboard the Quadra to examine her papers. Ford, her captain, one of the convicted defendants, refused to show his papers or to give any information until he had consulted counsel. The Shawnee officers then took charge of her. She was found to contain a large quantity of intoxicating liquor, and on refusal of Ford to take her by steam into San Francisco, the Shawnee towed her to that port and turned her cargo over to the United States customs officers, while her officers and crew, including Ford, were arrested.

The testimony for the government tended to show that the Quadra, when seized, was 5.7 nautical miles from the Farallon Islands, and that

---

[1] Compare the case of the Henry L. Marshall, 292 Fed. 486 (1923), in which the vessel was captured outside the three-mile limit while delivering its cargo by prearrangement into small boats belonging to others.

the motor boat C–55 could have traversed that distance in less than an hour.

The evidence for the government at the trial further showed there were three vessels, the Quadra, the Malahat, and the Coal Harbour, chartered by a cargo-owning corporation called the Consolidated Exporters' Corporation, Limited, of Canada, and loaded at Vancouver, British Columbia, with large cargoes of miscellaneous liquors; that the Malahat left Vancouver in May, officially destined to Buenaventura, Colombia; that the Coal Harbour left the same port in July, with a similar cargo officially destined to La Libertad, San Salvador, and the Quadra left there in September, officially destined to La Libertad. The captains of these vessels, while hovering near the Farallones, were constantly in touch with the convicted defendants Quartararo and Belanger at San Francisco, and acted to some extent under their orders and directions. Quartararo was the most active agent of the conspiracy on shore. Belanger was a director of the Canadian corporation above named. He arranged for and had sent from San Francisco to the Malahat burlap containers to be used for landing the bottled liquor, thence to be transferred to the Quadra, and also gave the order to transfer liquor from one vessel to another, and to bring designated liquor from the vessels' cargoes to the shore. The Quadra was supplied with fuel oil from the shore, pursuant to prearrangement. None of the seagoing vessels above named proceeded to their destinations officially described in their ship's papers, but cruised up and down between the Farallones and the Golden Gate, where the exchanges of liquor and sacks were made, and where the needed oil was delivered, and from which the liquor was carried by small boats to a landing place called Oakland Creek in San Francisco. The evidence of the conspiracy, the landing of the liquor, and the complicity of the convicted defendants therein was ample and practically undenied.

There was a preliminary motion to exclude and suppress the evidence of the ship and cargo. It was contended that the seizure was unlawful, because not within the zone of the high seas prescribed by the treaty, and the officers of the Quadra being prosecuted were protected against its use as evidence against them under the Fourth and Fifth Amendments to the federal Constitution. The motion was heard by the District Court without a jury, and was denied in an opinion reported in 3 Fed. (2d) 643. The evidence of the government showed that the Quadra was seized at a distance from the Farallon Islands of 5.7 miles, and a test made later of the speed of the motor boat C–55 caught carrying liquor from her showed that it could traverse 6.6 miles in an hour. There was a conflict as to the exact position of the Quadra at the time of the seizure. It was further objected that the speed of the motor boat was not made under the same conditions as those which existed at the time of the seizure. . . .

. . . The issue whether the ship was seized within the prescribed limit did not affect the question of the defendants' guilt or innocence. It only affected the right of the court to hold their persons for trial. It was necessarily preliminary to that trial. The proper way of raising the issue of fact of the place of seizure was by a plea to the jurisdiction. A plea to the jurisdiction must precede the plea of not guilty. Such a plea was not filed. The effect of the failure to file it was to waive the question of the jurisdiction of the persons of defendants. . . . It was not error, therefore, to refuse to submit to the jury on the trial the issue as to the place of the seizure.

There was a demurrer to the indictment, on the ground that it did not state facts sufficient to constitute an offense against the United States, that the court had no jurisdiction to try those who were on the Quadra because seized beyond the 3-mile limit, and that the acts charged were not within the jurisdiction of the court. The conspiracy was laid at the Bay of San Francisco, which was within the jurisdiction of the court. The conspiracy charged was undoubtedly a conspiracy to violate the laws of the United States under § 37 of the Criminal Code. The court had jurisdiction to try the offense charged in the indictment and the defendants were in its jurisdiction because they were actually in its custody.

The defendants contend that on the face of the indictment and the treaty they are made immune from trial. This requires an examination and construction of the treaty.

The preamble of the treaty recites that the two nations being desirous of avoiding any difficulties which might arise between them in connection with the laws in force in the United States on the subject of alcoholic beverages, have decided to conclude a convention for the purpose. The first four Articles are as follows:

"Article I.

"The high contracting parties declare that it is their firm intention to uphold the principle that 3 marine miles extending from the coast-line outwards and measured from low-water mark constitute the proper limits of territorial waters.

"Article II.

"(1) His Britannic Majesty agrees that he will raise no objection to the boarding of private vessels under the British flag outside the limits of territorial waters by the authorities of the United States, its territories or possessions in order that enquiries may be addressed to those on board and an examination be made of the ship's papers for the purpose of ascertaining whether the vessel or those on board are endeavoring to import or have imported alcoholic beverages into the United States, its territories or possessions in violation of the laws there in force. When such enquiries and examination show a reasonable ground for suspicion, a search of the vessel may be instituted.

"(2) If there is reasonable cause for belief that the vessel has committed or is committing or attempting to commit an offense against the laws of the United States, its territories or possessions prohibiting the importation of alcoholic beverages, the vessel may be seized and taken into a port of the United States, its territories or possessions for adjudication in accordance with such laws.

"(3) The rights conferred by this article shall not be exercised at a greater distance from the coast of the United States, its territories or possessions than can be traversed in one hour by the vessel suspected of endeavoring to commit the offense. In cases, however, in which the liquor is intended to be conveyed to the United States, its territories or possessions by a vessel other than the one boarded and searched, it shall be the speed of such other vessel and not the speed of the vessel boarded, which shall determine the distance from the coast at which the right under this article can be exercised.

"Article III.

"No penalty or forfeiture under the laws of the United States shall be applicable or attach to alcoholic liquors or to vessels or persons by reason of the carriage of such liquors, when such liquors are listed as sea stores or cargo destined for a port foreign to the United States, its territories or possessions on board British vessels voyaging to or from ports of the United States, or its territories or possessions or passing through the territorial waters thereof, and such carriage shall be as now provided by law with respect to the transit of such liquors through the Panama Canal, provided that such liquors shall be kept under seal continuously while the vessel on which they are carried remains within said territorial waters and that no part of such liquors shall at any time or place be unladen within the United States, its territories or possessions."

[Article 4 omitted.]

The treaty indicates a considerate purpose on the part of Great Britain to discourage her merchant ships from taking part in the illicit importation of liquor into the United States, and the further purpose of securing without objection or seizure the transportation on her vessels, through the waters and in ports of the United States, of sealed sea stores and sealed cargoes of liquor for delivery at other destinations than the United States. The counter consideration moving to the United States is the enlargement and a definite fixing of the zone of legitimate seizure of British hovering vessels seeking to defeat the laws against importation of liquor into this country from the sea. The treaty did not change the territorial jurisdiction of the United States to try offenses against its importation laws. That remained exactly as it was. If the ship could not have been condemned for such offenses before the treaty, it cannot be condemned now. If the persons on board could not have been convicted before the treaty, they cannot be convicted now. The treaty provides for the disposition of the vessel after seizure. It has to be taken into port for adjudication. What is to be adjudicated? The vessel. What does that include? The inference that both ship and those on board are to be subjected to prosecution on incriminating evidence is fully justified by paragraph 1 of Article II in specifically permitting examination of the ship papers and inquiries to those on board to ascertain whether not only the ship, but also those on board are endeavoring to import or have imported liquor into the United States. If those on board are to be excluded, then by the same narrow construction the cargo of liquor is to escape adjudication, though it is subject to search as the persons on board are to inquiry into their guilt. It is no straining of the language of the article therefore to interpret the phrase, "the vessel may be seized and taken into a port of the United States . . . . for adjudication in accordance with such laws," as intending that not only the vessel but that all and everything on board are to be adjudicated. The seizure and the taking into port necessarily include the cargo and persons on board. They cannot be set adrift or thrown overboard. They must go with the ship; they are identified with it. Their immunity on the high seas from seizure or being taken into port came from the immunity of the vessel by reason of her British nationality. When the vessel lost this immunity, they lost it, too; and when they were brought into a port of the United States and into the jurisdiction of its District Court, they were just as much subject to its adjudication as the ship. If they committed an offense against the United States and its liquor importation laws, they cannot escape conviction, unless the treaty affirmatively confers on them immunity from prosecution. There certainly are no express words granting such immunity. Why should it be implied? . . .

What reason could Great Britain have for a stipulation clothing with immunity either contraband liquor which should be condemned or the guilty persons aboard, when the very object of the treaty was to help the United States in its effort to protect itself against such liquor and such persons from invasion by the sea? To give immunity to the cargo and the guilty persons on board would be to clear those whose guilt should condemn the vessel and to restore to them the liquor, and thus release both for another opportunity to flout the laws of a friendly government, which it was the purpose of the treaty to discourage. The owner of the vessel would thus alone be subjected to penalty, and he would suffer for the primary guilt of the immunized owner of the liquor. Such implication of immunity leads to inconsistency and injustice. The palpable incongruity contended for is such that, without express words, we cannot attribute to the high contracting parties intention to bring it about.

Nor have we been advised that Great Britain has ever suggested that under this treaty a crew of a vessel lawfully seized could not be brought into port or tried according to our laws. Diligent as the representatives of that nation have always been in guarding the rights of their people, such a construction of the treaty has not been advanced. . . .

It is next objected that the convicted defendants taken from the Quadra were not triable under the indictment, because it charges an offense against them for which under the treaty neither they nor the Quadra could have been seized in the prescribed limit. It is very doubtful whether the objection was made in time and was not waived by the plea of not guilty; but we shall treat it as having been duly made. The contention of counsel on this point is that the treaty permits seizure only for the substantive offense of importing or attempting to import liquor illegally and not for a conspiracy to do so.

These defendants were indicted under § 37 of the Criminal Code of the United States for having conspired at the Bay of San Francisco to violate the National Prohibition Act and the Tariff Act of 1922. Section 37 of the Criminal Code provides that if two or more persons conspire to commit an offense against the United States, and one or more of such parties commit any act to effect the object of the conspiracy, each shall be punished.

The National Prohibition Act, c. 85, § 3, 41 Stat. 305, 308, enacted October 28, 1919, provides:

"No person shall on or after the date when the Eighteenth Amendment to the Constitution of the United States goes into effect, manufacture, sell, barter, transport, import, export, deliver, furnish or possess any intoxicating liquor except as authorized in this Act, and all the provisions of this Act shall be liberally construed to the end that the use of intoxicating liquor as a beverage may be prevented."

The Tariff Act of September 21, 1922, 42 Stat. c. 356, § 593 (b) provides that, if any person fraudulently or knowingly imports or brings into the United States, or assists in doing so, any merchandise contrary to law, he shall be fined or imprisoned. The importation of liquor into the United States is contrary to law, as shown by the Prohibition Act.

The indictment charged as overt acts that the defendants and each of them, on the 10th and 29th of September, and October 11th, by small boats from the Quadra, landed illegally in San Francisco substantial quantities of liquor, and on the 12th of October, the day of the seizure, attempted to land another lot of liquor but were defeated by the seizure. . . .

Considering the friendly purpose of both countries in making this treaty, we do not think any narrow construction should be given which would defeat it. The parties were dealing with a situation well understood by both. In effect they wished to enable the United States better to police its seaboard, by enabling it within an hour's sail from its coast, beyond its territorial jurisdiction, and on the high seas, to seize British actual or would-be smugglers of liquor and, if they were caught, to proceed criminally against them as if seized within the three-mile limit for the same offenses in reference to liquor importation. No particular laws by title or date were referred to in the treaty, but only the purpose and effect of them. Plainly it was the purpose of the contracting parties that vessels and men who are caught under the treaty and are proven to have violated any laws of the United States, by which the •importation of liquor is intended to be stopped through forfeiture or punishment, may be prosecuted after the seizure. The National Prohibition Act expressly punishes the importation of intoxicating liquor. The Tariff Act of 1922 declares it an offense to make any illegal importation and so makes it an offense to import intoxicating liquor. Section 37 of the Criminal Code makes it an offense to conspire to violate the Prohibition Act and the Tariff Act in respect to the importation of liquor, if the conspiracy is accompanied by overt acts in pursuance of it. The conspiracy act is the one most frequently used in the prosecution of liquor importations from the sea, because such smuggling usually necessitates a conspiracy in preparation for the landing. We think that any more limited construction would not satisfy the reasonable expectations of the two parties. Nothing in the words of the treaty makes such an interpretation a difficult one. The penalties under each act differ from those under the others. The Tariff Act and the conspiracy section each imposes a maximum penalty of two years, while that of the Prohibition Act is only six months, with a lower maximum of fine. The differences are clearly not sufficient to affect the construction. . . .

The judgment of conviction of the Court of Appeals is affirmed.[1]

---

[1] SUPPLEMENTARY CASES. In Rose v. Himely, 4 Cranch 241 (1808), the point at issue was the validity of a sale of goods, part of the cargo of the American schooner Sarah, made in a Spanish port under the authority of an agent representing the French government of Santo Domingo and subsequently confirmed by condemnation proceedings at Santo Domingo after the goods had been brought by the purchasers to the United States. The offense leading to the condemnation was the violation by the schooner of municipal regulations of Santo Domingo against trading with ports occupied by rebels. The Supreme Court, speaking through Chief Justice Marshall, held that the French court had no jurisdiction to condemn property seized on the high seas for the breach of a municipal regulation. "Of its own jurisdiction," said the court, "so far as depends on municipal rules, the court of a foreign nation must judge, and its decision must be respected. But if it exercises a jurisdiction which, according to the law of nations, its sovereign could not confer, however available its sentences may be within the dominions of the prince from whom the authority is derived, they are not regarded by foreign courts. This distinction is taken upon this principle, that the law of nations is the law of all tribunals in the society of nations, and is supposed to be equally understood by all. . . .

"It is conceded that the legislation of every country is territorial; that beyond its own territory, it can only affect its own subjects or citizens. It is not easy to conceive a power to execute a municipal law, or to enforce obedience to that law without the circle in which that law operates. A power to seize for the infraction of a law is derived from the sovereign, and must be exercised, it would seem, within those limits which circumscribe the sovereign power. The rights of war may be exercised on the high seas, because war is carried on upon the high seas; but the pacific rights of sovereignty must be exercised within the territory of the sovereign.

"If these propositions be true, a seizure of a person not a subject, or of a vessel not belonging to a subject, made on the high seas, for the breach of a municipal regulation, is an act which the sovereign cannot authorise. The person who makes this seizure, then, makes it on a pretext which, if true, will not justify the act, and is a marine trespasser. To a majority of the court it seems to follow, that such a seizure is totally invalid; that the possession, acquired by this unlawful act, is his own possession, not that of the sovereign; and that such possession confers no jurisdiction on the court of the country to which the captor belongs.

"This having been the fact in the case of The Sarah, and neither the vessel, nor the captain, supercargo, nor crew, having ever been brought within the jurisdiction of the court, or within the dominion of the sovereign whose laws were infracted, the jurisdiction of the court over the subject of its sentence never attached, the proceedings were entirely *ex parte,* and the sentence is not to be regarded." The sale was therefore held to be invalid.

In Hudson and Smith v. Guestier, 6 Cranch 281 (1810), involving the validity of a sale of the cargo of the brig Sea Flower made in a Spanish port in pursuance of condemnation proceedings by a French tribunal sitting at the French port of Guadalupe, the offense being the violation of municipal ordinances against trading with the revolted ports of the island of Hispaniola, the court held that the French tribunal had jurisdiction of the property even though present in the port of another nation, and if so, then the condemnation proceedings could not be questioned by the courts of another state even though the vessel was taken on the high seas. Chief Justice Marshall dissented, asserting that the principle of Rose v. Himely was now overruled.

Query, does the doctrine of "hot pursuit" apply to vessels which, after committing an illegal act, escape from territorial waters out to the high seas? In The Ship North v. The King, 37 Canada Sup. Ct. Rep. 385 (1906), involving the validity of the seizure on the high seas of an American fishing schooner for the offense of fishing within three miles of the seacoast of British Columbia without a license, the Supreme Court of the Dominion of Canada held that "the Admiralty Court when exercising its jurisdiction is bound to take notice of the law of nations, and that by that law when a vessel within foreign territory commits an infraction of its laws either for the protection of its fisheries or its revenues or coasts she may be immediately pursued into the open seas beyond the territorial limits and there taken. As Mr. Hall observes in the book upon International Law (4th Ed.) at page 267:

" 'It must be added that this can only be done when the pursuit is commenced while the vessel is still within the territorial waters or has only just escaped from them. The reason for the permission seems to be that pursuit under these circumstances is a continuation of an act of jurisdiction which has been begun or which but for the accident of immediate escape would have been begun within the territory itself and that it is necessary to permit it in order to enable the territorial jurisdiction to be efficiently exercised.'

"This clear terse statement of the law and the reason for it is amply sustained by the array of authorities cited by Martin, J., the local judge in admiralty in his judgment. The right of hot pursuit of a vessel found illegally fishing within the territorial waters of another nation being part of the law of nations was properly judicially taken notice of and acted upon by the learned judge in this prosecution."

The decision sustained the action of the lower court (11 B. C. Rep. 473) which had cited Hudson v. Guestier (above, p. 511) as settling the matter. Compare The Itata, above, p. 496, n. 1, in respect to hot pursuit into territorial waters.

In the case of Gillam v. United States, 27 F. (2d) 296 (1928), involving the assessment of penalties against the British schooner Vinces for violation of the United States Tariff Act of 1922, the vessel when signaled being about 7½ miles off the shore but not overtaken until about 12¾ miles from the shore, the Circuit Court of Appeals, citing Hudson v. Guestier and Ship North v. King, held that "no point is made that the vessel was actually overhauled and the seizure actually made beyond the hour's sailing distance and beyond the 12-mile limit, if she was within these limits when signaled; and we think it is clear, under the 'hot pursuit' doctrine, that if the right of seizure existed at the time the vessel was signaled, the right was not lost because she had succeeded in getting farther from shore in her attempt to run away. . . .

"While it is true, as contended, that the vessel never came within the 3-mile limit of the territorial waters of the United States, we think that, as she was bound for the United States with an unmanifested cargo and came within 12 miles, or 4 marine leagues, of the coast, her seizure was justified under the revenue statutes of the United States, and that these statutes constitute a valid exercise of the sovereign power of the government." The decree of the lower court assessing penalties was therefore upheld. Compare Cook v. United States, below, p. 564, and United States v. Ferris, below, p. 562.

In the case of the Elida, German Imperial Supreme Prize Court, 1915 [Translation in Am. Journal Int. Law, X (1916), 916], involving the seizure by a German warship of a Swedish steamer outside the three-mile limit but, as alleged, within the four-mile zone of neutrality proclaimed by Sweden, the court rejected the Swedish claim of an extension of territorial jurisdiction beyond the established three miles. While holding itself bound by the specific provisions of the German Prize Regulations, forbidding seizure within a zone of only three miles from neutral coasts, the court nevertheless maintained that the Prize Regulations in no way violated "the general principles of international law." "Heretofore," said the court, "the maritime boundary of states has been generally recognized in theory and practice as being three nautical miles distant from the coast. Originally, it was based on the carrying distance, corresponding to the gunnery technique of those times, of ships' and coast guns. It is true that now-a-days this reason is no longer applicable. Here however the axiom cessante ratione non cessat lex ipsa applies, and although numerous proposals and opinions have been put forward with regard to a different delimitation of the national waters, it cannot be asserted that any other method has in practice met with the general concurrence of the maritime states. This is also true of the view put forward in the above mentioned opinion, according to which each individual state is entitled to extend, by means of independent regulations, the boundary of its national waters beyond the three-mile zone as far as gun range, the former limit nevertheless to be regarded as a subsidiary international boundary. With the range of present day guns this would lead to quite intolerable conditions, and give to single states the possibility of including within their national territory extensive tracts of the open sea the freedom of which is in the interest of all maritime states. To a certain extent this is also acknowledged by Liszt in his opinion, for according thereto the regulation of the individual

D. Bays, gulfs, lakes.

No general rule can be laid down with regard to the territorial character of bays and gulfs. If the three-mile limit were strictly adhered to only bays six miles or less in width would be included within the territory of the state. But by custom a number of bays which are deep out of all proportion to their width have come to be regarded as territorial. Query, whether the term "bays" as used in treaties describing fishing rights should include any other bays than those six miles or less in width? [United States and Great Britain: The Schooner Washington; United States and Great Britain: North Atlantic Coast Fisheries Case.] Would a collision taking place in the Bristol Channel at a point where the Channel was twenty miles wide be within British territorial jurisdiction? [The Fagernes.]

UNITED STATES AND GREAT BRITAIN:
THE SCHOONER WASHINGTON.

Claims Commission under the Convention of February 8, 1853.

Report of Decisions, p. 170.

BATES, Umpire. The schooner Washington was seized by the revenue schooner Julia, Captain Darby, while fishing in the Bay of Fundy, ten

---

state is not alone sufficient; the absence of objection on the part of other states is also required. Thereby in reality the permissibility of an extension of the territorial waters is founded not so much upon the independent regulation by the single state, as upon the supposition of a tacit acknowledgment of such an extension by the other states. A mere failure to object, however, is not identical with a positive concurrence of the nations. Furthermore it must be remembered that even if the exercise by a maritime nation of certain official functions, such as those of the health and customs authorities, is tolerated beyond the three-mile zone, this by no means represents a concession to the effect that in all other respects the waters in question are included within the territorial jurisdiction." The vessel had, however, been released by the lower court on the ground that its cargo of wood, destined to Hull, England, was not contraband, and the higher court merely awarded compensation for the seizure.

In the I'm Alone case between the United States and Canada, decided January 9, 1935, by a mixed arbitration commission, involving a claim brought by Canada for damages due to the sinking of the I'm Alone on March 22, 1929, by a United States patrol boat after a chase begun when the I'm Alone was from twelve to fifteen miles from shore and continued to a distance of some two hundred and fifty miles out upon the high seas, the commissioners held the act of sinking the ship was an unlawful act and called for an apology and the payment of punitive damages to Canada and actual damages to the captain and members of the crew. In as much, however, as the I'm Alone, although a British ship of Canadian registry, was owned, controlled and at times managed by a group of persons who were citizens of the United States and engaged in an illegal conspiracy to smuggle liquor, no compensation was awarded for the loss of the ship or the cargo. [Dept. of State Press Release, Jan. 9, 1935.]

miles from the shore, on the 10th day of May, 1843, on the charge of violating the treaty of 1818. She was carried to Yarmouth, Nova Scotia, and there decreed to be forfeited to the Crown by the judge of the vice admiralty court, and with her stores ordered to be sold. The owners of the Washington claim for the value of the vessel and appurtenances, outfits, and damages, $2,483, and for eleven years' interest, $1,638, amounting together to $4,121. By the recent reciprocity treaty, happily concluded between the United States and Great Britain, there seems no chance for any future disputes in regard to the fisheries. It is to be regretted, that in that treaty, provision was not made for settling a few small claims of no importance in a pecuniary sense, which were then existing, but as they have not been settled, they are now brought before this commission.

The Washington fishing schooner was seized, as before stated, in the Bay of Fundy, ten miles from the shore, off Annapolis, Nova Scotia.

It will be seen by the treaty of 1783, between Great Britain and the United States, that the citizens of the latter, in common with the subjects óf the former, enjoyed the right to take and cure fish on the shores of all parts of her Majesty's dominions in America, used by British fishermen; but not to dry fish on the island of Newfoundland, which latter privilege was confined to the shores of Nova Scotia in the following words: "And American fishermen shall have liberty to dry and cure fish on any of the unsettled bays, harbors, and creeks of Nova Scotia, but as soon as said shores shall become settled, it shall not be lawful to dry or cure fish at such settlement, without a previous agreement for that purpose with the inhabitants, proprietors, or possessors of the ground."

The question turns, so far as relates to the treaty stipulations on the meaning given to the word "bays" in the treaty of 1783. By that treaty the Americans had no right to dry and cure fish on the shores and bays of Newfoundland, but they had that right on the coasts, bays, harbors, and creeks of Nova Scotia; and as they must land to cure fish on the shores, bays, and creeks, they were evidently admitted to the shores of the bays, etc. By the treaty of 1818, the same right is granted to cure fish on the coasts, bays, etc., of Newfoundland, but the Americans relinquished that right, and the right to fish within three miles of the coasts, bays, etc., of Nova Scotia. Taking it for granted that the framers of the treaty intended that the word "bay" or "bays" should have the same meaning in all cases, and no mention being made of headlands, there appears no doubt that the Washington, in fishing ten miles from the shore, violated no stipulations of the treaty.

It was urged on behalf of the British government, that by coasts, bays, etc., is understood an imaginary line, drawn along the coast from headland to headland, and that the jurisdiction of her Majesty extends three marine miles outside of this line; thus closing all the bays on the coast or shore, and that great body of water called the Bay of Fundy against Americans and others, making the latter a British bay. This doctrine of headlands is new, and has received a proper limit in the convention between France and Great Britain of 2d August, 1839, in which "it is agreed that the distance of three miles fixed as the general limit for the exclusive right of fishery upon the coasts of the two countries shall, with respect to bays, the mouths of which do not exceed ten miles in width, be measured from a straight line drawn from headland to headland."

The Bay of Fundy is from 65 to 75 miles wide, and 130 to 140 miles long, it has several bays on its coasts; thus the word bay, as applied to this great body of water, has the same meaning as that applied to the Bay of Biscay, the Bay of Bengal, over which no nation can have the right to assume the sovereignty. One of the headlands of the Bay of Fundy is in the United States, and ships bound to Passamaquoddy must sail through a large space of it. The island of Grand Menan (British) and Little Menan (American) are situated nearly on a line from headland to headland. These islands, as represented in all geographies, are situate in the Atlantic Ocean. The conclusion is, therefore, in my mind irresistible, that the Bay of Fundy is not a British bay, nor a bay within the meaning of the word as used in the treaties of 1783 and 1818.

The owners of the Washington, or their legal representatives, are therefore entitled to compensation, and are hereby awarded not the amount of their claim, which is excessive, but the sum of three thousand dollars, due on the 15th January, 1855.

UNITED STATES AND GREAT BRITAIN: NORTH ATLANTIC COAST FISHERIES CASE.

Tribunal of the Permanent Court of Arbitration, 1910.

Scott, Hague Court Reports, 146.

[In consequence of the termination of the provisions of the treaty of peace of 1783, in accordance with which Great Britain had granted certain fishing rights and liberties to the United States, a new treaty was entered into in 1818 by which Great Britain agreed (Article I) that the inhabitants of the United States should have forever, in common with the subjects of His Britannic Majesty, the "liberty" to take fish in certain waters along the coasts of Newfoundland and Labrador and also the "liberty" to dry and cure fish in any of the unsettled bays, creeks or harbors of those waters. At the same time the United States renounced "any liberty heretofore enjoyed or claimed by the inhabitants thereof, to take, dry, or cure fish on, or within three marine miles of any of the coasts, bays, creeks, or harbours of His Britannic Majesty's dominions in America not included within the abovementioned limits."

Differences having arisen as to the scope and meaning of this article and of the "liberties" referred to in it, the two governments by a special agreement of January 27, 1909, under the arbitration treaty of April 4, 1908, submitted seven questions to a tribunal of arbitration. The award of the tribunal was rendered on September 7, 1910. Only so much of it as deals with the question of the determination of what constitutes a "bay" within the meaning of the treaty is reproduced here.] [1]

[By the Tribunal.] . . . Question 5. From where must be measured the "three marine miles of any of the coasts, bays, creeks, or harbors" referred to in the said article?

In regard to this question, Great Britain claims that the renunciation applies to all bays generally, and

The United States contend that it applies to bays of a certain class or condition.

Now, considering that the treaty used the general term "bays" without qualification, the tribunal is of opinion that these words of the treaty must be interpreted in a general sense as applying to every bay on the coast in question that might be reasonably supposed to have been considered as a bay by the negotiators of the treaty under the general conditions then prevailing, unless the United States can adduce satisfactory proof that any restrictions or qualifications of the general use of the term were or should have been present to their minds. . . .

3d. The United States also contend that the term "bays of His Britannic Majesty's dominions" in the renunciatory clause must be read as including only those bays which were under the territorial sovereignty of Great Britain.

But the tribunal is unable to accept this contention:

(a) Because the description of the coast on which the fishery is to be exercised by the inhabitants of the United States is expressed throughout the treaty of 1818 in geographical terms and not by reference to political control; the treaty describes the coast as contained between capes;

(b) Because to express the political concept of dominion as equivalent to sovereignty, the word "dominion" in the singular would have been an adequate term and not "dominions" in the plural; this latter term having a recognized and well-settled meaning as descriptive of those portions of the earth which owe political allegiance to His Majesty; e. g., "His Britannic Majesty's dominions beyond the seas."

4th. It has been further contended by the United States that the renunciation applies only to bays six miles or less in width *inter fauces*

---

[1] An earlier part of the same award, dealing with the question whether any of the "liberties" claimed by the United States under the treaty of 1818 were of such a permanent character as to constitute "servitudes" and be as such exempt from local legislation, is reproduced below, p. 532.

terræ, those bays only being territorial bays, because the three-mile rule is, as shown by this treaty, a principle of international law applicable to coasts and should be strictly and systematically applied to bays.

But the tribunal is unable to agree with this contention:

(a) Because admittedly the geographical character of a bay contains conditions which concern the interests of the territorial sovereign to a more intimate and important extent than do those connected with the open coast. Thus conditions of national and territorial integrity, of de-fense, of commerce and of industry are all vitally concerned with the control of the bays penetrating the national coast line. This interest varies, speaking generally, in proportion to the penetration inland of the bay; but as no principle of international law recognizes any specified relation between the concavity of the bay and the requirements for con-trol by the territorial sovereignty, this tribunal is unable to qualify by the application of any new principle its interpretation of the treaty of 1818 as excluding bays in general from the strict and systematic appli-cation of the three-mile rule; nor can this tribunal take cognizance in this connection of other principles concerning the territorial sovereignty over bays such as ten-mile or twelve-mile limits of exclusion based on international acts subsequent to the treaty of 1818 and relating to coasts of a different configuration and conditions of a different character;

(b) Because the opinion of jurists and publicists quoted in the pro-ceedings conduce to the opinion that speaking generally the three-mile rule should not be strictly and systematically applied to bays; . . .

(f) Because from the information before this tribunal it is evident that the three-mile rule is not applied to bays strictly or systematically either by the United States or by any other Power;

(g) It has been recognized by the United States that bays stand apart, and that in respect of them territorial jurisdiction may be exercised farther than the marginal belt in the case of Delaware Bay by the re-port of the United States Attorney General of May 19, 1793; and the letter of Mr. Jefferson to Mr. Genet of November 8, 1793, declares the bays of the United States generally to be, "as being landlocked, within the body of the United States."

5th. In this latter regard it is further contended by the United States, that such exceptions only should be made from the application of the three-mile rule to bays as are sanctioned by conventions and es-tablished usage; that all exceptions for which the United States of America were responsible are so sanctioned; and that His Majesty's government are unable to provide evidence to show that the bays con-cerned by the treaty of 1818 could be claimed as exceptions on these grounds either generally, or except possibly in one or two cases, spe-cifically.

But the tribunal, while recognizing that conventions and established usage might be considered as the basis for claiming as territorial those bays which on this ground might be called historic bays, and that such claims should be held valid in the absence of any principle of international law on the subject; nevertheless is unable to apply this, *a contrario*, so as to subject the bays in question to the three-mile rule, as desired by the United States:

(a) Because Great Britain has during this controversy asserted a claim to these bays generally, and has enforced such claim specifically in statutes or otherwise, in regard to the more important bays such as Chaleurs, Conception and Miramichi; . . .

6th. It has been contended by the United States that the words "coasts, bays, creeks or harbors" are here used only to express different parts of the coast and are intended to express and be equivalent to the word "coast," whereby the three marine miles would be measured from the sinuosities of the coast and the renunciation would apply only to the waters of bays within three miles.

But the tribunal is unable to agree with this contention: . . .

(f) Because the tribunal is unable to understand the term "bays" in the renunciatory clause in other than its geographical sense, by which a bay is to be considered as an indentation of the coast, bearing a configuration of a particular character easy to determine specifically, but difficult to describe generally.

The negotiators of the treaty of 1818 did probably not trouble themselves with subtle theories concerning the notion of "bays"; they most probably thought that everybody would know what was a bay. In this popular sense the term must be interpreted in the treaty. The interpretation must take into account all the individual circumstances which for any one of the different bays are to be appreciated, the relation of its width to the length of penetration inland, the possibility and the necessity of its being defended by the state in whose territory it is indented; the special value which it has for the industry of the inhabitants of its shores; the distance which it is secluded from the highways of nations on the open sea and other circumstances not possible to enumerate in general.

For these reasons the tribunal decides and awards:

In case of bays the three marine miles are to be measured from a straight line drawn across the body of water at the place where it ceases to have the configuration and characteristics of a bay. At all other places the three marine miles are to be measured following the sinuosities of the coast.

But considering the tribunal cannot overlook that this answer to Question 5, although correct in principle and the only one possible in view of the want of a sufficient basis for a more concrete answer, is not entirely satisfactory as to its practical applicability, and that it leaves room for doubts and differences in practice. Therefore the tribunal considers it its duty to render the decision more practicable and to remove the danger of future differences by adjoining to it, a recommendation in virtue of the responsibilities imposed by Art. 4 of the special agreement.

Considering, moreover, that in treaties with France, with the North German Confederation and the German Empire and likewise in the North Sea convention, Great Britain has adopted for similar cases the rule that only bays of ten miles width should be considered as those wherein the fishing is reserved to nationals. And that in the course of the negotiations between Great Britain and the United States a similar rule has been on various occasions proposed and adopted by Great Britain in instructions to the naval officers stationed on these coasts. And that though these circumstances are not sufficient to constitute this a principle of international law, it seems reasonable to propose this rule with certain exceptions, all the more that this rule with such exceptions has already formed the basis of an agreement between the two Powers.

Now therefore this tribunal in pursuance of the provisions of Art. 4 hereby recommends for the consideration and acceptance of the high contracting Parties the following rules and method of procedure for determining the limits of the bays hereinbefore enumerated:

1. In every bay not hereinafter specifically provided for the limits of exclusion shall be drawn three miles seaward from a straight line across the bay in the part nearest the entrance at the first point where the width does not exceed ten miles. . . .

It is understood that nothing in these rules refers either to the Bay of Fundy considered as a whole apart from its bays and creeks or as to the innocent passage through the Gut of Canso, which were excluded by the agreement made by exchange of notes between Mr. Bacon and Mr. Bryce dated February 21, 1909, and March 4, 1909; or to Conception Bay, which was provided for by the decision of the Privy Council in the case of the Direct United States Cable Company v. The Anglo American Telegraph Company, in which decision the United States have acquiesced.

THE FAGERNES.

Great Britain, Court of Appeal, 1927.

L. R. [1927] Probate, 311.

Appeal by the defendants, the Società Nazionale di Navigazione, owners of the Italian steamship Fagernes, to set aside an order for service of notice of the writ in the action out of the jurisdiction.

On March 17, 1926, a collision occurred in the Bristol Channel between the steamship Cornish Coast, owned by the plaintiffs, and the

Fagernes. The Cornish Coast was damaged and the Fagernes was sunk. In these circumstances the plaintiffs brought their action for damage by collision *in personam* against the owners of the Italian steamship, and obtained an order in chambers giving leave under Order xi. r. l. (ee), to serve notice of the writ out of the jurisdiction. The defendants thereupon moved to set aside this order on the grounds that the collision occurred outside British territorial waters, and that the Court had no jurisdiction to try the case. The place of collision was 10½ or 12½ miles distant from the English coast and 9½ or 7½ miles from the Welsh coast, according to the respective cases, the distance across the channel being about twenty sea miles.

Hill, J., held that the waters of the Bristol Channel, at any rate above a line drawn from Bull Point, in Devonshire, to Port Eynon Head, in Glamorganshire, were *inter fauces terræ,* and were thus part of the territory of the State which owned the land on both sides, and therefore within the jurisdiction of the High Court. He accordingly held that the order for service of the notice of the writ out of the jurisdiction was rightly made.

The defendants appealed.

The appeal came before the Court on December 9, 1926, when their Lordships thought it raised questions on which the Crown might desire to be represented, and accordingly the case was adjourned for the attendance of the Attorney-General if so advised.

ATKIN, L. J. The question to be decided in this case is no less momentous than whether the Bristol Channel is part of the realm of England. What is the territory of the Crown is a matter of which the Court takes judicial notice. The Court has, therefore, to inform itself from the best material available; and on such a matter it may be its duty to obtain its information from the appropriate department of government. Any definite statement from the proper representative of the Crown as to the territory of the Crown must be treated as conclusive. A conflict is not to be contemplated between the Courts and the Executive on such a matter, where foreign interests may be concerned, and where responsibility for protection and administration is of paramount importance to the Government of the country. In these circumstances the Court requested the assistance of the Attorney-General who, after elaborate and valuable argument on the municipal and international law, so far as it affects the question, eventually informed the court that he had consulted the Home Secretary, and was by him instructed to say that the place of collision was not within the limits to which the territorial jurisdiction of His Majesty extends. I consider that statement binds the Court, and constrains it to decide that this portion of the Bristol Channel is not within British jurisdiction, and that the appeal must be allowed.

I think, however, that it is desirable to make it clear that this is not a decision on a point of law, and that no responsibility rests upon this Court save that of treating the statement of the Crown by its proper officer as conclusive. Speaking for myself alone, if I had to decide this case upon the materials before Hill, J., and the further authorities brought before us, I should have been inclined to come to the same conclusion as he did. It is quite certain that there is at present no such agreement in the practice of civilized States as to afford a definite rule to regulate territorial claims to the waters of gulfs and bays for the future; still less to determine what has been in fact the territorial jurisdiction in the past. It is also clear that whenever a rule can in the future be recognized as a principle of international law, it will have to admit exceptions where territorial jurisdiction has been effectively exercised beyond the limits of the general rule, whatever it may be; and in determining the existence of those exceptions, I do not know a better statement of the considerations that must be taken into account than is to be found in the Award of the Permanent Court of Arbitration at The Hague, in the *North Atlantic Coast Fisheries Arbitration,* in 1910: "The interpretation must take into account all the individual circumstances which, for any of the different bays are to be appreciated; the relation of its width to the length of penetration inland; the possibility and the necessity of its being defended by the State in whose territory it is indented; the special value which it has for the industry of the inhabitants of its shores; the distance which it is secluded from the highways of nations on the open sea and other circumstances not possible to enumerate in general." [Cd. 5396, Miscellaneous No. 3, 1910.]

One bears in mind that at this particular point the Channel is only about twenty miles wide, that it has on its north bank the teeming population of Glamorganshire with its coal ports, that it penetrates into the vitals of England, having towards the end of its course one of the oldest ports of the kingdom, Bristol. One has also to bear in mind that the whole of the Bristol Channel was part of one of the King's Chambers, which were delimited by an Order of James I in 1604, which will be found set out in Selden's Mare Clausum, Book II, ch. 22.

The statement of the Crown in this case makes it unnecessary to trace the history of the claim to the King's Chambers, but I think it relevant that though some modern writers on international law have doubted whether the claim to them would be maintained in these days, yet they were treated as material to the decision of cases in prize by Sir Leoline Jenkins in the cases of *St. Anne, Biscay, Hope,* and *De la Mothe,* from 1665 to 1675. . . . The existence of the territorial jurisdiction over them was maintained in the leading English work on international law of last century, Phillimore, throughout its editions; was admitted by Wheaton, the leading American authority of that century; and also by Major-General Halleck, of the United States of America; and was supported by the English Attorney-General in the *North Atlantic Coast Fisheries Arbitration* in 1910. The alleged limit of ten miles in width which the Attorney-General contended was the boundary of that part of the Channel which was wholly territorial (apart from the three miles' coast limit) is not yet accepted and undoubtedly has admitted exceptions in the case of British, American, French and other national waters. Finally, though neither Cunningham's Case [Bell's C. C. 72] nor Direct United States Cable Co. v. Anglo-American Telegraph Co. (the Conception Bay Case) [2 App. Cas. 394] determined this question as a matter of law, it seems to me plain that Cockburn, C. J., in the former case, and Lord Blackburn in the latter, treated the Bristol Channel as territorial waters in that part of it which is between Glamorgan and Somerset—i. e., at a width exceeding ten miles. In my view, also, considerable importance should be attached to the fact that Lundy Island, twenty miles to the westward of the *locus in quo,* is part of Devonshire. I mention these considerations, without further discussion of the various questions and authorities concerned, to support the statement that I have already made that, in arriving at its conclusion the Court is not purporting to do more than give effect to the authoritative pronouncement of the Government. The appeal must be allowed, and the order for service of notice of the writ and the service be set aside with costs here and below.

Appeal allowed.

[Opinions of BANKES and LAWRENCE, L. JJ., omitted.] [1]

---

[1] SUPPLEMENTARY CASES. In Regina v. Cunningham, Bell's Crown Cases, 86, involving the indictment of certain foreigners on board a foreign ship for a crime committed within the waters of Bristol Channel, the court held that the whole of that inland sea was by established usage to be considered as within the counties bounding its shores. Compare Mortensen v. Peters, above, p. 25, in respect to Moray Firth.

In Direct United States Cable Co. v. Anglo-American Telegraph Co., L. R. 2 App. Cas. 394 (1877), involving the validity of an injunction prohibiting the appellants from laying a telegraph cable within the waters of Conception Bay in infringement of exclusive rights granted to the respondents by the Newfoundland legislature, the Privy Council held that while jurists appeared to be in disagreement on the rules as to dimensions and configuration which determine whether a bay is or is not a part of the territory possessing the adjoining coasts, it seemed to their Lordships "that, in point of fact, the British government has for a long time exercised dominion over this bay, and that their claim has been acquiesced in by other nations, so as to show that the bay has been for a long time occupied exclusively by Great Britain, a circumstance which in the tribunals of any country would be very important."

In Manchester v. Massachusetts, 139 U. S. 240 (1891), involving a prosecution of Manchester, a citizen of Rhode Island, for fishing with a purse seine in the waters of Buzzard's Bay which is surrounded by the territory of Massachusetts, the Supreme Court held that as between nations it was established that "the minimum limit of the territorial jurisdiction of a nation over tide-waters is a marine league from its coast; that bays wholly within its territory not exceeding

E. Straits.

Straits, whether forming the boundary line between two states or separating the territory of a single state, are in general governed by the same rules that govern bays and may be territorial in character although subject to a servitude of innocent passage on the part of third states. Query, would the capture by a belligerent of an enemy vessel within a neutral territorial strait through which there exists a right of innocent passage be valid as between the belligerents in spite of the violation of neutral territorial sovereignty? [The Bangor.]

THE BANGOR.

Great Britain, High Court of Justice, Probate, Divorce, and Admiralty Division, 1916.

[1916] Probate, 181.

Suit for condemnation of a neutral vessel and her cargo on the ground that she was engaged in unneutral service. . . .

THE PRESIDENT (SIR SAMUEL EVANS). This is a flagrant case of a vessel flying the Norwegian flag, and commanded by a Norwegian master, being fitted and manned from New York for the purposes of

---

two marine leagues in width at the mouth are within this limit." Further, the court held that "the extent of the territorial jurisdiction of Massachusetts over the sea adjacent to its coast is that of an independent nation." The conviction of the offender was therefore sustained.

In United States v. Rodgers, 150 U. S. 249 (1893), involving a criminal prosecution for acts committed on board an American vessel in the Detroit river within the territorial limits of the Dominion of Canada, the Supreme Court interpreted the term "high seas," occurring in the section of the Revised Statutes upon which the criminal prosecution was founded, so as to include the Great Lakes and one of their connecting waters, the Detroit River. The plea of the defendant Rodgers to the jurisdiction of the court was therefore overruled.

The suit between El Salvador and Nicaragua before the Central American Court of Justice, Am. Journal of Int. Law, XI (1917), 674, involved a request by El Salvador for an injunction to prevent Nicaragua from carrying out the obligations undertaken by the Bryan-Chamorro treaty of August 5, 1914, by which Nicaragua granted to the United States in perpetuity the exclusive proprietary rights necessary to the construction of an inter-oceanic canal and at the same time leased to the United States the Great Corn and Little Corn Islands in the Caribbean Sea and granted the right to maintain a naval base on the territory of Nicaragua bordering upon the Gulf of Fonseca. The court held, inter alia, that the Gulf of Fonseca must be regarded as "an historic bay possessed of the characteristics of a closed sea" and therefore part of the territories of the three states bordering it, so that the concession of a naval base to the United States violated the "rights of condominium" of El Salvador in the gulf.

rendering services to German warships. Circumstances of aggravation of almost every kind attended her conduct and management. They are set out in the evidence to which the Attorney-General adverted. The master—one Hansen—attempted some kind of repudiation of the charges made against him. His efforts did not relieve the weight of those charges. He only added to his discredit the disgrace of giving false evidence.

It is unnecessary to make a statement of the facts; because counsel for the shipowners admitted that their vessel must suffer judgment of condemnation, unless she was immune from capture on the technical ground that she was at the time in waters alleged to be territorial waters of a neutral State.

The vessel was captured in the Strait of Magellan. According to the entry in the log the vessel was captured when she was in the middle of the strait opposite Port Tamar anchorage. This agreed with the statement of the British naval officers. The strait is admitted to be seven miles wide at that place. Strictly, therefore, the middle would not be within three miles of the land on either side.

The ship's master gave evidence that he took bearings which fixed his position much nearer the south shore than the line midway between the land on the north and south sides. His evidence is not worthy of any credence; and I cannot accept any part of it as being true. Accordingly, if it is material to establish that the capture took place within three miles, or a marine league, of either shore, the claimants have not proved to my satisfaction that it did.

The limits of territorial waters, in relation to national and international rights and privileges, have of recent years been subject to much discussion. It may well be that the old marine league, which for long determined the boundaries of territorial waters, ought to be extended by reason of the enlarged range of guns used for shore protection.

This case does not, in my view, call for any pronouncement upon that question. I am content to decide the question of law raised by the claimants upon the assumption that the capture took place within the territorial waters of the Republic of Chile. This assumption, of course, does not imply any expression of opinion as to the character of the Strait of Magellan as between Chile and other nations. This strait connects the two vast free oceans of the Atlantic and Pacific. As such, the strait must be considered free for the commerce of all nations passing between the two oceans.

In 1879 the Government of the United States of America declared that it would not tolerate exclusive claims by any nation whatsoever to the Strait of Magellan, and would hold responsible any Government that undertook, no matter on what pretext, to lay any impost on its commerce through the strait. Later, in 1881, the Republic of Chile entered into a treaty with the Argentine Republic by which the strait was declared to be neutralized forever, and free navigation was guaranteed to the flags of all nations.

I have referred to these matters in order to show that there is a right of free passage through the strait for commercial purposes. It is not inconsistent with this that, during war between any nations entitled to use them for commerce, the strait should be regarded in whole or in part as the territorial waters of Chile, whose lands bound it on both sides.

Upon the assumption made for the purposes of this case that the Bangor was in fact captured within the territorial waters of a neutral, the question is whether the vessel was immune from legal capture and its consequences according to the law of nations. In other words, can the owners of the vessel, who are, ex hypothesi, to be treated as enemies, rely upon the territorial rights of a neutral State and object to the capture? Or must the objection to the validity of the capture come from the neutral State alone?

No proposition in international law is clearer, or more surely established, than that a capture within the territorial waters of a neutral is, as between enemy belligerents, for all purposes rightful; and that it is only by the neutral State concerned that the legal validity of the capture can be questioned. It can only be declared void as to the neutral State, and not as to the enemy: see The Anne [(1818) 3 Wheaton, 435]; The Lilla [(1862) 2 Sprague, 177]; The Sir William Peel [(1866) 5 Wallace, 517]; The Adela [(1867) 6 Wallace, 266]. The proposition is neatly stated in The Sir William Peel [5 Wall. 536] as follows: "Neither an enemy, nor a neutral acting the part of an enemy, can demand the restitution of captured property on the sole ground of capture in neutral waters." . . .

For these reasons I decide that the objection made by the claimants to the validity of the capture, even if it took place in neutral territorial waters, is not well founded, and I disallow the claim with costs.

The judgment of the Court is that the vessel and her cargo be condemned as good and lawful prize.

CHAPTER XIV

JURISDICTION OVER TERRITORY: EASEMENTS AND SERVITUDES [1]

A. Rights of passage.

While the territorial jurisdiction of a state is in general absolute, in the sense of admitting no exercise of jurisdiction on the part of any other state, yet there are certain limited exceptions which have come to be recognized both by custom and by treaty. Among these exceptions are special obligations on the part of the state in possession of particular territory to permit a certain use to be made of it by other states. Such obligations are known as "servitudes," and the corresponding rights on the part of other states may be described as "easements," although that term has not yet found its way into international law. Query, where a servitude in the form of an obligation to permit a right of passage through a territorial canal has been created by treaty, would the territorial owner of the canal have the right, when neutral in time of war between two other states, to exclude a ship carrying munitions to one of the belligerents? [Great Britain et al. and Germany: Case of the Wimbledon.]

GREAT BRITAIN ET AL. AND GERMANY: CASE OF THE S. S. "WIMBLEDON."

Permanent Court of International Justice, 1923.

Publications of the Court, Series A, No. 1.

[By the Court.] The Governments of His Britannic Majesty, of the French Republic, of His Majesty the King of Italy and of His Majesty the Emperor of Japan, by means of an application instituting proceedings filed with the Registry of the Court on January 16th, 1923, in accordance with Article 40 of the Statute and Article 35 of the Rules

---

[1] For a more detailed study of this subject, see Fenwick, *op. cit.*, pp. 288–310; Hyde, *op. cit.*, §§ 152–198; Oppenheim, *op. cit.*, I, §§ 203–208; Reid, International Servitudes in Law and Practice; Váli, Servitudes of International Law; Smith, The Economic Uses of International Rivers; H. A. Smith, "The Chicago Diversion," British Year Book, X (1929), 144; R. E. Bacon, "British and American Policy and the Right of Fluvial Navigation," *ibid.*, XIII, (1932), 76.

of Court, brought before the Court the dispute which had arisen between these Governments and the Government of the German Empire by reason of the fact that on March 21st, 1921, the steamship "Wimbledon" was refused permission to pass through the Kiel Canal.

By this application it was submitted that:

1. The German authorities, on March 21st, 1921, were wrong in refusing free access to the Kiel Canal to the steamship "Wimbledon";

2. The German Government is under an obligation to make good the prejudice sustained as a result of this action by the said vessel and which is estimated at the sum of 174,082 frs. 86 centimes, with interest at six per cent per annum from March 20th, 1921. . . .

. On the other hand, the German Government, the respondent in this suit, requested the Court, in the conclusions contained in the Counter-case submitted by it on April 20th, 1923:

1. To declare that the German authorities were within their rights in refusing on March 21st, 1921, to allow the steamship "Wimbledon" to pass through the Kiel Canal.

2. To reject the claim for compensation. . . .

II. The facts, as stated in the course of the proceedings and in regard to which there appears to be no disagreement between the Parties, may be summarized as follows:

An English steamship, the "Wimbledon," had been time-chartered by the French Company, "Les Affréteurs réunis," whose offices are at Paris. . . .

The vessel, having been chartered in the manner indicated, had taken on board at Salonica 4,200 tons of munitions and artillery stores consigned to the Polish Naval Base at Danzig. On the morning of March 21st, 1921, it presented itself at the entrance to the Kiel Canal, but the Director of Canal Traffic refused to allow it to pass, basing his refusal upon the neutrality Orders issued by Germany in connection with the Russo-Polish war, and upon instructions which he had received.

On the next day but one, March 23rd, the French Ambassador at Berlin requested the German Government to withdraw this prohibition and to allow the S. S. "Wimbledon" to pass through the Kiel Canal in conformity with Article 380 of the Treaty of Versailles. Some days later, on March 26th, a reply was given to the effect that the German Government was unable to allow a vessel which had on board a cargo of munitions and artillery stores consigned to the Polish Military Mission at Danzig, to pass through the Canal, because the German Neutrality Orders of July 25th and 30th, 1920, prohibited the transit of cargoes of this kind destined for Poland or Russia, and Article 380 of the Treaty of Versailles was not an obstacle to the application of these Orders to the Kiel Canal.

On the evening of March 30th, the "Société des Affréteurs réunis" telegraphed to the captain of the S. S. "Wimbledon" ordering him to continue his voyage by the Danish Straits. The vessel weighed anchor on April 1st and, proceeding by Skagen, reached Danzig, its port of destination, on April 6th; it had been detained for eleven days, to which must be added two days for deviation.

In the meantime the "Wimbledon" incident had not failed to give rise to active negotiations between the Conference of Ambassadors and the Berlin Government; but these negotiations, in the course of which the contrast between the opposing standpoints had become apparent and the Allied Powers' protest had been met by a statement of Germany's alleged rights and obligations as a neutral in the war between Russia and Poland, led to no result, whereupon the Governments of His Britannic Majesty, the French Republic, His Majesty the King of Italy and His Majesty the Emperor of Japan decided to bring the matter which had given rise to the negotiations—thereby adopting a course suggested by the German Government itself in a letter from its Minister of Foreign Affairs, dated January 28th, 1922—before the jurisdiction instituted by the League of Nations to deal with, amongst other matters, any violation of Articles 380 to 386 of the Treaty of Versailles or any dispute as to their interpretation. This jurisdiction is the Permanent Court of International Justice which entered upon its duties at The Hague on February 15th, 1922. . . .

IV. The question upon which the whole case depends is whether the German authorities were entitled to refuse access to and passage through the Kiel Canal to the S. S. "Wimbledon" on March 21st, 1921, under the conditions and circumstances in which they did so.

The reply to this question must be sought in the provisions devoted by the Peace Treaty of Versailles to the Kiel Canal, in Part XII, entitled "Ports, Waterways and Railways," Section VI. This Section commences with a provision of a general and peremptory character, contained in Article 380, which is as follows:

"The Kiel Canal and its approaches shall be maintained free and open to the vessels of commerce and of war of all nations at peace with Germany on terms of entire equality."

Then follow various provisions intended to facilitate and regulate the exercise of this right of free passage. . . .

The idea which underlies Article 380 and the following articles of the Treaty is not to be sought by drawing an analogy from these provisions but rather by arguing a contrario, a method of argument which excludes them.

In order to dispute, in this case, the right of the S. S. "Wimbledon" to free passage through the Kiel Canal under the terms of Article 380, the argument has been urged upon the Court that this right really amounts to a servitude by international law resting upon Germany and that, like all restrictions or limitations upon the exercise of sovereignty, this servitude must be construed as restrictively as possible and confined within its narrowest limits, more especially in the sense that it should not be allowed to affect the rights consequent upon neutrality in an armed conflict. The Court is not called upon to take a definite attitude with regard to the question, which is moreover of a very controversial nature, whether in the domain of international law, there really exist servitudes analogous to the servitudes of private law. Whether the German Government is bound by virtue of a servitude or by virtue of a contractual obligation undertaken towards the Powers entitled to benefit by the terms of the Treaty of Versailles, to allow free access to the Kiel Canal in time of war as in time of peace to the vessels of all nations, the fact remains that Germany has to submit to an important limitation of the exercise of the sovereign rights which no one disputes that she possesses over the Kiel Canal. This fact constitutes a sufficient reason for the restrictive interpretation, in case of doubt, of the clause which produces such a limitation. But the Court feels obliged to stop at the point where the so-called restrictive interpretation would be contrary to the plain terms of the article and would destroy what has been clearly granted.

The argument has also been advanced that the general grant of a right of passage to vessels of all nationalities through the Kiel Canal cannot deprive Germany of the exercise of her rights as a neutral power in time of war, and place her under an obligation to allow the passage through the canal of contraband destined for one of the belligerents; for, in this wide sense, this grant would imply the abandonment by Germany of a personal and imprescriptable right, which forms an essential part of her sovereignty and which she neither could nor intended to renounce by anticipation. This contention has not convinced the Court; it conflicts with general considerations of the highest order. It is also gainsaid by consistent international practice and is at the same time contrary to the wording of Article 380 which clearly contemplates time of war as well as time of peace. The Court declines to see in the conclusion of any Treaty by which a State undertakes to perform or refrain from performing a particular act an abandonment of its sovereignty. No doubt any convention creating an obligation of this kind places a restriction upon the exercise of the sovereign rights of the State, in the sense that it requires them to be exercised in a certain way. But the right of entering into international engagements is an attribute of State sovereignty. . . .

The precedents therefore afforded by the Suez and Panama Canals invalidate in advance the argument that Germany's neutrality would have necessarily been imperiled if her authorities had allowed the passage of the "Wimbledon" through the Kiel Canal, because that vessel was carrying contraband of war consigned to a state then engaged in an armed conflict. Moreover they are merely illustrations of the general opinion according to which when an artificial waterway connecting two open seas has been permanently dedicated to the use of the whole world, such waterway is assimilated to natural straits in the sense that even the passage of a belligerent man-of-war does not compromise the neutrality of the sovereign State under whose jurisdiction the waters in question lie. . . .

From the foregoing, therefore, it appears clearly established that Germany not only did not, in consequence of her neutrality, incur the obligation to prohibit the passage of the "Wimbledon" through the Kiel Canal, but, on the contrary, was entitled to permit it. Moreover under Article 380 of the Treaty of Versailles, it was her definite duty to allow it. She could not advance her neutrality orders against the obligations which she had accepted under this Article. Germany was perfectly free to declare and regulate her neutrality in the Russo-Polish war, but subject to the condition that she respected and maintained intact the contractual obligations which she entered into at Versailles on June 28th, 1919. . . .

The Court having arrived at the conclusion that the respondent, Germany, wrongfully refused passage through the Canal to the vessel "Wimbledon," that country is responsible for the loss occasioned by this refusal, and must compensate the French Government, acting on behalf of the Company known as "Les Affréteurs réunis," which sustained the loss. . . .

V. For these reasons, the Court, having heard both parties,

Declares that the suit brought before it by the Governments of His Britannic Majesty, of the French Republic, of His Majesty the King of Italy and of His Majesty the Emperor of Japan, and in which the Government of the Polish Republic has intervened, has been validly submitted by all the parties; and passes judgment to the following effect:

1. That the German authorities on March 21st, 1921, were wrong in refusing access to the Kiel Canal to the S. S. "Wimbledon";

2. That Article 380 of the Treaty signed at Versailles on June 28th, 1919 between the Allied and Associated Powers and Germany, should have prevented Germany from applying to the Kiel Canal the Neutrality Order promulgated by her on July 25th, 1920;

3. That the German Government is bound to make good the prejudice sustained by the vessel and her charterers as the result of this action;

4. That the prejudice sustained may be estimated at the sum of 140,749 frs. 35 centimes with interest at 6% per annum from the date of this judgment;

5. That the German Government shall therefore pay to the Government of the French Republic, at Paris, in French francs, the sum of 140,749 frs. 35 centimes with interest at 6% per annum from the date of this judgment; payment to be effected within three months from this day;

6. And that each party shall bear its own costs. . . .

Dissenting opinion by M. SCHÜCKING. . . .

1. The right to free passage through the Kiel Canal, in my opinion, undoubtedly assumes the form of a *servitus juris publici voluntuaria*. This conception, which for centuries has proved extremely useful in international law, is, it is true, at the present time the subject of controversy amongst writers on international law, but its importance has in fact increased by the peace treaties following the World War. For in these treaties many legal situations have been created which can be placed in no other category than that of servitudes of international law.

If the right in question is regarded as a servitude, important consequences ensue with respect to the present case.

(a) According to the teaching of writers on international law, all treaties concerning servitudes must be interpreted restrictively in the sense that the servitude, being an exceptional right resting upon the territory of a foreign State, should limit as little as possible the sovereignty of that State. According to a purely literal construction of Article 380, the servitude is excluded from application only in cases where ships are concerned which belong to nations themselves at war with Germany. Serious doubts, however, arise as to whether Germany, in order to safeguard her interests, when placed in the position of a belligerent or neutral, should in fact, under Article 380, lose the right to take special measures as regards the canal, not provided for under Article 381, para. 2, also as against ships belonging to States other than her enemies. The canal is under the jurisdiction of Germany and it has not been neutralised as the Suez Canal had been, nor even in a still less complete form like the Panama Canal. Its use has rather been internationalised, like that of the great inland waterways. The right to take special measures in times of war or neutrality has not been expressly renounced; nor can such renunciation be inferred from the fact that the Canal is to be "maintained free and open." The fact that the right is granted in perpetuity does not in itself exclude the possibility of regulating or even of temporarily suspending its exercise, and the essential words which were used to provide for the neutralisation of the Suez Canal and which were reproduced in the treaty relating to the Panama Canal namely "in time of war as in time of peace," do not appear in Article 380. It is possible that a restrictive interpretation of the treaty establishing the servitude may infringe the purely literal meaning of Article 380, an interpretation, that is to say, according to which in time of war and neutrality the Reich, as possessing sovereignty over the canal zone, is entitled to take such measures against shipping as in normal times may not be taken by her under Article 380 and the following Articles. . . .

(b) Again, according to the teaching of writers on international law the States benefiting by the servitude are under the obligation *civiliter uti* as regards the State under servitude. The vital interests of the State under servitude must in all circumstances be respected. From this standpoint the benefiting State must allow its rights at times to be temporarily impaired. The vital interests of Germany at the moment made it necessary for her to observe a strict and absolute neutrality with regard to the war which was being waged in the immediate vicinity of her frontiers. . . . If it is possible to apply the doctrine of *civiliter uti* to a servitude of international law, then the German Government, in applying also to the Kiel Canal the prohibition against transit of contraband, did so in order to safeguard its vital interests. In doing this Germany did not allow a special right of necessity to prevail over her contractual obligations; she merely made use of the natural limitations to which every servitude is subjected. . . .

B. Profits à prendre.

Servitudes involving an obligation on the part of one state to permit another state or its citizens to enter its territory and take therefrom products of the soil or to carry on mining operations are occasionally created by treaty. Query, in such cases would the enjoyment of the privileges conferred be governed by the local laws of the territorial sovereign or by the laws of the state holding the easement? [United States and Great Britain: North Atlantic Coast Fisheries Case.]

UNITED STATES AND GREAT BRITAIN: NORTH ATLANTIC COAST FISHERIES CASE.[1]

Tribunal of the Permanent Court of Arbitration, 1910.

Scott, Hague Court Reports, 146.

PREAMBLE. Whereas a special agreement between the United States of America and Great Britain, signed at Washington the 27th January, 1909, . . . was concluded in conformity with the provisions of the general arbitration treaty between the United States of America and Great Britain, signed the 4th April, 1908, and ratified the 4th June, 1908; and . . . is as follows:

ARTICLE 1.

Whereas, by Article 1 of the convention signed at London on the 20th day of October, 1818, between Great Britain and the United States, it was agreed as follows:

Whereas, differences have arisen respecting the liberty claimed by the United States for the inhabitants thereof, to take, dry and cure fish

---

[1] Another part of the same case, dealing with the determination of what constituted a "bay" under the terms of the treaty, is reproduced above, p. 515.

on certain coasts, bays, harbors and creeks of His Britannic Majesty's dominions in America, it is agreed between the high contracting Parties, that the inhabitants of the said United States shall have forever, in common with the subjects of His Britannic Majesty, the liberty to take fish of every kind on that part of the southern coast of Newfoundland which extends from Cape Ray to the Rameau Islands, on the western and northern coast of Newfoundland, from the said Cape Ray to the Quirpon Islands, on the shores of Magdalen Islands, and also on the coasts, bays, harbors, and creeks from Mount Joly on the southern coast of Labrador, to and through the Straits of Belleisle and thence northwardly indefinitely along the coast, without prejudice, however, to any of the exclusive rights of the Hudson Bay Company; and that the American fishermen shall also have liberty forever, to dry and cure fish in any of the unsettled bays, harbors and creeks of the southern part of the coast of Newfoundland hereabove described, and of the coast of Labrador; but so soon as the same, or any portion thereof, shall be settled, it shall not be lawful for the said fishermen to dry or cure fish at such portion so settled, without previous agreement for such purpose with the inhabitants, proprietors, or possessors of the ground.—And the United States hereby renounce forever, any liberty heretofore enjoyed or claimed by the inhabitants thereof, to take, dry, or cure fish on, or within three marine miles of any of the coasts, bays, creeks, or harbors of His Britannic Majesty's dominions in America not included within the above-mentioned limits; provided, however, that the American fishermen shall be admitted to enter such bays and harbors for the purpose of shelter and of repairing damages therein, of purchasing wood, and of obtaining water, and for no other purpose whatever. But they shall be under such restrictions as may be necessary to prevent their taking, drying or curing fish therein, or in any other manner whatever abusing the privileges hereby reserved to them.

And, whereas, differences have arisen as to the scope and meaning of the said article, and of the liberties therein referred to, and otherwise in respect of the rights and liberties which the inhabitants of the United States have or claim to have in the waters or on the shores therein referred to:

It is agreed that the following questions shall be submitted for decision to a tribunal of arbitration constituted as hereinafter provided:

Question 1. To what extent are the following contentions or either of them justified?

It is contended on the part of Great Britain that the exercise of the liberty to take fish referred to in the said article, which the inhabitants of the United States have forever in common with the subjects of His Britannic Majesty, is subject, without the consent of the United States, to reasonable regulation by Great Britain, Canada, or Newfoundland in the form of municipal laws, ordinances, or rules, as, for example, to regulations in respect of (1) the hours, days, or seasons when fish may be taken on the treaty coasts; (2) the method, means, and implements to be used in the taking of fish or in the carrying on of fishing operations on such coasts; (3) any other matters of a similar character relating to fishing; such regulations being reasonable, as being, for instance—

(a) Appropriate or necessary for the protection and preservation of such fisheries and the exercise of the rights of British subjects therein and of the liberty which by the said Article 1 the inhabitants of the United States have therein in common with British subjects;

(b) Desirable on grounds of public order and morals;

(c) Equitable and fair as between local fishermen and the inhabitants of the United States exercising the said treaty liberty and not so framed as to give unfairly an advantage to the former over the latter class.

It is contended on the part of the United States that the exercise of such liberty is not subject to limitations or restraints by Great Britain, Canada, or Newfoundland in the form of municipal laws, ordinances, or regulations in respect of (1) the hours, days, or seasons when the inhabitants of the United States may take fish on the treaty coast, or (2) the method, means, and implements used by them in taking fish or in carrying on fishing operations on such coasts, or (3) any other limitations or restraints of similar character—

(a) Unless they are appropriate and necessary for the protection and preservation of the common rights in such fisheries and the exercise thereof; and

(b) Unless they are reasonable in themselves and fair as between local fishermen and fishermen coming from the United States, and not so framed as to give an advantage to the former over the latter class; and

(c) Unless their appropriateness, necessity, reasonableness and fairness be determined by the United States and Great Britain by common accord and the United States concurs in their enforcement. . . .

Now, therefore, this tribunal [Lammasch, De Savornin Lohman, Gray, Fitzpatrick, Drago] makes the following decisions and awards:

Question I, thus submitted to the tribunal, resolves itself into two main contentions:

1st. Whether the right of regulating reasonably the liberties conferred by the treaty of 1818 resides in Great Britain;

2nd. And, if such right does so exist, whether such reasonable exercise of the right is permitted to Great Britain without the accord and concurrence of the United States.

The treaty of 1818 contains no explicit disposition in regard to the right of regulation, reasonable or otherwise; it neither reserves that right in express terms, nor refers to it in any way. It is therefore incumbent on this tribunal to answer the two questions above indicated by interpreting the general terms of Article 1 of the treaty, and more especially the words "the inhabitants of the United States shall have, for ever, in common with the subjects of His Britannic Majesty, the liberty to take fish of every kind." This interpretation must be conformable to the general import of the instrument, the general intention of the parties to it, the subject matter of the contract, the expressions' actually used and the evidence submitted.

Now in regard to the preliminary question as to whether the right of reasonable regulation resides in Great Britain:

Considering that the right to regulate the liberties conferred by the treaty of 1818 is an attribute of sovereignty, and as such must be held to reside in the territorial sovereign, unless the contrary be provided; and considering that one of the essential elements of sovereignty is that it is to be exercised within territorial limits, and that, failing proof to the contrary, the territory is coterminous with the sovereignty, it follows that the burden of the assertion involved in the contention of the United States (viz., that the right to regulate does not reside independently in Great Britain, the territorial sovereign) must fall on the United States. And for the purpose of sustaining this burden, the United States have put forward the following series of propositions, each one of which must be singly considered. . . .

For the further purpose of such proof it is contended by the United States:

(2) That the liberties of fishery, being accorded to the inhabitants of the United States "for ever," acquire, by being in perpetuity and unilateral, a character exempting them from local legislation.

The tribunal is unable to agree with this contention:

(a) Because there is no necessary connection between the duration of a grant and its essential status in its relation to local regulation; a right granted in perpetuity may yet be subject to regulation, or, granted temporarily, may yet be exempted therefrom; or being reciprocal may yet be unregulated, or being unilateral may yet be regulated: as is evidenced by the claim of the United States that the liberties of fishery accorded by the reciprocity treaty of 1854 and the treaty of 1871 were exempt from regulation, though they were neither permanent nor unilateral;

(b) Because no peculiar character need be claimed for these liberties in order to secure their enjoyment in perpetuity, as is evidenced by the American negotiators in 1818 asking for the insertion of the words "for ever." International law in its modern development recognizes that a great number of treaty obligations are not annulled by war, but at most suspended by it;

(c) Because the liberty to dry and cure is, pursuant to the terms of treaty, provisional and not permanent, and is nevertheless, in respect of the liability to regulation, identical in its nature with, and never distinguished from, the liberty to fish.

For the further purpose of such proof, the United States allege:

(3) That the liberties of fishery granted to the United States constitute an international servitude in their favor over the territory of Great Britain, thereby involving a derogation from the sovereignty of Great Britain, the servient State, and that therefore Great Britain is deprived, by reason of the grant, of its independent right to regulate the fishery.

The tribunal is unable to agree with this contention:

(*a*) Because there is no evidence that the doctrine of international servitude was one with which either American or British statesmen were conversant in 1818, no English publicists employing the term before 1818, and the mention of it in Mr. Gallatin's report being insufficient;

(*b*) Because a servitude in the French law, referred to by Mr. Gallatin, can, since the code, be only real and can not be personal (*Code Civil*, art. 686);

(*c*) Because a servitude in international law predicates an express grant of a sovereign right and involves an analogy to the relation of a *prædium dominans* and a *prædium serviens;* whereas by the treaty of 1818 one State grants a liberty to fish, which is not a sovereign right, but a purely economic right, to the inhabitants of another State;

(*d*) Because the doctrine of international servitude in the sense which is now sought to be attributed to it originated in the peculiar and now obsolete conditions prevailing in the Holy Roman Empire of which the *domini terræ* were not fully sovereigns; they holding territory under the Roman Empire, subject at least theoretically, and in some respects also practically, to the courts of that Empire; their right being, moreover, rather of a civil than of a public nature, partaking more of the character of *dominium* than of *imperium,* and therefore certainly not a complete sovereignty. And because in contradistinction to this quasi-sovereignty with its incoherent attributes acquired at various times, by various means, and not impaired in its character by being incomplete in any one respect or by being limited in favor of another territory and its possessor, the modern State, and particularly Great Britain, has never admitted partition of sovereignty, owing to the constitution of a modern State requiring essential sovereignty and independence;

(*e*) Because this doctrine being but little suited to the principle of sovereignty which prevails in States under a system of constitutional government such as Great Britain and the United States, and to the present international relations of sovereign States, has found little, if any, support from modern publicists. It could therefore in the general interest of the community of nations, and of the parties to this treaty, be affirmed by this tribunal only on the express evidence of an international contract;

(*f*) Because even if these liberties of fishery constituted an international servitude, the servitude would derogate from the sovereignty of the servient State only in so far as the exercise of the rights of sovereignty by the servient State would be contrary to the exercise of the servitude right by the dominant State. Whereas it is evident that, though every regulation of the fishery is to some extent a limitation, as it puts limits to the exercise of the fishery at will, yet such regulations as are reasonable and made for the purpose of securing and preserving the fishery and its exercise for the common benefit, are clearly to be distinguished from those restrictions and "molestations," the annulment of which was the purpose of the American demands formulated by Mr. Adams in 1782, and such regulations consequently can not be held to be inconsistent with a servitude;

(*g*) Because the fishery to which the inhabitants of the United States were admitted in 1783, and again in 1818, was a regulated fishery. . . .

(*h*) Because the fact that Great Britain rarely exercised the right of regulation in the period immediately succeeding 1818 is to be explained by various circumstances and is not evidence of the non-existence of the right;

(*i*) Because the words "in common with British subjects" tend to confirm the opinion that the inhabitants of the United States were admitted to a regulated fishery;

(*j*) Because the statute of Great Britain, 1819, which gives legislative sanction to the treaty of 1818, provides for the making of "regulations with relation to the taking, drying and curing fish by inhabitants of the United States in 'common.'" . . .

In the course of the Argument it has also been alleged by the United States:

(5) That the treaty of 1818 should be held to have entailed a transfer or partition of sovereignty, in that it must in respect to the liberties of fishery be interpreted in its relation to the treaty of 1783; and that this latter treaty was an act of partition of sovereignty and of separation, and as such was not annulled by the war of 1812.

Although the tribunal is not called upon to decide the issue whether the treaty of 1783 was a treaty of partition or not, the questions involved therein having been set at rest by the subsequent treaty of 1818, nevertheless the tribunal could not forebear to consider the contention on account of the important bearing the controversy has upon the true interpretation of the treaty of 1818. In that respect the tribunal is of opinion:

(*a*) That the right to take fish was accorded as a condition of peace to a foreign people; wherefore the British negotiators refused to place the right of British subjects on the same footing with those of American inhabitants; and further, refused to insert the words also proposed by

Mr. Adams ("continue to enjoy") in the second branch of Art. 3 of the treaty of 1783;

(b) That the treaty of 1818 was in different terms, and very different in extent, from that of 1783, and was made for different considerations. It was, in other words, a new grant. . . .

It is finally contended by the United States:

That the United States did not expressly agree that the liberty granted to them could be subjected to any restriction that the grantor might choose to impose on the ground that in her judgment such restriction was reasonable. And that while admitting that all laws of a general character, controlling the conduct of men within the territory of Great Britain, are effective, binding and beyond objection by the United States, and competent to be made upon the sole determination of Great Britain or her colony, without accountability to anyone whomsoever; yet there is somewhere a line, beyond which it is not competent for Great Britain to go, or beyond which she cannot rightfully go, because to go beyond it would be an invasion of the right granted to the United States in 1818. That the legal effect of the grant of 1818 was not to leave the determination as to where that line is to be drawn to the uncontrolled judgment of the grantor, either upon the grantor's consideration as to what would be a reasonable exercise of its sovereignty over the British Empire, or upon the grantor's consideration of what would be a reasonable exercise thereof towards the grantee.

But this contention is founded on assumptions which this tribunal cannot accept for the following reasons in addition to those already set forth:— . . .

(e.) Because the right to make reasonable regulations, not inconsistent with the obligations of the treaty, which is all that is claimed by Great Britain, for a fishery which both Parties admit requires regulation for its preservation, is not a restriction of or an invasion of the liberty granted to the inhabitants of the United States. This grant does not contain words to justify the assumption that the sovereignty of Great Britain upon its own territory was in any way affected; nor can words be found in the treaty transferring any part of that sovereignty to the United States. Great Britain assumed only duties with regard to the exercise of its sovereignty. The sovereignty of Great Britain over the coastal waters and territory of Newfoundland remains after the treaty as unimpaired as it was before. But from the treaty results an obligatory relation whereby the right of Great Britain to exercise its right of sovereignty by making regulations is limited to such regulations as are made in good faith, and are not in violation of the treaty;

(f.) Finally, to hold that the United States, the grantee of the fishing right, has a voice in the preparation of fishery legislation involves the recognition of a right in that country to participate in the internal legislation of Great Britain and her colonies, and to that extent would reduce these countries to a state of dependence.

While therefore unable to concede the claim of the United States as based on the treaty, this Tribunal considers that such claim has been and is to some extent, conceded in the relations now existing between the two Parties. Whatever may have been the situation under the treaty of 1818 standing alone, the exercise of the right of regulation inherent in Great Britain has been, and is, limited by the repeated recognition of the obligations already referred to, by the limitations and liabilities accepted in the special agreement, by the unequivocal position assumed by Great Britain in the presentation of its case before this Tribunal, and by the consequent view of this Tribunal that it would be consistent with all the circumstances, as revealed by this record, as to the duty of Great Britain, that she should submit the reasonableness of any future regulation to such an impartial arbitral test, affording full opportunity therefor, as is hereafter recommended under the authority of Article IV of the special agreement, whenever the reasonableness of any regulation is objected to or challenged by the United States in the manner, and within the time hereinafter specified in the said recommendation.

Now therefore this Tribunal decides and awards as follows:

The right of Great Britain to make regulations without the consent of the United States, as to the exercise of the liberty to take fish referred to in Article I of the treaty of October 20th, 1818, in the form of municipal laws, ordinances or rules of Great Britain, Canada or Newfoundland is inherent to the sovereignty of Great Britain.

The exercise of that right by Great Britain is, however, limited by the said treaty in respect of the said liberties therein granted to the inhabitants of the United States in that such regulations must be made *bona fide* and must not be in violation of the said treaty.

Regulations which are (1) appropriate or necessary for the protection and preservation of such fisheries, or (2) desirable or necessary on grounds of public order and morals without unnecessarily interfering with the fishery itself, and in both cases equitable and fair as between local and American fishermen, and not so framed as to give unfairly an advantage to the former over the latter class, are not inconsistent with the obligation to execute the treaty in good faith, and are therefore reasonable and not in violation of the treaty. . . . [1]

---

[1] SUPPLEMENTARY CASES. In Aix-la-Chapelle-Maastricht R. R. Co. v. Thewis and Royal Dutch Government, Am. Journal of Int. Law, VIII (1914), 907, involving a suit by Thewis for damages by reason of injury to surface property caused by the operation by the railroad company of an underground mine, the court [Oberlandesgericht of Cologne] held that the assessment of damages was to be governed not by the law of Prussia, within whose territory the mine was located, but by Dutch law in consequence of the right to mine coal and other minerals retained by Holland when the territory in question was ceded to Prus-

C. Water rights: flow of rivers; level of lakes.

Where rivers flow from an upper state down into the territory of another state, controversies have arisen as to the extent to which the state in possession of the upper waters may divert their natural flow for purposes of consumption or irrigation. Query, has the lower state any right at international law, in the absence of treaty stipulations, to demand that the normal flow of a river continue uninterrupted? [Wyoming v. Colorado.] What if a state bordering on a lake should draw water from the lake in such quantities as to lower the level of the lake and injure the waterfront of other riparian states? [Wisconsin v. Illinois.]

STATE OF WYOMING v. STATE OF COLORADO ET AL.

United States, Supreme Court, 1922.

259 U. S. 419. [66 L. ed. 999; 42 S. Ct. 552.]

Mr. Justice Van Devanter delivered the opinion of the court.

This is an original suit in this court by the State of Wyoming against the State of Colorado and two Colorado corporations to prevent a proposed diversion in Colorado of part of the waters of the Laramie river, an interstate stream. . . . The case has been argued at the bar three times. The court directed one reargument because of the novelty and importance of some of the questions involved, and the other because of an intervening succession in the office of Chief Justice. As the United States appeared to have a possible interest in some of the questions, the court also directed that the suit be called to the attention of the Attorney General, and, by the court's leave, a representative of the United States participated in the subsequent hearings.

The Laramie is an unnavigable river which has its source in the mountains of Northern Colorado, flows northerly 27 miles in that state, crosses into Wyoming, and there flows northerly and northeasterly 150 miles to the North Platte river, of which it is a tributary. Both Colorado and Wyoming are in the arid region, where flowing waters are, and

---

sia. "Because of this fact," said the court, "a sort of international servitude has arisen by which Holland is as a state, entitled, now as previously, in the matter of this mine, to exercise its own legislative authority and police supervision; that is, it has real sovereign rights with respect to the object situated within the territory of the foreign state (see Ullman, Völkerrecht, p. 320 ff.)."

Compare also United States v. Winans, 198 U. S. 371 (1905), where the court held that fishing rights in the Columbia River secured to the Yakima Indians by the treaty of 1859 survived the private acquisition of lands bordering on the river by grants from the United States or the State of Washington and were not subordinate to the governmental powers acquired by the State of Washington at the time of its admission into the Union.

long have been, commonly diverted from their natural channels and used in irrigating the soil and making it productive. For many years some of the waters of the Laramie river have been subjected to such diversion and use, part in Colorado and part in Wyoming.

When this suit was brought, the two corporate defendants, acting under the authority and permission of Colorado, were proceeding to divert in that state a considerable portion of the waters of the river and to conduct the same into another watershed, lying wholly in Colorado, for use in irrigating lands more than 50 miles distant from the point of diversion. The topography and natural drainage are such that none of the water can return to the stream or ever reach Wyoming.

By the bill Wyoming seeks to prevent this diversion on two grounds: One that, without her sanction, the waters of this interstate stream cannot rightfully be taken from its watershed and carried into another, where she never can receive any benefit from them; and the other that through many appropriations made at great cost, which are prior in time and superior in right to the proposed Colorado diversion, Wyoming and her citizens have become and are entitled to use a large portion of the waters of the river in the irrigation of lands in that state and that the proposed Colorado diversion will not leave in the stream sufficient water to satisfy these prior and superior appropriations, and so will work irreparable prejudice to Wyoming and her citizens.

By the answers Colorado and her codefendants seek to justify and sustain the proposed diversion on three distinct grounds: First, that it is the right of Colorado as a state to dispose, as she may choose, of any part or all of the waters flowing in the portion of the river within her borders, "regardless of the prejudice that it may work" to Wyoming and her citizens; secondly, that Colorado is entitled to an equitable division of the waters of the river, and that the proposed diversion, together with all subsisting appropriations in Colorado, does not exceed her share; and, thirdly, that after the proposed diversion there will be left in the river and its tributaries in Wyoming sufficient water to satisfy all appropriations in that state whose origin was prior in time to the effective inception of the right under which the proposed Colorado diversion is about to be made.

Before taking up the opposing contentions a survey of several matters in the light of which they should be approached and considered is in order.

Both Colorado and Wyoming are along the apex of the Continental Divide, and include high mountain ranges where heavy snows fall in winter and melt in late spring and early summer; this being the chief source of water supply. Small streams in the mountains gather the water from the melting snow and conduct it to large streams below, which ultimately pass into surrounding States. The flow in all streams varies greatly in the course of the year, being highest in May, June, and

July, and relatively very low in other months. There is also a pronounced variation from year to year. . . . Both States have vast plains and many valleys of varying elevation, where there is not sufficient natural precipitation to moisten the soil and make it productive, but where, when additional water is applied artificially, the soil becomes fruitful—the reward being generous in some areas and moderate in others, just as husbandry is variously rewarded in states where there is greater humidity, such as Massachusetts, Virginia, Ohio, and Tennessee. Both states were territories long before they were admitted into the Union as states and while the territorial condition continued were under the full dominion of the United States. At first the United States owned all the lands in both, and it still owns and is offering for disposal millions of acres in each.

Turning to the decisions of the courts of last resort in the two States, we learn that the same doctrine respecting the diversion and use of the waters of natural streams has prevailed in both from the beginning, and that each state attributes much of her development and prosperity to the practical operation of this doctrine. The relevant views of the origin and nature of the doctrine, as shown in these decisions, may be summarized as follows: The common-law rule respecting riparian rights in flowing water never obtained in either state. It always was deemed inapplicable to their situation and climatic conditions. The earliest settlers gave effect to a different rule whereby the waters of the streams were regarded as open to appropriation for irrigation, mining, and other beneficial purposes. The diversion from the stream and the application of the water to a beneficial purpose constituted an appropriation, and the appropriator was treated as acquiring a continuing right to divert and use the water to the extent of his appropriation, but not beyond what was reasonably required and actually used. . . . This doctrine of appropriation, prompted by necessity and formulated by custom, received early legislative recognition in both territories and was enforced in their courts. When the states were admitted into the Union it received further sanction in their Constitutions and statutes and their courts have been uniformly enforcing it. . . .

The decision in Kansas v. Colorado, 206 U. S. 46, was a pioneer in its field. On some of the questions presented it was intended to be and is comprehensive, and on others it was intended to be within narrower limits, the court saying: "The views expressed in this opinion are to be confined to a case in which the facts and the local law of the two states are as here disclosed." On full consideration it was broadly determined that a controversy between two states over the diversion and use of waters of a stream passing from one to the other "makes a matter for investigation and determination by this court" in the exercise of its original jurisdiction, and also that the upper state on such a stream does not have such ownership or control of the waters flowing therein as entitles her to divert and use them regardless of any injury or prejudice to the rights of the lower state in the stream. And, on consideration of the particular facts disclosed and the local law of the two states, it was determined that Colorado was not taking more than what under the circumstances would be her share under an equitable apportionment. . . .

Like that case, the one now before us presents a controversy over the waters of an interstate stream. But here the controversy is between States in both of which the doctrine of appropriation has prevailed from the time of the first settlements, always has been applied in the same way, and has been recognized and sanctioned by the United States, the owner of the public lands. Here the complaining State is not seeking to impose a policy of her choosing on the other state, but to have the common policy which each enforces within her limits applied in determining their relative rights in the interstate stream. . . . And here the complaining State is not seeking to interfere with a diversion which has long been practiced and under which much reclamation has been effected, but to prevent a proposed diversion for the benefit of lands as yet unreclaimed.

With this understanding of the case in hand, and of some of the matters in the light of which it should be considered, we take up the several contentions, before noticed, which are pressed on our attention.

The contention of Colorado that she as a State rightfully may divert and use, as she may choose, the waters flowing within her boundaries in this interstate stream, regardless of any prejudice that this may work to others having rights in the stream below her boundary, cannot be maintained. The river throughout its course in both States is but a single stream, wherein each state has an interest which should be respected by the other. A like contention was set up by Colorado in her answer in Kansas v. Colorado and was adjudged untenable. Further consideration satisfies us that the ruling was right. . . .

The objection of Wyoming to the proposed diversion on the ground that it is to another watershed, from which she can receive no benefit, is also untenable. The fact that the diversion is to such a watershed has a bearing in another connection, but does not in itself constitute a ground for condemning it. In neither State does the right of appropriation depend on the place of use being within the same watershed. Diversions from one watershed to another are commonly made in both States and the practice is recognized by the decisions of their courts. . . .

We are thus brought to the question of the basis on which the relative rights of these States in the waters of this interstate stream should be determined. Should the doctrine of appropriation, which each recognizes and enforces within her borders, be applied? Or is there another basis which is more consonant with right and equity?

The lands in both States are naturally arid, and the need for irrigation is the same in one as in the other. The lands were settled under the same public land laws, and their settlement was induced largely by the prevailing right to divert and use water for irrigation, without which the lands were of little value. Many of the lands were acquired under the Desert Land Act, which made reclamation by irrigation a condition to the acquisition. The first settlers located along the streams where water could be diverted and applied at small cost. Others with more means followed, and reclaimed lands farther away. Then companies with large capital constructed extensive canals and occasional tunnels, whereby water was carried to lands remote from the stream and supplied, for hire, to settlers who were not prepared to engage in such large undertakings. Ultimately, the demand for water being in excess of the dependable flow of the streams during the irrigation season, reservoirs were constructed, wherein water was impounded when not needed and released when needed, thereby measurably equalizing the natural flow. Such was the course of irrigation development in both states. It began in territorial days, continued without change after statehood, and was the basis for the large respect always shown for water rights. These constituted the foundation of all rural home building and agricultural development, and, if they were rejected now, the lands would return to their naturally arid condition, the efforts of the settlers and the expenditures of others would go for naught, and values mounting into large figures would be lost.

In neither State was the right to appropriate water from this interstate stream denied. On the contrary, it was permitted and recognized in both. The rule was the same on both sides of the line. Some of the appropriations were made as much as 50 years ago, and many as much as 25. In the circumstances we have stated, why should not appropriations from this stream be respected, as between the two States, according to their several priorities, as would be done if the stream lay wholly within either state? By what principle of right or equity may either State proceed in disregard of prior appropriations in the other?

Colorado answers that this is not a suit between private appropriators. This is true, but it does not follow that their situation and what has been accomplished by them for their respective States can be ignored. As respects Wyoming, the welfare, prosperity, and happiness of the people of the larger part of the Laramie valley, as also a large portion of the taxable resources of two counties, are dependent on the appropriations in that State. Thus the interests of the state are indissolubly linked with the rights of the appropriators. To the extent of the appropriation and use of the water in Colorado a like situation exists there. . . .

We conclude that Colorado's objections to the doctrine of appropriation as a basis of decision are not well taken, and that it furnishes the only basis which is consonant with the principles of right and equity applicable to such a controversy as this is. The cardinal rule of the doctrine is that priority of appropriation gives superiority of right. Each of these States applies and enforces this rule in her own territory, and it is the one to which intending appropriators naturally would turn for guidance. The principle on which it proceeds is not less applicable to interstate streams and controversies than to others. Both States pronounce the rule just and reasonable as applied to the natural conditions in that region, and to prevent any departure from it the people of both incorporated it into their Constitutions. It originated in the customs and usages of the people before either State came into existence, and the courts of both hold that their constitutional provisions are to be taken as recognizing the prior usage rather than as creating a new rule. These considerations persuade us that its application to such a controversy as is here presented cannot be other than eminently just and equitable to all concerned. . . .

As the available supply is 288,000 acre-feet and the amount covered by senior appropriations in Wyoming is 272,500 acre-feet, there remain 15,500 acre-feet which are subject to this junior appropriation in Colorado. The amount sought to be diverted and taken under it is much larger.

A decree will accordingly be entered enjoining the defendants from diverting or taking more than 15,500 acre-feet per year from the Laramie river by means of or through the so-called Laramie-Poudre project.

It is so ordered.

STATE OF WISCONSIN ET AL. v. STATE OF ILLINOIS AND SANITARY DISTRICT OF CHICAGO.

United States, Supreme Court, 1929.

278 U. S. 367. [73 L. ed. 426; 49 S. Ct. 163.]

MR. CHIEF JUSTICE TAFT delivered the opinion of the Court:

These are amended bills by the States of Wisconsin, Minnesota, Michigan, Ohio, Pennsylvania, and New York, praying for an injunction against the State of Illinois and the Sanitary District of Chicago from continuing to withdraw 8,500 cubic feet of water a second from Lake Michigan at Chicago.

The Court referred the cause to Charles Evans Hughes as a Special Master, with authority to take the evidence, and to report the same to the court with his findings of fact, conclusions of law, and recommendations for a decree, all to be subject to approval or other disposal by the Court. The Master gave full hearings, and filed and submitted his report November 23, 1927, to which the complainants duly lodged exceptions, which have been elaborately argued.

When these bills were filed, there was pending in this Court an appeal by the Sanitary District of Chicago from a decree granted at the suit of the United States by the United States District Court for the Northern District of Illinois, against a diversion from the lake in excess of 250,000 cubic feet per minute, or 4,167 cubic feet per second. This amount had been permitted by the Secretary of War. In January, 1925, this Court affirmed the decree, without prejudice to the granting of a further permit by the Secretary of War according to law. 266 U. S. 405. On March 3, 1925, the Secretary of War, after that decree, enlarged the permit for a diversion not to exceed an annual average of 8,500 cubic feet per second, upon certain conditions hereafter to be noted.

The amended bills herein averred that the Chicago diversion had lowered the levels of Lakes Michigan, Huron, Erie and Ontario, their connecting waterways, and of the St. Lawrence River above tidewater, not less than 6 inches, to the serious injury of the complainant states, their citizens, and property owners; that the acts of the defendants had never been authorized by Congress, but were violations of the rights of the complainant states and their people; that the withdrawals of the water from Lake Michigan were for the purpose of taking care of the sewage of Chicago, and were not justified by any control Congress had attempted to exercise or could exercise in interstate commerce over the waters of Lake Michigan; and that the withdrawals were in palpable violation of the Act of Congress of March 3, 1899. The bills prayed that the defendants be enjoined from permanently diverting water from Lake Michigan or from dumping or draining sewage into its waterways which would render them unsanitary or obstruct the people of the complainant states in navigating them.

The State of Illinois filed a demurrer to the bills and the Sanitary District of Chicago an answer, which included a motion to dismiss. The States of Missouri, Kentucky, Tennessee, and Louisiana, by leave of court, became intervening codefendants, on the same side as Illinois, and moved to dismiss the bills. The demurrer of Illinois was overruled and the motions to dismiss were denied, without prejudice. Thereupon the intervening defendants and the defendants, the Sanitary District and the State of Illinois, filed their respective answers. The States of Mississippi and Arkansas were also permitted to intervene as defendants, and adopted the answers of the other interveners. The answers of the defendants denied the injuries alleged, and averred that authority was given for the diversion under the acts of the Legislature of Illinois and under acts of Congress and permits of the Secretary of War authorized by Congress in the regulation of interstate commerce. All the answers stressed the point that the diversion of water from Lake Michigan improved the navigation of the Mississippi river and was an aid to the commerce of the Mississippi Valley, and sought the preservation of this aid. . . .

We shall first consider in brief the parts taken by Congress and the State of Illinois and their respective agencies in the construction of the Sanitary District Canal and the creation of the Lake Michigan diversion.

By the Act of March 30, 1822, c. 14, Congress authorized Illinois to survey and mark, through the public lands of the United States, the route of a canal connecting the Illinois River with Lake Michigan, and granted certain lands in aid of the project. . . . The canal was completed in 1848. The canal crossed the continental divide between the Chicago and Des Plaines Rivers, on a summit level 8 feet above the Lake, and then paralleled the Des Plaines River and the Upper Illinois River to La Salle, Illinois, where it entered the latter stream. . . .

Before 1865, the Chicago River, being a sluggish stream in its lower reaches, had become so offensive because of receiving the sewage of the rapidly growing city, that for its immediate relief the municipal authorities and the canal commissioners agreed to pump water from the river in excess of the needs of navigation. . . .

The Sanitary District was organized under the Illinois Act of 1889. It was completed in 1890. It embraced an area of 185 square miles. By the later acts it was increased to approximately 438 square miles, extending from the Illinois state line on the south and east to the northern boundary of Cook County on the north, with about 34 miles of frontage on Lake Michigan, embracing the metropolitan area of Chicago, consisting of a total of fifty-four cities, towns, and villages.

The main drainage canal was begun in 1892, and was opened in January, 1900. Since that time the flow of the Chicago River has been reversed—that is, it has been made to flow away from Lake Michigan toward the Mississippi. . . .

In 1908, the Constitution of Illinois was amended to authorize the legislature to provide for the construction of a deep waterway or canal, from the water-power plant of the Sanitary District of Chicago, at or near Lockport, to a point on the Illinois River at or near Utica, and to provide that this power might be leased for the benefit of the state treasury. Meantime, all the sewage in the drainage district, including Evanston, was turned into the main channel, and the water directly abstracted from Lake Michigan by the Sanitary District was increased from 2,541 cubic feet a second in 1900 to 5,751 in 1909, to 7,228 in 1916, to 6,888 cubic feet a second in 1926, not including pumpage. . . .

The Master's findings on the subject of injury to the complainants are in effect as follows:

The diversion which has taken place through the Chicago Drainage Canal has been substantially equivalent to a diversion of about 8,500 cubic feet a second for a period of time sufficient to cause, and it has caused, the lowering of the mean levels of the lakes and connecting waterways, as follows: Lakes Michigan and Huron approximately 6 inches; Lakes Erie and Ontario approximately 5 inches; and of the connecting rivers, bays and harbors to the same extent respectively. A diversion of an additional 1,500 cubic feet per second, or a total diversion of 10,000 cubic feet a second, would cause an additional lowering in

Lakes Michigan and Huron of about 1 inch, and in Lakes Erie and Ontario a little less than 1 inch, with a corresponding additional lowering in the connecting waterways. The Master also finds that if the diversion at Chicago were ended, assuming that other diversions remained the same, the mean levels of the lakes and rivers affected by the Chicago drainage would be raised in the course of several years (about five years in the case of Lakes Michigan and Huron, and about one year in the case of Lakes Erie and Ontario) to the same extent as they had been lowered, respectively, by that diversion.

The Master finds that the damage due to the diversion at Chicago relates to navigation and commercial interests, to structures, to the convenience of summer resorts, to fishing and hunting grounds, to public parks and other enterprises, and to riparian property generally, but does not report that injury to agriculture is established. He says that the Great Lakes and their connecting channels form a natural highway for transportation, having a water surface of over 95,000 square miles, and a shore line of 8,300 miles, extending from Duluth-Superior, and from Chicago and Gary, to Montreal, at the head of deep-draft ocean navigation on the St. Lawrence; that there are approximately four hundred harbors on the Great Lakes and connecting channels, of which about one hundred have been improved by the Federal Government; . . .

The Master's report says that the water-borne traffic on the Great Lakes for the year 1923 consisted of 81,466,902,000 ton-miles of water haul, and that consideration of individual loaded boats and of their respective dimensions shows that, if water had been available for an additional 6 inches of draft, the fleet could have handled for the year 3,346,000 tons more than was actually transported, or, to put the matter in another light, the season's business could have been done with the elimination from service of about thirty freighters of the 2,000-3,000-ton class, and that the lost tonnage of the total through business of the lakes for 1923, incident to a 6-inch deficiency of draft, exceeded 4,000,000 tons, and that the average water-haul rate for the year was 88 cents per ton.

The great losses to which the complainant states and their citizens and their property owners have been subjected by the reductions of levels in the various Lakes and Rivers, except Lake Superior, are made apparent by these figures. . . .

The controversies have taken a very wide range. The exact issue is whether the State of Illinois and the Sanitary District of Chicago, by diverting 8,500 cubic feet from the waters of Lake Michigan, have so injured the riparian and other rights of the complainant States bordering the Great Lakes and connecting streams by lowering their levels as to justify an injunction to stop this diversion and thus restore the normal levels. . . .

The complainants, even apart from their constitutional objections, contend that Congress has not, by statute or otherwise, authorized the Lake

Michigan diversion, that it is therefore illegal, and that injuries by it to the complainant States and their people should be forbidden by decree of this Court. The diversion of 8,500 cubic feet a second is now maintained under a permit of the Secretary of War of March 3, 1925, acting under Section 10 of the Act of 1899, which it is contended by the complainants vests no such authority in him. They claim that the diversion is based on a purpose not to regulate navigation of the lake, but merely to get rid of the sewage of Chicago; that this is a State purpose, not a Federal function, and should be enjoined to save the rights of complainants. . . .

The normal power of the Secretary of War under Section 10 of the Act of March 3, 1899, is to maintain the navigable capacity of Lake Michigan, and not to restrict it or destroy it by diversions. . . . He could not make mere local sanitation a basis for a continuing diversion. Accordingly, he made the permit of March 3, 1925, both temporary and conditional—temporary in that it was limited in duration and revocable at will, and conditional in that it was made to depend on the adoption and carrying out by the district of other plans for disposing of the sewage.

It will be perceived that the interference which was the basis of the Secretary's permit, and which the latter was intended to eliminate, resulted directly from the failure of the Sanitary District to take care of its sewage in some way other than by promoting or continuing the existing diversion. It may be that some flow from the Lake is necessary to keep up navigation in the Chicago River, which really is part of the Port of Chicago, but that amount is negligible as compared with 8,500 second feet now being diverted. Hence, beyond that negligible quantity, the validity of the Secretary's permit derives its support entirely from a situation produced by the Sanitary District in violation of the complainants' rights; and but for that support complainants might properly press for an immediate shutting down by injunction of the diversion, save any small part needed to maintain navigation in the river. In these circumstances we think they are entitled to a decree which will be effective in bringing that violation and the unwarranted part of the diversion to an end. But in keeping with the principles on which courts of equity condition their relief, and by way of avoiding any unnecessary hazard to the health of the people of that section, our decree should be so framed as to accord to the Sanitary District a reasonably practicable time within which to provide some other means of disposing of the sewage, reducing the diversion as the artificial disposition of the sewage increases from time to time, until it is entirely disposed of thereby, when there shall be a final, permanent operative and effective injunction. . . .

The intervening States on the same side with Illinois, in seeking a recognition of asserted rights in the navigation of the Mississippi, have answered denying the rights of the complainants to an injunction. They really seek affirmatively to preserve the diversion from Lake Michigan in the interest of such navigation and interstate commerce, though they have made no express prayer therefor. In our view of the permit of March 3, 1925, and in the absence of direct authority from Congress for a waterway from Lake Michigan to the Mississippi, they show no rightful interest in the maintenance of the diversion. Their motions to dismiss the bills are overruled and so far as their answer may suggest affirmative relief, it is denied.

In increasing the diversion from 4,167 cubic feet a second to 8,500, the Sanitary District defied the authority of the National Government resting in the Secretary of War. And in so far as the prior diversion was not for the purposes of maintaining navigation in the Chicago river, it was without any legal basis, because made for an inadmissible purpose. It, therefore, is the duty of this Court by an appropriate decree to compel the reduction of the diversion to a point where it rests on a legal basis, and thus to restore the navigable capacity of Lake Michigan to its proper level. The Sanitary District authorities, relying on the argument with reference to the health of its people, have much too long delayed the needed substitution of suitable sewage plants as a means of avoiding the diversion in the future. Therefore, they can not now complain if an immediately heavy burden is placed upon the District because of their attitude and course. The situation requires the District to devise proper methods for providing sufficient money and to construct and put in operation with all reasonable expedition adequate plants for the disposition of the sewage through other means than the lake diversion.

Though the restoration of just rights to the complainants will be gradual instead of immediate, it must be continuous and as speedy as practicable, and must include everything that is essential to an effective project. . . .

To determine the practical measures needed to effect the object just stated and the period required for their completion there will be need for the examination of experts; and the appropriate provisions of the necessary decree will require careful consideration. For this reason, the case will be again referred to the Master for a further examination into the questions indicated. He will be authorized and directed to hear witnesses presented by each of the parties, and to call witnesses of his own selection, should he deem it necessary to do so, and then with all convenient speed to make report of his conclusions and of a form of decree.

It is so ordered.[1]

---

[1] Supplementary Cases. In the case of Kansas v. Colorado, 206 U. S. 46 (1907), involving a bill brought by Kansas to enjoin the diversion by Colorado of the water of the Arkansas River, the Supreme Court held inter alia that the rigid rule of the common law in respect to the rights of a lower riparian owner need not be held applicable to a controversy between two states; that in as

much as Kansas had by its local law recognized the appropriation of flowing waters for irrigation purposes, subject to the condition of an equitable division between riparian owners, it could not enjoin Colorado from diminishing the flow of the Arkansas River when the diversion resulted in reclaiming large areas of arid lands in Colorado yet worked little, if any, detriment to the great body of the Arkansas valley in Kansas, although perceptible injury to some portions of it.

In the case of Connecticut v. Massachusetts, 282 U. S. 660 (1931), involving a suit by Connecticut to enjoin a diversion of waters from the watershed of the Connecticut River to the use of the city of Boston and its neighboring towns, the Supreme Court of the United States held that the common-law rule which prevailed in both states, in accordance with which each riparian owner has a vested right to the use of flowing waters both as to quantity and quality, did not furnish a dependable basis for the decision of a controversy between states, but that the controversy must be decided by what appeared to be an equitable apportionment of the use of the water. Massachusetts was, accordingly, permitted to divert water for domestic uses so long as no substantial injury was done to navigation or power development along the lower reaches of the river as it flowed through Connecticut.

Query, may Congress, in the exercise of its power to regulate navigation along the lower reaches of a river, construct a dam which will be used for the additional purpose of furnishing water and power to one of two riparian states if the use of the dam as contemplated has the effect of diminishing possible future uses of water by the other boundary state? In Arizona v. California, 283 U. S. 423 (1931), involving a suit by Arizona to enjoin the carrying out of the Boulder Dam project authorized by Act of Congress, December 21, 1928, the Supreme Court of the United States held, inter alia, that the fact that purposes other than navigation were served by the dam did not invalidate the exercise of the authority of Congress; further, that the injunction asked for could not be granted where the waters to which the state might otherwise be entitled had not been and might never be appropriated.

CHAPTER XV

INTERNATIONAL TREATIES [1]

A. Legal form and effect of treaties.

Treaties are formal agreements between two states, or between a number of states, in accordance with which new rights and obligations are created. At times they define more specifically the general rights and obligations of international law, at other times they set up relationships outside the customary rules of international law. Certain formalities have traditionally attended the formation of treaties, one of which is that after the treaty has been duly signed by the diplomatic agents authorized to conclude the agreement it must be ratified by the appropriate governmental authority in the respective countries. Query, when a treaty is formally ratified does it come into effect from the date of signature or from the date of ratification, and what is the effect of the treaty upon rights which have vested before the date of ratification? [Haver v. Yaker.] Difficulties frequently arise in consequence of the conflict of the provisions of a treaty with the fundamental constitutional law of a state, or in consequence of the passage of legislation at a later date contrary to the provisions of the treaty. In such cases it is clear that, while the courts of a state may be under the necessity of upholding the constitution or the subsequent legislation, the treaty itself as an international obligation persists in spite of the action of the national legislature or the national courts. [Taylor v. Morton.] Query, has the Congress of the United States under the Constitution any powers with respect to the enforcement of a treaty which it does not possess apart from the treaty? [Missouri v. Holland.] What is the relative importance, in the United States, of treaties and statutes? To what extent will a statute be interpreted so as not to conflict with a prior treaty? [United States v. Ferris; Cook v. United States.]

---

[1] For a more detailed study of this subject, see Fenwick, *op. cit.*, pp. 326–359; Hyde, *op. cit.*, II, §§ 490–551; Oppenheim, *op. cit.*, I, §§ 491–554; A. D. McNair, "The Functions and Differing Legal Character of Treaties," British Year Book, XI (1930), 100; G. G. Fitzmaurice, "Do Treaties Need Ratification?" *ibid.*, XV (1934), 113; C. C. Hyde, "The Interpretation of Treaties by the Permanent Court of International Justice," Am. Journal Int. Law, XXIV (1930), 1; J. W. Garner, "The Doctrine of Rebus Sic Stantibus and the Termination of Treaties," *ibid.*, XXI (1927), 509; J. F. Williams, "The Permanence of Treaties," *ibid.*, XXII (1928), 89; Hudson, International Legislation, Vol. I, Introduction; Research in International Law: Draft Convention on Treaties.

HAVER v. YAKER.

United States, Supreme Court, 1869.

9 Wallace, 32. [19 L. ed. 571.]

Error to the Court of Appeals of Kentucky; the case being thus:

One Yaker, a Swiss by birth, who had come many years ago to the United States and become a naturalized citizen thereof, died in Kentucky in 1853, intestate, seized of real estate there. He left a widow, who was a resident and citizen of Kentucky, and certain heirs and next of kin, aliens and residents in Switzerland.

By the laws of Kentucky in force in 1853, the date of his death, aliens were not allowed to inherit real estate except under certain conditions, within which Yaker's heirs did not come, and if the matter was to depend on those laws, the widow was, by the laws then in force in Kentucky, plainly entitled to the estate.

However, in 1850, a treaty was "concluded and signed" by the respective plenipotentiaries of the two countries, between the Swiss Confederation and the United States [11 Stat. at Large 587] upon the proper construction of which, as Yaker's heirs asserted—although the widow denied that the construction put upon the treaty by the heirs was a right one—these heirs were entitled to take and hold the estate. The treaty provided by its terms that it should be submitted on both sides to the approval and ratification of the respective competent authorities of each contracting party, and that the ratifications should be exchanged at Washington as soon as circumstances should admit. It was so submitted, but was not duly ratified, nor were the respective ratifications exchanged in Washington till November 8, 1855, at which time the ratification and exchange was made. And on the next day the President, by proclamation—the treaty having been altered in the Senate—made the treaty public.

In 1859 the Swiss heirs, who had apparently not heard before of their kinsman's death, instituted proceedings to have the real estate of their kinsman, now in possession of the widow, assigned to them, and arguing that on a right construction of the treaty it was theirs.

But a preliminary question, and in case of one resolution of it, a conclusive objection to their claim was here raised; the question, namely, at what time the treaty of 1850-55, as it regarded private rights, became a law. Was it when it bore date, or was it only when the ratifications were exchanged between the parties to it? If not until it was ratified, then there was no necessity of deciding whether by its terms, the heirs of Yaker had any just claim to this real estate, because in no aspect of the case could the treaty have a retroactive effect so as to defeat the title of the widow, which vested in her, by the law of Kentucky of 1853, on the death of her husband.

The Court of Appeals of Kentucky, where the heirs set up the treaty as a basis of their title, decided that it took effect only when ratified, and so deciding against their claim, the case was now here for review under the twenty-fifth section of the Judiciary Act.

MR. JUSTICE DAVIS delivered the opinion of the court.

It is undoubtedly true, as a principle of international law, that, as respects the rights of either government under it, a treaty is considered as concluded and binding from the date of its signature. In this regard the exchange of ratifications has a retroactive effect, confirming the treaty from its date. [Wheaton's International Law, by Dana, 336, bottom paging.] But a different rule prevails where the treaty operates on individual rights. The principle of relation does not apply to rights of this character, which were vested before the treaty was ratified. In so far as it affects them, it is not considered as concluded until there is an exchange of ratifications, and this we understand to have been decided by this court, in Arredondo's case, reported in 6th Peters [p. 749]. The reason of the rule is apparent. In this country, a treaty is something more than a contract, for the Federal Constitution declares it to be the law of the land. If so, before it can become a law, the Senate, in whom rests the authority to ratify it, must agree to it. But the Senate are not required to adopt or reject it as a whole, but may modify or amend it, as was done with the treaty under consideration. As the individual citizen, on whose rights of property it operates, has no means of knowing anything of it while before the Senate, it would be wrong in principle to hold him bound by it, as the law of the land, until it was ratified and proclaimed. And to construe the law, so as to make the ratification of the treaty relate back to its signing, thereby divesting a title already vested, would be manifestly unjust, and cannot be sanctioned.

These views dispose of this case, and we are not required to determine whether this treaty, if it had become a law at an earlier date, would have secured the plaintiffs in error the interest which they claim in the real estate left by Yaker at his death.

Judgment affirmed.

TAYLOR v. MORTON.

United States, Circuit Court, District of Massachusetts, 1855.

2 Curtis, 454, 23 Fed. Cases, 784 (No. 13,799).

CURTIS, Circuit Justice. This is an action of assumpsit for money had and received, brought against the defendant as collector of the customs of the port of Boston, to recover back moneys alleged to have been illegally exacted by him in payment of duties, upon a quantity of hemp imported by the plaintiffs from Russia, while the tariff act of 1842 (5 Stat. 548) was in operation. The duties charged were at the rate of forty dollars per ton. The plaintiffs allege that twenty-five dollars per ton was the true rate. The commercial treaty between the United States and Russia of the 18th December, 1832, stipulated, in substance, that no higher rates of duty should be imposed on the products of Russia imported from that country into the United States, than on the like articles imported from other countries. The tariff act of 1842 imposed a duty of forty dollars per ton on all hemp excepting Manilla, Suera, and other hemps of India, on which a duty of twenty-five dollars only was to be levied.

The plaintiff's counsel insists, that the import now in question is, within the meaning of the treaty, an article "like" Bombay hemp; that congress has levied upon Bombay hemp a duty of twenty-five dollars per ton; that as soon as this lower duty had been levied on an article like Russian hemp, the stipulation in the treaty at once took effect, as part of our municipal law, and reduced the duty leviable on Russian hemp to twenty-five dollars per ton; and so, that under the laws of the United States, the amount beyond twenty-five dollars per ton, was illegally exacted, and can be recovered back in this action.

Several questions, involved in this position, require examination. One of them, when stated abstractly, is this,—if an act of congress should levy a duty upon imports, which an existing commercial treaty declares shall not be levied, so that the treaty is in conflict with the act, does the former or the latter give the rule of decision in a judicial tribunal of the United States, in a case to which one rule or the other must be applied? The second section of the fourth article of the constitution is: "This constitution, and the laws of the United States which shall be made in pursuance thereof, and all treaties made or which shall be made, under the authority of the United States, shall be the supreme law of the land." There is nothing in the language of this clause which enables us to say, that in the case supposed, the treaty, and not the act of congress, is to afford the rule. Ordinarily, treaties are not rules prescribed by sovereigns for the conduct of their subjects, but contracts, by which they agree to regulate their own conduct. This provision of our constitution has made treaties part of our municipal law. But it has not assigned to them any particular degree of authority in our municipal law, nor declared whether laws so enacted shall or shall not be paramount to laws otherwise enacted. No such declaration is made, even in respect to the constitution itself. It is named in conjunction with treaties and acts of congress, as one of the supreme laws, but no supremacy, is in terms assigned to one over the other. And when it became necessary to determine whether an act of congress repugnant to the constitution could be deemed by the judicial power an operative law, the solution of the question was found, by considering the nature and objects of each species of law, the authority from which each emanated, and the consequences of allowing or denying the paramount effect of the constitution. It is only ·by a similar course of inquiry that we can determine the question now under consideration.

In commencing this inquiry I think it material to observe, that it is solely a question of municipal, as distinguished from public law. The foreign sovereign between whom and the United States a treaty has been made, has a right to expect and require its stipulations to be kept with scrupulous good faith; but through what internal arrangements this shall be done, is, exclusively, for the consideration of the United States. Whether the treaty shall itself be the rule of action of the people as well as the government, whether the power to enforce and apply it shall reside in one department, or another, neither the treaty itself, nor any implication drawn from it, gives him any right to inquire. If the people of the United States were to repeal so much of their constitution as makes treaties part of their municipal law, no foreign sovereign with whom a treaty exists could justly complain, for it is not a matter with which he has any concern. We may approach this question therefore free from any of that anxiety respecting the preservation of our national faith, which can scarcely be too easily awakened, or too sensibly felt. For this question, in that aspect of it, is not, whether the act of congress is consistent with the treaty, but whether that is a judicial question to be here tried. If the act of congress, because it is the later law, must prescribe the rule by which this case is to be determined, we do not inquire whether it proceeds upon a just interpretation of the treaty, or an accurate knowledge of the facts of likeness or unlikeness of the articles, or whether it was an accidental or purposed departure from the treaty; and if the latter, whether the reasons for that departure are such as commend themselves to the just judgment of mankind. It is sufficient that the law is so written, and, if I mistake not, we shall find by further examination, great reasons for not entering into these inquiries. By the eighth section of the first article of the constitution, power is conferred on congress to regulate commerce with foreign nations, and to lay duties, and to make all laws necessary and proper for carrying those powers into execution. That the act now in question is within the legislative power of congress, unless that power is controlled by the treaty, is not doubted. It must be admitted, also, that in general, power to legislate on a particular subject, includes power to modify and repeal existing laws on that subject, and either substitute new laws in their place, or leave the subject without regulation, in those particulars to which the repealed laws applied. There is therefore nothing in the mere fact that a treaty is a law, which would prevent congress from repealing it. Unless it is for some reason distinguishable from other laws, the rule which it gives may be displaced by the legislative power, at its pleasure.

The first and most obvious distinction between a treaty and an act of congress is, that the former is made by the president and ratified by two thirds of the senators present; the latter by majorities of both houses of congress and the president, or by the houses only, by constitutional majorities, if the president refuses his assent. Ordinarily, it is certainly true, that the powers of enacting and repealing laws reside in the same persons. But there is no reason, in the nature of things, why it may not be otherwise. In the country from which we have derived many political principles, the king, by force of his prerogative makes laws for the colonies, which parliament repeals or modifies at its discretion. Campbell v. Hall, Cowp. 204. I think it is impossible to maintain that, under our constitution, the president and senate exclusively, possess the power to modify or repeal a law found in a treaty. If this were so, inasmuch as they can change or abrogate one treaty, only by making another inconsistent with the first, the government of the United States could not act at all, to that effect, without consent of some foreign government; for no new treaty, affecting, in any manner, one already in existence, can be made without the concurrence of two parties, one of whom must be a foreign sovereign. That the constitution was designed to place our country in this helpless condition, is a supposition wholly inadmissible. It is not only inconsistent with the necessities of a nation, but negatived by the express words of the constitution. . . .

. . . To refuse to execute a treaty, for reasons which approve themselves to the conscientious judgment of the nation, is a matter of the utmost gravity and delicacy; but the power to do so, is prerogative, of which no nation can be deprived, without deeply affecting its independence. That the people of the United States have deprived their government of this power in any case, I do not believe. That it must reside somewhere, and be applicable to all cases, I am convinced. I feel no doubt that it belongs to congress. That, inasmuch as treaties must continue to operate as part of our municipal law, and be obeyed by the people, applied by the judiciary and executed by the president, while they continue unrepealed, and inasmuch as the power of repealing these municipal laws must reside somewhere, and no body other than congress possesses it, then legislative power is applicable to such laws whenever they relate to subjects, which the constitution has placed under that legislative power. In conformity with these views was the action of congress in passing the act of July 7, 1798 (1 Stat. 578), declaring the treaties with France no longer obligatory on the United States. . . .

Is it a judicial question, whether a treaty with a foreign sovereign has been violated by him; whether the consideration of a particular stipulation in a treaty, has been voluntarily withdrawn by one party, so that it is no longer obligatory on the other; whether the views and acts of a foreign sovereign, manifested through his representative have given just occasion to the political departments of our government to withhold the

execution of a promise contained in a treaty, or to act in direct contravention of such promise? I apprehend not. These powers have not been
confided by the people to the judiciary, which has no suitable means to
exercise them; but to the executive and the legislative departments of
our government. They belong to diplomacy and legislation, and not to
the administration of existing laws. And it necessarily follows, that if
they are denied to congress and the executive, in the exercise of their
legislative power, they can be found nowhere, in our system of government. On the other hand, if it be admitted that congress has these powers, it is wholly immaterial to inquire whether they have, by the act in
question, departed from the treaty or not; or if they have, whether such
departure were accidental or designed, and if the latter, whether the
reasons therefor were good or bad. If by the act in question they have
not departed from the treaty, the plaintiff has no case. If they have,
their act is the municipal law of the country, and any complaint, either
by the citizen, or the foreigner, must be made to those, who alone are
empowered by the constitution, to judge of its grounds, and act as may
be suitable and just. . . .

The truth is, that this clause in the treaty is merely a contract, addressing itself to the legislative power. The distinction between such treaties,
and those which operate as laws in courts of justice, is settled in our
jurisprudence. It was clearly pointed out in Foster v. Neilson, 2 Pet.
314. . . .

For these reasons, I am of opinion that, inasmuch as the duty paid in
this case was duly assessed and levied pursuant to the act of congress,
there is no further or other question to be tried, and the plaintiffs cannot
recover. I desire to add, what perhaps is not necessary, that the various
suppositions of violation or departure from treaties by foreign sovereigns,
or by our country, which are put by way of argument in the course of
this opinion, have no reference whatever to the treaty now in question,
or to any actual case; that I have not formed, or intended to intimate,
any opinion, upon the question whether the duty levied upon hemp, the
product of Russia, is, or is not higher, than a just interpretation and
application of the treaty with the sovereign of that country would allow;
as, in my judgment, it belongs to the political department of the government of the United States to determine this question.

STATE OF MISSOURI v. HOLLAND, UNITED STATES GAME WARDEN.

United States, Supreme Court, 1920.

252 U. S. 416. [64 L. ed. 641; 40 S. Ct. 382.]

MR. JUSTICE HOLMES delivered the opinion of the court.

This is a bill in equity brought by the State of Missouri to prevent a game warden of the United States from attempting to enforce the Migratory Bird Treaty Act of July 3, 1918, c. 128, 40 Stat. 755, and the regulations made by the Secretary of Agriculture in pursuance of the same. The ground of the bill is that the statute is an unconstitutional interference with the rights reserved to the States by the Tenth Amendment, and that the acts of the defendant done and threatened under that authority invade the sovereign right of the State and contravene its will manifested in statutes. The State also alleges a pecuniary interest, as owner of the wild birds within its borders and otherwise, admitted by the Government to be sufficient, but it is enough that the bill is a reasonable and proper means to assert the alleged quasi sovereign rights of a State. Kansas v. Colorado, 185 U. S. 125, 142. Georgia v. Tennessee Copper Co., 206 U. S. 230, 237. Marshall Dental Manufacturing Co. v. Iowa, 226 U. S. 460, 462. A motion to dismiss was sustained by the District Court on the ground that the act of Congress is constitutional. 258 Fed. Rep. 479. Acc. United States v. Thompson, 258 Fed. Rep. 257; United States v. Rockefeller, 260 Fed. Rep. 346. The State appeals.

On December 8, 1916, a treaty between the United States and Great Britain was proclaimed by the President. It recited that many species of birds in their annual migrations traversed certain parts of the United States and of Canada, that they were of great value as a source of food and in destroying insects injurious to vegetation, but were in danger of extermination through lack of adequate protection. It therefore provided for specified close seasons and protection in other forms, and agreed that the two powers would take or propose to their law-making bodies the necessary measures for carrying the treaty out. 39 Stat. 1702. The above mentioned Act of July 3, 1918, entitled an act to give effect to the convention, prohibited the killing, capturing or selling any of the migratory birds included in the terms of the treaty except as permitted by regulations compatible with those terms, to be made by the Secretary of Agriculture. Regulations were proclaimed on July 31, and October 25, 1918. 40 Stat. 1812; 1863. It is unnecessary to go into any details, because, as we have said, the question raised is the general one whether the treaty and statute are void as an interference with the rights reserved to the States.

To answer this question it is not enough to refer to the Tenth Amendment, reserving the powers not delegated to the United States, because by Article II, § 2, the power to make treaties is delegated expressly, and by Article VI treaties made under the authority of the United States, along with the Constitution and laws of the United States made in pursuance thereof, are declared the supreme law of the land. If the treaty is valid there can be no dispute about the validity of the statute under Article I, § 8, as a necessary and proper means to execute the powers of the Government. The language of the Constitution as to the supremacy of treaties being general, the question before us is narrowed to an inquiry into the ground upon which the present supposed exception is placed.

It is said that a treaty cannot be valid if it infringes the Constitution, that there are limits, therefore, to the treaty-making power, and that one such limit is that what an act of Congress could not do unaided, in derogation of the powers reserved to the States, a treaty cannot do. An earlier act of Congress that attempted by itself and not in pursuance of a treaty to regulate the killing of migratory birds within the States had been held bad in the District Court. United States v. Shauver, 214 Fed. Rep. 154. United States v. McCullagh, 221 Fed. Rep. 288. Those decisions were supported by arguments that migratory birds were owned by the States in their sovereign capacity for the benefit of their people, and that under cases like Geer v. Connecticut, 161 U. S. 519, this control was one that Congress had no power to displace. The same argument is supposed to apply now with equal force.

Whether the two cases cited were decided rightly or not they cannot be accepted as a test of the treaty power. Acts of Congress are the supreme law of the land only when made in pursuance of the Constitution, while treaties are declared to be so when made under the authority of the United States. It is open to question whether the authority of the United States means more than the formal acts prescribed to make the convention. We do not mean to imply that there are no qualifications to the treaty-making power; but they must be ascertained in a different way. It is obvious that there may be matters of the sharpest exigency for the national well being that an act of Congress could not deal with but that a treaty followed by such an act could, and it is not lightly to be assumed that, in matters requiring national action, "a power which must belong to and somewhere reside in every civilized government" is not to be found. Andrews v. Andrews, 188 U. S. 14, 33. What was said in that case with regard to the powers of the States applies with equal force to the powers of the nation in cases where the States individually are incompetent to act. We are not yet discussing the particular case before us but only are considering the validity of the test proposed. With regard to that we may add that when we are dealing with words that also are a constituent act, like the Constitution of the United States, we must realize that they have called into life a being the development of which could not have been foreseen completely by the most gifted of its begetters. It was enough for them to realize or to hope that they had created an organism; it had taken a century and has cost their successors much sweat and blood to prove that they created a nation. The case before us must be considered in the light of our whole experience and not merely in that of what was said a hundred years ago. The treaty in question does not contravene any prohibitory words to be found in the Constitution. The only question is whether it is forbidden by some invisible radiation from the general terms of the Tenth Amendment. We must consider what this country has become in deciding what that Amendment has reserved.

The State as we have intimated founds its claim of exclusive authority upon an assertion of title to migratory birds, an assertion that is embodied in statute. No doubt it is true that as between a State and its inhabitants the State may regulate the killing and sale of such birds, but it does not follow that its authority is exclusive of paramount powers. To put the claim of the State upon title is to lean upon a slender reed. Wild birds are not in the possession of anyone; and possession is the beginning of ownership. The whole foundation of the State's rights is the presence within their jurisdiction of birds that yesterday had not arrived, tomorrow may be in another State and in a week a thousand miles away. If we are to be accurate we cannot put the case of the State upon higher ground than that the treaty deals with creatures that for the moment are within the state borders, that it must be carried out by officers of the United States within the same territory, and that but for the treaty the State would be free to regulate this subject itself.

As most of the laws of the United States are carried out within the States and as many of them deal with matters which in the silence of such laws the State might regulate, such general grounds are not enough to support Missouri's claim. Valid treaties of course "are as binding within the territorial limits of the States as they are elsewhere throughout the dominion of the United States." Baldwin v. Franks, 120 U. S. 678, 683. No doubt the great body of private relations usually fall within the control of the State, but a treaty may override its power. We do not have to invoke the later developments of constitutional law for this proposition; it was recognized as early as Hopkirk v. Bell, 3 Cranch, 454, with regard to statutes of limitation, and even earlier, as to confiscation, in Ware v. Hylton, 3 Dall. 199. It was assumed by Chief Justice Marshall with regard to the escheat of land to the State in Chirac v. Chirac, 2 Wheat. 259, 275. Hauenstein v. Lynham, 100 U. S. 483. Geofroy v. Riggs, 133 U. S. 258. Blythe v. Hinckley, 180 U. S. 333, 340. So as to a limited jurisdiction of foreign consuls within a State. Wildenhus's Case, 120 U. S. 1. See Ross v. McIntyre, 140 U. S. 453. Further illustration seems unnecessary, and it only remains to consider the application of established rules to the present case.

Here a national interest of very nearly the first magnitude is involved. It can be protected only by national action in concert with that of another power. The subject-matter is only transitorily within the State and has no permanent habitat therein. But for the treaty and the statute there soon might be no birds for any powers to deal with. We see nothing in the Constitution that compels the Government to sit by while a food supply is cut off and the protectors of our forests and our crops are destroyed. It is not sufficient to rely upon the States. The reliance is vain, and were it otherwise, the question is whether the United States is forbidden to act. We are of opinion that the treaty and statute must be upheld. Carey v. South Dakota, 250 U. S. 118.

Decree affirmed.

MR. JUSTICE VAN DEVANTER and MR. JUSTICE PITNEY dissent.

UNITED STATES v. FERRIS.

United States, District Court, Northern District of California, 1927.

19 F. (2d) 925.

BOURQUIN, District Judge. These indictments allege conspiracies to violate the Prohibition and Tariff Acts. Several defendants interpose pleas to the jurisdiction of the court, viz.: That March 1, 1927, they were of the crew of the steamer Federalship, then with their persons seized by United States Coast Guards some 270 miles off the west coast territory of the United States; that forcibly and against their will they were brought within the territory of the jurisdiction of the court and held to answer to these indictments; and that said steamer is of English ownership and Panaman registry.

Their contention is that the seizure is illegal, in that it is contrary to and prohibited by the treaty of 1924 between the United States and Panama (43 Stat. 1875), and that because thereof there can be no jurisdiction of their persons against their wills. This treaty is like to that between this country and England, involved in the Quadra Case (Ford v. United States, 47 S. Ct. 531). Amongst other things it provides that Panama "will not object" to search and seizure by the United States of vessels under the Panama flag and engaged in offenses against laws of the United States in respect to importation of alcoholic beverages, but that "the rights conferred by this article shall not be exercised at a greater distance" than one hour's sailing from the coast of the United States.

In the matter of search and seizure upon the high seas, to whatever extent the right exists, it is by virtue of international law, and is of vague, indefinite, and conflicting recognition. To settle the conflict, and to define the limit of the right in so far as illicit importation of alcoholic beverages is concerned, this and like treaties were negotiated. They modify and themselves are international law between their signatories, by the Constitution are declared to be of "the supreme law of the land,"

and in so far as they are self-executing and relate to private rights are to be given effect by the courts to the extent that they are capable of judicial enforcement. This treaty is the only law authorizing seizure on the high seas of Panaman vessels and crews offending as aforesaid, and it authorizes seizure only within one hour's sailing of the coast.

In and by it the right is "conferred," Panama concedes it, in consideration thereof the United States accepts and agrees to it as therein limited, abandons all claim of right exceeding it, and promises to comply with it. Hence, as the instant seizure was far outside the limit, it is sheer aggression and trespass (like those which contributed to the War of 1812), contrary to the treaty, not to be sanctioned by any court, and cannot be the basis of any proceeding adverse to defendants. The prosecution contends, however, that courts will try those before it, regardless of the methods employed to bring them there. There are many cases generally so holding, but none of authority wherein a treaty or other federal law was violated, as in the case at bar. That presents a very different aspect and case. "A decent respect for the opinions of mankind," national honor, harmonious relations between nations, and avoidance of war, require that the contracts and law represented by treaties shall be scrupulously observed, held inviolate, and in good faith precisely performed—require that treaties shall not be reduced to mere "scraps of paper." . . .

It seems clear that, if one legally before the court cannot be tried because therein a treaty is violated, for greater reason one illegally before the court, in violation of a treaty, likewise cannot be subjected to trial. Equally in both cases is there absence of jurisdiction.

In the Quadra Case (Ford v. United States) the Supreme Court indicates that this is the law; for in answer to the government's contention, like that of the prosecution here, it says the Ker Case [Ker v. Illinois, 119 U. S. 444, 7 S. Ct. 225] does not apply, in that therein the seizure of Ker "violated neither . . . a federal law, nor a treaty of the United States. . . . Here a treaty of the United States is directly involved, and the question is quite different." Thereupon it notes that the Quadra defendants, unlike defendants here, interposed no plea to the jurisdiction, and "the effect . . . was to waive the question of jurisdiction of the persons of defendants."

It further observes that defendants' "immunity on the high seas from seizure or being taken into port came from the immunity of the vessel"; that, coming within one hour's sailing of the coast, the vessel lost its immunity, and defendants theirs with it; and that, in consequence, they, being within the court's jurisdiction, were legally tried—which is but to say that, beyond one hour's sailing, vessel and crew were immune against seizure.

Defendants' pleas to the jurisdiction of the court over their persons are sustained.

COOK v. UNITED STATES.

United States, Supreme Court, 1933.

288 U. S. 102. [77 L. ed. 641; 53 S. Ct. 305.]

MR. JUSTICE BRANDEIS delivered the opinion of the Court:

The main question for decision is whether § 581 of the Tariff Act of [June 17], 1930, c. 497, 46 Stat. 590, 747, is modified, as applied to British vessels suspected of being engaged in smuggling liquors into the United States, by the Treaty between this country and Great Britain proclaimed May 22, 1924. (43 Stat. 1761.) That section—which is a re-enactment in identical language of § 581 of the Tariff Act of 1922, c. 356, 42 Stat. 858, 979,—declares that officers of the Coast Guard are authorized to stop and board any vessel at any place within four leagues [12 miles] of the coast of the United States "to examine the manifest and to inspect, search and examine" the vessel and any merchandise therein; and if it shall appear that any violation of any law of the United States has been committed by reason of which the vessel or merchandise is liable to forfeiture, it shall be the duty of such officers to seize the same.

On the evening of November 1, 1930, the British motor screw Mazel Tov—a vessel of speed not exceeding 10 miles an hour—was discovered by officers of the Coast Guard within four leagues of the coast of Massachusetts and was boarded by them at a point 11½ miles from the nearest land. The manifest was demanded and exhibited. Search followed, which disclosed that the only cargo on board, other than ship stores, was unmanifested intoxicating liquor which had been cleared from St. Pierre, a French possession. The vessel, ostensibly bound for Nassau, a British possession, had when boarded, been cruising off our coast with the intent that ultimately the liquor should be taken to the United States by other boats. But the evidence indicated that she did not intend to approach nearer than four leagues to our coast; and, so far as appeared, she had not been in communication with our shores and had not unladen any part of her cargo. The boarding officers seized the Mazel Tov at a point more than 10 miles from our coast; took her to the Port of Providence; and there delivered the vessel and cargo to the customs officials.

The Collector of Customs, acting pursuant to § 584 of the Tariff Act of 1930, assessed against Frank Cook, as master of the Mazel Tov, a penalty of $14,286.18 for failure to include the liquor in the manifest. By § 584, if merchandise not described in the manifest is found on board a vessel "bound to the United States," the master is subject to a penalty equal to its value, and the merchandise belonging or consigned to him is subject to forfeiture. By § 594, whenever a master becomes subject to a penalty, the vessel may be seized and proceeded against summarily by libel to recover the penalty. The Government proceeded, in the federal court for Rhode Island, to collect the assessed penalty by means of libels against both the cargo and the vessel. The cases were consolidated.

Cook, claiming as master and bailee of the vessel and as consignee and claimant of the cargo, alleged that the Mazel Tov was of British registry and owned by a Nova Scotia corporation. He answered to the merits; and excepted to the jurisdiction on the ground that the "vessel was not seized within the territorial limits of any jurisdiction of the United States, but, on the contrary, was captured and boarded at a point more than four (4) leagues from the coast," and that "it was not the intention at any time to enter any of the territorial limits of the United States."

The District Court, having found the facts above stated, dismissed the libels. 51 F. (2d) 292. The Government appealed to the Circuit Court of Appeals, which held that the Treaty did not "effect a change in the customs-revenue laws of the United States wherein Congress had fixed a four league protective zone;" reversed the judgments; and remanded the cases to the District Court for further proceedings. 56 F. (2d) 921. This Court granted certiorari.

Cook contends, among other things, that by reason of the Treaty between the United States and Great Britain proclaimed May 22, 1924 (43 Stat. 1761), the seizure was unlawful under the laws of the United States; that the authority conferred by § 581 of the Tariff Act of 1922 to board, search and seize within the four league limit, was, as respects British vessels, modified by the Treaty so as to substitute for four leagues from our coast, the distance which "can be traversed in one hour by the vessel suspected of endeavoring to commit the offense;" that Congress by re-enacting § 581 in the Tariff Act of 1930 intended to continue in force the modification effected by the Treaty; and, hence, that the Mazel Tov, being a British vessel of a speed not exceeding 10 miles an hour, could not be lawfully boarded, searched and seized at a distance of 11½ miles from the coast because suspected of "endeavoring to import or have imported alcoholic beverages into the United States in violation of the laws there in force."

The Government insists that the Treaty did not have the effect of so modifying § 581 of the Act of 1922; and that, if it did, the re-enactment of § 581 without change, by the Act of 1930, removed the alleged modification. It contends further that the validity of the seizure was not material; and if ever material had been waived.

The Treaty provides, among other things, as follows: . . .[1]

We are of opinion that the decrees entered by the District Court should have been affirmed.

First. It is suggested on behalf of the Government that the power to search and seize within the twelve-mile zone, conferred upon officers of

---

[1] For the text of Articles I and II of the treaty quoted by the court, see Ford v. United States, above, p. 213.

the Coast Guard by § 581 of the Tariff Act of 1922, was unaffected by the Treaty, save that the British Government agreed not to protest where the seizure was within an hour's sailing distance of the coast. The argument is that the Treaty settled the validity of the seizure only for those cases where it was made within the limits described in the Treaty; and that since this seizure was made beyond one hour's sailing distance from the coast the Treaty did not apply. In construing the Treaty its history should be consulted. Compare United States v. Texas, 162 U. S. 1; Oklahoma v. Texas, 260 U. S. 606; Nielsen v. Johnson, 279 U. S. 47, 52. Both its language and its history show that the high contracting parties did not intend so to limit its operation. The preamble states that they entered into the Treaty "being desirous of avoiding any difficulties which might arise between them in connection with the laws in force in the United States on the subject of alcoholic beverages." The history reveals that serious differences had arisen between the two Governments in that connection; and that, for the purpose of resolving them, the parties determined to deal completely with the subject of search and seizure, beyond our territorial limits, of British vessels suspected of smuggling liquors.

Prior to the Eighteenth Amendment the United States had never attempted, in connection with the enforcement of our customs laws, to board foreign vessels beyond the three-mile limit except where consent was implied from the fact that the vessel, being hailed, answered that she was bound for the United States, or where a vessel had been discovered violating our laws within the three-mile limit and, while endeavoring to escape, was hotly pursued. Although Hovering Acts conferring authority to board and search vessels, foreign and domestic, "within four leagues of the coast," had existed since the foundation of our Government, see Act of August 4, 1790, c. 35, § 31, 1 Stat. 145, 164, the authority therein conferred had, prior to the Tariff Act of 1922, been in terms limited to inbound vessels; and no statute had purported to confer authority to seize foreign vessels beyond our territorial waters for violation of any of our laws except in those few instances in which Congress acted pursuant to specific treaties. But soon after the Eighteenth Amendment took effect (January 16, 1920), vessels of British registry were found to be engaged in smuggling intoxicating liquors into the United States in violation of our laws. In the effort to prevent such violations British vessels were being boarded, searched and seized beyond the three-mile limit; and by § 581 of the Tariff Act of 1922 Congress undertook to sanction such action through enlarging the authority to board, search and seize beyond the three-mile limit so as to include foreign vessels although not inbound.

Both before and after the passage of the Tariff Act of 1922 it was the consistent policy of our Government to release, upon protest, all British vessels seized beyond the three-mile limit and not bound to the United

States, unless it appeared that the hovering vessel had, by means of her own small boats and crew, assisted in landing there contraband goods. Our Government deemed that exception an essential to the enforcement of our laws and consistent with the principles of international law. But the British Government declined to acquiesce in the propriety of the exception; declared that our practice of seizing vessels under those circumstances was not in harmony with the law of nations; protested against the seizure of any British vessel outside of the three-mile limit; and stated that insistence upon the practice would be regarded as creating "a very serious situation."

With a view to removing the British objections, the Secretary of State proposed, on June 26, 1922, that a treaty be entered into "under which the authorities of each nation would be authorized to exercise beyond the three-mile limit of territorial waters a measure of control over vessels belonging to the other" and which would include specifically "reciprocal provisions authorizing the authorities of each Government to exercise a right of search of vessels of the other beyond the three-mile limit of territorial waters to the extent of twelve miles from the shore." The British Government declined definitely to entertain any such proposal.

The decision rendered by this Court on April 30, 1923, in Cunard Steamship Co. v. Mellon, 262 U. S. 100, led to the resumption of negotiations. It was there decided that the National Prohibition Act applied to all merchant vessels, foreign or domestic, within the territorial waters of the United States, and that the carrying of intoxicating liquors, either as cargo or as sea stores, through the territorial waters or into the ports and harbors of the United States is forbidden by that Act and the Eighteenth Amendment. The embarrassment to British vessels and trade threatened by this decision was serious. Recognizing the urgent need of some arrangement between the two Governments which would permit the conduct by the British of legitimate trade and remove this obstacle to the operation of their vessels in the accustomed manner, the Secretary of State submitted to Great Britain, on June 11, 1923, the draft of a treaty designed to remove the friction between the two Governments. The draft did not refer specifically to intoxicating liquors. Article I. provided, in general terms, that the authorities of each country should "within the distance of twelve geographical miles from its coasts" be permitted to board and search private vessels of the other to ascertain whether such vessels were engaged in an attempt to violate its laws "prohibiting or regulating the unloading near, or importation into its territories of any article;" and "if there is reasonable cause for belief" that the vessel is so engaged to seize it. Article II. likewise, in general terms, provided that articles on private vessels of either nation listed as sea stores, or as cargo destined to a foreign port, the importation of which is prohibited, might be brought within the territorial waters of the other on condition that they be sealed "upon arrival of the vessel so destined within twelve geographical miles of the coasts'' and be kept sealed continuously thereafter while within the territorial waters.

This proposal of the Secretary of State also failed to meet with the approval of the British Government because it was regarded as involving an extension of the limits of the territorial waters. The negotiations were, however, continued; and ultimately the British Government submitted a counter-proposal, which sought to achieve the same results by different means. The British draft provided that the high contracting parties should declare ''their firm intention to uphold the principle that three marine miles measured from low watermark constitute the proper limits of territorial waters;'' and avoiding all language which could possibly indicate a contrary purpose, it made no reference to the twelve-mile limit. Moreover, the arrangement, instead of applying generally to merchandise subject to prohibitory or regulatory laws, was to be limited specifically to intoxicating liquors; and no reciprocal rights were to be conferred. Each country was to secure the immunity required to satisfy its peculiar need. The need of the United States was to be met by providing that His Britannic Majesty ''will raise no objection to the boarding,'' etc., outside the territorial waters at no ''greater distance from the coast of the United States than can be traversed in one hour by the vessel suspected of'' smuggling. The need of Great Britain was to be met by our allowing ''British vessels voyaging to or from the ports or passing through the waters of the United States to have on board alcoholic liquors listed as sea stores or as cargo destined for a foreign port, provided that such liquor is kept under seal while within the jurisdiction of the United States.''

The draft of treaty submitted by the British Government was accepted with a few purely verbal changes. Thereby, as stated in Ford v. United States, 273 U. S. 593, 609, 610, this country secured ''a definite fixing of the zone of legitimate seizure of hovering British vessels seeking to defeat the laws against the importation of liquor into this country from the sea.''

Second. The Treaty, being later in date than the Act of 1922, superseded, so far as inconsistent with the terms of the Act, the authority which had been conferred by § 581 upon officers of the Coast Guard to board, search and seize beyond our territorial waters. Whitney v. Robertson, 124 U. S. 190, 194. For in a strict sense the Treaty was self-executing, in that no legislation was necessary to authorize executive action pursuant to its provisions.

The purpose of the provisions for seizure in § 581, and their practical operation, as an aid in the enforcement of the laws prohibiting alcoholic liquors, leave no doubt that the territorial limitations there established were modified by the Treaty. This conclusion is supported by the course of administrative practice. Shortly after the Treaty took effect, the Treasury Department issued amended instructions for the Coast

Guard which pointed out, after reciting the provisions of § 581, that "in cases of special treaties, the provisions of those treaties shall be complied with;" and called attention particularly to the recent treaties dealing with the smuggling of intoxicating liquors. The Commandant of the Coast Guard, moreover, was informed in 1927, as the Solicitor General states, that all seizures of British vessels captured in the rum-smuggling trade should be within the terms of the Treaty and that seizing officers should be instructed to produce evidence, not that the vessel was found within the four-league limit, but that she was apprehended within one hour's sailing distance from the coast.

Third. The Treaty was not abrogated by re-enacting § 581 in the Tariff Act of 1930 in the identical terms of the Act of 1922. A treaty will not be deemed to have been abrogated or modified by a later statute unless such purpose on the part of Congress has been clearly expressed. Chew Heong v. United States, 112 U. S. 536; United States v. Payne, 264 U. S. 446, 448. Here, the contrary appears. The committee reports and the debates upon the Act of 1930, like the re-enacted section itself, make no reference to the Treaty of 1924. Any doubt as to the construction of the section should be deemed resolved by the consistent departmental practice existing before its re-enactment. . . . No change, in this respect, was made either by the Department of the Treasury or the Department of Justice after the Tariff Act of 1930.

Searches and seizures in the enforcement of the laws prohibiting alcoholic liquors are governed, since the 1930 Act, as they were before, by the provisions of the Treaty. Section 581, with its scope narrowed by the Treaty, remained in force after its re-enactment in the Act of 1930. The section continued to apply to the boarding, search and seizure of all vessels of all countries with which we had no relevant treaties. It continued also, in the enforcement of our customs laws not related to the prohibition of alcoholic liquors, to govern the boarding of vessels of those countries with which we had entered into treaties like that with Great Britain. . . .

The decree of the Circuit Court of Appeals is reversed.

MR. JUSTICE SUTHERLAND and MR. JUSTICE BUTLER are of opinion that in respect of British vessels engaged in smuggling intoxicating liquor into the United States the treaty of 1924 was not intended to cut down the rights claimed by the United States under the hovering statutes in force since the organization of our government, but that it was the purpose of both countries to extend and enlarge such rights to enable the United States more effectively to enforce its liquor laws and that therefore the decree of the Circuit Court of Appeals should be affirmed.[1]

---

[1] SUPPLEMENTARY CASES. In Foster and Elam v. Neilson, 2 Peters 253 (1829), involving a suit by the plaintiffs to recover a tract of land claimed under a grant made by the Spanish governor of Florida in 1804 within territory the

B. Interpretation of treaties.

An elaborate body of rules has been developed with respect to the proper interpretation of treaties. These rules bear many analogies to the rules governing the interpretation of contracts between individuals under national law. In general it is accepted that treaties must be interpreted so as to give effect to the original intention of the parties in so far as that can be discovered. Query, where the terms of the treaty are not clear should they be liberally or strictly construed? [Geofroy v. Riggs.] Should they be favorable to rights claimed under them or restrictive of such rights? [Asakura v. Seattle.] Treaties containing most-favored-nation clauses have given rise to special problems of interpretation. Query, should such clauses be interpreted conditionally, so as to grant favors only to those third states which are able and willing to meet the special conditions under which the favors in question have been granted to the particular state? [Whitney v. Robertson; Santovincenzo v. Egan.] Where treaties have been entered into with a political object in view, should the terms of the treaty be interpreted so as to secure that object even when to do so would be restrictive of the normal exercise of sovereignty by one of the parties? [France et al. and Austria: Austro-German Customs Régime.]

---

title to which was in dispute between the United States and Spain, the former asserting that the territory had been ceded by Spain to France in 1800 by the treaty of St. Ildefonso, and therefore passed to the United States by the Louisiana Purchase, the Supreme Court held that a question respecting the boundaries of nations was "more a political than a legal question; and in its discussion the courts of every country must respect the pronounced will of the legislature," in this case as expressed in specific acts of Congress. In answer to the demand that the court should interpret the treaty of 1818 between the United States and Spain by which grants of land were to be "ratified and confirmed to the persons in possession of the lands," the court held that this was the "language of contract" and called for an act of the legislature. "A treaty is in its nature," said the court, "a contract between two nations, not a legislative act. It does not generally effect, of itself, the object to be accomplished, especially so far as its operation is infra-territorial; but is carried into execution by the sovereign power of the respective parties to the instrument.

"In the United States a different principle is established. Our constitution declares a treaty to be the law of the land. It is, consequently, to be regarded in courts of justice as equivalent to an act of the legislature, whenever it operates of itself without the aid of any legislative provision. But when the terms of the stipulation import a contract, when either of the parties engages to perform a particular act, the treaty addresses itself to the political, not the judicial department; and the legislature must execute the contract before it can become a rule for the Court."

Query, where ratifications of a treaty have been exchanged, but one of the parties has failed to bring the treaty into force by the executive action required by national law, is the treaty binding upon the other party? See Factor v. Laubenheimer, above, p. 393.

GEOFROY v. RIGGS.

United States, Supreme Court, 1890.

133 U. S. 258. [33 L. ed. 642; 10 S. Ct. 295.]

On the 19th day of January, 1888, T. Lawrason Riggs, a citizen of the United States and a resident of the District of Columbia, died at Washington, intestate, seized in fee of real estate of great value in the District. The complainants are citizens and residents of France and nephews of the deceased. On the 12th of March, 1872, the sister of the deceased, then named Kate S. Riggs, intermarried with Louis de Geofroy, of France. She was at the time a resident of the District of Columbia and a citizen of the United States. He was then and always has been a citizen of France. The complainants are the children of this marriage, and are infants now residing with their father in France. One of them was born July 14, 1873, at Pekin, in China, whilst his father was the French minister plenipotentiary to that country, and was there only as such minister. The other was born October 18, 1875, at Cannes, in France. Their mother, who was a sister of all the defendants except Medora, wife of the defendant E. Francis Riggs, died February 7, 1881. The deceased, T. Lawrason Riggs, left one brother, E. Francis Riggs, and three sisters, Alice L. Riggs, Jane A. Riggs and Cecilia Howard, surviving him, but no descendants of any deceased brother or deceased sister, except the complainants.

The defendants, with the exception of Cecilia Howard, are, and always have been, citizens of the United States and residents of the District of Columbia. Cecilia Howard, in 1867, intermarried with Henry Howard, a British subject, and since that time has resided with him in England.

The real property described in the bill of complaint cannot be divided without actual loss and injury, and the interest of the complainants, if they have any, as well as of the defendants, in the property, would be promoted by its sale and a division of the proceeds.

To the bill of complaint setting up these facts and praying a sale of the premises described and a division of the proceeds among the parties to the suit according to their respective rights and interests, the defendants demurred, on the ground that the complainants were incapable of inheriting from their uncle any interest in the real estate. The Supreme Court of the District of Columbia sustained the demurrer and dismissed the bill. From the decree the case is brought to this court on appeal. . . .

Mr. Justice Field, after stating the case, delivered the opinion of the court. . . .

The question presented for solution, therefore, is whether the complainants, being citizens and residents of France, inherit an interest in the real estate in the District of Columbia of which their uncle, a citizen of the United States and a resident of the District, died seized. In more general terms the question is: can citizens of France take land in the District of Columbia by descent from citizens of the United States?

The complainants contend that they inherit an estate in the property described, by force of the stipulation of article 7 of the convention between the United States and France, concluded February 23, 1853, and the provisions of the act of Congress of March 3, 1887, to restrict the ownership of real estate in the Territories to American citizens. . . .

That the treaty power of the United States extends to all proper subjects of negotiation between our government and the governments of other nations, is clear. It is also clear that the protection which should be afforded to the citizens of one country owning property in another, and the manner in which that property may be transferred, devised or inherited, are fitting subjects for such negotiation and of regulation by mutual stipulations between the two countries. As commercial intercourse increases between different countries the residence of citizens of one country within the territory of the other naturally follows, and the removal of their disability from alienage to hold, transfer and inherit property in such cases tends to promote amicable relations. Such removal has been within the present century the frequent subject of treaty arrangement. The treaty power, as expressed in the Constitution, is in terms unlimited except by those restraints which are found in that instrument against the action of the government or of its departments, and those arising from the nature of the government itself and of that of the States. It would not be contended that it extends so far as to authorize what the Constitution forbids, or a change in the character of the government or in that of one of the States, or a cession of any portion of the territory of the latter, without its consent. Fort Leavenworth Railroad Co. v. Lowe, 114 U. S. 525, 541. But with these exceptions, it is not perceived that there is any limit to the questions which can be adjusted touching any matter which is properly the subject of negotiation with a foreign country. Ware v. Hylton, 3 Dall. 199; Chirac v. Chirac, 2 Wheat. 259; Hauenstein v. Lynham, 100 U. S. 483; 8 Opinions Attys. Gen. 417; The People v. Gerke, 5 California, 381. . . .

The seventh article of that Convention [of 1853] is as follows:

"In all the States of the Union, whose existing laws permit it, so long and to the same extent as the said laws shall remain in force, Frenchmen shall enjoy the right of possessing personal and real property by the same title and in the same manner as the citizens of the United States. They shall be free to dispose of it as they may please, either gratuitously or for value received, by donation, testament, or otherwise, just as those citizens themselves; and in no case shall they be subjected to taxes on transfer, inheritance, or any others different from those paid by the latter, or to taxes which shall not be equally imposed.

"As to the States of the Union, by whose existing laws aliens are not permitted to hold real estate, the President engages to recommend to them the passage of such laws as may be necessary for the purpose of conferring this right.

"In like manner, but with the reservation of the ulterior right of establishing reciprocity in regard to possession and inheritance, the government of France accords to the citizens of the United States the same rights within its territory in respect to real and personal property, and to inheritance, as are enjoyed there by its own citizens." 10 Stat. 996.

This article is not happily drawn. It leaves in doubt what is meant by "States of the Union." Ordinarily these terms would be held to apply to those political communities exercising various attributes of sovereignty which compose the United States, as distinguished from the organized municipalities known as Territories and the District of Columbia. And yet separate communities, with an independent local government, are often described as states, though the extent of their political sovereignty be limited by relations to a more general government or to other countries. Halleck on Int. Law, c. 3, §§ 5, 6, 7. The term is used in general jurisprudence and by writers on public law as denoting organized political societies with an established government. Within this definition the District of Columbia, under the government of the United States, is as much a State as any of those political communities which compose the United States. Were there no other territory under the government of the United States, it would not be questioned that the District of Columbia would be a State within the meaning of international law; and it is not perceived that it is any less a State within that meaning because other States and other territory are also under the same government. In Hepburn v. Ellzey, 2 Cranch, 445, 452, the question arose whether a resident and a citizen of the District of Columbia could sue a citizen of Virginia in the Circuit Court of the United States. The court, by Chief Justice Marshall, in deciding the question, conceded that the District of Columbia was a distinct political society, and therefore a State according to the definition of writers on general law; but held that the act of Congress in providing for controversies between citizens of different States in the Circuit Courts, referred to that term as used in the Constitution, and therefore to one of the States composing the United States. A similar concession, that the District of Columbia, being a separate political community, is, in a certain sense, a State, is made by this court in the recent case of Metropolitan Railroad Co. v. District of Columbia, 132 U. S. 1, 9, decided at the present term.

Aside from the question in which of these significations the terms are used in the convention of 1853, we think the construction of article 7 is free from difficulty. In some States aliens were permitted to hold real estate, but not to take by inheritance. To this right to hold real estate in some States reference is had by the words "permit it" in the first clause, and it is alluded to in the second clause as not permitted in others. This will be manifest if we read the second clause before the first. This construction, as well observed by counsel, gives consistency and harmony to all the provisions of the article, and comports with its character as an agreement intended to confer reciprocal rights on the citizens of each country with respect to property held by them within the territory of the other. To construe the first clause as providing that Frenchmen shall enjoy the right of possessing personal and real property by the same title and in the same manner as citizens of the United States, in States, so long as their laws permit such enjoyment, is to give a meaning to the article by which nothing is conferred not already possessed, and leaves no adequate reason for the concession by France of rights to citizens of the United States, made in the third clause. We do not think this construction admissible. It is a rule, in construing treaties as well as laws, to give a sensible meaning to all their provisions if that be practicable. "The interpretation, therefore," says Vattel, "which would render a treaty null and inefficient cannot be admitted;" and again, "it ought to be interpreted in such a manner as that it may have its effect, and not prove vain and nugatory." Vattel, Book II, c. 17. As we read the article it declares that in all the States of the Union by whose laws aliens are permitted to hold real estate, so long as such laws remain in force, Frenchmen shall enjoy the right of possessing personal and real property by the same title and in the same manner as citizens of the United States. They shall be free to dispose of it as they may please—by donation, testament, or otherwise—just as those citizens themselves. But as to the States by whose existing laws aliens are not permitted to hold real estate, the treaty engages that the President shall recommend to them the passage of such laws as may be necessary for the purpose of conferring that right.

In determining the question in what sense the terms "States of the Union" are used, it is to be borne in mind that the laws of the District and of some of the Territories, existing at the time the convention was concluded in 1853, allowed aliens to hold real estate. If, therefore, these terms are held to exclude those political communities, our government is placed in a very inconsistent position—stipulating that citizens of France shall enjoy the right of holding, disposing of, and inheriting, in like manner as citizens of the United States, property, real and personal, in those States whose laws permit aliens to hold real estate; that is, that in those States citizens of France, in holding, disposing of, and inheriting property, shall be free from the disability of alienage; and, in order that they may in like manner be free from such disability in those States whose existing laws do not permit aliens to hold real estate, engaging that the President shall recommend the passage of laws conferring that right; while, at the same time, refusing to citizens of France holding property in the District and in some of the Territories, where the power of the United States is in that respect unlimited, a like release from the

disability of alienage, thus discriminating against them in favor of
citizens of France holding property in States having similar legislation.
No plausible motive can be assigned for such discrimination.   A right
which the government of the United States apparently desires that
citizens of France should enjoy in all the States, it would hardly refuse
to them in the District embracing its capital, or in any of its own territorial dependencies.   By the last clause of the article the government
of France accords to the citizens of the United States the same rights
within its territory in respect to real and personal property and to
inheritance as are enjoyed there by its own citizens.   There is no limitation as to the territory of France in which the right of inheritance is
conceded.   And it declares that this right is given in like manner as the
right is given by the government of the United States to citizens of
France.   To ensure reciprocity in the terms of the treaty, it would be
necessary to hold that by "States of the Union" is meant all the political
communities exercising legislative powers in the country, embracing
not only those political communities which constitute the United States,
but also those communities which constitute the political bodies known
as Territories and the District of Columbia.   It is a general principle of
construction with respect to treaties that they shall be liberally construed, so as to carry out the apparent intention of the parties to secure
equality and reciprocity between them.   As they are contracts between
independent nations, in their construction words are to be taken in their
ordinary meaning, as understood in the public law of nations, and not
in any artificial or special sense impressed upon them by local law, unless
such restricted sense is clearly intended.   And it has been held by this
court that where a treaty admits of two constructions, one restrictive
of rights that may be claimed under it and the other favorable to them,
the latter is to be preferred.   Hauenstein v. Lynham, 100 U. S. 483, 487.
The stipulation that the government of France in like manner accords
to the citizens of the United States the same rights within its territory
in respect to real and personal property and inheritance as are enjoyed
there by its own citizens, indicates that that government considered
that similar rights were extended to its citizens within the territory of
the United States, whatever the designation given to their different
political communities.

We are, therefore, of opinion that this is the meaning of the article
in question—that there shall be reciprocity in respect to the acquisition
and inheritance of property in one country by the citizens of the
other, that is, in all political communities in the United States where
legislation permits aliens to hold real estate, the disability of Frenchmen
from alienage in disposing and inheriting property, real and personal, is
removed, and the same right, of disposition and inheritance of property,
in France, is accorded to citizens of the United States, as are there
enjoyed by its own citizens.   This construction finds support in the

first section of the act of March 3d, 1887. 24 Stat. 476, c. 340. That section declares that it shall be unlawful for any person or persons not citizens of the United States, or who have not declared their intention to become citizens, to thereafter acquire, hold or own real estate, or any interest therein, in any of the Territories of the United States or in the District of Columbia, except such as may be acquired by inheritance or in good faith in the ordinary course of justice in the collection of debts previously created. There is here a plain implication that property in the District of Columbia and in the Territories may be acquired by aliens by inheritance under existing laws; and no property could be acquired by them in the District by inheritance except by virtue of the law of Maryland as it existed when adopted by the United States during the existence of the convention of 1800 or under the 7th article of the convention of 1853. Our conclusion is, that the complainants are entitled to take by inheritance an interest in the real property in the District of Columbia of which their uncle died seized. The decree of the court below will, therefore, be reversed and the cause remanded, with direction to overrule the demurrer of the defendants; and it is so ordered.

ASAKURA v. CITY OF SEATTLE ET AL.

United States, Supreme Court, 1924.

265 U. S. 332. [68 L. ed. 1041; 44 S. Ct. 515.]

Error to a decree of the Supreme Court of Washington which sustained an ordinance of the City of Seattle restricting the business of pawnbroking, in a suit brought by Asakura to prevent its enforcement. . . .

MR. JUSTICE BUTLER delivered the opinion of the Court.

Plaintiff in error is a subject of the Emperor of Japan, and, since 1904, has resided in Seattle, Washington. Since July, 1915, he has been engaged in business there as a pawnbroker. The city passed an ordinance, which took effect July 2, 1921, regulating the business of pawnbroker and repealing former ordinances on the same subject. It makes it unlawful for any person to engage in the business unless he shall have a license, and the ordinance provides "that no such license shall be granted unless the applicant be a citizen of the United States." Violations of the ordinance are punishable by fine or imprisonment or both. Plaintiff in error brought this suit in the Superior Court of King County, Washington, against the city, its Comptroller and its Chief of Police to restrain them from enforcing the ordinance against him. He attacked the ordinance on the ground that it violates the treaty between the United States and the Empire of Japan, proclaimed April 5, 1911, 37 Stat. 1504;

violates the constitution of the State of Washington, and also the due process and equal protection clauses of the Fourteenth Amendment of the Constitution of the United States. He declared his willingness to comply with any valid ordinance relating to the business of pawnbroker. It was shown that he had about $5,000 invested in his business, which would be broken up and destroyed by the enforcement of the ordinance. The Superior Court granted the relief prayed. On appeal, the Supreme Court of the State held the ordinance valid and reversed the decree. The case is here on writ of error under § 237 of the Judicial Code.

Does the ordinance violate the treaty? Plaintiff in error invokes and relies upon the following provisions: "The citizens or subjects of each of the High Contracting Parties shall have liberty to enter, travel and reside in the territories of the other to carry on trade, wholesale and retail, to own or lease and occupy houses, manufactories, warehouses and shops, to employ agents of their choice, to lease land for residential and commercial purposes, and generally to do anything incident to or necessary for trade upon the same terms as native citizens or subjects, submitting themselves to the laws and regulations there established. . . . The citizens or subjects of each . . . shall receive, in the territories of the other, the most constant protection and security for their persons and property, . . ."

A treaty made under the authority of the United States "shall be the supreme law of the land; and the judges in every State shall be bound thereby, any thing in the constitution or laws of any State to the contrary notwithstanding." Constitution, Art. VI, § 2.

The treaty-making power of the United States is not limited by any express provision of the Constitution, and, though it does not extend "so far as to authorize what the Constitution forbids," it does extend to all proper subjects of negotiation between our government and other nations. Geofroy v. Riggs, 133 U. S. 258, 266, 267; In re Ross, 140 U. S. 453, 463; Missouri v. Holland, 252 U. S. 416. The treaty was made to strengthen friendly relations between the two nations. As to the things covered by it, the provision quoted establishes the rule of equality between Japanese subjects while in this country and native citizens. Treaties for the protection of citizens of one country residing in the territory of another are numerous, and make for good understanding between nations. The treaty is binding within the State of Washington. Baldwin v. Franks, 120 U. S. 678, 682–683. The rule of equality established by it cannot be rendered nugatory in any part of the United States by municipal ordinances or state laws. It stands on the same footing of supremacy as do the provisions of the Constitution and laws of the United States. It operates of itself without the aid of any legislation, state or national; and it will be applied and given authoritative effect by the courts. Foster v. Neilson, 2 Pet. 253, 314; Head Money Cases, 112 U. S. 580, 598; Chew Heong v. United States, 112 U. S. 536, 540;

Whitney v. Robertson, 124 U. S. 190, 194; Maiorano v. Baltimore & Ohio R. R. Co., 213 U. S. 268, 272.

The purpose of the ordinance complained of is to regulate, not to prohibit, the business of pawnbroker. But it makes it impossible for aliens to carry on the business. It need not be considered whether the State, if it sees fit, may forbid and destroy the business generally. Such a law would apply equally to aliens and citizens, and no question of conflict with the treaty would arise. The grievance here alleged is that plaintiff in error, in violation of the treaty, is denied equal opportunity.

It remains to be considered whether the business of pawnbroker is "trade" within the meaning of the treaty. Treaties are to be construed in a broad and liberal spirit, and, when two constructions are possible, one restrictive of rights that may be claimed under it and the other favorable to them, the latter is to be preferred. Hauenstein v. Lynham, 100 U. S. 483, 487; Geofroy v. Riggs, *supra*, 271; Tucker v. Alexandroff, 183 U. S. 424, 437. The ordinance defines "pawnbroker" to "mean and include every person whose business or occupation (it) is to take and receive by way of pledge, pawn or exchange, goods, wares or merchandise, or any kind of personal property whatever, for the repayment or security of any money loaned thereon, or to loan money on deposit of personal property"; and defines "pawnshop" to "mean and include every place at which the business of pawnbroker is carried on." The language of the treaty is comprehensive. The phrase "to carry on trade" is broad. That it is not to be given a restricted meaning is plain. The clauses "to own or lease . . . shops, . . . to lease land for . . . commercial purposes, and generally to do anything incident to or necessary for trade," and "shall receive . . . the most constant protection and security for their . . . property . . . " all go to show the intention of the parties that the citizens or subjects of either shall have liberty in the territory of the other to engage in all kinds and classes of business that are or reasonably may be embraced within the meaning of the word "trade" as used in the treaty.

By definition contained in the ordinance, pawnbrokers are regarded as carrying on a "business." A feature of it is the lending of money upon the pledge or pawn of personal property which, in case of default, may be sold to pay the debt. While the amounts of the loans made in that business are relatively small and the character of property pledged as security is different, the transactions are similar to loans made by banks on collateral security. The business of lending money on portable securities has been carried on for centuries. In most of the countries of Europe, the pledge system is carried on by governmental agencies; in some of them the business is also carried on by private parties. In England, as in the United States, the private pledge system prevails. In this country, the practice of pledging personal property for loans dates back to early colonial times, and pawnshops have been regulated by state laws for more than a century. We have found no state legislation abolishing or forbidding the business. Most, if not all, of the States provide for licensing pawnbrokers and authorize regulation by municipalities. While regulation has been found necessary in the public interest, the business is not on that account to be excluded from the trade and commerce referred to in the treaty. Many worthy occupations and lines of legitimate business are regulated by state and federal laws for the protection of the public against fraudulent and dishonest practices. There is nothing in the character of the business of pawnbroker which requires it to be excluded from the field covered by the above quoted provision, and it must be held that such business is "trade" within the meaning of the treaty. The ordinance violates the treaty. The question in the present case relates solely to Japanese subjects who have been admitted to this country. We do not pass upon the right of admission or the construction of the treaty in this respect, as that question is not before us and would require consideration of other matters with which it is not now necessary to deal. We need not consider other grounds upon which the ordinance is attacked.

Decree reversed.

WHITNEY v. ROBERTSON.

United States, Supreme Court, 1888.

124 U. S. 190. [31 L. ed. 386; 8 S. Ct. 456.]

This was an action to recover back duties alleged to have been illegally exacted. Verdict for the defendant and judgment on the verdict. The plaintiffs sued out this writ of error.

MR. JUSTICE FIELD delivered the opinion of the court.

The plaintiffs are merchants, doing business in the city of New York, and in August, 1882, they imported a large quantity of "centrifugal and molasses sugars," the produce and manufacture of the island of San Domingo. These goods were similar in kind to sugars produced in the Hawaiian Islands, which are admitted free of duty under the treaty with the king of those islands, and the act of Congress, passed to carry the treaty into effect. They were duly entered at the custom house at the port of New York, the plaintiffs claiming that by the treaty with the republic of San Domingo the goods should be admitted on the same terms, that is, free of duty, as similar articles, the produce and manufacture of the Hawaiian Islands. The defendant, who was at the time collector of the port, refused to allow this claim, treated the goods as dutiable articles under the acts of Congress, and exacted duties on them to the amount of $21,936. The plaintiffs appealed from the collector's decision to the Secretary of the Treasury, by whom the appeal was denied. They then paid under protest the duties exacted, and brought the present action to recover the amount.

The complaint set forth the facts as to the importation of the goods, the claim of the plaintiffs that they should be admitted free of duty because like articles from the Hawaiian Islands were thus admitted, the refusal of the collector to allow the claim, the appeal from his decision to the Secretary of the Treasury and its denial by him, and the payment under protest of the duties exacted, and concluded with a prayer for judgment for the amount. The defendant demurred to the complaint, the demurrer was sustained, and final judgment was entered in his favor, to review which the case is brought here.

The treaty with the king of the Hawaiian Islands provides for the importation into the United States, free of duty, of various articles, the produce and manufacture of those islands, in consideration, among other things, of like exemption from duty, on the importation into that country, of sundry specified articles which are the produce and manufacture of the United States. 19 Stat. 625. The language of the first two articles of the treaty, which recite the reciprocal engagements of the two countries, declares that they are made in consideration "of the rights and privileges" and "as an equivalent therefor," which one concedes to the other.

The plaintiffs rely for a like exemption of the sugars imported by them from San Domingo upon the 9th article of the treaty with the Dominican Republic, which is as follows: "No higher or other duty shall be imposed on the importation into the United States of any article the growth, produce, or manufacture of the Dominican Republic, or of her fisheries; and no higher or other duty shall be imposed on the importation into the Dominican Republic of any article the growth, produce, or manufacture of the United States, or their fisheries, than are or shall be payable on the like articles the growth, produce, or manufacture of any other foreign country, or its fisheries." 15 Stat. 473, 478.

In Bartram v. Robertson, decided at the last term, (122 U. S. 116,) we held that brown and unrefined sugars, the produce and manufacture of the island of St. Croix, which is part of the dominions of the King of Denmark, were not exempt from duty by force of the treaty with that country, because similar goods from the Hawaiian Islands were thus exempt. The first article of the treaty with Denmark provided that the contracting parties should not grant "any particular favor" to other nations in respect to commerce and navigation, which should not immediately become common to the other party, who should "enjoy the same freely if the concession were freely made, and upon allowing the same compensation if the concession were conditional." 11 Stat. 719. The fourth article provided that no "higher or other duties" should be imposed by either party on the importation of any article which is its produce or manufacture, into the country of the other party, than is payable on like articles, being the produce or manufacture of any other foreign country. And we held in the case mentioned that "those stipulations, even if conceded to be self-executing by the way of a proviso or exception to the general law imposing the duties, do not cover concessions like those made to the Hawaiian Islands for a valuable consideration. They were pledges of the two contracting parties, the United States and the King of Denmark, to each other, that in the imposition of duties on goods imported into one of the countries which were the produce or manufacture of the other, there should be no discrimination against them in favor of goods of like character imported from any other country. They imposed an obligation upon both countries to avoid hostile legislation in that respect. But they were not intended to interfere with special arrangements with other countries founded upon a concession of special privileges."

The counsel for the plaintiffs meet this position by pointing to the omission in the treaty with the Republic of San Domingo of the provision as to free concessions, and concessions upon compensation, contending that the omission precludes any concession in respect of commerce and navigation by our government to another country, without that concession being at once extended to San Domingo. We do not think that the absence of this provision changes the obligations of the United States. The 9th article of the treaty with that republic, in the clause quoted, is substantially like the 4th article in the treaty with the King of Denmark. And as we said of the latter, we may say of the former, that it is a pledge of the contracting parties that there shall be no discriminating legislation against the importation of articles which are the growth, produce, or manufacture of their respective countries, in favor of articles of like character, imported from any other country. It has no greater extent. It was never designed to prevent special concessions, upon sufficient considerations, touching the importation of specific articles into the country of the other. It would require the clearest language to justify a conclusion that our government intended to preclude itself from such engagements with other countries, which might in the future be of the highest importance to its interests.

But, independently of considerations of this nature, there is another and complete answer to the pretensions of the plaintiffs. The act of Congress under which the duties were collected authorized their exaction. It is of general application, making no exception in favor of goods of any Country. It was passed after the treaty with the Dominican Republic, and, if there be any conflict between the stipulations of the treaty and the requirements of the law, the matter must control. A treaty is primarily a contract between two or more independent nations, and is so regarded by writers on public law. For the infraction of its provisions a remedy must be sought by the injured party through reclamations upon the other. When the stipulations are not self-executing they can only be enforced pursuant to legislation to carry them into effect, and such legislation is as much subject to modification and repeal by Congress as legislation upon any other subject. If the treaty contains stipulations which are self-executing, that is, require no legislation to make them operative, to that extent they have the force and effect of a legislative enactment. Congress may modify such provisions, so far as they bind the United States, or supersede them altogether. By the Constitution a treaty is placed on the same footing, and made of like obligation, with an act of legislation. Both are declared by that instrument to be the supreme law of the land, and no superior efficacy is given to either over the other. When the two relate to the same subject, the courts will always endeavor to construe them so as to give effect to both, if that can be done without violating the language of either; but if the two are inconsistent, the one last in date will control the other, provided always the stipulation of the treaty on the subject is self-executing. If the country with which the treaty is made is dissatisfied with the action of the legislative department, it may present its complaint to the executive head of the government, and take such other measures as it may deem essential for the protection of its interests. The courts can afford no redress. Whether the complaining nation has just cause of complaint, or our country was justified in its legislation, are not matters for judicial cognizance. . . .

It follows, therefore, that when a law is clear in its provisions, its validity cannot be assailed before the courts for want of conformity to stipulations of a previous treaty not already executed. Considerations of that character belong to another department of the government. The duty of the courts is to construe and give effect to the latest expression of the sovereign will. In Head Money Cases, 112 U. S. 580, it was objected to an act of Congress that it violated provisions contained in treaties with foreign nations, but the court replied that so far as the provisions of the act were in conflict with any treaty, they must prevail in all the courts of the country; and, after a full and elaborate consideration of the subject, it held that "so far as a treaty made by the United States with any foreign nation can be the subject of judicial cognizance in the courts of this country, it is subject to such acts as Congress may pass for its enforcement, modification, or repeal."

Judgment affirmed.

SANTOVINCENZO, CONSUL OF THE KINGDOM OF ITALY AT NEW YORK, v. EGAN, PUBLIC ADMINISTRATOR, ET AL.

United States, Supreme Court, 1931.

284 U. S. 30. [76 L. ed. 151; 52 S. Ct. 81.]

MR. CHIEF JUSTICE HUGHES delivered the opinion of the Court.

Antonio Comincio, a native of Italy, died intestate in New York City sometime prior to March 10, 1925, when letters of administration were issued to the respondent as Public Administrator by the Surrogates' Court of New York County. Upon the judicial settlement of the administrator's account, the appellant, the Consul General of Italy at New York, presented the claim that the decedent at the time of his death was a subject of the King of Italy and had left no heirs or next of kin, and that, under Article XVII. of the Consular Convention of 1878 between the United States and Italy, the petitioner was entitled to receive the net assets of the estate for distribution to the Kingdom of Italy. The Attorney General of New York contested the claim. The Surrogates' Court, finding that the domicile of the decedent was in New York City, decreed that the balance of the estate, amounting to $914.64, after payment of debts and the sums allowed as commissions and as expenses of administration, be paid into the treasury of New York City for the use and benefit of the unknown kin of the decedent. The decree was affirmed by the Appellate Division of the Supreme Court of the State, First Department, and both the Appellate Division and the Court of Appeals of the State denied leave to appeal to the latter court. The case may be regarded as properly here on certiorari. Jud. Code, § 237 (c), U. S. C., Tit. 28, § 344 (c).

There is no controversy as to the facts. The decedent was never naturalized, and at the time of his death was an Italian subject. He had lived in New York for many years, and the finding that the decedent was domiciled there is not open to question. Nor were any heirs or next of kin discovered. The testimony introduced on behalf of the Italian Consul General, which was undisputed, stated that the decedent had no relatives, and the decree of the Surrogate's Court recited that next of kin were unknown. The decree was made pursuant to chapter 230 of the Laws of New York of 1898. The Surrogate said in his opinion: "Pursuant to our statutes this amount would be directed in the decree to be paid into the city treasury of the City of New York to await ascertainment of the next of kin. Ultimately the amount would find its way into the treasury of the State of New York."

The provision of the Consular Convention between the United States and Italy, under which the claim of the Italian Consul General was made, provides (20 Stat. 725, 732):

"Article XVII. The respective Consuls General, Consuls, Vice-Consuls and Consular Agents, as likewise the Consular Chancellors, Secretaries, Clerks or Attachés, shall enjoy in both countries, all the rights, prerogatives, immunities and privileges which are or may hereafter be granted to the officers of the same grade, of the most favoured nation.''

Pursuant to this agreement, the Italian Consul General sought the application of article VI. of the Treaty between the United States and Persia of 1856 as follows (11 Stat. 709, 710):

''Article VI. In case of a citizen or subject of either of the contracting parties dying within the territories of the other, his effects shall be delivered up integrally to the family or partners in business of the deceased; and in case he has no relations or partners, his effects in either country shall be delivered up to the consul or agent of the nation of which the deceased was a subject or citizen, so that he may dispose of them in accordance with the laws of his country.''

This Treaty with Persia was terminated on May 10, 1928, but, as this was subsequent to the death of the Italian national whose estate is in question, the termination does not affect the present case. . . .

We are not here concerned with questions of mere administration, nor is it necessary to determine that the loose phrasing of the provisions of Article VI. precludes an appropriate local administration to protect the rights of creditors. Nor have we to deal with a case of testamentary disposition. In this instance there is no will, administration has been had, creditors have been paid, proper steps have been taken, without success, to discover kin of the decedent, and, assuming the absence of relatives, the question is one of escheat, that is, whether the net assets shall go to Italy or to the State of New York. The provision of Article VI. of the Treaty with Persia does not contain the qualifying words ''conformably with the laws of the country'' (where the death occurred) as in the case of the Treaty between the United States and the Argentine Confederation of 1853 (Art. IX. 10 Stat. 1001, 1009; Rocca v. Thompson, 223 U. S. 317, 326, 330, 332); or the phrase ''so far as the laws of each country will permit,'' as in the Consular Convention between the United States and Sweden of [June 1] 1910 (Art. XIV. 37 Stat. 1479, 1487, 1488; Rocca v. Thompson, supra; Matter of D'Adamo, 212 N. Y. 214, 222, 223, 106 N. E. 81). The omission from Article VI. of the Treaty with Persia of a clause of this sort, so frequently found in treaties of this class, must be regarded as deliberate. In the circumstances shown, it is plain that effect must be given to the requirement that the property of the decedent ''shall be delivered up to the consul or agent of the nation of which the deceased was a subject or citizen, so that he may dispose of them in accordance with the laws of his country,'' unless a different rule is to apply simply because the decedent was domiciled in the United States.

The language of the provision suggests no such distinction and, if it is to be maintained, it must be the result of construction based upon the supposed intention of the parties to establish an exception of which their words give no hint. In order to determine whether such a construction is admissible, regard should be had to the purpose of the Treaty and to the context of the provision in question. The Treaty belongs to a class of commercial treaties the chief purpose of which is to promote intercourse, which is facilitated by residence. Those citizens or subjects of one party who are permitted under the Treaty to reside in the territory of the other party are to enjoy, while they are such residents, certain stipulated rights and privileges. Whether there is domiciliary intent, or domicile is acquired in fact, is not made the test of the enjoyment of these rights and privileges. The words "citizens" and "subjects" are used in several articles of the Treaty with Persia and in no instance are they qualified by a distinction between residence and domicile. Thus, in Article III, we find the following provision (11 Stat. 709):

"Article III. The citizens and subjects of the two high contracting parties, travellers, merchants, manufacturers, and others, who may reside in the territory of either country, shall be respected and efficiently protected by the authorities of the country and their agents, and treated in all respects as the subjects and citizens of the most favored nation are treated." It would be wholly inadmissible to conclude that it was the intention that citizens of the United States, making their residence in Persia under this Treaty, would be denied the benefit of Article III in case they acquired a domicile in Persia. The provision contemplated residence, nothing is said to indicate that domicile is excluded, and the clear import of the provision is that, so long as they retained their status as citizens of the United States, they would be entitled to the guaranty of Article III. The same would be true of Persians permitted to reside here under the Treaty.

Again, the provisions of Article V. of the Treaty were of special importance, as they provided for extraterritorial jurisdiction of the United States in relation to the adjudication of disputes. It would thwart the major purpose of the Treaty to exclude from the important protection of these provisions citizens of the United States who might be domiciled in Persia. The test of the application of every paragraph of Article V. with respect both to citizens of the United States and to Persian subjects, clearly appears to be that of nationality, irrespective of the acquisition of a domicile as distinguished from residence.

We find no warrant for a more restricted interpretation of the words "a citizen or subject of either of the contracting parties" in Article VI. than that which must be given to the similar description of persons throughout the other articles of the Treaty. The same intention which made nationality, without limitation with respect to domicile, the criterion in the other provisions, dominates this provision. The provision of Article VI. is reciprocal. The property of a Persian subject dying within the United States, leaving no kin, is to be dealt with in the same manner as the property of a citizen of the United States dying in Persia in similar circumstances.

It is not necessary to invoke the familiar rule with respect to the liberal construction of treaties, as the instant case merely calls for a reading of the provision as to "citizens" and "subjects" according to its terms. There is no applicable principle which permits us to narrow them. As treaties are contracts between independent nations, their words are to be taken in their ordinary meaning "as understood in the public law of nations." Geofroy v. Riggs, 133 U. S. 258, 271. . . .

Our conclusion is that, by virtue of the most-favored-nation clause of Article XVII. of the Consular Convention between the United States and Italy of 1878, the Italian Consul General was entitled in the instant case, being that of the death of an Italian national in this country prior to the termination of the Treaty between the United States and Persia of 1856, to the benefit of Article VI. of that Treaty, and that the net assets of the decedent should be delivered to him accordingly.

The decree is reversed, and the cause is remanded for further proceedings not inconsistent with this opinion.

Reversed.

FRANCE ET AL. AND AUSTRIA:
AUSTRO-GERMAN CUSTOMS RÉGIME.

Permanent Court of International Justice, 1931.

Publications of the Court, Series A/B, No. 41.

[By the Court.] On May 19, 1931, the Council of the League of Nations adopted the following Resolution:

"The Council of the League of Nations has the honor to request the Permanent Court of International Justice to give an advisory opinion, in accordance with Article 14 of the Covenant, on the following question:

" 'Would a régime established between Germany and Austria on the basis and within the limits of the principles laid down by the Protocol of March 19th, 1931, the text of which is annexed to the present request, be compatible with Article 88 of the Treaty of Saint-Germain and with Protocol No. I signed at Geneva on October 4th, 1922?'

" 'The Council requests that the Permanent Court will be so good as to treat the present request for an advisory opinion as a matter of urgency. . . .' "

Austria, owing to her geographical position in central Europe and by reason of the profound political changes resulting from the late war, is a sensitive point in the European system. Her existence, as determined by the treaties of peace concluded after the war, is an essential feature of the existing political settlement which has laid down in Europe the consequences of the break-up of the Austro-Hungarian Monarchy.

It was in view of these circumstances that the Treaty of Peace concluded at Saint-Germain on September 10, 1919, provided as follows:

"Article 88.

"The independence of Austria is inalienable otherwise than with the consent of the Council of the League of Nations. Consequently, Austria undertakes in the absence of the consent of the said Council to abstain from any act which might directly or indirectly or by any means whatever compromise her independence, particularly, and until her admission to membership of the League of Nations, by participation in the affairs of another Power."

It was, more particularly, in view of the same circumstances that, when Austria was given the financial and economic assistance necessary to her independence, the Protocols of October 4, 1922, were drawn up and signed at Geneva, of which Protocol No. I runs as follows:

"Protocol No. I.

(Translation.)

DECLARATION

THE GOVERNMENT OF HIS BRITANNIC MAJESTY, THE GOVERNMENT OF THE FRENCH REPUBLIC, THE GOVERNMENT OF HIS MAJESTY THE KING OF ITALY, AND THE GOVERNMENT OF THE CZECHOSLOVAK REPUBLIC,
Of the one part,

At the moment of undertaking to assist Austria in her work of economic and financial reconstruction,

Acting solely in the interests of Austria and of the general peace, and in accordance with the obligations which they assumed when they agreed to become Members of the League of Nations,

Solemnly declare:

That they will respect the political independence, the territorial integrity and the sovereignty of Austria;

That they will not seek to obtain any special or exclusive economic or financial advantage calculated directly or indirectly to compromise that independence; . . .

THE GOVERNMENT OF THE FEDERAL REPUBLIC OF AUSTRIA,

Of the other part,

Undertakes, in accordance with the terms of Article 88 of the Treaty of Saint-Germain, not to alienate its independence; it will abstain from

any negotiations or from any economic or financial engagement calculated directly or indirectly to compromise this independence.

This undertaking shall not prevent Austria from maintaining, subject
to the provisions of the Treaty of Saint-Germain, her freedom in the
matter of customs tariffs and commercial or financial agreements, and,
in general, in all matters relating to her economic régime or her commercial relations, provided always that she shall not violate her economic
independence by granting to any State a special régime or exclusive
advantages calculated to threaten this independence.

The present Protocol shall remain open for signature by all the States
which desire to adhere to it. . . . ''

Spain and Belgium acceded to this Protocol.

It will be seen that these provisions, without imposing any absolute
veto upon Austria, simply require her to abstain or, in certain circumstances, to obtain the consent of the League of Nations.

By a Protocol drawn up at Vienna on March 19, 1931, Germany and
Austria agreed to conclude a treaty with a view to assimilating the
tariff and economic policies of the two countries on the basis and principles laid down in that Protocol, thereby resulting in the establishment
of a customs union régime.

. . . the Court has not to consider the conditions under which the
Austro-German customs union might receive the Council's consent. The
only question the Court has to settle is whether, from the point of view
of law, Austria could, without the consent of the Council, conclude with
Germany the customs union contemplated in the Vienna Protocol of
March 19, 1931, without committing an act which would be incompatible with the obligations she has assumed under the provisions quoted
above.

I.—Firstly, as regards the undertakings assumed by Austria in Article 88 of the treaty of Saint-Germain:

When—as had previously been provided in Article 80 of the Treaty
of Peace concluded with Germany on June 28, 1919—the Treaty of
Saint-Germain laid down that the independence of Austria was inalienable, except with the consent of the Council of the League of Nations,
that Treaty imposed upon Austria, who in principle has sovereign control over her own independence, an obligation not to alienate that independence, except with the consent of the Council of the League of
Nations.

If we consider the general observations at the beginning of the present
Opinion concerning Austria's present status, and irrespective of the
definition of the independence of States which may be given by legal
doctrine or may be adopted in particular instances in the practice of
States, the independence of Austria, according to Article 88 of the
Treaty of Saint-Germain, must be understood to mean the continued
existence of Austria within her present frontiers as a separate State

with sole right of decision in all matters economic, political, financial or other, with the result that that independence is violated, as soon as there is any violation thereof, either in the economic, political, or any other field, these different aspects of independence being in practice one and indivisible. . . .

By "alienation," as mentioned in Article 88, must be understood any voluntary act by the Austrian State which would cause it to lose its independence or which would modify its independence in that its sovereign will would be subordinated to the will of Another Power or particular group of Powers, or would even be replaced by such will.

. . . the undertaking given by Austria to abstain from "any act which might directly or indirectly or by any means whatever compromise her independence" can only be interpreted to refer to "any act calculated to endanger" that independence, in so far, of course, as can reasonably be foreseen.

An act calculated to endanger cannot be assimilated to the danger itself, still less to the consummation of that danger, any more than a threatened loss or risk can be assimilated to a loss or risk which actually materializes. . . .

II.—As regards the Protocol signed at Geneva on October 4, 1922, by Austria, France, Great Britain, Italy and Czechoslovakia, and subsequently acceded to by Belgium and Spain, it cannot be denied that, although it took the form of a declaration, Austria did assume thereby certain undertakings in the economic sphere. . . .

That Austria's undertakings in the 1922 Protocol fall within the scope of the obligations undertaken by her in Article 88 of the Treaty of Saint-Germain appears from the express or implied reference made to that provision in this Protocol.

Accordingly, the "economic independence" expressly mentioned in the last paragraph of Austria's undertakings in the 1922 Protocol refers in the economic sphere to "the independence of Austria" within the meaning of Article 88 of the Peace Treaty, so that, as has been shown, a violation of this "economic independence" would be a violation of "the independence of Austria."

Thus also the grant of a special régime or exclusive advantages calculated to threaten Austria's independence within the meaning of the last paragraph of the 1922 Protocol would be one of these acts which might compromise Austria's independence within the meaning of Article 88.

But this in no way prevents the undertakings assumed by Austria in a special and distinct instrument open to the accession of all Powers, whether signatory to the Peace Treaty or not, and to which in fact a Power non-signatory to the Peace Treaty (i. e. Spain) did accede, from possessing their own value and on that account a binding force complete in itself and capable of independent application. . . .

In sum, the provisions of the 1922 Protocol create for Austria under-takings obligatory in themselves, special undertakings from the economic standpoint, i. e. undertakings not only not to alienate her independence, but, from the special economic standpoint, undertakings to abstain from any negotiations or from any economic or financial engagement cal-culated directly or indirectly to compromise that independence and still more precisely and definitely, undertakings not to violate her economic independence by granting to any State a special régime or exclusive advantages calculated to threaten this independence.

III.—That being so, a consideration of the Austro-German Protocol of March 19, 1931, the full text of which is annexed hereto, leads to the following results.

By the Protocol of Vienna of 1931, the German and Austrian Govern-ments agreed to enter into negotiations for a treaty "to assimilate the tariff and economic policies of their respective countries" *(Angleichung der zoll—und handelspolitischen Verhältnisse)* on the basis and within the limits of the principles laid down in that Protocol (Preamble).

While declaring that the independence of the two States and full respect for their international engagements are to be completely main-tained (Art. I) both Governments undertook (Art. II) to agree on a tariff law and customs tariff which are to be put into force simulta-neously and concordantly in Germany and Austria and the technical execution of which shall be uniform, although each country will enforce its application by means of its own administration (Art. V), the cus-toms receipts being apportioned according to a quota to be fixed (Art. VI, No. 2).

As between Germany and Austria, export and import duties are in principle to be removed (Art. III). There will be, subject to inevi-table exceptions necessary for public health and security, no import, export or transit prohibitions (Art. VII, No. 1). As regards exchange of goods between the two countries, the turnover tax and commodities forming the subject of monopolies or excise duties will provisionally be regulated by agreement (Art. IV).

As regards the economic treaty régime, Article IX, while declaring that both Governments retain in principle *(grundsätzlich)* the right to conclude commercial treaties "on their own behalf," provides on the other hand that the German and Austrian Governments will see that the interests of the other Party are not violated in contravention of the tenor and purpose of the customs union treaty, i. e. the assimilation of the tariff and economic policies of both countries; the negotiations, Article IX continues, will, as far as possible, be conducted jointly and, notwithstanding that treaties are to be signed and ratified separately, exchanges of ratifications are to be simultaneous (Art. IX, Nos. 2 and 3).

From the point of view of form, therefore, Austria will certainly possess commercial treaties concluded, signed and ratified by herself.

But in reality, and without its being necessary to consider in this connection whether Article IX does or does not imply that there may be limitations other than those set out in nos. 2 and 3, to the right of concluding "treaties" on her own account, it will suffice to note the provisions for joint negotiations, for regard for the interests of the other Party, and the undertaking to the effect that one Party will not ratify without the other.

Lastly, the necessary consequence of this new economic treaty régime, will be the modification of Austria's existing treaty régime, which must of course be brought into accord with the projected customs union treaty (Art. X). . . .

Lastly, the treaty, which is to be concluded for an unspecified duration, may be denounced after three years; it may be denounced before the conclusion of this period, should either of the two countries consider that a decision of the arbitral committee infringes its vital economic interests (Art. XII, and Art. XI, No. 3).

IV.—It is not and cannot be denied that the régime thus established certainly fulfils "the requirements of a customs union: uniformity of customs law and customs tariff; unity of the customs frontiers and of the customs territory vis-a-vis third States; freedom from import and export duties in the exchange of goods between the partner States; apportionment of the duties collected according to a fixed quota" (Austrian Memorial, p. 4).

Properly speaking, what has to be considered here is not any particular provision of the Protocol of 1931, but rather the Protocol as a whole or, better still—to use the actual terms of the question put by the Council—"the régime" to be established on the basis of this Protocol.

It can scarcely be denied that the establishment of this régime does not in itself constitute an act alienating Austria's independence, for Austria does not thereby cease, within her own frontiers, to be a separate State, with its own government and administration; and, in view, if not of the reciprocity in law, though perhaps not in fact, implied by the projected treaty, at all events of the possibility of denouncing the treaty, it may be said that legally Austria retains the possibility of exercising her independence.

It may even be maintained, if regard be had to the terms of Article 88 of the Treaty of Peace, that since Austria's independence is not strictly speaking endangered, within the meaning of that article, there would not be, from the point of view of law, any inconsistency with that article.

On the other hand, it is difficult to deny that the projected régime of customs union constitutes a "special régime" and that it affords Germany, in relation to Austria, "advantages" which are withheld from third Powers.

It is useless to urge that the Austro-German Protocol of 1931 (Art. I, No. 2) provides that negotiations are to be entered into for a similar arrangement with any other country expressing a desire to that effect.

It is clear that the contingency does not affect the immediate result of the customs union as at present projected between Germany and Austria.

Finally, if the régime projected by the Austro-German Protocol of Vienna in 1931 be considered as a whole from the economic standpoint adopted by the Geneva Protocol of 1922, it is difficult to maintain that this régime is not calculated to threaten the economic independence of Austria and that it is, consequently, in accord with the undertakings specifically given by Austria in that Protocol with regard to her economic independence.

FOR THESE REASONS,

The Court,
by eight votes to seven,
is of opinion that:
A régime established between Germany and Austria, on the basis and within the limits of the principles laid down by the Protocol of March 19th, 1931, would not be compatible with Protocol No. I signed at Geneva on October 4th, 1922.

[Seven of the eight judges were also of the opinion that the proposed customs régime would also be incompatible with Article 88 of the Treaty of Saint-Germain. A separate concurring opinion was delivered by Judge Anzilotti. A joint dissenting opinion was delivered by the seven dissenting judges.] [1]

---

[1] SUPPLEMENTARY CASES. In Tucker v. Alexandroff, 183 U. S. 424 (1902), involving a writ of habeas corpus issued upon the petition of a Russian seaman, Alexandroff, alleging his unlawful detention in Philadelphia as a deserter from a Russian ship of war upon which he had "never set his foot" as a seaman, the Supreme Court, interpreting the treaty of 1832 between the United States and Russia held that a ship which had been launched but not as yet finally accepted or taken possession of by the Russian government was nevertheless a ship of war in the sense of the treaty and that Alexandroff was a deserter therefrom even though he had been merely detailed to the ship without actually going on board it as a seaman. "As treaties," said the court, "are solemn engagements entered into between independent nations for the common advancement of their interests and the interests of civilization, and as their main object is not only to avoid war and secure a lasting and perpetual peace, but to promote a friendly feeling between the people of the two countries, they should be interpreted in that broad and liberal spirit which is calculated to make for the existence of a perpetual amity, so far as it can be done without the sacrifice of individual rights or those principles of personal liberty which lie at the foundation of our jurisprudence."

In Nielsen v. Johnson, 279 U. S. 47 (1929), involving an inheritance tax imposed by the state of Iowa upon the estate of an alien resident who died intestate leaving as his sole heir at law his mother, a resident and citizen of

C. Termination of treaties.

International law recognizes a number of ways in which treaties once legally entered into may terminate or become extinct. Executed treaties terminate by the performance of the specific acts which their terms call for; again, when executory in character, they may terminate by agreement of the parties; in rare instances one party to a treaty may declare it terminated because of a change in the circumstances under which the treaty was entered into. Query, would the abrogation of a treaty by one party because of alleged violation by another party automatically put an end to any rights which individual nationals of the abrogating state might otherwise have enjoyed? [Hooper v. United States.]

WILLIAM R. HOOPER, ADMINISTRATOR, v. THE UNITED STATES.

United States, Court of Claims, 1887.

22 Court of Claims, 408.

[This claim was brought by representatives of the owners of an American schooner seized on the high sea by a French frigate, February 1, 1800, and condemned by a French prize court at L'Orient.]

DAVIS, J. This court has now delivered three opinions upon general issues raised in the French Spoliations Cases. The first related to the broad questions as to the validity, against France, of the claims as

---

Denmark, Nielsen being the administrator of the estate and Johnson the state treasurer, the Supreme Court held that the discriminatory tax of 10% placed upon inheritances by non-resident as against resident aliens was in violation of the treaty of 1857 with Denmark providing that no higher taxes should be levied upon the property of their respective citizens upon the removal of the same from their territories reciprocally than upon property when removed by a citizen. When the meaning of treaty provisions is uncertain, said the court, "recourse may be had to the negotiations and diplomatic correspondence of the contracting parties relating to the subject-matter and to their own practical construction of it."

In the Japanese House Tax Case, between France, Germany and Great Britain on the one hand and Japan on the other, Scott, Hague Court Reports, 77, involving the interpretation of the provisions of three separate treaties between Japan and the states in controversy providing that, with the abolition of their extraterritorial privileges and the incorporation of their several foreign settlements in Japan with the respective Japanese communes, "the existing leases in perpetuity under which property is now held in the said settlements shall be confirmed, and no conditions whatever other than those contained in such existing leases shall be imposed in respect of such property," the arbitration tribunal constituted under a compromis of 1902 held (1905) that the provisions of the treaties precluded the imposition of a tax upon houses and improvements as well as upon the unimproved land to which Japan sought to confine the exemption.

a class, and the resulting liability of the United States to the claimants; the second was directed more especially to forms of pleading, the value of evidence, and rights of insurers; while the third disposed of a motion made by the defendants for a rehearing of the general questions discussed in the first opinion. (Gray, administrator, v. United States, 21 C. Cls. 340; Holbrook, administrator, v. United States, 21 C. Cls. R., p. 334; Cushing, administrator, v. United States, *ante,* p. 1.)

A large number of cases have since been argued and submitted to the court, and certain general questions are found raised in many of them. Those questions we shall now proceed to discuss, as well as two points which were sent back by the court for further argument.

It is urged by the claimants that the treaties of 1778 remained in force, notwithstanding the abrogating act of July 7, 1798, until the final ratification of the treaty of 1800, and that these treaties prescribe the rule by which all the spoliation claims are to be measured. This position is denied by the government.

For the purpose of this branch of the case, the period of the spoliations may be divided into two parts—that prior to July 7, 1798, and that subsequent thereto and prior to the ratification of the treaty of 1800.

As to the first period, we find the position on both sides to have been consistent, which a few citations covering different years will clearly show. . . .

The treaties of 1778, particularly the treaty of commerce, which is the important one for our purposes, were in existence until the passage of the abrogating act. Whatever disputes occurred between this country and France during the disturbed period following the conclusion of the Jay Treaty arose from differences of interpretation of various clauses of the Franco-American Treaty, and on neither side do we find seriously advanced a contention that the treaties were not in existence and were not binding upon both nations. The United States distinctly urged their enduring force, while the French departed from this position only in this (if it be a departure), that the Jay Treaty introduced a modification into their treaty with us of which they were entitled to the benefit.

We are of opinion that the treaties of 1778, so far as they modified the law of nations, constituted the rule by which all differences between the two nations were to be measured after February 6, 1778, and before July 7, 1798.

As to the period after July 7, 1798:

On that date the abrogating act passed by the Congress was approved by the President and became a law within the jurisdiction of the Constitution; a law replacing to that extent the treaties, and binding upon all subordinate agents of the nation, including its courts, but not necessarily final as the annulment of an existing contract between two sovereign powers.

A treaty which on its face is of indefinite duration, and which contains no clause providing for its termination, may be annulled by one of the parties under certain circumstances. As between the nations it is in its nature a contract, and if the consideration fail, for example, or if its important provisions be broken by one party, the other may, at its option, declare it terminated. The United States have so held in regard to the Clayton-Bulwer Treaty, as to which Mr. Frelinghuysen, then Secretary of State, wrote Mr. Hall, minister in Central America (July 19, 1884):

"The Clayton-Bulwer Treaty was voidable at the option of the United States. This I think, has been demonstrated fully upon two grounds. First, that the consideration of the treaty having failed, its object never having been accomplished, the United States did not receive that for which they covenanted; and, second, that Great Britain has persistently violated her agreement not to colonize the Central American coast."

Here concur two clear reasons for annulment, failure of consideration and an active breach of contract.

Abrogation of a treaty may occur by change of circumstances, as:

"When a state of things which was the basis of the treaty, and one of its tacit conditions, no longer exists. In most of the old treaties were inserted the *clausula rebus sic stantibus,* by which the treaty might be construed as abrogated when material circumstances on which it rested changed. To work this effect it is not necessary that the facts alleged to have changed should be material conditions. It is enough if they were strong inducements to the party asking abrogation.

"The maxim *'Conventio omnis intelligitur rebus sic stantibus'* is held to apply to all cases in which the reason for a treaty has failed, or there has been such a change of circumstances as to make its performance impracticable except at an unreasonable sacrifice." Wharton's Com. Am. Law, § 161.

"Treaties, like other contracts, are violated when one party neglects or refuses to do that which moved the other party to engage in the transaction. . . . When a treaty is violated by one party in one or more of its articles, the other can regard it as broken and demand redress, or can still require its observance." Woolsey, § 112.

The United States annulled, or.at least attempted to annul, the treaties with France upon the grounds, stated in the preamble of the statute, that the treaties had been repeatedly violated by France, that the claims of the United States for reparation of the injuries committed against them had been refused; that attempts to negotiate had been repelled with indignity and that there was still being pursued against this country a system of "predatory violence infracting the said treaties and hostile to the rights of a free and independent nation.'' Such were the charges upon which was based the enactment that ''the United States are of right freed and exonerated from the stipulations of the treaty and of the consular convention heretofore concluded between the United States and France, and that the same shall not henceforth be regarded as legally obligatory on the government or citizens of the United States.''

The treaties, therefore, ceased to be a part of the supreme law of the land, and when Chief Justice Marshall stated, in July, 1799 (Chirac v. Chirac, 2 Wheaton, 272), that there was no treaty in existence between the two nations, he meant only that within the jurisdiction of the Constitution the treaties had ceased to exist, and did not mean to decide, what it was exclusively within the power of the political branch of the government to decide, that, as a contract between two nations the treaties had ceased to exist by the act of one party, a result which the French ministers afterwards said could be reached only by a successful war.

The only question that we have now to consider is that of the international relation. The annulling act issued from competent authority and was the official act of the government of the United States. So far as it was in the power of one party to abrogate these treaties it was indisputably done by the act of July 7, 1798. Notwithstanding this statute, did not the treaties remain in effect to this extent, if no further, that they furnish a scale by which the acts of France, which we are charged to examine, are to be weighed; and in considering the legality of those acts are we not to follow the treaties where they vary the law of nations? The claimants in very learned and philosophical arguments contend for the affirmative. . . .

We are of the opinion that the circumstances justified the United States in annulling the treaties of 1778; that the act was a valid one, not only as a municipal statute, but as between the nations; and that thereafter the compacts were ended. We fail to find any agreement by France as to these claims to submit to the treaty rules after July 7, 1798, the treaties not being recognized by us, and we conclude that the validity of claims not expressly mentioned in the treaty of 1800, which arose after July 7, 1798, is to be ascertained by the principles of the law of nations, recognized at that time, and not by exceptional provisions found in the treaties of 1778. . . . [1]

---

[1] Supplementary Cases. The case between Belgium and China, Publications of the Court, Series A, No. 8, involved proceedings instituted by Belgium in 1926 under the Optional Clause of the Statute of the Permanent Court of International Justice, in which Belgium prayed for a judgment that the Chinese government was not entitled unilaterally to denounce a treaty of November 2, 1865, providing for extraterritorial privileges and other interests of Belgian nationals. The court issued an order providing for interim protection of Belgium's interests, but before jurisdiction could be further exercised the matter was diplomatically adjusted between the two countries.

CHAPTER XVI

AGENTS OF INTERNATIONAL INTERCOURSE [1]

A. Character of diplomatic agents.

The law regulating the character of diplomatic agents is one of the oldest branches of international law, with precedents reaching back into ancient Greece and Rome. Elaborate rules have developed regulating the extent to which states have a "right of representation," the classification of diplomatic agents, the formalities attending the appointment of particular agents, the credentials of their office and their reception by the foreign state. Query, in view of the peculiarly privileged position of diplomatic agents would the appointment of an agent in pursuance of a trade agreement be sufficient to confer upon him the status of diplomatic agent under circumstances where there was no regular representative? [Fenton Textile Association v. Krassin.] Special problems arise where there has been a change of governments and the new government has not been recognized by other states. Query, would the agent of a former *de jure* government continue to be regarded as the representative of his country until such time as the new *de facto* government has been recognized? [Lehigh Valley Railroad Co. v. State of Russia.]

FENTON TEXTILE ASSOCIATION, LTD., v. KRASSIN.

Great Britain, Court of Appeal, 1921.

38 Times Law Reports, 259.

This was an appeal by M. Krassin from an order of Mr. Justice Branson, dated August 2, 1921, allowing an appeal from the order of the Master. The action was brought by the plaintiffs against the defendants for £45,638 9s. 9d., the balance of the price of goods sold and delivered. The writ was issued and a conditional appearance entered by the defendant Krassin. On July 7, 1921, an application was made by Krassin to the Master in Chambers that service of the writ upon him be

---

[1] For a more detailed study of this subject, see Fenwick, *op. cit.*, pp. 360–387; Hyde, *op. cit.*, I, §§ 407–488; Oppenheim, *op. cit.*, I, §§ 358–442; Harvard Draft: Diplomatic Privileges, Consuls; Feller and Hudson, Diplomatic and Consular Laws and Regulations.

set aside on the ground that he was the authorized representative of a foreign State and was entitled as such to immunity from process.

On July 28, 1921, the master made an order that the service of the writ be set aside. The plaintiffs appealed to the Judge in Chambers, and on August 2, 1921, Mr. Justice Branson made an order allowing the appeal and extending the notice for the conditional appearance until the hearing of the appeal. The defendant Krassin appealed. . . .

Lord Justice Bankes said that M. Krassin had raised an important question, and it was desirable to obtain more evidence on the point raised. The Court proposed to communicate with the Foreign Office.
. . . .

At the adjourned hearing Mr. Leslie Scott said that their Lordships had been good enough to communicate to him the purport of the letter which they had received from the Foreign Office. That letter, which was written by Lord Curzon and was addressed to Lord Justice Bankes, read:

"I beg to acknowledge the receipt of your Lordship's letter of October 25, making certain inquiries with regard to the position of M. Krassin for the assistance of the Court in deciding the case of the Fenton Textile Association v. Krassin and Others. The specific questions which you ask me are:

"(1) Whether M. Krassin is received by his Majesty as chief assistant agent of the Soviet Government under the Trade Agreement for purposes other than the purposes of trade.

"(2) Whether M. Krassin since the date of the Trade Agreement was received by his Majesty as the representative of the Soviet Government in any capacity other than that of chief official agent under the Trade Agreement.

"(3) In reply, I beg to state that M. Krassin has not at any time been received by His Majesty. M. Krassin is present in this country in consequence of an agreement with the Soviet Government. It is not the practice of the Sovereign to receive the representative of States which have not been recognized *de jure*, and, further, quite apart from the question of M. Krassin's position, no representative of the Soviet Government would be received by his Majesty's Government because the Soviet Government has not been recognized *de jure* as a State.

"(4) Since the signature of the Russian Trade Agreement M. Krassin has been received by the officials of my department as the official agent of the Soviet Government under the provisions of article 5 of the Agreement for purposes covered by the agreement. This will, I think, give your Lordship the information in reply to your first question.

"(5) Apart from this, advantage has been taken of the presence of M. Krassin in London by the officials of this department, acting with my authority, on certain occasions, to discuss with him such questions as the repatriation of Russian refugees and the famine in Russia, and on one occasion during the temporary absence of M. Krassin his representative was invited to take part in the discussion at the Board of Trade on the subject of the credits required for famine relief. I trust that the above information may be sufficient for your Lordship's guidance.'' . . .

ATKIN, L. J. This action was commenced by writ dated June 23, 1921, in which the plaintiffs claim from the defendants, Leonid Krassin, the Russian Socialistic Federative Soviet Republic, and the All-Russian Cooperative Society, Limited, the sum of £45,638 9s. 9d., the balance of the price of goods sold and delivered. The Russian Government have not been served. The third-named defendants have been served and have appeared. The first-named defendant, M. Krassin, was served and thereupon applied to the Master to set aside the service of the writ upon him upon the ground that he is a public Minister of the Russian Government in this country and entitled to diplomatic immunity as such. The Master set aside the service of the writ, but on appeal Mr. Justice Branson reversed the Master's order. From that decision M. Krassin appeals.

In the view I take of the matter it is unnecessary to discuss the exact nature of the conditions which will entitle the agent of a foreign State to the diplomatic immunity which is given by the common law of this country in accordance with the usage of nations, and is confirmed by the Diplomatic Privileges Act 1708. The facts proved in this case do not bring M. Krassin within any definition of a diplomatic agent entitled to such privileges. At the time the writ was served M. Krassin was the chief official agent of the Russian Government appointed under clause 5 of the Trade Agreement made between that Government and the British Government and dated March 16, 1921. That agreement provides for certain rights and immunities being given to the official agents of either country in the territory of the other. It provides that the agents shall be exempted from all compulsory services whatsoever whether civil, naval, military, or other. Whether the immunity of official agents is subject to the qualification named in clause 4 "while sojourning therein for purposes of trade," I need not decide. I will assume that it is not. The agent is entitled to immunity from arrest and search; he has a right to couriers with sealed bags with, however, a limitation of 3 kilogrammes per week; and in this country he is to enjoy the same privileges in respect of taxation, central or local, as are accorded to the official representatives of other foreign governments. It is further provided that British official agents in Russia shall enjoy equivalent privileges which shall in no case be less than those accorded to the official agents of any other country. The duties of the official agents are not precisely defined, but I think that this is sufficiently indicated by the provision which entitles the agents to access to the authorities of the country in which they reside "for the purpose of facilitating the carrying out of this Agreement and of protecting the interests of their nationals," which, I think, must mean the interests in respect of the Trade Agreement. The Agreement provides for reciprocal rights of the agents of each contracting party in the territory of the other. I do not find it necessary to decide whether reciprocity is a condition of the grant of immunity, so that if the stipulated privileges are not given by the one party they could be withdrawn by the other, though at present I incline to that view. But it seems to me to be clear that in providing for the position of official agents under the Agreement the two contracting parties thought it advisable to try to remove the status of such agents from the realm of controversy, and for that purpose to provide for the exact degree of immunity that they should receive. In the provision made there is not included immunity from civil process other than arrest. It seems to follow that the parties did not intend their official agents to receive such immunity.

It was contended by the defendant that the British Legislature has made no provision exempting official agents from central or local taxation, and that the contracting parties must therefore have considered the official agents to be entitled to full diplomatic immunity, otherwise the provisions for such exemption are nugatory. It is a forcible argument, though we are not told whether the specified immunities are in practice withheld. On the other hand it is said for the plaintiffs that if the position of official agent was intended to be such as would give full diplomatic immunity there was no reason to make special provision for granting it in part. This is also a weighty argument, though possibly met by the special circumstances attending representation in Russia at the date of the Agreement. But it appears to me that even if the official agents when received in this country would, in the absence of agreement, have been entitled to full immunity, yet if the respective Governments by whom and to whom respectively they are sent choose to agree as to the precise immunity to be given them, such an agreement must prevail. I see no reason why Sovereign States should not come to an agreement as to the rights and duties of their respective envoys, ordinary or extraordinary, or why such agreements should not enlarge or restrict the immunities which otherwise would be due under the well established usage of nations. Here an agreement has been made clearly defining the status of the agents, and, as on ordinary principles of construction it clearly limits the immunity of the agent, such restricted immunity alone can be recognized by the municipal courts.

It was suggested, however, that the British Government recognized M. Krassin as a public Minister of his Government exercising functions outside those of an official agent under the Trade Agreement. I think that we must accept the facts as being those contained in the letter of the Secretary of State, dated November 7, 1921. I think the result of this is that the Government, having the chief official agent in this country, have taken the opportunity of discussing with him some questions outside the precise scope of the Agreement. I cannot think that this course can confer upon the official agent any different status or any larger immunity than he enjoys under the Agreement. Such a discussion might well take place between a foreign consul and the British or any other Government without conferring upon the consul the diplomatic immunity to which, as consul, he is not entitled. I think that Mr. Justice Branson's order was right and that this appeal should be dismissed.

[BANKES and SCRUTTON, L. JJ., concurred in separate judgments.]

LEHIGH VALLEY RAILROAD CO. v. STATE OF RUSSIA.

United States, Circuit Court of Appeals, Second Circuit, 1927.

21 F. (2d) 396.

In Error to the District Court of the United States for the Southern District of New York.

Action No. 1 by the State of Russia against the Lehigh Valley Railroad Company for breach of contract of carriage. Judgment for plaintiff. Defendant brings error. . . .

MANTON, Circuit Judge. The defendant in error has recovered a judgment against the plaintiff in error for loss of explosives and ammunition while in transit from the United States to Russia and while in its possession as carrier in its freight yards at Jersey City, N. J. The loss is due to a fire and explosion occurring July 30, 1916, and it is admitted that the fire was incendiary in its origin. The action by the defendant in error was instituted by the Russian government, and after the deposition of the then government of Russia, pursuant to an order granted, the action was continued in the name of the state of Russia.

Eight carloads of high explosives were on the same railroad siding, and, separated by a single car, on the same siding were seven cars of benzol and wet nitrocellulose; on an adjoining track were seven cars of ammunition of cannon. In the same vicinity were eight other cars of ammunition of cannon, two cars of combination fuses, and another car of benzol. A fire started in a car of ammunition prior to the first explosion, which occurred on a barge in the North River, which barge was also loaded with explosives, and then another explosion occurred in a car in the terminal. The barge was owned and operated by the Johnson Lighterage Company. After the fire started, no one, because of fear of the result that might follow from the explosive materials, attempted to put out the fire. Neither the railroad men, private detectives, nor the city firemen attempted to apply water or otherwise combat the fire, with one exception, a crew of the railroad men, who succeeded in removing some cars to a place of safety. Some lost their lives in this act. The railroad company failed to maintain a locomotive at the Black Tom Terminal, and the engine used in removing these cars was brought 2½ miles from Communipaw yards. At the time there was in force regulation No. 1906, which provided that in case of fire, to protect cars marked by placards "Inflammable," they should be quickly isolated. But in any case the explosions occurred before the engines arrived. Liability was imposed below because of the breach of the railroad's obligation as a common carrier, as supplemented by the Carmack Amendment (Comp. St. § 8604a [49 USCA § 20]), under the terms of the bills of lading issued. . . .

At the outset the railroad company attacks the right of the defendant in error to maintain the suit, and to do so in the courts of the United States. The right to recover damages for breach of this carrier's obligation became the property of the state of Russia on July 30, 1916, when the loss occurred. The government was then the Russian Imperial Government. The right of a foreign government to sue is now well recognized. Oetjen v. Central Leather Co., 246 U. S. 297, 38 S. Ct. 309, 62 L. Ed. 726; The Sapphire, 78 U. S. (11 Wall.) 164, 20 L. Ed. 127. It is equally a settled rule of law that the foreign relations of our government are committed by the Constitution to the executive and legislative departments of our government, and what is done by such departments is not subject to judicial inquiry or decision. In re Cooper, 143 U. S. 472, 12 S. Ct. 453, 36 L. Ed. 232; Williams v. Suffolk Ins. Co., 13 Pet. 420, 10 L. Ed. 226; United States v. Palmer, 3 Wheat. 610, 4 L. Ed. 471; The Penza (D. C.) 277 F. 91. Who may be the sovereign de jure or de facto of a territory is a political question; not judicial. Oetjen v. Central Leather Co., supra; Jones v. United States, 137 U. S. 212, 11 S. Ct. 80, 34 L. Ed. 691. The state is a community or assemblage of men, and the government the political agency through which it acts in international relations. State of Texas v. White, 7 Wall. 700, 19 L. Ed. 227; Cherokee Nation v. Georgia, 5 Pet. 52, 8 L. Ed. 25; Foulke, International Law, vol. 1, pp. 62, 82, 102, 192. The foreign state is the true or real owner of its property, and the agency the representative of the national sovereignty. The Sapphire, supra; The Rogdai (D. C.) 278 F. 294.

On July 5, 1917, Mr. Boris Bakhemeteff was recognized by our State Department as the accredited representative of the Russian government —the provisional Russian Government—as successor to the Imperial Russian Government. He continued as such until July 30, 1922. At that date he retired, and the custody of the property of the Russian government, for which Bakhemeteff was responsible, was recognized by the State Department to vest in Mr. Ughet, the financial attaché of the

Russian embassy. The Soviet government, which later secured control of the Russian government, was never recognized by our State Department, and ever since the diplomatic status with our government was never altered by the termination of the ambassador's duties. Therefore the provisional Russian Government is the last that has been recognized, and after its ambassador retired its property was considered by the State Department to vest in its financial attaché. Prior to his retirement, and while the accredited ambassador, Mr. Bakhemeteff authorized the suits here considered, which were commenced July 23, 1918.

Various preliminary attacks by motions to dismiss the complaint have been made, and the District Court has in each instance properly denied them, recognizing the principles of law referred to and their application to the fact that there has been no change recognized in the government or agency for Russia by the political branches of our government. Mr. Ughet, by the State Department's determination, is entitled to the custody in the United States of the property of Russia, and as part of that duty he was authorized to continue the suits for the state of Russia. This duty became obvious. It became important to avoid efforts to destroy the right of action as a basis of keeping its property, when motions to dismiss were made and delays occurred which would give rise to the bar of limitation to sue. The question of Mr. Ughet's power under his agency is generally important, because of the change in name of the plaintiff in the action to the state of Russia in substitution of the Imperial Russian Government. We must judicially recognize that the state of Russia survives.

Abatement of the action or a dismissal could only be sustained by reason of the nonexistence of the state, or the action of our government to no longer recognize the agency once accredited and never revoked. The action was properly started by an unquestioned agency. The attorneys and the agency thus employed were obliged to continue until some other government was recognized. It has been recognized that diplomatic agents of one state, while in another, may commence and maintain actions on behalf of their state while they are recognized as such. Republic of Mexico v. De Arangoiz, 12 N. Y. Super. Ct. 643. Proof of the agency or of the diplomat is dependent entirely upon the political fact of the recognition by the political department of the government. The courts may not independently make inquiry as to who should or should not be recognized. The argument of the plaintiff in error is directed entirely toward the court making its own investigation, in expectation that there would be some other government found, either de facto or de jure. This we may not do. Kennett v. Chambers, 14 How. 38, 14 L. Ed. 316; Agency of Canadian Car Co. v. American Can Co. (C. C. A.) 258 F. 363; 6 A. L. R. 1182; Russian Socialist Federated Republic v. Cibrario, 235 N. Y. 255, 139 N. E. 259. If it be a fact that there is a Russian Socialist Federated Republic now in charge of the government of Russia, it would bring no different result here.

Where there is a change of government, foreign states must of necessity judge for themselves whether they will continue their accustomed diplomatic relations with the prince whom they choose to regard as the legitimate sovereign. Wheaton on International Law, p. 332. It matters little whether the recognized state co-operates in it or not. Moore's Digest of International Law, vol. 1, p. 73. It is for the executive and legislative departments to say in what relations any other country stands toward it. Courts of justice cannot make the decision. Agency of Canadian Car Co. v. American Can Co., *supra;* Moore's International Law, vol. 1, p. 63. Nor does the personal withdrawal of an ambassador affect the relations with the government. Hyde, International Law, vol. 1, p. 731; Moore's Digest of International Law, vol. 4, p. 437. And, unless the political department of our government has decided otherwise, the judiciary recognizes the condition of things with respect to another country which once existed, and is still subsisting because of no other recognition. Phillips v. Payne, 92 U. S. 130, 23 L. Ed. 649; The Ambrose Light (D. C.) 25 F. 412.

"Changes in the government or the internal polity of a state do not as a rule affect its position in international law. A monarchy may be transformed into a republic, or a republic into a monarchy; absolute principles may be substituted for constitutional, or the reverse; but, though the government changes, the nation remains, with rights and obligations unimpaired." Moore, Digest International Law, vol. 1, p. 249.

The granting or refusal of recognition has nothing to do with the recognition of the state itself. If a foreign state refuses the recognition of a change in the form of government of an old state, this latter does not thereby lose its recognition as an international person. Oppenheim, International Law, p. 120; Moore, Digest of International Law, vol. 1, p. 298. The suit did not abate by the change in the form of government in Russia; the state is perpetual, and survives the form of its government. The Sapphire, *supra.* The recognized government may carry on the suit, at least until the new government becomes accredited here by recognition.

The argument that the plaintiff in error may at some future time, if the Soviet régime is recognized by our government, be compelled to pay again what it is obliged to pay now, is fallacious. It is only the acts performed in its own territory that can be validated by the retroactive effect of recognition. Acts theretofore performed outside its own territory cannot be validated by recognition. The former are illustrated in Underhill v. Hernandez, 168 U. S. 250, 18 S. Ct. 83, 42 L. Ed. 456, where the acts in question were performed in Venezuela; Oetjen v. Central Leather Co., *supra,* and Ricaud v. American Metal Co., 246 U. S. 304, 38 S. Ct.

312, 62 L. Ed. 733, where there were acts of confiscation in Mexico; and
the English case of Luther v. Sagor, [1921] 3 K. B. 532, acts performed
in Russia. The latter are illustrated by Kennett v. Chambers, *supra;*
U. S. v. Trumbull (D. C.) 48 F. 99; Agency of Canadian Car Co. v.
American Can Co., *supra.*

Following these principles, we agree with the contention of the defendant in error that the state of Russia, as a plaintiff, may continue the
prosecution through the agency vested in Mr. Ughet, and the plaintiff
in error will be protected as against any possible future claims of a subsequent recognized government of Russia, if payment be made as directed in this judgment. . . .

Judgment affirmed, with costs.

B. Privileges and immunities of diplomatic agents.

The privileges and immunities of diplomatic agents are so well established that few questions arise in connection with the head of the
diplomatic mission or his immediate subordinates. The old fiction of
the extraterritoriality of the embassy has given way to the more practical principle of recognizing certain definite exemptions belonging to
the diplomatic agent, based upon the necessity of securing to him the
fullest possible freedom in the discharge of his official duties. Query,
would a threat of violence offered to the secretary of a legation be
regarded as a more serious offense under the criminal law than a similar
threat offered to another person? [Respublica v. De Longchamps.]
May service of process be made upon the mere servant of a diplomatic
officer? [Heathfield v. Chilton.] What if a minister engages in business
activities? Would he be liable to suit in connection with his business
as distinct from his diplomatic functions? [Magdalena Steam Navigation Co. v. Martin.] Suppose a diplomatic agent on his way to or from
the country of his mission were to pass through a third state. Could
he be served with process in a civil suit in the courts of the third state?
[Holbrook, Nelson & Co. v. Henderson.]

RESPUBLICA v. DE LONGCHAMPS.

United States, Court of Oyer and Terminer at Philadelphia, 1784.

1 Dallas, 111.

Charles Julian De Longchamps, commonly called the Chevalier
De Longchamps, was indicted, that "he on the 17th of May, 1784, in
the dwelling-house of his Excellency the French Minister Plenipotentiary,
in the presence of Francis Barbe Marbois, unlawfully and insolently did

threaten and menace bodily harm and violence to the person of the said Francis Barbe Marbois, he being Consul General of France to the United States, Consul for the State of Pennsylvania, Secretary of the French Legation &c. resident in the house aforesaid, and under the protection of the law of nations and this Commonwealth.'' And that ''afterwards, to wit on the 19th of May in the public street &c. he the said Charles Julian De Longchamps unlawfully, premeditatedly and violently, in and upon the person of the said Francis Barbe Marbois under the protection of the laws of nations, and in the peace of this Commonwealth, then and there being, an assault did make, and him the said Francis Barbe Marbois unlawfully and violently did strike and otherwise &c. in violation of the laws of nations, against the peace and dignity of the United States and of the Commonwealth of Pennsylvania.''—To these charges the defendant pleaded *not guilty*.

The evidence, in support of the first Count, was, that on the 17th of May, De Longchamps went to the house of the Minister of France, and after some conversation with Monsieur Marbois, was heard to exclaim in a loud and menacing tone, *''Je vous deshonnerera, Poliçon, Coquin''*, addressing himself to that gentleman. That the noise being heard by the Minister, he repaired to the room from which it issued, and that in his presence the defendant repeated the insult offered to Monsieur Marbois in nearly the same terms.

In support of the second Count, it appeared, that De Longchamps and Monsieur Marbois, having met in Market Street, near the Coffee House, entered into a long conversation, in the course of which, the latter said that he would complain to the civil authority, and the former replied, ''you are a Blackguard.'' The witnesses generally deposed that De Longchamps struck the cane of Monsieur Marbois before that gentleman used any violent gestures, or even appeared incensed; but that as soon as the stroke was given, Monsieur Marbois employed his stick with great severity, till the spectators interfered and separated the parties. One of the witnesses, indeed, said, that previously to engaging with their canes, he observed the two gentlemen, at the same instant, lay their hands on each other's shoulders, in a manner so gentle, that he, who had heard it was customary among the French to part with mutual salutations, imagined a ceremony of that kind was about to take place, and was surprised to see De Longchamps step back, and strike the cane of Monsieur Marbois.

On the part of the defendant, evidence was produced of his having served with honour in the French armies, and his commission of Sub-Brigadier in the dragoons of Noailles, was read. It appeared that the occasion of his calling on Monsieur Marbois, was to obtain authentications of these, and some other papers relative to his family, his rank in France, and his military promotions, in order to refute several publications, which had been made in the news-papers, injurious to his character and pretensions. The refusal of Monsieur Marbois to grant the authentications required, was the ground of De Longchamps' resentment, and the immediate cause of his menaces at the Minister's house. . . .

The Jury, at first, found the defendant guilty of the Assault *only;* but, the Court desiring them to re-consider the matter, they returned with a verdict against him on both Counts. . . .

M'KEAN, Chief Justice.—Charles-Julian De Longchamps:—You have been indicted for unlawfully and violently threatening and menacing bodily harm and violence to the person of the honorable Francis-Barbe De Marbois, Secretary to the Legation from France, and Consul General of France to the United States of America, in the mansion-house of the Minister Plenipotentiary of France; and for an Assault and Battery committed upon the said Secretary and Consul, in a public street in the City of Philadelphia. To this Indictment you have pleaded, that you were not guilty, and for trial put yourself upon the country;—an unbiased Jury, upon a fair trial, and clear evidence, have found you guilty. . . .

The first crime in the indictment is an infraction of the law of Nations. This law, in its full extent, is part of the law of this State, and is to be collected from the *practice* of different Nations, and the *authority* of *writers.*

The *person* of a public minister is sacred and inviolable. Whoever offers any violence to him, not only affronts the Sovereign he represents, but also hurts the common safety and well-being of nations;—he is guilty of a crime against the whole world.

All the reasons, which establish the independency and inviolability of the *person* of a Minister, apply likewise to secure the immunities of his *house:* It is to be defended from all outrage; it is under a peculiar protection of the laws; to invade its freedom is a crime against the State and all other nations.

The *Comites* of a Minister, or those of his *train,* partake also of his inviolability. The independency of a Minister extends to all his household; *these* are so connected with him, that they enjoy his privileges and follow his fate. The Secretary to the Embassy has his commission from the Sovereign himself; he is the most distinguished character in the suite of a public Minister, and is in some instances considered as a kind of public Minister himself. Is it not then an extraordinary insult to use threats of bodily harm to his person in the domicil of the Minister Plenipotentiary? If this is tolerated, his freedom of conduct is taken away, the business of his Sovereign cannot be transacted, and his dignity and grandeur will be tarnished.

You then have been guilty of an atrocious violation of the law of nations; you have grossly insulted gentlemen, the peculiar objects of this law (gentlemen of amiable characters, and highly esteemed by the government of this State) in a most wanton and unprovoked manner: And it is now the interest as well as duty of the government, to animadvert upon your conduct with a becoming severity,—such a severity as may tend to reform yourself, to deter others from the commission of the like crime, preserve the honor of the State, and maintain peace with our great and good Ally, and the whole world.

A wrong opinion has been entertained concerning the conduct of Lord Chief Justice Holt and the Court of the King's-Bench in England, in the noted case of the Russian Ambassador. They detained the offenders, after conviction, in prison, from term to term, until the Czar Peter was satisfied, without ever proceeding to *judgment;* and from this it has been inferred, that the Court doubted, whether they could inflict *any punishment* for an infraction of the law of nations. But this was not the reason. The Court never doubted, that the law of nations formed a part of the law of England, and that a violation of this general law could be punished by them; but no punishment less than *death* would have been thought by the Czar an adequate reparation for the arrest of his Ambassador; *This* punishment they could not inflict, and such a sentence as they could have given, *He* might have thought a fresh insult. Another expedient was therefore fallen upon. However, the Princes of the world, at this day, are more enlightened, and do not require impracticable nor unreasonable reparations for injuries of this kind.

The second offence charged in the indictment, namely the Assault and Battery, needs no observations.

Upon the whole THE COURT, after a most attentive consideration of every circumstance in this case, do award, and direct me to pronounce the following sentence:—

That you pay a fine of one hundred French Crowns to the Commonwealth; that you be imprisoned until the 4th. day of July 1786, which will make a little more than two years imprisonment in the whole; that you then give good security to keep the peace, and be of good behaviour to all public Ministers, Secretaries to Embassies, and Consuls, as well as to all the liege people of Pennsylvania, for the space of seven years, by entering into a recognizance, yourself in a thousand pounds, and two securities in five hundred pounds each: that you pay the costs of this prosecution, and remain committed until this sentence be complied with.

HEATHFIELD v. CHILTON.

Great Britain, Court of King's Bench, 1767.

4 Burrow, 2015.

On showing cause why the defendant should not be discharged out of the custody of the marshal, (upon 7 Ann. c. 12) as a domestic servant to Paul Pierre Russell, minister from the Prince Bishop of Liege—he swore himself to be *bona fide English secretary* to him; and to have been *bona fide hired* by him as such; and to have *bona fide received wages* as they became due, at the rate of 30 l. per annum. Both the minister himself, and the relation of this man to him, were objected to.

But Chilton's own affidavit was positive, as to the service: and that it was real and not colourable; and it was confirmed by a Mr. Chamberlayne, who called himself Secretary. He also swore that he was not an object of the bankrupt laws. He had been house-steward to Lord Northington. No *certificate* was produced, under the hand and seal of the minister; though the present *application* was made (as the attorney alleged) on the *part* of the minister; nor was it sufficiently sworn that the defendant was in the service of the minister, *at the time* when he was arrested.

Lord Mansfield.—The privileges of public ministers and their retinue depend upon the law of *nations;* which is part of the common law of England. And the act of Parliament of 7 Ann. c. 12 did not *intend* to alter, nor *can* alter the law of nations. His Lordship recited the history of that act; and the occasion of it, and referred to the annals of that time. He said there is not one of the provisions in that act which is not warranted by the law of nations.

The law of nations will be carried as far in England as anywhere, because the Crown can do no particular favors, affecting the rights of suitors, in compliment to public ministers, or to satisfy their points of honor.

The law of nations, though it be liberal, yet does not give protections to screen persons who are not *bona fide* servants to public ministers, but only make use of that pretence in order to prevent their being liable to pay their just debts.

The law of nations does not take in consuls, or agents of commerce; though received *as such* by the courts to which they are employed. This was determined in Barbuit's Case in Canc. which was solemnly argued before and determined by Lord Talbot on considering and well-weighing Barbeyrac, Binkershoek [sic], Grotius, Wincquefort [sic] and all the foreign authorities: (for there is little said by our own writers on this subject.) In that case several curious questions were debated.

If I did not think there was enough in the present case, already appearing to the Court, to enable us to form an opinion, I should desire to know in what manner this minister was *accredited*. Certainly he is not an *ambassador;* which is the first rank. *Envoy*, indeed, is a second class; but he is not shown to be even an *envoy*. He is called *"Minister,"* it is true: but *Minister* (alone) is an equivocal term.

I find, this is not an application by the Attorney-General by the direction and at the expense of the Crown. That, indeed, would have shown that the Crown thought this person entitled to the character of a public minister. It now remains uncertain what his proper character is.

But *supposing* him to be a minister of such a kind as *intitles* him to privilege: yet I think this is *not a case* of privilege by the *law of nations:* for the defendant does not appear to have been in the service of the minister *at the time of the arrest.*

A public minister shall not *take* a man from the custody of the *law;* though the process of the law shall not take his menial servant out of his service.

Here, it is not sworn *when* the defendant came *into* the service. And upon the manner of swearing here used, the Court *must take it* ''That he was *not* in the minister's service at the time of the arrest.''

MR. JUSTICE YATES was not in Court.

MR. JUSTICE ASTON concurred. The rule laid down by Lord Mansfield is a very right one. The process of the law shall not, indeed, take a person *out* of the service of a public minister; but, on the other hand, a public minister cannot take a person out of the custody of the *law.* If a man has no such privilege *at the time* of his being arrested, no *subsequent* privilege can be given him, by being *afterwards* taken into the service of a public minister.

Therefore, as it does not appear here that the defendant was *then* in the service, he cannot be entitled to this privilege.

This is a true and right principle: and the establishing it may prevent many of these applications. . . .

Per cur. unanimously.

Rule discharged.

THE MAGDALENA STEAM NAVIGATION COMPANY v. MARTIN.

Great Britain, Court of Queen's Bench, 1859.

2 Ellis and Ellis, 94.

[The plaintiff company sued to recover from a shareholder the amount of a stock assessment levied upon the shares of a company in liquidation. The defendant, Martin, entered a plea to the jurisdiction of the Court on the ground that he was the public minister of a foreign state.]

LORD CAMPBELL, C. J. now delivered the judgment of the Court.

The question raised by this record is, whether the public minister of a foreign state, accredited to and received by Her Majesty, having no real property in England, and having done nothing to disentitle him to the privileges generally belonging to such public minister, may be sued, against his will, in the Courts of this country, for a debt, neither his person nor his goods being touched by the suit, while he remains such public minister. The defendant is accredited to and received by Her Majesty as Envoy Extraordinary and Minister Plenipotentiary for the Republics of Guatemala and New Granada respectively; and a writ has been sued out against him and served upon him, to recover an alleged debt, for the purpose of prosecuting this action to judgment against him whilst he continues such public minister. He says, by his plea to the jurisdiction of the Court, that, by reason of his privilege as such public minister, he ought not to be compelled to answer. We are of opinion that his plea is good, and that we are bound to give judgment in his favour. The great principle is to be found in Grotius *de Jure Belli et Pacis, lib.* 2, c. 18. s. 9., "Omnis coactio abesse a legato debet." He is to be left at liberty to devote himself body and soul to the business of his embassy. He does not owe even a temporary allegiance to the Sovereign to whom he is accredited, and he has at least as great privileges from suits as the Sovereign whom he represents. He is not supposed even to live within the territory of the Sovereign to whom he is accredited, and, if he has done nothing to forfeit or to waive his privilege, he is for all juridical purposes supposed still to be in his own country. For these reasons, the rule laid down by all jurists of authority who have written upon the subject is, that an ambassador is exempt from the jurisdiction of the Courts of the country in which he resides as ambassador. Whatever exceptions there may be, they acknowledge and prove this rule. The counsel for the plaintiffs, admitting that the person of an ambassador cannot be lawfully imprisoned in a suit, and that his goods cannot be taken in execution, contended that he might be cited and impleaded; and he referred to the decision of the tribunal at the Hague, in 1720, which is reported by Bynkershoek, and was the cause of that great jurist writing his valuable treatise *De Foro Legatorum.* But this case is to be found in chap. xiv., entitled "De Legato Mercatore," in which is explained the exception of an ambassador engaging in commerce for his private gain. The Envoy Extraordinary of the Duke of Holstein to the States General, leaving the Hague, where he ought to have resided, "Amsterdamum se confert, et strenuè mercatorem agit. Plurium debitor factus, Hagam revertitur, sed et plures curiam Hollandiæ adeunt, et impetrant mandatum arresti et in jus vocationis." The arrest was granted to operate on all goods, money and effects within the jurisdiction of the tribunal, with the exception of the movables, equipages and other things belonging to him in his character of ambassador. But this citation was entirely in respect of his having engaged in commerce, and shews that otherwise he would not have been subject to the jurisdiction of the Dutch Courts. Lord Coke's authority (4 Inst. 153) was cited, where, writing of the privileges of an ambassador, having said that "for any crime committed *contrà jus gentium,* as treason, felony, adultery, or any other crime which is against the law of nations, he loseth the privilege and dignity of an ambassador, as unworthy of so high a place," he adds, "and so of contracts that be good *jure gentium* he must answer here." There does not seem to be anything in the contract set out in this declaration contrary to the laws of nations; but Lord Coke, who is so great an authority as to our municipal law, is entitled to little respect as a general jurist.

Mr. Bovill, being driven from his supposition that the writ in this case might be sued out only to save the Statute of Limitations, by the fact that it had been served upon the defendant, and by the allegation in the plea that it was sued out for the purpose of prosecuting this action to judgment, strenuously maintained that at all events the action could be prosecuted to that stage, with a view to ascertain the amount of the debt, and to enable the plaintiffs to have execution on the judgment when the defendant may cease to be a public minister. But although this suggestion is thrown out in the discussion which took place in the Common Pleas, in Taylor v. Best [14 Com. B. 487. (per Maule, J.)], it is supported by no authority; the proceeding would be wholly anomalous; it violates the principle laid down by Grotius; it would produce the most serious inconvenience to the party sued; and it could hardly be of any benefit to the plaintiffs. In the first place, there is great difficulty in seeing how the writ can properly be served, for the ambassador's house is sacred, and is considered part of the territory of the sovereign he represents; nor could the ambassador be safely stopped in the street to receive the writ, as he may be proceeding to the Court of our Queen, or to negotiate the affairs of his Sovereign with one of her ministers. It is allowed that he would not be bound to answer interrogatories, or to obey a subpœna requiring him to be examined as a witness for the plaintiffs. But he must defend the action, which may be for a debt of 100,000 *l.*, or for a libel, or to recover damages for some gross fraud imputed to him. He must retain an attorney and counsel, and subpœna witnesses in his defence. The trial may last many days, and his personal attendance may be necessary to instruct his legal advisers. Can all this take place without "coactio" to the ambassador? Then, what benefit does it produce to the plaintiffs? There can be no execution upon it while the ambassador is accredited, nor even when he is recalled, if he only remains a reasonable time in this country after his recall. In countries where there may be a citation by seizure of goods, if an ambassador loses his privilege by engaging in commerce, he not only may be cited, but all his goods unconnected with his diplomatic functions may be arrested to force him to appear, and may afterwards, while he continues ambassador, be taken in execution on the judgment.

Reference was frequently made during the argument to stat. 7 Anne. c. 12.; but it can be of no service to the plaintiffs. The 1st and

3d sections are only declaratory of the law of nations, in conformity with what we have laid down; and the other sections, which regulate procedure, do not touch the extent of the immunity to which the ambassador is entitled. The Russian ambassador had been taken from his coach and imprisoned; but the statute cannot be considered as directed only against bailable process. The writs and processes described in the 3rd section are not to be confined to such as directly touch the person or goods of an ambassador, but extend to such as, in their usual consequences, would have this effect. At any rate, it never was intended by this statute to abridge the immunity which the law of nations gives to ambassadors, that they shall not be imputed in the Courts of the country to which they are accredited. . . .

Some inconveniences have been pointed out as arising from this doctrine, which, we think, need not be experienced. If the ambassador has contracted jointly with others, the objection that he is not joined as a defendant may be met by shewing that he is not liable to be sued. As to the difficulty of removing an ambassador from a house of which he unlawfully keeps possession, DeWicquefort, and other writers of authority on this subject, point out that in such cases there may be a specific remedy by injunction. Those who cannot safely trust to the honour of an ambassador, in supplying him with what he wants, may refuse to deal with him without a surety, who may be sued; and the resource is always open of making a complaint to the government by which the ambassador is accredited. Such inconveniences are trifling, compared with those which might arise were it to be held that all public ministers may be impleaded in our municipal Courts, and that judgment may be obtained against them in all actions, either *ex contractu* or *ex delicto*. It certainly has not hitherto been expressly decided that a public minister duly accredited to the Queen by a foreign state is privileged from all liability to be sued here in civil actions; but we think that this follows from well established principles, and we give judgment for the defendant.

Judgment for the defendant.

HOLBROOK, NELSON & CO. v. HENDERSON.

United States, Superior Court of City of New York, 1851.

4 Sandford, 619.

This was a motion to discharge the defendant from arrest, brought on at chambers, and by the direction of the judge sitting there, argued before the full bench. . . .

Oakley, J., delivered the decision of the court.

The defendant in this case is the ambassador of the Republic of Texas, sent by his government on a mission to the courts of France and England, and received and accredited as such at those courts. Having negotiated a treaty with France, he is now on his return to Texas, with the treaty, to lay it before the Congress of that country, now in session, for its ratification; and he has with him the regular credentials of his official station, which are to be considered as laid before us. On his arrival in this city he has been arrested and held to bail on civil process, issued out of this court, at the suit of the plaintiffs. It does not appear when or where the debt, on which the suit is founded, was contracted, nor is it necessary to inquire, according to the view I take of the case, any further than to infer, as I presume the fact is, that it has not been contracted since his late arrival in the United States.

Upon this state of the case, the question is submitted to us, whether the defendant is entitled to be discharged from this arrest, and whether the process against him ought to be set aside. The defendant contends that he is entitled to such discharge, because he is privileged from arrest, as an ambassador of a sovereign power, travelling through the country, in the execution of the duties assigned to him by his sovereign. On the other hand, it is contended, that such privilege applies only to an ambassador or public minister deputed to this country by a foreign state, and residing here as such.

It is not questioned that a resident minister, received and acknowledged by the executive of the United States, is not subject to the civil jurisdiction of our courts. It is clear that this privilege is founded, not on any municipal law of this country, but on the law of nations. The act of Congress of April, 1790 (which is in substance like the English act), cannot be construed as intended to confer this privilege. Its object is to enforce it, first, by declaring all process issued by any court against such minister void, and secondly, by inflicting punishment upon all persons who may be instrumental in violating the minister's privilege. . . .

Assuming, then, that the privileges of a foreign minister have their origin and support in the law of nations, it becomes necessary to inquire into the reasons on which that law is founded. They are, in substance, as I find them laid down in Vattel, that it is necessary for nations to treat with each other for the good of their affairs—that each has a right of free communication with others for that purpose—that such communication must, of necessity, be carried on by ministers or agents who are the representatives of their sovereign, and that each sovereign state has, therefore, a right to send and receive public ministers; that such being the rights of nations, a sovereign attempting to hinder another from sending or receiving a minister, does him an injury and offends against the law of nations. That, the minister representing the sovereign by whom he is deputed, the respect rendered to the minister is not personal, merely, but is, in truth, the respect due from one sovereign to another; and to withhold it is, therefore, an insult which may justly be resented, and thus the peace of nations may be endangered.

It is further laid down that the right of embassies being thus established, the inviolability of ambassadors is a certain consequence of that right, and is indispensable to the perfect enjoyment of it. That such inviolability may be complete, it is necessary that the ambassador should be free from the control or operation of the laws of the country to which he is sent, and from the jurisdiction of its courts, as without such freedom he might not be able to discharge his duty to his own sovereign with firmness and fidelity. It is further laid down that inasmuch as the minister is the representative of the dignity and independence of the sovereign, it is impossible to conceive that such sovereign in sending an ambassador intends to submit or subject him to the authority or jurisdiction of a foreign power.

Without dwelling further on this summary of the law of nations, relative to the rights and privileges of public ministers, it is sufficient to observe that the principles contained in it are not only obviously just, but that all the approved writers on international law, both before and since Vattel, concur fully with him as to their nature and extent.

Vattel, following out these principles, to what, I think, is their legitimate result, holds that an ambassador, passing through the territory of a friendly power, on a mission from his sovereign to another friendly power, is entitled to at least some of the rights and privileges of ambassadors. He says that, although the prince to whom the minister is sent, is under a particular obligation that he shall enjoy all the rights annexed to his character, yet others, through whose dominions he passes, are not to deny him those regards to which the minister of a sovereign is entitled, and which nations owe to each other. They especially owe him an entire safety. To insult him would be injuring his master, and the whole nation; to arrest him and offer violence to him, would be hurting the right of embassy which belongs to all sovereigns. According to Vattel's opinion, then, the principles of international law on which the rights and privileges of resident ministers rest, apply to a case like the one now before us, so far as to secure to the minister an entire personal safety, and freedom from arrest, and violence, or, in other words, from all restraint of his personal liberty, whereby he may be prevented from discharging his duties to his own sovereign.

This view of Vattel recommends itself very strongly to my judgment. It is founded in good sense and sound reason. It is difficult to designate any principle among those before stated, as sustaining the rights of a resident minister to be exempted from arrest or a restraint of his personal liberty, which does not apply to the case of one standing in the situation of this defendant. The ambassador of the republic of Texas, is travelling through our country, which is in amity with his own, in the actual discharge of a special duty, assigned to him by his sovereign. He is the representative of the dignity and independence of Texas as a sovereign state. Passing through our territory, on his route to his own country, to complete the mission with which he has been charged, he cannot be presumed to have laid aside his official character, and to have voluntarily submitted himself to the jurisdiction of our courts, as he could not do that without failing in his duty to his own sovereign. His arrest and detention, and perchance, his personal imprisonment for an indefinite period, might seriously interfere with the successful termination of his mission. The free right of embassy which Texas, in common with all other nations, enjoys, may thus be impaired, and she may feel that an insult has been offered to her dignity, and an injury to her rights, and thus a state of things may arise, which may endanger the national peace. It seems to me, that every principle of national courtesy, of a just observance of the rights and dignity of independent sovereign powers, and of a due regard to the preservation of public peace and of the maintenance of friendly intercourse with other nations, calls upon us to extend to the present case, the established rules of that law of nations, which, by the consent of all, secures the inviolability of a resident ambassador. The two cases seem to be equally within the reason of the law.

In thus adopting the doctrine of Vattel, I of course, have not overlooked the fact, that most, perhaps all the other writers on international law, to which we have been referred, have advanced different views. The most distinguished amongst them, Grotius and Wicquefort, unite in the opinion, that a public minister, passing through the territory of a third power, is not entitled to any privileges as such, and if my decision were to be governed by the mere weight of the opinions of learned men, I should probably arrive at a conclusion different from that which has resulted from my examination of the subject. But, as mere opinions, they do not address themselves to us with the authority of judicial decisions, and are to be regarded only as they seem consonant with sound reason. I am not satisfied with the grounds on which these writers sustain their opinions, or with the cases to which they refer for their support. Those cases cannot be considered, according to any reasonable view of the subject, as amounting to satisfactory evidence of the practice and usage of nations. The most that can be said of them is, that they are instances of violence, apparently acquiesced in, or to speak more properly, submitted to, in some cases after remonstrances against their legality, and, in all, from motives which cannot be known. They may have been motives of expediency merely, or motives springing from the necessary submission of the weak to the powerful. But in no case happening in times sufficiently modern to be entitled to respect as a precedent, do I find, that the violation of the person of an ambassador, travelling through the territory of a power at peace with his sovereign, has been acknowledged by that sovereign not to be a breach of the general law of nations. And after all, the practice of nations at a remote period, and the opinions of the old writers on national law, seem to me to be entitled of themselves to little weight with us. The law of nations, like other systems of law, is progressive. Its principles are expanded and liberalized by the spirit of the age and country in which we live. Cases, as they arise under it, must be brought to the test of enlightened reason and of liberal principles; and I should as soon think of going back to the times of the English star chamber, to search for the rules that ought to govern us in the protection of the personal liberty or rights of the private citizen, as of referring to the age of Charles V. or of Elizabeth, for the principles which ought to regulate the intercourse of nations.

It was urged, on the argument by the counsel for the plaintiffs, that the exemption claimed in this case could not rest on that necessity of preferring the free intercourse of nations, which alone can justify it, inasmuch as it was not necessary that the Texian ambassador should have entered our territory, on his return from Europe. And that therefore, his coming into our country was in fact voluntary, and a virtual submission, on his part, to the ordinary operation of our laws while within our borders.

It is true that the defendant might have returned to his own country without passing through ours; but we cannot but see that such a course would have been unusual, and probably highly inconvenient. He is returning by the ordinary and established route—that which, in practice, is adopted by almost all men, both public and private. There is at present little or no direct intercourse between Texas and Europe, and it would be treating the subject in a point of view altogether too narrow, to hold that the defendant, by adopting the ordinary and convenient mode of travelling to and from his place of destination, had thereby intended to abandon his official character, and to enter our territory as a mere private individual. It may happen, as in the case of some of the German states and of the Swiss Cantons, that a public minister, deputed to them, must, from absolute necessity, pass through the territory of a third power. In such a case, the refusal of a free passage through such territory would be a clear violation of that free right of embassy spoken of by Vattel. The obligation to permit such passage would therefore seem to be positive, and in the exercise of national courtesy it ought to be permitted by the usual and most convenient route. Any unnecessary impediment thrown in the way of the free passage of the minister impairs the right of embassy possessed by his sovereign. The same principle will justly apply to the case now before us. The right of free communication between nations, which has its foundation in public necessity, is in truth a right to be enjoyed according to a convenience exercised in good faith, and in reference to the usual and established modes of intercourse.

It was further contended on the argument, that the privilege claimed by the defendant is in conflict with the well-established right of every nation to exclude from its territories all persons at its pleasure. I do not consider it. Our government may undoubtedly, if it should see fit, send out of the country any resident minister. So may they do with the present defendant. They may direct him to leave our territory, but they cannot arrest and imprison him. In the one case he may return to his own country and complete the objects of his mission, in the other his mission would be interrupted, and, perchance, entirely defeated.

It is also contended, that before an ambassador, passing through our country, on a mission to another power, can claim an exemption from the ordinary operation of our laws, it should at least appear, that he had entered our territory by the permission of our government; and most of the writers on international law, who deny the right of a minister, in the situation of the present defendant, to the privilege claimed for him, seem to agree that if a minister thus situated obtain a passport or safe conduct, as such, from the sovereign of the territory through which he is about to pass, his right of protection by such sovereign becomes absolute. This must be so, according to every sound view of the case. If a sovereign invite or permit the representative of another power to enter his territory for any purpose, it is clear that he cannot, without a violation of all good faith, withhold from such representative all necessary protection. Now, may it not fairly be said that the present case falls within this principle? The practice of granting passports, or a safe conduct, to any person, except in time of war, is, as far as I am informed, unknown to our government. No man, I believe, being about to enter our country either to reside in it or pass through it, ever thinks of applying for permission to do so. Passports, though they may be named in our laws, are either entirely unknown in practice, or of extremely rare occurrence. The truth is, that every subject or citizen of a foreign power finds a passport for entrance into our country, in the nature and character of our political institutions. We hold out a standing invitation to all men to come freely among us, and it is doing no violence to good sense or sound reason to say, that foreigners enter our country, by, at least, the implied invitation of our government. The defendant, then, could not, in reason, be required to obtain any express consent of the government to come within our territory, in order that he might, when here, enjoy the privileges claimed by him as appertaining to his representative character; so long, at least, as that government permits him to remain.

In coming to the result at which I have arrived in this case, I have not considered, nor do I intend to say, what is the extent of the privileges which may be justly claimed by the defendant. It may be that many privileges clearly secured to a resident minister, as for example, those which refer to his domestic establishment, may not be necessary for the protection of a minister merely passing through the country, in the enjoyment of his personal freedom.

Nor do I intend to say whether the defendant may not, by his continuance in the country, or by his conduct while in it, divest himself of his representative character, so far as by his voluntary act to subject himself to the ordinary operation of our laws. These are questions not involved necessarily in the present inquiry.

I am of opinion, that the motion to set aside the process issued in this case and that the defendant be discharged, be granted. . . . [1]

---

[1] SUPPLEMENTARY CASES. Query, whether the fact that violence has been used by a public minister is justification for the issuance of a warrant of arrest? In United States v. Benner, 1 Baldwin 234, 24 Fed. Cas. 1084, No. 14,568 (1830), involving the indictment of a constable, Benner, who, under warrant of arrest issued by an alderman, arrested Louis Brandis, an attaché of the Danish legation, detained him and took him before the alderman to answer for a debt, the Supreme Court held that a certificate from the Secretary of State with respect to the public character of Mr. Brandis was conclusive evidence that he had been recognized by the President as such; further, that the arrest would not have been justified even if the defendant had as alleged, received a blow from Mr. Brandis. "But though the person of a minister is inviolable," said the court, "yet he is not exempted from the law of self-defense; if he unlawfully assaults another, the attack may be repelled by as much force as will prevent its continuance or repetition. The counsel for the defendant has endeavoured to bring his case within this principle, by evidence that he received a blow from Mr. Brandis; were the fact so, however, it would be no justification of the arrest on process, which is not a right of self-defense."

In Musurus Bey v. Gadban, [1894] 2 Q. B. 352, involving an action by the executor of a former ambassador from Turkey to Great Britain to recover money in the possession of Messrs. Gadban & Watson which the latter were holding as agent for the executor but which they refused to pay over until the satisfaction of a debt contracted by the ambassador in 1873, the Court of Appeal held that the debt of the ambassador was not barred by the Statute of Limitations since Gadban & Watson could not, during the residence of the ambassador in England, so much as sue out a writ of action against him even if it were not served, nor could they sue it during the two months of his stay in England after his recall or during the time of his subsequent residence in Turkey, so that their cause of action only arose when funds belonging to the estate of the ambassador happened to come into their possession after his death in 1890.

In the case of Parkinson v. Potter, 16 Q. B. Div. 152 (1885), involving the payment of parochial rates in England upon a house which had been sublet by Potter to an attaché of the Portuguese legation, the court held that the attaché was not liable to pay rates assessed upon him because of his occupation of the premises, with the result that since the landlord, Parkinson, was obliged under the law to pay them he might recover under his contract with Potter as the original lessee.

In Macartney v. Garbutt, 24 Q. B. Div. 368 (1890), involving a distress levied upon the furniture of a house in a claim for parochial rates, the court held that Macartney, although a British subject, was nevertheless entitled to share in the exemption of public ministers since he had been received by the Foreign Office as secretary to the Chinese Embassy in London without any reservation as to diplomatic privileges.

In Taylor v. Best, Drouet, Sperling and Clark, 14 C. B. Rep. 487 (1854), involving a suit by Taylor against the directors of a company, alleged to have been formed in Belgium, to recover money paid as a deposit on shares, the suit was allowed to go almost to trial, whereupon Drouet, after voluntarily submitting himself to the jurisdiction of the court, entered a motion to stay the proceedings, or to have his name stricken from them, on the ground that he was a public minister of the state of Belgium. The court held that while service of process could not have been made upon the minister against his will and a judgment could not be enforced against him, yet where he is sued as a joint-contractor and is a necessary party to an action to determine the liability of the other defendants proceedings will not be stayed where he has allowed the suit "to go on to an advanced stage without offering an objection, and where there does not appear to be any intention on the part of the plaintiff to interfere with either the person or the property of the ambassador."

By contrast, In re Republic of Bolivia Exploration Syndicate, Ltd., [1914] 1 Ch. 139, involving a summons by the liquidator issued against the directors of the company for damages for acts of misfeasance, one of the defendants, Lembcke, second secretary of the Peruvian legation, first entered an unconditional appearance, then swore an affidavit on the merits, stating his official position but not raising an objection to the jurisdiction, but at a later date insisted upon his diplomatic privilege, the objection to the jurisdiction being taken with the sanction and at the wish of the Peruvian legation. The Chancery Court, after a review of Taylor v. Best and other cases, held that the secretary had not by his earlier acts waived his privilege. "In the first place," said the court (Astbury, J.), "having regard to the earlier cases as to the absolute nullity of proceedings against foreign public ministers I am satisfied that waiver, if it be possible, must be strictly proved. It implies a knowledge of the rights waived, and I am not satisfied that R. E. Lembcke when he entered appearance and took the subsequent steps was aware of his privilege. Secondly, knowledge of our common and statute law cannot be imputed to a foreign subject residing here as diplomatic agent of a foreign State. Thirdly, I am far from satisfied that a subordinate secretary can effectually waive his privilege without the sanction of his Sovereign or Legation, and it is clear that, whatever knowledge R. E. Lembcke possessed, the objection on the ground of privilege is now taken with the sanction and at the instigation of the Peruvian Legation."

On the point whether a summons may be served upon a diplomatic officer of a foreign state when temporarily present in a third state en route to the state to which he is accredited, see also Wilson v. Blanco, 56 N. Y. Super. Ct. 582 (1889), involving a summons served in New York against Blanco, envoy from Venezuela to France, while he was temporarily in the city awaiting passage to France. A judgment was obtained against Blanco by default when he failed to put in appearance; but the higher court, citing Holbrook v. Henderson, granted a motion to vacate the judgment and set aside the service of summons. "The fact, rather suggested than positively averred in the complaint, that he was connected

C. Status of consuls.

Consuls, unlike diplomatic agents, do not "represent" their state before the foreign government but are merely custodians of certain domestic interests of their state which have been specially confided to them. Nevertheless, inasmuch as consuls are recognized by the foreign state as possessing an official character and are permitted by the foreign 'state to exercise official functions they have come to acquire a limited international status. Query, is the commercial agent of a foreign state entitled to exemption from civil suit? [Barbuit's Case.] Suppose a consul were actually performing the functions of a diplomatic agent although not formally appointed as such, would the exercise of such functions protect him from civil suit? [In re Baiz; Engelke v. Musmann.] Where the provisions of a consular convention grant a personal immunity to consuls in connection with official acts, would such immunity extend to acts associated with but not a necessary part of the official act? [Bigelow v. Princess Zizianoff.]

BARBUIT'S CASE.

Great Britain, Court of Chancery, 1737.

Williams, Cases in Equity during the Time of Lord Chancellor Talbot, 281.

Barbuit had a commission, as agent of commerce from the King of Prussia in Great Britain, in the year 1717, which was accepted here by the Lords Justices when the King was abroad. After the late King's demise his commission was not renewed until 1735, and then it was, and allowed in a proper manner; but with the recital of the powers given him in the commission, and allowing him as such. These commissions were directed generally to all the persons whom the same should concern and not to the King: and his business described in the commissions was, to do and execute what his Prussian Majesty should think fit to order with regard to his subjects trading in Great Britain; to present letters, memorials, and instruments concerning trade, to such persons, and at such places, as should be convenient, and to receive resolutions thereon; and thereby his Prussian Majesty required all persons to receive writings from his hands, and give him aid and assistance. Barbuit lived here near twenty years, and exercised the trade of a tallow-chandler, and claimed the privilege of an ambassador or foreign minister, to be free from arrests. After hearing counsel on this point,

---

as a partner in a mercantile business in New York," said the court, "is not material. It does not appear that the cause of action arose out of that mercantile relation, or business, or out of any contract or transaction which arose in the state of New York, or the United States."

LORD CHANCELLOR [TALBOT]. A bill was filed in this Court against
the defendant in 1725, upon which he exhibited his cross bill, stiling himself merchant. On the hearing of these causes the cross bill was dismissed; and in the other, an account decreed against the defendant. The
account being passed before the master, the defendant took exceptions
to the master's report, which were over-ruled; and then the defendant
was taken upon an attachment for non-payment, etc. And now, ten years
after the commencement of the suit, he insists he is a public minister, and
therefore all the proceedings against him null and void. Though this
is a very unfavourable case, yet if the defendant is truly a public minister, I think he may now insist upon it; for the privilege of a public
minister is to have his person sacred and free from arrests, not on his
own account, but on the account of those he represents, and this arises
from the necessity of the thing, that nations may have intercourse with
one another in the same manner as private persons, by agents, when they
cannot meet themselves. And if the foundation of this privilege is for
the sake of the prince by whom an ambassador is sent, and for sake of
the business he is to do, it is impossible that he can renounce such
privilege and protection: for, by his being thrown into prison the business must inevitably suffer. The question is, whether the defendant is
such a person as 7 Anne, cap. 10, describes, which is only declaratory
of the antient universal *jus gentium;* the words of the statute are
ambassadors or other public Ministers, and the exception of persons
trading relates only to their servants; the parliament never imagining
that the ministers themselves would trade. I do not think the words
ambassadors, or *other public ministers,* are synonymous. I think that
the word ambassadors in the act of parliament, was intended to signify
ministers sent upon extraordinary occasions, which are commonly called
ambassadors extraordinary; and *public ministers* in the act take in all
others who constantly reside here; and both are entitled to these privileges. The question is, whether the defendant is within the latter
words? It has been objected that he is not a public minister, because
he brings no credentials to the King. Now although it be true that this
is the most common form, yet it would be carrying it too far to say,
that these credentials are absolutely necessary; because all nations
have not the same forms of appointment. It has been said, that to
make him a public minister he must be employed about state affairs. In
which case, if state affairs are used in opposition to commerce, it is wrong:
but if only to signify the business between nation and nation the
proposition is right: for, trade is a matter of state, and of a public nature, and consequently a proper subject for the employment of an ambassador. In treaties of commerce those imployed are as much public
ministers as any others; and the reason for their protection holds as
strong: and it is of no weight with me that the defendant was not to
concern himself about other matters of state, if he was authorised as

a public minister to transact matters of trade. It is not necessary that a minister's commission should be general to intitle him to protection; but it is enough that he is to transact any one particular thing in that capacity, as every ambassador extraordinary is; or to remove some particular difficulties, which might otherwise occasion war. But what creates my difficulty is, that I do not think he is intrusted to transact affairs between the two crowns: the commission is, to assist his Prussian Majesty's subjects here in their commerce; and so is the allowance. Now this gives him no authority to intermeddle with the affairs of the King: which makes his employment to be in the nature of a consul. And although he is called only an agent of commerce, I do not think the name alters the case. Indeed there are some circumstances that put him below a consul; for, he wants the power of judicature, which is commonly given to consuls. Also their commission is usually directed to the prince of the country; which is not the present case: but at most he is only a consul.

It is the opinion of Barbeyrac, Wincquefort [sic] and others, that a consul is not intitled to the *Jus Gentium* belonging to ambassadors.

And as there is no authority to consider the defendant in any other view than as a consul, unless I can be satisfied that those acting in that capacity are intitled to the *Jus Gentium*, I cannot discharge him. . . .[1]

IN RE BAIZ, PETITIONER.

United States, Supreme Court, 1890.

135 U. S. 403. [34 L. ed. 222; 10 S. Ct. 854.]

[In answer to an action for libel brought against him in the United States District Court Jacob Baiz set up a plea to the jurisdiction alleging that in the absence of the Minister of the Republic of Guatemala, he was the acting minister of Guatemala and hence not within the jurisdiction of the court. Mr. Baiz was a citizen of the United States, and since 1887 had been Consul General of Guatemala in New York. In 1889, the Minister of Guatemala informed the Secretary of State that he was obliged to return to his home for a short time and said: "Meanwhile I beg your Excellency to please allow that the Consul General of Guatemala and Honduras in New York, Mr. Jacob Baiz, should communicate to the office of the Secretary of State any matter whatever relating to the peace of Central America, that should without delay be presented to the knowledge of your Excellency." Accordingly the Secretary of State informed Mr. Baiz, "Consul General of Guatemala

---

[1] Compare Triquet v. Bath, above, p. 31, which cites Buvot v. Barbuit as authority for the principle that international law is part of the law of the land.

and Honduras,'' that he would ''have pleasure in receiving any communication in relation to Central America, of which you may be made the channel, as intimated by Señor Lainfiesta.'' Upon the appointment of Mr. Blaine as Secretary of State official notice was sent to ''Señor Don Jacob Baiz, in charge of the legations of Guatemala, Salvador, and Honduras,'' who acknowledged receipt of the notice in a communication signed ''Jacob Baiz, Consul General.'' A month later, the Department of State addressed another communication to ''Señor Don Jacob Baiz, in charge of the business of the legations of Guatemala, Salvador and Honduras.'' In 1886 the Government of Honduras appointed Mr. Baiz to be its chargé d'affaires in the United States, but the Secretary of State declined to receive him in that capacity on the ground that it was contrary to American practice to recognize American citizens as the accredited diplomatic representatives of foreign powers. Later, when Mr. Baiz inquired whether he would be recognized as chargé d'affaires *ad hoc* or diplomatic agent of Honduras during the absence of the minister, the Secretary of State replied:

''. . . It is not the purpose of the Department to regard the substitutionary agency, which it cheerfully admits in your case, as conferring upon you personally any diplomatic status whatever. Your agency is admitted to be such only as is compatible with the continued existence of a vacancy in the diplomatic representation of Honduras in the United States. To recognize you as chargé d'affaires *ad hoc* would be to announce that the vacancy no longer existed, and that diplomatic representation was renewed in your person.

''It is a common thing to resort to a temporary agency, such as yours, in the conduct of the business of a mission. A foreign minister, on quitting the country, often leaves the affairs of his office in the friendly charge of the minister of another country, but the latter does not thereby become the diplomatic agent of the government in whose behalf he exerts his good offices. The relation established is merely one of courtesy and comity. The same thing occurs when the temporary good offices of a consul are resorted to. In neither case is a formal credence, *ad hoc* or *ad interim*, necessary.''

The District Court denied the defendant's motion to dismiss the suit for lack of jurisdiction; thereupon he made application to the Supreme Court for a rule to show cause why a writ of prohibition should not issue to the judge of the District Court prohibiting him from proceeding further in such action, or, in the alternative, for a writ of mandamus commanding the judge to enter an order dismissing the cause for the reason that the Supreme Court possessed sole jurisdiction thereof. A rule having issued to show cause, the judge of the District Court transmitted the record and opinion in the case and submitted to the Supreme Court whether he should take further cognizance of the case or should dismiss it.]

Mr. Chief Justice Fuller delivered the opinion of the court. . . .

Under section 2, Art. II, of the Constitution, the President is vested with power to "appoint ambassadors, other public ministers and consuls," and by section 3 it is provided that "he shall receive ambassadors and other public ministers."

These words are descriptive of a class existing by the law of nations, and apply to diplomatic agents whether accredited by the United States to a foreign power or by a foreign power to the United States, . . . These agents may be called ambassadors, envoys, ministers, commissioners, chargés d'affaires, agents, or otherwise, but they possess in substance the same functions, rights and privileges as agents of their respective governments for the transaction of its diplomatic business abroad. Their designations are chiefly significant in the relation of rank, precedence or dignity. 7 Opinions Atty. Gen. (Cushing), 186. . . .

But the scope of the words "public ministers" is defined in the legislation embodied in Title XLVII., "Foreign Relations," Rev. Stat., 2d ed. 783. Section 4062 provides that "every person who violates any safe conduct or passport duly obtained and issued under authority of the United States; or who assaults, strikes, wounds, imprisons or in any other manner offers violence to the person of a public minister, in violation of the law of nations, shall be imprisoned for not more than three years, and fined, at the discretion of the court." Section 4063 enacts that whenever any writ or process is sued out or prosecuted by any person in any court of the United States, or of a State, or by any judge or justice, whereby the person of any public minister of any foreign prince or state, authorized and received as such by the President, or any domestic or domestic servant of any such minister, is arrested or imprisoned, or his goods or chattels are distrained, seized or attached, such writ or process shall be deemed void. Section 4064 imposes penalties for suing out any writ or process in violation of the preceding section; and section 4065 says that the two preceding sections shall not apply to any case where the person against whom the process is issued is a citizen or inhabitant of the United States "in the service of a public minister," and process is founded upon a debt contracted before he entered upon such service; nor shall the preceding section apply to any case where the person against whom the process is issued is a "domestic servant of a public minister," unless the name of the servant has been registered and posted as therein prescribed.

Section 4130, which is the last section of the title, is as follows: "The word 'minister,' when used in this title, shall be understood to mean the person invested with, and exercising, the principal diplomatic functions. The word 'consul' shall be understood to mean any person invested by the United States with, and exercising, the functions of consul general, vice-consul general, consul or vice-consul." . . .

Was Consul General Baiz a person "invested with and exercising the principal diplomatic functions," within section 4130, or a "diplomatic officer," within section 1674? His counsel claim in their motion that he was "the acting minister or chargé d'affaires of the Republics of Guatemala, Salvador and Honduras in the United States," and so recognized by the State Department, and that he exercised diplomatic functions as such, and therefore was a public minister, within the statute.

By the Congresses of Vienna and Aix-la-Chapelle four distinct kinds of representation were recognized, of which the fourth comprised chargés d'affaires, who are appointed by the minister of foreign affairs, and not as the others, nominally or actually by the sovereign. Under the regulations of this Government the representatives of the United States have heretofore been ranked in three grades, the third being chargés d'affaires. Secretaries of legation act *ex officio* as chargés d'affaires *ad interim,* and in the absence of the secretary of legation the Secretary of State may designate any competent person to act *ad interim,* in which case he is specifically accredited by letter to the minister for foreign affairs. . . .

Diplomatic duties are sometimes imposed upon consuls, but only in virtue of the right of a government to designate those who shall represent it in the conduct of international affairs, 1 Calvo, Droit Int. 586, 2d ed., Paris, 1870, and among the numerous authorities on international laws, cited and quoted from by petitioner's counsel, the attitude of consuls, on whom this function is occasionally conferred, is perhaps as well put by De Clercq and De Vallat as by any, as follows:

"There remains a last consideration to notice, that of a consul who is charged for the time being with the management of the affairs of the diplomatic post; he is accredited in this case in his diplomatic capacity, either by a letter of the minister of foreign affairs of France to the minister of foreign affairs of the country where he is about to reside, or by a letter of the diplomatic agent whose place he is about to fill, or finally by a personal presentation of this agent to the minister of foreign affairs of the country." Guide Pratique des Consulats, Vol. I., p. 93.

That it may sometimes happen that consuls are so charged is recognized by section 1738 of the Revised Statutes, which provides:

"No consular officer shall exercise diplomatic functions, or hold any diplomatic correspondence or relation on the part of the United States, in, with, or to the government, or country to which he is appointed, or any other country or government when there is in such country any officer of the United States authorized to perform diplomatic functions therein; nor in any case, unless expressly authorized by the President so to do."

But in such case their consular character is necessarily subordinated to their superior diplomatic character. "A consul," observed Mr. Justice Story, in The Anne, 3 Wheat. 435, 445, "though a public agent, is supposed to be clothed with authority only for commercial purposes. He has an undoubted right to interpose claims for the restitution of property belonging to the subjects of his own country; but he is not considered as a minister, or diplomatic agent of his sovereign, intrusted by virtue of his office, with authority to represent him in his negotiations with foreign states, or to vindicate his prerogatives. There is no doubt that his sovereign may specially intrust him with such authority; but in such case his diplomatic character is superadded to his ordinary powers, and ought to be recognized by the government within whose dominions he assumes to exercise it."

When a consul is appointed chargé d'affaires, he has a double political capacity; but though invested with full diplomatic privileges, he becomes so invested as chargé d'affaires and not as consul, and though authorized as consul to communicate directly with the government in which he resides, he does not thereby obtain the diplomatic privileges of a minister. Atty. Gen. Cushing, 7 Opinions, 342, 345. . . .

We are of opinion that Mr. Baiz was not, at the time of the commencement of the suit in question, chargé d'affaires *ad interim* of Guatemala, or invested with and exercising the principal diplomatic functions, or in any view a "diplomatic officer." He was not a public minister within the intent and meaning of § 687; and the District Court had jurisdiction. . . .

The official circular issued by the Department of State, corrected to June 13, 1889, gives the names and description of the chargés d'affaires *ad interim,* in the case of countries represented by ministers who were absent and of countries having no minister, and the date of their presentation. In the instance of Portugal, the name is given of "Consul and acting Consul General, in charge of business of legation," and the fact of the presentation with the date appears in the list; while in the instance of Guatemala, Salvador and Honduras, the name of Mr. Baiz is referred to in a footnote, with the title of Consul General only; nor does it appear, nor is it claimed to be the fact, that he was ever presented. . . . But such presentation is undeniably evidence of the possession of diplomatic character, and so would be the formal reception of a chargé d'affaires *ad interim* by the Secretary of State. The inference is obvious, that if the Department of State had regarded Mr. Baiz as chargé d'affaires *ad interim,* or as "invested with and exercising the principal diplomatic functions," his name would have been placed in the list, with some indication of the fact, as the title of chargé, or, if he had been presented, the date of his presentation. Nor can a reason be suggested why the petitioner has not produced in this case a certificate from the Secretary of State that he had been recognized by the Department of State as chargé d'affaires *ad interim* of Guatemala, or as intrusted with diplomatic functions, if there had been such recognition. A certificate of his status was requested by the Guatemalan minister, and if the State Department had understood that Mr. Baiz was in any sense or in any way a "diplomatic representative," no reason is perceived why the Department would not have furnished a certificate to that effect; but instead of that, it contented itself with a courteous reply, giving what was in its judgment a sufficient résumé of the facts, the letter being in effect a polite declination to give the particular certificate desired, because that could not properly be done.

Mr. Baiz was a citizen of the United States and a resident of the city of New York. In many countries it is a state maxim that one of its own subjects or citizens is not to be received as a foreign diplomatic agent, and a refusal to receive, based on that objection, is always regarded as reasonable. The expediency of avoiding a possible conflict between his privileges as such and his obligations as a subject or citizen, is considered reason enough in itself. . . .

. . . The presumption, therefore, would ordinarily be against Mr. Baiz's contention, and, as matter of fact, we find that when, in 1886, he was appointed chargé d'affaires of the Republic of Honduras to the Government of the United States, Mr. Secretary Bayard declined receiving him as the diplomatic representative of the government of that country, because of his being a citizen of the United States, and advised him that: "It has long been the almost uniform practice of this Government to decline to recognize American citizens as the accredited diplomatic representatives of foreign powers. The statutory and jurisdictional immunities and the customary privileges of right attaching to the office of a foreign minister make it not only inconsistent, but at times even inconvenient, that a citizen of this country should enjoy so anomalous a position." . . . The objection which existed in 1886 to the reception of Mr. Baiz as chargé d'affaires *ad hoc* or *ad interim,* or according to him any diplomatic status whatever, whether temporary or otherwise, existed in 1889; and it is out of the question to assume that the State Department intended to concede the diplomatic status between January 16 and July 10, 1889, upon the request of Señor Lainfiesta that Consul General Baiz might be allowed to be a medium of communication during his absence, which it had refused to accord to the Republic of Honduras itself. It is evident that the statement of the Assistant Secretary, October 4, 1889, was quite correct, that "the business of the legation [of Guatemala] was conducted by Consul General Baiz, but without diplomatic character." . . .

Our conclusion is, as already stated, that the District Court had jurisdiction, and we accordingly discharge the rule and deny the writs.

ENGELKE, APPELLANT, v. MUSMANN, RESPONDENT.

Great Britain, House of Lords, 1928.

L. R. [1928] A. C. 433.

Appeal from an order of the Court of Appeal affirming an order of Shearman, J., in chambers.

The respondent issued a writ in the King's Bench Division against the appellant for payment of arrears of rent and dilapidations under a lease of a house in Hampstead. The appellant entered a conditional appearance and took out a summons to set aside the writ on the ground that he was in the service of the Ambassador of the German Empire. In support of his claim the appellant filed two affidavits to the following effect. He entered upon his duties on the staff of the German Embassy in London on November 25, 1920, and had been exclusively employed as a member of the Ambassador's staff ever since. He was employed in the commercial department of the Embassy, and in 1923 was promoted to the post of Consular Secretary. The duties which before the war were undertaken by a consul or consul-general were now in all towns where a German Ambassador was appointed performed by that Ambassador, and the appellant assisted in carrying out the duties of the Ambassador in that regard. Further, he was from time to time employed in the general duties of the Embassy, such as the coding and decoding of telegrams. His appointment as a member of the Embassy staff was notified to the British Foreign Office on November 30, 1920, by a letter of that date, and his name was on the Diplomatic List issued by the British Foreign Office. The respondent asked leave to cross-examine the appellant on his affidavits and filed an affidavit stating that to the best of his knowledge, information, and belief the appellant was a member of the consular staff and not of the diplomatic staff.

The Master refused leave to cross-examine the appellant, but Shearman, J., in chambers, reversed the order of the Master and ordered that the appellant should attend for cross-examination, but gave leave to appeal.

On the hearing of the appeal the Attorney General . . . informed the Court, on the instructions of the Secretary of State for Foreign Affairs, that the defendant had been appointed a member of the staff of the German Ambassador under the style of Consular Secretary, and that his position as a member of the Embassy was and had been since his appointment in 1920 recognized by the British Government without reservation or condition of any sort. . . .

The Court of Appeal by a majority (Scrutton and Sargant, L. JJ., Lord Hanworth, M. R., dissenting) affirmed the decision of the learned judge.

Scrutton, L. J., in whose judgment Sargant, L. J., concurred, declined to accept the Attorney General's statement as conclusive, as that would be to substitute a department of the Government for the Courts in a class of case where such substitution had never hitherto been recognized. In his opinion the question of immunity should only be decided after the relevant facts had been ascertained in the usual way, and the cross-examination of the appellant was necessary for that end.

The Attorney General obtained leave to intervene in the appeal to this House on the ground that the issues raised in these proceedings might affect the interests of His Majesty in the conduct of foreign affairs and his relations with foreign States. The contentions of the Attorney General were set out in the following paragraphs of his case:—

"26. The Attorney General submits that it is a necessary part of His Majesty's prerogative in his conduct of foreign affairs and his relations with foreign States and their representatives to accord or to refuse recognition to any person as a member of a foreign ambassador's staff exercising diplomatic functions. For this purpose a list of the members of his diplomatic staff is furnished from time to time to the Secretary of State by every foreign ambassador. . . . The list prepared by the Secretary of State and forwarded by him to the sheriffs for the purposes of the statute of Anne,[1] while it is based upon the list furnished in the first instance by the ambassador, is not . . . necessarily identical with it. . . .

"27. Since therefore it is for His Majesty alone, acting on the advice of His Secretary of State for Foreign Affairs, either to accord or refuse recognition to any particular person as a member of the diplomatic staff of a foreign ambassador, the Attorney General submits that a statement that recognition has been accorded made on behalf of His Majesty either by the Secretary of State or by H. M. Attorney General in person must necessarily be conclusive of the diplomatic status of that person. . . .

"28. If a statement made on behalf of His Majesty that a person has or has not been recognized as a member of the diplomatic staff of a foreign ambassador is not conclusive, and if the Court can go behind the statement and themselves seek to investigate the facts, compelling the person on behalf of whom immunity is claimed to submit to legal process for that purpose, it would be impossible for His Majesty to fulfil the obligations imposed on him by international law and the comity of nations, since the steps taken to investigate the claim would in themselves involve a breach of diplomatic immunity which in the event the Court might decide to have been established. . . .

LORD BUCKMASTER. My Lords, the privilege affording ambassadors and other accredited representatives of foreign countries immunity

---

[1] See Triquet v. Bath, above, p. 31.

from all writs and processes is an ancient doctrine of the common law declared in terms by the statute 7 Anne, c. 12.

No question is raised on this appeal affecting the existence or the extent of this protection. The sole point for determination is the method by which the status of any person who claims the benefit of this privilege is to be determined. For the appellant it is contended that the statement of the Attorney General on the instructions of the Foreign Office is for this purpose conclusive, while the respondent asserts that any such dispute should be ascertained in the ordinary way according to the usual rules of evidence. . . .

So far as the question of principle is concerned, the case decided in this House of Duff Development Co. v. Kelantan Government [1924] A. C. 797, is a clear authority that the method of proving the status either of the sovereigns or of the ambassadors who are their representatives is by the very method that is challenged in the present case. The statute, however, draws no distinction between the ambassadors and what, in the language of the Act of Parliament, is described as the "domestic or domestic servant of any such ambassador," and it seems difficult to understand when the principle is admitted with regard to the one that it should not apply in relation to the other, for the privilege is the same in each case. With regard to the sovereignty of a particular State and whether or not a particular person is a sovereign ruler, the case referred to makes the general principle plain. As Lord Finlay said [1924] A. C. 813, 820: "It has long been settled that on any question of the status of any foreign power the proper course is that the Court should apply to His Majesty's Government, and that in any such matter it is bound to act on the information given to them through the proper department. Such information is not in the nature of evidence; it is a statement by the Sovereign of this country through one of his Ministers upon a matter which is peculiarly within his cognizance." . . .

Now the acceptance and recognition of persons who form the staff of an ambassador are matters which, having regard to the practice in the conduct of foreign affairs, are equally based on the comity of nations and necessarily also within the cognizance of the Crown acting through the Foreign Office. They are in a position to know what are the duties performed and the persons who perform them, and it is plain that, though they trust the list put forward if it appears from their knowledge to be a list which might reasonably be accepted, yet the list itself is scrutinized, inquiries are made and, if necessary, persons are removed for sufficient reasons. . . . The list is not conclusive, nor is it the list itself on which reliance is to be placed, but on the statement of the Crown, speaking through the Attorney General, stating that a particular person at the critical moment is qualified to be upon the list. When this statement has been made it is difficult to see how it can be questioned without the introduction of proceedings which in the person of the ambassador himself, and equally of his wife and family and staff, it would obviously be undesirable to institute. . . .

It is, of course, obvious that the privilege claimed has serious results, as it excludes from their remedies in the Courts the people with whom members of the ambassador's staff may have incurred obligations, and it is possible that it is open to abuse. It is of the essence of all privilege that it may be abused, but that question has nothing to do with the matter we are called upon to decide; the merits of the dispute out of which this question has arisen are in no way before us for consideration. The privilege itself depends upon maintaining the obligations of international law and the comity of nations. It would, indeed, be unfortunate if, after recognition had been afforded by His Majesty through the Foreign Office to people as holding such posts on the ambassadorial staff as entitled them to the privilege and the statement as to their position had been afforded on behalf of the Crown through the Attorney General, it was to be disregarded by the judiciary, for, in such circumstances, the ensuing contest could not possibly inure to the public good.

My noble and learned friend Lord Blanesburgh concurs in the opinion I have just read.

[Other opinions omitted.]

Order of the Court of Appeal reversed, and declared that the appellant is entitled to diplomatic privilege. . . .

BIGELOW v. PRINCESS ZIZIANOFF ET AL.

France, Court of Appeal of Paris, 1928.

Gazette du Palais, May 4, 1928 (No. 125), as translated in Am. Journal of Int. Law, XXIII (1929), 172.

Mr. Bigelow, director of the Passport Service at the American Consulate General in Paris, has appealed from the judgment of the Correctional Tribunal of the Seine of April 5, 1927, which declared itself competent in a prosecution of him for defamation.

Attorney General Reynaud submitted the following conclusions: . . .

I. Princess Zizianoff, who had requested a visa of her passport in order to go to the United States, met with a refusal by the consulate, against which she had protested. Consul Bigelow, in order to explain the decision of his government, had, in the course of an interview in his office, furnished representatives of the press information concerning Princess Zizianoff which was reproduced in an American newspaper placed on sale in Paris, the *Boston Sunday Post*, where may be read in the issue of September 5, 1926, under the signature Robert Johnson, an article of which the essential sentences are as follows:

"Did Beauty Spy on U. S.? Princess Zizianoff is an international spy. She worked for the Germans in Russia during the World War and was deported to Siberia when she was caught. She was sent to America by Zinovieff last year to do espionage work among the American patriotic organizations, and her anti-Bolshevik activity was only a blind. In the past week she has twice secretly visited the Soviet embassy in Paris.''

In consequence of this article, Princess Zizianoff cited before the 12th Correctional Tribunal of the Seine for abusive language and libel Mr. Kahn, Paris representative of the said newspaper, two other collaborators, and also Mr. Bigelow, the latter as an accomplice, for having furnished the elements of the article.

Mr. Bigelow, having denied the competence of the French court, was overruled by the court, which declared itself competent in respect to him.

Appeal was entered against this judgment.

Two arguments are invoked in support of the contention of incompetence:

The first is drawn from the text of the convention of February 23, 1853, between France and the United States.

The second is based upon the general principles of public law and international law, which prohibit, even in the absence of any convention, citing a foreign consul before the courts of the country where he performs his duties for acts done in the performance of those duties.

II. On the first point the defense maintains that French tribunals have no jurisdiction over consuls of the United States both by reason of the provisions of the Consular Convention of February 23, 1853, between France and the United States, and those of the Consular Convention of January 7, 1876, between France and Greece, applicable to consuls of the United States in virtue of the most-favored-nation clause in the former convention.

The convention with the United States is in these terms:

''The consuls-general, consuls, vice-consuls or consular agents of the United States and France, shall enjoy in the two countries the privileges usually accorded to their offices, such as personal immunity, except in the case of crime. . . . If, however, the said consuls-general, consuls, vice-consuls or consular agents, are citizens of the country in which they reside; if they are, or become, owners of property there, or engage in commerce, they shall be subject to the same taxes and imposts, and with the reservation of the treatment granted to commercial agents, to the same jurisdiction, as other citizens of the country who are owners of property, or merchants.'' . . .

This first line of argument cannot be accepted. In public law it belongs to each state to interpret international conventions and its interpretation is final for courts under its sovereignty. A French court is bound by the sovereign opinion of the state in the name of which it renders justice. This opinion is a categorical command for the judge. The principle of the separation of powers requires it so.

Now, the French Government has made known its opinion in the case of the prosecution of Consul King, of the United States, and this opinion is to be found in a judgment of the Criminal Chamber of the Court of Cassation of February 23, 1912. (*Gaz. Pal.* 1912. 1. 454—*Bull. crim.* n. 111, p. 189). It is summed up in this brief formula: "The personal immunity granted to consuls by the convention does not exclude the competence of our courts in penal matters," and the letter addressed by the Minister of Foreign Affairs on October 26, 1926, to Mᵉ Thomas Olivera, *huissier* at Paris, confirms this doctrine by referring to the above-mentioned judgment.

This interpretation of the 1853 convention, to which the French courts ought to conform, is moreover the most reasonable one, and the arguments of the opposing thesis are by no means decisive. The expression "personal immunity" has different meanings, and to give it the meaning of immunity from jurisdiction would be an arbitrary assertion. . . .

III. The second argument, called subsidiary in the pleadings, should likewise be rejected.

A consul, the defense tells us, cannot be prosecuted even in the absence of any diplomatic convention before the judicial tribunals for acts done in his official capacity, nor even for misdeeds committed in the exercise of his functions. Now Mr. Bigelow was well within his functions when he explained the reasons which had led his government to refuse the visa requested by Princess Zizianoff. It is even added that he was performing an act proper to his functions when in his office, being charged with relations with the press, he issued a communiqué or gave an interview. Moreover, that is the opinion which has been stated in this matter by the Government of the United States. . . .

In what case does one find oneself in presence of an official act? In what case, on the other hand, can a personal act involving responsibility of the official before the ordinary tribunals be found? "If the injurious act is impersonal," writes Laferrière, "if it discloses an administrator, a mandatory of the state more or less subject to error, and not man with his feebleness, passions, and imprudences, the act remains administrative and cannot be brought before the courts. If, on the contrary, the personality of the agent is disclosed by acts in violation of law, by violence, or fraud, then the fault is chargeable to the functionary, not to his office. The act loses its administrative character and is no longer an obstacle to judicial cognizance." (Laferrière, *Tr. de juridiction administrative*, 2ᵉ éd., t. *I*, p. 648.)

"A gross mistake," he further says, "manifest usurpation, an inexcusable attack upon private rights, or even a serious fault as opposed to a mere administrative inaccuracy, may justify cognizance by the courts." Conclusions in the Laumonnier-Corrial (*Trib. conflits 5 Mai* 1877, D. 78. 3. 13.)

Likewise in M. Gaston Jèze's opinion, there is a personal fault "if the wrong committed consists in a serious error which by reason of his position the functionary should not be excused for having committed:" G. Jèze (*Rev. droit public*, 1909, p. 263, 268 *et suiv.; Les principes généraux du droit administratif*, 2ᵉ sect., p. 59, note 3, *et* p. 60, note 2); Duguit (*Tr. de droit constitutionnel, t. III*, p. 280.)

The criterion therefore should be sought in the element of intent and it is necessary to scrutinize the agent's intentions. Often the personal fault will consist in a sort of deceit, but it is necessary clearly to point out that jurisprudence follows doctrine on this point and does not limit the responsibility of officials to actions that are defined as deceit. There are faults which raise a presumption of deceit, and we often find in decrees the expression "serious fault amounting to deceit." . . .

Therefore the remarks imputed to Mr. Bigelow, remarks made after the refusal of a visa of the passport of Madam Zizianoff, appear quite materially distinct from the administrative act.

But even admit that they were made in the course of an official consular act, the relations with the press and the response to interviews being considered as essentially official attributions of consular agents. The alleged defamation will be found included in the act, but the personal fault will result from a serious unskillfulness susceptible of injuring private interests, a circumstance clearly detachable from the administrative act. The judgment to be rendered will not require in this case, according to a formula of a decision of the Supreme Court, "either consideration or examination of any administrative act." (*Cass. crim. 13 juillet* 1889. D. 90. 1. 330.)

The tribunal will limit itself to examining whether the constituted elements of the offences of insult and defamation are found united. The principle of the separation of powers will not be involved.

This appears to be a sound legal view. Moreover, French courts can not be bound by the opinion of the Government of the United States, which thinks that Consul Bigelow has acted within the scope of his duties, and they should apply the principles of French law. Neither the high consideration attaching to the viewpoint of a foreign authority, nor the traditions of the most perfect courtesy can have the consequence of subordinating the decision of our magistrates to this manner of viewing the subject.

In these conditions you will therefore doubtless hold that the jurisdiction of the Correctional Tribunal of the Seine with regard to Consul Bigelow is certain, and you will confirm the order of the judgment under appeal.

In conformity with the above argument, the court has rendered the following decree:

The Court,

Whereas, the defendant contends that the judges of first instance were in error in declaring themselves competent, on the ground, first, that they placed an incorrect interpretation upon the convention of February 23, 1853, of which Article 2, paragraph 1, conferring personal immunity upon American consular agents, did not permit a valid summons of Mr. Bigelow before the French tribunal, and, secondly, subsidiarily, even if it was proper to interpret the 1853 convention in the sense adopted by the judgment appealed from, Bigelow, having acted in his capacity as consul in the discharge of his duties, could not in any case be subject to the French tribunals for the act he is charged with, and to decide the contrary would be trespass upon the sovereignty of a foreign government;

But, whereas there is no need of deciding upon the principal arguments of Bigelow, the government, which alone is qualified to interpret diplomatic conventions, having previously made known its opinion with regard to the meaning which should be given to the provisions of the convention of February 23, 1853, and especially to the words "personal immunity"; and it appears from a decision of the Court of Cassation of February 23, 1912 (*Bull. crim.* n. 111, p. 189—*Gaz. Pal.* 1912. 1. 454), mentioned in the judgment appealed from, that this sentence concerning consular agents should be understood not as an immunity from personal jurisdiction in criminal matters, but only as an exemption from preliminary arrest and detention; and whereas the convention of 1853 has been neither modified nor denounced, this interpretation is obligatory upon the courts in virtue of the principle of separation of powers, and has even been repeated and confirmed as it appears from a letter from the Minister for Foreign Affairs dated October 26, 1926, addressed to the *huissier* Olivera, and produced at the hearing; and consequently, without there being need for making decisions on the other points raised and especially on that relating to the alleged secret documents, the present decision dealing only with the Cassation decision of 1912 and the letter mentioned, all immaterial points remaining undecided, the result is a declaration that the judges below have properly rejected the principal arguments of Bigelow;

Whereas, with regard to the subsidiary arguments, the judges below likewise acted justly in not entertaining them; referring to the conversations as charged in the original complaint, which tend to accuse Princess Zizianoff of having acted as a spy in Russia for the Germans, of having even been deported on that account, and of having later been a spy among the American patriotic societies for the Soviet Government, whose embassy she visited in Paris, we cannot discover a performance of an official act in the holding of such conversations;

Whereas, moreover, as the judgment below declares, the defendant is prosecuted, not for refusal of a passport, which would be an act in his consular capacity and would consequently be outside any jurisdiction of the courts, but only for having, in his communication of that decision of his country, delivered himself on the subject of said refusal of the above-

described comments, which were not its necessary and indispensable corollary; and as in these comments, viewed as apart from or included in
the official act itself, there is a serious wrong susceptible of injuring private interests and having a personal character; and this wrong, which is
clearly unconnected with the duty performed by Bigelow and is not at
all required in the examination of the said official act, would, if it is
established, involve him in penal liability by reason of the criminal elements which it appears to contain;

For these reasons, and those of the judges below not inconsistent
therewith;

And declaring that there is no legal reason for acceding to the requests of Bigelow, the present decision, dealing only with the documents already in evidence, confirms the judgment below in its declaration
of jurisdiction over the suit brought at the request of the civil party;

Consequently rejects the contention of Bigelow on appeal as ill-
founded;

Condemns Bigelow to the costs of the appeal.[1]

---

[1] SUPPLEMENTARY CASES. In Dainese v. Hale, 91 U. S. 13 (1875), above,
p. 222, the court discusses the judicial functions of consuls in non-Christian
countries.

Query, as to the liability of a consul to give bail-bond in a suit for debt?
In Viveash v. Becker, 3 M. & S. 284 (1814), involving the arrest in London of
the defendant for a debt and his application to have the bail bond required of
him delivered up on the ground that he was acting in the capacity of consul to
the Duke of Oldenburg, the court held that consuls were not entitled to the
jus gentium in respect to diplomatic privilege, and the application was refused.

Query, may a consul be compelled to attend as a witness in a criminal trial?
In United States v. Trumbull, 48 F. 94 (1891), involving the indictment of
Trumbull and another for violation of the neutrality laws, in connection with a
revolution in Chile, and a motion on the part of one Catton, vice-consul of Chile
at San Francisco, that he be discharged from process of subpoena to appear as
a witness against the defendants, the District Court held that while consuls were
not entitled under the law of nations to exemption from compulsory process to
attend as a witness in criminal proceedings, yet such exemption might be conceded by treaty provisions which in this case were found to apply in view of the
most-favored-nation clause in the treaty with Chile of 1832 and the subsequent
privileges granted to France by the treaty of 1853. The latter treaty was before
a District Court in 1854 in the case of In re Dillon, 7 Sawy. 561, involving the
service of a subpoena and the subsequent issue of an attachment against Dillon,
French consul at San Francisco, to appear as a witness at the trial of Señor
Del Valle, Mexican consul at San Francisco accused of violating the neutrality
laws. The court held that under the provisions of the treaty French consuls
were not amenable to the compulsory process of the courts, in spite of the provision of the United States Constitution giving to the accused the right to have
compulsory process for obtaining witnesses in his favor, the provision being
interpreted in the light of the implied exemption of ambassadors from service
of compulsory process although no specification of the exception was made in
the Constitution.

Query, may a consul, by treaty, be given jurisdiction over disputes between
master and crew of vessels flying the flag of his country? In The Cambitsis,

14 F. (2d) 236 (1926), involving a libel for wages brought in a port of the United States against a Greek vessel and an exception taken by the master of the vessel on the ground of jurisdiction, the District Court held that under the treaty of 1902 between the United States and Greece the jurisdiction of their respective courts was excluded in disputes such as the one before the court.

Query, as to the time of the termination of a consul's privileges? In People v. Savitch, 116 Misc. 531 (1921), involving a motion to dismiss an indictment against Savitch in the courts of the State of New York on the ground that the defendant was triable only in the Federal courts as being at the time of the commission of the alleged crime the consul general of a foreign power, namely, the Kingdom of the Serbs, Croats and Slovenes, the Court of General Sessions held that the revocation of the defendant's exequatur by the President terminated his consular status and that "as soon as he ceased to become a consul of a foreign power he became amenable to the state courts, at least for unofficial acts done by him during the time when he was serving as such consul."

CHAPTER XVII

ARBITRAL AND JUDICIAL PROCEDURE FOR THE SETTLEMENT OF INTERNATIONAL DISPUTES [1]

A. Arbitration.

As a procedure for the settlement of international disputes by peaceful methods arbitration is of ancient tradition. It may be defined, in terms of the Hague Convention for the Pacific Settlement of International Disputes adopted in 1899, as "the settlement of differences between states by judges of their own choice, and on the basis of respect for law." Numerous, however, as have been the arbitrations carried out, particularly since 1794, the rules of procedure applied in such cases have not developed into an established code, owing to the fact that special rules are regularly agreed upon in advance by the parties. On occasion it has happened that a state, believing it desirable that a controversy should be settled by arbitration, has agreed that the arbitral tribunal should be guided by certain principles in the particular case before it without being willing to concede that the principles thus accepted were rules of international law in force at the time the claims in question arose. [United States and Great Britain: Alabama Claims Case.]

THE UNITED STATES AND GREAT BRITAIN: ALABAMA CLAIMS.

Arbitration under the Treaty of May 8, 1871. 1872.

Treaties, Conventions, etc., between the United States and other Powers, I, 717.

[BY THE TRIBUNAL: ADAMS, SCLOPIS, STAMPFLI, D'ITAJUBA, (COCKBURN not signing the award).]

The United States of America and Her Britannic Majesty having agreed by Article I. of the treaty concluded and signed at Washington the 8th of May 1871, to refer all the claims "generically known as the

---

[1] For a more detailed study of this subject, see Fenwick, *op. cit.*, pp. 405–422; Hyde, *op. cit.*, II, §§ 559–585; Oppenheim, *op. cit.*, II, §§ 12–25g; Fachiri, The Permanent Court of International Justice, 2d ed.; Hudson, A Treatise on the Permanent Court of International Justice (1934); Scott, Hague Court Reports; Hudson, World Court Reports.

Alabama claims" to a tribunal of arbitration to be composed of five arbitrators. . . .

The tribunal having since [i.e. following its initial sessions] fully taken into their consideration the treaty and also the cases, counter-cases, documents, evidence, and arguments, and likewise all other communications made to them by the two parties during the progress of their sittings, and having impartially and carefully examined the same, has arrived at the decision embodied in the present award:

Whereas, having regard to the sixth and seventh articles of the said treaty, the arbitrators are bound under the terms of the said sixth article, "in deciding the matters submitted to them, to be governed by the three rules therein specified and by such principles of international law, not inconsistent therewith as the arbitrators shall determine to have been applicable to the case"; [1]

And whereas the "due diligence," referred to in the first and third of the said rules, ought to be exercised by neutral governments in exact proportion to the risks to which either of the belligerents may be exposed, from a failure to fulfill the obligations of neutrality on their part;

---

[1] The text of Article VI of the Treaty of Washington is as follows:

"In deciding the matters submitted to the Arbitrators, they shall be governed by the following three rules, which are agreed upon by the high contracting parties as rules to be taken as applicable to the case, and by such principles of international law, not inconsistent therewith, as the arbitrators shall determine to have been applicable to the case.

"A neutral government is bound—

"First, to use due diligence to prevent the fitting out, arming, or equipping, within its jurisdiction, of any vessel which it has reasonable ground to believe is intended to cruise or to carry on war against a power with which it is at peace; and also to use like diligence to prevent the departure from its jurisdiction of any vessel intended to cruise or carry on war as above, such vessel having been specially adapted, in whole or in part, within such jurisdiction, to warlike use.

"Secondly, not to permit or suffer either belligerent to make use of its ports or waters as the base of naval operations against the other, or for the purpose of the renewal or augmentation of military supplies or arms, or the recruitment of men.

"Thirdly, to exercise due diligence in its own ports and waters, and as to all persons within its jurisdiction, to prevent any violation of the foregoing obligations and duties.

"Her Britannic Majesty has commanded her high commissioners and plenipotentiaries to declare that Her Majesty's government cannot assent to the foregoing rules as a statement of the principles of international law which were in force at the time when the claims mentioned in article I arose, but that Her Majesty's government, in order to evince its desire of strengthening the friendly relations between the two countries and of making satisfactory provision for the future, agrees that in deciding the questions between the two countries, arising out of those claims, the arbitrators should assume that Her Majesty's government had undertaken to act upon the principles set forth in these rules.

"And the high contracting parties agree to observe these rules as between themselves in future, and to bring them to the knowledge of other maritime powers, and to invite them to accede to them."

And whereas the circumstances out of which the facts constituting the subject-matter of the present controversy arose were of a nature to call for the exercise on the part of Her Britannic Majesty's government of all possible solicitude for the observance of the rights and the duties involved in the proclamation of neutrality issued by Her Majesty on the 13th day of May, 1861;

And whereas the effects of a violation of neutrality, committed by means of the construction, equipment, and armament of a vessel are not done away with by any commission which the government of the belligerent power, benefited by the violation of neutrality, may afterwards have granted to that vessel; and the ultimate step, by which the offense is completed, cannot be admissible as a ground for the absolution of the offender, nor can the consummation of his fraud become the means of establishing his innocence;

And whereas the privilege of exterritoriality, accorded to vessels of war, has been admitted into the law of Nations, not as an absolute right, but solely as a proceeding founded on the principle of courtesy and mutual deference between different nations, and, therefore, can never be appealed to for the protection of acts done in violation of neutrality;

And whereas the absence of a previous notice cannot be regarded as a failure in any consideration required by the law of nations, in those cases in which a vessel carries with it its own condemnation;

And whereas in order to impart to any supplies of coal a character inconsistent with the second rule prohibiting the use of neutral ports or waters, as a base of naval operations for a belligerent, it is necessary that the said supplies should be connected with special circumstances, of time, of persons, or of place, which may combine to give them such character;

And whereas, with respect to the vessel called the Alabama, it clearly results from all the facts relative to the construction of the ship, at first designated by the number "290," in the port of Liverpool, and its equipment and armament in the vicinity of Terceira, through the agency of the vessels called the "Agrippina" and the "Bahama," dispatch[ed] from Great Britain to that end, that the British government failed to use due diligence in the performance of its neutral obligations, and especially that it omitted, notwithstanding the warnings and official representations made by the diplomatic agents of the United States during the construction of the said number "290," to take in due time any effective measures of prevention, and that those orders which it did give at last, for the detention of the vessel, were issued so late that their execution was not practicable;

And whereas, after the escape of that vessel, the measures taken for its pursuit and arrest were so imperfect as to lead to no result, and therefore cannot be considered sufficient to release Great Britain from the responsibility already incurred;

And whereas, in despite of the violations of the neutrality of Great Britain, committed by the "290," this same vessel, later known as the Confederate cruiser Alabama, was on several occasions freely admitted into the ports of colonies of Great Britain, instead of being proceeded against as it ought to have been in any and every port within British jurisdiction in which it might have been found;

And whereas the government of Her Britannic Majesty cannot justify itself for a failure in due diligence on the plea of insufficiency of the legal means of action which it possessed:

For [Four of] the arbitrators for the reasons above assigned and the fifth for the reasons separately signed by him,

Are of opinion—

That Great Britain has in this case failed by omission, to fulfill the duties prescribed in the first and third of the rules, established by the VIth article of the treaty of Washington.

And whereas, with respect to the vessel called the "Florida" . . .

And whereas, with respect to the vessel called the "Shenandoah," . . .

The tribunal, making use of the authority conferred upon it by article VII of the said treaty, by a majority of four voices to one awards to the United States a sum of $15,500,000 in gold as the indemnity to be paid by Great Britain to the United States, for the satisfaction of all the claims referred to the consideration of the tribunal, conformably to the provisions contained in article VII of the aforesaid treaty.

And, in accordance with the terms of article XI of the said treaty, the tribunal declares that "all the claims referred to in the treaty as submitted to the tribunal are hereby fully, perfectly, and finally settled."

Further it declares that "each and every one of the said claims, whether the same may or may not have been presented to the notice of, or made, preferred, or laid before the tribunal, shall henceforth be considered and treated as finally settled, barred, and inadmissible." . . .[1]

---

[1] Supplementary Cases.   Query, where a later arbitration is held to determine the effect of an earlier arbitration, would the principle of *res judicata* hold?   In the Pious Fund Case between the United States and Mexico, submitted to arbitration under an agreement of May 22, 1902, Scott, Hague Court Reports, p. 3, the issue was whether a claim, presented by the United States on behalf of the Archbishop of San Francisco and the Bishop of Monterey, to the annuities from a fund, originally created by private donors and subsequently taken over by the Mexican government as trustee, fell within the governing principle of *res judicata* in consequence of an earlier arbitral award of Sir Edward Thornton in 1875 in which the arbitrator held that annuities unpaid since 1848 were due to the amount of $904,700.79.   Mexico maintained that the payment of the sum fixed in the award of 1875 extinguished the whole claim.   The tribunal decided, October 14, 1902, that the award of 1875 recognized the validity of the claim and that under the principle of *res judicata* it could not now be contested.   Mexico was therefore held to pay a sum representing unpaid annuities and regular annuities in the future.

B. Judicial procedure before the Permanent Court of International Justice.

Procedure before the Permanent Court of International Justice is prescribed in detail in the Statute and Rules of the Court. On numerous occasions, however, questions have arisen that were not covered by the general provisions agreed upon by the signatories of the protocol, and it has remained for the Court to define its own jurisdiction, in accordance with the terms of the Statute. Query, where consent has been given by a state to the jurisdiction of the Court by a treaty drawn up in general terms, may the Court interpret those terms in the light of other international documents in order to determine their application in a specific case? [Greek Republic v. Great Britain: Mavrommatis Concessions Case.]

In addition to its function of rendering judgments in cases submitted to it by the parties in controversy the Court has, in accordance with the terms of Article 14 of the Covenant of the League of Nations, assumed the function of rendering advisory opinions to the Council of the League. In such cases the Court has adopted its own rules of procedure with respect to the conditions under which requests for advisory opinions will be entertained and the opinions themselves handed down. Query, where the Council of the League of Nations asks an opinion of the Court as to the legal obligations, under a particular treaty, of a non-member of the League, is it a necessary part of the procedure of the Court that both parties to the controversy, the member and the non-member alike, shall appear before the Court and state their cases after the manner of public hearings attending a judgment between the two parties? [Finland and Russia: Eastern Carelia Case.]

THE GOVERNMENT OF THE GREEK REPUBLIC, APPLICANT, v. THE GOVERNMENT OF HIS BRITANNIC MAJESTY, RESPONDENT.

CASE OF THE MAVROMMATIS PALESTINE CONCESSIONS.

Permanent Court of International Justice, 1924.

Publications of the Court, Series A, No. 2.

[On May 13, 1924, the Government of the Greek Republic submitted to the Permanent Court of International Justice a suit arising out of the alleged refusal on the part of the Government of Palestine, and consequently on the part of His Britannic Majesty's Government, in its capacity as Mandatory Power for Palestine, to recognize certain rights acquired by Mavrommatis, a Greek subject, under contracts concluded by him with the Ottoman Government in 1914. The concessions in question, relating to public works in Jerusalem and in Jaffa, were, it was alleged, rendered impossible of execution by the British authorities in Palestine, and new concessions were granted to Rutenberg which overlapped those claimed by Mavrommatis. Damages were claimed by the Greek Government for the losses sustained by its subject. In answer to the application of the Greek Government instituting the proceedings the British Government entered a preliminary objection on the ground that the Court had no jurisdiction to entertain the proceedings in question. The issue as to jurisdiction involved the following points: 1. Was the dispute a dispute between the Mandatory and another Member of the League of Nations? 2. Was it a dispute which could not "be settled by negotiation," as required by the terms of the Mandate? 3. Did the dispute relate "to the interpretation or the application of the terms of the Mandate"? 4. Were the Mavrommatis concessions affected by any international obligations arising out of Protocol XII of Lausanne relating to the "readaptation" to the new conditions in Palestine of certain concessionary contracts entered into by the Ottoman Government before October 29, 1914?]

The Court, . . . having heard the observations and conclusions of the Parties, delivers the following judgments:

The facts: . . .

The law:

Before entering on the proceedings in the case of the Mavrommatis concessions, the Permanent Court of International Justice has been made cognisant of an objection taken by His Britannic Majesty's Government to the effect that the Court cannot entertain the proceedings. . . . It appears in fact from the documents before the Court and from the speeches of Sir Cecil Hurst and of H. E. M. Politis that the preliminary question to be decided is not merely whether the nature and subject of the dispute laid before the Court are such that the Court derives from them jurisdiction to entertain it, but also whether the conditions upon which the exercise of this jurisdiction is dependent are all fulfilled in the present case.

The general basis of the jurisdiction given to the Permanent Court of International Justice is set down in Articles 34 and 36 of the Statute, according to which, in the first place, only States or Members of the League of Nations may appear before it and, in the second place, it has jurisdiction to hear and determine "all cases which the Parties refer to it and all matters specially provided for in Treaties and Conventions in force." . . .

Article 26 of the Mandate contains the following clause:

"The Mandatory agrees that, if any dispute whatever should arise between the Mandatory and another Member of the League of Nations relating to the interpretation or the application of the provisions of the Mandate, such dispute, if it cannot be settled by negotiation, shall be submitted to the Permanent Court of International Justice provided for by Article 14 of the Covenant of the League of Nations.''

The question therefore arises whether the conditions laid down by Article 26 in regard to the acceptance of the Court's jurisdiction, the absence of which would render such acceptance inoperative, are fulfilled in the case before the Court.

Before considering whether the case of the Mavrommatis concessions relates to the *interpretation* or *application* of the Mandate and whether consequently its nature and subject are such as to bring it within the jurisdiction of the Court as defined in the article quoted above, it is essential to ascertain whether the case fulfills all the other conditions laid down in this clause. Does the matter before the Court constitute a dispute between the Mandatory and another Member of the League of Nations? Is it a dispute which cannot be settled by negotiation?

I

A dispute is a disagreement on a point of law or fact, a conflict of legal views or of interests between two persons. The present suit between Great Britain and Greece certainly possesses these characteristics. The latter Power is asserting its own rights by claiming from His Britannic Majesty's Government an indemnity on the ground that M. Mavrommatis, one of its subjects, has been treated by the Palestine or British authorities in a manner incompatible with certain international obligations which they were bound to observe.

In the case of the Mavrommatis concessions it is true that the dispute was at first between a private person and a State—i. e. between M. Mavrommatis and Great Britain. Subsequently, the Greek Government took up the case. The dispute then entered upon a new phase; it entered the domain of international law, and became a dispute between two States. Henceforward therefore it is a dispute which may or may not fall under the jurisdiction of the Permanent Court of International Justice. . . .

It is an elementary principle of international law that a State is entitled to protect its subjects, when injured by acts contrary to international law committed by another State, from whom they have been unable to obtain satisfaction through the ordinary channels. By taking up the case of one of its subjects and by resorting to diplomatic action or international judicial proceedings on his behalf, a State is in reality asserting its own rights—its right to ensure, in the person of its subjects, respect for the rules of international law. . . .

II.

The second condition by which this article defines and limits the jurisdiction of the Permanent Court in questions arising out of the interpretation and application of the Mandate, *is that the dispute cannot be settled by negotiation.* It has been contended that this condition is not fulfilled in the present case; and leaving out of account the correspondence previous to 1924 between Mavrommatis or his solicitors and the British Government, emphasis has been laid on the very small number and brevity of the subsequent communications exchanged between the two Governments, which communications appear to be irreconcilable with the idea of negotiations properly so-called. The true value of this objection will readily be seen if it be remembered that the question of the importance and chances of success of diplomatic negotiations is essentially a relative one. Negotiations do not of necessity always presuppose a more or less lengthy series of notes and despatches; it may suffice that a discussion should have been commenced, and this discussion may have been very short; this will be the case if a deadlock is reached, or if finally a point is reached at which one of the Parties definitely declares himself unable, or refuses, to give way, and there can therefore be no doubt that *the dispute cannot be settled by diplomatic negotiation.* This will also be the case, in certain circumstances, if the conversation between the Governments are only the continuation of previous negotiations between a private individual and a government. . . .

III.

The Court has now to consider the condition which Article 26 of the Mandate imposes upon its jurisdiction when laying down that the dispute must relate "to the interpretation or the application of the provisions of the Mandate." The dispute may be of any nature; the language of the article in this respect is as comprehensive as possible (*any dispute whatever—tout différend, quel qu'il soit*); but in every case it must relate to the interpretation or the application of the provisions of the Mandate.

In the first place, the exact scope must be ascertained of the investigations which the Court must, under Article 36, last paragraph, of the Statute, pursue in order to arrive at the conclusion that the dispute before it does or does not relate to the interpretation or the application of the Mandate, and, consequently, is or is not within its jurisdiction under the terms of Article 26. Neither the Statute nor the Rules of Court contain any rule regarding the procedure to be followed in the event of an objection being taken *in limine litis* to the Court's jurisdiction. The Court therefore is at liberty to adopt the principle which it considers best calculated to ensure the administration of justice, most suited to procedure before an international tribunal and most in conformity with the fundamental principles of international law.

For this reason the Court, bearing in mind the fact that its jurisdiction is limited, that it is invariably based on the consent of the respondent and only exists in so far as this consent has been given, cannot content itself with the provisional conclusion that the dispute falls or not within the terms of the Mandate. The Court, before giving judgment on the merits of the case, will satisfy itself that the suit before it, in the form in which it has been submitted and on the basis of the facts hitherto established, falls to be decided by application of the clauses of the Mandate. For the Mandatory has only accepted the Court's jurisdiction for such disputes. . . .

In support of its application, the Greek Government cites Article II of the Mandate, which runs as follows:

"The Administration of Palestine shall take all necessary measures to safeguard the interests of the community in connection with the development of the country, and, subject to any international obligations accepted by the Mandatory, shall have full power to provide for public ownership or control of any of the natural resources of the country or of the public works, services and utilities established or to be established therein. . . ."

The Court feels that the present judgment should be based principally on the first part of paragraph I of Article II. . . .

The Mavrommatis concessions in themselves are outside the scope of Article II, but the question before the Court is whether, by granting the Rutenberg concessions—which cover at least a part of the same ground—the Palestine and British authorities have disregarded international obligations assumed by the Mandatory, by which obligations Greece is entitled to benefit. . . .

The conclusion which appears to follow from the preceding argument is that the Rutenberg concessions constitute an application by the Administration of Palestine of the system of "public control" with the object of developing the natural resources of the country and of operating public works, services and utilities. Thus envisaged, these concessions may fall within the scope of Article II of the Mandate. . . .

It now only remains to consider whether there are any international obligations arising out of Protocol XII of Lausanne—hereinafter called "Protocol XII"—which affect the Mavrommatis concessions. . . .

The fundamental principle of the Protocol is the maintenance of concessionary contracts concluded before October 29th, 1914. In territories detached from Turkey, the State which acquires the territory is subrogated as regards the rights and the obligations of Turkey. . .

The foregoing reasoning leads to the following conclusions:

(a) That the dispute between the British and Greek Governments concerning M. Mavrommatis' claim in respect of the Jerusalem concessions must be decided on the basis of the provisions of Article II of the Mandate and that consequently it is within the category of disputes for which the Mandatory has accepted the jurisdiction of the Court;

(b) that, on the other hand, the dispute between these Governments concerning M. Mavrommatis' claims in respect of the Jaffa concessions has no connection with Article II of the Mandate and consequently does not fall within the category of disputes for which the Mandatory has accepted the jurisdiction of the Court. . . .

The Court, having heard both Parties,

Upholds the preliminary objection submitted by His Britannic Majesty's Government in so far as it relates to the claim in respect of the works at Jaffa and dismisses it in so far as it relates to the claim in respect of the works at Jerusalem;

Reserves this part of the suit for judgment on the merits;

And instructs the President to fix, in accordance with Article 33 of the Rules of Court, the times for the deposit of further documents of the written proceedings. . . .[1]

FINLAND AND RUSSIA:
EASTERN CARELIA CASE.

Permanent Court of International Justice, 1923.

Publications of the Court, Series B, No. 5.

[BY THE COURT.] The Council of the League of Nations on April 21st, 1923, adopted the following Resolution:

"The Council of the League of Nations requests the Permanent Court of International Justice to give an advisory opinion on the following

---

[1] The question of jurisdiction decided, the Court, on March 26, 1925, delivered judgment on the merits of the case (Publications of the Court, Series A, No. 5) holding that the concessions granted to Mavrommatis under agreements, signed on January 27, 1914, between him and the City of Jerusalem regarding certain works to be carried out at Jerusalem were valid, and that the right granted to Rutenberg to require the annulment of the Mavrommatis concessions was in violation of the international obligations accepted by the Mandatory for Palestine. As a preliminary point the Court held that the erroneous description of Mavrommatis in the concessions as "an Ottoman subject" had no effect upon their validity since the nationality of Mavrommatis was not a condition of the contract.

Following the decision of the case upon its merits the Greek Government again instituted proceedings before the Court, this time alleging that, in consequence of delays on the part of the Mandatory Government in approving the plans submitted by Mavrommatis for the execution of his new concessions that had been substituted for those of 1914 and in consequence of the hostility displayed by certain British Authorities, Mavrommatis had been prevented from financing his project within the required time and had suffered "irreparable injury the responsibility for which rests with the British Government." In answer the British Government filed a preliminary objection to the jurisdiction of the Court, alleging inter alia that the jurisdiction of the Court under Article 11 of the Mandate did not extend to mere administrative delays obstructing the execution of a contract that had duly come into effect. On October 10, 1927, the Court gave judgment (Publications of the Court, Series A, No. 10) upholding the objection of the British Government to the jurisdiction of the Court, but in so doing it recorded the statements of the British Government, made at the hearing, that it was open to Mavrommatis to seek damages by process of law before the courts of England or Palestine.

question, taking into consideration the information which the various countries concerned may equally present to the Court:

" 'Do Articles 10 and 11 of the Treaty of Peace between Finland and Russia, signed at Dorpat on October 14th, 1920, and the annexed Declaration of the Russian Delegation regarding the autonomy of Eastern Carelia, constitute engagements of an international character which place Russia under an obligation to Finland as to the carrying out of the provisions contained therein?' . . .

The Court also heard, at the request of the Finnish Government, the statements of its representative, M. Rafael Erich, and received from him a document containing arguments supplementary to those statements. The Court had informed M. Erich before hearing his statement that it would be glad to have his views as to whether it had competence to give effect to the request for an advisory opinion upon the question of Eastern Carelia, submitted to it by the Council of the League of Nations.

The Secretary-General of the League was duly informed of the step taken by the Court in this respect.

M. Tchitcherin, the Russian People's Commissary for Foreign Affairs, on the 11th June despatched to the Court a telegram, which has been read in Court in full, and which is as follows [translation] : . . . "The Russian Government finds it impossible to take any part in the proceedings, without legal value either in substance or in form, which the Permanent Court intends to institute as regards the Carelian question. Whereas the Workers' Commune of Carelia is an autonomous portion of the Russian Federation; whereas its autonomy is based on the decree of the Pan-Russian Central Executive Council, dated June 8th, 1920, which was enacted before the examination of this question by the Russo-Finnish Peace Conference at Dorpat; furthermore, whereas the Treaty of Dorpat, in connection with another matter, refers to the autonomous territory of Carelia as already existing without imposing any obligation in this respect upon Russia; whereas the Russian Delegation at Dorpat declared each time that this question was raised that it was an internal question affecting the Russian Federation; furthermore, whereas Berzine, the President of the Russian Delegation, at the meeting of October 14th, 1920, brought the fact that Carelia was autonomous to the knowledge of the Finnish Delegation solely for their information; furthermore, whereas in a Note dated December 5th, 1920, and addressed to the Finnish Chargé d'affaires, Tchitcherin, the Commissary of the People, protested categorically against the action taken by the Finnish Government in placing the Eastern Carelian question before the League of Nations, a course which in the view of the Russian Government constituted an act of hostility to the Russian Federation and an intervention in its domestic affairs; furthermore, whereas, in an official communication published on June 18th, 1922, the Commissary of the People for Foreign Affairs declared that the Russian Government absolutely repudiated the claim of the so-called League of Nations to intervene in the question of the internal situation of Carelia and stated that any attempt on the part of any power to apply to Russia the article of the Covenant of the League relating to disputes between one of its Members and a non-participating State would be regarded by the Russian Government as an act of hostility to the Russian State: the Russian Government categorically refuses to take any part in the examination of this question by the League of Nations or by the Permanent Court.'' . . .

II. Eastern Carelia is a territory of considerable extent, lying between the White Sea and Lake Onega on the east and Finland on the west.

Finland became entirely separated from Russia in 1917. War broke out between the Soviet Government and Finland, the two countries being in controversy as to boundaries and as to a great many other questions which are enumerated in the Treaty of Dorpat, which was concluded on the 14th October, 1920, and came into force on the 1st January, 1921. While the hostilities were going on two of the Communes of Eastern Carelia Repola and Porajärvi were placed under the protection of Finland.

Articles 10 and 11 of the Treaty of Dorpat are as follows;

Article 10: ''Finland shall within a time limit of forty-five days, dating from the entry into force of the present Treaty, withdraw her troops from the Communes of Repola and Porajärvi. These Communes shall be re-incorporated in the State of Russia and shall be attached to the autonomous territory of Eastern Carelia, which is to include the Carelian population of the Governments of Archangel and Olonetz, and which shall enjoy the national right of self-determination.''

Article 11: ''The Contracting Powers have adopted the following provisions for the benefit of the local population of the Communes of Repola and Porajärvi, with a view to a more detailed regulation of the conditions under which the union of these Communes with the Autonomous Territory of Eastern Carelia referred to in the preceding article is to take place:

''1. The inhabitants of the Communes shall be accorded a complete amnesty, as provided in Article 35 of the present Treaty.

''2. The local maintenance of order in the territory of the Communes shall be undertaken by a militia organised by the local population for a period of two years, dating from the entry into force of the present Treaty.

''3. The inhabitants of these Communes shall be assured of the enjoyment of all their movable property situated in the territory of the Communes, also of the right to dispose and make unrestricted use of the fields which belong to or are cultivated by them and of all other immovable property in their possession, within the limits of the legislation in force in the Autonomous Territory of Eastern Carelia.

"4. All the inhabitants of these Communes shall be free, if they so desire, to leave Russia within a period of one month from the date upon which this Treaty comes into force. Those persons who leave Russia under these conditions shall be entitled to take with them all their personal possessions and shall retain, within the limits of the existing laws in the independent territory of Eastern Carelia, all their rights to any immovable property which they may leave in the territory of these Communes.

"5. Citizens of Finland and Finnish commercial and industrial associations shall be permitted, for the duration of one year from the date upon which this Treaty comes into force, to complete in these Communes the felling of forests to which they are entitled by contracts signed prior to June 1st, 1920, and to take away the wood felled."

The Treaty contains also a number of provisions upon other matters, e. g. boundaries, territorial waters, fishing, right of transit, neutralisation of waters and islands, customs, government property and debts, commercial relations and traffic, railways, posts and telegraphs. Article 37 provides for the appointment of a Russo-Finnish Mixed Commission, to see to the execution of the Treaty and to questions of public and private rights which might arise under it.

It will be observed that the Articles 10 and 11 describe the territory of Eastern Carelia as "autonomous," but, except as provided in these articles, there are not in the Treaty itself any provisions as to the nature and extent of the autonomy.

Certain other documents described as "Declarations inserted in the Procès-Verbal by the Finnish and Russian Peace Delegations at Dorpat, October 14th, 1920, at the meeting for the signature of the Treaty of Peace between the Republic of Finland and the Socialist Federative Republic of the Russian Soviets," were likewise presented to the Court; one of these documents is as follows [translation]:

"At the general meeting of Peace delegates on October 14th, the following declaration was inserted in the procès-verbal on behalf of the Russian Delegation:

"The Socialist Federative Republic of the Russian Soviets guarantees the following rights to the Carelian population of the Governments of Archangel and Olonetz (Aunus):

"(1) The Carelian population of the Governments of Archangel and Olonetz (Aunus) shall enjoy the right of self-determination.

"(2) That part of Eastern Carelia which is inhabited by the said population shall constitute, so far as its internal affairs are concerned, an autonomous territory united to Russia on a federal basis.

"(3) The affairs of this district shall be dealt with by national representatives elected by the local population, and having the right to levy taxes for the needs of the territory, to issue edicts and regulations with regard to local needs, and to regulate internal administration.

"(4) The local native language shall be used in matters of administration, legislation and public education.

"(5) The autonomous territory of Eastern Carelia shall have the right to regulate its economic life in accordance with its local needs, and in accordance with the general economic organization of the Republic.

"(6) In connection with the reorganization of the military defensive forces of the Russian Republic, there shall be organized in the autonomous territory of Eastern Carelia a militia system, having as its object the suppression of the permanent army and the creation in its place of a national militia for local defense."

III. It appears from the documents which have been supplied to the Court that the Government of Finland and the Soviet Government are in acute controversy with regard to the above-mentioned Declaration. The Finnish Government maintain that it forms part of the contract between the two countries and that the Treaty was signed on the terms that the Declaration was as binding as the Treaty itself. The Soviet Government maintain that the Declaration was not by way of contract, but was only declaratory of an existing situation and made merely for information. . . .

It appears from the documents presented to the Court that:

(a) Finland's contentions are:

(1) That Articles 10 and 11 of the Treaty of Dorpat and the Declaration inserted in the protocol relative thereto constitute executory obligations which Russia is bound to carry out.

(2) That Russia has not carried out those obligations.

(b) Russia's contentions are:

(1) That Russia considers the question relating to the Autonomy of Eastern Carelia as an internal matter, and that this was brought to the notice of the representatives of Finland at the time of the negotiation of the Treaty of Dorpat. The Declaration was given solely for information.

(2) That the autonomy mentioned under Articles 10 and 11 of the Treaty of Dorpat and in the Declaration refers only to the existing Workers' Commune of Carelia, established by Decree of June 7th, 1920, prior to the conclusion of the Treaty. . . .

The question whether this Declaration forms part of the obligations into which Russia entered, as Finland asserts, or was merely by way of information, as Russia contends, is, in the very nature of things, a question of fact. The question is, was such an engagement made? The real question put to the Court largely turns upon the Declaration as to autonomy inserted in the protocol of signature relative to the Treaty. If that Declaration forms part of the engagement between Finland and Russia, it would stand for this purpose on the same footing as the Treaty itself. . . .

There has been some discussion as to whether questions for an advisory opinion, if they relate to matters which form the subject of a pending dispute between nations, should be put to the Court without the consent of the parties. It is unnecessary in the present case to deal with this topic.

It follows from the above that the opinion which the Court has been requested to give bears on an actual dispute between Finland and Russia. As Russia is not a Member of the League of Nations, the case is one under Article 17 of the Covenant. According to this article, in the event of a dispute between a Member of the League and a State which is not a Member of the League, the State not a Member of the League shall be invited to accept the obligations of membership in the League for the purposes of such dispute, and, if this invitation is accepted, the provisions of Articles 12 to 16 inclusive shall be applied with such modifications as may be deemed necessary by the Council. This, rule, moreover, only accepts and applies a principle which is a fundamental principle of international law, namely, the principle of the independence of States. It is well established in international law that no State can, without its consent, be compelled to submit its disputes with other States either to mediation or to arbitration, or to any other kind of pacific settlement. Such consent can be given once and for all in the form of an obligation freely undertaken, but it can, on the contrary, also be given in a special case apart from any existing obligation. The first alternative applies to the Members of the League who, having accepted the Covenant, are under the obligation resulting from the provisions of this pact dealing with the pacific settlement of international disputes. As concerns States not members of the League, the situation is quite different; they are not bound by the Covenant. The submission, therefore, of a dispute between them and a Member of the League for solution according to the methods provided for in the Covenant, could take place only by virtue of their consent. Such consent, however, has never been given by Russia. On the contrary, Russia has, on several occasions, clearly declared that it accepts no intervention by the League of Nations in the dispute with Finland. The refusals which Russia had already opposed to the steps suggested by the Council have been renewed upon the receipt by it of the notification of the request for an advisory opinion. The Court therefore finds it impossible to give its opinion on a dispute of this kind.

It appears to the Court that there are other cogent reasons which render it very inexpedient that the Court should attempt to deal with the present question. The question whether Finland and Russia contracted on the terms of the Declaration as to the nature of the autonomy of Eastern Carelia is really one of fact. To answer it would involve the duty of ascertaining what evidence might throw light upon the contentions which have been put forward on this subject by Finland and Russia respectively, and of securing the attendance of such witnesses as might be necessary. The Court would, of course, be at a very great disadvantage in such an enquiry, owing to the fact that Russia refuses to take part in it. It appears, now to be very doubtful whether there would be available to the Court materials sufficient to enable it to arrive at any judicial conclusion upon the question of fact: What did the parties agree to? The Court does not say that there is an absolute rule that the request for an advisory opinion may not involve some enquiry as to facts, but, under ordinary circumstances, it is certainly expedient that the facts upon which the opinion of the Court is desired should not be in controversy, and it should not be left to the Court itself to ascertain what they are.

The Court is aware of the fact that it is not requested to decide a dispute, but to give an advisory opinion. This circumstance, however, does not essentially modify the above considerations. The question put to the Court is not one of abstract law, but concerns directly the main point of the controversy between Finland and Russia, and can only be decided by an investigation into the facts underlying the case. Answering the question would be substantially equivalent to deciding the dispute between the parties. The Court, being a Court of Justice, cannot, even in giving advisory opinions, depart from the essential rules guiding their activity as a Court.

It is with regret that the Court, the Russian Government having refused their concurrence, finds itself unable to pursue the investigation which, as the terms of the Council's Resolution had foreshadowed, would require the consent and co-operation of both parties. There are also the other considerations already adverted to in this opinion, which point to the same conclusion.

The Court cannot regret that the question has been put, as all must now realize that the Council has spared no pains in exploring every avenue which might possibly lead to some solution with a view to settling a dispute between two nations.

MM. WEISS, Vice-President, NYHOLM, DE BUSTAMANTE and ALTAMIRA, judges, declare that they are unable to share the views of the majority of the Court as to the impossibility of giving an advisory opinion on the Eastern Carelian question.[1]

---

[1] The opinion of the Court in this case has been a subject of much controversy, and it figured prominently in the debates in the United States Senate preceding the adoption of the Resolution of January 27, 1926, providing for the ratification of the Protocol of the Permanent Court of International Justice, subject to certain reservations. See Hudson, Permanent Court of International Justice (1925), Chap. V.

CHAPTER XVIII

FORCIBLE PROCEDURE SHORT OF WAR [1]

A. Reprisals.

Since arbitration, or the alternative procedure of conciliation, was not obligatory upon states until the adoption of the Covenant of the League of Nations, it frequently happened that the larger states, when they felt that the procedure of arbitration might not lead to satisfactory results, undertook to bring physical pressure to bear upon the opposing party without technically resorting to war. These methods of using force short of war were accepted by international law as legitimate measures of self-defense, and the only questions that arose were those relating to the rights of third parties, whether individual citizens whose property might be affected or states whose national interests might be involved. Query, would a court of claims, authorized to determine the validity of claims arising from "illegal captures," consider certain seizures of vessels as justified on the ground of the existence of open hostilities even when no formal declaration of war had been made? [Gray, Adm'r v. United States.]

WILLIAM GRAY, ADMINISTRATOR, v. THE UNITED STATES.

United States, Court of Claims, 1886.

21 Ct. Cl. 340.

[In 1885 Congress enacted a law authorizing American citizens having "valid claims to indemnity upon the French Government arising out of illegal captures, detentions, seizures, condemnations, and confiscations" prior to the treaty with France of September 30, 1800, to bring suit in the Court of Claims, and directing that court to "determine the validity and amount" thereof. Under this act the present suit was brought for indemnity for the loss of the Sally, a schooner owned and commanded by

---

[1] For a more detailed study of this subject, see Fenwick, *op. cit.*, pp. 433–440; Hyde, *op. cit.*, II, §§ 586–595; Oppenheim, *op. cit.*, II, §§ 26–49; Hindmarsh, Force in Peace; H. Lauterpacht, "Boycott in International Relations," British Year Book, XIV (1933), 125; C. C. Hyde, "The Boycott as a Sanction of International Law," Proceedings, Am. Society of Int. Law, 1933, p. 34.

Americans and laden with an American cargo, which, while on a voyage from Massachusetts to Spain, was seized on the high seas by a French privateer, taken to a French port and condemned for the violation of a French regulation "concerning the navigation of neutrals."]

Davis, J., delivered the opinion of the court:

This claim, one of the class popularly called "French Spoliations," springs from the policy of the French revolutionary government between the execution of King Louis XVI and the year 1801, a policy which led to the detention, seizure, condemnation, and confiscation of our merchant vessels peacefully pursuing legitimate voyages upon the high seas. . . .

The defendants contend that the seizures were justified, as war existed between this country and France during the period in question; and, as we could have no claim against France for seizure of private property in time of war, the claimants could have no resulting claim against their own Government; that is, the claims, being invalid, could not form a subject of set-off as it is urged these claims did in the second article of the treaty of 1800. It therefore becomes of great importance to determine whether there was a state of war between the two countries.

It is urged that the political and judicial departments of each Government recognized the other as an enemy; that battles were fought and blood shed on the high seas; that property was captured by each from the other and condemned as prize; that diplomatic and consular intercourse was suspended, and that prisoners had been taken by each Government from the other and "held for exchange, punishment, or retaliation, according to the laws and usages of war." While these statements may be in substance admitted and constitute very strong evidence of the existence of war, still they are not conclusive, and the facts, even if they existed to the extent claimed, may not be inconsistent with a state of reprisals straining the relations of the States to their utmost tension, daily threatening hostilities of a more serious nature, but still short of that war which abrogates treaties, and after conclusion of which parties must, as between themselves, begin international life anew.

The French issued decree after decree against our peaceful commerce, but, on the ground of military necessity incident to the war with Great Britain and her allies; they refused to receive our minister, but in that refusal, insolent though it was, there is nothing to show that war was intended, and the mere refusal to receive a minister does not in itself constitute a ground for hostilities. . . .

Congress enacted the various statutes hereinafter referred to in detail, and when one of them, the act providing an additional armament, was passed in the House, Edward Livingston, who opposed it, said:

"Let no man flatter himself that the vote which has been given is not a declaration of war. Gentlemen know that this is the case."

Those were times of great excitement; between danger of international contest and heat of internal partisan conflict statesmen could not look at the situation with the calmness possessed by their successors, and those successors, with some exceptions to be sure, regarded the relations between the countries as not amounting to war.

The question has been carefully examined by authorized and competent officers of the political department of the Government, and we may turn to their statements as expository of the view of that branch upon the subject. . . .

Mr. Livingston reported to the Senate in 1830 that—

"This was not a case of war, and the stipulations which reconciled the two nations was not a treaty of peace; it was a convention for the putting an end to certain differences. . . . Nowhere is the slightest expression on either side that a state of war existed, which would exonerate either party from the obligations of making those indemnities to the other. . . . The convention which was the result of these negotiations is not only in its form different from a treaty of peace, but it contains stipulations which would be disgraceful to our country on the supposition that it terminated a state of war. . . . Neither party considered then they were in a state of war." (Rep. 4, 445.) . . .

Mr. Sumner considered the acts of Congress as "vigorous measures," putting the country "in an attitude of defence;" and that the "painful condition of things, though naturally causing great anxiety, did not constitute war." (38th Cong., 1st sess., Rep. 41, 1864.)

The judiciary also had occasion to consider the situation, and the learned counsel for the defendants cites us to the opinion of Mr. Justice Moore, delivered in the case of Bass v. Tingy, (4 Dall. 37), wherein the facts were as follows: Tingy, commander of the public armed ship the Ganges, had libelled the American ship Eliza, Bass, master, setting forth that she had been taken on the high seas by a French privateer the 31st March, 1799, and retaken by him late in the following April, wherefore salvage was claimed and allowed below. Upon appeal the judgment was affirmed. Each of the four justices present delivered an opinion.

Justice Moore, answering the contention that the word "enemy" could not be applied to the French, says:

"How can the character of the parties engaged in hostility of war be otherwise described than by the denomination of enemies? It is for the honor and dignity of both nations, therefore, they should be called enemies; for it is by that description alone that either could justify or excuse the scene of bloodshed, depredation, and confiscation which has unhappily occurred, and surely Congress could only employ the language of the act of June 13, 1798, towards a nation whom she considered as an enemy."

Justice Washington considers the very point now in dispute, saying (p. 40):

"The decision of the question must depend upon . . . whether at the time of passing the act of Congress of the 2d of March, 1799, there subsisted a state of war between two nations. It may, I believe, be safely laid down that every contention by force between two nations, in external matters, under the authority of their respective Governments, is not only war, but public war. . . . But hostilities may subsist between two nations more confined in its nature and extent, being limited as to places, persons, and things, and this is more properly termed imperfect war, because not solemn, and because those who are authorized to commit hostilities act under special authority and can go no further than to the extent of their commission.'' . . .

Applying this rule he held that "an American and French armed vessel, combating on the high seas, were enemies," but added that France was not styled "an enemy" in the statutes, because "the degree of hostility meant to be carried on was sufficiently described without declaring war, or declaring that we were at war. Such a declaration by Congress might have constituted a perfect state of war which was not intended by the Government."

Justice Chase, who had tried the case below, said:

"It is a limited, partial war. Congress has not declared war in general terms, but Congress has authorized hostilities on the high seas by certain persons in certain cases. . . ."

Justice Patterson concurred, holding that the United States and France were "in a qualified state of hostility"—war "*quoad hoc.*" As far as Congress tolerated and authorized it, so far might we proceed in hostile operations and the word "enemy" proceeds the full length of this qualified war, and no further.

The Supreme Court, therefore, held the state of affairs now under discussion to constitute partial warfare, limited by the acts of Congress.

The instructions to Ellsworth, Davie, and Murray, dated October 22, 1799, did not recognize a state of war as existing, or as having existed, for they said the conduct of France would have justified an immediate declaration of war, but the United States, desirous of maintaining peace, contented themselves "with preparations for defence and measures calculated to defend their commerce." (Doc. 102, p. 561.) . . .

France did not consider that war existed, for the minister said that the suspension of his functions was not to be regarded as a rupture between the countries, "but as a mark of just discontent" (15 Nov., 1796, Foreign Relations, vol. I, p. 583); while J. Bonaparte and his colleagues termed it a "transient misunderstanding" (Doc. 102, p. 590), a state of "misunderstanding" which had existed "through the acts of some agents rather than by the will of the respective 'Governments,'" and which had not been a state of war, at least on the side of France. (Ib. 616.)

The opinion of Congress at the time is best gleaned from the laws which it passed. The important statute in this connection is that of May 28, 1798 (1 Stat. L., 561), entitled "An act more effectually to pro-

tect the commerce and coasts of the United States.'' Certainly there
was nothing aggressive or warlike in this title.

The act recites that, whereas French armed vessels have committed
depredations on American commerce in violation of the law of nations
and treaties between the United States and France, the President is
authorized—not to declare war, but to direct naval commanders to bring
into our ports, to be proceeded against according to the law of nations,
any such vessels ''which shall have committed, or which shall be found
hovering on the coasts of the United States for the purpose of committing, depredations on the vessels belonging to the citizens thereof; and
also to retake any ship or vessel of any citizen or citizens of the United
States which may have been captured by any such armed vessel.''

This law contains no declaration or threat of war; it is distinctly an
act to protect our coasts and commerce. It says that our vessels may
arrest a vessel raiding or intending to raid upon that commerce, and that
such vessel shall not be either held by an executive authority or confiscated, but turned over to the admiralty courts—recognized international tribunals—for trial, not according to municipal statutes, as was
being done in France, but according to the law of nations. . . .

. . . This statute is a fair illustration of the class of laws enacted at
this time; they directed suspension of commercial relations until the end
of the next session of Congress, not indefinitely (June 13, 1798, ib. § 4,
p. 566); they gave power to the President to apprehend the subjects of
hostile nations whenever he should make ''public proclamation'' of war
(July 6, 1798, ib. 577), and no such proclamation was made; they gave
him authority to instruct our armed vessels to seize French ''armed,''
not merchant, vessels (July 9, 1798, ib., 578), together with contingent
authority to augment the army in case war should break out in case of
imminent danger of invasion. (March 2, 1799, ib., 725.) Within a few
months after this last act of Congress the Ellsworth mission was on its
way to France to begin the negotiations which resulted in the treaty of
1800 and even the act abrogating the treaties of 1778 does not speak of
war as existing, but of ''the system of predatory violence . . . hostile
to the rights of a free and independent nation.'' (July 7, 1798, ib., 578.)

If war existed, why authorize our armed vessels to seize French armed
vessels? War itself gave that right, as well as the right to seize merchantmen, which the statutes did not permit. If war existed why empower the President to apprehend foreign enemies? War itself placed
that duty upon him as a necessary and inherent incident of military
command. Why, if there was war, should a suspension of commercial
intercourse be authorized, for what more complete suspension of that
intercourse could there be than the very fact of war? And why, if
war did exist, should the President, so late as March, 1799, be empowered
to increase the army upon one of two conditions, viz., that war should
break out or invasion be imminent, that is, if war should break out in the
future or invasion become imminent in the future? . . .

This legislation shows that war was imminent; that protection of our commerce was ordered, but distinctly shows that, in the opinion of the legislature, war did not in fact exist. . . .

There was no declaration of war; the tribunals of each country were open to the other—an impossibility were war in progress; diplomatic and commercial intercourse were admittedly suspended; but during many years there was no intercourse between England and Mexico, which were not at war; there was retaliation and reprisal, but such retaliations and reprisals have often occurred between nations at peace; there was a near approach to war, but at no time was one of the nations turned into an enemy of the other in such manner that every citizen of one became the enemy of every citizen of the other; finally, there was not that kind of war which abrogated treaties and wiped out, at least temporarily, all pending rights and contracts, individual and national.

In cases like this "the judicial is bound to follow the action of the political department of the Government, and is concluded by it" (Phillips v. Payne, 92 U. S. R. 130); and we do not find an act of Congress or of the Executive between the years 1793 and 1801 which recognizes an existing state of solemn war, although we find statutory provisions authorizing a certain course "in the event of a declaration of war," or "whenever there shall be declared war," or during the existing "differences." One act provides for the increase of the army "in case war shall break out," while another restrains this increase "unless war shall break out." (1 Stat. L., 558, 577, 725, 750; see also acts of Feb. 10, 1800, and May 14, 1800.)

We have already referred to the instructions of the Executive, which show that branch of the Government in thorough accord with the legislative on this subject, and the negotiations of our representatives hereinafter referred to were marked by the same views, while the treaty itself—a treaty of amity and commerce of limited duration—is strong proof that what were called "differences" did not amount to war. We are, therefore, of the opinion that no such war existed as operated to abrogate treaties, to suspend private rights, or to authorize indiscriminate seizures and condemnations; that, in short, there was no public general war, but limited war in its nature similar to a prolonged series of reprisals. . . . [1]

---

[1] SUPPLEMENTARY CASES. Query, will redress be made by a state to neutrals for property destroyed as an incident to reprisals? In Perrin v. United States, 4 Court of Claims Rep. 543 (1868), involving a claim for property destroyed in the bombardment of Greytown, Nicaragua, by a United States warship in 1854 because of the lawless acts of persons operating from that center, the claimant and her husband being French subjects temporarily domiciled at Greytown and the owners of merchandise stored there, the Court of Claims held that "the claimants' case must necessarily rest upon the assumption that the bombardment and destruction of Greytown was illegal and not justified by the law of nations." Questions such as these, said the court, were "international political questions"

B. Embargo.

A form of general reprisals frequently resorted to by states during the eighteenth and nineteenth centuries consisted in laying an embargo upon vessels of the offending state that happened at the time to be in the ports of the state seeking redress. Query, would a foreign vessel be confiscated absolutely if an embargo that was laid upon the vessels of that country should be followed by formal war? [The Boedes Lust.]

THE BOEDES LUST.

Great Britain, High Court of Admiralty, 1804.

5 C. Rob. 233.

[On May 16, 1803, the government of Great Britain imposed an embargo on all Dutch property in British ports. In consequence, the Boedes Lust, a vessel belonging to residents of the Dutch colony of Demerara, was seized. The next month war was declared between England and Holland. In December, 1803, the colony of Demerara was ceded to England. The original owners thereupon sought to recover the vessel on the ground that they were at the time of seizure, and of adjudication, "not enemies of the Crown of Great Britain."]

SIR WILLIAM SCOTT . . . The claim is given for several persons as inhabitants of Demerara, not settling there during the time of British possession, nor averring an intention of returning when that possession ceased. They are therefore to be treated under this general view as Dutch subjects, unless it can be shown that there are any other circumstances by which they are protected. It is contended that there are such circumstances and that they are these: That the property was taken in a state of peace, and that the proprietors are now become British subjects, and consequently that this property could not be considered as the property of an enemy, either at the time of capture or adjudication. Now, with respect to the first of these pleas, it must be admitted, that alone would not protect them, because the Court has, without any exception, condemned all other property of Dutchmen taken before the war—And upon what ground?—That the declaration had a retroactive effect, applying to all property previously detained, and rendering it liable to be considered as the property of enemies taken in time of war. This property was seized provisionally, an act hostile enough in the mere execution, but equivocal as to the effect, and liable to be varied by subsequent events, and by the conduct of the Government of Holland. If that conduct had been such as to reestablish the relations of peace, then the seizure, although made with the character of a hostile seizure, would

---

to be decided not by the courts but by the political department of the government, whose attitude in this case was expressed by a letter of the Secretary of State. The petition of the claimant was therefore dismissed.

have proved in the event a mere embargo, or temporary sequestration. The property would have been restored, as it is usual, at the conclusion of embargoes; a process often resorted to in the practice of nations, for various causes not immediately connected with any expectations of hostility. During the period that this embargo lasted, it is said, that the Court might have restored, but I cannot assent to that observation; because, on due notice of embargoes, this Court is bound to enforce them. It would be a high misprision in this Court, to break them, by re-delivery of possession to the foreign owner of that property, which the Crown had directed to be seized and detained for farther orders. The Court acting in pursuance of the general orders of the State, and bound by those general orders, would be guilty of no denial of justice, in refusing to decree restitution in such a case, for it has not the power to restore. Its functions are suspended by a binding authority, and if any injustice is done that is an account to be settled between the States. The Court has no responsibility, for it has no ability to act.

This was the state of the first seizure. It was at first equivocal; and if the matter in dispute had terminated in reconciliation, the seizure would have been converted into a mere civil embargo, so terminated. That would have been the retroactive effect of that course of circumstances. On the contrary, if the transactions end in hostility, the retroactive effect is directly the other way. It impresses the direct hostile character upon the original seizure. It is declared to be *no embargo*, it is no longer an equivocal act, subject to two interpretations; there is a declaration of the *animus*, by which it was done, that it was *done hostili animo*, and is to be considered as an hostile measure *ab initio*. The property taken is liable to be used as the property of persons, trespassers *ab initio*, and guilty of injuries, which they have refused to redeem by any amicable alteration of their measures. This is the necessary course, if no particular compact intervenes for the restitution of such property taken before a formal declaration of hostilities. No such convention is set up on either side, and the State, by directing proceedings against this property for condemnation, has signified a contrary intention. Accordingly the general mass of Dutch property has been condemned on this retroactive effect; and *this* property stands upon the same footing as to the seizure, for it was seized at the same time, and with the same intent. . . .

The Settlement [Demerara] has since surrendered to the British arms, and the parties are become British subjects; and this, it is said, takes off the hostile effect, although it might have attached. This argument to be effective, must be put in one of these two ways, either that the condemnation pronounced upon Dutch property went upon the ground that, though seized in time of neutrality, it could not be restored *only*, because the parties were not now in a condition to receive it; or else, that though seized at a time, that may to some effects be considered as time of war, yet the subjects, having become friends, are entitled to restitution. This latter position cannot be maintained for a moment. It is contradicted by all experience and practice, even in the case of those who had an original British character. . . . Where property is taken in a state of hostility, the universal practice has ever been to hold it subject to condemnation, although the claimants may have become friends and subjects prior to the adjudication. The plea of having again become British subjects, therefore, will not relieve them, and the other ground must be resorted to. That is equally untenable in point of fact; for the condemnation of the other Dutch property proceeded on no such ground as the mere incapacity of the proprietors to receive restitution. It proceeded on the other ground, which I have before mentioned, the retroactive effect of the declaration, which rendered their property liable to be treated as the property of enemies at the time of seizure. . . . The property, at the time of the capture, belonged to subjects of the Batavian Republic, and is as such or otherwise liable to confiscation.

C. Pacific blockade.

A blockade is said to be ''pacific'' when, without resorting to a declaration of war, a stronger state undertakes to surround a port or ports of the offending state and cut off communication with the outside world. It differs from hostile blockade not only in respect to the absence of a formal state of war but in respect to the relations of third states to the blockade. Query, if a number of states should have claims against a particular state and if certain of their number should resort to a pacific blockade to obtain their demands, would the latter acquire by reason of their measures of force any rights of priority in the settlement of the claims? [Germany et al. and Venezuela: Preferential Claims Case.]

GERMANY ET AL. AND VENEZUELA: PREFERENTIAL CLAIMS CASE.

Tribunal of the Permanent Court of Arbitration, 1904.

Scott, Hague Court Reports, 56.

[By the Tribunal. Mourawieff, Lammasch, de Martens, Arbitrators.] The tribunal of arbitration, constituted in virtue of the protocols signed at Washington on May 7, 1903, between Germany, Great Britain and Italy on the one hand and Venezuela on the other hand;

Whereas, other protocols were signed to the same effect by Belgium, France, Mexico, the Netherlands, Spain, Sweden and Norway and the United States of America on the one hand and Venezuela on the other hand;

Whereas, all these protocols declare the agreement of all the contracting parties with reference to the settlement of the claims against the Venezuelan Government;

Whereas, certain further questions, arising out of the action of the Governments of Germany, Great Britain and Italy concerning the settlement of their claims, were not susceptible of solution by the ordinary diplomatic methods;

Whereas, the Powers interested decided to solve these questions by submitting them to arbitration, in conformity with the dispositions of the Convention, signed at The Hague on July 29th, 1899, for the pacific settlement of international disputes; . . .

And whereas, in virtue of the protocols of Washington of May 7th, 1903, the above-named arbitrators, forming the legally constituted tribunal of arbitration, had to decide, in conformity with Article 1 of the protocols of Washington of May 7th, 1903, the following points:

The question as to whether or not Germany, Great Britain, and Italy are entitled to preferential or separate treatment in the payment of their claims against Venezuela, and its decision shall be final.

Venezuela having agreed to set aside thirty per cent. of the customs revenues of La Guaira and Puerto Cabello for the payment of the claims of all nations against Venezuela, the tribunal at The Hague shall decide how the said revenues shall be divided between the blockading Powers on the one hand and the other creditor Powers on the other hand, and its decision shall be final.

If preferential or separate treatment is not given to the blockading Powers, the tribunal shall decide how the said revenue shall be distributed among all the creditor Powers, and the parties hereto agree that the tribunal, in that case, shall consider, in connection with the payment of the claims out of the thirty per cent. any preference or pledges of revenues enjoyed by any of the creditor Powers, and shall accordingly decide the question of distribution so that no Power shall obtain preferential treatment, and its decision shall be final. . . .

Whereas, the tribunal, in its examination of the present litigation, had to be guided by the principles of international law and the maxims of justice;

Whereas, the various protocols signed at Washington since February 13th, 1903, and particularly the protocols of May 7th, 1903, the obligatory force of which is beyond all doubt, form the legal basis for the arbitral award; . . .

Whereas, the tribunal considers itself absolutely incompetent to give a decision as to the character or the nature of the military operations undertaken by Germany, Great Britain and Italy against Venezuela;

Whereas, also, the tribunal of arbitration was not called upon to decide whether the three blockading Powers had exhausted all pacific methods in their dispute with Venezuela in order to prevent the employment of force,

And it can only state the fact that since 1901 the Government of Venezuela categorically refused to submit its dispute with Germany and Great Britain to arbitration which was proposed several times and especially by the note of the German Government of July 16th, 1901;

Whereas, after the war between Germany, Great Britain and Italy on the one hand and Venezuela on the other hand no formal treaty of peace was concluded between the belligerent Powers;

Whereas, the protocols, signed at Washington on February 13th, 1903, had not settled all the questions in dispute between the belligerent parties, leaving open in particular the question of the distribution of the receipts of the customs of La Guaira and Puerto Cabello;

Whereas, the belligerent Powers in submitting the question of preferential treatment in the matter of these receipts to the judgment of the tribunal of arbitration, agreed that the arbitral award should serve to fill up this void and to ensure the definite reestablishment of peace between them;

Whereas, on the other hand, the warlike operations of the three great European Powers against Venezuela ceased before they had received satisfaction on all their claims, and on the other hand the question of preferential treatment was submitted to arbitration, the tribunal must recognize in these facts precious evidence in favor of the great principle of arbitration in all phases of international disputes;

Whereas, the blockading Powers, in admitting the adhesion to the stipulations of the protocols of February 13th, 1903, of the other Powers which had claims against Venezuela, could evidently not have the intention of renouncing either their acquired rights or their actual privileged position;

Whereas, the Government of Venezuela in the protocols of February 13th, 1903 (Article 1), itself recognizes *"in principle the justice of the claims"* presented to it by the Governments of Germany, Great Britain and Italy;

While in the protocol signed between Venezuela and the so-called neutral or pacific Powers the justice of the claims of these latter was not recognized in principle;

Whereas, the Government of Venezuela until the end of January, 1903 in no way protested against the pretension of the blockading Powers to insist on special securities for the settlement of their claims;

Whereas, Venezuela itself during the diplomatic negotiations always made a formal distinction between *"the allied Powers"* and *"the neutral Powers"*;

Whereas, the neutral Powers, who now claim before the tribunal of arbitration equality in the distribution of the thirty per cent of the customs receipts of La Guaira and Puerto Cabello, did not protest against the pretensions of the blockading Powers to a preferential treatment either at the moment of the cessation of the war against Venezuela or immediately after the signature of the protocols of February 13th, 1903;

Whereas, it appears from the negotiations which resulted in the signature of the protocols of February 13th and May 7th, 1903, that the German and British Governments constantly insisted on their being given guaranties for *"a sufficient and punctual discharge of the obligations"* (British memorandum of December 23rd, 1902, communicated to the Government of the United States of America);

Whereas, the plenipotentiary of the Government of Venezuela accepted this reservation on the part of the allied Powers without the least protest;

Whereas, the Government of Venezuela engaged, with respect to the allied Powers alone, to offer special guaranties for the accomplishment of its engagements;

Whereas, the good faith which ought to govern international relations imposes the duty of stating that the words *"all claims"* used by the representative of the Government of Venezuela in his conferences with the representatives of the allied Powers (statement left in the hands of Sir Michael Herbert by Mr. H. Bowen of January 23d, 1903) could only mean the claims of these latter and could only refer to them;

Whereas, the neutral Powers, having taken no part in the warlike operations against Venezuela, could in some respects profit by the circumstances created by those operations, but without acquiring any new rights;

Whereas, the rights acquired by the neutral or pacific Powers with regard to Venezuela remain in the future absolutely intact and guaranteed by respective international arrangements;

Whereas, in virtue of Article 5 of the protocols of May 7th, 1903, signed at Washington, the tribunal "shall also decide, subject to the general provisions laid down in Article 57 of the international Convention of July 29th, 1899, how, when and by whom the costs of this arbitration shall be paid";

For these reasons, the tribunal of arbitration decides and pronounces unanimously that:

1. Germany, Great Britain and Italy have a right to preferential treatment for the payment of their claims against Venezuela;

2. Venezuela having consented to put aside thirty per cent. of the revenues of the customs of La Guaira and Puerto Cabello for the payment of the claims of all nations against Venezuela, the three above-named Powers have a right to preference in the payment of their claims by means of these thirty per cent. of the receipts of the two Venezuelan ports above mentioned.

3. Each party to the litigation shall bear its own costs and an equal share of the costs of the tribunal.

The Government of the United States of America is charged with seeing to the execution of this latter clause within a term of three months.

. . .

CHAPTER XIX

PROCEDURE BY WAR: EFFECT OF WAR UPON NORMAL RELATIONS OF NATIONALS OF THE BELLIGERENT STATES [1]

A. Effect of war upon rights created by treaties.

Until the year 1920 the legal right of a state to declare war against another state as a measure of self-redress when other means of securing its alleged rights had failed was openly recognized by international law. Each state was the judge in its own case and its decision that it had a "just cause of war" did not have to be submitted to the collective judgment of the whole community of nations as to the merits of the case. The outbreak of war naturally put an end to the normal official relations of the contending states. Query, did war permanently abrogate or only temporarily suspend the various treaties between the two states? What was the effect of war upon private rights created by treaty and already vested before the outbreak of the war? [Society for the Propagation of the Gospel v. New-Haven.] What was the effect of war upon private rights not yet vested at the time of the war? [Techt v. Hughes; Karnuth v. United States.]

THE SOCIETY FOR THE PROPAGATION OF THE GOSPEL IN FOREIGN PARTS v. THE TOWN OF NEW-HAVEN, AND WILLIAM WHEELER.

United States, Supreme Court, 1823.

8 Wheaton, 464. [5 L. ed. 662.]

This case came before the Court upon a certificate of a division in opinion of the Judges of the Circuit Court for the District of Vermont. It was an action of ejectment, brought by the plaintiffs against the defendants, in that Court. . . .

By a charter granted by William III . . . . a number of persons, subjects of England . . . were incorporated by the name of "The

---

[1] For a more detailed study of this subject, see Fenwick, *op. cit.*, pp. 455–468; Hyde, *op. cit.*, II, §§ 605–637; Oppenheim, *op. cit.*, II, §§ 97–102b; Garner, International Law and the World War, I, Chaps. III–V, VIII–IX; E. M. Borchard, "Enemy Private Property," Am. Journal of Int. Law, XVIII (1924), 523.

Society for the Propagation of the Gospel in Foreign Parts." . . . The corporation has ever since existed, and now exists, as an organized body politic and corporate, in England, all the members thereof being subjects of the king of Great Britain.

On the 2d of November, 1761, a grant was made by the governor of the province of New Hampshire, in the name of the king, by which a certain tract of land . . . so granted, was to be incorporated into a town, by the name of New-Haven, and to be divided into sixty-eight shares, one of which was granted to "The Society for the Propagation of the Gospel in Foreign Parts." . . .

On the 30th of October, 1794, the Legislature of Vermont passed an act, declaring that the rights to land in that State, granted under the authority of the British government previous to the revolution, to "The Society for the Propagation of the Gospel in Foreign Parts," were thereby granted severally to the respective towns in which such lands lay, . . . Under this law, the selectmen of the town of New-Haven executed a perpetual lease of a part of the demanded premises, to the defendant, William Wheeler, . . . immediately after which, the said Wheeler entered upon the land so leased, and has ever since held the possession thereof. . . .

Mr. Justice Washington delivered the opinion of the Court, . . .

It has been contended by the counsel for the defendants,

1st. That the capacity of the plaintiffs, as a corporation, to hold lands in Vermont, ceased by, and as a consequence of, the revolution.

2dly. That the society being, in its politic capacity, a foreign corporation, it is incapable of holding land in Vermont, on the ground of alienage; and that its rights are not protected by the treaty of peace.

3dly. That if they were so protected, still the effect of the last war between the United States and Great Britain, was to put an end to that treaty, and, consequently, to rights derived under it, unless they have been revived by the treaty of peace, which was not done. . . .

2. The next question is, was this property protected against forfeiture, for the cause of alienage, or otherwise, by the treaty of peace? This question, as to real estates belonging to British subjects, was finally settled in this Court, in the case of Orr v. Hodgson (4 Wheat. Rep. 453), in which it was decided, that the 6th article of the treaty protected the titles of such persons, to lands in the United States, which would have been liable to forfeiture, by escheat, for the cause of alienage, or to confiscation, *jure belli*.

The counsel for the defendants did not controvert this doctrine, so far as it applies to natural persons; but he contends, that the treaty does not, in its terms, embrace corporations existing in England, and that it ought not to be so construed. The words of the 6th article are, "there shall be no future confiscations made, nor any prosecutions commenced, against any person or persons, for or by reason of the part which he or they may have taken in the present war; and that no person shall, on that account, suffer any future loss or damage, either in his person, liberty or property,'' &c.

The terms in which this article is expressed are general and unqualified, and we are aware of no rule of interpretation applicable to treaties, or to private contracts, which would authorize the Court to make exceptions by construction, where the parties to the contract have not thought proper to make them. Where the language of the parties is clear of all ambiguity, there is no room for construction. Now, the parties to this treaty have agreed, that there shall be no future confiscations in any case, for the cause stated. How can this Court say, that this is a case where, for the cause stated, or for some other, confiscation may lawfully be decreed? We can discover no sound reason why a corporation existing in England may not as well hold real property in the United States, as ordinary trustees for charitable, or other purposes; or as natural persons for their own use. We have seen, that the exemption of either, or all of those persons, from the jurisdiction of the Courts of the State where the property lies, affords no such reason.

It is said, that a corporation cannot hold lands, except by permission of the sovereign authority. But this corporation did hold the land in question, by permission of the sovereign authority before, during, and subsequent to the revolution, up to the year 1794, when the Legislature of Vermont granted it to the town of New-Haven; and the only question is, whether this grant was not void by force of the 6th article of the above treaty? We think it was. . . .

But even if it were admitted that the plaintiffs are not within the protection of the treaty, it would not follow, that their right to hold the land in question was devested by the act of 1794, and became vested in the town of New-Haven. At the time when this law was enacted, the plaintiffs, though aliens, had a complete, though defeasible, title to the land, of which they could not be deprived for the cause of alienage, but by an inquest of office; and no grant of the State could, upon the principles of the common law, be valid, until the title of the State was so established. (Fairfax's Devisee v. Hunter's Lessee, 7 Cranch's Rep. 503.) Nor is it pretended by the counsel for the defendants, that this doctrine of the common law was changed by any statute law of the State of Vermont, at the time when this land was granted to the town of New-Haven. This case is altogether unlike that of Smith v. The State of Maryland, (6 Cranch's Rep. 286,) which turned upon an act of that State, passed in the year 1780, during the revolutionary war, which declared, that all property within the State, belonging to British subjects, should be seized, and was thereby confiscated to the use of the State; and that the commissioners of confiscated estates should be taken as being in the actual seisin and possession of the estates so confiscated, without any office found, entry, or other act to be done. The law in question passed long after the treaty of 1783, and without confiscating or forfeiting this land, (even if that could be legally done,) grants the same to the town of New-Haven.

3. The last question respects the effect of the late war, between Great Britain and the United States, upon rights existing under the treaty of peace. Under this head, it is contended by the defendants' counsel, that although the plaintiffs were protected by the treaty of peace, still, the effect of the last war was to put an end to that treaty, and, consequently, to civil rights derived under it, unless they had been revived and preserved by the treaty of Ghent.

If this argument were to be admitted in all its parts, it nevertheless would not follow, that the plaintiffs are not entitled to a judgment on this special verdict. The defendants claim title to the land in controversy solely under the act of 1794, stated in the verdict, and contend, that by force of that law, the title of the plaintiffs was devested. But if the Court has been correct in its opinion upon the first two points, it will follow, that the above act was utterly void, being passed in contravention of the treaty of peace, which, in this respect, is to be considered as the supreme law. Remove that law, then, out of the case, and the title of the plaintiffs, confirmed by the treaty of 1794, remains unaffected by the last war, it not appearing from the verdict, that the land was confiscated, or the plaintiffs' title in any way devested, during the war, or since, by office found, or even by any legislative act.

But there is a still more decisive answer to this objection, which is, that the termination of a treaty cannot devest rights of property already vested under it.

If real estate be purchased or secured under a treaty, it would be most mischievous to admit, that the extinguishment of the treaty extinguished the right to such estate. In truth, it no more affects such rights, than the repeal of a municipal law affects rights acquired under it. If, for example, a statute of descents be repealed, it has never been supposed, that rights of property already vested during its existence, were gone by such repeal. Such a construction would overturn the best established doctrines of law, and sap the very foundation on which property rests.

But we are not inclined to admit the doctrine urged at the bar, that treaties become extinguished, *ipso facto,* by war between the two governments, unless they should be revived by an express or implied renewal on the return of peace. Whatever may be the latitude of doctrine laid down by elementary writers on the law of nations, dealing in general terms in relation to this subject, we are satisfied, that the doctrine contended for is not universally true. There may be treaties of such a nature, as to their object and import, as that war will put an end to them; but where treaties contemplate a permanent arrangement of territorial, and other national rights, or which, in their terms, are meant to provide for the event of an intervening war, it would be against every principle of just interpretation to hold them extinguished by the event of war. If such were the law, even the treaty of 1783, so far as it fixed our limits, and acknowledged our independence, would be gone, and we should have had again to struggle for both upon original revolutionary principles. Such a construction was never asserted, and would be so monstrous as to supersede all reasoning.

We think, therefore, that treaties stipulating for permanent rights and general arrangements, and professing to aim at perpetuity, and to deal with the case of war as well as of peace, do not cease on the occurrence of war, but are, at most, only suspended while it lasts; and unless they are waived by the parties, or new and repugnant stipulations are made, they revive in their operation at the return of peace.

A majority of the Court is of opinion, that judgment upon this special verdict ought to be given for the plaintiffs, which opinion is to be certified to the Circuit Court.

Certificate for the plaintiffs.

SARA E. TECHT, RESPONDENT, v. ELIZABETH L. HUGHES, APPELLANT, IMPLEADED WITH OTHERS.

United States, Court of Appeals of New York, 1920.

229 N. Y. 222.

Appeal, by permission, from a judgment of the Appellate Division of the Supreme Court in the first judicial department, entered January 30, 1920, affirming an interlocutory judgment in favor of plaintiff entered upon a decision of the court on trial at Special Term in an action for partition of real property.

The following question was certified: "Has the plaintiff herein an estate of inheritance in the trial property sought to be partitioned in this action?" . . .

CARDOZO, J. James J. Hannigan, a citizen of the United States, died intestate on December 27, 1917, seized in fee simple of real estate in the city of New York. Two daughters, the plaintiff, Sara E. Techt, and the defendant, Elizabeth L. Hughes, survived him. In November, 1911, the plaintiff became the wife of Frederick E. Techt, a resident of the United States, but a citizen of Austria-Hungary. On December 7, 1917, twenty days before the death of the plaintiff's father, war was declared between Austria-Hungary and the United States. The record contains a concession that neither the plaintiff nor her husband has been interned, nor has the loyalty of either been questioned by the government of state or nation, and that both, remaining residents of the United States, have kept the peace and obeyed the laws. The plaintiff's capacity on December 27, 1917, to acquire title by descent is the question to be determined. . . .

The rule at common law was that aliens might take lands by purchase, and hold until office found, but could take nothing by descent. . . . The plaintiff is indisputably an alien. . . . She is without capacity to inherit unless statute or treaty has removed the disability.

Both statute [State of New York] and treaty are invoked in her behalf. . . . The treaty says that "where, on the death of any person holding real property, or property not personal, within the territories of one party, such real property would, by the laws of the land, descend on a citizen or subject of the other, were he not disqualified by the laws of the country where such real property is situated, such citizen or subject shall be allowed a term of two years to sell the same; which term may be reasonably prolonged, according to circumstances; and to withdraw the proceeds thereof, without molestation, and exempt from any other charges than those which may be imposed in like cases upon the inhabitants of the country from which such proceeds may be withdrawn" (Art. II of Convention between United States and Austria, concluded May 8, 1848, and proclaimed October 25, 1850; 9 Stat. 944, extending the stipulations of the treaty of Commerce and Navigation, concluded August 27, 1829, and proclaimed February 10, 1831, 8 Stat. 398). . . .

(2) The support of the statute failing, there remains the question of the treaty. The treaty, if in force, is the supreme law of the land (U. S. art. 6) and supersedes all local laws inconsistent with its terms (Hauenstein v. Lynham, 100 U. S. 483; Geofroy v. Riggs, 133 U. S. 258; Chirac v. Chirac, 2 Wheat. 259; Kull v. Kull, 37 Hun, 476). . . .

The effect of war upon the existing treaties of belligerents is one of the unsettled problems of the law. The older writers sometimes said that treaties ended *ipso facto* when war came (3 Phillimore Int. L. 794). The writers of our own time reject these sweeping statements (2 Oppenheim Int. L. sec. 99; Hall Int. L. 398, 401; Fiore Int. L. (Borchard's Transl.) sec. 845). International law to-day does not preserve treaties or annul them regardless of the effects produced. It deals with such problems pragmatically, preserving or annulling as the necessities of war exact. It establishes standards, but it does not fetter itself with rules. When it attempts to do more, it finds that there is neither unanimity of opinion nor uniformity of practice. "The whole question remains as yet unsettled" (Oppenheim, *supra*). This does not mean, of course, that there are not some classes of treaties about which there is general agreement. Treaties of alliance fall. Treaties of boundary or cession, "dispositive" or "transitory" conventions, survive (Hall Int. L. pp. 398, 401; Westlake Int. L. II, 34; Oppenheim, *supra*). So, of course, do treaties which regulate the conduct of hostilities (Hall, *supra;* 5 Moore Dig. Int. L. 372; Society for Propagation of the Gospel v. Town of New Haven, 8 Wheat. 464, 494). Intention in such circumstances is clear. These instances do not represent distinct and final principles. They are illustrations of the same principle. They are applications of a standard. When I ask what that principle or standard is, and endeavor to extract it from the long chapters in the books, I get this, and nothing more, that provisions compatible with the state of hostilities, unless expressly terminated, will be enforced, and those incompatible rejected. "Treaties lose their efficacy in war only if their execution is incompatible with war. *Les traités ne perdent leur efficacité en temps de guerre que si leur exécution est incompatible avec la guerre elle-même*" (Bluntschli, Droit International Codifié, sec. 538.) That in substance was Kent's view, here as often in advance of the thought of his day. "All those duties of which the exercise is not necessarily suspended by the war, subsist in their full force. The obligation of keeping faith is so far from ceasing in time of war, that its efficacy becomes increased, from the increased necessity of it" (1 Kent Comm. p. 176). That, also, more recently, is the conclusion embodied by the Institute of International Law in the rules voted at Christiania in 1912 which defined the effects of war on International Conventions. . . .

This, I think, is the principle which must guide the judicial department of the government when called upon to determine during the progress of a war whether a treaty shall be observed in the absence of some declaration by the political departments of the government that it has been suspended or annulled. A treaty has a twofold aspect. In its primary operation, it is a compact between independent states. In its secondary operation, it is a source of private rights for individuals within states (Head Money Cases, 112 U. S. 580, 598). Granting that the termination of the compact involves the termination of the rights, it does not follow because there is a privilege to rescind that the privilege has been exercised. The question is not what states *may* do after war has supervened, and this without breach of their duty as members of the society of nations. The question is what courts are to presume that they have done. . . . President and senate may denounce the treaty, and thus terminate its life. Congress may enact an inconsistent rule, which will control the action of the courts (Fong Yue Ting v. U. S., 149 U. S. 698). The treaty of peace itself may set up new relations, and terminate earlier compacts either tacitly or expressly. The proposed treaties wtih Germany and Austria give the victorious powers the privilege of choosing the treaties which are to be kept in force or abrogated. But until some one of these things is done, until some one of these events occurs, while war is still flagrant, and the will of the political departments of the government unrevealed, the courts, as I view their function, play a humbler and more cautious part. It is not for them to denounce treaties generally, *en bloc*. Their part it is, as one provision or another is involved in some actual controversy before them, to determine whether, alone, or by force of connection with an inseparable scheme, the provision is inconsistent with the policy or safety of the nation in the emergency of war, and hence presumably intended to be limited to times of peace. The mere fact that other portions of the treaty are suspended or even abrogated is not conclusive. The treaty does not fall in its entirety unless it has the character of an indivisible act. *"Le traité tombe pour le tout quand il présente le caractère d'un acte indivisible"* (Rules of the Institute of Int. L. *supra*). To determine whether it has this character, it is not enough to consider its name or label. No general formula suffices. We must consult in each case the nature and purpose of the specific articles involved. *"Il faut . . . examiner dans chaque cas, si la guerre constitue par sa nature même un obstacle a l'exécution du traité"* (Bluntschli, *supra*).

I find nothing incompatible with the policy of the government, with the safety of the nation, or with the maintenance of the war in the enforcement of this treaty so as to sustain the plaintiff's title. We do not confiscate the lands or goods of the stranger within our gates. If we permit him to remain, he is free during good behavior to buy property and sell it (Trading with Enemy Act of Oct. 6, 1917; 40 St. 411, ch. 106). He is to be "undisturbed in the peaceful pursuit" of his life and occupation, and "accorded the consideration due to all peaceful and law-abiding persons" (President's Proclamation of Dec. 11, 1917). If we require him to depart, we assure to him, for the recovery, disposal and removal of his goods and effects and for his departure, the full time stipulated by any treaty then in force between the United States and the hostile nation of which he is a subject; and where no such treaty is in force, such time as may be declared by the President to be consistent with the public safety and the dictates of humanity and national hospitality (U. S. R. S. sec. 4068, re-enacting the act of July 6, 1798). A public policy not outraged by purchase will not be outraged by inheritance. The plaintiff is a resident; but even if she were a non-resident, and were within the hostile territory, the policy of the nation would not divest her of the title whether acquired before the war or later. Custody would then be assumed by the alien property custodian. The proceeds of the property, in the event of sale, would be kept within the jurisdiction. Title, however, would be unchanged, in default of the later exercise by Congress of the power of confiscation (40 Stat. ch. 106, pp. 416, 424), now seldom brought into play in the practice of enlightened nations (2 Westlake Int. L. 46, 47; Brown v. U. S., 8 Cranch, 110). Since the argument of this appeal, Congress has already directed, in advance of any treaty of peace, that property in the hands of the custodian shall be returned in certain classes of cases to its owners, and in particular where the owner is a woman who at the time of her marriage was a native-born citizen of the United States and prior to April 6, 1917, intermarried with a subject or citizen of Germany or Austria-Hungary (Act of June 5, 1920, amending sec. 9 of the act of Oct. 6, 1917). It follows that even in its application to aliens in hostile territory, the maintenance of this treaty is in harmony with the nation's policy and consistent with the nation's welfare. To the extent that there is conflict between the treaty and the statute (40 Stat. ch. 106), we have the same situation that arises whenever there is an implied repeal of one law by another. To the extent that they are in harmony, both are still in force. There is in truth no conflict here except in points of detail. In fundamental principle and purpose, the treaty remains untouched by later legislation. In keeping it alive, we uphold the policy of the nation, revealed in acts of Congress and proclamations of the President, "to conduct ourselves as belligerents in a high spirit of right and fairness" (President Wilson's Address to the Congress, April 2, 1917; Scott Diplomatic Correspondence between United States and Germany, p. 324), without hatred of race and without taint of self-seeking.

I do not overlook the statements which may be found here and there in the works of authors of distinction (Hall, *supra*; Halleck Int. L. (4th ed.) 314; Wheaton Int. L. (5th ed.) 377) that treaties of commerce and navigation are to be ranked in the class of treaties which war abrogates or at least suspends. Commerce is friendly intercourse. Friendly intercourse between nations is impossible in war. Therefore, treaties regulating such intercourse are not operative in war. But stipulations do not touch commerce because they happen to be embodied in a treaty which is styled one to regulate or encourage commerce. We must be on our guard against being misled by labels. Bluntschli's warning, already quoted, reminds us that the nature and not the name of covenants determines whether they shall be disregarded or observed. There is a line of division, fundamental in importance, which separates stipulations touching commerce *between* nations from those touching the tenure of land *within* the territories of nations (*Cf.* The Convention "as to tenure and disposition of real and personal property" between the U. S. & Great Britain dated March 2, 1899). Restrictions upon ownership of land by aliens have a history all their own, unrelated altogether to restrictions upon trade (Kershaw v. Kelsey, *supra*; Fairfax v. Hunter, *supra*). When removed, they cease to exist for enemies as well as friends, unless the statute removing them enforces a distinction (Kershaw v. Kelsey, Fairfax v. Hunter, *supra*).

More than that, the removal, when effected by treaty, gives reciprocal privileges to the subjects of each state, and is thus of value to one side as much as to the other. For this reason, the inference is a strong one, as was pointed out by the Master of the Rolls in Sutton v. Sutton (1 Russ. & M. 664, 675) that the privileges, unless expressly revoked, are intended to endure (*Cf.* 2 Westlake, p. 33; also Halleck Int. L., *supra*). There, as in Society for the Propagation of the Gospel v. Town of New Haven (8 Wheat. 464, 494), the treaty of 1794 between the United States and England protecting the citizens of each in the enjoyment of their landed property, was held not to have been abrogated by the war of 1812. Undoubtedly there is a distinction between those cases and this in that there the rights had become vested before the outbreak of the war. None the less, alike in reasoning and in conclusion, they have their value and significance. If stipulations governing the tenure of land survive the stress of war though contained in a treaty which is described as one of amity, it is not perceived why they may not also survive though contained in a treaty which is described as one of commerce. In preserving the right of inheritance for citizens of Austria when the land inherited is here, we preserve the same right for our citizens when the land inherited is there (Brown v. U. S., 8 Cranch, 110, 129). Congress has not yet commanded us, and the exigencies of war, as I view them, do not constrain us, to throw these benefits away.

No one can study the vague and wavering statements of treatise and decision in this field of international law with any feeling of assurance at the end that he has chosen the right path. One looks in vain either for uniformity of doctrine or for scientific accuracy of exposition. There are wise cautions for the statesman. There are few precepts for the judge. All the more, in this uncertainty, I am impelled to the belief that until the political departments have acted, the courts, in refusing to give effect to treaties, should limit their refusal to the needs of the occasion; that they are not bound by any rigid formula to nullify the whole or nothing; and that in determining whether this treaty survived the coming of war, they are free to make choice of the conclusion which shall seem the most in keeping with the traditions of the law, the policy of the statutes, the dictates of fair dealing, and the honor of the nation.

The judgment should be affirmed with costs, and the question certified answered in the affirmative. . . .

Judgment affirmed.

KARNUTH, DIRECTOR OF IMMIGRATION, ET AL. v. UNITED STATES OF AMERICA EX REL. ALBRO.

United States, Supreme Court, 1929.

279 U. S. 231.   [73 L. ed. 677; 49 S. Ct. 274.]

Certiorari, 278 U. S. 594, to review a judgment of the Circuit Court of Appeals which reversed, on appeal, a judgment of the District Court dismissing a writ of *habeas corpus*. The writ had been sued out [by Albro] on behalf of two aliens [Mary Cook and Antonio Danelon] who were detained by immigration officers.

MR. JUSTICE SUTHERLAND delivered the opinion of the court.

This case arose under § 3 of the Immigration Act of 1924, c. 190, 43 Stat. 153, 154, U. S. Code, Title 8, § 203 *et seq.*, which provides: "When used in this Act the term 'immigrant' means any alien departing from any place outside the United States destined for the United States, except . . . (2) an alien visiting the United States temporarily as a tourist or temporarily for business or pleasure. . . . " . . .

Neither respondent is a native of Canada. Mary Cook is a British subject, born in Scotland, who came to Canada in May, 1924. She is a spinner by occupation and resides at Niagara Falls, Ontario. Antonio Danelon is a native of Italy, who came to Canada in 1923. He also resides at Niagara Falls, Ontario. He alleges that he became a Canadian citizen by reason of his father's naturalization. Both sought admission to the United States on December 1, 1927, as non-immigrants under the excepting clause (2) above quoted. Prior thereto, Mary Cook had crossed from Canada to the United States daily for a period of three weeks to engage in work at which she was employed. On the occasion in question, she was out of employment, but desired admission to look for work. Danelon had been at work in the United States for more than a year crossing daily by the use of an identification card. He sought admission to resume work. Both were denied admission by the immigration authorities, on the ground that they were quota-immigrants within the meaning of the act, and did not come within the excepting clause, § 3 (2). The following departmental regulation, adopted under § 24 of the act, has been in force since September, 1925: "Temporary visits . . . for the purpose of performing labor for hire are not considered to be within the purview of section 3 (2) of the act." It is not disputed that both aliens were properly excluded if the validity of this regulation is established.

In a *habeas corpus* proceeding, brought in behalf of the two aliens, the federal District Court for the Western District of New York sustained the action of the immigration officials and dismissed the writ. On appeal, this judgment was reversed. The circuit court of appeals held that an alien crossing from Canada to the United States daily to labor for hire was not an immigrant but a visitor for business within the meaning of section 3 (2) of the act. 24 F. (2d) 649. In reaching that conclusion the court seemed of opinion that if the statute were so construed as to exclude the aliens, it would be in conflict with Article III of the Jay Treaty of 1794, 8 Stat. 116, 117, a result, of course, to be avoided if, reasonably, it could be done. Lem Moon Sing v. United States, 158 U. S. 538, 549.

We granted the writ of certiorari because of the far-reaching importance of the question. The decision below affects not only aliens crossing daily from Canada to labor in the United States, but, if followed, will extend to include those entering the United States for the same purpose from all countries, including Canada, who intend to remain for any period of time embraced within the meaning of the word "temporary." By the immigration rules, this time is defined as a reasonable fixed period to be determined by the examining officer, which may be extended from time to time, though not to exceed one year altogether from the date of original entry. Thus, if the view of the court below prevail, it will result that aliens—not native of Canada or any other American country named in § 4 (c)—whose entry as immigrants is precluded, may land as temporary visitors and remain at work in the United States for weeks or months at a time.

First. The pertinent provision of Article III of the Jay Treaty follows:

"It is agreed that it shall at all times be free to his Majesty's subjects, and to the citizens of the United States, and also to the Indians dwelling on either side of the said boundary line, freely to pass and repass by land or inland navigation, into the respective territories and countries of the two parties, on the continent of America (the country within the limits of the Hudson's Bay Company only excepted) and to navigate all the lakes, rivers and waters thereof, and freely to carry on trade and commerce with each other. . . . "

The position of the Government is that (1) there is no conflict between the treaty and the statute, but, (2) in any event, the treaty provision relied on was abrogated by the War of 1812. We pass at once to a consideration of the second contention, since if that be sustained, the first becomes immaterial and the statute open to construction unembarrassed by the treaty.

The effect of war upon treaties is a subject in respect of which there are widely divergent opinions. The doctrine sometimes asserted, especially by the older writers, that war *ipso facto* annuls treaties of every kind between the warring nations, is repudiated by the great weight of modern authority; and the view now commonly accepted is that "whether the stipulations of a treaty are annulled by war depends upon their intrinsic character." 5 Moore's Digest of International Law, § 779, p. 383. But as to precisely what treaties fall and what survive, under this designation, there is lack of accord. The authorities, as well as the practice of nations, present a great contrariety of views. The law of the subject is still in the making, and, in attempting to formulate principles at all approaching generality, courts must proceed with a good deal of caution. But there seems to be fairly common agreement that, at least, the following treaty obligations remain in force: stipulations in respect of what shall be done in a state of war; treaties of cession, boundary, and the like; provisions giving the right to citizens or subjects of one of the high contracting powers to continue to hold and transmit land in the territory of the other; and, generally, provisions which represent completed acts. On the other hand, treaties of amity, of alliance, and the like, having a political character, the object of which "is to promote relations of harmony between nation and nation," are generally regarded as belonging to the class of treaty stipulations that are absolutely annulled by war. *Id.*, p. 385, quoting Calvo, Droit Int. (4th Ed.) IV. 65, § 1931.

In Society, etc., v. New Haven, 8 Wheat. 464, a case involving the right of a British corporation to continue to hold lands in Vermont, this Court was called upon to determine the effect of the War of 1812 upon the Ninth Article of the Jay Treaty. . . .

It was held that the title to the property of the Society was protected by the Sixth Article of the Treaty of 1783, 8 Stat. 80, 83; was confirmed by the words of Article IX above quoted; and was not affected by the War of 1812. . . .

The English High Court of Chancery reached the same conclusion in Sutton v. Sutton, 1 Russ. & M. 663, 675:

"The relations, which had subsisted between Great Britain and America, when they formed one empire, led to the introduction of the ninth section of the treaty of 1794, and made it highly reasonable that the subjects of the two parts of the divided empire should, notwithstanding the separation, be protected in the mutual enjoyment of their landed property; and, the privileges of natives being reciprocally given, not only to the actual possessors of lands, but to their heirs and assigns, it is a reasonable construction that it was the intention of the treaty that the operation of the treaty should be permanent, and not depend upon the continuance of a state of peace."

These cases are cited by respondents and relied upon as determinative of the effect of the War of 1812 upon Article III of the treaty. This view we are unable to accept. Article IX and Article III relate to fundamentally different things. Article IX aims at perpetuity and deals with existing rights, vested and permanent in character, in respect of which, by express provision, neither the owners nor their heirs or assigns are to be regarded as aliens. These are rights which, by their very nature, are fixed and continuing, regardless of war or peace. But the privilege accorded by Article III is one created by the treaty, having no obligatory existence apart from that instrument, dictated by considerations of mutual trust and confidence, and resting upon the presumption that the privilege will not be exercised to unneighborly ends. It is, in no sense, a vested right. It is not permanent in its nature. It is wholly promissory and prospective and necessarily ceases to operate in a state of war, since the passing and repassing of citizens or subjects of one sovereignty into the territory of another is inconsistent with a condition of hostility. See 7 Moore's Digest of International Law, § 1135; 2 Hyde, International Law, § 606. The reasons for the conclusion are obvious—among them, that otherwise the door would be open for treasonable intercourse. And it is easy to see that such freedom of intercourse also may be incompatible with conditions following the termination of the war. Disturbance of peaceful relations between countries occasioned by war, is often so profound that the accompanying bitterness, distrust and hate indefinitely survive the coming of peace. The causes, conduct or result of the war may be such as to render a revival of the privilege inconsistent with a new or altered state of affairs. The grant of the privilege connotes the existence of normal peaceful relations. When these are broken by war, is wholly problematic whether the ensuing peace will be of such character as to justify the neighborly freedom of intercourse which prevailed before the rupture. It follows that the provision belongs to the class of treaties which does not survive war between the high contracting parties, in respect of which, we quote, as apposite, the words of a careful writer on the subject:

"Treaties of the fifth class are necessarily at least suspended by war, many of them are necessarily annulled, and there is nothing in any of them to make them revive as a matter of course on the advent of peace,—frequently in fact a change in the relations of the parties to them effected by the treaty of peace is inconsistent with a renewal of the identical stipulations." . . . Hall, International Law (5th Ed.), pp. 389–390.

Westlake classifies treaties not affected by war as (1) those providing what is to be done in a state of war, (2) transitory or dispositive treaties, including such as are intended to establish a permanent condition of things, such as treaties of cession, boundary, and recognition of independence, as well as those having no conceivable connection with the causes of war or peace, and (3) treaties establishing arrangements to which third powers are parties such as guarantees and postal and other unions. Westlake, International Law, Part II, pp. 29–32. He then says:

"Outside the exceptions which have been discussed, treaties between belligerents do not survive the outbreak of the war. At the peace there is no presumption that the parties will take the same view as before the war of their interests, political, commercial or other. It is for them to define on what terms they intend to close their interlude of savage life and to reenter the domain of law."

Fauchille, Traité de Droit International Public, 1921, Vol. II, p. 55, says that "a state of war puts an end to treaties concluded with a view to peaceful relations between the signatories and the object or end of which is to strengthen or maintain such peaceful relations, for example, treaties of alliance, subsidies, guarantees, commerce, navigation, customs union, etc. Those treaties from their very nature are subject to an implicit resolutory condition, namely a break in the state of peace. They cannot survive the outbreak of hostilities between the signatory States. War, to them, is a cause of final extinction and not of mere suspension. When peace is concluded, they do not spontaneously come out of a comatose state; they do not revive unless expressly renewed in the peace treaty."

These expressions and others of similar import which might be added, confirm our conclusion that the provision of the Jay Treaty now under consideration was brought to an end by the War of 1812, leaving the contracting powers discharged from all obligation in respect thereto, and, in the absence of a renewal, free to deal with the matter as their views of national policy, respectively, might from time to time dictate.

We are not unmindful of the agreement in Article XXVIII of the Treaty "that the first ten articles of this treaty shall be permanent, and that the subsequent articles, except the twelfth, shall be limited in their duration to twelve years." It is quite apparent that the word "permanent" as applied to the first ten articles was used to differentiate them from the subsequent articles—that is to say, it was not employed as a synonym for "perpetual" or "everlasting," but in the sense that those articles were not limited to a specific period of time, as was the case in respect of the remaining articles. Having regard to the context, such an interpretation of the word "permanent" is neither strained nor unusual. See Texas, etc., Railway Co. v. Marshall, 136 U. S. 393, 403; Bassett v. Johnson, 2 N. J. Eq. 154, 162.

It is true, as respondents assert, that citizens and subjects of the two countries continued after the War of 1812, as before, freely to pass and repass the international boundary line. And so they would have done if there never had been a treaty on the subject. Until a very recent period, the policy of the United States, with certain definitely specified exceptions, had been to open its doors to all comers without regard to their allegiance. This policy sufficiently accounts for the acquiescence of the Government in the continued exercise of the crossing privilege upon the part of the inhabitants of Canada, with whom we have always been upon the most friendly terms; and a presumption that such acquiescence recognized a revival of the treaty obligation cannot be indulged. . . .

Judgment reversed.[1]

---

[1] SUPPLEMENTARY CASES. In Sutton v. Sutton, 1 R. & M. 663 (1830), involving the right of an alien (American) to hold and convey real estate, under

B. Status of resident enemy aliens.

Apart from the protection given to resident enemy aliens by special treaty provisions their status has been an uncertain one. Down to the year 1914 enemy aliens were as a rule allowed to continue in residence without molestation, subject to good behavior. Query, have resident enemy aliens access to the courts for the prosecution of claims having no connection with the war? May they appeal if judgment has gone against them as defendants? May they carry on trade within the country as usual? May non-resident alien enemies be sued on contract or otherwise? If sued, may they defend? [Porter v. Freudenberg; Posselt v. D'Espard.]

PORTER v. FREUDENBERG.

Great Britain, Court of Appeal, 1915.

L. R. [1915] 1 K. B. 857.

[The defendant, Freudenberg, a German subject resident in Berlin, maintained a business establishment in London, which was carried on by his agent Barnes on premises leased from the plaintiff, Porter. On September 28, 1914, Barnes delivered the keys of the premises to the plaintiff and the next day removed the whole of the defendant's stock, fixtures and fittings. The plaintiff notified Barnes that the premises would be held at his disposal as agent of the defendant, and then brought suit for a quarter's rent. The trial justice gave leave to issue a concurrent writ, and to serve notice of it upon the defendant at Berlin. Such service being impracticable, the plaintiff appealed and asked for leave for substituted service of notice of the writ upon the defendant's agent in England.]

LORD READING, C. J. . . . Having now explained the meaning of "alien enemy" for civil purposes, and having decided that such alien enemy's right to sue or proceed either by himself or by any person on his behalf in the King's Courts is suspended during the progress of hostilities and until after peace is restored . . . the next point to consider is whether he is liable to be sued in the King's Courts during the war. To allow an alien enemy to sue or proceed during war in the civil Courts of the King would be, as we have seen, to give to the enemy the advantage of enforcing his rights by the assistance of the

---

the terms of the ninth article of the treaty of 1794 between the United States and Great Britain, notwithstanding the intervening war of 1812–1814, the British Court of Chancery held that it was "a reasonable construction that it was the intention of the treaty that the operation of the treaty should be permanent, and not depend upon the continuance of a state of peace."

King with whom he is at war. But to allow the alien enemy to be sued or proceeded against during war is to permit subjects of the King or alien friends to enforce their rights with the assistance of the King against the enemy. *Prima facie* there seems no possible reason why our laws should decree an immunity during hostilities to the alien enemy against the payment of just debts or demands due to British or neutral subjects. The rule of the law suspending the alien enemy's right of action is based upon public policy, but no consideration of public policy is apparent which would justify preventing the enforcement by a British or neutral subject of a right against the enemy. As was said by Bailhache, J., in Robinson & Co. v. Continental Insurance Co. of Mannheim, [1915] 1 K. B. 155, 159, "To hold that a subject's right of suit is suspended against an alien enemy is to injure a British subject and to favour an alien enemy and to defeat the object and reason of the suspensory rule." In our judgment the effect would be to convert that which during war is a disability, imposed upon the alien enemy because of his hostile character, into a relief to him during war from the discharge of his liabilities to British subjects. It is very noteworthy that when dealing with the rights of alien enemies there is no shadow of doubt suggested in the books as to the right to sue alien enemies. More often there is no mention of it, but sometimes it is the subject of express reference and then always to the same effect, that the alien enemy can be sued during the progress of hostilities. Bacon's Abridgment, 7th ed., vol. 1, p. 183, asserts this liability of the alien enemy without doubt or hesitation. "The plea of 'alien enemy' is a bar to a bill for relief in equity as well as to an action at law, but it would seem not sustainable to a mere bill for discovery for *as an alien enemy may be sued at law* and may have process to compel the appearance of his witnesses so he may have the benefit of a discovery." This is an important passage in other respects also, and in our judgment it is a correct statement of the law. . . .

The Supreme Court of the United States had to consider the position of an alien enemy defendant in McVeigh v. United States (1871) [11 Wallace, 259]. The United States, under a statute then in force, filed a libel of information in the District Court of Virginia for the forfeiture of certain real and personal property of McVeigh on the ground that he was "a resident of the City of Richmond within the Confederate lines and a rebel." McVeigh appeared by counsel and filed a claim to the property and an answer. The Attorney of the United States moved that the claim and answer and appearance be stricken from the files, and the Court granted the motion and the decree was made for forfeiture of the property. The case eventually was brought to the Supreme Court on writ of error. Swayne, J., in delivering the judgment of the court, said: "The order in effect denied the respondent a hearing. It was alleged he was in the position of an

alien enemy and hence could have no *locus standi* in that forum.   If
assailed there, he could defend there.   The liability and the right are
inseparable.   A different result would be a blot upon our jurisprudence
and civilization.   . . .   Whether the legal status of the plaintiff in
error was or was not that of an alien enemy is a point not necessary
to consider; because, apart from the views we have expressed, conceding the fact to be so, the consequences assumed would by no means
follow.   Whatever may be the extent of the disability of an alien enemy
to sue in the Courts of the hostile country, it is clear that he is liable
to be sued, and this carries with it the right to use all the means and
appliances of defence.''   The learned judge relied upon the above
mentioned passage in Bacon's Abridgment as an authority for this
proposition, and the Supreme Court acted upon it by reversing the
judgment of the District Court and the Circuit Court.   . . .

Once the conclusion is reached that the alien enemy can be sued, it
follows that he can appear and be heard in his defence, and may take
all such steps as may be deemed necessary for the proper presentment
of his defence.   If he is brought at the suit of a party before a Court
of justice he must have the right of submitting his answer to the Court.
To deny him that right would be to deny him justice and would be quite
contrary to the basic principles guiding the King's Courts in the administration of justice.

Equally it seems to result that, when sued, if judgment proceeded
against him, the appellate Courts are as much open to him as to any
other defendant.   It is true that he is the person who may be said
in one sense to initiate the proceedings in the appellate Court by giving
the notice of appeal, which is the first necessary step to bring the case
before that Court; but he is entitled to have his case decided according
to law, and if the judge in one of the King's Courts has erroneously
adjudicated upon it he is entitled to have recourse to another and an
appellate Court to have the error rectified.   Once he is cited to appear
he is entitled to the same opportunities of challenging the correctness
of the decision of the judge of first instance or other tribunal as any
other defendant.   The decision in McVeigh v. United States (1871) in
the Supreme Court of the United States is to the same effect.   In that
case the defendant, who was appellant in the circumstances already
stated, brought writ of error in respect of the judgment of the District and Circuit Courts and succeeded in reversing the judgments of
those Courts.

We must now consider whether the same conclusion is reached in
reference to appeals by an alien enemy plaintiff, that is, a person who
before the outbreak of war was a plaintiff in a suit and then by virtue
of his residence or place of business became an alien enemy.   As we
have seen, he could not proceed with his action during the war.   If
judgment had been pronounced against him before the war in an action

in which he was plaintiff, can he present an appeal to the appellate Courts of the King? We cannot see any distinction in principle between the case of an alien enemy seeking the assistance of the King to enforce a civil right in a Court of first instance and an alien enemy seeking to enforce such right by recourse to the appellate Courts. He is the "actor" throughout. He is not brought to the Court at the suit of another, it is he who invokes their assistance; and it matters not for this purpose that a judgment has been pronounced against him before the war. When once hostilities have commenced he cannot, so long as they continue, be heard in any suit or proceeding in which he is the person first setting the Courts in motion. If he had given notice of appeal before the war, the hearing of his appeal must be suspended until after the restoration of peace. . . .

ALFRED HUGO POSSELT ET AL. v. R. SEABURY D'ESPARD ET AL.

New Jersey, Court of Chancery, 1917.

87 N. J. Eq. 571.

On bill. On order to show cause. . . .

LANE, V. C. A preliminary objection is made to the prosecution of the cause upon the ground that the complainants are alien enemies. The facts are conceded. The individual complainant is a subject of Germany, resident in this country, and has taken out his first papers. The corporation complainant is a subject of, and resident in, Germany. The bill is for the preservation of the rights of the complainants as stockholders in a New Jersey corporation and also in the interest of the New Jersey corporation for the protection of its rights against the action of the defendants. The German corporation is a majority stockholder, practically the owner, of the New Jersey corporation. The charge is that the defendants have deliberately set about to wreck the New Jersey corporation. No money decree is prayed for. If I should deny relief upon the ground stated by the defendants, then the property of alien enemies within this country, acquired in time of peace, may be ruthlessly taken away from them, not by the government, but by individuals, subject only to the restraint of criminal law. I am familiar, of course, with the very many learned opinions of publicists of other days, and also with the opinions of the supreme court of the United States, but I think that at this time to attempt to consider them in detail would unduly extend this opinion, and in the view that I take of the present situation, would be wholly unwarranted. The right of government to confiscate property of alien enemies and close the doors of its courts to them, whether resident here or elsewhere, may be conceded. Whether that right is to be exercised is a matter of policy. The modern trend is to discourage interference with property rights, whether of friends or enemies in time of war, except so far as may be necessary to effectively accomplish the objects of the war. The solution of the problem now before me, I think, is found in the president's message to Congress, which, in view of the nature of its reception by Congress and the action of Congress under it, has become the voice of the country; and the president's proclamation declaring a state of war and defining rights of residents, an official act under authority of Congress. German residents who comply with needful regulations, and who properly conduct themselves, are assured that they will be undisturbed in the peaceful pursuit of their lives and occupations and be accorded the consideration due to all peaceful and law-abiding persons, except so far as restrictions may be necessary for their own protection and for the safety of the United States. To shut the door of the court in the face of an alien enemy resident here would be a distinct violation of not only the spirit but the letter of this proclamation.

With respect to the alien enemy resident in Germany the situation is somewhat different, but I think not essentially so. The president has very carefully distinguished between the German government and the German people, and the sins of that government ought not to be visited upon the people except so far as the legitimate interests of the United States require. I am convinced that there is no interest of the United States which requires the court, in advance of a definite command by the constituted authorities, to refuse to protect, at their instance, the rights of alien enemies resident abroad in property in this country. If it be said that this is in conflict with certain prior decisions, the answer is that the solution of the question depends upon public policy, and while it is not the function of the court to establish a public policy, it is the function and the duty of the court to determine, as a matter of fact, what the policy actually is, and it is the policy of the present day, not that of some years ago, that must be determined. Tolerance is the key-note of the president's proclamation, and by that I am bound. If the contention is made that to permit alien enemies resident abroad to sue in our courts would be to lend aid and comfort to the enemy, I think the answer is that either the court or the government may so act as to prevent any property coming into possession of the enemy. I am unwilling to concede that either the government or the courts are powerless to prevent aid and comfort being given to the enemy without exercising the drastic power of refusing absolutely at the instance of an alien enemy to protect property rights within this country. I think the doors of the court are still open to all persons who properly behave themselves.

The result is that the motion to stay the prosecution of this cause on the ground of alien enemy will be denied.

C. **Effect of war upon business relations between citizens and the enemy country.**

Since the outbreak of war suspends all legal relationships between the belligerent states, other than those entered into in contemplation of war, it has naturally resulted in municipal decrees and legislation forbidding trade between nationals and the enemy, while the courts of Great Britain and the United States have gone so far as to assert that such trade was forbidden by international law. [The Hoop.] Query, may a citizen who has been doing business in the enemy country before the outbreak of war retire with his property to his own country without being guilty of trading with the enemy? [The Rapid.] Query, what would be the effect of the outbreak of war upon a business partnership between a citizen and an enemy national resident in the enemy country? [Griswold v. Waddington.] Would a life insurance policy be invalidated by reason of the non-payment of premiums caused by the existence of a state of war? [New York Life Insurance Co. v. Statham.]

THE HOOP.

Great Britain, High Court of Admiralty, 1799.

1 C. Rob. 196.

This is a case of a claim of several British merchants for goods purchased on their account in Holland, and shipped on board a neutral vessel. . . . Mr. Malcolm of Glasgow, and several other merchants of North Britain, had, long prior to hostilities, been used to trade extensively with Holland; . . . after the irruption of the French into Holland, they had constantly applied for, and obtained special orders of his majesty in council permitting them to continue that trade; . . . after the passing of the acts of parliament 35 G. 3. c. 15. § 80., 36 G. 3. c. 76., 37 G. 3. c. 12 . . . it was apprehended in that part of Great Britain, that by these acts the importation of such goods was made legal: but for the greater security, they still made application to the commissioners of customs at Glasgow, to know what they considered to be the interpretation of the said acts, and whether his majesty's license was still necessary; and . . . were informed, under the opinion of the law advisers of the said commissioners, that no such orders of council were necessary, and that all goods brought from the United Provinces would in future be entered without them; and that in consequence of such information, they had caused the goods in question to be shipped at Rotterdam for their account; ostensibly documented for Bergen to avoid the enemy's cruisers. . . .

Sir W. Scott . . . It is said that these circumstances compose a case entitled to great indulgence; and I do not deny it. But if there is a rule of law on the subject binding the Court, I must follow where that rule leads me; though it leads to consequences which I may privately regret, when I look to the particular intentions of the parties.

In my opinion there exists such a general rule in the maritime jurisprudence of this country, by which all trading with the public enemy, unless with the permission of the sovereign, is interdicted. It is not a principle peculiar to the maritime law of this country; it is laid down by Bynkershoek as an universal principle of law.—*Ex naturâ belli commercia inter hostes cessare non est dubitandum. Quamvis nulla specialis sit commerciorum prohibitio, ipso tamen jure belli commercia esse vetita, ipsœ indictiones bellorum satis declarant,* &c. He proceeds to observe, that the interests of trade, and the necessity of obtaining certain commodities have sometimes so far overpowered this rule, that different species of traffic have been permitted, *prout e re suâ, subditorumque suorum esse censent principes* (Bynk. Q. J. P. B. 1, c. 3). But it is in all cases the act and permission of the sovereign. Wherever that is permitted, it is a suspension of the state of war *quoad hoc.* It is, as he expresses it, *pro parte sic bellum, pro parte pax inter subditos utriusque principis.* It appears from these passages to have been the law of Holland; Valin, l. iii., tit. 6, art. 3, states it to have been the law of France, whether the trade was attempted to be carried on in national or in neutral vessels; it will appear in a case which I shall have occasion to mention *(The Fortuna),* to have been the law of Spain; and it may, I think, without rashness be affirmed to have been a general principle of law in most of the countries of Europe.

By the law and constitution of this country, the sovereign alone has the power of declaring war and peace—He alone therefore who has the power of entirely removing the state of war, has the power of removing it in part, by permitting, where he sees proper, that commercial intercourse which is a partial suspension of the war. There may be occasions on which such an intercourse may be highly expedient. But it is not for individuals to determine on the expediency of such occasions on their own notions of commerce, and of commerce merely, and possibly on grounds of private advantage not very reconcilable with the general interest of the state. It is for the state alone, on more enlarged views of policy, and of all circumstances which may be connected with such an intercourse, to determine when it shall be permitted, and under what regulations. In my opinion, no principle ought to be held more sacred than that this intercourse cannot subsist on any other footing than that of the direct permission of the state. Who can be insensible to the consequences that might follow, if every person in a time of war had a right to carry on a commercial intercourse with the enemy, and under colour of that, had the means of carrying on any other species of intercourse he might think fit? The inconvenience to the public might be extreme; and where is the inconvenience on the other side, that the merchant should be compelled, in such a situation of the two countries, to carry on his trade between them (if necessary) under the eye and controul of the Government, charged with the care of the public safety?

Another principle of law, of a less politic nature, but equally general in its reception and direct in its application, forbids this sort of communication as fundamentally inconsistent with the relation at that time existing between the two countries; and that is, the total inability to sustain any contract by an appeal to the tribunals of the one country, on the part of the subjects of the other. In the law of almost every country, the character of alien enemy carries with it a disability to sue, or to sustain in the language of the civilians a *persona standi in judicio.* The peculiar law of our own country applies this principle with great rigour.—The same principle is received in our courts of the law of nations; they are so far British courts, that no man can sue therein who is a subject of the enemy, unless under particular circumstances that *pro hâc vice* discharge him from the character of an enemy; such as his coming under a flag of truce, a cartel, a pass, or some other act of public authority that puts him in the king's peace *pro hâc vice.* But otherwise he is totally *ex lex;* even in the case of ransoms which were contracts, but contracts arising *ex jure belli,* and tolerated as such, the enemy was not permitted to sue in his own proper person for the payment of the ransom bill; but the payment was enforced by an action brought by the imprisoned hostage in the courts of his own country, for the recovery of his freedom. A state in which contracts cannot be enforced, cannot be a state of legal commerce. If the parties who are to contract have no right to compel the performance of the contract, nor even to appear in a court of justice for that purpose, can there be a stronger proof that the law imposes a legal inability to contract? to such transactions it gives no sanction; they have no legal existence; and the whole of such commerce is attempted without its protection and against its authority. Bynkershoek expresses himself with great force upon this argument in his first book, chapter 7, where he lays down that the legality of commerce and the mutual use of courts of justice are inseparable: he says, that cases of commerce are undistinguishable from cases of any other species in this respect—*Si hosti semel permittas actiones exercere, difficile est distinguere ex quâ causâ oriantur, nec potui animadvertere illam distinctionem unquam usu fuisse servatam.*

Upon these and similar grounds it has been the established rule of law of this Court, confirmed by the judgment of the supreme court, that a trading with the enemy, except under a royal license, subjects the property to confiscation:—and the most eminent persons of the law sitting in the supreme courts have uniformly sustained such judgments. . . . [A number of English decisions are here reviewed.]

I omit many other cases of the last and the present war merely on this ground that the rule is so firmly established, that no one case exists which has been permitted to contravene it.—For I take upon me to aver, that all cases of this kind which have come before that tribunal have received an uniform determination. The cases which I have produced prove that the rule has been rigidly enforced,—where acts of parliament have on different occasions been made to relax the navigation-law and other revenue acts; where the government has authorized, under the sanction of an act of parliament, a homeward trade from the enemy's possessions, but has not specifically protected an outward trade to the same, though intimately connected with that homeward trade, and almost necessary to its existence; that it has been enforced, where strong claim not merely of convenience, but almost of necessity, excused it on behalf of the individual; that it has been enforced where cargoes have been laden before the war, but where the parties have not used all possible diligence to countermand the voyage after the first notice of hostilities; and that it has been enforced not only against the subjects of the crown, but likewise against those of its allies in the war, upon the supposition that the rule was founded on a strong and universal principle, which allied states in war had a right to notice and apply, mutually, to each other's subjects. Indeed it is the less necessary to produce these cases, because it is expressly laid down by Lord Mansfield, as I understand him, that such is the maritime law of England. . . .

. . . The Court has no power to depart from the law which has been laid down; and I am under the necessity of rejecting the claims.

THE RAPID, PERRY, MASTER.

United States, Supreme Court, 1814.

8 Cranch, 155. [3 L. ed. 520.]

This was an appeal from the sentence of the Circuit Court, for the District of Massachusetts. . . .

JOHNSON, J., delivered the opinion of the Court as follows:

This capture was made on the high seas, about a month after the declaration of war. The claimant, Harrison, had purchased a quantity of English goods, in England, "a long time," to use his own language, before the declaration of war, and deposited them on a small island, called Indian island, near to the line between Nova Scotia and these states. Upon the breaking out of the war, his agents in Boston hired the Rapid, a licensed vessel in the cod-fishery, to proceed to the place of deposit and bring away these goods. On her return, she was captured by the Jefferson privateer, and was condemned for trading with the enemy's country.

On the argument, it was contended, in behalf of the appellant, that this was not a trading, within the meaning of the cases cited, to support the condemnation; that, on the breaking out of a war, every citizen had a right, and it was the interest of the community to permit her citizens, to withdraw property lying in an enemy's country and purchased before the war; finally, that neither the declaration of war, nor the commission of the privateer authorized the capture of this vessel and cargo, as they were, in fact, American property.

It is understood, that the claim of the United States for the forfeiture is not now interposed. The Court, therefore, enters upon this consideration unembarrassed by a claim which would otherwise ride over every question now before us.

This is the first case, since its organization, in which this court has been called upon to assert the rights of war against the property of a citizen. It is, with extreme hesitation, and under a deep sense of the delicacy of the duty which we are called upon to discharge, that we proceed to adjudge the forfeiture of private right, upon principles of public law highly penal in their nature, and unfortunately too little understood.

But a new state of things has occurred—a new character has been assumed by this nation, which involves it in new relations, and confers on it new rights; which imposes a new class of obligations on our citizens, and subjects them to new penalties.

The nature and consequences of a state of war must direct us to the conclusions which we are to form on this case.

On this point, there is really no difference of opinion among jurists: there can be none among those who will distinguish between what it is, in itself, and what it ought to be, under the influence of a benign morality and the modern practice of civilized nations.

In the state of war, nation is known to nation only by their armed exterior; each threatening the other with conquest or annihilation. The individuals who compose the belligerent states, exist, as to each other, in a state of utter occlusion. If they meet, it is only in combat.

War strips man of his social nature; it demands of him the suppression of those sympathies which claim man for a brother; and accustoms the ear of humanity to hear with indifference, perhaps exultation, "that thousands have been slain."

These are not the gloomy reveries of the bookman. From the earliest time of which historians have written or poets imagined, the victor conquered but to slay, and slew but to triumph over the body of the vanquished. Even when philosophy had done all that philosophy could do, to soften the nature of man, war continued the gladiatorian combat: The vanquished bled, wherever caprice pronounced her fiat. To the benign influence of the Christian religion it remained to shed a few faint rays upon the gloom of war; a feeble light but barely sufficient to disclose its horrors. Hence, many rules have been introduced into modern warfare, at which humanity must rejoice, but which owe their existence altogether to mutual concession, and constitute so many voluntary relinquishments of the rights of war. To understand what it is in itself, and what it is under the influence of modern practice, we have but too many opportunities of comparing the habits of savage, with those of civilized warfare.

On the subject which particularly affects this case, there has been no general relaxation. The universal sense of nations has acknowledged the demoralizing effects that would result from the admission of individual intercourse. The whole nation are embarked in one common bottom, and must be reconciled to submit to one common fate. Every individual of the one nation must acknowledge every individual of the other nation as his own enemy—because the enemy of his country. It is not necessary to quote the authorities on this subject; they are numerous, explicit, respectable, and have been ably commented upon in the argument.

But after deciding what is the duty of the citizen, the question occurs, what is the consequence of a breach of that duty?

The law of prize is part of the law of nations. In it, a hostile character is attached to trade, independently of the character of the trader who pursues or directs it. Condemnation to the use of the captor is equally the fate of the property of the belligerent, and of the property found engaged in anti-neutral trade. But a citizen or ally may be engaged in a hostile trade, and thereby involve his property in the fate of those in whose cause he embarks.

This liability of the property of a citizen to condemnation as prize of war, may be likewise accounted for under other considerations. Everything that issues from a hostile country is, *prima facie,* the property of the enemy; and it is incumbent upon the claimant to support the negative of the proposition. But if the claimant be a citizen or an ally, at the same time that he makes out his interest, he confesses the commission of an offence which, under a well-known rule of the civil law, deprives him of his right to prosecute his claim.

This doctrine, however, does not rest upon abstract reason. It is supported by the practice of the most enlightened (perhaps we may say of all) commercial nations. And it affords us full confidence in our decision, that we find, upon recurring to the records of the Court of appeals in prize cases, established during the revolutionary war, that in various cases, it was reasoned upon as the acknowledged law of that Court. Certain it is, that it was the law of England, before the revolution, and therefore, constitutes a part of the admiralty and maritime jurisdiction conferred on this Court in pursuance of the constitution.

After taking this general view of the principal doctrine on this subject, we will consider the points made in behalf of the claimant in this case, and

1. Whether this was a trading, in the eye of the prize law, such as will subject the property to capture?

The force of the argument on this point depends upon the terms made use of. If by *trading*, in prize law, was meant that signification of the term which consists in negotiation or contract, this case would certainly not come under the penalties of the rule. But the object, policy and spirit of the rule is to cut off all communication or actual locomotive intercourse between individuals of the belligerent states. Negotiation or contract has, therefore, no necessary connection with the offence. *Intercourse* inconsistent with actual *hostility*, is the offence against which the operation of the rule is directed: and by substituting this definition for that of *trading with an enemy*, an answer is given to this argument.

2. Whether, on the breaking out of a war, the citizen has a right to remove to his own country with his property, is a question which we conceive does not arise in this case. This claimant certainly had not a right to leave the United States, for the purpose of bringing home his property from an enemy's country; much less could he claim it as a right to bring into this country, goods, the importation of which was expressly prohibited. As to the claim for the vessel, it is founded on no pretext whatever; for the undertaking, besides being in violation of two laws of the United States, was altogether voluntary and inexcusable. With regard to the importations from Great Britain about this time, it is well known that the forfeiture was released on grounds of policy and a supposed obligation induced by the assurances which had been held out by the American chargé d'affaires in England. But this claimant could allege no such excuse.

3. On the third point, we are of opinion that the foregoing observations furnish a sufficient answer.

If the right to capture property thus offending, grows out of the state of war, it is enough to support the condemnation in this case, that the act of Congress should produce a state of war, and that the commission of the privateer should authorize the capture of any property that shall assume the belligerent character.

Such a character we are of opinion this vessel and cargo took upon herself; or at least, she is deprived of the right to prove herself otherwise.

We are aware that there may exist considerable hardship in this case; the owners, both of vessel and cargo, may have been unconscious that they were violating the duties which a state of war imposed upon them. It does not appear that they meant a daring violation either of the laws or belligerent rights of their country. But it is the unenvied province

of this court to be directed by the head, and not by the heart. In deciding upon principles that must define the rights and duties of the citizen
and direct the future decisions of justice, no latitude is left for the exercise of feeling. . . .[1]

NATHANIEL L. GRISWOLD, AND GEORGE GRISWOLD, PLAIN-TIFFS IN ERROR, v. JOSHUA WADDINGTON, WHO IS IM-PLEADED WITH HENRY WADDINGTON, DEFENDANT IN ERROR.

New York, Court of Errors, 1819.

16 Johnson, 438.

[Prior to the War of 1812, Henry Waddington, an American citizen
resident in London, and Joshua Waddington, an American citizen resident in New York, were partners in a trading house in London. In the
course of the war one of the plaintiffs went to England and entered into
commercial relations with Henry Waddington. After the war the plaintiffs brought suit for the balance due on these transactions, and sought
to charge Joshua Waddington as a partner of Henry Waddington. The
judgment of the trial court in favor of the plaintiffs was reversed by
the Supreme Court, and the cause came before the Court of Errors on a
writ of error to the Supreme Court.]

The Chancellor [James Kent]. . . .[2]

It appears to me, that the declaration of war did, of itself, work a dissolution of all commercial partnerships existing at the time between
British subjects and American citizens. By dealing with either party,
no third person could acquire a legal right against the other, because
one alien enemy cannot, in that capacity, make a private contract binding upon the other. This conclusion would seem to be an inevitable
result from the new relations created by the war. It is a necessary consequence of the other proposition, that it is unlawful to have communication or trade with an enemy. To suppose a commercial partnership
(such as this was) to be continued, and recognized by law as subsisting,
when the same law had severed the subjects of the two countries, and
declared them enemies to each other, is to suppose the law chargeable
with inconsistency and absurdity. For what use or purpose could the
law uphold such a connection, when all further intercourse, communica-

---

[1] The vessel was subsequently condemned for violation of the Non-Intercourse
Act of 1809. See 8 Cranch 382.

[2] The first part of the opinion contains an exhaustive review of the authorities
on the effect of war upon commercial relations between subjects of belligerent
states.

tion, negotiation, or dealing between the partners, was prohibited, as unlawful? Why preserve the skeleton of the firm, when the sense and spirit of it has fled, and when the execution of any one article of it by either, would be a breach of his allegiance to his country? In short, it must be obvious to every one, that a state of war creates disabilities, imposes restraints, and exacts duties altogether inconsistent with the continuance of that relation. Why does war dissolve a charter-party, or a commercial contract for a particular voyage? Because, says Valin, (tom. 1, p. 626,) the war imposes an insurmountable obstacle to the accomplishment of the contract; and this obstacle arising from a cause beyond the control of the party, it is very natural, he observes, that the charter-party should be dissolved, as of course. Why should the contract of partnership continue by law when equally invincible obstacles are created by law to defeat it? If one alien enemy can go and bind his hostile partner, by contracts in time of war, when the other can have no agency, consultation, or control concerning them, the law would be as unjust as it would be extravagant. The good sense of the thing as applicable to this subject, is the rule prescribed by the Roman law, that a copartnership in any business ceased, when there was an end put to the business itself. *Item si alicujus rei societas sit, et finis negotio impositus est, finitur societas.* (Inst. 3, 26, 6).

The doctrine, that war does not interfere with private contracts, is not to be carried to an extent inconsistent with the rights of war. Suppose that H. & J. W. had entered into a contract before the war, which was to continue until 1814, by which one of them was to ship, half yearly, to London, consigned to the other, a cargo of provisions, and the other, in return, to ship to New York a cargo of goods. The war which broke out in 1812, would surely have put an end to the further operation of this contract, lawful and innocent as it was when made. No person could raise a doubt on this point; and what sanctity or magic is there in a contract of copartnership, that it must not yield to the same power?

If we examine, more particularly, the nature and objects of commercial partnerships, it would seem to be contrary to all the rules by which they are to be construed and governed, that they should continue to exist, after the parties are interdicted by the government, from any communication with each other, and are placed in a state of absolute hostility. It is of the essence of the contract that each party should contribute something valuable, as money, or goods, or skill and labour, on joint account, and for the common benefit; and that the object of the partnership should be lawful and honest business. . . . But how can the partners have any unity of interest, or any joint object that is lawful, when their pursuits, in consequence of the war, and in consequence of the separate allegiance which each owes to his own government, must be mutually hostile? The commercial business of each country, and of all its people, is an object of attack, and of destruction to the other. One party may be engaged in privateering, or in supplying the fleets and armies of his country with provisions, or with munitions of war; and can the law recognize the other partner as having a joint interest in the profits of such business? It would be impossible for the one partner to be concerned *in any commercial business,* which was not auxiliary to the resources and efforts of his country in a maritime war. And shall the other partner be lawfully drawing a revenue from such employment of capital, and such personal services directed against his own country? We cannot contemplate such a confusion of obligation between the law of partnership and the law of war, or such a conflict between his interest as a partner, and his duty as a patriot, without a mixture of astonishment and dread. Shall it be said that the partnership must be deemed to be abridged during war, to business that is altogether innoxious and harmless? But I would ask, how can we cut down a partnership in that manner without destroying it? The very object of the partnership, in this case, was, no doubt, commercial business between England and the United States, and which the hostile state of the two countries interdicted; or it may have been business in which the personal communication and advice of each partner was deemed essential, and without which the partnership would not have been formed. It is one of the principles of the law of partnership, that it is dissolved by the death of any one of its members, however numerous the association may be; and the reason is this: the personal qualities of each partner enter into the consideration of the contract, and the survivors ought not to be held bound without a new assent, when, perhaps, the character of the deceased partner was the inducement to the connection. . . . Shall we say that the partnership continues during war, in a quiescent state, and that the hostile partners do not share in each other's profits, made in carrying on the hostile commerce of each country? It would be then most unjust to make the party who did not share in profit to share in loss, and to be bound by the other's contracts; but if one partner does not share in profit, that alone destroys a partnership. It would be what the Roman lawyers called *Societas leonina,* in allusion to the fable of the lion, who, having entered into a partnership with the other animals of the forest in hunting, appropriated to himself all the prey. . . .

It is one of the fundamental principles of every commercial partnership, that each partner has the power to buy and sell, and pay and receive, and to contract and bind the firm. But then, again, as a necessary check to this power, each partner can interfere and stop any contract about to be made by any one of the rest. This is an elementary rule, derived from the civil law. *In re pari potiorem causam esse prohibentis constat.* . . . But if the partnership continues in war between hostile associates, this salutary power is withdrawn, and each partner is left defenceless. If the law continues the connection, after it has destroyed the check, the law is then cruel and unjust.

In speaking of the dissolution of partnerships, the French and civil law writers say, that partnerships are dissolved by a change of the condition of one of the parties which disables him to perform his part of the duty, as by a loss of liberty, or banishment, or bankruptcy, or a judicial prohibition to execute his business, or by confiscation of his goods. . . . The English law of partnership is derived from the same source; and as the cases arise, the same principles are applied. The principle here is, that when one of the parties becomes disabled to act, or when the business of the association becomes impracticable, the law, as well as common reason, adjudges the partnership to be dissolved. . . .

Another objection was raised, from the want of notice of the dissolution of the partnership. The answer to this is extremely easy, and perfectly conclusive. Notice is requisite when a partnership is dissolved by the act of the parties, but it is not necessary when the dissolution takes place, by the act of the law. The declaration of war, from the time it was duly made known to the nations, put an end to all future dealings between the subjects and citizens of the two countries, and, consequently, to the future operation of the copartnership in question. The declaration of war was, of itself, the most authentic and monitory notice. Any other notice in a case like this, between two public enemies, who had each his domicil in his own country, would have been useless. All mankind were bound to take notice of the war, and of its consequence. The notice, if given, could only be useless, as his countrymen could not hold any lawful intercourse with the enemy. It could not be given as a joint act, for the partners cannot lawfully commune together.

But, it was said, that the peace had a healing influence, and restored the parties to all their rights, and arrested all confiscations, and forfeitures, which had not previously and duly attached. I do not know that I differ from the counsel in any just application of this doctrine. As far as the war suspended the right of action existing in the adverse party prior to the war, that right revived; but if the contract in this case was unlawful, peace could not revive it, for it never had any legal existence. So too, the copartnership being once dissolved by the war, it was extinguished forever, except as to matters existing prior to the war. . . .

The judgment of the Supreme Court ought to be affirmed.

[Senator Van Vechten delivered a concurring opinion. Senator Livingston and Senator Seymour dissented.]

NEW YORK LIFE INSURANCE CO. v. STATHAM ET AL.

United States, Supreme Court, 1876.

93 U. S. 24. [23 L. ed. 789.]

The first of these cases is here on appeal from, and the second and third on writs of error to, the Circuit Court of the United States for the Southern District of Mississippi.

The first case is a bill in equity, filed to recover the amount of a policy of life insurance, granted by the defendant (now appellant) in 1851, on the life of Dr. A. D. Statham, of Mississippi, from the proceeds of certain funds belonging to the defendant attached in the hands of its agent at Jackson, in that state. It appears from the statements of the bill that the annual premiums accruing on the policy were all regularly paid, until the breaking out of the late civil war, but that, in consequence of that event, the premium due on the 8th of December, 1861, was not paid; the parties assured being residents of Mississippi, and the defendant a corporation of New York. Dr. Statham died in July, 1862. . . .

Each policy . . . contained various conditions, upon the breach of which it was to be null and void; and amongst others the following: "That in case the said [assured] shall not pay the said premium on or before the several days hereinbefore mentioned for the payment thereof, then and in every such case the said company shall not be liable to the payment of the sum insured, or in any part thereof, and this policy shall cease and determine." The Manhattan policy contained the additional provision, that, in every case where the policy should cease or become null and void, all previous payments made thereon should be forfeited to the company.

The non-payment of the premiums in arrear was set up in bar of the actions; and the plaintiffs respectively relied on the existence of the war as an excuse, offering to deduct the premiums in arrear from the amounts of the policies.

The decree and judgments below were against the defendants. . . . .

Mr. Justice Bradley . . . delivered the opinion of the court.

We agree with the court below, that the contract is not an assurance for a single year, with a privilege of renewal from year to year by paying the annual premium, but that it is an entire contract of assurance for life, subject to discontinuance and forfeiture for non-payment of any of the stipulated premiums. Such is the form of the contract, and such is its character. . . . Each instalment is, in fact, part consideration of the entire insurance for life. It is the same thing, where the annual premiums are spread over the whole life. . . .

The case, therefore, is one in which time is material and of the essence of the contract. Non-payment at the day involves absolute forfeiture, if such be the terms of the contract, as is the case here. Courts cannot with safety vary the stipulation of the parties by introducing equities for the relief of the insured against their own negligence.

But the court below bases its decision on the assumption that, when performance of the condition becomes illegal in consequence of the prevalence of public war, it is excused, and forfeiture does not ensue. It supposes the contract to have been suspended during the war, and to have revived with all its force when the war ended. Such a suspension and revival do take place in the case of ordinary debts. But have they ever been known to take place in the case of executory contracts in which time is material? If a Texas merchant had contracted to furnish some Northern explorer a thousand cans of preserved meat by a certain day, so as to be ready for his departure for the North Pole, and was prevented from furnishing it by the civil war, would the contract still be good at the close of the war five years afterwards, and after the return of the expedition? If the proprietor of a Tennessee quarry had agreed, in 1860, to furnish, during the two following years, ten thousand cubic feet of marble, for the construction of a building in Cincinnati, could he have claimed to perform the contract in 1865, on the ground that the war prevented an earlier performance?

The truth is, that the doctrine of the revival of contracts suspended during the war is one based on considerations of equity and justice, and cannot be invoked to revive a contract which it would be unjust or inequitable to revive.

In the case of life insurance, besides the materiality of time in the performance of the contract, another strong reason exists why the policy should not be revived. The parties do not stand on equal ground in reference to such a revival. It would operate most unjustly against the company. The business of insurance is founded on the law of averages; that of life insurance eminently so. The average rate of mortality is the basis on which it rests. By spreading their risks over a large number of cases, the companies calculate on this average with reasonable certainty and safety. Anything that interferes with it deranges the security of the business. If every policy lapsed by reason of the war should be revived, and all the back premiums should be paid, the companies would have the benefit of this average amount of risk. But the good risks are never heard from; only the bad are sought to be revived, where the person insured is either dead or dying. Those in health can get new policies cheaper than to pay arrearages on the old. To enforce a revival of the bad cases, whilst the company necessarily lose the cases, which are desirable, would be manifestly unjust. An injured person, as before stated, does not stand isolated and alone. His case is connected with and correlated to the cases of all others insured by the same company. The nature of the business, as a whole, must be looked at to understand the general equities of the parties.

We are of opinion, therefore, that an action cannot be maintained for the amount assured on a policy of life-insurance forfeited, like those in question, by non-payment of the premium, even though the payment was prevented by the existence of the war.

The question then arises, must the insured lose all the money which had been paid for premiums on their respective policies? If they must, they will sustain an equal injustice to that which the companies would sustain by reviving the policies. At the very first blush, it seems manifest that justice requires that they should have some compensation or return for the money already paid, otherwise the companies would be the gainers from their loss; and that from a cause for which neither party is to blame. The case may be illustrated thus: Suppose an inhabitant of Georgia had bargained for a house, situated in a Northern city, to be paid for by instalments, and no title to be made until all the instalments were paid, with a condition that on the failure to pay any of the instalments when due, the contract should be at an end, and the previous payments forfeited; and suppose that this condition was declared by the parties to be absolute and the time of payment material. Now, if some of the instalments were paid before the war, and others accruing during the war were not paid, the contract, as an executory one, was at an end. If the necessities of the vendor obliged him to avail himself of the condition, and to resell the property to another party, would it be just for him to retain the money he had received? Perhaps it might be just if the failure to pay had been voluntary, or could by possibility, have been avoided. But it was caused by an event beyond the control of either party,—an event which made it unlawful to pay. In such case, whilst it would be unjust, after the war, to enforce the contract as an executory one against the vendor contrary to his will, it would be equally unjust in him, treating it as ended, to insist upon the forfeiture of the money already paid on it. An equitable right to some compensation or return for previous payments would clearly result from the circumstances of the case. The money paid by the purchaser, subject to the value of any possession which he may have enjoyed, should, *ex æquo et bono,* be returned to him. This would clearly be demanded by justice and right.

And so, in the present case, whilst the insurance company has a right to insist on the materiality of time in the condition of payment of premiums, and to hold the contract ended by reason of non-payment, they cannot with any fairness insist upon the condition, as it regards the forfeiture of the premiums already paid; that would be clearly unjust and inequitable. The insured has an equitable right to have this amount restored to him, subject to a deduction for the value of the assurance enjoyed by him whilst the policy was in existence; in other words, he is fairly entitled to have the equitable value of his policy. . . .

We are of opinion, therefore, first, that as the companies elected to insist upon the condition in these cases, the policies in question must be regarded as extinguished by the non-payment of the premiums, though caused by the existence of the war, and that an action will not lie for the amount insured thereon.

Secondly, that such failure being caused by a public war, without the fault of the assured, they are entitled *ex æquo et bono* to recover the equitable value of the policies with interest from the close of the war. . . .

In estimating the equitable value of a policy, no deduction should be made from the precise amount which the calculations give, as is sometimes done where policies are voluntarily surrendered, for the purpose of discouraging such surrenders; and the value should be taken as of the day when the first default occurred in the payment of the premium by which the policy became forfeited. In each case the rates of mortality and interest used in the tables of the company will form the basis of the calculation.

The decree in the equity suit and the judgments in the actions at law are reversed, and the causes respectively remanded to be proceeded with according to law and the directions of this opinion.

[WAITE, C. J., and STRONG, CLIFFORD, and HUNT, JJ., dissented.] [1]

---

[1] SUPPLEMENTARY CASES. In Hanger v. Abbott, 6 Wallace 532 (1867), involving a suit by Abbott of New Hampshire against Hanger of Arkansas in assumpsit and a plea by the defendant that the suit was barred by the Statute of Limitations of Arkansas, the Supreme Court held that while war suspended intercourse between the citizens of the respective belligerent states it did not annul executed contracts, such as the debt in question, but merely suspended the remedy, so that upon the termination of the war suit might be brought without taking into account the period during which "the creditor is rendered incapable to sue." "The rule of the present day," said the court, "is that debts existing prior to the war, but which made no part of the reasons for undertaking it, remain entire, and the remedies are revived with the restoration of peace." Compare Williams v. Bruffy, above, p. 49, n. 1, for the effect of a law confiscating the credits of enemy aliens.

In Kershaw v. Kelsey, 100 Mass. 561 (1868), involving a suit by Kershaw, a citizen of Mississippi, against Kelsey, a citizen of Massachusetts, for breach of contract arising in connection with a lease of land in Mississippi made to the defendant when resident in that state during the war, the court held that while the "law of nations, as judicially declared, prohibits all intercourse between citizens of the two belligerents which is inconsistent with the state of war between their countries," yet this should be understood as referring to trading "from or to one of the countries at war," so that the contract in question was not within the prohibition and the plaintiff was allowed to recover the unpaid rent and the value of the corn delivered under the lease.

In Sutherland v. Mayer, 271 U. S. 272 (1926), involving a suit for an accounting brought by the Alien Property Custodian against Mayer who as a member of a partnership including German nationals held assets belonging to the firm at the time of its dissolution in 1917 when war broke out between the United States and Germany, the Supreme Court held that "the advent of a state of war put an end to the partnership and postponed all remedies relating to the dissolution; but it did not petrify rights and duties resulting therefrom. Its effect only was to suspend the enforcement of the obligation of each of the partners in respect of the assets and past transactions of the partnership; and the essential inquiry now is: What was the obligation which resulted from the dissolution?" This obligation the court found to consist in a liquidation equalizing the losses sustained by the German partners in consequence of the depreciation of the German mark before the resumption of commercial intercourse, since that depreciation would have affected Mayer's interest adversely just as much as if the German partners had liquidated the business in 1917 instead of continuing the business and setting aside Mayer's share of the profits which they did.

CHAPTER XX

PROCEDURE BY WAR: RIGHTS OF BELLIGERENT STATE OVER PROPERTY OF ENEMY NATIONALS [1]

A. Property on land.

Between the belligerents themselves in respect to their public property international law recognizes few limitations upon the extent to which each may seek to injure the other in order to attain the object of the war, whether by appropriating funds or other movable property of the enemy or by destroying such property as might weaken the enemy defenses. On the other hand, the rights of a belligerent over the property of individual enemy aliens as distinct from property of the enemy state itself are not so clear. Query, would the goods of an enemy alien found in the country at the beginning of the war be subject to confiscation and, if so, would the confiscation be automatic without a decree of the national legislature to that effect? [Brown v. United States.] Would the confiscation of private debts by a state operate to cancel the debt as between the individual debtor and a foreign creditor? [Wolff v. Oxholm.] May stocks and other securities owned by an enemy alien be confiscated? [In re Ferdinand.]

ARMITZ BROWN v. THE UNITED STATES.

United States, Supreme Court, 1814.

8 Cranch, 110. [3 L. ed. 504.]

This was an appeal from the sentence of the Circuit Court of Massachusetts, which condemned 550 tons of pine timber, claimed by Armitz Brown, the Appellant. . . .

MARSHALL, Ch. J. delivered the opinion of the Court, . . .

The Emulous owned by John Delano and others, citizens of the United States, was chartered to a company carrying on trade in Great Britain, one of whom was an American citizen, for the purpose of carrying a cargo

---

[1] For a more detailed study of this subject, see Fenwick, *op. cit.*, pp. 463–466, 510–523; Hyde, *op. cit.*, II, §§ 618–623, 761–772, 783–796; Oppenheim, *op. cit.*, II, §§ 102, 178, 186–188, 198–200; Garner, International Law and the World War, I, Chaps. IV, VIII.

from Savannah to Plymouth. After the cargo was put on board, the vessel was stopped in port by the embargo of the 4th of April, 1812. On the 25th of the same month, it was agreed between the master of the ship and the agent of the shippers, that she should proceed with her cargo to New Bedford, where her owners resided, and remain there without prejudice to the charter party. In pursuance of this agreement, the Emulous proceeded to New Bedford, where she continued until after the declaration of war. In October or November, the ship was unloaded and the cargo, except the pine timber, was landed. The pine timber was floated up a salt water creek, where, at low tide, the ends of the timber rested on the mud, where it was secured from floating out with the tide, by impediments fastened in the entrance of the creek. On the 7th of November, 1812, the cargo was sold by the agent of the owners, who is an American citizen, to the claimant, who is also an American citizen. On the 19th of April, a libel was filed by the attorney for the United States, in the district Court of Massachusetts, against the said cargo, as well on behalf of the United States of America as for and in behalf of John Delano and of all other persons concerned. It does not appear that this seizure was made under any instructions from the president of the United States; nor is there any evidence of its having his sanction, unless the libels being filed and prosecuted by the law officer who represents the government must imply that sanction.

On the contrary, it is admitted that the seizure was made by an individual, and the libel filed at his instance, by the district attorney who acted from his own impressions of what appertained to his duty. The property was claimed by Armitz Brown under the purchase made in the preceding November.

The District Court dismissed the libel. The Circuit Court reversed this sentence, and condemned the pine timber as enemy property forfeited to the United States. From the sentence of the Circuit Court, the claimant appealed to this Court.

The material question made at bar is this. Can the pine timber, even admitting the property not to be changed by the sale in November, be condemned as prize of war?

The cargo of the Emulous having been legally acquired and put on board the vessel, having been detained by an embargo not intended to act on foreign property, the vessel having sailed before the war, from Savannah, under a stipulation to re-land the cargo in some port of the United States, the re-landing having been made with respect to the residue of the cargo, and the pine timber having been floated into shallow water, where it was secured and in the custody of the owner of the ship, an American citizen, the court cannot perceive any solid distinction, so far as respects confiscation, between this property and other British property found on land at the commencement of hostilities. It will therefore be considered as a question relating to such property generally, and to be governed by the same rule.

Respecting the power of government no doubt is entertained. That war gives to the sovereign full right to take the persons and confiscate the property of the enemy wherever found, is conceded. The mitigations of this rigid rule, which the humane and wise policy of modern times has introduced into practice, will more or less affect the exercise of this right, but cannot impair the right itself. That remains undiminished, and when the sovereign authority shall choose to bring it into operation, the judicial department must give effect to its will. But until that will shall be expressed, no power of condemnation can exist in the court.

The questions to be decided by the Court are:

1st. May enemy's property, found on land at the commencement of hostilities, be seized and condemned as a necessary consequence of the declaration of war?

2d. Is there any legislative act which authorizes such seizure and condemnation?

Since, in this country, from the structure of our government, proceedings to condemn the property of an enemy found within our territory at the declaration of war, can be sustained only upon the principle that they are instituted in execution of some existing law, we are led to ask,

Is the declaration of war such a law? Does that declaration, by its own operation, so vest the property of the enemy in the government, as to support proceedings for its seizure and confiscation, or does it vest only a right, the assertion of which depends on the will of the sovereign power?

The universal practice of forbearing to seize and confiscate debts and credits, the principle universally received, that the right to them revives on the restoration of peace, would seem to prove that war is not an absolute confiscation of this property, but simply confers the right of confiscation.

Between debts contracted under the faith of laws, and property acquired in the course of trade, on the faith of the same laws, reason draws no distinction; and, although, in practice, vessels with their cargoes, found in port at the declaration of war, may have been seized, it is not believed that modern usage would sanction the seizure of the goods of an enemy on land, which were acquired in peace in the course of trade. Such a proceeding is rare, and would be deemed a harsh exercise of the rights of war. But although the practice in this respect may not be uniform, that circumstance does not essentially affect the question. The enquiry is, whether such property vests in the sovereign by the mere declaration of war, or remains subject to a right of confiscation, the exercise of which depends on the national will: and the rule which applies to one case, so far as respects the operation of a declaration of war on the thing itself, must apply to all others over which war gives an equal right. The right of the sovereign to confiscate debts being precisely the same with the right to confiscate other property found in the country, the operation of a declaration of war on debts and on other property found within the country must be the same. What then is this operation?

Even Bynkershoek, who maintains the broad principle, that in war every thing done against an enemy is lawful; that he may be destroyed, though unarmed and defenceless; that fraud, or even poison, may be employed against him; that a most unlimited right is acquired to his person and property; admits that war does not transfer to the sovereign a debt due to his enemy; and, therefore, if payment of such debt be not exacted, peace revives the former right of the creditor; "because," he says, "the occupation which is had by war consists more in fact than in law." He adds to his observations on this subject, "let it not, however, be supposed that it is only true of actions, that they are not condemned *ipso jure,* for other things also belonging to the enemy may be concealed and escape condemnation."

Vattel says, that "the sovereign can neither detain the persons nor the property of those subjects of the enemy who are within his dominions at the time of the declaration."

It is true that this rule is, in terms, applied by Vattel to the property of those only who are personally within the territory at the commencement of hostilities; but it applies equally to things in action and to things in possession; and if war did, of itself, without any further exercise of the sovereign will, vest the property of the enemy in the sovereign, his presence could not exempt it from this operation of war. Nor can a reason be perceived for maintaining that the public faith is more entirely pledged for the security of property trusted in the territory of the nation in time of peace, if it be accompanied by its owner, than if it be confided to the care of others.

Chitty, after stating the general right of seizure, says, "But, in strict justice, that right can take effect only on those possessions of a belligerent which have come to the hands of his adversary after the declaration of hostilities."

The modern rule then would seem to be, that tangible property belonging to an enemy and found in the country at the commencement of war, ought not to be immediately confiscated; and in almost every commercial treaty an article is inserted stipulating for the right to withdraw such property.

This rule appears to be totally incompatible with the idea that war does of itself vest the property in the belligerent government. It may be considered as the opinion of all who have written on the *jus belli,* that war gives the right to confiscate, but does not itself confiscate the property of the enemy; and their rules go to the exercise of this right.

The constitution of the United States was framed at a time when this rule, introduced by commerce in favor of moderation and humanity, was received throughout the civilized world. In expounding that constitution, a construction ought not lightly to be admitted which would give to a declaration of war an effect in this country it does not possess elsewhere, and which would fetter that exercise of entire discretion respecting enemy property which may enable the government to apply to the enemy the rule that he applies to us.

If we look to the constitution itself, we find this general reasoning much strengthened by the words of that instrument.

That the declaration of war has only the effect of placing the two nations in a state of hostility, of producing a state of war, of giving those rights which war confers; but not of operating, by its own force, any of those results, such as a transfer of property, which are usually produced by ulterior measures of government, is fairly deducible from the enumeration of powers which accompanies that of declaring war. "Congress shall have power" . . . "to declare war, grant letters of marque and reprisal, and make rules concerning captures on land and water." . . .

The proposition that a declaration of war does not, in itself, enact a confiscation of the property of the enemy within the territory of the belligerent, is believed to be entirely free from doubt. Is there in the act of Congress, by which war is declared against Great Britain, any expression which would indicate such an intention?

That act, after placing the two nations in a state of war, authorizes the President of the United States to use the whole land and naval force of the United States to carry the war into effect, and "to issue to private armed vessels of the United States, commissions or letters of marque and general reprisal against the vessels, goods and effects of the government of the United Kingdom of Great Britain and Ireland, and the subjects thereof."

That reprisals may be made on enemy property found within the United States at the declaration of war, if such be the will of the nation, has been admitted; but it is not admitted that, in the declaration of war, the nation has expressed its will to that effect.

It cannot be necessary to employ argument in showing that when the attorney for the United States institutes proceedings at law for the confiscation of enemy property found on land, or floating in one of our creeks, in the care and custody of one of our citizens, he is not acting under the authority of letters of marque and reprisal, still less under the authority of such letters issued to a private armed vessel.

The "act concerning letters of marque, prizes and prize goods," certainly contains nothing to authorize this seizure.

There being no other act of Congress which bears upon the subject, it is considered as proved that the legislature has not confiscated enemy property which was within the United States at the declaration of war, and that this sentence of condemnation cannot be sustained.

One view, however, has been taken of this subject which deserves to be further considered.

It is urged that, in executing the laws of war, the executive may seize and the courts condemn all property which, according to the modern law of nations, is subject to confiscation, although it might require an act of the legislature to justify the condemnation of that property which, according to modern usage, ought not to be confiscated.

This argument must assume for its basis the position that modern usage constitutes a rule which acts directly upon the thing itself by its own force, and not through the sovereign power. This position is not allowed. This usage is a guide which the sovereign follows or abandons at his will. The rule, like other precepts of morality, of humanity, and even of wisdom, is addressed to the judgment of the sovereign; and although it cannot be disregarded by him without obloquy, yet it may be disregarded.

The rule is, in its nature, flexible. It is subject to infinite modification. It is not an immutable rule of law, but depends on political considerations which may continually vary.

Commercial nations, in the situation of the United States, have always a considerable quantity of property in the possession of their neighbors. When war breaks out, the question, what shall be done with enemy property in our country, is a question rather of policy than of law. The rule which we apply to the property of our enemy, will be applied by him to the property of our citizens. Like all other questions of policy, it is proper for the consideration of a department which can modify it at will; not for the consideration of a department which can pursue only the law as it is written. It is proper for the consideration of the legislature, not of the executive or judiciary.

It appears to the court, that the power of confiscating enemy property is in the legislature, and that the legislature has not yet declared its will to confiscate property which was within our territory at the declaration of war. The court is therefore of opinion that there is error in the sentence of condemnation pronounced in the Circuit Court in this case, and doth direct that the same be reversed and annulled, and that the sentence of the District Court be affirmed.

[Dissenting opinion of STORY, J., omitted.] [1]

---

[1] Compare United States v. Chemical Foundation, 272 U. S. 1 (1926), involving the sale of German patents under the Trading with the Enemy Acts during the World War.

G. WOLFF AND OTHERS, ASSIGNEES OF J. WOLFF AND J. DORVILLE, BANKRUPTS, AGAINST OXHOLM.

Great Britain, Court of King's Bench, 1817.

6 Maule & Selwyn, 92.

[Assumpsit for money lent by the bankrupts, money paid, and money had and received. Oxholm, a Danish subject resident in Denmark, was indebted to the partnership of Wolff and Dorville, who assigned the debt to a third party who brought suit upon it in the courts of Denmark. Pending the suit war was declared between Denmark and Great Britain, and the government of Denmark thereupon sequestered debts due British subjects and ordered payment into the Danish treasury. Oxholm paid the debt to the Danish authorities pursuant to the order and received a receipt. Upon the presentation of this receipt the proceedings against him in the Danish court were quashed. After the war Oxholm went to Great Britain, where he was arrested and held to bail for the debt by the assignees in bankruptcy. For the plaintiffs three points were made; first, which was the principal point, that the Danish confiscatory ordinance was void, being contrary to the acknowledged practice and law of nations, and therefore affording no just ground of defence to this action.]

Lord Ellenborough, C. J., now delivered the judgment of the Court. This case was very ably argued before us at Serjeants' Inn. Upon the facts stated, it appears that the action was brought for the recovery of a debt contracted in England, by a Danish subject resident in Denmark, with a house of trade established here, and in a time of peace between the two countries. . . . It further appears, that with a view to deprive the defendant of some supposed claim of set off, which he was expected to make in the Danish courts against the suit of the original creditors, they had assigned the debt to a third person in trust for themselves; and that their assignee commenced a suit in his own name in one of the courts of Denmark against the defendant; who, in order to avoid the effect of this assignment, instituted a cross suit in the same court against them and their assignee, to which they appeared; and in this state of things a war broke out between the two countries, and no further proceedings were had in either of the suits for several years, nor until they were quashed upon the application of the defendant on the production of the commissioners' receipt mentioned in the case. . . . And this brings us to the consideration of what is the material question in the cause, viz. the legal effect of the Danish ordinance of confiscation promulgated on the 16th of August 1807, and the facts that took place after it, which constituted the main ground of the defence. If this ordinance is to be considered merely as a penal law, it is clear that the courts of this country ought not to take notice of it, because no country regards the penal laws of another. Folliott v. Ogden, 1 H. Black. 135. . . . But, it was contended, that this ordinance *was a proceeding founded upon and conformable to the law of nations,* and that as the defendant paid the debt to the persons appointed by the ordinance to receive the confiscated debts, he has a good discharge as to the debt itself according to the law of nations, to which the municipal courts of this country, as well as of all others, ought to give effect. To prove that this ordinance was grounded upon and conformable to the law of nations, two passages were cited from Vattel's treatise, the first from book 2. chap. 18. sect. 344., where, speaking on the subject of reprisals, the author says, "Between state and state whatever is the property of the members is considered as belonging to the body, and is answerable for the debts of the body; whence it follows, that in reprisals they seize the goods of the subject, in the same manner as those of the state or the sovereign. Every thing that belongs to the nation is subject to reprisals wherever it can be found, provided it be not a deposit entrusted to the public faith." The other passage is in book 3. ch. 5. sect. 77. "Among the rights belonging to the enemy, are likewise incorporeal things, all his rights, titles, and debts, excepting, however, those kind of rights granted by a third person, and in which the grantor is so far concerned that it is not a matter of indifference to him in what hands they are vested. Such, for instance, are the rights of commerce. But as debts are not of this number, war gives us the same rights over any sums of money due by neutral nations to our enemy, as it can give over his other property. When Alexander by conquest became absolute master of Thebes, he remitted to the Thessalians a hundred talents which they owed to the Thebans. The sovereign has naturally the same right over what his subjects may owe to enemies. He may therefore confiscate debts of this nature, if the term of payment happen in the time of war, or at least he may prohibit his subjects from paying while the war continues." To the proviso at the end of the first of these passages, the author himself immediately subjoins the following words: "As it is only in consequence of that confidence which the proprietor has placed in our good faith that we happen to have such deposit in our hands, it ought to be respected even in case of open war. Such is the conduct observed in France, England, and elsewhere, with respect to the money which foreigners have placed in the public funds." Now it is obvious that this reason will apply with equal force to a debt owing to an individual in the course of commerce; such individual trusted to the good faith of the individual with whom he dealt, and to the justice of the state of which that individual was a subject; and if it be contrary to good faith for a state to confiscate and convert to its own use debts owing by the state itself in its aggregate capacity, it cannot be less contrary to good faith to sequester and convert to the use of the state debts owing by its own subjects in their individual capacities. The concluding sentence of the second passage quoted by the defendant's counsel, and which was the main support of his argument, is expressed in such a manner as to shew that the author himself doubted of the right of confiscating debts due from individuals to individuals. He says, "at least the sovereign may prohibit his subjects from paying while the war continues." And, indeed, this is the actual limit of this right, viz. as it operates *in personam* upon the subject of the state, or upon his property, within the reach and controul of such state. And in the very next sentence the author further qualifies his doctrine, and adds, "But, at present, a regard to the advantage and safety of commerce had induced all the sovereigns of Europe to act with less rigour in this point. And as this custom has been generally received, he who should act contrary to it would violate the public faith; for strangers trusted his subjects only from a firm persuasion that the general custom would be observed." We have not, however, been able to discover that there ever was a time when greater rigour generally prevailed on this subject, as Vattel appears to have supposed. Some instances, indeed, of similar confiscations in the sixteenth and seventeenth centuries are mentioned by Bynkershoek in his *Questiones Juris Publici et Privati*, c. 7., and appear to be considered by that writer as warranted by the law of nations, and available to the debtor where payment has been actually enforced from him by the authority of his own government. And there was a decision about the middle of the sixteenth century by a court at Paris in favour of a Frenchman, against the claim of a Fleming, to recover a debt paid by the Frenchman to the treasury of his own country, in obedience to a French decree of this kind during a war between the two nations. It could not be expected that a French court should decide otherwise with reference to a decree of its own government. Sir Matthew Hale, also, in his *Pleas of the Crown*, vol. i. p. 95. says, "that by the law of England debts and goods found in this realm belonging to alien enemies belong to the king, and may be seized by him;" but the books referred to do not furnish an instance of the seizure of debts, or a decided case in support of the legality of such a seizure. And by the statute of Magna Charta, cap. 30. merchant strangers are, upon the breaking out of a war, to be attached and kept without harm to body or goods, until it shall be known how the English merchants are treated by the sovereign of their state, and if the latter are safe there, the former are to be safe here. So that foreign merchants could suffer nothing in England unless by way of retaliation and reprizal. So early as the time of Grotius opinions had been entertained against the right of confiscating incorporeal things; and there is nothing to be found in the great work of that very learned author which can give countenance to such a right. On the contrary, in lib. iii. c. 7. s. 4. of the Treatise *de Jure Gentium*, there is an allusion to the opinion of some *"qui dicunt incorporalia, belli jure, non acquiri;"* and Grotius himself does not controvert this opinion in general, but supposes it to admit of qualification in the case of a captive slave; and alludes to it in that way, after having remarked that, *"res omnes quæ captæ fuerant, cum persona acquiruntur domino.''* But the proposition last mentioned does not, in truth, furnish any qualification of the opinion to which Grotius alludes; for incorporeal things cannot be taken; and the dominion of corporeal things actually taken is in general acquired by the capture of them, and the title of the captor to them is not less valid where their owner is not taken, than where he is; as is observed by Puffendorff, at the end of the 22d sect. of lib. viii. c. 6. of the Treatise *de Jure Naturali et Gentium.* At the beginning of that section this learned author gives the rule as follows: *''Circa adquisitionem incorporalium in bello peculiariter observandum, ista non adquiri, nisi cum subjecto, cui inherent.''* . . . It was admitted that, notwithstanding all the violent measures to which recourse has been had during the extraordinary warfare, that we have witnessed in our own times, this ordinance of the Court of Denmark stands single and alone, not supported by any precedent, nor adopted as an example in any other state. The ordinance itself, however, so far as we can learn from this case, was not followed up by any practical measure of compulsion upon the subjects of Denmark. Nothing in the nature of process against the defendant to enforce the payment of this particular debt, nothing analogous to the seizure or condemnation of corporeal things taken in the time of war occurred on this occasion; and although the commissioners appointed under the ordinance to receive the sequestrated monies were informed of this debt as early as the year 1807, yet the defendant did not pay the money until 1812. . . . Considering, therefore, that the right of confiscating debts contended for on the authority of these citations from Vattel is not recognised by Grotius, and is impugned by Puffendorff and others, that such confiscation was not general at any period of time, and that no instance of it, except the ordinance in question, is to be found for something more than a century, we think our judgment would be pregnant of mischief to future times, if we did not declare, that in our opinion this ordinance, and the payment to the commissioners appointed under it, do not furnish a defence to the present action; and if they cannot do this of themselves, neither can they do so by the aid of the proceedings in the Danish court. The parties went into that court expecting justice, according to the then existing laws of the country, and are not bound by the quashing of their suit, in consequence of a *subsequent ordinance, not conformable to the usage of* nations, and which, therefore, they could not expect, nor are they or we bound to regard.

Postea to the plaintiffs.

IN RE FERDINAND, EX-TSAR OF BULGARIA.

Great Britain, Court of Appeal, 1920.

L. R. [1921] 1 Ch. 107.

LORD STERNDALE, M. R.   In this case the ex-Tsar of Bulgaria, who has obtained special leave for the purpose, appeals against two orders made on July 30,. 1919, and August 13, 1919, by Eve, J., and P. O. Lawrence, J., respectively.   By each order certain stocks and securities which formerly belonged to the appellant were vested in the Solicitor to the Treasury as trustee for H. M. King George V.   The appellant was by birth of German nationality, but according to his affidavit in 1887 he had become of Austro-Hungarian nationality by reason of holding a commission in the army of that country.   In that year he was elected Prince of Bulgaria and in 1908 he assumed the title of Tsar.   On being elected Prince of Bulgaria he became of Bulgarian nationality. War broke out between Bulgaria and this country in October, 1915, and the appellant thereupon became an enemy of His Majesty.   At that time the stocks and securities in question were held by Messrs. Coutts & Co. on behalf of the appellant, some of them being registered in his own name and some in the names of partners of Coutts & Co. who held them as trustees for the appellant.   After the outbreak of war Messrs. Coutts & Co., acting in accordance with the provisions of the Trading with the Enemy Amendment Act of 1914, gave notice to the custodian appointed under that act that they so held the said stocks and securities and also some bearer securities not the subject of this appeal.   They were required to deposit and did deposit them with the Bank of England to the order of the Solicitor to the Treasury, and the partners in whose names some of them were registered signed declarations that they held them also to the order of the Treasury.   No further step was taken in the matter until after the conclusion of an armistice with Bulgaria and the abdication of the appellant, which took place on September 29, and October 3, 1918, respectively.   After his abdication the appellant went to Germany and was resident there at the conclusion of the armistice with Germany on November 11, 1918.

On June 27, 1919, a commission was issued under the Great Seal by virtue of which on July 10, 1919, an inquisition was held by which it was found that the appellant was on the outbreak of war beneficially entitled to the stocks and securities and that the same became and remained forfeited to His Majesty.   The orders in question were then made on the dates before mentioned.   On November 19, 1919, an order was made by the Board of Trade under section 4 of the Trading with the Enemy Amendment Act, 1916, vesting the stocks and securities in the custodian, such order only to have effect in case of its being held that no forfeiture of them to His Majesty had taken place.

The points argued on the appeal were: (1) Was it ever the common law of England that the Crown had the right to seize and claim as forfeited to it private property including choses in action found in this kingdom belonging to subjects of an enemy state? (2) If so, had that right ceased to exist before the passing of the Trading with the Enemy Acts? (3) If not, has it been abandoned or ceased to exist by reason of the legislation contained in the various acts relating to trading with the enemy, so far as such legislation deals with the disposition of enemy property during the war? (4) Had the Crown lost the right to claim the forfeiture of such property, because no inquisition had been held before the conclusion of the armistice with Bulgaria? These stocks and securities were choses in action belonging to the appellant, and I do not think any distinction can be drawn between legal and equitable interests in such choses in action. The stocks and securities were the private property of the appellant and were in no way part of the national revenues or property of the state of Bulgaria. They would no doubt, if the appellant could have obtained possession of them, have been available for use by him in the promotion of the war against this country, but probably he had no intention of so using them, and I think that from the legal point of view they must be considered in the same light as the private property of any other national of the enemy state. The fact that they were the property of the enemy sovereign is only important from a moral or political point of view in influencing the crown to enforce the exercise of a right which it has not exercised for a long time, and probably would not have exercised against the property of a private person. I do not therefore think it necessary to discuss the question argued before us as to the position of the appellant as a sovereign under the constitution of Bulgaria, or the extent to which under that constitution he may be considered responsible for the war between this country and Bulgaria.

As to the first two questions I have no doubt that they should be answered against the appellant. I think the right to seize private enemy property existed and that nothing had occurred up to the beginning of the war with Bulgaria to deprive the Crown of that right unless that were the effect of the Trading with the Enemy Acts. The right is stated by Hale, C. J., in his Pleas of the Crown to have existed originally, and although it was argued with some force that the cases in the Year Books to which reference is there made do not fully bear out the statement and have been questioned in Rolle's Abridgment, 195, it has been recognized and repeated as a correct statement of the law many times since. It is so stated also by the writers on international law, in Wheaton, 8th ed., (by Dana) ss. 304–308, and notes 157 and 171; Phillimore, Part III, 132; Kent, Part. I, 65; Wheaton, 5th ed. (by Phillipson), p. 419; and Hall, 7th ed., pp. 460–464, and the notes to those pages. In Westlake's International Law, Part II, 47, the author after adducing strong arguments to show that such a right should not continue says: "The time is now fully ripe when a British Court should not lag behind the position taken by Governments, but should boldly follow Lord Ellenborough." The allusion to Lord Ellenborough refers to the case of Wolff v. Oxholm [6 M. & S. 92], with which I shall deal later. I have quoted Westlake's words, because they show that although the author strongly condemned the practice of seizing private property he did not consider that the law as then existing prohibited it, and earlier in the same passage he had referred to the decision of Dr. Lushington in The Johanna Emilie [Spinks' Prize Cas. 14], where the existence of the right was clearly stated. It was also so held in America in Brown v. United States [(1814) 8 Cranch, 110], though in the circumstances of that case the court decided that there was no right to seize the goods in question. The only statement to the contrary in a modern writer that I have found is in Oppenheim, vol. ii, s. 102, where he says that the right to seize private property is obsolete, and that there is a customary international law prohibiting the confiscation of private property and the annulment of enemy debts on the territory of a belligerent. If this only refers, as I think it does, to a general confiscation and annulment and not to a right in the Crown to seize in particular instances it is not, whether correct or not, opposed to what I think is the law. If it be intended to extend to the right to seize I think it is opposed to other authorities and incorrect.

Great reliance was however placed by the counsel for the appellant on the case of Wolff v. Oxholm [6 M. & S. 92] to which reference has already been made. In that case a Danish subject ordinarily resident in Denmark was sued for a debt due to the plaintiffs who were carrying on business in England. His defence was that he had during the war between England and Denmark paid the debt to commissioners appointed by the Danish government, by whose order all debts due to English subjects by Danes were sequestrated and made payable to the commissioners. Lord Ellenborough, delivering the judgment of the Court of King's Bench in 1817, held the defence bad and the ordinance to be contrary to the law of nations. The actual decision related to a general confiscation of mercantile debts, and Lord Ellenborough referred in his judgment to the protection given to merchants by Magna Charta, but he did use expressions which show that he considered that there was no right to seize any property of an incorporeal nature. This judgment has been the subject of criticism in Wheaton, 8th ed. (by Dana) s. 308, and is in my opinion, if it go to the length contended by the appellant's counsel, opposed to the decision I have already mentioned in The Johanna Emilie [Spinks' Prize Cas. 14] and also to Land v. Lord North [4 Doug. 266-274], where Lord Mansfield speaks of that summum jus which undoubtedly gives all enemies' property coming into this country to the King. In Furtado v. Rogers [3 Bos. & P. 191] also the right to seize property and debts seems to have been recognized by Lord Alvanley, though he does not expressly decide the question. It seems also clear that Lord Ellenborough was in error as to some of the historical facts upon which he relies in his judgment. It is pointed out in Hall's International Law, p. 462, note 1, that he was incorrect in stating that the ordinance in question "stood single and alone unsupported by any precedent and that no instance of such confiscation except the ordinance in question is to be found for more than a century," and instances are given in that note to the contrary. There were also produced before us in the argument instances of Exchequer special commissions in 1693, 1705, 1797, 1806, 1807 and 1812 under which inquisitions were found forfeiting to the crown private enemy property including choses in action, and in one case at least Government securities which would not now be seized. In one case, namely, that of the inquisition held in 1697, the matter came before the court in Attorney General v. Weeden [Parker, 267], where it was held that the inquisition was invalid because it was not held until after the conclusion of peace, but this decision was given: "upon long debate it was resolved first that choses in action which belonged to an alien enemy were forfeited to the crown." Lord Ellenborough seems to have been unaware of these inquisitions. I ought perhaps to mention that other inquisitions forfeiting property in 1854 were produced, but I attach no importance to them, because they related to certain steam vessels under construction for the Emperor of all the Russias during the Crimean War. These steam vessels may well have been considered enemy government property which might be used in the war. Taking these matters into consideration I do not think Wolff v. Oxholm displaces the other authorities to which I have referred. . . .

The third question raises very different considerations. I doubt whether such a right as in my opinion existed could be lost by mere disuse unless such disuse took place in circumstances which would raise the inference of an international compact, but I think it is quite clear that the Crown can abandon and give up a right if it choose to do so. The question here is whether by the various Acts called Trading with the Enemy Acts it has so abandoned the right. . . . It is fairly clear, I think, that the powers conferred by these Acts are in important respects inconsistent with the exercise of the common law right of forfeiture. If an order had been previously made by the Board of Trade vesting the property in the custodian I do not see how the right of forfeiture could be exercised or an inquisition held which could find that the property was enemy property forfeited to the Crown when it was already vested in the custodian to be disposed of according to Order in Council. The powers conferred by the Act no doubt afforded a readier and more convenient method of dealing with enemy property than the somewhat cumbrous method of procedure by inquisition, and were therefore useful to the Crown, but I do not think that is the only effect of the Act. It seems to me that a power to vest property in a custodian to be dealt with at the end of the war as His Majesty should by Order in Council direct is inconsistent with an intention of preserving a power to insist on an absolute forfeiture at common law. The one contemplates a discretion as to the disposal of the property which would no doubt be affected by the provisions of the treaty of peace, while the other works an absolute forfeiture following the exercise of a right still in existence but unexercised in late years. The right to forfeiture and the Trading with the Enemy legislation are concerned with all enemy property, and it must be remembered that the right to forfeit, although its existence is recognized, has been criticised and its exercise deprecated by practically all writers on international law in modern times. In these circumstances I think that if the Crown in taking powers in many respects inconsistent with that right meant also to preserve it the intention to do so should be clearly shown, and in my opinion that is not the case. Some confirmation of this view, though not perhaps very much, is obtained from section 14, sub-s. 1, of the Trading with the Enemy (Amendment) Act, 1914. This section contains a saving of certain powers of His Majesty existing apart from the Act, and does not mention this right of forfeiture.

The conclusion to which I have come seems to be in accordance with the view expressed by Bankes, L. J., in Stevenson v. Cartonnagen-Industrie [[1917] 1 K. B. 852], where he said: "The whole of the legislation which has been passed since the beginning of the war dealing with enemy property in this country rests on the assumption that the Crown is not insisting on any common law right to claim such property." . . .

I think, therefore, that on this ground the appeal should be allowed, and the orders appealed from discharged. . . .[1]

---

[1] Supplementary Cases. In Ware v. Hylton, 3 Dallas 199 (1796), involving an action by Ware (administrator of Jones, a British subject) against Hylton and others for a debt contracted in 1774, to which the defendants pleaded that the debt had been paid into the loan office of Virginia in pursuance of a law of 1777 sequestering British property and providing that such payment, and a receipt therefor, should discharge the debt, the Supreme Court held that the action taken by Virginia as an independent state in 1777 was consistent with the law of nations and was at the time a bar to the suit, but that Article 4 of the treaty of peace of 1783 nullified the law of Virginia, revived the debt and gave a right of recovery against the principal debtor notwithstanding the payment previously made under the law of 1777.

Query, would the property of a citizen, located in enemy territory, share in the fate of enemy property destroyed as an incident to military operations? In Juragua Iron Co., Ltd., v. United States, 212 U. S. 297 (1909), involving a claim brought by a Pennsylvania corporation for losses caused by an order of an American general in command of military operations in Cuba, in consequence of which buildings belonging to the plaintiff were destroyed to prevent the spread of yellow fever, the Supreme Court held that the claim was not

B. Property on the high seas.

As in the case of property on land, the right of a belligerent to confiscate or to destroy the public property of the other belligerent when found at sea is subject only to limitations of a humanitarian character. Many problems, however, have arisen in connection with the capture of the private property of individual enemy nationals. Unlike the rule in respect to private enemy property on land, the right of a belligerent to capture private enemy property on the high seas as "prize of war" has been universally recognized. Query, in respect to the determination of the enemy character of property, would goods shipped by a neutral citizen under contract to become enemy property on delivery in the enemy country be enemy property if captured in transit? [The Sally.] Would property belonging to a neutral be regarded as enemy property if the neutral were resident and doing business in the enemy country? [The Harmony.]   At what point does the title to property pass from the

---

admissible, on the ground that (quoting Miller v. United States, 11 Wall. 268) "the right to confiscate the property of all public enemies is a conceded right" and that an American corporation "which at the time and in reference to the property in question had a commercial domicile in the enemy's country" could not claim any other rights than those of a Spaniard residing there.

Query, where a treaty calls for the payment of damages for illegal acts, would losses of private persons due to bombardment from the air without warning be included? In Coenca Brothers v. Germany, Recueil des decisions des tribunaux arbitraux mixtes, VII, 683 (1927), involving a claim growing out of the alleged illegal bombardment of Salonika by Germany in 1916 and the consequent destruction of goods belonging to the claimants, the Greco-German Mixed Arbitration Tribunal held that the fact that the Allied Powers were in illegal occupation of Salonika, while it gave Germany the right to take military action against the town, did not absolve her of the duty of observing the laws of war in respect to bombardment one of which was that the authorities should be warned before commencing the bombardment. Germany was therefore held liable for the damage. (Annual Digest, 1927–1928, p. 570.)

Query, what is the status of citizens and their property when the territory of the home state is temporarily in occupation of the enemy? In United States v. Rice, 4 Wheaton 246 (1819), involving the liability of goods imported into Castine, Maine, during the occupation of that port by the British, to pay customs duties to the United States when the occupation by the enemy came to an end, the Supreme Court held the claim for duties could not be sustained. "By the surrender [of Castine]," said the court, "the inhabitants passed under a temporary allegiance to the British government, and were bound by such laws, and such only, as it chose to recognize and impose. From the nature of the case, no other laws could be obligatory upon them, for where there is no protection or allegiance or sovereignty, there can be no claim to obedience. Castine was, therefore, during this period, so far as respected our revenue laws, to be deemed a foreign port; and goods imported into it by the inhabitants, were subject to such duties only as the British government chose to require. Such goods were in no correct sense imported into the United States. The subsequent evacuation by the enemy, and resumption of authority by the United States, did not, and could not, change the character of the previous transactions." Compare Fleming v. Page, 8 Howard, 603 (1850).

neutral shipper to the enemy buyer when the goods have been shipped before the outbreak of war? [The Miramichi; The Odessa.] It was formerly the custom for governments to supplement their navies with privateers manned by individuals commissioned to make captures of enemy property on the high seas; but in such cases the title vested by international law immediately in the government, not in the individual captor. [United States v. The Active.] During the World War a new problem was presented by the fact that the submarine depended in large part for its success upon secrecy of attack and that it was unable to take on board the passengers and crew of the captured ship. Query, would it be illegal for a belligerent submarine to sink an enemy merchant vessel without warning when an attempt to warn might put the submarine at a disadvantage? [The Lusitania.]

THE SALLY.

Great Britain, The Lords Commissioners of Appeals, 1795.

3 C. Rob. 300, note.

The Sally, Griffiths [master], was a case of a cargo of corn shipped March 1793 by Steward and Plunket of Baltimore, ostensibly for the account and risk of Conyngham, Nesbit, and Co. of Philadelphia, and consigned to them *or their assigns:*—By an endorsement on the bill of lading, it was further agreed that the ship should proceed to Havre de Grace, and there wait such time as might be necessary, the orders of the consignee of the said cargo (the mayor of Havre), either to deliver the same at the port of Havre, or proceed therewith to any one port without the Mediterranean. . . .

Amongst the papers was a concealed letter from Jean Ternant, the minister of the French Republic to the United States, in which he informs the minister of foreign affairs in France, "The house of Conyngham and Co. already known to the ministers, by their former operations for France, is charged by me to procure without delay, a consignment of 22,000 bushels of wheat, 8,000 barrels of fine flour, 900 barrels of salted beef from New England. The conditions stipulated are the same as those of the contract of 2d November 1792 with the American citizens Swan and Co. . . . It has been moreover agreed, considering the actual reports of war, that the whole shall be sent as American property to Havre and to Nantes, with power to our government of sending the ships to other ports conditional on the usual freight. As you have not signified to me to whom these cargoes ought to be delivered in our ports, I shall provide each captain with a letter to the mayor of the place."

There was also a letter from J. Ternant to the mayor of the municipality of Havre. "Our government having ordered me to send supplies of provisions to your port, I inform you that the bearer of this, commanding the American ship the Sally, is laden with a cargo of wheat, of which he will deliver you the bill of lading.''

To the 12th and 20th interrogatories the master deposed, "that he believes the flour was the property of the French government, and, on being unladen, would have immediately become the property of the French government.'' . . .

The Court [present the Earl of Mansfield, Sir R. P. Arden, M. R., and Sir W. Wynne] said: It has always been the rule of the prize Courts, that property going to be delivered in the enemy's country, and under a contract to become the property of the enemy immediately on arrival, if taken *in transitu*, is to be considered as enemies' property. When the contract is made in time of peace or without any contemplation of a war, no such rule exists:—But in a case like the present, where the form of the contract was framed directly for the purpose of obviating the danger apprehended from approaching hostilities, it is a rule which unavoidably must take place. The bill of lading expresses account and risk of the American merchants; but papers alone make no proof, unless supported by the depositions of the master. Instead of supporting the contents of his papers, the master deposes, "that on arrival the goods would become the property of the French government," and all the concealed papers strongly support him in this testimony: The *evidentia rei* is too strong to admit farther proof. Supposing that it was to become the property of the enemy on delivery, *capture* is considered as *delivery:* The captors, by the rights of war, stand in the place of the enemy, and are entitled to a condemnation of goods passing under such a contract, as of enemy's property. On every principle on which Prize Courts can proceed, this cargo must be considered as enemy's property. Condemned.

THE HARMONY.

Great Britain, High Court of Admiralty, 1800.

2 C. Rob. 322.

This was one of several American vessels in which a claim had been reserved for part of the cargo, on further proof to be made of the national character of G. W. Murray, who appeared in the original case, as a partner of a house of trade in America, but personally resident in France; restitution had been decreed in the several claims to the house of trade in America, with a reservation of the share of this partner. . . . [It appeared in evidence that Murray, an American citizen, had gone to France in 1794 to dispose of a cargo belonging to his firm. He remained a year, and after a visit of about six months to America, he returned to France and four years later was still in that country. The court construed this as a continuous residence of six years in France. Murray argued that these facts did not show a domicile in France.]

Sir W. Scott—This is a question which arises on several parcels of property claimed on behalf of G. W. Murray; and it is in all of them a question of residence or domicil, which I have often had occasion to observe, is in itself a question of considerable difficulty, depending on a great variety of circumstances, hardly capable of being defined by any general precise rules: The active spirit of commerce now abroad in the world, still farther increases this difficulty by increasing the variety of local situations, in which the same individual is to be found at no great distance of time; and by that sort of extended circulation, if I may so call it, by which the same transaction communicates with different countries, as in the present cases, in which the same trading adventures have their origin (perhaps) in America, travel to France, from France to England, from England back to America again, without enabling us to assign accurately the exact legal effect of the local character of every particular portion of this divided transaction.

In deciding such cases, the necessary freedom of commerce imposes likewise the duty of a particular attention and delicacy; and strict principle of law must not be pressed too eagerly against it; and I have before had occasion to remark, that the particular situation of America, in respect to distance, seems still more particularly to entitle the merchants of that country to some favourable distinctions. They live at a great distance from Europe; they have not the same open and ready constant correspondence with individuals of the several nations of Europe, that these persons have with each other; they are on that very account more likely to have their mercantile confidence in Europe abused, and therefore to have more frequent calls for a personal attendance to their own concerns; and it is to be expected that when the necessity of their affairs calls them across the Atlantic, they should make rather a longer stay in the country where they are called, than foreign merchants who step from a neighboring country in Europe, to which every day offers a convenient opportunity of return. . . .

Of the few principles that can be laid down generally, I may venture to hold, that time is the grand ingredient in constituting domicil. I think that hardly enough is attributed to its effects; in most cases it is unavoidably conclusive; it is not unfrequently said, that if a person comes only for a special purpose, *that* shall not fix a domicil. This is not to be taken in an unqualified latitude, and without some respect had to the time which such a purpose may or shall occupy; for if the purpose be of a nature that *may, probably,* or *does actually* detain the person for a great length of time, I cannot but think that a general residence might grow upon the special purpose. A special purpose may lead a man to a country, where it shall detain him the whole of his life. A man comes here to follow a lawsuit; it may happen, and indeed is often used as a ground of vulgar and unfounded reproach, (unfounded as a matter of just reproach though the fact may be true), on the laws of this country, that it may last as long as himself. Some suits are famous in our juridical history for having even outlived generations of suitors. I cannot but think that against such a long residence, the plea of an original special purpose could not be averred; it must be inferred in such a case, that other purposes forced themselves upon him and mixed themselves with his original design and impressed upon him the character of the country where he resided. Suppose a man comes into a belligerent country at or before the beginning of a war; it is certainly reasonable not to bind him too soon to an acquired character, and to allow him a fair time to disengage himself; but if he continues to reside during a good part of the war, contributing, by payment of taxes, and other means, to the strength of that country, I am of opinion, that he could not plead his special purpose with any effect against the rights of hostility. If he could, there would be no sufficient guard against the fraud and abuses of masked, pretended, original, and sole purposes of a long continued residence. There is a time which will estop such a plea; no rule can fix the time *a priori,* but such a time there *must* be.

In proof of the efficacy of mere time, it is not impertinent to remark, that the same quantity of business, which would not fix a domicil in a certain space of time, would nevertheless have that effect, if distributed over a large space of time. Suppose an American comes to Europe, with six contemporary cargoes, of which he had the present care and management, meaning to return to America immediately; they would form a different case from that, of the same American, coming to any particular country of Europe, with one cargo, and fixing himself there, to receive five remaining cargoes, one in each year successively. I repeat, that time is the great agent in this matter; it is to be taken in a compound ratio, of the time and the occupation, with a great preponderance on the article of time: be the occupation what it may, it cannot happen, but with few exceptions, that mere length of time shall not constitute a domicil. . . . [The court here made an elaborate examination of the evidence as to Murray's residence in France, and found that the facts showed a domicil established in that country.]

I feel myself under the necessity . . . of condemning his share of the property in these several cargoes.

THE MIRAMICHI.

Great Britain, High Court of Justice, Admiralty, 1914.

L. R. [1915] Probate, 71.

[In June, 1914, an American firm contracted to sell 16,000 bushels of wheat to certain firms in Germany. The wheat was loaded upon the British ship Miramichi at Galveston, Texas, in July, 1914. The whole transaction was in entire innocence of any anticipation of war. The shippers obtained the bill of lading and drew a bill of exchange upon the buyers which was discounted by the Guaranty Trust Co. of New York, to whom the sellers delivered the bill of lading, which was to be delivered to the buyer on payment of the bill of exchange. En route to Rotterdam, the owners of the vessel ordered her to put into a British port because of the outbreak of war. While in a British port the cargo was seized as prize. The bill of exchange was presented to the buyers, who refused to accept it or to pay the sum due. The sellers and the Guaranty Trust Co. appeared as claimants and based their argument on the ground that the cargo was neutral property.]

SIR SAMUEL EVANS, President. . . . The question of law . . . is, was the cargo on September 1 subject to seizure or capture by or on behalf of the Crown, as droits of admiralty or as prize?

Before this question is dealt with, I desire to point out, and to emphasize, that nothing which I shall say in this case is applicable to capture or seizure at sea or in port of any property dealt with during the war, or in anticipation of the war. Questions relating to such property are on an entirely different footing from those relating to transactions initiated during the happier times of peace. The former are determined largely or mainly upon considerations of the rights of belligerents and of attempts to defeat such rights. . . .

In the case now before the Court there is no place for any idea of an attempt to defeat the rights of this country as a belligerent; and the case has to be determined in accordance with the principles by which rights of property are ascertained by our law in time of peace. . . .

Very difficult questions often arise at law as to when the property in goods carried by sea is transferred, or vests; and at whose risk goods are at a particular time, or who suffers by their loss.

These are the kind of questions which are often brushed aside in the Prize Court when the transactions in which they are involved take place during war or were embarked in when war was imminent or anticipated.

But where, as in the present case, all the material parts of the business transaction took place bona fide during peace, and it becomes necessary to decide questions of property, I hold that the law to be applied is the ordinary municipal law governing contracts for the sale and purchase of goods.

Where goods are contracted for to be sold and are shipped during peace without any anticipation of imminent war, and are seized or captured afloat after war has supervened, the cardinal principle is, in my opinion, that they are not subject to seizure or capture unless under the contract the property in the goods has by that time passed to the enemy.

It may be that the element of risk may legitimately enter into the consideration of the question whether the property has passed or has become transferred. But the incidence of risk or loss is not by any means the determining factor of property or ownership. . . . The main determining factor is whether, according to the intention of seller and buyer, the property had passed.

The question which governs this case, therefore, is, whose property were the goods at the time of seizure? . . .

In my opinion, the result of the many decisions . . . is that, in the circumstances of the present case, the goods had not, at the time of seizure, passed to the buyers; but that the sellers had reserved a right of disposal or a *jus disponendi* over them, and that the goods still remained their property, and would so remain until the shipping documents had been tendered to and taken over by the buyers, and the bill of exchange for the price had been paid.

It follows that the goods seized were the property of the American claimants, and were not subject to seizure; the Court decrees accordingly, and orders the goods to be released to the claimants. . . .

THE ODESSA.

Great Britain, Judicial Committee of the Privy Council, 1915.

L. R. [1916] 1 A. C. 145.

Consolidated Appeals from two decrees of the Prize Court (England) . . . reported as to the Odessa, [1915] P. 52. The appellants in both appeals were . . . bankers carrying on business in London. . . . The cargo [of the Odessa], consisting of nitrate of soda, was sold by a Chilean firm to a German company carrying on business at Hamburg, and was shipped in May, 1914, "bound for Channel for orders." In June, 1914, the appellants accepted bills of exchange for 41,153*l*. 1*s*. 5*d*. (the price of the cargo) drawn by the sellers, and as security received and held the bill of lading which made the cargo deliverable to them or to their assigns. On August 4, 1914, while the ship was on her voyage, war broke out between Great Britain and Germany, and on August 19, 1914, the ship was captured at sea. A writ was issued by the Procurator-General claiming that the ship and cargo belonged to enemies of the Crown and were liable to confiscation as lawful prize. The appellants claimed the cargo alleging that it was their property and/or as holders of the bill of lading for full value.

The President of the Probate, Divorce and Admiralty Division (Sir Samuel Evans), . . . held that the cargo was the property of the German company and that the appellants were merely pledgees and not entitled to have the cargo released to them; he therefore made a decree condemning the cargo as lawful prize.

LORD MERSEY. . . . Their Lordships are of opinion that the learned President was right in the inferences which he drew from the facts, namely, that the general property in the cargo was in the German company, and that the appellants were merely pledgees thereof at the date of the seizure. . . . The appellants indeed did not dispute the correctness of these inferences, but what they say is that, though correct, they do not justify a decree which has the effect of forfeiting their rights as pledgees. Thus the question in the appeal is whether in case of a pledge such as existed here a Court of Prize ought to condemn the cargo, and, if so, whether it should direct the appellants' claim to be paid out of the proceeds to arise from the sale thereof.

It is worth while to recall generally the principles which have hitherto guided British Courts of Prize in dealing with a claim by a captor for condemnation. All civilized nations up to the present time have recognized the right of a belligerent to seize, with a view to condemnation by a competent Court of Prize, enemy ships found on the high seas or in the belligerent's territorial waters and enemy cargoes. But seizure does not, according to British prize law, affect the ownership of the thing seized. Before that can happen the thing seized, be it ship or goods, must be brought into the possession of a lawfully constituted Court of Prize, and the captor must then act for and obtain its condemnation as prize. The suit may be initiated by the representative of the capturing State, in this country by the Procurator-General. It is a suit in rem, and the function of the Court is to inquire into the national character of the thing seized. If it is found to be of enemy character, the duty of the Court is to condemn it; if not, then to restore it to those entitled to its possession. The question of national character is made to depend upon the ownership at the date of seizure, and is to be determined by evidence. The effect of a condemnation is to divest the enemy subject of his ownership as from the date of the seizure and to transfer it as from that date to the Sovereign or to his grantees. The thing—the res—is then *his* for him to deal with as he thinks fit, and the proceeding is at an end.

As the right to seize is universally recognized, so also is the title which the judgment of the Court creates. The judgment is of international force, and it is because of this circumstance that Courts of Prize have always been guided by general principles of law capable of universal acceptance rather than by considerations of special rules of municipal law. Thus it has come about that in determining the national character of the thing seized the Courts in this country have taken ownership as the criterion, meaning by ownership the property or *dominium* as opposed to any special rights created by contracts or dealings between individuals, without considering whether these special rights are or are not, according to the municipal law applicable to the case, proprietary rights or otherwise. The rule by which ownership is taken as the criterion is not a mere rule of practice or convenience; it is not a rule of thumb. It lays down a test capable of universal application, and therefore peculiarly appropriate to questions with which a Court of Prize has to deal. It is a rule not complicated by considerations of the effect of the numerous interests which under different systems of jurisprudence may be acquired by individuals either in or in relation to chattels. All the world knows what ownership is, and that it is not lost by the creation of a security upon the thing owned. If in each case the Court of Prize had to investigate the municipal law of a foreign country in order to ascertain the various rights and interests of every one who might claim to be directly or indirectly interested in the vessel or goods seized, and if in addition it had to investigate the particular facts of each case (as to which it would have few, if any, means of learning the truth), the Court would be subject to a burthen which it could not well discharge.

There is a further reason for the adoption of the rule. If special rights of property created by the enemy owner were recognized in a Court of Prize, it would be easy for such owner to protect his own interests upon shipment of the goods to or from the ports of his own country. He might, for example, in every case borrow on the security of the goods an amount approximating to their value from a neutral lender and create in favour of such lender a charge or lien or mortgage on the goods in question. He would thus stand to lose nothing in the transaction, for the proceeds of the goods if captured would, if recovered by the lender, have to be applied by him in discharge of his debt. Again, if a neutral pledgee were allowed to use the Prize Court as a means of obtaining payment of his debt instead of being left to recover it in the enemy's Courts, the door would be opened to the enemy for obtaining fresh banking credit for his trade, to the great injury of the captor belligerent.

Acting upon the principle of this rule Courts of Prize in this country have from before the days of Lord Stowell refused to recognize or give effect to any right in the nature of a "special" property or interest or any mortgage or contractual lien created by the enemy whose vessel or goods have been seized. Liens arising otherwise than by contract stand on a different footing and involve different considerations; but even as to these it is doubtful whether the Court will give effect to them. Where the goods have been increased in value by the services which give rise to the possessory lien, it appears to have been the practice of this Court to make an equitable allowance to the national or neutral lien-holder in respect of such services. In the judgment in The Frances [8 Cranch, 418], speaking of freight, it is said: "On the one hand the captor by stepping into the shoes of the enemy owner of the goods is personally benefited by the labour of a friend, and ought in justice to make him proper compensation, and on the other, the shipowner, by not having carried the goods to the place of their destination, and this in consequence of the act of the captor, would be totally without remedy to recover his freight against the owner of the goods."

It is, however, unnecessary to deal with the question of liens arising apart from contract, the present case being one of pledge founded on a contract made with the enemy.

When the authorities are examined it will be found that they bear out the view that enemy ownership is the true criterion of the liability to condemnation. The case of The Tobago [5 C. Robinson, 218] is in point. There the claimant was a British subject. In time of peace he had honestly advanced money to a French shipowner to enable the latter to repair his ship which was disabled, and by way of security had taken from the owner a bottomry bond. Afterwards war broke out with France and the vessel was captured. In the proceedings in the Prize Court for condemnation the holder of the bottomry bond asked that his security might be protected, but Lord Stowell (then Sir William Scott), after observing that the contract of bottomry was one which the Admiralty Court regarded with great attention and tenderness, went on to ask: "But can the Court recognize bonds of this kind as titles of property so as to give persons a right to stand in judgment and demand restitution of such interests in a Court of Prize?" And he states that it had never been the practice to do so. He points out that a bottomry bond works no change of property in the vessel and says: "If there is no change of property there can be no change of national character. Those lending money on such security take this security subject to all the chances incident to it, and amongst the rest, the chances of war."

. . .

Lastly, the appellants urged that if the Court now applies the principles illustrated by the cases above referred to very serious injustice will be done to and serious loss incurred by neutrals or subjects who, before the commencement of the war and in the normal course of business, have made advances against bills of lading. It is to be observed that similar injustice and loss, though possibly on a less extensive scale, must have been occasioned by the application of the same rules in the eighteenth and early nineteenth centuries, and similar arguments were in fact addressed to Lord Stowell as a reason why they should not be applied in individual cases. The reason why such arguments cannot be sustained is fairly obvious. War must in its very nature work hardship to individuals, and in laying down rules to be applied internationally to circumstances arising out of a state of war it would be impossible to avoid it. All that can be done is to lay down rules which, if applied generally by civilized nations, will, without interfering with the belligerent right of capture, avoid as far as may be any loss to innocent parties. It is precisely because the recognition of liens or other rights arising out of private contracts would so seriously interfere with the belligerent rights of capture that the Courts have refused to recognize such liens or rights in spite of the hardship which may be occasioned to individuals from such want of recognition. . . .

For the foregoing reasons their Lordships will humbly advise His Majesty that the appeal should be dismissed. . . .[1]

UNITED STATES v. THE ACTIVE.[2]

United States, District Court, Territory of Mississippi, 1814.

24 Federal Cases, 755 (No. 14,420).

TOULMAN, J. This is the case of a vessel and cargo belonging to the enemy taken in sight of the fort at Mobile Point, by the troops stationed at that place under the command of Major Wm. Lawrence. . . . The libel prays the condemnation of the vessel and cargo as good and lawful prize to the United States. A plea, however, is filed by Lewis Judson (in the character of consignee and agent for the captors) to the jurisdiction of the court, on the ground that as this court has jurisdiction only in cases in which the United States are parties, it cannot legally entertain a suit in which the private captors (as it is alleged) are the only parties who have a right to claim the captured property. The said plea farther alleges that the "schooner Active and cargo were captured by Wm. Lawrence and others on the high seas, and not in the enemy's forts, camps, or barracks, and, therefore, by the usages of the laws of nations and the laws of war, as enemy's property, become forfeited to the said private captors."

. . . The most satisfactory mode, probably, of coming to a conclusion on this subject, will be to have recourse to general principles. . . .

1. What is war? "It is a contest," says Bynkershoek, "carried on between independent persons for the sake of asserting their rights."

---

[1] The decision in this case was criticised at the time as being unduly severe upon neutrals. It should be compared carefully with the decision in the case of the Miramichi, above, p. 722.

[2] In view of the abolition of privateering [see Hyde, *op. cit.*, II, § 704], the issue presented by this case is not likely to arise again. The case is given, however, because of the discussion of the nature of war incidental to the particular issue.

Where society does not exist—where there is no such institution as that which we call government—there individuals, being strictly independent persons, may carry on war against each other. But whenever men are formed into a social body, war cannot exist between individuals. The use of force among them is not war, but a trespass, cognizable by the municipal law. Bynk. War, p. 128. If war, then, be the act of the nation, whatever is done in the prosecution of it, must either expressly or implicitly be under the national authority. Whatever private benefits result from it must be from a national grant. "War," says Vattel (page 368), "is that state in which a nation prosecutes its right by force." The right of making war belongs alone to the sovereign power. Individuals cannot control operations of war, nor commit any hostility (except in self-defence), without the sovereign's order. The generals (adds that writer), the officers, the soldiers, the partizans, and those who fit out private ships of war, having all commissions from the sovereign, make war by virtue of a particular order. And the necessity of a particular order is so thoroughly established, that even after a declaration of war between two nations, if the peasants themselves commit any hostilities, the enemy, instead of sparing them, hangs them up as so many robbers or banditti. This is the case with private ships of war. It is only in virtue of a commission granted by the sovereign or his admiralty, that they are entitled to be treated like prisoners taken in a formal war. Vatt. Law Nat. pp. 365, 366. If, then, on the general principles of civil society, the whole operations of war depend upon the will and authority of the government, surely the appropriation and distribution of the property acquired in consequence of those operations must equally be subject to the control of the government, and depend on those regulations which it may establish.

2. What, indeed, is the object of war? Is it to aggrandize individuals, or is it to maintain the rights of the nation? "The just and lawful scope of every war," observes Vattel (page 280), "is to revenge or prevent injury. If, to accomplish this object, it is expedient to encourage individual warfare, by granting all the profits arising from it to the parties engaged, the nation has a right to promise this encouragement; but until this encouragement be actually offered, it must follow that everything which is required by individuals, whether acting as private persons or as a part of the public force, must belong to the nation under whose authority they act."

3. What rights are acquired by a state of war? "A nation," says Bynkershoek (page 4), "who has injured another is considered, with everything that belongs to it, as being confiscated to the nation which receives the injury." The rights accruing, therefore, are national altogether. They are not individual rights. The case seems analogous to that of the internal administration of justice. A civil society—a

nation—has the right of punishing those who are guilty of violating the public laws. Though the guilty be members of their own community, they may forfeit their property or their lives. But the right of the body politic does not attach itself to the individual members of it. The nation, indeed, might authorize individuals to take the lives or the property of known offenders; but, without an authority delegated by the nation, individuals have no such right. A right in private persons to avenge violations of the law does not follow as a natural consequence from the circumstance of their being members of the great political body. On the contrary, the very same act which would be retributive justice when emanating from the sovereign power would become murder or robbery in the individual. Why should it be otherwise, as it regards our intercourse with other nations? Why should a nation be less jealous of its rights with regard to hostile nations than with regard to hostile individuals? Why less jealous when they are encroached upon on a larger scale than when they are encroached upon on a scale truly small and insignificant? And even admitting that in the one case the public authority permits an individual to execute the sentence of the law, and in the other to attack and vanquish the public enemy, it will not follow that in either case the property of the enemy is to become the property of the individual by whom the national will is carried into execution. This, it should seem, must depend on express stipulations made in behalf of the nation. . . .

I have been more particular in stating the principles laid down by writers on the law of nations (or the dictates of justice and common sense, as applied to national intercourse,) because the attorney for the claimant, whilst acknowledging that the laws of the United States are silent on the present case, places a great reliance on the injunctions of national law. It is contended that the law of nations gives the booty in this case to the captors. . . .

What, indeed, is the law of nations? It is that rule of conduct which regulates the intercourse of nations with one another; or in the words of the author last cited, "the law of nations is the science of the law subsisting between nations or states, and of the obligations that flow from it." Vatt. Law Nat. 49. It is a law for the government of national communities as to their mutual relations, and not for the government of individuals of those communities in their relation towards one another—nor can it control the conduct of nations towards their own citizens, except in cases involving the rights of other nations. Property once transferred by capture must be subject to the laws of the nation by which the capture is made. The question whether it shall be public or private property must depend on the regulations adopted by the nation making the capture, and cannot naturally be regarded as subject to the control of a system of laws which has respect to the laws and duties of nations towards one another. What our author states as to the practice of nations towards their own citizens, is not, truly speaking, a delineation of the laws of nations. The conduct of nations towards their own citizens must depend on their own municipal regulations. It is by the laws of nations that we must determine the circumstances under which prizes may be taken, but what is to become of them when taken under the sanction of that law cannot depend upon the law of nations, but must depend upon the will of the nation by which the capture is made. Individuals of the capturing nation can have no right independent of the nation to which they belong. It is by a reliance on the authority of their nation, that they shelter themselves from the charge of robbery or piracy. The sovereign, however, may distribute the booty as he pleases. He may do it by a general law, or by special regulations, issued by his generals, subject to the emergency of the case; provided the form of government admits of such a delegation of authority. Even the property acquired by privateers depends on stipulations made with the supreme power of the country to which they belong. "Persons," says Vattel (page 367), "fitting out ships to cruise on the enemy, in recompense of their disbursements and risk they run, acquire the property of the capture; but they acquire it by grants of the sovereign who issues out commissions to them. The sovereign either gives up to them the whole capture or a part—this depends on the contract between them." Vatt. Law Nat. p. 367. As to those who without any authority from their sovereign, commit depredations by sea or land, they are regarded as pirates and plunderers, and things taken by them do not thereby undergo a change of property. Bynk. p. 127. . . .

The only question, then, which remains to be considered is, have the laws of the United States given to the military any share in prizes taken by troops so circumstanced? It may be desirable that they had done so. But this ground seems to be abandoned by the counsel for the army. . . .

As to the laws of the United States respecting property captured by the public force, the most material is the act of the 23d April, 1800, for the better government of the navy. This act gives to the captors the proceeds of vessels and goods taken on board of them when adjudged good prize. But this act is a law expressly for the government of the navy of the United States; and, indeed, it does not appear to be contended that it can by any rule of construction be extended to the army. Private commissioned vessels, in like manner, deserve their right to appropriate to themselves the prizes they make, from the "act concerning letters of marque, prizes, and prize goods," passed on the 26th day of June, 1812. This act, after stating the conditions on which authority should be given to our vessels to capture the vessels and property of the enemy, proceeds to vest the same, when taken under such authority, in the owners, officers, and crews of the vessels by which prizes should

be made. 11 Laws [Weightman's Ed.] p. 240 [2 Stat. 759]. . . .
. . . In the whole view of the case, therefore, now before the court,
it is adjudged and decreed, that the plea be overruled, and dismissed,
with costs in court occasioned by the plea, and that the schooner Active
and cargo be condemned as good and lawful prize to the United States.

THE LUSITANIA.

United States, District Court, Southern District of New York, 1918.

251 Fed. 715.

In Admiralty. In the matter of the petition of the Cunard Steamship
Company, Limited, as owner of the steamship Lusitania, for limitation
of its liability. Petition granted, and claims dismissed, without costs.
. . .

Mayer, District Judge. On May 1, 1915, the British passenger carrying merchantman Lusitania sailed from New York, bound for Liverpool, with 1,257 passengers and a crew of 702, making a total of 1,959
souls on board, men, women, and children. At approximately 2:10 on
the afternoon of May 7, 1915, weather clear and sea smooth, without
warning, the vessel was torpedoed and went down by the head in about
18 minutes, with an ultimate tragic loss of life of 1,195. Numerous
suits having been begun against the Cunard Steamship Company, Limited, the owner of the vessel, this proceeding was brought in familiar
form, by the steamship company, as petitioner, to obtain an adjudication as to liability, and to limit petitioner's liability to its interest in
the vessel and her pending freight, should the court find any liability.
. . .

So far as equipment went, the vessel was seaworthy in the highest
sense. . . .

The proof is absolute that she was not and never had been armed, nor
did she carry any explosives. She did carry some 18 fuse cases and
125 shrapnel cases, consisting merely of empty shells, without any
powder charge, 4,200 cases of safety cartridges, and 189 cases of infantry
equipment, such as leather fittings, pouches, and the like. All these
were for delivery abroad, but none of these munitions could be exploded
by setting them on fire in mass or in bulk, nor by subjecting them to
impact. . . .

On February 4, 1915, the Imperial German government issued a
proclamation as follows:

"Proclamation.

"1. The waters surrounding Great Britain and Ireland, including
the whole English Channel, are hereby declared to be war zone. On

and after the 18th of February, 1915, every enemy merchant ship found in the said war zone will be destroyed without its being always possible to avert the dangers threatening the crews and passengers on that account.

"2. Even neutral ships are exposed to danger in the war zone, as in view of the misuse of neutral flags ordered on January 31 by the British government, and of the accidents of naval war, it cannot always be avoided to strike even neutral ships in attacks that are directed at enemy ships.

"3. Northward navigation around the Shetland Islands, in the eastern waters of the North Sea, and in a strip of not less than 30 miles width along the Netherlands coast is in no danger.

"Von Pohl, Chief of the Admiral Staff of the Navy. "Berlin, February 4, 1915."

This was accompanied by a so-called memorial, setting forth the reasons advanced by the German government in support of the issuance of this proclamation, an extract from which is as follows:

"Just as England declared the whole North Sea between Scotland and Norway to be comprised within the seat of war, so does Germany now declare the waters surrounding Great Britain and Ireland, including the whole English Channel, to be comprised within the seat of war, and will prevent by all the military means at its disposal all navigation by the enemy in those waters. To this end it will endeavor to destroy, after February 18 next, any merchant vessels of the enemy which present themselves at the seat of war above indicated, although it may not always be possible to avert the dangers which may menace persons and merchandise. Neutral powers are accordingly forewarned not to continue to intrust their crews, passengers or merchandise to such vessels."

To this proclamation and memorial the government of the United States made due protest under date of February 10, 1915. . . .

It will be noted that nothing is stated in the German memorandum, *supra*, as to sinking enemy merchant vessels without warning, but, on the contrary, the implication is that settled international law as to visit and search, and an opportunity for the lives of passengers to be safeguarded, will be obeyed, "although it may not always be possible to avert the dangers which may menace persons and merchandise." . . .

On Saturday, May 1, 1915, the advertised sailing date of the Lusitania from New York to Liverpool on the voyage on which she was subsequently sunk, there appeared the following advertisement in the New York Times, New York Tribune, New York Sun, New York Herald, and New York World; this advertisement being, in all instances except one, placed directly over, under, or adjacent to the advertisement of the Cunard Line regarding the sailing of the Lusitania:

"Travelers intending to embark on the Atlantic voyage are reminded that a state of war exists between Germany and her allies and Great Britain and her allies. That the zone of war includes the waters adjacent to the British Isles. That in accordance with formal notice given by the Imperial German government vessels flying the flag of Great Britain or of any of her allies are liable to destruction in those waters and that travelers sailing in the war zone on ships of Great Britain or her allies do so at their own risk.

"April 22, 1915.

"Imperial German Embassy, Washington, D. C."

This was the first insertion of this advertisement, although it was dated more than a week prior to its publication. Capt. Turner, the master of the vessel, saw the advertisement or "something of the kind" before sailing and realized that the Lusitania was included in the warning. . . .

I now come to what seems to me the only debatable question of fact in the case; i. e., whether Capt. Turner was negligent in not literally following the Admiralty advices, and also in not taking a course different from that which he adopted. The fundamental principle in navigating a merchantman, whether in times of peace or of war, is that the commanding officer must be left free to exercise his own judgment. Safe navigation denies the proposition that the judgment and sound discretion of the captain of a vessel must be confined in a mental straitjacket. Of course, when movements are under military control, orders must be strictly obeyed, come what may. No such situation, however, was presented either to petitioner or Capt. Turner. The vessel was not engaged in military service, nor under naval convoy. True, she was, as between the German and British governments, an enemy ship as to Germany; but she was unarmed, and a carrier of not merely noncombatants, but, among others, of many citizens of the United States, then a neutral country, at peace with all the world. . . .

Let us now see what that responsibility was and how it was dealt with. The rules of naval warfare allowed the capture, and, in some circumstances, the destruction, of an enemy merchant ship; but, at the same time, it was the accepted doctrine of all civilized nations (as will be more fully considered *infra*), that, as Lord Mersey put it:

"There is always an obligation first to secure the safety of the lives of those on board."

The responsibility, therefore, of Capt. Turner, in his task of bringing the ship safely to port, was to give heed, not only to general advices advanced as the outcome of experience in the then developing knowledge as to submarine warfare, but particularly to any special information which might come to him in the course of the voyage.

Realizing that, if there was a due warning, in accordance with international law, and an opportunity, within a limited time, for the passengers to leave the ship, nevertheless that the operation must be quickly done, Capt. Turner, on May 6, had taken the full precautions, such as swinging out the boats, properly provisioned, which have been heretofore described. The principal features of the Admiralty advices were (1) to give the headlands a wide berth; (2) to steer a mid-channel course; (3) to maintain as high a speed as practicable; (4) to zigzag; and (5) to make ports, if possible, at dawn, thus running the last part of the voyage at night. . . .

I find, therefore, as a fact, that the captain, and, hence, the petitioner, were not negligent. The importance of the cause, however, justifies the statement of another ground which effectually disposes of any question of liability.

It is an elementary principle of law that, even if a person is negligent, recovery cannot be had, unless the negligence is the proximate cause of the loss or damage.

There is another rule, settled by ample authority, viz. that, even if negligence is shown, it cannot be the proximate cause of the loss or damage, if an independent illegal act of a third party intervenes to cause the loss. . . . The question, then, is whether the act of the German submarine commander was an illegal act.

The United States courts recognize the binding force of international law. As was said by Mr. Justice Gray in The Paquete Habana, 175 U. S. 677, 700, 20 Sup. Ct. 290, 299 (44 L. Ed. 320):

"International law is part of our law, and must be ascertained and administered by the courts of justice of appropriate jurisdiction as often as questions of right depending upon it are duly presented for their determination." . . .

Let us first see the position of our government, and then ascertain whether that position has authoritative support. Mr. Lansing, in his official communication to the German government, dated June 9, 1915, stated:

"But the sinking of passenger ships involves principles of humanity which throw into the background any special circumstances of detail that may be thought to affect the cases—principles which lift it, as the Imperial German government will no doubt be quick to recognize and acknowledge, out of the class of ordinary subjects of diplomatic discussion or of international controversy. Whatever be the other facts regarding the Lusitania, the principal fact is that a great steamer, primarily and chiefly a conveyance for passengers, and carrying more than a thousand souls, who had no part or lot in the conduct of the war, was torpedoed and sunk without so much as a challenge or a warning, and that men, women, and children were sent to their death in circumstances unparalleled in modern warfare. The fact that more than one hundred American citizens were among those who perished made it the duty of the government of the United States to speak of

these things, and once more, with solemn emphasis, to call the attention
of the Imperial German government to the grave responsibility which
the government of the United States conceives that it has incurred
in this tragic occurrence, and to the indisputable principle upon which
that responsibility rests.   The government of the United States is contending for something much greater than mere rights of property or
privileges of commerce.   It is contending for nothing less high and
sacred than the rights of humanity, which every government honors
itself in respecting, and which no government is justified in resigning on
behalf of those under its care and authority.   Only her actual resistance to capture, or refusal to stop when ordered to do so for the purpose of visit, could have afforded the commander of the submarine any
justification for so much as putting the lives of those on board the
ship in jeopardy. . . .   The government of the United States cannot admit that the proclamation of a war zone from which neutral
ships have been warned to keep away may be made to operate as in
any degree an abbreviation of the rights either of American shipmas-
ters or of American citizens bound on lawful errands as passengers
on merchant ships of belligerent nationality.'' . . .   White Book of
Department of State, entitled ''Diplomatic Correspondence with Belligerent Governments Relating to Neutral Rights and Duties, European War No. 2,'' at page 172.   Printed and distributed October 21,
1915.

The German government found itself compelled ultimately to recognize the principle insisted upon by the government of the United States,
for, after considerable correspondence, and on May 4, 1916 (after the
Sussex had been sunk), the German government stated:

''The German submarine forces have had, in fact, orders to conduct
submarine warfare in accordance with the general principles of visit
and search and destruction of merchant vessels as recognized by international law; the sole exception being the conduct of warfare against
the enemy trade carried on enemy freight ships that are encountered
in the war zone surrounding Great Britain. . . .   The German government, guided by this idea, notifies the government of the United
States that the German naval forces have received the following orders:
In accordance with the general principles of visit and search and destruction of merchant vessels recognized by international law, such
vessels, both within and without the area declared as naval war zone,
shall not be sunk without warning and without saving human lives,
unless these ships attempt to escape or offer resistance.''

See Official Communication by German Foreign Office to Ambassador
Gerard, May 4, 1916 (White Book No. 3 of Department of State,
pp. 302, 305).

There is, of course, no doubt as to the right to make prize of an
enemy ship on the high seas, and, under certain conditions, to destroy

her, and equally no doubt of the obligation to safeguard the lives of all persons aboard, whether passengers or crew. . . .

The rules recognized and practiced by the United States, among other things, provide:

"(10) In the case of an enemy merchantman it may be sunk, but only if it is impossible to take it into port, and provided always that the persons on board are put in a place of safety." U. S. White Book, European War, No. 3, p. 192.

These humane principles were practiced, both in the War of 1812 and during our own war of 1861–1865. Even with all the bitterness (now happily ended and forgotten) and all the difficulties of having no port to which to send a prize, Capt. Semmes, of the Alabama, strictly observed the rule as to human life, even going so far as to release ships because he could not care for the passengers. But we are not confined to American and English precedents and practices. . . .

Indeed, as late as May 4, 1916, Germany did not dispute the applicability of the rule, as is evidenced by the note written to our government by Von Jagow, of the German Foreign Office, an extract from which has been quoted *supra*. . . .

Thus, when the Lusitania sailed from New York, her owner and master were justified in believing that, whatever else had theretofore happened, this simple, humane, and universally accepted principle would not be violated. Few, at that time, would be likely to construe the warning advertisement as calling attention to more than the perils to be expected from quick disembarkation and the possible rigors of the sea, after the proper safeguarding of the lives of passengers by at least full opportunity to take to the boats. . . .

The fault, therefore, must be laid upon those who are responsible for the sinking of the vessel, in the legal as well as moral sense. It is therefore not the Cunard Line, petitioner, which must be held liable for the loss of life and property. The cause of the sinking of the Lusitania was the illegal act of the Imperial German government, acting through its instrument, the submarine commander, and violating a cherished and humane rule observed, until this war, by even the bitterest antagonists. . . .

But while, in this lawsuit, there may be no recovery, it is not to be doubted that the United States of America and her Allies will well remember the rights of those affected by the sinking of the Lusitania, and, when the time shall come, will see to it that reparation shall be made for one of the most indefensible acts of modern times.

The petition is granted, and the claims dismissed, without costs.[1,2]

---

[1] On the subject of the sinking of the Lusitania see, in particular, Garner, International Law and the World War, I, Chap. XV; Hyde, *op. cit.*, I, § 747.

[2] SUPPLEMENTARY CASES. Query, at what point may an enemy character acquired by "commercial domicile" be lost and the original national character of

the person be restored? In the case of the Indian Chief, 3 C. Rob. 12 (1801), involving the liability to confiscation of a vessel owned by an American citizen domiciled in London and captured by a British war-ship on a voyage from Batavia, a Dutch colony, to Hamburg, the ground for confiscation being the offense of trading with the enemy, the High Court of Admiralty held that the fact that the owner had actually left England with intent to return to' America revived his national character as an American and exempted his property from confiscation. "The character that is gained by residence," said the court, "ceases by residence: It is an adventitious character which no longer adheres to him, from the moment that he puts himself in motion, bona fide, to quit the country, *sine animo revertendi.*"

In the case of Murray v. The Charming Betsy, 2 Cranch 64 (1804), involving the liability to confiscation by the United States of a vessel owned by an American citizen domiciled in the island of St. Thomas, a Danish possession, on ground of the violation of the Non-Intercourse Act of 1800 prohibiting trade with France, the Supreme Court held that a citizen residing in a foreign country might acquire the privileges attaching to his domicile so as to be "exempted from the operation of an act expressed in such general terms as that now under consideration." [Ed. In this instance, however, the owner of the vessel had become a Danish subject and the question of the right of expatriation (see above, p. 159) entered into the decision so as to weaken its effect in respect to mere commercial domicile.]

In the case of the Venus, 8 Cranch 253 (1814) involving the liability to confiscation as enemy property of a vessel and cargo belonging to American citizens domiciled and doing business in Great Britain, the vessel having sailed from Liverpool to New York before the owners knew or could have known of the outbreak of hostilities, the Supreme Court held that the fact of domicile stamped a person with the "national character" of the state where he resided and subjected his property to capture as enemy property. The fact that the vessel left port in ignorance of the declaration of war was not allowed to affect the decision, since the owners were at the time of the capture in Great Britain and free to choose whether they would remain there during the war or return to their own country. Chief Justice Marshall dissented.

In the case of the Pedro, 175 U. S. 354 (1899), involving the liability to capture by the United States of a vessel flying the Spanish flag and operated by a company incorporated in Spain, the Supreme Court held that the fact that the shares of the company were owned by British citizens could not offset the character attaching to the ship by its registry and license.

In the case of the Roumanian, L. R. [1916] 1 A. C. 124 (1915), involving the liability to condemnation of a cargo of oil belonging to a German company, shipped from Texas on a British merchant vessel before the outbreak of war and captured en route to Hamburg by a British war-ship, the Judicial Committee of the Privy Council sustained the decision of the Prize Court condemning the property, and held that "it is the enemy character of the goods, and not the nationality of the ship on which they are embarked or the date of embarcation, which is the criterion of lawful prize." The provisions of the Declaration of Paris of 1856 with respect to enemy goods on neutral vessels were held not to apply to enemy goods on British ships.

In the case of the Lützow No. 4, II Br. & Col. Prize Cases 605 (1916), involving the ownership and liability to capture of goods bought in Germany by the Hamburg branch of a company incorporated in the United States on orders given by Japanese branches of the company and shipped to Japan before the outbreak of war on a German vessel, the Prize Court for Egypt before which the captured goods were brought held that the branch house of the company was a "separate entity" as a house of trade and that the goods were its property at the time of capture and so were liable to confiscation. In the course of an elaborate opinion the court adverted to the changed methods of modern trade which made it "the duty of the Court to see that its rules and practice keep in harmony with the general sentiment of civilized humanity; else it may subject itself to the reproach that it administers but a dry husk in lieu of a living law." The decision was, however, reversed, upon appeal, by the Judicial Committee, III Br. & Col. Prize Cases, 390, which regarded the Hamburg branch merely as agents for the purchasers and as having no property in the goods which might make them liable to capture as being German-owned.

Query, is private property of the enemy on the high seas subject to capture if it left a port of the enemy in ignorance of the outbreak of hostilities? In the case of the Buena Ventura, 175 U. S. 388 (1899), involving the liability to capture of a Spanish vessel which had left a port of the United States before the war began, the Supreme Court held that while there was in the President's proclamation of April 26, 1898, relative to vessels in port at the outbreak of war or subsequently arriving, no specification of the exemption of vessels on the high seas from capture, yet in view of the policy of the United States towards the exemption from capture of all private property of the enemy on the high seas "those vessels are clearly within the intention of the proclamation under the liberal construction we are bound to give to that document."

By contrast, in the case of the Perkeo, Br. and Col. Prize Cases, I, 136 (1914), involving the liability to capture by Great Britain of a German vessel which had left the neutral port of New York before the outbreak of hostilities, the British Prize Court held that while the vessel was the type of ship referred to in article 3 of the Hague Convention (VI) Relative to the Status of Enemy Merchant Ships at the Outbreak of Hostilities, yet the reservation entered by Germany to that article deprived German vessels of the exemption provided for.

Query, what exemptions are there to the general rule that enemy property is subject to capture on the high seas. In the case of the Paquete Habana, 175 U. S. 677 (1900), above, p. 12, the Supreme Court held that it was an established rule of customary international law that fishing vessels should be exempt from capture as prize of war. In the case of the Marquis de Somerueles, Stewart Adm. (Nova Scotia) 445 (1813), the prize court granted a petition for the restitution of a case of paintings and engravings owned by the Academy of Fine Arts in Philadelphia. "The same law of nations," said the court, "which prescribes that all property belonging to the enemy shall be liable to confiscation, has likewise its modifications and relaxations of that rule. The arts and sciences are admitted amongst all civilized nations, as forming an exception to the severe rights of warfare, and as entitled to favor and protection. They are considered, not as the peculium of this or that nation, but as the property of mankind at large, and as belonging to the common interests of the whole species." And he added that there had been "innumerable cases of the mutual exercise of this courtesy between nations in former wars."

In the case of the Amelia, 4 Phila. 417 (1861), a District Court of the United States, citing the Nova Scotia case of 1813, ordered two cases of books to be restored to the agent of a university in North Carolina. "Though this claimant," said the court, "as the resident of a hostile district, would not be entitled to restitution of the subject of a commercial adventure in books, the purpose of the shipment in question gives to it a different character. The United States, in prosecuting hostilities for the restoration of their constitutional authority, are compelled incidentally to confiscate property captured at sea, of which the pro-

C. Effect of acts of war.

The practice of issuing a formal declaration of war as a means of marking the opening of legal hostilities, while of ancient tradition and of strict obligation under the Hague Convention of 1907, was not always adhered to during the seventeenth and eighteenth centuries. In such cases the existence of a state of war was determined by the actual hostilities in progress between the two belligerents. Query, if war were declared by one party without a corresponding declaration by the other and there were only defensive acts on the part of the first state, would there be a state of legal war? [The Eliza Ann.] Recently the problem has been presented again in connection with reprisals which have taken the form of extensive military campaigns without being preceded by a declaration of war.[1]

THE ELIZA ANN, AND OTHERS.

Great Britain, High Court of Admiralty, 1813.

1 Dodson, 244.

These were three cases of American ships, laden with hemp, iron, and other articles, and seized in Hanoe Bay, on the 11th of August, 1812, by his Majesty's ship Vigo, which was then lying there, with other British ships of war. A claim was given, under the direction of the Swedish minister, for the ships and cargoes, ''as taken within one mile of the main land of Sweden, and within the territory of his Majesty the King of Sweden, contrary to and in violation of the law of nations, and the territory and jurisdiction of his said Majesty.''

Sir W. Scott.—These vessels came into Hanoe Bay, for the purpose of taking the benefit of British convoy, and were seized in conse-

---

ceeds would otherwise increase the wealth of that district. But the United States are not at war with literature in that part of their territory.''

Query, would the transfer of a vessel from belligerent to neutral ownership by sale in a neutral port or on the high seas exempt the vessel from capture by the enemy? In the case of the Dacia, French Council of State, 1916, Journal Official, January 14, 1917, p. 498, involving the liability to capture of a former Hamburg-American Company steamship that had been sold by its German owners to an American citizen while lying in an American port after the outbreak of war, the French court held that the transfer was void since the American purchaser had not, in accordance with the terms of Article 56 of the Declaration of London, proved that the sale ''was not caused principally by fear of seeing the vessel seized and captured by the navies of the Allied Powers from the moment of its first voyage.'' See also the earlier cases of the Noydt Gedacht, 2 C. Rob. 137 n. (1799) and the Benito Estenger, 176 U. S. 568 (1900).

[1] See, on this point, Q. Wright, ''When Does War Exist?'' and ''Responsibility for Losses at Shanghai,'' Am. Journal Int. Law, XXVI (1932), 362, 586.

quence of the order for the detention of American property. This order has been since followed up by a declaration of war; the ships, therefore, would be liable to condemnation, unless it can be shown that they are entitled to some special protection.

A claim has been given, by the Swedish consul, for these ships and cargoes, as having been taken within the territories of the King of Sweden, and in violation of his territorial rights. This claim could not have been given by the Americans themselves, for it is the privilege, not of the enemy, but of the neutral country, which has a right to see that no act of violence is committed within its jurisdiction. When a violation of neutral territory takes place, that country alone, whose tranquillity has been disturbed, possesses the right of demanding reparation for the injury which she has sustained. It is a principle which has been established by a variety of decisions, both in this and the superior Court, that the enemy, whose property has been captured, cannot himself give the claim, but must resort to the neutral for his remedy. . . .

Now, in order to support and give effect to this claim, two things are necessary to be established.—First, it is requisite that Sweden should appear to have been in a state of perfect neutrality at the time when the seizure was made.—Secondly, it must be shown that the act of violence was committed within the limits of Swedish territory. For, if the scene of hostility did not lie within the territories of the neutral state, then has there been no violation of its neutral rights, and consequently there exists no ground of complaint, and no foundation for the claim.

The first question then is, how far, in August, 1812, Sweden was to be considered as a neutral country.

It is not to be disputed that the conduct of Sweden towards this country had been, for a considerable time, of a very unfriendly description. Impelled by fear, or some other motive, she had excluded British ships from her ports, and had, either from choice or compulsion, adopted that course of policy which has been imposed by the French ruler on the other nations of Europe, and which has been termed the continental system. It is clear, too, that Sweden acted in this manner, not from any private views respecting her own municipal regulations, but in the execution of a plan auxiliary to the enemy of this country. Sweden, therefore, by her conduct, afforded to Great Britain a legitimate cause of war, and perfectly justified the seizure of Hanoe by the British admiral. The seizure of this place has been countenanced by the government of this country, the British flag has been hoisted, and every act of sovereignty exercised on the island and roadstead adjoining.

This was the state of things originally; British ships were excluded from the ports of Sweden, and the island of Hanoe was occupied by British forces.

After this, a declaration of war was issued by the government of Sweden; but it is said, that the two countries were not, in reality, in a state of war, because the declaration was *unilateral* only. I am, however, perfectly clear that it was not the less a war on that account, for war may exist without a declaration on either side. A declaration of war by one country only is not, as has been represented, a mere challenge, to be accepted or refused at pleasure by the other. It proves the existence of actual hostilities on one side at least, and puts the other party also into a state of war, though he may, perhaps, think proper to act on the defensive only. . . .

This war [between Great Britain and Sweden] has, however, been happily terminated by a treaty of peace, which was signed by the plenipotentiaries of the two countries, on the 18th of July, ratified by the Prince Regent of Great Britain on the 4th of August, and by the King of Sweden on the 17th of the same month. From the result of these dates it has been contended, that the war had ceased, and that friendship had been reëstablished before the time when these vessels were seized. The question, therefore, comes to this, whether a ratification is or is not necessary to give effect and validity to a treaty signed by plenipotentiaries. Upon abstract principles we know that, either in public or private transactions, the acts of those who are vested with a plenary power are binding upon the principal. But, as this rule was in many cases found to be attended with inconvenience, the latter usage of states has been to require a ratification, although the treaty may have been signed by plenipotentiaries. According to the practice now prevailing, a subsequent ratification is essentially necessary; and a strong confirmation of the truth of this position is, that there is hardly a modern treaty in which it is not expressly so stipulated; and, therefore, it is now to be presumed, that the powers of plenipotentiaries are limited by the condition of a subsequent ratification. The ratification may be a form, but it is an essential form; for the instrument, in point of legal efficacy, is imperfect without it. I need not add, that a ratification by one power alone is insufficient; that, if necessary at all, it must be mutual; and that the treaty is incomplete till it has been reciprocally ratified.

It is said, however, that the treaty, when ratified, refers back to the time of its signature by the plenipotentiaries, and that it does so in this case more especially on account of the terms in which it is drawn. The words in one of the articles of the treaty, "*Dès ce moment tout sujet de mésintelligence, qui ait pu subsister sera regardé comme entièrement cessant et détruit,*" have been pointed out, and from these it has been contended, that all hostilities were to cease the moment the treaty was signed. But I take that not to be the case; the positive and enacting part of the articles is, that there shall be a firm and inviolable peace between the two countries; the other part is descriptive only of the

pacific intention of the parties, and of their agreement to bury in oblivion all the causes of the war. It does not stand in the same substantive
way as the former part of the article; and must be considered as mere
explanatory description. The nature of a treaty of peace is well explained by Vattel [Book 4, c. 2], who lays it down that "a treaty of
peace can be no more than an agreement. Were the rules (he says)
of an exact and precise justice to be observed in it, each punctually
receiving all that belongs to him, a peace would become impossible."
He goes on to say, that "as in the most just cause we are never to lose
sight of the restoration of peace, but are constantly to tend towards this
salutary view, no other way is left than to agree on all the claims and
grievances on both sides, and to extinguish all differences by the most
equitable convention which the juncture will admit of." It is, therefore, an agreement to waive all discussion concerning the respective
rights of the parties, and to bury in oblivion all the original causes of
the war. It is an explanation of the nature of that peace and good
understanding which is to take place between the two countries, whenever that event shall be happily accomplished. It would be a stretch
beyond the limits to which a fair interpretation of these words could
be carried, to say they were intended to convey any other meaning.
I am of opinion, therefore, that the ratification is the point from which
the treaty must take effect. *Dès ce moment* must be referred to the
moment at which the treaty received its valid existence by mutual
ratification. It is perfectly clear that it was so considered on the part
of Sweden. The British officer who was sent to the Swedish coast was
still received with the same caution as in the time of war, and was
blindfolded before he was permitted to enter Carlsham. Hanoe remained in British possession, and the only communications between that
island and the main land of Sweden was by flags of truce. Though it
was reasonable to expect that Sweden would return to the relations of
amity with this country, yet it is quite clear that she had not at that
time confirmed the treaty, and, therefore, could not be entitled to the
benefit of a neutral character.

But, in order to give validity to the present claim, another proposition must necessarily be maintained: It must be shown that the place
of capture was within the Swedish territories; and I am of opinion that
it was not. . . .

. . . I am of opinion that the claim which has been given fails upon
the two essential points, both in respect of the neutrality of Sweden,
and of the neutrality of the place of capture, and consequently that
these ships and cargoes are liable to condemnation.

CHAPTER XXI

PROCEDURE BY WAR: RELATIONS BETWEEN BELLIGERENT AND NEUTRAL STATES [1]

A. Neutral rights as against belligerents.

The existence of a state of war between two or more belligerents regularly gives rise to new relations between the belligerents and third states not parties to the conflict. Until the adoption of the Covenant of the League of Nations in 1920 there was no recognition on the part of the community of nations as a whole of a collective responsibility for the maintenance of the general peace. Hence, when one state declared war on another, third states not directly concerned in the controversy proceeded to declare their neutrality, as a result of which they were recognized as having certain rights as against the belligerents and as being obligated to fulfill corresponding duties towards them. Query, would the capture of an enemy vessel in neutral territorial waters be valid as between the belligerents after allowing for redress to the neutral for the violation of its sovereignty? [The Florida.] May a prize of war be interned by a belligerent captor in a neutral port without violation of the neutrality of the state of asylum? [The Appam.]

THE FLORIDA.

United States, Supreme Court, 1879.

101 U. S. 37. [25 L. ed. 898.]

Appeal from the Supreme Court of the District of Columbia.

[On Oct. 7, 1864, the Confederate steamer Florida was captured by the American steamer Wachusett in the port of Bahia, Brazil. After having been brought to Hampton Roads the Florida was sunk in a collision. The act of the captain of the Wachusett was disavowed by the

---

[1] For a more detailed study of this subject, see Fenwick, *op. cit.,* pp. 536–547; 564–578; Hyde, *op. cit.,* II, §§ 844–888; Oppenheim, *op. cit.,* II, §§ 313–367; Garner, International Law and the World War, I. The future of the traditional rights and duties of neutrality in view of the obligations of the Covenant of the League of Nations, for those states that are members of the League, and of the Pact of Paris has been a subject of controversy. See, in particular, Proceedings, Am. Society of International Law, 1930, pp. 79 ff.; 1933, pp. 55 ff.

United States. The captain libelled the Florida as a prize of war, and when his libel was dismissed by the lower court, he appealed.]

MR. JUSTICE SWAYNE . . . delivered the opinion of the court.

The legal principles applicable to the facts disclosed in the record are well settled in the law of nations, and in English and American jurisprudence. Extended remarks upon the subject are, therefore, unnecessary. See Grotius, De Jure Belli, b. 3, c. 4, sect. 8; Bynkershoek, 61, c. 8; Burlamaqui, vol. ii. pt. 4, c. 5, sect. 19; Vattel, b. 3, c. 7, sect. 132; Dana's Wheaton, sect. 429 and note 208; 3 Rob. Ad. Rep. 373; 5 id. 21; The Anne, 3 Wheat. 435; La Amistad de Rues, 5 id. 385; The Santissima Trinidad, 7 id. 283, 496; The Sir William Peel, 5 Wall. 517; The Adela, 6 id. 266; 1 Kent, Com. (last ed.), pp. 112, 117, 121.

Grotius, speaking of enemies in war, says: "But that we may not kill or hurt them in a neutral country, proceeds not from any privileges attached to their persons, but from the right of the prince in whose dominions they are."

A capture in neutral waters is valid as between belligerents. Neither a belligerent owner nor an individual enemy owner can be heard to complain. But the neutral sovereign whose territory has been violated may interpose and demand reparation, and is entitled to have the captured property restored.

The latter was not done in this case because the captured vessel had been sunk and lost. It was, therefore, impossible.

The libellant was not entitled to a decree in his favor, for several reasons.

The title to captured property always vests primarily in the government of the captors. The rights of individuals, where such rights exist, are the results of local law or regulations. Here, the capture was promptly disavowed by the United States. They, therefore, never had any title.

The case is one in which the judicial is bound to follow the action of the political department of the government, and is concluded by it. Phillips v. Payne, 92 U. S. 130.

These things must necessarily be so, otherwise the anomaly would be possible, that, while the government was apologizing and making reparation to avoid a foreign war, the offending officer might, through the action of its courts, fill his pockets with the fruits of the offence out of which the controversy arose. When the capture was disavowed by our government, it became for all the purposes of this case as if it had not occurred.

Lastly, the maxim, "*ex turpi causa non oritur actio*," applies with full force. No court will lend its aid to a party who founds his claim for redress upon an illegal act.

The Brazilian Government was justified by the law of nations in demanding the return of the captured vessel and proper redress otherwise. It was due to its own character, and to the neutral position it had assumed between the belligerents in the war then in progress, to take prompt and vigorous measures in the case, as was done. The commander was condemned by the law of nations, public policy, and the ethics involved in his conduct.

Decree affirmed.

THE STEAMSHIP APPAM.[1]

United States, Supreme Court, 1917.

243 U. S. 124. [61 L. ed. 633; 37 S. Ct. 337.]

Appeals from the District Court of the United States for the Eastern District of Virginia. . . .

[On January 15, 1916 the British passenger steamer Appam, en route from West Africa to Liverpool, was captured on the high seas by the German cruiser Moewe. The point of capture was about 1590 miles from Emden, the nearest German port; 130 miles from Punchello in the Madeiras, the nearest available port; 1450 miles from Liverpool, and 3051 miles from Hampton Roads, Virginia. After remaining in the vicinity of the Moewe for two days, the vessel was placed under the command of a German officer who was ordered "to bring this ship into the nearest American harbor and there to lay up." A German prize crew was placed on board, dynamite bombs were distributed about the ship which the German commander was instructed to explode in case of "any trouble, mutiny or attempt to take the ship," and the crew of the Appam was compelled to navigate it to Hampton Roads where it arrived January 31, 1916. The German ambassador then informed the State Department that the vessel, in accordance with alleged treaty rights, would stay in an American port until further notice and requested the internment of the crew. This was denied, and the members of the crew were released with their personal effects. The owner and the master of the vessel then filed their libels in admiralty for the purpose of obtaining possession of the vessel and cargo, and the District Court decided in their favor. Appeals were taken by the German officer in charge of the vessel and by the German vice-consul at Newport News, Virginia.]

MR. JUSTICE DAY delivered the opinion of the court. . . . From the facts which we have stated, we think the decisive questions resolve

---

[1] Also reported as Hans Berg, Prize Master in Charge of the Prize Ship Appam, and L. M. von Schilling, Vice Consul of the German Empire, Appts., v. British and African Steam Navigation Co.

themselves into three: First, was the use of an American port, under the circumstances shown, a breach of this Nation's neutrality under the principles of international law? Second, was such use of an American port justified by the existing treaties between the German Government and our own? Third, was there jurisdiction and right to condemn the Appam and her cargo in a court of admiralty of the United States?

It is familiar international law that the usual course after the capture of the Appam would have been to take her into a German port, where a prize court of that Nation might have adjudicated her status, and, if it so determined, condemned the vessel as a prize of war. Instead of that, the vessel was neither taken to a German port, nor to the nearest port accessible of a neutral power, but was ordered to, and did, proceed over a distance of more than three thousand miles, with a view to laying up the captured ship in an American port.

It was not the purpose to bring the vessel here within the privileges universally recognized in international law, i. e., for necessary fuel or provisions, or because of stress of weather or necessity of repairs, and to leave as soon as the cause of such entry was satisfied or removed. The purpose for which the Appam was brought to Hampton Roads, and the character of the ship, are emphasized in the order which we have quoted to take her to an American port and there lay her up and in a note from His Excellency, The German Ambassador, to the Secretary of State, in which the right was claimed to keep the vessel in an American port until further notice, (Diplomatic Correspondence with Belligerent Governments Relating to Neutral Rights and Duties, Department of State, European War No. 3, p. 331,) and a further communication from the German Ambassador forwarding a memorandum of a telegram from the German Government concerning the Appam (*Idem*, p. 333), in which it was stated:

"Appam is not an auxiliary cruiser but a prize. Therefore she must be dealt with according to Article 19 of Prusso-American treaty of 1799. Article 21 of Hague Convention concerning neutrality at sea is not applicable, as this convention was not ratified by England and is therefore not binding in present war according to Article 28. The above-mentioned Article 19 authorizes a prize ship to remain in American ports as long as she pleases. Neither the ship nor the prize crew can therefore be interned nor can there be question of turning the prize over to English."

In view of these facts, and this attitude of the Imperial Government of Germany, it is manifest that the Appam was not brought here in any other character than as a prize, captured at sea by a cruiser of the German navy, and that the right to keep her here, as shown in the attitude of the German Government and in the answer to the libel, was rested principally upon the Prussian-American Treaty of 1799.

The principles of international law recognized by this Government, leaving the treaty aside, will not permit the ports of the United States to be thus used by belligerents. If such use were permitted, it would constitute of the ports of a neutral country harbors of safety into which prizes, captured by one of the belligerents, might be safely brought and indefinitely kept.

From the beginning of its history this country has been careful to maintain a neutral position between warring governments, and not to allow the use of its ports in violation of the obligations of neutrality; nor to permit such use beyond the necessities arising from the perils of the seas or the necessities of such vessels as to sea-worthiness, provisions and supplies. Such usage has the sanction of international law, Dana's Note to Wheaton on International Law, 1866, 8th American Edition, § 391, and accords with our own practice. Moore's Digest of International Law, vol. 7, 936, 937, 938.

A policy of neutrality between warring nations has been maintained from 1793 to this time. In that year President Washington firmly denied the use of our ports to the French Minister for the fitting out of privateers to destroy English commerce. This attitude led to the enactment of the Neutrality Act of 1794, afterwards embodied in the Act of 1818, enacting a code of neutrality, which among other things inhibited the fitting out and arming of vessels; the augmenting or increasing of the force of armed vessels; or the setting on foot in our territory of military expeditions; and empowering the President to order foreign vessels of war to depart from our ports and compelling them so to do when required by the law of nations. Moore on International Arbitrations, vol. 4, 3967 *et seq.*

This policy of the American Government was emphasized in its attitude at the Hague Conference of 1907. Article 21 of the Hague Treaty provides:

"A prize may only be brought into a neutral port on account of unseaworthiness, stress of weather, or want of fuel or provisions.

"It must leave as soon as the circumstances which justified its entry are at an end. If it does not, the neutral Power must order it to leave at once; should it fail to obey, the neutral Power must employ the means at its disposal to release it with its officers and crew and to intern the prize crew."

Article 22 provides:

"A neutral Power must, similarly, release a prize brought into one of its ports under circumstances other than those referred to in Article 21."

To these articles, adherence was given by Belgium, France, Austria-Hungary, Germany, the United States, and a number of other nations. They were not ratified by the British Government. This Government refused to adhere to Article 23, which provides:

"A neutral Power may allow prizes to enter its ports and roadsteads, whether under convoy or not, when they are brought there to be seques-

trated pending the decision of a Prize Court. It may have the prize taken
to another of its ports.

"If the prize is convoyed by a war-ship, the prize crew may go on
board the convoying ship.

"If the prize is not under convoy, the prize crew are left at liberty."

And in the proclamation of the convention the President recited the
resolution of the Senate adhering to it, subject to the "reservation and
exclusion of its Article 23 and with the understanding that the last clause
of Article 3 of the said Convention implies the duty of a neutral power
to make the demand therein mentioned for the return of a ship captured
within the neutral jurisdiction and no longer within that jurisdiction."
36 Stat., Pt. II, p. 2438.

While this treaty may not be of binding obligation, owing to lack of
ratification, it is very pursuasive as showing the attitude of the American Government when the question is one of international law; from
which it appears clearly that prizes could only be brought into our ports
upon general principles recognized in international law, on account of
unseaworthiness, stress of weather, or want of fuel or provisions, and we
refused to recognize the principle that prizes might enter our ports and
roadsteads, whether under convoy or not, to be sequestrated pending the
decision of a prize court. From the history of the conference it appears
that the reason for the attitude of the American delegates in refusing to
accept Article 23 was that thereby a neutral might be involved in participation in the war to the extent of giving asylum to a prize which the
belligerent might not be able to conduct to a home port. See Scott on
Peace Conferences, 1899–1907, vol. II, p. 237 *et seq.*

Much stress is laid upon the failure of this Government to proclaim
that its ports were not open to the reception of captured prizes, and it is
argued that having failed to interdict the entrance of prizes into our
ports permission to thus enter must be assumed. But whatever privilege
might arise from this circumstance it would not warrant the attempted
use of one of our ports as a place in which to store prizes indefinitely,
and certainly not where no means of taking them out are shown except
by the augmentation of her crew, which would be a clear violation of
established rules of neutrality. . . .

It remains to inquire whether there was jurisdiction and authority in
an admiralty court of the United States, under these circumstances, to
order restoration to an individual owner of the vessel and cargo. . . .

It is insisted that these cases [cited by the court] involve illegal captures at sea, or violations of neutral obligation, not arising because of the
use of a port by sending in a captured vessel and keeping her there in
violation of our rights as a neutral. But we are at a loss to see any
difference in principle between such cases and breaches of neutrality of
the character here involved in undertaking to make of an American port
a depository of captured vessels with a view to keeping them there in-

definitely. Nor can we consent to the insistence of counsel for appellant that the Prize Court of the German Empire has exclusive jurisdiction to determine the fate of the Appam as lawful prize. The vessel was in an American port and under our practice within the jurisdiction and possession of the District Court which had assumed to determine the alleged violation of neutral rights, with power to dispose of the vessel accordingly. The foreign tribunal under such circumstances could not oust the jurisdiction of the local court and thereby defeat its judgment. The Santissima Trinidad, *supra,* p. 355.

Were the rule otherwise than this court has frequently declared it to be, our ports might be filled in case of a general war such as is now in progress between the European countries, with captured prizes of one or the other of the belligerents, in utter violation of the principles of neutral obligation which have controlled this country from the beginning.

The violation of American neutrality is the basis of jurisdiction, and the admiralty courts may order restitution for a violation of such neutrality. In each case the jurisdiction and order rests upon the authority of the courts of the United States to make restitution to private owners for violations of neutrality where offending vessels are within our jurisdiction, thus vindicating our rights and obligations as a neutral people.

It follows that the decree in each case must be affirmed.[1]

B. Neutral duties towards belligerents.

The duties imposed on a state as a condition of the neutral position it has assumed may be divided into two classes: those which consist in the abstention by the neutral government from any official act which might have the effect of favoring one belligerent more than the other and those which consist in the prevention of acts, whether on the part of the belligerents themselves or on the part of individuals in their interest,

---

[1] SUPPLEMENTARY CASES. In the case of the Anne, 3 Wheaton 435 (1818), involving a claim interposed in behalf of the Spanish consul on account of the violation of the neutral territory of Spain by reason of the capture of a British vessel by an American privateer in Spanish waters, and a claim by the British owner brought subsequent to the treaty of peace, the Supreme Court held that the claim of the Spanish consul must be dismissed as not having been authorized by his government and the claim of the owner had no standing in its own right. "A capture made in neutral waters," said the court, "is, as between enemies, deemed, to all intents and purposes, rightful; it is only by the neutral sovereign that its legal validity can be called in question; and as to him and him only, is it to be considered void. The enemy has no rights whatsoever; and if the neutral sovereign omits or declines to interpose a claim, the property is condemnable, *jure belli,* to the captors. This is the clear result of the authorities; and the doctrine rests on well established principles of public law." A similar conclusion was reached by the British Prize Court in the case of the Eliza Ann, above, p. 739, and in that of the Bangor, above, p. 523.

which might compromise the neutrality of the state. Query, as respects acts of the belligerents themselves, what action would a neutral government be obligated to take in the event that one belligerent should attack a vessel belonging to the other in neutral territorial waters? [United States and Portugal: The General Armstrong Case.] As respects the acts of individuals within the neutral state international law has drawn a distinction between those acts which, although favoring one belligerent more than the other, the neutral state is not obligated to prevent because of their commercial character, such as the sale of munitions of war, and other acts more directly designed to furnish aid to one of the belligerents. Query, would the sale of a merchant vessel by a neutral citizen to a belligerent come within the class of acts to be prevented? [The Santissima Trinidad.] Suppose the neutral state were to permit a vessel to be built in its ports knowing that such vessel, although unarmed at the time, was later to be armed and used in the service of one of the belligerents against the other? [United States and Great Britain: Alabama Claims Case.]

UNITED STATES AND PORTUGAL: CASE OF THE BRIG GENERAL ARMSTRONG.

Arbitration under the Convention of February 26, 1851.

Moore, International Arbitrations, II, p. 1094.

We, Louis Napoleon, President of the French Republic [Arbitrator]: The Government of the United States and that of Her Majesty the Queen of Portugal and of the Algarves, having, by the terms of a convention signed at Washington on the 26th of February, 1851, asked us to pronounce as arbiter upon a claim relative to the American privateer General Armstrong, which was destroyed in the port of Fayal, on the 27th of September, 1814,

After having caused ourself to be correctly and circumstantially informed in regard to the facts which have been the cause of the difference, and after having maturely examined the documents duly signed, in the name of the two parties, which have been submitted to our inspection by the representatives of both powers,

Considering that it appears as a fact that, the United States being at war with Her Britannic Majesty, and Her Most Faithful Majesty preserving neutrality, the American brig General Armstrong, commanded by Captain Reid, legally provided with letters of marque, and armed as a privateer, having sailed from the port of New York, did, on the 26th September, 1814, cast anchor in the port of Fayal, one of the Azores Islands, constituting part of Her Most Faithful Majesty's dominions;

That it is equally clear that, on the evening of the same day, an English squadron commanded by Commodore Lloyd, entered the same port;

That it is no less certain that, during the following night, without respect for the rights of sovereignty and of neutrality of Her Most Faithful Majesty, a bloody encounter took place between the Americans and the English, and that, on the 27th September, one of the vessels belonging to the English squadron ranged herself alongside the American privateer, for the purpose of cannonading her; that this demonstration, accompanied by the act, caused Captain Reid, together with his crew, to abandon his vessel and destroy her;

Considering that, if it be clear that, on the night of the 26th of September, some English longboats, commanded by Lieutenant Robert Fausset, of the British navy, approached the American brig, the General Armstrong, it is not clear that the men who manned the boats were provided with arms and ammunition;

That it appears as a fact, from the documents which have been produced, that, those longboats having approached the American brig, the crew of the latter, after having hailed them and summoned them to haul off, immediately fired upon them, and that some men were killed on board the English boats, and others wounded, some of them mortally, without any attempt having been made on the part of the crew of the boats to repel, immediately, force by force;

Considering that the report of the governor of Fayal proves that the American captain did not apply to the Portuguese government for protection until blood had already been shed, and that when the fire had ceased the brig General Armstrong came to anchor under the castle, at the distance of a stone's throw; that the governor affirms that it was only then that he was informed of what was passing in the port;

That he several times interposed with Commodore Lloyd, with a view to obtain a cessation of hostilities and to complain of the violation of neutral territory;

That he effectively prevented some American sailors, who were on land, from embarking on board the American brig, for the purpose of prolonging a conflict which was contrary to the law of nations;

That the weakness of the garrison of the island, and the undoubted decay of the guns in the forts, rendered all armed intervention on his part impossible;

Considering, in this state of things, that Captain Reid, not having applied, in the beginning, for the intervention of the neutral sovereign, and having had recourse to arms for the purpose of repelling an unjust aggression of which he claimed to be the object, thus failed to respect the neutrality of the territory of the foreign sovereign, and released that sovereign from the obligation to afford him protection by any other means than that of a pacific intervention;

From which it follows that the government of Her Most Faithful Majesty cannot be held responsible for the results of a collision, which took place in contempt of her rights of sovereignty, in violation of the neutrality of her territory, and without the local officers or lieutenants having been requested in proper time and warned to grant aid and protection to those to whom it was due:

Therefore, we have decided and we declare that the claim presented by the government of the United States against Her Most Faithful Majesty has no foundation, and that no indemnity is due by Portugal, in consequence of the loss of the American brig, the privateer General Armstrong. . . .

THE SANTISSIMA TRINIDAD, AND THE ST. ANDRE.

United States, Supreme Court, 1822.

7 Wheaton, 283. [5 L. ed. 454.]

Appeal from the Circuit Court of Virginia.

This was a libel filed by the consul of Spain, in the district court of Virginia, in April, 1817, against eighty-nine bales of cochineal, two bales of jalap, and one box of vanilla, originally constituting part of the cargoes of the Spanish ships, Santissima Trinidad and St. Andre, and alleged to be unlawfully and piratically taken out of those vessels, on the high seas, by a squadron consisting of two armed vessels, called the Independencia del Sud, and the Altravida, and manned and commanded by persons assuming themselves to be citizens of the United Provinces of the Rio de la Plata. The libel was filed, in behalf of the original Spanish owners, by Don Pablo Chaçon, consul of his Catholic Majesty for the port of Norfolk; and as amended, it insisted upon restitution, principally for three reasons: 1. That the commanders of the capturing vessels, the Independencia and the Altravida, were native citizens of the United States, and were prohibited by our treaty with Spain of 1795, from taking commissions to cruise against that power. 2. That the said capturing vessels were owned in the United States, and were originally equipped, fitted out, armed and manned in the United States, contrary to law. 3. That their force and armament had been illegally augmented within the United States. . . .

The District Court, upon the hearing of the cause, decreed restitution to the original Spanish owners. That sentence was affirmed in the Circuit Court, and from the decree of the latter the cause was brought by appeal to this court.

MR. JUSTICE STORY delivered the opinion of the Court.

Upon the argument at the bar several questions have arisen, which have been deliberately considered by the court; and its judgment will now be pronounced. The first in the order in which we think it most convenient to consider the cause, is, whether the Independencia is, in point of fact, a public ship, belonging to the government of Buenos Ayres. The history of this vessel, so far as is necessary for the disposal of this point, is briefly this: She was originally built and equipped at Baltimore, as a privateer, during the late war with Great Britain, and was then rigged as a schooner, and called the Mammoth, and cruised against the enemy. After the peace, she was rigged as a brig, and sold by her original owners. In January, 1816, she was loaded with a cargo of munitions of war, by her new owners (who are inhabitants of Baltimore), and being armed with twelve guns, constituting a part of her original armament, she was despatched from that port, under the command of the claimant, on a voyage, ostensibly to the north-west coast, but in reality to Buenos Ayres. By the written instructions given to the supercargo on this voyage, he was authorized to sell the vessel to the government of Buenos Ayres, if he could obtain a suitable price. She duly arrived at Buenos Ayres, having exercised no act of hostility, but sailed under the protection of the American flag, during the voyage. At Buenos Ayres, the vessel was sold to Captain Chaytor and two other persons; and soon afterwards, she assumed the flag and character of a public ship, and was understood by the crew to have been sold to the government of Buenos Ayres: and Captain Chaytor made known these facts to the crew, and asserted that he had become a citizen of Buenos Ayres; and had received a commission to command the vessel, as a national ship; and invited the crew to enlist in the service; and the greater part of them accordingly enlisted. From this period, which was in May 1816, the public functionaries of our own and other foreign governments at that port, considered the vessel as a public ship of war, and such was her avowed character and reputation. . . .

The next question growing out of this record, is, whether the property in controversy was captured, in violation of our neutrality, so that restitution ought, by the law of nations, to be decreed to the libellants. Two grounds are relied upon to justify restitution: *First*, that the Independencia and Altravida were originally equipped, armed, and manned as vessels of war, in our ports; secondly, that there was an illegal augmentation of the force of the Independencia, within our ports. Are these grounds, or either of them, sustained by the evidence? . . .

The question as to the original illegal armament and outfit of the Independencia may be dismissed in a few words. It is apparent, that though equipped as a vessel of war, she was sent to Buenos Ayres on a commercial adventure, contraband, indeed, but in no shape violating our laws or our national neutrality. If captured by a Spanish ship of war, during the voyage, she would have been justly condemnable as good prize, for being engaged in a traffic prohibited by the law of nations. But there is nothing in our laws, or in the law of nations, that forbids our citizens from sending armed vessels, as well as munitions of war, to foreign ports for sale. It is a commercial adventure, which no nation is bound to prohibit; and which only exposes the persons engaged in it to the penalty of confiscation. Supposing, therefore, the voyage to have been for commercial purposes, and the sale at Buenos Ayres to have been a *bona fide* sale (and there is nothing in the evidence before us to contradict it), there is no pretence to say, that the original outfit on the voyage was illegal, or that a capture made after the sale was, for that cause alone, invalid.

The more material consideration is, as to the augmentation of her force, in the United States, at a subsequent period. . . .

. . . The court is, therefore, driven to the conclusion, that there was an illegal augmentation of the force of the Independencia, in our ports, by a substantial increase of her crew; and this renders it wholly unnecessary to enter into an investigation of the question, whether there was not also an illegal increase of her armament. . . .

And here we are met by an argument on behalf of the claimant, that the augmentation of the force of the Independencia within our ports, is not an infraction of the law of nations, or a violation of our neutrality; and that so far as it stands prohibited by our municipal laws, the penalties are personal, and do not reach the case of restitution of captures made in the cruise, during which such augmentation has taken place. It has never been held by this Court, that an augmentation of force or illegal outfit affected any captures made after the original cruise was terminated. By analogy to other cases of violations of public law, the offence may well be deemed to be deposited at the termination of the voyage, and not to affect future transactions. But as to captures made during the same cruise, the doctrine of this Court has long established, that such illegal augmentation is a violation of the law of nations, as well as of our own municipal laws, and as a violation of our neutrality, by analogy to other cases, it infects the captures subsequently made with the character of torts, and justifies and requires a restitution to the parties who have been injured by such misconduct. It does not lie in the mouth of wrongdoers, to set up a title derived from a violation of our neutrality. The cases in which this doctrine has been recognized and applied, have been cited at the bar, and are so numerous and so uniform, that it would be a waste of time to discuss them, or to examine the reasoning by which they are supported: more especially as no inclination exists on the part of the Court to question the soundness of these decisions. If, indeed, the question were entirely new, it would deserve very grave consideration, whether a claim founded on a violation of our neutral jurisdiction, could be asserted by private persons, or in any other manner than a direct intervention of the government itself. In the case of a capture made within a neutral territorial jurisdiction, it is well settled, that as between the captors and the captured, the question can never be litigated. It can arise only upon a claim of the neutral sovereign, asserted in his own Courts, or the courts of the power having cognisance of the capture itself for the purposes of prize. And by analogy to this course of proceeding, the interposition of our own government might seem fit to have been required, before cognisance of the wrong could be taken by our Courts. But the practice from the beginning, in this class of causes, a period of nearly 30 years, has been uniformly the other way; and it is now too late to disturb it. If any inconvenience should grow out of it, from reasons of state policy or executive discretion, it is competent for Congress to apply at its pleasure the proper remedy. . . .

An objection . . . has been urged at the bar . . . that public ships of war are exempted from the local jurisdiction, by the universal assent of nations; and that as all property captured by such ships, is captured for the sovereign, it is, by parity of reasoning, entitled to the like exemption; for no sovereign is answerable for his acts to the tribunals of any foreign sovereign. . . .

. . . But there is nothing in the law of nations which forbids a foreign sovereign, either on account of the dignity of his station, or the nature of his prerogative, from voluntarily becoming a party to a suit, in the tribunals of another country, or from asserting there, any personal, or proprietary, or sovereign rights, which may be properly recognised and enforced by such tribunals. It is a mere matter of his own good will and pleasure; and if he happens to hold a private domain, within another territory, it may be, that he cannot obtain full redress for any injury to it, except through the instrumentality of its Courts of justice. It may, therefore, be justly laid down, as a general proposition, that all persons and property within the territorial jurisdiction of a sovereign, are amenable to the jurisdiction of himself or his Courts: and that the exceptions to this rule are such only as, by common usage and public policy, have been allowed, in order to preserve the peace and harmony of nations, and to regulate their intercourse in a manner best suited to their dignity and rights. . . . We are of opinion, that the objection cannot be sustained; and that whatever may be the exemption of the public ship herself, and of her armament and munitions of war, the prize property which she brings into our ports is liable to the jurisdiction of our Courts, for the purpose of examination and inquiry, and if a proper case be made out, for restitution to those whose possession has been divested by a violation of our neutrality; . . .

Upon the whole, it is the opinion of the Court, that the decree of the Circuit Court be affirmed, with costs.[1]

---

[1] The change in the law in the decades following this decision found expression in the "Three Rules of the Treaty of Washington" of 1871, which were applied in the arbitration of the Alabama Claims. See above, p. 640, n. 1.

UNITED STATES AND GREAT BRITAIN: ALABAMA CLAIMS
CASE, 1872.

[For the text of the award in this case, see Chap. XVII, where the
case appears in illustration of the application by an arbitral tribunal
of special principles of law accepted by the parties for the particular
controversy.]

CHAPTER XXII

PROCEDURE OF WAR: RELATIONS BETWEEN BELLIGERENT STATES AND NEUTRAL CITIZENS [1]

A. Neutral goods on enemy vessels.

The most serious ground of conflict between belligerent and neutral rights has been in connection with the commercial intercourse between neutral citizens and one or other of the enemy countries. While international law has recognized that neutral states are under no obligation to prevent their citizens from continuing normal commercial intercourse with the belligerents, or even from selling munitions of war to them, at the same time it has recognized the right of either belligerent to take certain measures to prevent such supplies from reaching the enemy. Query, what if neutral goods should be found in an enemy vessel captured by a belligerent as prize of war? Would such goods lose their neutral character and become liable to confiscation along with the enemy vessel? [The Nereide.]

THE NEREIDE, BENNETT, MASTER.

United States, Supreme Court, 1815.

9 Cranch, 388. [3 L. ed. 769.]

[The Nereide, a vessel belonging to a British subject, was chartered in London August 26, 1813, by Manuel Pinto, a Spanish citizen residing in Buenos Ayres, for a voyage from London to Buenos Ayres and return. The cargo was owned in part by British and in part by Spanish subjects. On her outward voyage, while in the vicinity of Madeira, the ship was captured by an American privateer and brought into the port of New York, where both vessel and cargo were libelled and condemned. The Circuit Court for the district of New York affirmed the decision of the District Court. Pinto, on behalf of himself and other Spanish subjects, appealed from that part of the decision which applied to so much of the cargo as was their property.]

---

[1] For a more detailed study of this subject, see Fenwick, *op. cit.*, 548–563; Hyde, *op. cit.*, II, §§ 797–837; Oppenheim, *op. cit.*, II, 364–447; Garner, Prize Law during the World War; Briggs, The Doctrine of Continuous Voyage; A. P. Higgins, "Retaliation in Naval Warfare," British Year Book, VIII (1927) 129.

MARSHALL, CH. J., ... delivered the opinion of the court. . . .

2. Does the treaty between Spain and the United States subject the goods of either party, being neutral, to condemnation as enemy property, if found by the other in the vessel of an enemy? That treaty stipulates that neutral bottoms shall make neutral goods, but contains no stipulation that enemy bottoms shall communicate the hostile character to the cargo. It is contended by the captors that the two principles are so completely identified that the stipulation of the one necessarily includes the other.

Let this proposition be examined.

The rule that the goods of an enemy found in the vessel of a friend are prize of war, and that the goods of a friend found in the vessel of an enemy are to be restored, is believed to be a part of the original law of nations, as generally, perhaps universally, acknowledged. Certainly it has been fully and unequivocally recognized by the United States. This rule is founded on the simple and intelligible principle that war gives a full right to capture the goods of an enemy, but gives no right to capture the goods of a friend. In the practical application of this principle, so as to form the rule, the propositions that the neutral flag constitutes no protection to enemy property, and that the belligerent flag communicates no hostile character to neutral property, are necessarily admitted. The character of the property, taken distinctly and separately from all other considerations, depends in no degree upon the character of the vehicle in which it is found.

Many nations have believed it to be their interest to vary this simple and natural principle of public law. They have changed it by convention between themselves as far as they have believed it to be for their advantage to change it. But unless there be something in the nature of the rule which renders its parts unsusceptible of division, nations must be capable of dividing it by express compact, and if they stipulate either that the neutral flag shall cover enemy goods, or that the enemy flag shall infect friendly goods, there would, in reason, seem to be no necessity for implying a distinct stipulation not expressed by the parties. Treaties are formed upon deliberate reflection. Diplomatic men read the public treaties made by other nations and cannot be supposed either to omit or insert an article, common in public treaties, without being aware of the effect of such omission or insertion. Neither the one nor the other is to be ascribed to inattention. And if an omitted article be not necessarily implied in one which is inserted, the subject to which that article would apply remains under the ancient rule. That the stipulation of immunity to enemy goods in the bottoms of one of the parties being neutral does not imply a surrender of the goods of that party being neutral, if found in the vessel of an enemy, is the proposition of the counsel for the claimant, and he powerfully sustains that proposition by arguments arising from the nature of the two stipulations. The agreement that neutral bottoms shall make neutral goods is, he very justly remarks, a concession made by the belligerent to the neutral. It enlarges the sphere of neutral commerce, and gives to the neutral flag a capacity not given to it by the law of nations.

The stipulation which subjects neutral property, found in the bottom of an enemy, to condemnation as prize of war, is a concession made by the neutral to the belligerent. It narrows the sphere of neutral commerce, and takes from the neutral a privilege he possessed under the law of nations. The one may be, and often is, exchanged for the other. But it may be the interest and the will of both parties to stipulate the one without the other; and if it be their interest, or their will, what shall prevent its accomplishment? A neutral may give some other compensation for the privilege of transporting enemy goods in safety, or both parties may find an interest in stipulating for this privilege, and neither may be disposed to make to, or require from, the other the surrender of any right as its consideration. What shall restrain independent nations from making such a compact? And how is their intention to be communicated to each other or to the world so properly as by the compact itself?

If reason can furnish no evidence of the indissolubility of the two maxims, the supporters of that proposition will certainly derive no aid from the history of their progress from the first attempts at their introduction to the present moment.

For a considerable length of time they were the companions of each other—not as one maxim consisting of a single indivisible principle, but as two stipulations, the one, in the view of the parties, forming a natural and obvious consideration for the other. The celebrated compact termed the armed neutrality attempted to effect by force a great revolution in the law of nations. The attempt failed, but it made a deep and lasting impression on public sentiment. The character of this effort has been accurately stated by the counsel for the Claimants. Its object was to enlarge, and not in any thing to diminish the rights of neutrals. The great powers, parties to this agreement, contended for the principle, that free ships should make free goods; but not for the converse maxim; so far were they from supposing the one to follow as a corollary from the other, that the contrary opinion was openly and distinctly avowed. The king of Prussia declared his expectation that in future neutral bottoms would protect the goods of an enemy, and that neutral goods would be safe in an enemy bottom. There is no reason to believe that this opinion was not common to those powers who acceded to the principles of the armed neutrality.

From that epoch to the present, in the various treaties which have been formed, some contain no article on the subject and consequently leave the ancient rule in full force. Some stipulate that the character of the cargo shall depend upon the flag, some that the neutral flag shall protect the goods of an enemy, some that the goods of a neutral in the vessel of a friend shall be prize of war, and some that the goods of an enemy in a neutral bottom shall be safe, and that friendly goods in the bottom of an enemy shall also be safe.

This review which was taken with minute accuracy at the bar, certainly demonstrates that in public opinion no two principles are more distinct and independent of each other than the two which have been contended to be inseparable.

Do the United States understand this subject differently from other nations? It is certainly not from our treaties that this opinion can be sustained. The United States have in some treaties stipulated for both principles, in some for one of them only, in some that neutral bottoms shall make neutral goods and that friendly goods shall be safe in the bottom of an enemy. It is therefore clearly understood in the United States, so far as an opinion can be formed on their treaties, that the one principle is totally independent of the other. They have stipulated expressly for their separation, and they have sometimes stipulated for the one without the other.

But in a correspondence between the secretary of state of the United States and the minister of the French republic in 1793, Prussia is enumerated among those nations with whom the United States had made a treaty adopting the entire principle that the character of the cargo shall be determined by the character of the flag.

Not being in possession of this correspondence the Court is unable to examine the construction it has received. It has not deferred this opinion on that account, because the point in controversy at that time was the obligation imposed on the United States to protect belligerent property in their vessels, not the liability of their property to capture if found in the vessel of a belligerent. To this point the whole attention of the writer was directed, and it is not wonderful that in mentioning incidentally the treaty with Prussia which contains the principle that free bottoms made free goods, it should have escaped his recollection that it did not contain the converse of the maxim. On the talents and virtues which adorned the cabinet of that day, on the patient fortitude with which it resisted the intemperate violence with which it was assailed, on the firmness with which it maintained those principles which its sense of duty prescribed, on the wisdom of the rules it adopted, no panegyric has been pronounced at the bar in which the best judgment of this Court does not concur. But this respectful deference may well comport with the opinion, that an argument incidentally brought forward by way of illustration, is not such full authority as a decision directly on the point might have been. . . .

[A further portion of the opinion, dealing with the effect of resistance on the part of the vessel to visit and search, is reproduced below, p. 795.] [1]

---

[1] This case should be read in the light of the provisions of the Declaration of Paris of 1856, Higgins, Hague Peace Conferences, p. 1; Hyde, *op. cit.*, II, § 762.

B. Blockade.

It has long been recognized that as a measure of bringing pressure to bear upon the enemy belligerents have the right to establish a blockade of the enemy coast and thus cut off as far as possible the importation of goods of whatever character from neutral countries. But a blockade, to be legal, must conform to certain conditions. Query, would a mere proclamation by a belligerent that a certain enemy port was blockaded be sufficient to constitute a valid blockade? [The Betsey.] Would a blockade otherwise valid justify the capture of goods not of a contraband character during their passage from one neutral port to another if the evidence indicated that they were to be transshipped to a smaller vessel which would attempt to violate the blockade? [The Springbok.] Would conveyance to the enemy by an inland route affect the liability of the goods to capture? [The Peterhoff.] To what extent might a belligerent stretch the law of blockade as a measure of retaliation for illegal practices of the enemy? [The Stigstad.]

THE BETSEY.

Great Britain, High Court of Admiralty, 1798.

1 C. Rob. 93.

This was a case of a ship and cargo, taken by the English, at the capture of Guadaloupe, April the 13th, 1794, and retaken, together with that island, by the French, in June following. . . . The first seizure was defended on a suggestion, that The Betsey had broken the blockade at Guadaloupe.

Judgment.

SIR W. SCOTT— . . . On the question of blockade, three things must be proved, 1st, The existence of an actual blockade; 2dly, The knowledge of the party; and, 3dly, Some act of violation, either by going in, or by coming out with a cargo laden after the commencement of blockade: The time of shipment would on this last point be very material; for although it might be hard to refuse a neutral liberty to retire with a cargo already laden, and by that act already become neutral property; yet, after the commencement of a blockade, a neutral cannot, I conceive, be allowed to interpose in any way to assist the exportation of the property of the enemy. After the commencement of the blockade, a neutral is no longer at liberty to make any purchase in that port.

It is necessary, however, that the evidence of a blockade should be clear and decisive. In this case there is only an affidavit of one of the captors, and the account which is there given is, "that on the arrival of the British forces in the West Indies, a proclamation issued, inviting the inhabitants of Martinique, St. Lucie, and Guadaloupe, to put themselves under the protection of the English; that on a refusal, hostile operations were commenced against them all;'' though it cannot be meant that they began immediately against all at once; for it is notorious that they were directed against them separately and in succession. It is farther stated, ''that in January 1794, (but without any more precise date,) Guadaloupe was summoned, and was then put into a state of complete investment and blockade.''

The word *complete* is a word of great energy; and we might expect from it to find, that a number of vessels were stationed round the entrance of the port to cut off all communication. But from the protest, I perceive, that the captors entertained but a very loose notion of the true nature of a blockade; for it is there stated, ''that on the 1st of January, after a general proclamation to the French islands, they were put into a state of *complete* blockade.'' It is a term, therefore, which was applied to all those islands, at the same time, under the first proclamation.

The Lords of Appeal have determined that such a proclamation was not in itself sufficient to constitute a legal blockade: It is clear, indeed, that it could not in reason be held to produce the effect, which the captors erroneously ascribed to it. From the misapplication of these phrases in one instance, I learn, that we must not give too much weight to the use of them on this occasion; and from the generality of these expressions, I think we must infer, that there was not that actual blockade, which the law is now distinctly understood to require.

But it is attempted to raise other inferences on this point, from the manner in which the master speaks of the difficulty and danger of entering; and from the declaration of the Municipality of Guadaloupe, which states ''the island to have been in a state of siege.'' It is evident that the American master speaks only of the difficulty of avoiding the English cruisers generally in those seas; and as to the other phrase, it is a term of the new jargon of France, which is sometimes applied to domestic d'sturbances; and certainly is not so intelligible as to justify me in concluding, that the island was in that state of investment, from a foreign enemy, which we require to constitute blockade. I cannot, therefore, lay it down, that a blockade did exist, till the operations of the forces were actually directed against Guadaloupe in April.

It would be necessary for me, however, to go much farther, and to say that I am satisfied also that the parties had knowledge of it: but this is expressly denied by the master. He went in without obstruction. Mr. Incledon's statement of *his belief* of the notoriety of the blockade is not such evidence, as will alone be sufficient to convince me of it. With respect to the shipment of the cargo, it does not appear exactly under what circumstances or what time it was taken in: I shall therefore dismiss this part of the case. . . .[1]

THE SPRINGBOK.

United States, Supreme Court, 1866.

5 Wallace, 1. [18 L. ed. 480.]

Appeal from a decree of the District Court of the United States for the Southern District of New York. . . .

[The Springbok, a British vessel, was chartered in November, 1862, to T. S. Begbie of London to take a cargo of merchandise and "proceed to Nassau, or as near thereunto as she may safely get, and deliver same." The brokers charged with the lading, acting for Isaac, Campbell & Co., instructed the master in December, 1862: "You will proceed at once to the port of Nassau, N. P., and on arrival report yourself to Mr. B. W. Hart there, who will give you orders as to the delivery of your cargo." By the bills of lading the cargo was made deliverable to order or assigns. The Springbok was captured February 3, 1863 by an American war vessel about 150 miles from Nassau. It was a matter of common knowledge that Nassau was then used as a port for the transshipment of cargoes destined for blockaded ports in the Confederate States. At the hearing in the District Court evidence introduced in the cases of the Stephen Hart captured January 28, 1863 and the Gertrude captured April 16, 1863, was invoked whereby it appeared that the cargoes in the three vessels consisted in whole or in part of contraband and were owned largely by the same persons. In the case of the Springbok, the District Court condemned both the ship and the cargo.]

The CHIEF JUSTICE [CHASE] delivered the opinion of the court. . . .

We have already held in the case of the Bermuda, where goods, destined ultimately for a belligerent port, are being conveyed between two neutral ports by a neutral ship, under a charter made in good faith for that voyage, and without any fraudulent connection on the part of her owners with the ulterior destination of the goods, that the ship, though liable to seizure in order to the confiscation of the goods, is not liable to condemnation as prize.

We think that the Springbok fairly comes within this rule. . . .

The case of the cargo is quite different from that of the ship. . . .

---

[1] This case should be read in the light of the provisions of the Declaration of Paris of 1856 and of the Declaration of London of 1909. See Higgins, Hague Peace Conferences, 540 ff.

The bills of lading disclosed the contents of six hundred and nineteen, but concealed the contents of thirteen hundred and eighty-eight, of the two thousand and seven packages which made up the cargo. Like those in the Bermuda case they named no consignee, but required the cargo to be delivered to order or assigns. The manifest of the cargo also, like that in the Bermuda case, mentioned no consignee, but described the cargo as delivered to order. Unlike those bills and that manifest, however, these concealed the names of the real owners as well as the contents of more than two-thirds of the packages.

Why were the contents of the packages concealed? The owners knew that they were going to a port in the trade with which the utmost candor of statement might be reasonably required. The adventure was undertaken several months after the publication of the answer of Earl Russell to the Liverpool shipowners. . . . In that answer the British foreign secretary had spoken of allegations by the American government that ships had been sent from England to America with fixed purpose to run the blockade, and that arms and ammunition had thus been conveyed to the Southern States to aid them in the war; and he had confessed his inability either to deny the allegations or to prosecute the offenders to conviction; and he had then distinctly informed the Liverpool memorialists that he could not be surprised that the cruisers of the United States should watch with vigilance a port which was said to be the great entrepôt of this commerce. For the concealment of the character of a cargo shipped for that entrepôt, after such a warning, no honest reason can be assigned. The true reason must be found in the design of the owners to hide from the scrutiny of the American cruisers the contraband character of a considerable portion of the contents of those packages.

And why were the names of those owners concealed? Can any honest reason be given for that? None has been suggested. But the real motive of concealment appears at once when we learn, from the claim, that Isaac, Campbell & Co., and Begbie were the owners of the cargo of the Springbok, and from the papers involved, that Begbie was the owner of the steamship Gertrude, laden in Nassau in April, 1863, with a cargo corresponding in several respects with that now claimed by him and his associates, and dispatched on a pretended voyage to St. John's, New Brunswick, but captured for unneutral conduct and abandoned to condemnation without even the interposition of a claim in the prize court; and when we learn further from the same papers that Isaac, Campbell & Co., were the sole owners of the cargo of the Stephen Hart, consisting almost wholly of arms and munitions of war, and sent on a pretended destination to Cardenas, but with a real one for the States in rebellion. Clearly the true motive of the concealment must have been the apprehension of the claimants, that the disclosure of their names as owners would lead to the seizure of the ship in order to the condemnation of the cargo.

We are next to ascertain the real destination of the cargo, for their concealments do not, of themselves, warrant condemnation. If the real intention of the owners was that the cargo should be landed at Nassau and incorporated by real sale into the common stock of the island, it must be restored, notwithstanding this misconduct.

What then was this real intention? That some other destination than Nassau was intended may be inferred, from the fact that the consignment, shown by the bills of lading and the manifest, was to order or assigns. Under the circumstances of this trade, already mentioned, such a consignment must be taken as a negation that any sale had been made to any one in Nassau. It must also be taken as a negation that any such sale was intended to be made there; for had such sale been intended, it is most likely that the goods would have been consigned for that purpose to some established house named in the bills of lading.

This inference is strengthened by the letter of Speyer & Haywood to the master, when about to sail from London. That letter directs him to report to B. W. Hart, the agent of the charterers at Nassau, and receive his instructions as to the delivery of the cargo. The property in it was to remain unchanged upon delivery. The agent was to receive it and execute the instructions of his principals.

What these instructions were may be collected, in part, from the character of the cargo.

A part of it, small in comparison with the whole, consisted of arms and munitions of war, contraband within the narrowest definition. Another and somewhat larger portion consisted of articles useful and necessary in war, and therefore contraband within the construction of the American and English prize courts. These portions being contraband, the residue of the cargo, belonging to the same owners, must share their fate. [The Immanuel, 2 Robinson, 196; Carrington v. Merchants' Insurance Co., 8 Peters, 495.]

But we do not now refer to the character of the cargo for the purpose of determining whether it was liable to condemnation as contraband, but for the purpose of ascertaining its real destination; for, we repeat, contraband or not, it could not be condemned, if really destined for Nassau and not beyond; and, contraband or not, it must be condemned if destined to any rebel port, for all rebel ports were under blockade.

Looking at the cargo with this view, we find that a part of it was specially fitted for use in the rebel military service, and a larger part, though not so specially fitted, was yet well adapted to such use. Under the first head we include the sixteen dozen swords, and the ten dozen rifle-bayonets, and the forty-five thousand navy buttons, and the one hundred and fifty thousand army buttons; and, under the latter, the seven bales of army cloth and the twenty bales of army blankets and other similar goods. We cannot look at such a cargo as this, and doubt that a considerable portion of it was going to the rebel States, where alone it could be used; nor can we doubt that the whole cargo had one destination.

Now if this cargo was not to be carried to its ultimate destination by the Springbok (and the proof does not warrant us in saying that it was), the plan must have been to send it forward by transshipment. And we think it evident that such was the purpose. We have already referred to the bills of lading, the manifest, and the letter of Speyer & Haywood, as indicating this intention; and the same inference must be drawn from the disclosures by the invocation, that Isaac, Campbell & Co. had before supplied military goods to the rebel authorities by indirect shipment, and that Begbie was owner of the Gertrude and engaged in the business of running the blockade.

If these circumstances were insufficient grounds for a satisfactory conclusion, another might be found in the presence of the Gertrude in the harbor of Nassau with undenied intent to run the blockade, about the time when the arrival of the Springbok was expected there. It seems to us extremely probable that she had been sent to Nassau to await the arrival of the Springbok and to convey her cargo to a belligerent and blockaded port, and that she did not so convey it, only because the voyage was intercepted by the capture.

All these condemnatory circumstances must be taken in connection with the fraudulent concealment attempted in the bills of lading and the manifest, and with the very remarkable fact that not only has no application been made by the claimants for leave to take further proof in order to furnish some explanation of these circumstances, but that no claim, sworn to personally, by either of the claimants, has ever been filed.

Upon the whole case we cannot doubt that the cargo was originally shipped with intent to violate the blockade; that the owners of the cargo intended that it should be transshipped at Nassau into some vessel more likely to succeed in reaching safely a blockaded port than the Springbok: that the voyage from London to the blockaded port was, as to cargo, both in law and in the intent of the parties, one voyage; and that the liability to condemnation, if captured during any part of that voyage, attached to the cargo from the time of sailing.

The decree of the District Court must, therefore, be reversed as to the ship . . . and must be affirmed as to the cargo.[1] . . .

---

[1] This decision, although sharply criticized at the time, ultimately brought about a change in the law, and was in turn relied upon by Great Britain in extending still further the doctrine of continuous voyage during the World War. Compare, also, in this respect, The Peterhoff, below, p. 767.

THE PETERHOFF.

United States, Supreme Court, 1866.

5 Wallace, 28.   [18 L. ed. 564.]

Appeal from a decree of the District Court for the Southern District of New York. . . .

[On April 19, 1862 the President proclaimed a blockade of the "whole coast from the Chesapeake Bay to the Rio Grande." About forty miles up the Rio Grande, on the American side of the river, is the town of Brownsville. On the opposite bank in Mexico is the city of Matamoras. While the blockade was in force, the Peterhoff, a British vessel, sailed from London for Matamoras, with a miscellaneous cargo part of which was the property of the owner of the vessel. In the Caribbean Sea to the south of Cuba, she was captured by an American war vessel and taken to New York where the vessel and cargo were condemned for intent to violate the blockade by sending her cargo in lighters up the river Rio Grande to the city of Matamoras, from which point much of her cargo was to be sent into Texas.]

The CHIEF JUSTICE [CHASE] delivered the opinion of the court. . . .
. . . It was maintained in argument (1) that trade with Matamoras, at the time of the capture, was made unlawful by the blockade of the mouth of the Rio Grande; and if not, then (2) that the ulterior destination of the cargo was Texas and the other States in rebellion, and that this ulterior destination was in breach of the blockade. . . .

In determining the question whether this blockade was intended to include the mouth of the Rio Grande, the treaty with Mexico in relation to that river must be considered. It was stipulated in the 5th article that the boundary line between the United States and Mexico should commence in the Gulf, three leagues from land opposite the mouth of the Rio Grande, and run northward from the middle of the river. And in the 7th article it was further stipulated that the navigation of the river should be free and common to the citizens of both countries without interruption by either without the consent of the other, even for the purpose of improving the navigation.

The mouth of the Rio Grande was, therefore, for half its width, within Mexican territory, and, for the purposes of navigation, was, altogether, as much Mexican as American. It is clear, therefore, that nothing short of an express declaration by the Executive would warrant us in ascribing to the government an intention to blockade such a river in time of peace between the two Republics. . . .

. . . And we are the less inclined to say it, because we are not aware of any instance in which a belligerent has attempted to blockade the mouth of a river or harbor occupied on one side by neutrals, or in which such a blockade has been recognized as valid by any court administering the law of nations. . . .

We come next to the question whether an ulterior destination to the rebel region, which we now assume as proved, affected the cargo of the Peterhoff with liability to condemnation. We mean the neutral cargo: reserving for the present the question of contraband. . . .

It is an undoubted general principle, recognized by this court in the case of The Bermuda, and in several other cases, that an ulterior destination to a blockaded port will infect the primary voyage to a neutral port with liability for intended violation of blockade.

The question now is whether the same consequences will attend an ulterior destination to a belligerent country by inland conveyance. And upon this question the authorities seem quite clear.

During the blockade of Holland in 1799, goods belonging to Prussian subjects were shipped from Edam, near Amsterdam, by inland navigation to Emden, in Hanover, for transshipment to London. Prussia and Hanover were neutral. The goods were captured on the voyage from Emden, and the cause [The Stert, 4 Robinson, 65] came before the British Court of Admiralty in 1801. It was held that the blockade did not affect the trade of Holland carried on with neutrals by means of inland navigation. "It was," said Sir William Scott, "a mere maritime blockade effected by force operating only at sea." He admitted that such trade would defeat, partially at least, the object of the blockade, namely, to cripple the trade of Holland, but observed, "If that is the consequence, all that can be said is that it is an unavoidable consequence. It must be imputed to the nature of the thing which will not admit of a remedy of this species. The court cannot on that ground take upon itself to say that a legal blockade exists where no actual blockade can be applied. . . . It must be presumed that this was foreseen by the blockading state, which, nevertheless, thought proper to impose it to the extent to which it was practicable."

The same principle governed the case of The Ocean, [3 Robinson, 297] made also in 1801. At the time of her voyage Amsterdam was blockaded, but the blockade had not been extended to the other ports of Holland. Her cargo consisted partly or wholly of goods ordered by American merchants from Amsterdam and sent thence by inland conveyance to Rotterdam, and there shipped to America. It was held that the conveyance from Amsterdam to Rotterdam, being inland, was not affected by the blockade, and the goods, which had been captured, were restored.

These were cases of trade from a blockaded to a neutral country by means of inland navigation, to a neutral port or a port not blockaded. The same principle was applied to trade from a neutral to a blockaded country by inland conveyance from the neutral port of primary destination to the blockaded port of ulterior destination in the case of the

Jonge Pieter [4 Id. 79], adjudged in 1801. Goods belonging to neutrals going from London to Emden, with ulterior destination by land or an interior canal navigation to Amsterdam were held not liable to seizure for violation of the blockade of that port. . . .

These cases fully recognize the lawfulness of neutral trade to or from a blockaded country by inland navigation or transportation. . . .

And the general doctrines of international law lead irresistibly to the same conclusion. We know of but two exceptions to the rule of free trade by neutrals with belligerents: the first is that there must be no violation of blockade or siege: and the second, that there must be no conveyance of contraband to either belligerent. And the question we are now considering is, "Was the cargo of the Peterhoff within the first of these exceptions?" We have seen that Matamoras was not and could not be blockaded; and it is manifest that there was not and could not be any blockade of the Texan bank of the Rio Grande as against the trade of Matamoras. . . .

We must say, therefore, that trade, between London and Matamoras, even with attempt to supply, from Matamoras, goods to Texas, violated no blockade, and cannot be declared unlawful. . . .[1]

THE STIGSTAD.

Great Britain, Judicial Committee of the Privy Council, 1918.

L. R. [1919] A. C. 279.

(See **D. Reprisals**, below, p. 785.) [2]

---

[1] Another part of the opinion, dealing with the question of contraband, is reproduced below, p. 773.

[2] SUPPLEMENTARY CASES. In the case of the Franciska, 10 Moore P. C. 37 (1855), involving the condemnation of a neutral Danish vessel for breach of blockade of the port of Riga in 1854, the British Privy Council held that the relaxation of the blockade by an Order in Council in favor of Russian vessels, accompanied by a corresponding concession from the Russian government in favor of British vessels, was sufficient to invalidate the blockade as a whole, so that "this ship cannot be considered to have had notice of any blockade of Riga at the time when she sailed for that port; for, in truth, no legal blockade was then in existence."

In the case of the Olinde Rodriguez, 174 U. S. 510 (1899), involving the liability to confiscation of a French vessel for breach of blockade of the port of San Juan in Puerto Rico, the Supreme Court held that under the circumstances a single cruiser was adequate to maintain an effective blockade. The captured vessel was, however, released for lack of evidence of intent to enter the blockaded port, but payment of costs and expenses incident to its custody was imposed upon it because of the suspicious circumstances under which it was captured.

In the case of the Adula, 176 U. S. 361 (1900), involving the liability to confiscation for breach of blockade of a British vessel seeking to enter the port

C. Contraband.

In addition to the right to maintain a blockade of the enemy country belligerents have by long tradition been permitted to confiscate certain classes of neutral goods when captured on their way to the enemy. Absolute contraband, that is, goods contraband under all conditions, consists of military supplies and the materials for their manufacture. Conditional contraband consists of supplies susceptible of use in war as well as for purposes of peace, so that the condition of their confiscation is that they shall be destined to the army or navy of the enemy or to the enemy government. Absolute contraband need only be destined to the enemy country to be subject to confiscation; conditional contraband must show evidence of intended use in the enemy country. Query, would foodstuffs, being conditional contraband, be said to be intended for military use simply because they were destined to an enemy port of naval equipment? [The Jonge Margaretha.] Would military supplies, being absolute contraband, be subject to capture en route to a neutral port on the ground that their character indicated that they were to be transshipped to an ulterior enemy destination?   [The Peterhoff.] Would goods be subject to capture if they were consigned "to order" in the neutral country so as to suggest probable ulterior enemy destination? [The Kim.] Would the fact that the goods, in the form of raw materials, were to be converted in the neutral country into manufactured articles which were to be sold in the enemy country, or, if not directly sold to the enemy, make possible the exportation from the neutral country to the enemy of other similar articles, make the goods liable to confiscation?   [The Bonna.]

---

of Guantanamo, Cuba, in 1898, the Supreme Court held that, while no blockade of that port had ever been proclaimed by the President, it was competent for the admiral of the fleet to establish a "simple or actual blockade" at Guantanamo as an adjunct to naval operations off Santiago, and since the charterer of the Adula and its officers knew of the blockade the vessel was liable to condemnation.

Query, what form must the notification of a blockade take to raise a presumption of knowledge of the blockade by a neutral vessel? In the case of the Neptunus, 2 C. Rob. 110 (1799), involving the liability to confiscation of a vessel sailing from Danzig and captured when about to enter the blockaded port of Havre in 1798, the British High Court of Admiralty held the official notification by the British government of the blockade of that port raised an absolute presumption of knowledge on the part of the neutral captain. "It is the duty of foreign governments," said the court, "to communicate the information to their subjects, whose interests they are bound to protect." In view, however, of the fact that a captain of the British fleet had by mistake informed the captain of the Neptunus that Havre was not blockaded, the vessel and cargo were restored.

THE JONGE MARGARETHA.

Great Britain, High Court of Admiralty, 1799.

1 C. Rob. 189.

This was a case of a Papenberg ship, taken on a voyage from Amsterdam to Brest with a cargo of cheese, April 1797. . . .

Sir Wm. Scott—There is little reason to doubt the property in this case, and therefore passing over the observations which have been made on that part of the subject, I shall confine myself to the single question of law; Is this a legal transaction in a neutral, being the transaction of a Papenberg ship carrying Dutch cheeses from Amsterdam to Brest, or Morlaix, (as it is said) but certainly to Brest? or as it may be otherwise described, the transaction of a neutral carrying a cargo of provisions, not the product and manufacture of his own country, but of the enemy's ally in the war—of provisions which are a capital ship's store—and to the great port of naval equipment of the enemy.

If I adverted to the state of Brest at this time, it might be no unfair addition to the terms of the description, if I noticed, what was notorious to all Europe, that there was in that port a considerable French fleet in a state of preparation for sallying forth on a hostile expedition; its motions at that time watched with great anxiety by a British fleet which lay off the harbour for the purpose of defeating its designs. Is the carriage of such a supply, to such a place, and on such an occasion, a traffic so purely neutral, as to subject the neutral trader to no inconvenience?

If it could be laid down as a general position, in the manner in which it has been argued, that cheese being a provision is universally contraband, the question would be readily answered; but the Court lays down no such position. The catalogue of contraband has varied very much, and sometimes in such a manner as to make it very difficult to assign the reason of the variations, owing to particular circumstances, the history of which has not accompanied the history of the decisions. In 1673, when many unwarrantable rules were laid down by public authority respecting contraband, it was expressly asserted by Sir R. Wiseman, the then King's Advocate, upon a formal reference made to him, that by the practice of the English Admiralty, corn, wine, and oil, were liable to be deemed contraband. "I do agree," says he, reprobating the regulations that had been published, and observing that rules are not to be so hardly laid down as to press upon neutrals, "that corn, wine, and oil, will be deemed contraband."

These articles of provisions then were at that time confiscable, according to the judgment of a person of great knowledge and experience in the practice of this Court. In much later times many other sorts of provisions have been condemned as contraband. In 1747, in the Jonge

Andreas, butter, going to Rochelle, was condemned; how it happened that cheese at the same time was more favourably considered, according to the case cited by Dr. Swabey, I do not exactly know; the distinction appears nice; in all probability the cheeses were not of the species which is intended for ship's use. Salted cod and salmon were condemned in the Jonge Frederick, going to Rochelle, in the same year; in 1748, in the Joannes, rice and salted herrings were condemned as contraband. These instances shew that articles of food have been so considered, at least where it was probable that they were intended for naval or military use.

I am aware of the favourable positions laid down upon this matter by Wolfius and Vattel, and other writers of the continent, although Vattel . . . expressly admits that provisions may, under circumstances, be treated as contraband. And I take the modern established rule to be this, that generally they are not contraband, but may become so under circumstances arising out of the particular situation of the war, or the condition of the parties engaged in it. The Court must therefore look to the circumstances under which this supply was sent.

Among the causes of exception which tend to prevent provisions from being treated as contraband, one is, that they are of the growth of the country which exports them. In the present case, they are the product of another country, and that a hostile country; the claimant has not only gone out of his way for the supply of the enemy, but he has assisted the enemy's ally in the war by taking off his surplus commodities.

Another circumstance to which some indulgence, by the practice of nations, is shewn, is, when the articles are in their native and unmanufactured state. Thus iron is treated with indulgence, though anchors and other instruments fabricated out of it are directly contraband. Hemp is more favourably considered than cordage; and wheat is not considered as so noxious a commodity as any of the final preparations of it for human use. In the present case, the article falls under this unfavourable consideration, being a manufacture prepared for immediate use.

But the most important distinction is, whether the articles were intended for the ordinary use of life, or even for mercantile ships' use; or whether they were going with a highly probable destination to military use? Of the matter of fact, on which the distinction is to be applied, the nature and quality of the port to which the articles were going, is not an irrational test; if the port is a general commercial port, it shall be understood that the articles were going for civil use, although occasionally a frigate or other ships of war, may be constructed in that port. On the contrary, if the great predominant character of a port be that of a port of naval military equipment, it shall be intended that the articles were going for military use, although merchant ships resort to the same place, and although it is possible that the articles might have been applied to civil consumption; for it being impossible to ascertain the final application of an article *ancipitis usus,* it is not an injurious rule which deduces both ways the final use from the immediate destination; and the presumption of a hostile use, founded on its destination to a military port, is very much inflamed, if at the time when the articles were going, a considerable armament was notoriously preparing, to which a supply of those articles would be eminently useful.

In the case of the Eendraght, cited for the claimant, the destination was to Bourdeaux; and though smaller vessels of war may be occasionally built and fitted out there, it is by no means a port of naval military equipment in its principal occupation, . . . in the same manner as Brest is universally known to be.

The Court, however, was unwilling, in the present case, to conclude the claimant on the mere point of destination, it being alleged that the cheeses were not fit for naval use, but were merely luxuries for the use of domestic tables. It therefore permitted both parties to exhibit affidavits as to their nature and quality. The claimant has exhibited none; but there are authentic certificates from persons of integrity and knowledge, that they are exactly such cheeses as are used in British ships, when foreign cheeses are used at all; and that they are such as are exclusively used in French ships of war.

Attending to all these circumstances, I think myself warranted to pronounce these cheeses to be contraband, and condemn them as such. As, however, the party has acted without dissimulation in the case, and may have been misled by an inattention to circumstances, to which in strictness he ought to have adverted, as well as by something like an irregular indulgence on which he has relied; I shall content myself with pronouncing the cargo to be contraband, without enforcing the usual penalty of the confiscation of the ship, belonging to the same proprietor.[1]

THE PETERHOFF.

United States, Supreme Court, 1866.

5 Wallace, 28. [18 L. ed. 564.]

(Part of the opinion, dealing with the question whether the vessel and cargo were liable to condemnation for breach of blockade, is reproduced above, p. 767.)

The CHIEF JUSTICE [CHASE]. . . .

Thus far we have not thought it necessary to discuss the question of actual destination beyond Matamoras. . . . Destination in this case

---

[1] This case should be read in the light of the provisions of the Declaration of London, of 1909. See Higgins, Hague Peace Conferences, 540 ff.; Oppenheim, *op. cit.,* II, §§ 393, 394.

becomes specially important only in connection with the question of contraband.

And this brings us to the question: was any portion of the cargo of the Peterhoff contraband?

The classification of goods as contraband or not contraband has much perplexed text-writers and jurists. A strictly accurate and satisfactory classification is perhaps impracticable; but that which is best supported by American and English decisions may be said to divide all merchandise into three classes. Of these classes, the first consists of articles manufactured and primarily and ordinarily used for military purposes in time of war; the second, of articles which may be and are used for purposes of war or peace, according to circumstances; and the third, of articles exclusively used for peaceful purposes. [Lawrence's Wheaton, 772–6, note; The Commercen, 1 Wheaton, 382; Dana's Wheaton, 629, note; Parsons', Mar. Law, 93–4.] Merchandise of the first class, destined to·a belligerent country or places occupied by the army or navy of a belligerent, is always contraband; merchandise of the second class is contraband only when actually destined to the military or naval use of a belligerent; while merchandise of the third class is not contraband at all, though liable to seizure and condemnation for violation of blockade or siege.

A considerable portion of the cargo of the Peterhoff was of the third class, and need not be further referred to. A large portion, perhaps, was of the second class, but is not proved, as we think, to have been actually destined to belligerent use, and cannot therefore be treated as contraband. Another portion was, in our judgment, of the first class, or, if of the second, destined directly to the rebel military service. This portion of the cargo consisted of the cases of artillery harness, and of articles described in the invoices as "men's army bluchers," "artillery boots," and "government regulation gray blankets." These goods come fairly under the description of goods primarily and ordinarily used for military purposes in time of war. They make part of the necessary equipment of an army.

It is true that even these goods, if really intended for sale in the market of Matamoras, would be free of liability: for contraband may be transported by neutrals to a neutral port, if intended to make part of its general stock in trade. But there is nothing in the case which tends to convince us that such was their real destination, while all the circumstances indicate that these articles, at least, were destined for the use of the rebel forces then occupying Brownsville, and other places in the vicinity.

And contraband merchandise is subject to a different rule in respect to ulterior destination than that which applies to merchandise not contraband. The latter is liable to capture only when a violation of blockade is intended; the former when destined to the hostile country, or to the actual military or naval use of the enemy, whether blockaded or not. The trade of neutrals with belligerents in articles not contraband is absolutely free, unless interrupted by blockade; the conveyance by neutrals to belligerents of contraband articles is always unlawful, and such articles may always be seized during transit by sea. Hence, while articles, not contraband, might be sent to Matamoras and beyond to the rebel region, where the communications were not interrupted by blockade, articles of a contraband character, destined in fact to a State in rebellion, or for the use of the rebel military forces, were liable to capture, though primarily destined to Matamoras.

We are obliged to conclude that the portion of the cargo which we have characterized as contraband must be condemned.

And it is an established rule that the part of the cargo belonging to the same owner as the contraband portion must share its fate. This rule is well stated by Chancellor Kent, thus: "Contraband articles are infectious, as it is called, and contaminate the whole cargo belonging to the same owners, and the invoice of any particular article is not usually admitted, to exempt it from general confiscation."

So much of the cargo of the Peterhoff, therefore, as actually belonged to the owner of the artillery harness, and the other contraband goods, must be also condemned. . . .

THE KIM. THE ALFRED NOBEL.

THE BJORNSTERJNE BJORNSON. THE FRIDLAND.

Great Britain, High Court of Justice, Probate, Divorce and Admiralty Division, 1915.

L. R. [1915] Probate, 215.

The PRESIDENT (SIR SAMUEL EVANS). The cargoes which have been seized, and which are claimed in these proceedings, were laden on four steamships belonging to neutral owners, and were under time charters to an American corporation, the Gans Steamship Line. . . . The four ships . . . [three Norwegian and one Swedish] all started within a period of three weeks in October and November, 1914, on voyages from New York to Copenhagen with very large cargoes of lard, hog and meat products, oil stocks, wheat and other foodstuffs; two of them had cargoes of rubber and one of hides. They were captured on the high seas, and their cargoes were seized on the ground that they were conditional contraband, alleged to be confiscable in the circumstances, with the exception of one cargo of rubber which was seized as absolute contraband.

The Court is now asked to deal only with the cargoes. All questions relating to the capture and confiscability of the ships are left over to be argued and dealt with hereafter. . . .

Denmark is a country with a small population of less than three millions; and is, of course, as regards foodstuffs, an exporting, and not an importing country. Its situation, however, renders it convenient to transport goods from its territory to German ports and places like Hamburg, Altona, Lübeck, Stettin, and Berlin.

The total cargoes in the four captured ships bound for Copenhagen within about three weeks amounted to 73,237,796 lbs. in weight. . . . Portions of these cargoes have been released, and other portions remain unclaimed. The quantity of goods claimed in thèse proceedings is very large. Altogether the claims cover 32,312,479 lbs. (exclusive of the rubber and hides). The claimants did not supply any information as to the quantities of similar products which they had supplied or consigned to Denmark previous to the war. Some illustrative statistics were given by the Crown, with regard to lard of various qualities, which are not without significance, and which form a fair criterion of the imports of these and like substances into Denmark before the war; and they give a measure for comparison with the imports of lard consigned to Copenhagen after the outbreak of war upon the four vessels now before the Court.

The average annual quantity of lard imported into Denmark during the three years 1911–1913 from all sources was 1,459,000 lbs. The quantity of lard consigned to Copenhagen on thèse four ships alone was 19,252,000 lbs. Comparing these quantities, the result is that these vessels were carrying towards Copenhagen within less than a month more than thirteen times the quantity of lard which had been imported annually to Denmark for each of the three years before the war. . . .

With regard to the general character of the cargoes, evidence was given by persons of experience that all the foodstuffs were suitable for the use of troops in the field; that some, e. g., the smoked meat or smoked bacon, were similar in kind, wrapping, and packing to what was supplied in large quantities to the British troops, and were not ordinarily supplied for civilian use; that others, e. g., canned or boiled beef in tins, were of the same brand and class as had been offered by Armour & Co. for the use of the British forces in the field; and that the packages sent by these ships could only have been made up for the use of troops in the field. As against this, there was evidence that goods of the same class had been ordinarily supplied to and for civilians.

As to the lard, proof was given that glycerine (which is in great demand for the manufacture of nitro-glycerine for high explosives) is readily obtainable from lard. Although this use is possible, there was no evidence before me that any lard had been so used in Germany; and I am of opinion that the lard comprised ought to be treated upon the footing of foodstuffs only. It is largely used in German army rations.

As to the fat backs (of which large quantities were shipped), there was also proof that they could be used for the production of glycerine.

. . . In fact no evidence . . . was offered for the shippers of fat backs. Mr. Nuttall, a deponent for one of them . . . says the fat backs shipped by them were not in a condition which was suitable for eating; but he may have meant only that they required further treatment before they became edible.

There was no market for these fat backs in Denmark. The Procurator-General deposed as a result of inquiries that the Germans were very anxious to obtain fat backs merely for the glycerine they contain. In these circumstances it is not by any means clear that fat backs should be regarded merely as foodstuffs in these cases, and in the absence of evidence to the contrary, it is fair to treat them as materials which might either be required as food, or for the production of glycerine.

The convenience of Copenhagen for transporting goods to Germany need hardly be mentioned. It is in evidence that the chief trade between Copenhagen and Germany since the war was through Lübeck, Stettin, and Hamburg.

The sea-borne trade of Lübeck has increased very largely since this war. It was also sworn in evidence that Lübeck was a German naval base. Stettin is a garrison town, and is the headquarters of army corps. It has also shipbuilding yards where warships are constructed and repaired. It is Berlin's nearest seaport. It will be remembered that one of the big shipping companies asked a Danish firm to become nominal consignees for goods destined for Stettin. Hamburg and Altona had ceased to be the commercial ports dealing with commerce coming through the North Sea. They were the headquarters of various regiments. Copenhagen is also a convenient port for communication with the German naval arsenal and fortress of Kiel and its canal, and for all places reached through the canal. These ports may properly be regarded, in my opinion, as bases of supply for the enemy, and the cargoes destined for these might on that short ground be condemned as prize; but I prefer, especially as no particular cargo can definitely be said to be going to a particular port, to deal with the cases upon broader grounds.

Before stating the inferences and conclusions of fact, it will be convenient to investigate and ascertain the legal principles which are to be applied according to international law, in view of the state of things as they were in the year 1914.

While the guiding principles of the law must be followed, it is a truism to say that international law, in order to be adequate, as well as just, must have regard to the circumstances of the times, including "the circumstances arising out of the particular situation of the war, or the condition of the parties engaged in it:" *vide* The Jonge Margaretha [(1799), 1 C. Rob. 189; and Chancellor Kent's Commentaries, p. 139.]

Two important doctrines familiar to international law come prominently forward for consideration: the one is embodied in the rule as to "continuous voyage," or continuous "transportation"; the other relates to the ultimate hostile destination of conditional and absolute contraband respectively.

The doctrine of "continuous voyage," was first applied by the English Prize Courts to unlawful trading. There is no reported case in our Courts where the doctrine is applied in terms to the carriage of contraband; but it was so applied and extended by the United States Courts against this country in the time of the American Civil War; and its application was acceded to by the British Government of the day: and was, moreover, acted upon by the International Commission which sat under the Treaty between this country and America, made at Washington on May 8, 1871, when the commission, composed of an Italian, an American, and a British delegate, unanimously disallowed the claims in The Peterhoff [(1866), 5 Wallace, 28], which was the leading case upon the subject of continuous transportation in relation to contraband goods. . . .

I am not going through the history of it, but the doctrine was asserted by Lord Salisbury at the time of the South African war with reference to German vessels carrying goods to Delagoa Bay, and as he was dealing with Germany, he fortified himself by referring to the view of Bluntschli as the true view as follows: "If the ship or goods are sent to the destination of a neutral port only the better to come to the aid of the enemy, these will be contraband of war, and confiscation will be justified."

It is essential to appreciate that the foundation of the law of contraband, and the reason for the doctrine of continuous voyage which has been grafted into it, is the right of a belligerent to prevent certain goods from reaching the country of the enemy for his military use. Neutral traders, in their own interest, set limits to the exercise of this right as far as they can. These conflicting interests of neutrals and belligerents are the causes of the contests which have taken place upon the subject of contraband and continuous voyages.

A compromise was attempted by the London Conference in the unratified Declaration of London. The doctrine of continuous voyage or continuous transportation was conceded to the full by the conference in the case of absolute contraband, and it was expressly declared that "it is immaterial whether the carriage of the goods is direct, or entails transshipment, or a subsequent transport by land."

As to conditional contraband, the attempted compromise was that the doctrine was excluded in the case of conditional contraband, except when the enemy country had no seaboard. As is usual in compromises, there seems to be an absence of logical reason for the exclusion. If it is right that a belligerent should be permitted to capture absolute contraband proceeding by various voyages or transport with an ultimate destination for the enemy territory, why should he not be allowed to capture goods which though not absolutely contraband, become contraband by reason of a further destination to the enemy Government or its armed forces?

And with the facilities of transportation by sea and by land which now exist the right of a belligerent to capture conditional contraband would be of a very shadowy value if a mere consignment to a neutral port were sufficient to protect the goods. It appears also to be obvious that in these days of easy transit, if the doctrine of continuous voyage or continuous transportation is to hold at all, it must cover not only voyages from port to port at sea, but also transport by land, until the real, as distinguished from the merely ostensible, destination of the goods is reached.

In connection with this subject, note may be taken of the communication of January 20, 1915, from Mr. Bryan, as Secretary of State for the United States Government, to Mr. Stone, of the Foreign Relations Committee of the Senate. . . .

"The rights and interests of belligerents and neutrals are opposed in respect to contraband articles and trade. . . . The record of the United States in the past is not free from criticism. When neutral, this Government has stood for a restricted list of absolute and conditional contraband. As a belligerent, we have contended for a liberal list, according to our conception of the necessities of the case.

"The United States has made earnest representations to Great Britain in regard to the seizure and detention of all American ships or cargoes bona fide destined to neutral ports. . . . It will be recalled, however, that American Courts have established various rules bearing on these matters. The rule of 'continuous voyage' has been not only asserted by American tribunals, but extended by them. They have exercised the right to determine from the circumstances whether the ostensible was the real destination. They have held that the shipment of articles of contraband to a neutral port 'to order' (this was of course before the Order in Council of October 29.), from which, as a matter of fact, cargoes had been transshipped to the enemy, is corroborative evidence that the cargo is really destined to the enemy instead of to the neutral port of delivery. It is thus seen that some of the doctrines which appear to bear harshly upon neutrals at the present time are analogous to or outgrowths from policies adopted by the United States when it was a belligerent. The Government, therefore, cannot consistently protest against the application of rules which it has followed in the past, unless they have not been practiced as heretofore. . . ."

It is not necessary to dilate further upon the history of the doctrine in question.

I have no hesitation in pronouncing that, in my view, the doctrine of continuous voyage, or transportation, both in relation to carriage by sea and to carriage over land, had become part of the law of nations at the commencement of the present war, in accordance with the principles of recognized legal decisions, and with the view of the great body of modern jurists, and also with the practice of nations in recent maritime warfare.

The result is that the Court is not restricted in its vision to the primary consignments of the goods in these cases to the neutral port of Copenhagen; but is entitled, and bound, to take a more extended outlook in order to ascertain whether this neutral destination was merely ostensible and, if so, what the real ultimate destination was.

As to the real destination of a cargo, one of the chief tests is whether it was consigned to the neutral port to be there delivered for the purpose of being imported into the common stock of the country. . . . Another circumstance which has been regarded as important in determining the question of real or ostensible destination at the neutral port was the consignment "to order or assigns" without naming any consignee.

In the celebrated case of The Springbok (1866) [5 Wallace, 1] the Supreme Court of the United States acted upon inferences as to destination (in the case of blockade) on this very ground. . . .

I am not unmindful of the argument that consignment "to order" is common in these days. But a similar argument was used in The Springbok, supported by the testimony of some of the principal brokers in London, to the effect that a consignment "to order or assign" was the usual and regular form of consignment to an agent for sale at such a port as Nassau. . . .

The argument still remains good, that if shippers, after the outbreak of war, consign goods of the nature of contraband to their own order without naming a consignee, it may be a circumstance of suspicion in considering the question whether the goods were really intended for the neutral destination, and to become part of the common stock of the neutral country, or whether they had another ultimate destination. Of course, it is not conclusive. The suspicion arising from this form of consignment during war might be dispelled by evidence produced by the shippers. . . .

Upon this branch of the case—for reasons which have been given when dealing with the consignments generally, and when stating the circumstances with respect to each claim—I have no hesitation in stating my conclusion that the cargoes (other than the small portions acquired by persons in Scandinavia whose claims are allowed) were not destined for consumption or use in Denmark or intended to be incorporated into the general stock of that country by sale or otherwise; that Copenhagen was not the real bona fide place of delivery; but that the cargoes were on their way at the time of capture to German territory as their actual and real destination. . . .

Having decided that the cargoes, though ostensibly destined for Copenhagen, were in reality destined for Germany, the question remains whether their real ultimate destination was for the use of the German Government or its naval or military forces.

If the goods were destined for Germany, what are the facts and the law bearing upon the question whether they had the further hostile destination for the German Government for military use?

In the first place, as has already been pointed out, they were goods adapted for such use; and further, in part, adapted for immediate warlike purposes in the sense that some of them could be employed for the production of explosives. They were destined, too, for some of the nearest German ports like Hamburg, Lübeck, and Stettin, where some of the forces were quartered, and whose connection with the operations of war has been stated. It is by no means necessary that the Court should be able to fix the exact port. . . .

Regard must also be had to the state of things in Germany during this war in relation to the military forces, and to the civil population, and to the method described in evidence which was adopted by the Government in order to procure supplies for the forces.

The general situation was described by the British Foreign Secretary in his Note to the American Government on February 10, 1915, as follows:—

"The reason for drawing a distinction between foodstuffs intended for the civil population and those for the armed forces or enemy Government disappears when the distinction between the civil population and the armed forces itself disappears. In any country in which there exists such a tremendous organization for war as now obtains in Germany, there is no clear division between those whom the Government is responsible for feeding and those whom it is not. Experience shows that the power to requisition will be used to the fullest extent in order to make sure that the wants of the military are supplied, and however much goods may be imported for civil use it is by the military that they will be consumed if military exigencies require it, especially now that the German Government have taken control of all the foodstuffs in the country."— I am not saying that the last sentence is applicable to the circumstances of this case.—. . .

Now as to the question of the proof of intention on the part of the shippers of the cargoes.

It was argued that the Crown as captors ought to show that there was an original intention by the shippers to supply the goods to the enemy Government or the armed forces at the inception of the voyage as one complete commercial transaction, evidenced by a contract of sale or something equivalent to it.

It is obvious from a consideration of the whole scheme of conduct of the shippers that if they had expressly arranged to consign the cargoes to the German Government for the armed forces, this would have been done in such a way as to make it as difficult as possible for belligerents to detect it.

If the captors had to prove such an arrangement affirmatively and absolutely, in order to justify capture and condemnation, the rights of belligerents to stop articles of conditional contraband from reaching the hostile destination would become nugatory. . . .

It is not necessary that an intention at the commencement of the voyage should be established by the captors either absolutely or by inference. . . . If at the time of the seizure the goods were in fact on their way to the enemy Government or its forces as their real ultimate destination, by the action of the shippers, whenever the project was conceived, or however it was to be carried out; if, in truth, it is reasonably certain that the shippers must have known that that was the real ultimate destination of the goods (apart of course from any genuine sale to be made at some intermediate place), the belligerent had a right to stop the goods on their way, and to seize them as confiscable goods. . . .

For the many reasons which I have given in the course of this judgment and which do not require recapitulation, or even summary, I have come to the clear conclusion from the facts proved, and the reasonable and, indeed, irresistible inferences from them, that the cargoes claimed by the shippers as belonging to them at the time of seizure were not on their way to Denmark to be incorporated into the common stock of that country by consumption, or bona fide sale, or otherwise; but, on the contrary, that they were on their way not only to German territory, but also to the German Government and their forces for naval and military use as their real ultimate destination.

To hold the contrary would be to allow one's eyes to be filled by the dust of theories and technicalities, and to be blinded to the realities of the case. . . .

[Some of the claims were allowed; others were disallowed. The vessels themselves were subsequently condemned.]

THE BONNA.

Great Britain, High Court of Justice, Probate, Divorce and Admiralty Division, 1918.

L. R. [1918] Probate, 123.

In this case, which governed a number of others, the Procurator-General, on behalf of the Crown, claimed the condemnation of 416 tons of cocoanut oil seized at Bristol on August 27, 1916, ex the Norwegian steamship Bonna.

The claimants, the Nya Margarin A/B. Svea, of Kalmar, Sweden, claimed the release of the oil on the ground that it had been bought by them for the purpose of the manufacture, in their own factory, of margarine for sale and consumption in Sweden.

The case is reported on the alternative question argued on behalf of the Crown that, assuming the claimants established that the oil was destined solely for the Swedish factory, it should be deemed to have an enemy destination on the ground that it helped to form part of a reservoir of edible fats part of which went to Germany, or that the margarine manufactured from it would, to the knowledge of the claimants, be consumed in Sweden in substitution for butter exported to Germany. On this latter point it appeared from an affidavit by the Controller of the War Trade Statistical Department that before the war Sweden exported about 76 per cent. of her surplus butter to the United Kingdom and Denmark, and that the quantity exported to Germany was 2.3 per cent. After the outbreak of war the export to the United Kingdom, and in a lesser degree to Denmark, decreased, until by June, 1916, it had dwindled to less than 0.4 per cent., while Germany was receiving 98 per cent. of the total export. During the second half of 1916 large quantities of edible fats and oils suitable for margarine manufacture were seized as prize, with the result that, whereas in July, 1916, 1716 tons of butter were exported, 1701 of which went to Germany, in December, 1916, less than one ton was exported, and from January to October, 1917, only one and a half tons were exported to Germany. . . .

THE PRESIDENT (SIR SAMUEL EVANS). . . . Apart from these questions of fact, counsel for the Crown rested their case upon a broader ground. Statistics were given in evidence to show the increase of the importation into Sweden of raw materials for margarine and of the production and sale of margarine, and to show the simultaneous increase of the export of butter from Sweden to Germany. They were interesting, and beyond doubt they proved that the more margarine was made for the Swedes the more butter was supplied by them to the Germans; and that when by reason of the naval activity of this country the imports of margarine production became diminished, the Swedish butter was kept for consumption within Sweden itself and ceased to be sent to the enemy.

Upon these facts counsel for the Crown formulated and founded their logical proposition. That proposition may be translated in practical terms, in relation to the facts of this case, perhaps more usefully than if it were stated in abstract language. So translated it may be stated thus: "Margarine and butter are of the same class of food, one being used as a substitute for, or even as an equivalent of, the other. Margarine was produced in Sweden—by the claimants among others—with the result that, to the knowledge of the manufacturers, the butter of the country was being sent to Germany, where it would pass under the control of the Government. There was, so to speak, one reservoir of the edible fats, butter and margarine. As one part of the contents—the butter—was conveyed away for consumption in Germany, the other part—margarine—was sent in to take its place for consumption in Sweden. If the one part could be captured as conditional contraband, the other was subject to capture also; and not only that part when completely manufactured, but the raw materials for it as well."

No authority was, or could be, adduced for the proposition formulated in such an argument; but it was contended, nevertheless, that it logically followed principles recognized by international law.

Before pronouncing the decision of the Court I think it right to say that, if it were established that raw materials were imported by a neutral for the manufacture of margarine with an intention to supply the enemy with the manufactured article, I should be prepared to hold that the doctrine of continuous voyage applied so as to make such raw materials subject to condemnation as conditional contraband with an enemy destination.

I should go even further and hold that, if it were shown that in a neutral country particular manufacturers of margarine were acting in combination with particular producers or vendors of butter, and that the intention and object of their combination was to produce the margarine in order to send the butter to the enemy, the same doctrine would be applicable with the same results.

But there is a long space between those two supposed cases and the one now before the Court; and this space, in my view, cannot be spanned by the application of the accepted principles of the law of nations.

I do not consider that it would be in accordance with international law to hold that raw materials on their way to citizens of a neutral country to be converted into a manufactured article for consumption in that country were subject to condemnation on the ground that the consequence might, or even would, necessarily be that another article of a like kind, and adapted for a like use, would be exported by other citizens of the neutral country to the enemy.

I therefore allow the claim, and order that the goods seized, or the proceeds if sold, be released to the claimants.[1]

---

[1] SUPPLEMENTARY CASES. In the controversy between France and Italy over the detention of the steamship Carthage, submitted to arbitration before a tribunal of the Hague Permanent Court of Arbitration, [Scott, Hague Court Reports, 329] the ground of detention being the presence on board the ship of an aeroplane destined to Tunis which the Italian government claimed to be contraband destined ultimately to Turkey, the tribunal held, May 6, 1913, that the Italian government did not have such evidence of the hostile destination of the aeroplane as to warrant detention of the vessel and the removal of the aeroplane. Damages were accordingly awarded.

In the case of the Louisiana and Other Ships, L. R. [1918] A. C. 461, involving the liability to condemnation as conditional contraband of cargoes of fodder

D. Reprisals.

An alleged violation of the laws of war by one of the belligerents frequently leads the other belligerent to resort to measures of retaliation or reprisal. Query, what if such measures should interfere with neutral commerce with the enemy? May the neutral be made to bear the burden of restrictions justified only by the alleged illegal acts of the belligerent with whom he is trading? [The Stigstad.]

---

stuffs shipped from the United States to a Swedish port, the Judicial Committee of the Privy Council held that in view of the evidence showing that the consignees were merely "intermediary tools" acting on behalf of agents of the German government in America it was "the intention of the German Government which must be looked for," and this might be presumed to be a German military destination.

In the case of the Noordam, L. R. [1919] P. 57, involving the liability of a cargo of cotton piece goods to confiscation as contraband destined for Germany, the goods having been shipped from New York by an American firm and consigned to a Dutch firm for delivery to a Dutch purchaser, the British Prize Court held that since the Dutch purchaser was shown to have sold large quantities of cotton goods to Germany the captured cargo had a presumptive destination to Germany and it was of no consequence that the neutral shippers were not parties to such ultimate destination. "I do not think," said the court, "the enemy destination—which is a fact—can depend upon the intention of the shipper when he puts the goods on board." The fact that the consignee, acting as intermediary, might have endeavored to frustrate the enemy destination was held to be irrelevant.

In the case of the Baron Stjernblad, L. R. [1918] A. C. 173, involving a claim for costs incurred by a neutral Swedish corporation by reason of the seizure and detention of a cargo of cocoa beans released by the Prize Court as not being contraband, the Judicial Committee of the Privy Council held that there were, in the increase of the export trade from Sweden to Germany in the particular commodity, "circumstances of suspicion calling for further inquiry and amply sufficient to justify the seizure" even though the goods were subsequently released.

Query, what acts are included under the head of "unneutral service," so as to subject the vessel engaged in it to confiscation? In the case of the Atalanta, 6 C. Rob. 440 (1808), involving the liability to confiscation of a vessel captured on a voyage from Batavia to Bremen, having come last from the Isle de France where a packet of despatches from the government of the Isle to the minister of Marine at Paris was taken on board with the knowledge of the master and of one of the supercargoes the British prize court held that the offense was so serious as to warrant confiscation of both vessel and cargo. In the case of the Orozembo, 6 C. Rob. 430 (1807), an American vessel was condemned by the British prize court for the offense of carrying a number of Dutch officers from Lisbon to Batavia. In the case of the Manouba, Scott, Hague Court Reports, 341, decided in 1913, the Hague Court of Arbitration held that Italy was justified in stopping a French steamer in 1912 and demanding the surrender of certain Turkish passengers believed to be enemy soldiers.

THE STIGSTAD.

Great Britain, Judicial Committee of the Privy Council, 1918.

L. R. [1919] A. C. 279.

Appeal from a judgment of the President of the Admiralty Division (in Prize) [[1916] P. 123].

[In retaliation for measures taken by the German Government, the British Government, on March 11, 1915, issued an Order in Council providing that every merchant ship on its way to a port other than a German port and carrying goods with an enemy destination might be required to discharge the goods at a British port. No provision was made for compensation. The Stigstad, a Norwegian vessel bound from a Norwegian port to Rotterdam with iron-ore briquettes the property of neutrals but destined to Germany, was stopped and required to discharge at a British port. The claimants put in a claim for freight, detention and expenses consequent upon the seizure and discharge. The President, Sir Samuel Evans, holding the Order in Council valid, allowed the freight but dismissed the claims for detention and special expenses. The claimants appealed.]

LORD SUMNER. . . . With the fullest recognition of the rights of neutral ships, it is impossible to say that owners of such ships can claim damages from a belligerent for putting into force such an Order in Council as that of March 11, 1915, if the Order be valid. The neutral exercising his trading rights on the high seas and the belligerent exercising on the high seas rights given him by Order in Council or equivalent procedure, are each in the enjoyment and exercise of equal rights; and, without an express provision in the Order to that effect, the belligerent does not exercise his rights subject to any overriding rights in the neutral. The claimants' real contention is, and is only, that the Order in Council is contrary to international law, and is invalid.

Upon this subject two passages in The Zamora, [[1916] 2 A. C. 77, 95, 98] are in point. The first is at p. 95, and relates to Sir William Scott's decision in The Fox [Edw. 311]. "The decision proceeded upon the principle that, where there is just cause for retaliation, neutrals may by the law of nations be required to submit to inconvenience from the act of a belligerent power greater in degree than would be justified had no just cause for retaliation arisen, a principle which had been already laid down in The Lucy [(1809) Edw. 122]."

Further, at p. 98, are the words "An order authorising reprisals will be conclusive as to the facts which are recited as showing that a case for reprisals exists, and will have due weight as showing what, in the opinion of His Majesty's advisers, are the best or only means of meeting the emergency; but this will not preclude the right of any party aggrieved to contend, or the right of the Court to hold, that these means are unlawful, as entailing on neutrals a degree of inconvenience unreasonable, considering all the circumstances of the case.'' . . .

What is here in question is not the right of the belligerent to retaliate upon his enemy the same measure as has been meted out to him, or the propriety of justifying in one belligerent some departure from the regular rules of war on the ground of necessity arising from prior departures on the part of the other, but it is the claim of neutrals to be saved harmless under such circumstances from inconvenience or damage thereout arising. If the statement above quoted from The Zamora be correct, the recitals in the Order in Council sufficiently establish the existence of such breaches of law on the part of the German Government as justify retaliatory measures on the part of His Majesty, and, if so, the only question open to the neutral claimant for the purpose of invalidating the Order is whether or not it subjects neutrals to more inconvenience or prejudice than is reasonably necessary under the circumstances.

Their Lordships think that such a rule is sound, and indeed inevitable. From the nature of the case the party who knows best whether or not there has been misconduct calling such a principle into operation, is a party who is not before the Court, namely, the enemy himself. The neutral claimant can hardly have much information about it, and certainly cannot be expected to prove or disprove it. His Majesty's Government, also well aware of the facts, has already, by the fact as well as by the recitals of the Order in Council, solemnly declared the substance and effect of that knowledge, and an independent inquiry into the course of contemporary events, both naval and military, is one which a Court of Prize is but ill-qualified to undertake for itself. Still less would it be proper for such a Court to inquire into the reasons of policy, military or other, which have been the cause and are to be the justification for resorting to retaliation for that misconduct. Its function is, in protection of the rights of neutrals, to weigh on a proper occasion the measures of retaliation which have been adopted in fact, and to inquire whether they are in their nature or extent other than commensurate with the prior wrong done, and whether they inflict on neutrals, when they are looked at as a whole, inconvenience greater than is reasonable under all the circumstances. If follows that a Court of Prize, while bound to ascertain, from the terms of the Order itself, the origin and the occasion of the retaliatory measures for the purpose of weighing those measures with justice as they affect neutrals, nevertheless ought not to question, still less to dispute, that the warrant for passing the Order, which is set out in its recitals, has in truth arisen in the manner therein stated. Although the scope of this inquiry is thus limited in law, in fact their Lordships cannot be blind to what is notorious to all the world and is in the recollection of all men, the outrage namely committed by the enemy, upon law, humanity, and the rights, alike of belligerents and neutrals, which led to, and indeed compelled, the adoption of some such policy as is embodied in this Order in Council. In considering whether more inconvenience is inflicted upon neutrals than the circumstances involve, the frequency and the enormity of the original wrongs are alike material, for the more gross and universal those wrongs are, the more are all nations concerned in their repression, and bound for their part to submit to such sacrifices as that repression involves. It is right to recall that, as neutral commerce suffered and was doomed to suffer gross prejudice from the illegal policy proclaimed and acted on by the German Government, so it profited by, and obtained relief from, retaliatory measures, if effective to restrain, to punish and to bring to an end such injurious conduct. Neutrals, whose principles or policy lead them to refrain from punitory or repressive action of their own, may well be called on to bear a passive part in the necessary suppression of courses which are fatal to the freedom of all who use the seas.

The argument principally urged at the bar ignored these considerations, and assumed an absolute right in neutral trade to proceed without interference or restriction, unless by the application of the rules heretofore established as to contraband traffic, unneutral service and blockade. The assumption was that a neutral, too pacific or too impotent to resent the aggressions and lawlessness of one belligerent, can require the other to refrain from his most effective, or his only, defence against it, by the assertion of an absolute inviolability for his own neutral trade, which would thereby become engaged in a passive complicity with the original offender. For this contention no authority at all was forthcoming. Reference was made to the Orders in Council of 1806 to 1812, which were framed by way of retaliation for the Berlin and Milan decrees. There has been much discussion of these celebrated instruments on one side or the other, though singularly little in decided cases or in treatises of repute; and, according to their nationality or their partisanship, writers have denounced the one policy or the other, or have asserted their own superiority by an impartial censure of both. The present Order, however, does not involve for its justification a defence of the very terms of those Orders in Council. It must be judged on its merits and, if the principle is advanced against it that such retaliation is wrong in kind, no foundation in authority has been found on which to rest it. Nor is the principle itself sound. The seas are the highway of all, and it is incidental to the very nature of maritime war that neutrals, in using that highway, may suffer inconvenience from the exercise of their concurrent rights by those who have to wage war upon it. Of this fundamental fact the right of blockade is only an example. It is true that contraband, blockade, and unneutral service are branches of international law which have their own history, their own illustrations, and their own development. Their growth has been unsystematic, and the assertion of right under these different heads has not been closely connected or simultaneous. Nevertheless, it would be illogical to regard them as being in themselves disconnected topics or as being the subject of rights and liabilities which have no common connexion. They may also be treated, as in fact they are, as illustrations of the broad rule that belligerency and neutrality are states so related to one another that the latter must accept some abatement of the full benefits of peace in order that the former may not be thwarted in war in the assertion and defence of what is the most precious of all the rights of nations, the right to security and independence. The categories of such cases are not closed. To deny to the belligerent under the head of retaliation any right to interfere with the trade of neutrals beyond that which, quite apart from circumstances which warrant retaliation, he enjoys already under the heads of contraband, blockade, and unneutral service, would be to take away with one hand what has formally been conceded with the other. As between belligerents acts of retaliation are either the return of blow for blow in the course of combat, or are questions of the laws of war not immediately falling under the cognizance of a Court of Prize. Little of this subject is left to Prize Law beyond its effect on neutrals and on the rights of belligerents against neutrals, and to say that retaliation is invalid as against neutrals, except within the old limits of blockade, contraband, and unneutral service, is to reduce retaliation to a mere simulacrum, the title of an admitted right without practical application or effect.

Apart from The Zamora, the decided cases on this subject, if not many, are at least not ambiguous. Of The Leonora [[1918] P. 182], decided on the later Order in Council, their Lordships say nothing now, since they are informed that it is under appeal to their Lordships' Board, and they desire on the present occasion to say no more, which might affect the determination of that case, than is indispensable to the disposal of the present one.

Sir William Scott's decisions on the retaliatory Orders in Council were many, and many of them were affirmed on appeal. He repeatedly, and in reasoned terms, declared the nature of the right of retaliation and its entire consistency with the principles of international law. Since then discussion has turned on the measures by which effect was then given to that right, not on the foundation of the principle itself, and their Lordships regard it as being now too firmly established to be open to doubt.

Turning to the question which was little argued, if at all, though it is the real question in the case, whether the Order in Council of March 11, 1915, inflicts hardship excessive either in kind or in degree upon neutral commerce, their Lordships think that no such hardship was shown. It might well be said that neutral commerce under this Order is treated with all practicable tenderness, but it is enough to negative the contention that there is avoidable hardship. Of the later Order in Council they say nothing now. If the neutral shipowner is paid a proper price for the service rendered by his ship, and the neutral cargo-owner a proper

price according to the value of his goods, substantial cause of complaint
can only arise if considerations are put forward which go beyond the
ordinary motives of commerce and partake of a political character, from
a desire either to embarrass the one belligerent or to support the other.
In the present case the agreement of the parties as to the amount to be
allowed for freight disposes of all question as to the claimants' rights to
compensation for mere inconvenience caused by enforcing the Order in
Council. Presumably that sum took into account the actual course and
duration of the voyage and constituted a proper recompense alike for
carrying and for discharging the cargo under the actual circumstances
of that service. The further claims are in the nature of claims for
damages for unlawful interference with the performance of the Rotterdam charter party. They can be maintained only by supposing that a
wrong was done to the claimants, because they were prevented from
performing it, for in their nature these claims assume that the shipowners are to be put in the same position as if they had completed the
voyage under that contract, and are not merely to be remunerated on
proper terms for the performance of the voyage, which was in fact
accomplished. In other words, they are a claim for damages, as for
wrong done by the mere fact of putting in force the Order in Council.
Such a claim cannot be sustained. Their Lordships will humbly advise
His Majesty that the appeal should be dismissed with costs.[1]

E. Angary.

The presence of neutral citizens and their property within the territory of one or the other of the belligerents has at times given rise to
controversy. In general, with the exception of liability to military service, resident neutral aliens are subject to the same burdens as nationals
of the belligerent state, while their property is subject to the same special
taxes and requisitions. Query, what of property belonging to neutrals
which happens to be temporarily present in the belligerent state? Would
a neutral cargo be subject to requisition if the vessel carrying it stopped
at a belligerent port en route to the neutral country? [The Zamora.]

------

[1] SUPPLEMENTARY CASES. In the case of the Leonora, L. R. [1919] A. C. 974,
involving the liability to condemnation of a Dutch vessel and its cargo of coal
captured en route from Rotterdam to Stockholm by a British warship in pursuance of the provisions of an Order in Council of 1917 known as the second
retaliatory order, the Judicial Committee of the Privy Council reaffirmed the
doctrine of retaliation set forth in The Stigstad and held that "the assertion of
a particular right [of retaliation] arising out of a particular provocation in
the course of the war" on the part of one of the belligerents came within the
jurisdiction of prize courts quite as much as violations of the more normal
rights of belligerents in respect to contraband and blockade.

THE ZAMORA.

Great Britain, Judicial Committee of the Privy Council, 1916.

L. R. [1916] 2 A. C. 77.

(The case is given below, p. 799, under the head of Prize Courts.)

F. Visit and search.

As a means of enforcing the belligerent right to capture neutral vessels for breach of blockade or to confiscate neutral goods of a contraband character when destined to the enemy, international law recognizes the further right of the belligerent to visit and search all vessels encountered on the high seas. Resistance by neutral vessels to visit and search, or the attempt to escape by flight, subjects them to the same penalties which are inflicted upon belligerent vessels. Query, would a neutral vessel sailing under the convoy of a neutral warship be condemned on the ground of sharing impliedly in the resistance offered by the warship? [The Maria.] Would resistance to capture on the part of an enemy merchant ship justify condemnation of neutral goods carried in the vessel if the neutral owner did not directly participate in the resistance? [The Nereide.]

THE MARIA.

Great Britain, High Court of Admiralty, 1799.

1 C. Rob. 340.

This was the leading case of a fleet of Swedish merchantmen, carrying pitch, tar, hemp, deals, and iron to several ports of France, Portugal, and the Mediterranean; and taken, Jan. 1798, sailing under convoy of a ship of war; and proceeded against for resistance of visitation and search by British cruisers. . . .

Judgment.

Sir W. Scott—. . . In forming that judgment [of the case], I trust that it has not escaped my anxious recollection for one moment, what it is that the duty of my station calls for from me; namely, to consider myself as stationed here, not to deliver occasional and shifting opinions to serve present purposes of particular national interest, but to administer with indifference that justice which the law of nations holds out without distinction to independent states, some happening to be neutral and some to be belligerent. The seat of judicial authority is, indeed, locally here, in the belligerent country, according to the known law and practice of nations: but the law itself has no locality. It is the duty of the person who sits here to determine this question exactly as he would determine the same question if sitting at Stockholm;—to assert no pretensions on the part of Great Britain, which he would not allow to Sweden in the same circumstances, and to impose no duties on Sweden, as a neutral country, which he would not admit to belong to Great Britain in the same character. If, therefore, I mistake the law in this matter, I mistake that which I consider, and which I mean should be considered, as the universal law upon the question; a question regarding one of the most important of belligerent rights relatively to neutrals. . . .

Removing mere civility of expression, what is the real import of these instructions [given by the Swedish government to the commander of the convoying ship]? Neither more nor less than this, according to my apprehension:—"If you meet with the cruisers of the belligerent states, and they express an intention of visiting and searching the merchant-ships, you are to *talk* them out of their purpose if you can; and if you can't, you are to *fight* them out of it." That is the plain English, and, I presume, the plain Swedish of the matter. . . .

This being the *actual* state of facts, it is proper for me to examine, 2dly, what is their legal state, or, in other words, to what considerations they are justly subject according to the law of nations; for which purpose I state a few principles of that system of law which I take to be incontrovertible.

1st, That the right of visiting and searching merchant-ships upon the high seas, whatever be the ships, whatever be the cargoes, whatever be the destinations, is an incontestible right of the lawfully commissioned cruisers of a belligerent nation. I say, be the ships, the cargoes, and the destinations what they may, because, till they are visited and searched, it does not appear what the ships, or the cargoes, or the destinations are; and it is for the purpose of ascertaining these points that the necessity of this right of visitation and search exists. This right is so clear in principle, that no man can deny it who admits the legality of maritime capture; because if you are not at liberty to ascertain by sufficient inquiry whether there is property that can legally be captured, it is impossible to capture. Even those who contend for the inadmissible rule, that *free ships make free goods*, must admit the exercise of this right at least for the purpose of ascertaining whether the ships are free ships or not. The right is equally clear in practice; for practice is uniform and universal upon the subject. The many European treaties which refer to this right, refer to it as pre-existing, and merely regulate the exercise of it. All writers upon the law of nations unanimously acknowledge it, without the exception even of Hubner himself, the great champion of neutral privileges. In short, no man in the least degree conversant in subjects of this kind has ever, that I know of, breathed a doubt upon it.

The right must unquestionably be exercised with as little of personal harshness and of vexation in the mode as possible; but soften it as much as you can, it is still a right of force, though of lawful force—something in the nature of civil process, where force is employed, but a lawful force, which cannot lawfully be resisted. For it is a wild conceit that wherever force is used, it may be forcibly resisted; a lawful force cannot lawfully be resisted. The only case where it can be so in matters of this nature, is in the state of war and conflict between two countries, where one party has a perfect right to attack by force, and the other has an equally perfect right to repel by force. But in the relative situation of two countries at peace with each other, no such conflicting rights can possibly coexist.

2dly, That the authority of the Sovereign of the neutral country being interposed in any manner of mere force cannot *legally* vary the rights of a lawfully-commissioned belligerent cruiser; I say *legally*, because what may be given, or be fit to be given, in the administration of this species of law, to considerations of comity or of national policy, are views of the matter which, sitting in this Court, I have no right to entertain. All that I assert is, that *legally* it cannot be maintained, that if a Swedish commissioned cruiser, during the wars of his own country, has a right by the law of nations to visit and examine neutral ships, the King of England, being neutral to Sweden, is authorized by that law to obstruct the exercise of that right with respect to the merchant-ships of his country. I add this, that I cannot but think that if he obstructed it by force, it would very much resemble (with all due reverence be it spoken) an opposition of illegal violence to legal right. Two sovereigns may unquestionably agree, if they think fit, as in some late instances they have agreed [It is made an article of treaty between America and Holland an. 1782; Article 10. Mart. Tr. vol. ii. p. 255.], by special covenant, that the presence of one of their armed ships along with their merchant-ships shall be mutually understood to imply, that nothing is to be found in that convoy of merchant-ships inconsistent with amity or neutrality; and if they consent to accept this pledge, no third party has a right to quarrel with it, any more than with any other pledge which they may agree mutually to accept. But surely no sovereign can legally compel the acceptance of such a security by mere force. The only security known to the law of nations upon this subject, independent of all special covenant, is the right of personal visitation and search, to be exercised by those who have the interest in making it. I am not ignorant, that amongst the loose doctrines which modern fancy, under the various denominations of philosophy and philanthropy, and I know not what, have thrown upon the world, it has been within these few years advanced, or rather insinuated, that it might possibly be well if such a security were accepted. Upon such unauthorized speculations it is not necessary for me to descant: the law and practice of nations (I include particularly the practice of Sweden when it happens to be belligerent) give them no sort of countenance; and until that law and practice are new-modelled in such a way as may surrender the known and ancient rights of some nations to the present convenience of other nations, (which nations may perhaps REMEMBER to *forget* them, when they happen to be themselves belligerent), no reverence is due to them; they are the elements of that system which, if it is consistent, has for its purpose an entire abolition of capture in war—that is, in other words, to change the nature of hostility, as it has ever existed amongst mankind, and to introduce a state of things not yet seen in the world, that of a military war and a commercial peace. If it were fit that such a state should be introduced, it is at least necessary that it should be introduced in an avowed and intelligible manner, and not in a way which, professing gravely to adhere to that system which has for centuries prevailed among civilized states, and urging at the same time a pretension utterly inconsistent with all its known principles, delivers over the whole matter at once to eternal controversy and conflict, at the expense of the constant hazard of the harmony of states, and of the lives and safeties of innocent individuals.

3dly, That the penalty for the violent contravention of this right is the confiscation of the property so withheld from visitation and search. For the proof of this I need only refer to Vattel, one of the most correct and certainly not the least indulgent of modern professors of public law. In Book III. c. vii., sect. 114, he expresses himself thus: ''On ne peut empecher le transport des effets de contrebande, si l'on ne visite pas les vaisseaux neutres que l'on rencontre en mer. On est donc en droit de les visiter. Quelques nations puissantes ont refusé en différents tems de se soumettre à cette visite, *aujourd'hui un vaisseau neutre, qui refuseroit de souffrir la visite, se seriot condammer par cela seul, comme etant de bonne prise.''* Vattel is here to be considered not as a lawyer merely delivering an opinion, but as a witness asserting the fact—the fact that such is the existing practice of modern Europe. And to be sure the only marvel in the case is, that he should mention it as a law merely modern, when it is remembered that it is a principle, not only of the civil law, (on which great part of the law of nations is founded,) but of the private jurisprudence of most countries in Europe,—that a contumacious refusal to submit to fair inquiry infers all the penalties of convicted guilt. . . . But I stand with confidence upon all fair principles of reason,—upon the distinct authority of Vattel,—upon the Institutes of other great maritime countries, as well as those of our own country, when I venture to lay it down that by the law of nations, as now understood, a deliberate and continued resistance to search, on the part of a neutral vessel, to a lawful cruiser, is followed by the legal consequence of confiscation. . . .[1]

THE NEREIDE, BENNETT, MASTER.

United States, Supreme Court, 1815.

9 Cranch, 388. [3 L. ed. 769.]

(Part of this case, dealing with the question whether neutral goods are liable to condemnation if found by a belligerent in the vessel of an enemy, is reproduced above, p. 757. The fourth point raised by the captors deals with the effect upon the neutral cargo of the resistance of the vessel to capture.)

MARSHALL, CH. J. . . . .

4. Has the conduct of Manuel Pinto and of the Nereide been such as to impress the hostile character on that part of the cargo which was in fact neutral?

In considering this question the Court has examined separately the parts which compose it.

The vessel was armed, was the property of an enemy, and made resistance. How do these facts affect the claim?

Had the vessel been armed by Pinto, that fact would certainly have constituted an important feature in the case. But the Court can perceive no reason for believing she was armed by him. He chartered, it is true, the whole vessel, and that he might as rightfully do as contract for her partially; but there is no reason to believe that he was instrumental in arming her. . . .

Whether the resistance, which was actually made, is in any degree imputable to Mr. Pinto, is a question of still more importance.

It has been argued that he had the whole ship, and that, therefore, the resistance was his resistance. . . .

. . . His control over the ship began and ended with putting the cargo on board. He does not appear ever to have exercised any authority in the management of the ship. So far from exercising any during the battle, he went into the cabin where he remained till the conflict was over. . . .

The next point to be considered is the right of a neutral to place his goods on board an armed belligerent merchantman.

---

[1] During the World War the advent of the submarine into naval warfare presented new conditions which raised the question of the applicability of the existing rules as to the visit and search of vessels and the removal of passengers to a place of safety. See Fenwick, *op. cit.*, pp. 517 ff.; Hyde, *op. cit.*, II, §§ 731, 732.

That a neutral may lawfully put his goods on board a belligerent ship for conveyance on the ocean, is universally recognized as the original rule of the law of nations. It is, as has already been stated, founded on the plain and simple principle that the property of a friend remains his property wherever it may be found. "Since it is not," says Vattel, "the place where a thing is which determines the nature of that thing, but the character of the person to whom it belongs, things belonging to neutral persons which happen to be in an enemy's country, or on board an enemy's ships, are to be distinguished from those which belong to the enemy."

Bynkershoek lays down the same principles in terms equally explicit; and in terms entitled to the more consideration, because he enters into the enquiry whether a knowledge of the hostile character of the vessel can affect the owner of the goods.

The same principle is laid down by other writers on the same subject, and is believed to be contradicted by none. It is true there were some old ordinances of France declaring that a hostile vessel or cargo should expose both to condemnation. But these ordinances have never constituted a rule of public law.

It is deemed of much importance that the rule is universally laid down in terms which comprehend an armed as well as an unarmed vessel; and that armed vessels have never been excepted from it. Bynkershoek, in discussing a question suggesting an exception, with his mind directed to hostilities, does not hint that this privilege is confined to unarmed merchantmen.

In point of fact, it is believed that a belligerent merchant vessel rarely sails unarmed, so that this exception from the rule would be greater than the rule itself. At all events, the number of those who are armed and who sail under convoy, is too great not to have attracted the attention of writers on public law; and this exception to their broad general rule, if it existed, would certainly be found in some of their works. It would be strange if a rule laid down, with a view to war, in such broad terms as to have universal application, should be so construed as to exclude from its operation almost every case for which it purports to provide, and yet that not a *dictum* should be found in the books pointing to such construction.

The antiquity of the rule is certainty not unworthy of consideration. It is to be traced back to the time when almost every merchantman was in a condition of self-defence, and the implements of war were so light and so cheap that scarcely any would sail without them.

A belligerent has a perfect right to arm in his own defence; and a neutral has a perfect right to transport his goods in a belligerent vessel. These rights do not interfere with each other. The neutral has no control over the belligerent right to arm—ought he to be accountable for the exercise of it?

By placing neutral property in a belligerent ship, that property, according to the positive rules of law, does not cease to be neutral. Why should it be changed by the exercise of a belligerent right, universally acknowledged and in common use when the rule was laid down, and over which the neutral had no control?

The belligerent answers, that by arming his rights are impaired. By placing his goods under the guns of an enemy, the neutral has taken part with the enemy and assumed the hostile character.

Previous to that examination which the Court has been able to make of the reasoning by which this proposition is sustained, one remark will be made which applies to a great part of it. The argument which, taken in its fair sense, would prove that it is unlawful to deposit goods for transportation in the vessel of an enemy generally, however imposing its form, must be unsound, because it is in contradiction to acknowledged law.

It is said that by depositing goods on board an armed belligerent the right of search may be impaired, perhaps defeated.

What is this right of search? Is it a substantive and independent right wantonly, and in the pride of power, to vex and harass neutral commerce, because there is a capacity to do so? or to indulge the idle and mischievous curiosity of looking into neutral trade? or the assumption of a right to control it? If it be such a substantive and independent right, it would be better that cargoes should be inspected in port before the sailing of the vessel, or that belligerent licenses should be procured. But this is not its character.

Belligerents have a full and perfect right to capture enemy goods and articles going to their enemy which are contraband of war. To the exercise of that right the right of search is essential. It is a mean justified by the end. It has been truly denominated a right growing out of, and ancillary to the greater right of capture. Where this greater right may be legally exercised without search, the right of search can never arise or come into question.

But it is said that the exercise of this right may be prevented by the inability of the party claiming it to capture the belligerent carrier of neutral property.

And what injury results from this circumstance? If the property be neutral, what mischief is done by its escaping a search? In so doing there is no sin even as against the belligerent, if it can be effected by lawful means. The neutral cannot justify the use of force or fraud, but if by means, lawful in themselves, he can escape this vexatious procedure, he may certainly employ them.

To the argument that by placing his goods in the vessel of an armed enemy, he connects himself with that enemy and assumes the hostile character; it is answered that no such connexion exists.

The object of the neutral is the transportation of his goods. His connexion with the vessel which transports them is the same, whether that vessel be armed or unarmed. The act of arming is not his—it is the act of a party who has a right to do so. He meddles not with the armament nor with the war. Whether his goods were on board or not, the vessel would be armed and would sail. His goods do not contribute to the armament further than the freight he pays, and freight he would pay were the vessel unarmed.

It is difficult to perceive in this argument anything which does not also apply to an unarmed vessel. In both instances it is the right and the duty of the carrier to avoid capture and to prevent a search. There is no difference except in the degree of capacity to carry this duty into effect. The argument would operate against the rule which permits the neutral merchant to employ a belligerent vessel without imparting to his goods the belligerent character.

The argument respecting resistance stands on the same ground with that which respects arming. Both are lawful. Neither of them is chargeable to the goods or their owner, where he has taken no part in it. They are incidents to the character of the vessel; and may always occur where the carrier is belligerent. . . .

If the neutral character of the goods is forfeited by the resistance of the belligerent vessel, why is not the neutral character of the passengers forfeited by the same cause? The master and crew are prisoners of war, why are not those passengers who did not engage in the conflict also prisoners? That they are not would seem to the Court to afford a strong argument in favor of the goods. The law would operate in the same manner on both.

It cannot escape observation, that in argument the neutral freighter has been continually represented as arming the Nereide and impelling her to hostility. He is represented as drawing forth and guiding her warlike energies. The Court does not so understand the case. The Nereide was armed, governed, and conducted by belligerents. With her force, or her conduct, the neutral shippers had no concern. They deposited their goods on board the vessel, and stipulated for their direct transportation to Buenos Ayres. It is true that on her passage she had a right to defend herself, and might have captured an assailing vessel; but to search for the enemy would have been a violation of the charter party and of her duty.

With a pencil dipped in the most vivid colors, and guided by the hand of a master, a splendid portrait has been drawn exhibiting this vessel and her freighter as forming a single figure, composed of the most discordant materials, of peace and war. So exquisite was the skill of the artist, so dazzling the garb in which the figure was presented, that it required the exercise of that cold investigating faculty which ought always to belong to those who sit on this bench, to discover its only imperfection; its want of resemblance.

The Nereide has not that centaur-like appearance which has been ascribed to her. She does not rove over the ocean hurling the thunders of war while sheltered by the olive branch of peace. She is not composed in part of the neutral character of Mr. Pinto, and in part of the hostile character of her owner. She is an open and declared belligerent; claiming all the rights, and subject to all the dangers of the belligerent character. She conveys neutral property which does not engage in her warlike equipments, or in any employment she may make of them; which is put on board solely for the purpose of transportation, and which encounters the hazard incident to its situation; the hazard of being taken into port, and obliged to seek another conveyance should its carrier be captured.

In this it is the opinion of the majority of the Court there is nothing unlawful. The characters of the vessel and cargo remain as distinct in this as in any other case. The sentence, therefore, of the Circuit Court must be reversed, and the property claimed by Manuel Pinto for himself and his partners, and for those other Spaniards for whom he has claimed, be restored, and the libel as to that property, be dismissed.

[Mr. Justice Johnson delivered a concurring opinion, and Mr. Justice Story, for himself and one other, delivered a dissenting opinion.]

G. Jurisdiction and function of prize courts.

In each of the belligerent states prize courts are set up to determine the legality of the capture by the belligerent of enemy or neutral merchant vessels. While these courts are domestic tribunals the rules which they apply to the cases coming before them are rules of international law, except in so far as national legislation may have prescribed a special interpretation of the more general rule. Query, would Orders in Council made in pursuance of a grant of power to prescribe the "procedure and practice" of British prize courts justify the Crown in Council in issuing imperative directions to the prize courts? [The Zamora.]

THE ZAMORA.

Great Britain, Judicial Committee of the Privy Council, 1916.

L. R. [1916] 2 A. C. 77.

The judgment of their Lordships was delivered by

Lord Parker of Waddington. On April 8, 1915, the Zamora, a Swedish steamship bound from New York to Stockholm with a cargo of grain and copper, was stopped by one of His Majesty's cruisers between the Faroe and Shetland Islands and taken for purposes of search first to the Orkney Islands and then to Barrow-in-Furness. She was seized as prize in the latter port on April 19, 1915, and in due course placed in the custody of the marshal of the Prize Court. It is admitted, on the one hand, that the copper was contraband of war, and, on the other hand, that the steamship was ostensibly bound for a neutral port. The question whether either steamship or cargo was lawful prize must therefore depend on whether the steamship had a concealed or ulterior destination in an enemy country, or whether the copper was by means of transshipment or otherwise, in fact, destined for the enemy.

On May 14, 1915, a writ was issued by His Majesty's Procurator-General claiming confiscation of both vessel and cargo, and on June 14, 1915, the President, at the instance of the Procurator-General, made an order under Order XXIX., r. 1, of the Prize Court Rules giving leave to the War Department to requisition the copper, but subject to an undertaking being given in accordance with the provisions of Order XXIX., r. 5. This appeal is from the President's order of June 14, 1915.

It will be convenient in the first place to consider the precise terms of Order XXIX. of the Prize Court Rules. In so doing it must be borne in mind that though the Order in terms applies to ships only, it is by virtue of Order I., r. 2, of the Prize Court Rules equally applicable to goods. The first rule of Order XXIX. provides that where it is made to appear to the judge on the application of the proper officer of the Crown that it is desired to requisition, on behalf of his Majesty, a ship in respect of which no final decree of condemnation has been made, he shall order that the ship be appraised, and upon an undertaking being given in accordance with r. 5 of the Order, the ship shall be released and delivered to the Crown. . . . The 5th rule of the Order provides that in every case of requisition under the Order an undertaking in writing shall be filed by the proper officer of the Crown for payment into Court on behalf of the Crown of the appraised value of the ship or of the amount fixed under r. 4 of the Order, as the case may be, at such time or times as the Court shall declare that the same or any part thereof is required for the purpose of payment out of Court.

The first observation which their Lordships desire to make on this Order is that the provisions of r. 1 are prima facie imperative. The judge is to act in a certain way whenever it is made to appear to him that it is desired to requisition the vessel or goods in question on His Majesty's behalf. If this be the true construction of the rule and the judge is, as a matter of law, bound thereby, there is nothing more to be said and the appeal must fail. If, however, it appear that the rule so construed is not, as a matter of law, binding on the judge, it will have, if possible, to be construed in some other way. Their Lordships propose, therefore, to consider in the first place whether the rule construed as an imperative direction to the judge is to any and what extent binding.

The Prize Court Rules derive their force from Orders of His Majesty in Council. These Orders are expressed to be made under the powers vested in His Majesty by virtue of the Prize Court Act, 1894, or otherwise. The Act of 1894 confers on the King in Council power to make rules as to the procedure and practice of the Prize Courts. So far, therefore, as the Prize Court Rules relate to procedure and practice they have statutory force and are, undoubtedly, binding. But Order xxix., r. 1, construed as an imperative direction to the judge is not merely a rule of procedure or practice. It can only be a rule of procedure or practice if it be construed as prescribing the course to be followed if the judge is satisfied that according to the law administered in the Prize Court the Crown has, independently of the rule, a right to requisition the vessel or goods in question, or if the judge is minded in exercise of some discretionary power inherent in the Prize Court to sell the vessel or goods in question to the Crown. If, therefore, Order xxix., r. 1, construed as an imperative direction be binding, it must be by virtue of some power vested in the King in Council otherwise than by virtue of the Act of 1894. It was contended by the Attorney-General that the King in Council has such a power by virtue of the Royal prerogative, and their Lordships will proceed to consider this contention.

The idea that the King in Council, or indeed any branch of the Executive, has power to prescribe or alter the law to be administered by Courts of law in this country is out of harmony with the principles of our Constitution. It is true that, under a number of modern statutes, various branches of the Executive have power to make rules having the force of statutes, but all such rules derive their validity from the statute which creates the power, and not from the executive body by which they are made. No one would contend that the prerogative involves any power to prescribe or alter the law administered in Courts of Common Law or Equity. . . .

In the first place, all those matters upon which the Court is authorized to proceed are, or arise out of, acts done by the sovereign power in right of war. It follows that the King must, directly or indirectly, be a party to all proceedings in a Court of Prize. . . . Rights based on sovereignty are waived and the Crown for most purposes accepts the position of an ordinary litigant. A Prize Court must of course deal judicially with all questions which come before it for determination, and it would be impossible for it to act judicially if it were bound to take its orders from one of the parties to the proceedings.

In the second place, the law which the Prize Court is to administer is not the national or, as it is sometimes called, the municipal law, but the law of nations—in other words, international law. It is worth while dwelling for a moment on this distinction. Of course, the Prize Court is a municipal Court, and its decrees and orders owe their validity to municipal law. The law it enforces may therefore, in one sense, be considered a branch of municipal law. Nevertheless, the distinction between municipal and international law is well defined. A Court which administers municipal law is bound by and gives effect to the law as laid down by the sovereign State which calls it into being. It need inquire only what that law is, but a Court which administers international law must ascertain and give effect to a law which is not laid down by any particular State, but originates in the practice and usage long observed by civilized nations in their relations towards each other or in express international agreement. It is obvious that, if and so far as a Court of Prize in this country is bound by and gives effect to Orders of the King in Council purporting to prescribe or alter the international law, it is administering not international but municipal law; for an exercise of the prerogative cannot impose legal obligation on any one outside the King's dominions who is not the King's subject. If an Order in Council were binding on the Prize Court, such Court might be compelled to act contrary to the express terms of the commission from which it derived its jurisdiction.

There is yet another consideration which points to the same conclusion. The acts of a belligerent Power in right of war are not justiciable in its own Courts unless such Power, as a matter of grace, submit to their jurisdiction. Still less are such acts justiciable in the Courts of any other Power. As is said by Story J. in the case of The Invincible [2 Gall. 28, 44], "the acts done under the authority of one Sovereign can never be subject to the revision of the tribunals of another Sovereign; and the parties to such acts are not responsible therefor in their private capacities." It follows that but for the existence of Courts of Prize no one aggrieved by the acts of a belligerent Power in times of war could obtain redress otherwise than through diplomatic channels and at the risk of disturbing international amity. An appropriate remedy is, however, provided by the fact that, according to international law, every belligerent Power must appoint and submit to the jurisdiction of a Prize Court to which any person aggrieved by its acts has access, and which administers international as opposed to municipal law—a law which is theoretically the same, whether the Court which administers it is constituted under the municipal law of the belligerent Power or of the Sovereign of the person aggrieved, and is equally binding on both parties to the litigation. It has long been well settled by diplomatic usage that, in view of the remedy thus afforded, a neutral aggrieved by any act of a belligerent Power cognizable in a Court of Prize ought, before resorting to diplomatic intervention, to exhaust his remedies in the Prize Courts of the belligerent Power. A case for such intervention arises only if the decisions of those Courts are such as to amount to a gross miscarriage of justice. It is obvious, however, that the reason for this rule of diplomacy would entirely vanish if a Court of Prize, while nominally administering a law of international obligation, were in reality acting under the direction of the Executive of the belligerent Power.

It cannot, of course, be disputed that a Prize Court, like any other Court, is bound by the legislative enactments of its own sovereign State. A British Prize Court would certainly be bound by Acts of the Imperial Legislature. But it is none the less true that if the Imperial Legislature passed an Act the provisions of which were inconsistent with the law of nations, the Prize Court in giving effect to such provisions would no longer be administering international law. It would in the field covered by such provisions be deprived of its proper function as a Prize Court. Even if the provisions of the Act were merely declaratory of the international law, the authority of the Court as an interpreter of the law of nations would be thereby materially weakened, for no one could say whether its decisions were based on a due consideration of international obligations, or on the binding nature of the Act itself. The fact, however, that the Prize Courts in this country would be bound by Acts of the Imperial Legislature affords no ground for arguing that they are bound by the executive orders of the King in Council. . . .

The Attorney-General was unable to cite any case in which an Order of the King in Council had as to matters of law been held to be binding on a Court of Prize. He relied chiefly on the judgment of Lord Stowell in the case of The Fox. [Edw. 311; 2 Eng. P. C. 61.] The actual decision in that case was to the effect that there was nothing inconsistent with the law of nations in certain Orders in Council made by way of reprisals for the Berlin and Milan Decrees, though if there had been no case for reprisals the Orders would not have been justified by international law. . . .

There are two further points requiring notice in this part of the case. The first arises on the argument addressed to the Board by the Solicitor-General. It may be, he said, that the Court would not be bound by an Order in Council which is manifestly contrary to the established rules of international law, but there are regions in which such law is imperfectly ascertained and defined; and, when this is so, it would not be unreasonable to hold that the Court should subordinate its own opinion to the directions of the Executive. This argument is open to the same objection as the argument of the Attorney-General. If the Court is to decide judicially in accordance with what it conceives to be the law of nations, it cannot, even in doubtful cases, take its directions from the Crown, which is a party to the proceedings. It must itself determine what the law is according to the best of its ability, and its view, with whatever hesitation it be arrived at, must prevail over any executive order. Only in this way can it fulfil its function as a Prize Court and justify the confidence which other nations have hitherto placed in its decisions.

The second point requiring notice is this. It does not follow that, because Orders in Council cannot prescribe or alter the law to be administered by the Prize Court, such Court will ignore them entirely. On the contrary, it will act on them in every case in which they amount to a mitigation of the Crown rights in favour of the enemy or neutral, as the case may be. . . . Further, the Prize Court will take judicial notice of every Order in Council material to the consideration of matters with which it has to deal, and will give the utmost weight and importance to every such Order short of treating it as an authoritative and binding declaration of law. Thus, an Order declaring a blockade will prima facie justify the capture and condemnation of vessels attempting to enter the blockaded ports, but will not preclude evidence to show that the blockade is ineffective and therefore unlawful. An Order authorizing reprisals will be conclusive as to the facts which are recited as showing that a case for reprisals exists, and will have due weight as showing what, in the opinion of His Majesty's advisers, are the best or only means of meeting the emergency; but this will not preclude the right of any party aggrieved to contend, or the right of the Court to hold, that these means are unlawful, as entailing on neutrals a degree of inconvenience unreasonable, considering all the circumstances of the case. Further, it cannot be assumed, until there be a decision of the Prize Court to that effect, that any executive order is contrary to law, and all such orders, if acquiesced in and not declared to be illegal, will, in the course of time, be themselves evidence by which international law and usage may be established: see Wheaton's International Law, 4th English ed., pp. 25 and 26.

On this part of the case, therefore, their Lordships hold that Order xxix., r. 1, of the Prize Court Rules, construed as an imperative direction to the Court, is not binding. Under these circumstances the rule must, if possible, be construed merely as a direction to the Court in cases in which it may be determined that, according to international law, the Crown has a right to requisition the vessel or goods of enemies or neutrals. . . .

The next question which arises for decision is whether the order appealed from can be justified under any power inherent in the court as to the sale or realization of property in its custody pending decision of the question to whom such property belongs. It cannot, in their Lordships' opinion, be held that the court has any such inherent power as laid down by the President in this case. . . .

It remains to consider the third, and perhaps the most difficult, question which arises on this appeal—the question whether the Crown has, independently of Order xxix, r. 1, any and what right to requisition vessels or goods in the custody of the Prize Court pending the decision of the court as to their condemnation or release. . . .

On the whole question their Lordships have come to the following conclusion: A belligerent power has by international law the right to requisition vessels or goods in the custody of its Prize Court pending a decision of the question whether they should be condemned or released, but such right is subject to certain limitations. First, the vessel or goods in question must be urgently required for use in connection with the defence of the realm, the prosecution of the war, or other matters involving national security. Secondly, there must be a real question to be tried, so that it would be improper to order an immediate release. And, thirdly, the right must be enforced by application to the Prize Court, which must determine judicially whether, under the particular circumstances of the case, the right is exercisable. . . .

It remains to apply what has been said to the present case. In their Lordships' opinion the order appealed from was wrong, not because, as contended by the appellants, there is by international law no right at all to requisition ships or goods in the custody of the court, but because the judge had before him no satisfactory evidence that such a right was exercisable. . . .

The proper course, therefore, in the present case, is to declare that upon the evidence before the President he was not justified in making the order the subject of this appeal, and to give the appellants leave, in the event of their ultimately succeeding in the proceedings for condemnation, to apply to the court below for such damages, if any, as they may have sustained by reason of the order and what has been done under it. Their Lordships will humbly advise His Majesty accordingly; but inasmuch as the case put forward by the appellants has succeeded in part only, they do not think that any order should be made as to the costs of the appeal.[1]

---

[1] This case should be read in the light of the Hague convention of 1907, relative to the establishment of an International Prize Court. See Higgins, Hague Peace Conferences, pp. 407 ff.

INDEX

[REFERENCES ARE TO PAGES]

A

B